Analyzing Moral Issues

Analyzing Moral Issues

SECOND EDITION

JUDITH A. BOSS

Brown Medical School

Boston   Burr Ridge, IL   Dubuque, IA   Madison, WI   New York
San Francisco   St. Louis   Bangkok   Bogotá   Caracas   Kuala Lumpur
Lisbon   London   Madrid   Mexico City   Milan   Montreal   New Delhi
Santiago   Seoul   Singapore   Sydney   Taipei   Toronto

McGraw-Hill Higher Education

*A Division of The **McGraw-Hill** Companies*

Copyright © 2002, 1999 by The McGraw-Hill Companies, Inc. All rights reserved. Printed in the United States of America. Except as permitted under the United States Copyright Act of 1976, no part of this publication may be reproduced or distributed in any form or by any means, or stored in a data base or retrieval system, without the prior written permission of the publisher.

2 3 4 5 6 7 8 9 0 MAL/MAL 0 9 8 7 6 5 4 3 2

Library of Congress Cataloging-in-Publication Data
Boss, Judith A.,
    Analyzing moral issues / Judith A. Boss.—2nd ed.
        p.   cm.
    Includes bibliographical references and index.
    ISBN 0-7674-2022-5
    1. Ethical problems.   2. Applied ethics.   I. Title.
BJ1031 .B68   2001
170—dc21   2001030427

Sponsoring editor, Kenneth King; production, Hockett Editorial Service; manuscript editor, Regina Knox; design manager, Violeta Diaz; cover designer, Glenda King; manufacturing manager, Randy Hurst. Cover image: © Diana Ong. The text was set in 9.5/12 New Baskerville by G&S Typesetters, Inc. and printed on acid-free 50# Champion Offset by Malloy Lithographing, Inc.

Text credits appear following the Endnotes on a continuation of the copyright page, pages C-1–C-2.

www.mhhe.com

To my ethics students at Brown Medical School

Preface

Although there are several approaches to teaching college ethics, the use of moral issues is probably the most popular as well as the most appealing to students. The moral issues approach, on its own, however, has some drawbacks. It often fails to provide students with the analytical tools necessary for making real-life moral decisions. Students may also come to confuse "ideology," or the holding of certain views on issues, with morality itself. This, in turn, may contribute to "moral passivity" in which

> . . . great numbers of people, the young and educated especially, feel they have an adequate moral identity merely because they hold the "right" views on such matters as ecology, feminism, socialism, and nuclear energy. They may lead narrow, self-indulgent lives . . . yet still feel a moral advantage over those who actively work to help the needy but who are, in their eyes, ideologically unsound.*

Analyzing Moral Issues provides a corrective to these drawbacks by combining the appeal and strengths of the moral issues approach with a solid foundation in moral theory and moral reasoning. In addition to giving an overview of some of the major moral issues in our society, it (1) gives students the hands-on skills necessary to recognize and analyze moral arguments, (2) introduces students to both Western and non-Western moral theories, and (3) teaches students how to write a paper in moral philosophy as well as how to productively debate moral issues.

THE ORGANIZATION OF THE BOOK

The Moral Theory Chapter

This chapter covers the major moral theories. It also includes a section on moral development. When grounded in moral theory, the moral issues approach can engage the students' interest and connect abstract moral theory to what is going on in the world around them. Connecting moral theory to real-life moral decisions encourages students to accept personal responsibility for their moral choices rather than substituting ideology for character development. This chapter is followed by short readings from ten major world philosophers.

---

*Christiana Sommers, "Where Have All the Good Deeds Gone?" *Hastings Center Report,* August 1982, pp. 13–14.

The Moral Reasoning Chapter

Knowing how to use logical arguments in discussions of different viewpoints on an issue encourages lively and thoughtful classroom discussion. In this chapter students learn how to analyze and construct moral arguments as well as how to recognize logical fallacies.

The Reading Selections

The reading selections following Chapters 3 to 12 begin with a bridge between moral theory and moral issues by showing students how to apply moral reasoning to an actual philosophical reading on a moral issue—Judith Jarvis Thomson's "A Defense of Abortion." They include readings from traditional Western moral philosophers as well as readings that represent non-Western, multicultural, feminist, religious, and legal perspectives. The readings have been selected to introduce students to diverse and opposing viewpoints regarding the particular issue under discussion.

The Ten Issues Chapters

Chapters 3–12 each cover a different contemporary moral issue. Each issue is related, when possible, to the students' everyday experience, thus connecting their lives as college students to wider societal issues. While students' lives may not be directly affected by broader issues such as capital punishment, as citizens in a democratic society they will be directly responsible for formulating policy regarding these issues. Bringing in broader social issues also requires students to extend their range of moral concern beyond their immediate community, which is one of the goals of a college education.

The introduction to each chapter includes a historical background of the issue and an overview of the traditional philosophical perspectives on the issue presented. Following is a summary of each of the ten chapters.

Chapter 3, Abortion: Despite its legalization, abortion remains one of the most divisive moral issues. This chapter looks at the history of the abortion debate and some of the key moral issues underlying this debate, such as women's rights and the moral status of the fetus. It also raises the issue of selective abortion and discrimination.

Chapter 4, Genetic Engineering and Cloning: Cloning entered the ethics spotlight in 1997 with the announcement of the birth of Dolly, the first mammal to be cloned from an adult cell. This chapter explores some of the moral issues raised by cloning and other forms of genetic engineering. In doing so it also addresses the issue of personhood as well as the morality of trying to control what it means to be a human.

Chapter 5, Euthanasia and Assisted Suicide: Euthanasia has become an important moral issue mainly because of advances in medical technology that permit physicians to extend life. The demand for legalized euthanasia is also a reflection of the emphasis on personal autonomy and freedom in modem society. This chapter focuses primarily on the question of voluntary, active euthanasia and the debate over physician-assisted suicide.

Chapter 6, Punishment and the Death Penalty: The issue of punishment, and in particular capital punishment, touches on the most basic questions of justice and what is meant by the moral value of human life. This chapter looks at both the legal and moral issues involved in the debate over capital punishment. In addition to questions regarding the morality of the death penalty, it also challenges students to think about the more basic question of the morality of punishing wrongdoers.

Chapter 7, Drug and Alcohol Use: Drug and alcohol use among college students has increased dramatically since 1990. This chapter looks at some of the moral issues involved in the use of both legal and illegal drugs. It also includes an examination of the disease model and the moral model of addiction.

Chapter 8, Homosexuality and Same-Sex Marriage: Most Americans regard homosexuality as violations of both religious and moral norms. This chapter provides students with background information on the debate over the morality of homosexuality. Homosexuality is also examined in the context of same-sex marriage.

Chapter 9, Freedom of Speech: Rather than being an absolute right, freedom of speech needs to be considered in context and in light of other values that may conflict with it. In this chapter, freedom of speech is analyzed primarily in the context of hate speech, especially on college campuses, and of restrictions on speech in cyberspace. Also examined are the moral underpinnings of the First Amendment and the implications of the First Amendment for regulating these types of speech.

Chapter 10, Sexism, Pornography, and Violence Against Women: Sexism can manifest itself in several forms including sexual discrimination, pornography, rape, sexual harassment, and domestic violence. These practices are rooted in philosophical views and myths that define the roles and relationships between men and women in society. This chapter examines and critically analyzes the nature and implications of these views.

Chapter 11, Racism and Affirmative Action: Racism, the belief that certain groups of people are morally inferior simply because of their race, is perpetuated and reinforced at both the institutional and the individual level. This chapter examines the roots of racism in Western philosophy and American culture and the policies, such as affirmative action, that are designed to overcome the effects of racism.

Chapter 12, Nonhuman Animals and the Environment: This chapter explores questions regarding the moral status of nonhuman animals and the environment, as well as our obligations toward other animals and nonhuman nature. In particular, it challenges students to rethink anthropocentrism and to question whether human practices such as meat-eating, animal experimentation, hunting, and deforestation are morally acceptable.

The Critical Reading and Discussion Questions

Analyzing Moral Issues encourages students to apply critical thinking and reading skills to each reading through the use of critical thinking and discussion questions. Each reading is preceded by a short introduction and a set of critical reading questions related to the main points raised in the reading. The discussion questions at the end of each reading require students to think deeper about the arguments and concepts raised in that particular reading. The discussion questions also encourage students to relate these concepts and arguments to the different moral theories and other readings in the book as well as to real-life moral issues in their own lives.

Case Studies

Each moral issues chapter includes, at the end, several case studies related to the particular moral issue. The majority of these case studies are based on real-life events. By placing the issue within a context, students are encouraged to apply theory and moral reasoning to actual situations that they might encounter in their own lives.

Some of the case studies involve moral dilemmas that force students to defend a particular position on a controversial issue. Discussion of real-life moral dilemmas has been shown to enhance a student's ability to engage in effective moral reasoning. On the other hand, exclusive focus on dilemmas runs the danger of leaving students with the impression that there are no right and wrong answers and that morality is all relative. Therefore, other cases focus on issues that are fairly straightforward but which require introspection and reflection.

The Appendixes

The two appendixes, "Writing a Paper in Moral Philosophy," and "Debating Moral Issues," give students step-by-step guidance in researching and preparing a carefully thought out and well-reasoned argument on a moral issue.

ACKNOWLEDGMENTS

I thank the reviewers for their helpful suggestions: Martin Andic, University of Massachusetts, Boston; Ann E. Lange, Bentley College; Dennis Outwater, Suffolk University, Boston; Charles Padrón, Nashville Tech; James E. Roper, Michigan State University; Glenn M. Sanford, Sam Houston State University; and Lara Trout, Spring Hill College.

Thanks to my editor, Ken King, and his assistant, Georgia Gero-Chen, for their enthusiastic support and suggestions. Heartfelt thanks also go to Rachel Youngman of Hockett Editorial Service, for managing the project and keeping me on schedule, and to Regina Knox for her excellent job of editing the second edition. I would also like to express my appreciation to Marty Granahan, permission editor, for her patience and assistance in obtaining permissions for the new reading selections in this edition. In addition, I am grateful to the many authors who gave me permission to use their writings in this edition. My deepest gratitude also goes out to the many people, including Michael Jackson, reference librarian at Brown University, and my daughter Alyssa Boss, Esq., who assisted me with my research and provided feedback on the manuscript. Thanks also to Kelvin Chan for his assistance in preparing the second edition. Last, but not least, I would like to thank my former assistant, James Nuzum, for his continuing enthusiasm, his dedication to this project, and his invaluable input and assistance in putting this text together.

Contents

CHAPTER 5   **Euthanasia and Assisted Suicide**   199

CHAPTER 6   **Punishment and the Death Penalty**   253

CHAPTER 10   Sexism, Pornography, and Violence Against Women   464

CHAPTER 11   Racism and Affirmative Action   520

CHAPTER 12   **Nonhuman Animals and the Environment**   580

Analyzing Moral Issues

C H A P T E R 1

Moral Theory

A favorite theory is a possession for life.
—William Hazlitt, *Characteristics* (1837)

Adolf Hitler once said, "What good fortune for those in power that people do not think." In the early 1960s, Yale psychologist Stanley Milgram conducted an experiment on obedience to determine if Americans would be as ready to blindly follow the orders of an authority figure as were the Nazis.

In Milgram's experiment, subjects, many of whom were college-educated professionals, were led to believe that they were delivering a series of increasingly painful electric shocks as part of an experiment on the effect of punishment on learning. In fact, the person who was playing the role of the learner was an accomplice of the experimenter and was not actually receiving the shocks.

When the subjects balked upon hearing the screams of pain from the learner, they were urged to continue by an experimenter wearing a white lab coat. Despite the feigned protests of the learner, about two-thirds of the subjects obeyed the experimenter and continued delivering what they believed were potentially fatal electric shocks.

The findings of this experiment suggest that people can be persuaded to torture, and perhaps even kill, another person simply at the urging of an authority figure. A film made of the experiment revealed that those who were most likely to give in to the urging of the authority figure knew that what they were doing was wrong but were unable to articulate *why* it was wrong.[1] Those who were able to resist the authority figure, on the other hand, were able to provide justifications, in the form of moral principles and moral theory, for their refusal; they were able to say *why* continuing to deliver the shocks was wrong. Milgram wrote of his findings:

> Ordinary people, simply doing their jobs, and without any particular hostility on their part, can become agents in a terribly destructive process. Moreover, even when the destructive effects of their work become patently clear, and they are asked to carry out actions incompatible with fundamental standards of morality, relatively few people have the resources needed to resist.[2]

Like the subjects in the Milgram experiment, many of us also lack the resources necessary to critically analyze moral issues. For example, in a study of how college students judge social issues, such as abortion, pornography, and homosexuality, researchers found that many students had inconsistent "informational assumptions"; they were unable to offer a well-reasoned justification for their position on an issue, shifting positions depending on the questions asked.[3] Although the outcome of this research may not be as dramatic as the Milgram experiment, this inability hinders many of us from engaging in thoughtful discussions of issues such as euthanasia, abortion, capital punishment, animal rights, and environmental ethics. Like the Milgram subjects, simply deferring to those in authority or refusing to take a stand can contribute to a life-and-death decision for those affected.

MORAL PHILOSOPHY

Moral philosophy is the study of the values and guidelines by which we live, as well as the justification of these values and guidelines. There are two traditional subdivisions in moral philosophy: (1) applied or normative ethics and (2) theoretical ethics.

Applied or *normative ethics* is concerned with the study of the values and guidelines by which we live. Normative ethics also includes the study of moral issues—the primary focus of this text. *Theoretical ethics,* also known as *metaethics,* is concerned with the justification of these values and guidelines. These justifications involve skill in *moral reasoning* and critical thinking. In other words, while we can legitimately study theoretical ethics on its own, the study of moral issues and applied or normative ethics is built on an understanding of moral reasoning and theoretical ethics.

APPLIED ETHICS
(moral issues)

THEORETICAL ETHICS   MORAL REASONING

If we simply begin debating moral issues without first establishing this foundation, our arguments may be weak and can easily collapse like the proverbial house built on the sand. Without the ability to critically analyze or offer theoretical underpinning for our position on a given moral issue, we are unable to effectively defend it or respond to others' arguments.

This inability contributes to the feelings that our position on a moral issue is simply a matter of personal opinion. "Well," we may say with a shrug of the shoulders, "we all have a right to our opinions." Having a right to our own opinion, however, is not the same as saying that all opinions are equally reasonable.

Or, in our frustration, we may resort to using logical fallacies, glaring at our opponents in an attempt to intimidate them, or attacking their character; we may make wild generalizations that we are unable to back up, or we may simply change the topic. We see this especially in highly polarized issues such as the current abortion debate that seems to go nowhere but where emotions run high.

The moral rightness or wrongness of a position or action, such as delivering potentially lethal shocks to another subject in an experiment, is not a matter of personal feeling or opinion but of reason. The study of moral theory and moral reasoning helps us recognize and organize these general principles and moral concerns. It is up to us as critical thinkers to decide which arguments are the strongest and to come up with a well-reasoned position that takes into account the strengths of both sides of the argument.

WHAT IS THE PURPOSE OF MORAL THEORIES?

Most people, if given a choice, would prefer to skip moral theory and get on with discussions of real-life moral issues. Theory is often contrasted with action. This is a false dichotomy, since it is theory that informs our actions. Knowing how to ground discussions of moral issues in moral theory and good moral reasoning will make us less vulnerable to persuasive, but logically incorrect, thinking.

A theory is a conceptual framework for explaining a set of facts or concepts. In moral philosophy, theory *explains* why a certain action—such as torturing babies—is wrong and why we *ought* to act in certain ways and be a certain type of person. Moral theory also helps us *clarify, critically analyze,* and *rank* the moral concerns raised by particular moral issues.

A good theory should also be able to explain the whole range or scope of morality, not just particular types of actions. For example, the theory that morality is a private choice is inadequate for dealing with choices such as rape, torture, and genocide, since these actions affect other people. In addition, a theory should take into account what we, upon reflection, believe to be right. Aristotle (384–322 B.C.E.), for example, takes as the starting point in developing his moral theory the moral intuitions of ordinary people. Moral theory, however, goes beyond our everyday notions about morality. It requires consistency in our thinking and the weeding out of those commonly held beliefs about morality that are inconsistent or superfluous.

Moral theories can be compared to road maps. A good theory offers *guidance* or signposts for thinking about and resolving moral issues. Although we may just happen to come upon a good solution, a moral theory, like a road map, makes it more likely that we will reach our destination with the least amount of wrong turns and aggravation. By providing guidelines, moral theories help us identify conflicts and contradictions in our thinking and make more satisfactory moral decisions.

Like maps, not all theories are equally good. Some may be good as far as they go, but they leave out too much. In this case we may want to combine them with other theories or "maps." Other moral theories, such as ethical subjectivism, lead us down dead ends. Knowing about the strengths and weaknesses of the different moral theories can save us from heading down these dead ends!

Theories provide us with a framework for discussing real-life moral issues; they also shape our worldviews or interpretations of our experiences. We all approach the world with certain assumptions that, loosely, form our theories about what to expect in the world. In any culture there are certain theories that are so embedded in the cultural worldview that they are uncritically assumed to be true. For example, in Western culture the theory that humans are superior to and separate from other animals (anthropocentrism) is rarely questioned. This is reflected in our language, where the common use of the term *animal* does not include humans. Anthropocentrism is also implicit in the assumption of ethical relativists that humans are the ultimate source of what is right and wrong. Rather than uncritically adopting the prevailing theories of our culture, we need to ask first if their assumptions can be justified or if they embody false views.

THE TYPES OF MORAL THEORIES

There are two main types of moral theories: (1) ethical relativism and (2) universalist or objectivist. *Ethical relativist moral theories* state that morality is different for different people. An ethical relativist claims that morality is invented or created by people; therefore morality, like fashion, can vary from time to time and from person to person. *Universalist* or *objectivist moral theories,* in contrast, state that there are fundamental, objective moral principles and values that are universally true for all people, independent of their personal beliefs or culture.

In his study of moral development, psychologist Lawrence Kohlberg found that when it comes to moral theory, 90 percent of adult Americans, while they may acknowledge universal moral principles such as equality, believe, for the most part, that morality is relative to or created by society.[4] In other words, being morally good, for the majority of Americans, means following the norms and values of their society or culture—whether this be their peer culture, their church,[5] their country, or a combination of these. The theory that morality is relative to societal norms is known in moral philosophy as *cultural relativism.*

Many college students, on the other hand, claim that morality is relative to the individual and is different for every person depending on what they feel.[6] This theory is known in philosophy as *ethical subjectivism.* Philosopher Stephen Satris maintains, however, that students' relativism is not a genuine philosophical position but a way of avoiding critical analysis of their opinions. Indeed, critical analysis of these two theories uncovers implications that few people would be willing to accept. Rather than promote tolerance as a universal moral value, ethical relativism breeds suspicion of those who are different and allows exploitation of the weak by the powerful.

Because of this it is important that we learn how to analyze different moral theories. As critical thinkers and students of moral philosophy, we cannot be content with simply accepting the norms of our culture or dismissing morality as a matter of personal opinion. Rather than depend on the opinions of others and risk getting off course, we can use theory as a guide as we make our way through the often bewildering morass of moral issues that confront us in modern life.

EXERCISES

1. What do you mean when you say that something is morally right or morally wrong?
2. Make a list of guidelines and values that you use in making moral decisions. Are your values and guidelines consistent? Where did you get these guidelines and values? Do they give you sufficient guidance in resolving difficult moral issues? Explain.

3. Choose a moral issue that is important to you. Discuss how the guidelines and values you listed in the previous answer help shape your position on that issue.

RELATIVISM IN ETHICS

There is one thing a professor can be absolutely certain of: almost every student entering the university believes, or says he believes, that truth is relative . . .

—Allan Bloom, *The Closing of the American Mind*

The fact of moral disagreement among individuals and between cultures raises the question of whether there are really any objective or universal moral principles. Cultural and individual disagreements, fueled by popular clichés such as "morality is all relative," "do what you feel is right," "don't force your values on me," and "who am I to judge?" create serious doubts in people's minds about whether moral issues can ever be resolved, or whether meaningful dialogue between those holding opposing positions is even possible.

Ethical relativism is one of the most popular moral theories among college students. According to ethical relativists, there are no independent or objective moral standards. Instead, morality is *created* by people. In other words, humans, either individually or collectively, are the ultimate measure of what is right and wrong.

Ethical Subjectivism

What I feel is right is right. What I feel is wrong is wrong.

—Jean-Jacques Rousseau

Ethical relativism can be subdivided into ethical subjectivism and cultural relativism. Ethical subjectivists claim that individual people create their own morality. There are no objective moral truths—only individuals' opinions or preferences. What is right for you may be wrong for me, depending on our respective feelings. You may feel that racism is wrong; I may feel that white supremacy is morally right. You may feel that it is wrong to eat meat; I may feel it is right for me. The rightness or wrongness of our actions depends solely on how each of us *feels* about racism or meat-eating.

Do not confuse ethical subjectivism with the obviously true and trivial statement that "whatever a person believes is right for him or her is what that person believes is right for him or her." Ethical subjectivism goes beyond this by claiming that sincerely believing or feeling that something is right makes it right for the individual. Because morality is merely a matter of personal opinion, we can never be mistaken about what is right and wrong. In other words, my actions in terrorizing black students on campus are morally commendable and perhaps even morally obligatory, so long as I personally feel that what I am doing is right.

When asked if he thought what he did was wrong, convicted serial killer Craig Price calmly replied, "Morality is a private choice." If morality is simply a matter of personal opinion, there is no point in trying to use rational arguments to convince the racist or the serial killer that what he did was wrong, anymore than it would make sense to try to convince me that I really don't like cashew nuts. Similarly, there would not be any point in proceeding further in a moral-issues course.

If morality is based only on personal feelings or opinion, no one can ever be mistaken about what is morally correct or incorrect. The correct position on a moral issue is simply a matter of personal feeling, rather than reason or shared values. When peoples' views come into conflict, those who are strongest will be able to impose their agenda on others, as Craig Price did. Under ethical subjectivism we do not have to tolerate other people's views or even their lives unless, of course, we feel that tolerance is right for us.

What Would the World Be Like if We Took Ethical Subjectivism Seriously?   Ethical subjectivism is one of the weakest moral theories. If taken seriously, it permits people to exploit and hurt others without having to justify their actions. As a theory, it does not provide a correct explanation for why certain actions are wrong. In real life we generally make moral judgments independently of anyone's feelings toward the action. Indeed, the fact that a serial killer enjoys torturing and killing his victims or that a child molester sincerely believes that his young victims enjoyed being raped only makes their actions more horrific. If ethical subjectivism were true, the opposite would be the case: Our moral heroes would be psychopaths—people who act solely on their feelings, without concern for any universal moral principles.

Cultural Relativism

We recognize that morality differs in every society, and is a convenient term for socially approved habits.

—Ruth Benedict (1933)

The modern theory of cultural relativism developed primarily out of late-nineteenth- and early-twentieth–century studies of simple cultures by prominent anthropologists such as Ruth Benedict, Emile Durkheim, William Graham Sumner, and Franz Boas. Like ethical subjectivists, *cultural relativists* maintain that standards of right and wrong are created by people. It is societal norms, however, rather than the opinions of isolated individuals, that form the basis of morality. Public opinion, not private opinion, determines what is right and wrong. There are no objective universal moral standards that hold for all people in all cultures, only different cultural customs.

Cultural relativists are not merely arguing that some moral values are relative to culture. They claim that *all* moral values are nothing more than cultural customs. Because there are no universal moral standards, the moral values of one culture cannot be judged to be any better or worse than those of any other culture. Headhunting, for example, is right or wrong only within a particular cultural context. In some New Guinea cultures, it is morally commendable for a young man to give his sweetheart a shrunken head as a trophy. In our country such an action would be regarded as highly immoral and even evidence of serious mental illness. Similarly, if a culture believes that women should be kept in subjection, women have a moral obligation to be submissive to their fathers or husbands, and men have a moral right, and perhaps even a moral duty, to use brute force should their women deviate from the cultural norm. It is wrong in our culture for men to beat their wives, but, according to a cultural relativist, it is wrong *only* because it goes against cultural norms.

Cultural Relativism Is Not the Same as Sociological Relativism   Cultural relativism is a moral theory about what *ought to be. Sociological relativism* is simply the observation that there is disagreement among cultures regarding moral values. Unlike cultural relativism, sociological relativism draws no conclusions about the rightness or wrongness of these values. Sociological relativists leave open the possibility that a culture may be mistaken about its moral values (such as Nazi Germany or the headhunting cultures) and that there *may* be universal moral principles that all cultures ought to respect. Cultural relativism, on the other hand, claims that if a culture believes something is morally right, that in itself makes it morally right. Because morality is nothing more than custom, there are no legitimate grounds for criticizing the moral practices of other cultures.

Morality may also change within a culture over time, much like laws and fashions. Slavery is now considered highly immoral in the United States. Two hundred years ago, however, slavery was not only *believed to be* morally acceptable by the majority, it *was,* according to cultural relativists, morally acceptable. If morality is synonymous with conformity to cultural norms, it was the abolitionists, not the slaveholders, who were immoral. Similarly, Martin Luther King Jr. was immoral for protesting the segregation laws of the South.

For cultural relativists, if something is legal, whether it be slavery, apartheid, abortion, capital punishment, affirmative action, or pornography, it is, by definition, morally acceptable. Things that are illegal—such as recreational drug use, human cloning, assisted suicide, and, in some states, homosexual activity—are, by definition, immoral according to the cultural relativist.

Cultural Relativism Is Based on Faulty Reasoning   Cultural relativism argues from the fact that a culture believes something, such as slavery, *is* moral, to the conclusion that that is the way things *ought to be.* In logic this type of faulty reasoning is known as the naturalist fallacy. The *naturalist fallacy* draws a conclusion about what ought to be, based on what is. As noted earlier, the fact that people believe something to be true, whether it be the flatness of the earth or the morality of slavery, does not make it true or moral. Yet even though the reasoning behind cultural relativism is faulty, the conclusion that it is the correct description of morality may still just happen to be true.

What If Cultural Relativism Is True?   Further analysis of cultural relativism, however, reveals that, like ethical subjectivism, it is wrought with problems and contradictions.

Cultural relativism offers no criteria for distinguishing between reformers, such as Martin Luther King Jr. and Susan B. Anthony, who may break the law as an act of conscience, and common criminals. Both the social reformer and the criminal break cultural norms; both, therefore, are immoral. Identifying what is moral with what is legal is problematic, however, since there are some laws—such as laws supporting slavery or prohibiting women from voting—that are clearly unjust and that reasonable people believe should be changed.

Because it identifies morality with maintaining the status quo, cultural relativism cannot explain moral progress. Yet most people believe that the abolition of slavery in the United States, the civil rights movement, and granting women full rights of citizenship all represented moral progress. Similarly, cultural relativism cannot account for the fact that most people believe that there are ways in which their own society can be improved. Not only does cultural relativism prevent criticism of other cultures, it also rules out the possibility of engaging in a rational critique of one's own cultural customs.

Cultural relativism encourages blind conformity to cultural norms rather than rational analysis of moral issues. Rather than using dialogue, we resolve a moral issue simply by taking a poll or calling a lawyer. But surely this is not an accurate description of how we make moral decisions. We do not resolve moral issues by checking the law books or taking a hand count. Legalizing abortion and capital punishment did not stop moral debate over those two issues; and outlawing the cloning of humans in the United States will not end moral discussion on the matter. Futhermore, the fact that most Americans eat meat is irrelevant to someone who is struggling with the morality of meat-eating.

Cultural relativism does not work in pluralistic cultures. Although it may have been possible a century ago for anthropologists to identify the cultural norms of simple, relatively isolated and static cultures, in the rapidly changing modern world it is becoming more and more difficult to draw sharp distinctions between cultures or even to figure out what our own cultural norms are. Most of us are members of several cultures or subcultures. We may be members of a Catholic, Cambodian, Native American, African American, feminist, or homosexual subculture whose values may conflict with those of the wider culture. Indeed, the so-called dominant cultural values are sometimes simply the values held by a small group of people who happen to hold the power in that culture.

We also cannot assume that simply because the majority holds a certain value that it is desirable. In his essay "On Liberty," John Stuart Mill (1806–1873) argues that basing public policy on the will of the people can result in the "tyranny of the majority." Suppression of freedom of speech and religion, censorship of the press, and discrimination against minorities have all, at some time, had the blessing of the majority. Aristotle likewise warns that majority rule is not necessarily in the best interests of the community.

The belief that there are no shared universal moral values can lead to suspicion and mistrust of people from other cultures or subcultures, rather than tolerance and a sense of community. We may feel that "they" do not share our respect for life; that people from other cultures may even have dangerous values. Because cultural relativism rules out the possibility of rational discussion when cross-cultural values come into conflict and persuasion fails, groups may resort to either apathy and isolationism when the values of other cultures are not a threat, or to violence when another culture's values or actions create a threat to one's own way of life.

The Positive Aspects of Cultural Relativism   Most theories, even though they may not stand up under the scrutiny of critical analysis, contain at least a grain of truth. Cultural relativism reminds us that culture and history are important in the moral life. Our traditions, our religious values, and our political and social institutions all shape the way in which we apply moral values. In their concern to disavow ethical relativism, too many philosophers have divorced morality from the actual historical and cultural settings in which we make our moral decisions, but cultural relativism takes this observation too far. Although the *application* of specific moral principles is relative to cultures (as noted in the Eskimo example later in this chapter), this does not imply that these moral principles are the *creation* of cultures.

Cultural relativism is also a reminder of how easily we can confuse custom and tradition with morality. Because of this, we need to be able to critically analyze not just issues that are considered moral controversies, but also customs that society accepts as perfectly moral, such as meat-eating.

Ethical Relativism and Doublethink   The simplicity and popularity of the two types of ethical relativism theories make them particularly seductive. Ethical subjectivism absolves people of ever having to deliberate before making a moral judgment, whereas cultural relativism absolves people from moral responsibility so long as they follow the crowd. At the same time, almost everyone wants others to treat them with respect and be held morally culpable for their hurtful actions.

Some people try to hold on to ethical relativism by jumping back and forth between the different theories, depending on what is more expedient in a particular situation. For example, some students may argue that morality is a private choice when it comes to something they are doing, such as binge drinking or cheating on a test or using hate speech. At the same time, they may be morally critical of teachers who break cultural norms by coming to class drunk or who use sexist or racist language in class or play favorites in grading tests. Ethical subjectivism and cultural relativism, however, are mutually exclusive theories. A person cannot consistently believe both that morality is created by individuals and that morality is a cultural creation.

Some people who claim that they are relativists may also bring universal moral principles concerning justice and respect in through the back door. They may argue that sexist and racist language is disrespectful or that playing favorites in grading is unfair. They may even cite the Golden Rule or some form of it. Because the two types of theories are based on contradictory claims regarding the source of morality, however, both forms of ethical relativism are incompatible with universalist theories.

What About Moral Disagreement?

But, you may ask, if ethical relativism is incorrect, how can we explain the lack of agreement among individuals and cultures over moral values? The fact that people disagree does not necessarily mean that there are no objective moral principles. People can disagree for a number of reasons. They may be mistaken about their facts. At one time most people believed that the earth was flat, but it turns out they were mistaken. Physicians used to routinely lie to dying cancer patients, believing that the truth would be so upsetting that it might kill them. It wasn't until the 1970s that studies were carried out that showed physicians to be wrong. There may also be objective moral standards, even though we may have yet to discover them, or at least their exact nature.

Disagreement can also occur because natural conditions and religious beliefs influence the expression of a particular moral value. In 1941 Gontran de Poncins wrote the following about the Kabloona, an Eskimo culture living in the Canadian arctic.

> One observer was told of an Eskimo who was getting ready to move camp and was concerned about what to do with his blind and aged father, who was a burden to the family. One day the old man expressed a desire to go seal hunting again, something he had not done for many years. His son readily assented to this suggestion, and the old man was dressed warmly and given his weapons. He was then led out to the seal grounds and was walked into a hole in the ice into which he disappeared.[7]

Is cultural relativism the only way to explain the difference between the Kabloona and modern Americans? Modern Americans can hire caregivers or put their ailing parents or grandparents in nursing homes. The Kabloona, on the other hand, were a nomadic people; there were no nursing homes or hospitals or spare bedrooms in the house for grandparents. As nomadic people their lives depended on following the seal herds. To take a blind and ailing parent on one of these treks could have resulted in starvation, not just of the elderly parent, but of the whole family. In addition, the son, as was the tradition, respected his father's autonomy, waiting until he requested the "hunting" trip.

What was different here, in other words, were not the fundamental moral values of respect for life, family loyalty, and personal autonomy, but different conditions that placed limitations on how these values could best be *applied*. Saving the lives of many took precedence over prolonging the father's life. The question of when, if ever, it is morally permissible to assist a terminally ill person in taking his or her life is not one limited to the Kabloona culture. The introduction of medical technology that can prolong the lives of the elderly and the dying has brought the issues of death with dignity and assisted suicide to the forefront in our own culture.

People may also disagree about moral issues not because they hold fundamentally different moral values, but because they *rank* or prioritize them differently. Both Aristotle and the Confucians give a high ranking to community and social values. In his article "Law, Morality, and 'Sexual Orientation,'" John Finnis opposes homosexual marriage on the grounds that it is destructive to the common good. Libertarians, on the other hand, like most Americans, place a higher value on individual autonomy and freedom. Michael Nava and Robert Dawidoff defend gay marriage as being a private choice. Moral theory helps us recognize and rank these values and in so doing helps us come to a resolution that honors as many moral values as possible.

Relativism, Personhood, and Moral Community

Variations in cultural norms can also occur because of differences in how cultures define their moral communities. According to anthropologist Clyde Kluckholn, there are universal moral values that are recognized by all cultures. No culture, for example, approves of indiscriminate lying, cheating, or stealing. Random violence is also prohibited universally. Every culture also makes arrangements for the care of its children. These moral values, however, apply only to members of a particular culture's *moral community*, that is, to those who are seen as having moral value. Headhunters, for example, always select their victims from outside their immediate community.

Beings who have moral worth are known in moral philosophy as *persons*. Persons are worthy of respect as valuable in themselves, rather than simply because of their usefulness or value to someone else. The widespread identification of *person* with *human being* in our culture betrays our anthropocentric bias in defining moral community; the use of the term *man* for all humans also shows our patriarchal bias. In coming up with a rational and consistent definition of the moral community, it is important to look beyond culturally biased terms.

Cultural Relativism and Ethnocentrism   Cultural relativism defines moral community in ethnocentric terms: Someone, or something, has moral value only because society grants this status. There is no source of moral value other than one's culture. Those who are granted moral status by their culture receive the protection and support of the community. Moreover, those who are closer to the center of the moral community—such as white males in our culture—receive more privileges and protection. Those who are *marginalized*—such as women, homosexuals, blacks, and Hispanics—have less access to economic and social benefits. When members of a marginalized group transgress cultural norms, they are not given the same protection as those in power. For example, in the United States, blacks are more likely to receive the death penalty.[8] Beings who are outside the moral community—such as nonhuman animals, fetuses, and the environment in our culture—on the other hand, can be treated as a "means only" and disposed of, eaten, or exploited solely for the benefit of those within the moral community.

In Buddhist cultures and some of the Native American cultures, the moral community is defined very broadly to include all living beings—human and nonhuman. Other cultures define their moral community more narrowly. For a group of beings to be excluded from the moral community, they first have to be "depersonalized." Before embarking on their "final solution," for example, the German Supreme Court in 1936 ruled that "the Jew is only a rough copy of a human being, with human like facial traits but nonetheless . . . lower than any animal . . . otherwise nothing." In the 1857 *Dred Scott v. Sanford* decision, the United States Supreme Court reaffirmed that the slave was "property in the strictest sense of the word" and an "inferior being that had no rights which the white man was bound to respect." In the 1973 *Roe v. Wade* decision, which legalized abortion, the Court declared that "the word 'person,' as used in the Fourteenth Amendment, does not include the unborn."

Discussions of whether these exclusions were or are morally justified should be based on reason, not cultural or legal tradition. The cultural definition of the moral community is, to a large extent, politically and economically motivated and serves to maintain the status quo. By protecting the interests of those in power and morally sanctioning the marginalization and exploitation of other groups, cultural relativism promotes ethnocentrism and legitimates hatred and discrimination. Problems such as racism and sexism, which are based on long traditions of discrimination against blacks and women, exist in our culture, in part, because the majority of American adults are cultural relativists.

The power of our cultural worldview is much more pervasive in our moral thinking than most of us realize. Many people, while giving lip service to the universal principle of equality, in their everyday lives tacitly adopt the prevailing cultural view of the moral community. In the study mentioned earlier of how college students judge social issues, researchers found that slightly more than half of the students interviewed, for example, evaluated homosexuality in a positive light, stating that it was a personal preference just as heterosexuality was a personal preference.[9] When the same students were presented with a hypothetical example of their own child being homosexual, however, 92 percent shifted their position, stating that this would not be morally acceptable or desirable. In other words, they shifted from a definition of the moral community based on the principle of equality to the cultural definition of the moral community that marginalizes homosexuals. To avoid getting mired in doublethink, it is important to be aware of how the cultural definition of the moral community shapes viewpoints on moral issues.

Unlike cultural relativism, universalist theories of morality require rational criteria for personhood and, most important, that the exclusion of a particular group of people or beings from the moral community be justified. Much of the dissension over abortion, animal rights, and environmental ethics stems from disagreement over the definition of moral community and personhood. Thus, any debate on these issues must be based on a rational and consistent definition of these key terms. Mary Anne Warren in her article on abortion, for example, devotes considerable space to defining personhood. As with slavery, justifying practices such as meat-eating, commodification of the environment, or abortion on the grounds of tradition or legality just won't do.

EXERCISES

1. Philosopher Stephen Satris argues that the ethical relativism of most college students is intended not as a well-thought-out philosophical theory but as an "invincible suit of armor" to "prevent or close off dialogue and thought."[10] Do you agree? Discuss an instance when you, or someone else, used ethical subjectivism as a means of ending the discussion on a moral issue.
2. Do your views on the issues covered in this chapter coincide, for the most part, with those of your culture or subculture? To what extent do you use widespread agreement as support for the "rightness" of your position on issues such as abortion or capital punishment?
3. In his book *1984,* George Orwell coined the term *doublethink* to describe when people simultaneously hold two contradictory views and believe both to be true. He predicted that doublethink would become more and more prevalent as people lost the ability to think critically. Do you agree with Orwell? What are some instances of doublethink in debates on moral issues?
4. What criteria do you use to decide who or what is included and who or what is excluded from the moral community? Are you satisfied with your criteria? How does your definition of personhood affect your views on the moral issues included in this text?

MOVING BEYOND ETHICAL RELATIVISM

Moral thought, then, seems to behave like all other kinds of thought. Progress through the moral levels and stages is characterized by increasing differentiation and increasing integration, and hence is the same kind of progress that scientific theory represents.

—Lawrence Kohlberg, *The Philosophy of Moral Development* (1971)

French novelist André Gide (1869–1951) once wrote: "Culture, born of life, ultimately kills life." Just as children must one day leave their parents and strike out on their own if they are to continue maturing, so too must we put behind us the dictates of our peer group or culture as the ultimate moral authority and seek a more solid and reliable foundation for everyday moral decisions.

Both types of ethical relativism—ethical subjectivism and cultural relativism—are inadequate as explanations of how we make real-life moral decisions and as guides for what we ought to do. Universalist moral theories offer an alternative to ethical relativism. These theories claim that morality is universal and objective and, as such, exists independently of personal or cultural opinions.

The Stage Theory of Moral Development

According to developmental psychologists, there are innate cognitive structures that are fundamental to all humans. These structures include—among others—causality, time and space, and moral excellence. In his study of moral reasoning, psychologist Lawrence Kohlberg found that humans move through distinct stages of moral development. These stages are universal and cross-cultural and represent "transformations in the organization of thought, rather than increasing knowledge of cultural values." The earlier stages are not so much replaced by higher stages as incorporated into them—much like elementary school arithmetic becomes part of understanding complex statistical analysis. People move on to the next or "higher" stage of moral development only when they find their current type of moral reasoning inadequate. This generally occurs when they encounter a crisis that their current mode of thinking is unable to satisfactorily resolve.

Young children use primarily egoistic or preconventional moral reasoning. Morality is simply a matter of satisfying their own needs. In the second or conventional stage of moral reasoning, people look to others, whether it be their peers or societal norms, for their moral values. In other words, they reject egoism and adopt cultural relativism. The transition to the conventional stage generally takes place during early adolescence. While egoistic reasoning may be effective in helping the young child get what he or she wants, in high school and college, egoism is more likely to irritate others and alienate the egoist from his or her peers.

Conventional moral reasoners are concerned with pleasing others and respecting social rules. Their position on a moral issue is generally determined by what their peers believe, or, at the higher level of conventional reasoning, what is legal. As a developmental stage, conventional moral reasoning helps to socialize young people and move them beyond egoism to a concern for community values and the needs of others.

The final stage, according to Kohlberg, is that of principled reasoning. In justifying this as a more desirable or higher stage than the previous stages, Kohlberg points out that people at this stage prefer it to their earlier stages of moral reasoning. In addition, most world philosophers have long held that autonomous moral reasoning, universality and impartiality, and compassion and a concern for justice for all are the hallmarks of sound moral reasoning.

Kohlberg used only males in formulating his theory on moral development. Not surprisingly, his stage theory has been criticized for not taking into account the way women think about moral issues. Through her interviews with women and a study of women in literature, Harvard psychologist Carol Gilligan concluded that women's moral development tends to follow a different path than men's: Men tend to be duty- and principle-oriented; women are more context-oriented and tend to view the world in a more emotional and personal way.[11] Women's moral judgment, Gilligan found, is characterized by concern for themselves and others, accepting and maintaining responsibility within relationships, attachment, and self-sacrifice.

Although Gilligan's and Kohlberg's theories emphasize different aspects of moral development, and Kohlberg divides each stage into two levels, their stages are roughly parallel. The preconventional stage in both their theories includes the egoists and ethical subjectivists who put their needs before those of others. Conventional moral reasoners, in both theories, are cultural relativists. The different descriptions of the conventional stage are not surprising given the different ways in which men and women are socialized in our culture. Men, for the most part, are socialized to be the upholders of law and order—whether it be the law of the land or the rules laid down by their fraternity. Women, on the other hand, are taught that being a good woman involves self-sacrifice and placing the welfare of others before her own. As Susan Wolf points out in her article on feminism and euthanasia, this can make women more vulnerable to pressure to choose euthanasia.

In both theories the postconventional stage is represented by autonomous moral reasoning, where a person looks to transcultural universal values—whether these are in the form of abstract principles of justice and respect or sentiments such as compassion and empathy. These two theories or perspectives are not mutually exclusive. Indeed, scores on Kohlberg's Moral Judgment Interview are significantly related to those of the Ethic of Care Interview.[12] Developing an awareness that respect applies to all persons involves being able to empathize with others. Psychopaths, who lack the ability to empathize, also lack any sense of moral duty. In addition, Gilligan's postconventional stage entails that women realize that principles of justice and respect apply to themselves as well as to other people.

Recent research has shown that most people—men and women alike—use both the care and the justice perspective in their moral reasoning. Neither perspective is better than the other; both Gilligan and Kohlberg came to acknowledge that moral maturity involves the development and integration of both perspectives.[13]

The preference for one of the two perspectives can show up in how students debate different moral issues. Women, as well as some men, at the conventional stage of moral reasoning may fail to speak up or challenge someone for fear of offending them. Men, as well as some women, at the conventional stage may conform to the rules of their peer culture or confuse what is moral with what is legal. These stages also influence how students make real-life moral decisions. Studies of drinking on campuses, for example, show that freshmen men are more likely than women to succumb to peer pressure to engage in heavy drinking and drug use. Female freshmen, in contrast, are more likely to refrain from drinking and drug use, because of concern for how it will affect their families.[14]

Being wary of peer pressure and being concerned about the impact of our actions on our relationships are both important in moral decision making. Being aware of your own moral-decision-making style, and the fact that it may differ in emphasis from that of others, can help you cultivate your own strengths and overcome your weaknesses. It will also encourage you to appreciate the strengths and contributions of other perspectives in moral decision making and in group discussions of moral issues.

College and Moral Development

When young people begin college, they may discover that what they thought were clear-cut cultural norms and values are not so uncontroversial after all. Their cherished world-views may come into conflict with those of others, especially people from different cultural backgrounds. This, in turn, leads them to question the morality of some of their own cultural norms. During this transition period, students are torn between the rejection of moral values that are culturally relative and the reluctance to commit to universal moral principles (postconventional moral reasoning). This conflict can manifest itself in hedonistic disregard for any moral values—either relative or universal.[15]

STAGES OF MORAL REASONING

Stage	Kohlberg[16]	Gilligan[17]
Preconventional	Punishment (avoid punishment) Egoist (satisfy one's own needs; consider the needs of others only if it benefits you)	Self-centered (view one's own needs as all that matters)
Conventional	Good boy/nice girl (please and help others; concern for earning others' approval; conformity to peer norms) Society-maintaining (respect authority and social rules; maintain the existing social order)	Self-sacrificing (view others' needs as more important)
Postconventional	Social contract or legalistic (obey useful social rules; appeal to social consensus and majority rule as long as minimal basic rights are safeguarded) Conscience and universal principles (autonomously recognize universal rules, such as justice and equality; respect for equal human rights and the dignity of each individual)	Mature care ethics (balance one's own needs and the needs of others)

Moral maturity entails making our own well-reasoned moral decisions rather than simply following the dictates of the crowd or going with our selfish desires. At the same time, moral maturity involves integrating into our moral reasoning the strengths of these earlier stages; in particular, a sensitivity to cultural and historical norms in *applying* moral principles and a realization that our desires and needs count as much as anyone else's.

Unfortunately, most college students do not complete the transition to postconventional moral reasoning, but instead move into a higher level of conventional moral reasoning. Although they may become less dependent on the opinions of their peers, the trade-off is that they become more conforming to wider societal norms. Rather than making the transition from cultural relativism to postconventional (principled) moral reasoning, they simply accept the norms and laws of their culture as the final word in what is right or wrong. While this may serve a person well in a just society, blind obedience to cultural norms can lead to disasters like the Holocaust in Nazi Germany, the slave trade, and the massacre of Native Americans.

The Importance of Moral Development and Ethics Education

Could such culturally approved holocausts happen today in the United States? Most people would like to think that they would draw the line at participating in such atrocities.

If laws were enacted ordering, let's say, the euthanasia of all people over 65, or mandatory prenatal genetic testing and the destruction of all genetically "imperfect" fetuses, or mandatory "reprogramming" of the brains of racists or sexists, would we go along with these laws? Most of us would like to think that we would draw the line at participating in atrocities such as genocide and mind control. Although these practices may make us feel uncomfortable, if we identify morality with cultural norms, on what grounds are we going to oppose them?

One of the primary purposes of ethics education is to help students make the transition to postconventional moral reasoning by providing them with the resources to make effective moral decisions that they will not come to regret later. Unlike moral indoctrination, ethics education is not about telling people what is right and wrong. Most people, with the exception of psychopaths, "know" right from wrong.[18]

In the Milgram experiment, for example, many of the subjects were openly distressed and "knew" that what they were doing was wrong, but they were unable to say why. Ethics education helps us articulate moral values. It also teaches us how to effectively apply moral theory and moral reasoning to a particular issue or real-life moral decision. Because the majority of subjects in the Milgram experiment could not support their intuition with moral principles and moral reasoning, they instead defaulted to the authority figure.[19]

MORAL THEORY AND PRAXIS

The study of moral theory and the reasoning underlying moral issues also help motivate people. Research has found that people who are morally mature and better at moral reasoning are more motivated to act on their beliefs.[20] People at the higher stages of moral development not only sympathize with those who are suffering, but take active steps to help alleviate that suffering. They are willing to speak out on behalf of themselves and others when they witness an injustice and will take effective and well-thought-out action to correct the injustice.

The ability to effectively analyze moral issues, such as those addressed in this text, should motivate students to take moral action, also known as *praxis*, rather than simply being content to subscribe to the "correct" ideology. Praxis can take many forms, whether it be engaging in a letter-writing campaign regarding an issue such as capital punishment, assisting women who have unwanted pregnancies, speaking up when confronted with a sexist or racist comment or action, joining an animal rights or environmental group, or working in a campus drug-and-alcohol awareness program.

Praxis involves not only *doing* the right thing, but striving to *be* the best person we can be. Virtuous people, those who regard morality as an important aspect of their self-identity, are more likely to do the right thing and to get involved in social action.[21] Taking a class in ethics helps us on our journey to becoming the best people we can be.

EXERCISES

1. Which perspective—Kohlberg's justice perspective or Gilligan's care perspective—most accurately describes the way you approach discussions of moral issues? To what extent do you draw from both perspectives? Illustrate your answer with specific examples.

2. Has the college experience enhanced your moral development? Has your strategy for making moral decisions changed at all since you started college? If so, are you more satisfied with your current strategy? Explain using specific examples.
3. Have your views on any of the issues covered in this chapter changed or been called into doubt as a result of your college experience? Explain using specific examples.
4. Discuss a time when you went along with others even though you "knew" that what they were doing was morally questionable.
5. Discuss ways in which you are engaged in moral action or praxis. Illustrate your answer with an example.

MORALITY AND RELIGION

> *A list of virtues or duties drawn up by a Buddhist would not differ very greatly from one drawn up by a Christian, a Confucianist, a Muhammadan or a Jew. Formally all of the ethico-religious systems are universalist in scope.*
>
> —Morris Ginsberg, *Reason and Unreason in Society* (1947)

Many people look to religion for moral guidance. The concept of God in the major world religions—Hinduism, Judaism, Christianity, and Islam—is intimately connected with that of moral goodness.[22] People worship God, in part, because God represents perfect goodness. Worshipping reaffirms these moral values.

This raises the question of the connection between religion and morality. Is morality dependent on religion or does it exist independently of religion? In other words, is something moral because God approves of it, or does God approve of something because it is moral?[23]

The Divine Command Theory

The first position, that something is moral merely because God approves of it, is known as the *divine command theory*. Just as morality for the cultural relativist is relative to cultural norms, for the divine command theorist morality is relative to what God commands or wills. There are no independent, universal moral standards by which to judge God's commands. No other justification is necessary for an action to be right other than God's commanding it. For example, Israeli law student Yigal Amir shot and killed Israeli prime minister Yitshak Rabin as Rabin was leaving a peace rally. When apprehended, Amir told police, "I acted alone on God's orders and I have no regrets." In another case a woman put her baby in a microwave oven and turned it on; she too defended her actions on the grounds that God had commanded her to kill her child. If we respond that God would not have commanded anyone to do something so horrible, we are implying that there are independent moral standards by which we can judge God's commands.

If we accept the divine command theory, the only way to resolve a moral issue such as cloning or affirmative action, or to decide if we should kill someone, would be to wait for God to speak to us. There are no other criteria for deciding right from wrong. If someone claims that God spoke to her and commanded her to oppose cloning, we have no independent criteria for judging whether she, in fact, heard God or not. Under the divine command theory, God's commands are arbitrary; they are based only on divine whim. Most of us, however, including most religious people, believe that actions such as rape or genocide are not arbitrary but a matter of reason.

Natural Law Theory

Natural law theorists disagree with the divine command theory. They maintain that God commands something *because* it is moral, not the other way around. Whereas religious teachings may affirm universal moral principles, morality exists independently of religion and God's commands. Morality is universally binding on everyone, no matter what their religion or lack thereof. Many, if not most, modern theologians and religious ethicists, including Martin Luther King Jr., subscribe to some form of natural law theory and reject divine command theory. Because natural law theory is based on universal principles, rather than on particular religious doctrines, it will be discussed in greater depth in the section on "Universal Moral Theories."

UNIVERSALITY AND RELIGIOUS ETHICS

In discussing moral issues, it may be tempting to dismiss a particular position as a religious issue, especially if we are unsure of how to defend our own position. For example, anti-slavery arguments were dismissed for many years as the rantings of fanatic Quakers who were trying to force their religious views on the southerners. Today certain moral positions on abortion and homosexuality are dismissed as religious views. The fact that a specific religion, however, whether it be Quaker or Roman Catholic or Hindu, takes an official stand on a certain moral issue such as slavery, abortion, or homosexuality does not imply that these issues are religious rather than moral issues. In discussing these and similar issues, we must be careful to separate the moral issues involved from specific religious doctrines.

Most theologians and philosophers maintain that morality exists independently of religion—that religious ethics is not fundamentally different from philosophical ethics. Although a moral code is incorporated into the doctrine of most religions, moral issues can be discussed without appealing to religion. When people who are religious use the terms *right* and *wrong,* they generally mean the same thing as someone who is not religious. Religious differences tend to fall away in most serious discussion of moral issues, such as slavery and abortion, not because religion isn't important to the participants but because moral disputes can be discussed and even resolved without bringing religion into the equation.[24]

EXERCISES

1. How, if at all, have your religious beliefs shaped your morality? Is there a difference between religious and secular morality in your life? What happens when your religion and your culture take radically different positions on a particular moral issue? How do you resolve the conflict?
2. Discuss a case in which someone justified a position that most people would consider immoral, such as mandatory euthanasia of a particular group of people, on the grounds that God commanded him or her to take this position. How would you respond to such a person?

3. Choose a controversial topic, such as abortion, euthanasia, or homosexuality, that is sometimes regarded as a religious issue. Can the morality of these practices be discussed without bringing in religious doctrine? Support your answer.

UNIVERSAL MORAL THEORIES

Two things fill the mind with ever new and increasing admiration and awe, the oftener and more steadily we reflect on them: the starry heavens above and the moral law within.

—Immanuel Kant, *Critique of Practical Reason* (1788)

Like natural law theorists, most moral philosophers believe that there are moral principles that are universal and objective. There are several different universalist theories, including natural law theory, utilitarianism, deontology, rights ethics, and virtue ethics. They all agree, however, that there are universal moral principles that are binding on all people regardless of their personal opinions, culture, or religion. These moral principles are *discovered* rather than created by people. Although individual interests or cultural customs, as noted in the example about the Kabloona, can influence how a particular moral principle is applied, fundamental moral principles are universal and transcultural.

Just as scientists disagree about the origin of the universe or the nature of gravity, people may disagree about the source and nature of these principles and sentiments. Some philosophers believe that we intuitively know what is morally right and wrong; others argue that reason is the primary source of moral knowledge. The fact of disagreement, however, does not mean that objective universal moral principles do not exist, anymore than it follows that disagreement about the source of the universe or the nature of gravity means that the universe and gravity do not exist.

There is a great deal of overlap between the different universalist theories. Instead of being mutually exclusive, like ethical subjectivism and cultural relativism, universalist theories, for the most part, emphasize one particular aspect of morality. In addition, almost all ethicists include aspects of more than one of these theories in their moral philosophy.

NATURAL LAW THEORY

According to the natural law theory, morality is grounded in rational human nature rather than in God's commands or personal feelings or cultural norms. We act morally for the same reasons God does. According to Thomas Aquinas (c. 1225–1274), it is through the "light of natural reason," which was given to us by God, that humans discern moral or natural law. These moral laws are very general and exist in the form of guidelines, such as the Golden Rule, the Ten Commandments, or respect for persons. Moral law is also teleological; it directs us toward a particular purpose or goal of the natural order. It is incumbent upon us as rational humans to discern how these moral laws apply at a particular time in history and in a particular case.

Although natural law theory is often identified with the Catholic Church, one need not be Catholic—or even believe in God—to subscribe to this theory. Aristotle believed that, rather than being created by God, the moral law has always been part of the natural order. Variations of natural law theory are also found in non-Western cultures, such as the Akan tribe of Ghana.[25]

Natural law ethicists reject cultural relativism. According to them a human or civil law (legislation) or tradition is moral only to the extent that it is in accord with natural or moral law. If a law is unjust, we may have a moral obligation to disobey it. A human law is unjust if it is degrading to humans, such as laws that permit torture or slavery. Laws that are discriminatory, such as segregation laws and, perhaps, affirmative action, may also be unjust. In engaging in civil disobedience, the dissident can use only moral means and must be nonviolent and open about his or her actions. Civil disobedience, on the grounds of obedience to a higher moral law, has a long history in this country. Members of animal liberation groups break into laboratories and set animals free; anti-abortionists block women from entering abortion clinics; anti-nuclear activists block roads leading to nuclear power plants and military establishments; during the Vietnam War, college students openly burned their draft cards to protest the war; and in the back of his Volkswagen van, Dr. Jack Kevorkian—despite repeated warnings from the courts—continued to assist terminally ill people in ending their lives. In each of these cases, the people engaged in civil disobedience justified their actions on the grounds of a higher moral law.

UTILITARIANISM

The happiness of the individuals, of whom a community is composed, that is their pleasures and their security, is the end and the sole end which the legislator ought to have in view.

—Jeremy Bentham, *Principles of Morals and Legislation* (1789)

Modern utilitarian theory was developed by English jurist, philosopher, and social reformer Jeremy Bentham (1748–1832) in response to the flagrant injustices and the desperate needs of workers. The industrial revolution, coupled with the widespread political unrest that culminated in the American and French revolutions, brought about tremendous changes in Western society. Bentham's goal was to develop a practical ethical theory that could provide a secure, scientific foundation for developing social policy and legislation.

Jeremy Bentham: Father of Modern Utilitarian Theory

Bentham's utilitarian theory was inspired primarily by the theories of Epicurus (341–270 B.C.E.) and David Hume (1711–1776). Hume and Epicurus both argued that certain traits are virtues because of their utility, or usefulness. Those traits that promote happiness have the greatest utility. Bentham took this one step further by arguing that utility provides the *only* source of political obligation for the state; it is utility alone that proved the test of what a law ought to be and which laws ought to be obeyed.

According to utilitarian theory, the morality of an action is determined solely by its consequences. Utilitarians maintain that the desire for happiness is universal and that we intuitively recognize it as the greatest good. Happiness, they argue, is synonymous with pleasure; unhappiness with pain. Actions are right, therefore, to the extent that they tend to promote overall happiness, and wrong to the extent that they tend to promote overall unhappiness. What counts is not just individual or even human happiness, but the sum of the happiness of the whole community of *sentient beings*—that is, those beings who are capable of feeling pleasure and pain.

The Principle of Utility: Promoting Happiness and Minimizing Pain

In determining which action or policy has the greatest utility (produces the greatest amount of happiness) we cannot rely on a majority vote, since people's choices are not always well informed. The majority, either because of ignorance about the nuances of a particular issue or because of irrational traditions and prejudice, may be mistaken about what is the best course of action. Nor can we rely on feelings alone, such as sympathy, because feelings can also mislead us. Instead we need a rational principle by which to guide our actions and choices. This principle is the *principle of utility,* or the *greatest happiness principle:*

> Actions are right in proportion as they tend to promote happiness, wrong as they tend to produce the reverse of happiness.[26]

In deciding which action is the most morally compelling, we need only measure the total amount of pleasure and the total amount of pain involved in the alternatives, and choose the alternative with the greatest net pleasure. Because the interests of all sentient beings count, the pain caused by human practices to other animals—such as animal agriculture, logging, and research using nonhuman animals—also has to be taken into consideration.

John Stuart Mill's Reformulation of Utilitarianism

Jeremy Bentham advocated equality and impartiality. He argued that all pleasures, whether those of a pig or a human, are equal. Equality, according to him, is not a description of actual equality of ability; rather, it is a moral ideal or prescription of how we ought to treat all sentient beings. The happiness of any one individual is no more or less important than that of any other.

Utilitarian John Stuart Mill disagreed with Bentham regarding the equality of pleasures, arguing instead that some pleasures are higher or more desirable than others. In particular, he claimed that the intellectual pleasures, such as listening to a symphony or reading a great book, are *qualitatively* better than those of the body, such as eating or enjoying a day basking in the sun. In other words, the intellectual pleasures experienced by humans, though they are less intense at times, are morally preferable to the simple pleasures of a pig. This is not to say that the pleasures of the pig should not count at all. In fact, utilitarians, such as Peter Singer, continue to be in the forefront of the animal-welfare movement.

Utilitarianism and Social Reform

Utilitarian theory has had a profound influence over the past two hundred years on social reform and the shaping of public policy. Jeremy Bentham was an advocate of animal welfare and prison reform. John Stuart Mill spoke out eloquently on behalf of equal opportunities for women, freedom of the press, and the legalization of homosexual acts between consenting adults. Contemporary discussions of capital punishment, euthanasia, animal welfare, genetic engineering, pornography, legalization of drugs, and environmental ethics all have utilitarian components.

Unlike most moral theories, utilitarian theory adopts a practical bottom-up approach. It begins with the actual happiness of the people and other sentient beings rather than imposing morality and social ideals on them from above. The principle of utility requires that we do not take refuge in ideological slogans, cultural traditions, or personal opinion, but that we instead examine our position on moral issues in light of the actual consequences. This entails overcoming our ignorance regarding the extent to which our lifestyle is built upon the suffering of other people or animals.

Utilitarianism requires that we first do our research. For example, is capital punishment, in fact, an effective deterrent? Does viewing pornography and violence, in fact, cause people to behave more violently? Does permitting people who are openly homosexual to teach in schools, in fact, make children more likely to become homosexuals?

We also need to look at possible consequences of our decisions. Would censorship of hate speech and pornography cause more harm than allowing hate speech and access to pornography? Would legalizing recreational drugs result in more or in less drug abuse and drug-related crime? Would condoning voluntary euthanasia put us on the slippery slope toward involuntary euthanasia? The slippery-slope argument applies to issues with large gray areas in which it is difficult to draw a distinct line between what is morally acceptable and what is morally unacceptable. In "The Question of Human Cloning," John Robertson raises the question of whether seemingly valid uses of cloning might open the door to undesirable uses of the technology.

Finally, we need to balance harm and benefit. Is the harm that human activities cause to the environment and to other animals justified by the benefit the products bring to humans? Would permitting parents to genetically engineer their children result in more overall happiness for society, or less?

The Strengths and Limitations of Utilitarianism

Utilitarian theory is a powerful tool for formulating social policies. It is also a reminder that tradition alone cannot serve as a foundation for morality.

One of the greatest strengths of utilitarian theory is that it challenges us to rethink our traditional notions about moral community. If we are going to exclude or marginalize people or other animals, we have to offer a rational justification for our decision. For example, we cannot exclude other animals from moral consideration based on irrational religious doctrines that claim that only humans are created in the image of God. Nor can we justify expending expensive limited resources on humans who are no longer sentient simply on the grounds that they are human.

The utilitarian insistence on equality and impartiality is both one of its greatest strengths and one of its weaknesses. Justice as impartiality assumes that people living in a community share a common conception of the good. In reality, however, people have different needs and goals. The capitalist's idea of happiness, for example, is not the same as that of the religious contemplative. John Rawls (b. 1921), a critic of utilitarian theory, also points out that justice demands not only impartiality, but also that we treat people fairly and in proportion to their needs and merits. A person who works hard deserves a raise or reward simply because he has done a good job. Utilitarians, in contrast, are not con-

UTILITARIAN GUIDELINES FOR THINKING ABOUT MORAL ISSUES

- **Determine who or what will be affected:** Who will be caused pain or pleasure?
- **Look at the possible consequences:** What are both the long-term and short-term consequences of the different alternatives?
- **Maximize happiness:** Which solution will bring about the greatest net happiness?
- **Minimize pain:** Which solution will cause the least pain and suffering to those affected by the decision?

cerned with what a person deserves, but whether giving rewards based on merit produces the most utility.

There are other desirable goals in life besides pleasure. Another criticism of utilitarian theory is its claim that pleasure is the only intrinsic good. Most people agree that goals such as friendship, spiritual growth, and appreciation of the aesthetic are also desirable. On the other hand, utilitarian theory reminds us that one of the primary purposes of morality is not to make our lives more tedious or to make us feel more guilt-ridden, but to improve the quality of our lives by promoting ideals and behavior that provide optimal conditions for us to flourish, both as individuals and as a community.

By claiming that only consequences count, utilitarianism underplays the importance of individual integrity and personal responsibility. In considering only consequences when determining the rightness and wrongness of an action, utilitarian theory may sometimes require us to act in ways that violate our integrity and our conscience. For example, say that a particularly heinous murder, which the community believes to have been racially motivated, has created racial tension, looting, and killing in that community. The police have been unable to find the murderer. It also seems fairly certain that the community rampage will continue until someone is brought to "justice" and given the death penalty. In desperation the police arrest a man—an unsavory character who has a history of petty crime—whom they know is not guilty of the murder. As a judge, you can bring about more pleasure and restore social harmony by convicting the man and giving him the death penalty. What should you do? The utilitarian would probably have to say: Send the man to the electric chair as a means of restoring social order. But our actions do not happen just as part of a wider context of the general good; each of us is also responsible for what we do as individuals.

Because only pleasure has intrinsic value, utilitarian theory allows us to use people as a means toward that end, rather than requiring us to respect people as ends in themselves. In the previous example, the accused man was used as a means to social harmony, as was the judge. In addition, to pressure the judge into bringing about the death of an innocent person to prevent the death of others is to treat the judge as a means only.

Utilitarian theory is not so much wrong as incomplete. Despite its limitations utilitarian theory provides valuable guidelines for discussions of issues in social ethics. Although other moral philosophers may regard other moral considerations as more fundamental than the principle of utility, as deontologist John Rawls writes: "all ethical doctrines worth our attention take consequences into account in judging rightness. One which did not would simply be irrational, crazy."[27]

EXERCISES

1. Utilitarian theory is frequently used to formulate social policies regarding issues like AIDS testing and distribution of social benefits such as scholarships and medical care. Find some examples of utilitarian thinking in current public or college policies. Explain why these policies represent utilitarian thinking.
2. Does social ethics require a different strategy than personal moral decision making? If so, how do the two strategies differ? On what grounds can you justify these differences?
3. Do you agree with Mill that human intellectual pleasures have greater moral value than the pleasures of other animals? Discuss how adopting either Bentham's or Mill's position would influence public policy on the use of nonhuman animals to benefit humans.
4. Both Confucianism and modern care ethics teach that our concern should be strongest for our family and friends. Utilitarian theory, in contrast, teaches that our concern for others' happiness should be impartial. Discuss these two competing concepts of moral obligation. Do we have as strong a moral obligation to benefit or increase the happiness of people we don't know as we do to our own friends and family? Support your answer using examples from your own life.

DEONTOLOGY: THE ETHICS OF DUTY

> *Look to your own duty; do not tremble before it . . .*
> —Bhagavad Gita

Deontological theories regard duty as the basis of morality. *Duty,* or doing what is right for its own sake, is the foundation of morality. There are strong strands of deontology in Confucianism and Hindu ethics as well as in many Western philosophies.

Immanuel Kant and the Categorical Imperative

Deontologist Immanuel Kant (1724–1804) believed that we should do our duty purely out of the good will, not because of rewards or punishment or other consequences. A person of good will can be depended upon to do what is right, even when other motives are absent. An action that is done out of sympathy or because one enjoys helping others, rather than out of a sense of duty, may be praiseworthy, but according to Kant it has no moral value.

Kant also argued that if there is a universal moral law and if it is to be morally binding, it must be based on reason. According to Kant, the most fundamental moral principle is the *categorical imperative.* He came up with two formulations of the categorical imperative. The first formulation states:

> Act only on that maxim by which you can at the same time will that it should become a universal law.

Kant believed that all rational beings would recognize the categorical imperative as universally binding. Because reason provides the foundation of morality, this makes humans and other rational beings very special in Kant's mind. Whereas rational beings have free will, everything else in nature operates according to physical laws. Because autonomy is essential for dignity, only rational beings have intrinsic worth. Rational beings can therefore never be treated as expendable, but must be treated with dignity as ends in themselves. This ideal is summed up in the second formulation of the categorical imperative:

> So act as to treat humanity, whether in thine own person or in that of any other, in every case as an end in itself, never as a means only.

The categorical imperative is a formal principle that provides a framework for deriving moral maxims or duties, such as "Do not lie" and "Help others in distress," that can be applied in specific situations. When deciding if a particular maxim creates a moral duty, we need only ask, keeping in mind that rational beings must be treated with dignity, whether we would will that it be a universal law.

The *Golden Rule* in Judeo-Christian ethics, and the *law of reciprocity* in Confucian ethics are both similar to the categorical imperative. The Golden Rule states, "Do unto others as you would have them do unto you." Similarly, when Confucius (551–479 B.C.E.) was asked if there was a single principle that can be used as a guide to conduct in our lives, he replied, "Do not impose on others what you yourself do not desire."[28]

Universalization

Universalization is one of the trademarks of morality: Moral maxims or duties, by their very nature, apply to everyone and under all circumstances. It is inconsistent, for example, to argue that it is wrong for others to lie but that it is okay for us. If it is wrong to lie, it is wrong for everyone. If we could make an exception of ourselves whenever it is to our advantage, the moral rule "Do not lie" would be meaningless.

Many people become easily confused in discussions of moral issues because their basic moral assumptions do not meet the standard of universality. They may feel tricked and frustrated when what they believed was a carefully thought-out argument ends up supporting a position they never intended to support.

For example, in the study of how college students judge social issues, 35 percent of students stated that abortion is immoral because life starts at conception; therefore, abortion violates the moral maxim "It is wrong to take an innocent life."[29] When asked whether abortion would be morally permissible for a woman who was raped, however, many students said yes. Others in the pro-life group stated that abortion was morally wrong because the fetus was a person, but at the same time added that abortion should be legal because it is a personal choice. Their inconsistency can be further exposed by asking whether killing children after birth should also be a personal choice.

Twenty-seven percent of students in the study responded that abortion is not immoral because "abortion is a personal choice." Like the pro-life students, however, many of the pro-choice students were inconsistent when it came to universalizing their fundamental moral maxims or assumptions. When asked if abortion was morally acceptable for sex selection, many of the pro-choice students said no. In other words, they were unwilling to universalize their moral maxim "Abortion is a personal choice."

Effective analysis and discussion of moral issues requires that we first examine our basic assumptions about what is a good moral maxim. A good moral maxim must be consistent with the demands of the categorical imperative. Are we willing, in good conscience, to consistently apply our moral maxims? If not, why not? If we are unwilling to universalize a particular moral maxim—that is, apply it consistently in all similar cases—we should either modify the maxim or toss it out.

Unlike the categorical imperative itself, specific moral maxims are open for debate. For example, many people question whether we would want to universalize, as did Kant, a maxim that states, "Do not commit suicide." Kant, of course, was writing in the days before medical technology could artificially extend the dying process. Besides problems with universality, some people believe that refusing to help someone die who is suffering terribly and is unable to carry out his own suicide is disrespectful and, hence, violates the second formulation of the categorical imperative. What moral maxims, then, can we come up with for shaping a policy on euthanasia and assisted suicide? Would we want to universalize a maxim that states, "Physicians have a duty to carry out the requests of their patients"? This may sound good in some situations, but there may be others in which it would not be, such as when a student who is temporarily depressed because she got a poor grade on an exam requests medical assistance in committing suicide. What if a patient demands an expensive and potentially dangerous treatment for a minor illness? In fact, further consideration of this maxim reveals so many exceptions that it proves to be of little use in making moral decisions.

W. D. Ross: Duties Are Prima Facie

Kant argued that universalizing moral maxims requires that they be absolutely binding in all circumstances. If it is wrong to lie, then, according to him, it is *always* wrong to lie, no matter what the circumstance. He also believed that because morality is based on reason, there could never be a conflict between moral duties.

Most moral philosophers, while agreeing with Kant that moral duties or maxims are universal, disagree that they are also absolute. Moral duties are prima facie rather than absolute. *Prima facie* duties are moral duties that may on occasion be overridden by stronger moral claims.

According to W. D. Ross (1877–1971), moral duties cannot be absolute, because there are particular situations in which they come into conflict. The moral duty of nonmaleficence, for example, could conflict with the moral duty to keep a promise when keeping that promise could result in death or injury. Because duties are context-bound, the particular circumstances and possible consequences will affect which moral duties are most important in any given situation.

Unlike Kant, Ross also believed that consequences matter when applying moral principles. Moral duties, however, cannot be overridden by nonmoral duties or considerations such as obeying the law, financial success, or getting good grades in college. When there is a conflict between moral and nonmoral duties, we ought to do what is morally right.

Seven Prima Facie Duties

Ross came up with a list of seven prima facie duties that he claimed we intuitively know. These include duties concerning the consequences of our actions, such as the duty of *nonmaleficence* (do no harm) and the duty of *beneficence* (increase happiness). These two

---

 W. D. ROSS'S SEVEN PRIMA FACIE DUTIES

Future-Looking Duties
Beneficence the duty to do good acts and to promote happiness
Nonmaleficence the duty to do no harm and to prevent harm

Duties Based on Past Obligations
Fidelity duties arising from past commitments and promises
Reparation duties that stem from past harms to others
Gratitude duties based on past favors and unearned services

Ongoing Duties
Self-Improvement the duty to improve our knowledge and virtue
Justice the duty to give each person equal consideration

---

duties are also recognized by utilitarians. *Ahimsa,* or the principle of nonviolence, in Buddhist ethics, is a version of the principle of nonmaleficence and is the most fundamental moral principle in Buddhist ethics. Buddhists oppose meat-eating because it violates this principle.

Although almost all ethicists agree that we have a positive duty to refrain from harming others, they disagree about whether we have a positive duty of beneficence—that is, to perform altruistic actions. Both Judith Jarvis Thomson in her essay "A Defense of Abortion" and Margaret Pabst Batten in "The Case for Euthanasia" discuss the question of whether we have a positive duty of beneficence, and, if so, what the limits of this duty are.

We also have duties that stem from past obligations. The duty of *fidelity* arises from past commitments and promises. We have a commitment to our fellow students, to our parents, and to our children, independent of the pleasure we may get from them at the moment. The duty of fidelity or filial piety is particularly important in Confucian ethics and generally takes precedence over individual liberty rights. Some philosophers argue that part of the physician's commitment to his or her patients is to assist dying patients who request assistance in committing suicide. Others, such as Daniel Callahan, argue that the duty of nonmaleficence is more compelling in this case and that physicians should refuse to carry out actions that cause lethal harm to their patients.

The duty of *gratitude* is evoked when we receive gifts or unearned favors and services from others. Some environmental ethicists argue that we have a duty of gratitude toward the earth which nourishes us.

The duty of *reparation* is also based on past actions. Reparation requires that we make up for past harms we have caused others. Affirmative action is an attempt to make up for past harms to women and minorities. Some philosophers argue that affirmative action is unjust and that justice in this case is a more compelling duty than reparation.

Finally, there are two ongoing duties: self-improvement and justice. *Self-improvement,* as a moral duty, entails striving to improve our moral knowledge and our virtue. Self-improvement requires that we work to overcome our ignorance by becoming well informed about moral issues. It also requires that we be open to new ideas. In addition, being a virtuous person requires that we use our moral knowledge to make this world a better place.

Justice

Justice is the seventh prima facie duty. Many philosophers consider justice to be our most important social duty. The ongoing duty of *justice* requires that we give each person equal consideration. Because laws and social institutions are generally the agencies for balancing conflicting interests, the issue of justice is closely tied with that of "the good society." As noted earlier, however, not all laws are just, nor are all demands for justice addressed by law.

There are two types of justice: retributive justice and distributive justice. *Retributive justice* requires punishment for wrongdoing in proportion to the magnitude of the crime. Both Immanuel Kant and Ernest van den Haag argue that the only suitable punishment for murder is the death penalty. Hugo Adam Bedeau and Helen Prejean, on the other hand, in their readings at the end of Chapter 6 claim that the death penalty is immoral because it violates the underlying moral principle of respect for persons. Buddhist philosophers also oppose the death penalty as being in conflict with the principle of nonviolence *(ahimsa)*.

Distributive justice refers to the fair distribution of benefits and burdens in a society. Benefits include education, medical care, police protection, legal representation, and economic opportunities. Taxes, jury duty, and military conscription are examples of shared burdens. Distributive justice becomes a concern when (1) there are conflicts of interest and (2) people have competing claims for certain limited or scarce societal goods. Because there are not enough good jobs, college scholarships, and medical care for everyone, the distribution of these goods is an issue of justice. For example, John Hardwig supports euthanasia on the grounds that it is unjust that those who are dying long, lingering deaths get such a disproportionate share of medical and other resources. He claims that in cases such as these, we have a duty to die.

Distributive justice also requires impartiality. We should treat equals equally and unequals in proportion to their differences. In a just society, we all deserve a fair opportunity to pursue our goals. Charles R. Lawrence III argues that hate speech creates an atmosphere on campuses in which certain groups of people are denied this opportunity. Aristotle, on the other hand, focuses more on merit as the key criterion in distributive justice. He was opposed to democracy, preferring instead an oligarchy, or an elitist political system based on merit. Those who are most talented and most virtuous, and who have contributed most to society, ought to get a greater share of the privileges and opportunities.

John Rawls and Justice as Fairness

In his book *A Theory of Justice,* John Rawls maintains that justice requires not only impartiality but also treating people fairly and in proportion to their needs as well as their merits. There are inequalities of birth and natural endowment (what Rawls calls the "natural lottery") and historic circumstances, such as slavery, that create undeserved disadvantages for certain people. Simply redistributing opportunities or wealth does not solve the root problem as long as the underlying conditions that disadvantage certain people still exist. What is needed, Rawls argues, is a change in the social system so that it does not permit these injustices to occur in the first place.

Rawls's solution is to base justice upon a social contract that is unbiased and impartial. To do this Rawls proposes that we use a conceptual device that he calls the "veil of ignorance," where everyone is ignorant of the advantages or disadvantages he or she will receive in this life. Under these conditions, Rawls argues, all rational people would agree upon the following two principles of justice:

1. Each person is to have an equal right to the most extensive basic liberty compatible with a similar liberty for others.

2. Social and economic inequalities are to be arranged so that both are (a) reasonably expected to be to everyone's advantage and (b) attached to positions and offices open to all.

Rawls's theory of justice has been used to reform social institutions and to develop policy in areas such as health-care reform and education. Sissela Bok, for example, argues that we must first alleviate the extraordinary inequalities in the way medical care is distributed to people at the end of their lives before we can think of moving toward legalizing voluntary euthanasia. While it is, of course, impossible to truly forget our advantages and disadvantages in this life, the "veil of ignorance" provides a powerful conceptual tool for thinking about different moral issues from an impartial point of view.

Moral Dilemmas and Resolving Moral Issues

Any of the above duties can come into conflict with one another. When moral duties and other moral concerns come into conflict, we have a *moral dilemma.* Because moral duties are prima facie, when we have an issue that involves a moral conflict, we must carefully weigh each duty, decide which duties are the most compelling for that particular issue, and try to arrive at a resolution that honors as many duties as possible.

According to Ross, there is no set formula for determining which action we should take in a moral dilemma. Whereas the general duties themselves may be self-evident, judgment about our duties in a particular case is not. Because of this we need to use reason and creativity in making judgments about our duty in a particular case. Ross believed that this lack of clarity is due to the nature of moral decision making, which, he claims, is more like creating a work of art than solving a mathematical problem. When there is a moral dilemma, no solution is going to be completely satisfactory. Different people may come to different solutions because they prioritize duties differently. The purpose of moral deliberation in these cases is to arrive at the *best* solution or, if this doesn't occur, the best possible alternatives.

Strengths and Limitations of Deontology

Kant's deontology, because of its abstractness and lack of specificity, suffered a decline in popularity during the past century. It is currently making a comeback, however, in part because of disillusionment with ethical relativism. Many contemporary philosophers, such as John Rawls and Sissela Bok, while adopting the basic premises of deontology, have revised it or combined it with the strengths of other theories, such as social contract theory and utilitarianism, so it is more useful in everyday moral decision making.

DEONTOLOGY: CONSIDERATIONS FOR THINKING ABOUT MORAL ISSUES

- **Universality:** Are we willing to universalize our rules and assumptions?
- **Reciprocity:** How would we want to be treated in a similar situation?
- **Respect:** Is our position on an issue respectful of all persons affected, or does it entail treating some as a means only?
- **Impartiality:** Are we treating equals equally?
- **Identify relevant duties:** What are the relevant duties in this particular issue?
- **Prioritize duties:** If there is a conflict of duties, which duties are the most important?

Kantian deontology, with its claim that duties are absolute and that there are no conflicts between moral rules, is unable to provide guidance in situations where there is a moral dilemma. A good moral theory, as noted earlier, should provide guidance for making real-life moral decisions. Although prima facie deontology has overcome this limitation to some extent, it has been criticized for failing to provide a strategy for ranking conflicting duties.

Deontology sacrifices community in the name of individual autonomy. In Kantian deontology in particular, the private life replaces the public life as the sphere of moral actions. According to philosophers such as Confucius and Aristotle, humans are first and foremost social or political beings; humans need the community in order to be virtuous. German philosopher Georg Hegel (1770–1831), Kant's contemporary, also questioned Kant's belief that individual autonomy and rationality are possible prior to membership in an ethical community. Kant's assumption that people are basically autonomous, private units who are free to carry out the moral law fails to take into consideration that we are all part of a wider social network of relationships that places restraints on the actions of some people and bestows privilege on others.

The deontologist's overriding concern with duty and justice fails to take into account the role of sentiment and care in morality. Feminist care ethicists, such as Carol Gilligan and Nel Noddings, claim that deontology, or what they call the "justice perspective," is a distinctly male approach that ignores caring in relationships. Practical morality, they argue, is constructed dialectically through interaction with others, not merely by an autonomous examination of the dictates of reason. Care ethicists also claim that reason alone is insufficient both to provide us with practical guidance and to motivate us to act morally. Indeed, as studies with psychopaths have shown, reason without the ability to empathize with others seems unable to produce the categorical imperative or to inspire us to respect others.

Deontology ignores consequences. Kant's denial that consequences are morally relevant has been criticized by utilitarians as well as by modern deontologists. Even if we agree that consequences are not as important as duty, most philosophers still believe that they must be taken into consideration. Indeed, John Stuart Mill points out that the categorical imperative by its very nature requires that we take consequences into account when adopting moral rules. According to Mill, rational people would not universalize a moral rule that would harm, rather than benefit, the moral community.

Few philosophers accept Kant's deontology in its entirety; nevertheless, Kantian deontology is one of the most, if not *the* most, influential and fertile moral philosophies in modern history. Despite its shortcomings, the strengths and richness of deontology far outshine its weaknesses.

It would be a mistake to consider any philosophical, or even scientific, theory a finished or complete statement about a particular phenomenon. One of the characteristics of a good theory is that it is open-ended and generates further thought. In this respect deontology has made important contributions to the study of ethics. In particular, with its emphasis on the dignity of the individual, deontology has had a major influence on the development of rights ethics in Western and non-Western philosophies.

EXERCISES

1. List some of the fundamental moral assumptions or maxims that you use in discussing moral issues such as capital punishment, affirmative action, or animal rights. Examine each of these maxims in light of the imperative of universality.
2. Select a moral issue that involves a moral dilemma. List the duties that support the "pro" side of the issue, then list the moral duties that support the "con" side of the issue. Which duties are the most compelling? Discuss possible solutions that take the most duties into account.
3. Is it morally acceptable to euthanize people who have terminal illnesses and who request physician-assisted suicide? Is it morally acceptable to euthanize people with burdensome illnesses, such as coma or severe brain damage, who are unable to give their consent? Discuss the contributions both utilitarians and deontologists would make to a debate on this issue.
4. In 1997 Ron Fitzsimmons, executive director of the National Coalition of Abortion Providers, confessed that he had lied about the number of late-term abortions performed, which are far more frequent than the public had been led to believe. He and his colleagues also admitted that many of these abortions were being performed on healthy women, not only those who were dying or whose fetuses had severe deformities. Some pro-choice advocates defended Fitzsimmons, arguing that the means—lying—justified the ends—keeping late-term abortions legal and available to all women. How would both Kantian and prima facie deontologists respond to Fitzsimmons's actions? Compare and contrast their responses with that of a utilitarian.

RIGHTS-BASED ETHICS

> *We hold these truths to be self-evident, that all men are created equal, that they are endowed by their Creator with certain inalienable Rights, that among these are Life, Liberty and the Pursuit of Happiness.*
>
> —*United States Declaration of Independence* (July 4, 1776)

Before the eighteenth century, the focus of moral theory was primarily on duty. The language of rights in Western philosophy emerged primarily in the context of the growing confrontation with the principle of absolute sovereignty. Rights ethics enjoyed a revival following World War II and the Holocaust. In 1948 the United Nations issued the Universal Declaration of Human Rights as "a common standard of achievement for all peoples and all nations." Its preamble states that human rights are not simply a Western creation but belong to people everywhere.

Moral rights are not the same as legal rights, although in a just society the two would overlap. Moral rights instead are generally seen as either (1) natural and existing independently or (2) derived from duties.

John Locke's Natural Rights Ethics

The philosophical doctrine of natural rights first appeared in Western philosophy in the seventeenth century as a demand for equality for all people. According to natural rights ethicists such as John Locke (1632–1704), these rights stem from our human nature and are self-evident and God-given. Humans alone have moral rights because of our creation in the image of God. These natural rights include a right to own property, a right to marry and have children, and a right to punish someone who has wronged us. The right of private punishment, which exists in a state of nature, is turned over to the state when we agree to form a civil society. The freedom or right to pursue our interests without interference is limited to legitimate interests; that is, those interests that do not harm other people by violating their similar and equal interests.

The doctrine of natural rights had a profound influence on the thinking of Thomas Jefferson, who drafted the Declaration of Independence. The influence of natural rights in the United States is especially evident in the way that moral rights are generally equated with human rights and are discussed without any reference to correlative duties. For example, freedom of speech, especially in the cases of pornography and hate speech, is sometimes depicted as a natural right that exists independently of any duty of nonmaleficence or concerns for the harm caused to others by the speech.

Whether hate speech constitutes a legitimate interest that should be protected is up for debate. In Chapter 9, Jonathan Rauch argues that hate speech should be protected but Charles R. Lawrence III argues that we do not have a right to use hate speech because it causes harm to those targeted by it.

Ayn Rand and Laissez-Faire Capitalism

Ayn Rand (1905–1982) is one of the foremost contemporary defenders of natural rights ethics. According to her, the doctrine of natural rights created the possibility of free societies. The United States, she argued, has the honor of being the first society created upon natural rights ethics; only through free enterprise and laissez-faire capitalism can individual rights and a free society be sustained.

Like Locke, Rand believed that rights exist independently of duties. Moral rights define and protect our freedoms without imposing obligations on anyone else. For example, the right to property does not entail an obligation to provide people with property; the right to life does not entail an obligation to provide people with the necessities of life.

Although she agreed with John Locke that rights exist prior to and independent of duties, she disagreed with him about the source of these rights. The source of our rights, she argues, is not God, but man's rational nature. Moral rights, according to Rand, define and protect our freedoms without imposing obligations on anybody else. According to Rand, humans are fundamentally solitary individuals, each pursuing his or her own rational self-interests. The ideal society, consequently, is one that protects people's individual liberty rights so they can freely pursue their interests.

Rights and Duties

Most philosophers disagree with natural rights ethics. They maintain that moral rights do not stand on their own but are linked to or even, some deontologists argue, derived from duties. For example, the duty of nonmaleficence requires that people refrain from interfering with other people's rights to pursue their interests. Rights, as noted earlier, are also limited by the duty of nonmaleficence. The duty of fidelity entails a right to expect others to keep their promises and the right of children to receive proper care from their parents. Utilitarians, deontologists, natural law ethicists, and Buddhist ethicists all see rights as entailing duties. According to duty-based rights ethics, rights are something to which we are *entitled*. Rights protect us as persons who ought to be treated with respect. Because we are entitled to certain rights, others have a duty to honor these rights.

Natural rights ethicists like Locke, in contrast, maintain that our possession of a right does not imply that someone else has a duty to honor that right. Under natural rights ethics, being able to actually claim our rights boils down to having the power—generally political or economic power—to assert ourselves. Because the environment and nonhuman animals lack the power of assertion, they lack rights.

Unlike John Locke, philosophers such as Tom Regan argue that rights stem from interests. Regan maintains that because nonhuman animals have interests, such as not being confined or eaten, they also have rights that we have a duty to respect. Similarly, Catharine MacKinnon argues that women have a right not to be raped, molested, and used solely for pleasure and profit; therefore, publishers have a corresponding duty not to produce hard-core pornography.

Liberty and Welfare Rights

Moral rights are generally divided into liberty rights and welfare rights. *Welfare rights* entail the right to receive certain social goods such as education, medical care, and police protection. Welfare rights are important because without a minimal standard of living or education, we cannot pursue our legitimate interests. Socialist and Marxist countries place more emphasis on welfare rights.

Liberty rights, in contrast, entail the right to be left alone to pursue our legitimate interests without interference from the government or other people. Liberty rights include autonomy, privacy, freedom of speech, freedom to own property, freedom from harassment and confinement, and freedom to choose our own career. Our "legitimate interests" are those that do not violate other people's similar and equal interests. For example, a misogynist may have an interest in keeping women out of the workplace, but this does not give him the right to discriminate in hiring, because doing so would violate women's rights to equal opportunity.

In the United States, we tend to place more emphasis on liberty rights. Our privacy rights, freedom of speech, and right to own property, for example, are carefully protected. People, such as Ayn Rand, who emphasize liberty rights are known as *libertarians*. Libertarians believe that personal *autonomy*—the freedom to make our own decisions—is the highest moral value. According to libertarians, respect for others means allowing them freedom to develop and exercise the capacities that are necessary for them to pursue their concept of the good. This includes freedom of speech and privacy as well as freedom from coercive interference from the government. Robertson likewise argues that since cloning does not harm anyone or violate their legitimate interests, it should be permitted.

According to deontologists our liberty rights are limited by our duty to respect ourselves; we do not have a right to harm ourselves or neglect our own welfare. Kant, for example, regarded suicide as "an abomination because it involves the misuse of freedom to destroy oneself and one's freedom."[30] In contrast, Dr. Jack Kevorkian, a libertarian, considers suicide to be one of our most fundamental rights.

The emphasis on liberty rights at the expense of welfare rights, however, tends to handicap those who are unable to assert their liberty rights either because of natural disadvantages or because of traditional roles that limit their options. Supporters of affirmative action, such as Bernard Boxill, point out that merely being granted access to societal goods, such as jobs and education, will not ensure that people will actually be able to purchase the goods they need or pursue an education without facing discrimination or harassment.

Like duties, most rights are prima facie. Rights may come into conflict with one another or with duties. A white man's right to a college education may conflict with a duty of reparation toward African Americans who have been harmed by our public education system. The welfare rights of nonhuman animals, if they have rights, may come into conflict with our search for a cure for cancer using nonhuman animals as subjects.

The Strengths and Limitations of Rights Ethics

Rights ethics is an important component of a comprehensive moral theory. Nevertheless, there are some shortcomings, especially with natural rights ethics, which claims that rights ethics can stand on its own.

The theological basis of natural rights ethics, which privileges humans as a special creation, is difficult, if not impossible, to justify on either rational philosophical or empirical grounds. Natural rights ethics has given a moral blessing to the exploitation of other animals and the environment. The reduction of nonhuman animals and the environment to the status of resources for humans has had a devastating effect on the environment.

The separation of rights from duties fails to take into account the limitations placed on marginalized groups by societal traditions. The claim that all people are created equal has too often been treated as a description rather than a moral ideal. Natural rights ethicists such as Rand and Locke assume that in a free society everyone is equally able to pursue their concept of the good life. Not all people are equally capable of asserting their rights, however. Traditional roles, for example, give men and people born into wealthy families greater access to resources, thus disadvantaging women and poorer people in a free marketplace. If the right to accumulate property is not constrained by the duty of distributive justice, the gap between the haves and have-nots will become greater and greater.

The claim that pursuing liberty rights does not impose obligations on others is false. The libertarian model of rights actually depends upon the backing of an extensive and expensive legal and police system. Liberty rights to own property and businesses, for example, are protected by tax monies, most of which are forcibly taken from people who are too poor to own property.

RIGHTS ETHICS: CONSIDERATIONS FOR THINKING ABOUT MORAL ISSUES

- **Identify the relevant rights:** What are the liberty rights in the moral issue? What welfare rights are at stake in the issue?
- **Identify the legitimate interests:** Does exercising any of these rights infringe on the equal and similar rights of others?
- **Prioritize rights and duties:** If there is a conflict of rights and/or duties, which ones are most important?

The assertion by natural rights ethicists that rights are self-evident leaves us with no criteria for determining which claims are legitimate rights. The belief that rights need no justification has led to a proliferation of demands for certain rights. Former U.S. ambassador to the United Nations Jeane Kirkpatrick (b. 1926) compares the current proliferation of rights declarations to "writing letters to Santa Claus"; they are based on wishful thinking rather than any reasonable expectations.[31] Without any criteria for justifying rights, there is no way to decide which rights are frivolous and which should be taken seriously. For this reason most philosophers argue that rights must be grounded in duties and, in particular, from the fundamental duty of respect for the dignity of others.

Although rights ethics is problematic if it is used as a complete explanation of morality, rights are important because they protect our dignity as persons. If we do not have rights, all our claims to be treated with respect simply amount to requests for favors and privileges. If there are no rights to freedom and equal opportunity, we need to make a case for having our freedom or equal opportunities.

Although few philosophers deny that rights are morally meaningful, the origin and nature of rights have been the focus of considerable debate. The claim that rights are based on the principle of equality has prompted animal rights advocates such as Tom Regan to question why this principle should not also be extended to other animals. Buddhist ethicists go even further and extend the concept of rights to all of nature. The extension of the concept of rights to all humans—and even to nonhumans—has been a difficult endeavor, but one that has been very fruitful in calling our attention to the dignity of those who are different from us.

EXERCISES

1. Are rights self-evident, as natural rights ethicists argue? List some rights that you consider to be important in making moral decisions. On what grounds do you justify these rights?
2. Referring to the list of rights you created in question 1, which are welfare rights? Which are liberty rights?
3. Do you agree with Ayn Rand that capitalism is the only system that can protect our individual freedoms? Does capitalism benefit not only the powerful but also those who have the least power in our society? Or does it merely further empower those who are already privileged? Support your answers.
4. Do we have a moral right to property and inheritance acquired through someone else's forced labor, such as slave labor and the exploitation of people living under

conditions of poverty? If not, do we have a duty of reparation to those who were forced to work to provide us with our property? Explain.

5. Select a moral issue that involves a conflict between rights or between rights and duties. List the rights and duties that support the "pro" side of the issue, then list the rights and duties that support the "con" side of the issue. Which rights and/or duties are the most compelling? Discuss possible solutions that take the greatest number of rights into account.

VIRTUE ETHICS

The rule of virtue can be compared to the Pole Star which commands the homage of the multitude of Stars without leaving its place.

—Confucius, *The Analects,* book 4:4

Virtue ethics emphasizes right being over right action. The sort of people we are constitutes the heart of our moral life. More important than the rules or principles we follow is our character. Virtue ethics, however, is not an alternative to ethical theories that stress right conduct, such as utilitarianism and deontological theories. Rather, virtue ethics and theories of right action complement each other.

A *virtue* is an admirable character trait or disposition to habitually act in a manner than benefits ourselves and others. The actions of virtuous people stem from a respect and concern for the well-being of themselves and others. Compassion, courage, generosity, loyalty, and honesty are all examples of virtues.

Virtues are often spoken of as though they were discrete, individual traits; but virtue is more correctly defined as an overarching quality of goodness that gives unity and integrity to a person's character. Because virtuous people are motivated to act in ways that benefit society, the cultivation of a virtuous character is an important aspect of social ethics. For example, generous people are more likely to act in ways that benefit those who are least well-off in society. Honesty is an important social virtue because without honest communication, society would soon collapse. According to both Aristotle and Confucius, a good social policy or resolution to a social issue is one that encourages the development of virtue among people. "If the will be set on virtue," Confucius taught, "there will be no practice of wickedness."[32]

Buddhism, care ethics, and the moral philosophies of David Hume, Aristotle, and Jesus of Nazareth are often classified as virtue ethics. Confucian ethics has strong strands of both virtue ethics and deontology. The ancient Greek ethicists, like most Eastern ethicists, focused primarily on virtue and character rather than on duty and principles.

Aristotle: Reason and Virtue

Aristotle divided virtues into two broad categories: intellectual virtues and moral virtues. The intellectual virtues are cultivated through growth and experience; the moral virtues through habit. Wisdom is the most important virtue because it makes all other virtues (intellectual and moral) possible. The role of habituation, including repeated exposure to particular types of stimuli and behavior, in the development of virtuous and

---

🖋 ARISTOTLE'S DOCTRINE OF THE MEAN [33]

Deficit (Vice)	Mean (Virtue)	Excess (Vice)
cowardice	courage	foolhardiness
inhibition	temperance	overindulgence/ intemperance
miserliness	liberality	prodigality/extravagance
shabbiness	magnificence	bad taste/vulgarity
unambitiousness	proper pride	ambitiousness
poor spiritedness	gentleness	irascibility
peevishness/surlyness	friendliness	obsequiousness/flattery
malice	righteous indignation	envy
irony	truthfulness	boastfulness
boorishness	wittiness	buffoonery
shamelessness	modesty	shame

---

vicious behavior is one of the questions involved in censorship of pornography and campus restrictions on drinking and drug use.

Aristotle believed that all life has a function that is peculiar to its particular life-form. The function peculiar to human life, he claimed, is the exercise of reason. The function of the excellent man, therefore, "is to exert such activities well." Virtue, which is essential to the good life, involves living according to reason. Only by living in accord with reason, which is our human function, can we achieve happiness and inner harmony.

Aristotle also believed that people by nature are political animals, and that the state is a natural form of society. Humans need community in order to be virtuous. The purpose of the state is to promote the virtuous or good life. Justice is the primary virtue of the state; unless a state is just and encourages the development of virtue in its citizens, it has no power to make its citizens good.

According to Aristotle most virtues entail finding the mean between excess and deficiency. For example, courage is the mean between cowardice (a deficit) and foolhardiness (an excess); truthfulness lies between irony and boastfulness.

This doctrine of the mean should not be misinterpreted as advising us to be wishy-washy or to compromise our moral standards. Aristotle was not suggesting that we seek consensus or take a moderate position on moral issues. The doctrine of the mean is meant to apply to virtues, not to our positions on social issues. By suggesting that we seek the mean, Aristotle was not referring to being lukewarm or a fence-straddler but to seeking what is *reasonable*. Indeed, the most effective moral reformers have taken positions that differed sharply from the status quo. The abolitionists, as well as the early feminists, for example, were considered extremists and fanatics. Instead, Aristotle writes, "virtue discovers the means and deliberately chooses it."

The doctrine of the mean is found in moral philosophies throughout the world. Confucians as well as Buddhist ethicists teach that the mean is that which is consistent with harmony and equilibrium, or the Way (Tao).

Confucian Virtue Ethics

Confucius is one of the most important Chinese philosophers. Although Confucius died one century before the birth of Aristotle, there are remarkable similarities between the ethics of the two men. Both taught that virtue, in general, involves hitting the mean between excess and deficit, both emphasized the role of habituation in the cultivation of virtue, and both believed that virtue was essential for individual and social harmony. A deontologist as well, Confucius also taught that a virtuous person is a person of goodwill who puts duty first.

Like Aristotle, Confucius believed that a virtuous society and individual virtue are inseparable. It is the rulers, therefore, who have the greatest power to promote virtue in society and individuals. People are happiest and most virtuous when they are living in a just and well-ordered society. If the actions and policies of the government are consistent with the Way, the common people will also be good, and there will be no need for the government to use punishment to maintain order.

Buddhist Virtue Ethics

Buddhist ethics affirms the absolute worth of the individual and the community of all living beings. Buddhism rejects individualism as an illusion; we exist only as members of a community. Because we are all part of the same web of being, to be true to ourselves is to extend concern for everything that lies in our path of experience. The virtuous person is motivated not by self-interest, but by a concern to benefit all living beings.

Like Aristotle and Confucius, Buddhists believe that good and evil—virtue and vice—are expressed in our actions. Engaging in destructive actions makes it more likely that we'll repeat that behavior in the future; engaging in virtuous actions makes it more likely that we'll repeat that behavior in the future. A good society encourages the development of moral wisdom and virtue. We cannot resolve the problems that plague modern society by encouraging an individualism, such as that advocated by natural rights ethics, that allows people to pursue their concept of good at the expense of other human and nonhuman beings. Without moral progress, modern Buddhists warn, our rapid technological advances could lead us down the path to disaster.

Care Ethics

Care ethics emphasizes caring over considerations of justice and impartiality. Care ethics, as a moral theory, developed primarily out of Carol Gilligan's study of women's moral reasoning. It has also been influenced by David Hume's ethics, which emphasize moral sentiment over moral reasoning.

According to Hume, it is sympathy rather than reason that motivates us to act morally. Sympathy opens us up to others by breaking down the "we/them" barriers that impede the development of caring relationships.

Gilligan also stresses the importance of sympathy in moral decision making. In her interviews with women and through her study of women in literature, Gilligan concluded that women's moral development tends to follow a different path than men's. Men, she found, tend to base their moral decisions on duty and principle-oriented moral theories; women are more context-oriented and concerned with relationship.

According to care ethicist Nel Noddings, we are at our moral best when we are "caring and being cared for." Whereas Noddings limits her moral community to humans, arguing that nonhuman animals are incapable of being in a caring relationship, ecofeminist Karen Warren expands care ethics to include all living creatures and all of nature. Unlike abstract moral principles, sympathy joins us to others and breaks down barriers. It is care, not rational calculations or an abstract sense of duty, that creates moral obligations. Caring is also ranked highly in Confucian ethics, where traditional family ties and loyalty are extremely important.

An inclination to care, however, is not enough. When our personal inclination to care is lacking, our commitment to an ideal or principle of caring motivates us to do what is right. On this point care ethicists and deontologists find common ground. A person of goodwill—a person who is truly virtuous and caring—can be counted on to act out of a sense of duty even when the immediate emotional inclination to do so is lacking.

Care ethicists maintain that, rather than being limited to personal relationships, moral sentiments such as compassion and sympathy are forms of knowledge that should be taken seriously in discussing social issues and formulating social policy. Philosopher Virginia Held, for example, disagrees with the traditional division wherein justice as a value belongs to the public sphere and care to the private domain of family, friends, and charity.[34] Just as justice is needed in the family, so is the care perspective badly needed in the public domain. Care ethics plays a central role in the hospice movement's opposition to euthanasia and its belief that we should work on providing a more caring and supportive environment for those who are dying. In her book *Dead Man Walking*, Helen Prejean enjoins her readers to see condemned to death row prisoners from a care perspective as well as a justice perspective.

Care ethicists do not want to dispense with justice; rather, they want to see the two approaches used together in formulating social policy. Care ethics serves as a corrective to our traditional views by demanding that we recognize welfare rights as basic rights. It also requires that we see others in relationship as individuals with their own needs and dignity, rather than adopting a paternalistic attitude toward them.

Although care ethics is often associated with feminism, some feminists reject it on the grounds that it reinforces traditional stereotypes of women's roles in the family and in society.

The Strengths and Limitations of Virtue Ethics

The primary criticism of virtue ethics is that it is incomplete. It has also been criticized for its lack of coherence as a bag-of-virtues approach. This criticism is based on a misunderstanding of the nature of virtue, however. Virtue ethicists do not mean virtue to imply a list of unrelated character traits, but rather a unity of character—a unity that most of us are still striving to achieve.

Virtue ethics does not offer sufficient guidance for making real-life moral decisions. While a virtuous character may be enough to motivate the saint and those at the higher stages of moral development, most of us also need formal guidelines. Indeed, according to Kant, to a person of perfect goodwill (God), the concept of duty no longer applies.

On the other hand, virtue ethicists do not toss out abstract principles regarding duties and rights; instead they give them a personal face. Virtue ethicists are not suggesting that we

---

  VIRTUE ETHICS: CONSIDERATIONS FOR THINKING ABOUT MORAL ISSUES

- **Seeking the mean:** Does the trait we are encouraging represent a balance between excess and deficiency?
- **Social policies and the promotion of virtue:** Does this social policy or resolution to a social issue encourage the development of virtue in the people affected by it?
- **Relationships:** What relationships are involved in this moral issue?
- **Caring and caring for:** How can we best nurture these relationships both as the "ones-caring" and the "ones-cared-for"?

---

ignore moral principles; they are saying that virtue ethics is more fundamental than duty ethics. Nor does virtue ethics entail discarding reason and relying solely on our "good" feelings. In the virtuous person, reason and feeling, as Hume himself pointed out, complement and confirm one another.

Virtue ethics goes beyond pure duty and rights-based ethics. They directly challenge the individual to rise above ordinary moral demands and to work toward creating a society in which it is easy for everyone to be virtuous and enjoy the good life.

EXERCISES

1. Which motivates you more to take action, a sense of justice or a feeling of sympathy for other persons? Illustrate your answer.
2. Discuss possible social policies for dealing with an issue such as hate speech, pornography, or alcohol and drug use on campus. Which policies are most likely to promote virtue in citizens? Support your answer.
3. Select a specific moral issue that is covered in this text. Discuss ways in which the care perspective might help in coming up with a resolution.

CONCLUSION

Moral issues are complex. No one theory offers the complete truth or perfect solution to a moral issue. On the other hand, theories can work together to provide us with more comprehensive tools for effectively analyzing moral issues. Theories help us recognize and prioritize moral principles and concerns. We should not simply discard a theory because it has limitations, but adopt a multidimensional approach that draws from the strengths of each of the theories. Whether the theory is deontological and oriented toward autonomy and the careful delineation of rules and rights; or utilitarian and concerned with consequences and mazimizing benefits; or virtue-based and focused on making us better, more caring people—all theories have the same ultimate goal: to provide a rational basis for making better moral decisions.

It is up to each of us, as critical thinkers, to apply moral theory to real-life moral decisions. In addition, although moral theory offers guidance, theory alone does not offer specific solutions. An understanding of the relevant facts, cultural traditions and conditions, practical wisdom, and sound moral reasoning are all necessary adjuncts to theory.

ARISTOTLE

Nicomachean Ethics

Aristotle was born in Stagira, a Greek colony north of Athens. He spent most of his childhood in Macedonia, where his father, Nicomachus, was a court physician and scholar. Unlike his forerunners Socrates and Plato, Aristotle had a fondness for luxury and wealth, owned several slaves, and hobnobbed with the rich and powerful.

A true Renaissance man, Aristotle was a scientist, philosopher, logician, poet, and psychologist who wrote hundreds of works, including poems, treatises, and books. *Nicomachean Ethics* is one of Aristotle's best-known works. In *Nicomachean Ethics,* Aristotle argues that living the good life—the life of virtue—is our most important human activity. Because the peculiar function of humans is the exercise of reason, virtue involves living according to reason. Only by living in accord with reason can we achieve happiness, inner harmony, and a well-ordered society.

Much of Aristotle's writing on the state is in response to the views of his teacher, Plato. Aristotle joined Plato's academy in Athens as a teenager and remained there for twenty years, until Plato's death at the age of eighty-one.

After the death of Plato, Aristotle took on the education of Alexander the Great, future king of Macedonia. The young ruler took Aristotle's teachings about world political unity to heart and, upon coming to the throne, set out to conquer the world, much to the chagrin of the Greeks. Given Aristotle's close association with the Macedonian conqueror, the Athenians had mixed feelings about him. Alexander the Great's untimely death in 323 B.C.E. unleashed a flood of anti-Macedonian feeling in Athens. Soon after, Aristotle was charged with impiety. Rather than take a chance that "the Athenians should sin a second time against philosophy" (they had put Plato's teacher Socrates to death for impiety in 399 B.C.E.), Aristotle fled to Euboea. He died in Babylon a year later.

Aristotle is sometimes dismissed as being too much of an elitist to be relevant for today's democracies. His critique of democracy, however, is a timely warning against the dangers of relying on majority rule as the criterion for deciding what is just.

Critical Reading Questions

1. How does Aristotle go about analyzing the term *good*?
2. According to Aristotle, what is the most important human activity? What is the final end of human activity?
3. What is the relationship between morality and happiness?
4. What is virtue? What are the two types of virtue?
5. What does Aristotle mean by habituation? What does habituation have to do with becoming virtuous? What is the role of the state in helping citizens become virtuous?

Nicomachean Ethics, from Richard McKeon (ed.), *The Basic Works of Aristotle* (New York: Random House, 1941). Copy of an earlier translation by Benjamin Jowett (1817–1893). Notes have been omitted.

6. What does Aristotle mean when he says that goodness is the quality that hits the mean? Is virtue always a matter of hitting the mean?
7. What are some examples of excesses and deficits? How do we avoid them?

Book I

CHAPTER 1

Every art and every inquiry, and similarly every action and pursuit, is thought to aim at some good; and for this reason the good has rightly been declared to be that at which all things aim. But a certain difference is found among ends; some are activities, others are products apart from the activities that produce them. Where there are ends apart from the actions, it is the nature of the products to be better than the activities. . . .

CHAPTER 7

Let us again return to the good we are seeking, and ask what it can be. It seems different in different actions and arts; it is different in medicine, in strategy, and in the other arts likewise. What then is the good of each? Surely that for whose sake everything else is done. In medicine this is health, in strategy victory, in architecture a house, in any other sphere something else, and in every action and pursuit the end; for it is for the sake of this that all men do whatever else they do. Therefore, if there is an end for all that we do, this will be the good achievable by action, and if there are more than one, these will be the goods achievable by action.

So the argument has by a different course reached the same point; but we must try to state this even more clearly. Since there is evidently more than one end, and we choose some of these (e.g., wealth, flutes, and in general instruments) for the sake of something else, clearly not all ends are final ends; but the chief good is evidently something final. Therefore, if there is only one final end, this will be what we are seeking, and if there are more than one, the most final of these will be what we are

seeking. Now we call that which is in itself worthy of pursuit more final than that which is worthy of pursuit for the sake of something else, and that which is never desirable for the sake of something else more final than the things that are desirable both in themselves and for the sake of that other thing, and therefore we call final without qualification that which is always desirable in itself and never for the sake of something else.

Now such a thing happiness, above all else, is held to be; for this we choose always for itself and never for the sake of something else, but honour, pleasure, reason, and every virtue we choose indeed for themselves (for if nothing resulted from them we should still choose each of them), but we choose them also for the sake of happiness, judging that by means of them we shall be happy. Happiness, on the other hand, no one chooses for the sake of these, nor, in general, for anything other than itself. . . .

Presumably, however, to say that happiness is the chief good seems a platitude, and a clearer account of what it is is still desired. This might perhaps be given, if we could first ascertain the function of man. For just as for a flute-player, a sculptor, or any artist, and, in general, for all things that have a function or activity, the good and the "well" is thought to reside in the function, so would it seem to be for man, if he has a function. Have the carpenter, then, and the tanner certain functions or activities, and has man none? Is he born without a function? Or as eye, hand, foot, and in general each of the parts evidently has a function, may one lay it down that man similarly has a function apart from all these? What then can this be? Life seems to be common even to plants, but we are seeking what is peculiar to man. Let us exclude, therefore, the life of nutrition and growth. Next there would be a life of perception, but *it* also seems to be common even to the horse, the ox, and every animal. There remains, then, an active life of the element that has a rational principle; of this, one part has such a principle in the sense of being obedient to one, the other in the sense of possessing one and exercising thought. And, as "life of the rational element" also has two meanings, we must state that life in the sense of activity is what we mean; for this seems to be the more proper sense of the term. Now if the function of man is an activity of soul which follows or implies a rational principle, . . . : if this is the case, [and we state the function of man to be a certain kind of life, and this to be an activity or actions of the soul implying a rational principle, and the function of a good man to be the good and noble performance of these, and if any action is well performed when it is performed in accordance with the appropriate excellence: if this is the case,] human good turns out to be activity of soul in accordance with virtue, and if there are more than one virtue, in accordance with the best and most complete.

But we must add "in a complete life". For one swallow does not make a summer, nor does one day; and so too one day, or a short time, does not make a man blessed and happy. . . .

Book II

CHAPTER 1

Virtue, then, being of two kinds, intellectual and moral, intellectual virtue in the main owes both its birth and its growth to teaching (for which reason it requires experience and time), while moral virtue comes about as a result of habit, whence also its name *ethike* is one that is formed by a slight variation from the word *ethos* (habit). From this it is also plain that none of the moral virtues arises in us by nature, for nothing that exists by nature can form a habit contrary to its nature. For instance the stone which by nature moves downwards cannot be habituated to move upwards, not even if one tries to train it by throwing it up ten thousand times; nor can fire be habituated to move downwards, nor can anything else that by nature behaves in one way be trained to behave in another. Neither by nature, then, nor contrary to nature do

the virtues arise in us; rather we are adapted by nature to receive them, and are made perfect by habit.

Again, of all the things that come to us by nature we first acquire the potentiality and later exhibit the activity (this is plain in the case of the senses; for it was not by often seeing or often hearing that we got these senses, but on the contrary we had them before we used them, and did not come to have them by using them); but the virtues we get by first exercising them, as also happens in the case of the arts as well. For the things we have to learn before we can do them, we learn by doing them, e.g. men become builders by building and lyre-players by playing the lyre; so too we become just by doing just acts, temperate by doing temperate acts, brave by doing brave acts.

This is confirmed by what happens in states; for legislators make the citizens good by forming habits in them, and this is the wish of every legislator, and those who do not effect it miss their mark, and it is in this that a good constitution differs from a bad one.

Again, it is from the same causes and by the same means that every virtue is both produced and destroyed, and similarly every art; for it is from playing the lyre that both good and bad lyre-players are produced. And the corresponding statement is true of builders and of all the rest; men will be good or bad builders as a result of building well or badly. For if this were not so, there would have been no need of a teacher, but all men would have been born good or bad at their craft. This, then, is the case with the virtues also; by doing the acts that we do in our transactions with other men we become just or unjust, and by doing the acts that we do in the presence of danger, and being habituated to feel fear or confidence, we become brave or cowardly. The same is true of appetites and feelings of anger; some men become temperate and good-tempered, others self-indulgent and irascible, by behaving in one way or the other in the appropriate circumstances. Thus, in one word, states of character arise out of like activities. This is why the activities we exhibit must be of a certain kind; it is because the states of character correspond to the differences between these. It makes no small difference, then, whether we form habits of one kind or of another from our very youth; it makes a very great difference, or rather *all* the difference.

CHAPTER 2

Since, then, the present inquiry does not aim at theoretical knowledge like the others (for we are inquiring not in order to know what virtue is, but in order to become good, since otherwise our inquiry would have been of no use), we must examine the nature of actions, namely how we ought to do them; for these determine also the nature of the states of character that are produced, as we have said. Now, that we must act according to the right rule is a common principle and must be assumed—it will be discussed later, i.e. both what the right rule is, and how it is related to the other virtues. . . .

First, then, let us consider this, that it is the nature of such things to be destroyed by defect and excess, as we see in the case of strength and health (for to gain light on things imperceptible we must use the evidence of sensible things); both excessive and defective exercise destroys the strength, and similarly drink or food which is above or below a certain amount destroys the health, while that which is proportionate both produces and increases and preserves it. So too is it, then, in the case of temperance and courage and the other virtues. For the man who flies from and fears everything and does not stand his ground against anything becomes a coward, and the man who fears nothing at all but goes to meet every danger becomes rash; and similarly the man who indulges in every pleasure and abstains from none becomes self-indulgent, while the man who shuns every pleasure, as boors do, becomes in a way insensible; temperance and courage, then, are destroyed by excess and defect, and preserved by the mean.

But not only are the sources and causes of their origination and growth the same as those of their destruction, but also the sphere of their actualization will be the same; for this is also true of the things which are more evident to sense, e.g. of strength; it is produced by taking much food and undergoing much exertion, and it is the strong man that will be most able to do these things. So too is it with the virtues; by abstaining from pleasures we become temperate, and it is when we have become so that we are most able to abstain from them; and similarly too in the case of courage; for by being habituated to despise things that are terrible and to stand our ground against them we become brave, and it is when we have become so that we shall be most able to stand our ground against them. . . .

CHAPTER 5

Next we must consider what virtue is. Since things that are found in the soul are of three kinds—passions, faculties, states of character, virtue must be one of these. By passions I mean appetite, anger, fear, confidence, envy, joy, friendly feeling, hatred, longing, emulation, pity, and in general the feelings that are accompanied by pleasure or pain; by faculties the things in virtue of which we are said to be capable of feeling these, e.g. of becoming angry or being pained or feeling pity; by states of character the things in virtue of which we stand well or badly with reference to the passions, e.g. with reference to anger we stand badly if we feel it violently or too weakly, and well if we feel it moderately; and similarly with reference to the other passions.

Now neither the virtues nor the vices are *passions,* because we are not called good or bad on the ground of our passions, but are so called on the ground of our virtues and our vices, and because we are neither praised nor blamed for our passions (for the man who feels fear or anger is not praised, nor is the man who simply feels anger blamed, but the man who feels it in a certain way), but for our virtues and our vices we *are* praised or blamed.

Again, we feel anger and fear without choice, but the virtues are modes of choice or involve choice. . . . Further, in respect of the passions we are said to be moved, but in respect of the virtues and the vices we are said not to be moved but to be disposed in a particular way.

For these reasons also they are not *faculties;* for we are neither called good nor bad, nor praised nor blamed, for the simple capacity of feeling the passions; again, we have the faculties by nature, but we are not made good or bad by nature; we have spoken of this before.

If, then, the virtues are neither passions nor faculties, all that remains is that they should be *states of character.*

Thus we have stated what virtue is in respect of its genus.

CHAPTER 6

We must, however, not only describe virtue as a state of character, but also say what sort of state it is. We may remark, then, that every virtue or excellence both brings into good condition the thing of which it is the excellence and makes the work of that thing be done well; e.g. the excellence of the eye makes both the eye and its work good; for it is by the excellence of the eye that we see well. Similarly the excellence of the horse makes a horse both good in itself and good at running and at carrying its rider and at awaiting the attack of the enemy. Therefore, if this is true in every case, the virtue of man also will be the state of character which makes a man good and which makes him do his own work well. . . .

Virtue, then, is a state of character concerned with choice, lying in a mean, i.e. the mean relative to us, this being determined by a rational principle, and by that principle by which the man of practical wisdom would determine it. Now it is a mean between two vices, that which depends on excess and that which depends on defect; and again it is a mean because the vices respectively fall short of or exceed what is right in both passions and actions, while virtue both finds and chooses that which is intermediate. Hence in respect of its substance and the definition which states its essence virtue is a mean, with regard to what is best and right an extreme.

But not every action nor every passion admits of a mean; for some have names that already imply badness, e.g. spite, shamelessness, envy, and in the case of actions adultery, theft, murder; for all of these and suchlike things imply by their names that they are themselves bad, and not the excesses or deficiencies of them. It is not possible, then, ever to be right with regard to them; one must always be wrong. Nor does goodness or badness with regard to such things depend on committing adultery with the right woman, at the right time, and in the right way, but simply to do any of them is to go wrong. It would be equally absurd, then, to expect that in unjust, cowardly, and voluptuous action there should be a mean, an excess, and a deficiency; for at that rate there would be a mean of excess and of deficiency, an excess of excess, and a deficiency of deficiency. But as there is no excess and deficiency of temperance and courage because what is intermediate is in a sense an extreme, so too of the actions we have mentioned there is no mean nor any excess and deficiency, but however they are done they are wrong; for in general there is neither a mean of excess and deficiency, nor excess and deficiency of a mean.

Discussion Questions

1. Do you agree with Aristotle that every act and inquiry aims at some good (goal)? Is there a single end toward which all human behavior is directed? If so, does this justify the regulation of people's behavior, including restrictions on viewing media violence and pornography, by the government so they are more likely to achieve this end? Use specific examples to support your answer.
2. Do colleges have a duty to help students become virtuous people by creating an atmosphere in which good behavior becomes habitual for them? Support your answer. Should campus administrations prohibit certain excessive behaviors in order to make it easier for students to become good people? Discuss your answer in light of regulations on hate speech, cheating, and drug and alcohol abuse.
3. Aristotle warned against the rule of the many, arguing that "the many are more

corruptible than the few." Is the fact that the United States is a democracy an impediment to getting the United States to comply with international policies regarding environmental protection? Discuss whether important public policies, especially those that affect the international community, should be left up to the experts or to majority rule.

 THOMAS AQUINAS

Summa Theologica

Thomas Aquinas (c. 1225–1274) was the most important scholar and philosopher of the medieval period. Born into nobility, Thomas was named after his grandfather, who had been commander of the imperial forces. Young Thomas, however, showed little interest in the battles for political power that characterized the thirteenth century, preferring instead to sit quietly at the feet of the friars who visited his parents' castle and listen to their stories of spirituality.

A bright student and original thinker, Thomas entered the university at the age of fourteen. After graduating from the University of Naples in 1244, instead of going into the military or politics, he joined the newly established evangelical Dominican Order over his parents' protest.

Distressed by their youngest son's defiance—especially after the zealous Dominican monks refused to let the mother visit her son—his parents arranged to have his brothers kidnap him. They locked Thomas in a tower in the family castle, where he remained for the next year. In an effort to cure him of his "madness," his family brought him racy books and spicy foods and even tried to tempt him with a beautiful prostitute. Eventually, they gave up on trying to convert Thomas to the ways of the world and let him go. Following his release, Aquinas continued his studies in philosophy and theology in Paris.

In 1256 Aquinas completed his magistrate (doctorate) in theology and was appointed professor of theology at the University of Paris. It was here that he undertook a serious study of the philosophy of Aristotle. Aristotle's works had been rediscovered by the Arabs in the Middle Ages and made their way into Western Europe across the Spanish border with the Muslims. Aquinas readily took to Aristotle's philosophy, reinterpreting it in the light of Christian doctrine and referring to Aristotle in his writings as, simply, "the philosopher."

Aquinas returned to Italy in 1272, where he taught at the University of Naples for about a year until illness forced him to discontinue his teaching and writing. He was canonized by the Roman Catholic Church in 1323. His authority as the leading philosopher of the Church was officially established in 1879 by Pope Leo XIII.

An active teacher and writer throughout his career, Aquinas produced several large treatises on theological and philosophical issues. His most important scholastic work, the

---

Summa Theologica, translated by Fathers of the English Dominican Province (1911). Republished in 1948 by Benzinger Brothers, Inc. Notes have been omitted.

Summa Theologica (1265–1273), brings together Christian doctrine and the teachings of Aristotle. In the following selection, Aquinas argues that moral law is grounded in human nature which, in turn, was created by God as part of His divine plan for the universe. God is the perfectly rational being. Moral law, also known as natural law, applies to all rational beings: God and humans, religious people and atheists—all are bound by the same moral principles. If human law or customs conflict with natural or moral law, we have a moral duty to put natural law first.

Critical Reading Questions

1. What is the source of natural (moral) law?
2. How do we know right from wrong?
3. What is virtue? What is the role of lawmakers in promoting virtue in people?
4. Which is more important to Aquinas—the individual or the common good?
5. How, according to Aquinas, should we make decisions on moral issues such as assisted suicide or cloning?
6. What is the relationship between human law and natural law?
7. What is our moral duty when a human law, such as a law on abortion or capital punishment, is in conflict with natural law?

Question 91
– Of the Various Kinds of Law

FIRST ARTICLE
Whether There Is an Eternal Law?

. . . A law is nothing else but a dictate of practical reason emanating from the ruler who governs a perfect community. Now it is evident, granted that the world is ruled by Divine Providence, as was stated in the First Part (Q. 22, AA. 1, 2), that the whole community of the universe is governed by Divine Reason. Wherefore the very Idea of the government of things in God the Ruler of the universe, has the nature of a law. And since the Divine Reason's conception of things is not subject to time but is eternal, according to Prov. viii. 23, therefore it is that this kind of law must be called eternal. . . .

It is evident that all things partake somewhat of the eternal law, in so far as, namely, from its being imprinted on them, they derive their respective inclinations to their proper acts and ends. Now among all others, the rational creature is subject to Divine Providence in the most excellent way, in so far as it partakes of a share of providence, by being provident both for itself and for others. Wherefore it has a share of the Eternal Reason, whereby it has a natural inclination to its proper act and end: and this participation of the eternal law in the rational creature is called the natural law. Hence the Psalmist after saying (Ps. iv. 6): *Offer up the sacrifice of justice,* as though someone asked what the works of justice are, adds: *Many say, Who showeth us good things?* in answer to which question he says: *The light of Thy countenance, O Lord, is signed upon us:* thus implying that the light of natural reason, whereby we discern what is good and what is evil, which is the function of the natural law, is nothing else than an imprint on us of the Divine light. It is therefore evident that the natural law is nothing else than the rational creature's participation of the eternal law. . . .

Question 92
– Of the Effects of Law

FIRST ARTICLE
Whether an Effect of Law Is to Make Men Good?

. . . A law is nothing else than a dictate of reason in the ruler by whom his subjects are governed. Now the virtue of any subordinate thing consists in its being well subordinated to that by which it is regulated: thus we see that the virtue of the irascible and concupiscible faculties consists in their being obedient to reason; and accordingly *the virtue of every subject consists in his being well subjected to his ruler,* as the Philosopher says (*Polit.* i). But every law aims at being obeyed by those who are subject to it. Consequently it is evident that the proper effect of law is to lead its subjects to their proper virtue: and since virtue is *that which makes its subject good,* it follows that the proper effect of law is to make those to whom it is given, good, either simply or in some particular respect. . . .

Virtue is twofold, as explained above (Q. 63, A. 2), viz., acquired and infused. Now the fact of being accustomed to an action contributes to both, but in different ways; for it causes the acquired virtue; while it disposes to infused virtue, and preserves and fosters it when it already exists. And since law is given for the purpose of directing human acts; as far as human acts conduce to virtue, so far does law make men good. Wherefore the Philosopher says in the second book of the *Politics* (*Ethic.* ii) that *lawgivers make men good by habituating them to good works.* It is not always through perfect goodness of virtue that one obeys the law but sometimes it is through fear of punishment, and sometimes from the mere dictates of reason, which is a beginning of virtue, as stated above (Q. 63, A. 1).

The goodness of any part is considered in comparison with the whole; hence Augustine says (*Conf.* iii) that *unseemly is the part that harmonizes not with the whole.* Since then every man is a part of the state, it is impossible that a man be good unless he be well proportionate to the common good: nor can the whole be well consistent unless its parts be proportionate to it. Consequently the common good of the state cannot flourish, unless the citizens be virtuous, at least those whose business it is to govern. But it is enough for the good of the community, that the other citizens be so far virtuous that they obey the commands of their rulers. Hence the Philosopher says (*Polit.* iii. 2) that *the virtue of a sovereign is the same as that of a good man, but the virtue of any common citizen is not the same as that of a good man.*

A tyrannical law, through not being according to reason, is not a law, absolutely speaking, but rather a perversion of law; and yet in so far as it is something in the nature of a law, it aims at the citizens' being good. For all it has in the nature of a law consists in its being an ordinance made by a superior to his subjects, and aims at being obeyed by them, which is to make them good, not simply, but with respect to that particular government.

Discussion Questions

1. Some natural law theorists argue that homosexuality is contrary to natural law. Does this follow? Is homosexuality irrational? What if a person is by nature homosexual? Furthermore, even if we do agree with Aquinas that the union of man and woman is an expression of the divine, does this necessarily exclude union between same-sex partners as also being an expression of the divine? Discuss how a natural law theorist such as Aquinas might respond to these questions. Are you satisfied with the response? Support your answer.

2. The Catholic Church has taken a stand, based on natural law theory, against physician-assisted suicide. If you agreed that assisted suicide is contrary to moral law and you were living in a country where assisted suicide is legal, what would your moral obligation be as a citizen or a physician?

3. Like Aristotle, Aquinas believed that the proper effect of law is to make people virtuous. Discuss what policies Aquinas and Aristotle might propose for dealing with drinking on college campuses.

JOHN STUART MILL

Utilitarianism

John Stuart Mill (1806–1873) was educated at home by his father James Mill, with the help of Jeremy Bentham, to carry on the utilitarian tradition. When Mill was about twenty, he experienced a nervous breakdown and sank into a deep depression that lasted for two years. During this time, he began to question some of the tenets of Bentham's utilitarian theory, particularly Bentham's insistence on the equality of pleasures.

Like Bentham, Mill was interested in legislation and social reform. However, unlike Bentham, Mill believed that certain pleasures should count more than others.

Critical Reading Questions

1. What is the principle of utility, and what are the only things that the principle of utility regards as desirable moral ends?
2. Which pleasures does Mill regard as superior?
3. What method does Mill use for determining which pleasures are of a higher quality?
4. Whose interests should be taken into account when determining the utility of an action?
5. What is the relationship between the principle of utility and the golden rule?

The creed which accepts as the foundation of morals, Utility, or the Greatest Happiness Principle, holds that actions are right in proportion as they tend to promote happiness, wrong as they tend to produce the reverse of happiness. By happiness is intended pleasure, and the absence of pain; by unhappiness, pain, and the privation of pleasure. To give a clear view of the moral standard set up by the theory, much more requires to be said; in particular, what things it includes in the ideas of pain and pleasure; and to what extent this is left an open question. But these supplementary explanations do not affect the theory of life on which this theory of morality is grounded—namely, that pleasure, and freedom from pain, are the only things desirable as ends; and that all desirable things (which are as numerous in the utilitarian as in any other scheme) are desirable either for the pleasure inherent in themselves, or as means to the promotion of pleasure and the prevention of pain. . . .

It is quite compatible with the principle of utility to recognise the fact, that some *kinds* of pleasure are more desirable and more valuable than others. It would be absurd that while, in estimating all other things, quality is considered as well as quantity, the estimation of pleasures should be supposed to depend on quantity alone.

If I am asked, what I mean by difference of quality in pleasures, or what makes one pleasure more valuable than another, merely as a pleasure, except its being greater in amount, there is but one possible answer. Of two pleasures, if there be one to which all or almost all who have experience of both give a decided preference, irrespective of any feeling of moral obligation to prefer it, that is the more desirable pleasure. If one of the two is, by those who

Originally published in three installments in Fraser's magazine, 1861.

are competently acquainted with both, placed so far above the other that they prefer it, even though knowing it to be attended with a greater amount of discontent, and would not resign it for any quantity of the other pleasure which their nature is capable of, we are justified in ascribing to the preferred enjoyment a superiority in quality, so far outweighing quantity as to render it, in comparison, of small account.

Now it is an unquestionable fact that those who are equally acquainted with, and equally capable of appreciating and enjoying, both, do give a most marked preference to the manner of existence which employs their higher faculties. Few human creatures would consent to be changed into any of the lower animals, for a promise of the fullest allowance of a beast's pleasures; no intelligent human being would consent to be a fool, no instructed person would be an ignoramus, no person of feeling and conscience would be selfish and base, even though they should be persuaded that the fool, the dunce, or the rascal is better satisfied with his lot than they are with theirs. . . . It is better to be a human being dissatisfied than a pig satisfied; better to be Socrates dissatisfied than a fool satisfied. And if the fool, or the pig, are of a different opinion, it is because they only know their own side of the question. The other party to the comparison knows both sides.

. . .

According to the Greatest Happiness Principle, as above explained, the ultimate end, with reference to and for the sake of which all other things are desirable (whether we are considering our own good or that of other people), is an existence exempt as far as possible from pain, and as rich as possible in enjoyments, both in point of quantity and quality; the test of quality, and the rule for measuring it against quantity, being the preference felt by those who in their opportunities of experience, to which must be added their habits of self-consciousness and self-observation, are best furnished with the means of comparison. This, being, according to the utilitarian opinion, the end of human action, is necessarily also the standard of morality; which may accordingly be defined, the rules and precepts for human conduct, by the observance of which an existence such as has been described might be, to the greatest extent possible, secured to all mankind; and not to them only, but, so far as the nature of things admits, to the whole sentient creation.

. . .

I must again repeat, what the assailants of utilitarianism seldom have the justice to acknowledge, that the happiness which forms the utilitarian standard of what is right in conduct, is not the agent's own happiness, but that of all concerned. As between his own happiness and that of others, utilitarianism requires him to be as strictly impartial as a disinterested and benevolent spectator. In the golden rule of Jesus of Nazareth, we read the complete spirit of the ethics of utility. To do as you would be done by, and to love your neighbour as yourself, constitute the ideal perfection of utilitarian morality. As the means of making the nearest approach to this ideal, utility would enjoin, first, that laws and social arrangements should place the happiness, or (as speaking practically it may be called) the interest, of every individual, as nearly as possible in harmony with the interest of the whole; and secondly, that education and opinion, which have so vast a power over human character, should so use that power as to establish in the mind of every individual an indissoluble association between his own happiness and the good of the whole; especially between his own happiness and the practice of such modes of conduct, negative and positive, as regard for the universal happiness prescribes; so that not only he may be unable to conceive the possibility of happiness to himself, consistently with conduct opposed to the general good, but also that a direct impulse to promote the general good may be in every individual one of habitual motives of action, and the sentiments connected therewith may fill a large and prominent place in every human being's sentient existence. If the impugners of the utilitarian morality represented it to their own minds in this its true character, I know not what recommendation possessed by any other morality they could possibly affirm to be wanting to it; what more beautiful or more exalted developments of human nature any other ethical system can be supposed to foster, or what springs of action, not accessible to the utilitarian, such systems rely on for giving effect to their mandates. . . .

Discussion Questions

1. Do you agree with Mill that the life of an unhappy human is preferable to that of a satisfied pig? On what grounds does Mill make such an assertion? Is this distinction between the different pleasures justified? If so, on what basis?
2. How does Mill's concept of pleasure differ from that of Bentham's? Which definition is most useful? Apply Mill's concept of the quality of pleasures to moral issues involving nonhuman animals, for example, meat-eating versus vegetarianism, keeping animals in zoos, and the use of nonhuman animals in medical experimentation and cosmetic experimentation.
3. What is "sentience"? Why does Mill use sentience as a criterion for determining whose interests should be taken into account? Do you agree with this criterion? Using this criterion what would Mill's position most likely be regarding euthanasia and "partial-birth" abortions?
4. Discuss the legalization of drugs and pornography in light of Mill's theory.

IMMANUEL KANT

Fundamental Principles of the Metaphysic of Ethics

An intellectual giant, German philosopher Immanuel Kant (1724–1804) stood barely five feet tall as an adult. Born with a deformed chest, Kant was plagued with health problems his entire life. Because of his poor health, Kant maintained a strict regimen; his daily walks were so regular that people could set their watches by the time he walked past their houses.

After completing his studies, Kant worked for several years as a tutor to the children of Prussian aristocrats. In 1755 he got a job as privatdocent at the University of Konigsberg, making Kant the first of the major philosophers to be a professional university teacher. As a privatdocent Kant was licensed to give lectures. He was not paid by the university, however, but by the students. Kant lectured as many as twenty-one hours a week on subjects ranging from fireworks and physical geography to metaphysics. As a lecturer he was witty and inspiring. One of his students later wrote that they "never left a single lecture in his ethics without having become better men." Despite his popularity as a teacher, Kant remained poor for many years.

In 1770, after many years of trying to get a permanent teaching position at the university, Kant was finally appointed professor of logic and metaphysics. He remained at

Fundamental Principles of the Metaphysic of Ethics, trans. by Thomas Kingsmill Abbott (London: Longmans, Green and Co., Ltd., 1926). Notes have been omitted.

the university as a professor until poor health forced him to retire in 1796. In his later years, Kant gained fame as a sort of oracle, and Konigsberg became a shrine of philosophy. People came from all over to consult Kant on all sorts of issues, including the lawfulness of vaccinations. He died in 1804, having spent his entire life in Konigsberg.

Kant's first great work in philosophy, *Critique of Pure Reason,* was not published until 1781, when he was in his late fifties. It was followed in relatively quick succession by other great works, including the *Fundamental Principles of the Metaphysic of Morals* in 1785.

Unlike the utilitarians, Kant was more concerned with establishing a metaphysical foundation for morality than in coming up with an ethical system that could be used for formulating social policy. He believed that only reason could provide this foundation. If moral law is to be morally compelling, he argued, it must be logically consistent as well as absolutely binding. Kant's concepts of the good will and the categorical imperative—the most fundamental moral principle—continue to be two of the most useful concepts in discussion of moral issues.

Critical Reading Questions

1. What is the good will? What is the relevance of the good will in making decisions regarding social policy?
2. What gives an action moral worth?
3. Why does Kant reject utilitarianism as the foundation of morality?
4. What is the source of moral knowledge?
5. Why does Kant argue that moral maxims must be universal rather than relative?
6. What is the categorical imperative? How does it differ from a hypothetical imperative? Give examples of both types of imperatives.
7. What does it mean for a being to be an "end in itself"? What gives a being value as an end in itself?
8. What is the difference between treating a being as an end in itself and treating a being as a means only? Why is it wrong to treat persons as means only?

Nothing can possibly be conceived in the world, or even out of it, which can be called good without qualification, except a Good Will. Intelligence, wit, judgment, and the other *talents* of the mind, however they may be named, or courage, resolution, perseverance, as qualities of temperament, are undoubtedly good and desirable in many respects; but these gifts of nature may also become extremely bad and mischievous if the will which is to make use of them, and which, therefore, constitutes what is called *character,* is not good. It is the same with the *gifts of fortune.* Power, riches, honour, even health, and the general well-being and contentment with one's condition which is called *happiness,* inspire pride, and often presumption, if there is not a Good Will to correct the influence of these on the mind, and with this also to rectify the whole principle of acting, and adapt it to its end. . . .

A Good Will is good not because of what it performs or effects, not by its aptness for the attainment of some proposed end, but simply by virtue of the volition, that is, it is good in itself, and considered by itself is to be esteemed much higher than all that can be brought about by it in favour of any inclination, nay, even of the sum total of all inclinations. Even if it should happen that, owing to special disfavour of fortune, or the niggardly provision of a step-motherly nature, this will should wholly lack power to accomplish its purpose, if with its greatest efforts it should yet achieve nothing, and there should remain only the Good Will (not, to be sure, a mere wish, but the summoning of all means in our power), then, like a jewel, it would still shine by its own light, as a thing which has its whole value in itself. Its usefulness or fruitlessness can neither add to nor take away anything from this value. . . .

To be beneficent when we can is a duty; and besides this, there are many minds so sympathetically constituted that, without any other motive of vanity or self-interest, they find a pleasure in spreading joy around them, and can take delight in the satisfaction of others so far as it is their own work. But I maintain that in such a case an action of this kind, however proper, however amiable it may be, has nevertheless no true moral worth, but is on a level with other inclinations, *e.g.* the inclination to honour, which, if it is happily directed to that which is in fact of public utility and accordant with duty, and consequently honourable, deserves praise and encouragement, but not esteem. For the maxim lacks the moral import, namely, that such actions be done *from duty,* not from inclination. Put the case that the mind of that philanthropist was clouded by sorrow of his own extinguishing all sympathy with the lot of others, and that while he still has the power to benefit others in distress, he is not touched by their trouble because he is absorbed with his own; and now suppose that he tears himself out of his dead insensibility, and performs the action without any inclination to it, but simply from duty, then first has his action its genuine moral worth. . . .

Thus the moral worth of an action does not lie in the effect expended from it, not in any principle of action which requires to borrow its motive from this expected effect. For all these effects—agreeableness of one's condition, and even the promotion of the happiness of others—could have been also brought about by other causes, so that for this there would have been no need of the will of a rational being; whereas it is in this alone that the supreme and unconditional good can be found. The preeminent good which we call moral can therefore consist in nothing else than *the conception of law* in itself, *which certainly is only possible in a rational being,* in so far as this conception, and not the expected effect, determines the will. . . .

But what sort of law can that be, the conception of which must determine the will, even without paying any regard to the effect expected from it, in order that this will may be called good absolutely and without qualification? As I have deprived the will of every impulse which could arise to it from obedience to any law, there remains nothing but the universal conformity of its actions to law in general, which alone is to serve the will as a principle, *i.e.* I am never to act otherwise than *so that I could also will that my maxim should become a universal law.* Here now, it is the simple conformity to law in general, without assuming any particular law applicable to certain actions, that serves the will as its principle, and must so serve it, if duty is not to be a vain delusion and a chimerical notion. The common reason of men in its practical judgments perfectly coincides with this, and always has in view the principle here suggested. Let the question be, for example: May I when in distress make a promise with the intention not to keep it? I readily distinguish here between the two significations which the question may have: Whether it is prudent, or whether it is right, to make a false promise? The former may undoubtedly often be the case. . . . The shortest way, however, and an unerring one, to discover the answer to this question whether a lying promise is consistent with duty, is to ask myself, Should I be content that my maxim (to extricate myself from difficulty by a false promise) should hold good as a universal law, for myself as well as for others? and should I be able to say to myself, "Every one may make a deceitful promise when he finds himself in a difficulty from which he cannot otherwise extricate himself"? Then I presently become aware that while I can will the lie, I can by no means will that lying should be a univeral law. For with such a law there would be no promises at all, since it would be in vain to allege my intention in regard to my future actions to those who would not believe this allegation, or if they overhastily did so would pay me back in my own coin. Hence my maxim, as soon as it should be made a universal law, would necessarily destroy itself. . . .

I do not indeed as yet *discern* on what this respect is based (this the philosopher may inquire), but at least I understand this, that it is an estimation of the worth which far outweighs all worth of what is recommended by inclination, and that the necessity of acting from *pure* respect for the practical law is what constitutes duty, to which every other motive must give place, because it is the condition of a will being good *in itself,* and the worth of such a will is above everything. . . .

Everything in nature works according to laws. Rational beings alone have the faculty of acting according *to the conception* of laws, that is according to principles, *i.e.* have a *will.* Since the deduction of actions from principles requires *reason,* the will is nothing but practical reason. . . .

The conception of an objective principle, in so far as it is obligatory for a will, is called a command (of reason), and the formula of the command is called an Imperative.

All imperatives are expressed by the word *ought* [or *shall*], and thereby indicate the relation of an objective law of reason to a will, which from its subjective constitution is not necessarily determined by it (an obligation). They say that something would be good to do or to forbear, but they say it to a will which does not always do a thing because it is conceived to be good to do it. . . .

Now all *imperatives* command either *hypothetically* or *categorically.* The former represent the practical necessity of a possible action as means to something else that is willed (or at least which one might possibly will). The categorical imperative would be that which represented an action as necessary of itself without reference to another end, *i.e.* as objectively necessary.

Since every practical law represents a possible action as good, and on this account, for a subject who is practically determinable by reason, necessary, all imperatives are formulæ determining an action which is necessary according to the principle of a will good in some respects. If now the action is good only as a means *to something else,* then the Imperative is *hypothetical;* if it is conceived as good *in itself* and consequently as being necessarily the principle of a will which of itself conforms to reason, then it is *Categorical.* . . .

An imperative which commands a certain conduct immediately, without having as its condition any other purpose to be attained by it . . . is Categorical. It concerns not the matter of the action, or

its intended result, but its form and the principle of which it is itself a result; and what is essentially good in it consists in the mental disposition, let the consequence be what it may. This Imperative may be called that of Morality. . . .

When I conceive a hypothetical imperative in general I do not know beforehand what it will contain until I am given the condition. But when I conceive a Categorical Imperative I know at once what it contains. For as the imperative contains besides the law only the necessity that the maxims* shall conform to this law, while the law contains no conditions restricting it, there remains nothing but the general statement that the maxim of the action should conform to a universal law, and it is this conformity alone that the imperative properly represents as necessary.

There is therefore but one Categorical Imperative, namely this: *Act only on that maxim whereby thou canst at the same time will that it should become a universal law.*

Now if all imperatives of duty can be deduced from this one imperative as from their principle, then, although it should remain undecided whether what is called duty is not merely a vain notion, yet at least we shall be able to show what we understand by it and what this notion means.

Since the universality of the law according to which effects are produced constitutes what is properly called *nature* in the most general sense (as to form), that is, the existence of things so far as it is determined by general laws, the Imperative of duty may be expressed thus: *Act as if the maxim of thy action were to become by thy will a Universal Law of Nature.* . . .

A man reduced to despair by a series of misfortunes feels wearied of life, but is still so far in possession of his reason that he can ask himself whether it would not be contrary to his duty to himself to take his own life. Now he inquires whether the maxim of

---

* A MAXIM is a subjective principle of action, and must be distinguished from the *objective principle,* namely, practical law. The former contains the practical rule set by reason according to the conditions of the subject (often its ignorance or its inclinations), so that it is the principle on which the subject *acts;* but the law is the objective principle valid for every rational being, and is the principle on which it *ought to act,* that is, an imperative.

his action could become a universal law of nature. His maxim is: From self-love I adopt it as a principle to shorten my life when its longer duration is likely to bring more evil than satisfaction. It is asked then simply whether this principle founded on self-love can become a universal law of nature. Now we see at once that a system of nature of which it should be a law to destroy life by means of the very feeling whose special nature it is to impel to the improvement of life would contradict itself, and therefore could not exist as a system of nature; hence that maxim cannot possibly exist as a universal law of nature, and consequently would be wholly inconsistent with the supreme principle of all duty. . . .

We have thus established at least this much, that if duty is a conception which is to have any import and real legislative authority for our actions, it can only be expressed in Categorical, and not at all in hypothetical imperatives. We have also, which is of great importance, exhibited clearly and definitely for every practical application the content of the Categorical Imperative, which must contain the principle of all duty if there is such a thing at all. . . .

If then there is a supreme practical principle or, in respect of the human will, a Categorical Imperative, it must be one which, being drawn from the conception of that which is necessarily an end for every one because it is *an end in itself,* constitutes an *objective* principle of will, and can therefore serve as a universal practical law. The foundation of this principle is: *rational nature exists as an end in itself.* Man necessarily conceives his own existence as being so: so far then this is a *subjective* principle of human actions. But every other rational being regards its existence similarly, just on the same rational principle that holds for me: so that it is at the same time an objective principle, from which as a supreme practical law all laws of the will must be capable of being deduced. Accordingly the practical imperative will be as follows: *So act as to treat humanity,* *whether in thine own person or in that of any other, in every case as an end withal, never as means only.* We will now inquire whether this can be practically carried out.

To abide by the previous examples:

Firstly, under the head of necessary duty to oneself: He who contemplates suicide should ask himself whether his action can be consistent with the idea of humanity *as an end in itself.* If he destroys himself in order to escape from painful circumstances, he uses a person merely as a *mean* to maintain a tolerable condition up to the end of life. But a man is not a thing, that is to say, something which can be used merely as means, but must in all his actions be always considered as an end in himself. I cannot, therefore, dispose in any way of a man in my own person so as to mutilate him, to damage or kill him. (It belongs to ethics proper to define this principle more precisely so as to avoid all misunderstanding, *e.g.* as to the amputation of the limbs in order to preserve myself; as to exposing my life to danger with a view to preserve it, &c. This question is therefore omitted here.)

Secondly, as regards necessary duties, or those of strict obligation, toward others; he who is thinking of making a lying promise to others will see at once that he would be using another man *merely as a mean,* without the latter containing at the same time the end in himself. For he whom I propose by such a promise to use for my own purposes cannot possibly assent to my mode of acting towards him, and therefore cannot himself contain the end of this action. This violation of the principle of humanity in other men is more obvious if we take in examples of attacks on the freedom and property of others. For then it is clear that he who transgresses the rights of men, intends to use the person of the others merely as means, without considering that as rational beings they ought always to be esteemed also as ends, that is, as beings who must be capable of containing in themselves the end of the very same action.

Discussion Questions

1. Kant formulated his views on suicide long before medical technology was developed that could be used to extend the dying process. What would Kant's position most likely be on physician-assisted suicide? Is physician-assisted suicide always incompatible with the categorical imperative? Support your answers.

2. The categorical imperative requires that we treat persons as ends in themselves and never as means only. Develop a policy on affirmative action for college admissions that is based on the categorical imperative.

3. Can hate speech ever be compatible with the categorical imperative? Why or why not? If not, what is your moral duty, as a person of good will, if you witness or are the victim of hate speech? Support your answers.

4. Discuss how Kant's definition of personhood and the moral community would influence his position on vegetarianism or environmental issues such as the destruction of the Amazon rain forests. Although Kant excluded nonhuman animals from the moral community, he was opposed to cruelty to other animals on the grounds that it makes us more likely to be cruel to people. Is enjoying the products of animals agriculture, particularly animals raised on land that used to be rain forest, morally acceptable so long as we are not directly involved or do not witness the pain or extinction of other species? Support your answer.

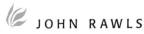 JOHN RAWLS

A Theory of Justice

Harvard philosopher and political theorist John Rawls (b. 1921), like the utilitarians, is primarily concerned with providing a theoretical framework for formulating social policy. Rawls argues that utilitarian theory is too obscure and simplistic to deal with many of the issues facing modern society. In his book *A Theory of Justice,* he offers an alternative to utilitarian social theory by combining deontology with a social contract approach to social ethics.

Social contract theory has its roots in classical Greek philosophy. Elements of social contract theory are also found in the philosophies of John Locke, Jean-Jacques Rousseau, and Immanuel Kant. A social contract is an agreement between individuals and a governing power in which the individuals freely surrender some personal liberties in exchange for the advantages of living in a well-organized society.

According to Rawls, justice as fairness is the most basic requirement of the social contract. This element of justice, he argues, is absent in strict utilitarian theory. In order to determine which principles of justice should govern a society, Rawls came up with a hypothetical device he calls the "veil of ignorance." The veil of ignorance provides an objective and impartial viewpoint from which we can view our place in society and come up with principles of justice that are fair for everyone. Rawls believes that under the veil of ignorance, people in the "original position," the time prior to the founding of the social contract, will come up with two principles of justice outlined in the reading. By applying these two principles, we can resolve disputes in social ethics and formulate social policies that are just.

A Theory of Justice (Cambridge, Mass.: Harvard University Press, 1971). Some notes have been omitted.

Rawls's theory of justice has been tremendously influential in discussions of public policy in areas such as health care and welfare reform.

Critical Reading Questions

1. What is "the first virtue of social institutions"?
2. What does Rawls mean by a "social contract" and what is its relevance to resolving moral issues?
3. What is the "original position of equality"? Does this position actually exist or has it ever existed in the past?
4. What is the "veil of ignorance" and what is its purpose?
5. What does Rawls mean by "justice as fairness"?
6. What, according to Rawls, are the two principles of justice that would be chosen in the original position? How are these principles to be applied in resolving social issues?
7. Why does Rawls reject the principle of utility as one that would be chosen in the original position?
8. What are the basic rights, according to Rawls? Does he place more emphasis on liberty rights or on welfare rights?

Justice as Fairness

THE ROLE OF JUSTICE

Justice is the first virtue of social institutions, as truth is of systems of thought. A theory however elegant and economical must be rejected or revised if it is untrue; likewise laws and institutions no matter how efficient and well-arranged must be reformed or abolished if they are unjust. Each person possesses an inviolability founded on justice that even the welfare of society as a whole cannot override. . . .

A society is a more or less self-sufficient association of persons who in their relations to one another recognize certain rules of conduct as binding and who for the most part act in accordance with them. Suppose further that these rules specify a system of cooperation designed to advance the good of those taking part in it. Then, although a society is a cooperative venture for mutual advantage, it is typically marked by a conflict as well as by an identity of interests. There is an identity of interests since social cooperation makes possible a better life for all than any would have if each were to live solely by his own efforts. There is a conflict of interests since persons are not indifferent as to how the greater benefits produced by their collaboration are distributed, for in order to pursue their ends they each prefer a larger to a lesser share. A set of principles is required for choosing among the various social arrangements which determine this division of advantages and for underwriting an agreement on the proper distributive shares. These principles are the principles of social justice: they provide a way of assigning rights and duties in the basic institutions of society and they define the appropriate distribution of the benefits and burdens of social cooperation. . . .

THE MAIN IDEA OF THE THEORY OF JUSTICE

My aim is to present a conception of justice which generalizes and carries to a higher level of abstraction the familiar theory of the social contract as found, say, in Locke, Rousseau, and Kant. In order to do this we are not to think of the original contract as one to enter a particular society or to set up a particular form of government. Rather, the guiding idea is that the principles of justice for the basic structure of society are the object of the original agreement. They are the principles that free and rational persons concerned to further their own interests would accept in an initial position of equality as defining the fundamental terms of their association. These principles are to regulate all further agreements; they specify the kinds of social cooperation that can be entered into and the forms of government that can be established. This way of regarding the principles of justice I shall call justice as fairness.

Thus we are to imagine that those who engage in social cooperation choose together, in one joint act, the principles which are to assign basic rights and duties and to determine the division of social benefits. Men are to decide in advance how they are to regulate their claims against one another and what is to be the foundation charter of their society. . . .

In justice as fairness the original position of equality corresponds to the state of nature in the traditional theory of the social contract. This original position is not, of course, thought of as an actual historical state of affairs, much less as a primitive condition of culture. It is understood as a purely hypothetical situation characterized so as to lead to a certain conception of justice. Among the essential features of this situation is that no one knows his place in society, his class position or social status, nor does any one know his fortune in the distribution of natural assets and abilities, his intelligence, strength, and the like. . . . The principles of justice are chosen behind a veil of ignorance. This ensures that no one is advantaged or disadvantaged in the choice of principles by the outcome of natural chance or the contingency of social circumstances. Since all are similarly situated and no one is able to design principles to favor his particular condition, the principles of justice are the result of a fair agreement or bargain. . . . The original position is, one might say, the appropriate initial status quo, and thus the fundamental agreements reached in it are fair. This explains the propriety of the name "justice as fairness": it conveys the idea that the principles of justice are agreed to in an initial situation that is fair. . . .

In working out the conception of justice as fairness one main task clearly is to determine which principles of justice would be chosen in the original position. To do this we must describe this situation in some detail and formulate with care the problem of choice which it presents. . . . It may be observed, however, that once the principles of justice are thought of as arising from an original agreement in a situation of equality, it is an open question whether the principle of utility would be acknowledged. Offhand it hardly seems likely that persons who view themselves as equals, entitled to press their claims upon one another, would agree to a principle which may require lesser life prospects for some simply for the sake of a greater sum of advantages enjoyed by others. . . .

I shall maintain instead that the persons in the initial situation would choose two rather different principles: the first requires equality in the assignment of basic rights and duties, while the second holds that social and economic inequalities, for example inequalities of wealth and authority, are just only if they result in compensating benefits for everyone, and in particular for the least advantaged members of society. These principles rule out justifying institutions on the grounds that the hardships of some are offset by a greater good in the aggregate. . . .

TWO PRINCIPLES OF JUSTICE

I shall now state in a provisional form the two principles of justice that I believe would be chosen in the original position. . . .

The first statement of the two principles reads as follows.

First: each person is to have an equal right to the most extensive basic liberty compatible with a similar liberty for others.

Second: social and economic inequalities are to be arranged so that they are both (a) reasonably expected to be to everyone's advantage, and (b) attached to positions and offices open to all. . . .

By way of general comment, these principles primarily apply, as I have said, to the basic structure of society. They are to govern the assignment of rights and duties and to regulate the distribution of social and economic advantages. As their formulation suggests, these principles presuppose that the social structure can be divided into two more or less distinct parts, the first principle applying to the one, the second to the other. They distinguish between those aspects of the social system that define and secure the equal liberties of citizenship and those that specify and establish social and economic inequalities. The basic liberties of citizens are, roughly speaking, political liberty (the right to vote and to be eligible for public office) together with freedom of speech and assembly; liberty of conscience and freedom of thought; freedom of the person along with the right to hold (personal) property; and freedom from arbitrary arrest and seizure as defined by the concept of the rule of law. These liberties are all required to be equal by the first principle, since citizens of a just society are to have the same basic rights.

The second principle applies, in the first approximation, to the distribution of income and wealth and to the design of organizations that make use of differences in authority and responsibility, or chains of command. While the distribution of wealth and income need not be equal, it must be to everyone's advantage, and at the same time, positions of authority and offices of command must be accessible to all. One applies the second principle by holding positions open, and then, subject to this constraint, arranges social and economic inequalities so that everyone benefits.

These principles are to be arranged in a serial order with the first principle prior to the second. This ordering means that a departure from the institutions of equal liberty required by the first principle cannot be justified by, or compensated for, by greater social and economic advantages. The distribution of wealth and income, and the hierarchies of authority, must be consistent with both the liberties of equal citizenship and equality of opportunity. . . .

Discussion Questions

1. Is the "veil of ignorance" a useful conceptual device for formulating public policy on issues of social justice? Do you agree with Rawls that people under the veil of ignorance would come up with his two principles of justice? Explain why or why not.
2. How should social benefits, such as a college education, be distributed? Apply Rawls's two principles of justice in developing a public policy on affirmative action in college admissions.
3. Does pornography violate Rawls's first principle of justice? Support your answer.
4. Given that genetic engineering and cloning will probably be an option only for well-off parents, discuss whether it is fair to use public tax money to fund research on cloning and genetic engineering. Support your answer.

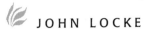 JOHN LOCKE

Two Treatises of Civil Government

British philosopher John Locke (1632–1704) was born into a liberal Puritan family that was heavily involved in political activism. His father, a country attorney, fought on the parliamentary side in the first rebellion against King Charles I.

Locke's theory of natural rights emerged primarily as a protest against the idea that the king possessed divine rights. A deeply religious man, Locke believed that God created the earth as a resource for humans. These natural rights ethics had a profound effect on the founders of the United States, especially Thomas Jefferson. Locke maintained that our natural rights include life, liberty, and property.

In the following selection, from *Two Treatises of Civil Government,* Locke defends our right to own property and explains why people in a state of nature come together to form a political society.

Critical Reading Questions

1. How does Locke define political power?
2. What is the state of nature? What rights do humans have in a state of nature?
3. What is the law of nature?
4. On what grounds does Locke argue that civil society is preferable to a state of nature?
5. According to Locke, why do humans as a group have a right to the resources of the earth?
6. How do humans, as individuals, make these resources their property?
7. What are the limits on what we can claim as our property?
8. According to Locke, why do people come together to form a political society?
9. What are the advantages and disadvantages of living in a political society?

OF THE STATE OF NATURE

4. To understand political power aright, and derive it from its original, we must consider what estate all men are naturally in, and that is, a state of perfect freedom to order their actions, and dispose of their possessions and persons as they think fit, within the bounds of the law of Nature, without asking leave or depending upon the will of any other man.

A state also of equality, wherein all the power and jurisdiction is reciprocal, no one having more than another, there being nothing more evident than that creatures of the same species and rank, promiscuously born to all the same advantages of Nature, and the use of the same faculties, should also be equal one amongst another, without subordination or subjection, unless the lord and master of them all should, by any manifest declaration of

"Natural Rights," from *Two Treatises of Civil Government* (London: A & J Churchill, 1698). Notes have been omitted.

his will, set one above another, and confer on him by an evident and clear appointment an undoubted right to dominion and sovereignty.

. . .

6. But though this be a state of liberty, yet it is not a state of license; though man in that state have an uncontrollable liberty to dispose of his person or possessions, yet he has not liberty to destroy himself, or so much as any creature in his possession, but where some nobler use than its bare preservation calls for it. The state of nature has a law of nature to govern it, which obliges everyone; and reason, which is that law, teaches all mankind who will but consult it, that, being all equal and independent, no one ought to harm another in his life, health, liberty, or possessions. For men being all the workmanship of one omnipotent and infinitely wise Maker, they are his property, . . .

. . .

15. . . . "for as much as we are not by ourselves sufficient to furnish ourselves with competent store of things needful for such a life as our Nature doth desire, a life fit for the dignity of man, therefore to supply those defects and imperfections which are in us, as living single and solely by ourselves, we are naturally induced to seek communion and fellowship with others; this was the cause of men uniting themselves as first in politic societies." But I, moreover, affirm that all men are naturally in that state, and remain so till, by their own consents, they make themselves members of some politic society, . . .

OF PROPERTY

. . .

25. God, who hath given the world to men in common, hath also given them reason to make use of it to the best advantage of life and convenience. The earth and all that is therein is given to men for the support and comfort of their being. And though all the fruits it naturally produces, and beasts it feeds, belong to mankind in common, as they are produced by the spontaneous hand of Nature, and

nobody has originally a private dominion exclusive of the rest of mankind in any of them, as they are thus in their natural state, yet being given for the use of men, there must of necessity be a means to appropriate them some way or other before they can be of any use, or at all beneficial, to any particular men. . . .

26. Though the earth and all inferior creatures be common to all men, yet every man has a "property" in his own "person." This nobody has any right to but himself. The "labour" of his body and the "work" of his hands, we may say, are properly his. Whatsoever, then, he removes out of the state that Nature hath provided and left it in, he hath mixed his labour with it, and joined to it something that is his own, and thereby makes it his property. It being by him removed from the common state Nature placed it in, it hath by this labour something annexed to it that excludes the common right of other men. For this "labour" being the unquestionable property of the labourer, no man but he can have a right to what that is once joined to, at least where there is enough, and as good left in common for others.

OF THE BEGINNING OF POLITICAL SOCIETIES

95. Men being, as has been said, by nature all free, equal, and independent, no one can be put out of this estate and subjected to the political power of another without his own consent, which is done by agreeing with other men, to join and unite into a community for their comfortable, safe, and peaceable living, one amongst another, in a secure enjoyment of their properties, and a greater security against any that are not of it. This any number of men may do, because it injures not the freedom of the rest; they are left, as they were, in the liberty of the state of Nature. When any number of men have so consented to make one community or government, they are thereby presently incorporated, and make one body politic, wherein the majority have a right to act and conclude the rest.

96. For, when any number of men have, by the consent of every individual, made a community, they have thereby made that community one body, with a power to act as one body, which is only by the will and determination of the majority.

. . .

99. Whosoever, therefore, out of a state of Nature unite into a community, must be understood to give up all the power necessary to the ends for which they unite into society to the majority of the community, unless they expressly agreed in any number greater than the majority. And this is done by barely agreeing to unite into one political society, which is all the compact that is, or needs be, between the individuals that enter into or make up a commonwealth. And thus, that which begins and actually constitutes any political society is nothing but the consent of any number of freemen capable of majority, to unite and incorporate into such a society. And this is that, and that only, which did or could give beginning to any lawful government in the world. . . .

Discussion Questions

1. Do you agree with Locke that people can exist outside of civil society in a "state of nature"? Support your answer.
2. Do you agree with Locke that there is a law of nature that gives individuals living in a state of nature the right to punish transgressors? Does the lack of an international government mean that nations are living in a state of nature? Discuss whether this justifies, for example, the use of war against nations that violate our property rights.
3. Natural rights ethicists claim that human equality is self-evident. What does this mean? What are the implications of this belief for public policy on gay rights?
4. Discuss how an animal-rights proponent such as Tom Regan might respond to Locke's claim that only humans have moral rights.
5. Ralph Waldo Emerson once said that "people say law but they mean wealth." In the United States 90 percent of the resources are owned by 10 percent of the people. Compare and contrast the capitalist system of property ownership, as supported by Ayn Rand, with Locke's philosophy. Use specific examples to illustrate your answer.

AYN RAND

Man's Rights

Philosopher, novelist, and playwright Ayn Rand (1905–1982) is one of the foremost contemporary defenders of natural rights ethics. Born in St. Petersburg, Russia, Rand immigrated to the United States in 1931. Her rights ethics developed, in part, as a result of her experience living under both the Soviet and the U.S. systems of government. Rand became disillusioned with the demoralizing effects of collectivism and Soviet communism and concluded that the blend of natural rights ethics and ethical egoism underlying laissez-faire capitalism is the only philosophy compatible with respect for the integrity and the reality of the individual human.

The sole purpose of government is the protection of our individual rights. Having the freedom to choose how to use our property, to choose our careers, and to choose where we buy and sell our goods and labor is essential to Rand's concept of the good life. Welfare rights, on the other hand, are not true rights, because they involve forcibly taking goods from people who earned them and giving them to people who have neither earned nor deserve them.

In the selection from her essay "Man's Rights," Rand compares and contrasts her notion of liberty rights with the current notion of economic or welfare rights. Freedom of speech, she argues, has already been curtailed in the name of welfare rights. Affirmative action is another example of welfare rights taking precedence over liberty rights. Rand concludes that the promotion of economic or welfare rights can occur only at the expense of individual freedom.

Critical Reading Questions

1. What, according to Rand, is the relationship between capitalism and individual rights?
2. How does Rand define the term *rights?*
3. What is our most fundamental right? Why?
4. Which political/economic system, according to Rand, is the best at promoting and protecting rights? Why?
5. Why does Rand consider the United States to be a great nation? What does she have to say about the Declaration of Independence and the Bill of Rights?
6. What is the distinction between economic rights and political rights?
7. On what grounds does Rand criticize the Democratic platform of 1960?

"Man's Rights," from *The Virtue of Selfishness* (New York: Signet, 1964).

If one wishes to advocate a free society—that is, capitalism—one must realize that its indispensable foundation is the principle of individual rights. If one wishes to uphold individual rights, one must realize that capitalism is the only system that can uphold and protect them. . . .

"Rights" are a moral concept—the concept that provides a logical transition from the principles guiding an individual's actions to the principles guiding his relationship with others—the concept that preserves and protects individual morality in a social context—the link between the moral code of a man and the legal code of a society, between ethics and politics. *Individual rights are the means of subordinating society to moral law. . . .*

The most profoundly revolutionary achievement of the United States of America was *the subordination of society to moral law.*

The principle of man's individual rights represented the extension of morality into the social system—as a limitation on the power of the state, as man's protection against the brute force of the collective, as the subordination of *might* to *right*. The United States was the first *moral* society in history.

All previous systems had regarded man as a sacrificial means to the ends of others, and society as an end in itself. The United States regarded man as an end in himself, and society as a means to the peaceful, orderly *voluntary* coexistence of individuals. All previous systems had held that man's life belongs to society, that society can dispose of him in any way it pleases, and that any freedom he enjoys is his only by favor, by the *permission* of society, which may be revoked at any time. The United States held that man's life is his by *right* (which means: by moral principle and by his nature), that a right is the property of an individual, that society as such has no rights, and that the only moral purpose of a government is the protection of individual rights.

A "right" is a moral principle defining and sanctioning a man's freedom of action in a social context. There is only *one* fundamental right (all the others are its consequences or corollaries): a man's right to his own life. Life is a process of self-sustaining and self-generated action; the right to life means the right to engage in self-sustaining and self-generated action—which means: the freedom to take all the actions required by the nature of a rational being for the support, the furtherance, the fulfillment and the enjoyment of his own life. (Such is the meaning of the right to life, liberty and the pursuit of happiness.)

The concept of a "right" pertains only to action—specifically, to freedom of action. It means freedom from physical compulsion, coercion or interference by other men.

Thus, for every individual, a right is the moral sanction of a *positive*—of his freedom to act on his own judgment, for his own goals, by his own *voluntary, uncoerced* choice. As to his neighbors, his rights impose no obligations on them except of a *negative* kind: to abstain from violating his rights.

The right to life is the source of all rights—and the right to property is their only implementation. Without property rights, no other rights are possible. Since man has to sustain his life by his own effort, the man who has no right to the product of his effort has no means to sustain his life. The man who produces while others dispose of his product, is a slave.

Bear in mind that the right to property is a right to action, like all the others: it is not the right *to an object,* but to the action and the consequences of producing or earning that object. It is not a guarantee that a man *will* earn any property, but only a guarantee that he will own it if he earns it. It is the right to gain, to keep, to use and to dispose of material values.

The concept of individual rights is so new in human history that most men have not grasped it fully to this day. In accordance with the two theories of ethics, the mystical or the social, some men assert that rights are a gift of God—others, that rights are a gift of society. But, in fact, the source of rights is man's nature. . . .

To violate man's rights means to compel him to act against his own judgment, or to expropriate his values. Basically, there is only one way to do it: by the use of physical force. There are two potential violators of man's rights: the criminals and the government. The great achievement of the United States was to draw a distinction between these two—by forbidding to the second the legalized version of the activities of the first.

The Declaration of Independence laid down the principle that "to secure these rights, governments are instituted among men." This provided the only valid justification of a government and defined its only proper purpose: to protect man's rights by protecting him from physical violence.

Thus the government's function was changed from the role of ruler to the role of servant. The government was set to protect man from criminals—and the Constitution was written to protect man from the government. The Bill of Rights was not directed against private citizens, but against the government—as an explicit declaration that individual rights supersede any public or social power. . . .

Altruism is incompatible with freedom, with capitalism and with individual rights. One cannot combine the pursuit of happiness with the moral status of a sacrificial animal.

It was the concept of individual rights that had given birth to a free society. It was with the destruction of individual rights that the destruction of freedom had to begin. . . .

The Democratic Party platform of 1960 summarizes the switch boldly and explicitly. It declares that a Democratic Administration "will reaffirm the economic bill of rights which Franklin Roosevelt wrote into our national conscience sixteen years ago."

Bear clearly in mind the meaning of the concept of *"rights"* when you read the list which that platform offers:

"1. The right to a useful and remunerative job in the industries or shops or farms or mines of the nation.

2. The right to earn enough to provide adequate food and clothing and recreation.

3. The right of every farmer to raise and sell his products at a return which will give him and his family a decent living.

4. The right of every businessman, large and small, to trade in an atmosphere of freedom from unfair competition and domination by monopolies at home and abroad.

5. The right of every family to a decent home.

6. The right to adequate medical care and the opportunity to achieve and enjoy good health.

7. The right to adequate protection from the economic fears of old age, sickness, accidents and unemployment.

8. The right to a good education."

A single question added to each of the above eight clauses would make the issue clear: *At whose expense?*

Jobs, food, clothing, recreation (!), homes, medical care, education, etc., do not grow in nature. These are man-made values—goods and services produced by men. *Who* is to provide them?

If some men are entitled *by right* to the products of the work of others, it means that those others are deprived of rights and condemned to slave labor.

Any alleged "right" of one man, which necessitates the violation of the rights of another, is not and cannot be a right.

No man can have a right to impose an unchosen obligation, an unrewarded duty or an involuntary servitude on another man. There can be no such thing as *"the right to enslave."*

A right does not include the material implementation of that right by other men; it includes only the freedom to earn that implementation by one's own effort.

Observe, in this context, the intellectual precision of the Founding Fathers: they spoke of the right to *the pursuit* of happiness—*not* of the right to happiness. It means that a man has the right to take the actions he deems necessary to achieve his happiness; it does *not* mean that others must make him happy. . . .

The right to property means that a man has the right to take the economic actions necessary to earn property, to use it and dispose of it; it does *not* mean that others must provide him with property.

The right of free speech means that a man has the right to express his ideas without danger of suppression, interference or punitive action by the government. It does *not* mean that others must provide him with a lecture hall, a radio station or a printing press through which to express his ideas.

Any undertaking that involves more than one man, requires the *voluntary* consent of every participant. Every one of them has the *right* to make his own decision, but none has the right to force his decision on the others. . . .

And while people are clamoring about "economic rights," the concept of political rights is vanishing. It is forgotten that the right of free speech means the freedom to advocate one's views and to bear the possible consequences, including disagreement with others, opposition, unpopularity and lack of support. The political function of "the right of free speech" is to protect dissenters and un-

popular minorities from forcible suppression—*not* to guarantee them the support, advantages and rewards of a popularity they have not gained. . . .

Such is the state of one of today's most crucial issues: *political* rights versus "*economic* rights." It's either-or. One destroys the other. But there are, in fact, no "economic rights," no "collective rights," no "public-interest rights." The term "individual rights" is a redundancy: there is no other kind of rights and no one else to possess them.

Those who advocate *laissez-faire* capitalism are the only advocates of man's rights.

Discussion Questions

1. Discuss how Rand would approach the issue of affirmative action. Explain why. Relate your answer to the concepts of liberty rights and welfare rights.
2. Discuss how Rand might approach the issue of hate speech on campus.
3. What concerns would Rand have regarding the regulation of violence in children's television programs and hard-core pornography? Would it matter to her if it could be shown that exposure to television violence and hard-core pornography increases violent behavior in viewers?
4. How might Rand reconcile her support for laissez-faire capitalism and free enterprise with the increasing problem of industrial pollution and the destruction of the environment? Develop a policy for dealing with global warming based on Rand's rights ethics. Are you satisfied with this policy? Why or why not?

  NEL NODDINGS

Caring: A Feminine Approach to Ethics and Moral Education

American philosopher and virtue ethicist Nel Noddings is a professor at Stanford University. Noddings's care ethics integrates the personal and the analytical. The mother of ten children, five of her own and five that she and her husband adopted, Noddings asked herself how she could bring together her personal life, particularly her life as a mother, and her analytical training in philosophy. This question changed the direction of her work. Shortly after, she published her first article on care ethics.

Care ethics, which expands on Carol Gilligan's studies of women's moral reasoning, is currently one of the most influential feminist theories in moral philosophy. Unlike the

---

Caring: A Feminine Approach to Ethics and Moral Education (Berkeley: University of California Press, 1984).

analytical approach of most earlier philosophers, care ethics stresses the contextual aspect of morality. Care, according to Noddings, is an active virtue. We are at our moral best when we are caring and being cared for in relationships. It is care, not an abstract sense of duty, that creates moral obligations.

In the selection from her book *Caring: A Feminine Approach to Ethics and Moral Education*, Noddings illustrates the role of feelings or sentiment in morality, using the example of the natural care a mother feels for her child. Ethical caring in relationships builds on and strives to maintain this feeling of natural care. Thus, caring becomes an ethical ideal.

Although Noddings does not altogether reject the use of principled moral reasoning, she believes that as an ideal, care offers us guidance in actual situations and relationships that an abstract ethics of duty cannot provide. Care ethics requires that we consider issues such as abortion, physician-assisted suicide, and gay marriage from within the context of actual caring relationships, rather than simply from the perspective of abstract universal principles.

Critical Reading Questions

1. What does Noddings mean by the term *care?*
2. How do we demonstrate caring for others?
3. What are the limitations on caring? Do we, for example, have a moral obligation to care for people we do not know or people we do not like?
4. What is the difference between natural caring and ethical caring? What are some examples of each type?
5. What, according to Noddings, is the "ethical ideal" or "vision of the best self"?
6. Why does Noddings consider the ethical ideal of caring preferable to moral principles as a guide to moral actions?
7. Why does Noddings reject the principle of universality? In particular, why does she reject the principle of universal love?
8. On what grounds does Noddings claim that we do not have moral obligations to other animals?
9. What does Noddings mean when she says that an ethic of care is a "feminine," as opposed to a "masculine," ethic?

From Natural to Ethical Caring

David Hume long ago contended that morality is founded upon and rooted in feeling—that the "final sentence" on matters of morality, "that which renders morality an active virtue"—". . . this final sentence depends on some internal sense or feeling, which nature has made universal in the whole species. For what else can have an influence of this nature?"

What is the nature of this feeling that is "universal in the whole species"? I want to suggest that morality as an "active virtue" requires two feelings and not just one. The first is the sentiment of natural caring. There can be no ethical sentiment without the initial, enabling sentiment. In situations where we act on behalf of the other because we want to do so, we are acting in accord with natural caring. A mother's caretaking efforts in behalf of her child are not usually considered ethical but natural. Even maternal animals take care of their offspring, and we do not credit them with ethical behavior. . . .

Recognizing that ethical caring requires an effort that is not needed in natural caring does not commit us to a position that elevates ethical caring over natural caring. Kant has identified the ethical with that which is done out of duty and not out of love, and that distinction in itself seems right. But an ethic built on caring strives to maintain the caring attitude and is thus dependent upon, and not superior to, natural caring. The source of ethical behavior is, then, in twin sentiments—one that feels directly for the other and one that feels for and with that best self, who may accept and sustain the initial feeling rather than reject it.

We shall discuss the ethical ideal, that vision of best self, in some depth. When we commit ourselves to obey the "I must" even at its weakest and most fleeting, we are under the guidance of this ideal. It is not just any picture. Rather, it is our best picture of ourselves caring and being cared for. . . .

I feel the moral "I must" when I recognize that my response will either enhance or diminish my ethical ideal. It will serve either to increase or decrease the likelihood of genuine caring. My response affects me as one-caring. In a given situation with someone I am not fond of, I may be able to find all sorts of reasons why I should not respond to his need. I may be too busy. He may be undiscerning. The matter may be, on objective analysis, unimportant. But, before I decide, I must turn away from this analytic chain of thought and back to the concrete situation. Here is this person with this perceived need to which is attached this importance. I must put justification aside temporarily. Shall I respond? How do I feel as a duality about the "I" who will not respond?

I am obliged, then, to accept the initial "I must" when it occurs and even to fetch it out of recalcitrant slumber when it fails to awake spontaneously. The source of my obligation is the value I place on the relatedness of caring. This value itself arises as a product of actual caring and being cared-for and my reflection on the goodness of these concrete caring situations. . . .

Let me say here, however, why it seems preferable to place an ethical ideal above principle as a guide to moral action. It has been traditional in moral philosophy to insist that moral principles must be, by their very nature as moral principles, universifiable. If I am obligated to do X under certain conditions, then under sufficiently similar conditions you also are obligated to do X. But the principle of universifiability seems to depend, as Nietzsche pointed out, on a concept of "sameness." In order to accept the principle, we should have to establish that human predicaments exhibit sufficient sameness, and this we cannot do without abstracting away from concrete situations those qualities that seem to reveal the sameness. In doing this, we often lose the very qualities or factors that gave rise to the moral question in the situation. That condition which makes the situation different and thereby induces genuine moral puzzlement cannot be satisfied by the application of principles developed in situations of sameness.

This does not mean that we cannot receive any guidance from an attempt to discover principles that seem to be universifiable. We can, under this sort of plan, arrive at the doctrine of "prima facie duty" described by W. D. Ross. Ross himself, however, admits that this doctrine yields no real guidance for moral conduct in concrete situations. It guides us in abstract moral thinking; it tells us, theoretically, what to do, "all other things being equal." But other things are rarely if ever equal. . . .

Our obligation is limited and delimited by relation. We are never free, in the human domain, to abandon our preparedness to care; but, practically, if we are meeting those in our inner circles adequately as ones caring and receiving those linked to our inner circles by formal chains of relation, we shall limit the calls upon our obligation quite naturally. We are not obliged to summon the "I must" if there is no possibility of completion in the other. I am not obliged to care for starving children in Africa, because there is no way for this caring to be completed in the other unless I abandon the caring to which I am obligated. I may still choose to do something in the direction of caring, but I am not obliged to do so. When we discuss our obligation to animals, we shall see that this is even more sharply limited by relation. We cannot refuse obligation in human affairs by merely refusing to enter relation;

we are, by virtue of our mutual humanity, already and perpetually in potential relation. Instead, we limit our obligation by examining the possibility of completion. In connection with animals, however, we may find it possible to refuse relation itself on the grounds of a species-specific impossibility of any form of reciprocity in caring. . . .

One under the guidance of an ethic of caring is tempted to retreat to a manageable world. Her public life is limited by her insistence upon meeting the other as one-caring. So long as this is possible, she may reach outward and enlarge her circles of caring. When this reaching out destroys or drastically reduces her actual caring, she retreats and renews her contact with those who address her. If the retreat becomes a flight, an avoidance of the call to care, her ethical ideal is diminished. Similarly, if the retreat is away from human beings and toward other objects of caring—ideas, animals, humanity-at-large, God—her ethical ideal is virtually shattered. This is not a judgment, for we can understand and sympathize with one who makes such a choice. It is more in the nature of a perception: we see clearly what has been lost in the choice.

Our ethic of caring—which we might have called a "feminine ethic"—begins to look a bit mean in contrast to the masculine ethics of universal love or universal justice. But universal love is illusion. Under the illusion, some young people retreat to the church to worship that which they cannot actualize; some write lovely poetry extolling universal love; and some, in terrible disillusion, kill to establish the very principles which should have entreated them not to kill. Thus are lost both principles and persons.

Discussion Questions

1. Compare and contrast the moral philosophies of Nel Noddings and Immanuel Kant. In particular, what is the source and role of duty or moral obligation in care ethics?
2. Do you agree with Noddings that care requires reciprocity in a relationship? Discuss the implications of her ethics for issues such as abortion and euthanasia. If moral obligation requires reciprocal relationships, does a pregnant woman have a moral obligation to her fetus? Do families have a moral obligation to care for members who are severely retarded or senile, or is euthanasia morally permissible for members of a family who are unable to reciprocate caring?
3. Discuss how a care ethicist might approach issues in environmental ethics such as global warming and preservation of wildlife. Is care ethics adequate for dealing with these issues? Support your answer.
4. Pornography takes women out of relationships and objectifies them. While a care ethicist might be morally opposed to pornography because of this, how would this translate into a public policy regarding pornography in the media? Support your answer.
5. Some judges hear victims' statements before passing sentences. To what extent should a sentence depend on the willingness of the family and friends of the victim to express care for the guilty party? Is capital punishment permissible if no one wants to be in a caring relationship with the guilty party? If so, is it fair that one's moral worth as a person is judged by others' willingness to care? Support your answers.

CONFUCIUS

The Analects

Confucius (551–479 B.C.E.) is the most revered philosopher in China. He lived during the period of the "hundred philosophers" (the late-sixth to the early-third centuries B.C.E.). This period in history was paralleled by the golden age in Greek philosophy; indeed, Confucius died only ten years before the birth of Socrates, the "father of Western philosophy."

As a young man, Confucius had trouble holding on to a job because he was too outspoken about the proper conduct of rulers, so he gave up his dream of becoming a government official and settled for being a teacher. Confucius traveled for many years with his pupils, teaching and trying to influence rulers. Much of the writing in *The Analects* is directed toward the rulers, since it is the rulers who have the most power to advance virtue in society and individuals.

As a teacher Confucius radically changed Chinese philosophy by focusing on our duties to humanity rather than on spiritual concerns. Confucian moral philosophy is a blend of deontology, virtue ethics, and communitarianism; it emphasizes duties over rights, virtue over self-interest, and the well-being of the community over individual interests. Like Aristotle, Confucius believed that humans were happiest and found it easiest to be virtuous when they were living in a just and well-ordered society. Righteousness demands that we do what is right simply because it is our moral duty, not because it benefits us personally.

Confucian philosophy is not incompatible with expanding human rights in China; unlike Western natural rights ethics, however, where rights exist independently of our duties, rights exist in Confucian ethics only in the context of, and are derived from, our duty to the wider community. Freedom of speech, for example, should not be extended to the point that it threatens the harmony of the community. Freedom of speech should be extended, however, to permit criticism of the government and demand for social reform.

Critical Reading Questions

1. What does Confucius mean by "benevolence"?
2. Does Confucius think that virtue or benevolence is relative to the individual or culture? Or does he believe that it is the same for all people?
3. What does Confucius mean by the terms *gentleman* and *small man?*
4. Which does Confucius value the most—personal freedom or social harmony?
5. What duties do children have toward their parents?
6. What does Confucius mean when he says that the "gentleman is not invariably for or against anything. He is on the side of what is moral"?
7. Why is trust the most important social virtue?

The Analects, trans. by D. C. Lau (New York: Penguin Books, 1979). Notes have been omitted.

8. What is the root of injustice?

9. What does Confucius say about punishment?

10. Why do we have crime? What is the role of government and social policy in promoting virtuous behavior?

Book I

. . . 2. Yu Tzu said, "It is rare for a man whose character is such that he is good as a son and obedient as a young man to have the inclination to transgress against his superiors; it is unheard of for one who has no such inclination to be inclined to start a rebellion. The gentleman devotes his efforts to the roots, for once the roots are established, the Way will grow therefrom. Being good as a son and obedient as a young man is, perhaps, the root of a man's character."

3. The Master said, "It is rare, indeed, for a man with cunning words and an ingratiating face to be benevolent."

4. Tseng Tzu said, "Every day I examine myself on three counts. In what I have undertaken on another's behalf, have I failed to do my best? In my dealings with my friends have I failed to be trustworthy in what I say? Have I passed on to others anything that I have not tried out myself?"

5. The Master said, "In guiding a state of a thousand chariots, approach your duties with reverence and be trustworthy in what you say; avoid excesses in expenditure and love your fellow men; employ the labour of the common people only in the right seasons."

6. The Master said, "A young man should be a good son at home and an obedient young man abroad, sparing of speech but trustworthy in what he says, and should love the multitude at large but cultivate the friendship of his fellow men. If he has any energy to spare from such action, let him devote it to making himself cultivated." . . .

8. The Master said, "A gentleman who lacks gravity does not inspire awe. A gentleman who studies is unlikely to be inflexible.

"Make it your guiding principle to do your best for others and to be trustworthy in what you say. Do not accept as a friend anyone who is not as good as you.

"When you make a mistake, do not be afraid of mending your ways." . . .

Book IV

1. The Master said, "Of neighbourhoods benevolence is the most beautiful. How can the man be considered wise who, when he has the choice, does not settle in benevolence?"

2. The Master said, "One who is not benevolent cannot remain long in straitened circumstances, nor can he remain long in easy circumstances.

"The benevolent man is attracted to benevolence because he feels at home in it. The wise man is attracted to benevolence because he finds it to his advantage." . . .

4. The Master said, "If a man sets his heart on benevolence, he will be free from evil."

5. The Master said, . . . "If the gentleman forsakes benevolence, in what way can he make a name for himself? The gentleman never deserts benevolence, not even for as long as it takes to eat a meal. If he hurries and stumbles one may be sure that it is in benevolence that he does so."

6. The Master said, "I have never met a man who finds benevolence attractive or a man who finds unbenevolence repulsive. A man who finds benevolence attractive cannot be surpassed. A man who finds unbenevolence repulsive can, perhaps, be counted as benevolent, for he would not allow what is not benevolent to contaminate his person. . . .

7. The Master said, "In his errors a man is true to type. Observe the errors and you will know the man."

8. The Master said, "He has not lived in vain who dies the day he is told about the Way."

9. The Master said, "There is no point in seeking the views of a Gentleman who, though he sets his heart on the Way, is ashamed of poor food and poor clothes."

10. The Master said, "In his dealings with the world the gentleman is not invariably for or against anything. He is on the side of what is moral."

11. The Master said, "While the gentleman cherishes benign rule, the small man cherishes his native land. While the gentleman cherishes a respect for the law, the small man cherishes generous treatment."

12. The Master said, "If one is guided by profit in one's actions, one will incur much ill will." . . .

13. The Master said, "The gentleman understands what is moral. The small man understands what is profitable." . . .

15. The Master said, "In serving your father and mother you ought to dissuade them from doing wrong in the gentlest way. If you see your advice being ignored, you should not become disobedient but remain reverent. You should not complain even if in so doing you wear yourself out." . . .

Book XII

. . . 2. Chung-kung asked about benevolence. The Master said, "When abroad behave as though you were receiving an important guest. When employing the services of the common people behave as though you were officiating at an important sacrifice. Do not impose on others what you yourself do not desire. In this way you will be free from ill will whether in a state or in a noble family." . . .

7. Tzu-kung asked about government. The Master said, "Give them enough food, give them enough arms, and the common people will have trust in you."

Tzu-kung said, "If one had to give up one of these three, which should one give up first?"

"Give up arms."

Tzu-kung said, "If one had to give up one of the remaining two, which should one give up first?"

"Give up food. Death has always been with us since the beginning of time, but when there is no trust, the common people will have nothing to stand on." . . .

10. Tzu-chang asked about the exaltation of virtue and the recognition of misguided judgement. The Master said, "Make it your guiding principle to do your best for others and to be trustworthy in what you say, and move yourself to where rightness is, then you will be exalting virtue. When you love a man you want him to live and when you hate him you want him to die. . . .

16. The Master said, "The gentleman helps others to realize what is good in them; he does not help them to realize what is bad in them. The small man does the opposite."

17. Chi K'ang Tzu asked Confucius about government. Confucius answered, "To govern (cheng) is to correct (cheng). If you set an example by being correct, who would dare to remain incorrect?" . . .

19. Chi K'ang Tzu asked Confucius about government, saying, "What would you think if, in order to move closer to those who possess the Way, I were to kill those who do not follow the Way?"

Confucius answered, "In administering your government, what need is there for you to kill? Just desire the good yourself and the common people will be good. The virtue of the gentleman is like wind; the virtue of the small man is like grass. Let the wind blow over the grass and it is sure to bend." . . .

21. Fan Ch'ih was in attendance during an outing to the Rain Altar. He said, "May I ask about the exaltation of virtue, the reformation of the de-

praved and the recognition of misguided judgement?" The Master said, "What a splendid question! To put service before the reward you get for it, is that not exaltation of virtue? To attack evil as evil and not as evil of a particular man, is that not the way to reform the depraved? To let a sudden fit of anger make you forget the safety of your own person or even that of your parents, is that not misguided judgement?"

22. Fan Ch'ih asked about benevolence. The Master said, "Love your fellow men."

He asked about wisdom. The Master said, "Know your fellow men." Fan Ch'ih failed to grasp his meaning. The Master said, "Raise the straight and set them over the crooked. This can make the crooked straight." . . .

23. Tzu-kung asked about how friends should be treated. The Master said, "Advise them to the best of your ability and guide them properly, but stop when there is no hope of success. Do not ask to be snubbed." . . .

Book XIII

11. The Master said, "How true is the saying that after a state has been ruled for a hundred years by good men it is possible to get the better of cruelty and to do away with killing."

12. The Master said, "Even with a true king it is bound to take a generation for benevolence to become a reality."

13. The Master said, "If a man manages to make himself correct, what difficulty will there be for him to take part in government? If he cannot make himself correct, what business has he with making others correct?" . . .

19. Fan Ch'ih asked about benevolence. The Master said, "While at home hold yourself in a respectful attitude; when serving in an official capacity be reverent; when dealing with others do your best. These are qualities that cannot be put aside, even if you go and live among the barbarians." . . .

Discussion Questions

1. In light of what Confucius says about the relative importance of personal freedom and social harmony, discuss concerns he would have regarding the regulation of hate speech and pornography. Compare and contrast his approach with that of John Stuart Mill.
2. Discuss whether filial duty requires us to carry out a parent's or grandparent's wish for assistance in committing suicide. If so, is the duty to carry out these types of requests absolute or prima facie? Support your answer.
3. Compare the Confucian principle of reciprocity (book XII–2) to Kant's categorical imperative.
4. Why is Confucius opposed to capital punishment? What would he say about why capital punishment is legal in the United States? Discuss alternatives to capital punishment that Confucius might propose.

P. DON PREMASIRI

The Relevance of the Noble Eightfold Path to Contemporary Society

Buddhist moral philosopher P. Don Premasiri is a philosophy professor at the University of Peradeniya in Sri Lanka. In his paper he argues that Buddha's noble eightfold path offers valuable guidance for addressing and resolving contemporary moral issues. He suggests that Buddhist ethics offers a vision of the good society that may have even greater relevance for today's technologically advanced world than it did in Buddha's time.

Indian philosopher Siddhartha Gautama (c. 563–c. 483 B.C.E.), better known as Buddha or the "enlightened one," lived at the same time as Confucius. Buddha was born into a wealthy family in India, near Nepal. At the age of twenty-nine, he left his family and fortune in a quest for truth. After six years of fasting, meditation, and study, he received enlightenment while sitting under a bodhi tree.

Leading a moral and virtuous life is central to Buddhist philosophy. Right livelihood involves above all adopting right view and avoiding behavior that harms others. Only through encouraging the development of virtue through right living and right thinking can we as a society achieve moral progress and a resolution of the many social problems that plague modern society.

Unlike Hinduism and most Western ethics, Buddhism is nonhierarchical, emphasizing the interrelatedness and moral value of all living beings. Right living, therefore, includes compassion and an attitude of nonviolence toward all of nature. Buddha's rejection of the Hindu caste system and his imperative that we treat all beings with dignity has brought attention to the dignity of the poor and has inspired great leaders such as Mohandas Gandhi. Buddhism has also played a prominent role in both the animal-rights and environmental ethics movements.

Critical Reading Questions

1. On what grounds does Premasiri claim that the Buddhist eightfold path is relevant in addressing contemporary social issues?
2. How have advances in science and technology contributed to an increase in moral problems?
3. Why is our current approach to morality inadequate for resolving moral issues?
4. What is the noble eightfold path?
5. What does Buddha mean by "moral wisdom"?
6. What is the relationship between an individual's moral development (or lack thereof) and the prevalence of injustice and moral problems in society?
7. What, according to Buddha, is the primary source of suffering and corruption?

"The Relevance of the Noble Eightfold Path to Contemporary Society," from Charles Wei-hsun Fu and Sandra A. Wawrytko (eds.), *Buddhist Ethics and Modern Society* (New York: Greenwood Press, 1991), pp. 134–139. Notes have been omitted.

8. What is "right view"? Why is it important, in order for moral progress to occur, to embrace "right view"?
9. What does Buddha mean when he says that "evil dispositions are expressed in behavioral terms"?
10. What does Buddha mean by "right livelihood"?
11. How can we cultivate in ourselves an attitude that will contribute to moral progress and a better understanding of social issues?

THE CONTEMPORARY HUMAN CONDITION

In many respects the present age cannot be compared with Buddha's time. Today, human beings have made enormous progress in scientific knowledge. They have increased their knowledge about the nature of their own physical existence and the nature of their physical environment. With this increased theoretical knowledge, their technological capabilities to control and manipulate the physical environment have increased correspondingly. There is no doubt that we are making rapid and ongoing progress in the areas of scientific knowledge and technological skill. However, reflection on another aspect of our contemporary situation makes it evident that no corresponding progress has been achieved in practical wisdom. All the progress humanity has made appears to be endangered by the very technological skills that humans have achieved. We live in an age in which the evils that humans inflict on others have reached unparalleled extremes of barbarism. . . .

According to Buddhism, society can never be totally free of immorality and the resulting tensions and conflicts, for the predominant factors that generally govern human behavior, untutored by spiritual nurture and impelled purely by the baser instincts of human nature, are greed, hatred, and confusion. Buddhism considers these three psychological dispositions to be the roots of evil and human misery. Scientific progress has not made it possible for humanity to overcome these roots. Consequently, we are placed in a more precarious predicament when the discoveries and inventions based on our own intelligence threaten us with destruction. . . .

Technological progress has been utilized to feed human greed, with no limits set for human wants and patterns of consumption. Ecologists and environmental scientists foresee devastating effects from modern technology on the natural environment, as is now becoming apparent.

Associated with the above trends is a growth of other types of social evils, such as the spread of alcoholism and drug addiction. The younger generation, who have moved away from traditional religious values, appears to be seeking a new kind of salvation in the hallucinatory and escapist experiences evoked by alcohol and psychedelic drugs. This has resulted in a dulling of reason and intellect and a debilitation of sound judgment, contributing further to the growing trends of violence, insanity, and irresponsible behavior. . . .

Today, morality is often believed to belong to the sphere of the nonrational. This has given rise to an intellectual climate in which morality is seen as devoid of a rational foundation. It came to be believed that no universally acceptable standards of morality could be rationally discovered. Consequently, the possibility of moral knowledge and moral truth has been denied.

THE NOBLE EIGHTFOLD PATH IN A CONTEMPORARY CONTEXT

Buddhism does not subscribe to this view. It believes that what is indispensable in the life of humanity is moral wisdom. Those who lack moral wisdom are said to be stupid and deluded (*mando, momuho*). Each step in the Noble Eightfold Path of the Buddha is characterized morally and evaluatively as "right" (*sammā*). This path is the quintessence of Buddhist morality. . . .

Social harmony, peace, and justice depend largely on the moral development of the individual members constituting a society. Where this is lacking, we enter the vicious circle of morally degenerate individuals and a corrupt social order. Moral progress must reduce the intensity of the roots of evil. Our contemporary situation amply testifies to the fact that, although we have progressed in material science and technology, there has been no improvement, but rather a regression, in the moral sphere. Technological skill devoid of moral consciousness leads only to more effective expressions of cruelty and viciousness. . . .

RIGHT VIEWS

Right views (*sammā ditthi*) is the first step of the Noble Path, and there is an important reason why. It brings into focus the need for a wholesome ideological orientation or worldview, as a prerequisite for anyone who embarks on the search for the meaning of life and wishes to make intelligent choices regarding the way one ought to conduct oneself. However, the Buddhist notion of right views does not imply a dogmatic clinging to an ideological position. Attachment to a view (*ditthi rāga*) is as much a hindrance to moral progress as attachment to a material thing. The Buddha cautioned his disciples against converting his teachings into a dogma. Dogmatic clinging to an ideology can create conflicts not only among those with a diversity of aims and interests, but also among those whose aims and interests are the same. Fanaticism and intolerance often result from the delusion that, "this alone is the truth and everything else is false" (*idam eva saccam mogham aññam*), causing people to commit atrocities in the name of "truth." This applies to any ideological commitment—religious, moral, or political. . . .

Buddhism believes in personal survival after death, while the moral law of *kamma* is conducive to moral restraint. The materialist worldview is for Buddhism a life devoid of moral, spiritual, or religious concerns (*abrahmacariyāvāsa*). In the age of science it is felt that scientific humanism, which is essentially the adoption of a utilitarian norm coupled with the conviction that individual existence is limited to this life, is sufficient to guide human behavior. There is good reason to question this based on modern day experience. The Buddhist position is that human beings can be motivated to lead a moral life only if they can be urged to act on enlightened self-interest, especially in the initial stages of their spiritual development. The belief in *kamma* and rebirth, and the prudential concept of merit (*puñña*) serves an important role in the moral life of the Buddhist. . . .

Right Thought, Right Speech, and Right Action

Buddhism recognizes three modes in which evil dispositions are expressed in behavioral terms: physical, verbal, and mental acts. Three steps of the Noble Path, right thought (*sammā sankappa*), right speech (*sammā vācā*), and right action (*sammā kammanta*), are specifically meant to prevent these evils. Buddhism attaches great significance to our mental life. Moral progress becomes possible only when a person acquires the ability to bring the mental processes under the direction of the will. . . .

Methods and schemes of moral development recommended by Buddhism appear to be based on an understanding of the mutual relationship between overt behavior and psychological dispositions. . . . Every verbal and bodily act creates a disposition toward repetition, thus contributing to the formation of a general pattern of behavior. Recognizing this fact, Buddhism emphasizes the importance of cultivating right speech and right action. Right speech consists first of avoiding false speech (*musā-vāda*), while cultivating truthfulness and trustworthiness. Second, it involves avoiding slanderous speech (*pisunāvācā*) intent on causing dissension among people, and cultivating speech that heals divisiveness and strengthens the bonds of those already united in bonds of friendship. Third, it involves the avoidance of harsh speech (*pharusāvacā*) and the cultivation of pleasant speech. Fourth, it involves abstention from frivolous or vain talk (*samphappalāpa*) and the cultivation of meaningful, purposeful, useful, and timely speech.

In right action (*sammā kammanta*), one is expected to abstain from injury to life, from violence and acts of terrorism, laying aside all weapons that cause injury to living beings. It also involves the positive cultivation of a mind filled with love and compassion, leading to compassionate action. . . .

Right Livelihood

Another step in the Noble Path that has considerable contemporary relevance is right livelihood (*sammā ājiva*). . . . At the level of the ordinary layperson, *sammā ājiva* draws attention to the necessity of adopting a morally acceptable means of livelihood and avoiding occupations that might be materially productive but morally reprehensible. These occupations include trading in weapons (*satthāvanijjā*), living beings (*sattavanijja*), flesh (*mamsavanijjā*), intoxicants or drugs (*majjavanijjā*) and poisons (*visavanijjā*). Almost all these forms of trade are practiced today on a global scale purely to satisfy commercial interests, without regard for their harmful social consequences. Most destructive of all is the trade in military weapons and addictive drugs. Commercial interests associated with excessive greed hinder responsible people from taking effective measures to prevent the miseries resulting from these social menaces. . . .

Right Effort, Right Mindfulness, and Right Contemplation

The sixth step, right effort (*sammāvāyāma*) recommends initiative and effort to prevent the growth of evil dispositions, cultivate healthy attitudes, and stabilize the wholesome dispositions of character already acquired. The moral agent constantly experiences inner conflict when choosing between what is considered to be the right thing to do and what passions, emotions, instincts, and inclinations prompt us to do. Right effort is considered to be the most effective means of overcoming those natural impulses, [and] is possible only if one does not resign oneself to external causes due to a false belief in fatalism or strict determinism.

The seventh step, right mindfulness (*sammāsati*), stands for watchfulness over the overall functioning of one's personality, both mental and physical. . . .

The eighth step of the path, right contemplation (*sammā samādhi*), stands for the clear and composed mind that is a prerequisite for the understanding that leads to moral perfection. Right contemplation is no doubt much needed by contemporary humanity; we are constantly bombarded by a dizzying variety of sensuous stimuli from our material environment, driving us to the brink of insanity. Those who have had the unsettling experience of sensory overload and excessive sensuous gratification suffer subsequent spells of boredom and depression, leading them to seek solace in psychedelic drugs that promise temporary states of altered consciousness, rapture, or mental ecstasy. Unfortunately, they are forms of false contemplation . . .

Most human suffering, of which human volition itself is the cause, springs from the actions of people whose minds are confused. Confused minds seem to be operative at all levels of contemporary society, from the topmost levels of decision-making to the lowest levels in the social hierarchy. In Buddhist theory, moral corruption or moral growth tends to flow from higher levels of the social hierarchy to the lower levels. It is imperative that we entrust the guidance of the destinies of the world to individuals who have cultivated the kind of right contemplation that Buddhism prescribes in its Noble Path if we are to avert the global annihilation that ominously looms before us.

Discussion Questions

1. Compare and contrast Buddha's beliefs about the role of leaders in moral progress with those of Confucius and Aristotle.
2. Like Aristotle, Buddha believed that engaging in destructive behavior makes us more likely to repeat that behavior in the future. Discuss the implications of his teachings regarding the morality of drug and alcohol use, pornography, and hate speech.

3. If Buddha were giving a speech to freshmen on your campus, what advice would he mostly likely give them for how to achieve moral wisdom and live the virtuous life?

4. Discuss what Buddha would most likely think about the morality of professions that involve animal agriculture, clearing of wildlife habitats for commercial use, or cloning. Apply the concept of "right livelihood" to your own career choice.

5. Many people believe that science is morally neutral and that, therefore, there is no problem in developing technology independent of considerations of the moral implications of such technology. Buddhists, on the other hand, warn against rapid technological advances that are not accompanied by similar progress in practical wisdom. Which position do you find most compelling from a moral point of view? Discuss the proposal a Buddhist ethicist would most likely make regarding the regulation of scientific research in cloning and genetic engineering.

C H A P T E R   2

Moral Reasoning

We get our . . . habits and opinions from outside influences; . . . Our manners change from time to time, but the changes are not reasoned out; . . . as a rule we do not think, we only imitate . . . what we mistake for standards are only fashions.

—Mark Twain, "Corn-Pone Opinions"

I believe that in this generation those with the courage to enter the moral conflict will find themselves with companions in every corner of the world.

—Senator Robert F. Kennedy, "Day of Affirmation,"
address at the University of Capetown, South Africa (June 6, 1966)

We have probably all heard the expression "The road to Hell is paved with good intentions." Without correct reasoning, people who have good intentions may end up actually causing harm. This is because, although people may be strongly motivated to do what is right, they cannot always figure out what is the best way to achieve this goal.

Policy makers in pre–Civil War America, for example, hoped to achieve harmony among the Northern and Southern states by means of the 1820 Missouri Compromise. After much bitter debate, Missouri was admitted to the Union as a slave state in order to maintain equal numbers of slave and free states. Although the intentions of the policy makers may have been good, their moral analysis of slavery and what constituted a fair and just policy was not. Moral reasoning involves more than simply following the majority viewpoint or trying to placate opposing sides through compromise.

Some people are so emotionally invested in certain moral issues that they may unwittingly manipulate their arguments in order to "prove" a conclusion that does not logically follow from their premise. When confronted with objections to their position, they often resort to resistance and fallacies as a way of shielding their "argument" from critical analysis. An understanding of logic and moral reasoning can help us break through these patterns of resistance. By sharpening our analytical skills, we can become more independent in our thinking and less susceptible to opinions that foster narrow-mindedness and bigotry.

THE THREE LEVELS OF THINKING

The thinking process used in moral reasoning can be broken down into three levels: experience, interpretation, and analysis. Keep in mind that this division is artificial. We never have *pure* experience or engage in *pure* analysis. All three levels overlap and interact with one another.

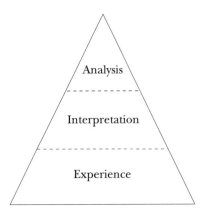

Experience

Experience, the first level of thinking, goes beyond the five senses; it also includes indirect experience. We may be gay or know people who are gay; we may read about the depletion of the ozone layer; we may hear about a murderer who was released from prison and who killed again; we may experience a feeling of moral repugnance when we see pictures of animals being used in lab experiments.

At this level of moral reasoning, we simply describe our experiences using neutral language. We do not, at least in theory, pass judgment on these experiences or draw any conclusions. The following are examples of statements at the level of experience:

1. Gay couples are not allowed to marry.
2. About 40 percent of college students engage in binge drinking (consuming more than five drinks in a short period of time).[1]
3. The sea level has risen several inches in the past century.[2]
4. Some lab experiments cause pain to nonhuman animals.
5. Affirmative action discriminates against white men.
6. Although black males represent only 6 percent of the U.S. population, they make up 50 percent of the prison inmates.[3]

Experience forms the foundation of moral reasoning. For this reason it is important that we first have our facts straight. When statistics or other findings are cited, they should be backed up with reliable sources. Ambiguous key terms, such as *binge drinking,* should also be clearly defined.

Interpretation

Interpretation involves trying to make sense of our experiences. The following are some possible interpretations of the experience that gay couples are not allowed to marry:

INTERPRETATION

If the law says it is wrong, it is wrong.
The Bible says that homosexuality is a sin.
It's not fair that gay people cannot enjoy the privileges of marriage.
Homosexuality is unnatural and should not have social or legal recognition.
The purpose of marriage is to have children, and gay people can't have children.
If gay marriage were allowed it would encourage homosexuality among young people.

— —

EXPERIENCE

Gay couples are not allowed to marry.

The interpretations of our experience, taken together, form what is known as our *worldview*. Most people like to think that they came up with their worldview on their own. In reality, our worldview or interpretations of moral issues are strongly influenced by our upbringing, our peers, and our culture. In addition to cultural norms, our worldview is also shaped by metaphysical assumptions regarding the nature of reality and the relationship of humans to the rest of the natural world. Our experiences not only contribute to our worldview; our worldview or interpretation of events also shapes the way we experience the world. For example, in a study of stereotyping, college students were shown a picture of a white thug beating up a black man in a business suit. When students were later asked to describe what they saw, the majority reported that they saw a black thug beating up a white businessman!

By not analyzing our views, we can get caught up in a sort of self-fulfilling prophecy, or vicious cycle, whereby we interpret our experience through the filter of a particular worldview, and our "experience," in turn, further confirms our distorted worldview. Because interpretations can be one-sided or distorted, it is important that we remain open-minded when listening to different people's interpretations of a moral issue. Of course, some of these interpretations may turn out to be better than others, but we should decide this based on analysis rather than prejudice or prejudging the issue.

Analysis

Analysis is the heart of moral reasoning. Many people rely on opinion, or a blend of fact and opinion, in formulating their views on moral issues. It is important to learn how to distinguish between the two. An *opinion* is a statement that is based on feeling rather than on fact. Unless we can back up our interpretations with facts, they are merely opinions, whether they be those of the majority or personal ones.

Analysis of moral issues requires not only beginning with correct facts but examining the possible interpretations of our experiences in light of fundamental moral principles and sentiments. As such, it often begins with a series of questions. Analysis of the issue of gay marriage, for example, might include the following questions: What is the purpose of marriage? Do people have a moral right to marry, or is marriage a privilege? If it is a right, what is the basis of this right? Is sexual orientation a morally relevant criteria for excluding people from marriage? Does the fact that something is illegal necessarily make it immoral? What are the consequences to society of sanctioning gay marriages? Does sanctioning gay marriage, in fact, encourage homosexuality among young people, and, if so, is this necessarily a harm? Is homosexuality unnatural? Is the naturalness or unnaturalness of homosexuality morally relevant? On what grounds does the Bible claim that homosexuality is an abomination? Are these grounds morally relevant when it comes to prohibiting or sanctioning gay marriage?

Analysis requires that we provide good reasons for why we support or reject a particular interpretation or worldview. It also requires a willingness to challenge our own views as well as those of others. Those interpretations that can stand up to the challenge of critical analysis can become part of our argument. Those that cannot should be discarded, no matter how dear to our hearts they may be.

EXERCISES

1. Discuss the quote from Mark Twain at the beginning of this chapter. How can we know whether our interpretations—our "habits and opinions"—are based on reason and analysis or whether they are merely based on "fashion"? Use specific examples to illustrate your answers.
2. Choose one of your own experiences, or use one of the six experiences listed earlier in this chapter. Working in small groups, list the possible interpretations of the experience. The interpretations do not have to be ones that you or members of your group accept. Also include on your list the prevailing cultural interpretations of the experience. Next analyze the different interpretations, asking: Which ones are merely opinions? Which ones can be backed up with good reasons?
3. How did you respond when other members of your group in the previous exercise challenged an interpretation with which you strongly agreed? Discuss how your reaction affected, if at all, your ability to engage in critical analysis of the issue.
4. What does Robert F. Kennedy mean, in the quote at the beginning of this chapter, by having "the courage to enter the moral conflict"? Why might some people be afraid to enter into moral conflict? Discuss your answers in light of your feelings about entering into a debate in which there is a moral conflict.

RESISTANCE

Most of us hate to be proven wrong. To avoid having our views or interpretations challenged, we may resort to a type of defense mechanism known as *resistance*. Everyone uses resistance at times to keep from feeling overwhelmed. A problem arises, however, when resistance becomes a habitual way of responding to challenges. When this happens, resistance acts a barrier to any critical analysis of our worldview. There are societal as well as more personal, psychological forms of resistance. We need to be aware of both forms in our lives.

To move past interpretation to analysis, we need to break down this barrier of resistance. We may rely primarily on one type of resistance, or we may have a wide repertoire

---

  TYPES OF RESISTANCE

Resistance is a defense mechanism used by people to avoid having their interpretations analyzed.

- **Ignorance** choosing not to learn about a particular issue.
- **Avoidance** staying away from situations in which our views may be challenged.
- **Anger** responding with anger when our view is challenged.
- **Clichés** dismissing challenges to our views with trite sayings.
- **Conformity/Superficial tolerance** going along with the crowd rather than risking rejection.
- **Struggling** struggling with an issue to avoid taking a stand.
- **Distractions** using distractions, such as television, to block out thoughts.

---

of types, depending on the situation. The following (shown also in the box) are just a few of the types of resistance that people may use when their moral views are challenged. In reading about the different types, ask yourself which you are most likely to use in discussing a moral issue. Recognizing and acknowledging our biases is the first step to breaking through our resistance.

Ignorance

There are situations in which we are ignorant because information is not available. For example, we do not know if people in comas are suffering, or what the long-term effects of cloning may be. Sometimes, however, we avoid learning about particular issues because we just do not want to know, rationalizing to ourselves that not knowing excuses us from having to think about an issue or take a stand. We may, for example, prefer to remain comfortably ignorant about the destructive effects on the environment of our individual and collective lifestyles. Society, through the use of media and political rhetoric, may choose to remain ignorant of the humanity of the "enemy" or of the extent of racism and sexism. An act of omission—failure to act or take a stand—however, is as much a moral decision as taking action. Millions of Jews died because Germans and other Europeans in Nazi-occupied countries chose to remain ignorant about the extent of the atrocities going on in their own backyards. Even today hundreds of thousands of people around the world are starving and being tortured by their own governments while most of the rest of the world prefers to remain comfortably ignorant about their plight. Animal agriculture and factory farming not only cause tremendous suffering to animals we raise to satisfy our taste for meat but are responsible for much of the current environmental crisis.

Avoidance

Rather than welcoming feedback from people who have different points of view, we may avoid people who disagree with us. Some people who hold strong opinions about certain moral issues, such as abortion, yet are insecure in the face of challenges to their position, read only literature that supports their opinion and associate only with people who agree with them. The tendency to avoid controversial situations can lead to a serious lack of communication and even hostility between people who hold widely opposing views. Avoidance can also stem from the fear of offending or angering others through disagreement with them.

Anger

We cannot always avoid people who disagree with us, especially if we are taking a class in ethics! When challenged about our view, we may respond by getting angry. Anger may also serve as a cover for our ignorance regarding a particular issue. Anger may be expressed overtly in physical violence or threats or by storming out of the room, or it may be expressed more subtly in glares, snubs, sarcastic remarks, or angry phrases such as "Don't force your views on me." Anger as a form of resistance is most effective in thwarting disagreement when the angry person has greater social or physical power, which leaves the more vulnerable person feeling threatened and intimidated.

Clichés

"Don't force your views on me." "It's all relative." "To each his own." "Things always work out for the best." "There are two sides to every story." "I have a right to my own opinion." Used sparingly, clichés can be useful for illustrating a point, but their habitual use in response to challenges to our views trivializes issues and, hence, acts as a barrier that keeps us from having to think seriously about those issues.

Conformity/Superficial Tolerance

Many people are afraid they will not be accepted by their peers if they disagree with them, so even when they do disagree they go along with the group anyway rather than risk rejection. Others who engage in superficial tolerance really do not have a point of view of their own, or they may confuse fairness with not taking sides. The expression "I can see both sides of the issue" often masks a reluctance to analyze contradictory views of a moral issue. Italian poet Dante Alighieri (1265–1321) took a dim view of people who used this type of resistance. In his *Divine Comedy,* Dante reserved the "darkest place in Hell" for those who remained neutral when confronted with a moral conflict.

"I'm Struggling"

During the Nazi occupation of France in World War II, the thirty-five hundred people of the village of Le Chambon provided refuge for Jews who were fleeing the Nazis. Many years later the villagers were asked by a television reporter from the United States why they did this when other people in France were still struggling with the issue. One elderly gentleman replied: "Those who struggle don't act; those who act don't struggle." It is appropriate to wrestle with moral issues before reaching at least a tentative stand, but for some people the "struggle" is used to avoid taking a stand while creating an appearance of being concerned.

Distractions

We all use distractions at some time in our lives to block out conflicting and troubling thoughts, but some people do this habitually. They may turn on the television or have loud music playing whenever they are alone. Alcohol, drugs, food, partying, work, or shopping for things we don't really need can also serve as a means of keeping our minds preoccupied. In class this type of resistance may take the form of sitting in the back of the room and whispering to another student, staring out the window, or reading a novel or newspaper during discussions of controversial moral issues.

People who habitually engage in resistance may unwittingly get caught up in "doublethink." Coined by George Orwell in his novel *1984, doublethink* involves holding two contradictory views at the same time and believing both to be true. When young people come to college, they often hold certain contradictory views regarding morality. Many college students, as noted in the previous chapter, hold contradictory views regarding the morality of homosexuality and abortion. In his book *The Closing of the American Mind,* Allan Bloom noted that many college students claim that morality is all relative while at the same time holding the opposite view that equality and tolerance are universal moral values. He writes:

> There is one thing a professor can be absolutely certain of: Almost every student entering the university believes, or says he believes, that truth is relative . . . students nowadays are unified only in their relativism and their allegiance to equality. . . . The danger they have been taught to fear from absolutism is not error but intolerance. . . . The point is not to correct the mistake and be really right; rather it is not to think you are right at all.[4]

Putting aside our resistance in discussions of controversial moral issues may bring up uncomfortable feelings and ideas. Breaking through resistance, consequently, can create disequilibrium and confusion. Although we may believe that by avoiding conflict life will be more tranquil and enjoyable, in fact, habitual resistance takes a lot of energy. When we shut out ideas and experiences that conflict with our cherished worldview, we also shut out much of the richness of life. The use of resistance in response to challenges to our views not only shuts off analysis and makes us vulnerable to doublethink, it also impedes our moral development.[5] In addition, habitual resistance can create a sense of boredom and general anxiety with life. It can also numb us to the needs of others and leave us unprepared to make effective moral decisions.

EXERCISES

1. What type of resistance are you most likely to use when your moral views are challenged? Illustrate your answer with a specific example of a time when you used this type of resistance during a discussion of a moral issue. What can you do to make yourself less prone to using this type of resistance?
2. According to Martin Luther King Jr., conformity and superficial tolerance are epidemic among Americans. "Many people fear nothing more terribly," he once wrote, "than to take a position which stands out sharply and clearly from prevailing opinion. The tendency of most is to adopt a view that is so ambiguous that it will include everything, and so popular that it will include everyone." Do you agree with King? Use specific examples to support your answer.
3. What are some examples of doublethink in your own life? Do you agree with Allan Bloom that most college students are caught up in doublethink when it comes to morality? Support your answer.

RECOGNIZING ARGUMENTS

Before we can engage in analysis, we first need to know how to recognize arguments as well as how to distinguish between good and bad arguments.

The Components of an Argument

An *argument* is made up of two or more propositions, one of which is supported by the others. A *proposition,* in logic, is a statement that expresses a complete thought; it can be true or false, and the same proposition can be stated in different ways. For example, "Torturing children is wrong," "It is wrong to torture children," and "Kinder zu qualen ist unmoralisch" are the same proposition because they all express the same thought.

The *conclusion* is the proposition that is affirmed or denied on the basis of the other propositions. The conclusion of an argument can appear anywhere in the argument. The *premise* is the proposition that provides reasons or support for the conclusion. An argument can have more than one premise. The process by which we move from the premise to the conclusion is known as *inference.*

$$\text{Premise(s)} \xrightarrow{\text{ inference }} \text{Conclusion}$$

The premises form the foundation of the argument. In a good argument, the premises must be strong enough to support the conclusion. A well-constructed argument, like a well-built house, must be able to withstand challenges. If the premises are weak, the whole argument may collapse like the proverbial house built on sand.

Premises can take several forms, including descriptive (factual) statements, definitions of key terms, prescriptive (value) statements, and analogies:

- *Descriptive statements* tell us what *is.* As Detective Joe Friday said in *Dragnet,* "Just the facts, ma'am."
- *Prescriptive statements* deal with values; they tell us what *ought* to be. Moral principles and normative judgments are prescriptive statements.
- Sometimes *definitions* of ambiguous key terms are included in the premises.
- An *analogy* is a comparison based on similarities between two things or events. In logic, analogies are used to support the conclusion that because things are similar in some important respects, they are also similar in other respects.

An argument may or may not contain terms known as *premise indicators* and *conclusion indicators* that can help us identify the premises and conclusion. Words such as *because, for, since,* and *as shown by* can serve as premise indicators. Words such as *therefore, thus, hence,* and *consequently,* can serve as conclusion indicators. Unfortunately, not all arguments contain premise indicators or conclusion indicators. Many of the words that serve as indicators can also appear in other contexts. For example, *because* and *therefore* are also used in explanations.

Rhetoric

Many people mistake rhetoric for logical argument. *Rhetoric* is a means of defending a particular worldview or opinion rather than analyzing it.[6] In logical arguments, we *end* with the conclusion; rhetoric, in contrast, *begins* with a pseudo-conclusion or opinion. Rhetoricians use only statements that support their particular opinion, disregarding any statements or facts that do not. The purpose of rhetoric is to win your opponents over through the power of persuasive speech; the purpose of a logical argument is to discover the truth.

Breaking Down Arguments

Breaking down an argument into its component parts makes it easier to analyze. In breaking down an argument, look for any premise and conclusion indicators. Circle the indicators, putting a *p.i.* above premise indicators, and a *c.i.* above conclusion indicators.

If there are no indicators, begin by identifying the conclusion, which can appear anywhere in an argument. In identifying the conclusion, ask yourself: What is this person trying to prove? What position is this person defending? Draw two lines under the conclusion.

Next identify the premises. Ask yourself: What support is this person offering for his or her conclusion? Draw one line under each premise.

The following is an example of an argument that has been broken down into its component parts. Note that the conclusion appears in the middle of the argument:

> We ought to treat people with equal respect. Therefore, racism is wrong because racism involves treating certain groups of people with less respect.

If there are no indicators and you are unsure whether a particular proposition is a premise or a conclusion, try putting the word *therefore* or *because* in front of it. If the meaning of the argument remains the same when you insert *therefore,* the proposition is a conclusion. If the meaning of the argument remains the same when you insert *because,* the proposition is a premise.

Moral Dilemmas

Sometimes moral arguments contain conflicting premises, each of which is morally compelling. A situation in which we have a conflict between moral values is known as a *moral dilemma.* In a moral dilemma, no matter what conclusion we draw or what solution we choose, it will involve doing something wrong in order to do what is right.

The great majority of moral issues are straightforward and do not need to be subjected to critical analysis in order to know what is right and wrong. Moral decision making is such a normal part of everyday life that we generally don't give it a second thought. For example, we don't need to lay out premises and engage in logical analysis to know that we shouldn't run down pedestrians—even though they may be jaywalking. We don't need to struggle over whether it would be morally acceptable to clobber the person sitting next to us and steal his book just because we forgot ours. We don't need to debate the morality of adults having sexual relations with young children, or the morality of genocide, or the morality of torturing dogs just for the fun of it.

Sometimes, however, we encounter a situation in which the right thing to do is not so clear-cut. We may be torn between our loyalty to a friend and telling the truth—

particularly when the truth involves bad news. A physician be may torn between wanting a cancer patient to seek further treatment and the patient's request to die. A college president may be torn between wanting to see hate speech stopped on campus and her belief in freedom of speech. A high school principal may be torn between wanting minority teachers and discriminating against white males. Parents may be torn between wanting a healthy, intelligent child and concerns about the unforeseen effects of genetic engineering.

The conclusions of arguments involving moral dilemmas are neither right nor wrong, only better or worse. With a dilemma, we have to prioritize the competing moral values and concerns and seek a solution or conclusion that takes into account as many of the important moral values as possible. For example, is there a solution to the problem of hate speech on campus that would reduce hate speech without infringing on students' freedom of speech? In most cases the best we can hope for is a solution that causes the least amount of harm or restriction.

Most of the issues covered in this text contain moral dilemmas. Practice at resolving moral dilemmas has been found to be an effective means of improving our skill at moral reasoning. Issues involving moral dilemmas, by their very nature, demand that we sort out and take a closer look at moral values and learn how to analyze the arguments on all sides of the issue.

Constructing Moral Arguments

When constructing an argument, begin by listing possible premises or interpretations. In doing this it is generally most productive to work with others, especially those who may disagree with you. According to Socrates and other philosophers, it is through ongoing dialogue that we get to try out our views, respond to challenges, and, in the process, hopefully come closer to discovering the truth.

The following is a summary of the steps for constructing an argument:

1. *Compile a list of premises.* In a good argument, the premises are relatively uncontroversial and should be acceptable to all or most reasonable people. Identify in your premises the relevant moral principles and ideals in the issue. If there are conflicting moral values, prioritize them. Make sure your factual statements are supported with reliable sources. Any ambiguous terms should be clearly defined.

2. *Eliminate weak or irrelevant premises.* After listing possible premises or interpretations, go back over them and eliminate any that are weak or irrelevant. Resist the temptation to engage in rhetoric—to eliminate premises simply because they do not support your personal opinion on this issue. Also, make sure there are no obvious gaps in the premises.

3. *Come to a conclusion.* The next step is inference, or drawing the conclusion. The conclusion should take into account the information contained in the premises, but it should not state more than what was contained therein. If your argument involves conflicting prescriptive premises, the conclusion should take into account as many of the important moral values as possible. Also check for fallacies in the inference process. If there are fallacies, or if your conclusion is too narrow (ignores some of the important premises) or too broad (states more than what was in the premises), redo the inference process.

 TIPS FOR RECOGNIZING AND BREAKING DOWN ARGUMENTS

- The entire argument may appear in either one sentence or several sentences.
- The conclusion can appear anywhere in the argument.
- Identify the conclusion first. Ask yourself: What is this person trying to prove?
- The conclusion is often, though not always, preceded by words or phrases known as conclusion indicators, such as:

therefore	which shows that
hence	for these reasons
thus	consequently

- The premises are often, though not always, preceded by words or phrases known as premise indicators, such as:

because	may be inferred that
for	the reason is that
since	as shown by

- Underline, or highlight, the conclusion and the premises.

---

4. *Try out the argument on others.* The final step is to try out your argument on others. This is a good opportunity to see if your argument can stand up to critical analysis as well as to find out if you have overlooked important premises that should have been included. Once again, if any problems with your argument arise, go back and revise it.

EXERCISES

1. Break down each of the following arguments into its component parts. Identify the conclusion and premise(s) that support it. Circle any conclusion or premise indicators.
   a. The law of retribution states "An eye for an eye and a tooth for a tooth." For this reason, people who murder should get the death penalty.
   b. Physician-assisted suicide is immoral because death is the ultimate harm, and a doctor's first duty is to do no harm.
   c. It is wrong for parents to lie to their children. Therefore, it is wrong for parents to tell their children that Santa Claus is a real, living person.
   d. It is wrong to use rabbits in cosmetic experiments because causing unnecessary pain is immoral, and animals are capable of feeling pain.
   e. People need to pass a driving test to get a license to drive. People should also have to take a test and get a license before they can become parents. After all, parenting is a greater responsibility and requires more skill than driving.
2. Choose a controversial issue, such as physician-assisted suicide, cloning, abortion, or banning alcohol on campus. Working in groups, follow the four steps described in the previous section for constructing an argument.
3. Choose an unresolved moral dilemma from your own life. Write a paragraph describing the facts or experience. Next list the competing moral values and possible consequences. Underline those moral values that are most important, then list possible

resolutions to the dilemma. Choose the solution or conclusion that takes into account the most important values and consequences. Carry out your solution.

AVOIDING LOGICAL FALLACIES

There are several ways in which an argument can be weak or invalid. An argument that is psychologically or emotionally persuasive but logically incorrect contains what logicians call an informal *fallacy*. Fallacies can be used as a form of resistance to keep ourselves or others from analyzing our position. We are most likely to use fallacies when we are unsure of how to support our position. The use of fallacies may be effective in the short run, but thoughtful people will eventually begin to question our faulty reasoning.

Knowing how to recognize fallacies makes us less likely to fall victim to them, or to unwittingly using them, in an argument. The following are some of the fallacies that are most likely to appear in arguments on moral issues.

Equivocation

Some terms have several meanings. Most often, the context of a particular word or phrase tells us which definition is being used, but this is not always the case. When the meaning of a particular term is unclear, we refer to it as an ambiguous term. The *fallacy of equivocation* occurs when a word changes meaning in the course of an argument, as in the following example:

> People do not have a right to do or say things that infringe upon others' pursuit of their legitimate interests. The Constitution guarantees us the right of freedom of speech. Hate speech is a type of speech. Therefore, hate speech does not infringe on other peoples' pursuit of their legitimate interests.

In this argument the term *right* has shifted meaning between the first and second premises. In the first sentence, *right* means a moral right; in the second sentence, the term refers to a legal or constitutional right. The two terms are not synonymous, however. Some legal rights, such as the right to own slaves, are not moral rights. Because there is an equivocation on the term *right* in the premises, the conclusion does not logically follow. To avoid this fallacy, the key terms should be clearly defined and used in a consistent manner throughout the argument.

Abusive Fallacy

The *abusive fallacy* occurs when we disagree with someone's conclusion but, instead of addressing her argument, we attack her character. In so doing, we attempt to evoke a feeling of disapproval toward the person, so that the feeling will overflow into disapproval of her argument:

> LILA: I think abortion is morally wrong.
> CHLOE: You pro-lifers are just a bunch of narrow-minded, anti-choice religious fanatics who think they have a right to force their religious morality on others.
> LILA: Oh, yeah? Well you so-called pro-choice people are nothing but a bunch self-centered, anti-life baby-killers whose only concern is being politically correct.

In this argument the issue of abortion has been completely sidestepped. Instead, Lila and Chloe get caught up in slandering each other's character because they hold an opposing view. The abusive fallacy can take the form of name calling, cutting humor, sarcastic remarks, eye rolling, or scoffing. Although it may be tempting to respond in kind, as Lila did, a person skilled in logic will calmly bring the discussion back to the subject at hand rather than fall for such diversionary tactics.

Circumstantial Fallacy

The *circumstantial fallacy* occurs when we argue that our opponent should accept a certain position because of his or her personal situation, such as a particular lifestyle or membership in a group based on race, ethnicity, gender, nationality, or religion. The circumstantial and abusive fallacies are also known collectively as the *ad hominem fallacy,* because they both entail attacking the opponent rather than addressing his or her argument. The following is an example of the circumstantial fallacy:

> Granted, you may be a vegetarian, but you certainly can't argue against the killing of animals. After all, you wear leather shoes and use products that are tested on animals.

A person can use animal products, however, and still argue against the very practice in which they engage. Parents who are heavy smokers or drinkers, for example, can still give their children sound arguments regarding the evils of drug and alcohol abuse. Although it may damage our credibility, being a hypocrite or engaging in doublethink does not invalidate our argument.

Appeal to Force

The *appeal to force fallacy* occurs when we use or threaten to use muscle—whether physical, psychological, or legal—in an attempt to coerce another person into accepting our conclusion. The proverb "Might makes right" summarizes the reasoning (or lack of it) behind this fallacy. In classroom discussions of moral issues, this fallacy is likely to take a subtle form, such as glaring, adopting a menacing pose, or snubbing those who disagree. The following is an example of this fallacy:

> Don't disagree with me! Remember who's paying your way through college.

The parent, in this case, uses the threat of withholding money for college expenses in order to silence their child.

Although this fallacy may prove effective at arousing fear in the heart of your opponent, as well as in ending debate on a moral issue, its effectiveness in classroom discussions is often short-lived. The "winners" are likely to be avoided by their intended victims rather than admired for their intellectual prowess.

Popular Appeal

This fallacy is committed when we use the fact that the majority of people agree with a particular position as support for the truth of that position. Also known as the *bandwagon approach,* the *popular appeal fallacy* assumes that a certain conclusion is right simply because "everyone" is doing it or "everyone" believes it:

> Seventy percent of Americans support capital punishment, so it must be morally acceptable.

The fact that the majority of people agree with a certain practice, however, does not mean it is right. After all, the majority of people once believed that the Earth was flat and that slavery was morally acceptable.

According to John Stuart Mill, one of the dangers of living in a democracy is the "tyranny of the majority." In 1826 historian Alexis de Tocqueville visited the United States, where he made the observation that although democracy may have liberated us from tradition, the great democratic danger is enslavement to public opinion. In fact, as noted earlier, most Americans define morality in terms of what the majority believes is right or wrong.

Appeal to Inappropriate Authority

In discussions of moral issues, it is appropriate to use the testimony of someone who is an expert in the field. It is reasonable, for example, to obey the authority of a police officer directing traffic at a busy intersection, or to consult a geneticist to learn more about the possible long-term consequences of genetic engineering. We commit a fallacy, however, when we appeal to an expert or authority in a field other than the one under debate, as in the following example:

> My priest says that genetic engineering and cloning are dangerous. Therefore, all experimentation in this field should be discontinued immediately.

In this example the person cited is an authority in theology rather than in the medical field. Titles such as *Reverend, Doctor, General,* and *Professor* increase our perception of a person's authority. We tend to believe and obey these authority figures even when they overextend their authority to the point where it would be appropriate to question it. This was poignantly demonstrated in the Milgram study on obedience to authority, in which two-thirds of the subjects continued to follow the orders of an authority figure even though they thought doing so might result in the injury or death of another person.[7]

Ignorance

The *fallacy of ignorance* does not imply that we are stupid, it simply means that we are ignorant of how to go about proving something. This fallacy occurs whenever we argue that our conclusion is true simply because it has not been proven false, or that it is false simply because it has not been proven true. For example, in defense of his position that black people are innately inferior to white people, biologist Arthur Jensen writes:

> No one has yet produced any evidence based on a properly controlled study to show that representative samples of negro and white children can be equalized in intellectual ability through statistical control of environment and education.[8]

It does not logically follow from *lack* of evidence that "negro and white children" cannot be "equalized in intellectual ability," a conclusion Jensen later draws. Similarly, we cannot conclude that life does not exist in other galaxies simply on the basis of *lack* of evidence for its existence. The most we can conclude in both cases is that we don't know.

Begging the Question

Also known as *circular reasoning,* the *fallacy of begging the question* occurs when a premise and conclusion are rewordings of the same proposition. In other words, when presenting our argument we *assume* the truth of our conclusion rather than offer proof for it. In some cases the premise simply defines the key term in the conclusion rather than offering support for it.

This fallacy is often difficult to recognize, because the premise and conclusion are worded differently. At first glance it may seem to be an airtight argument because the premise appears to support that conclusion so perfectly, as in the following argument:

> Voluntary euthanasia is morally acceptable because people have the right to choose when and how they will end their lives.

Rather than offering support for the conclusion that "voluntary euthanasia is morally acceptable," the premise simply defines the key term *euthanasia.* If we reverse the premise and the conclusion, we can see that they are the same proposition: "Voluntary euthanasia is morally acceptable, *therefore,* people have a right to choose when and how they will end their lives."

Hasty Generalization

When used properly, generalization can be a valuable tool for gathering information in both the physical and social sciences. A generalization is valid if it is based on observations of a representative sampling of a group. The *fallacy of hasty generalization* occurs when we use only unusual or atypical cases to support our conclusion. Stereotypes are often based upon hasty generalization:

> My father abused me, and my boyfriend in high school hit me too; all men are scum.

In this example the woman is making a hasty generalization about all men from her limited experience with only two men. One of the dangers of this fallacy is that, rather than be proven wrong, many people will choose only experiences that fit with their stereotypes. If the woman in this above example is unwilling to subject her interpretation to critical analysis, she may continue to seek out men who fit in with her negative worldview.

Slippery Slope

The *slippery slope fallacy* is committed when a person argues that a position or proposal, which may not in itself be bad, should be rejected because it may set off a chain of events that will lead to a situation that is dangerous or undesirable. One seemingly innocent step down the slippery slope, it is argued, will send us hurtling toward disaster. When Mary Wollstonecraft published her *Vindication of the Rights of Woman* in 1792, her views were received by most people with ridicule. One critic, Thomas Taylor, wrote in response to her tract that

> if equality should apply to women, then why should it not be applied also to dogs, cats, horses, and other "brutes"?

Since this, he suggested, was patently absurd, it would be ludicrous to extend equal rights to women. Taylor's response may seem absurd to us today, but at the time it seemed to make good sense to most people.

We have since come to realize that Taylor's alarmist response was not grounded in a realistic assessment of the situation. When properly used the slippery slope argument can be a valid and compelling form of argument like the hasty generalization. However, most situations are not slippery slopes—we *can* stop or draw lines.

The slippery slope fallacy also may be based on a weak analogy. For example, the euthanasia by the Nazis of insane and mentally retarded people has been used against the legalization of active voluntary euthanasia in the United States. If we legalize active voluntary euthanasia, it is argued, we will start down the slippery slope toward involuntary euthanasia of people who are "inconvenient." In deciding whether this argument contains this fallacy, we need to first determine if this is a good analogy or if the two situations are sufficiently different to render the argument fallacious.

Irrelevant Conclusion

The *fallacy of irrelevant conclusion* occurs when we support or reject one conclusion using premises that are directed at a different conclusion. We may try to avoid a specific topic that makes us feel uncomfortable by changing the topic to something more general or less controversial. In other words, we throw in a red herring in an attempt to divert attention from the real issue:

> ANA: I think that gay marriage ought to be recognized by the church and the law.
> BEN: We should respect the private sex lives of consenting adults, whatever their sexual orientation.

In this argument Ben deflected discussion of public acknowledgment of gay relationships by changing the topic to a less controversial topic—tolerance of people's private sex lives. Many people who agree with Ben, however, still oppose gay marriage. When this fallacy happens in a discussion of a moral issue, you should immediately bring the discussion back to the topic at hand.

This fallacy may also take the form of setting up a "straw man," an argument that is easy to knock down, in order to divert attention from the real argument. For example, in a discussion of "partial-birth" abortion a person who is antiabortion may change the topic to the moral permissibility of infanticide. Or, a person who is pro–abortion rights may change the topic to the abuse of unwanted children—something few people support.

Naturalistic Fallacy

This fallacy is a specific type of irrelevant conclusion. We commit the *naturalistic fallacy* when we assume that because something *is* the case, it *ought to be* the case, as in the following example:

> Men are larger and naturally more aggressive than women. Therefore, men ought to be the dominant partner in a relationship.

People who use the naturalistic fallacy may also cite the natural activities of other animals. But it does not logically follow from the fact that other animals eat meat, or that they sometimes kill and eat their young, or that most animals have several sexual partners (and a few even eat their partner after mating!) that it is morally acceptable for

---

 THIRTEEN INFORMAL FALLACIES

Informal fallacies are psychologically persuasive but incorrect arguments.

Equivocation A key term shifts meaning during the course of an argument

Abusive We attack our opponent's character rather than address her conclusion

Circumstantial We argue that our opponent should accept a particular position because of his lifestyle or membership in a particular group

Appeal to force Force or threat of force is used to coerce our opponent into accepting our conclusion

Popular appeal The opinion of the majority is used as support for a conclusion

Appeal to inappropriate authority The testimony of someone who is an authority in a different field is used as support for our conclusion

Ignorance We argue that a certain position is true because it hasn't been proven false, or that it is false because it hasn't been proven true

Begging the question The premise and conclusion are different wordings of the same proposition

Hasty generalization Our conclusion is based on atypical cases

Slippery Slope A position or proposal is rejected, without sufficient evidence, on the grounds that it will set off a chain of events that will lead to a situation that is dangerous or undesirable

Irrelevant conclusion Our argument is directed at a different conclusion than the one under discussion

Naturalistic We argue from an "is" to an "ought"

Appeal to tradition We argue that something is moral because it is traditional

---

humans to do the same. The morality of these behaviors must be evaluated on grounds other than that they are natural.

Appeal to Tradition

Like the naturalistic fallacy, the *fallacy of appeal to tradition* also involves going from an "is" to an "ought" statement. Instead of trying to justify a particular practice on the grounds that it is natural, however, it is argued a certain practice is moral because it is traditional. Cultural relativists are most likely to use this fallacy.

> It is morally acceptable to own handguns because the right to own guns is protected by the Constitution.

In debates on moral issues, this fallacy may take the form of the argument that a particular practice is moral because it is legal or constitutional, but the U.S. Constitution is a legal document, not a moral one. The Constitution also permitted slavery for almost a century and prohibited women from voting for even longer.

EXERCISES

1. Which fallacy are you most likely to use in a discussion of a moral issue? Give an example of a time when you used this fallacy. Which fallacy are you most likely to fall for in a discussion of a moral issue? Give an example of a time when this fallacy was used on you. What can you do to make yourself less prone to using or falling for these particular fallacies in discussions of moral issues?

2. Identify the fallacies found in the interpretations of the gay marriage experience in the "Interpretation" section (see p. 81) in this chapter.

3. Identify the fallacy in each of the following arguments:

   a. A universal set of moral principles obviously does not exist. After all, no one has been able to come to any definite agreement on what it is.

   b. Of course there is a Santa Claus. But he brings toys only to good girls and boys who do what their parents ask them to do.

   c. Abortion is morally acceptable because it is a woman's constitutional right.

   d. Smoking isn't all that bad for your health. After all, my grandfather began smoking when he was thirteen and he's ninety-three years old now and still in good health!

   e. Capital punishment is morally acceptable because murderers should be put to death.

   f. Why all this concern about people who are starving in Africa? Look at all the poverty we have right here in our own country.

   g. A recent poll found that the majority of Americans feel that openly homosexual men and women should not be allowed to serve in the military. Therefore, the current "Don't ask, don't tell" policy in the military is morally acceptable.

   h. My parents used to get into arguments all the time and they ended up getting divorced. Logic teaches people how to make arguments. Therefore, if you want a happy marriage, you should stay away from logic.

   i. Euthanasia is wrong because it interferes with the natural dying process. We should wait until it is our time to die.

   j. So you're going to argue in class that alcohol should be banned on campus. Well, this is the last time we're going to ask you to go out with us on the weekend.

   k. I'm opposed to affirmative action because I don't agree with preferential treatment based on race or gender.

   l. Date rape is just a ploy for bitter women like Kim to get back at some guy who spurns them. Why, just last week it was found out that Joe, the guy Kim accused of raping her, had broken off the relationship the day before she brought rape charges against him.

   m. You can't prove definitively that violence in the media has a direct effect on people's actual behavior. Therefore, banning violence in the media cannot be morally justified.

   n. My dentist doesn't think that the loss of animal and plant species due to the destruction of rain forests is going to permanently upset the balance of nature.

Therefore, it is morally acceptable to continue clearing rain forests for cattle grazing.

o. I'm not surprised that you're arguing that hate speech should not be banned on campus. You're one of the most hateful, racist, and insensitive people I've ever met. Why, you couldn't care less about the effect of hate speech on its intended victims.

p. How can you argue in favor of cloning? After all, you're a Catholic and the Church recently issued a statement calling for a ban of human cloning.

q. The use of cloning for infertile couples should not be legalized. Once we allow this form of human cloning it will lead to large-scale cloning of humans for use as organ donors and drones.

CRITICAL READING SKILLS

Learning how to recognize and analyze arguments is at the heart of critical reading. Now that you can recognize fallacies and break down arguments into their component parts, the next step is to learn how to apply these skills to critical reading. Critical-reading skills provide a framework by which you can evaluate arguments. The following are some recommendations for effective critical reading.

Preparing to Read

1. *Set aside enough time.* The arguments in most of the reading selections work together to support the final conclusion or thesis of the paper, so allow enough time to read through each selection without interruption. To get the most out of each reading, also set aside time between the readings to evaluate and reflect on the arguments.

2. *Get in the right frame of mind.* The first step in reading moral philosophy is to take on the perspective of the philosopher. This involves setting aside your own prejudices and preconceptions in order to be objective. As a philosopher you should be willing to question your own beliefs and interpretations as well as those of others.

3. *Be aware of your own reactions.* Being objective requires controlling, or at least being aware of, your emotional reactions to the readings. If you are aware of what type of resistance you are most likely to use, you can take steps to overcome these defenses when reading a selection that challenges your particular interpretation of the moral issue.

4. *Read the critical reading questions.* Before you start reading, look over the critical-reading questions at the beginning of the selection. These questions serve as guideposts that point out important ideas and arguments in the reading. They also make it easier for you to answer the discussion questions and evaluate the case studies.

First Reading: Identifying the Key Parts

The key parts of the first article, "A Defense of Abortion" by Judith Jarvis Thomson, have been identified for you by way of illustration.

1. *Identify the conclusion.* Readings on moral issues often contain several arguments that work together to support the final conclusion or thesis. The conclusion may be

stated in the title of the paper or in the introductory paragraph. It can also be found in the closing paragraph(s). To identify the conclusion or thesis of a paper, ask yourself: What is the main purpose of the argument? What is the writer trying to prove? What position is the writer trying to get me to accept?

Thomson's thesis—that abortion is morally defensible—is summarized in the title of her paper. It is also repeated in other parts of her paper. Repeating the thesis statement helps keep the reader focused on the argument.

In critical reading it is helpful to underline or highlight the conclusion or thesis whenever it appears. If it is clearly marked, you, as a critical reader, will be less likely to be thrown off by any distractions or irrelevant material.

2. *Identify the premises.* To identify the premises, ask yourself: What is the writer offering in support of his or her conclusion? Bracket or mark each premise.

Sometimes a premise is followed by a long explanation or description, as in Thomson's analogy of the unconscious violinist. Most of the premises in position papers support subconclusions which, in turn, support the main conclusion or thesis statement. Thomson's violinist analogy, for example, depends on the premise that we do not have a moral obligation to be a Good Samaritan.

The same premise may also appear later in the paper. Number or write a quick summary of each premise in the margin so you can keep track of them. If you have any questions about the soundness of a particular premise, put a question mark in the margin.

Premises that writers consider obvious may be unstated. In critical reading it is important that you learn how to read between the lines. Although some of the unstated assumptions or premises may be factual, others are based on cultural and religious biases or incorrect data.

3. *Identify the key terms.* In a good argument, the key terms, such as *person* in Thomson's argument, are clearly defined at the beginning of the paper. Circle the key terms and their definitions. Identifying the key terms will make it easier for you to follow the argument as well as to make sure that the writer does not commit the fallacy of equivocation.

4. *Identify the objections or counterarguments.* Rather than simply list the premises, some writers formulate their premises as a response to counterarguments. Consequently, you may need to sort out the writer's position and the one he or she is disputing. Draw a line or make a notation, such as putting the letters *CA* beside each counterargument.

Counterarguments may occur anywhere in the paper. They are frequently woven in and out of the arguments in support of the thesis statement. For example, Thomson introduces and responds in the first part of her paper to what she sees as the pro-lifers' primary counterargument—that abortion is wrong because the fetus is a person and that every person has a right to life. A second, related counterargument is that the right to life is stronger than a mother's right to decide what to do with her body. These two counterarguments turn up again and again throughout Thomson's paper.

The Second Reading: Critical Analysis

Once you have identified the various parts of the reading, you are ready to engage in critical analysis of the argument. In going back over the reading, ask yourself the following questions:

1. *Are the key terms and concepts clearly defined?* Are definitions omitted, or are they too vague to be useful? Are the definitions used in a consistent manner throughout the paper?

2. *Are the premises acceptable?* Although an argument may be logically flawless, some of the premises may be based on incorrect data. Which of the premises are based on empirical facts? Is adequate support offered for the empirical claims in these premises?

Are the prescriptive premises—those based on moral principles—consistent with our most fundamental moral beliefs and intuitions? Have all the relevant moral premises been included? Does Thomson, for example, take the personhood of the fetus and the familial relationship between the fetus and the mother seriously enough? Does she focus too much on rights and the autonomy of the woman?

3. *Do the premises support the conclusion?* In a good argument, the premises must be strong enough to support the conclusion. If any of the key premises are based on incorrect data or unacceptable prescriptive statements, the whole argument is weak, no matter how compelling the conclusion may seem.

An argument can also be weak because it contains fallacies. Remember that informal fallacies by their very nature are psychologically convincing. Therefore, check the argument carefully for fallacies

If analogies are used, are the similarities morally relevant? Or are there too many dissimilarities between the two situations being compared? For example, is there sufficient similarity between a woman being pregnant and a person being plugged into a violinist to draw a conclusion about the morality of abortion based on this analogy? Is the similarity between children and "person plants" close enough to justify abortion of a pregnancy resulting from failed contraception?

4. *Are you satisfied with the writer's response to the objections or counterarguments?* Does the writer take the counterarguments seriously, or dismiss them too quickly? Thomson gives considerable space to the pro-life counterarguments. Indeed, rather than reject the premises of the counterargument that fetuses are persons and that all persons have a right to life, Thomson accepts these premises and from there argues that these premises can be used in defense of abortion.

5. *What are the implications of the arguments?* This last step involves doing a reality check on the analysis. Has the writer considered the practical implications of his or her conclusion? Thomson, for example, looks at the implications of her argument on the permissibility of late-term abortions. Are there other implications that should be considered? If so, are you willing to accept these implications?

6. *Is it a good argument?* Go back over your answers to the first five questions. Can the argument still stand on its own if you weed out the weak, contradictory, and fallacious premises? If an argument cannot stand on its own, it should be rejected, no matter how much you agree with the thesis. This does not mean that the conclusion is necessarily false, only that the writer has failed to offer support for it.

Abortion

There is probably no more controversial issue in bioethics today, or one that touches so many lives, as abortion. An estimated 43 percent of American women will have an abortion by age forty-five.[1] Prior to the early 1960s, however, there was little public debate over the morality of abortion or support for reform of the restrictive abortion laws that had been on the books in the United States since the turn of the century.

In 1962 Sherri Finkbine, the star of a popular Arizona children's show and mother of four small children, discovered much to her horror that the drug thalidomide, which she had taken early in her pregnancy to help her sleep, could cause birth defects such as missing limbs or seal-like flippers, paralysis, and malformed internal organs. After much tortured soul-searching, the Finkbines decided that the best course of action for them was abortion. Because it was not sold in the United States, the devastating effects of thalidomide on unborn children had not received as much coverage in the American press as it had in the European press.

Shortly before the scheduled day for her abortion, Sherri Finkbine decided to go public in order to warn other women about the dangers of thalidomide. Although she requested that her name not be used by the press, the newspaper article made her identity relatively easy to figure out. As a result of the publicity, the hospital, fearful of legal prosecution, withdrew its consent to perform the abortion. Sherri Finkbine eventually obtained an abortion in Sweden. The fetus was severely deformed. Sherri Finkbine's tragic ordeal helped galvanize public support for abortion reform and a relaxing of laws regulating therapeutic abortions.

BACKGROUND

Abortion was legalized in the United States in January 1973 by the U.S. Supreme Court *Roe v. Wade* ruling. Between 1973, when 760,000 abortions were performed, and 1980, the national abortion rate increased rapidly every year. The abortion rate continued to increase at a slower rate between 1980 and 1988, the year when the number of reported abortions reached 1,600,000. The abortion rate began declining in the 1990s, reaching, by the end of the decade, its lowest point since 1975.[2] In the United States today, about 25 percent of pregnancies are ended by abortion.[3] Of these, 85 to 90 percent are terminated in the first twelve weeks of pregnancy.[4]

The drop in abortion rates has been attributed to a combination of factors, including changes in contraceptive and sexual practices, reduced access to abortion services with fewer doctors and medical centers willing to perform abortions, changes in attitude toward abortion with more people trying to avoid it, greater acceptance of unmarried mothers, and a decline in the overall number of pregnancies.[5] There is also less acceptability of abortion among younger people. According to the American Council of Education and University of California national college freshman survey, freshman support for legalized abortion has declined steadily since 1993. In 1999 50.9 percent of freshmen supported legalized abortion compared to 53.5 percent in 1997 and 64.9 percent in 1990.[6]

While the abortion rate has been dropping in the United States, it has been increasing worldwide. According to the World Health Organization, 45 million abortions were performed in 1995, up from 25 million in 1990.

THE HISTORY OF ABORTION IN THE UNITED STATES

Abortion was not uncommon in America during the colonial period up until the late 1800s. When abortion was mentioned, it was not the abortion itself that was usually condemned but the violation of other social taboos, such as sexual relations outside of marriage, that led to the abortion.[7] Many middle- and upper-class women also used abortion as a means of birth control.

During the early 1820s, American physicians began to take an interest in medical law and the legal regulation of abortion.[8] In 1821, Connecticut passed the country's first antiabortion law. Early-nineteenth-century antiabortion laws, for the most part, applied only to women "quick with child." Before the mid-nineteenth century, it was generally believed that the unborn child or fetus did not come to life until "quickening"—the moment, generally between sixteen and eighteen weeks, when the pregnant woman first feels the movement of her fetus. Despite laws against abortion, folk remedies and patented medicines continued to be widely available to women.

In the mid-nineteenth century, the newly founded American Medical Association (AMA) spearheaded a movement to outlaw abortion. In an 1859 resolution, the AMA condemned abortion as an "unwarranted destruction of human life," calling upon state legislators to pass or toughen their existing antiabortion laws.[9]

Although many people, including physicians, blamed the prevalence of abortion on feminist ideas, the early feminists disapproved of abortion, which they considered to be "a revolting outrage against . . . our common humanity" and a form of infanticide.[10] Unlike the physicians, however, the feminists did not think that outlawing abortion without getting to the root cause of abortion—the oppression of women—would have the desired effect. Instead they wanted the *need* for abortion to be eliminated. "We want prevention, not merely punishment," Susan B. Anthony wrote in 1869. "We must reach the root of the evil, and destroy it."[11] Elizabeth Cady Stanton also regarded abortion as just one more result of degradation of women.[12]

Between 1855 and 1880, most states passed antiabortion laws. By 1900 every state had laws prohibiting or restricting abortion; all but six included a "therapeutic exception" in their abortion laws. These laws remained virtually unchanged until the 1960s.

Several events during the 1960s led to an increasing dissatisfaction with the restrictive abortion laws. These included an increase in the number of women in the workforce, a desire for smaller families, increased publicity about the dangers of illegal abortion, improvements in the safety of surgical abortion, and a series of front-page stories chronicling the desperate circumstances of women such as Sherri Finkbine who were denied legal therapeutic abortions. The thalidomide tragedy was closely followed by a German measles epidemic in the United States. Many pregnant women who came down with German measles were unable to obtain legal abortions in the United States. As a result of this outbreak, 15,000 babies were born with birth defects—including blindness, mental retardation, and heart problems—between 1963 and 1966.

Fueled by the publicity generated by the thalidomide and German measles tragedies, the push for legal reform came primarily from the medical and legal professions. Although most people supported more liberal laws regarding the regulation of therapeutic abortions, there was little public support in the late 1960s for non-therapeutic abortions or "abortion on demand"—what later became known as the pro-choice position.[13]

In 1969 Planned Parenthood, which had historically been opposed to abortion, reversed its position and came out in support of repealing all antiabortion laws. The following year the AMA followed suit, voting to support a physician's right to perform abortions if the woman's social and economic circumstances would make it difficult for her to have a baby. These changes, together with the first legal acknowledgment of a constitutional "right to privacy" in the 1965 Supreme Court *Griswold v. Connecticut* case, provided lawyers with the grist they needed to turn the wheels of reform by challenging the constitutionality of existing antiabortion laws.

Between 1967 and 1970, twelve states, including California, Hawaii, New York, Alaska, and Washington, repealed their restrictive abortion laws. The failures in liberalizing state abortion laws outnumbered the successes, however, due in part to a lack of public support as well as to the efforts of the fledgling right-to-life movement.

THE U.S. SUPREME COURT *ROE V. WADE* DECISION

A major turning point in the abortion-reform movement came when the battleground moved to the federal courts. In January 1973 the Supreme Court in *Roe v. Wade* ruled that the Texas antiabortion law violated a woman's fundamental constitutional right to privacy as implied in the Fourteenth Amendment. It also ruled that the fetus was not a person according to the Fourteenth Amendment. The effect of this ruling was to legalize abortion, at least prior to viability, throughout the United States. After viability, set at twenty-eight weeks, the state has a legitimate interest in "potential life" and can pass laws to regulate abortion, except for abortions to preserve the life and health of the mother. Selections from the *Roe v. Wade* majority ruling can be found on pages 104–105.

Rather than settling the abortion question once and for all, *Roe v. Wade* has left Americans deeply divided. Positions regarding the moral permissibility of abortion range from the pro-life view that all abortions are wrong except to save the life of the mother, to the pro-choice view that abortion is morally acceptable for any reason at any time during the pregnancy. A 2000 Gallup Poll found that 28 percent of Americans polled thought abortion should be legal under any circumstances, 51 percent thought it should be legal only under certain circumstances, while 19 percent thought it should be illegal under all circumstances. Support for abortion is strongest, 81 percent, when the woman's life or physical health is endangered; it is lowest for abortions performed after the first term with 66 percent of those polled opposing the legalization of "partial-birth" abortions, also known as intact dilation and extraction or IDX.[14] (See page 107 for a description of this procedure.) The challenge to *Roe v. Wade* comes not only from the pro-life movement but also from the pro-choice groups who would like to see all restrictions on abortion removed.

Although the percentage of Americans who identify themselves as moderates has remained relatively stable between 1980 and the mid-1990s, nationwide there has been a trend toward wanting more restrictions placed on abortion, particularly abortions after the first trimester and those for social or economic reasons.[15] A 1998 ABC News poll found a marked shift since 1994 away from acceptance of abortion as a woman's right toward wanting more restrictions on abortion. This shift has been attributed, in part, to advances in prenatal technology, such as real-time ultrasound, that allow us to visualize the fetus, and growing concerns over late-term abortions. The rise in violence against abortion clinics and abortion providers and the reluctance of younger doctors to perform abortions (two-thirds of abortion providers are now over the age of sixty-five)[16] has also contributed to a decline in the number of facilities providing abortions and the number of doctors who are willing to perform them. In 1995 only 33 percent of obstetrician-gynecologists, compared with 42 percent in 1983, were performing abortions.[17]

Since 1973 several states have passed legislation that places restrictions on abortion. Thirty-seven states enacted laws restricting abortion in 1997 alone. These restrictions include parental and spousal notification requirements, mandatory waiting periods, and bans on federal funding for abortions. Several bills for a constitutional amendment that would overturn *Roe v. Wade* have been introduced, including the Human Life Amendment, which would extend "personhood" or legal protection to "all human beings." However, with the election of George W. Bush in 2000, it is likely that more restrictions will be placed on abortion rights.

In the 2000 *Stenberg v. Carhart* case, the U.S. Supreme Court struck down, in a 5 to 4 ruling, a Nebraska law that banned "partial-birth" abortion. This was the first time in eight years that the Supreme Court took up laws on abortion. About thirty states at the time had similar laws banning "partial-birth" abortion. The court ruled that the Nebraska law placed an "undue burden" on women since it failed to include an exception in which the health of the pregnant woman was at risk.

The following month the U.S. Supreme Court, in *Hill v. Colorado,* ruled in favor of a Colorado statute that restricted protesters from coming within eight feet of women who were within one hundred feet of an entrance to an abortion clinic. Three years previously the Court had upheld a New York law that established buffer zones around abortion clinics in which antiabortion demonstrations are prohibited.

The fact that abortion is currently legal does not mean that it is moral; nor does believing that abortion is immoral necessarily imply that it ought to be outlawed. On the other hand, the resolution of most moral issues that confront us as a society involves not just discerning right from wrong, but determining how best to embody this moral wisdom in a just public policy. This involves balancing concerns about abortion with other concerns such as equal economic rights for women. As both Confucius and Aristotle maintain, good laws and public policy are important because they make it easier for people to be virtuous.

✐ *ROE V. WADE*: EXCERPTS FROM THE MAJORITY OPINION

[Justice Blackmun delivered the opinion of the Court]

It is . . . apparent that at common law, at the time of the adoption of our Constitution, and throughout the major portion of the nineteenth century, abortion was viewed with less disfavor than under most American statutes currently in effect. Phrasing it another way, a woman enjoyed a substantially broader right to terminate a pregnancy than she does in most states today. . . .

Three reasons have been advanced to explain historically the enactment of criminal abortion laws in the nineteenth century and to justify their continued existence.

[First] It has been argued occasionally that these laws were the product of a Victorian special concern to discourage illicit sexual conduct. . . .

A second reason is concerned with abortion as a medical procedure. When most criminal abortion laws were first enacted, the procedure was a hazardous one for the woman. . . . Modern medical techniques have altered this situation. . . .

The third reason is the state's interest—some phrase it in terms of duty—in protecting prenatal life. Some of the argument for this justification rests on the theory that a new human life is present from the moment of conception. . . . Only when the life of the pregnant mother herself is at stake, balanced against the life she carries within her, should the interest of the embryo or fetus not prevail. Logically, of course, a legitimate state interest in this area need not stand or fall on acceptance of the belief that life begins at conception or at some other point prior to live birth. In assessing the state's interest, recognition may be given to the less rigid claim that as long as at least *potential* life is involved, the state may assert interests beyond the protection of the pregnant woman alone. . . .

The Constitution does not explicitly mention any right of privacy. . . . [Earlier Supreme Court] decisions make it clear that only personal rights that can be deemed "fundamental" or "implicit in the concept of ordered liberty" . . . are included in this guarantee of personal privacy. They also make it clear that the right has some extension to activities relating to marriage . . . [and] procreation. . . .

ABORTION AND RELIGION

Although the pro-life stand is often labeled as the "religious" position, religious views on abortion vary widely. Muslims believe that human life is sacred and that the fetus is a person with rights under the law from the moment of "ensoulment." This is tempered by practical concerns, however, and Islamic law generally permits early abortions on medical and health grounds.[18]

In Hinduism the killing of a conscious fetus carries the same penalty as the murder of a learned Brahman. However, the current emphasis on having sons in many Asian countries, including India, has led to a high rate of selective abortion for gender, despite laws in some countries specifically prohibiting abortion for sex selection.

We therefore conclude that the right of personal privacy includes the abortion decision, but that this right is not unqualified and must be considered against important state interests in regulation.

. . . [N]o case could be cited that holds that a fetus is a person within the meaning of the Fourteenth Amendment. . . . All this, together with our observation, *supra*, that throughout the majority portion of the nineteenth century prevailing legal abortion practices were far freer than they are today, persuades us that the word "person," as used in the Fourteenth Amendment, does not include the unborn. . . .

There has always been strong support for the view that life does not begin until live birth. . . . Physicians and their scientific colleagues have. . . . tended to focus either upon conception or upon live birth or upon the interim point at which the fetus becomes "viable," that is, potentially able to live outside the mother's womb, albeit with artificial aid. Viability is usually placed at about seven months (28 weeks) but may occur earlier, even at 24 weeks. . . .

With respect to the state's important and legitimate interest in the health of the mother, the compelling point, in the light of present medical knowledge, is at approximately the end of the first trimester. This is so because of the now established medical fact . . . . that until the end of the first trimester mortality in abortion is less than mortality in normal childbirth. It follows that, from and after this point, a state may regulate the abortion procedure to the extent that the regulation reasonably relates to the preservation and protection of maternal health. Examples of permissible state regulation in this area are requirements as to the qualifications of the person who is to perform the abortion. . . .

With respect to the state's important and legitimate interest in potential life, the "compelling" point is at viability. This is so because the fetus then presumably has the capability of meaningful life outside the mother's womb. State regulation protective of fetal life after viability thus has both logical and biological justifications. If the state is interested in protecting fetal life after viability, it may go so far as to proscribe abortion during that period except when it is necessary to preserve the life or health of the mother. . . .

There is little mention of abortion in the Bible, and what there is is ambiguous. Orthodox Jews emphasize passages in Genesis that teach that, because we are created in the image of God, all human life is inviolable and sacred. Thus abortion is prohibited except to save the life of the mother. Liberal and reform Jews, on the other hand, point out that Adam did not become a living being or fully human until God breathed life into him. Likewise, the infant does not become a *nephesh,* or a person with a soul, until he or she takes the first breath of air. Abortion, therefore, is morally permissible at any time during the pregnancy.

The position of the early Christian Church was similar to that of the Orthodox Jews. The *Didache,* written no later than A.D. 100, contains a prohibition against abortion, calling those who procure abortions "destroyers of God's image." This prohibition was reiterated by the early Christian writers. The only exception to the prohibition was abortion to save the life of the mother.

Unlike the early Church, Thomas Aquinas set the time of ensoulment at forty days for males and eighty days for females. Based on this distinction, for centuries the Church regarded late-term abortions as more sinful than early abortions. The belief that early abortions are less morally problematic is still common today. In the nineteenth century, the Roman Catholic Church changed its position, returning to the early Christian prohibition against abortion at any time of the pregnancy.

Unlike their Catholic contemporaries, who permitted early abortions, both John Calvin (1509–1564) and Martin Luther (1483–1546) were emphatic in their opposition to abortion, believing that one is fully human from the moment of conception. The reaction of modern Protestants to abortion is varied. Most fundamentalist, evangelical, and African American Protestant churches take a position similar to that of the Roman Catholics, whereas most of the mainstream Protestant churches take a moderate stand, supporting abortion prior to viability.

The moral controversy over abortion cannot be resolved simply by uncritically accepting religious dogma. At the same time, the arguments used by the different religions should not be dismissed offhand, because they are generally based on philosophical rather than purely theological arguments. Good ethical analysis, while eschewing arguments based solely on faith, entails being open to, listening to, and subjecting to critical analysis, the moral arguments put forth by the various religions.

STAGES OF FETAL DEVELOPMENT

Discussions on the morality of abortion often focus on the level of development of the fetus. The following are some of the milestones in prenatal human development:

Day 1: Conception. The egg and sperm, each containing twenty-three chromosomes, unite to form one cell with forty-six chromosomes. The newly fertilized egg is known as the zygote.

Day 2 to week 2: Blastocyst. The fertilized egg, or blastocyst, travels down the fallopian tube and implants in the uterus. The blastocyst is composed of an embryonic disk, which will develop into an embryo after implantation, and two cavities, an amniotic cavity and the yolk sac.

Weeks 2 to 8: Embryo. The germ layers of the embryonic disk develop into the principle organ systems. At this stage of development, the cells are rapidly dividing and transforming into specialized cells such as eye, skin, and muscle cells. Brain waves are detectable between six and eight weeks. By eight weeks the embryo is 23 millimeters long.

Week 8 to birth: Fetus. By eight weeks all organs and structural features are in place and the fetus resembles a very small newborn child. Between twenty and twenty-four weeks, the fetus becomes viable and is able to survive outside the womb.

Week 40: Birth.

METHODS OF ABORTION

There are three primary types of abortion: medical abortions, surgical abortions, and medical induction of uterine contractions. The method used depends primarily on the time of gestation.

Medical Abortions

Medical abortions include the morning-after pill and mifepristone, popularly known as RU 486. Medical abortions can be done only early in pregnancy.

The morning-after pill. The morning-after pill is actually a high dose of birth control pills taken at two intervals over the three days following intercourse. The doses prevent the blastocyst from implanting in the uterine wall. This method is 75-percent successful at preventing implantation.

Mifepristone (RU 486). Mifepristone, popularly known as RU 486, was developed in France and approved by the U.S. Food and Drug Administration (FDA) in September 2000 for sale to the public, thus decreasing the need for surgical abortions in early pregnancies. Mifepristone induces menstruation, thus expelling the implanted embryo. It is more than 90 percent effective in terminating pregnancies of less than seven weeks' gestation. In 10 to 20 percent of the cases, it takes more than two weeks for the fetus to be expelled.[19]

Surgical Abortions

Most abortions are performed surgically. The 98- to 99-percent success rate of surgical abortion is much higher than that of medical abortion.

Dilation and curettage (D & C). Dilation and curettage used to be one of the most popular methods of abortion. It involves expanding the cervix of the uterus so a spoon-shaped curette can be inserted to scrape the surface of the uterine wall. This method has since fallen out of favor because of the risk of puncturing the uterus, which, in turn, can cause maternal hemorrhaging and even death.

Vacuum aspiration (D & E). The development in China in the early 1960s of the safer vacuum aspiration method was accompanied by a sharp decline in the death rate in women from abortions. Also known as dilation and evacuation (D & E), vacuum aspiration was first used in the United States in the late 1960s. This method is similar to D & C, but the fetus is suctioned rather than scraped out of the uterus. Today more than 90 percent of abortions in the United States are vacuum aspirations.

Intact dilation and extraction (IDX or "partial-birth" abortion). This method is used only in late-term abortions. After partially delivering an intact fetus feet-first, the doctor punctures the fetus's skull, suctions out the brains, and then crushes the skull so the fetus can fit easily through the woman's birth canal. An estimated five thousand "partial-birth" abortions are performed annually.[20]

Hysterectomy and hysterontomy. Surgical removal of the fetus is generally reserved for late-term abortions. A hysterectomy entails the surgical removal of the whole uterus; a hysterontomy, the removal of the fetus through an incision in the uterus. Because of the large number of fetuses who survive these procedures and the high incidence of maternal complications, these methods are rarely used anymore except in emergencies.

Medical Induction of Uterine Contractions

Abortions between sixteen and twenty weeks can be carried out using either surgical removal of the fetus or medical induction of uterine contractions.

Saline solution. With a saline abortion, about 200 milliliters of amniotic fluid is withdrawn from the amniotic sac and replaced with a similar amount of saline solution. The fetus's heartbeat usually stops within sixty to ninety minutes after the injection, and the fetus is expelled from the womb within seventy-two hours. Although the saline solution is meant to kill the fetus, this method occasionally results in a live birth.

Prostaglandins. This method involves an intramuscular or intravaginal injection of prostaglandins to induce labor. The use of prostaglandins, or a combination of prostaglandins and saline solution, is associated with fewer live births than using just saline solution.

THE MORAL ISSUES

The Moral Status of the Fetus

The question of fetal personhood is important because persons have rights that we ought to respect. Is a fetus ever a person? If so, is there a distinct point when embryos or fetuses achieve personhood, or do they gradually achieve this status based on developmental criteria?

John Noonan maintains that there is no distinction between biological humanhood and personhood. We have moral value simply because we have a human genotype, no matter what our age or stage of development. Therefore, even the zygote is a person with moral standing. Mary Anne Warren, in contrast, argues that at no stage does the fetus meet the criteria of personhood. A fetus does not become a person until sometime after birth, when the infant becomes a "socially responsive member of a human community."

Most definitions of personhood fall between these extremes. According to utilitarians, only sentient beings need to be given moral consideration. Abortion, therefore, becomes a moral issue only after the fetus is able to experience pain. While there is considerable controversy over whether the older embryo and young fetus are able to feel pain or whether they are simply responding reflexively to external stimuli, most physicians agree that by thirteen weeks the fetus is able to experience pain.[21] A related developmental milestone that has been suggested as marking the beginning of personhood is the presence of brainwaves, which occurs at about six weeks.[22] This criterion has the advantage of being symmetrical with definitions of the end of personhood. On the other hand, an adult whose brainwaves have ceased is no longer alive and developing, whereas an embryo, despite lack of a brain, is.

Viability—"the capacity to survive disconnection from the placenta"[23]—replaced quickening after the 1973 *Roe v. Wade* ruling as the most widely accepted point for granting the fetus moral rights. Viability is problematic as a criteria, however, because personhood becomes dependent on medical technology rather than on any characteristic of the fetus. In 1950, viability occurred at about thirty weeks' gestation. When the *Roe v. Wade* decision was handed down in 1973, medical technology had advanced to the point where viability occurred at twenty-four weeks. Now fetuses as young as twenty weeks are surviving. If an artificial womb, or another means for the young fetus to breathe and survive outside the womb, is created, viability could occur much earlier, making *Roe v. Wade* a pro-life ruling.

A final criterion is that of potentiality, according to which the potential to develop into a full-fledged adult confers personhood on a fertilized egg. Noonan's definition of personhood embraces this criterion. Thomson, on the other hand, rejects it in her analogy between human development and the development of an acorn into an oak tree.

Some people, frustrated with the lack of consensus on a definition of personhood, argue that it is better left to personal or religious opinion. To say that one's definition of personhood is a matter of opinion, however, is to mire the debate in ethical subjectivism. Not only is abortion morally permissible, if in one's opinion a fetus is not a person, but so is infanticide, slavery, and genocide, so long as the perpetrators of these practices believe, or their religions teach, that their victims are not persons.

On the other hand, it is possible to argue that even though a fetus is a person, abortion is still morally permissible. If a fetus is a person who can feel pain, however, the method used for abortion becomes a moral concern, since it is wrong to cause unnecessary pain. Don Marquis, in his article "Why Abortion Is Immoral," argues that the killing of human beings who are able to enjoy their future experiences is wrong because it deprives them of the value of their future. Because the fetus, like an adult human, has a future which he or she can value—a future that is destroyed by abortion—abortion, according to Marquis, is immoral.

The Rights and Autonomy of the Mother

Some people think that the emphasis in the abortion debate on the personhood of the fetus has been at the expense of concerns about the rights of the woman. Judith Jarvis Thomson shifts the debate from the moral status of the fetus to the rights of the mother. She agrees that trying to prove that the fetus is not a person is fraught with difficulties; therefore, she gives the fetus the benefit of the doubt. From here she argues that even though the fetus may have moral standing, the rights of the mother, in most cases, outweigh those of the fetus.

Mary Anne Warren likewise maintains that a woman's liberty rights, or autonomy, is paramount; women should have the right to make decisions about their own bodies. To deny women this basic right, according to Warren, is to treat them as a means only. Opponents of abortion, in response, argue that autonomy is not an absolute right. While women have a moral right to control their bodies, this right does not extend to abortion, because abortion involves destroying the body of an unborn child.

The extent to which women have a right to control their own bodies is an issue not just in abortion. It also arises in the debate over whether women have a responsibility to refrain from prenatal behaviors, such as drug and alcohol use, that may harm fetuses.

Justice

According to some pro-life feminists, we need to move from focusing on the rights of women to a more inclusive ideal of justice. Pitting women's rights against fetal rights, she argues, has prevented women from fully developing since the rights of women and children are linked. The principle of justice requires that all persons, including unborn children, be given equal consideration. So long as abortion is legal and freely available, unjust social structures that drive women to seek abortions will not be changed.

Advocates of abortion, on the other hand, point out that as long as we have a patriarchal society in which pregnant women and mothers are socially and economically disadvantaged, abortion must remain a legitimate alternative. To have it otherwise is to deny women full and equal participation in society. Because women need to have the option of abortion, justice is also an issue in access to abortion services. Restrictive abortion laws, lack of money to pay for an abortion, unavailability of a clinic in one's area, and the presence of pro-life harassment outside of abortion clinics—all contribute to a situation in which some women, especially poor women, do not have the same access to abortion.

Selective Abortion and the Principle of Discrimination

Injustice based on discrimination is one of the key issues in selective abortion. Unlike elective abortion, in which the pregnancy itself is unwanted, in selective abortion it is the particular fetus, rather than the pregnancy, that is unwanted. About 7 percent of infants are born with a physical and/or mental disorder. Prenatal diagnosis provides parents with information about most of these disorders as well as the gender of the fetus. The overwhelming majority of pregnancies in which the fetus is diagnosed as having a genetic disorder are terminated by selective abortion.

In countries where a daughter is considered a greater burden than a son with a handicap, selective abortion is more likely to be used for sex selection than for genetic disorders. Because of this, there is a great discrepancy in some parts of India and China between the number of males and the number of females.[24] In South Korea the abortion rate of female fetuses in later pregnancy is as high as 40 percent.[25] According to the *Journal of Family Welfare*, of eight thousand abortions in Bombay in which the sex of the fetus was known, all but one of the aborted fetuses was female.[26]

There is a clear trend toward approval of selective abortion for sex selection in the United States as well as in countries like India and China. In the great majority of cases, including within the United States, where there is a preference for sons as firstborn and only children, selective abortion is used to dispose of unwanted female fetuses. In a 1987 study, the United States was one of only three nations in which the majority of geneticists surveyed said they would perform prenatal diagnosis for sex selection.[27] With increasing knowledge of the human genome, geneticists may soon be able to prenatally diagnose tendencies toward obesity, cancer, and homosexuality—to name only a few traits that most Americans consider undesirable in their children.[28]

The principle of nondiscrimination states that humans not be denied benefits or equal treatment for morally irrelevant reasons, such as sex or skin color or physical abilities. Does selective abortion involve discrimination against females, people with handicaps, and other socially unacceptable people? Even if it does involve discrimination, this has to be weighed against women's autonomy as well as against the social consequences of having "undesirable" children who will be a burden on their parents and on society.

Consequentialist Arguments

Those who favor a permissive public policy on abortion point to the harmful consequences to women, and society in general, of restrictive abortion policies. These include complications and deaths from self-induced and illegal abortions, overpopulation, the burden on women of mandatory motherhood, and the burden on society when unwanted children are neglected or abandoned.

On the flip side, Judith Boss argues that permissive abortion policies may be contributing to a devaluation of children. While not arguing for the outlawing of abortion, she points out that we need to take into consideration the possible harmful consequences of abortion on children, pro-life feminists likewise argue that permissive abortion policies, rather than contributing to the liberation of women, have held women back.

CONCLUSION

As members of a pluralistic society, can we ever reach a resolution to the current abortion debate? Indeed, should we even bother to try? Why can't we just be tolerant of other people's views: "If you don't believe in abortion, don't have one." Unfortunately, the hands-off approach doesn't work, because those who are opposed to abortion are not merely expressing a personal opinion about abortion; they are saying that abortion is wrong because it goes against universal moral principles. Furthermore, to claim that we should be tolerant of other people's moral opinions is to advocate tolerance not only of abortion but also of other practices. Few of us would be willing to carry a bumper sticker sporting the slogan "If you don't believe in slavery, don't own slaves."

Ethical analysis should not be a matter of personal opinion or majority consensus. It should be logical, consistent, and universal in its application. Until we can approach the moral issue of abortion rationally, the issue is unlikely to be resolved. The following readings are an invitation to rethink the abortion issue with an open and analytical mind.

JUDITH JARVIS THOMSON

A Defense of Abortion

Judith Jarvis Thomson is a professor of philosophy at the Massachusetts Institute of Technology. Her article "A Defense of Abortion," published two years before *Roe v. Wade*, has become a classic in the abortion debate. Rather than attempt to refute the premises that the fetus is a person and that every person has a right to life, Thomson argues that abortion may be morally permissible even if these premises are true. Using her now-famous violinist analogy, Thomson attempts to show that even if the fetus has a right to life, this right does not entail the right to have whatever one needs—including use of a woman's body—to stay alive.

Critical Reading Questions

1. What is Thomson's position regarding the personhood of the fetus?
2. How does Thomson use the violinist analogy to illustrate the relationship between the fetus and the woman?
3. What conclusion regarding the rights of the fetus, the rights of the mother, and the moral permissibility of abortion does Thomson draw based on the violinist analogy?
4. Why does Thomson reject the "extreme" pro-life view of abortion?
5. Which position on abortion is Thomson addressing when she uses the analogy of a person being trapped in a tiny house with a rapidly growing child?
6. How does Thomson respond to the pro-life argument that if the fetus has a right to life, abortion is unjust killing?
7. What analogy does Thomson use to justify abortion in cases of contraceptive failure?
8. Are there any circumstances, according to Thomson, in which abortion is not morally permissible?
9. What is the difference between a Minimally Decent Samaritan and a Good Samaritan? What is the relevance of this distinction in the abortion debate?
10. On what grounds does Thomson draw a moral distinction between the right to have an abortion and the right to secure the death of an unborn child?

Most opposition to abortion relies on the premise that the fetus is a human being, a person, from the moment of conception. The premise is argued for, but, as I think, not well. Take, for example, the most common argument. We are asked to notice that the development of a human being from conception through birth into childhood is continuous; then it is said that to draw a line, to choose a point in this development and say "before this point the thing is not a person, after this point it is a person" is to make an arbitrary choice, a choice for which in the nature of things no good reason can be given. It is concluded that

[margin note: CA 1: Fetus is a person]

[margin note: J. T.'s response to CA 1]

"A Defense of Abortion," *Philosophy and Public Affairs* 1, no. 1 (1971): 47–66. Notes have been omitted.

Oak tree analogy

the fetus is, or anyway that we had better say it is, a person from the moment of conception. But this conclusion does not follow. [Similar things might be said about the development of an acorn into an oak tree, and it does not follow that acorns are oak trees, or that we had better say they are.] Arguments of this form are sometimes called "slippery slope arguments"—the phrase is perhaps self-explanatory—and it is dismaying that opponents of abortion rely on them so heavily and uncritically.

J.T.'s response to CA 1

Definition of key term "person"

I am inclined to agree, however, that the prospects for "drawing a line" in the development of the fetus look dim. I am inclined to think also that [we shall have to agree that the fetus has already become (a human person) well before birth.] Indeed, it comes as a surprise when one first learns how early in its life it begins to acquire human characteristics. By the tenth week, for example, it already has a face, arms and legs, fingers and toes; it has internal organs, and brain activity is detectable. On the other hand, I think that the premise is false, that the fetus is not a person from the moment of conception. A newly fertilized ovum, a newly implanted clump of cells, is no more a person than an acorn is an oak tree. But I shall not discuss any of this. For it seems to me to be of great interest to ask what happens if, for the sake of argument, we allow the premise. . . .

Premise #1: Fetus is a person

Explanation of premise #1

I propose, then, that [we grant that the fetus is a person from the moment of conception.] How does the argument go from here? Something like this, I take it. [Every person has a right to life.] So the fetus has a right to life. No doubt the [mother has a right to decide what shall happen in and to her body;] everyone would grant that. But surely a person's right to life is stronger and more stringent than the mother's right to decide what happens in and to her body, and so outweighs it. [So the fetus may not be killed; an abortion may not be performed.]

Premise #1 and premise #2: Fetus has a right to life
Premise #3: The mother has a right to life

CA 2: The fetus may not be killed

J.T.'s response to CA 2: Violinist analogy

It sounds plausible. But let me ask you to imagine this. You wake up in the morning and find yourself back to back in bed with an unconscious violinist. A famous unconscious violinist. He has been found to have a fatal kidney ailment, and the Society of Music Lovers has canvassed all available medical records and found that you alone have the right blood type to help. They have therefore kidnapped you, and last night the violinist's circulatory system was plugged into yours, so that your kidneys can be used to extract poisons from his blood as well as your own. The director of the hospital now tells you, "Look, we're sorry the Society of Music Lovers did this to you—we would have never permitted it if we had known. But still, they did it, and the violinist is now plugged into you. To unplug you would be to kill him. But never mind, it's only for nine months. By then he will have recovered from his ailment, and can be safely unplugged from you." Is it morally incumbent on you to accede to this situation? No doubt it would be very nice of you if you did, a great kindness. But do you *have* to accede to it? What if it were not nine months, but nine years? Or longer still? What if the director of the hospital says, "Tough luck, I agree, but you've now got to stay in bed, with the violinist plugged in to you, for the rest of your life. Because remember this. All persons have a right to life, and violinists are persons. Granted you have a right to decide what happens in and to your body, but a person's right to life outweighs your right to decide what happens in and to your body. So you cannot ever be unplugged from him." [I imagine you would regard this as

Rejection of CA 2

violinist analogy

outrageous, which suggests that something really is wrong with that plausible-sounding argument I mentioned a moment ago.]   *Rejection of CA 2*

In this case, of course, you were kidnapped; you didn't volunteer for the operation that plugged the violinist into your kidneys. Can those who oppose abortion on the ground I mentioned make an exception for a pregnancy due to rape? Certainly. They can say that persons have a right to life only if they didn't come into existence because of rape; or they can say that all persons have a right to life, but that some have less of a right to life than others, in particular, that those who came into existence because of rape have less. But these statements have a rather unpleasant sound. Surely the question of whether you have a right to life at all, or how much of it you have, shouldn't turn on the question of whether or not you are the product of a rape. And in fact the people who oppose abortion on the ground I mentioned do not make this distinction, and hence do not make an exception in case of rape. . . .   *Explanation*

Some won't even make an exception for a case in which continuation of the pregnancy is likely to shorten the mother's life; they regard abortion as impermissible even to save the mother's life. Such cases are nowadays very rare, and many opponents of abortion do not accept this extreme view. All the same, it is a good place to begin: a number of points of interest come out in respect to it.

CA 3: Extreme pro-life view

1. Let us call the view that abortion is impermissible even to save the mother's life "the extreme view." I want to suggest first that it does not issue from the argument I mentioned earlier without the addition of some fairly powerful premises. Suppose a woman has become pregnant, and now learns that she has a cardiac condition such that she will die if she carries the baby to term. What may be done for her? The fetus, being a person, has a right to life, but as the mother is a person too, so has she a right to life. Presumably they have an equal right to life. How is it supposed to come out that an abortion may not be performed? If mother and child have an equal right to life, shouldn't we perhaps flip a coin? Or should we add to the mother's right to life her right to decide what happens in and to her body, which everybody seems to be ready to grant—the sum of her rights now outweighing the fetus' right to life?

J. T.'s response to extreme view

The most familiar argument here is the following. We are told that performing the abortion would be directly killing the child, whereas doing nothing would not be killing the mother, but only letting her die. Moreover, in killing the child, one would be killing an innocent person, for the child has committed no crime, and is not aiming at his mother's death. . . .

Premise #4: It is not murder to perform an abortion to save your life

If directly killing an innocent person is murder, and thus is impermissible, then the mother's directly killing the innocent person inside her is murder, and thus is impermissible. But [it cannot seriously be thought to be murder if the mother performs an abortion on herself to save her life. It cannot seriously be said that she *must* refrain, that she *must* sit passively by and wait for her death.] Let us look again at the case of you and the violinist. There you are, in bed with the violinist, and the director of the hospital says to you, "It's all most distressing, and I deeply sympathize, but you see this is putting an additional strain on your kidneys, and you'll be dead within the month. But you *have* to stay where you are all the same. Because unplugging you would be directly killing an in-   *violinist analogy explanation of premise #4* nocent violinist, and that's murder, and that's impermissible." If anything in the world is true, it is that you do not commit murder, you do not do what is impermissible, if you reach around to your back and unplug yourself from that violinist to save your life.

The main focus of attention in writings on abortion has been on what a third party may or may not do in answer to a request from a woman for an abortion. This is in a way understandable. Things being as they are, there isn't much a woman can safely do to abort herself. So the question asked is what a third party may do, and what the mother may do, if it is mentioned at all, is deduced, almost as an afterthought, from what is concluded that third parties may do. But it seems to me that to treat the matter in this way is to refuse to grant to the mother that very status of person which is so firmly insisted on for the fetus. For we cannot simply read off what a person may do from what a third party may do. Suppose you find yourself trapped in a tiny house with a growing child. I mean a very tiny house, and a rapidly growing child—you are already up against the wall of the house and in a few minutes you will be crushed to death. The child on the other hand won't be crushed to death; if nothing is done to stop him from growing he'll be hurt, but in the end he'll simply burst open the house and walk out a free man. Now I could well understand it if a bystander were to say, "There's nothing we can do for you. We cannot choose between your life and his, we cannot be the ones to decide who is to live, we cannot intervene." But it cannot be concluded that you too can do nothing, that you cannot attack it to save your life. However innocent the child may be, you do not have to wait passively while it crushes you to death. Perhaps a pregnant woman is vaguely felt to have the same status of house, to which we don't allow the right of self-defense. But if the woman houses the child, it should be remembered that she is a person who houses it. . . .

In sum, [a woman surely can defend her life against the threat to it posed by the unborn child, even if doing so involves its death.] And this shows also that the extreme view of abortion is false, and so we need not canvass any other possible ways of arriving at it from the argument I mentioned at the outset.

2. The extreme view should of course be weakened to say that while abortion is permissible to save a mother's life, it may not be performed by a third party, but only by the mother herself. But this cannot be right either. For what we have to keep in mind is that the mother and the unborn child are not like two tenants in a small house which has, by an unfortunate mistake, been rented to both: the mother *owns* the house. The fact that she does adds to the offensiveness of deducing that the mother can do nothing from the supposition that third parties can do nothing. But it does nothing more than this: it casts a bright light on the supposition that third parties can do nothing. Certainly it lets us see that a third party who says "I cannot choose between you" is fooling himself if he thinks this is impartiality. If Jones has found and fastened on a certain coat, which he needs to keep from freezing, but which Smith also needs to keep him from freezing, then it is not impartiality that says "I cannot choose between you" when Smith owns the coat. Women have said again and again "This body is *my* body!" and they have reason to feel angry, reason to feel that it has been like shouting in the wind. . . .

Margin notes:

Rejection of CA 3: Extreme pro-life position

Sub conclusion and Premise #6: A woman can defend herself against threats from the unborn child even if it results in child's death

CA 4: Self-defense allows only mother to perform abortion

Explanation of rejection of CA 3 Analogy of house with growing child

Premise #5: A pregnant woman's body is her own

J.T.'s rejection of CA 4: Smith owns the coat

We should really ask what it is that says "no one may choose" in the face of the fact that the body that houses the child is the mother's body. It may be simply a failure to appreciate this fact. But it may be something more interesting, namely the sense that one has a right to refuse to lay hands on people, even where it would be just and fair to do so, even where justice seems to require that somebody do so. This justice might call for somebody to get Smith's coat back from Jones, and yet you have a right to refuse to be the one to lay hands on Jones, a right to refuse to do physical violence to him. This, I think, must be granted. But then what should be said is not "no one may choose," but only "*I cannot choose,*" and indeed not even this, but "*I will not act,*" leaving it open that somebody else can or should, and in particular that anyone in a position of authority, with the job of securing people's rights, both can and should. So this is no difficulty. I have not been arguing that any given third party must accede to the mother's request that he perform an abortion to save her life, but only that he may. . . .

J.T.'s rejection of CA 4: Smith owns the coat

3. Where the mother's life is not at stake, the argument I mentioned at the outset seems to have a much stronger pull. "Everyone has a right to life, so the unborn person has a right to life." And isn't the child's right to life weightier than anything other than the mother's own right to life, which she might put forward as ground for an abortion?

CA 5: The child's right to life is stronger than the mother's rights

This argument treats the right to life as if it were unproblematic. It is not, and this seems to me to be precisely the source of the mistake.

For we should now, at long last, ask what it comes to, to have a right to life. In some views having a right to life includes having a right to be given at least the bare minimum one needs for continued life. But suppose that what in fact *is* the bare minimum a man needs for continued life is something he has no right at all to be given? If I am sick unto death, and the only thing that will save my life is the touch of Henry Fonda's cool hand on my fevered brow, then all the same, I have no right to be given the touch of Henry Fonda's cool hand on my fevered brow. It would be frightfully nice of him to fly in from the West Coast to provide it. It would be less nice, though no doubt meant well, if my friends flew out to the West Coast and carried Henry Fonda back with them. But I have no right at all against anybody that he should do this for me. Or again, to return to the story told earlier, the fact that for continued life that violinist needs the continued use of your kidneys does not establish that he has a right to be given the continued use of your kidneys. He certainly has no right against you that *you* should give him continued use of your kidneys. For [nobody has any right to use your kidneys unless you give him such a right; and nobody has the right against you that you shall give him this right—if you do allow him to go on using your kidneys, this is a kindness on your part, and not something he can claim from you as his due. . . .

J.T.'s reply to CA 5: Henry Fonda analogy

But I would stress that I am not arguing that people do not have the right to life—quite to the contrary, it seems to me that the primary control we must place on the acceptability of an account of rights is that it should turn out in that account to be a truth that all persons have a right to life.[I am arguing only that having a right to life does not guarantee having either a right to be given the use of or a right to be allowed continued use of another person's body—even if one

Premise #1: It is a kindness rather than an obligation to let someone else use our body

needs it for life itself.] So the right to life will not serve the opponents of abortion in the very simple and clear way in which they seem to have thought it would.

4. There is another way to bring out the difficulty. In the most ordinary sort of case, [to deprive someone of what he has a right to is to treat him unjustly.] Suppose a boy and his small brother are jointly given a box of chocolates for Christmas. If the older boy takes the box and refuses to give his brother any of the chocolates, he is unjust to him, for the brother has been given a right to half of them. But suppose that, having learned that otherwise it means nine years in bed with that violinist, you unplug yourself from him. You surely are not being unjust to him, for you gave him no right to use your kidneys, and no one else can have given him any such right. But we have to notice that in unplugging yourself, you are killing him; and violinists, like everybody else, have a right to life, and thus in the view we were considering just now, the right not to be killed. So here you do what he supposedly has a right you shall not do, but you do not act unjustly to him in doing it.

Premise #8: It is unjust to deprive someone of something to which they have a right

Explanation of premise #8

The emendation which may be made at this point is this: [the right to life consists not in the right not to be killed, but rather in the right not to be killed unjustly.] This runs a risk of circularity, but never mind: it would enable us to square the fact that the violinist has a right to life with the fact that you do not act unjustly toward him in unplugging yourself, thereby killing him. For if you do not kill him unjustly, you do not violate his right to life, and it is no wonder you do him no injustice.

Premise #9: The right to life consists only of the right not to be killed unjustly

But if this emendation is accepted, the gap in the argument against abortion stares us plainly in the face: it is no means enough to show that the fetus is a person, and to remind us that all persons have a right to life—we need to be shown also that killing the fetus violates its right to life, i.e., that abortion is unjust killing. And is it?

I suppose we may take it as a datum that in a case of pregnancy due to rape the mother has not given the unborn person a right to the use of her body for food and shelter. Indeed, in what pregnancy could it be supposed that the mother has given the unborn person such a right? It is not as if there were unborn persons drifting about the world, to whom a woman who wants a child says "I invite you in."

But it might be argued that there are other ways one can have acquired a right to the use of another person's body than by having been invited to use it by that person. Suppose a woman voluntarily indulges in intercourse, knowing that the chance it will issue in pregnancy, and then she does become pregnant; is she not in part responsible for the presence, in fact the very existence, of the unborn person inside her? No doubt she did not invite it in. But doesn't her partial responsibility for its being there itself give it a right to the use of her body? If so, then her aborting it would be more like the boy's taking away the chocolates, and less like your unplugging yourself from the violinist—doing so would be depriving it of what it does have a right to, and thus would be doing it an injustice. . . .

CA 6: If mother "invites" fetus to use her body, it is unjust to then kill the fetus

The first thing to be said about this is that it is something new. Opponents of abortion have been so concerned to make out the independence of the fetus, in order to establish that it has a right to life, just as its mother does, that they have tended to overlook the possible support they might gain from making out [that the fetus is *dependent* on the mother, in order to establish that she has a special kind of responsibility for it,] a responsibility that gives it rights against her which are not possessed by any independent person—such as an ailing violinist who is a stranger to her.

Premise #10: The fetus is dependent on the mother

On the other hand, this argument would give the unborn person a right to its mother's body only if her pregnancy resulted from a voluntary act, undertaken in full knowledge of the chance a pregnancy might result from it. It would leave out entirely the unborn person whose existence is due to rape. Pending the availability of some further argument, then, we would be left with the conclusion that unborn persons whose existence is due to rape have no right to the use of their mothers' bodies, and thus that aborting them is not depriving them of anything they have a right to and hence is not unjust killing.

J.T.'s response to CA 6 people seeds analogy

And we should also notice that it is not at all plain that this argument really does not go even as far as it purports to. For there are cases and cases, and the details make a difference. If the room is stuffy, and I therefore open a window to air it, and a burglar climbs in, it would be absurd to say, "Ah, now he can stay, she's given him a right to the use of her house—for she is partially responsible for his presence there, having voluntarily done what enabled him to get in, in full knowledge that there are such things as burglars, and that burglars burgle." It would be still more absurd to say this if I had had bars installed outside my windows, precisely to prevent burglars from getting in, and a burglar got in only because of a defect in the bars. It remains equally absurd if we imagine it is not a burglar who climbs in, but an innocent person who blunders or falls in. Again, suppose it were like this: people-seeds drift about in the air like pollen, and if you open your windows, one may drift in and take root in your carpets or upholstery. You don't want children, so you fix up your windows with fine mesh screens, the very best you can buy. As can happen, however, and on very, very rare occasions does happen, one of the screens is defective; and a seed drifts in and takes root. Does the person-plant who now develops have a right to the use of your house? Surely not—despite the fact that you voluntarily opened your windows, you knowingly kept carpets and upholstered furniture, and you knew that screens were sometimes defective. Someone may argue that you are responsible for its rooting, that it does have a right to your house, because after all you *could* have lived out your life with bare floors and furniture, or with sealed windows and doors. But this won't do—for by the same token anyone can avoid a pregnancy due to rape by having a hysterectomy, or anyway by never leaving home without a (reliable!) army.

It seems to me that the argument we are looking at can establish at most that [there are *some* cases in which the unborn person has a right to the use of its mother's body,] and therefore [*some* cases in which abortion is unjust killing.] There is room for much discussion and argument as to precisely which, if any. But I think we should sidestep this issue and leave it open, for at any rate the argument certainly does not establish that all abortion is unjust killing.

Premise #11: There are some cases where the fetus has a right to the mother's body

Sub conclusion and premise #12: There are some cases where abortion is unjust killing

5. There is room for yet another argument here, however. [We surely must all grant that there may be cases in which it would be morally indecent to detach a

person from your body at the cost of his life.] Suppose you learn that what the violinist needs is not nine years of your life, but only one hour: all you need to do to save his life is to spend one hour in that bed with him. Suppose also that letting him use your kidneys for that one hour would not affect your health in the slightest. Admittedly you were kidnapped. Admittedly you did not give anyone permission to plug him into you. Nevertheless it seems to me plain you *ought* to allow him to use your kidneys for that one hour—it would be indecent to refuse.

Explanation of premise #10: The violinist analogy revisited

Again, suppose pregnancy lasted only an hour, and constituted no threat to your life or health. And suppose that a woman becomes pregnant as a result of rape. Admittedly she did not voluntarily do anything to bring about the existence of a child. Admittedly she did nothing at all which would give the unborn person a right to the use of her body. All the same it might well be said, as in the newly emended violinist story, that she *ought* to allow it to remain for that hour—that it would be indecent in her to refuse.

Now some people are inclined to use the term "right" in such a way that it follows from the fact that you ought to allow a person to use your body for the hour he needs, that he has the right to use your body for the hour he needs, even though he has not been given that right by any person or act. They may say that it follows also that if you refuse, you act unjustly toward him. This use of the term is perhaps so common that it cannot be called wrong; nevertheless it seems to me to be an unfortunate loosening of what we would do better to keep a tight rein on. Suppose the box of chocolates I mentioned earlier had not been given to both boys jointly, but was given only to the older boy. There he sits, stolidly eating his way through the box, his small brother watching enviously. Here we are likely to say "You ought not to be so mean. You ought to give your brother some of those chocolates." My own view is that it just does not follow from the truth of this that the brother has any right to any of the chocolates. If the boy refuses to give his brother any, he is greedy, stingy, callous—but not unjust. . . .

Premise #13: Even if there are cases in which the mother ought to allow the unborn child to use her body, this does not mean the child has a right to her body

So my own view is that even though you ought to let the violinist use your kidneys for the one hour he needs, we should not conclude that he has a right to do so—we should say that if you refuse, you are, like the boy who owns all the chocolates and will give none away, self-centered and callous, indecent in fact, but not unjust. And similarly, that even supposing a case in which a woman pregnant due to rape ought to allow the unborn person to use her body for the hour he needs, we should not conclude that he has a right to do so; we should conclude that she is self-centered, callous, indecent, but not unjust, if she refuses. The complaints are no less grave; they are just different. . . .

Explanation of two types of Samaritans

6. We have in fact to distinguish between two kinds of Samaritan: the Good Samaritan and what we might call the Minimally Decent Samaritan. . . . The Good Samaritan went out of his way, at some cost to himself, to help one in need of it. . . . [in Luke 10:30–35]

Key terms: Good Samaritan and Minimally Decent Samaritan

These things are a matter of degree, of course, but there is a difference, and it comes out perhaps most clearly in the story of Kitty Genovese, who, as you will remember, was murdered while thirty-eight people watched or listened, and did nothing at all to help her. A Good Samaritan would have rushed out to give direct assistance against the murderer. Or perhaps we had better allow that

Explanation of two types of Samaritan

it would have been a Splendid Samaritan who did this, on the ground that it would have involved a risk of death for himself. But the thirty-eight not only did not do this, they did not even trouble to pick up a phone to call the police. Minimally Decent Samaritanism would call for doing at least that, and their not having done it was monstrous.

After telling the story of the Good Samaritan, Jesus said "Go, and do thou likewise." Perhaps he meant that we are morally required to act as the Good Samaritan did. Perhaps he was urging people to do more than is morally required of them. At all events it seems plain that[it was not morally required of

Premise #14: We are only morally required to be Minimally Decent Samaritans

any of the thirty-eight that he rush out to give direct assistance at the risk of his own life,]and that[it is not morally required of anyone that he give long stretches of his life—nine years or nine months—to sustaining that life of a person who has no special right (we were leaving open the possibility of this) to demand it.]

Premise #15: Being a Minimally Decent Samaritan does not require us to give long stretches to sustain the life of someone who has no special rights

Indeed, with one rather striking class of exceptions, no one in any country in the world is *legally* required to do anywhere near as much as this for anyone else. The class of exceptions is obvious. My main concern here is not the state of the law in respect to abortion, but it is worth drawing attention to the fact that in no state in this country is any man compelled by law to be even a Minimally Decent Samaritan to any person; there is no law under which charges could be brought against the thirty-eight who stood by while Kitty Genovese died. . . .

Explanation of premises #14 and #15

I should think, myself, that Minimally Decent Samaritan laws would be one thing, Good Samaritan laws quite another, and in fact highly improper. But we are not here concerned with the law. What we should ask is not whether anybody should be compelled by law to be a Good Samaritan, but whether we must accede to a situation in which somebody is being compelled—by nature, perhaps—to be a Good Samaritan. We have, in other words, to look now at third-party interventions. I have been arguing that no person is morally required to make large sacrifices to sustain the life of another who has no right to demand them, and this even where the sacrifices do not include life itself; we are not morally required to be Good Samaritans or anyway Very Good Samaritans to one another. But what if a man cannot extricate himself from such a situation? What if he appeals to us to extricate him? It seems to me plain that there are cases in which we can, cases in which a Good Samaritan would extricate him. There you are, you were kidnapped, and nine years in bed with that violinist lie ahead of you. You have your own life to lead. You are sorry, but you simply cannot see giving up so much of your life to the sustaining of his. You cannot extricate yourself, and ask us to do so. I should have thought that—in light of his having no right to the use of your body—it was obvious that we do not have to accede to your being forced to give up so much. We can do what you ask. There is no injustice to the violinist in our doing so.

CA 1: The woman has a special kind of obligation toward her fetus because she is the mother

7. Following the lead of opponents of abortion, I have throughout been speaking of the fetus merely as a person, and what I have been asking is whether or not the argument we began with, which proceeds only from the fetus' being a person, really does not establish its conclusion. I have argued that it does not.

But of course there are arguments and arguments, and it may be said that I have simply fastened on the wrong one. It may be said that what is important is not merely the fact that the fetus is a person, but that it is a person for whom the woman has a special kind of responsibility issuing from the fact that she is the mother. And it might be argued that all my analogies are therefore irrelevant—for you do not have that special responsibility for that violinist, Henry Fonda does not have that special kind of responsibility for me. And our attention might be drawn to the fact that men and women both *are* compelled by law to provide support for their children.

I have in effect dealt (briefly) with this argument in section 4 above; but a (still briefer) recapitulation now may be in order. Surely we do not have any such "special responsibility" for a person unless we have assumed it, explicitly or implicitly. If a set of parents do not try to prevent a pregnancy, do not obtain an abortion, and then at the time of birth of the child do not put it out for adoption, but rather take it home with them, then they have assumed responsibility for it, they have given it rights, and they cannot *now* withdraw support from it at the cost of its life because they now find it difficult to go on providing for it. But if they have taken all reasonable precautions against having a child, they do not simply by virtue of their biological relationship to the child who comes into existence have a special responsibility for it. They may wish to assume responsibility for it, or they may not wish to. And I am suggesting that if assuming responsibility for it would require large sacrifices, then they may refuse. . . .

8. My argument will be found unsatisfactory on two counts by many of those who want to regard abortion as morally permissible. First, while I do argue that abortion is not impermissible, I do not argue that it is always permissible. There may well be cases in which carrying the child to term requires only Minimally Decent Samaritanism of the mother, and this is a standard we must not fall below. I am inclined to think it a merit of my account precisely that it does *not* give a general yes or a general no. It allows for and supports our sense that, for example, a sick and desperately frightened fourteen-year-old schoolgirl, pregnant due to rape, may *of course* choose abortion, and that any law which rules this out is an insane law. And it also allows for and supports our sense that in other cases resort to abortion is even positively indecent. It would be indecent in the woman to request an abortion, and indecent in a doctor to perform it, if she is in her seventh month, and wants the abortion to avoid the nuisance of postponing a trip abroad. The very fact that the arguments I have been drawing attention to treat all cases of abortion, or even all cases of abortion in which the mother's life is not at stake, as morally on a par ought to have made them suspect at the outset.

Secondly, while I am arguing for the permissibility of abortion in some cases, I am not arguing for the right to secure the death of the unborn child. It is easy to confuse these two things in that up to a certain point in the life of the fetus it is not able to survive outside the mother's body; hence removing it from her body guarantees its death. But they are importantly different. I have argued that you are not morally required to spend nine months in bed, sustaining the life of that violinist; but to say this is by no means to say that if, when you unplug yourself, there is a miracle and he survives, you then have to turn around and slit his throat. You may detach yourself even if this costs him his life; you have no right to be guaranteed his death, by some other means, if unplugging yourself does not kill him. There are some people who will feel dissatisfied by this feature of

Margin notes:

J.T.'s response to CA 1

Premise #16: We do not have a responsibility for another person unless we have assumed it

Part 1 of conclusion: Abortion is permissible except in cases where it falls beneath the standard of Minimally Decent Samaritan

Part 2 of conclusion: The woman does not have a right to secure the death of her child, but only to remove it from her body my argument. A woman may be utterly devastated by the thought of a child, a bit of herself, put out for adoption and never seen or heard of again. She may therefore want not merely that the child be detached from her, but more, that it die. Some opponents of abortion are inclined to regard this as beneath contempt—thereby showing insensitivity to what is surely a powerful source of despair. All the same, I agree that the desire for the child's death is not one which anybody may gratify, should it turn out to be possible to detach the child alive.

At this place, however, it should be remembered that we have only been pretending throughout that the fetus is a human being from the moment of conception. A very early abortion is surely not the killing of a person, and so is not dealt with by anything I have said here.

Discussion Questions

1. Do you agree with Thomson that abortion is morally defensible even if the fetus is a person? In her analogies does Thomson take the presumption of the personhood of the fetus as seriously as she does the personhood of the mother? Support your answers.

2. Imagine that you find a baby or toddler in your winter cabin. There is no one else around to help care for the child and, because of heavy snows, no way to get to town for the next eight months. Assuming that you have enough food in the cabin for both of you, do you have a moral obligation, as a Minimally Decent Samaritan, to let the child share your cabin for the next eight months? Would it be morally permissible for you to put the child outside even though you knew she would certainly die of exposure if you did? Discuss the analogy between this case and that of abortion.

3. Using the Aristotelean and Confucian doctrine of the mean, discuss whether being a Minimally Decent Samaritan is sufficient for living the good and virtuous life.

4. Does Thomson's argument that the fetus has no right to the mother's womb justify killing the fetus? Does Thomson do an adequate job of distinguishing between the right of a mother to have an abortion and the moral injunction against taking the life of the fetus? Support your answers.

5. Thomson argues that we have no responsibility for another person unless we have voluntarily assumed it. Do you agree? What are the implications of Thomson's argument for cases in which the woman chose to continue her pregnancy when the father did not want to have the child? Does the father have any moral obligation toward the child in terms of child support and sharing in the care of the child? Support your answers.

6. Discuss how Thomson would most likely stand in the debate over late-term "partial-birth" abortions.

JOHN T. NOONAN JR.

An Almost Absolute Value in History

John Noonan is a professor of law at the University of California in Berkeley. Like Thomson's "A Defense of Abortion," Noonan's 1970 article on abortion remains one of the classics in abortion debates. Both Noonan and Thomson begin with the presumption that the fetus is a person with moral standing. Unlike Thomson, however, Noonan draws the conclusion that abortion is rarely, if ever morally justified. After rejecting the various criteria of personhood used by defenders of abortion, he concludes that anyone conceived by human parents is a person.

Critical Reading Questions

1. What, according to Noonan, is the most fundamental question in the abortion debate?
2. What does Noonan mean by "ensoulment"? Why does he claim that the notion of ensoulment does not require a theological basis?
3. On what grounds does Noonan reject viability as the point that distinguishes persons from nonpersons? What are the implications, according to Noonan, of using independence as a criterion for personhood?
4. On what grounds does Noonan reject experience and the possession of memories as an argument in support of abortion? What are some of the implications of this argument that Noonan finds unacceptable?
5. On what grounds does Noonan reject both parental feelings toward the fetus and social visibility as morally irrelevant to the moral status of the fetus?
6. What criterion does Noonan use to define personhood? What support does he offer for his definition?
7. What analogy does Noonan offer to support his argument that even if we are not sure that the fetus is a person, we should give the fetus the benefit of the doubt?
8. How does Noonan use "biological probabilities" to support his argument that the fetus is a person?
9. How does Noonan suggest that we resolve conflicts between the rights of the fetus and the rights of the mother? Under what conditions does Noonan permit abortion?
10. What philosophical principle is, according to Noonan, equivalent to the scriptural command to "love your neighbor as yourself"? How does this principle apply to the fetus?

"An Almost Absolute Value in History," *The Morality of Abortion: Legal and Historical Perspectives* (Cambridge, Mass.: Harvard University Press, 1970), 51–59. Notes have been omitted.

The most fundamental question involved in the long history of thought on abortion is: how do you determine the humanity of a being? To phrase the question that way is to put in comprehensive humanistic terms what the theologians either dealt with as an explicitly theological question under the heading of "ensoulment" or dealt with implicitly in their treatment of abortion. The Christian position as it originated did not depend on a narrow theological or philosophical concept. . . . The theological notion of ensoulment could easily be translated into humanistic language by substituting "human" for "rational soul"; the problem of knowing when a man is a man is common to theology and humanism.

If one steps outside the specific categories used by the theologians, the answer they gave can be analyzed as a refusal to discriminate among human beings on the basis of their varying potentialities. Once conceived, the being was recognized as man because he had man's potential. The criterion for humanity, thus, was simple and all-embracing: if you are conceived by human parents, you are human.

The strength of this position may be tested by a review of some of the other distinctions offered in the contemporary controversy over legalizing abortion. Perhaps the most popular distinction is in terms of viability. Before an age of so many months, the fetus is not viable, that is, it cannot be removed from the mother's womb and live apart from her. To that extent, the life of the fetus is absolutely dependent on the life of the mother. This dependence is made the basis of denying recognition to its humanity.

There are difficulties with this distinction. One is that the perfection of artificial incubation may make the fetus viable at any time: it may be removed and artificially sustained. Experiments with animals already show that such a procedure is possible. This hypothetical extreme case relates to an actual difficulty: there is considerable elasticity to the idea of viability. Mere length of life is not an exact measure. The viability of the fetus depends on the extent of its anatomical and functional development. . . .

The most important objection to this approach is that dependence is not ended by viability. The fetus is still absolutely dependent on someone's care

in order to continue existence; indeed a child of one or three or even five years of age is absolutely dependent on another's care for existence; uncared for, the older fetus or the younger child will die as surely as the early fetus detached from the mother. The unsubstantial lessening in dependence at viability does not seem to signify any special acquisition of humanity.

A second distinction has been attempted in terms of experience. A being who has had experience, has lived and suffered, who possesses memories, is more human than one who has not. Humanity depends on formation by experience. The fetus is thus "unformed" in the most basic human sense. . . .

This distinction is not serviceable for the embryo which is already experiencing and reacting. The embryo is responsive to touch after eight weeks and at least at that point is experiencing. At an earlier stage the zygote is certainly alive and responding to its environment. The distinction may also be challenged by the rare case where aphasia has erased adult memory: has it erased humanity? More fundamentally, this distinction leaves even the older fetus or the younger child to be treated as an unformed inhuman thing. Finally, it is not clear why experience as such confers humanity. It could be argued that certain central experiences such as loving or learning are necessary to make a man human. But then human beings who have failed to love or to learn might be excluded from the class called man.

A third distinction is made by appeal to the sentiments of adults. If a fetus dies, the grief of the parents is not the grief they would have for a living child. The fetus is an unnamed "it" till birth, and is not perceived as personality until at least the fourth month of existence when movements in the womb manifest a vigorous presence demanding joyful recognition by the parents.

Yet feeling is notoriously an unsure guide to the humanity of others. Many groups of humans have had difficulty in feeling that persons of another tongue, color, religion, sex are as human as they. Apart from reactions to alien groups, we mourn the loss of a ten-year-old boy more than the loss of his one-day-old brother or his 90-year-old grandfather. The difference felt and the grief expressed vary with the potentialities extinguished, or the experience wiped out; they do not seem to point to any substantial difference in the humanity of baby, boy, or grandfather.

Distinctions are also made in terms of sensation by the parents. The embryo is felt within the womb only after about the fourth month. The embryo is seen only at birth. What can be neither seen nor felt is different from what is tangible. If the fetus cannot be seen or touched at all, it cannot be perceived as man.

Yet experience shows that sight is even more untrustworthy than feeling in determining humanity. By sight, color became an appropriate index for saying who was a man, and the evil of racial discrimination was given foundation. Nor can touch provide the test; a being confined by sickness, "out of touch" with others, does not thereby seem to lose his humanity. To the extent that touch still has appeal as a criterion, it appears to be a survival of the old English idea of "quickening"—a possible mistranslation of the Latin *animatus* used in the canon law. To that extent touch as a criterion seems to be dependent on the Aristotelian notion of ensoulment, and to fall when this notion is discarded.

Finally, a distinction is sought in social visibility. The fetus is not socially perceived as human. It cannot communicate with others. Thus, both subjectively and objectively, it is not a member of society. As moral rules are rules for the behavior of members of society to each other, they cannot be made for behavior toward what is not yet a member. Excluded from the society of men, the fetus is excluded from the humanity of men.

By force of the argument from the consequences, this distinction is to be rejected. It is more subtle than that founded on an appeal to physical sensation, but it is equally dangerous in its implications. If humanity depends on social recognition, individuals or whole groups may be dehumanized by being denied any status in their society. Such a fate is fictionally portrayed in *1984* and has actually been the lot of many men in many societies. In the Roman empire, for example, condemnation to slavery meant the practical denial of most human rights; in the Chinese Communist world, landlords have been classified as enemies of the people and so treated as nonpersons by the state. Humanity does not depend on social recognition, though often the failure of society to recognize the prisoner, the alien, the heterodox as human has led to the destruction of human beings. Anyone conceived by a man and a woman is human. Recognition of this condition by society follows a real event in the objective order, however imperfect and halting the recognition. Any attempt to limit humanity to exclude some group runs the risk of furnishing authority and precedent for excluding other groups in the name of the consciousness or perception of the controlling group in the society.

A philosopher may reject the appeal to the humanity of the fetus because he views "humanity" as a secular view of the soul and because he doubts the existence of anything real and objective which can be identified as humanity. One answer to such a philosopher is to ask how he reasons about moral questions without supposing that there is a sense in which he and the others of whom he speaks are human. Whatever group is taken as the society which determines who may be killed is thereby taken as human. A second answer is to ask if he does not believe that there is a right and wrong way of deciding moral questions. If there is such a difference, experience may be appealed to: to decide who is human on the basis of the sentiment of a given society has led to consequences which rational men would characterize as monstrous. . . .

There is a kind of continuity in all life, but the earlier stages of the elements of human life possess tiny probabilities of development. Consider for example, the spermatozoa in any normal ejaculate: there are about 200,000,000 in any single ejaculate, of which one has a chance of developing into a zygote. Consider the oocytes which may become ova: there are 100,000 to 1,000,000 oocytes in a female infant, of which a maximum of 390 are ovulated. But once spermatozoon and ovum meet and the conceptus is formed, such studies as have been made show that roughly in only 20 percent of the cases will spontaneous abortion occur. In other words, the chances are about 4 out of 5 that this new being will develop. At this stage in the life of the being there is a sharp shift in probabilities, an immense jump in potentialities. . . .

It may be asked, What does a change in biological probabilities have to do with establishing humanity? The argument from probabilities is not aimed at establishing humanity but at establishing an objective discontinuity which may be taken into account in moral discourse. As life itself is a matter of probabilities, as most moral reasoning is an estimate of probabilities, so it seems in accord with the structure of reality and the nature of moral thought to found a moral judgment on the change in probabilities at conception. The appeal to probabilities is the most commonsensical of arguments, to a greater or smaller degree all of us base our actions on probabilities, and in morals, as in law, prudence and negligence are often measured by the account one has taken of the probabilities. If the chance is 200,000,000 to 1 that the movement in the bushes into which you shoot is a man's, I doubt if many persons would hold you careless in shooting; but if the chances are 4 out of 5 that the movement is a human being's, few would acquit you of blame. Would the argument be different if only one out of ten children conceived came to term? Of course this argument would be different. This argument is an appeal to probabilities that actually exist, not to any and all states of affairs which may be imagined.

The probabilities as they do exist do not show the humanity of the embryo in the sense of a demonstration in logic any more than the probabilities of the movement in the bush being a man demonstrate beyond all doubt that the being is a man. The appeal is a "buttressing" consideration, showing the plausibility of the standard adopted. The argument focuses on the decisional factor in any moral judgment and assumes that part of the business of a moralist is drawing lines. One evidence of the nonarbitrary character of the line drawn is the difference of probabilities on either side of it. If a spermatozoon is destroyed, one destroys a being which had a chance of far less than 1 in 200 million of developing into a reasoning being, possessed of the genetic code, a heart and other organs, and capable of pain. If a fetus is destroyed, one destroys a being already possessed of the genetic code, organs, and sensitivity to pain, and one which had an 80 percent chance of developing further into a baby outside the womb who, in time, would reason.

The positive argument for conception as the decisive moment of humanization is that at conception the new being receives the genetic code. It is this genetic information which determines his characteristics, which is the biological carrier of the possibility of human wisdom, which makes him a self-evolving being. A being with a human genetic code is man. . . .

Even with the fetus weighed as human, one interest could be weighed as equal or superior: that of the mother in her own life. The casuists between 1450 and 1895 were willing to weigh this interest as superior. Since 1895, that interest was given decisive weight only in the two special cases of the cancerous uterus and the ectopic pregnancy. In both of these cases the fetus itself had little chance of survival even if the abortion were not performed. As the balance was once struck in favor of the mother whenever her life was endangered, it could be so struck again. The balance reached between 1895 and 1930 attempted prudentially and pastorally to forestall a multitude of exceptions for interests less than life.

The perception of the humanity of the fetus and the weighing of fetal rights against other human rights constituted the work of the moral analysts. But what spirit animated their abstract judgments? For the Christian community it was the injunction of Scripture to love your neighbor as yourself. The fetus as human was a neighbor; his life had parity with one's own. The commandment gave life to what otherwise would have been only rational calculation.

The commandment could be put in humanistic as well as theological terms: do not injure your fellow man without reason. In these terms, once the humanity of the fetus is perceived, abortion is never right except in self-defense. When life must be taken to save life, reason alone cannot say that a mother must prefer a child's life to her own. With this exception, now of great rarity, abortion violates the rational humanist tenet of the equality of human lives.

Discussion Questions

1. Noonan argues that parents' feelings toward their fetus are morally irrelevant. Discuss how a care ethicist, such as Nel Noddings, might respond to Noonan's argument.
2. According to Noonan, "anyone conceived by a man and a woman is human [a person]." Do you agree? Critically evaluate the premises that Noonan offers in support of this definition of personhood.
3. Discuss Noonan's criterion of personhood in light of the fact that it is now possible to clone human beings.[29]
4. Imagine a conversation between Noonan and Thomson. How might Noonan respond to Thomson's defense of abortion? How might Thomson respond to Noonan's claim that abortion is never right except in cases of self-defense?
5. While Noonan supports the Catholic position on abortion, he points out that this position can be supported on rational philosophical or humanistic premises. Has Noonan done an adequate job of supporting his position on abortion using only philosophical premises? Support your answer.

 MARY ANNE WARREN

The Moral Significance of Birth

Mary Anne Warren is a professor of philosophy at San Francisco State University. Warren defends a pro-choice position on abortion: Women have a fundamental right to make their own decisions about their bodies. After rejecting the traditional criteria of personhood, including that used by Noonan, Warren argues that personhood does not begin until after birth. Because the fetus is not a person, abortion can be justified under any circumstances. Her definition of personhood also permits infanticide under some circumstances.

Critical Reading Questions

1. According to Warren, what is the relationship between moral and legal rights?
2. What are Warren's arguments against the use of the "intrinsic-properties assumption" and the "single-criterion assumption" as the foundation of moral rights?
3. Why does Warren reject both sentience and viability as sufficient conditions for personhood?
4. What arguments does Warren use in support of self-awareness as a condition for personhood?
5. Why does Warren consider early infanticide morally preferable to infanticide after a few weeks, even though the two-week-old infant is not yet a person?

"The Moral Significance of Birth," *Hypatia* 4, no. 3 (Fall 1989): 46–65. Notes have been omitted.

6. What arguments does Warren use to support her claim that, in our society, we should extend protection to human infants even though they are not yet persons? What are some of the problems involved in extending the same protection to sentient, late-term fetuses?

7. What is the relationship, according to Warren, between personhood and being a member of a community? Does personhood require that one be a member of a social community?

8. What does Warren mean when she says that granting legal personhood to the fetus is "necessarily incompatible" with respect for the personhood of women? How does Warren deal with the conflict between maternal autonomy and protection of the fetus?

Does birth make a difference to the moral right of the fetus/ infant? Should it make a difference to its legal rights? Most contemporary philosophers believe that birth cannot make a difference to moral rights. If this is true, then it becomes difficult to justify either a moral or a legal distinction between late abortion and infanticide. I argue that the view that birth is irrelevant to moral rights rests upon two highly questionable assumptions about the theoretical foundations of moral rights. If we reject these assumptions, then we are free to take account of the contrasting biological and social relationships that make even relatively late abortion morally different from infanticide.

English common law treats the moment of live birth as the point at which a legal person comes into existence. Although abortion has often been prohibited, it has almost never been classified as homicide. In contrast, infanticide generally is classified as a form of homicide, even where (as in England) there are statutes designed to mitigate the severity of the crime in certain cases. But many people—including some feminists—now favor the extension of equal legal rights to some or all fetuses (S. Callahan 1984, 1986). The extension of legal personhood to fetuses would not only threaten women's right to choose abortion, but also undermine other fundamental rights. I will argue that because of these dangers, birth remains the most appropriate place to mark the existence of a new legal person. . . .

THE DENIAL OF THE MORAL SIGNIFICANCE OF BIRTH

The view that birth is irrelevant to moral rights is shared by philosophers on all points of the spectrum of moral views about abortion. For the most conservative, birth adds nothing to the infant's moral rights, since all of those rights have been present since conception. Moderates hold that the fetus acquires an equal right to life at some point after conception but before birth. The most popular candidates for this point of moral demarcation are (1) the stage at which the fetus becomes viable (i.e., capable of surviving outside the womb, with or without medical assistance), and (2) the stage at which it becomes sentient (i.e., capable of having experiences, including that of pain). For those who hold a view of this sort, both infanticide and abortion at any time past the critical stage are forms of homicide, and there is little reason to distinguish between them either morally or legally.

Finally, liberals hold that even relatively late abortion is sometimes morally acceptable, and that at no time is abortion the moral equivalent of homicide. However, few liberals wish to hold that infanticide is not—at least sometimes—morally comparable to homicide. Consequently, the presumption that being born makes no difference to one's moral rights creates problems for the liberal view of abortion. Unless the liberal can establish some grounds for a general moral distinction between late abortion and early infanticide, she must either retreat to a moderate position on abortion, or else conclude that infanticide is not so bad after all.

To those who accept the intrinsic-properties assumption, birth can make little difference to the moral standing of the fetus/infant. For birth does not seem to alter any intrinsic property that could reasonably be linked to the possession of a strong right to life. Newborn infants have very nearly the same intrinsic properties as do fetuses shortly before birth. . . .

Prenatal neurophysiology and behavior suggest that human fetuses begin to have rudimentary sensory experiences at some time during the second trimester of pregnancy. . . .

These two theories are worth examining, not only because they illustrate the difficulties generated by the intrinsic-properties and single-criterion assumptions, but also because each includes valid insights that need to be integrated into a more comprehensive account. Both Sumner and Tooley are partially right. Unlike "genetic humanity"— a property possessed by fertilized human ova— sentience and self-awareness are properties that have some general relevance to what we may owe another being in the way of respect and protection. However, neither the sentience criterion nor the self-awareness criterion can explain the moral significance of birth.

THE SENTIENCE CRITERION

Both newborn infants and late-term fetuses show clear signs of sentience. For instance, they are apparently capable of having visual experiences. Infants will often turn away from bright lights, and those who have done intrauterine photography have sometimes observed a similar reaction in the late-term fetus when bright lights are introduced in its vicinity. Both may respond to loud noises, voices, or other sounds, so both can probably have auditory experiences. They are evidently also responsive to touch, taste, motion, and other kinds of sensory stimulation.

The sentience of infants and late-term fetuses makes a difference to how they should be treated, by contrast with fertilized ova or first-trimester fetuses. Sentient beings are usually capable of experiencing painful as well as pleasurable or effectively neutral sensations. . . . Thus, sentient beings may plausibly be said to have a moral right not to be deliberately subjected to pain in the absence of any compelling reason. For those who prefer not to speak of rights, it is still plausible that a capacity for sentience gives an entity some moral standing. . . .

But it is not clear that sentience is a sufficient condition for moral equality, since there are many clearly-sentient creatures (e.g., mice) to which most of us would not be prepared to ascribe equal moral standing. . . .

The 1973 *Roe v. Wade* decision treats the presumed viability of third-trimester fetuses as a basis for permitting states to restrict abortion rights in order to protect fetal life in the third trimester, but not earlier. Yet viability is relative, among other things, to the medical care available to the pregnant woman and her infant. Increasingly sophisticated neonatal intensive care has made it possible to save many more premature infants than before, thus altering the average age of viability. Someday it may be possible to keep even first-trimester fetuses alive and developing normally outside the womb. The viability criterion seems to imply that the advent of total ectogenesis (artificial gestation from conception to birth) would automatically eliminate women's right to abortion, even in the earliest stages of pregnancy. At the very least, it must imply that as many aborted fetuses as possible should be kept alive through artificial gestation. But the mere technological possibility of providing artificial wombs for huge numbers of human fetuses could not establish such a moral obligation. A massive commitment to ectogenesis would probably be ruinously expensive, and might prove contrary to the interests of parents of children. The viability criterion forces us to make a hazardous leap from the technologically possible to the morally mandatory.

The sentience criterion at first appears more promising as a means of defending a moderate view of abortion. It provides an intuitively plausible distinction between early and late abortion. Unlike the viability criterion, it is unlikely to be undermined by new biomedical technologies. . . .

The strong version of the sentience criterion treats sentience as a sufficient condition for having full and equal moral standing. The weak version treats sentience as sufficient for having some moral standing, but not necessarily full and equal moral standing. . . .

[According to the strong version] any being which has even minimal capacities for sensory experience is the moral equal of any person. If we accept this theory, then we must conclude that not only is late abortion the moral equivalent of homicide, but so is the killing of such sentient nonhuman beings as mice. . . . [According to the weak version] all sentient beings have some moral standing, but beings that are more highly sentient have greater moral standing than do less highly sentient beings. This weaker version of the sentience criterion leaves room for a distinction between the moral standing of mice and that of sentient humans—provided, that is, that mice can be shown to be less highly sentient. However, it will not support the moral equality of late-term fetuses, since the relatively undeveloped condition of fetal brains almost certainly means that fetuses are less highly sentient than older human beings. . . .

THE SELF-AWARENESS CRITERION

Although newborn infants are regarded as persons in both law and common moral conviction, they lack certain mental capacities that are typical of persons. They have sensory experiences, but, as Tooley points out, they probably do not yet think, or have a sense of who they are, or a desire to continue to exist. It is not unreasonable to suppose that these facts make some difference to their moral standing. Other things being equal, it is surely worse to kill a self-aware being that wants to go on living than one that has never been self-aware and that has no such preference. If this is true, then it is hard to avoid the conclusion that neither abortion nor infanticide is quite as bad as the killing of older human beings.

And indeed many human societies seem to have accepted that conclusion. . . .

But if infanticide is to be considered, it is better that it be done immediately after birth, before the bonds of love and care between the infant and the mother (and other persons) have grown any stronger than they may already be. Postponing the question of the infant's acceptance for weeks or months would be cruel to all concerned. Although an infant may be little more sentient or self-aware at two weeks of age than at birth, its death is apt to be a greater tragedy—not for it, but for those who have come to love it. I suspect that this is why, where infanticide is tolerated, the decision to kill or abandon an infant must usually be made rather quickly. If this consideration is morally relevant—and I think it is—then the self-awareness criterion fails to illuminate some of the morally salient aspects of infanticide. . . .

WHY PROTECT INFANTS?

I have already mentioned some of the reasons for protecting human infants more carefully than we protect most comparably-sentient nonhuman beings. Most people care deeply about infants, particularly—but not exclusively—their own. Normal human adults (and children) are probably "programmed" by their biological nature to respond to human infants with care and concern. For the mother, in particular, that response is apt to begin well before the infant is born. But even for her it is likely to become more intense after the infant's birth. The infant at birth enters the human social world, where, if it lives, it becomes involved in social relationships with others, of kinds that can only be dimly foreshadowed before birth. It begins to be known and cared for, not just as a potential member of the family or community, but as a socially present and responsive individual. . . . The newborn is not yet self-aware, but it is already (rapidly becoming) a social being.

Thus, although the human newborn may have no intrinsic properties that can ground a moral right to life stronger than that of a fetus just before birth, its emergence into the social world makes it appropriate to treat it as if it had such a stronger right. This, in effect, is what the law has done, through the doctrine that a person begins to exist at birth. . . .

Another reason for condemning infanticide is that, at least in relatively privileged nations like our own, infants whose parents cannot raise them can usually be placed with people who will love them and take good care of them. This means that infanticide is rarely in the infant's own best interests, and would often deprive some potential adoptive individual or family of a great benefit. . . .

But have I not left the door open to the claim that infanticide may still be justified in some places, e.g., where there is severe poverty and a lack of accessible adoption agencies or where women face exceptionally harsh penalties for "illegitimate" births? I have, and deliberately. The moral case against the toleration of infanticide is contingent upon the existence of morally preferable options. Where economic hardship, the lack of contraception and abortion, and other forms of sexual and political oppression have eliminated all such options, there will be instances in which infanticide is the least tragic of a tragic set of choices. In such circumstances, the enforcement of extreme sanctions against infanticide can constitute an additional injustice.

WHY BIRTH MATTERS

I have defended what most regard as needing no defense, i.e., the ascription of an equal right to life to human infants. Under reasonably favorable conditions that policy can protect the rights and interests of all concerned, including infants, biological parents, and potential adoptive parents.

But if protecting infants is such a good idea, then why is it not a good idea to extend the same strong protections to sentient fetuses? The question is not whether sentient fetuses ought to be protected: of course they should. Most women readily accept the responsibility of doing whatever they can to ensure that their (voluntarily continued) pregnancies are successful, and that no avoidable harm

comes to the fetus. Negligent or malevolent actions by third parties which result in death or injury to pregnant women or their potential children should be subject to moral censure and legal prosecution. A just and caring society would do much more than ours does to protect the health of all its members, including pregnant women. The question is whether the law should accord to late-term fetuses *exactly the same* protections as are accorded to infants and older human beings.

The case for doing so might seem quite strong. . . .

But there is one crucial consideration which this argument leaves out. It is impossible to treat fetuses *in utero* as if they were persons without treating women as if they were something less than persons. The extension of equal rights to sentient fetuses would inevitably license severe violations of women's basic rights to personal autonomy and physical security. In the first place, it would rule out most second-trimester abortions performed to protect the women's life or health. Such abortions might sometimes be construed as a form of self-defense. But the right to self-defense is not usually taken to mean that one may kill innocent persons just because their continued existence poses some threat to one's own life or health. If abortion must be justified as self-defense, then it will rarely be performed until the woman is already in some extreme danger, and perhaps not even then. Such a policy would cost some women their lives, while others would be subjected to needless suffering and permanent physical harm.

Other alarming consequences of the drive to extend more equal rights to fetuses are already apparent in the United States. In the past decade it has become increasingly common for hospitals or physicians to obtain court orders requiring women in labor to undergo Caesarean sections, against their will, for what is thought to be the good of the fetus. . . . Forced Caesareans threaten to reduce women to the status of inanimate objects—containers which may be opened at the will of others in order to get at their contents. . . .

Another danger in extending equal legal protections to sentient fetuses is that women will increasingly be blamed, and sometimes legally prosecuted, when they miscarry or give birth to premature, sick, or abnormal infants. It is reasonable to hold the caretakers of infants legally responsible if their charges are harmed because of their avoidable negligence. But when a woman miscarries or gives birth to an abnormal infant, the cause of harm might be traced to any of an enormous number of actions or circumstances which would not normally constitute any legal offense. She might have gotten too much exercise or too little, eaten the wrong foods or the wrong quantity of the right ones, or taken or failed to take certain drugs. She might have smoked, consumed alcohol, or gotten too little sleep. She might have "permitted" her health to be damaged by hard work, by unsafe employment conditions, by the lack of affordable medical care, by living near a source of industrial pollution, by a physically or mentally abusive partner, or in any number of other ways.

Are such supposed failures on the part of pregnant women potentially to be construed as child abuse or negligent homicide? If sentient fetuses are entitled to the same legal protections as infants, then it would seem so. . . .

Such an approach to the protection of fetuses authorizes the legal regulation of virtually every aspect of women's public and private lives, and thus is incompatible with even the most minimal right to autonomy. Moreover, such laws are apt to prove counterproductive, since the fear of prosecution may deter poor or otherwise vulnerable women from seeking medical care during pregnancy. I am not suggesting that women whose apparent negligence causes prenatal harm to their infants should always be immune from criticism. However, if we want to improve the health of infants we would do better to provide the services women need to protect their health, rather than seeking to use the law to punish those whose prenatal care has been less than ideal. . . .

Such arguments will not persuade those who deeply believe that fetuses are already persons, with equal moral rights. How, they will ask, is denying legal equality to sentient fetuses different from denying it to any other powerless group of human beings? If some human beings are more equal than

others, then how can any of us feel safe? The answer is twofold.

First, pregnancy is a relationship different from any other, including that between parents and already-born children. It is not just one of innumerable situations in which the rights of one individual may come into conflict with those of another; it is probably the *only* case in which the legal personhood of one human being is necessarily incompatible with that of another. Only in pregnancy is the organic functioning of one human individual biologically inseparable from that of another. This organic unity makes it impossible for others to provide the fetus with medical care or any other presumed benefit, except by doing something to or for the woman. To try to "protect" the fetus other than through her cooperation and consent is effectively to nullify her right to autonomy, and potentially to expose her to violent physical assaults such as would not be legally condoned in any other type of case. The uniqueness of pregnancy helps to explain why the toleration of abortion does not lead to the disenfranchisement of other groups of human beings, as opponents of abortion often claim. . . .

But, granting the uniqueness of pregnancy, why is it *women's* rights that should be privileged? If women and fetuses cannot both be legal persons then why not favor the fetus, e.g., on the grounds that they are more helpless, or more innocent, or have a longer life expectancy? It is difficult to justify this apparent bias towards women without appealing to the empirical fact that women are already persons in the usual, nonlegal sense—already thinking, self-aware, fully social beings—and fetuses are not. Regardless of whether we stress the intrinsic properties of persons, or the social and relational dimensions of personhood, this distinction remains. Even sentient fetuses do not yet have either the cognitive capacities or the richly interactive social involvements typical of persons.

This "not yet" is morally decisive. It is wrong to treat persons as if they do not have equal basic rights. Other things being equal, it is worse to deprive persons of their most basic moral and legal rights than to refrain from extending such rights to beings that are not persons. This is one important element of truth in the self-awareness criterion. If fetuses were already thinking, self-aware, socially responsive members of communities, then nothing could justify refusing them the equal protection of the law. In that case, we would sometimes be forced to balance the rights of the fetus against those of the woman, and sometimes the scales might be almost equally weighted. However, if women are persons and fetuses are not, then the balance must swing toward women's rights.

CONCLUSION

Birth is morally significant because it marks the end of one relationship and the beginning of others. It marks the end of pregnancy, a relationship so intimate that it is impossible to extend the equal protection of the law to fetuses without severely infringing women's most basic rights. Birth also marks the beginning of the infant's existence as a socially responsive member of a human community. Although the infant is not instantly transformed into a person at the moment of birth, it does become a biologically separate human being. As such, it can be known and cared for as a particular individual. It can also be vigorously protected without negating the basic rights of women. There are circumstances in which infanticide may be the best of a bad set of options. But our own society has both the ability

and the desire to protect infants, and there is no reason why we should not do so.

We should not, however, seek to extend the same degree of protection to fetuses. Both late-term fetuses and newborn infants are probably capable of sentience. Both are precious to those who want children; and both need to be protected from a variety of possible harms. All of these factors contribute to the moral standing of the late-term fetus, which is substantial. However, to extend equal legal rights to fetuses is necessarily to deprive pregnant women of the rights to personal autonomy, physical integrity, and sometimes life itself. *There is room for only one person with full and equal rights inside a single human skin.* That is why it is birth, rather than sentience, viability, or some other prenatal milestone that must mark the beginning of legal parenthood.

REFERENCES

Callahan, Sidney. 1984. Value choices in abortion. In *Abortion: Understanding differences*. Sidney Callahan and Daniel Callahan, eds. New York and London: Plenum Press.

Callahan, Sidney. 1986. Abortion and the sexual agenda. *Commonweal*, April 25, 232–238.

Tooley, Michael. 1983. *Abortion and infanticide*. Oxford: Oxford University Press.

Discussion Questions

1. Does Warren confuse cultural norms and legal rights with moral rights? Can she defend her position without reference to cultural norms and legal rights? Use specific examples to support your answers.
2. Discuss Warren's claim that deontology, rights ethics, and care ethics all support abortion and early infanticide. Would a utilitarian also agree with Warren's position on abortion? How would a Buddhist respond to Warren's argument? Support your answers.
3. Do you agree with Warren that self-concept is necessary for personhood? How can we determine if a being has a self-concept and a desire for a future? Support your answers. What are the implications of accepting this criterion for the moral standing of infants and brain-damaged, senile, and comatose humans? Would Warren permit euthanasia for these groups of humans? What are the implications of her criteria for how we should treat adult nonhuman mammals?
4. Massachusetts Institute of Technology psychology professor Steven Pinker claims that the killing of newborn babies is perfectly natural and has been practiced and accepted

in most cultures. "To a biologist," he points out, "birth is as arbitrary a milestone as any other . . . so how do you provide grounds for outlawing neonaticide? The facts don't make it easy."[30] Discuss how Warren might respond to Pinker's claim. What is the moral relevance, if any, of their claim that infanticide is natural and, in some cultures, acceptable?

5. The United Nations Population Fund advocates abortion as a means of population control, especially in areas of the world that are already plagued by overpopulation, such as China and India.[31] Discuss what Warren would most likely think of this policy.

 DON MARQUIS

Why Abortion Is Immoral

Don Marquis is a professor of philosophy at the University of Kansas. Marquis disagrees with philosophers such as Warren who believe that birth is morally significant in terms of the value of a human's life. He argues instead that the moral presumption against killing a fetus is as strong as the moral presumption against killing an adult human or newborn because both involve the murder of humans after birth, and abortion deprives the victims of the value of the activities, experiences, and enjoyments of their future. He concludes that while abortion may sometimes be morally permissible, it is prima facie seriously immoral.

Critical Reading Questions

1. What is the major presumption of Marquis's argument that abortion is immoral?
2. Why, according to Marquis, is it wrong to kill adult humans?
3. What does Marquis mean by the phrase a "future like ours"?
4. What are the implications of Marquis's argument for the killing of nonhuman animals? What are the implications of Marquis's argument for euthanasia?
5. On what grounds does Marquis dismiss arguments against abortion that depend on the category of personhood?
6. Why is a "future like ours" of value to the fetus? Why is it wrong to deprive a fetus of this future?
7. What are the implications of Marquis's argument for the use of contraception?

Don Marquis, "Why Abortion is Immoral," *Journal of Philosophy*, vol. 86, April 1989. Some notes have been omitted.

The view that abortion is, with rare exceptions, seriously immoral has received little support in the recent philosophical literature. No doubt most philosophers affiliated with secular institutions of higher education believe that the anti-abortion position is either a symptom of irrational religious dogma or a conclusion generated by seriously confused philosophical argument. The purpose of this essay is to undermine this general belief. This essay sets out an argument that purports to show, as well as any argument in ethics can show, that abortion is, except possibly in rare cases, seriously immoral, that it is in the same moral category as killing an innocent adult human being.

The argument is based on a major assumption. Many of the most insightful and careful writers on the ethics of abortion—such as Joel Feinberg, Michael Tooley, Mary Anne Warren, H. Tristram Engelhardt, Jr., L. W. Sumner, John T. Noonan, Jr., and Philip Devine*—believe that whether or not abortion is morally permissible stands or falls on whether or not a fetus is the sort of being whose life it is seriously wrong to end. The argument of this essay will assume, but not argue, that they are correct.

Also, this essay will neglect issues of great importance to a complete ethics of abortion. Some anti-abortionists will allow that certain abortions, such as abortion before implantation or abortion when the life of a woman is threatened by a pregnancy or abortion after rape, may be morally permissible. This essay will not explore the casuistry of these hard cases. The purpose of this essay is to develop a general argument for the claim that the over-whelming majority of deliberate abortions are seriously immoral. . . .

A necessary condition of resolving the abortion controversy is a more theoretical account of the wrongness of killing. After all, if we merely believe, but do not understand, why killing adult human beings such as ourselves is wrong, how could we conceivably show that abortion is either immoral or permissible?

In order to develop such an account, we can start from the following unproblematic assumption concerning our own case: it is wrong to kill *us*. Why is it wrong? Some answers can be easily eliminated. It might be said that what makes killing us wrong is that a killing brutalizes the one who kills. But the brutalization consists of being inured to the performance of an act that is hideously immoral; hence, the brutalization does not explain the immorality. It might be said that what makes killing us wrong is the great loss others would experience due to our absence. Although such hubris is understandable, such an explanation does not account for the wrongness of killing hermits, or those whose lives are relatively independent and whose friends find it easy to make new friends.

A more obvious answer is better. What primarily makes killing wrong is neither its effect on the murderer nor its effect on the victim's friends and relatives, but its effect on the victim. The loss of one's life is one of the greatest losses one can suffer. The loss of one's life deprives one of all the experiences, activities, projects, and enjoyments that would otherwise have constituted one's future. Therefore, killing someone is wrong, primarily because the killing inflicts (one of) the greatest possible losses on the victim. To describe this as the loss of life can be misleading, however. The change in my biological state does not by itself make killing me wrong. The effect of the loss of my biological life is the loss to me of all those activities, projects, experiences, and enjoyments which would otherwise have constituted my future personal life. These activities, projects, experiences, and enjoyments are either valuable for their own sakes or are means to something else that is valuable for its own sake. Some parts of my future are not valued by me now, but will come to be

* Feinberg, "Abortion," in *Matters of Life and Death: New Introductory Essays in Moral Philosophy*, Tom Regan, ed. (New York: Random House, 1986), pp. 256–293; Tooley, "Abortion and Infanticide," *Philosophy and Public Affairs*, II, 1 (1972): 37–65, Tooley, *Abortion and Infanticide* (New York: Oxford, 1984); Warren, "On the Moral and Legal Status of Abortion," *The Monist*, I.VII, 1 (1973): 43–61; Engelhardt, "The Ontology of Abortion," *Ethics*, I.XXXIV, 3 (1974): 217–234; Sumner, *Abortion and Moral Theory* (Princeton: University Press, 1981); Noonan, "An Almost Absolute Value in History," in *The Morality of Abortion: Legal and Historical Perspectives*, Noonan, ed. (Cambridge: Harvard, 1970); and Devine, *The Ethics of Homicide* (Ithaca: Cornell, 1978).

valued by me as I grow older and as my values and capacities change. When I am killed, I am deprived both of what I now value which would have been part of my future personal life, but also what I would come to value. Therefore, when I die, I am deprived of all of the value of my future. Inflicting this loss on me is ultimately what makes killing me wrong. This being the case, it would seem that what makes killing *any* adult human being prima facie seriously wrong is the loss of his or her future. . . .

The view that what makes killing wrong is the loss to the victim of the value of the victim's future gains additional support when some of its implications are examined. In the first place, it is incompatible with the view that it is wrong to kill only beings who are biologically human. It is possible that there exists a different species from another planet whose members have a future like ours. Since having a future like that is what makes killing someone wrong, this theory entails that it would be wrong to kill members of such a species. Hence, this theory is opposed to the claim that only life that is biologically human has great moral worth, a claim which many anti-abortionists have seemed to adopt. This opposition, which this theory has in common with personhood theories, seems to be a merit of the theory.

In the second place, the claim that the loss of one's future is the wrong-making feature of one's being killed entails the possibility that the futures of some actual nonhuman mammals on our own planet are sufficiently like ours that it is seriously wrong to kill them also. Whether some animals do have the same right to life as human beings depends on adding to the account of the wrongness of killing some additional account of just what it is about my future or the futures of other adult human beings which makes it wrong to kill us. No such additional account will be offered in this essay. Undoubtedly, the provision of such an account would be a very difficult matter. Undoubtedly, any such account would be quite controversial. Hence, it surely should not reflect badly on this sketch of an elementary theory of the wrongness of killing that it is indeterminate with respect to some very difficult issues regarding animal rights.

In the third place, the claim that the loss of one's future is the wrong-making feature of one's being killed does not entail, as sanctity of human life theories do, that active euthanasia is wrong. Persons who are severely and incurably ill, who face a future of pain and despair, and who wish to die will not have suffered a loss if they are killed. It is, strictly speaking, the value of a human's future which makes killing wrong in this theory. This being so, killing does not necessarily wrong some persons who are sick and dying. Of course, there may be other reasons for a prohibition of active euthanasia, but that is another matter. Sanctity-of-human-life theories seem to hold that active euthanasia is seriously wrong even in an individual case where there seems to be good reason for it independently of public policy considerations. This consequence is most implausible, and it is a plus for the claim that the loss of a future of value is what makes killing wrong that it does not share this consequence.

In the fourth place, the account of the wrongness of killing defended in this essay does straightforwardly entail that it is prima facie seriously wrong to kill children and infants, for we do presume that they have futures of value. Since we do believe that it is wrong to kill defenseless little babies, it is important that a theory of the wrongness of killing easily account for this. Personhood theories of the wrongness of killing, on the other hand, cannot straightforwardly account for the wrongness of killing infants and young children.* Hence, such theories must add special ad hoc accounts of the wrongness of killing the young. The plausibility of such ad hoc theories seems to be a function of how desperately one wants such theories to work. The claim that the primary wrong-making feature of a killing is the loss to the victim of the value of its future accounts for the wrongness of killing young children and infants directly; it makes the wrongness of such acts as obvious as we actually think it is. . . .

The claim that the primary wrong-making feature of a killing is the loss to the victim of the value of its future has obvious consequences for the eth-

---

* Feinberg, Tooley, Warren, and Engelhardt have all dealt with this problem.

ics of abortion. The future of a standard fetus includes a set of experiences, projects, activities, and such which are identical with the futures of adult human beings and are identical with the futures of young children. Since the reason that is sufficient to explain why it is wrong to kill human beings after the time of birth is a reason that also applies to fetuses, it follows that abortion is prima facie seriously morally wrong.

This argument does not rely on the invalid inference that, since it is wrong to kill persons, it is wrong to kill potential persons also. The category that is morally central to this analysis is the category of having a valuable future like ours; it is not the category of personhood. The argument to the conclusion that abortion is prima facie seriously morally wrong proceeded independently of the notion of person or potential person or any equivalent. . . .

Of course, this value of a future-like-ours argument, if sound, shows only that abortion is prima facie wrong, not that it is wrong in any and all circumstances. Since the loss of the future to a standard fetus, if killed, is, however, at least as great a loss as the loss of the future to a standard adult human being who is killed, abortion, like ordinary killing, could be justified only by the most compelling reasons. The loss of one's life is almost the greatest misfortune that can happen to one. Presumably abortion could be justified in some circumstances, only if the loss consequent on failing to abort would be at least as great. Accordingly, morally permissible abortions will be rare indeed unless, perhaps, they occur so early in pregnancy that a fetus is not yet definitely an individual. Hence, this argument should be taken as showing that abortion is presumptively very seriously wrong, where the presumption is very strong—as strong as the presumption that killing another adult human being is wrong.

How complete an account of the wrongness of killing does the value of a future-like-ours account have to be in order that the wrongness of abortion is a consequence? This account does not have to be an account of the necessary conditions for the wrongness of killing. Some persons in nursing homes may lack valuable human futures, yet it may be wrong to kill them for other reasons. Furthermore, this account does not obviously have to be the sole reason killing is wrong where the victim did have a valuable future. This analysis claims only that, for any killing where the victim did have a valuable future like ours, having that future by itself is sufficient to create the strong presumption that the killing is seriously wrong. . . .

In this essay, it has been argued that the correct ethic of the wrongness of killing can be extended to fetal life and used to show that there is a strong presumption that any abortion is morally impermissible. If the ethic of killing adopted here entails, however, that contraception is also seriously immoral, then there would appear to be a difficulty with the analysis of this essay.

But this analysis does not entail that contraception is wrong. Of course, contraception prevents the actualization of a possible future of value. Hence, it follows from the claim that futures of value should be maximized that contraception is prima facie immoral. This obligation to maximize does not exist, however; furthermore, nothing in the ethics of killing in this paper entails that it does. The ethics of killing in this essay would entail that contraception is wrong only if something were denied a human future of value by contraception. Nothing at all is denied such a future by contraception, however.

Candidates for a subject of harm by contraception fall into four categories: (1) some sperm or other, (2) some ovum or other, (3) a sperm and an ovum separately, and (4) a sperm and an ovum together. Assigning the harm to some sperm [or ovum] is utterly arbitrary, . . . One might attempt to avoid these problems by insisting that contraception deprives both the sperm and the ovum separately of a valuable future like ours. On this alternative, too many futures are lost. Contraception was supposed to be wrong, because it deprived us of one future of value, not two. One might attempt to avoid this problem by holding that contraception deprives the combination of sperm and ovum of a valuable future like ours. But here the definite article misleads. At the time of contraception, there are hundreds of millions of sperm, one (released) ovum and millions of possible combinations of all of these. There is no actual combination at all. Is the subject of the loss to be a merely possible combination? Which one? This alternative does not yield an actual subject of harm either. Accordingly, the immorality of contraception is not entailed by the loss of a future-like-ours argument simply because there is no nonarbitrarily identifiable subject of the loss in the case of contraception.

The purpose of this essay has been to set out an argument for the serious presumptive wrongness of abortion subject to the assumption that the moral permissibility of abortion stands or falls on the moral status of the fetus. Since a fetus possesses a property, the possession of which in adult human beings is sufficient to make killing an adult human being wrong, abortion is wrong. This way of dealing with the problem of abortion seems superior to other approaches to the ethics of abortion, because it rests on an ethics of killing which is close to self-evident, because the crucial morally relevant property clearly applies to fetuses, and because the argument avoids the usual equivocations on "human life," "human being," or "person." The argument rests neither on religious claims nor on Papal dogma. It is not subject to the objection of "speciesism." Its soundness is compatible with the moral permissibility of euthanasia and contraception. It deals with our intuitions concerning young children.

Finally, this analysis can be viewed as resolving a standard problem—indeed, *the* standard problem —concerning the ethics of abortion. Clearly, it is wrong to kill adult human beings. Clearly, it is not wrong to end the life of some arbitrarily chosen single human cell. Fetuses seem to be like arbitrarily chosen human cells in some respects and like adult humans in other respects. The problem of the ethics of abortion is the problem of determining the fetal property that settles this moral controversy. The thesis of this essay is that the problem of the ethics of abortion, so understood, is solvable.

Discussion Questions

1. Without bringing in the concept of "personhood," discuss why it is wrong to kill newborns and adult humans. Apply your criteria to the killing of fetuses.
2. Break down Marquis's argument into its premises and conclusion. Analyze the argument. Are the premises acceptable? Are the premises complete? Does the conclusion follow from the premises? If not, come up with a counterargument that addresses Marquis's concerns.
3. Apply Marquis's argument to the use of RU 486. Discuss whether his argument against abortion would or would not preclude the use of the early abortion pill.
4. In his essay, Marquis does not address the future of the pregnant woman who wants an abortion. Even if we accept Marquis's claim that abortion is a prima facie wrong because it destroys the future of the fetus, are there circumstances where continuing the pregnancy might damage the value of the woman's future to such an extent that it overrides the value of her fetus's future? How about situations in which the fetus has a severe genetic anomaly associated with a life of suffering and/or death shortly after birth? Role-play a situation where you are discussing these possible exceptions with Marquis.
5. Discuss how both Thomson and Warren might respond to Marquis's argument.

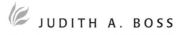

JUDITH A. BOSS

Pro-Child/Pro-Choice: An Exercise in Doublethink?

Judith A. Boss is a philosopher, author, and assistant director of curriculum affairs at the Brown University School of Medicine. Most of the abortion debate focuses on the conflict between the purported rights of a fetus and the rights of a woman. Boss examines the morality of abortion from the perspective of its consequences on another group of people—children after birth. In a review of studies on the well-being of children since *Roe v. Wade,* she finds that most of the utilitarian claims regarding the benefits of legalized abortion to children have not been substantiated. Boss concludes that the pro-choice position cannot be justified on the grounds that it benefits children.

Critical Reading Questions

1. What is "doublethink"? Why is doublethink logically incorrect? How, according to Boss, has doublethink been used in the abortion debate?
2. What, according to Boss, is the position of many pro-choice advocates regarding the benefits of legalized abortion to children? Why does Boss reject this reasoning?
3. What do studies show regarding the well-being of children since 1973? Why, according to these studies, might abortion be a contributing factor in the rise of child abuse?
4. Why does Boss think that viewing abortion as a woman's private choice does not empower women? What evidence does Boss use to debunk the notion that abortion is freely chosen?
5. What are the effects, according to studies, of abortion on some women?
6. What is a "disenfranchised death"?
7. What is the "aborted sibling factor"?
8. Why does Boss argue that the slogan "Every child a wanted child" devalues children?

George Orwell in his novel *1984* envisioned a society controlled not only by watchful posters of Big Brother, but by doublethink—a type of mental gymnastics which involves the capacity for "holding two contradictory beliefs in one's mind simultaneously and accepting both of them."[1] The purpose of doublethink is the destruction of human thought and dignity and, hence, the capacity of dissenting with those in power.

Doublethink is maintained by a refusal to examine the assumptions and facts supporting one's beliefs. This insidious, and for the most part unconscious, process is closely related to "newspeak" in which vocabulary is pared down to a minimum so that whole ideologies are expressed in a single slogan such as, to use some of Orwell's examples, "War is peace" and "Ignorance is strength." In the ongoing battle of "newspeak" type slogans between

"Pro-Child/Pro-Choice: An Exercise in Doublethink?" *Public Affairs Quarterly,* no. 2 (April 1993): 85–91. Some notes have been omitted.

"pro-life" advocates and "pro-choice" advocates, who support a policy of abortion-on-demand, one frequently sees bumper-stickers and buttons sporting the slogan "PRO-CHILD/PRO-CHOICE." Is this an example of doublethink or can one truly be both pro-child and pro-choice simultaneously?

The assumption underlying this slogan is that the exclusion of humans prior to birth from the protection of the moral and legal community, thereby leaving the choice of carrying a pregnancy to term entirely up to the woman, benefits children. The children who are supposedly being benefited might be divided into two categories: 1) the fetus whose abortion will spare him or her a life of misery, and 2) born children who can enjoy a higher quality of life and parental love unhindered by the presence of burdensome siblings who were unwanted and "unchosen" by Mom.

While not all unwanted pregnancies are aborted, nor does the pro-choice position advocate that they should be, the first claim, that abortion-on-demand benefits unwanted fetal-children by causing their death, certainly seems like a good candidate for doublethink. Morally it constitutes paternalism at its worse. In no other case do we kill potential victims of a crime for their own sake. To do so contradicts all that for which our criminal justice system stands. However, defenders of the "pro-child/pro-choice" stance could counter that since the fetus is not really a person, let alone a child, they cannot be benefited or harmed. But, even if one denies that the fetus is a person, this still leaves us with the second category of children who might be benefited by abortion-on-demand—children after birth.

The assumption that the availability of abortion-on-demand benefits these children has rarely been questioned, let alone been subjected to scientific scrutiny, despite the fact that developments since the legalization of abortion in 1973 have failed to bear out the optimistic prognosis of the pro-choice movement. While the general well-being of the nation as a whole remained relatively stable in the 1970s, declining significantly in the first part of the 1980s under the umbrella of Reaganomics, the "social health" of children and youth began a steady course of decline beginning

in 1974.[2] At the same time the abortion rate began rising rapidly, increasing in every state after 1973 and in many cases tripling.[3] . . .

The concurrent decline in children's well-being has touched almost all facets of children's lives including dramatic rises in teen suicide, children living under the poverty level, and drug abuse. However, the problem area that has worsened most significantly in the past seventeen years, and which continues to get worse each year, is child abuse.

The rate of child abuse has increased dramatically, without exception, every year since 1973, when abortion was first legalized. Prior to 1973 the reported rate of child abuse was relatively stable. Between 1977 and 1980 alone there was a 566% increase in reported incidents of child abuse.[4] This increase cannot be attributed solely to better reporting of child abuse cases since most of the improvement in reporting techniques took place in the early 1980s, in response to the alarming increase in child abuse, rather than the mid-1970s.[5] This phenomenon is not limited to the United States but is found in several other countries, such as Canada, Britain and Japan, which have liberalized their abortion laws to permit, for all practical purposes, abortion-on-demand.[6] . . .

While suggestive, the fact that a rapid increase in child abuse followed closely on the footsteps of legalized abortion does not prove, without controlled studies, a cause-effect relationship between the two. Johns Hopkins Hospital, using the mothers of 532 physically abused children aged four and under who were reported to the Baltimore (Maryland) Department of Social Services, conducted a study to identify perinatal factors that contribute to the risk that a woman will abuse her child. They found that "abusive families appeared at significantly higher risk for increased number of stillbirths or abortions before the current birth." Unfortunately the birth certificates did not distinguish between stillbirths and abortions so the two variables could not be studied separately. However, the study conjectures that if the previous abortions were primarily elective, it is possible mothers may have used that option because of negative feelings about that pregnancy, or because they felt unprepared to care for a child either economically, physically or socially. Abuse of the child of a subsequent pregnancy could reflect similar feelings or concerns in the absence of a similar option.

Unfortunately there is a "similar option" to abortion for dealing with a child who evokes similar negative feelings after birth. The easy availability of abortion for dealing with negative feelings prior to birth, consequently, needs to be assessed in terms of the harm that the practice may be causing when parents attempt the same problem-solving strategy with their troublesome born children. In a society where the small size and dependency of the unborn human are often used, especially by laypeople, as reasons to deny them equal moral worth, it is not difficult to notice that infants and young children after birth are also much smaller and more dependent than their adult caretakers. Indeed, one of the alarming findings regarding current child abuse is the young age of the victims. In the Johns Hopkins study, for example, 48% of the abused children were under the age of two and 25% under the age of one. Abuse of a small child can lead to permanent disability or death. In 1986 there was a 23% increase over the previous year in the number of deaths caused by child abuse.[7] Death at the hands of one's caretakers is now one of the leading causes of death of children between eighteen months and two years.

[Psychiatrist Philip] Ney suggests that by legitimating the death of the child in utero we have weakened the normal instinctual restraint and social taboo against the use of violence against those dependent on our care.[8] Other researchers have found that abortion hinders the normal maternal-fetal bonding in later pregnancies and births.[9] This may also be a contributing factor to the rise in child abuse.

Many people assume that the mere presence of "choice" in decisions involving abortion eliminates, or at least significantly reduces, the anguish and grief suffered by the family. However, the anticipation of death or loss does not necessarily diminish the actual grief after the loss occurs.[10] Also, a policy of abortion-on-demand does not necessarily entail that women presently getting abortions perceive their decisions to have an abortion as freely chosen. . . . In a study of women's perception of their abortion experience, Mary Zimmerman found that the overwhelming number of women interviewed portrayed themselves as victims, as "'having no choice' in the matter of abortion, of being 'forced' to have the abortion."[11] . . .

Social worker Mary Parthun, in her study of the psychological effects of induced abortion, concluded that "abortion ruptures the mother-child dyad but also the family constellation, affecting family relationships, present and future."[12] In another study of the psychosocial aspects of the stress following abortion, 73% of women who had abortions reported having feelings of "grief, jealousy or extreme guilt in the presence of small children and infants."[13] Feelings of guilt are also frequently accompanied by low self-esteem.

Feelings of guilt and low self-esteem are two of the major contributing factors in child abuse as well as other forms of domestic violence.[14] A Canadian study on the psychological sequelae of abortion found that women who had induced abortions were 40.8% more likely to suffer from mental disorders as well as 25% more likely to be seen for treatment resulting from accidents and violence.[15] Abortion is also frequently associated with a deterioration in the relationship with the partner.[16] In these cases the women's resentment and anger at having been "forced" to have an abortion, and her fear of sex that sometimes follows an abortion experience,[17] may bring retaliation from her partner in the form of spousal abuse. The woman may, in turn, displace the anger and resentment she feels onto her children by abusing them.[18]

These negative feelings may be exacerbated by or contribute to what one team of researchers terms the "aborted sibling factor." According to their study ". . . there is increasing evidence that even very young children may be aware of maternal abortions despite family attempts at secrecy."[19] Another study on the effects of selective abortion on a family found that, even when the child was unaware of their mother's abortion, almost all parents noted some change in their children's behavior in the weeks following the abortion. These changes included regressed behavior, anxiety attacks, sudden outbursts of fear or hatred of the mother, sadness, disappointment and feelings of guilt.[20] It has been suggested that this behavior may in part be a re-action on the part of the child to the parent's guilt and resulting overcompensation, a reaction which may in turn increase the parent's guilt and resent-ment and, consequently, provoke them into abus-ing the child.

One of the corollaries of the "pro-child/pro-choice" ideology is the slogan: "Every child a wanted child." This reflects a belief that if women only have to bear children who are wanted, these children will be treated with respect. However, a 1976 study of abused children and their families found that it is not the so-called "unwanted" chil-dren who are at greatest risk of abuse, but those whose parents expressed a significantly higher than average desire for the pregnancy.[21] One hypothesis put forth to explain this phenomenon is that par-ents who have high expectations of their "wanted" children are more likely to get frustrated when their children do not live up to these expectations.

Few people would doubt that the sentiment that every child be both wanted and loved for whom she or he is is morally commendable. How-ever, this does not imply that it is morally desirable or even morally acceptable to abort unwanted fe-tuses. Many "unwanted" pregnancies are carried to term and the child either given up for adoption or raised by the birth parent(s) who have come to want and cherish the child over the course of the pregnancy. The sentiment that every child be a wanted child is interpreted, in these cases, as a chal-lenge to parents and society to provide homes where children will be loved and nurtured, just as the ideal that every child be a healthy child chal-lenges society to provide adequate medical care to all children, not just those of privileged parents.

However, unlike the slogan "Every child a healthy child," the slogan "Every child a wanted child" in the context of abortion-on-demand judges the worth of a child solely in terms of their value to another person. Thus, the expression—"every child a wanted child"—reduces children to objects which have only instrumental worth. They have a right to exist only if someone in power over them "wants" or is pleased by them.

In her book *When the Bough Breaks: The Cost of Neglecting Our Children*, Sylvia Ann Hewlett points

out that over the past twenty-five years "American society has been tilting in an ominous new direc-tion—toward the devaluation of children." It is in-teresting to also note that basic in the child abuser's attitude is the conviction, mostly unconscious, that "children exist to satisfy parental needs—that chil-dren are essentially property of parents who have the right to deal with their offspring as they see fit, without interference."[22] Ney likewise warns that with parental love being no longer "unqualified" but a parental choice, "children are becoming in-creasingly aware . . . that they exist only because their mothers chose them and chose them only be-cause they were desirable. Since their fate once hung on their desirability they tend to feel secure only when they are pleasing to their parents."[23]

Too often philosophical discussions of moral is-sues take place in a vacuum devoid of reference to the "real" or empirical world. The "Pro-Child/Pro-Choice" slogan fails to live up to its most basic premise: that abortion on demand benefits chil-dren. To believe so in the face of contradictory evi-dence is to be involved in doublethink.

Few people would question the assertion that women in our male-dominated society are in need of empowerment. But the pro-choice position on abortion seeks to empower women at the expense of their children. Perhaps the price is unavoidable. However, if we want to maintain our pro-choice stance let us not, at least, delude ourselves into thinking we are doing it to benefit children, but instead be willing to examine our real motives and to back up our position with viable and consistent arguments.

NOTES

1. George Orwell, *1984* (New York: New American Library, 1949), p. 264.

2. Marc Miringoff, *The Index of Social Health, 1989. Measuring the Social Well-Being of Children* (New York: Fordham Institute for Innovation in So-cial Policy, Fordham University, 1989), p. 8.

3. Martha Goldsmith, "Researchers Amass Abor-tion Data," *JAMA* vol. 26 (September 15, 1989), pp. 1431–1432.

4. Barbara Kantrowitz, "How to Protect Abused Children," *Newsweek* (November 23, 1987), pp. 70–71.

5. Marc Miringoff, *The Index of Social Health, 1989. Measuring the Social Well-Being of Children,* p. 7.

6. David Reardon, *Aborted Women: Silent No More* (Chicago: Loyola University Press, 1987), p. 225.

7. Barbara Kantrowitz, "How to Protect Abused Children," p. 71.

8. Philip Ney, "Infant Abortion and Child Abuse: Cause and Effect," in *The Psychological Aspects of Abortion,* David Mall and Walter Watts, eds. (Washington, DC, University Publications of America, 1979), p. 26.

9. M. H. Klaus and J. H. Kennell, *Maternal Bonding* (St. Louis: C. V. Mosby Co., 1976).

10. Lynn de Spelder and Albert Strickland, *The Last Dance* (Palo Alto, CA: Mayfield Publishing Co., 1987), p. 222.

11. Mary Zimmerman, *Passage Through Abortion: The Personal and Social Reality of Women's Experiences* (New York: Praeger Publishers, 1977), p. 201.

12. Mary Parthun, "The Psychological Effects of Induced Abortion," in *Abortion's Aftermath,* Mary Parthun, Heather Morris and Lorraine Williams. (Toronto, Ontario, Canada: Human Life Research Institute, 1985), p. 16.

13. Anne Speckhard, *The Psychosocial Aspects of Stress Following Abortion* (Kansas City, MO: Sheed & Ward, 1987), p. 48.

14. Lewis Okun, *Woman Abuse* (Albany, NY: State University of New York Press, 1986), 51; and

R. Emerson Dobash and Russell P. Dobash, *Violence Against Wives* (New York: Free Press, 1979).

15. Mary Parthun, "The Psychological Effects of Induced Abortion," p. 11.

16. Mary Parthun, "The Psychological Effects of Induced Abortion," p. 11; and Mary Zimmerman, *Passage Through Abortion,* p. 188.

17. Anne Speckhard, *The Psychological Aspects of Stress Following Abortion,* pp. 45–47.

18. Gail Goodman and Mindy Rosenberg, "The Child Witness to Family Violence: Clinical and Legal Considerations," in *Domestic Violence on Trial,* Daniel Jay Sonkin, ed. (New York: Springer Publishing Co., 1987), p. 99.

19. Anita Weiner and Eugene Weiner, "The Aborted Sibling Factor," *Clinical Social Work Journal* (1984), p. 209.

20. Regina Furlough and Rita Black, "Pregnancy Termination for Genetic Indications: The Impact on Families," *Social Work in Health Care,* vol. 10 (1984), p. 25; and Mary Parthun, "The Psychological Effects of Induced Abortion," p. 17.

21. E. F. Lenoski, "Translating Injury Data in Preventive Health Care Services: Physical Child Abuse," unpubl. ms. (University of Southern California, Department of Pediatrics, 1976).

22. James Burtchaell, *Rachel Weeping* (Kansas City: Andrews and McMeel, Inc., 1982), p. 79.

23. Philip Ney, "A Consideration of Abortion Survivors," *Child Psychiatry and Human Development,* vol. 13 (1983), pp. 171–72.

Discussion Questions

1. Does Boss's utilitarian argument militate against abortion under all circumstances? Even if a causal link could be established between child abuse and abortion, does this necessarily imply that abortion is morally impermissible? Explain.

2. Discuss how Warren might respond to Boss's claim that abortion on demand is wrong because it is harmful to the parent/children relationship. Compare and contrast their arguments regarding the effect of the pro-choice ideology on empowering women.

3. Boss notes that feelings of guilt and low self-esteem are two of the major contributing factors in child abuse. Some pro-choice advocates argue, however, that the guilt felt by women following an abortion is not true moral guilt but socially imposed guilt

caused by pro-life rhetoric. Can people who have done nothing wrong be *made* to feel guilty? If even *some* of this guilt is socially imposed, should women seeking abortions be protected from antiabortion demonstrators? Support your answers.

4. Do you agree with Boss that abortion contributes to the belief that children exist to satisfy parental needs? Given that most abusive parents believe this, discuss what Boss's position most likely is on selective abortion for genetic defects or sex selection.

5. A 1997 AMA report on abortion states: "The demands for abortions, with the exception of those indicated by serious fetal anomalies or conditions that threaten the life or health of the pregnant women, represent failures in the social environment and education."[32] What does this mean? Discuss whether Boss would agree with this statement. Discuss how Warren might respond to this statement.

6. Discuss the arguments on the morality of abortion presented by Boss, Marquis, Warren, Thomson, and Noonan in light of the Buddhist concept of "right livelihood." Which position regarding the morality of abortion would a Buddhist find most acceptable? Support your answer.

CASE STUDIES

1. THE UNWANTED DAUGHTERS

Chandra and Ramdas Malik were poor farmers who lived in a small village outside of Bombay. They had one son and one daughter. Although they would have welcomed the birth of another son, they did not want another daughter, because giving the required dowry to her future husband's family would have been financially crippling for the Maliks. Sons also provided the best social security for elderly parents, because daughters were absorbed into their husbands' families. The Maliks decided that they would have an abortion if the fetus was a female. In India minivans carrying ultrasound equipment cruise the countryside, providing prenatal diagnosis of the sex of fetuses. Although the price of an ultrasound was high, it was worth it to the Maliks.[33] "Better 800 rupees now for an abortion," Ramdas Malik said before the procedure, "than tens of thousands of rupees later for a dowry." The ultrasound operator informed them that the child was a boy. Malik let out a sigh of relief.

Chandra Malik's second cousin, Indira, had emigrated to Canada in 1979. Two years later she married a successful engineer, John Sarava, whose grandparents immigrated to Canada from India in the 1920s. With her son and daughter now in high school, Indira Sarava decided to return to college to complete her degree in business administration. She had just started her first semester when she found out she was pregnant. Because she is forty, Indira has amniocentesis at sixteen weeks to see if the fetus has any genetic disorders. The following week Dr. Lee calls her and says, "Congratulations. You're going to have a healthy baby girl!" Two weeks later Indira calls Dr. Lee back and asks him to perform an abortion. She explains that although she would have continued the pregnancy had the fetus been a boy, she is not interested in having another daughter. Her husband is opposed to the abortion. He points out that having another daughter would not be a burden for the family since they are financially secure, and because he is semiretired, he is also willing to do most of the child care.

Discussion Questions

1. Discuss how a cultural relativist would respond to each of the above scenarios. Are you satisfied with the answers? Explain.
2. Would it have made a difference if either the Chandras or Indira Sarava had requested the abortion because amniocentesis revealed that their children had Down syndrome?
3. Although the Maliks did not have an abortion, they intended to had the fetus been a girl. What is the role of intention in moral responsibility? Discuss what Thomson and Boss would think regarding the morality of the Maliks's actions in seeking prenatal diagnosis for sex selection. If it is morally irresponsible to have prenatal diagnosis for sex selection, does this create a moral obligation on the part of physicians administering prenatal diagnosis to withhold information about the gender of the fetus? Support your answers.
4. Does the father have any rights when it comes to deciding whether a pregnancy should be terminated? Support your answer using the Sarava case study.
5. Sometimes, because of the position of the fetus or material floating in the amniotic fluid, ultrasound misdiagnoses the sex of the fetus. Imagine, much to the Maliks's dismay, that their son turns out to be a girl. They wrap the newborn in a rag and abandon her in a ditch beside a road. Is their action morally acceptable? Would your answer be different if the Canadian couple had done the same? Support your answers.
6. Although most Americans disapprove of abortion for sex selection, they regard abortion for genetic disorders, such as Down syndrome, as morally permissible. Is this distinction morally justified? Should the principle of equality apply to people born with physical or mental handicaps as well as to females? Support your answers.

---

2. JENNIFER JOHNSON: MATERNAL DRUG USE AND FETAL RIGHTS

When twenty-three-year-old Jennifer Johnson arrived to give birth to her fourth child, hospital drug tests found traces of cocaine in her blood. It was later revealed that her other children had all been cocaine-affected babies. In 1989 Johnson was arrested in a crack house. A Florida judge found her guilty of delivery (through the umbilical cord) of a controlled substance to a child. Johnson was sentenced to fifteen years' probation, drug treatment, random drug testing, and educational and vocational training. She was also ordered to participate in an intensive prenatal care program if she should ever become pregnant again.[34]

A 1988 survey of hospitals in the United States found that every year as many as 375,000 infants are adversely affected by maternal cocaine use during pregnancy. The cost of medical treatment for a baby exposed to drugs can run as high as $150,000.[35] In response, several states have passed civil child abuse and neglect laws, which state that taking illicit drugs or alcohol during pregnancy constitutes child abuse. As a result of these laws, thousands of women have lost custody of their children and some have even been jailed.

In February 2000 the U.S. Supreme Court agreed, in the case of *Whitner v. South Carolina,* to review a South Carolina law that allowed public hospitals to test pregnant women for drug use and to then give the results to the police without the woman's consent. So far over thirty women have been arrested under the South Carolina law. As in the case of Jennifer Johnson, addicted women can avoid arrest by agreeing to undergo drug treatment.[36]

Discussion Questions

1. Discuss whether hospitals that routinely perform drug tests on any pregnant woman "suspected of being a drug user" are violating the privacy rights of the woman. Discuss how both Ayn Rand and Mary Anne Warren might respond to this question. How might a utilitarian respond?

2. In South Carolina a viable fetus is considered a person under law. Opponents of these laws argue that they are based on the mistaken "image of the fetus as separate from the mother-to-be" and a patriarchal worldview in which women are reduced to a "passive receptacle in reproduction."[37] Do you agree? Discuss whether holding women liable for prenatal conduct that may harm the fetus depends on accepting the premise that the fetus is a separate person with rights that can come into conflict with the rights of the mother.

3. Do pregnant women who plan to carry their fetus to term have a moral obligation to refrain from using substances that are harmful to the fetus? If so, does such an obligation depend on the personhood or moral status of the fetus? If the young fetus is not a person, to whom does the pregnant woman have the obligation? Can we have a duty to refrain from behavior that might harm persons who do not yet exist? If so, what is the moral basis of this duty?

4. Some people who oppose holding mothers legally responsible for prenatal behavior argue that punishing women who use drugs during pregnancy will not change their behavior or help babies. They point out that many women who use drugs during pregnancy come from families characterized by drug and alcohol abuse, as well as sexual abuse and domestic violence. Instead of punishment, these women need to be empowered through counseling, low-cost housing, and residential treatment facilities. Others argue that women should be held responsible and that the view that women cannot be expected to handle adversity is based on a degraded view of women. Which position do you find most compelling? What position would Marquis most likely take in this debate? Support your answers.

5. Should a pregnant woman's behavior that is potentially harmful to the fetus be regulated by law? Discuss how Warren and Boss would each stand on the morality of passing laws to protect the fetus from the mother's use of toxic substances during pregnancy. What would a utilitarian philosopher say?

6. Come up with a public policy for resolving the conflict between maternal and fetal rights. Consider the views of Confucius, Aristotle, rights ethicists, utilitarians, and care ethicists in coming to your solution.

---

3. THE LIMITS OF PROTEST: BOMBING OF ABORTION CLINICS

Between 1977 and 2000, antiabortion activists have committed more than two thousand four hundred acts in at least twenty-eight states and the District of Columbia including bombings, assaults, death threats, and even murders.[38] On January 16, 1997, a bomb blast ripped through a family-planning clinic in Atlanta, Georgia, sending terrified people scattering in all directions. An hour later a second bomb went off in another part of the building. Six people were injured by the blasts; windows in nearby buildings were blown out, and the clinic was left in ruins. President Clinton condemned the bombing as "a vile and malevolent act" of terrorism. "No one has the right to use violence in America to advance their own convictions over the rights of others."[39]

The same clinic, then in a different location, had reportedly been attacked by a firebomb in 1984. In 1992 and 1993, Rachelle Shannon set fire to and vandalized six abortion clinics in California, Nevada, and Oregon. In 1993 Shannon attempted to kill Wichita, Kansas, gynecologist George Tiller. That same year Dr. David Gunn was shot and killed by another abortion foe outside a Pensacola, Florida, clinic. In 1994 John Salvi killed two receptionists at clinics in Massachusetts, and former minister Paul Hill shot and killed two men outside another Pensacola clinic. During 1995 and 1996, abortion-related crime at clinics declined somewhat only to rise again in 1997. During 1997 alone there were six bombings, sixty-five acts of vandalism, and sixty-two cases of stalking.[40]

Discussion Questions

1. The people who are protesting at the clinics believe that *Roe v. Wade* is unjust and that abortion is murder. They compare the abortion clinics to the death camps in Nazi Germany. Is this analogy accurate? Support your answer.

2. Do you agree with Clinton that people in America do not have a right to use violence to advance their own convictions over the rights of others? Is violence, including war against nations such as Nazi Germany, ever justified as a means of achieving an end? Discuss how a utilitarian might answer this question.

3. What are the limits of protest against what is seen as an unjust law? Discuss the morality of vandalism, harassment, stalking, bombing clinics, and causing injury to abortion providers as forms of protest.

4. About one-third of the approximately 200 clinics offering abortion in the United States now have buffer zones that require protesters to stay a certain distance from the clinic.[41] In 1998 a U.S. district court ruled that antiabortion protesters violated federal racketeering laws; and in 2000 the U.S. Supreme Court upheld as constitutional a state law that created a buffer zone around abortion clinics prohibiting antiabortion protesters from being within one hundred feet of the entrance. Antiabortion activists argue that these laws restrict their freedom of speech, because they prevent them from having a one-on-one conversation with or passing out leaflets to women entering the clinics. Discuss how a rights ethicist would balance the rights of the protesters against those of the people who want to use the services of the clinic.

4. TEEN PREGNANCY, RAPE, AND ABORTION

Lisa, an eighteen-year-old high school honor student, attends a fraternity party with her nineteen-year-old boyfriend, Derek, a college sophomore. Although alcohol is forbidden on campus, there is plenty of liquor at the party. Derek and his roommate, a twenty-one-year-old junior and social chair of the fraternity, have already started drinking when Lisa arrives. Lisa says she is not interested in drinking. "Come on," her boyfriend chides her, "don't be such a baby." Lisa reluctantly agrees to join them in a drink. After a few drinks, she becomes so tipsy that she can't stand up, so she lies down on Derek's bed. Derek's roommate winks and tells him to "go for it." Then he leaves the room. Derek then has sex with Lisa, who neither consents nor protests.

The next morning Lisa deeply regrets what has happened. She tells Derek that she is worried she might be pregnant. He gives her the name of an out-of-town doctor and reassures her that the doctor will take care of everything. Lisa goes to the doctor that morning. The doctor gives her the morning-after pill and suggests that, because of the circumstances and because she is so upset, she consider seeing a rape crisis counselor.

Lisa doesn't tell anyone else what has happened, nor does she keep her follow-up appointment with the doctor. When her periods don't return and she begins putting on weight, she dismisses the changes as stress and the effects of the morning-after pill. After all, she reassures herself, she couldn't be pregnant because she took the morning-after pill and she hasn't had sex since the fraternity party.

Six months after the incident, Lisa she goes to the doctor for what she thinks are stomach problems or possibly a tumor. After examining her, the doctor tells her that she is six months' pregnant.

Discussion Questions

1. A disproportionate number of late-term abortions are performed on teenagers, because many teens do not recognize the early signs of pregnancy. Would a late-term "partial-birth" abortion be morally justified in Lisa's case? State why or why not.

2. Is using the morning-after pill contraception or abortion? Support your answer. Discuss how Thomson, Noonan, Warren, and Marquis would each answer this question. If the morning-after pill is an abortifacient, is there any difference morally between using the morning-after pill and having a late-term abortion?

3. Is this a case of rape? Support your answer. Is this relevant in regard to whether the abortion is morally permissible?

4. Discuss the responsibility, if any, of the other people involved. Should the boyfriend be punished for having sex with Lisa when she was drunk? Is the fact that he was also drunk morally relevant? Should he have to pay for or share Lisa's medical expenses? Should he be compelled to provide support for the child if she decides not to have a late-term abortion? To what extent is the college or fraternity responsible for what happened? Should they owe Lisa a duty of reparation?

5. Discuss the responsibility of physicians in cases where the patient is a minor. If Lisa had been under eighteen, should the physician have given her the morning-after pill? Did the doctor have a moral responsibility to follow up when Lisa failed to keep her second appointment?

6. The United States has one of the highest teen pregnancy, birth, and abortion rates in the world. Only Russia has a higher rate of teen pregnancy. The teen pregnancy and abortion rate is well above that of other Western nations which, unlike the United States, promote a "safe-sex or no sex" approach and provide confidential and acces-

sible contraceptive services to the teenagers. Discuss the moral issues involved in policies, including access to confidential abortion services, aimed at discouraging teen pregnancies. Discuss how a utilitarian, a rights ethicist, and a virtue ethicist might respond to these policies.

---

5. PARTIAL BIRTH ABORTION

When a family immigrated from India to a suburb of Detroit, Michigan, in 1997 they moved into a two-bedroom apartment, where the sixteen-year-old son and eleven-year-old daughter shared a bedroom. The following spring the girl, now twelve, began complaining of abdominal pains. At first her physician passed them off as digestion problems. However, the pains were not in her stomach. It turned out that she was 27 weeks pregnant. Furthermore, the father of the baby was the girl's brother. The family requested an abortion. After an anguished court battle, the girl finally obtained a "partial-birth" abortion at a Wichita clinic, even though there is a ban on them in Kansas.

An ultrasound in Vikki Stella's thirty-second week of pregnancy revealed that something was very wrong with her baby. More tests revealed that the fetus had several abnormalities, including a fluid-filled cranium with no brain tissue at all. A diabetic, Stella's pregnancy also put a strain on her health, and she did not wish to continue a pregnancy with a fetus who had no chance of survival after birth. She also had a "partial-birth" abortion.

Discussion Questions

1. What are the moral issues involved in the above two cases? Discuss what you might say to each of the two women if you were on the hospital ethics board and they came to you for advice. Develop an argument to support your position, using the steps listed beginning on page 108.
2. Dr. Martin Haskell, who has performed over 1,000 "partial-birth" abortions indicated in a 1995 testimony before the U.S. Senate Judiciary Committee that about 80 percent are purely elective and performed on a healthy woman with a healthy fetus.[42] According to a 1998 *U.S. News and World Report,* only 10 percent of late (post-twenty weeks) abortions are for medical reasons.[43] Most late abortions, including "partial-birth" abortions, are on women who don't know until late that they are pregnant; including young teenagers who still have irregular menstrual cycles and women in their later years who mistake the missed menstrual cycles for menopause. Discuss the morality of using "partial-birth" abortion in these cases. Are the reasons for the abortion morally relevant? Support your answer. Compare these cases to the two in the above case study as well as to the case of Lisa in the previous case study.
3. According to the American College of Obstetricians and Gynecologists, after viability, "partial-birth" abortion is rarely, if ever, necessary to save the health and life of the mother. Nevertheless, they oppose a ban on the procedure arguing that the decision regarding a third-term abortion should be made within the context of the patient–physician relationship, not by legislators. Provide a moral analysis of their position.

4. Some ethicists consider "partial-birth" abortion infanticide, or at least well down the slippery slope toward infanticide. They maintain that the right to an abortion provides only for the termination of a pregnancy, not a dead child. Abortion is a right because of the burden of being pregnant, not because having a living child is a burden (since adoption is an option). The most a woman can claim is a severance right to be freed from the excessive burdens of pregnancy, not a right to have someone else kill her child. After viability a woman can be freed of the burden of pregnancy without the death of the child. Discuss the strengths and weaknesses of this position.

C H A P T E R   4

Genetic Engineering and Cloning

It was one of the most controversial and startling birth announcements in history: On February 23, 1997, Ian Wilmut and a team of scientists at the Roslin Institute in Edinburgh, Scotland, announced to the world that they had created the first genetic clone of an adult mammal. The new arrival was a lamb called Dolly, reportedly named after Dolly Parton. Dolly looked like any other frolicking lamb; however, unlike any other mammal ever born, Dolly was created asexually from a single cell from her mother's udder. Dolly's genetic makeup is, for all practical purposes, identical to her mother's. The announcement of Dolly's birth set off a flurry of debate over the morality of using cloning on humans. Giving greater urgency to the debate is the recent completion of the Human Genome Project, which is expected to revolutionize both medicine and society.

THE HISTORY OF GENETIC ENGINEERING

Until recently, humans created new offspring the old-fashioned, natural way. Our children may not have been perfect, but we accepted them, for the most part, as they were. The desire to improve humans through genetic engineering, however, goes back at least to the time of Plato (c. 427–347 B.C.E.). In his *Republic,* Plato proposed the use of selective breeding as a means of improving society.[1]

The term *eugenics* was first used by English scientist Francis Galton, a cousin of Charles Darwin, to describe the study of human improvement by genetic means. Eugenics fell out of favor in the mid-twentieth century as a result of the eugenic programs that used sterilization to prevent the reproduction of people who were deemed unfit. Although the eugenics programs in the United States never reached the magnitude and level of coerciveness of those in Nazi Germany, memories of the state-run programs of involuntary sterilization left Americans feeling uneasy with talk of genetic engineering.

In 1962 James Watson and Francis Crick won a Nobel Prize for their discovery of the molecular structure of DNA. Each human cell, with the exception of germ or reproductive cells, contain forty-six chromosomes; each chromosome contains thousands of pairs of four different nucleotides or bases. Altogether, each human cell contains about 3 billion base-pairs of nucleotides, which can be roughly divided into about a hundred thousand sequences known as genes. There are also intervening sequences which, as yet, have an unknown purpose.

During the latter part of the twentieth century, reproductive technology focused primarily on the problem of infertility and prenatal diagnosis of birth defects. The development of amniocentesis in 1966 provided a method for diagnosing chromosomal disorders in the fetus.

The birth of Louise Brown, the first "test-tube baby," in England in 1978 heralded a new era of reproductive technology. Conception was no longer limited to the bedroom, so to speak; it could now take place in a petri dish or test tube in a laboratory without the presence of either parent. *In vitro fertilization* ("fertilization in a glass") soon became a popular means of overcoming the problem of infertility. Surrogate motherhood, in which a woman agrees to bear a child for a couple, hit the front pages in 1986 when surrogate mother Mary Beth Whitehead, who was also the baby's natural mother, went to court to get custody of the child she had contracted to have for William Stern, the biological father, and his wife. This case raised a public outcry over treating children, and women's reproductive capacities, as commercial commodities, an outcry that has gained renewed vigor in 2000, with the completion of the mapping of the human genome.[2] The ability to genetically engineer and even clone humans has awakened fears of a resurgence of large-scale human eugenics programs. Matt Ridley, author of *Genome: The Autobiography of a Species in 23 Chapters,* addresses this issue later in this chapter in his article entitled "The New Eugenics."

THE HUMAN GENOME PROJECT

The number of disorders that can now be diagnosed prenatally has increased dramatically since the beginning in 1990 of the Human Genome Project, a worldwide cooperative effort to map the entire human genetic makeup.

There is a staggering array of reproductive options based on this knowledge. Parents may soon be able to have their fetuses tested for genes that incline the child to obesity, shortness, nearsightedness, depression, alcoholism, Alzheimer's disease, sexual preference, and even "risk-taking behavior." Parents theoretically could seek genetic therapy or enhancement to alter the genetic makeup of their fetus or preimplant embryo by overriding or replacing these "undesirable" genes with more "desirable" ones. Parents may even be able to choose the genetic traits they want in their children or have children who are clones of themselves or some famous person.

The ability to identify and manipulate a person's genome has raised myriad ethical questions. Is it moral to tamper with our genetic makeup? If so, are there limits that should be placed on the use of genetic engineering and cloning? Can information about human DNA be owned? Indeed, what does it mean to be human?

GENETIC ENGINEERING

Genetic engineering includes both gene therapy, in which a new gene is introduced to override a defective gene, and genetic enhancement. Genetic enhancement involves the manipulation of the germ cell—in this case the egg—to improve the genetic code of a being. In this chapter we are concerned only with the second type of genetic engineering.

By the late 1980s, scientists were genetically altering food by taking genetic material from fish, bacteria, viruses, and insects and adding it to fruits, grains, and vegetables to improve durability and quality. *Transgenic* animals and plants are those with introduced genes, sometimes from another species. In 1992 the FDA declared that genetically engineered food is safe and does not need FDA approval before marketing. Scientists also began experimenting in the 1990s with mass-producing drugs by inserting human genes into bacteria. Scientists are also experimenting with chimeras—embryos created from the genetic material of two different species.

In late 1997 the same institute that had produced Dolly announced that by blending the two technologies—cloning and genetic engineering—it had created five almost-identical transgenic lambs with human genes that produce factor IX, a blood-clotting substance used in treating hemophilia.

The possibility of using genetic engineering in conjunction with cloning to produce "perfect" humans raises the ante in the debate.

There are two types of gene therapy: somatic cell therapy and germ cell therapy. In *somatic cell therapy,* normal genes are introduced to produce something, such as an enzyme or protein, that is lacking because of a genetic defect. Somatic cell therapy is a treatment; it does not get rid of the defective gene, nor does it change a person's genotype. Therefore, the defective gene can still be passed on to future generations.

Germ line therapy, in contrast, actually alters the genetic structure of germ line cells—the sperm and the ova—so that the genotype of future generations is also altered. It is even possible to synthesize completely *new genes and chromosomes,* thus overriding the human genetic code itself. It may soon be possible to protect offspring against AIDS or certain types of cancer through the use of germ line therapy.

Both of these types of genetic engineering can also be used for genetic enhancement. Geneticists are now able to create artificial genes and even whole chromosomes that can be passed on to offspring.[3] Some computer scientists are even talking of "upgrading" humans by combining genetic engineering with robotics. Dr. Gregory Stock writes that "In the not-too-distant future, it will be looked at as kind of foolhardy to have a child by normal conception."[4]

The capacity to create "designer babies," while good news to some, also raises the thorny moral question of "What is a human?". In his article "Genetics and Human Malleability," W. French Anderson, one of the pioneers of human genetic engineering, argues that gene therapy and genetic engineering should be used only for serious illness because of the associated medical risks and inherent moral problems they pose.

CLONING

Cloning is the process of producing genetically identical individuals through asexual reproduction. There are currently two types of cloning: (1) blastocyst (embryo) splitting and (2) nuclei transfer. Nuclei transfer can be further subdivided into nuclei transfer using embryonic or fetal cells and nuclei transfer using adult cells.

In *blastocyst (embryo) splitting,* the blastocyst, or preembryo, consists of two to eight cells. At this stage in development, cells are not yet specialized into different organ systems. Each cell is still capable of reproducing an entire organism, as occurs naturally in the case of identical twins or triplets. In 1993 researchers at George Washington University announced that they had created the first clones of human embryos. This event

---

🍃 PROPOSED USES OF GENETIC ENGINEERING AND CLONING TECHNOLOGY

- **A solution to infertility:** Couples who are infertile could clone one of themselves in order to have a child that is genetically related to at least one parent.
- **Replacement children:** Parents can clone a child to replace one that has died or is dying.
- **Replicating desirable genomes:** Nuclei transfer from adult cells could be used to create clones of people of great genius, talent, and beauty, such as Michael Jordan, Bill Gates, Mother Teresa, or Cindy Crawford.
- **Genetic testing and gene therapy:** Genetic tests could predict genetic diseases and gene therapy used to override or replace the defective gene(s).
- **Prolonging human life:** The identification of the genes responsible for aging may help us to expand the average human life span to ninety or even one hundred years or more.
- **Directing our evolution:** Scientists predict that by the year 2040 we will be able to direct our own evolution, as well as that of other species, by replacing selected genes or adding new genes.[5]
- **Agriculture:** Scientists could genetically engineer and clone animals and plants that produce high-quality food.
- **Medicinal animals:** Genetically engineered animals with human genetic material could be cloned to be used as drug factories for humans or as models for human diseases.
- **Research tools:** Cloned animals could be infected with diseases such as AIDS or cancer, and different therapies could be tried on them. Because all the animals are genetically identical, the research results would be more accurate.
- **Organ donors:** Nonhuman animals could be genetically altered so their organs would be compatible with human organs. Human clones could also be produced for organ transplants.
- **Endangered and extinct species:** Endangered species could be cloned to ensure their survival. Extinct animals could also be cloned if viable cells (generally frozen) are obtainable.

---

touched off the first round of debates on the morality of human cloning. John Robertson's article focuses primarily on this type of cloning in humans.

In the type of cloning known as *nuclei transfer using embryonic and fetal cells,* the nucleus from an early embryo is transferred to an unfertilized egg from which the original nucleus has been removed. Nuclei transfer using embryonic cells has also been used in cloning mice, rabbits, sheep, and cattle. The first successful cloning in vertebrate animals (animals with backbones), using nuclei transfer from tadpoles rather than embryonic cells, was accomplished in 1952.

In 1984 Danish embryologist Steen Willadsen succeeded in cloning the first lamb from embryonic cells. In 1997 Don Wolf at the Oregon Regional Primate Research Center created two monkey clones from embryonic cells. Bernie Harford of Monash University in Australia informed the world that his team had created 470 identical cattle

SELECTIONS FROM *CLONING HUMAN BEINGS: THE REPORT AND RECOMMENDATIONS OF THE NATIONAL BIOETHICS ADVISORY COMMISSION (NBAC), JUNE 1997*

In its deliberation, NBAC reviewed the scientific developments which preceded the Roslin announcement, as well as those likely to follow in its path. It also considered the many moral concerns raised by the possibility that this technique could be used to clone human beings. Much of the initial reaction to this possibility was negative. Careful assessment of that response revealed fears about harms to the children who may be created in this way, particularly psychological harms associated with a possibly diminished sense of individuality and personal autonomy. Others expressed concern about a degradation in the quality of parenting and family life.

In addition to concern about specific harms to children, people have frequently expressed fears that the widespread practice of somatic cell nuclear transfer cloning would undermine important social values by opening the door to a form of eugenics or by tempting some to manipulate others as if they were objects instead of persons. Arrayed against these concerns are other important social values, such as protecting the widest possible sphere of personal choice, particularly in matters pertaining to procreation and child rearing; maintaining privacy and the freedom of scientific inquiry; and encouraging the possible development of new biomedical breakthroughs . . .

Within this overall framework the Commission came to the following conclusions and recommendations:

I. The Commission concludes that at this time it is morally unacceptable for any-one in the public or private sector, whether in a research or clinical setting, to attempt to create a child using somatic cell nuclear transfer cloning. We have reached a consensus on this point because current scientific information indicates that this technique is not safe to use in humans at this time . . . The Commission, therefore, recommends the following for immediate action:
   - A continuation of the current moratorium on the use of federal funding in support of any attempt to create a child by somatic cell nuclear transfer.
   - An immediate request to all firms, clinicians, investigators, and professional societies in the private and non-federally-funded sectors to comply voluntarily with the intent of the federal moratorium . . .
II. The Commission further recommends that:
   - Federal legislation should be enacted to prohibit anyone from attempting, whether in a research or clinical setting, to create a child through somatic cell nuclear cloning . . .
III. The Commission also concludes that:
   - The United States government should cooperate with other nations and international organizations to enforce any common aspects of their respective policies on the cloning of human beings.

embryos, which they planned to use to produce herds of high-quality livestock.[6] Since 1997 most scientists have focused on the second method of cloning using adult cells.

Nuclei transfer using adult cells involves taking the nucleus from the cell of an adult and transferring it into a mature egg from which the nucleus has been removed. Prior to the cloning of Dolly, this type of cloning had never succeeded. Since the birth of Dolly in 1997, mice, cows, pigs, and even human embryos have been cloned using this method. Because the new nucleus has the full complement of forty-six chromosomes, the renucleated egg and the individual who contributed the new nucleus will be virtually genetically identical, with the exception of a very small contribution of DNA material from the mitochondria[7] of the host egg. Unlike blastocyst splitting, which is limited by the number of cells in a blastocyst, using nuclei transfer from adult cells, anyone—man or woman, adult or child—can be cloned in any quantity. With the ability to store cells that outlive their donors, as apparently happened in the case of Dolly's donor, it may someday even be possible to clone the dead.

Shortly after the birth of Dolly, an advertisement appeared on the Internet from a Bahamas-based group called Clonaid, which offered to clone people for $200,000 or to save a person's cells after death for future cloning. Early in 1998 American Richard Seed announced his intention to open a human cloning clinic in the United States.[8] Because human cloning is outlawed by the U.S. Food and Drug Administration (FDA), Seed refuses to comment on whether he has succeeded in cloning humans. "The less everyone knows the better," he told a reporter.[9] However, he did say that he and his wife Gloria plan to have a child who is a clone of her, perhaps as early as 2001. Meanwhile, Clonaid has announced that it too plans to produce the first cloned human before the end of 2001.

Putting the Brakes on the Research of Human Cloning

Because technological progress is way ahead of the debate over the morality of cloning, many countries have established temporary bans on human-cloning research. In the weeks that followed the announcement of Dolly's birth, human-cloning research was banned in Spain, Italy, Norway, Germany, Canada, Denmark, Great Britain, and the United States. The European Commission on the Ethical Implications of Biotechnology also came out in 1997 with a statement of "condemnation of human reproductive cloning."[10]

The 1997 Cloning Prohibition Act in the United States outlaws for a period of five years the use of cloning for the creation of humans. This law affects only research using federal money, however. The private sector is still able to engage in human-cloning research, as well as human cloning itself. Some legislators are calling for a permanent ban on cloning. In his article, "The Question of Human Cloning," John Robertson concludes that such a ban cannot be morally justified. As of the year 2000, three states have outlawed human cloning.

Most religious organizations are opposed to human cloning. Catholic theologian Reverend Albert Moraczewski of the National Council of Catholic Churches claims that cloning is "intrinsically wrong" because it is an attempt to "play God," and it robs people of their uniqueness. Islam scholar Adculaziz Sachedina adds that cloning violates religious teachings about the family and the traditional role of the father in creating children. Rabbi Richard Address of the Union of American Hebrew Congregations also opposes human cloning because "it violates the mystery of what it means to be human."

MORAL ISSUES OF GENETIC ENGINEERING AND CLONING

Human Dignity

According to Kant, human dignity requires that humans be treated as ends in themselves. Cloning, in particular, Leon Kass argues, treats humans as means to an end—a commodity—rather than as ends in themselves, because clones are valued only for their desirable genome. Because it is wrong to use a human to carry out someone else's desires, cloning is not morally acceptable. The fact that we value our children—whether they are clones or "natural" children—for their desirable genomes does not mean that we do not also respect them for who they are. Robertson points out that the argument that it is undignified for one person to have the same genome as another is questionable, given that we do not consider it an affront to dignity to be one of a set of identical twins. Clones are merely "delayed" twins.

On the other hand, it is argued, cloning violates human dignity in a way that natural twinning does not, because cloning reduces people to their genetic codes. In 1672 British philosopher and scientist Robert Boyle (1627–1691) expressed the following view of the human body: "I think the physician is to look upon the patient's body as an engine that is out of order, but yet so constituted that, by his concurrence with . . . the parts of the automaton itself, it may be brought to a better state."

The idea that the human body can be reduced to an elaborate machine with parts that can be manipulated and analyzed continues to dominate medicine and medical research to this day. In defense of the Vatican's 1987 statement condemning artificial fertilization and generation of human life outside the body, Cardinal Joseph Ratzinger told a news conference at the Vatican: "We encourage scientific research, but science is not [an] absolute, to which everything must be subordinated and eventually scarified, including the dignity of man."[11] Reductionism removes the human body from its social and personal context and reduces it to an object to be studied and manipulated. To have someone else define who we are, as occurs in cloning, removes our sense of self-control over our bodies, which is essential to our self-identity and well-being.

Because cloning involves the destruction of surplus embryos, it also raises the same issues of personhood found in the abortion debate. Some philosophers, such as Robertson, maintain that embryos are not persons and therefore do not deserve our moral concern. Bioethicist Richard McCormick argues that cloning collapses the person into genetic data, thus shattering our "wonder at human diversity and uniqueness."[12] Indeed, it is even suggested that cloning might constitute a "wrongful life." Genetic enhancement, especially germ line therapy, has also been condemned *as tampering with a child's self-identity and right to choose their own future.* However, other bioethicists point out that parents make environmental interventions—including making the child eat a healthy diet, sending the child to school and dance classes, signing them up for sports, and getting them vaccinated against certain diseases—that benefit the children by modifying their phenotype. If it is laudable on the part of parents to control their child's environment in order to produce the "best" offspring possible, why not also use genetic interventions to attain the same goals? Why are genetic interventions regarded as a violation of the child's dignity or essence while environmental ones are not? Bioethicists Allen Buchanan, Dan Brock, Norman Daniels, and Daniel Wikler write:

> Part of what may disturb us is the (mistaken) belief that genotypic interventions modify the essence of essential features of the individual, whereas environmental interventions only modify accidental features. The idea seems to be that genetic interventions result in a different individual, whereas environmental interventions merely modify the same individual . . . our compunctions about genetic interventions seem to rest on some underlying confusion about genetic determinism (we are essentially what our genes make us).[13]

Thus, the critics of reductionism and genetic engineering are using as a premise the very assumption they reject ("we are essentially our genes") to support their conclusion. McCormick, for example, argues that cloning violates the personhood and dignity of pre-embryos. There is also concern that clones, because they are human inventions, may be denied the rights of full personhood. Clones could be mass produced to act as drones for the "real" humans. On the other hand, clones, because of their more desirable genomes, might become a new master race, while "natural" humans are relegated to an inferior role.

Gene Patents and Owning Life

Another potential threat to autonomy is the patenting of genetic material, a trend that has been accelerated by the Human Genome Project. In the United States human cells that have been genetically modified can be owned and patented. Several companies have already obtained patents on individual genes as well as on genetically engineered animals such as Harvard's oncomouse, which has a gene for cancer. Can we, or should we, draw the line at patenting genetically engineered humans? Laws against slavery prohibit the ownership of humans, but how great a deviation from the human genome is required before we can legally consider a genetically engineering being a nonhuman, and hence, a nonperson that can be used as a means only?

While corporations may not be able to own us in entirety, they can hold patents on parts of us. Questions have already been raised by lawyers about whether genetically enhanced "designer" children will need permission from the company that owns the patent on their designer genes before they can legally pass the genes on to children of their own. And what about those "superior" genes that we possess naturally? Will they be ours? Or will they be the property of a private corporation?

Scientists and biotech companies are also scouting the globe in search of rare genetic traits that may have future market potential. The Human Genome Diversity Project (HGCP), an offshoot of the Human Genome Project, was established to expand the scope of genome research by collecting blood samples from groups of isolated indigenous people. The project, dubbed the "Vampire Project" by its critics, has been heavily criticized, especially by indigenous groups, as an extension of white colonialism that treats the bodies of indigenous people as commodities to be exploited. Ethicists Lori Andrews and Dorothy Nelkin in their article, "Whose Body is it Anyway? Disputes Over Body Tissue in a Biotechnology Age," explore the moral issues surrounding the commercialization of human tissue.

Defining "Perfection" and "Disease"

Then there is the question of what it means to be a "perfect" human. Who determines this? Should we define *perfect* in terms of the consequences for the wider community and the species? Or is what constitutes a "perfect" child a private decision that should be left up to parents? By being allowed to impose their concept of perfection on their offspring, the parent generation will control the destiny of subsequent generations. The world, however, does not sit still. Talents that may be appropriate today may be passé in years to come. The reject of today may be the genius of tomorrow's world.

Like the concepts of "perfection" and "health," the concept of "disease" is difficult to define. In his article on "Genetics and Human Malleability," W. French Anderson asks the question of what distinguishes a disease from discomfort or the suffering caused by the variations that exist in the cultural norms. Is shortness or homosexuality a disease? While recognizing that there is a large gray area, Anderson also maintains that there are some severe disorders that are clearly diseases and, as such, are morally permissible candidates for gene therapy.

We also need to ask if cloning and genetic enhancement are the best uses of our limited medical resources. Genetically engineering animals that can produce valuable drugs and organs for humans may drastically reduce that cost of manufacturing these drugs. On the other hand, a utilitarian would balance this against the pain and suffering caused to these animals.

The Right to Be Unique

President Clinton, in announcing the federal ban on funding for research on human cloning, affirmed that "human life is unique, born of a miracle, a 'profound gift.'"[14] Cloning, in particular, is regarded by many of its opponents as a violation of a purported "right to be unique." Cloning, it is argued, robs the clone of his or her sense of uniqueness. The fact that twins occur naturally does not give us the right to impose sameness on other people. Kass, for example, expresses concern that clones will be burdened with genetic identities—those of their parents—that have already lived, thus creating a serious self-identity problem.

Natural twins, however, have a sense of self-identity. Although genes provide the building blocks for individuals, they do not determine who we are. Who we are is the result of the interaction between our genetic inheritance and our social and cultural environment. Thus the idea that we could clone an army of identical Hitlers, or any group of people, who lack a unique identity has no scientific basis.

Genetic engineering too brings up the issue of uniqueness. Defenders of a right to be unique point out that children are unique individuals rather than projections of their parents' plans and wishes. If it becomes widespread, cloning of genetically engineered humans would allow one generation to makes its descendants as it pleases. All subsequent generations, now cleansed of unacceptable genes, would remain subject to that power.

Interfering with Nature

Upon hearing of the completion of the Human Genome Project, President Bill Clinton said, "Today we are learning the language in which God created life." There are two strands to the argument that genetic engineering is wrong because it interferes with nature. The first states that nature and the right to create new life belongs to God and that we should not encroach on God's domain. This objection is somewhat vague: What exactly do we mean by "creating" as opposed to "reproducing" life? What exactly is included in God's domain? This argument is also irrelevant to those who do not believe in God.

The second strand implicit in this argument is the assumption that "natural" and "good" are invariably linked. However, we are constantly interfering with nature in the name of morality. This argument, which is based on the naturalistic fallacy, is one of the weakest arguments against cloning. What is meant by "unnatural"? Is it unnatural for humans to develop and use technology? Indeed, the primary purpose of medicine is to prevent diseases by interfering with their natural courses.

A related argument is that species have integrity as biological units and we should not disrupt the natural boundaries between species. Again this argument assumes that *natural* and *good* are synonymous. The species-integrity argument is also reminiscent of the racial-purity argument. Just what is the moral value in keeping groups biologically separate? In addition, the distinction between species is not as distinct as biologists once thought. Genetic exchange between species occurs in nature without human interference as well as in cloning combined with genetic engineering.

Proposals are already afoot to use cloning to revive extinct species, such as the woolly mammoth (see Case Study 5 at the end of this chapter) and to preserve endangered species such as the giant panda, which experts predict may be extinct by 2010.[15]

Redefining Parenthood and Family

Kass argues that cloning would wreak havoc with our ideas of parenting and family. In particular, he questions the wisdom of separating reproduction from sexuality and the family, which is the fundamental unit of all societies. Without grounding parenting in the family, the care of children loses its natural grounding. The act of conjugal love, therefore, is the only method of human procreation consistent with the dignity of man.

Clones break this connection between family and children, because a clone comes from a single parent who, unless the child's genome was also genetically engineered, may also be that parent's identical twin. What's more, cloning will make men reproductively superfluous. A woman who wants to clone herself would not need a man. On the other hand, a man who wanted to clone himself would need a woman to provide both the egg and a womb.

Kass's critics maintain that the right to have two parents is an artificial right, not a genuine one. As for making men superfluous, cloning would not make social fatherhood obsolete. Clones could still have two social parents. Also, cloning may be the only chance for some couples to have a child who is genetically related to them. The father could provide the nucleus and the mother the egg. That way the mother would at least contribute some material—the DNA from her mitochondria—to their child.

Autonomy and Reproductive Rights

Randolfe Wicke is head of Clone Rights United Front, a New York City group founded in 1997 in the wake of Dolly's birth. Wicke believes that "human cloning is a reproductive option and should be available to all."[16] Cloning, he says, is not the business of government any more than "a woman's decision to have an abortion is."

According to many people, including Matt Ridley, autonomy is one of the most fundamental human rights. Ridley maintains that the right to procreate, including procreation through genetic engineering and cloning, is part of this fundamental right. The desire of parents to have a child who is "their own genetic child" is already widely accepted. In cases of infertility or serious genetic disorders, cloning may provide a way for parents to realize this dream. Although Anderson supports the use of germ line therapy and genetic engineering for serious genetic disorders, he also warns that the successful use of gene therapy for disease could lead us down the slippery slope by opening the door for enhancement genetic therapy.

Like Kass, we may find repugnant or arrogant the idea of people cloning themselves, or of parents using genetic engineering to produce the "perfect" child; however, it is argued, these feelings do not, in themselves, make these practices morally wrong so long as the children's interests are protected after birth.

On the other hand, given the high cost of genetic engineering and cloning, making it available could severely curtail reproductive freedom for parents who cannot afford the technology. Parents who had a less-than-perfect child in a society full of perfect children would put their child at risk for failure and discrimination. In the 1980 case *Curlander v. Bio-Science Laboratories*, a California appellate court ruled that a child with a genetic defect could bring a "wrongful life" suit against her parents for not undergoing prenatal screening and aborting her. This case could set a precedent for children who do not meet certain social and physical standards to sue their parents because their parents did not choose to have their genome genetically engineered to remove "flaws."

There is also the danger that medical care and social services would be withheld from families that do not avail themselves of the new reproductive technologies—a trend that has also begun with private medical insurance companies. Thus what began as a reproductive right could turn into a duty to have "perfect" children.

Justice as Fairness

Rejection is the flip side of perfection. What will happen to those people who do not meet certain standards of perfection? Genetic engineering might give children who are products of this technology an unfair advantage. This could draw even tighter boundaries around membership in privileged classes and further increase the gap between the rich, who can afford such technology, and the poor, who cannot. The fact that technology that nullifies the need to have "inferior" children exists may render policy makers less sympathetic to those who are disadvantaged.

John Rawls acknowledges that eugenics could create a caste system that divides society into separate biological populations. He also points out, however, that justice as fairness entails that the talents of those with greater abilities would have to be used for the common advantage. Whether this would happen in actual practice is another question.

Another related issue is the use of genetic tests to identify harmful genes, such as genes that increase the risk of breast cancer, alcoholism, manic-depressive disorder, or Huntington's disease. Is it fair for potential employers, colleges, and medical insurance companies to use these tests to screen people? Mandatory genetic testing by employers or insurance companies could lead to discrimination against people who carry "flawed" genes and could also constitute a violation of their privacy rights.

Consequentialist Arguments

These arguments weigh the harms of genetic engineering and cloning against the benefits. For example, because we have no experience with human cloning, we have to rely for the most part on speculation in determining whether the harms outweigh the benefits.

Even research to improve our knowledge has its own dangers. In 1999, eighteen-year-old Jesse Glesinger died following a gene therapy experiment at the University of Pennsylvania that was thought by the researchers to be relatively safe. A subsequent FDA investigation revealed that several experiments in gene research at other institutes did not follow preapproved research protocol and failed to report harmful effects on human subjects.

Some bioethicists maintain that because the possibility for misuse of cloning is so great, all human cloning ought to be banned. Kass, for example, fears that cloning and genetic engineering may lead to the mass production of children and the breakdown of parent/child relationships. Others point to the benefits of cloning to infertile couples, noting that cloning does not harm the offspring, because the clone owes his or her very existence to the cloning process.

Some biologists are concerned that cloning will undermine human diversity. French philosopher Emmanuel Levinas maintains that diversity is one of the key values in social interaction. The primary challenge in social interaction is accepting other people—including our children—precisely as other, rather than as mirror, images of ourselves.

Diminished genetic diversity may also affect our very survival. Almost all of us carry several recessive genes that are potentially debilitating or even fatal. Will cleaning up the gene pool by getting rid of these harmful genes amount to throwing the baby out with the bathwater? By culling genes that may be harmful today, we become less flexible genetically. This in turn makes us less capable, as a species, of adapting to sudden climate changes or of resisting new diseases. A case in point is the gene for sickle-cell anemia. In this genetic disorder, found primarily in people of African descent, the red blood cells have a tendency to become distorted into a sickle shape. These distortions can precipitate a "sickle-cell crisis," which is characterized by severe pain. On the other hand, sickle-cell anemia also provides a measure of immunity against malaria—a potentially deadly disease. Although malaria is no longer a threat in most parts of the world, the deletion of this gene from the human gene pool could make us less resistant to future diseases.

On the other hand, genetic technology is now capable of manufacturing and inserting artificial genes and even an entire chromosome. Thus, as Ridley points out in his article, we now have the potential of creating unlimited biodiversity.

There is also concern about the breeding of cloned herds of agricultural animals and plants—a practice that results in a genetically homogeneous population. In these cases genetic diversity, which is necessary for adaptation, may fall below an acceptable limit and the whole herd or crop could be wiped out by a single disease. In 1970 half of the maize crop in the United States was lost to one disease—the southern corn leaf blight. The loss was attributed to lack of genetic diversity in the plant.

The trend in genetic engineering in agriculture, however, is toward increasingly genetically homogeneous populations of plants and livestock. For example, ProLinia Inc., a biotech company associated with the University of Georgia, was to clone livestock, particularly cattle and hogs, on a large scale using the genes from superior animals—"superior" being defined as having traits most appealing to the human palate. The current process of breeding, says a company spokesman, is "time-consuming" and "unreliable . . . the [superior] genes eventually become diluted through generations of mixing and mating."[17] Some ethicists fear that this reasoning will some day be applied to the currently "unreliable" method of human breeding. What will happen when we have the technology to guaranteed to have a "superior" child? Kass maintains that access to genetic engineering may lead to the commodification of children. Ridley, on the other hand, argues that genetic engineering and cloning is unlikely to be used to mass produce superior children.

We also do not yet know the effect of using adult cells to create clones. Although the incident of death among the fetuses and offspring of clones is higher than normal, this problem may be resolved with better cloning technology. Initially there were also fears that cells cloned from an adult animal would age prematurely.[18] However, a recent study found that cells from clones actually have longer life spans than the original cells.[19] One two-year-old cloned cow has the teleomeres of a calf, teleomeres being the tips of DNA that determine a cell's longevity. Obviously much more research is needed on the effects of cloning.

We also need to take into account the risks associated with genetic engineering and gene therapy. Because of these risks, Anderson insists that gene therapy should be restricted to the treatment of serious disease.

The Rights of Nonhuman Animals

In our belief that humans exist outside and above the natural world, we often forget that we are not just *like* animals—we *are* animals. One of the surprising findings of the Human Genome Project is how much humans are genetically like other animals and even plants. There are also more parallels between human development and the development of "lower" animals than was previously assumed.[20] In fact, several animals, including sheep like Dolly and man's best friend the dog, have more chromosomes than humans do.[21]

What are we to make of this? In light of these findings, can we continue to justify the moral wedge between humans and nonhuman animals? Does our animal status lessen the moral value of humans; or does the close relationship of humans to other animals mean that we should extend moral respect to all animals, as Buddhists and animal-rights advocates do?

Currently fewer than one in three people who need a transplant receive one. The use of xenotransplants—organs from another species—may be a solution to this problem. On the other hand, it also raises the problem of the moral status of nonhuman animals, including animals genetically engineered with human genes so that their organs are more compatible with ours. This conflict may eventually be resolved if human stem-cell research finds a method for growing new organs from the recipient's own cloned cells.[22] Some current researchers are infusing human DNA with a cow egg, which is used as a cellular incubator for the human embryo, in an attempt to grow human embryonic stem cells.[23] This method, in addition to using another species to benefit humans, raises issues of its own, including the destruction of human embryos in order to use their "spare parts" for transplantation and the possibility of inadvertently introducing viruses from the donor cow egg. If other animals have moral status, can we justify the cloning and genetic engineering of animals as a means to benefit humans?

Another issue is the inclusion of human genetic material in other animals. Do other animals with human genetic material deserve the moral respect now reserved only for humans? What are the moral implications of the breeding of transgenic animals for species integrity? Will the concept of species someday become morally irrelevant? Cloning and genetic engineering may bring an end to the traditional line now drawn between humans and other species of animals; indeed it may even obliterate the concept of species. Whether this is morally desirable remains to be seen.

CONCLUSION

The ability to genetically engineer and clone humans is a milestone in history. How are we, as morally responsible citizens, going to respond to this new technology? We must resist the temptation to use the temporary ban on cloning as an opportunity to sweep the moral issues under the rug or to dismiss cloning offhand as too bizarre to be morally acceptable. Such a head-in-the-sand approach may simply encourage the development of unregulated back-alley cloning clinics.

There are compelling and broad-based arguments on both sides of the cloning debate. These moral concerns also address issues related to abortion and the use of non-human animals in medical experiments. How should we balance the different moral concerns? During the five years of the temporary ban, college students and new college graduates will have an opportunity to actively engage in policy making.

 M A T T   R I D L E Y

The New Eugenics

Better than the old

Matt Ridley is former editor of the *Economist* and author of *Genome: The Autobiography of a Species in 23 Chapters*. In his article "The New Eugenics," Ridley explores the use of eugenics in light of its history as well as the successful completion of Human Genome Project. He concludes that the use of eugenics in genetic engineering will not undermine the fundamental moral principle of respect for persons.

Critical Reading Questions

1. What is the history of eugenics? In light of its history, why do many people have misgivings about eugenics?

Matt Ridley, "The New Eugenics," *National Review,* July 31, 2000, Vol. 52, Issue 14, pp. 34–36.

2. How are we currently practicing eugenics?
3. What is the difference between medical genetic engineering and cosmetic genetic engineering?
4. Why does "everybody" agree that human genetic engineering is wrong?
5. On what grounds does Ridley disagree with his colleague Tom Shakespeare's objection to genetic engineering to correct preventable disabilities such as dwarfism?
6. What are the similarities, according to Ridley, between historic attitudes toward in vitro fertilization and current attitudes toward genetic engineering?
7. What is Ridley's position on the use of cosmetic engineering by parents? On what grounds does he support his position?

The entire human genome has been read. Even ten years ago, that seemed a distant goal; but last month, scientists announced that they have completed reading a "rough draft" of the complete recipe for a human being. It will soon be available on compact disc for anybody to read: a book 800 times longer than the Bible. This breakthrough will open an amazing world of possibilities for medicine—including the prediction, prevention, and treatment of many diseases, from kidney stones to cancer.

But why stop at disease? Instead of merely eliminating the negative, why not accentuate the positive—by tinkering with the text to improve it? After all, in pursuit of the perfect human being, we have willingly tried every weapon that falls into our hands, from prayer to psychoanalysis to breast implants. Will we—and should we—do the same with genes? . . .

A SAD LEGACY

Discussions of these issues are burdened by a complicated history. A century ago, progressive social reformers were obsessed by the new agenda of "eugenics." There was a sense of urgency in their desire to improve the human race by selective breeding. It had worked well enough in cattle and chickens, but we human beings were not only failing to breed from the best specimens; we were allowing the worst to have the most children.

"Some day," said Theodore Roosevelt in 1910, "we will realize that the prime duty, the inescapable duty, of the good citizen of the right type is to leave his or her blood behind him in the world." In the same year, Winston Churchill lobbied for compulsory sterilization of the mentally handicapped: "I feel that the source from which the stream of madness is fed should be cut off and sealed up before another year has passed."

Britain never did pass such a law, thanks to determined opposition from a libertarian member of parliament named Josiah Wedgwood. In America, however, states began to pass laws allowing mandatory sterilization. In 1927, the Supreme Court upheld Virginia's eugenic-sterilization law in *Buck v. Bell*. Carrie Buck, whom the state wished to sterilize, lived in a colony for "epileptics and the feeble minded" in Lynchburg, with her mother Emma and her daughter Vivian. After a cursory examination, Vivian was declared an imbecile—she was six months old at the time!—and Carrie was ordered sterilized to prevent her from bringing more imbeciles into the world. Supreme Court Justice Oliver Wendell Holmes thundered that "Three generations of imbeciles are enough!" Compulsory-sterilization laws were thenceforth upheld in many states; more than 100,000 Americans were sterilized under them.

The tragedy of that story lies not in the science behind eugenics, but in the politics: It is the *coercion* that was wrong. An individual who volunteers for sterilization is doing no harm, whatever his or her motives; one who orders another to be sterilized against his or her will is doing wrong. It is that simple.

The eugenic movement began with the best of intentions. Many of its most strident advocates were socialists, who saw eugenics as enlightened state planning of reproduction. But what it actually achieved, when translated into policies, was a human-rights catastrophe: the rejection of many immigrants, the sterilization of many people whose only crime was to have below-average intelligence, and eventually, in Germany, the murder of millions of people.

But now, a century later, we are once again practicing a sort of eugenics: We abort fetuses that would be born with Down syndrome or inherited disorders. In New York, Ashkenazi Jews who carry the Tay-Sachs mutation can avoid marrying each other through blood testing organized by the Committee for the Prevention of Jewish Genetic Disease. We also stand on the brink of cosmetic genetic engineering.

Are we simply repeating the mistakes of the past? No. The principal difference is that whereas eugenics, as conceived in the early part of the 20th century, was a public project, modern genetic screening is a private matter. Only China still preaches eugenics for the good of society; everywhere else, modern eugenics is about individuals applying private criteria to improve their own offspring by screening their genes. The benefits are individual, and any drawbacks are social—exactly the opposite of the old eugenics.

Another difference is precision: The selective breeding of the past worked slowly and unpredictably—but today, we can insert a gene into an organism and be all but certain what the effect will be: For example, inserting the genetic phrase "Make insulin!" into a bacterium transforms the life of a diabetic.

Genetic engineering of plants and animals is now routine. Only the genetic engineering of human beings is forbidden.

It would work: Of this, there is no doubt. Take a simple example: the gene on chromosome 4 that is associated with Huntington's disease, a terrible mental affliction of middle age. You could go into the gene in a fertilized egg, find the crucial phrase "CAG"—which, in affected people, is repeated more than 39 times in the middle of the gene—and remove about half of the repeats. It would not be easy, but it could probably be done. The result would be a healthy person with no risk of Huntington's, and no risk of passing it on to her children. . . .

It is not just medical genetic engineering that is feasible; cosmetic genetic engineering could also begin tomorrow, though it would still be very primitive. There is a gene on chromosome 17 called the ACE gene, which comes in two equally common varieties, long and short. On average, people who inherit two long ACE genes (one from each parent) are better athletes than people who inherit two short versions. . . .

It would be comparatively trivial to engineer a human embryo so that it had two long ACE genes. The result would be a child slightly more likely to win long-distance running races. There would be no risk of unpredictable consequences, because about one in four of us have two long ACE genes already; it is not unnatural. It would not be cruel to the child, and it would have no consequences for society. But should it be allowed? . . .

NO NIGHTMARE SCENARIOS

Yet even at this "easy" end of the spectrum, there are uncomfortable questions. Cures might seem uncontroversial, but they are not. My colleague, the sociologist Tom Shakespeare, is achondroplasic, but he regards his inherited short stature as a disability only to the extent that society imposes that prejudice on him. With a first-class degree from Cambridge University and a good career, he does not see his genetic disorder as a reason for eliminating future people like him.

He sees genetic engineering as undermining society's respect for people like him, because it sends the message that disability could be—and therefore perhaps *should* be—eliminated. In a genetically engineered society, the parents of a genetically disabled child would feel social opprobrium for not having "done something about it."

I see his point, but I do not fully agree with it, for the following reason: I see nothing in history to suggest that the ability to cure a condition lessens compassion or respect towards its sufferers. Indeed, society's respect for people with "preventable" disabilities has surely never been greater than now: People with Down syndrome, for example, were once abandoned or shunned; they are now treated with much more respect.

I suspect it will prove impossible in practice to draw a line between cure and enhancement, between medical and cosmetic genetic engineering. One person's cure is another person's enhancement. Is an inherited weight problem a disease? Would it be a cosmetic enhancement to "cure" dyslexia?

Assume that one day, genetic alleles that predict homosexuality are discovered—a wild assumption, but not inconceivable. To a heterosexual couple, disabling the "gay genes" in their potentially homosexual child might seem like a "cure" that prevents an "abnormal" life. But if so, then for a homosexual couple trying to procreate through a surrogate mother, disabling the "straight genes" in their child might also seem to be a "cure."

James Watson famously remarked a few years ago that if a mother, following a prenatal diagnosis, wanted to avoid having a gay child, that was up to her. After all, more than 95 percent of abortions are carried out for the convenience of the mother and are of "normal" fetuses. . . .

Another objection to genetic engineering is that it would drive out diversity, as people converge on the "ideal." Again, I think this argument is mistaken. Far from threatening diversity, genetic engineering may actually increase it. Supposing cosmetic genetic engineering became accepted, musical people might seek out musical genes for their children; athletes might seek athletic genes; etc. It is very unlikely that everybody would choose the same priority.

If diversity is not threatened by genetic engineering, then another argument—that in a genetically engineered world, there would be an underclass of those who could not afford the procedure —also evaporates. In this scare scenario, the rich might buy themselves an even better start in life with the best genes. But this argument applies only if genetic engineering becomes commonplace, and

it is at least partly undermined if everybody is using different criteria of perfection. After all, just by choosing our marriage partners we have been practicing private eugenics ever since we became human: Dark good looks, a slender figure, a winning personality, or a quick mind—in considering these attributes in potential mates, we are, at least partly, selecting genes. Yet diversity is not threatened, because each of us has different criteria. . . .

IVF (in vitro fertilization) is actually an instructive precedent for the current debate: When it was invented in the 1970s, society as a whole largely disapproved, finding the procedure unnatural and abhorrent. It gained acceptance because mild disapproval by the many was matched by fierce demand from the few; it took off because infertile individuals demanded it, not because society as a whole decided they could have it. It was an individual decision, not a collective one.

Just as infertile people demanded access to IVF, even before it had been fully tested for safety, it is possible that people who carry fatal genes will demand access to genetic engineering; but this is not very likely. Unlike infertile people, they already have an alternative: pre-implantation genetic diagnosis, which can spot and discard affected embryos in favor of unaffected ones. And if these people, for whom a "bad" gene is the difference between misery and happiness, do not need genetic engineering, why would anybody else need it? It is true that a few people might wish for a blue-eyed boy, but would they really be prepared to abandon the easy business of natural conception for a painful and exhausting test-tube conception instead?

My point is that cosmetic genetic engineering would attract a very small—and probably half-hearted—clientele, even if it were made legal and safe. I simply cannot think of a single feature of my own children that I would have liked to fix in advance. People do not want particular types of children; they just want their own children, and they want them to be a bit like themselves. . . .

The history of eugenics teaches that nobody should be forced to engineer her children's genes—but, by implication, neither should anyone be forced *not* to. To regulate such decisions with heavy-handed state intervention would be to fall into the very trap that caught the do-gooder eugenicists of 1910. I am not against all regulation: At the very least, governments can step in to ensure standards among practitioners (something they are quite good at). But they would be unwise to try to specify in detail what people can and cannot decide to do for themselves. As Thomas Jefferson said: "I know no safe depository of the ultimate powers of the society but the people themselves; and if we think them not enlightened enough to exercise their control with a wholesome discretion, the remedy is not to take it from them, but to inform their discretion."

Discussion Questions

1. Examine your own reaction toward the term *eugenics*. To what extent are your concerns influenced by historic uses of eugenics? Discuss what fallacies, if any, are involved in your conclusions about eugenics. Discuss also how Matt Ridley would most likely respond to your concerns.
2. Critique Ridley's position on the moral permissibility of cosmetic genetic engineering by parents. Discuss how a natural rights ethicist, a natural law ethicist, and a care ethicist would most likely respond to Ridley's argument.
3. Compare and contrast the positions of Ridley and his colleague Tom Shakespeare on the use of genetic engineering to correct genetic disabilities. Which position do you find most morally compelling and why? Discuss how Ayn Rand might respond to each of their arguments.
4. Using both utilitarian theory and Rawls's two principles of justice, develop a public policy on the use of eugenics and genetic engineering by both parents and biotech corporations.

 W. FRENCH ANDERSON

Genetics and Human Malleability

W. French Anderson is professor of biochemistry and pediatrics at the University of Southern California School of Medicine. Anderson is also one of the pioneers in gene therapy. In the following selection, Anderson supports the use of gene therapy for serious diseases. However, he rejects enhancement genetic engineering as both medically hazardous and morally precarious.

W. French Anderson, "Genetics and Human Malleability," *Hastings Center Report*, vol. 20, January/February 1990, pp. 21–24. Notes have been omitted.

Critical Reading Questions

1. What, according to Anderson, are the key questions that must be answered before we can determine the moral permissibility of genetic engineering?
2. What is the difference between gene therapy and genetic enhancement? According to Anderson, why does gene therapy open the door for the latter?
3. What is the difference between somatic gene therapy and germ line therapy? On what grounds does Anderson draw a moral distinction between these two types of gene therapy?
4. Why does Anderson have stronger misgivings about the use of germ line therapy?
5. On what grounds does Anderson reject the use of genetic enhancement?
6. What is the distinction between a serious disease, a minor disease, and a cultural discomfort?

Just how much can, and should we change human nature . . . by genetic engineering? Our response to that hinges on the answers to three further questions: (1) What *can* we do now? Or more precisely, what *are* we doing now in the area of human genetic engineering? (2) What *will* we be able to do? In other words, what technical advances are we likely to achieve over the next five to ten years? (3) What *should* we do? I will argue that a line can be drawn and should be drawn to use gene transfer only for the treatment of serious disease, and not for any other purpose. Gene transfer should never be undertaken in an attempt to enhance or "improve" human beings. . . .

WHAT WILL WE BE ABLE TO DO?

But successful somatic cell gene therapy opens the door for enhancement genetic engineering, that is, for supplying a specific characteristic that individuals might want for themselves (somatic cell engineering) or their children (germ-line engineering) which would not involve the treatment of a disease. The most obvious example at the moment would be the insertion of a growth hormone gene into a normal child in the hope that this would make the child grow larger. Should parents be allowed to choose (if the science should ever make it possible) whatever useful characteristics they wish for their children?

WHAT SHOULD WE DO?

A line can and should be drawn between somatic cell gene therapy and enhancement genetic engineering. Our society has repeatedly demonstrated that it can draw a line in biomedical research when necessary. . . . Our responsibility is to determine how and where to draw lines with respect to genetic engineering.

Somatic cell gene therapy for the treatment of severe disease is considered ethical because it can be supported by the fundamental moral principle of beneficence: It would relieve human suffering. Gene therapy would be, therefore, a moral good. Under what circumstances would human genetic engineering not be a moral good? In the broadest sense, when it detracts from, rather than contributes to, the dignity of man. . . .

Somatic cell enhancement engineering would threaten important human values in two ways: It could be medically hazardous, in that the risks could exceed the potential benefits and the procedure therefore cause harm. And it would be morally precarious, in that it would require moral decisions our society is not now prepared to make, and it could lead to an increase in inequality and discriminatory practices.

Medicine is a very inexact science. We understand roughly how a simple gene works and that there are many thousands of housekeeping genes, that is, genes that do the job of running a cell. We predict that there are genes which make regulatory messages that are involved in the overall control and regulation of the many housekeeping genes. Yet we have only limited understanding of how a body organ develops into the size and shape it does. . . .

Even though we do not understand how a thinking, loving, interacting organism can be derived from its molecules, we are approaching the time when we can change some of those molecules. Might there be genes that influence the brain's organization or structure or metabolism or circuitry in some way so as to allow abstract thinking, contemplation of good and evil, fear of death, awe of a "God"? What if in our innocent attempts to improve our genetic make-up we alter one or more of those genes? . . . If we caused a problem that would affect the individual or his or her offspring, could we repair the damage? . . .

My concern is that, at this point in the development of our culture's scientific expertise, we might be like the young boy who loves to take things apart. He is bright enough to disassemble a watch, and maybe even bright enough to get it back together again so that it works. But what if he tries to "improve" it? Maybe put on bigger hands so that the time can be read more easily. But if the hands are too heavy for the mechanism, the watch will run slowly, erratically, or not at all. . . . Attempts on his part to improve the watch will probably only harm it. We are now able to provide a new gene so that a property involved in a human life would be changed, for example, a growth hormone gene. If we were to do so simply because we could, I fear we would be like that young boy who changed the watch's hands. We, too, do not really understand what makes the object we are tinkering with tick.

In summary, it could be harmful to insert a gene into humans. In somatic cell gene therapy for an already existing disease the potential benefits could outweigh the risks. In enhancement engineering, however, the risks would be greater while the benefits would be considerably less clear.

Yet even aside from the medical risks, somatic cell enhancement engineering should not be performed because it would be morally precarious. Let us assume that there were no medical risks at all from somatic cell enhancement engineering. There would still be reasons for objecting to this procedure. To illustrate, let us consider some examples. What if a human gene were cloned that could produce a brain chemical resulting in markedly increased memory capacity in monkeys after gene transfer? Should a person be allowed to receive such a gene on request? Should a pubescent adolescent whose parents are both five feet tall be provided with a growth hormone gene on request? Should a worker who is continually exposed to an industrial toxin receive a gene to give him resistance on his, or his employer's request?

These scenarios suggest three problems that would be difficult to resolve: What genes should be provided; who should receive a gene; and, how to prevent discrimination against individuals who do or do not receive a gene.

We allow that it would be ethically appropriate to use somatic cell gene therapy for treatment of serious disease. But what distinguishes a serious disease from a "minor" disease from cultural "discomfort"? What is suffering? What is significant suffering? Does the absence of growth hormone that results in a growth limitation to two feet in height represent a genetic disease? What about a limitation to a height of four feet, to five feet? Each observer might draw the lines between serious disease, minor disease, and genetic variation differently. But all can agree that there are extreme cases that produce significant suffering and premature death. Here then is where an initial line should be drawn for determining what genes should be provided: treatment of serious disease.

If the position is established that only patients suffering from serious diseases are candidates for gene insertion, then the issues of patient selection are no different than in other medical situations: the determination is based on medical need within a supply and demand framework. But if the use of gene transfer extends to allow a normal individual to acquire, for example, a memory-enhancing gene, profound problems would result. On what basis is the decision made to allow one individual to receive the gene but not another[?] . . .

Discrimination can occur in many forms. If individuals are carriers of a disease (for example, sickle cell anemia), would they be pressured to be treated? Would they have difficulty in obtaining health insurance unless they agreed to be treated? These are ethical issues raised also by genetic screening and by the Human Genome project. But the concerns would become even more troublesome if there were the possibility for "correction" by the use of human genetic engineering.

Finally, we must face the issue of eugenics, the attempt to make hereditary "improvements." The abuse of power that societies have historically demonstrated in the pursuit of eugenic goals is well doc-umented. Might we slide into a new age of eugenic thinking by starting with small "improvements"? It would be difficult, if not impossible, to determine where to draw a line once enhancement engineering had begun. Therefore, gene transfer should be used only for the treatment of serious disease and not for putative improvements.

Our society is comfortable with the use of genetic engineering to treat individuals with serious disease. On medical and ethical grounds we should draw a line excluding any form of enhancement engineering. We should not step over the line that delineates treatment from enhancement.

Discussion Questions

1. Discuss how W. French Anderson addresses the problem of the slippery slope in his endorsement of genetic therapy. Does Anderson do an adequate job in drawing the line between acceptable and nonacceptable uses of genetic therapy? Support your answer.

2. Do you agree with Anderson's moral distinction between germ line and somatic gene therapy? Why? Discuss how a utilitarian might respond to Anderson.

3. What does Anderson mean when he says that enhancement engineering is "morally precarious"? Do you agree with Anderson? Support your answer.

4. Compare and contrast the positions of Anderson with that of Matt Ridley on the morality of genetic enhancement. Which person presents the stronger argument? Support your answer.

5. Define the term *disease*. Is it possible to draw a clear distinction between a "disease" and a "cultural discomfort" and, correspondingly, between gene therapy and genetic enhancement? If not, does this invalidate Anderson's moral distinction between gene therapy and genetic enhancement? Support your answers.

6. Discuss Anderson's concerns about the use of both gene therapy and genetic enhancement on discrimination. Discuss how both Rawls and a rights ethicist might respond to Anderson.

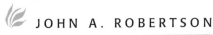

JOHN A. ROBERTSON

The Question of Human Cloning

John A. Robertson is a bioethicist and professor of law at the University of Texas. Robertson considers some of the ethical issues raised by human cloning. After looking at some of the possible applications of human cloning, he concludes that no one who deserves our moral respect is harmed by it, and some people may benefit from it. Cloning, therefore, is a morally acceptable reproductive choice.

Critical Reading Questions

1. What are the two types of cloning? Does Robertson think that the first type is likely to be developed for mammals?
2. What was the study at George Washington University Hospital, and why did it raise public fears and concerns about the morality of cloning?
3. What were some of the concerns raised by religious organizations regarding human cloning?
4. What, according to Robertson, is the most prevalent moral concern regarding cloning? How does he respond to this concern?
5. What are some of the potential applications of human cloning? Which of these applications does Robertson regard as morally acceptable?
6. How does Robertson respond to the objection that cloning is wrong because it involves the destruction of embryos?
7. On what grounds does Robertson dismiss the argument that producing identical clones, either at the same time or as later-born twins, is not wrong?
8. Should research on cloning be restricted according to Robertson, and, if so, under what conditions?

Accustomed though we are to advances in medical technology, a 24 October 1993 news report that human embryos had been cloned astonished many persons. A *New York Times* story, "Researcher Clones Embryos of Humans in Fertility Effort," was the feature that Sunday morning in many newspapers throughout the country. Media coverage continued for several days, with debates about cloning on editorial pages, *Nightline,* and *Larry King Live.*

Within a week the issue had faded from media consciousness, aided in part by *Time* and *Newsweek* stories that stressed the huge gap between the reported research and the *Jurassic Park*-type fears of cloned human beings that initially spurred national coverage. Bioethicists and lawmakers, however, must still contend with the ethical and policy issues that even limited cloning of humans presents. Should researchers be free to continue cloning research? May infertile couples and their physicians employ cloning to form families? Or should government prevent cloning research or discourage some or all of its later applications?

"The Question of Human Cloning," *Hastings Center Report* 24, no. 2 (1994): 6–14. Some notes have been omitted.

As with many biomedical developments, these questions present a mix of issues that need careful sorting. They involve, among others, questions of the propriety of embryo research, the validity of deliberately creating twins, and the importance of nature versus nurture in forming human beings. They also raise slippery slope concerns: should otherwise seemingly valid uses of a new technique be stopped to prevent later undesirable uses from occurring? To address those issues we must first describe the cloning research that has touched off the furor and the concerns that it presents. . . .

The study that generated the recent interest in cloning involved a small but essential step toward cloning human beings by embryo splitting. Researchers at George Washington University Hospital in Washington, D.C., separated cells or blastomeres from seventeen two- to eight-celled preembryos and showed that, to a limited extent, they would divide and grow in culture. . . .

The study thus demonstrated that experimental cloning or twinning of human embryos is potentially feasible as an aid to relieving infertility, though much additional work remains before offspring are produced, and there is uncertainty whether the technique will ever work at all. . . .

FEARS AND CONCERNS

Some commentators saw nothing particularly unethical or disturbing in the George Washington research. This was simply another step toward improving the efficacy and efficiency of IVF (in vitro fertilization), particularly for those couples who produce too few eggs or embryos to initiate pregnancy.

Many news reports, however, highlighted the disturbing or possibly unethical features of cloning and quoted ethicists who found the practice troubling. They described hypothetical scenarios in which embryos would be cloned for sale or to produce organs and tissue for existing children who need transplants. One ethicist termed cloning as "contrary to human values"; others saw it as "an opportunity for mischief" that called for "governmental and societal debate and, perhaps, prohibitions

and restraints." The Vatican newspaper termed it a step into "a tunnel of madness," while the United Methodist Church called for an executive order banning cloning in all federally financed institutions. A poll a week after the first story reported that 60 percent of Americans opposed cloning.*

The fears and concerns about cloning have several strands. Some of them arise from the artificial nature of assisted laboratory reproduction. Others are tied to discomfort with the manipulation and destruction of embryos that cloning research, if not the procedure itself, will inevitably cause. The most prevalent ethical concern, however, arises from the dangers that intentional creation of identical twins or multiples of one genome might pose to resulting offspring. The fear is that cloning will violate the inherent uniqueness and dignity of individuals, as well as create unrealistic parental expectations for their children. It also opens the door to identical embryos being created and sold because of their genetic desirability, as cattle embryos now are sold to increase animal yield and profitability. A worst-case scenario envisages the mass production of identical embryos to be sold to persons seeking desirable children. Finally, there are fears that embryos will be created to provide organs and tissue for existing children who need transplants. . . .

As micromanipulation of eggs and embryos is a rapidly growing practice, the ability to excise blastomeres from an embryo will easily be within the reach of many IVF physicians and embryologists. If shown to be safe and effective, physicians in many fertility centers will then offer the procedure to patients.

These possibilities engender a recurring disquietude about new reproductive technologies. Scientific zeal and the profit motive combine with the desire of infertile couples for biological offspring to create an enormous power to manipulate

---

* *New York Times*, 1 November 1993. Fifty-eight percent of respondents believe that "it was morally wrong to clone a human being." Sixty-three percent believe cloning was against God's will. Fewer than one in five respondents thought that cloning should be allowed to continue.

the earliest stages of human life in infertility centers across the country. . . .

Some persons would argue that the idea of creating exact replicas of other human beings is so novel that there should be a moratorium on further research and development until a national consultative body evaluates the ethical acceptability of the procedure and develops guidelines for research and use of the technique. At the very least, to prevent abuses there should be strict rules about the circumstances in which cloning by embryo splitting occurs, and about the uses made of cloned embryos. . . .

To assess the ethics of embryo splitting and the need for regulation, we must first ask who would use this technique if it were available and why, and then analyze the ethical issues that the likely demand for cloning would generate. We can then address the need for regulation of the embryo research that is essential if cloning by blastomere separation is to occur, and of the uses to which cloning techniques will be put.

THE DEMAND FOR CLONING

The news accounts of the George Washington University research emphasized many speculative uses of cloning, thereby slighting the most likely uses of the technique. The immediate impetus to develop cloning—and its most likely future use—is to enable infertile couples going through IVF to have a child.

To Increase the Number of Embryos Transferred

Initially the main demand for embryo splitting would come from couples undergoing IVF who cannot produce enough viable embryos to initiate pregnancy. In basic IVF practice, the highest rates of pregnancy occur with transfer of three to four embryos. . . .

If they produce only one embryo and embryo splitting has been shown to be safe and effective, they may opt to divide that embryo. Depending on the embryonic stage at which splitting is most suc-

cessful, this could produce two embryos (if split at the two-cell stage), four (if split at the four-cell stage), or even eight (if two embryos are both split at the four-cell stage). . . .

If they produce four or more viable embryos by blastomere separation, three or four might then be transferred to the uterus in the hopes of having one child, with the rest frozen for later use. . . .*

However, this scenario also opens the door to having "twins" (or even "triplets" or "quadruplets") born several years apart. This would occur if one or two children were born as a result of the first transfer cycle. Three years later, perhaps, the couple wishes to have a second child, and rather than go through IVF again, opts to have the remaining cloned embryos thawed and transferred to the wife's uterus. The period between births of children with the same genome could vary from a year or two to several years. . . .

Embryo Splitting as a Form of Life or Health Insurance

An often-cited though highly unlikely demand for embryo cloning could arise from couples seeking insurance against disaster for any children that they have. That is, a couple might request that one or more blastomeres be split from embryos that will be transferred, so that the resulting clone can be frozen for later use in case the child born from the source embryo later dies or needs an organ or tissue transplant. In that case, embryos that are genetically identical to the child already born can be thawed and implanted in the mother (or a surrogate) to produce a genetically identical child to replace the dead child, or to serve as an organ or tissue donor for an existing child.

This scenario could occur, but it is unlikely for several reasons. First, few couples not otherwise undergoing IVF would choose to do so just to gain the

---

* However, it is possible that three or even all four embryos transferred will implant. In that case, the couple will face the issue of selective reduction of the pregnancy to twins. Depending on the number of children who are born, cloning by separation could lead to twins or even triplets as a result of intentional cloning.

hypothetical protection that identical backup embryos might provide. Second, couples that experience the death of a child may not, because of the sadness that it will engender, want to replace that child with a genetic twin, much less plan even before the first child is born to create a replica for that purpose. Third, couples undergoing IVF who produce enough embryos for transfer may not want to risk their viability by separating blastomeres for hypothetical insurance purposes. Fourth, a genetic replica of an existing child might not be necessary to provide needed organs or tissue, or there may not be sufficient time once organ failure in a child occurs to thaw, implant, and bring to term the cloned embryo to serve as an organ or tissue donor. . . .

Because so few couples—even those otherwise going through IVF—will request embryo splitting for this purpose, the use of cloned embryos as backup protection for existing children is likely to arise only with embryos that were created to enhance the efficiency of IVF. In situations of this kind, where the embryonic clones were *not* produced with the specific intention of insuring against disaster, parents might occasionally be glad of the opportunity to avail themselves to the stored cloned embryos to obtain tissue for transplant for an existing child, or to replace a child who has already died. Such scenarios are not impossible, but for the reasons stated above, they are not likely to be frequent.

Embryo Splitting to Obtain a Desirable Genome

Ethicists have speculated that cloning by embryo splitting might occur to facilitate, or might result in, the selection of stored embryos deemed to be particularly desirable. They envisage scenarios whereby parents will try to sell clones of desirable children to other couples, or where an attractive or successful couple will clone many embryos for later sale or dissemination.

These speculations are highly fanciful. Most couples are not in the market for other peoples' genetic offspring, but prefer to have their own. If so, they can exercise some control over the genetic characteristics of offspring by mate or gamete se-

lection, or by preimplantation or prenatal genetic analysis. Few couples who can have their own children would be so obsessed with having a perfect child that they would eschew their own reproduction in order to obtain a cloned embryo that appears to have a desirable genome. . . .

ETHICAL ISSUES: DESTRUCTION OF EMBRYOS

Cloning by blastomere separation raises a number of ethical issues. Some ethical concerns derive from the stark interference with natural reproduction, or the manipulation and destruction of embryos that cloning necessarily entails. However, those concerns are not unique to cloning and have been voiced about embryo research, freezing, and discard, and about IVF generally. Since they are not deemed sufficient to justify banning or restricting those accepted forms of assisted reproduction, they should not be sufficient to ban cloning either.

Yet persons who believe fertilized eggs and embryos are already persons with rights will object that embryo splitting goes beyond the manipulations ordinarily involved in IVF. In this case a new unique individual will be intentionally split to serve other ends. The very process of blastomere separation could destroy embryos that would have developed normally, thus denigrating and undermining the value of human life. Because human life at all stages is a preeminent value, cloning by blastomere separation is an unethical procedure and should be banned.

There may be no way to answer the objections of persons who think that embryos are themselves persons and must be protected at all costs. . . . One can only point to the prevailing moral and legal consensus that views early embryos as too rudimentary in neurological development to have interests or rights. On this view, splitting embryos can no more harm them than freezing or discarding them can. Nor is splitting embryos to enable one or more of them to implant and come to term inherently degrading or disrespectful of human life. Cloning embryos thus poses no greater harm to embryos than other IVF practices and should be permitted to the same extent that they are.

ETHICAL ISSUES: DELIBERATE TWINNING

Ethical objections that are unique to cloning arise from a concern that the intentional creating of genetic replicas of an existing person denies the uniqueness of resulting offspring. This could occur from causing more than one child with the same genome to be born simultaneously. It could also occur from causing more than one child with the same genome to be born at different points in time.

Is the intentional creation of twins who are born simultaneously morally objectionable? Identical twinning occurs naturally and is not generally thought to be harmful or disadvantageous to twins. If anything, being a twin appears to create close emotional bonds that confer special advantages. If this is true, then having twins as a result of embryo splitting should be no more harmful to offspring than having twins naturally. . . .

ETHICAL ISSUES: LATER BORN TWINS

The second ethical issue unique to cloning by embryo splitting is the possibility of genetically identical siblings being born years apart in the same or different families. Are later born children harmed because a twin or triplet already exists? The claim rests on the notion that the later born child lacks the uniqueness or individuality that we deem essential to human worth and dignity, and that human individuality is largely determined by nature or genome rather than by nurture and environmental factors. Because phenotype and genotype do diverge, and because the environment in which the child will be raised will be different from that of his older twin, the child will still have a unique individuality. Physical characteristics alone do not define individuals, and there is no reason to think that personal identity will be wholly controlled by having an older twin.

Still, there could be special problems faced by such a child. Its path through life might be difficult

if the later born child is seen merely as a replica of the first and is expected to develop and show the skills and traits of the first. This might be a special danger if the later born child is used as a replacement for an earlier born child who has died. However, it will be some years before the later born child is even aware of his genetic identity relative to an older sibling and the special expectations his parents might have.

But it is also as likely that the later born child will be loved and wanted for his own sake. His status as a later born twin (or triplet) could be seen as a special status, indeed, a unique or novel status that confers attention and love. It could also lead to close ties with the older twin, if the special bond that twins feel is genetically based. However, it could also lead to unique forms of sibling rivalry. Will the older twin feel that he is deficient because his parents wanted a newer version of him, or will he feel special and proud that his parents wanted another child like him? In any event, it is difficult to conclude that later or earlier born twins or triplets are likely to have such serious psychological problems that they should never be born at all. Even if one did so conclude, this would counsel against implanting cloned embryos only when a twin already exists, not against implanting two cloned embryos simultaneously or splitting embryos at all.

ETHICAL ISSUES: CLONING AS LIFE OR HEALTH INSURANCE

Although cloning for the explicit purpose of providing parents with a replica for a lost child or as a source of organs or tissue for transplant for an earlier born child will not frequently occur, couples who have split embryos to treat infertility might occasionally be faced with thawing a cloned embryo for those purposes. Consider, for example, parents who request cloning to protect against the loss or death of a child, or who wish to thaw a cloned embryo to replace a dead child. Wanting a child to replace one who has died is not itself unethical. Nor does it become so merely because the new child will be a twin of the first. Although the parents may hope that the new child will develop and show the same traits as her deceased twin, they should very rapidly learn that the second child is different in some respects and similar in others, and would ordinarily come to treat and accept her as the individual that she is.

The use of cloned embryos as insurance against organ and tissue failure in an existing child presents a different set of issues. Here the concern is that the cloned embryo will be treated as an instrument or means to serve the needs of an older twin and will not be loved or respected for his own sake. . . .

If this is so, thawing cloned embryos to provide tissue or organs for an existing child should also be ethically acceptable. The key is whether the child will be loved and accepted by the family that brings her into the world, not how or why she was conceived, nor even whether she was cloned for that purpose. As long as the child's interests are protected after birth occurs, it is hard to see how being cloned or thawed to provide organs for a twin is any worse than being conceived for that purpose. . . .

ETHICAL ISSUES: EMBRYO SPLITTING FOR GENETIC SELECTION

. . . It is true that the small subset of infertile couples who are candidates for embryo donation might wish to know the actual characteristics of existing twins or triplets of the embryos they seek to "adopt." However, neither having nor satisfying this wish is itself immoral. Indeed, the right of adoptive parents to receive as full information as possible about the children whom they seek to adopt is increasingly recognized. There is no reason why the same principle should not apply to embryo "adoptions." Even though the couple seeking the embryos will be choosing them on the basis of expected characteristics, such a choice is neither invalid nor immoral. As long as the parents are realistic about what the information signifies, do not have unrealistic expectations about the child's perfection, and love the child for itself, seeking and providing such information prior to embryo donation should be ethically acceptable. If it were not, providing such information could be banned without requiring that embryo splitting to treat infertility also be banned. . . .

THE PERMISSIBILITY OF CLONING

The idea of cloning human beings initially sounds so bizarre and dangerous that one would think that such practices should be closely regulated, if permitted at all. Yet this survey of ethical and policy issues in cloning by embryo splitting suggests that the procedure has fewer risks and more benefits than first appeared and would be ethically permissible in most cases. The most unappealing applications of the technique are highly speculative and could be restricted without also stopping more valid uses.

Cloning by embryo splitting thus presents a regulatory situation that often arises with new reproductive technologies. An immediate step that seems justified to meet the legitimate needs of infertile couples could open the door to future applications that are much less defensible. If we ban the immediate steps in order to prevent potentially harmful future applications, infertile couples lose the benefits of the procedure without clear showing that future harms would necessarily have occurred. . . .

As a result, we are left to elucidate and resolve on a reality basis the ethical dilemmas that each new innovation presents. Cloning by embryo splitting is another example of this policymaking process. Unless there are greater risks from its use than are now apparent, the case for adding the technique to the armamentarium of infertility treatments is a reasonable one. Its novelty will not prevent parents from loving and acting in the best interests of children born in this way.

REFERENCES

Michael Waldholz, "Scientists Halt Research to Duplicate Human Embryos after Furor Erupts," *Wall Street Journal,* 27 October 1993; Gina Kolata, "Cloning Human Embryos: Debate Erupts over Ethics," *New York Times,* 26 October 1993.

Time, 5 November 1993; "Cleric Asks President for a Curb on Cloning," *New York Times,* 30 October 1993.

Judith Thomson, "The Trolley Problem," *Yale Law Journal* 94 (1985): 1395–1415.

American Fertility Society, "Ethical Considerations of the New Reproductive Technologies," special supplement, *Fertility and Sterility* 46 (1986); John A. Robertson, "In the Beginning: The Legal Status of the Early Embryo," *Virginia Law Review* 76 (1990): 437–517, at 440–50.

John A. Robertson, "Embryos, Families, and Procreative Liberty: The Legal Structure of the New Reproduction," *Southern California Law Review* 59 (1986): 939–1041.

American Fertility Society, "Ethical Considerations of the New Reproductive Technologies."

Federal Register 59, no. 10 (14 January 1994): 2414. See also, Joseph Palca, "A Word to the Wise," in this issue (p. 5).

Discussion Questions

1. In his discussion of the two types of cloning. Robertson argues that the first type appears unlikely to be accomplished with mammals "even in the mid-range future." Since he wrote his article, however, this type of cloning has been accomplished with sheep. Does Robertson underestimate the power of science? Does his argument for cloning support nuclei transfer cloning as well? Or is he able to support only blastocyst splitting because of its inherent limitations? Support your answers.

2. Discuss Robertson's claim that the interests both of parents and offspring are benefited, or at least not harmed, by cloning.

3. Would John Noonan agree with Robertson regarding the moral status of the embryo? Discuss what Noonan's position would most likely be on the morality of cloning.

4. Robertson assumes that cloning will be used primarily to help parents overcome infertility. Is this assumption realistic? Support your answer.

5. One of the arguments against cloning is that people have a right to a unique identity—a right destroyed by cloning. Are twins or triplets harmed by being identical? If possible, use examples from your experience to illustrate your answer. Would there be a cutoff point at, say, a hundred or a thousand identical clones, where this might be an issue? How would Robertson respond to this scenario?

LEON KASS

The Wisdom of Repugnance:
Why We Should Ban the Cloning of Humans

Leon Kass is on the Committee on Social Thought at the University of Chicago. In the late 1960s and 1970s, Kass, who has an MD in internal medicine and a PhD in biochemistry, was one of the first scholars to openly express concern about the morality of human cloning. He argues that people should trust their initial feeling of repugnance toward cloning. Cloning violates some of the most important human values and turns children into commodities. The manufacture of humans by cloning, therefore, should be prohibited.

Critical Reading Questions

1. What does Kass mean when he says that cloning is "the perfect embodiment of the ruling opinions of our new age"?
2. Why does Kass claim that cloning is dehumanizing?
3. What, according to Kass, is the most common reaction of people regarding the prospect of cloning humans? What is the source of this reaction?
4. According to Kass, what are some of the moral values violated by cloning? What are some of the inherent dangers?
5. Why, in Kass's view, is sexual reproduction morally preferable to cloning? What effects would cloning have on parent/child and husband/wife relationships?
6. On what grounds does Kass claim that the independence of clones would be subverted by their maker?
7. How does "making" differ from "begetting"? What is the moral significance of these differences?
8. Why does Kass reject Robertson's "right to reproduction" as a justification of cloning?
9. Why is Kass concerned about cloning taking us down a "slippery slope"?

TAKING CLONING SERIOUSLY, THEN AND NOW

Cloning first came to public attention roughly thirty years ago, following the successful asexual production, in England, of a clutch of tadpole clones by the technique of nuclear transplantation. . . .

Much has happened in the intervening years. It has become harder, not easier, to discern the true meaning of human cloning. We have in some sense been softened up to the idea—through movies, cartoons, jokes and intermittent commentary in the mass media, some serious, most lighthearted. We have become accustomed to new practices in human reproduction: not just in vitro fertilization, but also embryo manipulation, embryo donation and surrogate pregnancy. Animal biotechnology has yielded transgenic animals and a burgeoning science of genetic engineering, easily and soon to be transferable to humans.

"The Wisdom of Repugnance: Why We Should Ban the Cloning of Humans," *The New Republic* 216, no. 22 (1997): 17–26.

Even more important, changes in the broader culture make it now vastly more difficult to express a common and respectful understanding of sexuality, procreation, nascent life, family, and the meaning of motherhood, fatherhood and the links between the generations. . . .

Cloning turns out to be the perfect embodiment of the ruling opinions of our new age. Thanks to the sexual revolution, we are able to deny in practice, and increasingly in thought, the inherent procreative teleology of sexuality itself. But, if sex has no intrinsic connection to generating babies, babies need have no necessary connection to sex. Thanks to feminism and the gay rights movement, we are increasingly encouraged to treat natural heterosexual difference and its preeminence as a matter of "cultural construction." But if male and female are not normatively complementary and generatively significant, babies need not come from male and female complementarity. Thanks to the prominence and the acceptability of divorce and out-of-wedlock births, stable, monogamous marriage as the ideal home for procreation is no longer the agreed-upon cultural norm. For this new dispensation, the clone is the ideal emblem: the ultimate "single-parent child."

Thanks to our belief that all children should be *wanted* children (the more high-minded principle we use to justify contraception and abortion), sooner or later only those children who fulfill our wants will be fully acceptable. Through cloning, we can work our wants and wills on the very identity of our children, exercising control as never before. Thanks to modern notions of individualism and the rate of cultural change, we see ourselves not as linked to ancestors and defined by traditions, but as projects for our own self-creation, not only as self-made men but also man-made selves; and self-cloning is simply an extension of such rootless and narcissistic self-re-creation.

Unwilling to acknowledge our debt to the past and unwilling to embrace the uncertainties and the limitations of the future, we have a false relation to both: cloning personifies our desire fully to control the future, while being subject to no controls ourselves. Enchanted and enslaved by the glamour of technology, we have lost our awe and wonder before the deep mysteries of nature and of life. We cheerfully take our own beginnings in our hands and, like the last man, we blink. . . .

Human cloning, though it is in some respects continuous with previous reproductive technologies, also represents something radically new, in itself and in its easily foreseeable consequences. The stakes are very high indeed. I exaggerate, but in the direction of the truth, when I insist that we are faced with having to decide nothing less than whether human procreation is going to remain human, whether children are going to be made rather than begotten, whether it is a good thing, humanly speaking, to say yes in principle to the road which leads (at best) to the dehumanized rationality of *Brave New World.* This is not business as usual, to be fretted about for a while but finally to be given our seal of approval. We must rise to the occasion and make our judgments as if the future of our humanity hangs in the balance. For so it does.

THE STATE OF THE ART

. . . For the tens of thousands of people already sustaining over 200 assisted reproduction clinics in the United States and already availing themselves of in vitro fertilization, intracytoplasmic sperm injection and other techniques of assisted reproduction, cloning would be an option with virtually no added fuss (especially when the success rate improves). Should commercial interests develop in "nucleus-banking," as they have in sperm-banking; should famous athletes or other celebrities decide to market their DNA the way they now market their autographs and just about everything else; should techniques of embryo and germline genetic testing and manipulation arrive as anticipated, increasing the use of laboratory assistance in order to obtain "better" babies—should all this come to pass, then cloning, if it is permitted, could become more than a marginal practice simply on the basis of free reproductive choice, even without any social encouragement to upgrade the gene pool or to replicate superior types. Moreover, if laboratory research on human cloning proceeds, even without any intention to produce cloned humans, the existence of cloned human embryos in the laboratory, created to begin with only for research purposes, would surely pave the way for later baby-making implantations.

In anticipation of human cloning, apologists and proponents have already made clear possible uses of the perfected technology, ranging from the sentimental and compassionate to the grandiose. They include: providing a child for an infertile couple; "replacing" a beloved spouse or child who is dying or who has died; avoiding the risk of genetic disease; permitting reproduction for homosexual men and lesbians who want nothing sexual to do with the opposite sex; securing a genetically identical source of organs or tissues perfectly suitable for transplantation; getting a child with a genotype of one's own choosing, not excluding oneself; replicating individuals of great genius, talent or beauty—having a child who really could "be like Mike"; and creating large sets of genetically identical humans suitable for research on, for instance, the question of nature versus nurture, or for special missions in peace and war (not excluding espionage), in which using identical humans would be an advantage. Most people who envision the cloning of human beings, of course, want none of these scenarios. That they cannot say why is not surprising. What is surprising, and welcome, is that, in our cynical age, they are saying anything at all.

THE WISDOM OF REPUGNANCE

"Offensive." "Grotesque." "Revolting." "Repugnant." "Repulsive." These are the words most commonly heard regarding the prospect of human cloning. Such reactions come both from the man or woman in the street and from the intellectuals, from believers and atheists, from humanists and scientists. Even Dolly's creator has said he "would find it offensive" to clone a human being.

People are repelled by many aspects of human cloning. They recoil from the prospect of mass production of human beings, with large clones of look-alikes, compromised in their individuality; the idea of father-son or mother-daughter twins; the bizarre prospects of a woman giving birth to and rearing a genetic copy of herself, her spouse or even her deceased father or mother; the grotesqueness of conceiving a child as an exact replacement for another who has died; the utilitarian creation of embryonic genetic duplicates of oneself, to be frozen away or created when necessary, in case of need for homologous tissues or organs for transplantation; the narcissism of those who would clone themselves and the arrogance of others who think they know who deserves to be cloned or which genotype any child-to-be should be thrilled to receive; the Frankensteinian hubris to create human life and increasingly to control its destiny; man playing God. Almost no one finds any of the suggested reasons for human cloning compelling; almost everyone anticipates its possible misuses and abuses. Moreover, many people feel oppressed by the sense that there is probably nothing we can do to prevent it from happening. This makes the prospect all the more revolting.

Revulsion is not an argument; and some of yesterday's repugnancies are today calmly accepted—though, one must add, not always for the better. In crucial cases, however, repugnance is the emotional expression of deep wisdom, beyond reason's power fully to articulate it. Can anyone really give an argument fully adequate to the horror which is father-daughter incest (even with consent), or having sex with animals, or mutilating a corpse, or eating human flesh, or even just (just!) raping or murdering another human being? Would anybody's failure to give full rational justification for his or her revulsion at these practices make that revulsion ethically suspect? Not at all. On the contrary, we are suspicious of those who think that they can rationalize away our horror, say, by trying to explain the enormity of incest with arguments only about the genetic risks of inbreeding.

The repugnance of human cloning belongs in this category. We are repelled by the prospect of cloning human beings not because of the strangeness or novelty of the undertaking, but because we intuit and feel, immediately and without argument, the violation of things that we rightfully hold dear. Repugnance, here as elsewhere, revolts against the excesses of human willfulness, warning us not to transgress what is unspeakably profound. Indeed, in this age in which everything is held to be permissible so long as it is freely done, in which our given human nature no longer commands respect, in which our bodies are regarded as mere instruments of our autonomous rational wills, repugnance may be the only voice left that speaks up to defend the central core of our humanity. Shallow are the souls that have forgotten how to shudder. . . .

THE PROFUNDITY OF SEX

To see cloning in its proper context, we must begin not, as I did before, with laboratory technique, but with the anthropology—natural and social—of sexual reproduction.

Sexual reproduction—by which I mean the generation of new life from (exactly) two complementary elements, one female, one male, (usually) through coitus—is established (if that is the right term) not by human decision, culture or tradition, but by nature; it is the natural way of all mammalian reproduction. By nature, each child has two complementary biological progenitors. Each child thus stems from and unites exactly two lineages. In natural generation, moreover, the precise genetic constitution of the resulting offspring is determined by a combination of nature and chance, not by human design: each human child shares the common natural human species genotype, each child is genetically (equally) kin to each (both) parent(s), yet each child is genetically unique.

These biological truths about our origins foretell deep truths about our identity and about our human condition altogether. Every one of us is at once equally human, equally enmeshed in a particular familial nexus of origin, and equally individuated in our trajectory from birth to death. . . . Though less momentous than our common humanity, our genetic individuality is not humanly trivial. It shows itself forth in our distinctive appearance through which we are everywhere recognized; it is revealed in our "signature" marks of fingerprints and our self-recognizing immune system; it symbolizes and foreshadows exactly the unique, never-to-be-repeated character of each human life.

Human societies virtually everywhere have structured child-rearing responsibilities and systems of identity and relationship on the bases of these deep natural facts of begetting. The mysterious yet ubiquitous "love of one's own" is everywhere culturally exploited, to make sure that children are not just produced but well cared for and to create for everyone clear ties of meaning, belonging and obligation. But it is wrong to treat such naturally rooted social practices as mere cultural constructs (like left- or right-driving, or like burying or cremating the dead) that we can alter with little human cost. What would kinship be without its clear natural grounding? And what would identity be without kinship? We must resist those who have begun to refer to sexual reproduction as the "traditional method of reproduction," who would have us regard as merely traditional, and by implication arbitrary, what is in truth not only natural but most certainly profound.

Asexual reproduction, which produces "single-parent" offspring, is a radical departure from the natural human way, confounding all normal understandings of father, mother, sibling, grandparent, etc., and all moral relations tied thereto. It becomes even more of a radical departure when the resulting offspring is a clone derived not from an embryo, but from a mature adult to whom the clone would be an identical twin; and when the process occurs not by natural accident (as in natural twinning), but by deliberate human design and manipulation; and when the child's (or children's) genetic constitution is preselected by the parent(s) (or scientists). Accordingly, as we will see, cloning is vulnerable to three kinds of concerns and objections, related to these three points: cloning threatens confusion of identity and individuality, even in small-scale cloning; cloning represents a giant step (though not the first one) toward transforming procreation into manufacture, that is, toward the increasing depersonalization of the process of generation and, increasingly, toward the "production" of human children as artifacts, products of human will and design (what others have called the problems of "commodification" of new life); and cloning—like other forms of eugenic engineering of the next generation—represents a form of despotism of the cloners over the cloned, and thus (even in benevolent cases) represents a blatant violation of the inner meaning of parent-child relations, of what it means to have a child, of what it means to say "yes" to our own demise and "replacement."

Human procreation, in sum, is not simply an activity of our rational wills. It is a more complete activity precisely because it engages us bodily, erotically and spiritually, as well as rationally. There is wisdom in the mystery of nature that has joined the pleasure of sex, the inarticulate longing for union, the communication of the loving embrace and the deep-seated and only partly articulate desire for children in the very activity by which we continue the chain of human existence and participate in the renewal of human possibility. Whether or not we know it, the severing of procreation from sex, love and intimacy is inherently dehumanizing, no matter how good the product.

We are now ready for the more specific objections to cloning.

THE PERVERSITIES OF CLONING

First, an important if formal objection: any attempt to clone a human being would constitute an unethical experiment upon the resulting child-to-be. As the animal experiments (frog and sheep) indicate, there are grave risks of mishaps and deformities. Moreover, because of what cloning means, one cannot presume a future cloned child's consent to be a clone, even a healthy one. Thus, ethically speaking, we cannot even get to know whether or not human cloning is feasible.

I understand, of course, the philosophical difficulty of trying to compare a life with defects against nonexistence. Several bioethicists, proud of their philosophical cleverness, use this conundrum to embarrass claims that one can injure a child in its conception, precisely because it is only thanks to that complained-of conception that the child is alive to complain. But common sense tells us that we have no reason to fear such philosophisms. For we surely know that people can harm and even maim children in the very act of conceiving them, say, by paternal transmission of the AIDS virus, maternal transmission of heroin dependence or, arguably, even by bringing them into being as bastards or with no capacity or willingness to look after them properly. And we believe that to do this intentionally, or even negligently, is inexcusable and clearly unethical.

The objection about the impossibility of presuming consent may even go beyond the obvious and sufficient point that a clonant, were he subsequently to be asked, could rightly resent having been made a clone. At issue are not just benefits and harms, but doubts about the very independence needed to give proper (even retroactive) consent, that is, not just the capacity to choose but the disposition and ability to choose freely and well. It is not at all clear to what extent a clone will truly be a moral agent. For, as we shall see, in the very fact of cloning, and of rearing him as a clone, his makers subvert the cloned child's independence, beginning with that aspect that comes from knowing that one was an unbidden surprise, a gift, to the world, rather than the designed result of someone's artful project.

Cloning creates serious issues of identity and individuality. The cloned person may experience concerns about his distinctive identity not only because he will be in genotype and appearance identical to another human being, but, in this case, because he may also be twin to the person who is his "father" or "mother"—if one can still call them that. What would be the psychic burdens of being the "child" or "parent" of your twin? The cloned individual, moreover, will be saddled with a genotype that has already lived. He will not be fully a surprise to the world. People are likely always to compare his performances in life with that of his alter ego. True, his nurture and his circumstances in life will be different; genotype is not exactly destiny. Still, one must also expect parental and other efforts to shape the new life after the original—or at least to view the child with the original version always firmly in mind. Why else did they clone from the star basketball player, mathematician and beauty queen—or even dear old dad—in the first place?

Since the birth of Dolly, there has been a fair amount of doublespeak on this matter of genetic identity. Experts have rushed in to reassure the public that the clone would in no way be the same person, or have any confusions about his or her identity: as previously noted, they are pleased to point out that the clone of Mel Gibson would not be Mel Gibson. Fair enough. But one is shortchanging the truth by emphasizing the additional importance of the intrauterine environment, rearing and social setting: genotype obviously matters plenty. That, after all, is the only reason to clone, whether human beings or sheep. The odds that clones of Wilt Chamberlain will playing in the NBA are, I submit, infinitely greater than they are for clones of Robert Reich.

Curiously, this conclusion is supported, inadvertently, by the one ethical sticking point insisted on by friends of cloning: no cloning without the donor's consent. Though an orthodox liberal objection, it is in fact quite puzzling when it comes from people who also insist that genotype is not identity or individuality, and who deny that a child could reasonably complain about being made a genetic copy. If the clone of Mel Gibson would not be Mel Gibson, why should Mel Gibson have grounds to object that someone had been made his clone? We already allow researchers to use blood and tissue samples for research purposes of no benefit to their sources: my falling hair, my expectorations, my urine and even my biopsied tissues are "not me" and not mine. Courts have held that the profit gained from uses to which scientists put my discarded tissues do not legally belong to me. Why, then, no cloning without consent—including, I assume, no cloning from the body of someone who just died? What harm is done the donor, if genotype is "not me"? Truth to tell, the only powerful justification for objecting is that genotype really does have something to do with identity, and everybody knows it. If not, on what basis could Michael Jordan object that someone cloned "him," say, from cells taken from a "lost" scraped-off piece of his skin?

The insistence on donor consent unwittingly reveals the problem of identity in all cloning.

Genetic distinctiveness not only symbolizes the uniqueness of each human life and the independence of its parents that each human child rightfully attains. It can also be an important support for living a worthy and dignified life. Such arguments apply with great force to any large-scale replication of human individuals. But they are sufficient, in my view, to rebut even the first attempts to clone a human being. One must never forget that these are human beings upon whom our eugenic or merely playful fantasies are to be enacted. . . .

Human cloning would also represent a giant step toward turning begetting into making, procreation into manufacture (literally, something "handmade"), a process already begun with in vitro fertilization and genetic testing of embryos. With cloning, not only is the process in hand, but the total genetic blueprint of the cloned individual is selected and determined by the human artisans. To be sure, subsequent development will take place according to natural processes; and the resulting children will still be recognizably human. But we here would be taking a major step into making man himself simply another one of the man-made things. Human nature becomes merely the last part of nature to succumb to the technological project, which turns all of nature into raw material at human disposal, to be homogenized by our rationalized technique according to the subjective prejudices of the day.

How does begetting differ from making? In natural procreation, human beings come together, complementarily male and female, to give existence to another being who is formed, exactly as we were, *by what we are:* living, hence perishable, hence aspiringly erotic, human beings. In clonal reproduction, by contrast, and in the more advanced forms of manufacture to which it leads, we give existence to a being not by what we are but by what we intend and design. As with any product of our making, no matter how excellent, the artificer stands above it, not as an equal but as a superior, transcending it by his will and creative prowess. Scientists who clone animals make it perfectly clear that they are engaged in instrumental making; the animals are, from the start, designed as means to serve rational human purposes. In human cloning, scientists and prospective "parents" would be adopting the same technocratic mentality to human children: human children would be their artifacts.

Such an arrangement is profoundly dehumanizing, no matter how good the product. Mass-scale cloning of the same individual makes the point vividly; but the violation of human equality, freedom and dignity are present even in a single planned clone. And procreation dehumanized into manufacture is further degraded by commodification, a virtually inescapable result of allowing baby-making to proceed under the banner of commerce. Genetic and reproductive biotechnology companies are already growth industries, but they will go into commercial orbit once the Human Genome Project nears completion. . . .

Finally, and perhaps most important, the practice of human cloning by nuclear transfer—like other anticipated forms of genetic engineering of the next generation—would enshrine and aggravate a profound and mischievous misunderstanding of the meaning of having children and of the parent-child relationship. When a couple now chooses to procreate, the partners are saying yes to the emergence of new life in its novelty, saying yes not only to having a child but also, tacitly, to having whatever child this child turns out to be. In accepting our finitude and opening ourselves to our replacement, we are tacitly confessing the limits of our control. In this ubiquitous way of nature, embracing the future by procreating means precisely that we are relinquishing our grip, in the very activity of taking up our own share in what we hope will be the immortality of human life and the human species. This means that our children are not *our* children: they are not our property, not our possessions. Neither are they supposed to live our lives for us, or anyone else's life but their own. To be sure, we seek to guide them on their way, imparting to them not just life but nurturing, love, and a way of life; to be sure, they bear our hopes that they will live fine and flourishing lives, enabling us in small measure to transcend our own limitations. Still, their genetic distinctiveness and independence are the natural foreshadowing of the deep truth that they have their own and never-before-enacted life to live. They are sprung from a past, but they take an uncharted course into the future.

Much harm is already done by parents who try to live vicariously through their children. Children are sometimes compelled to fulfill the broken dreams of unhappy parents: John Doe Jr. or the III is under the burden of having to live up to his forebear's name. Still, if most parents have hopes for their children, cloning parents will have expectations. In cloning, such overbearing parents take at the start a decisive step which contradicts the entire meaning of the open and forward-looking nature of parent-child relations. The child is given a genotype that has already lived, with full expectation that this blueprint of a past life ought to be controlling of the life that is to come. Cloning is inherently despotic, for it seeks to make one's children (or someone else's children) after one's own image (or an image of one's choosing) and their future according to one's will. In some cases, the despotism may be mild and benevolent. In other cases, it will be mischievous and downright tyrannical. But despotism—the control of another through one's will—it inevitably will be.

MEETING SOME OBJECTIONS

The defenders of cloning, of course, are not wittingly friends of despotism. Indeed, they regard themselves mainly as friends of freedom: the freedom of individuals to reproduce, the freedom of scientists and inventors to discover and devise and to foster "progress" in genetic knowledge and technique. They want large-scale cloning only for animals, but they wish to preserve cloning as a human option for exercising our "right to reproduce"— our right to have children, and children with "desirable genes." As law professor John Robertson points out, under our "right to reproduce" we already practice early forms of unnatural, artificial and extramarital reproduction, and we already practice early forms of eugenic choice. For this reason, he argues, cloning is no big deal.

We have here a perfect example of the logic of the slippery slope, and the slippery way in which it already works in this area. Only a few years ago, slippery slope arguments were used to oppose artificial insemination and in vitro fertilization using unrelated sperm donors. Principles used to justify these practices, it was said, will be used to justify more artificial and more eugenic practices, including cloning. Not so, the defenders retorted, since we can make the necessary distinctions. And now, without even a gesture at making the necessary distinctions, the continuity of practice is held by itself to be justificatory.

The principle of reproductive freedom as currently enunciated by the proponents of cloning logically embraces the ethical acceptability of sliding down the entire rest of the slope—to producing children ectogenetically from sperm to term (should it become feasible) and to producing children whose entire genetic makeup will be the product of parental eugenic planning and choice. If reproductive freedom means the right to have a child of one's own choosing, by whatever means, it knows and accepts no limits.

But, far from being legitimated by a "right to reproduce," the emergence of techniques of assisted reproduction and genetic engineering should compel us to reconsider the meaning and limits of such a putative right. In truth, a "right to reproduce" has always been a peculiar and problematic notion. Rights generally belong to individuals, but this is a right which (before cloning) no one can exercise alone. Does the right then inhere only in couples? Only in married couples? Is it a (woman's) right to carry or deliver or a right (of one or more parents) to nurture and rear? Is it a right to have your own biological child? Is it a right only to attempt reproduction, or a right also to succeed? Is it a right to acquire the baby of one's choice?

The assertion of a negative "right to reproduce" certainly makes sense when it claims protection against state interference with procreative liberty, say, through a program of compulsory sterilization. But surely it cannot be the basis of a tort claim against nature, to be made good by technology, should free efforts at natural procreation fail. Some insist that the right to reproduce embraces also the right against state interference with the free use of all technological means to obtain a child. Yet such a position cannot be sustained: for

reasons having to do with the means employed, any community may rightfully prohibit surrogate pregnancy, or polygamy, or the sale of babies to infertile couples, without violating anyone's basic human "right to reproduce." When the exercise of a previously innocuous freedom now involves or impinges on troublesome practices that the original freedom never was intended to reach, the general presumption of liberty needs to be reconsidered. . . .

Though I recognize certain continuities between cloning and, say, in vitro fertilization, I believe that cloning differs in essential and important ways. Yet those who disagree should be reminded that the "continuity" argument cuts both ways. Sometimes we establish bad precedents, and discover that they were bad only when we follow their inexorable logic to places we never meant to go. Can the defenders of cloning show us today how, on their principles, we will be able to see producing babies ("perfect babies") entirely in the laboratory or exercising full control over their genotypes (including so-called enhancement) as ethically different, in any essential way, from present forms of assisted reproduction? Or are they willing to admit, despite their attachment to the principle of continuity, that the complete obliteration of "mother" or "father," the complete depersonalization of procreation, the complete manufacture of human beings and the complete genetic control of one generation over the next would be ethically problematic and essentially different from current forms of assisted reproduction? If so, where and how will they draw the line, and why? I draw it at cloning, for all the reasons given.

BAN THE CLONING OF HUMANS

What, then, should we do? We should declare that human cloning is unethical in itself and dangerous in its likely consequences. In so doing, we shall have the backing of the overwhelming majority of our fellow Americans, and of the human race, and (I believe) of most practicing scientists. Next, we should do all that we can to prevent the cloning of human beings. We should do this by means of an international legal ban if possible, and by a unilateral national ban, at a minimum. . . .

Discussion Questions

1. Feeling repugnance does not, in itself, signal that the object of our repugnance is immoral; repugnance can arise from cultural conditioning as well. For example, people once felt deep repugnance at the thought of interracial marriage. Discuss whether Kass provides a convincing argument for his claim that our repugnance at the prospect of human cloning is based on "deep wisdom" rather than cultural constructs.
2. One of Kass's objections to cloning is that there are too many risks of mishaps and deformities. Would cloning be morally acceptable if it were perfected to the point where the chances of mishaps and deformities were significantly less than relying on sexual reproduction? How would Kass answer this question? How would a utilitarian philosopher respond?
3. Are Kass's concerns regarding the autonomy and identity of a clone well founded? Discuss how Ridley might respond to Kass's concerns. Who presents the most compelling argument—Kass or Ridley? Support your answer.
4. Kass argues that whereas using preimplantation to create a healthy child may be morally acceptable, the use of cloning to produce a healthy child never is. Is this distinction justified? Support your answer.

 LORI ANDREWS AND DOROTHY NELKIN

Whose Body Is It Anyway? Disputes over Body Tissue in a Biotechnology Age

Lori Andrews is a professor of law and director of the Institute of Science, Law and Technology at Chicago-Kent College of Law. Dorothy Nelkin is a professor of sociology and a law professor at New York University. In the following selection, Andrews and Nelkin explore the gap between scientific and social views of the body in the increasing commercialization of bodily tissue. In particular, they raise the question of whether individuals have a right to know what use will be made of their bodily tissue for genetic tests and gene patents.

Critical Reading Questions

1. What are some of the historic precedents for the collection and use of bodily tissues by scientists and physicians?
2. What is the biotechnology age? What are some of the ways interest in the use of bodily tissues has changed in the biotechnology age?
3. Define the scientific view and the social view of the body. What is the basis of each view? What are some examples of these views?

Lori Andrews and Dorothy Nelkin, "Whose Body Is it Anyway? Disputes Over Body Tissue in a Biotechnology Age," *Lancet,* Vol. 352, Issue 9095, January 3, 1998, pp. 53–57. Some notes have been omitted.

4. Which view of the body, the scientific or the social, prevails in the biotechnology age?
5. Why is the Human Genome Diversity Project (HGDP) interested in studying the bodily tissue of indigenous people? In what ways does the HGDP's view of the body conflict with those of many indigenous groups?
6. According to Andrews and Nelkin, what rights are at stake in the use of patients' tissues for genetic testing and patents?
7. What are some of the U.S. court decisions regarding the conflict between the use of bodily tissue by scientists and physicians and the rights of the patients?
8. What policies have been proposed for regulating the commercial use of bodily tissue?

The collection and use of human body tissue—from 18th century practices of dissection to 20th century organ transplantation—have evoked concerns about the use of body parts without consent; the psychological, social, and religious impact of breaking down the integrity of the body; and, especially, the potential exploitation of the individuals who are the sources of organs and tissues. Physicians and scientists have been accused of profiteering, insensitivity to the emotions of patients or family members, and secrecy about unseemly practices as they sought out cadavers and body parts.

Recent disputes—over the taking,[1] use,[2] and distribution[3] of body tissue; the genetic testing of previously collected samples;[4,5] and the patentability of human genes[6]—are taking place in an increasingly commercial context. They are often viewed in terms of a narrow practical question: are individuals entitled to know about, and have a say in, the uses that are made of their body tissue? But the proliferation and diversity of disputes over body tissue are symptomatic of a much larger problem—a growing divide between scientific and social views of the body in the commercial context of the biotechnology age. This gap is the focus of our analysis.

THE GROWTH OF INTEREST IN HUMAN TISSUE

Human tissue has always provided clues to health status. But the body in the biotechnology age is speaking in new ways. DNA analysis of waste tissue such as hair, blood, or saliva can reveal intimate and detailed information about a person. Genetic testing of tissue can indicate an individual's future health, information that may open beneficial therapeutic or remedial options, but also the possibility of employment or insurance discrimination.[7] And, according to recent scientific claims, human tissue can reveal information about behavioral traits,[8] race,[9] or sexual preference.[10]

Human tissue has also become a source of raw material for products (such as cell lines and diagnostic tests). The market for skin, blood, placenta, gametes, biopsied tissue, and genetic material is expanding,[11] driven partly by commercial incentives fostered by legal developments in the 1980s. . . . A landmark US Supreme Court case in 1980 granted a patent on a life-form (a bacterium) setting the stage for the patenting of human genes.[12] . . .

As the market for human tissue has increased, so have disputes in which scientific and commercial ideas about the proper uses of tissue confront social and personal understandings about the body. Whereas scientists seek greater access to bodily materials, others defend their cultural values and individual rights. Scientists need to pay greater heed to such social claims, for they reflect legitimate interests and further other important social values and activities. Indeed, courts and other policy-making bodies are struggling to develop systems to accommodate productive use of bodily materials while respecting cultural associations and individual rights. And they are increasingly incorporating social meanings of the body into their decisions.

THE SCIENTIFIC VIEW OF THE BODY

In 1772, Robert Boyle expressed a view of the body that has characterized much of medical practice: "I think the physician is to look upon the patient's body as an engine that is out of order, but yet so constituted that, by his concurrence with . . . the parts of the automaton itself, it may be brought to a better state."[13] This mechanical view of the body as a set of parts that can be manipulated, analyzed, and enhanced has reached the ultimate in genetics in which the very object manipulated, assessed, turned into a product, and enhanced, is the DNA itself. . . .

Expanding commercial interests in the biotechnology age have reinforced this trend, but not without costs. Biologist Ernest Chargaff warns that the growth of human tissue research can be a slippery slope to social disaster, "an Auschwitz in which valuable enzymes, hormones, and so on will be extracted instead of gold teeth."[14] Others see the search for human tissue as a modern-day form of body snatching. The body is clearly more than an abstract object, a project, a resource to be mined.

THE SOCIAL MEANING OF THE BODY

Just as the scientific view of the body serves certain functions for scientists and for society, so personal and social views of the body serve certain functions for individuals and their communities. A person's control over what is done to his or her body, or its parts, is important to the individual's psychological development and well-being. It is also a means to establish identity and convey values to others. But body tissue has social importance beyond the individual.[15] Social conceptions of the body establish community identification, encourage socially responsible behaviors, and set acceptable priorities for group activities. . . .

Because the body is also a means to express personal values, some people want to place limits on the use of their body parts. Some men who donate sperm only want it used by married couples. Some women will serve as a surrogate mother for

women with infertility problems, but not for those who want to avoid pregnancy for career reasons. During the Nazi occupation of the Netherlands, many citizens, as a form of social protest, refused to take part in blood transfusions for Nazi soldiers. Some African-American women, recalling past research abuses, refuse to allow amniotic tissue to be collected for prenatal diagnosis out of concern about the uses that could be made of this tissue.[16] Other people have objected to the use of their tissue in the commercialized setting of biotechnology firms. The decisions people make about the body and its parts convey important messages about identity, values, and interests.

Body tissue also has important social meaning. In some developing world societies, blood, hair, and placenta are important in social rituals, defining community identification and reinforcing the values and rules that govern accepted behavior.[17] But even in contemporary western societies, the treatment of body parts can define community and reinforce social values. People signal their identification with their community by the way they display and manipulate their body. Sensitive questions emerge when genetic analysis of body tissue is used to reveal community identity. Through tissue analysis, a person may (whether that person wishes to or not) be identified according to particular genetic criteria as a member of a certain family, a certain race, a certain culture, or a certain sex. Some patients do not want their tissue used (even without their names attached) for research on race and intelligence, race and crime, or sex and mathematical ability because the findings of the research could label and stigmatize their group. . . .

Control over the use of body tissue is also critical for establishing religious identity and demonstrating religious beliefs. Navajo Indians believe that placenta should be buried, rather than regarded as "waste" that is available for research. Voicing opposition to the patenting of genes, some religious leaders insist that the body be valued as a fulfillment of divine purpose: the body belongs to God.[18] . . .

The norms that guide the disposition of body tissue reflect community ideals; the highest priorities for body use in a social sense are not always the same as those advocated by scientists. Giving blood and body tissue rather than selling it, for example, is a way to encourage altruism and affirm social cohesion by linking donors to strangers and donations to the public good. A dispute over the development of private cord-blood banks and the patenting of the cord-blood stem-cell extraction technique resulted from a conflict between community ideals and the encouragement of commerce. Those who believe that cord-blood should be a public resource, freely available to those in need of therapy, have challenged commercial interests that see patenting and privatization as essential for investment in research.

The wide range of social meanings placed upon the body—in defining community, reinforcing acceptable behavior, and establishing priorities—have converged in disputes surrounding the Human Genome Diversity Project (HGDP). In some cases, the opposition to the Project's collection of blood and tissue for DNA analysis reflects ritual beliefs in the communal importance of body tissue. But the opposition also follows from historically informed resentment of exploitation.

HGDP scientists insist that blood is replenishable, that taking it does no harm. But indigenous groups with little reason to trust western science have other priorities that can be expressed through controlling the use of their bodies: the major threat to their health is not genetic disease, but disorders such as diarrhea.[19] They see the harvesting of genes from people from developing countries as "biocolonialism," providing cures for diseases in the developed world and products affordable only in wealthy countries. They believe that the project might threaten their future. Scientists want to "immortalize" the cell lines of groups that are going to become extinct.[20] But members of indigenous groups fear that preservation of their DNA could eliminate the incentives to improve social conditions that would ensure their survival. They derive little comfort from the reductionist idea that their DNA lives on while their descendants perish. In 1993, the World Council of Indigenous Peoples unanimously voted to "categorically reject and con-

demn the Human Genome Diversity Project as it applies to our rights, lives and dignity."[21]

SCIENTISTS' RESPONSES

The gap between scientific and social perspectives of the body has been exacerbated by the often dismissive or defensive reactions of scientists. . . .

The most powerful arguments made by scientists seeking unimpeded access to human tissue have to do with contributions to scientific and medical progress. They argue that restraints on their ability to gain access to, manipulate, and commercialize tissue will impede the progress of research and deprive society of useful medical benefits. But that argument is wearing thin. The "advances" in genetic diagnosis of late-onset disorders have meant that many currently healthy people live under the sword of Damocles—of knowing they are at enhanced risk for later illnesses, such as breast cancer or Alzheimer's disease. . . .

Moreover, claims about the potential benefits from unrestricted access to patient-tissue have been exaggerated. A federally appointed committee investigating gene therapy found that, even though 567 Americans had undergone gene therapy, in about 100 different experiments, "there is still little or no evidence of therapeutic benefit [of gene therapy] in patients or even animal models." The panel condemned most of the efforts as "pure hype" and expressed concern that in the rush to undertake gene therapy, the development of other easier-to-achieve conventional treatments for the same disease was likely to be ignored.[22]

INTEGRATED CULTURAL MEANING INTO POLICY

The potential contribution of unfettered research to scientific and medical progress has had significant influence on legal and policy decisions. For example, in *Moore v Regents of the University of California,*[23] a patient sued his physician and a biotechnology company for using his biopsied tissue without his consent and transforming it into a patented commercial cell line, and the court sided with the interests of the defendant. Its reasoning was that giving the patient a property right to his tissue would impede progress and "destroy the economic incentive to conduct important medical research."

However, in recent decisions, the federal government, professional societies, institutional review boards, and courts have begun to apply values other than mere scientific progress. Some institutional review boards, for example, have integrated cultural values into the protocols for tissue retrieval and use, giving patients increased rights to control the uses made of their body material. . . .

The personal feelings of individuals about maintaining body integrity are increasingly recognized by the courts. In one case, a man with a strong fear of fire had his leg amputated.[24] 4 weeks later, he inquired about the disposal of the leg. When he learned that it had been incinerated, he suffered psychological "shock." The court did not allow him to sue the hospital for shock because he did not voice his concerns in a timely manner. But the court did indicate that patients have the right to make specific reservations about demands on, or objections to, a hospital's normal procedures for disposal of tissue.

Even in the *Moore* case, the California Supreme Court held that the physician had violated his fiduciary duty by not telling the patient in advance of surgery that the physician had a commercial interest in the tissue: "A physician who treats a patient in whom he also has a research interest has potentially conflicting loyalties."[23] . . .

Cultural norms, too, are beginning to influence the treatment of body tissue. The North American Advisory Group to the HGDP has emphasized the importance of sensitivity to community values in the collection of tissue from indigenous groups. They would require that the current process be handled in a culturally appropriate way, including the need for consent from a representative or the leader of the group or tribe, not only from the individuals being sampled. . . .

Policies governing the use of patients' tissues for genetic testing, product development, and transplantation are currently being debated. The proliferation of disputes suggest that social conceptions of the body serve important purposes for individuals and society. Ignoring them may be hazardous—to the psychological well-being of individuals, to the maintenance of important social values, and to the future of science itself.

NOTES

1. *Mayfield v Dalton,* 901 F.Supp. 300 (1995); US Court of Appeals, 9th Cir. 95-16626.

2. *Moore v Regents of the University of California,* 793 P.2d 479 (Cal. 1990).

3. Mitchell P. European researchers condemn US firm's cord-blood-storage patent. *Lancet* 1997; **349:** 1232.

4. *Norman-Bloodsaw v Lawrence Berkeley Nat'l Lab,* No. C95-03220 (N.D. Cal. Filed Sept 12, 1995).

5. Clayton EW, Steinberg KK, Khoury MJ, et al. Informed Consent for Genetic Research on Stored Tissue Samples. *JAMA* 1995; **274:** 1786–92.

6. Eisenberg RS. "Patenting the Human Genome," 39 *Emory LJ* 721 (1990).

7. Nelkin D, Tancredi L. Dangerous diagnostics, 2nd ed. Chicago: University of Chicago Press, 1995.

8. Kelner K, Benditt J. Genes and Behaviour. *Science* 1994; **264:** 1685–97.

9. Genes in Black and White. *New Scientist* July 8, 1995: 34–37.

10. Hamer D, Copeland P. The science of desire. New York: Simon and Schuster, 1995.

11. Kimbrell A. The human body shop: the engineering and marketing of life. San Francisco: Harper, 1993.

12. *Diamond v Chakabarty,* 447 US 303 (1980).

13. Robert Boyle, Works, vol 5, 1772 p 236. In: Feher M, ed. Fragments for a History of the Human Body 3. New York: Zone Books, 1989.

14. Quoted in Kimbrell A. The Human Body Shop 284. San Francisco: Harper's 1993.

15. Douglas M. Purity and danger. London: Routledge, 1966 (reprinted 1996).

16. Rapp R. Refusing Pre-natal Diagnosis: The Uneven Meanings of Bioscience in a Multicultural World. *Science, Technology and Human Values.* Fall 1997.

17. Turner V. The forest of symbols. Ithaca, New York: Cornell University Press, 1967.

18. Pope John Paul II. "Address to the Pontifical Academy of Sciences." October 8, 1994, quoted in *Family Resource Center News* (Winter 1996).

19. Lappé M. Broken code 80. San Francisco: Sierra Club Books, 1994.

20. Bowcock A, Cavilli-S Forza L. The study of variation in the human genome. *Genomics* 1991; **11:** 191–98.

21. World Council of Indigenous People's "Resolution on the HGDP." Native Net Archive Page, <http://broc09.uthscsa.edu/natnet/archive/nl/hgdp.html>.

22. "Report and Recommendations of the Panel to Assess the NIH Investment and Research on Gene Therapy" 9, 32 (Stuart H Orkin and Arno G Motulsky, co-chairs, Dec 7, 1995).

23. *Moore v Regents of the University of California,* 271 Cal. Rptr. 146, 151 (Cal 1990).

24. *Browning v Norton Children's Hospital,* 504 S.W.2d 713 (Ky. 1974).

Discussion Questions

1. Discuss the social and scientific views of the the human body in light of the concepts of genetic determinism.

2. Discuss the moral implications of the social and scientific views of the body for genetic testing and genetic engineering. Are these the only two ways of viewing the human body, and if not, what are some other ways of viewing the human body? What view of the human body is most compatible with the fundamental moral principles of respect for persons?

3. Gus Stokes has been HIV positive for over twenty years, yet he has developed no symptoms of AIDS. His physician, Dr. Sharma, thinks that Stokes might have a genetic antibody to AIDS. If this gene could be identified, it is possible that it could be reproduced and used in somatic gene therapy, thus possibly saving the lives of millions of people who are HIV positive. When Dr. Sharma asks Stokes for permission to use a sample of his blood for research Stokes refuses. "This body is my own," he says, "and I don't want anyone messing with my genes and giving them to other people."

   Dr. Sharma already has several samples of Stokes's blood left over from routine medical tests. Should she use the samples and not tell Stokes; indeed, does she have a moral obligation to do so? Or does Stokes have a moral right to refuse to let scientists use his tissue for a possible cure for AIDS? What would you do if you were Stokes's physician?

   Discuss how Andrews and Nelkin, as well as a utilitarian and a rights ethicist, might each respond to the above scenario.

4. Discuss how both Ridley and Kass would most likely respond to Andrews's and Nelkin's concerns about the commercialization of the human tissue, including the use of genetic material from indigenous people.

5. Formulate a public policy for the use of patients' tissues for genetic testing, research, and transplantation, as well as for gene patents. Evaluate and revise, when appropriate, your policy in light of the universal moral theories presented in Chapter 1.

CASE STUDIES

1. RICHARD SEED: HUMAN CLONES FOR SALE

Now that scientists can clone sheep, retired physicist Richard Seed thinks cloning humans is an idea whose time has come. Indeed, Seed went so far as to brag to the news media that he was going to produce "half-a-dozen bounding babies, happy, smiling clones" for infertile couples by the year 2000.[24]

Critics claim that not only is Dr. Seed unqualified to clone humans, he is also a dangerous man—a "modern-day Frankenstein."[25] One *New York Times* editorial compared Dr. Seed to Dr. Kevorkian: "The main difference is that Dr. Kevorkian is reckless in bringing about the end of life, whereas Dr. Seed plans to be reckless in the creation of life."[26] Despite the flurry of criticism, Dr. Seed's brother, Randolph Seed, says he believes that his brother could be successful at cloning.

While the turn of the millennium has come and gone, and several countries have outlawed or placed temporary bans on human cloning, Seed remains undeterred. "We've had calls from people who want to be cloned," he tells reporters.[27] Because of the ban on human cloning in the United States, Seed is somewhat reluctant to talk about his plans; but he has hinted that he and his wife Gloria are hoping to have a child who is her clone.

The blessed moment, however, may come too late for the Seeds to claim the honor of being the first parents of a bouncing baby clone. In September 2000, the biotech company Clonaid announced that it was planning to produce the first cloned human. A U.S. couple has offered the company $500,000 for cloning their infant who died from an infection at the age of ten months. The couple was just one of many people clamoring for Clonaid's service. Clonaid has announced that it has cloned human embryos and that, if all goes well, the first cloned baby will be born in December 2001 or in early 2002.[28]

Discussion Questions

1. Is Seed acting immorally? Support your answer. Discuss how Robertson would most likely respond to this question.
2. Is cloning a liberty right? Would we be interfering with the American couple's reproductive rights if we denied them the opportunity to be cloned? Would we be interfering with Dr. Seed's and Clonaid's legitimate interests by forbidding them the opportunity to open a cloning clinic? Discuss how Robertson, Kass, and Ridley might each respond to these questions. Discuss how Ayn Rand might respond.
3. The couple who offered Clonaid money to clone their dead infant have other children and are not infertile. According to a spokesperson at Clonaid: "They just want to give this particular genome another chance."[29] Is this a morally acceptable reason for using cloning? Discuss your answer in light of some of the arguments for and against cloning put forth in this chapter.
4. Joe Palca, the National Public Radio science reporter whose January 7, 1998, interview with Dr. Seed hurled Seed into the limelight, replied to criticisms against his focus on someone who is not a trained geneticist: "If somebody was going to try this, it was going to be someone like Seed, not someone from the mainstream, establishment scientific community."[30]

   According to philosopher Thomas Kuhn in his landmark work *The Structure of Scientific Revolutions* those who challenge the paradigm or worldview of "normal science" must either work in isolation or join a fringe group.[31] Consequently, most new ideas come from people who are new to the field or who are outside the field. Rather than engaging in open and critical analysis of novel ideas, those who control the worldview of a particular science through textbooks and mainstream publications often attempt to suppress new ideas that threaten their worldview and discredit those who go public with such ideas. Is this happening in the case of Richard Seed? Discuss the negative response to Dr. Seed's proposal in light of the three levels of thinking discussed in Chapter 2, "Moral Reasoning."

2. DOLLY AND HER SISTERS: GENETICALLY ENGINEERING ANIMALS WITH HUMAN GENES

In December 1997 the same scientists who brought Dolly into the limelight achieved another breakthrough with the birth of five almost-identical Dorset lambs. The lambs were created by fusing a fetal lamb cell, which was altered by the addition of human genetic material, into the nucleus of a cell from a sheep's ovary. The lambs carry a gene to produce factor IX, a blood-clotting substance used in treating a rare form of hemophilia known as hemophilia B or Christmas disease. People with hemophilia B lack factor IX, a component of blood plasma.

The Edinburgh-based firm PPL Therapeutics, which helped fund the research, announced that it wants to eventually establish herds of sheep carrying human genes to produce proteins and blood products for treating diseases such as hemophilia and osteoporosis.

In 1998 George and Charlie, two Holsteins, were born. They were cloned from genetically engineered fetal cells that included human genes so their milk would contain valuable human proteins such as factor IX.[32]

Two years later five piglets were cloned from an adult female by PPL Therapeutics.[33] PPL plans to use them to develop and clone genetically modified pigs whose organs can be used for transplantation into humans.

Discussion Questions

1. Is it morally acceptable to use other animals as a means only? Given that humans are a lot more like other animals than we previously believed, should moral respect be extended to other animals? Is cloning an affront to the dignity of other animals? Can cloning ever be a benefit to them? Discuss the implications of your answers for the morality of cloning and genetic engineering projects that use nonhuman animals.

2. What does it mean to be human? How many human genes must beings have before they merit the respect accorded to persons? Are the genetically engineered animals mentioned in the above case study part human because they carry human genes? If so, how does that affect the moral respect we should show them?

3. Many countries have banned the use of public money for research involving human cloning. Should this ban also include cloning animals with human genetic material? Should private firms be prohibited from cloning? Support your answers.

4. Discuss how a utilitarian might think about the practice of genetically engineering and cloning lambs to produce factor IX to benefit humans with hemophilia B and genetically engineering pigs so their organs can be used by humans.

---

3. USING CLONES AS ORGAN DONORS

One of the proposed uses of genetic engineering is the creation of human organs for transplantation to use as an alternative to xenoplants. One method of doing this would be to clone a person's own cells and then using the embryonic stem cells to grow the needed tissue or organ.

Jeremy has been waiting for a kidney transplant for two years and despairs of ever getting one.[34] He knows that his odds of getting the kidney he so badly needs from a compatible human donor is probably only about 5 percent. He has heard that physicians have been conducting experiments using xenoplants from pigs with limited success. Jeremy, however, feels uneasy about having a xenoplant, in part because of rumors that those people who have received the transplants have been infected with a potentially deadly virus from the transplanted organs (a rumor vehemently denied by the scientists running the experiments).

His physician tells him of an experiment using embryonic stem cells to grow organs. The process entails creating a clone of Jeremy and then aborting the embryo so that the embryo's stem cells can be harvested. The process, the physician tells him, can be carried out in vitro in a newly created "artificial womb." However, the success rate in getting the stem cells to differentiate into a functional kidney is very low, and it may take many attempts before the procedure is successful, if at all. Jeremy is opposed to abortion but also realizes that this may be his only chance for survival.

Discussion Questions

1. Because Jeremy is opposed to abortion he is faced with a moral dilemma. Role-play a situation in which Jeremy comes to you, an ethics student, for assistance in resolving his moral dilemma. Have one student play the role of Jeremy and the other the role of the ethics student. When you are finished, share your insights with the class.
2. The cloning of embryos for transplantation tissue raises the issue of abortion since the embryo must be aborted before the stem cells can be harvested. Is the abortion of embryos in order to obtain tissue for transplantation morally different than elective abortion for the reason that the woman doesn't want the pregnancy? Support your answer.
3. Discuss whether the use of cloned human embryos for organ transplants and medical research is morally preferable to the current practice of using sentient non-human animals for organ transplants and medical experimentation.
4. Many people consider a brain a prerequisite for personhood. Biologists have already succeeded in creating mouse embryos that fail to develop a head. According to British biologist Jonathan Slack we could do the same with human embryos.[35] These headless and, hence, nonsentient humans, he says, could serve as "organ sacs" for organ transplants as well as subjects for medical research. Discuss the moral issues involved

in genetically engineering and cloning headless humans for organ transplants and medical research.

---

4. PATENT NO. EP-0695351B1: HUMANS AS INVENTIONS

Humans have long set themselves apart from other animals as morally superior, a special creation. However, as philosopher Mary Midgley once put it, "We are not just like other animals; we are animals." In 1999 the University of Edinburgh in Scotland, where Darwin once studied and where Dolly was cloned, inadvertently received a patent for humans created in their lab.[36] While this was not the intention of the office that issued the patent, according to lawyers, the term *animal cell* in the patent covers human cells.

Biopatents are relatively recent and are based mostly on the patent of the transgenic Harvard University Oncomouse. Since then biotech investors have patented cows, pigs, and other mammals, but never humans. The scientists at the University of Edinburgh who received the patent say they only want to patent methods for growing stem cells that might be useful in fighting diseases such as Parkinson's. However, the potential exists for its use in more ambitious human projects. Both President Clinton and Prime Minister Tony Blair of Britain have proposed that data from the Human Genome Project be available to the public. Biotechnologists, in response, argue that it is difficult to justify pouring millions of dollars into research on something like a breast cancer gene, and gene therapy cure, if the results of their research can be used by anyone.

An appeals process for overturning Patent No. EP-0695351B1 is underway, but it could take years. Meanwhile, the European patent office is being more vigilant in reviewing the over 6,000 biopatents it now receives every year.

Discussion Questions

1. Does the belief that we are creators of life reinforce the view that humans and human activities are outside of and above nature rather than part of it? Analyze the following argument: Humans are not a special creation but simply another species of mammal. It is morally acceptable to patent genetically engineered mammals such as mice. Therefore, it is also morally acceptable to genetically engineer and patent human life forms.

2. Religious leaders denounced the 1980 Supreme Court's decision, calling for a moratorium on the patenting of life forms. They argue that genetic engineers are not playing God, nor can they design new organisms from scratch. To grant patents on animal or plant genomes is to usurp the "ownership rights of God." Are human beings "creating" other beings? Do you agree that there should be a moratorium on patenting life forms? Support your answers.

3. In his *Second Treatise of Government*, John Locke argues that ownership is a consequence of authorship. Locke adds that only God can create a living being. Parents do not create their offspring or own them; rather they are "but occasions of their being." Are genetically engineered animals (or humans for that matter) created by scientists, and hence their property; or do the scientists merely serve as "the occasions of their being"? To the extent that they use their own ideas rather than ideas found in nature

to design these genetically engineered animals, are the scientists the owners of these animals? Support your answers.

4. Discuss the moral issues raised by giving patents on human genes. How might Ridley as well as Andrews and Nelkin respond to this question? Relate your answers to the above case as well as to the issues raised on pages 158–159.

---

5. *JURASSIC PARK* REVISITED

One of the proposed uses for cloning is to save endangered species by creating multiple clones of the few remaining members of the species. If this is morally acceptable, and even perhaps morally desirable, is it also morally acceptable to clone species that have already passed into extinction?

In his book *Jurassic Park,* author Michael Creighton envisions a world where extinct dinosaur species are resurrected by cloning DNA from fossils. On March 8, 1998, British newspapers announced that the DNA from 8,000-year-old human remains, which had been found in a cave in 1903, had been genetically linked to Adrian Targett, a living descendent of the cave dweller. In the not too distant future, it may be possible to clone DNA from prehistoric human remains or to use DNA fragments to alter the genes of a human or animal cell. Doing so might provide valuable information about human evolution and about other earlier species of humanoids.

In 1999 a team of scientists recovered a 23,000-year-old woolly mammoth that was embedded in 26 tons of permafrost 477 miles north of the Arctic Circle.[37] Scientists hope that some of the cells are well preserved enough to be used for cloning. While the prospect of bringing back the woolly mammoth is exciting for some, others are concerned that reintroducing extinct species will upset the balance of nature. Some people also fear that cloning programs for preserving endangered species may divert resources from efforts to save the natural habitats of these species.

Discussion Questions

1. If you have read the book or seen the movie *Jurassic Park,* discuss the moral issues it raises about cloning extinct animals such as dinosaurs. Does the knowledge we might acquire from cloning now extinct species justify it? Would it make a difference, morally, if the species under question were human rather than dinosaurs? Support your answers.

2. Analyze the arguments for and against cloning extinct animals. Would it be morally relevant if it could be shown, as some paleontologists believe is the case, that it was prehistoric human hunting that led to the extinction of the woolly mammoth? Support your answer.

3. Is it morally acceptable to use cloning to preserve endangered species? Is there a morally relevant difference between preserving species who are on their way to extinction and resurrecting extinct species?

4. Does Adrian Targett, as a direct descendent of the "cave dweller," have a reproductive right to clone his or her DNA? Support your answer. Discuss how Andrews and Nelkin might respond to this question.

5. Would a clone of an extinct species of humans be harmed by cloning, given that cloning is the only means of resurrecting the species? Does the fact that such a clone would not share the genotype of another living person overcome the objection that cloning violates the right of a person to have his or her own genotype? Support your answers. Discuss how Robertson would respond to these questions.

---

6. MY FATHER, MY SON[38]

Dianne's father was on his deathbed. Her father was an only child, and neither she nor her brother had any children, so Dianne decided she wanted to have her "father" as a baby. She wrote to a British geneticist, asking for information on cloning her father. "My father," she explained, "is a remarkable man and I intend to see that he goes on in the world. . . . I am writing in the hope that you can help me find information on where human cloning may be performed now. There must be organizations that are actively pursuing cloning, and I want to contact them and see if there is a possibility of cloning my father. I have little time left to pursue this venture, and I would greatly appreciate your assistance." Dianne offered to be the host mother for the clone of her father.

Derek, who had an opportunity to read Dianne's correspondence on the Internet, was horrified at her request. "The desire to clone a passed-on loved one," he responded, "seems to me to be grotesque. It brings to mind the Stephen King book *Pet Semetary*. The clone would be a disappointment to the donor's relatives, in that the original personality could never be completely duplicated. Additionally, the clone would not be able to live its own life; it would be forced to live in a predefined, unattainable role."

Discussion Questions

1. Discuss how you might respond to Dianne if she came to you, a geneticist, with her request. Discuss how Robertson might respone to Dianne if she came to him with her request.
2. Discuss Derek's initial reaction to Dianne's request. How might Kass explain Derek's repugnance toward Dianne's request? How would Ridley most likely respond to Dianne's request?
3. Are Derek's misgivings valid? Does the fact that the relative's donors might be disappointed, or the concern that the clone may be deprived of an open future, override Dianne's reproductive autonomy? If so, should this criteria be considered anytime a woman wants to have a child, through sexual procreation, to carry as a replica of herself and the father of the child?
4. Discuss whether the clone of Dianne's father would be harmed by being a clone. Would it make a difference morally if Dianne's father had concurred with her request? Support your answer.

C H A P T E R   5

Euthanasia and Assisted Suicide

In 1975 twenty-one-year-old Karen Ann Quinlan went into a coma after having a few drinks at a party. Apparently, she had eaten very little in the days before the party and had also taken some drugs—perhaps tranquilizers. She was rushed to the hospital, where doctors restored her breathing and connected her to a respirator. Unfortunately, by this time the lack of oxygen had caused permanent brain damage. Her parents, convinced that Karen would not have wanted to be kept alive by artificial means, asked the hospital to disconnect her from the respirator machine. The hospital refused.

The resulting controversy and court battles brought the issue of euthanasia to the public's attention. In 1976 the New Jersey Supreme Court ruled that Karen Quinlan's right to privacy had been violated by the hospital. As a result, she was removed from the machine and moved to a nursing home to die in peace. To most people's surprise, she continued to live with the assistance of feeding tubes. She remained there in a vegetative state until when she died in 1985.

WHAT IS EUTHANASIA?

The term *euthanasia* comes from the Greek *eu* and *thanatos* meaning "good death." In modern usage euthanasia has come to mean painlessly bringing about the death of a person who is suffering from a terminal or incurable disease or condition.

Euthanasia can be classified as active or passive, voluntary or involuntary:

Voluntary euthanasia: A competent, rational person requests or gives informed consent about a particular action or withholding of treatment that will lead to his or her death.

Involuntary euthanasia: Bringing about people's deaths without their consent, although the consent of relatives may be obtained.

Active euthanasia: Taking direct action, such as a lethal injection, to kill a person; also known as "mercy killing."

Passive euthanasia: Allowing patients to die by withholding life support or medical treatment that would prolong their lives.

Combining these two continuums, a particular act of euthanasia can fall into one of four categories: active voluntary, passive voluntary, active involuntary, and passive involuntary.

view is echoed in the modern Protestant prohibition of active euthanasia, although most Protestants agree that it is morally acceptable to withhold or discontinue treatment and life support that is merely prolonging the dying process.

Immanuel Kant regarded suicide and voluntary euthanasia as immoral. Suicide does not fulfill the requirements of the categorical imperative because it involves a contradiction—that of exercising our autonomy to destroy our autonomy by destroying ourselves. People who want to end their lives also show a lack of respect for themselves by viewing their lives as a means only rather than an end. The prohibition of euthanasia, bolstered by the Hippocratic oath, Judeo-Christian teachings, and the philosophies of such greats as Aquinas, Locke, and Kant, remained pretty much unchallenged right up to the end of the nineteenth century.[2]

THE CONTEMPORARY DEBATE OVER EUTHANASIA

It was not until the end of the nineteenth century that the public began questioning the prohibition of euthanasia. Public debate over euthanasia turned to horror when it was learned that in Nazi Germany up to a hundred thousand mentally ill and disabled children and adults "considered incurable according to the best available human judgment" were, to use official language, "granted a mercy death."[3] The memory of this terrible event still haunts Germany, which now prohibits euthanasia.

The public debate over euthanasia resumed after the 1950s with the development of new life-sustaining technologies such as the mechanical respirator, which had first been used in the 1930s. Along with these advances came a growing concern over the increasing control of technology over life and death.

In 1957, troubled by the ethical problems involved in resuscitating unconscious individuals, the International Congress of Anesthesiology sought moral guidance from Pope Pius XII. The Pope responded that physicians should not act without the consent of the family. Physicians also have a moral duty to use ordinary, but not "extraordinary," measures to prolong life. The Pope's position was supported by the Church's "principle of double effect." This principle states that if an act has two effects, one intended (in this case to end pain and suffering) and the other unintended (the death of the patient), terminating treatment may be not only morally permissible but morally advisable if it is the only way to bring about the intended effect. This distinction between passive euthanasia, where death is an unintended effect, and active euthanasia, where the intention is to directly bring about the death of the patient, has remained unchallenged for years.

Public opinion began shifting in favor of legalized euthanasia in the early 1970s. As of 1996, 69 percent of Americans were in favor of permitting doctors to perform euthanasia if a person has an incurable disease.[4] In a recent 2000 survey of 30,000 Americans over the age of 55, 65 percent said that people with a terminal illness have the right to hasten their deaths with the assistance of a physician.[5] Support for legalizing euthanasia and physician-assisted suicide tends to be higher in other Western countries. Three-quarters of both Canadians and Australians support active euthanasia, including assisted suicide, for terminal illnesses.[6] Eighty-two percent of the British would like to see euthanasia, although not necessarily assisted suicide, legalized.[7] Support for euthanasia is especially high in France and in the Netherlands where active, voluntary euthanasia has been legal for several years.[8] In China, although euthanasia is illegal, 80 percent of people surveyed in a 1988 poll stated that they were in favor of euthanasia.[9] Although Japanese views on euthanasia have been influenced by the Buddhist repugnance of killing, the influence of the Shinto religion's glorification of self-willed death for the benefit of the country has led to a more permissive attitude toward euthanasia than in other Buddhist countries.

EUTHANASIA LEGISLATION

The 1976 California Natural Death Act became the first law in the United States to address the issue of decision making on the part of incompetent individuals. The act allowed individuals, under certain circumstances, to make decisions in advance about the kind of treatment they would receive at the end of their lives.

Most people, however, do not have a living will. A 1997 study of 4,804 terminally ill patients found that only 14 percent had either prepared written directives regarding their medical care or appointed a durable power of attorney for health care. Of the directives, only 0.5 percent were as detailed as they should have been. Thus it is not surprising that more than 50 percent of patients end up in a "highly undesirable state"— that is, being kept alive despite their apparent wishes or despite family requests to terminate treatment.[10]

In the 1990 landmark case *Cruzan v. Director, Missouri Department of Health,* the U.S. Supreme Court ruled that every competent individual has a constitutional liberty right to be free of unwanted medical treatment if there is "clear and convincing evidence" of the patient's desire to have the medical treatment withdrawn. The Court left it up to the states to decide for incompetent individuals. The following year Washington State's Initiative 119 "Death with Dignity" proposal failed to pass.

In 1994 the citizens of Oregon approved Ballot Measure 16 (the "Oregon Death with Dignity Act"), which would legalize euthanasia under certain conditions. The Oregon Death with Dignity Act took effect in 1997 following a lengthy appeal process in which the appeal court upheld the Act by a 60 to 40 percent vote.[11] At least thirty-four states have outlawed physician-assisted suicide. In October 1999, in the wake of the controversy generated by the Kevorkian trial, the Oregon Death with Dignity Act was effectively blocked by a bill passed by the United States House of Representatives.

In 1995 the Northern Territory in Australia passed a law that permitted active euthanasia under careful controls. In 1997, however, the Australian Senate struck down the Northern Territory's law.

The debate over euthanasia is perhaps nowhere so intense as in the Netherlands. Although active euthanasia is illegal there, it has been tolerated for many years. In 1993 the Dutch Parliament reaffirmed the illegal status of euthanasia but added that doctors would be immune from prosecution if they met the following four requirements:

- The patient is in intolerable pain.
- The patient has repeatedly asked to die.
- Two doctors agree on the procedure.
- Relatives are consulted.

Many people are critical of this new law on the grounds that it has too much potential for abuse. Germans, who are adamantly opposed to legalized euthanasia, believe that the

CRUZAN V. MISSOURI DEPARTMENT OF HEALTH (1990):
EXCERPTS FROM THE MAJORITY OPINION

Chief Justice Rehnquist delivering the opinion of the court:

Petitioner Nancy Beth Cruzan was rendered incompetent as a result of severe injuries sustained during an automobile accident. Copetitioners Lester and Joyce Cruzan, Nancy's parents and coguardians, sought a court order directing the withdrawal of their daughter's artificial feeding and hydration equipment after it became apparent that she had virtually no chance of recovering her cognitive faculties. The Supreme Court of Missouri held that because there was no clear and convincing evidence of Nancy's desire to have life sustaining treatment withdrawn under such circumstances, her parents lacked authority to effectuate such a request. . . .

At common law, even the touching of one person by another without consent and without legal justification was a battery . . . This notion of bodily integrity has been embodied in the requirement that informed consent is generally required for medical treatment. . . . The logical corollary of the doctrine of informed consent is that the patient generally possesses the right not to consent, that is, to refuse treatment. . . .

Whether or not Missouri's clear and convincing evidence requirement comports with the United States Constitution depends in part on what interests the State may properly seek to protect in this situation. . . . As a general matter, the States—indeed, all civilized nations—demonstrate their commitment to life by treating homicide as a serious crime. Moreover, the majority of States in this country have laws imposing criminal penalties on one who assists another to commit suicide. We do not think a State is required to remain neutral in the fact of an informed and voluntary decision by a physically able adult to starve to death. . . . We believe Missouri may legitimately seek to safeguard the personal element of this choice through the imposition of heightened evidentiary requirements. . . .

In our view, Missouri has permissibly sought to advance these interests through the adoption of a "clear and convincing" standard of proof to govern such proceedings. . . .

In sum, we conclude that a State may apply a clear and convincing evidence standard in proceedings where a guardian seeks to discontinue nutrition and hydration of a person diagnosed to be in a persistent vegetative state. We note that many courts which have adopted some sort of substituted judgment procedure in situations like this, whether they limit consideration of evidence to the prior expressed wishes of the incompetent individual, or whether they allow

more general proof of what the individual decision would have been, require a clear and convincing standard of proof for such evidence. The Supreme Court of Missouri held that in this case the testimony adduced at trial did not amount to clear and convincing proof of the patient's desire to have hydration and nutrition withdrawn.

The judgment of the Supreme Court of Missouri is Affirmed.

Justice O'Connor concurring . . . The liberty interest in refusing medical treatment flows from decisions involving the States' invasions into the body. Because our notions of liberty are inextricably entwined with our idea of physical freedom and self-determination, the Court has often deemed state incursions into the body repugnant. . . .

The State's artificial provision of nutrition and hydration implicates identical concerns. Artificial feeding cannot readily be distinguished from other forms of medical treatment . . . Feeding a patient by means of a nasogastric tube requires a physician to pass a long flexible tube through the patient's nose, throat, and esophagus and into the stomach. Because of the discomfort such a tube causes, many patients need to be restrained forcibly and their hands put into large mittens to prevent them from removing the tube . . . Requiring a competent adult to endure such procedures against her will burdens the patient's liberty, dignity, and freedom to determine the course of her own treatment.

I . . . also emphasize that the Court does not today decide the issue whether a State must also give effect to the decision of a surrogate decisionmaker. In my view, such a duty may well be constitutionally required to protect the patient's liberty interest in refusing medical treatment. Few individuals [however] provide explicit oral and written instructions regarding their interest to refuse medical treatment should they become incompetent. States which decline to consider any evidence to other than such instructions may frequently fail to honor a patient's intent. Such failures might be avoided if the State considered an equally probative source of evidence: the patient's appointment of a proxy to make health care decisions on her behalf. [Cruzan neither left instructions nor appointed a proxy.]

Today's decision does not preclude a future determination that the Constitution requires the State to implement the decisions of a patient's duly appointed surrogate. Nor does it prevent States from developing other approaches for protecting an incompetent individual's liberty interest in refusing medical treatment. . . . Today we decide only that one State's practice does not violate the Constitution; the more challenging task of crafting appropriate procedures for safeguarding incompetents' liberty interests is entrusted to the "laboratory" of the States. . . .

Dutch have already begun the slide down the proverbial slippery slope. Indeed, Daniel Callahan points out that an estimated 30 percent of the cases of euthanasia in the Netherlands are involuntary. Active euthanasia is involved in an estimated 3 to 5 percent of deaths in the Netherlands.[12] In July 2000, because of public opposition, the Dutch government withdrew proposed legislation, known as the "child paragraph," that would give children aged twelve to sixteen "in a situation of hopeless suffering, the right to choose euthanasia, even if their parents opposed this wish."[13]

PHYSICIAN-ASSISTED SUICIDE

Americans are split over whether physician-assisted suicide should be legal.[14] However, public support for physician-assisted suicide is softening. Because of laws against euthanasia, most physicians who help patients die do not go public. One notable exception is Dr. Jack Kevorkian, a retired pathologist and trained physician. In 1990 Kevorkian helped Janet Adkins, an Oregon women who was suffering from the early stages of Alzheimer's disease, to end her life. The vision of Adkins lying dead on the crisp white sheets in the back of Kevorkian's rusting '68 Volkswagen van has become permanently etched onto the American psyche. Since 1990, Kevorkian has presided over the deaths of over one hundred other people, including one that was televised live on national television in September 1998. In April 1999 a Michigan judge sentenced Kevorkian to ten to twenty-five years in prison for second-degree murder.

The publicity surrounding Kevorkian has sparked intense debate over the morality of physician-assisted suicide. Kevorkian's detractors dubbed him "Dr. Death." Surgeon General C. Everett Koop denounced him as "a serial killer who should be put away."[15] Kevorkian's opponents also point out that he is a pathologist, not a psychiatrist. Unlike health-care workers, who know their patients for a long time, Kevorkian hardly knows his; he knew Janet Adkins only two days before participating in her death. Kevorkian, on the other hand, sees himself as a defender of liberty.

On June 26, 1997, the U.S. Supreme Court declared that there is no constitutional right to the aid of a physician in dying and that states had the right to outlaw assisted suicide. Echoing the sentiment of most of the jurists, Justice William Rehnquist expressed concern about the slippery slope and "a possible slide towards voluntary and perhaps involuntary euthanasia."

THE HOSPICE MOVEMENT

The number one fear of most people is not fear of dying or of pain, but of loss of control and dignity.[16] The modern hospice movement was founded in 1967 by British physician Cicely Saunders to help people die confidently and with dignity rather than with fear. The first hospice program in the United States opened in 1974. The philosophy behind hospice is to provide palliative care—pain relief, comfort, and compassion—to the dying. As such, hospice has been active in the development of pain control. Hospice also emphasizes attention to the emotional needs of the patient and the patient's family.

Hospice is opposed to the legalization of euthanasia. "If one of our patients requests euthanasia," Saunders once wrote, "it means we are not doing our job." Saunders continued:

> We are not so poor a society that we cannot afford time and trouble and money to help people live until they die. We owe it to all those for whom we can kill the pain which traps them in fear and bitterness. To do this we do not have to kill them . . . To make voluntary [active] euthanasia lawful would be an irresponsible act, hindering help, pressuring the vulnerable, abrogating our true respect and responsibility to the frail and the old, the disabled and dying.[17]

Hospice believes that providing terminally ill people with better palliative care allows them to live their last days in relative comfort and dignity.[18] Advocates of euthanasia, on the other hand, maintain that while the hospice program is wonderful for many people, there are still cases in which pain cannot be controlled, and euthanasia should be an option.

THE MORAL ISSUES

The Sanctity of Life

Most Western philosophers believe that human life has intrinsic worth and, therefore, ought to be respected and cherished. Legalizing euthanasia will weaken this respect for life. If life has intrinsic worth, our right not to be killed cannot be overridden, even at our own request.

A variation of this theme is the religious argument that our lives are a gift from God and, therefore, we are not free to end them on our own terms. In their role as healers, however, physicians are continuously working to prevent death and suffering. Does this interfere with God's will?

Furthermore, those who do not believe in God, or God's "ownership" of humans, argue that people are not owned by God, or anyone else for that matter. As beings with intrinsic moral worth, we have inalienable rights that cannot be waived by anyone else—including God. One of the most fundamental of these rights is the right of autonomy.

Autonomy and Self-Determination

Autonomy requires two conditions: freedom from outside control and moral agency. According to Margaret Pabst Battin, autonomy is one of the two key principles in the euthanasia debate. Autonomy requires that, in general, physicians respect a competent person's choices in determining his or her medical treatment, including euthanasia. If euthanasia is a positive right, as Battin claims, physicians may have a duty to assist their patients in dying.

Daniel Callahan, on the other hand, argues that autonomy and self-determination have been given too much weight in the euthanasia debate. People do not have a right to do anything they want to do. He also notes that the leap between claiming that people have a right to end their lives based on autonomy and the claim that it is morally acceptable for physicians to assist in this process is not as self-evident as most advocates of active euthanasia would have us believe.

There is also the danger that making euthanasia available will compromise our autonomy. Some people may feel pressured by circumstances, such as lack of medical insurance or family support, into requesting euthanasia. Susan Wolf, in her article at the end of this chapter, argues that, given the traditional view of women as self-sacrificing, not only are women especially vulnerable to these sorts of pressures, but physicians will be more likely to carry out their requests.

Nonmaleficence and the Principle of *Ahimsa*

The principle of nonmaleficence or "do no harm" is one of the strongest moral principles. In the Buddhist prohibition against euthanasia *ahimsa* is the deciding principle. Battin, on the other hand, argues that the principle of nonmaleficence and the duty to relieve pain and suffering may, at times, require euthanasia.

The Principle of Mercy

The principle of mercy is based on the duty of nonmaleficence. It states that we have a duty both (1) not to cause further pain and suffering and (2) to relieve pain and suffering. Most philosophers agree that the first part of this duty justifies refusal of futile and painful treatment, even though withdrawing or withholding such treatment may result in an earlier death for the patient, but philosophers disagree on the practical implications of the second part of this duty. Both Rachels and Battin agree that pain relief is a universal duty of physicians and that this duty may entail a positive obligation to use active euthanasia when it is the only way to end pain and suffering. Callahan, on the other hand, maintains that the appropriate response to suffering is compassionate care, not conceding to a patient's request to be put to death.

Death with Dignity

The expressions "death with dignity" and the "good death" are often heard in euthanasia debates. Advocates of euthanasia argue that respect for the dignity of life entails allowing a person to *die* with dignity as well, rather than spend the last days of life hooked up to machines and wasting away in agony. Some opponents of euthanasia believe that the good death involves courageously accepting the suffering entailed in dying.

Quality of Life: Pain and Suffering

Human life is more that mere biological existence. Battin points out that the ability to be in relationship with family and friends, to have hopes for the future, and to live without constant pain are all basic goods. When isolation, pain, and suffering outweigh any expectation of enjoying the goods of life, the quality of that life becomes a negative value and death may be preferable.

Pain, however, such as that associated with cancer, can be relieved in up to 90 percent of cases. A 1994 study at Stanford University found that more than half of terminally ill patients spend their last days in agony. They blame this, in part, not on the lack of effective pain relievers, but on Western society's opiophobia—fear of drug addiction and abuse.[19]

Canadian bioethicist Peter Singer maintains that improving the quality of end-of-life care is a more important issue than euthanasia. According to Singer, "Euthanasia and

physician-assisted suicide at best address a very small percentage of the dying population; there are still more than 95 percent of people who die who need to be given quality care and the focus must shift to identifying and addressing their needs."[20] Indeed, a recent study found that "Substantive palliative interventions lead some—but not all—patients to change their minds about assisted suicide."[21] To address this issue, as well as the finding that technical difficulties occur in almost a fifth of all cases of physician-assisted suicide, the Dutch government spends about US$3 million dollars to train general physicians as "euthanasia consultants."[22] Part of the role of these consultants will be the improvement of the quality of end-of-life care, including better palliative care for pain management.

On the other hand, why should only physical pain count? There are other types of suffering, such as lifelong disability, loneliness, and depression. Should there be a moral distinction between wanting to die because one is depressed or facing chronic illness, as is the case with many of Dr. Kevorkian's patients, and the pain associated with a terminal illness?

Another quality of life issue is determining the quality of life of incompetent patients, such as people in comas and children with disabilities. Who, if anyone, should decide if their lives are worth living? If we answer that euthanasia should be voluntary only, we have to ask ourselves, as Callahan does, if it is fair that incompetent people be doomed to lives of suffering and hopelessness.

Ordinary Versus Extraordinary Treatment

The AMA, while opposing euthanasia, allows the withdrawal of extraordinary treatment. Ordinary medical treatment includes measures that have a reasonable hope of benefiting the patient, whereas extraordinary treatments are measures that provide no reasonable hope of benefiting the patient. They are frequently excessively expensive, as well. This brings up the sticky question of just when treatment becomes extraordinary. How should we draw the line between prolonging life and prolonging the dying process? Is withholding surgery that could save the life of a child with severe disabilities ordinary or extraordinary treatment? Is using chemotherapy on an ailing eighty-five-year-old with cancer ordinary or extraordinary treatment? Also, what counts as a reasonable hope? Is continuing to keep a patient in a coma on artificial life support, even though there is only slight hope of recovery, ordinary or extraordinary treatment?

The Principle of Double Effect: Letting Die Versus Actively Killing

The traditional distinction between active and passive euthanasia rests on intention. According to this argument, in active euthanasia the intention is to cause the death of another person. In the latter case, there is a "double effect": the death of the person is an unintended consequence of the intended effect—the elimination of pain and suffering.

Some philosophers claim that this distinction is hypocritical. Physicians are morally responsible for both intended and foreseen consequences. The double-effect argument is simply a cover for engaging in slow euthanasia. Rachels argues that knowing that high doses of painkillers may hasten a person's death is an action as much as is administering a lethal injection on request. Both involve decision and action on the part of the physician. Indeed, there may be cases in which active euthanasia is the more humane alternative.

The Physician's Role as Healer

Some opponents of physician-assisted suicide and euthanasia argue that expecting physicians to be agents of death runs contrary to their training as healers and comforters and may damage trust in the patient/physician relationship. This argument does not rule out euthanasia. The act of euthanasia could instead be left to others, perhaps people like Dr. Kevorkian or "death technicians," who specialize in it.

Patient Competence

Two of the problems in deciding who should be a candidate for euthanasia are (1) determining if a patient is rational and competent to make such a decision and (2) whether it is a sincere request for death or simply a cry for help. What, in other words, are the patient's real intentions? Furthermore, if the patient is incompetent, how do we determine what is in the patient's best interests? Some people argue that physicians or close family members can usually be counted on to respect a patient's self-determination, whereas others, such as Wolf, question the insidious effect of cultural biases on these decisions. How are we to know that a particular euthanasia decision is based on the doctor's judgment that the request is justified because the patient's life is no longer worth living?

To some the term *assisted suicide* is an oxymoron. They claim that the request, especially in cases in which the patient is able to carry out the suicide without assistance, is often a cloaked request for help. Suicide prevention workers point out that people who are suicidal often feel a sense of depression, hopelessness, and despair. Rather than seeking to end their lives, the request to die is really an expression of that despair and, as such, is a cry for help.

Justice and the Principle of Equality

Some opponents of euthanasia maintain that it is always unjust because it involves the death of an innocent person. Battin, on the other hand, maintains that the duty of justice may require euthanasia, especially in cases in which keeping a person alive is tremendously expensive.

Wolf expresses concern that euthanasia may be unjust because it unfairly targets certain groups. In a society that holds up self-sacrifice as a virtue for women, women are especially vulnerable to gender-biased pressures to put the needs and desires of others before their own. The physician-assisted death of Judith Curren, who was later alleged to have been abused by her husband, is just one case in point.

Another concern is our society's negative view of people who are disabled and the tendency to devalue their lives. While it may be countered that disabled people fall outside the scope of euthanasia because they are not terminally ill, the facts show that infants and children with disabilities, such as Baby Doe, are also vulnerable to euthanasia. A study of infant deaths at the special-care unit of the Yale–New Haven Hospital between 1970 and 1972 revealed that of 299 deaths, 14 percent were associated with the withholding or withdrawal of treatment in cases of severe congenital disorders.[23]

Burdens to Society

A study published in January 2000 found that a majority of Dutch and American doctors favor physician-assisted suicide for a patient in excruciating pain.[24] However, they differ in their justifications of euthanasia. Dutch doctors are more likely to support physician-assisted suicide in cases in which a patient finds life meaningless; American physicians are more likely to consider a patient's fear of being a burden as a justification for euthanasia.

Both Hardwig and Battin argue that when costly medical resources are needed to sustain a human life, the principle of justice may warrant involuntary, active euthanasia. There are about twenty-five thousand terminally ill Americans annually. Treatment in an intensive care unit can cost $1,000 a day or more.[25] There are also an estimated ten thousand people in the United States in vegetative comas. The annual cost of caring for these people ranges from $1.2 million to $1.2 billion.[26] In contrast, it costs only a few dollars to deliver a lethal injection.

On the other hand, there are cases in which a patient comes out of a coma or makes a miraculous recovery despite a prognosis of imminent death or irreversible brain damage. Jackie Cole, to give one example, suffered a stroke and massive bleeding in her brain. The doctors predicted that without artificial life support she would be dead within a few days. Shortly before slipping into a coma, she had made it clear that she did not want to be kept alive by artificial means. The court, however, refused her husband's petition to have life support withdrawn. Six days later Cole awoke from the coma and slowly began to recover from her stroke.[27] What is a reasonable cost of sustaining hope? Do cases like Jackie Cole's justify spending millions of dollars keeping comatose people alive in hopes that a few of them will come out of it?

The ailing elderly population also puts a strain on medical and social resources. Are these resources well spent? Do the elderly have what Hardwig calls "a duty to die"?

A Duty to Die

While rejecting what he calls a "crass" utilitarian calculus, Hardwig nevertheless argues that burden to family and society creates a duty to die. According to him, there comes a time in life when we have a duty to let go. In a nonegalitarian society, however, where the lives of certain groups are valued less than others, a duty to die might come into conflict with the principle of justice by unfairly targeting certain people, such as women and the disabled.

Slippery Slope Argument

Even if it can be shown that euthanasia, in principle, can be morally justified, there may still be problems when it comes to legalizing it, because of the difficulty of drawing the line between who should and who should not be eligible. If there is no definite line to stop abuses, it will be easy to slip down the slope toward greater and greater acceptance of euthanasia. For example, how do we know if a person's request for euthanasia is genuine and not influenced by outside pressures and cultural biases? Battin argues that evidence that this will happen is weak at best, but a report from the Netherlands states that Dutch physicians "sometimes act without patient requests in performing euthanasia and that there was a sense among some patients that they had a duty to die."[28] The right to euthanasia, in other words, can easily slip into a duty to die. In a society in which euthanasia is an option, it will also be easy to redefine chronic medical conditions as terminal illnesses to justify the euthanasia of people who have Alzheimer's or of children with genetic disorders, a practice that has already begun to some extent.[29]

CONCLUSION

The moral issues surrounding euthanasia are complex. Many of the relevant principles come into conflict with one another and need to be carefully weighed. A further complication is the uncertainty of medical prognoses and the presence of subjective factors in assessing patients' requests for euthanasia. Nevertheless, this does not mean that the issue cannot be resolved.

In addition, public policies on euthanasia need to be drafted within the wider social context. As with abortion, the judgment that euthanasia, or at least certain types of it, is morally acceptable does not imply that the law should permit it.

 JAMES RACHELS

Active and Passive Euthanasia

James Rachels is a professor of philosophy at the University of Alabama. In his celebrated article "Active and Passive Euthanasia," which first appeared in the *New England Journal of Medicine* in 1975, Rachels argues that the traditional distinction between active and passive euthanasia cannot be morally justified. He also points out that there are cases in which active euthanasia may be morally preferable to passive euthanasia, especially when passive euthanasia would result in unnecessary suffering and slow and painful, rather than quick and painless, death for terminally ill people.

Critical Reading Questions

1. What is the AMA's position on euthanasia?
2. What is the distinction between active and passive euthanasia? In Rachels's view is this distinction morally relevant?
3. Why is passive euthanasia worse in some cases, according to Rachels, than active euthanasia? What cases does he use to illustrate this?
4. What does Rachels think of the practice of allowing newborns with Down's syndrome to die?
5. What point is Rachels illustrating with the analogy of Smith and Jones and the death of their six-year-old cousin?
6. How important, in Rachels's view, is the role of intention in determining if euthanasia is morally justified in a particular case?
7. According to Rachels, what is the crucial issue in euthanasia?
8. Why does Rachels claim that the AMA position as well as the current laws on euthanasia are inconsistent?

"Active and Passive Euthanasia," *New England Journal of Medicine* (January 9, 1975): 78–81.

The distinction between active and passive euthanasia is thought to be crucial for medical ethics. The idea is that it is permissible, at least in some cases, to withhold treatment and allow a patient to die, but it is never permissible to take any direct action designed to kill the patient. This doctrine seems to be accepted by most doctors, and it is endorsed in a statement adopted by the House of Delegates of the American Medical Association on December 4, 1973:

> The intentional termination of the life of one human being by another—mercy killing—is contrary to that for which the medical profession stands and is contrary to the policy of the American Medical Association.
>
> The cessation of the employment of extraordinary means to prolong the life of the body when there is irrefutable evidence that biological death is imminent is the decision of the patient and/or his immediate family. The advice and judgement of the physician should be freely available to the patient and/or his immediate family.

However, a strong case can be made against this doctrine. In what follows I will set out some of the relevant arguments, and urge doctors to reconsider their views on this matter.

To begin with a familiar type of situation, a patient who is dying of incurable cancer of the throat is in terrible pain, which can no longer be satisfactorily alleviated. He is certain to die within a few days, even if present treatment is continued, but he does not want to go on living for those days since the pain is unbearable. So he asks the doctor for an end to it, and his family joins in the request.

Suppose the doctor agrees to withhold treatment, as the conventional doctrine says he may. The justification for his doing so is that the patient is in terrible agony, and since he is going to die anyway, it would be wrong to prolong his suffering needlessly. But now notice this. If one simply withholds treatment, it may take the patient longer to die, and so he may suffer more than he would if more direct action were taken and a lethal injection given. This fact provides strong reason for thinking that, once the initial decision not to prolong his agony has been made, active euthanasia is actually preferable to passive euthanasia, rather than the reverse. To say otherwise is to endorse the option that leads to more suffering rather than less, and is contrary to the humanitarian impulse that prompts the decision not to prolong his life in the first place.

Part of my point is that the process of being "allowed to die" can be relatively slow and painful, whereas being given a lethal injection is relatively quick and painless. Let me give a different sort of example. In the United Sates about one in 600 babies is born with Down's syndrome. Most of these babies are otherwise healthy—that is, with only the usual pediatric care, they will proceed to an otherwise normal infancy. Some, however, are born with congenital defects such as intestinal obstructions that require operations if they are to live. Sometimes, the parents and the doctor will decide not to operate, and let the infant die. Anthony Shaw describes what happens then:

> . . . When surgery is denied [the doctor] must try to keep the infant from suffering while natural forces sap the baby's life away. As a surgeon whose natural inclination is to use the scalpel to fight off death, standing by and watching a salvageable baby die is the most emotionally exhausting experience I know. It is easy at a conference, in a theoretical discussion, to decide that such infants should be allowed to die. It is altogether different to stand by in the nursery and watch as the dehydration and infection wither a tiny being over hours and days. This is a terrible ordeal for me and the hospital staff—much more so than for the parents who never set foot in the nursery.*

I can understand why some people are opposed to all euthanasia, and insist that such infants must be allowed to live. I think I can also understand why other people favor destroying these babies quickly and painlessly. But why should anyone favor letting "dehydration and infection wither a tiny being over

---

* Shaw A: "Doctor, Do We Have a Choice?" *The New York Times Magazine,* January 30, 1972, p. 54.

hours and days?" The doctrine that says that a baby may be allowed to dehydrate and wither, but may not be given an injection that would end its life without suffering, seems so patently cruel as to require no further refutation. The strong language is not intended to offend, but only to put the point in the clearest possible way.

My second argument is that the conventional doctrine leads to decisions concerning life and death made on irrelevant grounds.

Consider again the case of the infants with Down's syndrome who need operations for congenital defects unrelated to the syndrome to live. Sometimes, there is no operation, and the baby dies, but when there is no such defect, the baby lives on. Now, an operation such as that to remove an intestinal obstruction is not prohibitively difficult. The reason why such operations are not performed in these cases is, clearly, that the child has Down's syndrome and the parents and doctor judge that because of that fact it is better for the child to die.

But notice that this situation is absurd, no matter what view one takes of the lives and potentials of such babies. If the life of such an infant is worth preserving, what does it matter if it needs a simple operation? Or, if one thinks it better that such a baby should not live on, what difference does it make that it happens to have an unobstructed intestinal tract? In either case, the matter of life and death is being decided on irrelevant grounds. It is the Down's syndrome, and not the intestines, that is the issue. The matter should be decided, if at all, on that basis, and not be allowed to depend on the essentially irrelevant question of whether the intestinal tract is blocked.

What makes this situation possible, of course, is the idea that when there is an intestinal blockage, one can "let the baby die," but when there is no such defect there is nothing that can be done, for one must not "kill" it. The fact that this idea leads to such results as deciding life or death on irrelevant grounds is another good reason why the doctrine should be rejected.

One reason why so many people think that there is an important moral difference between active and passive euthanasia is that they think killing someone is morally worse than letting someone die.

But is it? Is killing, in itself, worse than letting die? To investigate this issue, two cases may be considered that are exactly alike except that one involves killing whereas the other involves letting someone die. Then, it can be asked whether this difference makes any difference to the moral assessments. It is important that the cases be exactly alike, except for this one difference, since otherwise one cannot be confident that it is this difference and not some other that accounts for any variation in the assessment of the two cases. So, let us consider this pair of cases:

In the first, Smith stands to gain a large inheritance if anything should happen to his six-year-old cousin. One evening while the child is taking his bath, Smith sneaks into the bathroom and drowns the child, and then arranges things so that it will look like an accident.

In the second, Jones also stands to gain if anything should happen to his six-year-old cousin. Like Smith, Jones sneaks in planning to drown the child in his bath. However, just as he enters the bathroom Jones sees the child slip and hit his head, and fall face down in the water. Jones is delighted; he stands by, ready to push the child's head back under if it is necessary, but it is not necessary. With only a little thrashing about, the child drowns all by himself, "accidentally," as Jones watches and does nothing.

Now Smith killed the child, whereas Jones "merely" let the child die. That is the only difference between them. Did either man behave better, from a moral point of view? If the difference between killing and letting die were in itself a morally important matter, one should say that Jones's behavior was less reprehensible than Smith's. But does one really want to say that? I think not. In the first place, both men acted from the same motive, personal gain, and both had exactly the same end in view when they acted. It may be inferred from Smith's conduct that he is a bad man, although that judgment may be withdrawn or modified if certain further facts are learned about him—for example, that he is mentally deranged. But would not the very same thing be inferred about Jones from his conduct? And would not the same further considerations also be relevant to any modification of this judgment? Moreover, suppose Jones pleaded, in his own defense, "After all, I didn't do anything except just stand there and watch the child drown. I didn't kill him; I only let him die." Again, if letting die were in itself less bad than killing, this defense should have at least some weight. But it does not. Such a "defense" can only be regarded as a grotesque perversion of moral reasoning. Morally speaking, it is no defense at all.

Now, it may be pointed out, quite properly, that the cases of euthanasia with which doctors are concerned are not like this at all. They do not involve personal gain or the destruction of normal healthy children. Doctors are concerned only with cases in which the patient's life is of no further use to him, or in which the patient's life has become or will soon become a terrible burden. However, the point is the same in these cases: the bare difference between killing and letting die does not, in itself, make a moral difference. If a doctor lets a patient die, for humane reasons, he is in the same moral position as if he had given the patient a lethal injection for humane reasons. If his decision was wrong—if, for example, the patient's illness was in fact curable—the decision would be equally regrettable no matter which method was used to carry it out. And if the doctor's decision was the right one, the method used is not itself important.

The AMA policy statement isolates the crucial issue very well; the crucial issue is "the intentional termination of the life of one human being by another." But after identifying this issue, and forbidding "mercy killing," the statement goes on to deny that the cessation of treatment is the intentional termination of a life. This is where the mistake comes in, for what is the cessation of treatment, in these circumstances, if it is not "the intentional termination of the life of one human being by another?" Of course it is exactly that, and if it were not, there would be no point to it.

Many people will find this judgment hard to accept. One reason, I think, is that it is very easy to conflate the question of whether killing is, in itself, worse than letting die, with the very different question of whether most actual cases of killing are more reprehensible than most actual cases of letting die. Most actual cases of killing are clearly ter-

rible (think, for example, of all the murders reported in the newspapers), and one hears of such cases every day. On the other hand, one hardly ever hears of a case of letting die, except for the actions of doctors who are motivated by humanitarian reasons. So one learns to think of killing in a much worse light than of letting die. But this does not mean that there is something about killing that makes it in itself worse than letting die, for it is not the bare difference between killing and letting die that makes the difference in these cases. Rather, the other factors—the murderer's motive of personal gain, for example, contrasted with the doctor's humanitarian motivation—account for different reactions to the different cases.

I have argued that killing is not in itself any worse than letting die; if my contention is right, it follows that active euthanasia is not any worse than passive euthanasia. What arguments can be given on the other side? The most common, I believe, is the following:

> The important difference between active and passive euthanasia is that, in passive euthanasia, the doctor does not do anything to bring about the patient's death. The doctor does nothing, and the patient dies of whatever ills already afflict him. In active euthanasia, however, the doctor does something to bring about the patient's death: he kills him. The doctor who gives the patient with cancer a lethal injection has himself caused the patient's death; whereas if he merely ceases treatment, the cancer is the cause of death.

A number of points need to be made here. The first is that it is not exactly correct to say that in passive euthanasia the doctor does nothing, for he does do one thing that is very important: he lets the patient die. "Letting someone die" is certainly different, in some respects, from other types of action—mainly in that it is a kind of action that one may perform by way of not performing certain other actions. For example, one may let a patient die by way of not giving medication, just as one may insult someone by way of not shaking his hand. But for any purpose of moral assessment, it is a type of action nonetheless. The decision to let a patient die is subject to moral appraisal in the same way that a decision to kill him would be subject to moral appraisal: it may be assessed as wise or unwise, compassionate or sadistic, right or wrong. If a doctor deliberately let a patient die who was suffering from a routinely curable illness, the doctor would certainly be to blame for what he had done, just as he would be to blame if he had needlessly killed the patient. Charges against him would then be appropriate. If so, it would be no defense at all for him to insist that he didn't "do anything." He would have done something very serious indeed, for he let his patient die.

Fixing the cause of death may be very important from a legal point of view, for it may determine whether criminal charges are brought against the doctor. But I do not think that this notion can be used to show a moral difference between active and passive euthanasia. The reason why it is considered bad to be the cause of someone's death is that death is regarded as a great evil—and so it is. However, if it has been decided that euthanasia—even passive euthanasia—is desirable in a given case, it has also been decided that in this instance death is no greater an evil than the patient's continued existence. And if this is true, the usual reason for not wanting to be the cause of someone's death simply does not apply.

Finally, doctors may think that all of this is only of academic interest—the sort of thing that philosophers may worry about but that has no practical bearing on their own work. After all, doctors must be concerned about the legal consequences of what they do, and active euthanasia is clearly forbidden by the law. But even so, doctors should also be concerned with the fact that the law is forcing upon them a moral doctrine that may well be indefensible, and has a considerable effect on their practices. Of course, most doctors are not now in the position of being coerced in this matter, for they do not regard themselves as merely going along with what the law requires. Rather, in statements such as the AMA policy statement that I have quoted, they are endorsing this doctrine as a central point of medical ethics. In that statement, active euthanasia is condemned not merely as illegal but as "contrary to that for which the medical profession stands," whereas passive euthanasia is approved. However, the preceding considerations suggest that there is really no moral difference between the two, considered in themselves (there may be important moral differences in some cases in their *consequences*, but, as I pointed out, these differences may make active euthanasia, and not passive euthanasia, the morally preferable option). So, whereas doctors may have to discriminate between active and passive euthanasia to satisfy the law, they should not do any more than that. In particular, they should not give the distinction any added authority and weight by writing it into official statements of medical ethics.

Discussion Questions

1. Do you agree with Rachels that withholding treatment or assistance is the moral equivalent of intentional termination of life? Discuss whether withholding treatment, as in the case of an infant with Down's syndrome, is the same as causing the patient's death.

2. What would Rachels think of the hospice policy of using large doses of morphine to alleviate pain, knowing that it might shorten a patient's life? Is this practice an example of euthanasia? Support your answers.

3. Are we are morally responsible for acts of omission as we are for acts of commission? For example, we can save the lives of dying children in Third World countries through our donations of money and medical supplies. Are we responsible for the deaths of these children because we withhold assistance that we know could have saved their lives? Is the fact that we do not desire their deaths morally relevant, given that the outcome is the same in both cases? Support your answers.

MARGARET PABST BATTIN

The Case for Euthanasia

Margaret Pabst Battin is a professor of philosophy and adjunct professor of internal medicine, Division of Medical Ethics, at the University of Utah. She is also author of the book *The Least Worst Death* (1994). Battin argues that the moral values of mercy, justice, and autonomy support the legalization of euthanasia. The principle of mercy may even impose a positive duty on the physician, in some cases, to assist patients to end their lives.

Critical Reading Questions

1. Why is euthanasia "one of the most acute and uncomfortable problems in medical ethics"?
2. What is the principle of mercy? What two duties does this principle establish for physicians and caregivers? What common medical practices, in Battin's view, go against this principle?
3. According to Battin, does the principle of mercy justify both passive and active euthanasia? What examples does Battin use to illustrate this?
4. What is Battin's response to the argument that euthanasia is no longer necessary because of advances in pain control and palliative care?
5. What is Battin's response to the argument that life itself is a benefit and ought to be preserved? How should we determine when life is no longer a benefit to someone?
6. What is the principle of autonomy, and why is it fundamental to the euthanasia debate? How, according to Battin, is the principle of autonomy conceptually tied to the principle of mercy in the euthanasia debate?
7. What objections to the principle of autonomy does Battin consider? How does she respond to these objections?
8. What is "limited paternalism"? When is it responsible for physicians to deny patient requests for euthanasia? When is it irresponsible?
9. What is the basic premise of "extended paternalism"? Does Battin accept or reject this premise?
10. According to Battin, does patient autonomy create a moral obligation for physicians to perform euthanasia? What examples does Battin use to support her position?
11. How does the principle of justice, according to Battin, support euthanasia?
12. What is Battin's response to those who argue that legalizing euthanasia will take us down the slippery slope to a Nazi-type scenario?
13. What is Battin's position on physician-assisted suicide?

"The Case for Euthanasia," from *Health Care Ethics*, ed. by D. VanDeVeer and Tom Regan (Philadelphia, Penn.: Temple University Press, 1987), 58–95. Some notes have been omitted.

Because it arouses questions about the morality of killing, the effectiveness of consent, the duties of physicians, and equity in the distribution of resources, the problem of euthanasia is one of the most acute and uncomfortable contemporary problems in medical ethics. It is not a new problem; euthanasia has been discussed—and practiced—in both Eastern and Western cultures from the earliest historical times to the present. But because of medicine's new technological capacities to extend life, the problem is much more pressing than it has been in the past, and both the discussion and practice of euthanasia are more widespread. Despite this, much of contemporary Western culture remains strongly opposed to euthanasia: doctors ought not kill people, its public voices maintain, and ought not let them die if it is possible to save life.

I believe that this opposition to euthanasia is in serious moral error—on grounds of mercy, autonomy, and justice. I shall argue for the rightness of granting a person a humane, merciful death, if he or she wants it, even when this can be achieved only by a direct and deliberate killing. . . .

THE CASE FOR EUTHANASIA, PART I: MERCY

The case for euthanasia rests on three fundamental moral principles: mercy, autonomy, and justice.

The principle of mercy asserts that *where possible, one ought to relieve the pain or suffering of another person, when it does not contravene that person's wishes, where one can do so without undue costs to oneself, where one will not violate other moral obligations, where the pain or suffering itself is not necessary for the sufferer's attainment of some overriding good, and where the pain or suffering can be relieved without precluding the sufferer's attainment of some overriding good.* This principle might best be called the principle of medical mercy, to distinguish it from principles concerning mercy in judicial contexts. . . . Contexts that require mercy sometimes require euthanasia as a way of granting mercy—both by direct killing and by letting die. . . .

"Relief of pain is the least disputed and most universal of the moral obligations of the physician," writes one doctor. "Few things a doctor does are

more important than relieving pain," says another.[1] These are not simply assertions that the physician ought "do no harm," as the Hippocratic oath is traditionally interpreted, but assertions of positive obligation. . . .

This principle of mercy establishes two component duties:

1. the duty not to cause further pain or suffering; and
2. the duty to act to end pain or suffering already occurring.

Under the first of these, for a physician or other caregiver to extend mercy to a suffering patient may mean to refrain from procedures that cause further suffering—provided, of course, that the treatment offers the patient no overriding benefits. So, for instance, the physician must refrain from ordering painful tests, therapies, or surgical procedures when they cannot alleviate suffering or contribute to a patient's improvement or cure. . . .

Of course, whether a painful test or therapy will actually contribute to some overriding good for the patient is not always clear. Nevertheless, the principle of mercy directs that where such procedures can reasonably be expected to impose suffering on the patient without overriding benefits for him or her, they ought not be done. . . .

In such cases, the principle of mercy demands that the "treatments" no longer be imposed, and that the patient be allowed to die.

But the principle of mercy may also demand "letting die" in a still stronger sense. Under its second component, the principle asserts a duty to act to end suffering that is already occurring. Medicine already honors this duty through its various techniques of pain management. . . . But there are some difficult cases in which pain or suffering is severe but cannot be effectively controlled, at least as long as the patient remains sentient at all. Classical examples include tumors of the throat (where agonizing discomfort is not just a matter of pain but of inability to swallow, "air hunger," or acute shortness of breath), tumors of the brain or bone, and so on. Severe nausea, vomiting, and exhaustion may increase the patient's misery. In these cases, continuing life—or at least continuing consciousness—may mean continuing pain. Consequently, mercy's demand for euthanasia takes hold here: mercy demands that the pain, even if with it the life, be brought to an end.

Ending the pain, though with it the life, may be accomplished through what is usually called "passive euthanasia," withholding or withdrawing treatment that could prolong life. In the most indirect of these cases, the patient is simply not given treatment that might extend his or her life—say, radiation therapy in advanced cancer. . .

But the second component of the principle of mercy may also demand the easing of pain by means more direct than mere allowing to die; it may require *killing*. This is usually called "active euthanasia," and despite borderline cases (for instance, the ancient Greek practice of infanticide by exposure), it can in general be conceptually distinguished from passive euthanasia. In passive euthanasia, treatment is withheld that could support failing bodily functions, either in warding off external threats or in performing its own processes; active euthanasia, in contrast, involves the direct interruption of ongoing bodily processes that otherwise would have been adequate to sustain life. However, although it may be possible to draw a conceptual distinction between passive and active euthanasia, this provides no warrant for the ubiquitous view that killing is morally worse than letting die. Nor does it support the view that withdrawing treatment is worse than withholding it. If the patient's condition is so tragic that continuing life brings only pain, and there is no other way to relieve the pain than by death, then the more merciful act is not one that merely removes support for bodily processes and waits for eventual death to ensue; rather, it is one that brings the pain—and the patient's life—to an end *now*. . . .

But, it may be objected, the cases we have mentioned to illustrate intolerable pain are classical ones; such cases are controllable now. Pain is a thing of the medical past, and euthanasia is no longer necessary, though it once may have been, to relieve pain. . . . Particularly impressive are the huge advances under the hospice program in the amelioration of both the physical and emotional pain of terminal illness, and our culturewide fears of pain in terminal cancer are no longer justified: cancer pain, when it occurs, can now be controlled in virtually all cases. We can now end the pain without also ending the life.

This is a powerful objection, and one very frequently heard in medical circles. Nevertheless, it does not succeed. It is flatly incorrect to say that all pain, including pain in terminal illness, is or can be controlled. Some people still die in unspeakable agony. With superlative care, many kinds of pain can indeed be reduced in many patients, and adequate control of pain in terminal illness is often quite easy to achieve. Nevertheless, complete, universal, fully reliable pain control is a myth. Pain is not yet a "thing of the past," nor are many associated kinds of physical distress. . . . Finally, there are cases in which pain control is theoretically possible but for various extraneous reasons does not occur. Some deaths take place in remote locations where there are no pain-relieving resources. Some patients are unable to communicate the nature or extent of their pain. And some institutions and institutional personnel who have the capacity to control pain do not do so, whether from inattention, malevolence, fears of addiction, or divergent priorities in resources.

In all these cases, of course, the patient can be sedated into unconsciousness; this does indeed end the pain. But in respect of the patient's experience, this is tantamount to causing death: the patient has no further conscious experience and thus can achieve no goods, experience no significant communication, satisfy no goals. Furthermore, adequate sedation, by depressing respiratory function, may hasten death. . . .

The principle of mercy holds that suffering ought to be relieved—unless, among other provisos, the suffering itself will give rise to some overriding benefit or unless the attainment of some benefit would be precluded by relieving the pain. But it might be argued that life itself is a benefit, always an overriding one. Certainly life is usually a benefit, one that we prize. But unless we accept certain metaphysical assumptions, such as "life is a gift from God," we must recognize that life is a benefit because of the experiences and interests associated with it. . . . Philippa Foot treats this as a conceptual point: "Ordinary human lives, even very hard lives, contain a minimum of basic goods, but when these are absent the idea of life is no longer linked to that of good."[2]

Such basic goods, she explains, include not being forced to work far beyond one's capacity; having the support of a family or community; being able to more or less satisfy one's hunger; having hopes for the future; and being able to lie down to rest at night. When these goods are missing, she asserts, the connection between *life* and *good* is broken, and we cannot count it as a benefit to the person whose life it is that his life is preserved.

These basic goods may all be severely compromised or entirely absent in the severely ill or dying patient. . . . Yet even for someone lacking all of what Foot considers to be basic goods, the experiences associated with life may not be unrelievedly negative. We must be very cautious in asserting of someone, even someone in the most abysmal-seeming conditions of the severely ill or dying, that life is no longer a benefit, since the way in which particular experiences, interests, and "basic goods" are valued may vary widely from one person to the next. . . .

It is true that contemporary pain management techniques do make possible the control of pain to a considerable degree. But unless pain and discomforting symptoms are eliminated altogether without loss of function, the underlying problem for the principle of mercy remains: how does *this* patient value life, how does he or she weigh death against pain? We are accustomed to assume that only patients suffering extreme, irremediable pain could be candidates for euthanasia at all and do not consider whether some patients might choose death in preference to comparatively moderate chronic pain, even when the condition is not a terminal one. Of course, a patient's perceptions of pain are extremely subject to stress, anxiety, fear, exhaustion, and other factors, but even though these perceptions may vary, the underlying weighing still demands respect. This is not just a matter of differing sensitivities to pain, but of differing values as well: for some patients, severe pain may be accepted with resignation or even pious joy, whereas for others mild or moderate discomfort is simply not worth enduring. . . .

If the sufferer is the best judge of the relative values of that suffering and other benefits to himself, then his own choices in the matter of mercy ought to be respected. To impose "mercy" on someone who insists that despite his suffering life is still valuable to him would hardly be mercy; to withhold mercy from someone who pleads for it, on the basis that his life could still be worthwhile for him, is insensitive and cruel. Thus, the principle of mercy is conceptually tied to that of autonomy, at least insofar as what guarantees the best application of the principle—and hence, what guarantees the proper response to the ostensive premise in the argument from mercy—is respect for the patient's own wishes concerning the relief of his suffering or pain.

To this issue we now turn.

THE CASE FOR EUTHANASIA, PART II: AUTONOMY

The second principle supporting euthanasia is that of (patient) autonomy: *one ought to respect a competent person's choices, where one can do so without undue costs to oneself, where doing so will not violate other moral obligations, and where these choices do not threaten harm to other persons or parties.* This principle of autonomy, though limited by these provisos, grounds a person's right to have his or her own choices respected in determining the course of medical treatment, including those relevant to euthanasia: whether the patient wishes treatment that will extend life, though perhaps also suffering, or whether he or she wants the suffering relieved, either by being killed or by being allowed to die. It would of course also require respect for the choices of the person whose condition is chronic but not terminal, the person who is disabled though not dying, and the person not yet suffering at all, but facing senility or old age. Indeed, the principle of autonomy would require respect for self-determination in the matter of life and death in any condition at all, provided that the choice is freely and rationally made and does not harm others or violate other moral rules. Thus, the principle of autonomy would protect a much wider range of life-and-death acts than those we call euthanasia, as well as those performed for reasons of mercy. . . .

It is often objected that autonomy in euthanasia choices should not be recognized in practice, whether or not it is accepted in principle, because such choices are often erroneously made. One version of this argument points to physician error. . . . People diagnosed as dying rapidly of inexorable cancers have survived, cancer-free, for dozens of years; people in cardiac failure or long-term irreversible coma have revived and regained full health. . . .

A second argument pointing to the possibility of erroneous choice on the part of the patient asserts the very great likelihood of impairment of the patient's mental processes when seriously ill. Impairing factors include depression, anxiety, pain, fear, intimidation by authoritarian physicians or institutions, and drugs used in medical treatment that affect mental status. Perhaps a person in good health would be capable of calm, objective judgment even in such serious matters as euthanasia, so this view holds, but the person as patient is not. Depression, extremely common in terminal illness, is a particular culprit: it tends to narrow one's view of the possibilities still open; . . . A choice of euthanasia in terminal illness, this view holds, probably reflects largely the gloominess of the depression, not the gravity of the underlying disease or any genuine intention to die.

If this is so, ought not the euthanasia request of a patient be ignored for his or her own sake? According to a limited paternalistic view (sometimes called "soft" or "weak" paternalism), intervention in a person's choices for his or her own sake is justified if the person's thinking is impaired. Under this principle, not every euthanasia request should be honored; such requests should be construed, rather as pleas for more sensitive physical and emotional care.

It is no doubt true that many requests to die are pleas for better care or improved conditions of life. But this still does not establish that all euthanasia requests should be ignored, because the principle of paternalism licenses intervention in a person's choices just *for his or her own good*. Sometimes the choice of euthanasia, though made in an impaired, irrational way, may seem to serve the person's own good better than remaining alive. Thus, since the paternalist, in intervening, must act for the sake of the person in whose liberty he or she interferes, the paternalist must take into account not only the costs for the person of failing to interfere with a euthanasia decision when euthanasia was not warranted (the cost is death, when death was not in this person's interests) but also the costs for that person of interfering in a decision that was warranted (the cost is continuing life—and continuing suffering—when death would have been the better choice). The likelihood of these two undesirable outcomes must then be weighed. To claim that "there's always hope" or to insist that "the diagnosis could be wrong" in a morally responsible way, one must weigh not only the cost of unnecessary death to the patient but also the costs to the patient of dying in agony if the diagnosis is right and the cure does not materialize. . . .

As with limited paternalism, extended "strong" or "hard" paternalism—permitting intervention not merely to counteract impairment but also to avoid great harm—provides a special case when applied to euthanasia situations. The hard paternalist may be tempted to argue that because death is the greatest of harms, euthanasia choices must always be thwarted. But the initial premise of this argument is precisely what is at issue in the euthanasia dispute itself, as we've seen: is death the worst of harms that can befall a person, or is unrelieved, hopeless suffering a still worse harm? The principle of mercy obliges us to relieve suffering when it does not serve some overriding good; but the principle itself cannot tell us whether sheer existence—life—is an overriding good. In the absence of an objectively valid answer, we must appeal to the individual's own preferences and values. . . .

To claim that an incessantly pain-racked but conscious person cannot make a rational choice in matters of life and death is to misconstrue the point: he or she, better than anyone else, can make such a choice, based on intimate acquaintance with pain and his or her own beliefs and fears about death. If the patient wishes to live, despite such suffering, he or she must be allowed to do so; or the patient must be granted help if he or she wishes to die.

But this introduces a further problem. The principle of autonomy, when there are no countervailing considerations on paternalistic grounds or on grounds of harm to others, supports the practice of voluntary euthanasia and, in fact, any form of rational, voluntary suicide. We already recognize a patient's right to refuse any or all medical treatment and hence correlative duties of noninterference on the part of the physician to refrain from treating the patient against his or her will. But does the patient's right of self-determination also give rise to any positive obligation on the part of the physician or other bystander to actively produce death? . . . Although we usually recognize only that the principle of autonomy generates rights to noninterference, in some circumstances a right of self-determination does generate claims to assistance or to the provision of goods. . . .

Some singularly sympathetic cases—like that of the completely paralyzed cerebral palsy victim Elizabeth Bouvier—have brought this issue to public attention. But notice that in euthanasia situations, most persons are handicapped with respect to producing for themselves an easy, "good," merciful death. The handicaps are occasionally physical, but most often involve lack of knowledge of how to bring this about and lack of access to means for so doing. . . . Full autonomy is not achieved until one can both choose and act upon one's choices. It is here, in these cases of "handicap" that afflict many or most patients, that rights to self-determination may generate obligations on the part of physicians (provided, perhaps, that they do not have principled objections to participation in such activities themselves). The physician's obligation is not only to respect the patient's choices but also to make it possible for the patient to act upon his or her choices. This means supplying the knowledge and equipment to enable the person to stay alive, if he or she so chooses; this is an obligation physicians now recognize. But it may also mean providing the knowledge, equipment, and help to enable the patient to

die, if that is his or her choice; this is the other part of the physician's obligation, not yet recognized by the medical profession or the law in the United States.

This is not to say that any doctor should be forced to kill any person who asks that: other contravening considerations—particularly that of ascertaining that the request is autonomous and not the product of coerced or irrational choice, and that of controlling abuses by unscrupulous physicians, relatives, or patients—would quickly override. Nor would the physician have an obligation to assist in "euthanasia" for someone not severely ill. But when the physician is sufficiently familiar with the patient to know the seriousness of the condition and the earnestness of the patient's request, when the patient is sufficiently helpless, and when there are no adequate objections on grounds of personal scruples or social welfare, then the principle of autonomy—like the principle of mercy—imposes on the physician the obligation to help the patient in achieving an easy, painless death.

THE CASE FOR EUTHANASIA, PART III: JUSTICE

Although the term "euthanasia" traditionally was employed in cases in which "good death" meant the avoidance of suffering, in recent years use of the term has been extended to cover cases in which the patient is neither suffering nor capable of choosing to die. . . .

This argument from justice is usually employed only to justify the denial of treatment, that is, to justify passive euthanasia; but similar considerations also favor active euthanasia. Passive euthanasia is often practiced upon unsalvageable patients by withholding treatment if a medical crisis occurs: for instance, no-code orders are issued, or pneumonias are not treated, or electrolyte imbalances not corrected if they occur. If justice demands that, despite the prima facie claims of these patients, the resources allocated to their care are better assigned somewhere else, then we must notice that *passive* euthanasia does not provide the most just redistribution of these resources. To "allow" the patient to die may still involve enormous expenditures of money, scarce supplies, or caregiver time. This is most evident in cases of "irretrievably inaccessible" patients, for whom no considerations of mercy or autonomy override the demands of justice in weighing claims. . . . The total cost of maintaining a permanently comatose woman, who was injured in a riding accident in 1956 at age twenty-seven and died eighteen years later, has been estimated at just over $6,000,000; this care provided her with not a single moment of conscious life.[3] The record survival for a coma patient is thirty-seven years and 111 days.[4] The argument from justice demands that these patients, since their claims for care are so weak as to have virtually no force at all, be killed, not simply allowed to die.

OBJECTION TO THE ARGUMENT FROM JUSTICE: THE SLIPPERY SLOPE

But if justice, under the distributive principle employed here, licenses the killing of permanently comatose patients, will it not also license the killing of still-conscious, still-competent dying patients, perhaps still salvageable, close or not so close to death? What extensions of the scope of this principle might be made, should resources become still more scarce? These concerns introduce the "wedge" or "slippery slope" argument, which holds that although some acts of euthanasia may be morally permissible (say, on grounds of mercy or autonomy), to allow them to occur will set a logical precedent for, or will causally result in, consequences that are morally repugnant. Just as Hitler's 1938 "euthanasia" program for mentally defective, senile, and terminally ill Aryans paved the way for the establishment of the extermination camps several years later, it is argued, so permissive euthanasia policies invite irreversible descent down that slippery slope that leads to mass murder. . . .

As it is usually posed, the form of the argument that points to the Nazi experience does not succeed: the forces that brought the mass extermination camps into being were not *caused* by the earlier euthanasia program, and, other things being equal, the extermination camps for Jews would no doubt have been established had there been no euthana-

sia program at all. To argue that permitting euthanasia now will lead to death camps like Hitler's is to overlook the many other political, social, and psychological factors of the Nazi period. Yet the wedge argument cannot be simply discarded; the factors operating to favor the slide from morally warranted euthanasia to murder are probably much stronger than we realize. They are best seen, I think, as misunderstandings or corruptions of the very principles that favor euthanasia: mercy, autonomy, and perhaps most prominently, justice.

A contemporary version of the wedge argument holds that to permit euthanasia at all—including cases justified on grounds of mercy, autonomy, or justice—will in the presence of strong financial incentives lead to circumstances in which people are killed who are not suffering or who do not wish to die. Furthermore, to permit some doctors to allow their patients to die or to kill them would invite cavalier attitudes concerning the lives of the patients and, in addition to financial incentives, ordinary greed, insensitivity, hastiness, and self-interest, would cause some doctors to let their patients die—or kill them—when there was no moral warrant for doing so. Doctors treating difficult or unresponding patients would find an easy way out. Medical blunders could be more easily covered up, and doctors might use euthanasia as a way of avoiding criticism in cases that were medically difficult to treat. Particularly important, perhaps, are societal and political pressures, most evident in cost-containment policies, to which doctors might respond. After all, to permit earlier, less expensive death would ease the enormous pressures on third-party insurers, public welfare, and the Social Security system: euthanasia is less expensive than continuing medical care. . . .

Is there any reason to think such practices would actually occur? The reasons are closer to hand than one might imagine. Rather than predicting the future, we need simply look to our present practices for evidence that violations of the moral limits to euthanasia can occur. . . .

The wedge argument assumes, without adequate justification, that the rights of those who may become the victims of abuses of a practice outweigh the rights of those who become victims if a practice is prohibited to whose benefits they are morally entitled and urgently need.

To protect those who might wrongly be killed or allowed to die might seem a stronger obligation than to satisfy the wishes of those who desire release from pain, analogous perhaps to the principle in law that "better ten guilty men go free than one be unjustly convicted." . . . But to require the person who chooses to die to stay alive in order to protect those who might unwillingly be killed sometime in the future is to impose an extreme harm—intolerable suffering—on that person, which he or she must bear for the sake of others. Furthermore, since, as we've seen, the question of which is worse, suffering or death, is person-relative, we have no independent, objective basis for protecting the class of persons who might be killed at the expense of those who would suffer intolerable pain; perhaps our protecting ought to be done the other way around. . . .

CONCLUSION: EUTHANASIA AND SUICIDE

It may be objected that requiring the patient to choose between death and life, insofar as the patient must antecedently consider treatment decisions that affect the circumstances and timing of his or her own demise, is equivalent to requiring the patient's consideration of suicide. In a sense, it is; but this is also the more general solution to the euthanasia problem. Although euthanasia is indeed warranted on grounds of mercy, autonomy, and justice, these principles can be more effectively and safely honored by permitting suicide, perhaps assisted by the physician who has care of the patient or a family member under the advice of the physicians, and supplemented by nonvoluntary euthanasia *only* when the patient is permanently comatose or otherwise irretrievably inaccessible. Not only do practical reasons like avoiding greed and manipulation on the part of the physicians or the institutions controlling them speak for preferring physician-assisted suicide to physician-initiated eu-

thanasia, but there are conceptual reasons as well. The conditions that distinguish morally permissible euthanasia from impermissable murder all involve matters that the patient, not the physician, is in a privileged position to know. To extend mercy, the physician must know how the patient weights suffering against death, and at what point *for the patient* death becomes the lesser of two evils. To respect the patient's autonomy, the physician must know what his or her preferences are, given the alternatives available, in the matter of dying. And to exercise justice, the physician must know what treatment the patient realistically desires. . . . Consequently, since the risk of misinterpretation is great and the possibility of manipulation or coercion high, the physician should not be the one to *initiate* the choice. Rather, he or she must be prepared to assist the patient who chooses death, just as he or she is prepared to assist the patient who chooses continuing life. . . .

NOTES

1. Edmund D. Pellegrino, M.D., "The Clinical Ethics of Pain Management in the Terminally Ill," *Hospital Formulary* 17 (November 1982): 1,495–1,496; and Marcia Angell, "The Quality of Mercy," *New England Journal of Medicine* 306 (January 1982): 98–99.

2. Philippa Foot, "Euthanasia," *Philosophy & Public Affairs* 6 (Winter 1977): 95.

3. This case, originally presented in the *Illinois Medical Journal* and reprinted in *Connecticut Medicine* with commentary from medical, ethical, and legal experts, is summarized in *Concern for Dying* 8 (Summer 1982): 3.

4. President's Commission for the Study of Ethical Problems in Medicine and Biomedical and Behavioral Research, *Defining Death: Medical, Legal, and Ethical Issues in the Determination of Death* (Washington, D.C.: Government Printing Office, 1981), 18, citing the *Guiness Book of World Records* regarding the case of Elaine Esposito.

Discussion Questions

1. Dr. Jack Kevorkian claimed that his mission was one of mercy. He also claimed that by allowing patients to administer the lethal injections themselves, he was respecting their autonomy. Discuss whether Battin would approve of Kevorkian's "mercy killings" given her support of both limited paternalism and physician-assisted suicide.

2. In a note in her article, Battin asks us to try the following thought experiment. Discuss the questions at the end of the experiment.

   Imagine that you have been captured by a gang of ruthless and superlatively clever criminals, whom you know with certainty will never be caught or change their minds. They plan either to execute you now or to torture you unremittingly for the next twenty years and then put you to death. Which would be worse? Does your view change if the length of the torture period is reduced to twenty days or twenty minutes, and, if so, why? How severe must the torture be?

3. Battin's use of the principles of autonomy and mercy in her support of euthanasia is primarily deontological. Is her claim that life has worth only if it is a benefit and contains "a minimum of basic goods" consistent with the deontological principle that rational beings have intrinsic worth? How has Battin modified the strict Kantian deontological position? Discuss which interpretation of the value of rational human life, Battin's or Kant's, you find most compelling.

4. Are you satisfied with Battin's response to the slippery slope or wedge argument against legalizing euthanasia? Support your answer. Discuss what limits, if any, Battin might place on a public policy regarding euthanasia.

5. David Lewis, an AIDS counselor in Vancouver, British Columbia, revealed in 1990 that he had helped eight friends with AIDS take lethal doses of drugs that had been prescribed earlier by a doctor. The men had begged to die; none of them wanted to suffer anymore, he told a reporter. "To refuse to help them would be criminal."[30] Did Lewis make the morally right decision? Support your answer using the principles of mercy and autonomy as well as Battin's concept of limited paternalism.

6. Discuss Battin's claim that distributive justice supports involuntary, active euthanasia in cases in which costly medical resources are needed to sustain life. Discuss what other considerations might be relevant in a utilitarian calculus regarding euthanasia in cases like these.

DANIEL CALLAHAN

"Aid-in-Dying": The Social Dimensions

Daniel Callahan is co-founder and director of the Hastings Center as well as author of several books and articles in bioethics. Like Hardwig, Callahan argues that euthanasia is not a matter of private self-determination but a social issue; however, Callahan draws a much different conclusion regarding the morality of euthanasia. Euthanasia, Callahan points out, puts absolute power of life and death in the hands of another person, and thus the resulting inequality of power in this relationship is incompatible with respect for human dignity. In addition, the criteria used for euthanasia decisions are necessarily arbitrary and subjective. Therefore, euthanasia should remain illegal.

Critical Reading Questions

1. What, according to Callahan, is one of the greatest fears people have about dying? Does Callahan think that permitting euthanasia is a reasonable response to that fear?
2. On what grounds does Callahan argue that euthanasia and assisted suicide are more than a personal matter of self-determination?
3. Why is Callahan opposed to the legalization of euthanasia?
4. What are the two classic arguments in favor of euthanasia and assisted suicide?
5. How does Callahan respond to the argument that a right to euthanasia is simply an extension of the right to control our own lives and our own bodies?
6. Does John Stuart Mill's principle of freedom support Callahan's position?
7. Why does Callahan claim that there is a contradiction between euthanasia and the principle of autonomy or sovereignty over our lives? What point is Callahan making when he draws a comparison between slavery and euthanasia?
8. What are some of the problems, according to Callahan, of using pain and suffering as a standard for justifying euthanasia?
9. What are some of the problems of requiring patient competence for euthanasia?
10. Do doctors have a duty to relieve suffering by carrying out a patient's request for euthanasia? Why, according to Callahan, is it unfair to burden a physician with the moral decision to end a patient's life?

The fear of dying is powerful. Even more powerful sometimes is the fear of not dying, of being forced to endure destructive pain, or to live out a life of unrelieved, pointless suffering. The movement to legalize euthanasia and assisted suicide is a strong and, seemingly, historically inevitable response to that fear. It draws part of its strength from the failure of modern medicine to reassure us that it can manage our dying with dignity and comfort. It draws another part from the desire to be masters of our fate. Why must we endure that which need not be endured? If medicine cannot always bring us the kind of death we might like through its technical skills, why can it not use them to give us a quick and merciful release? . . .

"'Aid-in-Dying': The Social Dimensions." *Commonweal,* August 9, 1991.

If it should happen to be impossible for us to so easily bring about our own death, would it not be reasonable to ask someone else, specifically a doctor, to help us to die? Would it not, moreover, be an act of mercy for a doctor to give us that kind of a release? Is not the relief of suffering a high moral good?

To say "no" in response to questions of that kind seems both repressive and cruel. They invoke our cherished political values of liberty and self-determination. They draw upon our deep and long-standing moral commitment to the relief of suffering. They bespeak our ancient efforts to triumph over death, to find a way to bring it to heel.

Nonetheless, we should as a society say no, and decisively so, to euthanasia and assisted suicide. . . . If a death marked by pain or suffering is a nasty death, a natural biological evil of a supreme kind, euthanasia and assisted suicide are wrong and harmful responses to that evil. To directly kill another person in the name of mercy (as I will define "euthanasia" here), or to assist another to commit suicide (which seems to me logically little different from euthanasia), would add to a society already burdened with man-made evils still another.

Euthanasia is mistakenly understood as only a personal matter of self-determination, the control of our own bodies, just a small step beyond the removal of legal prohibitions against suicide. Unlike suicide, euthanasia should be understood as of its nature a social act. It is social because, by definition, it requires the assistance of someone else, as the expression "aid-in-dying" itself makes clear.

Legalization would also provide an important social sanction for euthanasia, affecting many aspects of our society beyond the immediate relief of suffering individuals. The implications of that sanction are profound. . . .

All civilized societies have developed laws to reduce the occasions on which one person is allowed to kill another person. All have resisted the notion that private agreements can be reached allowing one person to take the life of another to serve the interests of one or both parties. Traditionally, only three circumstances have been acceptable for the taking of life: killing in self-defense or to protect another life, killing in the course of a just war, and, in the case of capital punishment, killing by agents of the state. . . .

The proposal for "aid-in-dying" is nothing less than a proposal to add a new category of acceptable killing to those already socially accepted. To do so would be to reverse the long-developing trend to limit the occasions of legally sanctioned killing (most notable in the campaigns to abolish capital punishment and to limit access to firearms). Civilized societies have slowly come to understand how virtually impossible it is to control even legally sanctioned killing. It seems of its nature to invite abuse. Most notably, the proposal would reinstate private killings. By a "private" killing I mean one in which the agreement of one person to kill another is ratified in private by the persons themselves, not by public authorities (even if it is made legal and safeguards are put into effect). Do we want to give one person the right to kill another for the sake of the relief of pain and suffering? That is the question before us. . . .

Yet if we generally accept in our society a right to control our own life and body, why has the extension of that right to private killing been denied? The most obvious reason is a reluctance to give one person absolute and irrevocable power over the life of another, whether there is consent or not. That prohibition is a way of saying that the social stakes in the legitimization of killing are extraordinarily high. It is to recognize that a society should—for the mutual protection of all—be exceedingly parsimonious about conferring a right to kill on anyone, for whatever reason.

John Stuart Mill, in his classic essay *On Liberty*, noted that civilized societies do not grant individuals a legal right to sell themselves into slavery, even though that denial is a limitation on self-determination. "The principle of freedom," he wrote, "cannot require that he should be free not to be free. It is not freedom to be allowed to alienate his freedom."

Yet it is not just the ceding of freedom that is problematic. The absolute power that is put into the hands of another, I would add—the right to be a slaveholder—is not compatible with respect for our human dignity. Both the slaveholder and the enslaved are corrupted by the relationship, even if both have the good of the other as their motive. The one gives up too much, and the other has too much given him.

A similar consideration applies in the case of killings authorized in the name of mercy: they give one person an absolute power over another. . . .

We cannot, I believe, transfer our sovereignty to another without contradicting it. A sovereignty that can legally and morally be given away is fragile and contingent, not sovereignty at all. To allow another person to kill us is the most radical relinquishment of sovereignty imaginable, not just one more way of exercising it. Our life belongs no longer to us, but to the person into whose power we give it. No person should have that kind of power over another, freely gained or not. . . .

There is another problem. If the person who is to kill is to do so in a responsible fashion, then he or she must have some independent standards for determining when to honor such requests. This becomes all the more important when it is argued, as it sometimes is, that a doctor has not just a right to respond to a request for euthanasia but that, in the name of a duty to relieve suffering, there can be a positive obligation to do so.

We come here to a striking pitfall of the common argument for euthanasia and assisted suicide. Once the key premises of that argument are accepted, there will remain no logical way in the future to: (1) deny euthanasia to anyone who requests it for whatever reason, terminal illness or not; or to (2) deny it to the suffering incompetent, even if they do not request it. . . .

Where are the flaws here? Recall that there are two classical arguments in favor of euthanasia and assisted suicide: our right of self-determination, and our claim upon the mercy of others, especially doctors, to relieve our suffering if they can do so. These two arguments are typically spliced together and presented as a single contention. Yet if they are considered independently—and there is no inherent reason why they must be linked—they display serious problems. Consider, first, the argument for our right of self-determination. It is said that a competent, adult person should have a right to euthanasia for the relief of suffering. But why must the person be suffering? Does not that stipulation already compromise the right of self-determination? How can self-determination have any limits? Why are not the person's desires or motives, whatever they may be, sufficient? How can we satisfy this arbitrary limitation of self-determination? The standard arguments for euthanasia offer no answers to those questions.

Consider next the person who is suffering but not competent, who is perhaps demented or mentally retarded. The standard argument (and the proposed Washington state law) would deny euthanasia to that person. But why? If a person is suffering but not competent, then it would seem grossly unfair to deny relief simply because that person lacks competence. Are the incompetent less entitled to relief from suffering than the competent? Will it only be affluent middle-class people, mentally fit and able, who can qualify? Will those who are incompetent but suffering be denied that which those who are intellectually and emotionally better off can have? Would that be fair? Do they suffer less for being incompetent? . . .

My contention is that the joining of those two requirements is perfectly arbitrary, a jerry-rigged combination if ever there was one. Each has its own logic, and each could be used to justify euthanasia. But in the nature of the case that logic, it seems evident, offers little resistance to denying any competent person the right to be killed, sick or not; and little resistance to killing the incompetent, so long as there is good reason to believe they are suffering. There is no principled reason to reject that logic, and no reason to think it could long remain suppressed by the expedient of arbitrary legal stipulations.

There is a related problem worth considering. If the act of euthanasia, conventionally understood, requires the request and consent of the patient, it no less requires that the person to do the killing have his or her own independent moral standards for acceding to the request. The doctor must act with integrity. How can a doctor who voluntarily brings about, or is instrumental in, the death of another legitimately justify that to herself? Would the mere claim of self-determination on the part of someone be sufficient—"it is my body. Doctor, and, I request that you kill me"? There is a widespread resistance to that kind of claim, and doctors quite rightly have never been willing to do what patients want just because they want it. There is surely a legitimate fear that, if such a claim were sanctioned, there would be no reason to forbid any two competent persons from entering into an agreement for one to kill the other. Perhaps it arises out of a reluctance to put doctors in the role of taking life simply as a means of advancing patient self-determination, quite apart from any medical reasons for doing so.

The most likely reason for resistance to a pure self-determination standard is that we have, traditionally, defined the appropriate role of the physician as someone whose duty it is to relieve suffering. . . . A doctor will not cut off my healthy arm simply because I decide my autonomy and well-being would thereby be enhanced. But the additional requirement that the physician also be relieving suffering carries with it the problem mentioned above. How can a physician determine, much less diagnose in any traditional medical sense, genuine and unrelievable suffering?

The doctor will not be able to use a medical standard. He or she will only be able to use a moral standard. Faced with a patient reporting great suffering, a doctor cannot, therefore, justify euthanasia on purely medical grounds (because suffering is unmeasurable and scientifically undiagnosable). To maintain professional and personal integrity, the doctor will have to justify it on his or her own moral grounds. The doctor must believe that a life of subjectively experienced intense suffering is not worth living. He must believe that himself if he is to be justified in taking the decisive and ultimate step of killing the patient; it must be his moral reason to act, not the patient's reason (even though they may coincide). But if he believes that a life of some forms of suffering is not worth living, then how can he deny the same relief to a person who cannot request it, or who requests it but whose competence

is in doubt? This is simply a different way of making the point that there is no self-evident reason why the supposed duty to relieve suffering must be limited to competent patients claiming self-determination. Or why patients who claim death as their right under self-determination must be either suffering or dying.

There is, moreover, the possibility that what begins as a right of doctors to kill under specified conditions will soon become a duty to kill. On what grounds could a doctor deny a request by a competent person for euthanasia? . . .

Our duty to relieve suffering cannot justify the introduction of new evils into society. The risk of doing just that in the legalization of "aid-in-dying" is too great, particularly since the number of people whose pain and suffering could not be relieved would never be a large one (so even most euthanasia advocates recognize). It is too great because it would take a disproportionate social change to bring it about, one whose implications extend far beyond the sick and dying. It is too great because, as the history of the twentieth century should demonstrate, killing is a contagious disease, not easy to stop once unleashed in society. It is too great a risk because it would offer medicine too convenient a way out of its hardest cases, those where there is ample room for further, more benign reforms. We are far from exhausting the known remedies for the relief of pain (frequently, even routinely, underused), and a long way from providing decent psychological support for those who suffer from despair and a sense of futility in continuing life.

Pain and suffering in the critically ill and dying are great evils. The attempt to relieve them by the introduction of euthanasia and assisted suicide is even greater. Those practices threaten the future security of the living. They no less threaten the dying themselves. Once a society allows one person to take the life of another based on their mutual private standards of a life worth living, there can be no safe or sure way to contain the deadly virus thus introduced. It will go where it will thereafter.

Discussion Questions

1. Callahan's argument against euthanasia is based on his definition of euthanasia as "aid-in-dying." Dr. Jack Kevorkian claims that he has overcome this moral objection to euthanasia with the invention of his Mercitron, a device that allows patients to kill themselves with a self-administered lethal injection.[31] Discuss whether the Mercitron overcomes Callahan's objection to aiding another person in dying. Would Callahan approve of the Mercitron? Support your answer.

2. Callahan argues that linking the criteria of suffering and competence excludes some people who may well be deserving of euthanasia, such as incompetent terminally ill people who are suffering greatly. On the other hand, applying each criterion separately can lead to too many abuses. Because these criteria entail unfairness and can come into conflict with one another, they should be discarded and, therefore, euthanasia should be rejected. Do you agree with Callahan's reasoning? Support your answer. Discuss how both Battin and Hardwig would respond to Callahan's objection.

3. Callahan argues that it is morally unacceptable to make euthanasia decisions based on subjective criteria. Euthanasia, therefore, is morally unacceptable, because there is no way a physician can objectively determine whose requests for euthanasia should be honored. Such a decision ultimately requires subjective moral judgments on the part of the physician. Do you agree with Callahan? Are medical decisions regarding a patient's treatment, especially those based on dialogue between a patient and doctor, always objective, or are such decisions necessarily partly subjective? If decisions regarding a patient's treatment are based, at least in part, on subjective criteria, shouldn't subjective criteria be permitted in euthanasia decisions as well? Support your answers. Discuss how Callahan might respond to this objection.

4. Discuss whether Callahan's argument that legalizing euthanasia would change the role of the doctor sufficiently takes into account the fact that, with modern medical technology, the role of the doctor has already changed.

 J O H N   H A R D W I G

Is There a Duty to Die?

John Hardwig is a professor of philosophy and medical ethics at East Tennessee State University. Hardwig rejects the current emphasis on patient autonomy as the critical issue in euthanasia, because it does not take into account family interests in the care of the patient. Because of modern technology, more and more elderly people are saved from acute illness only to eventually die lingering and costly deaths from chronic illnesses. Adopting a position similar to Plato and the early Stoics, Hardwig argues that when this happens and we become a burden on our family and loved ones, we may have a duty to die.

"Is There a Duty to Die?" *Hastings Center Report* 27, no. 2 (1997): 34–42. Notes have been omitted.

Critical Reading Questions

1. Why does Hardwig claim that most of us probably do believe in the existence of a duty to die? What examples does he use to support his claim?
2. What are some of the developments in modern medicine that have made the duty to die an important issue?
3. According to Hardwig, what "American fantasy" has lead bioethics to see euthanasia as a private decision?
4. How does Hardwig answer the question: Whose life is it, anyway?
5. What are some of the burdens imposed on loved ones who have to care for an old, ailing family member? What obligations, if any, do these families have toward their old and ailing members?
6. What, according to Hardwig, are some of the most serious objections to the idea that there is a duty to die? How does he respond to these objections?
7. What are some of the guidelines Hardwig gives for deciding if someone has a duty to die? Who should make the decision about when a person has a duty to die?
8. According to Hardwig, how does a duty to die affirm rather than compromise our moral agency and human dignity?
9. Why does our fear of death, according to Hardwig, prevent us from finding meaning in death?

When Richard Lamm made the statement that old people have a duty to die, it was generally shouted down or ridiculed. The whole idea is just too preposterous to entertain. Or too threatening. In fact, a fairly common argument against legalizing physician-assisted suicide is that if it were legal, some people might somehow get the idea that they have a duty to die. These people could only be the victims of twisted moral reasoning or vicious social pressure. It goes without saying that there is no duty to die.

But for me the question is real and very important. I feel strongly that I may very well some day have a duty to die. I do not believe that I am idiosyncratic, morbid, mentally ill, or morally perverse in thinking this. I think many of us will eventually face precisely this duty. But I am first of all concerned with my own duty. . . .

CIRCUMSTANCES AND A DUTY TO DIE

Do many of us really believe that no one ever has a duty to die? I suspect not. I think most of us probably believe that there is such a duty, but it is very

uncommon. Consider Captain Oates, a member of Admiral Scott's expedition to the South Pole. Oates became too ill to continue. If the rest of the team stayed with him, they would all perish. After this had become clear, Oates left his tent one night, walked out into a raging blizzard, and was never seen again. That may have been a heroic thing to do, but we might be able to agree that it was also no more than his duty. It would have been wrong for him to urge—or even to allow—the rest to stay and care for him.

This is a very unusual circumstance—a "lifeboat case"—and lifeboat cases make for bad ethics. But I expect that most of us would also agree that there have been cultures in which what we would call a duty to die has been fairly common. These are relatively poor, technologically simple, and especially nomadic cultures. In such societies, everyone knows that if you manage to live long enough, you will eventually become old and debilitated. Then you will need to take steps to end your life. The old people in these societies regularly did precisely that. Their cultures prepared and supported them in doing so.

Those cultures could be dismissed as irrelevant to contemporary bioethics; their circumstances are so different from ours. But if that is our response, it is instructive. It suggests that we assume a duty to die is irrelevant to us because our wealth and technological sophistication have purchased exemption for us . . . except under very unusual circumstances like Captain Oates's.

But have wealth and technology really exempted us? Or are they, on the contrary, about to make a duty to die common again? We like to think of modern medicine as all triumph with no dark side. Our medicine saves many lives and enables us to live longer. That is wonderful, indeed. We are all glad to have access to this medicine. But our medicine also delivers most of us over to chronic illnesses and it enables many of us to survive longer than we can take care of ourselves, longer than we know what to do with ourselves, longer than we even are ourselves.

The costs—and these are not merely monetary—of prolonging our lives when we are no longer able to care for ourselves are often staggering. If further medical advances wipe out many of today's "killer diseases"—cancer, heart attacks, strokes, ALS, AIDS, and the rest—then one day most of us will survive long enough to become demented or debilitated. These developments could generate a fairly widespread duty to die. . . .

Let me be clear. I certainly believe that there is a duty to refuse life-prolonging medical treatment and also a duty to complete advance directives refusing life-prolonging treatment. But a duty to die can go well beyond that. There can be a duty to die before one's illnesses would cause death, even if treated only with palliative measures. In fact, there may be a fairly common responsibility to end one's life in the absence of any terminal illness at all. Finally, there can be a duty to die when one would prefer to live. . . .

THE INDIVIDUALISTIC FANTASY

Because a duty to die seems such a real possibility to me, I wonder why contemporary bioethics has dismissed it without serious consideration. I believe that most bioethics still shares in one of our deeply embedded American dreams: the individualistic fantasy. This fantasy leads us to imagine that lives are separate and unconnected, or that they could be so if we chose. . . .

Within a health care context, the individualistic fantasy leads us to assume that the patient is the only one affected by decisions about her medical treatment. If only the patient were affected, the relevant questions when making treatment decisions would be precisely those we ask: What will benefit the patient? Who can best decide that? The pivotal issue would always be simply whether the patient wants to live like this and whether she would consider herself better off dead. "Whose life is it, anyway?" we ask rhetorically.

But this is morally obtuse. We are not a race of hermits. Illness and death do not come only to those who are all alone. Nor is it much better to think in terms of the bald dichotomy between "the interests of the patient" and "the interests of society" (or a third-party payer), as if we were isolated individuals connected only to "society" in the abstract or to the other, faceless members of our health maintenance organization.

Most of us are affiliated with particular others and most deeply, with family and loved ones. Families and loved ones are bound together by ties of care and affection, by legal relations and obligations, by inhabiting shared spaces and living units, by interlocking finances and economic prospects, by common projects and also commitments to support the different life projects of other family members, by shared histories, by ties of loyalty. This life together of family and loved ones is what defines and sustains us; it is what gives meaning to most of our lives. We would not have it any other way. We would not want to be all alone, especially when we are seriously ill, as we age, and when we are dying.

But the fact of deeply interwoven lives debars us from making exclusively self-regarding decisions, as the decisions of one member of a family may dramatically affect the lives of all the rest. The impact of my decisions upon my family and loved ones is the source of many of my strongest obligations and also the most plausible and likeliest basis of a duty to die. "Society," after all, is only very marginally affected by how I live, or by whether I live or die.

A BURDEN TO MY LOVED ONES

Many older people report that their one remaining goal in life is not to be a burden to their loved ones. Young people feel this, too: when I ask my undergraduate students to think about whether their death could come too late, one of their very first responses always is, "Yes, when I become a burden to my family or loved ones." Tragically, there are situations in which my loved ones would be much better off—all things considered, the loss of a loved one notwithstanding—if I were dead.

The lives of our loved ones can be seriously compromised by caring for us. The burdens of providing care or even just supervision twenty-four hours a day, seven days a week are often overwhelming. When this kind of caregiving goes on for years, it leaves the caregiver exhausted, with no time for herself or life of her own. . . .

I am not advocating a crass, quasi-economic conception of burdens and benefits, nor a shallow, hedonistic view of life. Given a suitably rich understanding of benefits, family members sometimes do benefit from suffering through the long illness of a loved one. Caring for the sick or aged can foster growth, even as it makes daily life immeasurably harder and the prospects for the future much bleaker. Chronic illness or drawn-out death can also pull a family together, making the care for each other stronger and more evident. If my loved ones are truly benefiting from coping with my illness or debility, I have no duty to die based on burdens to them.

But it would be irresponsible to blithely assume that this always happens, that it will happen in my family, or that it will be the fault of my family if they cannot manage to turn my illness into a positive experience. Perhaps the opposite is more common: . . .

Our families and loved ones also have obligations, of course—they have the responsibility to stand by us and to support us through debilitating illness and death. They must be prepared to make significant sacrifices to respond to an illness in the family. I am far from denying that. Most of us are aware of this responsibility and most families meet it rather well. . . .

OBJECTIONS TO A DUTY TO DIE

To my mind, the most serious objections to the idea of a duty to die lie in the effects on my loved ones of ending my life. But to most others, the important objections have little or nothing to do with family and loved ones. Perhaps the most common objections are: (1) there is a higher duty that always takes precedence over a duty to die; (2) a duty to end one's own life would be incompatible with a recognition of human dignity or the intrinsic value of a person; and (3) seriously ill, debilitated, or dying people are already bearing the harshest burdens and so it would be wrong to ask them to bear the additional burden of ending their own lives. . . .

An example of the first line of argument would be the claim that a duty to God, the giver of life, forbids that anyone take her own life. It could be argued that this duty always supersedes whatever obligations we might have to our families. But what convinces us that we always have such a religious duty in the first place? And what guarantees that it always supersedes our obligations to try to protect our loved ones? . . .

Secondly, religious considerations aside, the claim could be made that an obligation to end one's own life would be incompatible with human dignity or would embody a failure to recognize the intrinsic value of a person. But I do not see that in thinking I had a duty to die I would necessarily be failing to respect myself or to appreciate my dignity or worth. Nor would I necessarily be failing to respect you in thinking that you had a similar duty. There is surely also a sense in which we fail to respect ourselves if in the face of illness or death, we stoop to choosing just what is best for ourselves. Indeed, Kant held that the very core of human dignity is the ability to act on a self-imposed moral law, regardless of whether it is in our interest to do so. We shall return to the notion of human dignity.

A third objection appeals to the relative weight of burdens and thus, ultimately, to considerations of fairness or justice. The burdens that an illness creates for the family could not possibly be great enough to justify an obligation to end one's life—the sacrifice of life itself would be a far greater burden than any involved in caring for a chronically ill family member.

But is this true? Consider the following case:

An 87-year-old woman was dying of congestive heart failure. Her APACHE score predicted that she had less than a 50 percent chance to live for another six months. She was lucid, assertive, and terrified of death. She very much wanted to live and kept opting for rehospitalization and the most aggressive life-prolonging treatment possible. That treatment successfully prolonged her life (though with increasing debility) for nearly two years. Her 55-year-old daughter was her only remaining family, her caregiver, and the main source of her financial support. The daughter duly cared for her mother. But before her mother died, her illness had cost the daughter all of her savings, her home, her job, and her career.

This is by no means an uncommon sort of case. Thousands of similar cases occur each year. Now, ask yourself which is the greater burden:

a) To lose a 50 percent chance of six more months of life at age 87?

b) To lose all your savings, your home, and your career at age 55?

Which burden would you prefer to bear? Do we really believe the former is the greater burden? . . .

I think most of us would quickly agree that (b) is a greater burden. That is the evil we would more hope to avoid in our lives. . . .

This point does not depend on a utilitarian calculus. Even if death were the greatest burden (thus disposing of any simple utilitarian argument), serious questions would remain about the moral justifiability of choosing to impose crushing burdens on loved ones in order to avoid having to bear this burden oneself. . . .

WHO HAS A DUTY TO DIE?

Suppose, then, that there can be a duty to die. Who has a duty to die? And when? To my mind, these are the right questions, the questions we should be asking. Many of us may one day badly need answers to just these questions. . . .

Some may object that it would be wrong to put a loved one in a position of having to say, in effect, "You should end your life because caring for you is too hard on me and the rest of the family." Not only will it be almost impossible to say something like that to someone you love, it will carry with it a heavy load of guilt. On this view, you should decide by yourself whether you have a duty to die and approach your loved ones only after you have made up your mind to say good-bye to them. Your family could then try to change your mind, but the tremendous weight of moral decision would be lifted from their shoulders.

Perhaps so. But I believe in family decisions. Important decisions for those whose lives are interwoven should be made together, in a family discussion. Granted, a conversation about whether I have a duty to die would be a tremendously difficult conversation. The temptations to be dishonest could be enormous. Nevertheless, if I am contemplating a duty to die, my family and I should, if possible, have just such an agonizing discussion. It will act as a check on the information, perceptions, and reasoning of all of us. But even more importantly, it affirms our connectedness at a critical juncture in our lives and our life together. Honest talk about difficult matters almost always strengthens relationships. . . .

I cannot say when someone has a duty to die. Still, I can suggest a few features of one's illness, history, and circumstances that make it more likely that one has a duty to die. I present them here without much elaboration or explanation.

1. A duty to die is more likely when continuing to live will impose significant burdens—emotional burdens, extensive caregiving, destruction of life plans, and, yes, financial hardship—on your family and loved ones. . . .

2. A duty to die becomes greater as you grow older. As we age, we will be giving up less by giving up our lives, if only because we will sacrifice fewer remaining years of life and a smaller portion of our life plans. . . .

3. A duty to die is more likely when you have already lived a full and rich life. You have already had a full share of the good things life offers.

4. There is greater duty to die if your loved ones' lives have already been difficult or impoverished, if they have had only a small share of the good things that life has to offer (especially if through no fault of their own).

5. A duty to die is more likely when your loved ones have already made great contributions—perhaps even sacrifices—to make your life a good one. Especially if you have not made similar sacrifices for their well-being or for the well-being of other members of your family.

6. To the extent that you can make a good adjustment to your illness or handicapping condition, there is less likely to be a duty to die. A good adjustment means that smaller sacrifices will be required of loved ones and there is more compensating interaction for them. . . .

7. There is less likely to be a duty to die if you can still make significant contributions to the lives of others, especially your family. . . .

8. A duty to die is more likely when the part of you that is loved will soon be gone or seriously compromised. Or when you soon will no longer be capable of giving love. Part of the horror of dementing disease is that it destroys the capacity to nurture and sustain relationships, taking away a person's agency and the emotions that bind her to others.

9. There is a greater duty to die to the extent that you have lived a relatively lavish lifestyle instead of saving for illness or old age. . . . It is a greater wrong to come to your family for assistance if your need is the result of having chosen leisure or a spendthrift lifestyle. . . .

CAN THE INCOMPETENT HAVE A DUTY TO DIE?

. . . I am tempted to simply bypass the entire question by saying that I am talking only about competent persons. But the idea of a duty to die clearly raises the specter of one person claiming that another—who cannot speak for herself—has such a duty. So I need to say that I can make no sense of the claim that someone has a duty to die if the person has never been able to understand moral obligation at all. To my mind, only those who were formerly capable of making moral decisions could have such a duty.

But the case of formerly competent persons is almost as troubling. Perhaps we should simply stipulate that no incompetent person can have a duty to die, not even if she affirmed belief in such a duty in an advance directive. . . .

But for me personally, very urgent practical matters turn on their resolution. If a formerly competent person can no longer have a duty to die (or if other people are not likely to help her carry out this duty), I believe that my obligation may be to die while I am still competent, before I become unable to make and carry out that decision for myself. Surely it would be irresponsible to evade my moral duties by temporizing until I escape into incompetence. And so I must die sooner than I otherwise would have to. One the other hand, if I could count on others to end my life after I become incompetent, I might be able to fulfill my responsibilities while also living out all my competent or semi-competent days. Given our society's reluctance to permit physicians, let alone family members, to perform aid-in-dying, I believe I may well have a duty to end my life when I can see mental incapacity on the horizon.

There is also the very real problem of sudden incompetence—due to a serious stroke or automobile accident, for example. For me, that is the real nightmare. If I suddenly become incompetent, I will fall into the hands of a medical-legal system that will conscientiously disregard my moral beliefs and do what is best for me, regardless of the consequences for my loved ones. And that is not at all what I would have wanted!

SOCIAL POLICIES AND A DUTY TO DIE

The claim that there is a duty to die will seem to some a misplaced response to social negligence. If our society were providing for the debilitated, the chronically ill, and the elderly as it should be, there would be only very rare cases of a duty to die. . . .

I cannot claim to know whether in some abstract sense a society like ours should provide care for all who are chronically ill or debilitated. But the fact is that we Americans seem to be unwilling to pay for this kind of long-term care, except for ourselves and our own. In fact, we are moving in precisely the opposite direction—we are trying to shift the burdens of caring for the seriously and chronically ill onto families in order to save costs for our health care system. As we shift the burdens of care onto families, we also dramatically increase the number of Americans who will have a duty to die.

I must not, then, live my life and make my plans on the assumption that social institutions will protect my family from my infirmity and debility. To do so would be irresponsible. More likely, it will be up to me to protect my loved ones.

A DUTY TO DIE AND THE MEANING OF LIFE

A duty to die seems very harsh, and often it would be. It is one of the tragedies of our lives that someone who wants very much to live can nevertheless have a duty to die. It is both tragic and ironic that it is precisely the very real good of family and loved ones that gives rise to this duty. Indeed, the genuine love, closeness and supportiveness of family members is a major source of this duty: we could not be such a burden if they did not care for us. Finally, there is deep irony in the fact that the very successes of our life-prolonging medicine help to create a widespread duty to die. . . .

We do not even ask about meaning in death, so busy are we with trying to postpone it. But we will not conquer death by one day developing a technology so magnificent that no one will have to die. Nor can we conquer death by postponing it ever longer. We can conquer death only by finding meaning in it.

Although the existence of a duty to die does not hinge on this, recognizing such a duty would go some way toward recovering meaning in death. . . .

First, recognizing a duty to die affirms my agency and also my moral agency. I can still do things that make an important difference in the lives of my loved ones. Moreover, the fact that I still have responsibilities keeps me within the community of moral agents. My illness or debility has not reduced me to a mere moral patient (to use the language of the philosophers). . . .

To treat me as if I had no moral responsibilities when I am ill or debilitated implies that my condition has rendered me morally incompetent. Only small children, the demented or insane, and those totally lacking in the capacity to act are free from moral duties. There is dignity, then, and a kind of meaning in moral agency, even as it forces extremely difficult decisions upon us.

Second, recovering meaning in death requires an affirmation of connections. If I end my life to spare the futures of my loved ones, I testify in my death that I am connected to them. It is because I love and care for precisely these people (and I know they care for me) that I wish not to be such a burden to them. By contrast, a life in which I am free to choose whatever I want for myself is a life unconnected to others. . . .

This need not be connections with other people. Some people are deeply tied to land (for example, the family farm), to nature, or to a transcendent reality. But for most of us, the connections that sustain us are to other people. . . .

I don't know about others, but these reflections have helped me. I am now more at peace about facing a duty to die. Ending my life if my duty required might still be difficult. But for me, a far greater horror would be dying all alone or stealing the futures of my loved ones in order to buy a little more time for myself. I hope that if the time comes when I have a duty to die, I will recognize it, encourage my loved ones to recognize it too, and carry it out bravely.

Discussion Questions

1. Discuss how Aristotle would reply to Hardwig's argument that there is a duty to die once we have become burdensome. Compare and contrast Aristotle's likely public policy on euthanasia with the one proposed by Hardwig.
2. Hardwig protests that he is "not advocating a crass, quasi-economic conception of burdens and benefits." Much of his argument for a duty to die, however, is based on utilitarian considerations of consequences. Discuss ways, if any, in which Hardwig's argument differs from, or goes beyond, that of pure utilitarianism.
3. Hardwig draws a comparison between modern society and primitive societies. Looking back at the example of the Kabloona Eskimo in Chapter 1, would Hardwig approve of the practice of walking elderly people into holes in the ice? Compare and contrast this situation with that of an elderly person with a chronic illness in a modern hospital. What would Hardwig suggest had the ailing father refused to walk out on the ice to his death? What would Hardwig suggest if the elderly American on a respirator refused to give permission to be disconnected?
4. Hardwig claims that the duty to die is consistent with Immanuel Kant's claim that "human dignity rests on the capacity for moral agency within a community of those who respect the demands of morality." Kant, however, was opposed to suicide and euthanasia. Discuss how Hardwig might reconcile his claim with Kant's opposition to euthanasia.
5. Discuss whether Noddings would agree with Hardwig that the duty to die is consistent with an ethics of care.
6. Would Battin agree with Hardwig that there are times when we have a duty to die? Discuss your answer using her three principles of autonomy, mercy, and justice.

S U S A N   M .   W O L F

A Feminist Critique of Physician-Assisted Suicide

Susan Wolf is an associate professor of law and medicine at the University of Minnesota Law School and an associate at the University of Minnesota's Center for Biomedical Ethics. In her essay Wolf argues that euthanasia practices are gender-biased. The traditional view of women as self-sacrificing puts subtle pressures on women to request euthanasia, as well as on doctors to comply with their requests.

"A Feminist Critique of Physician-Assisted Suicide," from Susan M. Wolf, "Gender, Feminism, and Death: Physician-Assisted Suicide and Euthanasia," in *Feminism and Bioethics,* ed. by Susan M. Wolf (New York: Oxford University Press, 1996), 282–317. Copyright 1996 the Hastings Center. Some notes have been omitted.

Critical Reading Questions

1. What arguments does Wolf use to support her claim that there are gender differences that might contribute to women being more affected than men by the legalization of euthanasia?
2. What are some of the implications of the research findings of Lawrence Kohlberg and Carol Gilligan on the euthanasia debate?
3. How does Wolf use the "Debbie" case as well as the Kevorkian cases to support her argument that euthanasia is gender-biased?
4. According to Wolf, why did Kevorkian's female patients request his assistance in their suicides? What is it about the nature of the male-physician/female-patient relationship that makes it both more likely that female patients will request euthanasia and that male doctors will be more likely to comply with their requests?
5. What are some of the traditional female virtues? How, according to Wolf, do these traditional views of women contribute to the greater likelihood that women will request euthanasia?
6. What are the three objections Wolf raises to the rights-based argument for euthanasia?
7. Why does Wolf reject the argument that euthanasia can be based on a physician's duty of beneficence?
8. According to Wolf, why does linking an ethics of justice to an ethics of care require that euthanasia remain illegal?
9. Why does Wolf, despite her opposition to euthanasia, claim that "physicians must honor patients' requests to be free of unwanted life-sustaining treatment"? How does she use care ethics to justify her position?

The debate in the United States over whether to legitimate physician-assisted suicide and active euthanasia has reached new levels of intensity. . . .

Yet the debate over whether to legitimate physician-assisted suicide and euthanasia (by which I mean active euthanasia, as opposed to the termination of life-sustaining treatment) is most often about a patient who does not exist—a patient with no gender, race, or insurance status. This is the same generic patient featured in most bioethics debates. Little discussion has focused on how differences between patients might alter the equation.

Even though the debate has largely ignored this question, there is ample reason to suspect that gender, among other factors, deserves analysis. The cases prominent in the American debate mostly feature women patients. This occurs against a backdrop of a long history of cultural images revering women's sacrifice and self-sacrifice. . . .

What sort of gender effects might we expect? There are four different possibilities. First, we might anticipate a higher incidence of women than men dying by physician-assisted suicide and euthanasia in this country. This is an empirical claim that we cannot yet test; we currently lack good data in the face of the illegality of the practices in most states and the condemnation of the organized medical profession. . . .

There may, however, be a second gender effect. Gender differences may translate into women seeking physician-assisted suicide and euthanasia for somewhat different reasons than men. Problems we know to be correlated with gender—difficulty getting good medical care generally, poor pain relief, a higher incidence of depression, and a higher rate of poverty—may figure more prominently in women's motivation. Society's persisting sexism may figure as well. And the long history of valorizing women's self-sacrifice may be expressed in women's requesting assisted suicide or euthanasia.

The well-recognized gender differences in suicide statistics also suggest that women's requests for physician-assisted suicide and euthanasia may more often than men's requests be an effort to change an oppressive situation rather than a literal request for death. . . .

Third, gender differences may also come to the fore in physicians' decisions about whether to grant or refuse requests for assisted suicide or euthanasia. The same historical valorization of women's self-sacrifice and the same background sexism that may affect women's readiness to request may also affect physicians' responses. Physicians may be susceptible to affirming women's negative self-judgments. This might or might not result in physicians agreeing to assist; other gender-related judgments (such as that women are too emotionally labile, or that their choices would not be taken seriously) may intervene.[1] But the point is that gender may affect not just patient but physician.

Finally, gender may affect the broad public debate. The prominent U.S. cases so far and related historical imagery suggest that in debating physician-assisted suicide and euthanasia, many in our culture may envision a woman patient. . . .

The debate over physician-assisted suicide and euthanasia so starkly raises questions of rights, caring, and context that at this point it would take determination *not* to bring to bear a literature that has been devoted to understanding those notions. Indeed, the work of Lawrence Kohlberg bears witness to what an obvious candidate this debate is for such analysis. It was Kohlberg's work on moral development, of course, that provoked Carol Gilligan's *In A Different Voice,* criticizing Kohlberg's vision of progressive stages of moral maturation as one that was partial and gendered. Gilligan proposed that there were really two different approaches to moral problems, one that emphasized generalized rights and universal principles, and the other that instead emphasized contextualized caring and the maintenance of particular human relationships. She suggested that although women and men could use both approaches, women tended to use the latter and men the former. . . .

The euthanasia debate thus demands analysis along the care, rights, and context axes that the Kolhberg-Gilligan debate has identified. Kolhberg himself used this problem to reveal how well respondents were doing in elevating general principles over the idiosyncrasies of relationship and context. It is no stretch, then, to apply the fruits of more than a decade of feminist critique. . . .

GENDER IN CASES, IMAGES, AND PRACTICE

The tremendous upsurge in American debate over whether to legitimate physician-assisted suicide and euthanasia in recent years has been fueled by a series of cases featuring women. The case that seems to have begun this series is that of Debbie, published in 1988 by the *Journal of the American Medical Association (JAMA).*[2] *JAMA* published this now infamous, first-person, and anonymous account by a resident in obstetrics and gynecology of performing euthanasia. Some subsequently queried whether the account was fiction. Yet it successfully catalyzed an enormous response.

The narrator of the piece tells us that Debbie is a young woman suffering from ovarian cancer. The resident has no prior relationship with her, but is called to her bedside late one night while on call and exhausted. Entering Debbie's room, the resident finds an older woman with her, but never pauses to find out who that second woman is and what relational context Debbie acts within. Instead, the resident responds to the patient's clear discomfort and to her words. Debbie says only one sentence, "Let's get this over with." It is unclear whether she thinks the resident is there to draw blood and wants that over with, or means something else. But on the strength of that one sentence, the resident retreats to the nursing station, prepares a lethal injection, returns to the room, and administers it. The story relates this as an act of mercy under the title, "It's Over, Debbie," as if in caring response to the patient's words.

The lack of relationship to the patient; the failure to attend to her own history, relationships, and resources; the failure to explore beyond the patient's presented words and engage her in conversation;

the sense that the cancer diagnosis plus the patient's words demand death; and the construal of that response as an act of mercy are all themes that recur in later cases. The equally infamous Dr. Jack Kevorkian has provided a slew of them.

They begin with Janet Adkins, a 54-year-old Oregon woman diagnosed with Alzheimer's disease. Again, on the basis of almost no relationship with Ms. Adkins, on the basis of a diagnosis by exclusion that Kevorkian could not verify, prompted by a professed desire to die that is a predictable stage in response to a number of dire diagnoses, Kevorkian rigs her up to his "Mercitron" machine in a parking lot outside Detroit in what he presents as an act of mercy.

Then there is Marjorie Wantz, a 58-year-old woman without even a diagnosis. Instead, she has pelvic pain whose source remains undetermined. By the time Kevorkian reaches Ms. Wantz, he is making little pretense of focusing on her needs in the context of a therapeutic relationship. Instead, he tells the press that he is determined to create a new medical specialty of "obitiatry." Ms. Wantz is among the first six potential patients with whom he is conferring. When Kevorkian presides over her death there is another woman who dies as well, Sherry Miller. Miller, 43, has multiple sclerosis. Thus neither woman is terminal.

The subsequent cases reiterate the basic themes. And it is not until the ninth "patient" that Kevorkian finally presides over the death of a man. By this time, published criticism of the predominance of women had begun to appear.

Kevorkian's actions might be dismissed as the bizarre behavior of one man. But the public and press response has been enormous, attesting to the power of these accounts. Many people have treated these cases as important to the debate over physician-assisted suicide and euthanasia. Nor are Kevorkian's cases so aberrant—they pick up all the themes that emerge in "Debbie." . . .

Prevailing values have imbued women's deaths with a specific meaning. Indeed, Carol Gilligan builds on images of women's suicides and sacrifice in novels and drama, as well as on her own data, in finding a psychology and even an ethic of self-sacrifice among women. Gilligan finds one of the "conventions of femininity" to be "the moral equation of goodness with self-sacrifice." "[V]irtue for women lies in self-sacrifice. . . ."[3]

Given this history of images and the valorization of women's self-sacrifice, it should come as no surprise that the early cases dominating the debate about self-sacrifice through physician-assisted suicide and euthanasia have been cases of women. In Greek tragedy only women were ever candidates for sacrifice and self-sacrifice, and to this day self-sacrifice is usually regarded as a feminine not masculine virtue. . . .

Analyzing the early cases against the background of this history also suggests hidden gender dynamics to be discovered by attending to the facts found in the accounts of these cases, or more properly the facts not found. What is most important in these accounts is what is left out, how truncated they are. We see a failure to attend to the patient's context, a readiness on the part of these physicians to facilitate death, a seeming lack of concern over why these women turn to these doctors for deliverance. A clue about why we should be concerned about each of these omissions is telegraphed by data from exit polls on the day Californians defeated a referendum measure to legalize active euthanasia. Those polls showed support for the measure lowest among women, older people, Asians, and African Americans, and highest among younger men with postgraduate education and incomes over $75,000 per year.[4] The *New York Times* analysis was that people from more vulnerable groups were more worried about allowing physicians actively to take life. This may suggest concern not only that physicians may be too ready to take their lives, but also that these patients may be markedly vulnerable to seeking such relief. Why would women, in particular, feel this?

Women are at greater risk for inadequate pain relief.[5] Indeed, fear of pain is one of the reasons most frequently cited by Americans for supporting legislation to legalize euthanasia.[6] Women are also at greater risk for depression.[7] And depression appears to underlie numerous requests for physician-assisted suicide and euthanasia.[8] These factors suggest that women may be differentially driven to consider requesting both practices.

That possibility is further supported by data showing systematic problems for women in relationship to physicians. As an American Medical Association report on gender disparities recounts, women receive more care even for the same illness, but the care is generally worse. Women are less likely to receive dialysis, kidney transplants, cardiac catheterization, and diagnostic testing for lung cancer. The report urges physicians to uproot "social or cultural biases that could affect medical care" and "presumptions about the relative worth of certain social roles."[9]

This all occurs against the background of a deeply flawed health care system that ties health insurance to employment. . . . In the U.S. two-tier health care system, men dominate in the higher-quality tier, women in the lower. . . .

Women may also be driven to consider physician-assisted suicide and euthanasia out of fear of otherwise burdening their families. . . . The history and persistence of family patterns in this country in which women are expected to adopt self-sacrificing behavior for the sake of the family may pave the way too for the patient's request for death. Women requesting death may also be sometimes seeking something other than death. The dominance of women among those attempting but not completing suicide in this country suggests that women may differentially engage in death-seeking behavior with a goal other than death. Instead, they may be seeking to change their relationships or circumstances.

In analyzing why women may request physician-assisted suicide and euthanasia, and why indeed the California polls indicate that women may feel more vulnerable to and wary of making that request, we have insights to bring to bear from other realms. Those insights render suspect an analysis that merely asserts women are choosing physician-assisted suicide and active euthanasia, without asking why they make that choice. The analogy to other forms of violence against women behind closed doors demands that we ask why the woman is there, what features of her context brought her there, and why she may feel there is no better place to be. Finally, an analogy [to domestic violence] counsels us that the patient's consent does not resolve the question of whether the physician acts properly in deliberately taking her life through physician-assisted suicide or active euthanasia. The two people are separate moral and legal agents.

This leads us from consideration of why women patients may feel vulnerable to these practices, to the question of whether physicians may be vulnerable to regarding women's requests for physician-assisted suicide and euthanasia somewhat differently from men's. There may indeed be gender-linked reasons for physicians in this country to say "yes" to women seeking assistance in suicide or active euthanasia. In assessing whether the patient's life has become "meaningless," or a "burden," or otherwise what some might regard as suitable for extinguishing at her request, it would be remarkable if the physician's background views did not come into play on what makes a woman's life meaningful or how much of a burden on her family is too much.[10]

Second, there is a dynamic many have written about operating between the powerful expert physician and the woman surrendering to his care. It is no accident that bioethics has focused on the problem of physician paternalism. Instead of an egalitarianism or what Susan Sherwin calls "amicalism,"[11] we see a vertically hierarchical arrangement built on domination and subordination. When the patient is female and the doctor male, as is true in most medical encounters, the problem is likely to be exacerbated by the background realities and history of male dominance and female subjugation in the broader society. Then a set of psychological dynamics are likely to make the male physician vulnerable to acceding to the woman patient's request for active assistance in dying. . . .

FEMINISM AND THE ARGUMENTS

. . . Advocacy of physician-assisted suicide and euthanasia has hinged to a great extent on rights claims. The argument is that the patient has a right to self-determination or autonomy that entitles her to assistance in suicide or euthanasia. The strategy is to extend the argument that self-determination entitles the patient to refuse unwanted life-sustaining treatment by maintaining that the same rationale supports patient entitlement to more active physician assistance in death. Indeed, it is sometimes argued that there is no principled difference between the termination of life-sustaining treatment and the more active practices.

The narrowness and mechanical quality of this rights thinking, however, is shown by its application to the stories recounted above. That application suggests that the physicians in these stories are dealing with a simple equation: given an eligible rights bearer and her assertion of the right, the correct result is death. What makes a person an eligible rights bearer? Kevorkian seems to require neither a terminal disease nor thorough evaluation of whether the patient has non-fatal alternatives. Indeed, the Wantz case shows he does not even require a diagnosis. Nor does the Oregon physician-assisted suicide statute require evaluation or exhaustion of non-fatal alternatives; a patient could be driven by untreated pain, and still receive physician-assisted suicide. And what counts as an assertion of the right? For Debbie's doctor, merely "Let's get this over with." Disease plus demand requires death. . . .

Feminist critiques suggest three different sorts of problems with the rights equation offered to justify physician-assisted suicide and euthanasia. First, it ignores context, both the patient's present context and her history. The prior and surrounding failures in her intimate relationships, in her resources to cope with illness and pain, and even in the adequacy of care being offered by the very same physician fade into invisibility next to the bright light of a rights bearer and her demand. In fact, her choices may be severely constrained. . . .

Second, in ignoring context and relationship, the rights equation extols the vision of a rights bearer as an isolated monad and denigrates actual dependencies. Thus it may be seen as improper to ask what family, social, economic, and medical supports she is or is not getting; this insults her individual self-governance. Nor may it be seen as proper to investigate alternatives to acceding to her request for death; this too dilutes self-rule. Yet feminists have reminded us of the actual embeddedness of persons and the descriptive falseness of a vision of each as an isolated individual.[12] . . . Indeed,

the very meaning of the patient's request for death is socially constructed; that is the point of the prior section's review of the images animating the debate. If we construe the patient's request as a rights bearer's assertion of a right and deem that sufficient grounds on which the physician may proceed, it is because we choose to regard background failures as irrelevant even if they are differentially motivating the requests of the most vulnerable. We thereby avoid real scrutiny of the social arrangements, governmental failures, and health coverage exclusions that may underlie these requests. We also ignore the fact that these patients may be seeking improved circumstances more than death. We elect a myopia that makes the patient's request and death seem proper. We construct a story that clothes the patient's terrible despair in the glorious mantle of "rights." . . .

In fact, there are substantial problems with grounding advocacy for the specific practices of physician-assisted suicide and euthanasia in a rights analysis, even if one accepts the general importance of rights and self-determination. I have elsewhere argued repeatedly for an absolute or near-absolute moral and legal right to be free of unwanted life-sustaining treatment. Yet the negative right to be free of unwanted bodily invasion does not imply an affirmative right to obtain bodily invasion (or assistance with bodily invasion) for the purpose of ending your own life.

Moreover, the former right is clearly grounded in fundamental entitlements to liberty, bodily privacy, and freedom from unconsented touching; in contrast there is no clear "right" to kill yourself or be killed. Suicide has been widely decriminalized, but decriminalizing an act does not mean that you have a positive right to do it and to command the help of others. . . .

There are even less grounds for concluding that there is a right to be killed deliberately on request, that is, for euthanasia. There are reasons why a victim's consent has traditionally been no defense to an accusation of homicide. . . . Similarly, acceding to a patient's request to be killed wipes out the possibility of her future exercise of her liberty. The capacity to command or permit another to take your life deliberately, then, would seem beyond the bounds of those things which you have a right grounded in notions of liberty. . . .

Finally, the rights argument in favor of physician-assisted suicide and euthanasia confuses two separate questions: what the patient may do, and what the physician may do. After all, the real question in these debates is not what patients may request or even do. It is not at all infrequent for patients to talk about suicide and request assurance that the physician will help or actively bring on death when the patient wants; that is an expected part of reaction to serious disease and discomfort. The real question is what the doctor may do in response to this predictable occurrence. That question is not answered by talk of what patients may ask; patients may and should be encouraged to reveal everything on their minds. Nor is it answered by the fact that decriminalization of suicide permits the patient to take her own life. The physician and patient are separate moral agents. Those who assert that what a patient may say or do determines the same for the physician, ignore the physician's separate moral and legal agency. They also ignore the fact that she is a professional, bound to act in keeping with a professional role and obligations. They thereby avoid a necessary argument over whether the historic obligations of the physician to "do no harm" and "give no deadly drug even if asked" should be abandoned. Assertion of what the patient may do does not resolve that argument.

The inadequacy of rights arguments to legitimate physician-assisted suicide and euthanasia has led to a different approach, grounded on physicians' duties of beneficence. This might seem to be quite in keeping with feminists' development of an ethics of care.[13] Yet the beneficence argument in the euthanasia context is a strange one, because it asserts that the physician's obligation to relieve suffering permits or even commands her to annihilate the person who is experiencing the suffering. Indeed, at the end of this act of beneficence, no patient is left to experience its supposed benefits. . . .

What does feminism have to offer these debates? Feminists too have struggled extensively with the question of method, with how to integrate detailed attention to individual cases with rights, justice, and principles. Thus in criticizing Kohlberg

and going beyond his vision of moral development, Carol Gilligan argued that human beings should be able to utilize both an ethics of justice and an ethics of care. "To understand how the tension between responsibilities and rights sustains the dialectic of human development is to see the integrity of two disparate modes of experience that are in the end connected. . . . In the representation of maturity, both perspectives converge. . . ."[14] What was less clear was precisely how the two should fit together. And unfortunately for our purposes, Gilligan never took up Kohlberg's mercy killing case to illuminate a care perspective or even more importantly, how the two perspectives might properly be interwoven in that case. . . .

Here we find the beginning of an answer to our dilemma. It appears that we must attend to both context and abstraction, peering through the lens of both care and justice. Yet our approach to each will be affected by its mate. Our apprehension and understanding of context or cases inevitably involves categories, while our categories and principles should be refined over time to apply some contexts and not others. Similarly, our understanding of what caring requires in a particular case will grow in part from our understanding of what sort of case this is and what limits principles set to our expressions of caring; while our principles should be scrutinized and amended according to their impact on real lives, especially the lives of those historically excluded from the process of generating principles. . . .

Against this background, arguments for physician-assisted suicide and euthanasia—whether grounded on rights or beneficence—are automatically suspect when they fail to attend to the vulnerability of women and other groups. . . .

To institute physician-assisted suicide and euthanasia at this point in this country—in which many millions are denied the resources to cope with serious illness, in which pain relief and palliative care are by all accounts woefully mishandled, and in which we have a long way to go to make proclaimed rights to refuse life-sustaining treatment and to use advanced directives working realities in clinical settings—seems, at the very least, to be premature. Were we actually to fix those other problems, we have no idea what demand would remain for these more drastic practices and in what category of patients. . . .

The required interweaving of principles and caring, combined with attention to the heightened vulnerability of women and others, suggests that the right answer to the debate over legitimating these practices is at least "not yet" in this grossly imperfect society and perhaps a flat "no." Beneficence and caring indeed impose positive duties upon physicians, especially with patients who are suffering, despairing, or in pain. Physicians must work with these patients intensively; provide first-rate pain relief, palliative care, and symptomatic relief; and honor patients' exercise of their rights to refuse life-sustaining treatment and use advance directives. Never should the patient's illness, deterioration, or despair occasion physician abandonment. Whatever concerns the patient has should be heard and explored, including thoughts of suicide, or requests for aid or euthanasia.

Such requests should redouble the physician's efforts, prompt consultation with those more expert in pain relief or support care, suggest exploration of the details of the patient's circumstances, and a host of other efforts. What such requests should not do is prompt our collective legitimation of the physician's saying "yes" and actively taking the patient's life. The mandates of caring fail to bless killing the person for whom one cares. Any such practice in the United States will inevitably reflect enormous background inequities and persisting societal biases. And there are special reasons to expect gender bias to play a role. . . .

CONCLUSION

Some will find it puzzling that elsewhere we seek to have women's voices heard and moral agency respected, yet here I am urging that physicians not accede to the request for assisted suicide and euthanasia. Indeed, as noted above, I have elsewhere maintained that physicians must honor patients' requests to be free of unwanted life-sustaining treatment. In fact, attention to gender and feminist argument would urge some caution in both realms. . . . Finally there is a difference between the two domains. As I have argued above, there is a strong right to be free of unwanted bodily invasion. Indeed, for women, a long history of being harmed specifically through unwanted bodily invasion such as rape presents particularly compelling reasons for honoring a woman's refusal of invasion and effort to maintain bodily intactness. When it comes to the question of whether women's suicides should be aided, however, or whether women should be actively killed, there is no right to command physician assistance, the dangers of permitting assistance are immense, and the history of women's subordination cuts the other way. Women have historically been seen as fit objects for bodily invasion, self-sacrifice, and death at the hands of others. The task before us is to challenge all three. . . .

NOTES

1. Compare Jecker, "Physician-Assisted Death," 676, on reasons physicians might differentially refuse women's requests.
2. See "It's Over, Debbie," *Journal of the American Medical Association* 259 (1988): 272.
3. Carol Gilligan, *In a Different Voice,* 70.
4. See Peter Steinfels, "Help for the Helping Hands in Death," *New York Times,* February 14, 1993, sec. 4, pp. 1, 6.
5. See Charles S. Cleeland et al., "Pain and Its Treatment in Outpatients with Metastatic Cancer," *New England Journal of Medicine* 330 (1994): 592–96.
6. See Robert J. Blendon, U. S. Szalay, and R. A. Knox, "Should Physicians Aid Their Patients in Dying?" *Journal of the American Medical Association* 267 (1992): 2658–62.
7. See William Coryell, Jean Endicott, and Martin B. Keller, "Major Depression in a Non-Clinical Sample of Demographic and Clinical Risk Factors for First Onset," *Archives of General Psychiatry* 49 (1992): 117–25.
8. See Susan D. Block and J. Andrew Billings, "Patient Requests to Hasten Death: Evaluation and Management in Terminal Care," *Archives of Internal Medicine* 154 (1994): 2039–47.

9. Council on Ethical and Judicial Affairs, American Medical Association, "Gender Disparities in Clinical Decision Making," *Journal of the American Medical Association* 266 (1991): 559–62, 561–62.

10. As noted above, though, Nancy Jecker speculates that a physician's tendency to discount women's choices may also come into play. See Jecker, "Physician-Assisted Death," 676. Compare Silvia Sara Canetto, "Elderly Women and Suicidal Behavior," in Canetto and Lester, eds., *Women and Suicidal Behavior,* 215–33, 228, asking whether physicians are more willing to accept women's suicides.

11. Sherwin, *No Longer Patient,* 157.

12. See, for example, Naomi Scheman, "Individualism and the Objects of Psychology," In Sandra Harding and Merrill B. Hintikka, eds., *Discovering Reality: Feminist Perspectives on Episte-* *mology, Metaphysics, Methodology, and the Philosophy of Science* (Boston, MA: D. Reidel, 1983), 225–40, 240.

13. See Leslie Bender, "A Feminist Analysis of Physician-Assisted Dying and Voluntary Active Euthanasia," *Tennessee Law Review* 59 (1992): 519–46, making a "caring" argument in favor of "physician-assisted death."

14. See Gilligan, *In A Different Voice,* 174. Lawrence Blum points out that Kohlberg himself stated that "the final, most mature stage of moral reasoning involves an 'integration of justice and care that forms a single moral principle,'" but that Kohlberg, too, never spelled out what the integration would be. See Lawrence A. Blum, "Gilligan and Kohlberg: Implications for Moral Theory," *Ethics* 98 (1988): 472–91, 482–83.

Discussion Questions

1. Do you agree with Wolf that women are more likely than men to request as well as receive euthanasia? If so, does this necessarily imply that euthanasia is gender-biased? Does the fact that women live longer and may feel freer to seek assistance from others account for at least some of the gender discrepancy? Support your answers.

2. Are the women in your class more likely than the men to say that they would choose euthanasia should they become a burden to their families? If so, how do they justify their decisions? Are women more likely than men to use care ethics to justify their decisions? Which of Gilligan's levels of moral reasoning does the reasoning represent? Does conventional moral reasoning contribute to injustice? Discuss.

3. Discuss how Wolf might reply to Battin's argument that, for the most part, we can trust the physician to serve as a check in preventing "ill-considered" physician-assisted suicide and involuntary euthanasia.

4. Would Wolf support physician-assisted suicide in an egalitarian society? If not, what other conditions would she require? Discuss the specific steps we would have to take in the United States before legalizing euthanasia.

5. Ayn Rand claims that "our right to our own life" is "the one fundamental right." Rand also thinks that the United States is the freest country in the world. Should euthanasia be prohibited simply because some women run into sexist attitudes? Discuss how Rand might respond to this question. Which person, Rand or Wolf, presents the most convincing argument? Support your answers.

CASE STUDIES

1. NANCY CRUZAN: SEVEN YEARS IN A PERSISTENT VEGETATIVE STATE

In 1983 twenty-five-year-old Nancy Cruzan's car crashed after skidding out of control on a patch of ice. She was thrown from the car and landed facedown in a ditch, where she nearly suffocated. Although paramedics restored her breathing, her brain had gone without oxygen for thirteen minutes. When doctors told Nancy's parents that she was in a vegetative state, they requested that the hospital disconnect all life supports, including the feeding tubes in her stomach. They told the doctors that they knew she would not want to be kept alive with machines. Although the hospital complied with the request that Nancy be taken off the respirator, it decided not to remove the feeding tube, arguing that food and water were not medical treatment or artificial life support but merely part of basic care. To not provide food and water would be tantamount to killing Nancy by starvation and dehydration.

The Cruzans turned to the courts for help. In 1990, after Nancy had been in a vegetative state for seven years, the case reached the U.S. Supreme Court *(Cruzan v. Missouri Department of Health)*. The Supreme Court ruled that a person has a constitutional right to refuse life-support treatment, including food and water. The court also ruled, however, that the state could limit that right for incompetent people by requiring that the surrogate decision makers provide "clear and convincing" proof of the "patient's desire to have hydration and nutrition withdrawn." Barred by this requirement from removing their daughter's feeding tube, the Cruzans recruited several of Nancy's co-workers to testify that she had clearly stated that she did not want to be kept alive by artificial means. On December 14, 1990, a Missouri court finally gave the Cruzans permission to remove the feeding tube. Nancy died twelve days later.

Discussion Questions

1. Read the excerpts on pages 204–205 from the United States Supreme Court opinion on *Cruzan v. Missouri Department of Health.* If you had been one of the Supreme Court justices would you have concurred with the ruling or dissented? Explain your position in a paragraph giving your opinion, as a Supreme Court justice, of the case.
2. Does providing food and water to a person in a coma constitute artificial life support? Discuss the statement by the hospital that withholding food and water is the same as killing someone.
3. In Rachels's view, did Nancy Cruzan die in the best possible way, given her condition? Is it morally relevant that Nancy did not seem to be in any pain? Support your answers.
4. Are the principles of autonomy and mercy relevant in this case? Does the physician have a moral obligation to Nancy? If so, do these principles apply to the physician's relationship with the parents?
5. Discuss how Battin's principle of limited paternalism applies to the physician, the parents, and the judge in this case.
6. Compare and contrast the recommendations Battin, Hardwig, and Callahan would each have made in this case. What would you have done had you been Nancy's physician? Support your position.

7. Discuss who should make the decision in cases in which incompetent people have not made their wishes explicitly known in a document such as a living will.

---

2. DR. KEVORKIAN AND THE ASSISTED SUICIDE OF JUDITH CURREN [32]

On August 15, 1996, Judith Curren, a forty-two-year-old mother of two young daughters, comitted suicide with the assistance of Dr. Jack Kevorkian. Unlike most of Kevorkian's clients, Curren was not terminally ill; she was suffering from depression, chronic fatigue syndrome, and fibromyalgia—a benign but painful inflammation of fibromuscular tissue.

Curren's husband, psychiatrist Franklin Curren, who was present at his wife's death, was a strong supporter of physician-assisted suicide and his wife's choice to end her life.[33] Kevorkian was surprised when he read a press release a few days later stating that Dr. Curren had been charged with assaulting his wife just three weeks earlier. This was not the first domestic assault charge that had been brought against Curren by his wife.[34]

When questioned about the role that domestic violence may have played in Judith Curren's decision to end her life, Kevorkian replied he had asked the Currens if there had been any trouble in the family and that they had said no. "You can't know what goes on domestically," Kevorkian added in defense of his action.

Kevorkian is currently serving a ten- to twenty-five year jail sentence for assisting in the 1998 suicide of a Tom Youk, who was suffering from amyotrophic lateral sclerosis.

Discussion Questions

1. Kevorkian justifies his actions on the grounds that it would be immoral, similar to torture, not to help people in excruciating pain who request his help. How would Battin respond to this argument?
2. Kevorkian claims that he has never caused a death, but merely helped people exercise their last civil right. Kevorkian's supporters claim that he is a "prisoner of conscience," a "martyr to the cause of the right to choose to die." They argue that the assisted suicide of Tom Youk should have been ruled an "act of mercy" rather than murder. Derek Humphry, founder of the Hemlock Society wrote following Kevorkian's conviction: "The severity of the sentence on Kevorkian will drive the practice of voluntary euthanasia and assisted suicide even further underground. It will not stop it . . . Kevorkian's martyrdom—self-imposed as it is—will speed up the day when voluntary euthanasia for the dying is removed from the legal classification of 'murder' and recognized as a justifiable act of compassion."[35] Do you agree with Kevorkian and his supporters? Or did Kevorkian "get what he deserved" in court? Support your answer.
3. Judith Curren was not terminally ill at the time of her death. Should physician-assisted suicide be extended to anyone who desires it? Support your answer. Discuss how you would respond if someone you knew who was depressed and/or suffering from a chronic illness asked you to assist in his or her suicide.
4. Both Callahan and Wolf argue that many people consider euthanasia because they lack adequate pain control medication or medical insurance to seek proper treatment and care, or because they feel they have become a burden to their friends and

family and that the world would be better off without them. Discuss these objections to euthanasia in light of the Judith Curren case.

5. According to research, women who adopt traditional views of women as self-sacrificing are more likely to be victims of domestic violence. Discuss this finding in light of the Judith Curren case. Is physician-assisted suicide in these cases simply an extension of violence against women? Discuss how both Wolf and Nel Noddings (Chapter 1) might answer this question.

6. John Stuart Mill argues that security and a safe environment are "the most indispensable of all necessaries after physical nutriment. . . ."[36] Would allowing physicians to assist in the suicide of their terminally ill patients damage this sense of security and safety in a physician/patient relationship? Or would it expand the freedom of the dying patient to choose his or her own destiny? Support your answer.

---

3. "FINAL EXIT": HOW TO COMMIT SUICIDE

In February 2000, "Final Exit," a show on how to commit suicide, was aired on late-night cable television in two Oregon cities. The program, which was produced by Hemlock Society founder Derek Humphry, laid out in detail the tools and drugs needed to end one's life quickly and painlessly. It also offered practical advice on "keeping clear of the law" and, for the friends and family of the deceased, "dealing with the aftermath." The show was also intended to raise public support against proposed federal legislation that would impose sanctions on physicians who prescribe lethal drugs to their terminally ill patients.

Although physician-assisted suicide is legal in Oregon, Barbara Coombs Lee, who led the initiative to get the bill passed, criticized the video as "irresponsible and potentially dangerous for some people . . . There is information about how a person could die using very readily available tools and drugs, and for some people who may be mentally unbalanced or acting impulsively, that could be dangerous information."[37]

In response, the cable station and the producers of the show pointed out that this information is already widely available. The program was based on Humphry's book, *Final Exit*, which has sold over 1 million copies and is available in twelve languages. The book is also available on audiocassette and on Humphry's Internet site. "I feel strongly," says Cindy Noblitt, co-producer of the video, "that if we are truly free, that an individual should have the right to decide when and how to end their lives . . . I think it's a central role of the media to provide complete and accurate information to the public that they may need to make those hard decisions in their lives."[38]

Discussion Questions

1. Analyze the arguments put forth by both Lee and Noblitt. What premises do they use, or could they use, to support their conclusions? Which person presents the stronger argument and why?

2. Should there be limits on freedom of speech when it comes to publicizing methods for killing oneself or others? Analyze the case study using Ross's prima facie duties. Present your conclusion in the form of a policy statement for the media.

3. In her article Battin argues that a patient's autonomy may be compromised because of lack of knowledge about humane methods for ending his or her life. Discuss whether the principle of autonomy creates a moral obligation for physicians to provide patients who request it with information on how to die. Role-play a scenario in which you are a physician and a patient comes to you requesting the video "Final Exit." Would it make a difference if the patient was not terminally ill? If the patient were an adolescent? If the patient seemed depressed? If it was the relative of a comatose patient? Support your answers.
4. Discuss what Kant's position would most likely be regarding the above case.

---

4. DONALD COWART: "PLEASE, LET ME DIE"

In 1973 twenty-six-year-old jet pilot and sometime rodeo performer Donald Cowart was standing in a field with his father when there was a violent explosion caused by leaking gas. The explosion killed his father and sent Donald, whose body was engulfed in flames, running for half a mile. When a farmer found him, Cowart, who was in excruciating pain from burns covering more than 65 percent of his body, asked for a gun so he could kill himself. The farmer refused his request and called an ambulance. Cowart asked the paramedics not to drive him to the hospital but to leave him in the field to die. They instead administered lifesaving measures and took him to the hospital.

At the hospital Cowart was subjected to daily baths in a chlorine bleach solution to clean his sores. He lost both his eyes and all his fingers and underwent several operations for skin grafts and amputations. After he was released from the hospital, Cowart attempted suicide several times. Eventually, he completed a law degree. Cowart frequently speaks at medical conferences on issues relating to euthanasia. He still insists that the hospital staff who treated him for his burns violated his right to self-determination in keeping him alive.

Discussion Questions

1. Discuss whether the paramedics did the morally right thing in treating Cowart, even though he asked them not to. What moral principles and concerns are relevant to this decision?
2. Imagine that you are Cowart's best friend and that you, rather than the farmer, found him. What is your moral duty as his friend? Discuss whether the fact that you are his friend, rather than a stranger or a medical professional, is relevant in making your decision to end his suffering or call an ambulance. Would your decision have been different if this incident had occurred in a war, or in the wilderness where there was no medical assistance available?
3. Some people argue that suicide attempts are really a cry for help. Does the fact that Cowart never successfully committed suicide, despite repeated attempts, suggest that he was mistaken about his own wishes to end his life? Can people be sincerely mistaken about their desires? How can a physician determine if a request for euthanasia is genuine? If physicians cannot be sure, how should they respond to these requests? How might Battin and Callahan each respond to this question?

4. Many people think that euthanasia is morally acceptable only when a person is dying. Is the fact that Cowart did not have a terminal condition relevant? Support your answer.

---

5. THE DEATH OF "BABY DOE"

When Baby Doe was born in an Indiana hospital in 1982, his parents were at first overjoyed. Their joy turned to dismay, however, when they learned that their son had Down syndrome. It was later found that the baby also had a malformed esophagus, which prevented food from entering his stomach. Whereas a blockage in the esophagus can be easily corrected by surgery, there is no cure for Down syndrome. The parents, believing that their son might be severely retarded, refused to give approval for the surgery. Without the surgery or a feeding tube, the baby would starve to death. The hospital administration took the case to court. The judge who heard the case concluded that Baby Doe's parents had the right to make an informed decision regarding the course of treatment for their child. Baby Doe died, five days after his birth, of starvation and dehydration.

Discussion Questions

1. What are the limits of parental rights? Do parents have a right to make euthanasia decisions for children who are not terminally ill? Is the assumption that parents will act in the best interests of their children justified?
2. Rachels uses the Baby Doe case to illustrate how passive euthanasia can sometimes cause more suffering than active euthanasia. If it is morally permissible for parents to allow their infants to die, should active euthanasia be used instead?
3. The death of Baby Doe created an uproar, especially from people concerned about the rights of the disabled. Columnist George Will, himself the father of a child with Down syndrome, accused the parents of being cruel and treating their child and those like him as less than human. Do you agree with Will? Support your answer. Would the judge have acknowledged the parents' right to refuse lifesaving surgery for the child had Baby Doe been, for example, an unwanted but otherwise perfectly normal baby of the "wrong" gender? What if the parents had refused the surgery because they had not wanted another son? Discuss whether there is a morally relevant difference between refusing lifesaving surgery for a child with a disability and refusing lifesaving surgery for child because he or she is the "wrong" gender.
4. Anencephaly is a congenital disorder in which the brain fails to develop; it is almost always fatal at or very shortly after birth. In 1996 a couple who gave birth to an anencephalic baby had her placed on life support so her organs could be harvested for organ transplants. This way at least some good would come out of their tragedy.

    Proposals have been made recently to the AMA to allow the harvesting of organs from anencephalic infants before death. Should infants who are going to die or be euthanized be harvested for their organs? Whose decision should this be—the parents' or the hospital's? Do parents give up their right to make decisions about their child's future once they request his or her death, as in the Baby Doe case? How would a utilitarian respond to a hospital policy of using these infants for organ transplants? How would Callahan respond to such a policy? Support your answers.

---

6. ROBERT LATIMER: MURDERER OR ANGEL OF MERCY?

In a courtroom in the quiet farming community of Battleford, Saskatchewan, twelve jurors declared Robert Latimer guilty of second-degree murder. Fours years earlier, on October 24, 1993, Latimer, a canola and wheat farmer, had trudged through the snow with his severely disabled twelve-year-old daughter, Tracy, cradled in his arms and placed her gently in the cab of the family pickup truck. He watched through the window as the cab filled with deadly carbon monoxide fumes. Seven minutes later Tracy was dead.

Twelve days earlier Laura Latimer, Tracy's mother, had taken Tracy to the doctor, who recommended the removal of her right thigh bone to ease her pain. She was horrified at the thought of her daughter being mutilated. Both she and Robert broke down and cried as they thought about their daughter's prospects for the future. They had already tried placing her in a group home but she was so unhappy she lost a sixth of her weight. "It would be better for Tracy if she died," Laura told her husband. She was relieved when, twelve days later, she came home and found Tracy dead.

Was this an act of mercy or a cold-blooded murder? As a result of his actions, Latimer received a life sentence with no access to parole for at least ten years.

His supporters argue that Latimer is "a loving man and a decent father" who acted out of compassion; he deserves leniency, not a prison sentence. If the proper legal and social supports for mercy killing had been in place, Latimer would not have taken the law into his own hands.

Many disabled-rights activists see things differently, however. "What that [granting leniency] says is that it's all right to kill your child with a disability because she may encounter some discomfort," says a spokesperson for the Council of Canadians with Disabilities.[39] "What's happened to Tracy Latimer," said Shivawn Wolfe, a severely disabled thirteen-year-old who testified on behalf of the prosecution, "was not an act of love. She was killed the day the love ran out."

Discussion Questions

1. Mercy killing is usually seen as justified only when there is no other way to relieve pain and suffering. According to witnesses at the trial, however, Tracy Latimer experienced no more pain than many other people with disabilities. Six days before Tracy's death, her mother had written in her journal that Tracy had "eaten well" and was "quite cheerful." "You will not find that she was in constant pain or that she had no joy in her last year," the prosecutor told the jury. "Pain is a condition of life, not a reason for death. Must a person like Tracy die because another person cannot bear to watch her fight?"

   How would you respond to the prosecution's position? Should other kinds of suffering besides unremitting pain, including the suffering of the caregivers, be taken into account in justifying mercy killing?

2. Compare and contrast this case with that of the 1982 Baby Doe case. Would it have made a difference if it had been Tracy's physician, rather than her father, who had euthanized her? Would it have made a difference if they had withheld medical treatment rather than actively killed her? Is it morally relevant that Baby Doe was allowed to die, whereas Tracy was actively killed? How would Rachels respond to these two case studies?

3. Two-thirds of Americans support physician-assisted suicide and euthanasia for terminally ill people, but only 37 percent of respondents felt that relatives or friends should be allowed to commit the deed. Is this distinction morally relevant? Discuss in light of the Robert Latimer case study.

4. Discuss what suggestions Daniel Callahan might make to the Latimers regarding their daughter Tracy.

C H A P T E R   6

Punishment and
the Death Penalty

Fred Simmons and Bob Moore were on their way from Florida to Georgia when they stopped to pick up two hitchhikers, Tony Gregg and Floyd Allen. They later picked up another hitchhiker, Dennis Weaver, whom they dropped off in Atlanta. At a rest stop outside of Atlanta, Gregg told Allen that he was going to rob Simmons and Moore. As Simmons and Moore were returning to the car, Gregg pulled a gun and fired three shots at them. The two men fell into a ditch. Gregg then got out of the car and shot them both point-blank in the head. When Weaver heard about the shootings, he contacted the police and gave them a description of Gregg and Allen as well as of the car they had stolen.

Gregg was found guilty of two counts of armed robbery and two counts of murder and given the death penalty. Gregg appealed his sentence. The death penalty had been ruled unconstitutional in 1972 by the U.S. Supreme Court in *Furman v. Georgia* on the grounds that it had been arbitrarily administered. In response the State of Georgia, as well as Florida and Texas, overhauled their death penalty laws to make them less arbitrary. In 1976 the U.S. Supreme Court in *Gregg v. Georgia* ruled that the revised statutes of Georgia were constitutional, thus overturning the 1972 ruling that had banned the death penalty.

HISTORY OF THE DEATH PENALTY

In the Middle Ages, the purpose of punishment, including the death penalty, was as much to save the criminal's soul as to protect society from harm. Torture instruments, isolation, hard labor, horrendous living conditions, the gallows, and burning at the stake were used to terrorize criminals to the point that they would repent their evil ways and cry out for God's mercy.

During the nineteenth century, public executions were abolished in most of Europe and North America. Citizen participation in the modern democracy depended on people becoming rational participants in public life and restraining their desires for revenge as well as the sadistic and bawdy behavior often displayed at public executions. Rather than abolish the death penalty, however, societies simply moved executions behind the walls of an impersonal penal system. It wasn't until the mid-twentieth century that there was a worldwide movement to abolish the death penalty.

THE DEATH PENALTY TODAY

During the 1970s and 1980s, many countries abolished the death penalty. In 1983 the European Convention of Human Rights was amended to prohibit the death penalty during peacetime. Although in 2000 ninety countries still had the death penalty on their books, it has ceased to be used in eighty-five of these countries, including virtually all of Western Europe, as well as Canada, Australia, and most Latin American, South American, and African countries. In fact, admission to the European Union is contingent on abolishing capital punishment. The United States is the only Western democracy that still retains and practices the death penalty. According to Amnesty International, a human rights organization, of the 1,813 people executed in thirty-one countries in 1999, almost 85 percent occurred in just five countries—China, Iran, the Democratic Republic of the Congo, the United States, and Saudi Arabia.[1]

Punishment for offenses under Islamic law, as is the case in Saudi Arabia, can be swift and severe. Although the death penalty is used in most Islamic countries, the Qur'an's ancient law of retributive justice or *lex talionis*—"an eye for an eye and a tooth for a tooth"—has been softened to permit the payment of "blood money" in some cases. The imposition of the Islamic penal code and the death penalty on both Muslims and non-Muslims has become a controversial issue in Malaysia and other Asian countries that have both Islamic and non-Islamic populations such as Buddhists, Hindus, and Christians.

Unlike Islamic law, Jewish law interprets the Old Testament law of retributive justice to prohibit capital punishment. According to the Jewish Mishnah, it is murder for the courts to execute a person. The death penalty was a last resort and rarely used in ancient Israel and Judah after A.D. 70.

Most Christian churches likewise regard capital punishment as being inconsistent with the sanctity of human life. Capital punishment is illegal in almost all Protestant and Catholic countries, with the exception of the United States. The papal encyclical *Evangelium Vitae* expressly forbids abortion, capital punishment, and euthanasia. Although the U.S. bishops issued statements in 1973 and again in 1980 opposing the death penalty, the majority of U.S. Catholics support capital punishment.[2]

Whereas, as was just noted, the death penalty has been abolished in all other Western democracies, it is currently being expanded in the United States. Of the thirty-eight states that have the death penalty, Texas has the highest execution rate. The number of inmates on death row has also increased dramatically since 1980. In 1998 3,452 prisoners were living under the sentence of death.[3]

Prior to the 1970s, there was not much public support for the death penalty in the United States. In a 1971 Roper poll, Americans overwhelmingly responded that society had a duty to reform criminals and give them a second chance.[4] Only 15 percent responded that the primary purpose of prisons was to punish criminals.

The death penalty was ruled unconstitutional in the U.S. Supreme Court 1972 *Furman v. Georgia* case. The Court ruled that the unlimited discretion given to judges and juries to impose the death penalty led to its capricious and arbitrary use. Justice William O. Douglas, in concurring with the opinion of the Court, wrote: "A law which . . . reaches that [discriminatory] result in practice has no more sanctity than a law which in terms provides the same since it is inconsistent with the equal protection of the laws" [provided in the Fourteenth Amendment].

Between 1967 and 1977, there were no executions in the United States. The escalating violent crime rate in the 1970s, however, led to increasing public support for swift and severe punishment, including the death penalty for murder, in place of rehabilitation. The number of executions have more than tripled between 1994 and 1999 when ninety-eight people were executed.[5] At the beginning of the year 1999 there were 3,452 prisoners under the sentence of death in thirty-seven state and federal prisons, an increase of 4 percent over the previous year.[6]

In 1976 the U.S. Supreme Court in *Gregg v. Georgia* reversed the earlier ruling, saying that Georgia's new "guided discretion" laws had removed the arbitrariness of sentencing from the death penalty.

Between 1960 and 1992, the reported rate of violent crime rose by more than 350 percent.[7] The media's extensive coverage of the most brutal and horrific cases, and the onslaught of violent crime on television and in movies, intensified people's fear of and anger over violent crime and their demand for harsher punishment.

By 1994 Americans no longer saw rehabilitation as the goal of prison; instead the majority regarded stricter punishment as the most effective means of dealing with criminals.[8] All but fifteen states had reinstated the death penalty. A decline in violent crime beginning in the late 1990s futher convinced many Americans that strict punishment, including capital punishment, was the solution to the nation's crime rate. The number of people in prison and on death row continued to increase in the late 1990s and into the new millennium. The U.S. Supreme Court has also issued several rulings in the previous twenty years that make it more difficult for inmates on death row to have their sentences overturned on appeal. Despite greater emphasis on punishment, the inmate population has nearly doubled since 1983. The United States in 1999 has the second highest rate of incarceration in the world. At 682 inmates per 100,000 population we are only slightly behind Russia.[9]

While the number of executions continues to increase, public support for the death penalty is beginning to wane. Support for the death penalty for a person convicted of murder began rising in the 1980s and peaked in 1994 at 80 percent. A June 2000 Gallup poll reported that support dropped to 66 percent with the majority of those stating that they supported it "with reservations."[10] Half of those polled responded that they thought the "death penalty is applied unfairly in this country today." There is also increasing support for using "life imprisonment with absolutely no possibility of parole" instead of the death penalty for murder.

Despite continuing support for capital punishment, the vast majority of murderers do not receive the death penalty. Of the 20,000 homicides that occur in an average year in the United States, fewer than 300 convicted murderers are sentenced to death.[11] Of the people sentenced to death row, 99 percent are poor and have to rely on public defenders.[12] While blacks make up only 12 percent of the U.S. population, they represent 43 percent of death row inmates.

Race, gender, and education have the most significant effect on a person's position on the death penalty. Men are more likely than women to support capital punishment; and people who have been to college are far more likely to support it than people who did not graduate from high school. The most striking difference is based on race, however, with white people being more than twice as likely as black people to support the death penalty.[13]

U.S. SUPREME COURT *GREGG V. GEORGIA* (1976):
EXCERPTS FROM THE MAJORITY OPINION*

[Justice Potter Stewart delivered the opinion of the Court.]

The issue in this case is whether the imposition of the sentence of death for the crime of murder under the law of Georgia violates the Eighth and Fourteenth Amendments . . .

The Court on a number of occasions has both assumed and asserted the constitutionality of capital punishment. In several cases that assumption provided a necessary foundation for the decision, as the Court was asked to decide whether a particular method of carrying out a capital sentence would be allowed to stand under the Eighth Amendment. But until *Furman v. Georgia,* 408 U.S. 238 (1972), the Court never confronted squarely the fundamental claim that the punishment of death always, regardless of the enormity of the offense or the procedure followed in imposing the sentence, is cruel and unusual punishment in violation of the Constitution. Although this issue was presented and addressed in Furman, it was not resolved by the Court . . . We now hold that the punishment of death does not invariably violate the Constitution.

The phrase ["cruel and unusual" punishment] first appeared in the English Bill of Rights of 1689 . . . The American draftsman, who adopted the English phrasing in drafting the Eighth Amendment, were primarily concerned with proscribing "tortures" and other "barbarous" methods of punishment . . .

In the earliest cases raising Eighth Amendment claims, the Court focused on particular methods of execution to determine whether they were too cruel to pass constitution muster. The constitutionality of the sentence of death itself was not at issue, and the criterion used to evaluate the mode of the sentence of death itself was not at issue . . .

But the Court has not confined the prohibition embodied in the Eighth Amendment to "barbarous" methods that were generally outlawed in the 18th century. Instead, the Amendment has been interpreted in a flexible and dynamic manner. The Court early recognized that "a principle to be vital must be capable of wider application than the mischief which gave it birth" *Weems v. United States* (1910). Thus the Clause forbidding "cruel and unusual" punishments

THE DEATH PENALTY AND JUVENILE OFFENDERS

In addition to the apparent racial and socioeconomic disparities in the application of the death penalty, the rise in violent crime among juveniles has raised the moral issue of whether people under eighteen should be put to death. While crime in general is down, teenagers are more violent than ever.[14] Although overall criminal victimization at school

---

* Footnotes omitted.

"is not fastened to the obsolete but may acquire meaning as public opinion becomes enlightened by a humane justice." . . .

But our cases also make clear that public perceptions of standards of decency with respect to criminal sanctions are not conclusive. A penalty also must accord with "the dignity of man," which is the "basic concept underlying the Eighth Amendment." This means, at least, that the punishment not be "excessive." . . . First, the punishment must not involve the unnecessary and wanton infliction of pain *Furman v. Georgia* (1972) . . .

In the discussion to this point we have sought to identify the principles and considerations that guide a court in addressing an Eighth Amendment claim. We now consider specifically whether the sentence of death for the crime of murder is a per se violation of the Eighth and Fourteenth Amendments to the Constitution. We note first that history and precedent strongly support a negative answer to this question.

The imposition of the death penalty for the crime of murder has a long history of acceptance in the United States and in England.

It is apparent from the text of the Constitution itself that the existence of capital punishment was accepted by the framers. At the time the Eighth Amendment was ratified, capital punishment was a common sanction in every state. Indeed, the first Congress of the United States enacted legislation providing death as the penalty for specified crimes . . .

The death penalty is said to serve two principle social purposes: retribution and deterrence of capital crimes by prospective offenders.

In part, capital punishment is an expression of society's moral outrage at particularly offensive conduct. This function may be unappealing to many, but it is essential in an ordered society that asks its citizens to rely on legal processes rather than self-help to vindicate their wrongs. . . .

Capital punishment may be the appropriate sanction in extreme cases as an expression of the communities' belief that certain crimes are themselves so grievous an affront to humanity that the only adequate response may be the death penalty.

is down, according to a 1999 government report,[15] violent victimization rose during the 1990s. And although the total number of school-associated homicides has come down in recent years, the total number of multiple homicide events in schools has increased. Should children who kill be subjected to the same penalties as adults?

Despite the fact that international treaties and the American Convention on Human Rights prohibits the death penalty for people under eighteen, the U.S. Supreme Court in both *Stanford v. Kentucky* and *Wilkins v. Missouri* ruled that it was not unconstitutional to execute juveniles who were sixteen or seventeen at the time of their crime. The United

States, along with Iran, Iraq, Bangladesh, and Pakistan, has one of the highest rates of juvenile executions. In 1985 Charles Rumbaugh of Texas became the first juvenile to be executed in the United States since 1964. About half the states now permit underage executions. In the wake of increasing school violence, many state and federal politicians are calling for harsher penalties for violent juvenile offenders. In 1998 Texas State Representative Jim Pitts submitted a proposal to lower the state's age for the death penalty to eleven.[16]

THE MEDICALIZATION OF EXECUTIONS

The gas chamber, firing squads, and hanging have all been used in the past twenty years in the United States and continue to be used in some other countries. Lethal injection and the electric chair, however, are the two most common methods in the United States, accounting for more than 96 percent of the executions since 1977.[17]

The electric chair was first used in the United States in August 1890 as a more humane means of execution. Lethal injection was adopted in Oklahoma and Texas in 1977. Lethal injection involves intravenous injection of a lethal dose of a barbiturate mixture that causes paralysis, suppression of breathing, and death by asphyxiation. Death generally occurs within minutes.

The adoption of lethal injection as the preferred method of execution in most states has led to what some call "medicalized execution."[18] Although it is claimed that lethal injection is more humane than the earlier methods of execution, the use of medical knowledge to kill people has created a conflict between medical professionals and penal officials. In 1980 the American Medical Association (AMA) adopted a resolution that states that "A physician, as a member of a profession dedicated to the preservation of life . . . should not be a participant in a legally authorized execution." In a 2000 resolution the AMA rejected a moratorium on the death penalty, although it reaffirmed its existing policy that precludes physician participation in executions.

Despite consensus on the part of every national and international physicians' organization that physician participation in an execution violates medical ethics, twenty-eight states require the presence of a physician in the death chamber.[19] To protect physicians from censure by their colleagues, some prisons keep the identity of participating physicians secret, even paying them in cash in order to thwart attempts to identify them.

In California, one of the states that requires a physician's presence at executions, a group of physicians is suing the state prison system, charging that requiring physicians to participate in executions forces them to violate their professional code of ethics— "First of all, do no harm."[20] Dr. Janet Kirsch, one of the physicians involved in the suit, points out that "at Nuremberg, the Nazi doctors were found guilty of crimes against humanity for using medical skills to harm by order of the state."

But then who should carry out executions? Dr. Kirsch has an answer: "Anyone can learn to start an IV from a training film. Let Governor [Pete] Wilson do it. He might miss [the vein] and cause a bruise, but he plans to kill that person anyway." Those who support the law requiring physician's presence counter that a physician is needed in case something goes wrong; between 1982 and 1997, states have botched some twenty executions.[21] Having a physician present makes it less likely that the condemned prisoner will have to endure extra suffering.

THE PHILOSOPHERS ON THE DEATH PENALTY

The morality of capital punishment became an issue during the Enlightenment Period. In the eighteenth century, with its increasing emphasis on individual rights and the inherent dignity of the individual.

According to natural rights ethicist John Locke, the right to life is the primary human right. This right, however, can be forfeited if we violate another person's right to life. Locke writes in his *Second Treatise of Government:*

> Every Man hath a right to punish the Offender, and be Executioner of the Law of Nature. . . . Thus it is, that every Man in the State of Nature, has a Power to kill a Murderer, both to deter others from doing the like injury, which no Reparation can compensate . . . and also to secure Men from the attempts of a Criminal, who having renounced Reason . . . hath by the unjust Violence and Slaughter he hath committed upon one, declared War against all Mankind, and therefore may be destroyed as a *Lyon* or a *Tyger,* one of those wild Savage Beasts, with whom Men can have no Society nor Security: And upon this is grounded the great Law of Nature, *Who so sheddeth Man's Blood, by Man shall his Blood be shed.*[22]

The right to punish, including the right to administer the death penalty, is transferred to the state when people enter a social contract. Governments assume the prerogative to punish wrongdoers in order to prevent society from degrading into a state of disorder and anarchy, or what Locke refers to as a "state of nature." For more on the social contract see the reading from John Locke at the end of Chapter 1.

The main objection to capital punishment came from social reformers such as Karl Marx and utilitarian Jeremy Bentham. Bentham opposed the death penalty as well as punishment in general, because punishment subtracts from the total happiness of the community. "All punishment is mischief," he wrote. "All punishment is evil." The deliberate infliction of suffering on a person who has committed an evil, such as murder, he argued, merely adds more evil and suffering to the world. Punishment, therefore, can be justified only if it is the *only* way to remove an even greater evil.[23] As an alternative to punishment, Bentham proposed a prison system based on reform and rehabilitation. Although his plan for a model prison was sanctioned by an act of Parliament in 1791, the prison was never built.

Not all utilitarians oppose the death penalty. Unlike Bentham, John Stuart Mill believed that the benefits of capital punishment outweighed the harms. In a 1868 speech delivered in the British House of Commons, Mill called the death penalty appropriate for brutal crimes, arguing that it has a deterrent effect.[24] The deterrent argument is still one of the most popular arguments for the death penalty. Both Ernest van den Haag and Hugo Adam Bedau examine this argument in their readings at the end of this chapter.

Immanuel Kant rejected all consequentialist arguments for capital punishment. A murderer must die, he argued, not because of any social benefits that will accrue as a result of the execution, but because this is the only way to satisfy the requirement of retributive justice. Kant writes:

> The penal law is a categorical imperative; and woe to him who creeps through the serpent-windings of utilitarianism to discover some advantage that may discharge him from the justice of punishment, or even from the due measure of it. . . . For if justice and righteousness perish, human life would no longer have any value in the world . . .
>
> But what is the mode and measure of punishment which public justice takes as its principle and standard? It is just the principle of equality, by which the pointer of the scale of justice is made to incline no more to the one side than the other. It may be rendered by saying that the undeserved evil which any one commits on another, is to be regarded as perpetrated on himself. ". . . if you strike another, you strike yourself; if you kill another, you kill yourself." This is the right of retaliation (jus talionis). . . whoever has committed murder must die.[25]

Kant maintained that not only does the state have a right to punish; wrongdoers also have a right to *be* punished. Punishment, including the death penalty, Kant argued, affirms the criminals' dignity by acknowledging that, unlike children and "animals," they are responsible for their actions. Denying people the right to punishment is to deny that they are rational beings capable of responsibility for their own decisions. Jeffrey Reiman, in his article at the end of this chapter, rejects Kant's conclusion that moral respect and retributivism create a duty for the state to give the death penalty for murder. He argues that there are other types of punishment that can meet these moral requirements.

Marx, likewise, rejected the Kantian justification of capital punishment based on retributive justice. He argued that an abstract theory, like the theory of retributive justice, is unable to take into account the unfair relations among different groups of people in a community, and, especially, in a capitalist society. Capital punishment may work in theory, but in actual practice it is applied unjustly and, hence, is immoral. Helen Prejean addresses this issue in the selection from her book *Dead Man Walking* at the end of this chapter.

Both Buddhist and Confucian philosophers reject the death penalty. Buddhists oppose capital punishment because it violates the principle of *ahimsa,* which requires that both individuals and society refrain from harming living beings. It is through encouraging individuals to cultivate right thinking and embrace the noble eightfold path that society overcomes injustice, not by violent punishment of wrongdoers.

Confucius believed that crime is a symptom of a disordered state, rather than an individual problem. It is the rulers, rather than individual citizens, who have the most power to advance virtue in society and individuals. Because it is easiest for people to be virtuous when they are living in a just and well-ordered society, a state where there is a problem with crime needs to work on developing social policy that is more conducive to individual virtue and social harmony.

The reintroduction of the death penalty in the United States in 1976 after so many years of decline has once again raised questions regarding the morality of capital punishment. Contemporary philosophers are divided over capital punishment. Van den Haag and Christopher Morris both support it. Bedau, Reiman, and Prejean, on the other hand, while believing that criminals ought to be punished, call for the abolition of the death penalty.

MORAL ISSUES

Deterrence

Van den Haag argues that the threat of death is the ultimate deterrent. The deterrence argument is based on the assumption that the more severe the punishment for an action, the less likely people are to engage in it. If the fear of punishment is removed, ordinarily law-abiding citizens may become violent and lawless and ruled by mob mentality.

Not all arguments that appear to be intuitively obvious or logical are true, however. For example, it seems intuitively obvious that if a heavy and a light ball are both dropped from the Tower of Pisa at the same time, the heavy one will hit the ground first. In fact, they both hit the ground at the same time. Similarly, it may seem obvious that the more severe the punishment, the greater the deterrent effect, but this does not mean that the two are logically connected or that the proposition is true. As with dropping the two balls from the tower, we need to examine empirical evidence to see if there really is a causal connection between severity of punishment and deterrence.

Abolitionists of the death penalty point out that studies have not found any connection between the use of capital punishment and the rate of violent crime. Indeed, in Canada, for example, the homicide rate peaked in 1975, the year before the reintroduction of the death penalty, and then continued to decline for the next ten years.[26] In the United States, by contrast, two of the states with the most executions since 1979 have had an increase in murder rates following the reinstitution of the death penalty.[27] Because capital punishment has not been shown to have a deterrent effect, we are not saving innocent lives, but rather adding to the loss of human life.

Incapacitation

Whereas deterrence has a broader social goal of keeping others from committing similar crimes, incapacitation is aimed only at the specific person who was convicted of the crime. This defense of capital punishment is based on an analogy between capital punishment and self-defense. The death penalty, it is argued, is the only way to ensure that a murderer will never kill again. Just as people have the right to use lethal force to protect themselves, so too does the government have the right to use the death penalty to protect society from dangerous criminals.

Opponents of capital punishment, such as Prejean and Bedau, disagree. They maintain that life imprisonment, including the use of restraints and the isolation of those who pose a threat to guards and fellow inmates, is sufficient to incapacitate a would-be repeat murderer. Incapacitation justifies the killing of a wrongdoer only during the commission of a violent crime, such as a police officer or potential murder victim killing to prevent grievous harm from occurring.

Retributive Justice

Many supporters of the death penalty, including Kant, Locke, and van den Haag state that it doesn't really matter whether capital punishment is a deterrent or if there are other effective ways to incapacitate a murderer. Retributive justice alone justifies the death penalty. Retribution is not the same as revenge. Revenge is based on a personal desire for retaliation; retribution, on the other hand, is the impersonal carrying out of punishment to "cancel out" an evil act. A person who commits a crime creates a debt that must be paid to society. This debt is due regardless of whether the victim desires it.

One of the underlying principles of retributive justice is *proportionality*. Retributive justice requires that the severity of the punishment be proportionate to the crime, what Kant called the "equality of crime and punishment." The only appropriate payment for murder is death of the murderer. The murderer is "getting what he deserves" or "what is coming to him." As long as the debt remains unpaid, there is a sort of imbalance in the community or universe—a state of injustice exists until the debt is paid. Kant also argues that rather than denying the criminal's worth and dignity, retributive justice assumes moral worth and dignity by acknowledging that the criminal is a rational person who can be held morally responsible for his or her actions.

Some philosophers, including Bentham, question whether there really is a moral duty of retribution. How can one act of violence cancel out another evil act? Although both Bedau and Reiman accept the principle of retributive justice, they argue that it does not require an exact fit between the crime and the punishment. We do not rape rapists or burn the homes of arsonists; the deliberate killing of a murderer is also an inappropriate punishment. Instead the appropriate moral response to wrongdoing is to demand that wrongdoers provide restitution to their victims. The goals of restitution are incompatible with capital punishment, because death removes all possibility of victim compensation.

Furthermore, many opponents of capital punishment question Kant's assumption that retributive justice is required on the grounds that murder is based on a rational decision. Evidence indicates that very few murderers engage in any sort of analysis of their actions before committing murder. Rather than being a rational decision, as Kant presumes, evidence suggests that the great majority of murders are carried out impulsively, in the heat of passion, with little deliberation over the possible consequences. If murder is not based on a rational decision, murderers cannot be held morally responsible for their actions. Hence, the requirement of retributive justice that the murderer have a particular state of mind, when applied in practice, rules out capital punishment in most if not all cases.

Human Dignity and the Sanctity of Human Life

Some opponents of capital punishment, including Prejean and the Buddhists, claim that all deliberate taking of human life is wrong. The use of the death penalty diminishes the value of human life and lowers us to the level of the criminal. Prejean rejects the retributivist argument that the death penalty affirms human dignity, arguing instead that it is degrading and inconsistent with respect for the dignity of persons. Because humans have intrinsic moral value, it is wrong to deprive them of their lives.

Human Rights and Moral Standing

Both the United Nations and Amnesty International oppose the death penalty on the grounds that it violates human rights, including the right to life. The human-rights argument has also been used to *support* capital punishment. Like Locke, Morris acknowledges that humans have certain fundamental rights, such as the right to life; but Morris also argues that by intentionally violating the social contract, wrongdoers lose some of their moral standing and, hence, forfeit some of their moral rights. Those who violate other people's right to life by murdering them in turn forfeit their own right to life. Because they have forfeited this right, capital punishment cannot be said to violate it.

Some opponents of capital punishment, such as Prejean, question the logic of this argument, which is known as *reciprocity retributivism,* concluding, like Marx, that it does not take into account unfairness in society. Thus, rather than setting wrongs right, capital punishment can further perpetuate an unfair status quo that denies certain groups of people full rights.

Distributive Justice and the Principle of Equality

There has been considerable concern that capital punishment is unfairly distributed. For example, Tibetans are disproportionately represented on death row in China.

In the United States, blacks are six times more likely than whites to end up on death row. In addition, although less than half of murder victims are white, 80 percent of people executed in the past two decades killed whites.[28] Poorer defendants are also more likely to get the death penalty, because they cannot afford good defense lawyers.

Some opponents of capital punishment argue that it is an extension of the slavery mentality, whereby the death penalty was frequently used on slaves who committed crimes against whites. They point out that all of the states who executed eight or more prisoners in the years since the Supreme Court declared capital punishment to be constitutional were Confederacy states. Furthermore, although all sixteen states that formed the Confederacy have the death penalty, outside of the former slave-owning states more than half have either abolished it or do not use it even though it is still on the books.

Others disagree with this analysis, maintaining that although racism used to be a problem, the proportion of white and black convicted murderers who get the death penalty is about the same.[29] Furthermore, the distribution-of-justice argument is irrelevant in terms of the morality of capital punishment. Van den Haag maintains that the principle of equality requires not the abolition of the death penalty, but that all those guilty of murder—whether white or black—receive it. Even if the death penalty is applied in a discriminatory manner, this does not mean that capital punishment itself is wrong; it means that too many murderers who deserve the death penalty are getting off.

Some Marxist philosophers, on the other hand, argue that capital punishment is inherently unjust. The flaw is not in the way the death penalty is administered, but in the theory of retributive justice itself. Retribution cannot provide a foundation for punishment, because it is unable to take into account the unfair relationships among different groups of people in a community.

Utilitarian (Consequentialist) Arguments

The primary purpose of punishment is to harm convicted criminals, whether through incapacitation or depriving them of rights. Because pain is essential to punishment, utilitarians maintain that punishment is permissible only if it leads to an overall decrease in pain and an increase in pleasure for society. Studies have not shown this to be the case, however.

First of all, capital punishment has not been proven to have a deterrent effect. In addition, the cost of the death penalty can be expensive. A 1982 study found that the death penalty costs three to six times as much as life imprisonment.[30] Most of these costs are incurred prior to and during trials, as trials for capital offenses are much more costly and time-consuming.

Capital punishment has also been denounced as cruel and inhumane. Amnesty International, a group opposed to the use of torture on criminals, writes: "International law states that torture or cruel, inhuman, or degrading punishments can never be justified. The cruelty of the death penalty is self-evident." Amnesty International classifies lethal injection, justified by supporters of the death penalty as a more humane method of execution, as a type of deliberate poisoning that is inflicted on people against their will. In *Dead Man Walking*, Prejean also vividly describes the cruelty of the death penalty, both during the actual execution and during the long wait before the final moment. In a 1983 electrocution in Alabama, it took three attempts and fourteen minutes to kill the prisoner. Death from lethal injection can also take several minutes, during which time the prisoner is suffocating.

The suffering of the criminal awaiting execution also has to be considered in a utilitarian calculus. The average time spent on death row before execution in this country is ten years. French writer Albert Camus (1913–1960) once wrote that the moral contradiction inherent in a punishment that imitates the violence that it claims to abhor is only made worse by the premeditated nature of capital punishment:

> Many laws consider a premeditated crime more serious than a crime of pure violence. . . . For there to be equivalence, the death penalty would have to punish a criminal who had warned his victim of the date at which he would inflict a horrible death on him and who, from the moment onward, had confined him at his mercy for months. Such a monster is not encountered in private life.[31]

According to social contract theory, governments are formed because of the need for people to band together to protect themselves against danger. Therefore, one of the primary purposes of capital punishment is to protect society against dangerous people such as murderers. Some opponents of the death penalty, however, argue that it actually reduces public safety by draining public resources that could be used for crime prevention and drug treatment.

The death penalty has repercussions that reach far beyond the death chamber. Not only is the executioner affected by the action; the ripple effect reaches out to the family and friends of both the murder victim and the condemned person, as well as to society in general. Does capital punishment ease the grief of the murder victim's family? What is the effect of participating in an execution on medical professionals, who are sworn to save lives? Does violent punishment reinforce or legitimate violence in society in general?

Finality and the Risk of Errors

The death penalty removes all possibility of restitution or repentance. Even if repentance does occur between the sentencing and the actual execution, as in the case study of Karla Faye Tucker, the death penalty ignores it.

Furthermore, it assumes that the judgment about the person's guilt is infallible. A 1993 House of Representatives subcommittee report found instances of forty-eight executions of people later found to be innocent.[32] Van den Haag dismisses these mistakes as part of the cost of doing justice, whereas others, such as Bedau and Prejean, find this risk to be morally unacceptable.

In a 2000 Gallup Poll, 80 percent of those polled thought that innocent people had been executed in the last five years. Since 1982 more than seventy inmates have been found not guilty through DNA evidence, including eight on death row. Errors can also occur because of flaws in the legal procedure. A Columbia University Law School study released in June 2000 found that between 1973 and 1995 over two-thirds of the death sentences had been overturned in the appeal process because of "procedural flaws or unsound evidence."[33] The report concluded that the American capital punishment system is "fraught with error" mainly due to three factors: incompetent defense lawyers, flawed instructions to jurors, and procedural misconduct such as suppressed evidence.

Flaws in the legal procedure as well as better scientific tests for establishing innocence have led some hard-core supporters of capital punishment to rethink their position. For example, Governor George Ryan of Illinois imposed a moratorium on capital punishment in January 2000 after thirteen wrongly convicted men were released from Illinois's death row. Several months later Ricky McGinn, who was only eighteen minutes from death by lethal injection in a Texas execution chamber, received word that he had a thirty-day reprieve to prove his innocence through advanced DNA testing. McGinn's case has led to demands that all death row inmates who are eligible for DNA testing receive it.

Care Ethics

Prejean claims that one reason people favor the death penalty is that we don't identify with the condemned persons; we don't see them as humans like us. Before we can discuss the morality of capital punishment, we first have to see those who are condemned from a care perspective rather than a pure justice perspective.

Adopting Jesus Christ as her role model, Prejean maintains that we ought to love and care for people despite what they may have done. We should return compassion and good for evil, rather than evil for evil as the retributivists claim.

Why Punish?

This raises the question of whether punishment is ever morally acceptable. Most discussions of capital punishment begin with the assumption that punishment is the appropriate moral response to wrongdoing. Good moral reasoning, however, requires that we critically examine the premises of an argument as well as the soundness of the reasoning. This requires asking, "Why punishment?" Does justice require punishment as the retributive justice theorists claim? Or is the punishment paradigm actually counterproductive and harmful to society?

One of the greatest frustrations of our criminal justice system is that criminals often come out in worse shape than when they went in. A 1972 study found that prisoners and guards interacted primarily at the lowest level of moral development—avoiding coercion and punishment. With one another, however, they interacted primarily at Kohlberg's stage two of moral development—mutual benefit. The researchers concluded that prison life tends to mold prisoners into a morality lower than their "private best," that is, their moral development outside the prison environment. In other words, the punishment paradigm, rather than making society safer, may actually be harming society by turning out more-hardened criminals.[34]

CONCLUSION

Although few students will ever be directly faced with decisions involving the death penalty, the moral assumptions underlying both positions affect their daily interaction with one another. Capital punishment raises the issue of the moral value and dignity of humans who, apparently, are at the most despicable end of the spectrum, who have little or no respect for the dignity of those whom they brutally massacre.

The debate over the death penalty also needs to return to the assumption that punishment is justified. We need to question the very punishment paradigm that underlies capital punishment. In addition, even if the death penalty can be morally justified in theory, it does not necessarily follow that it should be used in practice. Creating a just public policy regarding capital punishment requires balancing moral theory with the realities of human nature and society.

ERNEST VAN DEN HAAG

The Ultimate Punishment: A Defense of Capital Punishment

Ernest van den Haag is a retired professor of jurisprudence and public policy at Fordham University. A well-known advocate of the death penalty, van den Haag is author of *Punishment Criminals* and *The Death Penalty: A Debate*. Like Kant, van den Haag argues that the primary purpose of capital punishment is to satisfy the demands of retributive justice. The often-cited objection that capital punishment is applied in a discriminatory manner, therefore, does not make capital punishment *itself* immoral, but rather the manner in which it is currently meted out. In response to the objection that innocent people are sometimes executed, van den Haag points out that almost all human activities cost the lives of some innocent bystanders. As for lack of proof that it works as a deterrent, the primary purpose of capital punishment, he reminds us, is not deterrence but retribution.

Critical Reading Questions

1. How does van den Haag respond to the argument that capital punishment is morally wrong because it is applied in a discriminatory manner?
2. According to van den Haag, which is the most important value—equality or justice—and why?
3. On what grounds does van den Haag argue that justice requires the death penalty?
4. How does van den Haag respond to the objection that sometimes innocent people are executed?
5. Does van den Haag think that capital punishment is an effective deterrent? Does his argument depend on capital punishment being an effective deterrent?
6. What are some of the "incidental" issues in the capital punishment debate?
7. What is the "rule of retaliation"? What, according to van den Haag, is the relevance of retaliation to the capital punishment debate?
8. How does van den Haag respond to the argument that capital punishment legitimates killing?
9. According to van den Haag, why does the principle of retribution require capital punishment for some crimes?
10. How does van den Haag respond to the argument that capital punishment is degrading to human dignity? Which philosophers does he use to support his position?

"The Ultimate Punishment: A Defense of Capital Punishment," *The Harvard Law Review* 99 (1986): 1662–1669. Notes have been omitted.

In an average year about 20,000 homicides occur in the United States. Fewer than 300 convicted murderers are sentenced to death. But because no more than thirty murderers have been executed in any recent year, most convicts sentenced to death are likely to die of old age. Nonetheless, the death penalty looms large in discussions: it raises important moral questions independent of the number of executions.

The death penalty is our harshest punishment. It is irrevocable: it ends the existence of those punished, instead of temporarily imprisoning them. Further, although not intended to cause physical pain, execution is the only corporal punishment still applied to adults. These singular characteristics contribute to the perennial, impassioned controversy about capital punishment.

I. DISTRIBUTION

Consideration of the justice, morality, or usefulness of capital punishment is often conflated with objections to its alleged discriminatory or capricious distribution among the guilty. Wrongly so. If capital punishment is immoral *in se*, no distribution among the guilty could make it moral. If capital punishment is moral, no distribution would make it immoral. Improper distribution cannot affect the quality of what is distributed, be it punishments or rewards. Discriminatory or capricious distribution thus could not justify abolition of the death penalty. Further, maldistribution inheres no more in capital punishment than in any other punishment.

Maldistribution between the guilty and the innocent is, by definition, unjust. But the injustice does not lie in the nature of the punishment. Because of the finality of the death penalty, the most grievous maldistribution occurs when it is imposed upon the innocent. However, the frequent allegations of discrimination and capriciousness refer to maldistribution among the guilty and not to the punishment of the innocent.

Maldistribution of any punishment among those who deserve it is irrelevant to its justice or morality. Even if poor or black convicts guilty of capital offenses suffer capital punishment, and other convicts equally guilty of the same crimes do not, a more equal distribution, however desirable, would merely be more equal. It would not be more just to the convicts under sentence of death.

Punishments are imposed on persons, not on racial or economic groups. Guilt is personal. The only relevant question is: does the person to be executed deserve the punishment? Whether or not others who deserve the same punishment, whatever their economic or racial group, have avoided execution is irrelevant. If they have, the guilt of the executed convicts would not be diminished, nor would their punishment be less deserved. To put the issue starkly, if the death penalty were imposed on guilty blacks, but not on guilty whites, or, if it were imposed by a lottery among the guilty, this irrationally discriminatory or capricious distribution would neither make the penalty unjust, nor cause anyone to be unjustly punished, despite the undue impunity bestowed on others.

Equality, in short, seems morally less important than justice. And justice is independent of distributional inequalities. The ideal of equal justice demands that justice be equally distributed, not that it be replaced by equality. Justice requires that as many of the guilty as possible be punished, regardless of whether others have avoided punishment. To let these others escape the deserved punishment does not do justice to them, or to society. But it is not unjust to those who could not escape. . . .

Recent data reveal little direct racial discrimination in the sentencing of those arrested and convicted of murder. The abrogation of the death penalty for rape has eliminated a major source of racial discrimination. Concededly, some discrimination based on the race of murder victims may exist; yet, this discrimination affects criminal victimizers in an unexpected way. Murderers of whites are thought more likely to be executed than murderers of blacks. Black victims, then, are less fully vindicated than white ones. However, because most black murderers kill blacks, black murderers are spared the death penalty more often than are white murderers. They fare better than most white murderers. The motivation behind unequal distribution of the death penalty may well have been to discriminate against blacks, but the result has favored them. Maldistribution is thus a straw man for empirical as well as analytical reasons.

II. MISCARRIAGES OF JUSTICE

In a recent survey Professors Hugo Adam Bedau and Michael Radelet found that 7000 persons were executed in the United States between 1900 and 1985 and that 25 were innocent of capital crimes. Among the innocents they list Sacco and Vanzetti as well as Ethel and Julius Rosenberg. Although their data may be questionable, I do not doubt that, over a long enough period, miscarriages of justice will occur even in capital cases.

Despite precautions, nearly all human activities, such as trucking, lighting, or construction, cost the lives of some innocent bystanders. We do not give up these activities, because the advantages, moral or material, outweigh the unintended losses. Analogously, for those who think the death penalty just, miscarriages of justice are offset by the moral benefits and the usefulness of doing justice. For those who think the death penalty unjust even when it does not miscarry, miscarriages can hardly be decisive.

III. DETERRENCE

Despite much recent work, there has been no conclusive statistical demonstration that the death penalty is a better deterrent than are alternative punishments. However, deterrence is less than decisive for either side. Most abolitionists acknowledge that they would continue to favor abolition even if the death penalty were shown to deter more murders than alternatives could deter. Abolitionists appear to value the life of a convicted murderer or, at least, his non-execution, more highly than they value the lives of innocent victims who might be spared by deterring prospective murderers.

Deterrence is not altogether decisive for me either. I would favor retention of the death penalty as retribution even if it were shown that the threat of execution could not deter prospective murderers not already deterred by the threat of imprisonment. Still, I believe the death penalty, because of its finality, is

more feared than imprisonment, and deters some prospective murderers not deterred by the threat of imprisonment. Sparing the lives of even a few prospective victims by deterring their murderers is more important than preserving the lives of convicted murderers because of the possibility, or even the probability, that executing them would not deter others. Whereas the lives of the victims who might be saved are valuable, that of the murderer has only negative value, because of his crime. Surely the criminal law is meant to protect the lives of potential victims in preference to those of actual murderers.

Murder rates are determined by many factors; neither the severity nor the probability of the threatened sanction is always decisive. However, for the long run, I share the view of Sir James Fitzjames Stephen: "Some men, probably, abstain from murder because they fear that if they committed murder they would be hanged. Hundreds of thousands abstain from it because they regard it with horror. One great reason they regard it with horror is that murderers are hanged." Penal sanctions are useful in the long run for the formation of the internal restraints so necessary to control crime. The severity and finality of the death penalty is appropriate to the seriousness and finality of murder.

IV. INCIDENTAL ISSUES: COST, RELATIVE SUFFERING, BRUTALIZATION

Many nondecisive issues are associated with capital punishment. Some believe that the monetary cost of appealing a capital sentence is excessive. Yet most comparisons of the cost of life imprisonment with the cost of execution, apart from their dubious relevance, are flawed at least by the implied assumption that life prisoners will generate no judicial costs during their imprisonment. At any rate, the actual monetary costs are trumped by the importance of doing justice.

Others insist that a person sentenced to death suffers more than his victim suffered, and that this (excess) suffering is undue according to the *lex talionis* (rule of retaliation). We cannot know whether the murderer on death row suffers more than his victim suffered; however, unlike the murderer, the victim deserved none of the suffering inflicted. Further, the limitations of the *lex talionis* were meant to restrain private vengeance, not the social retribution that has taken its place. Punishment—regardless of the motivation—is not intended to revenge, offset, or compensate for the victim's suffering, or to be measured by it. Punishment is to vindicate the law and the social order undermined by the crime. This is why a kidnapper's penal confinement is not limited to the period for which he imprisoned his victim; nor is a burglar's confinement meant merely to offset the suffering or the harm he caused his victim; nor is it meant only to offset the advantage he gained.

Another argument heard at least since Beccaria is that, by killing a murderer, we encourage, endorse, or legitimize unlawful killing. Yet, although all punishments are meant to be unpleasant, it is seldom argued that they legitimize the unlawful imposition of identical unpleasantness. Imprisonment is not thought to legitimize kidnapping; neither are fines thought to legitimize robbery. The difference between murder and execution, or between kidnapping and imprisonment, is that the first is unlawful and undeserved, the second a lawful and deserved punishment for an unlawful act. The physical similarities of the punishment to the crime are irrelevant. The relevant difference is not physical, but social.

V. JUSTICE, EXCESS, DEGRADATION

We threaten punishments in order to deter crime. We impose them not only to make the threats credible but also as retribution (justice) for the crimes that were not deterred. Threats and punishments are necessary to deter and deterrence is a sufficient practical justification for them. Retribution is an independent moral justification. Although penalties can be unwise, repulsive, or inappropriate, and those punished can be pitiable, in a sense the infliction of legal punishment on a guilty person cannot be unjust. By committing the crime, the criminal volunteered to assume the risk of receiving a legal punishment that he could have avoided by not committing the crime. The punishment he suffers is

the punishment he voluntarily risked suffering and, therefore, it is no more unjust to him than any other event for which one knowingly volunteers to assume the risk. Thus, the death penalty cannot be unjust to the guilty criminal.

There remain, however, two moral objections. The penalty may be regarded as always excessive as retribution and always morally degrading. To regard the death penalty as always excessive, one must believe that no crime—no matter how heinous—could possibly justify capital punishment. Such a belief can neither be corroborated nor refuted; it is an article of faith.

Alternatively, or concurrently, one may believe that everybody, the murderer no less than the victim, has an imprescriptible (natural?) right to life. The law therefore should not deprive anyone of life. I share Jeremy Bentham's view that any such "natural and imprescriptible rights" are "nonsense upon stilts."

Justice Brennan has insisted that the death penalty is "uncivilized," "inhuman," inconsistent with "human dignity" and with "the sanctity of life," that it "treats members of the human race as nonhumans, as objects to be toyed with and discarded," that it is "uniquely degrading to human dignity" and "by its very nature, [involves] a denial of the executed person's humanity." Justice Brennan does not say why he thinks execution "uncivilized." Hitherto most civilizations have had the death penalty, although it has been discarded in Western Europe, where it is currently unfashionable probably because of its abuse by totalitarian regimes.

By "degrading," Justice Brennan seems to mean that execution degrades the executed convicts. Yet philosophers, such as Immanuel Kant and G. F. W. Hegel, have insisted that, when deserved, execution, far from degrading the executed convict, affirms his humanity by affirming his rationality and his responsibility for his actions. They thought that execution, when deserved, is required for the sake of the convict's dignity. (Does not life imprisonment violate human dignity more than execution, by keeping alive a prisoner deprived of all autonomy?)

Common sense indicates that it cannot be death—our common fate—that is inhuman.

Therefore, Justice Brennan must mean that death degrades when it comes not as a natural or accidental event, but as a deliberate social imposition. The murderer learns through his punishment that his fellow men have found him unworthy of living; that because he has murdered, he is being expelled from the community of the living. This degradation is self-inflicted. By murdering, the murderer has so dehumanized himself that he cannot remain among the living. The social recognition of his self-degradation is the punitive essence of execution. To believe, as Justice Brennan appears to, that the degradation is inflicted by the execution reverses the direction of causality.

Execution of those who have committed heinous murders may deter only one murder per year. If it does, it seems quite warranted. It is also the only fitting retribution for murder I can think of.

Discussion Questions

1. Do you agree with van den Haag that retributive justice is more important than equality? Support your answer. Discuss how John Rawls might respond to van den Haag's claim.
2. Are you satisfied with van den Haag's argument that miscarriages of justice, in which innocent people are executed, are offset by the moral benefits of retributive justice? Discuss whether his response is consistent with human dignity and the categorical imperative, which state that we should never treat a person as a means only.
3. Clarence Darrow, U.S. lawyer and criminal defense attorney (1857–1938), was renowned for his outspoken opposition to the death penalty. Darrow believed that human behavior is determined by circumstances out of our control and, therefore, does not deserve to be punished. In his "Address to the Prisoners in the Chicago County Jail," Darrow told the inmates:

   > In one sense, everybody is equally good and equally bad. We all do the best we can under the circumstances . . . there were circumstances that drove you to do exactly the thing which you did. You could not help it any more than we outside can help taking the positions we take. . . .
   >
   > I will guarantee to take from this jail, or any jail in the world, five hundred men who have been the worst criminals and law-breakers who ever got into jail, and I will go down to our lowest streets and take five hundred of the most abandoned prostitutes, and go out somewhere where there is plenty of good land, and will give them a chance to make a living, and they will be as good people as the average in the community.[35]

   Do you agree with Darrow? Discuss how van den Haag might respond to Darrow's claim that criminals are simply products of their environments.
4. Discuss how a care ethicist, such as Carol Gilligan or Nel Noddings, might respond to van den Haag's justice-based argument. Is van den Haag's justification of capital punishment consistent with a care ethics approach? Support your answer.

CHRISTOPHER W. MORRIS

Punishment and Loss of Moral Standing

Christopher Morris is a professor of philosophy at Bowling Green University in Ohio. In his article Morris presents a social contract theory of punishment. In social contractarianism, justice is a more compelling moral concern than benevolence. Morris argues that people who intentionally violate the social contract by engaging in wrongdoing lose some moral standing and, hence, forfeit some of their moral rights. Those who murder forfeit their right to life. Because they have forfeited this right, capital punishment cannot be said to violate it.

Critical Reading Questions

1. How does Morris answer the question: "By what authority do we punish?"
2. According to Morris, what is the moral status of a wrongdoer? Does wrongdoing affect a person's rights?
3. How does Morris define punishment? What is the purpose of punishment according to Morris?
4. What distinction does Morris make between justice and benevolence? Which of these moral duties is more relevant to the question of punishment?
5. How does Morris define justice? Why, according to him, should we act justly?
6. What is the "doctrine of the circumstances of justice"?
7. According to Morris, what does it mean for someone to have "moral standing"?
8. What are the differences among "moral subjects," "direct moral objects," and "indirect moral objects"?
9. What is the "forfeiture justification of punishment"?
10. According to Morris, why would a rational person choose to be just?
11. What are some of the objections to the forfeiture justification of punishment? How does Morris respond to these objections?

"Punishment and Loss of Moral Standing," *Canadian Journal of Philosophy* 21, no. 1 (March 1991): 53–80. Some notes have been omitted.

When any man, even in political society, renders himself by his crimes obnoxious to the public, he is punished by the laws in his goods and person; that is, the ordinary rules of justice are, with regard to him, suspended for a moment, and it becomes equitable to inflict on him, for the *benefit* of society, what otherwise he could not suffer without wrong or injury.[1]

By what authority do we punish? What permits us to deprive people of their liberty or possessions for some wrong that they have committed? Normally we may not do to people what we do when we punish wrongdoers. What exactly allows us to treat the latter as we do? . . .

I. THE MORAL JUSTIFICATION OF PUNISHMENT

. . . I shall argue that wrongdoers do not possess moral rights that stand in the way of their being punished. Thus punishment of wrongdoers will not be unjust.

What is punishment? The matter of the definition of punishment is complicated, as well as controversial. It will suffice for my purposes to have a general characterization of the notion. As such, punishment is the intentional imposition of some pain, unpleasantness, or deprivation for an offense committed by the culprit. It may be imposed so as to teach the offender a lesson, to deter others from similar acts, or to exact retribution. . . .

Criminal penalties are often recommended or defended as effective deterrents, or as appropriate means of retribution for certain offenses or at least of expressing the seriousness with which we view them. It is usually, and quite naturally, assumed that such penalties must consequentially be justified— that is, *morally* justified—if they are to be inflicted. In particular, it is usually thought that a particular kind of moral justification is required in the standard cases of punishment—namely, justification with reference to *justice*.

It is common to think of morality as having different parts or virtues. It is controversial how to understand these parts or even how to distinguish them. But it is widely thought that justice is differ-

ent from the virtues of friendship, courage, moderation, and the like. More importantly, justice is usually distinguished from charity or benevolence, although there is less agreement here. The standard distinction is to understand justice to pertain to what individuals are *owed,* to what they may *claim,* to what they have a *right.* Benevolence, by contrast, is a virtue that attaches itself directly to the well-being of others. It is exemplified by taking an interest in others' welfare independently of that to which they have a claim. . . .

Typically, infringements of liberty or intentional infliction of pain violate moral rights to be free and not to be harmed. Thus, it would normally be thought that punishment requires a rationale in terms of justice. The state's involvement, it is usually thought, will only strengthen this requirement.

Now the moral rights of criminals do not stand in the way of punishment if we may justifiably *infringe* or *override* them. I do not, however, wish to defend either of these two possibilities. Instead I shall argue that punishment will not be unjust when wrongdoers lose the moral rights that would otherwise protect them against harm or loss. I turn now to the conception of justice that will be the basis of my approach to punishment.

II. JUSTICE BY CONVENTION

Justice is the moral virtue that is concerned with what is *owed* or *due* to individuals. It is that to which individuals appeal when they claim that to which they have a moral *right* (though this is not to say that the domain of rights exhausts that of justice). Recent discussions of justice have focused largely on principles of distributive justice, but this narrow focus should not let us lose sight of the larger virtue.

There is a long western tradition, dating back to Antiphon, Glaucon, and Epicurus, developed by Hobbes, Hume, and Rousseau, and continued in various ways by Rawls, Harsanyi, Mackie, Harman, Scanlon, Gauthier, and Kavka that understands justice to be a type of mutually agreeable convention. According to this tradition, justice consists of principles, rules, and norms that ideally serve to advance the interests and aims of all in certain situations. This tradition is dubbed "contractarian" as it often understands the terms of justice to be the outcome of a hypothetical bargain or "social contract." It might be less misleading to think of contemporary representatives of this tradition as offering a "rational choice" conception of morality after John Rawls's famous remark, "The theory of justice is a part, perhaps the most significant part, of the theory of rational choice."[2]

The account of justice offered by this tradition is designed to answer two traditional questions: what does justice require? and why be just? . . .

The indirect advantages of justice may normally be such that few individuals can wish to forego them. The advantages of injustice may, however, be sufficiently great that individuals are tempted to act unjustly. When then is it rational to be just? The principles of conduct that would emerge from the hypothetical bargain that rational choice ethicists use to determine the requirements of justice are those to which it is rational to agree. For such principles, if complied with, secure everyone's advantage. Without them, life would be nasty, brutish, and short, depending on the efficacy of alternative means of social control (e.g., law, superstition, kinship relations). However, granting that we have a reason to agree to such principles—even to grant that they define what justice is—what reason do we have to comply with their requirements?

We have reason to be just because if we have reason to accept certain principles of conduct, then we have reason to comply with them, provided the conditions under which we accepted the principles remain unchanged. . . .

One of the conditions—one of the "circumstances of justice," to use Rawls's phrase—giving rise to the need for justice is the possibility of mutual benefit. Others are the capacity and willingness of rational beings to impose constraints on their behavior. In the absence of such conditions, one has no reason to abide by the constraints of justice in one's conduct toward others. This is important, for it effectively means that in the absence of (1) mutual benefit or of (2) the capacity or (3) willingness to be just, individuals are not constrained by justice

in their behavior toward one another. The answer that contractarian theorists give to the question "why be just?" commits them to the view just expressed, that in the absence of certain conditions there is no reason to act justly; we may call this view "the *doctrine* of the circumstances of justice." This doctrine is crucial to my understanding of the justification of punishment. I turn now to a brief account of *moral standing*.

Let us say that a *moral object* is something that is an object of moral consideration. A *direct* moral object is something *to* which (or to whom) that consideration is paid or owed; an *indirect* moral object is something *about* or *concerning* which moral consideration is paid. The latter is a *beneficiary* of the moral consideration. . . .

To have *moral standing* is to be owed (some) moral consideration, that is, to be a direct moral object. To be a mere indirect moral object is *not* to possess moral standing. In terms of these notions and distinctions, people typically are direct moral objects and have moral standing. Protected natural sites, national monuments, significant works of art might be examples of indirect moral objects. When we destroy the latter, we may be understood to fail in our duties to other people. . . .

We may contrast the notion of a moral object with that of a *moral subject*. The latter is something that has moral duties or may be expected to give moral consideration to direct moral objects. We usually understand adult humans to be moral subjects, while non-human animals and young infants are not so regarded; presumably *agency* would be necessary to being a moral subject.

Supposing that the "circumstances of justice" be satisfied, rational choice or contractarian moral theory understands rational humans, capable and willing to impose moral constraints on their conduct toward others, as moral subjects and direct moral objects. Thus, for this theory, as for most others, in normal circumstances adult humans have moral obligations and are owed certain moral considerations. However, it is important to note that "having moral standing" is a relation; something has moral standing in its relations to some other entity(ies). It should not be assumed that the relation holds universally, as we shall see. . . .

Now contractarian moral theory will imply that in the circumstances of justice all humans capable and willing to impose constraints on their behavior toward others have full moral standing. . . .

III. WRONGDOING AND LOSS OF MORAL STANDING

To have moral standing is to be owed (some) moral consideration. Justice consists in part of a set of moral rights, the most important of which, we may assume, are those to life, liberty, and property. To lose some such rights is to lose some of one's moral standing. I wish to argue that wrongdoers lose some of their rights and some of their moral standing, and that some wrongdoers lose all of their rights (or never possessed the full set) and retain at most what I have called partial moral standing. In other words, I shall defend a type of forfeiture theory, one according to which part (but only part) of the justification for punishment rests in the fact that wrongdoers lack certain rights, the presence of which would normally suffice to block the appropriate punishment. . . .

The first way in which wrongdoers can lose rights is less controversial or novel than the second; so I shall spend less time developing it. We may suppose that the conventions that determine justice, according to the contractarian tradition, have built into them provisions for penalties in the event of violation. Consider a club or organization established for the benefit of its members. It will have rules, respect of which will further the ends of the members. Without supposing duplicity on the part of the latter, it would be reasonable for them to include sanctions, however mild, for the violation of these rules; sanctions may provide assurance that others will not take advantage of one's cooperative behavior. Similarly, we may suppose that the rules of morality have built into them penalties, which may be applied whenever individuals act wrongly, that is, in violation of the rules.

The conception of justice characteristic of the contractarian tradition is that of an "artificial" system—to use the predicate favored by Hobbes and Hume—which ideally serves the interests of members of society. Given the imperfections of human rationality, it would be unwise to desire a system without sanctions for violations of its norms. That is, since we may expect that ordinary humans, without manifesting unwillingness to abide by the constraints of justice, will violate these constraints on occasion, when the temptation proves to be difficult to resist, we build into these constraints penalties for violations. . . .

The normal rights of individuals, then, are suspended whenever they violate the constraints of justice. The *act* of wrongdoing may cause the wrongdoer to lose, if only temporarily, certain rights. . . .

Criminal acts, then, insofar as they manifest the agent's unwillingness to comply with the requirements of justice, lead to (some) loss of moral standing. This is a simple consequence of the conditional nature of contractarian justice. What rights are thus lost? Alan H. Goldman makes the following suggestion:

> if we ask which rights are forfeited in violating rights of others, it is plausible to answer just those rights that one violates (or an equivalent set). One continues to enjoy rights only as long as one respects those rights in others: violation constitutes forfeiture. But one retains those rights which one has continued to respect in others.[3]

Wrongdoers, then, may lose (some of) their rights by their acts. The act alone may cause this loss insofar as the conventions of justice have penalties and the requisite suspension of duties built in. Further, the act, insofar as it manifests an unwillingness to abide by the constraints of justice, will bring about this loss; in some cases, the unwillingness revealed by the act may show that we mistakenly cooperated with the wrongdoer. Inflicting pain or deprivation of property or liberty on wrongdoers as a response to their acts is not unjust for they have lost, through their acts, the moral rights that would otherwise stand in the way of such treatment. Their status is analogous to exile; they are banished, not from a physical space but from a moral space. They have lost, at least in part, their membership in the moral community.

The forfeiture account may be independently appealing for retributive and other reasons. It may be thought that loss of the rights that wrongdoers violate is actually a most appropriate punishment for individuals unwilling to respect the requirements of justice. The intuitive appeal here may be similar to that of *lex talionis* in retributive theories. Further, it might be argued that punishing wrongdoers in ways that emphasize the relation between the rights they have violated and those they have thereby lost best *expresses* the community's outrage or anger at the wrongful act. Insofar as punishment has an expressive function, the criminal's forfeiture of moral rights would be both a consequence of his or her wrong doing and an expression of the moral community's consequent outrage. . . .

IV. THE DEATH PENALTY

The forfeiture account may be illustrated by an application to the death penalty. A discussion of capital punishment in light of the forfeiture thesis may provide a different understanding of the issues than is usually found in the contemporary literature. Consider the cases of contract killers, war criminals, tyrants, and certain terrorists who are unwilling to abide by the constraints of justice in their conduct toward others. . . .

Such people clearly lack full moral standing on a contractarian account of justice. They show by their conduct that they are unwilling to abide by the constraints of justice with most others. With respect to the latter, they themselves lack the protection that justice normally affords people. Suppose that they are apprehended, tried, and convicted of their crimes. Would it be *unjust* to execute them? No, for they lack full moral standing and thus the protection of justice. By their unwillingness to impose the constraints of justice on their conduct toward others, they lose the protection of justice. . . .

[W]e have no moral obligations of justice to contract killers, war criminals, tyrants, and genuine terrorists, or other individuals who place themselves outside the constraints of justice. Were it to be wrong to execute them, we would not be wronging *them* were we to do so; *they* would have no grounds of justice to complain.

We normally possess moral rights to life and to liberty. It is a controversial matter among ethicists exactly how these rights are to be understood, thus the contemporary debates over abortion, euthanasia, nuclear deterrence, and other issues. But at least part of the content of such moral rights is the obligation of others to refrain from intentionally taking one's life or from interfering with one's liberty when such is not necessary in order to protect the equal liberty of others or to serve some other important good. Such characterizations are imprecise, but they will serve my purpose.

Justice gives us our basic moral rights to life and liberty. Most theories of justice, contractarian or other, should have little trouble accounting for these rights, at least as I have characterized them. Thus, normally when we intentionally take another's life or interfere with their liberty, we must justify our actions with reference to justice, given their rights to life and liberty. Since taking or thus restricting another's life or liberty appear to be violations of their moral rights to life or liberty, a moral justification, one which makes reference to justice, seems required. Usually we will seek to show that the rights in question were *overridden* by some moral consideration. . . .

In the cases of the contract killers, war criminals, tyrants, and terrorists, I am suggesting that their moral rights to life or liberty are not overridden. (Indeed, I believe that this is not possible with respect to the moral right to life since I believe that this right is not *defeasible,* though I do not propose to argue this here.) Instead I am arguing that we do not have to give standard *moral* justifications for executing contract killers, war criminals, tyrants, or terrorists because so killing them would neither be a violation nor an overriding of their moral rights to life or liberty. Rather, they no longer have, or never had, such moral rights. Thus we merely need sufficient reason to execute them. To use Hobbes' language, such individuals have only the "right" of nature, that is, mere Hohfeldian liberties that entail no correlative obligations on the part of others. . . .

V. OBJECTIONS

Many will find my account counter-intuitive and will reject the idea that some humans, no matter how amoral, lose their rights and moral standing. And there are many objections that will be, and have been, made. I shall discuss some of these.

Much crime is committed by the destitute in the urban underclass. It may be argued that the account I have offered "does not apply" to them, as "they are *outside* of the circumstances of justice to begin with and have nothing to forfeit." It is unclear what exactly the objection is, for if individuals who commit crimes lack certain rights to begin with, then no rights stand in the way of their being punished for their acts, and the first part of a justification for punishment is complete. This criticism might be the same as that which finds the very idea of someone without full moral standing objectionable. Now there *is* a serious question about the implications of our moral theories for the plight of those in our cities who have no or little stake in the social order. My view is that there are compelling contractarian arguments for some redistribution to the poor and destitute to give them a stake in the social order and bring them into the circumstances of justice. But that would seem to be another matter entirely than the subject of this essay.

It might be argued that the forfeiture account would permit various forms of cruel punishment—for instance, the death penalty—and that this constitutes an objection. If cruelty involves indifference to another's pain or suffering, then punishment as I have characterized it may well be cruel. However, if cruelty involves taking pleasure in another's suffering, then cruelty is not part of the account that I am offering. For on the view that I am defending, the reasons for punishment are independent of the grounds for the permissibility of punishment.

It is a criticism, however, of many of our institutions to point out that our motivations are mixed and include elements of cruelty or malice. Were we to dispose of certain amoral criminals by imprisoning or executing them, accepting the account I have offered, but do so largely from malice and revenge, then our practices would be vulnerable to criticism. Supposing that the criminal in question lacks the moral rights that justice accords, then cruelty will be an objection only insofar as (1) it is contrary to benevolence or some other virtue, (2) it is bad public policy, or (3) we have obligations to others that prohibit us from treating any human cruelly. It is likely that, e.g., torture will virtually always be ruled out for these reasons, though I do not propose to argue this here. . . .

VI. CONCLUSION

Punishment, I have argued, is justified in part because wrongdoers lose the moral rights that would otherwise stand in the way of their being harmed in the manner that we do when we punish. Moral standing is to some degree lost, and moral rights are to some degree forfeited, by wrongdoers.

It might be argued that the position I have put forward does not take justice seriously. I disagree. The forfeiture account I have developed links in a certain way being a direct moral object with being a moral subject. Rational humans who are not willing to impose the constraints of justice on their conduct toward others are not themselves protected by these constraints. In my view, *that* is to take justice seriously.

NOTES

1. David Hume, *Inquiry Concerning the Principles of Morals,* Section III, "Of Justice," Part I, paragraph 10.

2. *A Theory of Justice* (Cambridge, MA: Harvard University Press, 1971), 16; see also 172. It is clear from his most recent writings, if not from some of the elements of *A Theory of Justice,* that Rawls does not really endorse the view of moral theory expressed by his remark.

3. Alan H. Goldman, "The Paradox of Punishment," *Philosophy & Public Affairs* **9** (1979): 44.

Discussion Questions

1. Does Morris make a convincing argument for why it benefits people to behave justly? Consider the story of Gyges's ring recounted by Glaucon in Plato's *Republic*. In a debate with Socrates over justice, Glaucon argues that people are naturally selfish and will behave unjustly whenever they have the opportunity. To illustrate his point, Glaucon tells the story of a shepherd named Gyges. Gyges takes a ring off a dead body, and the ring makes him invisible. Delighted with his discovery, Gyges takes advantage of his invisibility to murder the king and seize the throne. Glaucon argues that everyone would behave unjustly like Gyges if they knew they could get away with it.

   Do people behave justly only to avoid punishment or public censure, as Glaucon claims? Or do people behave justly because it mutually benefits them, as Morris claims? Support your answer. Does the story of Gyges's ring weaken Morris's argument?

2. In a footnote to his article, Morris draws an analogy between forfeiture of rights and exile or banishment of criminals. Someone "violates certain fundamental norms of society (or displeases the rulers) and is stripped of citizenship and banished from the land." Socrates, he notes, was offered the choice of exile or the death penalty; he chose the latter. Most people, now believe, however, that the execution of Socrates by the state was not morally justified. Does the death of Socrates and others who question societal norms and laws demonstrate a flaw in the contractual concept of justice? How might a natural law theorist such as Aquinas respond to this question? Discuss how Morris might respond.

3. In 1945, following World War II, the tribunal at the United Nations Nuremberg Trials compiled a charter with a list of universal standards of justice. Between 1945 and 1949, almost 200 Nazis were tried under this new charter. Of these 161 were found guilty and 36 sentenced to death. Discuss how a social contractarian such as Morris would respond to the use of the death penalty for the Nazi war criminals. Because the Nazis did not violate their own community's social contract, and the Nuremberg charter was not written until after the war, did the United Nations act unjustly by punishing the Nazis for being "good" citizens?

4. Inmates on death row are sometimes put on "suicide watch" so they cannot take their own lives. Retributivists claim that the death penalty is not about revenge but about justice, so is there some doublethink inherent in trying to prevent condemned prisoners from taking their own lives? If retribution stems from a respect for the dignity of persons rather than a desire for revenge, wouldn't it be preferable for murderers to voluntarily end their own lives in payment for their crimes rather than be involuntarily executed? Support your answers. Discuss how Kant, Morris, and van den Haag might respond to these questions.

HUGO ADAM BEDAU

Capital Punishment

Hugo Adam Bedau is a professor of philosophy at Tufts University and a well-known opponent of capital punishment. In the following selection, Bedau examines the death penalty in light of important relevant moral values, such as the sanctity of life and the right to life. Bedau rejects Locke's argument that the right to life can be forfeited by murder, arguing that the concept of forfeiture of one's right to life is inconsistent with human dignity. Bedau also rejects Kant's claim that retributive justice requires the death penalty for murder, as well as a utilitarian approach to determining the morality of capital punishment. From here Bedau goes on to question the morality of punishment.

Critical Reading Questions

1. What, according to Bedau, is one of the most important moral values?
2. What is the relationship between the sanctity of human life and the right to life? Why, according to Bedau, is the death penalty inconsistent with these two values?
3. Why does Bedau reject Locke's argument that the right to life is forfeited by murderers?
4. On what grounds does Bedau reject Kant's claim that retributive justice requires capital punishment for murder?
5. According to Kant, in what state of mind must a murderer be to be held morally responsible for his or her actions? Why does Bedau reject Kant's reasoning on this point?
6. On what grounds does Bedau reject utilitarian arguments for capital punishment?
7. What is the nature and purpose of punishment, according to Bedau?
8. Why does Bedau conclude that the death penalty violates the dignity of persons?
9. On what grounds does Bedau reject the social defense argument for the death penalty?
10. On what grounds does Bedau reject consequentialist arguments, such as deterrence, incapacitation, and crime prevention, for the death penalty?
11. What are the two leading principles that underlie retributive justice?
12. On what grounds does Bedau argue that retributive justice does not require the death penalty for murder?
13. According to Bedau, why does capital punishment demean society as well as the criminal being executed?

"Capital Punishment," ed. by Tom Regan, *Matters of Life and Death* (New York: McGraw-Hill, 1993), 160–192. Some notes have been omitted.

INTRODUCTION

When we confront the task of evaluating punishments from the moral point of view, a host of questions immediately arises: Who should be punished? What offenses and harms should be made liable to punishment? What is involved in making the punishment fit the crime? Are some punishments too cruel or barbaric to be tolerated no matter how effective they may be in preventing crime? Are some criminals so depraved or dangerous that no punishment is too severe for them? What moral principles should govern our thinking about crime and punishment?

To give reasonable answers to such questions, we need to appeal to a wide variety of empirical facts. We will want to know, for example, what would happen to the crime rate if no one were punished at all, or if all offenders were punished more leniently or more severely than is now usual. We would want to know whether the system of criminal justice operates with adequate efficiency and fairness when it metes out punishment, or whether the severest punishments tend to fall mainly on some social, racial, or economic classes. But we will want to settle other things besides these matters of fact. Social values, moral ideals, ethical principles are also involved, and we will want to know which values and which ideals they are and how to evaluate them as well. Central among these ethical considerations are the value, worth, and dignity of persons—the victims of crime, the offenders, and the rest of society. How, exactly, does our belief in the value of human life, the worth of each person, our common humanity and our common dignity, bear on the nature and methods of punishment as seen from the moral point of view?

There is no better setting in which to examine these questions than the one provided by the controversy over the morality of capital punishment (the death penalty). From an historical perspective, one of the most important relevant ethical values is the idea of *the sanctity of human life*. . . .

Distinct as the sanctity of human life and the right to life are, they are held together by a common bond. Each expresses the view that it is morally wrong to take a purely instrumental view of human life. By "instrumental view of human life" I mean any view that makes it permissible to kill persons in order to protect some other value (e.g., property) or in order to advance some social or political goal (e.g., national liberation). . . .

So far as the death penalty is concerned, it might seem that once it is granted that human life is sacred or that everyone has an equal right to life, the death penalty is morally indefensible. Such a punishment seems obviously inconsistent with such ideals as human worth and value. The opposite, however, is true if we let history be our guide. Chief among the traditional defenders of capital punishment have been religious and secular thinkers who sincerely believed in these ideals. In fact, these thinkers usually invoked the sanctity of human life and the right to life as part of their defense and justification of death for murderers and other criminals. To see how such a seemingly paradoxical doctrine can be maintained, as well as to begin our examination of the major issues involved in the moral evaluation of the death penalty, we must scrutinize the traditional doctrine of the right to life.

I. THE RIGHT TO LIFE AND CAPITAL PUNISHMENT

The Doctrine of Natural Rights

The general idea shared by many philosophers, beginning in the seventeenth century, was that each person by nature—that is, apart from the laws of the state and simply by virtue of being born a human being—had the right to live. It followed from this that it was a violation of this right to murder another person, and that it was the responsibility of government to protect human rights, prohibit murder, and try to arrest, convict, and punish anyone guilty of this crime. Thus, the right to life can be thought of, first, as underlying the prohibition against murder common to the criminal law of all countries. . . .

The right to life seems to pose a problem for a policy of capital punishment. Even if a person has committed murder (so the argument runs) and has therewith intentionally violated another's right to life, the criminal still has his or her own right to life.

Would it not be a violation of the murderer's right for him or her to be put to death as punishment? If so, must not capital punishment be morally wrong? . . .

Forfeiting the Right to Life

Locke argued that although a person's right to life is natural and inalienable, it can be "forfeited" and *is* forfeited whenever one person violates that right in another. [W. D. Ross] has put the point clearly: "The offender, by violating the life, liberty, or property of another, has lost his own right to have his life, liberty, or property respected. . . ."[1] The idea is a familiar one, although there are troubling and unanswered questions: To whom is it forfeited? Can this right, once forfeited, ever be restored? If so, by whom and under what conditions? Thanks to the doctrine of forfeiture, it was possible for Locke to assert without apparent contradiction both that everyone has a natural and inalienable right to life and that the death penalty for a murderer does not violate that right.

Locke's actual reasoning was somewhat more complex and less plausible but more revealing than the account of it so far given. According to Locke, a person forfeits the right to life whenever he or she commits a criminal act that "deserves death."[2] What criterion does Locke use to decide whether a crime deserves death or some lesser penalty? He seems not to have given any thought to the problem. . . .

Difficulties with Locke's Theory

There are various objections to the classic theory of the right to life, two of which deserve to be mentioned here. First, underlying Locke's doctrine of natural rights and wholly independent of it are two important assumptions. One is that punishment under law is necessary for social defense. (By "social defense" is meant the prevention of crime, by means of deterrence and incapacitation, as well as by the reduction of incentives and opportunities for the commission of crimes. Thus, prisons, police forces, controlling the sale of firearms, locks on doors, and threats of punishment can all be regarded as methods of social defense.) The other

is that justice requires retribution—criminals deserve to be punished, and the punishment must fit the crime. Such beliefs lead to the conclusion that the punishment for murder and other crimes should be death, and they force Locke to make some accommodation in his theory of natural rights. The device he hit upon, as we have just seen, and one that generations of later thinkers have also adopted, is to declare that the right to life could be forfeited under certain conditions.

Against Locke's doctrine several objections deserve to be considered. First of all, there are other alternatives. . . . [S]uppose it is argued that although punishments typically constitute harms or deprivations to the person who undergoes them, the quality and extent of the deprivations [are] an open question. What is necessary is that the deprivation be imposed on the offender regardless or his or her preferences and choice. On this view, while it would be necessary for the offender to forfeit some rights in order to be punished, it would not be necessary to forfeit the right to life. Yet another possibility is to regard the right to life as an absolute right, one that it is always wrong to violate. Whether any of these alternatives can be better supported than the doctrine of forfeiture need not be resolved here. They do show that forfeiture of rights as Locke presents it is not the only way to permit punishment under a theory of natural rights.

Another difficulty with Locke's doctrine is that it seems to collapse two distinct issues into one. It is one thing to appeal to forfeiting rights in order to permit society to punish the guilty offender in the first place. It is quite another to appeal to forfeiture of rights in order to decide which among the available punishments is the appropriate one. . . . There is no intrinsic feature of any natural right, including the right to life, that makes it subject to loss through forfeiture. The only basis for supposing that any right is forfeited rather than grossly violated by society when it punishes an offender by death is that just retribution and social defense together require the death penalty for offenders guilty of a crime of this sort. If this requirement turns out to be false, unsubstantiated, or doubtful, then the claim that a criminal's right to life has been forfeited turns out to be equally false, unsubstantiated, or doubtful. . . .

Even if it is concluded that a murderer or violent criminal does forfeit the natural right to life, it does not follow that a murderer *must* be put to death. The doctrine of forfeiture does not involve the idea that once a person forfeits a right to *x*, those to whom it is forfeited have a *duty* to take *x* away from that person. This is often overlooked by those who insist that the death penalty is justified because murderers forfeit their lives. Forfeiting one's *right* to life is not identical with forfeiting one's life. . . .

Finally, we should note that Locke's doctrine of forfeiture makes his theory of natural rights vulnerable to utilitarian reasoning, and with devastating effect. The chief attraction of the idea of natural rights is that it provides each of us with moral armor (our rights) to protect us against burdens and deprivations that might be imposed on the ground that they are in the interests of the many or good for society in the long run. . . .

The Dignity of Persons

Although Kant by no means repudiated the doctrine of natural rights, he elevated to primary importance a different idea, the supreme worth or dignity of each person. The most famous single passage in which this doctrine and Kant's views on the punishment of murder are brought together runs as follows:

> If . . . he has committed a murder, he must die. In this case, there is no substitute that will satisfy the requirements of legal justice. There is no sameness of kind between death and remaining alive even under the most miserable conditions, and consequently there is no equality between the crime and the retribution unless the criminal is judicially condemned and put to death. But the death of the criminal must be kept entirely free of any maltreatment that would make an abomination of the humanity residing in the person suffering it.[3] . . .

For Kant, that idea of the dignity of man enters explicitly only to rule out any aggravations and brutality accompanying the sentence of death and its execution. For Kant, the dignity of man underlies the whole idea of society of free and rational persons

choosing to submit themselves to a common rule of law that includes the punishment of crimes. Accordingly, in punishment, "a human being can never be manipulated merely as a means to the purposes of someone else. . . . His innate personality protects him against such treatment. . . ."[4] Kant must therefore also reject the idea that a murderer should be punished by death because by doing so we prevent him from killing again and also discourage others from murder. Kant's appeal to the dignity of man requires him to rule out any role for social defense in the justification of capital punishment.

As the above passage also shows, underlying Kant's belief in the appropriateness of punishing murder with death is a principle of just retribution. This is reminiscent of Locke's view. . . . The chief difference between Kant and Locke is that Locke thinks it is proper to take into account not only just retribution but also social defense to determine proper punishments, whereas Kant unequivocally rules out the latter. What Kant has done is to present us with two moral ideas—the dignity or worth of each person as a rational creature, and the principle of retribution—that he regards as inextricably tied together. The latter principle he explained in the following way:

> What kind and what degree of punishment does public legal justice adopt as its principle and standard? None other than the principle of equality . . . , that is, the principle of not treating one side more favorably than the other. Accordingly, any undeserved evil that you inflict on someone else among the people is one that you do to yourself. Only the Law of retribution . . . can determine exactly the kind and degree of punishment.[5] . . .

Kant, as is obvious from his remarks, thought that retribution *required* the death penalty for murder. He is not alone in holding this view; it has widespread appeal even today. . . .

Difficulties with Kant's Theory

In the course of presenting Kant's views, we have already identified three respects in which his theory is vulnerable. One is that, like Locke's, it assumes that just retribution *requires* capital punishment for murder, an assumption that may be unnecessary and in any case is not proved. Another difficulty is that, unlike Locke's theory, Kant's seems to make no room whatever for the role of social defense in the justification of punishment. . . .

Finally, the third objection follows from the fact that Kant's theory is so obviously abstract and unempirical from beginning to end. If we really take seriously the idea of the dignity of the human person, then it may be that we will be led in case after case of actual crime to reject Kant's reasoning on the ground that it is inapplicable in light of the actual facts of the case. Kant's theory tells us what to do only with ideally rational killers; what we need is a theory that tells us how to cope with the actual persons who kill, and how to do that in a way that acknowledges our common humanity with both the victim and the offender, as well as the injustices to which all social systems are prone and the wisdom of self-restraint in the exercise of violence, especially when undertaken deliberately and in the name of justice.

Utilitarianism and the Death Penalty

. . . Just as Kant disregarded considerations of consequences in evaluating the morality of capital punishment, so utilitarians disregard any appeals to natural rights or the dignity of the human person. For them, these ideas at best mask a reference to social benefits, more likely, they are moral standards independent of (and thus potentially in conflict with) the principle of utility. At worst, they are rhetorical phrases of dubious content. The utilitarian, therefore, regards the death penalty as justified by the degree to which it advances the general welfare. Accordingly, its justification proceeds in the following manner: (1) Consider the practice of the death penalty and all its present and future consequences—for the executed offenders, for the victims of crime, their friends and families, and the rest of society. (2) Consider each of the alternative modes of punishment that might be imposed and the consequences of each were it to be employed. (3) Decide in favor of the death penalty rather than any alternative only if, in light of all of the facts, its

practice would have the greatest net balance of benefit over burden for everyone affected by it.

Two things are noteworthy about such a pattern of reasoning. First, everything depends on the facts, and diverse issues of fact are always in question. Moreover, these facts are not likely to remain constant in a given society decade after decade, much less from one society to another. The result is that it may be very difficult to reach agreement on all of them, as the unending debate over the deterrent efficacy of executions attests. When that happens, reasonable utilitarians will have to agree to disagree with each other over whether the death penalty should be retained, modified, or abolished for this or that crime. We have, in fact, a perfect illustration of precisely such a disagreement between the two most influential classic utilitarian philosophers. Jeremy Bentham (1748–1832) strongly opposed the death penalty throughout his life and in one of his last essays argued forcefully for its complete abolition in England and France. His student, John Stuart Mill (1806–1873), however, when he was a member of Parliament in the 1860s, argued with comparable firmness against abolition of the death penalty for murder in the England of his day. Thus, within the space of a generation, Bentham and Mill, professing utilitarians, disagreed over the desirability of abolishing the death penalty. . . .

A second point of interest is that the general welfare is an extremely abstract, remote, and elusive end-state to serve as the good to be aimed at in choosing among alternative penal policies. Utilitarians have devoted much energy to trying to give shape and content to this idea, or to what they regard as better-defined alternative conceptions. Still, even the utilitarian may have to be content, as a practical compromise, to rely on some intermediate moral principles less comprehensive in their scope than the principle of utility and more directly applicable to the problem of punishment and the death penalty controversy. . . .

II. THE MORALITY OF PUNISHMENT

As a first step toward providing a fresh setting for the rest of our discussion, it is useful to have a general sketch before us of why it is rational for society to have a system of punishment at all, quite apart from whether the death penalty is used as one of the modes of punishment. We are not likely to assess the morality of capital punishment correctly unless we understand the morality of punishment in general. . . .

The Right to Punish

Society is organized by reference to common norms that forbid anyone and everyone to engage in certain sorts of harmful conduct. When someone deliberately, willfully, and knowingly violates such rules, and therewith harms the innocent, the offender has violated the rights of others and immediately becomes liable to a punitive response. Since the norms were originally designed to provide protection to every person, and since (so we also assume) the culprit knew in advance that his or her conduct was prohibited because it would be injurious to others, and since he or she freely and knowingly chose nevertheless to violate the norm, society cannot simply ignore the violation and continue to treat the offender as if no wrong had been done. It must attempt to bring the offender to judgment. The reason is twofold. First, it is inconsistent for society to establish a set of fair rules, with penalties for their violation, and then to ignore them when actual violations occur. Second, it is unfair for the law-abiding to have to suffer both the undeserved harms inflicted on them by lawbreakers and the inconvenience of complying with laws that they, too, might like to violate, while the criminals indulge their lawless inclinations and suffer nothing in return. . . .

Punishment, therefore, serves the complex function of reinforcing individual compliance with a set of social norms deemed necessary to protect the rights of all the members of society. Once it has been determined that one of these norms has been deliberately violated, then there is no alternative but to set in motion the system of criminal justice that culminates in the punishment of the guilty offender.

Such a system is essentially retributive in at least two respects. Crime must be punished, and the punishment must fit the crime. The theory relied upon here certainly acknowledges the first of these contentions. Punishment by its nature pays back an offender who has inflicted suffering and indignity on an innocent victim by inflicting suffering and indignity on the offender. Justice, more than any other consideration (social defense, reform of the offender), dictates that all crimes be liable to punishment, and that a reasonable portion of social resources (public expenditures) be allocated to the arrest, conviction, and punishment of offenders. . . .

Modes of Punishment

What sorts of punishments are available to society to inflict on offenders? What are the sorts of things any person could be deprived of that would count as punishment? Obviously, one could have one's money or property confiscated, or be deprived of the right to future earnings or an inheritance. But because so much crime against property and against the person is committed by the poor and untalented, by persons with no property and no prospects of any, and because the stolen property is so often disposed of prior to the offender's arrest, it is often pointless to levy punishments in the form of fines or confiscations. . . .

For reasons such as these society has long preferred to take other things of intrinsic value from persons in the name of punishment—notably their freedom and their bodily integrity. Everybody, rich and poor, young and old, male and female, has life and limb and some degree of liberty to lose. Historically, the objection to making punishments mainly a deprivation of liberty was that considerable tax revenues were needed to build and staff prisons. Partly for just such economic reasons the earliest punishments were neither pecuniary nor incarcerative, but corporal: flogging, branding, maiming, and killing. Inexpensive and quick to administer, acutely painful for the offender—it is hardly any wonder that every society today is heir to punitive practices involving widespread and varied use of corporal punishments. . . .

III. THE SEVERITY AND INDIGNITY OF THE DEATH PENALTY

Is Capital Punishment an Untimely and Undignified Death?

Some defenders of capital punishment have complained that opposition to the death penalty entails an overestimation of the value of human life; it tends to ignore that we will all die eventually. All that capital punishment does, according to this objection, is to schedule a person's death at a definite time and place, by a definite mode, and for a definite reason. This raises a new question for us, namely, how the idea of the value, worth, dignity, or sanctity of human life can be made consistent with human mortality.

Even though death is a fact of life, emphasizing the worth of human life is a way of giving sense to the familiar notions of "untimely" death and of an "undignified" death. These terms are admittedly vague and have application in a wide variety of settings, but they also have a place where crime and punishment are concerned. Other things being equal, if a death is brought about by one person killing another, as in murder, then it is an untimely death. If a death is brought about in a way that causes terror during the dying or disfigurement of the body, then it is an undignified death. This, of course, is exactly what murder and capital punishment both typically do. . . .

Why Death Is More Severe than Imprisonment

. . . Roughly, of two punishments, one is more severe than the other depending on its duration and on its interference with things a person so punished might otherwise do. Death is interminable, whereas it is always possible to revoke or interrupt a life sentence. Death also makes compensation impossible, whereas it is possible to compensate a prisoner in some way for wrongful confinement even if it is not possible to give back any of the liberty that was taken away. Of most importance, death permits of no concurrent experiences or activities, whereas even a life-term prisoner can read a book, watch television, perhaps even write a book or repair a television set, and experience various social relations with other people. Death eliminates the presupposition of all experience and activity: life itself. For these reasons, the death penalty is unquestionably the more severe punishment, no matter what a few despondent life-term prisoners or sentimental observers may think they would prefer, and no matter how painless and dignified the mode of execution might be. . . .

The Indignity of Corporal Punishments

In addition to the severity of the death penalty, the killing of persons as punishment shares certain important features with other modes of corporal punishment—maiming, flogging, branding— once widely practiced in our society but now abandoned. All these other methods of corporal punishment have been adandoned in part because they are now seen to violate the dignity of the person being punished. . . .

Why has death as a punishment escaped the nearly universal condemnation visited on all these other punishments with which it is historically and naturally associated? In part, it may be owing to a failure of imagination. Whereas we all know or can easily and vividly imagine the pain and humiliation involved in other corporal punishments, executions today are carried out away from public view, they are quickly over, and the person punished by death is no longer in our midst as a constant reminder. Other factors come into play, too. One is the belief that in some cases there is truly no alternative, because if the criminal were not killed there would be too much risk that he or she would repeat the crime. If so, then neither retribution nor deterrence, but rather incapacitation turns out to be the last line of defense. . . .

IV. CAPITAL PUNISHMENT AND SOCIAL DEFENSE

The Analogy with Self-Defense

Capital punishment, it is sometimes said, is to the body politic what self-defense is to the individual. If the latter is not morally wrong, how can the former be? To assess the strength of this analogy, we need first to inspect the morality of self-defense.

Except for absolute pacifists, who believe it is morally wrong to use violence even to defend themselves or others from undeserved aggression, most of us believe that it is not morally wrong and may even be our moral duty to use violence to prevent aggression directed against either ourselves or innocent third parties. The law has long granted persons the right to defend themselves against the unjust aggressions of others, even to the extent of using lethal force to kill an assailant. . . .

The foregoing account assumes that the person acting in self-defense is innocent of any provocation of the assailant. It also assumes that there is no alternative to victimization except resistance. In actual life, there may be a third alternative: escape, or removing oneself from the scene of the imminent aggression. Hence, the law imposes on us the "duty to retreat." . . . The rule is this: Use of deadly force is justified only to prevent loss of life in immediate jeopardy where a lesser use of force cannot reasonably be expected to save the life that is threatened. . . .

The rationale for self-defense as set out above illustrates two moral principles of great importance to our discussion. One is that if a life is to be risked, then it is better that it be the life of someone who is guilty (in this context, the initial assailant) rather than the life of someone who is not (the innocent potential victim). It is not fair to expect the innocent prospective victim to run the added risk of severe injury or death in order to avoid using violence in self-defense to the extent of possibly killing his or her assailant. Rather, fairness dictates that the guilty aggressor ought to be the one to run the risk.

The other principle is that taking life deliberately is not justified so long as there is any feasible alternative. One does not expect miracles, of course, but in theory, if shooting a burglar through the foot will stop the burglar and enable one to call the police for help, there is no reason to shoot to kill. Likewise, if the burglar is unarmed, there is no reason to shoot at all. . . . In these ways the law shows a tacit regard for the life even of a felon and discour-

ages the use of unnecessary violence even by the innocent; morality can hardly do less.

Deterrence, Incapacitation, and Crime Prevention

The analogy with self-defense leads naturally to the empirical and the conceptual questions surrounding the death penalty as a method of crime prevention. Notice first that crimes can be prevented without recourse to punishment; we do that when we take weapons from offenders, protect targets by bolts and alarms, and educate the public to be less vulnerable to victimization. As for punishment, it prevents crimes by *incapacitation* and by *deterrence.* The two are theoretically independent because they achieve prevention very differently. Executing a murderer prevents crimes by means of *incapacitation* to the extent that the murderer would have committed further crimes if not executed. Incapacitating a murderer will not have any preventative benefits, however, unless the murderer would otherwise have committed some further crimes. (In fact relatively few murderers turn out to be homicidal recidivists.) Nor is killing persons the only way to incapacitate them; isolation and restraints will suffice. Executing a murderer prevents crimes by means of *deterrence* to the extent that others are frightened into not committing any capital crimes by the knowledge that convicted offenders are executed. Thus, successful deterrence is prevention by a psychologically effective threat; incapacitation, if it prevents crimes at all, does so by physically disabling the offender.

The Death Penalty and Incapacitation

Capital punishment is unusual among penalties because its incapacitative effects limit its deterrent effects. The death penalty can never deter an executed person from further crimes. At most, it incapacitates the executed person from committing them. . . . But incapacitation is not identical with prevention. Prevention by means of incapacitation occurs only if the executed criminal would have committed other crimes if he or she had not been executed and had been punished only in some less incapacitative way (e.g., by imprisonment). . . .

This is the nub of the problem. There is no way to know in advance which if any of the incarcerated or released murderers will kill again. It is useful in this connection to remember that the only way to guarantee that no horrible crimes ever occur is to execute *everyone* who might conceivably commit such a crime. Similarly, the only way to guarantee that no convicted murderer ever commits another murder is to execute them all. No modern society has ever done this, and for two hundred years Western societies have been moving steadily in the opposite direction.

These considerations show that our society has implicitly adopted an attitude toward the risk of murder rather like the attitude it has adopted toward the risk of fatality from other causes, such as automobile accidents, lung cancer, or drowning. Since no one knows when or where or upon whom any of these lethal events will fall, it would be too great an invasion of freedom to undertake the severe restrictions that alone would suffice to prevent any such deaths from occurring. It is better to take the risks and keep our freedom than to try to eliminate the risks altogether and lose our freedom in the process. Hence, we have lifeguards at the beach, but swimming is not totally prohibited; smokers are warned, but cigarettes are still legally sold; pedestrians may have the right of way in a crosswalk, but marginally competent drivers are still allowed to operate motor vehicles. Some risk is thereby imposed on the innocent; in the name of our right to freedom, we do not insist on having society protect us at all costs.

The Death Penalty and Deterrence

. . . For half a century, social scientists have studied the questions whether the death penalty is a deterrent and whether it is a better deterrent than the alternative of imprisonment. Their verdict, while not unanimous, is nearly so. Whatever may be true about the deterrence of lesser crimes by other penalties, the deterrence achieved by the death penalty for murder is not measurably any greater than the deterrence achieved by long-term imprisonment. . . .

If the death penalty and long-term imprisonment are equally effective (or ineffective) as deterrents to murder, then the argument for the death penalty on grounds of deterrence is seriously weakened. One of the moral principles identified earlier now comes into play: Unless there is a good reason for choosing a more rather than a less severe punishment for a crime, the less severe penalty is to be preferred. This principle obviously commends itself to anyone who values human life and who concedes that, all other things being equal, less pain and suffering is always better than more. . . .

A Cost/Benefit Analysis of the Death Penalty

A full study of the costs and benefits involved in the practice of capital punishment would not be confined solely to the question of whether it is a better deterrent or preventive of murder than imprisonment. Any thoroughgoing utilitarian approach to the death-penalty controversy would need to examine carefully other costs and benefits as well, because maximizing the balance of all the social benefits over all the social costs is the sole criterion of right and wrong according to utilitarianism. Let us consider, therefore, some of the other costs and benefits to be calculated. Clinical psychologists have presented evidence to suggest that the death penalty actually incites some persons of unstable mind to murder others, either because they are afraid to take their own lives and hope that society will punish them for murder by putting them to death, or because they fancy that they, too, are killing with justification analogously to the lawful and presumably justified killing involved in capital punishment. If such evidence is sound, capital punishment can serve as a counterpreventive or even an incitement to murder; such incited murders become part of its social cost. Imprisonment, however, has not been known to incite any murders or other crimes of violence in a comparable fashion. . . . The risks of executing the innocent are also part of the social cost. The historical record is replete with innocent persons arrested, indicted, convicted, sentenced, and occasionally legally executed for crimes they did not commit. . . . Nor is this all. The high costs of a capital trial and the inevitable appeals, the costly methods of custody most prisons adopt for convicts on "death row," are among the straightforward economic costs that the death penalty incurs. Conducting a valid cost/benefit analysis of capital punishment would be extremely difficult; nevertheless, on the basis of the evidence we have, it is quite possible that such a study would show that abolition of all death penalties is much less costly than their retention. . . .

V. CAPITAL PUNISHMENT AND RETRIBUTIVE JUSTICE

No discussion of the morality of punishment would be complete without taking into account the two leading principles of retributive justice relevant to the capital punishment controversy. One is the principle that crimes ought to be punished. The other is the principle that the severity of a punishment ought to be proportional to the gravity of the offense. These are moral principles of recognized weight. Leaving aside all questions of social defense, how strong a case for capital punishment can be made on their basis? How reliable and persuasive are these principles themselves?

Crime Must Be Punished

. . . Fortunately, this principle need not be in dispute between proponents and opponents of the death penalty. Even defenders of the death penalty must admit that putting a convicted murderer in prison for years is a punishment of that criminal. The principle that crime must be punished is neutral to our controversy, because both sides acknowledge it.

The other principle of retributive justice is the one that seems to be decisive. Under *lex talionis*, it must always have seemed that murderers ought to be put to death. Proponents of the death penalty, with rare exceptions, have insisted on this point, and even opponents of the death penalty must give grudging assent to the seeming fittingness of demanding capital punishment for murder. The strategy for opponents of the death penalty is to argue either that (1) this principle is not really a principle of justice after all, or that (2) to the extent it is,

it does not require death for murderers, or that (3) in any case it is not the only principle of punitive justice. As we shall see, all these objections have merit. . . .

Is Death Sufficiently Retributive?

Those who advocate capital punishment for murder on retributive grounds must face the objection that, on their own principles, the death penalty in some cases is morally inadequate. How could death in the electric chair or the gas chamber or before a firing squad or by lethal injection suffice as just retribution, given the savage, brutal, wanton character of so many murders? How can retributive justice be served by anything less than equally savage methods of execution? From a retributive point of view, the oft-heard exclamation, "Death is too good for him!," has a certain truth. Are defenders of the death penalty willing to embrace this consequence of their own doctrine?

If they were, they would be stooping to the squalor of the murderer. Where the quality of the crime sets the limits of just methods of punishment, as it will if we attempt to give exact and literal implementation to *lex talionis,* society will find itself descending to the cruelties and savagery that criminals employ. What is worse, society would be deliberately authorizing such acts, in the cool light of reason, and not (as is usually true of vicious criminals) impulsively or in hatred and anger or with an insane or unbalanced mind. Moral constraints, in short, prohibit us from trying to make executions perfectly retributive. Once we grant that such constraints are proper, it is unreasonable to insist that the principle of "a life for a life" nevertheless by itself justifies the execution of murderers. . . .

As the French writer Albert Camus once remarked:

> For there to be an equivalence, the death penalty would have to punish a criminal who had warned his victim of the date at which he would inflict a horrible death on him and who, from that moment onward, had confined him at his mercy for months. Such a monster is not encountered in private life.[6]

Differential Severity Does Not Require Executions

What, then, emerges from our examination of retributive justice and the death penalty? If retributive justice is thought to consist in *lex talionis,* all one can say is that this principle has never exercised more than a crude and indirect effect on the actual punishments meted out by society. Other moral principles interfere with a literal and single-minded application of this one. Some homicides seem improperly punished by death at all; others would require methods of execution too horrible to inflict. . . .

But retributive justice need not be identified with *lex talionis.* One may reject that principle as too crude and still embrace the retributive principle that the severity of punishments should be graded according to the gravity of the offense. Even though one need not claim that life imprisonment (or any kind of punishment other than death) "fits" the crime of murder, one can claim that this punishment is the proper one for murder. To do this, the schedule of punishments accepted by society must be arranged so that this mode of imprisonment is the most severe penalty used. Opponents of the death penalty can embrace this principle of retributive justice, even though they must reject a literal *lex talionis.*

Equal Justice and Capital Punishment

During the past generation, the strongest practical objection to the death penalty has been the inequity with which it has been applied. As the late Supreme Court Justice William O. Douglas once observed, "One searches our chronicles in vain for the execution of any member of the affluent strata of the society." One does not search our chronicles in vain for the crime of murder committed by the affluent. All the sociological evidence points to the conclusion that the death penalty is the poor man's justice; hence the slogan, "Those without the capital get punishment." The death penalty is also racially sensitive. . . .

Let us suppose that the factual basis for such a criticism is sound. What follows for the morality of capital punishment? Many defenders of the death penalty have been quick to point out that since there is nothing intrinsic about the crime of murder or rape dictating that only the poor or only racial-minority males will commit it, and since there is nothing overtly racist about the statutes that authorize the death penalty for murder or rape, capital punishment itself is hardly at fault if in practice it falls with unfair impact on the poor and the black. There is, in short, nothing in the death penalty that requires it to be applied unfairly and with arbitrary or discriminatory results. At worst such results stem from defects in the system of administering criminal justice. . . .

We can look at these statistics in another way to illustrate the same point. If we could be assured that the nearly four thousand persons executed were the worst of the bad, repeated offenders impossible to incarcerate safely (much less to rehabilitate), the most dangerous murderers in captivity—the ones who had killed more than once and were likely to kill again, and the least likely to be confined in prison without chronic danger to other inmates and the staff—then one might accept half a million murders and a few thousand executions with a sense that rough justice had been done. But the truth is otherwise. Persons are sentenced to death and executed not because they have been found to be uncontrollably violent or hopelessly poor risks for safe confinement and release. Instead, they are executed because at trial they had a poor defense (inexperienced or overworked counsel); they had no funds to bring sympathetic witnesses to court; they are transients or strangers in the community where they are tried; the prosecuting attorney wanted the publicity that goes with "sending a killer to the chair"; there were no funds for an appeal or for a transcript of the trial record; they are members of a despised racial or political minority. In short, the actual study of why particular persons have been sentenced to death and executed does not show any careful winnowing of the worst from the bad. It shows that those executed were usually the unlucky victims of prejudice and discrimination, the losers in an arbitrary lottery that could just as well have spared them, the victims of the disadvantages that almost always go with poverty. A system like this does not enhance human life; it cheapens and degrades it. However heinous murder and other crimes are, the system of capital punishment does not compensate for or erase those crimes. It tends only to add new injuries of its own to the catalogue of human brutality.

VI. CONCLUSION

Our discussion of the death penalty from the moral point of view shows that there is no one moral principle that has paramount validity and that decisively favors one side of the controversy. Rather, we have seen how it is possible to argue either for or against the death penalty, and in each case to be appealing to moral principles that derive from the worth, value, or dignity of human life. . . .

My own view of the controversy is that, given the moral principles identified in the course of our discussion (including the overriding value of human life), and given all the facts about capital punishment, the balance of reasons favors abolition of the death penalty. The alternative to capital punishment that I favor, as things currently stand, is long-term imprisonment. Such a punishment is retributive and can be made more or less severe to reflect the gravity of the crime. It gives adequate (though hardly perfect) protection to the public.

It is free of the worst defect to which the death penalty is liable: execution of the innocent. It tacitly acknowledges that there is no way for a criminal, alive or dead, to make complete amends for murder or other grave crimes against the person. Last but not least, long-term imprisonment has symbolic significance. The death penalty, more than any other kind of killing, is done by officials in the name of society and on its behalf. Each of us, therefore, has a hand in such killings. Unless they are absolutely necessary they cannot be justified. Thus, abolishing the death penalty represents extending the hand of life even to those who by their crimes have "forfeited" any right to live. A penal policy limiting the severity of punishment to long-term incarceration acknowledges that we must abandon the folly and pretense of attempting to secure perfect justice in an imperfect world. . . .

NOTES

1. W. D. Ross, *The Right and the Good.* Oxford: Clarendon Press, 1930, pp. 60–61.
2. John Locke, *Second Treatise of Government* (1690), §23, §172.
3. Immanuel Kant, *The Metaphysical Elements of Justice* (1797), Indianapolis, Ind.: Bobbs-Merrill (1965), translated by John Ladd, p. 102.
4. Ibid., p. 100.
5. Ibid., p. 101.
6. Albert Camus, *Resistance, Rebellion, and Death.* New York: Knopf, 1961, p. 199.

Discussion Questions

1. Bedau maintains that the forfeiture-of-rights argument is problematic because it can be used to justify the death penalty for almost any crime. Do you agree with Bedau? Use the execution of Socrates to illustrate your answer.
2. Bedau claims that Kant's criteria for determining a murderer's "state of mind" at the time of the crime are too ambiguous to be of much practical use. Do you agree? Make up a list of criteria that a judge or jury might use in determining if a murderer should be held morally blameworthy. Make a list of criteria that a judge or jury might use in determining if a murderer should get the death penalty. Are the two lists the same? Discuss why or why not.
3. Compare and contrast the arguments of Bedau and van den Haag regarding the morality of capital punishment. Which person presents the most compelling argument? Support your answer.

4. In his *Philosophy of Law,* Kant argues that "even if a civil society were to dissolve itself by common agreement of all its members . . . the last murderer remaining in prison must first be executed, so that everyone will duly receive what his actions are worth . . . " What if a society were dissolved, not by common agreement, but because of a natural disaster that led to the collapse of the government and, with it, the penal system. Discuss whether Bedau would permit the death penalty in situations in which there is no other effective means of incapacitating dangerous criminals.

 JEFFREY REIMAN

Why the Death Penalty Should Be Abolished in the United States

Jeffrey Reiman is a professor of philosophy at American University. In this selection from his essay "Why the Death Penalty Should be Abolished," Reiman analyzes the retributivist argument for the death penalty. He concludes that one can accept retributivism, as well as the claim that the murderers deserve to die for their offense, without accepting the claim that murderers ought to receive the death penalty. Instead there are forms of punishment that are both less harsh and less morally questionable that satisfy the requirements of retributivism, justice, and deterrence.

Critical Reading Questions

1. What are the two arguments used by advocates of the death penalty?
2. What does Reiman mean when he says the "desert creates a *right to punish,* not a duty to do so"?
3. What is the standard problem confronting those who justify retributivism?
4. What is the "retributivist principle," and how is it related to the justice of *lex talionis*?
5. What is the relationship between *lex talionis* and the Golden Rule?
6. What is the Hegelian approach to retributivism? How does it differ from the utilitarian view of retributivism?
7. What is the Kantian approach to retributivism? What is the role of reason and will in Kant's approach? What is Kant's view of the Golden Rule?
8. What conclusion does Reiman draw about retributive justice from the Hegelian and Kantian approaches?
9. Why is it important to figure out what penalties are equivalent to the crimes?
10. According to Reiman, when is the desire for revenge rational?

Jeffrey Reiman, "Why the Death Penalty Should be Abolished," from Louis P. Pojman and Jeffrey Reiman, *The Death Penalty: For and Against* (Lanham, MD: Rowman & Littlefield Publishers, Inc., 1998), from pages 67, 87–100.

11. Why is acceptance of the retributivist principle, and the question of the exacting a particular type of punishment, two different questions?
12. According to Reiman, what types of punishment are monstrous and unacceptable?
13. Who has the right to punish in a civil state?
14. How does Reiman determine the top and the bottom of the range of acceptable punishment? What is the role of deterrence in setting these limits?
15. How does "proportional retributivism" modify the requirements of *lex talionis*? What are the implications of this modification for the use of the death penalty as punishment?

Death penalty advocates commonly press two claims in favor of executing murderers. The first is that the death penalty is a just punishment for murder, a murderer's just deserts. On this line of thought, we do injustice to the victims of murder if we do not execute their murderers. The second claim is that the death penalty is necessary to deter potential murderers. Here, the suggestion is that we do injustice to potential victims of murder if we do not execute actual ones. I accept that the death penalty is a just punishment for some murders—some murderers' just deserts—and that, if the death penalty were needed to deter future murders, it would be unjust to future victims not to impose it. Notice, then, that I accept two of the strongest points urged in favor of the death penalty. If, granting these strong points, I can show that it would still be wrong to impose the death penalty, that should be a strong argument indeed. . . .

DEATH AND DESERT

In this section, I aim to show that execution is justly deserved punishment for some murders, *as a step toward arguing that it is not unjust to punish murder less harshly.* Note, then, that the fact that a punishment is justly deserved does not, in my view, entail that someone has a duty to impose that punishment. Rather, I shall argue in this section that desert creates *a right to punish*, not a duty to do so. To prepare the ground for this argument, I present here three commonplace observations that support the view that desert does not entail a duty to give what is deserved: First, the victim of an offense has the moral right to forgive the offending party rather than pun-

ish him though he deserves to be punished; second, we have no duty (not even a prima facie duty) to torture torturers even if they deserve to be tortured; and third, though great benefactors of humanity deserve to be rewarded, no one necessarily has a duty to provide that reward. At most, there is a very weak and easily overridden duty to provide the reward. On the other hand, I will claim that, when the state punishes a criminal, the state has a duty to punish in a way that does not trivialize the harm suffered by the criminal's victim. However, we shall see that this duty is compatible with administering punishment that is less than the full amount deserved. . . .

1. Retributivism, *Lex Talionis,* and Just Desert

There is nothing self-evident about the justice of the *lex talionis* or, for that matter, of retributivism.[1] The standard problem confronting those who would justify retributivism is that of overcoming the suspicion that it does no more than sanctify the victim's desire to hurt the offender back. Since serving that desire amounts to hurting the offender simply for the satisfaction that the victim derives from seeing the offender suffer, and since deriving satisfaction from the suffering of others seems primitive, the policy of imposing suffering on the offender for no other purpose than giving satisfaction to his victim seems primitive as well. Consequently, defending retributivism requires showing that the suffering imposed on the wrongdoer has some worthy point beyond the satisfaction of victims. In what follows, I shall try to identify a proposition—which I call the *retributivist principle*—that I take to be the nerve of retributivism. I think this principle accounts for the justice of the *lex talionis* and indicates the point of the suffering demanded by retributivism. . . .

I think that we can see the justice of the *lex talionis* by focusing on the striking affinity between it and the Golden Rule. The Golden Rule mandates, "Do unto others as you would have others do unto you," while the *lex talionis* counsels, "Do unto others as they have done unto you." It would not be too far-fetched to say that the *lex talionis* is the law enforcement arm of the Golden Rule, at least in the sense that if people were actually treated as they treated others, then everyone would necessarily follow the Golden Rule, because then people could only willingly act toward others as they were willing to have others act toward them. This is not to suggest that the *lex talionis* follows from the Golden Rule, but rather that the two share a common moral inspiration: the equality of persons. Treating others as you *would* have them treat you means treating others as equal to you, because it implies that you count their suffering to be as great a calamity as your own suffering, that you count your right to impose suffering on them as no greater than their right to impose suffering on you, and so on. The notion of the equality of persons leads to the *lex talionis* by two approaches that start from different points and converge.

I call the first approach "Hegelian" because Hegel held (roughly) that crime upsets the equality among persons and that retributive punishment restores that equality by "annulling" the crime.[2] As we have seen, acting according to the Golden Rule implies treating others as your equals. Conversely, violating the Golden Rule implies the reverse: Doing to another what you would *not* have that other do to you violates the equality of persons by asserting a right toward the other that the other does not possess toward you. Doing back to you what you did "annuls" your violation by reasserting that the other has the same right toward you that you assert toward him. Punishment according to the *lex talionis* cannot heal the injury that the other has suffered at your hands; rather, it rectifies the indignity he has suffered, by restoring him to equality with you.

This Hegelian account of retributivism provides us with a nonutilitarian conception of crime and punishment. This is so because "equality of per-

sons" here does not mean equality of concern for their happiness, as it might for a utilitarian. On a utilitarian understanding of equality, imposing suffering on a wrongdoer equivalent to the suffering she has imposed would have little point (unless such suffering were exactly what was needed to deter future would-be offenders). Rather, equality of concern for people's happiness would lead us to impose as little suffering on the wrongdoer as is compatible with promoting the happiness of others. Instead of seeing morality as administering doses of happiness to individual recipients, the Hegelian retributivist envisions morality as maintaining the relations appropriate to equally sovereign individuals.[3] . . . The victim (or his representative, the state) . . . has the right to rectify this loss of standing relative to the criminal by meting out a punishment that reduces the criminal's sovereignty to the degree to which she vaunted it above her victim's. It might be thought that this is a duty, not just a right, but that is surely too much. The victim has the right to forgive the violator without imposing punishment. This suggests that it is by virtue of having the right to punish the violator—having authority over the violator's fate equivalent to the authority over the victim's fate that the violator wrongly took—rather than having the duty to punish the violator, that the victim's equality with the violator is restored.

I call the second approach "Kantian" because Kant held (roughly) that, since reason (like justice) is no respecter of the sheer difference among individuals, when a rational being decides to act in a certain way toward his fellows, he implicitly authorizes similar action by his fellows toward him.[4] A version of the Golden Rule, then, is a requirement of reason: Acting rationally, one always acts as he would have others act toward him.[5] Consequently, to act toward a person as he has acted toward others is to treat him as a rational being, that is, as if his act were the product of a rational decision. From this, it may be concluded that we have a duty to do to offenders what they have done, since this amounts to according them the respect due rational beings. And Kant asserts as much.[6] Here, too, however, the assertion of a duty to punish seems excessive, since, if this duty arose because doing to people what they have done to others is necessary to accord them the respect due rational beings, then we would have a duty to do to all rational persons *everything*—good, bad, or indifferent—that they do to others. The point, rather, is that, by his acts, a rational being *authorizes* others to do the same to him; he doesn't *compel* them to. Here, again, the argument leads to a right, rather than a duty, to exact the *lex talionis*. It should be clear that the Kantian argument, like the Hegelian one, rests on the equality of persons. A rational agent implicitly authorizes having done to him action similar to what he has done to another only if he and the other are similar in the relevant ways.

The Hegelian and Kantian approaches arrive at the same destination from opposite sides. . . . Taken together, these approaches support the following proposition: *The equality and rationality of persons imply that an offender deserves, and his victim has the right to impose on him, suffering equal to that which he imposed on the victim.* This is the proposition I call the *retributivist principle.* This principle provides that the *lex talionis* is the criminal's just desert and the victim's—or, as her representative, the state's—right. . . .

I do not contend that it is easy or even always possible to figure out what penalties are equivalent to the harms imposed by offenders. Hugo Bedau, for example, has observed that, apart from murder and possibly some other crimes against the person, "we have no clear intuitions at all about what such equivalences consist in."[7] Even if this is so, however, it is still worth knowing what the criterion of deserved punishment is. . . . [K]nowing what criminals deserve according to *lex talionis* gives us something at which to aim, a target in light of which we might eventually sharpen our intuitions.

When I say that, with respect to the criminal, the point of retributive punishment is to impress upon him his equality with his victim, I mean to be understood quite literally. If the sentence is just and the criminal rational, then the punishment should normally *force* upon him recognition of his equality with his victim, recognition of their shared vulnerability to suffering and their shared desire to avoid it, as well as recognition of the fact that he counts for no more than his victim in the eyes of their fellows. For this reason, the retributivist requires that

the offender be sane not only at the moment of his crime, but also at the moment of his punishment—while this latter requirement would be largely pointless (if not downright malevolent) to a utilitarian. Incidentally, it is, I believe, the desire that the offender be forced by suffering punishment to recognize his equality with his victim, rather than the desire for that suffering itself, that constitutes what is rational in the desire for revenge. . . .

It seems, then, reasonable to take the equality and rationality of persons as implying moral desert in the way asserted in the retributivist principle. I shall assume henceforth that the retributivist principle is true.

2. The Top and the Bottom End of the Range of Just Punishments

The truth of the retributivist principle establishes that *lex talionis* is the offender's just desert; but, since it establishes this as a right of the victim rather than the victim's duty, it does not settle the question of whether or to what extent the victim or the state ought to exercise this right and exact the *lex talionis.* This is a separate moral question because strict adherence to the *lex talionis* amounts to allowing criminals, even the most barbaric of them, to dictate our punishing behavior. . . . It seems certain that there are at least some crimes, such as rape or torture, that we ought not to try to match. And this is not merely a matter of imposing an alternative punishment that produces an equivalent amount of suffering, as, say, some number of years in prison that might "add up" to the harm caused by a rapist or a torturer. Even if no amount of time in prison would add up to the harm caused by a torturer, it still seems that we ought not to torture him even if this were the only way of making him suffer as much as he has made his victim suffer. Or consider someone who has committed several murders in cold blood. On the *lex talionis,* it would seem that such a criminal might justly be brought to within an inch of death and then revived (or to within a moment of execution and then reprieved) as many times as he has killed (minus one), and then finally executed. But surely this is a degree of cruelty that would be monstrous.

Since the retributivist principle establishes the *lex talionis* as the victim's right, it might seem that the question of how far this right should be exercised is "up to the victim." Indeed, this would be the case in the state of nature. But once, for all the good reasons familiar to readers of Locke, the state comes into existence, public punishment replaces private, and the victim's right to punish reposes in the state. With this, the decision as to how far to exercise this right goes to the state as well. . . .

I suspect that it will be widely agreed that the state ought not to administer punishments of the sort described above even if required by the letter of the *lex talionis* and that, thus, even granting the justice of *lex talionis*, there are occasions on which it is morally appropriate to diverge from its requirements. . . .

The implication of the notion that justice permits us to avoid extremely cruel punishments is that there is a range of just punishments that includes some that are just though they exact less than the full measure of the *lex talionis*. What are the top and bottom ends of this range? . . . [A]ll punishments within the range of just punishments must be sufficient to deter rational people generally from the crime in question. Assume, then, for purposes of simplicity, that we are trying to identify the range of just punishments from within a series of punishments of increasing harshness all of which suffice to provide adequate deterrence.

Within this series of punishments, the top end of the range of just punishments is given by *lex talionis*, and the bottom end is, in a way, as well. Based on the argument of the previous section, the top end, the point after which more or harsher punishment is undeserved and thus unjust, is reached when we impose a punishment that is equivalent to the harm caused by the criminal (including both the harm done to his immediate victim and the harm done to the law-abiding by his unfair taking of advantage). As for the bottom end, recall that, if the retributivist principle is true, then denying that the offender deserves suffering equal to that which she imposed amounts to denying the equality and rationality of persons. From this, it follows that we fall below the bottom end of the range of just punishments when we act in ways that are incompatible with the *lex tal-*

ionis at the top end. We do injustice to the victim when we treat the offender in a way that is no longer compatible with sincerely believing that she deserves to have done to her what she has done to her victim. In this way, the range of just punishments remains faithful to the victim's right.

This way of understanding just punishment enables us to formulate proportional retributivism so that it is compatible with acknowledging the justice of the *lex talionis*. If we take the *lex talionis* to spell out the offender's just desert, and if other moral considerations require us to refrain from matching the injury caused by the offender while still allowing us to punish justly, then surely we impose just punishment if we impose the closest morally acceptable approximation to the *lex talionis*. Proportional retributivism, then, in requiring that the worst crime be punished by the society's worst punishment and so on, could be understood as translating the offender's just desert into its nearest equivalent in the society's table of morally acceptable punishments. Then, the two versions of retributivism (*lex talionis* and proportional) are related in that the first states what just punishment would be if nothing but the offender's just desert mattered and the second locates just punishment at the meeting point of the offender's just desert and the society's moral scruples.

Inasmuch as proportional retributivism modifies the requirements of the *lex talionis* only in light of other moral considerations, it is compatible with believing that the *lex talionis* spells out the offender's just desert, much in the way that modifying the obligations of promisers in light of other moral considerations is compatible with believing in the binding nature of promises. That a person is justified in failing to keep a promised appointment because she acted to save a life is compatible with still believing that promises are binding. So, too, justifiably doing less than *lex talionis* requires in order to avoid cruelty is compatible with believing that offenders still deserve what *lex talionis* would impose.

Proportional retributivism so formulated preserves the point of retributivism and remains faithful to the victim's right that is its source. Since it punishes with the closest morally acceptable approximation to the *lex talionis*, it effectively says to the offender: You deserved the equivalent of what you did to your victim, and you are getting less only to the degree that our moral scruples limit us from duplicating what you have done. Such punishment, then, affirms the equality of persons by respecting, *as far as seems morally permissible,* the victim's right to impose suffering on the offender equal to what she received, and it affirms the rationality of the offender by treating him as authorizing others to do to him what he has done, though they take him up on it only *as far as it seems to them morally permissible.* Needless to say, the alternative punishments must in some convincing way be comparable in gravity to the crimes that they punish, or else they will trivialize the harms those crimes caused and be no longer compatible with sincerely believing that the offender deserves to have done to him what he has done to his victim and no longer capable of impressing upon the criminal his equality with the victim. . . .

To sum up: When, because we are simply unable to duplicate the criminal's offense, we modify the *lex talionis* to call for imposing on the offender as nearly as possible what he has done, we are still at the top end of punishment justified via *lex talionis,* modifying the *lex talionis* only for reasons of practical possibility. When, because of our own moral scruples, we do less than this, we still act justly as long as we punish in a way that is compatible with sincerely believing that the offender deserves the full measure of the *lex talionis.* If this is true, then it is not unjust to spare murderers as long as they can be punished in some other suitably grave way. For example, a natural life sentence with no chance of parole might be a civilized equivalent of the death penalty—after all, people sentenced to life imprisonment have traditionally been regarded as "civilly dead."[8]

It might be objected that no punishment short of death will serve the point of retributivism with respect to murderers because no punishment short of death is commensurate with the crime of murder. For, while some number of years of imprisonment may add up to the amount of harm done by rapists or assaulters or torturers, no number of years will add up to the harm done to the victim of murder. But justified divergence from the *lex talionis* is not limited only to changing the form of punishment while maintaining equivalent severity. . . . If justice

allows us to refrain from these penalties, then justice allows punishments that are not equal in suffering to their crimes. It seems to me that if the objector grants this much, then she must show that a punishment less than death is not merely incommensurate to the harm caused by murder, but so far out of proportion to that harm that it trivializes the harm and thus effectively denies the equality and rationality of persons. . . .

I take it, then, that the justice of the *lex talionis* implies that it is just to execute murderers, but not that it is unjust to spare them as long as they are systematically punished in some other suitably grave way—and as long as the deterrence requirement can be satisfied. . . .

NOTES

1. "[T]o say 'it is fitting' or 'justice demands' that the guilty should suffer is only to affirm that punishment is right, not to give grounds for thinking so" (Stanley I. Benn, "Punishment," *The Encyclopedia of Philosophy,* ed. Paul Edwards [New York: Macmillan, 1967], vol. 7, p. 30).

2. "The sole positive existence which the injury [i.e., the crime] possesses is that it is the particular will of the criminal [i.e., it is the criminal's intention that distinguishes criminal injury from, say, injury due to an accident]. Hence to injure (or penalize) this particular will as a will determinately existent is to annul the crime, which otherwise would have been held valid, and to restore the right" (G. W. F. Hegel, *The Philosophy of Right,* trans. T. M. Knox [Oxford: Clarendon Press, 1962; originally published 1821], 69).

3. For this reason, I think this account of crime and punishment is especially appropriate to a liberal moral theory, and I have defended it as such. See my *Justice and Modern Moral Philosophy* (New Haven, CT: Yale University Press, 1990), 187–99, 306–07; and my *Critical Moral Liberalism: Theory and Practice* (Lanham, MD: Rowman & Littlefield, 1997), 235–70, esp. 240.

4. According to Kant, "any undeserved evil that you inflict on someone else among the people is one that you do to yourself. If you vilify him, you vilify yourself; if you steal from him, you steal from

yourself; if you kill him, you kill yourself." Since Kant held that "[i]f what happens to someone is also willed by him, it cannot be a punishment," he took pains to distance himself from the view that the offender *wills* his punishment. "The chief error contained in this sophistry," Kant wrote, "consists in the confusion of the criminal's [i.e., the murderer's] own judgment (which one must necessarily attribute to his reason) that he must forfeit his life with a resolution of the will to take his own life" (Kant, "Metaphysical Elements of Justice," 101, 105–106).

5. Cf. Kant, *Grounding for the Metaphysics of Morals,* 37n. Kant thinks that the Golden Rule, as commonly stated, places too much emphasis on what an agent *wants,* rather than on what he rationally endorses. Nonetheless, Kant affirms that the Golden Rule is derived from his own central moral principle, the categorical imperative.

6. "Even if a civil society were to dissolve itself by common agreement of all its members . . . , the last murderer remaining in prison must first be executed, so that everyone will duly receive what his actions are worth" (Kant, Metaphysical Elements of Justice," 102).

7. Hugo Bedau, personal correspondence to author.

8. I am indebted to my colleague Robert Johnson for this suggestion. Prisoners condemned to spend their entire lives in prison, Johnson writes, "experience a permanent civil death, the death of freedom. The prison is their cemetery, a 6′ by 9′ cell their tomb. Interred in the name of justice, they are consigned to mark the passage of their lives in the prison's peculiar dead time, which serves no larger human purpose and yields few rewards. In effect, they give their civil lives in return for the natural lives they have taken" (Robert Johnson, *Death Work: A Study of the Modern Execution Process* [Belmont, CA: Wadsworth Publishing, 1990], 158).

Discussion Questions

1. Discuss how Morris would most likely respond to Reiman's claim that the principle of retributivism does not require the death penalty for murder. Which person presents the stronger argument? Support your answer.

2. Break down Reiman's article into its premises and conclusion. Are his premises sound? Eliminate any false or weak premises. Does the conclusion logically follow from the remaining premises, or does the conclusion go beyond the premises? Support your answer.

3. One of Reiman's premises is that all people are moral equals. However, in practice, certain groups of people are denied full and equal rights and have been morally degraded by social practices and attitudes. This inequality is reflected in the greater likelihood that blacks and people from disadvantaged backgrounds will end up in prison. Discuss whether prejudice and lack of social and economic equality should be taken into consideration in determining the top and bottom of the range of punishment in a particular case since the criminal from a disadvantaged background has started from an unequal moral status. How might Reiman most likely respond to this question?

4. Read the quote from lawyer Clarence Darrow in question 3 on page 271. Role-play a conversation between Reiman and Darrow regarding Darrow's claim that criminals are simply products of their environment.

5. Examine how the principle of retributivism, as explicated by Reiman, would apply to children and teenagers that kill. For example, should the boys responsible for the Columbine High School killings, had they lived, received the same punishment as an adult would receive? Support your answer.

HELEN PREJEAN

Dead Man Walking

Helen Prejean is a member of the Sisters of St. Joseph of Medaille in Louisiana. Through her work with inner-city residents in New Orleans, she became involved in ministry to death row inmates at the Louisiana State Prison in Angola. Prejean is also founder of *Survive,* a victims' advocacy group. Prejean, who is opposed to the death penalty, relies primarily on narrative and consciousness-raising to make her argument. Rather than appeal to our sense of justice, as do van den Haag, and Bedau to a lesser extent, Prejean instead appeals to our sense of care and empathy. By inviting us to share in her experiences as a spiritual adviser to prisoners on death row, Prejean seeks to enhance our moral sensitivity to the brutality of capital punishment as well to raise our collective consciousness about the issue. Her vivid account of the suffering of all the participants as well as her description of an actual execution serves to break down our resistance by forcing us to question our worldviews about capital punishment.

Critical Reading Questions

1. Why does Prejean argue that capital punishment by electrocution is cruel, rather than a painless "euthanasia by electrocution"?
2. What are some types of suffering experienced by prisoners on death row?
3. On what grounds does Prejean argue that rage and grief experienced by the family and friends of a murder victim do not justify the death penalty?
4. Why does Prejean oppose giving the government the power to execute murderers?
5. According to Prejean, why do executioners prefer to remain anonymous?
6. On what grounds does Prejean reject the argument, used by some Christians, that retaliation and the death penalty are consistent with biblical teachings?
7. What is Prejean's position on the use of long-term imprisonment to incapacitate violent criminals?
8. According to Prejean, is the public's fear of crime realistic? What fuels this fear?
9. What utilitarian arguments does Prejean use against capital punishment?
10. Does Prejean believe in retribution and punishment?
11. How does Prejean respond to the grief and desire for retribution felt by the families and friends of murder victims? Does she sympathize with the families, or does she feel they are being unreasonable?
12. Why does Prejean maintain that capital punishment diminishes the crime victim and instead focuses attention on the murderer?
13. What is Gandhi's concept of *satyagraha*? Why were both Mohandas Gandhi and Martin Luther King Jr. opposed to the use of violence in response to violence?
14. In what ways is capital punishment costly to the American people? What are some of the steps proposed by Prejean to make Americans more aware of the violence and costliness of the death penalty?

Dead Man Walking (New York: Vintage Books, 1993).

15. Why is political commentator George Will in favor of capital punishment? How does Prejean respond to his arguments?
16. Why, according to Camus, are executions performed in secret?
17. What were the findings of Bedau and Radelet's study on capital punishment? How did van den Haag respond to these findings?

. . . Death by electrocution was introduced in the United States in 1890 at Auburn Prison in upstate New York, when William Kemmler was killed by the state of New York. The *New York Times* described the new method as "euthanasia by electricity," and the U.S. Supreme Court, upholding the state appellate court's decision that death by electricity was not cruel and unusual punishment, had concluded: "It is in easy reach of the electrical science at this day to so generate and apply to the person of the convict a current of electricity of such known and sufficient force as certainly to produce instantaneous and therefore painless death."

A reporter for the *New World* newspaper who witnessed Kemmler's execution reported:

"The current had been passing through his body for 15 seconds when the electrode at the head was removed. Suddenly the breast heaved. There was a straining at the straps which bound him. A purplish foam covered the lips and was spattered over the leather head band. The man was alive.

"Warden, physician, guards . . . everybody lost their wits. There was a startled cry for the current to be turned on again. . . . An odor of burning flesh and singed hair filled the room, for a moment, a blue flame played about the base of the victim's spine. This time the electricity flowed four minutes. . . ."

That was in 1890.

On October 16, 1985, the electrocution of William Vandiver by the state of Indiana took seventeen minutes, requiring five charges of electricity.

On April 22, 1983, as the state of Alabama electrocuted John Louis Evans, the first electrical charge burned through the electrode on the leg and the electrode fell off. The prison guards repaired it and administered another charge of electricity. Smoke and flame erupted from Evans's temple and leg but the man was still alive. Following the second jolt, Evans's lawyer demanded that Governor George C. Wallace halt the proceedings. The governor refused. Another jolt was administered. It took fourteen minutes for Evans to die. . . .

Later, in the months ahead, Patrick Sonnier will confide his terror to me of the death that awaits him, telling me of a recurring nightmare, always the same: the guards coming for him, dragging him screaming toward the chair, strapping him in with the wide leather straps, covering his face with the hood, and he is screaming, "No, no, no . . ." For him there can never again be restful, unbroken sleep, because the dream can always come. Better, he says, to take short naps and not to sink into deep sleep.

I cannot accept that the state now plans to kill Patrick Sonnier in cold blood. But the thought of the young victims haunts me. Why do I feel guilty when I think of them? Why do I feel as if I have murdered someone myself?

In prayer I sort it out.

I know that if I had been at the scene when the young people were abducted, I would have done all in my power to save them.

I know I feel compassion for their suffering parents and family and would do anything to ease their pain if I knew how. I also know that nothing can ease some pain.

I know I am trying to help people who are desperately poor, and I hope I can prevent some of them from exploding into violence. Here my conscience is clean and light. No heaviness, no guilt.

Then it comes to me. The victims are dead and the killer is alive and I am befriending the killer.

Have I betrayed his victims? Do I have to take sides? I am acutely aware that my beliefs about the death penalty have never been tested by personal loss. Let Mama or my sister, Mary Ann, or my brother, Louie, be brutally murdered and then see how much compassion I have. My magnanimity is gratuitous. No one has shot my loved ones in the back of the head.

If someone I love should be killed, I know I would feel rage, loss, grief, helplessness, perhaps for the rest of my life. It would be arrogant to think I can predict how I would respond to such a disaster. But Jesus Christ, whose way of life I try to follow, refused to meet hate with hate and violence with violence. I pray for the strength to be like him. I cannot believe in a God who metes out hurt for hurt, pain for pain, torture for torture. . . .

In sorting out my feelings and beliefs, there is, however, one piece of moral ground of which I am absolutely certain: if I were to be murdered I would not want my murderer executed. I would not want my death avenged. *Especially by government*—which can't be trusted to control its own bureaucrats or collect taxes equitably or fill a pothole, much less decide which of its citizens to kill.

Albert Camus' "Reflections on the Guillotine" is for me a moral compass on the issue of capital punishment. He wrote this essay in 1957 when the stench of Auschwitz was still in the air, and one of his cardinal points is that no government is ever innocent enough or wise enough or just enough to lay claim to so absolute a power as death.

> Society proceeds sovereignly to eliminate the evil ones from her midst as if she were virtue itself. . . . To assert, in any case, that a man must be absolutely cut off from society because he is absolutely evil amounts to saying that society is absolutely good, and no one in his right mind will believe this today.

I ask [Warden Phelps] to tell me about the execution process that he has designed, and he shows me a copy of Department Regulation Number 10–25, issued April 6, 1981. I glance at the document and notice headings: Purpose, Responsibility, Legal Authority, Incarceration Prior to Execution, Media Access, Time and Place of Execution . . .

"From a personal standpoint it is very, very bizarre to design a process like this," he says, "because you find yourself approaching an execution the same way you approach putting on a rodeo or any other special event." Before designing the process, he says, he made field trips to talk to corrections officials in other states that use the electric

chair, and he engaged the services of an electrical engineer—"he worked for free, he refused to be paid"—to devote his attention to "the technical aspects of the apparatus."

Inwardly I translate the terms, *technical aspects of the apparatus,* and I think of how silent it was there in the room as the guard screwed the rubber-coated wire to the top of the metal cap on Pat's shaved head.

Setting up the "process," Phelps explains, involved hiring an executioner.

"We hired a man, an electrician, who filled out a civil service application for the job. Frank Blackburn, the warden at Angola at the time, interviewed the prospective candidate for the job in some depth because we obviously wanted somebody who was screwed down pretty tight and very, very firm in his convictions, not just someone with a morbid interest. We were looking for—this may sound strange—somebody professional. We didn't want a mafia-type executioner." . . . He agreed to be paid $400 per execution. It was a verbal agreement, not written.

I make a mental note of the anonymity of the executioner and the reluctance to sign a contract specifying fee for service. I log it alongside something that Phelps mentioned earlier: that the electrician who wired the chair refused to be paid—the intuitive recognition that this is "blood money," this is "death for hire."

The fact that anonymity is granted to the executioner intrigues me. I've heard that in Utah, when Gary Gilmore was executed by a firing squad, blanks were inserted into one of the rifles so that those firing the guns would not know for certain if they killed the man. No doubt, the uncertainty helps diffuse responsibility.

Phelps says that for him, the most "troublesome" aspect of the "process" has been the selection of witnesses. With the resumption of executions, some victims' families asked if they might witness, and he says he "pondered" this a long time but "couldn't think of a reason why they shouldn't. Our position in the D.O.C. is that I am not the 'keeper of the morals' but merely the enforcer of the law, and if there is no legal reason barring a victim's family, I see no reason to deny them."

Phelps says that he emphasizes to all witnesses—victims' families included—that during an execution there must be "no emotional outbursts, no obscenities uttered, no undignified behavior of any kind." They have designed a process, he says, that "protects everyone's rights," including those of the one being executed. "They have a family too. A circus atmosphere is not in anyone's interest."

I am listening to all this and I keep picturing Pat's dead body in the chair, the fingers of his right hand curling upward, the doctor's light shining into vacant eyes.

I say that I disagree that the rights of the man being killed are protected because the witnesses to his death are expected to be polite.

"Pat Sonnier was tortured, Mr. Phelps," I say. "I'm not sure what he felt physically when the nineteen hundred volts hit him, but certainly he agonized emotionally and psychologically—preparing to die, anticipating it, dreaming about it. Amnesty International defines torture as an extreme physical and mental assault on a person who has been rendered defenseless. That is what happened to Patrick Sonnier, isn't it, Mr. Phelps? . . .

Yes, I cared for Patrick Sonnier. Despite his terrible crime, he was a human being and deserved to be treated with dignity and, yes, I was emotionally distraught watching him die. "Who wouldn't be," I ask [Warden Blackburn], "watching someone killed in such a cold, calculated way right in front of your eyes? You and the others are part of a process that shields you from natural, human emotions. The raw truth is that you're killing a fellow human being whose hands and feet are tied, and who wants to admit he's doing that?"

There is silence for a short moment, and then Blackburn says, "We can't let feelings dominate our actions or we couldn't carry out our responsibilities. . . .

I challenge him: "But you're a Christian, a minister in your church, a man who professes to follow the way of life that Jesus taught. Yet you are the one who, with a nod of your head, signals the executioner to kill a man. Do you really believe that Jesus, who taught us not to return hate for hate and evil for evil and whose dying words were, 'Father, for-give them,' would participate in these executions? Would Jesus pull the switch?" . . .

"Nope," he says, "I don't experience any contradiction with my Christianity. Never thought about it too much, really. Executions are the law, and Christians are supposed to observe the law, and that's that." And then he adds, "My wife, she's a good Christian woman, and she supports the death penalty, and believe me, you can't find a better Christian woman than my wife."

How is it, I wonder, that the mandate and example of Jesus, so clearly urging compassion and nonviolence, could so quickly become *accommodated*? Over the centuries "lawful authorities"—supposedly in God's name and with God's blessing—have hanged, shot, guillotined, drawn and quartered, burned, gassed, electrocuted, lethally injected—criminals. Over the years the crimes meriting death might change, but, for the most part, the blessing of God on retaliatory punishment has been unquestioned. Of course, those who justify retaliation can cite as authority numerous passages in the Bible, where divine vengeance is meted out to guilty and innocent alike: the Great Flood, the destruction of Sodom and Gomorrah, the slaying of the firstborn sons of the Egyptians (God's "lesson" to a recalcitrant Pharaoh), to mention just a few examples. Even the Pauline injunction "Vengeance is mine, says the Lord, I will repay" can be interpreted as a command and a promise—the command to restrain individual impulses toward revenge in exchange for the assurance that God will be only too pleased to handle the grievance—in spades. That God wants to "get even" like the rest of us does not seem to be in question.

One intractable problem, however, is that divine vengeance (barring natural disasters, so-called acts of God) can only be interpreted and exacted by human beings. *Very* human beings.

I can't accept that.

First, I can't accept that God has fits of rage and goes about trucking in retaliation. Second, I can't accept that any group of human beings is trustworthy enough to mete out so ultimate and irreversible a punishment as death. And, third, I can't accept that it's permissible to kill people provided you "prepare" them with good spiritual counsel to "meet their Maker." . . .

The swath of violence cut by Christians across the centuries is long and wide and bloodstained: inquisitions, crusades, witch burnings, persecutions of Jewish "Christ-killers." Now, in the last decade of the twentieth century, U.S. government officials kill citizens with dispatch with scarcely a murmur of resistance from the Christian citizenry. In fact, surveys of public opinion show that those who profess Christianity tend to favor capital punishment slightly more than the overall population—Catholics more than Protestants. True, in recent years leadership bodies of most Christian denominations have issued formal statements denouncing the death penalty, but generally that opposition has yet to be translated into aggressive pastoral initiatives to educate clergy and membership on capital punishment. And the U.S. Catholic Bishops in their "Statement on Capital Punishment," while strongly condemning the death penalty because of the "unfair and discriminatory" manner in which it is imposed, its continuance of the "cycle of violence," and its fundamental disregard for the "unique worth and dignity of each person," nevertheless uphold the "right" of the state to kill. But if we are to have a society which protects its citizens from torture and murder, then torture and murder must be off-limits to *everyone*. No one, for any reason, may be permitted to torture and kill—and that includes government. Before prisons existed, executions might have been justified as society's only means of defense against crazed, violent killers. But today in the United States, following the example of other modern industrialized countries, we can incapacitate violent criminals through long-term imprisonment. . . .

We know that one of the key issues we must address is the fear of crime which fuels the death penalty. Actually, the public (not by accident) has an exaggerated perception of the risk of felony-type murders (murders which occur in the course of another felony which may be punishable by death). The risk varies, of course, according to one's neighborhood—inner-city residents have *good* reason to fear felony-type murders—but nationwide, according to 1989 statistics, a very small percentage,

2.0 persons in 100,000, die of felony-type murders each year, roughly the same percentage as those who die from drowning or accidental poisoning. In contrast, the probability of dying in an automobile accident is 47.9 per 100,000, and the probability of dying from heart disease is 765.5 per 100,000. But the public's view of crime is largely shaped by the media, which are prone to emphasize death from violence while downplaying more prevalent and commonplace threats to life. . . .

I also point out that execution of a prisoner costs more than life imprisonment. That's because capital trials require more expert witnesses and more investigators, a longer jury-selection process (those who oppose the death penalty must be screened out), the expenses of sequestering a jury, not one but two trials because of the required separate sentencing trial, and appeals in state and federal courts. . . . In Florida, which may be typical, each death sentence is estimated to cost approximately $3.18 million, compared to the cost of life imprisonment (40 years) of about $516,000. Another reason for swollen costs is the added expense of incarcerating prisoners on death row. Most states segregate death-row prisoners in maximum security units and must hire additional security personnel. Nor are most death-row prisoners allowed to work, which prevents them from helping to pay for their upkeep.

Besides the expense there is also a "distortion cost" which capital trials and appellate proceedings impose on the court system. State supreme court judges in some death-penalty jurisdictions report that they spend a disproportionate amount of their judging time tending to capital punishment business.

To these utilitarian arguments I add others in these media interviews—that the death penalty is too selective and capricious to serve as a deterrent, that it is racially biased—but the argument I always save for last is this one: if we believe that murder is wrong and not admissible in our society, then it has to be wrong for everyone, not just individuals but governments as well. And I end by challenging people to ask themselves whether we can continue to allow the government, subject as it is to every imaginable form of inefficiency and corruption, to have such power to kill. . . .

It's my first time meeting people in the media. I notice how friendly many of them are. After the interviews I always shake hands and thank them for coming out, the reporters and the camera people too; and before the walk is over I have quite a collection of their personal cards, which I file so I can call on them in the future. Reflecting back after ten years, I realize now, even more than I did then, just how crucial the media are to public education on this issue, and I am struck by how many reporters and journalists become sympathetic to the cause of abolition once they become knowledgeable about the issue.

We walk in the sunshine. It's October, one of Louisiana's clearest, driest months. The sky is cobalt blue. The trees and grass are still mostly green, but the swamp maples have turned orange-red. It feels good to be walking out on the open road. Bill Quigley is at the head of the line, setting the pace. We'll do twenty-five miles each day. When people drop behind the crowd (people such as me, with short legs), a van picks us up and brings us to the front. That way we keep a brisk pace. Everybody's full of chatter. Some sing. . . .

Many people, barreling along the highway, energetically signal their response to our cause: they put thumbs down; they flip us the middle finger; they shout "Fry the bastards"; they call us "bleeding-heart liberals"; they call us "commies." But every now and then we hear a horn and see a thumb up, and we all wave and cheer. . . .

For three days we walk.

We arrive in Baton Rouge as the sun is setting. The darkness is fast descending and streetlights have come on and give a furry amber glow. As we approach the capitol steps we spot a small group holding up posterboard signs. Supporters coming to join us for the rally? Getting closer, we can make out what the signs say: "What about the victims?" "Justice, *even* for victims." It's a counter-demonstration group. How will we deal with them? Ignore them? Talk to them? The steering committee huddles. We decide to send a couple of people on a "peacekeeping" mission.

We hold the rally. The press gives us good coverage. The "peacekeeping" mission is successful, and we are not interrupted by the counter-demonstrators. . . .

I wonder what will ever be able to heal the Harveys' pain and bring them peace. No, there is no replacing the unique universe of Faith Hathaway. Even if Robert Willie is destroyed, the aching void can never be filled.

I understand the Harveys' desire for retribution. Their lives have been violated by Robert Willie and they want to see him punished. They want to see him made accountable for his actions. They want to see him pay for what he did. So did I. In an ideal world, there would be no need for retribution. But in real societies, punishing the guilty is as integral to the function of law as exonerating the innocent and preventing crime.

Susan Jacoby, in her insightful book *Wild Justice: The Evolution of Revenge,* maintains, and I agree, that the retribution which society metes out should be *measured.* Her objection to capital punishment is that such "eye-for-an-eye" retribution is as excessive as the original crime it punishes. But she also finds it excessive that those convicted of so heinous and irrevocable a crime as murder should be made to serve only a few short years in prison. The Bureau of Justice Statistics reveals that in 1986 the average amount of time served on a life sentence in the United States was six years, nine months.

Jacoby holds that the public's desire to see serious punishment consistently meted out for serious crimes is legitimate and that to ignore it encourages "the boundless outrage that generates demands for boundless retribution." But she says that punishment should be tempered: . . .

Such measured retribution is attained, I believe, by sentencing which requires *nonnegotiable* long-term imprisonment for first-degree murder (also termed *aggravated* or *capital* murder). At least forty states in recent years have revised criminal codes to require life without parole or lengthy mandatory minimum years served for convictions they deem most serious. In a growing number of states— twenty-five as of 1992, including Louisiana—life-without-parole sentences are *true* life sentences. . . .

This evening's encounter with the Harveys has to count as one of the most painful of my life. Never have I met such unrequited grief. What, I wonder, can I possibly do to ease their pain? I am out of my depth. Driving across these dark waters of Lake Pontchartrain, I realize how vulnerable we all are. Faith Hathaway—dead. Loretta Bourque—dead. David LeBlanc—dead. Children snatched from their parents in the night. I think of my sister, Mary Ann. I think of Mama. I think of Mary Ann and Charlie's five children, especially Helen, my namesake. I think of Julie and Marcy, my brother Louie's little girls. When I get home I will telephone Mama. I want to hear that everyone is safe.

This Robert Willie, who is he? I recoil at the thought of him. How dare he calmly read law books and concoct arguments in his defense? He should fall on his knees, weeping, begging forgiveness from these parents. He should spend every moment of his life repenting his heinous deed. But, judging from my first visit, he seems to be in a world of his own, oblivious to the pain he has caused others. . . . *Someone is trying to kill him,* and this must rivet his energies on his own survival, not the pain of others.

My hope for the Harveys is that eventually they will be able to overcome their terrible grief and once again live positive lives. How I can help them I am not sure, but I want to try. And Robert Willie? What can I possibly do for him? I will do what Millard Farmer asked me to do—accompany him, treat him with dignity—but I will also challenge him to take responsibility for his crime and to ask forgiveness of the Harveys.

Emotionally it's confusing to think of the Harveys and their needs alongside Robert Willie and his. Hearing the details of Faith's vicious murder, I find myself sucked into the Harveys' rage. But then I think of the death the state has in store for Robert Willie.

A few days after visiting the Harveys I visit Robert for the second time. I have a notebook on the front seat of the car. I'm not allowed to take it into the prison (only attorneys and news reporters can bring writing materials inside), but afterward I'll jot down notes from our conversation. I'm much more alert now than I was with Pat Sonnier. When the Pardon Board hearing comes up, facts about Robert's family life and background will be important. I feel that there isn't much time.

Robert comes into the visiting room. He is wearing a black knitted hat. He walks with a little bounce, poising momentarily on the balls of his feet. I dispense with preliminaries.

"I went to visit the Harveys," I say. "They told me about Faith's death. Robert, you raped and stabbed that girl and left her to rot in the woods. Why?" . . .

Unfortunately, the exercise of power practiced by Christians in alliance with the Roman Empire—with its unabashed allegiance to the sword—soon bore no resemblance to the purely moral persuasion that Jesus had taught.

In the fifth century, . . . Augustine provided the theological rationale the church needed to justify the use of violence by church and state governments. Augustine persuaded church authorities that "original sin" so damaged every person's ability to make moral choices that external control by church and state authorities over people's lives was necessary and justified. The "wicked" might be "coerced by the sword" to "protect the innocent," Augustine taught. And thus was legitimated for Christians the authority of secular government to "control" its subjects by coercive and violent means—even punishment by death.

In the latter part of this century, however, two flares of hope—Mohandas K. Gandhi and Martin Luther King—have demonstrated that Jesus' counsel to practice compassion and tolerance even toward one's enemies can effect social change. Susan Jacoby, analyzing the moral power that Gandhi and King unleashed in their campaigns for social justice, finds a unique form of aggression:

"'If everyone took an eye for an eye,' Gandhi said, 'the whole world would be blind.' But Gandhi did not want to take anyone's eye; he wanted to force the British out of India . . .'"

The writings of both men are filled with references to love as a powerful force against oppression, and while the two leaders were not using the term "force" in the military sense, they certainly regarded nonviolence as a tactical weapon as well as an expression of high moral principle. The root meaning of Gandhi's concept of *satyagraha* . . . is "holding on to truth." . . . Gandhi also called *satyagraha* the "love force" or "soul force" and explained that he had discovered "in the earliest stages that pursuit of truth did not permit violence being inflicted on one's opponent, but that he must be weaned from error by patience and sympathy." . . .

King was even more explicit on this point: the purpose of civil disobedience, he explained many times, was to force the defenders of segregation to commit brutal acts in public and thus arouse the conscience of the world on behalf of those wronged by racism. King and Gandhi did not succeed because they changed the hearts and minds of southern sheriffs and British colonial administrators (although they did, in fact, change some minds) but because they *made the price of maintaining control too high for their opponents* [emphasis mine].

That, I believe, is what it's going to take to abolish the death penalty in this country: we must persuade the American people that government killings are too costly for us, not only financially, but— more important—morally.

The death penalty *costs* too much. Allowing our government to kill citizens compromises the deepest moral values upon which this country was conceived: the inviolable dignity of human persons.

I have no doubt that we will one day abolish the death penalty in America. . . . The secrecy surrounding executions makes it possible for executions to continue. I am convinced that if executions were made public, the torture and violence would be unmasked, and we would be shamed into abolishing executions. We would be embarrassed at the brutalization of the crowds that would gather to watch a man or woman be killed. And we would be humiliated to know that visitors from other countries—Japan, Russia, Latin America, Europe—were watching us kill our own citizens—we, who take pride in being the flagship of democracy in the world.

And here I am driving to Baton Rouge from the death house, where tomorrow a man is going to be executed. . . .

As soon as I arrive, a technician, working quickly, hooks the microphone onto the lapel of my coat, hands me a small hearing device to insert into my ear, and in a few short moments I am hooked up to New York. Before we go on the air, Peter Jennings practices saying "Prejean"—"Pray-zshawn." He recognizes that it's French and wants to make sure he pronounces it correctly. To tell you the truth, he tells me, they want my viewpoint because they are featuring the Harveys and they don't want to present only one side of the issue. . . .

The story opens showing the Harveys outside the prison after the execution. Someone is holding a sign that says "Have 'Faith' in the Justice System."

Vernon says he wishes every victim could have the opportunity he had tonight. Lizabeth says that since Robert Willie saw Faith die, her parents should see him die. Warden Blackburn is shown announcing that Robert Willie was pronounced dead at 12:15 A.M. and then Robert's last statement is read. Then they go back to Elizabeth and Vernon Harvey, and Vernon says he feels it was too easy and quick for Willie, "he didn't suffer no pain, and my daughter had to." . . .

Jennings asks if I feel it would be a good thing for people to be exposed to executions, and I say yes, because then they would see the violence unmasked and this would lead them to abolish executions. I say that an execution is a brutal and horrible thing, and that I heard Mr. Harvey say Robert experienced no pain, but that the pain came every time he looked at his watch, knowing that in a few days, a few hours he would die.

Jennings thanks me and turns to George Will, the political commentator, and asks whether he thinks people should be able to witness executions.

George Will says the American people favor capital punishment, not primarily because they believe it's an effective deterrent, but because it satisfies a deeply felt moral intuition that there are some crimes for which death is the only proportionate punishment, and this murder certainly seems to be one of those crimes. That is what the American people feel, he says, and he thinks they're right and that vengeance, far from being shameful, can be noble. . . .

[Walter Burns, a death-penalty advocate], too, fears that public viewing of such events would have a "coarsening" effect upon the populace: "No ordinary person can be required to witness [executions], and it would be better if some people not be permitted to witness them—children, for example, and the sort of persons who would, if permitted, happily join a lynch mob. Executions should not be televised, both because of the unrestricted character of the television audience and the tendency of television to make a vulgar spectacle of the most *dignified event*" [italics mine].

But it's not the presence of television cameras or the composition of the crowd or even whether the crowd acts politely or not that makes the execution of a human being ugly. An execution is ugly because the premeditated killing of a human being is ugly. Torture is ugly. Gassing, hanging, shooting, electrocuting, or lethally injecting a person whose hands and feet are tied is ugly. And hiding the ugliness from view and rationalizing it numbs our minds to the horror of what we are doing. This is what truly "coarsens" us.

I think of the moment when Warden Ross Maggio stood at the microphone to announce the time of Pat Sonnier's execution. His eyes happened to meet mine, and he lowered his eyes. It was instinctive. He had helped kill a man. There was nothing noble about it.

Camus held that executions are performed in secret because they are shameful deeds. State governments, he said, who wish executions to continue, know to keep them hidden from view, not only physically but also symbolically in the euphemistic language used to describe them. . . .

Louisiana became the nineteenth state to use lethal injection to kill prisoners since the state of Oklahoma inaugurated its use in 1977. The method is preferred because it virtually eliminates visible, bodily pain. There is only the "uncomfortableness" of a needle prick into a vein. There remains, however, one dimension of suffering that can never be eliminated when death is imposed on a conscious human being: the horror of being put to death against your will and the agony of anticipation. As if, when they strap you down on the gurney, your arms outstretched, waiting for the silent deadly fluid to flow—the sodium pentothol, which comes first to make you unconscious so you do not feel the pancuronium bromide when it paralyzes your dia-

phragm and stops your breathing and the potassium chloride which causes cardiac arrest and stops your heart—as if you feel the terror of death any less because chemicals are being used to kill you instead of electricity or bullets or rope?

There is an elaborate ruse going on here, a pitiful disguise. Killing is camouflaged as a medicinal act. The attendant will even swab the "patient's" arm with alcohol before inserting the needle—*to prevent infection*. . . .

A two-year study of capital punishment in the U.S. by Hugo A. Bedau of Tufts University and Michael L. Radelet of the University of Florida documents that in this century 417 people were wrongly convicted of capital offenses and 23 were actually executed. . . .

Ernest van den Haag, a professor of jurisprudence and public policy at Fordham University, when asked to respond to the Bedau-Radelet study showing that innocent people have actually been executed in this country, said: "All human activities—building houses, driving a car, playing golf or football—cause innocent people to suffer wrongful death, but we don't give them up because on the whole we feel there's a net gain. Here [executions], a net gain in justice is being done."

A handful of relatives and friends gather at the Brown-McGeehee Funeral Home in Covington to bury Robert Lee Willie. When I see Elizabeth she holds me tight and cries and I try to comfort her, telling her about the last hours of her son and how bravely he had met his death.

The three boys hover close to their mother, and Junior is here, too. Little Todd keeps taking his mother's hand and holding it.

I walk over to the open casket and look down at what remains of Robert Lee Willie. His body is dressed in blue jeans and a white T-shirt, and I notice a couple of tattoos on his arms that I hadn't noticed before—a peacock and marijuana leaves. It is a shock to see him so quiet and still like this, his eyes closed, his lips not moving.

There is a flutter of commotion and some laughter when word spreads that Robert's aunt Bessie, waving her shoe, just chased away a reporter who tried to enter the funeral home.

When the funeral director announces that the last good-byes are to be said, Elizabeth approaches the casket. "Oh, Robert, Robert, my boy, O God, help me," she says, weeping. "Oh, Robert, how much I loved you." . . .

Discussion Questions

1. Prejean maintains that all humans have intrinsic moral value—"Nobody is disposable human waste." She writes, "Yes, I cared for Patrick Sonnier. Despite his terrible crime, he was a human being and deserved to be treated with dignity."[36] Do you agree with Prejean? Does moral respect require that people be treated with dignity even when they treat others as "disposable human waste"? Support your answers.
2. Discuss the methods Prejean used to protest capital punishment. Is her protest of civil law consistent with natural law ethics? If you believe that capital punishment is immoral, how should you go about protesting it? Explain using specific examples.
3. Prejean argues that capital punishment is contrary to the moral teachings of Jesus of Nazareth, "who taught us not to return hate for hate and evil for evil." Many Christians disagree with this interpretation of Christian ethics. Indeed, in the United States, Christians are more likely to support the death penalty than are non-Christians. Discuss the relative merits of the two interpretations of Christian ethics.
4. According to psychologist Carol Gilligan, moral maturity entails integrating the justice and the care perspectives. Develop a policy on capital punishment that draws from both perspectives.
5. According to care ethicist Nel Noddings, it is being in a caring relationship that gives people moral value. If someone on death row is cared for by others, such as Robert Lee Willie, should that person's life be spared? Is the death penalty more justified if the condemned person is not in a caring relationship of any sort? Support your answers.

CASE STUDIES

1. KARLA FAYE TUCKER: THE REPENTANT MURDERER

There's no question that thirty-eight-year-old Karla Faye Tucker of Texas is guilty of murder. In 1983 while strung out on drugs, Tucker hacked her two helpless victims to death with a pickax. She even boasted afterward that the killing gave her a sexual thrill. So why is she appealing her death sentence?

Tucker has since come to regret her deeds. She has found God, she says, and is a changed person. "God reached down inside of me and literally uprooted all of that stuff and took it out and poured himself in." Tucker is now involved in a prison-run program counseling young people to stay away from crime. "The world per se may not believe I deserve forgiveness," she told the world in an ABC interview, "but God says He's forgiven me."

More than one hundred people gathered outside the Texas prison on February 3, 1998, the day of her scheduled execution, some protesting the death penalty and hoping for a stay of execution, others rallying in support of her execution. Despite pleas for her pardon, Tucker was executed that evening by lethal injection.

Discussion Questions

1. Texas has not executed a woman since the Civil War; only one woman has been executed in the United States since the death penalty was reinstated twenty years ago. Is the fact that the vast majority of violent crime is committed by young men relevant to the practical application of capital punishment? Because women, in general, do not need deterring, can capital punishment be justified in Tucker's case?

2. A 1997 survey of seven hundred death row inmates found that most share certain characteristics. Seven out of ten began their criminal careers as children, going on to commit more and more serious crimes, crimes which often included killing, before the murder that landed them on death row. Nine out of ten also had childhoods marred by poverty, drugs, abuse, alcoholism, broken families, or lack of high school education. Despite their crimes, the survey found that most death row inmates "view themselves as normal people caught up in abnormal circumstances."[37] Like most inmates on death row, Tucker had a rough childhood. A former prostitute, she was using marijuana by age eight and heroin at age eleven. She was on drugs when she committed the murders. Is any of this relevant to her moral responsibility for her action?

3. One of the arguments against the death penalty is that people change, that retributive justice and rehabilitation are, therefore, contradictory goals. Capital punishment denies people the opportunity for growth whereas other types of punishment do not. It is generally years before a death sentence is finally carried out. Meanwhile some people, like Tucker, go through major changes and moral growth. Should this be taken into consideration? Is it fair to punish people for a crime they committed during a different "stage" in their lives? Support your answers.

4. Discuss how both Kant and van den Haag might respond to the argument that capital punishment and rehabilitation are contradictory goals. Discuss how each would most likely have responded to Tucker's pleas for pardon. Discuss how Morris and Kant might each respond to Tucker's execution.

---

2. THE OKLAHOMA CITY BOMBER[38]

Shortly after 9:00 A.M. on April 19, 1995, a fireball ripped through the plate-glass doors of the Oklahoma City Federal Building in Oklahoma City, collapsing all nine floors on the north side.

Patrolman Charlie Hanger was outside of town patrolling for speeders when he heard about the explosion on his police radio. About 10:34 A.M. Hanger stopped a car for having no license plates. When he approached the driver, Hanger noticed a semi-automatic pistol poking out of the driver's shoulder strap. Hanger arrested him for driving an unregistered car and carrying an unregistered handgun and took him to the Noble County Jail. The driver, as it turned out, was twenty-seven-year-old Timothy McVeigh.

The explosion killed 168 people and injured 850. In June 1997 McVeigh was found guilty of murder and conspiracy and sentenced to death for his role in the bombing. McVeigh appealed the conviction claiming that the testimony of a former government militia informer had been excluded from his trial and that the jury was not impartial. His appeal was rejected by a U.S. Court of Appeals in February 1998. McVeigh is currently on death row, scheduled for execution in May 2001. His accomplice, Terry Nichols, is serving a life sentence for involuntary manslaughter and murder.

Discussion Questions

1. Prejean argues that capital punishment is inconsistent with the intrinsic value of human life. Nobody, she writes, is disposable human waste . . . Despite their terrible crimes, murderers are human beings and deserve to be treated with dignity. Do you agree? Does morality require that people like McVeigh, who allegedly treat others as "disposable human waste," be treated with dignity?

2. McVeigh, a decorated Gulf War veteran, saw the U.S. government as an enemy force responsible for killing eighty Branch Davidians near Waco, Texas. Compare and contrast the morality of McVeigh's actions as a terrorist with those of the pilots who bombed Baghdad during the Gulf War or dropped the atomic bomb on Hiroshima. Should soldiers who kill civilians during wartime be held morally accountable for their actions? Support your answers.

3. French existentialist Albert Camus claimed that there is a moral contradiction in a policy, such as capital punishment, that imitates the violence it is claiming to hate.[39] Do you agree with Camus? Are we as a community made a little less virtuous by executing McVeigh? Support your answers.

4. Kant maintained that if a person makes a rational decision to kill another person, respect for the murderer's dignity and free will requires that we in turn execute him. Although the vast majority of murders are carried out impulsively without previous rational analysis, McVeigh seem to be an exception to this rule. Does the fact that McVeigh carefully planned his crime make him more morally culpable than people who murder on impulse?

5. Discuss McVeigh's appeal in light of the recent study (see page 265) that over two-thirds of sentences had been overturned in the appeal process because of "procedural flaws or unsound evidence."[40] Does even the slightest possibility of error in the sentencing process justify the abolition of the death penalty? Support your answer.

---

3. CHILDREN WHO KILL

In 1999, in one of the worst school shootings in history, Eric Harris and Dylan Klebold opened fire on their classmates at Columbine High School in Littleton, Colorado. Thirteen people were killed and twenty-one others wounded before the two boys finally turned the guns on themselves ending both the rampage and their own lives. This is just one among many incidences in what ABC recently called an "explosion of violence" in U.S. schools.

Killings by children are not limited to the school. In 1989, fifteen-year-old Craig Price murdered three of his neighbors. When the police arrived at the Heaton home in Warwick, Rhode Island, they found three mutilated bodies. Joan Heaton, thirty-nine, had been stabbed with a knife eleven times, strangled, and bitten in the face. Her daughter Jennifer, ten, had been stabbed sixty-two times. Melissa, eight, had been stabbed eight times and her skull crushed. "We think of what these little kids went through . . .

that screaming . . . that unmerciful attack." Police Captain Kevin Collins shudders re-calling that grisly night in September.[41]

Price was arrested shortly after the bodies were found. Police later discovered that two years earlier Price had murdered another neighbor. He also had a record of assaults, burglaries, and other crimes.

Does Price think what he did was immoral? When asked about the murders, Price shrugged his shoulders and responded: "Morality is a private choice." According to Collins, who witnessed Price's confessions to the four murders, "He just loves to kill. There's no doubt . . . that he's going to kill again."[42]

Rhode Island does not have the death penalty. In addition, because Price was fifteen he could not be tried as an adult. Under Rhode Island law, the maximum sentence for juveniles, regardless of their crime, is detention in the training school until they are twenty-one.

Discussion Questions

1. Many societies draw a line at age eighteen, when people are suddenly held to be fully responsible for their actions. Is this practice justifiable? Or should children who kill be treated and punished like adults? Is it a violation of their dignity to deny them an equal "right to punishment"? Support your answers. Discuss how Reiman would most likely respond to these questions.

2. Many schools are tightening up security. While several students have been expelled for bringing weapons to school, others have been expelled simply for making threatening statements to classmates. Critics of this practice maintain that it violates these students' freedom of speech. Discuss ways in which schools and society in general might best respond to the problem of school violence, taking into consideration both utilitarian theory and rights ethics in formulating your policy.

3. People are still searching for an answer to why Harris and Klebold turned killers. One explanation being put forth is that their rage was fueled by vengeance against Columbine High School athletes whose taunting and bullying and harassment of other students at the school, including Harris and Klebold, was generally tolerated. Indeed, Harris and Klebold opened fire on their classmates with the words, "All the jocks stand up." To what extent, if any, do the athletes who engaged in this behavior, bear responsibility for the killings. Should athletes who engage in this type of behavior be punished? How about school officials who generally turned a blind eye to the athletes' behavior. Discuss how a virtue ethicist might respond to these questions.

4. In 1986 there were thirty-seven teenage killers on death row. A 1986 Justice Department study commission recommended that youths fifteen and older be treated as adult killers. Given that most people on death row began their life of crime as children and that most violent acts are committed by men under thirty, wouldn't execution of young killers make more sense as a deterrent than execution of adults? Discuss also how juvenile murderers should be handled in states, such as Rhode Island, that have no death penalty.

5. A 1988 study of fourteen juveniles on death row concluded that they had brain abnormalities, low IQs, and psychiatric problems and had suffered severe head injuries as children. Price, however, did not fit this profile. There is nothing unusual about Price's background: He came from what seemed to be a good family and lived in a

middle-class neighborhood. Does the fact that Price did not apparently act out of past conditioning make him more morally blameworthy than if he had grown up amidst poverty and violence? Support your answer.

6. Studies of prisoners' moral development have found that their level of moral reasoning is equivalent to that of thirteen year olds. Should murderers' level of moral development be taken into consideration before sentencing them to death? If not, what is the morally relevant difference between using the death penalty on a thirteen year old and on an adult who operates at a similar low level of moral reasoning? Support your answers.

7. Some psychologists believe that Craig Price, a brutal serial killer, is a psychopath. Psychopaths lack any sense of moral duty or moral right or wrong. Because they lack a conscience, they can maim and murder with impunity. Given that psychopaths lack the ability to distinguish between right and wrong, should they be held morally accountable for their actions? Does their inability mean that the concept of retributive justice and punishment, including the use of capital punishment, is inapplicable to them? Support your answers. Discuss how van den Haag might respond to these questions.

---

4. IS THERE A CRIMINAL GENE?

The popular science fiction thriller *Alien 3* opens with *Alien* veteran Lieutenant Ripley (Sigourney Weaver) crash-landing on the planet Fiorina "Fury" 161, a decommissioned maximum-security correctional facility for "double-Y-chromosome" offenders.[43] Upon regaining consciousness, Lieutenant Ripley is promptly warned by the prison superintendent not to leave the infirmary without an escort, because these prisoners are presumably unable to control their violent sexual urges in the presence of a woman. As the movie unfolds, it becomes clear that these twenty-five prisoners are a violent and obscene lot—social misfits of the worst sort—"all thieves, rapists, murderers, child molesters—all scum." They are not part of the mainstream human race but, in the words of the prison doctor, "alternative people" set apart from others by their genome and the bar codes indelibly tattooed on their heads. The moviegoer leaves the theater with the uneasy feeling that if these "double-Y-chromosome" men are such a threat, perhaps we ought to be seeking them out and destroying them with the same fervor that the brave Lieutenant Ripley pursued those nasty aliens.

The notion of a criminal gene that will allow us to sort out the chaff from the wheat is not a new one. The observation that young men commit the great majority of violent crimes as well as the finding that 80 percent of youth violence is committed by 7 percent of the youth population suggest that some people may have a genetic predisposition toward violent behavior. In the decade that followed the 1961 discovery of the XYY disorder, researchers found that maximum-security prison hospitals have a much higher than normal incidence of XYY males. They also noted that these men tend to be taller and more aggressive than other prisoners. These findings lead to speculations, which were sensationalized by the press, that there might be a criminal gene.

Although more-recent studies have found that the great majority of XYY males do not engage in any sort of violent criminal activity, interest in a possible genetic basis for violent crime has resurfaced in the wake of the Human Genome Project. Dr. Louis Sullivan, the Bush administration's secretary of Health and Human Services from 1989 to 1993, maintains that violence is a public-health issue. In the early 1990s, philosopher David Wasserman made the observation that genetic research suggests there are "genetic factors in crime." His statement was promptly denounced for fostering prejudice and a "modern-day version of eugenics." Federal funding for research on a genetic basis for crime was withdrawn. Other scientists who have sought to find a genetic link to violence have also been reprimanded.

Discussion Questions

1. Is life imprisonment on a desolate planet preferable to the death penalty? Or should the remaining twenty-five prisoners on planet Fiorina "Fury" 161 be executed? Does the fact that these prisoners have a chromosomal disorder excuse what they did? If so, what is the morally appropriate response to their crimes? Support your answers.

2. Despite the taboo on any suggestion that crime has a genetic link, some scientists have cautiously suggested that genes influencing serotonin production may make certain people, particularly young men, who are most likely to have low levels of serotonin, more susceptible to impulsive and aggressive behavior as well as to alcohol and drug abuse.[44] Should murderers who have an extra Y chromosome, a low level of serotonin, or a genetic predisposition to addictive behavior be held morally responsible for their crimes? Should they be "treated" rather than punished?

3. Being a psychopath seems to be, at least in part, genetically based. There is strong evidence that the frontal-lobe cortex in the brain, which is abnormal in a psychopath, plays a key role in moral decision making.[45] If this is the case, is it fair to hold psychopaths morally responsible for their crimes? Is punishment based on retribution inappropriate even though psychopaths are some of the most dangerous criminals? Support your answers. Role-play a discussion between van den Haag, Morris, and Reiman on these questions.

4. Although researchers say that they expect their findings to be used to screen people who have a predisposition toward violence in order to treat them, there is fear that screening will be used to discriminate against these people or to selectively abort fetuses with genetic predispositions toward violence. Should research on a criminal gene be banned or restricted?

---

5. INSIDE A TEXAS DEATH CHAMBER

Texas has been dubbed "the execution capital of the free world." The frequency of executions in some of the prisons has made them routine. How does participation in capital punishment affect those who carry it out or witness it?

Journalist Michael Graczyk of the Houston bureau of The Associated Press has witnessed about seventy executions. "It's my job," he says. "It's like going to cover a baseball game or a basketball game." Executions are no longer big news in Texas. In the past, executions were scheduled for midnight; now they are held at 6 P.M. for the convenience of those involved. As the prisoner is ushered into the death chamber, guards stand around talking about their kids, Little League, and what they're going to do on their day off.

There is no blood, no sense of horror, no scream of anguish as the needle is inserted into the inmate's arm. When the act is over, it just looks like the inmate went to sleep. Graczyk wrote, after the execution of brutal murderer Billy Joe Woods, "It was bizarre to look around and see all these people just doing their job. It was just another day at the office."[46]

Outside was a handful of anti-death penalty advocates crying, "Murderer!"—not at the man about to be executed, but at the gray-shirted guards. Later they chanted into a megaphone, "God bless Billy Woods. God bless Billy Woods."

Discussion Questions

1. Does the death penalty brutalize and numb all those who participate in it, as abolitionists claim? Discuss how van den Haag might respond to this objection to capital punishment.
2. Prejean argues that capital punishment creates sympathy for the murderer, as in the case of Billy Woods. Does it weaken respect for the authority of the law if the state is seen as the murderer and the death row inmate as the victim? Support your answer. Discuss how a social contractarian would answer this question.
3. Executions involving lethal injection generally require the presence of a physician. Should physicians participate in executions, or does this require them to go against their professional code of ethics, as the AMA claims? Does the principle of nonmaleficence, or "Do no harm," forbid doctors from witnessing or participating in the execution of murderers? If not physicians, who should carry out executions? Does the principle of nonmaleficence forbid anyone from executing another person? Support your answers.
4. Prejean suggests making executions public. It is the secrecy surrounding executions, she maintains, that keeps the public from realizing just how brutal capital punishment really is. Discuss the relative merits of having executions open to the public.

Drug and Alcohol Use

Scott Krueger had graduated near the top of his high school class and was looking forward to balancing the challenging demands of an engineering major at MIT, early-morning crew practice, and an active social life at Phi Gamma Delta, one of the thirty fraternities at MIT. In the fall of 1997, however, the fraternity pledge passed out during a Greek Week celebration after downing sixteen drinks in an hour. Krueger's fraternity brothers carried him back to the fraternity house. When they noticed he was having trouble breathing, they called an ambulance.

When rescue workers arrived, Krueger was already comatose. His blood alcohol level was later found to be more than five times the legal driving limit. A few days later, Krueger's distraught parents had him removed from life support. He died shortly thereafter. Krueger is only one of hundreds of college students whose lives are cut short or devastated every year as a result of drug and alcohol abuse.

In September 2000 Krueger's parents were awarded a $6 million settlement by the university. This unprecedented financial settlement and MIT's declared commitment to change the college conditions that contributed to Krueger's death has spurred other colleges to make similar commitments to create a safer and more secure campus environment for students.

WHAT IS A DRUG?

Drugs, for the purpose of this chapter, are defined as chemicals that enter the bloodstream and are easily transported to the brain, where they alter the way we feel, with predictable results. Alcohol, by this definition, is a type of drug. Drugs can be smoked, taken by needle, snorted, or swallowed.

Drug abuse is defined as "taking a drug or drugs for purposes other than those for which the drug or drugs were intended, and/or the illicit use of a drug or drugs which can cause harm (not necessarily physical) to oneself and/or others."[1] One of the risks of alcohol and drug use is addiction. *Addiction* is "a behavioral pattern of drug use, characterized by overwhelming involvement with the use of a drug [compulsive use], the securing of its supply, and a high tendency to relapse after withdrawal."[2]

🖋 DRUG CLASSIFICATIONS

Classification	Drugs	Effects[3]
Stimulants	Amphetamines, cocaine, prescription diet pills, nicotine, caffeine	Alertness; a sense of power; enhanced performance[4]
Depressants	Alcohol, anti-anxiety drugs and sleeping pills containing benzodiazepine and barbiturates	Drowsiness and sedation
Opiates	Prescription painkillers, codeine, heroin, Demerol, methadone, morphine	Diminished or no pain; sense of euphoria
Hallucinogens	LSD, "magic mushrooms," peyote, MDMA ("ecstasy"), mescaline	Intensified perception and sense experience; hallucinations
Cannabinals	All forms of marijuana	Mellowness
Inhalants/ Solvents	Acetone, aerosol gases, glue, paint thinner, correction fluid	Giddiness and confusion
Performance enhancement	Anabolic and androgenic steroids	Increased muscle mass

---

THE HISTORY OF DRUG AND ALCOHOL USE

Alcohol is the most widely used drug in North America. Wine and beer have been used since ancient times for their pleasurable effects, in medicine, with meals, and in religious ceremonies. Even the *Mayflower* carried a good supply of "bere."

Distilled spirits were first produced in Europe about 1300 and were often referred to as "aqua vitae" because of their purported powers to prolong life. In 1606, alarmed by the increase in drunkenness, the British government made intoxication a statutory offense with the Act of Repression of the Odious and Loathsome Sin of Drunkedness.

Laws in the colonies were relatively lenient and geared primarily toward controlling drunkenness and disorderly conduct. A Connecticut law prohibited drinking for more than one-half hour at a time. A 1760 Virginia law prohibited ministers from "drinking to excess and inciting riots."

There were no large-scale temperance movements in North America until the mid-nineteenth century. The first temperance movement was fired by the sermons of reformers such as the Reverend Lyman Beecher, who denounced all alcohol as inherently evil. For a short period in the mid-1850s, several states as well as the Canadian provinces of Nova Scotia and New Brunswick enacted prohibition laws. Following this, alcohol consumption reached a low point.

Alcohol consumption hit another peak in the United States around the turn of the century. The temperance movement of the late-nineteenth and early-twentieth centuries was spearheaded by groups such as the Women's Christian Temperance Union (WCTU) and the Anti-Saloon League. The WCTU opposed drinking primarily because of its destructive effect on the family. The problem was also blamed on the influx of immigrants from Europe and Ireland, with their decadent European drinking habits.

In 1919 the Eighteenth Amendment to the Constitution outlawed the sale and consumption of alcohol. Despite lack of unanimous support for the amendment, most prohibitionists thought that Americans would not violate their Constitution. They were mistaken. The ratification of the Eighteenth Amendment ushered in an era of organized crime and a vast illegal liquor trade, known as "bootlegging," under the control of such notorious gangsters as Al Capone. Large quantities of alcohol were smuggled in from countries such as Canada and England, which did not have prohibition laws.

Although alcohol consumption declined during the first few years of prohibition, it began to climb again during the 1920s. The cost of trying to stamp out illegal drinking soared into the many millions of dollars. It soon became apparent that prohibition was too unpopular and too expensive to enforce. The Eighteenth Amendment was repealed in 1933 by the Twenty-first Amendment, although some states continued to have local prohibition laws as late as 1966.

Alcohol consumption hit another peak about 1980. Once again the tide of public opinion turned against alcohol. This time it was the medical profession that led the crusade. Rather than denounce alcohol as a moral failing or the work of the devil, as had the early prohibitionists, the medical establishment declared alcoholism to be a disease. The disease model continues to dominate attitudes toward alcohol use in the United States today.

Attitudes toward drug use have followed a similar course. Hallucinogenic drugs have been used since antiquity both for pleasure and religious purposes. Apparently, the techniques of ecstatic trances used by some Hindu yogis involved the use of drugs. The peyote cult of Mexico also used drug-induced ecstasy in mystical and religious rituals. LSD, which was popular in North America in the 1960s, has been similarly credited with helping users get in touch with a deeper mystical wisdom. Western philosophers and psychologists, with their emphasis on reason as the source of knowledge, tend to dismiss these experiences as merely drug induced and, hence, unreal.

Drugs have also been widely used for medicinal purposes. Opium was available in a crude form prior to 1800 and was valued by physicians for its calming effect and as a cure for gastrointestinal illnesses. Noted nineteenth-century physician George Wood wrote that opium produces "an exaltation of our better mental qualities, a warmer glow of benevolence, a disposition to do great things, but nobly and beneficently, a higher devotional spirit, and withal a stronger self-reliance, and consciousness of power."[5]

Morphine, a derivative of opium, became a popular painkiller after 1870. When heroin, a derivative of morphine, was introduced into medical practice in the late 1800s, it was actively promoted by the American Medical Association (AMA) and pharmaceutical companies as a cure for many ailments. The easy availability of these drugs in the late-nineteenth century was accompanied by a substantial increase in the number of drug addicts.[6] This increase, however, could not be attributed solely to easier access to drugs. These same drugs were also widely available in France, Germany, Great Britain, Russia,

SECTION 1 OF THE EIGHTEENTH AMENDMENT TO THE UNITED STATES CONSTITUTION

[Adopted January 29, 1919]

Section 1. After one year from the ratification of this article the manufacture, sale, or transportation thereof into, or the exportation thereof from the United States and all territories subject to the jurisdiction thereof for beverage purposes is hereby prohibited.

and Italy, yet these countries did not experience similar increases in numbers of drug addicts.

Cocaine was first isolated from the coca leaf in the mid-nineteenth century. It was popular as a general tonic and for sinusitis and hay fever. Even psychoanalyst Sigmund Freud used cocaine as a tonic. The exhilarating effects of cocaine made it a popular additive in medicine, soda, and wine. In the United States, blacks were blamed by prohibitionists for the "cocaine problem." It was feared that euphoric black cocaine users might forget their place in life and begin attacking white society. Despite the fact that studies at the time failed to confirm the widespread use of cocaine by blacks, the fear of an uprising was used, in part, to justify an era of lynchings and legal segregation.

LEGAL AND ILLEGAL DRUGS

State laws regulating the use of morphine and cocaine were first enacted in the United States in the 1890s. Federal prohibition of drugs was not attempted initially because it was thought to be unconstitutional. Libertarians, physicians, and the major pharmaceutical societies also protested the outlawing in the United States of opiates, cocaine, and cannabis, substances they relied heavily on for symptom relief. Despite support for the medicinal use of drugs, by the mid-1920s the federal government moved to eliminate all heroin use.

The Pure Food and Drug Act of 1906 was the first federal legislation to regulate the use of opium. Blacks were not the only oppressed group in the United States to be scapegoated by drug prohibitionists. Because opium was exported from China, opposition to the recreational use of opium was used to reinforce anti-Chinese sentiment and the persecution of Chinese immigrants.

It is sometimes assumed that the division between legal and illegal drugs is based on rational criteria, but this clearly isn't the case. Alcohol, nicotine (tobacco), and marijuana are currently the three most frequently used drugs in the United States. Yet marijuana, which rarely causes physiological addiction or serious illness, is illegal whereas alcohol and tobacco are not. According to an AMA study, tobacco is the number one "actual cause of death" in the United States; alcohol is number three. Tobacco is responsible for 430,000 deaths a year and alcohol for another 100,000 deaths. The abuse of legal over-the-counter or prescription drugs, inhalants, or solvents can also lead to addiction, serious health problems, and even death. Heroin, morphine, and cocaine, in contrast, are responsible for fewer than 8,500 a year, while marijuana has yet to be implicated as responsible in anyone's death.[7]

The most recent wave of antidrug laws comes at a time when the public is divided over the wisdom of drug prohibition. Does the state have a right to prohibit or protect adults from using drugs? Is drug abuse a moral, legal, medical, or religious issue? Which drugs should be prohibited and which allowed?

DRUG AND ALCOHOL USE TODAY

When the George H. W. Bush administration declared an official "war on drugs," it had strong public support. Illicit drug use had already begun declining during the 1980s. However, despite tougher laws and some initial victories, the success of the "war" was short-lived. During the mid-1990s, drug use began rising again, especially among young people. The marketing of illicit drugs has also become more sophisticated. In the fall of 1997, the Royal Canadian Mounted Police in Vancouver raided one of the largest and most sophisticated drug-producing operations in North America. The hidden lab, which produced "designer drugs," had computer links to drug networks throughout North America and Europe.[8]

By 1994 polls showed that approximately 19 percent of eighth-graders, 36 percent of high school seniors, and 75 percent of people in their twenties had tried illicit drugs.[9] Of this sample, 28 percent were binge drinkers—that is, had five or more drinks in a row in the two weeks preceding the survey.[10] Between 1997 and 1999 the use of illegal drugs by children age twelve to seventeen declined; at the same time it increased among people eighteen to twenty-five. The number of high school students who were binge drinkers also increased slightly to 30 percent in 1999.[11]

There is growing concern about the high rate of marijuana and tobacco use among young people, because both are regarded by some as "gateway drugs" that may lead to the use of so-called hard drugs. While smoking has declined among the adult population, from 43 percent in 1972 to 23 percent in 1999,[12] it has risen among people under age twenty-five, especially females. According to an October 2000 Centers for Disease Control (CDC) report on teenage smoking, about 13 percent of middle school students use tobacco in some form.[13] The CDC also found that one out of every four middle and high school students who don't smoke will, in all likelihood, start smoking within a year. By the time students reach high school 35 percent of them are using tobacco, up from 30 percent in 1994.[14]

Cocaine, the second most popular illicit drug in the United States, is still regarded by many as primarily a problem among inner-city blacks. In actual fact, white males, at 12 percent, are twice as likely to use cocaine as black, Hispanic, and Native American males. African Americans, on the other hand, are more likely to use heroin. Because heroin-related offenses in the United States receive much more severe legal penalties than cocaine use or alcohol-related crimes such as drunk driving, blacks bear a disproportionate burden with respect to enforcement of drug laws. Blacks are also more likely than whites to receive convictions for similar drug-related offenses.[15]

Both cigarette and alcohol use are substantially higher among white and Native American young people than among blacks and Asian Americans. White and Hispanic college students are almost three times more likely to engage in binge drinking than black students.[16] Men also binge-drink more than women. In a September 1999 Gallup Poll, 36 percent of Americans responded that drinking has been a cause of trouble in their families, up from 14 percent in 1950 and 23 percent in 1990.

DRUG AND ALCOHOL USE AMONG COLLEGE STUDENTS

Drug and alcohol use among college students has risen dramatically since the early 1990s. A 1997 *Time* magazine article described American colleges as "among the nation's most alcohol-drenched institutions."[17] American undergraduates drink 4 billion cans of beer a year and spend an average of $446 on alcoholic beverages—more than they spend on soft drinks and textbooks combined.[18]

Binge drinking is a serious problem on many campuses in both the United States and Canada.[19] A 1994 survey of 140 campuses in the United States revealed that 51 percent of college students are heavy drinkers, with 44 percent of them being binge drinkers.[20] Of these students, those who do not consider themselves to be problem drinkers are the most likely to experience alcohol-related problems as well as to cause problems for others.[21] Indeed, alcohol-related automobile accidents are one of the leading killers of young people. Of the 25,000 annual accidental deaths among teenagers, 40 percent are alcohol-related.

Peer pressure to drink is one of the greatest barriers to giving up binge drinking. Members of fraternities and sororities are at the highest risk of excessive drinking, because intoxication is viewed as an acceptable aspect of Greek life.[22] Of students who live in fraternities and sororities, 84 percent engage in binge drinking.[23] Excessive alcohol use in fraternity hazing is once again on the upswing as well. Peer pressure is also a factor in the increased use of steroids by college athletes and young people who want to improve their appearance.[24]

In addition to such problems as poor concentration, lower grade-point average (GPA), and health risks, binge drinking among college students is associated with behaviors that harm others.[25] Of students who do not engage in binge drinking, 87 percent reported problems caused by students who do. These problems ranged from unwanted sexual advances and property damage to having sleep or studying interrupted.[26] About half of all date rapes on campuses are associated with alcohol consumption.[27] The excessive use of drugs and alcohol has also lead to an increase in violent crime on campuses, 95 percent of which involve alcohol and/or drugs.[28]

In the mid-1980s the drinking age was raised from eighteen to twenty-one throughout the United States in an attempt to curb drunk-driving accidents. However, the drinking-age laws have had little effect on the actual drinking habits of college students. Forty-five percent of students under twenty-one binge-drink compared with only 28 percent of students over twenty-four.[29] In a 1996 study, 46 percent of college students surveyed reported that they used fake IDs to obtain alcohol; fraternity and sorority members were much more likely to use fake IDs.[30] The use of illicit drugs among young people age eighteen to twenty-five has also increased from 14.7 percent in 1997 to 18.8 percent in 1999.[31]

Although freshmen beer and wine drinking in 1999 was lower than it has been in over thirty-three years, those who do drink are drinking more. Binge drinking has worsened on college campuses leaving fraternities paying out several million dollars in liability costs associated with drunken parties.[32]

DRUGS IN SPORTS

Two weeks after the close of the summer Olympics in Sydney, Australia, the International Olympic Committee medical commission recommended that German wrestler Alexander Leipold be stripped of his gold medal. Leipold had tested positive for the steroid nandrolone after defeating American Brandon Slay in freestyle wrestling. Leipold's sample contained 20 nanograms of nandrolone per milliliter of urine, ten times more than the acceptable level of 2 nanograms. He denies taking the steroid and said he had no idea of how he could have tested positive. Leipold is only one of forty-seven athletes who were suspended from the Sydney games for doping offenses, the highest number ever in the history of the Olympics.

Anabolic steroids, such as nandrolone, are testosterone-based drugs that stimulate muscle growth and help athletes recover faster from injuries. However, use of these steroids also increases by fivefold the risk of heart attacks and strokes and may also contribute to the development of liver disease.

Despite the harms associated with performance enhancement drugs, their use in sports appears to be on the increase. According to one estimate, between 20 and 40 percent of major league baseball players use testosterone-based drugs.[33] Unlike the Olympics, the National Football League, and college athletics policies, random testing of major league baseball players for steroids or other illicit performance enhancement drugs is forbidden by the current collective bargaining agreement.

Creatine, a legal and readily available muscle-building nutritional supplement that is similar to anabolic steroids, is especially popular among high school athletes. A recent survey found that 5.6 percent of sixth to twelfth graders has used creatine. Forty-four percent of the high school students surveyed reported using the performance-enhancing substances. While creatine is most popular among boys engaged in power sports such as football, wrestling, and hockey, it is also used by girls who participate in gymnastics and cheerleading.

The use of performance-enhancing drugs raises several moral issues. Does the duty of self-improvement require that athletes refrain from using drugs that will harm their bodies over the long run? Is it fair that athletes who use these drugs have a competitive advantage? Should drug testing be mandatory; or does mandatory drug-testing violate the autonomy of the athlete? Is the use of performance-enhancing drugs in sports inherently coercive since it puts pressure on athletes to use drugs if they want to win? Thomas Murray explores these questions in his article on "Drugs, Sports, and Ethics" at the end of this chapter.

THE DISEASE MODEL OF ADDICTION

The therapeutic revolution in the mid-twentieth century involved relabeling certain behaviors, previously attributed to moral weakness, as diseases. The disease model views addiction primarily as an individual medical problem rather than a social or moral problem. Drug use is discussed in medical terminology; there is a heroin or cocaine "epidemic."

According to this model, it is not lack of willpower or moral character that separates addicts from nonaddicts. Addiction is a pathological state. Addicts abuse drugs or alcohol, not because they are bad people or weak willed, but because they are ill; they are biologically different from nonaddicts. People who harm others or break the law while under the influence of alcohol or drugs should receive treatment or therapy, not punishment, because they were no more in control of what they did when "under the influence" than an epileptic having a seizure.

The disease model of alcoholism was first articulated in the 1940s by Elvine M. Jellinek of the Yale Center of Alcoholic Studies.[34] Since then this view of alcohol and drug addiction has become the official view of both the AMA and the World Health Organization (WHO). In 1956 the AMA recognized drug addiction as a "chemical dependency" and, therefore, a disease like diabetes or cancer. Addicts are not bad people; they are chemically dependent. In 1977 the AMA added alcoholism to its list of illnesses, defining it as "an illness characterized by significant impairment that is directly associated with persistent and excessive use of alcohol. Impairment may involve physiological, psychological, or social dysfunction." Recent advances in genetics lend weight to the disease model of addiction.[35]

Because the cause of the disease lies in the drugs, people with an "addictive personality" will simply substitute one drug for another. And though abstinence may arrest the disease of addiction, the disease itself can never be cured because it is biologically based. Abstinence from all drugs, therefore, is the ideal. This ideal is reflected in laws that seek to ban all addictive drugs because, it is believed, addicts will simply switch to another drug if the one they are using is no longer available.

Alcoholics Anonymous (AA) is based primarily on the disease model of addiction. A fundamental assumption of the AA Twelve Steps program is that healing can occur only when alcoholics admit their powerlessness over addiction and turn the healing process over to a "higher power." The "one disease [addiction], one treatment [abstinence]" approach of AA currently dominates the medical field.

THE MORAL MODEL OF ADDICTION

Many philosophers and bioethicists, such as Thomas Szasz, question the validity of the medical model of addiction and call for a return to the moral model. Addiction, according to the moral model, is a freely chosen vice. Resisting or overcoming addiction is simply a matter of willpower. The religious view that alcoholism is a sin, the prohibition legislation of the early-twentieth century, and the current "Just Say No" campaign are all based on the moral model of addiction.

Most positions on addiction lie somewhere between the two extremes. Although AA is based primarily on the disease model, accepting moral responsibility for one's actions is also part of the recovery process. Similarly, most supporters of the moral model acknowledge that there are social, personal, and genetic factors that make it more likely that certain people will become addicts. They also maintain, however, that a predisposition toward addiction is not the same as a predetermination that one will become addicted. Unlike predispositions to other diseases, such as breast cancer and diabetes, a person who is genetically predisposed to addiction can avoid it altogether by avoiding the substances that may lead to addiction. Therefore, people who harm others while under the influence of alcohol or drugs should be held morally responsible for their choices and actions. Under the moral model, punishment is an appropriate response to drug-related crime.

The disease model has been called into question by scientific studies as well. A Rand Corporation study in the late 1970s and early 1980s suggested that recovering alcoholics can resume moderate or responsible drinking.[36] The claim made by supporters of the disease model that addiction knows no social class, race, gender, or ethnic background also runs contrary to empirical findings. Jews, for example, have one of the lowest, if not *the* lowest, rates of alcoholism.[37]

THE PHILOSOPHERS ON DRUG AND ALCOHOL ABUSE

According to Aristotle, virtue entails acting according to reason. Wisdom is the greatest intellectual virtue and ignorance the greatest vice. People who are drunk are "acting in ignorance." Thus, addicts give up their essential humanity by giving up control of their actions. Aristotle rejects the disease model of addiction, however. We need have no sympathy for a person whose health is destroyed by excessive drinking or drug abuse. Unlike a person whose illness is involuntary, a drunkard is responsible for his ignorance "since it was open to him to refrain from getting drunk."[38]

Although Aristotle would probably not object to the use of drugs and alcohol in moderation, many Buddhists are morally opposed to any use of drugs and alcohol. The eight-fold path requires a "clear and composed mind" in order to achieve moral perfection and enlightenment. Seeking solace or distraction in mind-altering drugs is a form of false contemplation. According to Buddha, all human suffering is caused by people whose minds are confused and their reason dulled. Buddhist philosopher Don Premasiri maintains that many of the contemporary social evils, such as violence, irresponsible behavior, and moral corruption, are the result of the spread of alcoholism and drug addiction.

Muslims are also opposed to the use of alcohol and drugs. Alcohol use is a moral failing similar to slander. According to Muslim philosophy, "When a person drinks he becomes intoxicated; when he is intoxicated he raves; and when he raves he falsely accuses."[39]

Libertarians, on the other hand, favor a permissive policy on drug and alcohol use. John Stuart Mill opposed the American prohibition laws of the 1850s as an unjustified interference with people's liberty. He wrote, "Over himself, over his own body and mind, the individual is sovereign."[40] Although Mill acknowledged that drug or alcohol users can harm others by rendering themselves incapable of working, this does not justify prohibiting drugs, because society can afford to absorb these losses for the sake of liberty. The benefits of liberty, in other words, outweigh the harms caused by alcohol and drug use.

MORAL ISSUES

Virtue Ethics and the Good Life

According to virtue ethicists, we have a moral obligation to improve our character through self-examination and the practice of virtuous behavior. The Buddhist virtue of right effort, for example, requires that we live deliberately rather than impulsively. Addiction interferes with our ability to engage in philosophical self-examination and to seek the higher good.

Virtue, in most cases, requires us to seek the mean between excess and deficit. The doctrine of the mean requires that we know ourselves and our limitations and that we use our reason to discern where the mean is, for us, between excess and deficit. According to the disease model, the use of any amount of a drug is an excess for addicts. On the other hand, for other people, moderation may be appropriate and consistent with the good and virtuous life. Recent studies at Harvard University have found that moderate drinkers are healthiest and live the longest. Anti-anxiety drugs can also help people who are depressed by offering them a respite and an opportunity for self-examination; on the other hand, they can also be used as a crutch for avoiding self-analysis. Morphine is another drug where excess for one person may be a deficiency for another. Although morphine can be addictive, to refuse a dying cancer patient morphine because of fear of addiction is to err on the side of deficiency.

Confucius believed that government bears the primary responsibility for promoting virtue in citizens. The purpose of laws and public policy is to make it easier for people to be virtuous. James Q. Wilson argues that if drugs are legal, many people will prefer the pleasure of drug excess over treatment and virtuous behavior. Douglas Husak counters that it is not the place of government to impose on citizens an ideal of human excellence. It is up to each of us to responsibly determine our own concept of the good life.

Human Dignity and the Categorical Imperative

Kant's categorical imperative states that we should never use ourselves as a means only. Addicts debase themselves by using themselves as a means only—to get a fix through the ingestion of drugs or alcohol. Addiction is tempting because it tranquilizes; it "fixes" our disquiet and malaise. We become dependent on this fix. Addiction distracts us from our lives and relieves us of the burden, the frustration, the boredom, and the search for meaning in our lives. Addiction *becomes* the meaning of life. Because drug abuse and addiction prevent us from being fully human, they are incompatible with human dignity.

As rational moral agents, we are responsible for our choices and actions. The disease model is problematic in that it places the burden of "curing" addiction on physicians rather than on the individual using the drugs, thus allowing addicts to abdicate personal responsibility for their behavior. The medical model also invites blaming other people (known as "co-dependents") for the addict's behavior. Passing off responsibility for our destructive and disrespectful behavior is inconsistent with human dignity and freedom.

Autonomy, Liberty Rights, and the Principle of Noninterference

Autonomy involves our ability to make free choices. Autonomous people lead rational and self-critical lives. Our autonomy is violated if we are prevented from doing what we have a moral right to do.

Both Szasz and Husak argue that prohibiting recreational drug use violates our autonomy. Enforcement procedures are not only futile, but an infringement on people's liberty rights. They also reject the disease model of addiction. Drug addicts are autonomous, because any person of "reasonable firmness" can stop using drugs. Szasz likewise argues that the "right of self-medication" is a fundamental right.

Not everyone agrees that adult drug users are acting autonomously, however. Murray, for example, maintains that the use of performance-enhancing drugs in sports is "inherently coercive." In sports, in which one's professional success may ride on using performance-enhancing drugs, the pressure to use these drugs may seriously compromise the athlete's autonomy. The principle of noninterference states that interference with adults' free choice must be justified. Interference in the case of minors may also justify interference in adult drug and alcohol use, because most people become addicted as children, before they are able to make fully informed, rational decisions. In the United States, the average age is twelve for the first alcohol use and thirteen for the first use of illicit drugs.[41] Because those who desire to quit often cannot, addiction is a form of slavery. According to natural rights ethicists such as John Locke, our liberty rights do not permit us to sell ourselves into slavery. Using this analogy, it is also wrong to turn our lives over to drugs, as in doing so we give up ownership over our lives.

Pleasure

Pleasure is by far the most common reason college students give for using alcohol and drugs.[42] According to some utilitarians, the use of drugs for pleasure is not necessarily at odds with the good life and may even contribute to it in some cases. On the other hand, most philosophers, including utilitarians, draw the line at drug use that interferes with living the good life.

Paternalism and Harm to Self

Most people's position on the morality of drug and alcohol use depends primarily on whether they believe that drugs are harmful. Paternalism permits interfering with people's choices for their own good. Drugs and alcohol can be harmful to self. The life of an average alcoholic, for example, is fifteen years shorter than that of a nonalcoholic.[43]

The belief that drug and alcohol abuse is a disease promotes a paternalistic approach toward drug and alcohol regulation. Laws prohibiting alcohol and tobacco use by children are generally based on the principle of paternalism. Given that most untimely adult deaths involve drugs and alcohol abuse, however, shouldn't paternalism extend to adults as well? If prohibition is justified for minors on the grounds that it is harmful and irrational for children to use drugs and alcohol, why is it not the same for adults who abuse drugs? If adults use drugs in a manner that is harmful toward themselves, isn't their "decision" to do so by definition irrational and, hence, not a free and autonomous choice?

Prohibition based on paternalism can come into conflict with the principle of autonomy. The use of coercion—even paternalistic "well-meaning" coercion—in an attempt to regulate another person's character is an affront to human dignity and freedom. Should we prohibit drugs for all because drugs seriously impair the autonomy of some? The belief that people use drugs "against their will" or have "lost control of their lives" or that drug users are "morally deficient" is demeaning. It may be better to let addicts continue harming themselves rather than deny them at least some control over their lives.

Furthermore, because people do not like to be told what to do, paternalism can backfire. There was a dramatic increase in drug use, especially among young people, following Bush's declaration of war on drugs. Studies also suggest that raising the drinking age from eighteen to twenty-one throughout the United States may actually have exacerbated the bingeing problem on campuses. In addition to the lure of forbidden fruit, students are now more likely to drink in private places like their dorms and fraternities or in bars that are lax on checking for proper ID.[44]

"Harm reduction," which attempts to minimize the harms of addictive behavior without engaging in paternalism, is currently a popular approach to controlling such behavior.[45] This alternative to a prohibitionist/criminal approach is used in the Netherlands. Instead of prosecuting drug users, the Dutch policy in general preserves the liberty right to use drugs while minimizing harm by providing sterile needles.

Nonmaleficence and Preventing Harm to Others

One of the most common arguments for drug prohibition is protection of public health and safety. Although restrictions based on paternalism are often considered an affront to personal dignity, most people acknowledge that coercion is justified to prevent people from harming one another.

Wilson argues that the harms of legalizing drugs outweigh those of prohibition. Drug abuse, he points out, is hardly a victimless crime. It is associated with health problems, reduced job productivity, family violence, crime, fetal alcohol syndrome, drug-addicted newborns, and suicide. Many of these costs are passed on to society. Twenty percent of Medicare funds, for example, go to the treatment of problems stemming from alcohol and drug abuse. Indeed, elderly patients are more likely to be hospitalized for conditions related to alcohol abuse than for heart attacks.[46] The cost of treating infants born to cocaine/crack mothers is estimated to be $500 million a year.[47] Is it fair that others are forced to pick up these costs?

Drug-related crimes cost taxpayers more than $30 billion a year. In 1994 about 60 percent of federal prisoners were incarcerated for drug offenses[48]; 81 percent of juvenile offenders are also "substance abusers."[49] Canada is not far behind the United States in the number of drug-related arrests per capita.[50] According to John Edwards, commissioner of the Correctional Service of Canada, convicted drug traffickers simply continue their lucrative business in prison, and many inmates become addicted to drugs while incarcerated, thus making them less fit to be members of society than before they were imprisoned.

Drugs can also be used to bolster courage prior to committing a non-drug-related crime. Of frequent cocaine users, 40 percent engage in property and violent crimes.[51] A 1997 study of alcohol use at college parties found that "heavy drinking during the parties tempered moral condemnation of criminal acts, enhanced the desirability of criminal behavior, and relaxed perceptions of risk regarding crime."[52]

On the other hand, as Husak reminds us, we also have to consider the costs associated with criminalizing drugs. Harm to others is a powerful argument for working toward decreasing drug and alcohol abuse, but it is not obvious that legal prohibition is the best solution; drug education may be more effective. Making drugs illegal forces up the prices of drugs, thus encouraging users to resort to crime to pay for their habits. Much of the street violence in our cities is attributable to the illicit sale of drugs rather than to the actual effects of the drugs themselves. Also, deaths due to overdose reactions and AIDS are in part due to impurities in the street drugs and to contaminated needles. In addition, because street dealers are already criminals, drug prohibition brings young people seeking drugs into contact with the criminal element.

Advocates of more legal restrictions on drugs and alcohol, such as Wilson, counter that the claim that legalizing currently illegal drugs will decrease violence is speculation. Yet, despite the media attention given to the violence associated with illegal drugs, it is legal drugs that are the most deadly. The violence of illegal drugs may be more visible, but there are hidden costs of alcoholism in terms of domestic violence and the breakup of families. In addition, the cost of health care for alcoholics is more than double that of nonalcoholics; much of this cost is borne by taxpayers and employers. Smokers also use more medical resources and have longer hospital stays than nonsmokers. Indeed, lung cancer has now become the leading cause of all cancer deaths in women.[53]

CONCLUSION

Drug and alcohol use raises two concerns. The first relates to virtue ethics: We have a personal responsibility to abstain from harmful drugs or drugs that are addictive to us. If addiction is a disease, virtue dictates that addicts or potential addicts are morally responsible for avoiding drugs and/or alcohol and for seeking a cure, or at least avoiding situations in which they could harm others. On the other hand, the moderate use of certain drugs may actually enhance the good life. Knowing the difference between excess and moderation involves the development of wisdom and character.

The second issue relates to social policy. Some philosophers maintain that drugs should be prohibited. Others, while not supporting drug use, argue that banning drugs is wrong. Sometimes what initially appears to be a moral disagreement turns out to be a factual dispute. This is often the case in debates over appropriate policies on drugs and alcohol. Most people agree that harm to others is a strong justification for restricting drug use; however, they disagree over the best means to achieve the objective of minimizing harm.

T H O M A S   S Z A S Z

The Ethics of Addiction

Thomas Szasz is a professor of psychiatry at the State University of New York Upstate Medical Center and author of several books on psychiatry, including *The Myth of Mental Illness* and *The Manufacture of Madness*. In this article Szasz rejects the disease model of addiction and the argument that people who use drugs and/or alcohol lack control over that aspect of their lives. Citing John Stuart Mill's principle of no harm, Szasz argues that drug laws do not respect the right of citizens to exercise control over their own lives. Therefore, all prohibition laws should be repealed, at least for adults.

Critical Reading Questions

1. What is the World Health Organization definition of drug abuse? Why does Szasz maintain that this definition is a moral judgment rather than a medical or technical judgment?
2. According to Szasz, what "propaganda" is used by proponents of the disease model of addiction to justify the prohibition of drug use?
3. Why does Szasz reject the prohibition argument that some drugs are dangerous?
4. According to Szasz, why do people become addicted? Why does Szasz reject the prohibition argument that drug addiction is different from addiction to other substances and stimuli?
5. According to Szasz, what are the primary reasons people take drugs? Which of these reasons is identified with "drug abuse"?
6. Why, according to Szasz, is there so much opposition to the concept of free trade in drugs?
7. What arguments does Szasz use to support his position for the legalization of drugs?
8. On what grounds does Szasz argue that the "right of self-medication" is a fundamental right? Should there be any limitations on this right, and, if so, what are some possible limitations?
9. Why does Szasz support the prohibition of drug and alcohol sales to minors?
10. What are the two principal methods of legitimizing policy in the United States? How have these two methods been used to legitimize the prohibition of drugs?
11. On what grounds does Szasz reject the current medical concept of drug abuse and drug treatment programs?
12. According to Szasz, why are we in need of a "medical reformation"?
13. On what grounds does Szasz argue that we have a constitutional right to use drugs and alcohol?
14. How does Szasz use John Stuart Mill's philosophy to support his position?

"The Ethics of Addiction," *Harper's Magazine* 244, April 1972, 74–79.

AN ARGUMENT IN FAVOR OF LETTING AMERICANS TAKE ANY DRUG THEY WANT TO TAKE

To avoid cliches about "drug abuse," let us analyze its official definition. According to the World Health Organization, "Drug addiction is a state of periodic or chronic intoxication detrimental to the individual and to society, produced by the repeated consumption of a drug (natural or synthetic). Its characteristics include: 1) an overpowering desire or need (compulsion) to continue taking the drug and to obtain it by any means, 2) a tendency to increase the dosage, and 3) a psychic (psychological) and sometimes physical dependence on the effects of the drug."

Since this definition hinges on the harm done to both the individual and society, it is clearly an ethical one. Moreover, by not specifying what is "detrimental," it consigns the problem of addiction to psychiatrists who define the patient's "dangerousness to himself and others."

Next, we come to the effort to obtain the addictive substance "by any means." This suggests that the substance must be prohibited, or is very expensive, and is hence difficult for the ordinary person to obtain (rather than that the person who wants it has an inordinate craving for it). If there were an abundant and inexpensive supply of what the "addict" wants, there would be no reason for him to go to "any means" to obtain it. Thus by the WHO's definition, one can be addicted only to a substance that is illegal or otherwise difficult to obtain. This surely removes the problem of addiction from the realm of medicine and psychiatry, and puts it squarely into that of morals and law.

In short, drug addiction or drug abuse cannot be defined without specifying the proper and improper uses of certain pharmacologically active agents. The regular administration of morphine by a physician to a patient dying of cancer is the paradigm of the proper use of a narcotic; whereas even its occasional self-administration by a physically healthy person for the purpose of "pharmacological pleasure" is the paradigm of drug abuse.

I submit that these judgments have nothing whatever to do with medicine, pharmacology, or psychiatry. They are moral judgments. Indeed, our present views on addiction are astonishingly similar to some of our former views on sex. Until recently, masturbation—or self-abuse, as it was called—was professionally declared, and popularly accepted, as both the cause and the symptom of a variety of illnesses. Even today, homosexuality—called a "sexual perversion"—is regarded as a disease by medical and psychiatric experts as well as by "well-informed" laymen.

To be sure, it is now virtually impossible to cite a contemporary medical authority to support the concept of self-abuse. Medical opinion holds that whether a person masturbates or not is medically irrelevant; and that engaging in the practice or refraining from it is a matter of personal morals or life-style. On the other hand, it is virtually impossible to cite a contemporary medical authority to oppose the concept of drug abuse. Medical opinion holds that drug abuse is a major medical, psychiatric, and public health problem; that drug addiction is a disease similar to diabetes, requiring prolonged (or lifelong) and careful, medically supervised treatment; and that taking or not taking drugs is primarily, if not solely, a matter of medical responsibility.

Thus the man on the street can only believe what he hears from all sides—that drug addiction is a disease, "like any other," which has now reached "epidemic proportions," and whose "medical" containment justifies the limitless expenditure of tax monies and the corresponding aggrandizement and enrichment of noble medical warriors against this "plague."

PROPAGANDA TO JUSTIFY PROHIBITION

Like any social policy, our drug laws may be examined from two entirely different points of view: technical and moral. Our present inclination is either to ignore the moral perspective or to mistake the technical for the moral.

Since most of the propagandists against drug use seek to justify certain repressive policies because of the alleged dangerousness of various drugs, they often falsify the facts about the pharma-

cological properties of the drugs they seek to prohibit. They do so for two reasons: first, because
many substances in daily use are just as harmful as
the substances they want to prohibit; second, because they realize that dangerousness alone is never
a sufficiently persuasive argument to justify the prohibition of any drug, substance, or artifact. Accordingly, the more they ignore the moral dimensions
of the problem, the more they must escalate their
fraudulent claims about the dangers of drugs.

To be sure, some drugs are more dangerous
than others. It is easier to kill oneself with heroin
than with aspirin. But is also easier to kill oneself by
jumping off a high building than a low one. In the
case of drugs, we regard their potentiality for self-
injury as justification for their prohibition; in the
case of buildings, we do not.

Furthermore, we systematically blur and confuse
the two quite different ways in which narcotics may
cause death: by a deliberate act of suicide or by accidental overdosage.

Every individual is capable of injuring or killing
himself. This potentiality is a fundamental expression of human freedom. Self-destructive behavior
may be regarded as sinful and penalized by means
of informal sanctions. But it should not be regarded
as a crime or (mental) disease, justifying or war-
ranting the use of the police powers of the state for
its control.

Therefore, it is absurd to deprive an adult of a
drug (or of anything else) because he might use it
to kill himself. To do so is to treat everyone the way
institutional psychiatrists treat the so-called suicidal
mental patient: they not only imprison such a person but take everything away from him—shoelaces,
belts, razor blades, eating utensils, and so forth—
until the "patient" lies naked on a mattress in a
padded cell—lest he kill himself. The result is degrading tyrannization.

Death by accidental overdose is an altogether
different matter. But can anyone doubt that this
danger now looms so large precisely because the
sale of narcotics and many other drugs is illegal?
Those who buy illicit drugs cannot be sure what
drug they are getting or how much of it. Free trade
in drugs, with governmental action limited to safeguarding the purity of the product and the veracity

of the labeling, would reduce the risk of accidental
overdose with "dangerous drugs" to the same levels
that prevail, and that we find acceptable, with respect to other chemical agents and physical artifacts
that abound in our complex technological society.

This essay is not intended as an exposition
on the pharmacological properties of narcotics
and other mind-affecting drugs. However, I want
to make it clear that in my view, *regardless* of their
danger, all drugs should be "legalized" (a misleading term I employ reluctantly as a concession to
common usage). Although I recognize that some
drugs—notably heroin, the amphetamines, and
LSD, among those now in vogue—may have undesirable or dangerous consequences, I favor free
trade in drugs for the same reason the Founding Fathers favored free trade in ideas. In an open society,
it is none of the government's business what idea a
man puts into his mind; likewise, it should be none
of the government's business what drug he puts
into his body.

WITHDRAWAL PAINS FROM TRADITION

It is a fundamental characteristic of human beings
that they get used to things: one becomes habituated, or "addicted," not only to narcotics, but to
cigarettes, cocktails before dinner, orange juice for
breakfast, comic strips, and so forth. It is similarly a
fundamental characteristic of living organisms that
they acquire increasing tolerance to various chemical agents and physical stimuli: the first cigarette
may cause nothing but nausea and headache; a year
later, smoking three packs a day may be pure joy.
Both alcohol and opiates are "addictive" in the
sense that the more regularly they are used, the
more the user craves them and the greater his tolerance for them becomes. Yet none of this involves
any mysterious process of "getting hooked." It is
simply an aspect of the universal biological propensity for *learning*, which is especially well developed
in man. The opiate habit, like the cigarette habit or
food habit, can be broken—and without any medical assistance—provided the person wants to break
it. Often he doesn't. And why, indeed, should he,
if he has nothing better to do with his life? Or, as

happens to be the case with morphine, if he can live an essentially normal life while under its influence?

Actually, opium is much less toxic than alcohol. Just as it is possible to be an "alcoholic" and work and be productive, so it is (or, rather, it used to be) possible to be an opium addict and work and be productive. . . .

I am not citing this evidence to recommend the opium habit. The point is that we must, in plain honesty, distinguish between pharmacological effects and personal inclinations. Some people take drugs to help them function and conform to social expectations; others take them for the very opposite reason, to ritualize their refusal to function and conform to social expectations. Much of the "drug abuse" we now witness—perhaps nearly all of it—is of the second type. But instead of acknowledging that "addicts" are unfit or unwilling to work and be "normal," we prefer to believe that they act as they do because certain drugs—especially heroin, LSD, and the amphetamines—make them "sick." If only we could get them "well," so runs this comforting view, they would become "productive" and "useful" citizens. To believe this is like believing that if an illiterate cigarette smoker would only stop smoking, he would become an Einstein. With a falsehood like this, one can go far. No wonder that politicians and psychiatrists love it.

The concept of free trade in drugs runs counter to our cherished notion that everyone must work and idleness is acceptable only under special conditions. In general, the obligation to work is greatest for healthy, adult, white men. We tolerate idleness on the part of children, women, Negroes, the aged, and the sick, and even accept the responsibility to support them. But the new wave of drug abuse affects mainly young adults, often white males, who are, in principle at least, capable of working and supporting themselves. But they refuse: they "drop out"; and in doing so, they challenge the most basic values of our society.

The fear that free trade in narcotics would result in vast masses of our population spending their days and nights smoking opium or mainlining heroin, rather than working and taking care of their responsibilities, is a bugaboo that does not deserve to be taken seriously. Habits of work and idleness are deep-seated cultural patterns. Free trade in abortions has not made an industrious people like the Japanese give up work for fornication. Nor would free trade in drugs convert such a people from hustlers to hippies. Indeed, I think the opposite might be the case: it is questionable whether, or for how long, a responsible people can tolerate being treated as totally irresponsible with respect to drugs and drug-taking. In other words, how long can we live with the inconsistency of being expected to be responsible for operating cars and computers, but not for operating our own bodies?

Although my argument about drug-taking is moral and political, and does not depend upon showing that free trade in drugs would also have fiscal advantages over our present policies, let me indicate briefly some of its economic implications.

The war on addiction is not only astronomically expensive; it is also counterproductive. On April 1, 1967, New York State's narcotics addiction control program, hailed as "the most massive ever tried in the nation," went into effect. "The program, which may cost up to $400 million in three years," reported the *New York Times,* "was hailed by Governor Rockefeller as 'the start of an unending war.'" . . . In short, the detection and rehabilitation of addicts is good business. We now know that the spread of witchcraft in the late Middle Ages was due more to the work of witchmongers than to the lure of witchcraft. Is it not possible that the spread of addiction in our day is due more to the work of addictmongers than to the lure of narcotics?

Let us see how far some of the monies spent on the war on addiction could go in supporting people who prefer to drop out of society and drug themselves. Their "habit" itself would cost next to nothing; free trade would bring the price of narcotics down to a negligible amount. . . .

. . . free trade in narcotics would be more economical for those of us who work, even if we had to support legions of addicts, than is our present program of trying to "cure" them. Moreover, I have not even made use, in my economic estimates, of the incalculable sums we would save by reducing crimes now engendered by the illegal traffic in drugs.

THE RIGHT OF SELF-MEDICATION

Clearly, the argument that marijuana—or heroin, methadone, or morphine—is prohibited because it is addictive or dangerous cannot be supported by facts. For one thing, there are many drugs, from insulin to penicillin, that are neither addictive nor dangerous but are nevertheless also prohibited; they can be obtained only through a physician's prescription. For another, there are many things, from dynamite to guns, that are much more dangerous than narcotics (especially to others) but are not prohibited. As everyone knows, it is still possible in the United States to walk into a store and walk out with a shotgun. We enjoy this right not because we believe that guns are safe but because we believe even more strongly that civil liberties are precious. At the same time, it is not possible in the United States to walk into a store and walk out with a bottle of barbiturates, codeine, or other drugs.

I believe that just as we regard freedom of speech and religion as fundamental rights, so we should also regard freedom of self-medication as a fundamental right. Like most rights, the right of self-medication should apply only to adults; and it should not be an unqualified right. Since these are important qualifications, it is necessary to specify their precise range.

John Stuart Mill said (approximately) that a person's right to swing his arm ends where his neighbor's nose begins. And Oliver Wendell Holmes said that no one has a right to shout "Fire!" in a crowded theater. Similarly, the limiting condition with respect to self-medication should be the inflicting of actual (as against symbolic) harm on others.

Our present practices with respect to alcohol embody and reflect this individualistic ethic. We have the right to buy, possess, and consume alcoholic beverages. Regardless of how offensive drunkenness might be to a person, he cannot interfere with another person's "right" to become inebriated so long as that person drinks in the privacy of his own home or at some other appropriate location, and so long as he conducts himself in an otherwise law-abiding manner. In short, we have a right to be intoxicated—in private. Public intoxication is considered an offense to others and is therefore a violation of the criminal law. It makes sense that what is a "right" in one place may become, by virtue of its disruptive or disturbing effect on others, an offense somewhere else.

The right to self-medication should be hedged in by similar limits. Public intoxication, not only with alcohol but with any drug, should be an offense punishable by the criminal law. Furthermore, acts that may injure others—such as driving a car—should, when carried out in a drug-intoxicated state, be punished especially strictly and severely. The right to self-medication must thus entail unqualified responsibility for the effects of one's drug-intoxicated behavior on others. For unless we are willing to hold ourselves responsible for our own behavior, and hold others responsible for theirs, the liberty to use drugs (or to engage in other acts) degenerates into a license to hurt others.

Such, then, would be the situation of adults, if we regarded the freedom to take drugs as a fundamental right similar to the freedom to read and worship. What would be the situation of children? Since many people who are now said to be drug addicts or drug abusers are minors, it is especially important that we think clearly about this aspect of the problem.

I do not believe, and I do not advocate, that children should have a right to ingest, inject, or otherwise use any drug or substance they want. Children do not have the right to drive, drink, vote, marry, or make binding contracts. They acquire these rights at various ages, coming into their full possession at maturity, usually between the ages of eighteen and twenty-one. The right to self-medication should similarly be withheld until maturity.

In short, I suggest that "dangerous" drugs be treated, more or less, as alcohol is treated now. Neither the use of narcotics, nor their possession, should be prohibited, but only their sale to minors. Of course, this would result in the ready availability of all kinds of drugs among minors—though perhaps their availability would be no greater than it is now, but would only be more visible and hence more easily subject to proper controls. This arrangement would place responsibility for the use of all drugs by children where it belongs: on parents and their children. This is where the major responsibility rests for the use of alcohol. It is a tragic symptom of our refusal to take personal liberty and responsibility seriously that there appears to be no public desire to assume a similar stance toward other "dangerous" drugs.

Consider what would happen should a child bring a bottle of gin to school and get drunk there. Would the school authorities blame the local liquor stores as pushers? Or would they blame the parents and the child himself? There is liquor in practically every home in America and yet children rarely bring liquor to school. Whereas marijuana, Dexedrine, and heroin—substances children usually do not find at home and whose very possession is a criminal offense—frequently find their way into the school.

Our attitude toward sexual activity provides another model for our attitude toward drugs. Although we generally discourage children below a certain age from engaging in sexual activities with others, we do not prohibit such activities by law. What we do prohibit by law is the sexual seduction of children by adults. The "pharmacological seduction" of children by adults should be similarly punishable. In other words, adults who give or sell drugs to children should be regarded as offenders. Such a specific and limited prohibition—as against the kinds of generalized prohibitions that we had under the Volstead Act or have now with respect to countless drugs—would be relatively easy to enforce. Moreover, it would probably be rarely violated, for there would be little psychological interest and no economic profit in doing so.

THE TRUE FAITH: SCIENTIFIC MEDICINE

What I am suggesting is that while addiction is ostensibly a medical and pharmacological problem, actually it is a moral and political problem. We ought to know that there is no necessary connection between facts and values, between what is and what ought to be. Thus, objectively quite harmful acts, objects, or persons may be accepted and tolerated—by minimizing their dangerousness. Conversely, objectively quite harmless acts, objects, or persons may be prohibited and persecuted—by exaggerating their dangerousness. It is always necessary to distinguish—and especially so when dealing with social policy—between description and prescription, fact and rhetoric, truth and falsehood.

In our society, there are two principal methods of legitimizing policy: social tradition and scientific judgment. More than anything else, time is the supreme ethical arbiter. Whatever a social practice might be, if people engage in it, generation after generation, that practice becomes acceptable.

Many opponents of illegal drugs admit that nicotine may be more harmful to health than marijuana; nevertheless, they urge that smoking cigarettes should be legal but smoking marijuana should not be, because the former habit is socially accepted while the latter is not. This is a perfectly reasonable argument. But let us understand it for what it is—a plea for legitimizing old and accepted practices, and for illegitimizing novel and unaccepted ones. It is a justification that rests on precedent, not evidence.

The other method of legitimizing policy, ever more important in the modern world, is through the authority of science. In matters of health, a vast and increasingly elastic category, physicians play important roles as legitimizers and illegitimizers. This, in short, is why we regard being medicated by a doctor as drug use, and self-medication (especially with certain classes of drugs) as drug abuse.

This, too, is a perfectly reasonable arrangement. But we must understand that it is a plea for legitimizing what doctors do, because they do it with "good therapeutic" intent; and for illegitimatizing what laymen do, because they do it with bad self-abusive ("masturbatory" or mind-altering) intent. This justification rests on the principles of professionalism, not of pharmacology. Hence we applaud the systematic medical use of methadone and call it "treatment for heroin addiction," but decry the occasional nonmedical use of marijuana and call it "dangerous drug abuse."

Our present concept of drug abuse articulates and symbolizes a fundamental policy of scientific medicine—namely, that a layman should not medicate his own body but should place its medical care under the supervision of a duly accredited physician. Before the Reformation, the practice of True Christianity rested on a similar policy—namely, that a layman should not himself commune with God but should place his spiritual care under the supervision of a duly accredited priest. The self-interests of the church and of medicine in such policies are obvious enough. What might be less obvious is the interest of the laity: by delegating responsibility for the spiritual and medical welfare of the people to a class of authoritatively accredited specialists, these policies—and the practices they ensure—relieve individuals from assuming the burdens of responsibility for themselves. As I see it, our present problems with drug use and drug abuse are just one of the consequences of our pervasive ambivalence about personal autonomy and responsibility.

I propose a medical reformation analogous to the Protestant Reformation: specifically, a "protest" against the systematic mystification of man's relationship to his body and his professionalized separation from it. The immediate aim of this reform would be to remove the physician as intermediary between man and his body and to give the layman direct access to the language and contents of the pharmacopoeia. If man had unencumbered access to his own body and the means of chemically altering it, it would spell the end of medicine, at least as we now know it. This is why, with faith in scientific medicine so strong, there is little interest in this kind of medical reform. Physicians fear the loss of their privileges; laymen, the loss of their protections. . . .

LIFE, LIBERTY, AND THE PURSUIT OF HIGHS

Sooner or later we shall have to confront the basic moral dilemma underlying this problem: does a person have the right to take a drug, any drug—not because he needs it to cure an illness, but because he wants to take it?

The Declaration of Independence speaks of our inalienable right to "life, liberty, and the pursuit of happiness." How are we to interpret this? By asserting that we ought to be free to pursue happiness by playing golf or watching television, but not by drinking alcohol, or smoking marijuana, or ingesting pep pills?

The Constitution and the Bill of Rights are silent on the subject of drugs. This would seem to imply that the adult citizen has, or ought to have, the right to medicate his own body as he sees fit. Were this not the case, why should there have been a need for a Constitutional Amendment to outlaw drinking? But if ingesting alcohol was, and is now again, a Constitutional right, is ingesting opium, or heroin, or barbiturates, or anything else, not also such a right? If it is, then the Harrison Narcotic Act is not only a bad law but is unconstitutional as well, because it prescribes in a legislative act what ought to be promulgated in a Constitutional Amendment.

The questions remain: as American citizens, should we have the right to take narcotics or other drugs? If we take drugs and conduct ourselves as responsible and law-abiding citizens, should we have a right to remain unmolested by the government? Lastly, if we take drugs and break the law, should we have a right to be treated as persons accused of crime, rather than as patients accused of mental illness?

These are fundamental questions that are conspicuous by their absence from all contemporary discussions of problems of drug addiction and drug abuse. The result is that instead of debating the use of drugs in moral and political terms, we define our task as the ostensibly narrow technical problem of protecting people from poisoning themselves with substances for whose use they cannot possibly assume responsibility. This, I think, best explains the frightening national consensus against personal responsibility for taking drugs and for one's conduct while under their influence. . . .

To me, unanimity on an issue as basic and complex as this means a complete evasion of the actual problem and an attempt to master it by attacking and overpowering a scapegoat—"dangerous drugs" and "drug abusers." There is an ominous resemblance between the unanimity with which all "reasonable" men—and especially politicians, physicians, and priests—formerly supported the protective measures of society against witches and Jews, and that with which they now support them against drug addicts and drug abusers.

After all is said and done, the issue comes down to whether we accept or reject the ethical principle John Stuart Mill so clearly enunciated: "The only purpose [he wrote in *On Liberty*] for which power can be rightfully exercised over any member of a civilized community, against his will, is to prevent harm to others. His own good, either physical or moral, is not a sufficient warrant. He cannot rightfully be compelled to do or forbear because it will make him happier, because in the opinions of others, to do so would be wise, or even right. . . . In the part [of his conduct] which merely concerns himself, his independence is, of right, absolute. Over himself, over his own body and mind, the individual is sovereign."

By recognizing the problem of drug abuse for what it is—a moral and political question rather than a medical or therapeutic one—we can choose to maximize the sphere of action of the state at the expense of the individual, or of the individual at the expense of the state. In other words, we could commit ourselves to the view that the state, the representative of many, is more important than the individual; that it therefore has the right, indeed the duty, to regulate the life of the individual in the best interests of the group. Or we could commit ourselves to the view that individual dignity and liberty are the supreme values of life, and that the foremost duty of the state is to protect and promote these values.

In short, we must choose between the ethic of collectivism and individualism, and pay the price of either—or of both.

Discussion Questions

1. What, according to Szasz, are some of the myths surrounding the notion of drug addiction? Would an advocate of the disease model of addiction agree that these are myths? Discuss how Elvine Jellinek might respond to Szasz. Which person presents the stronger argument? Support your answers.

2. Do you agree with Szasz that people under eighteen or twenty-one are not mature enough to use drugs and alcohol? Is Szasz being logically consistent or is he using doublethink in his rejection of legal access to drugs and alcohol for teenagers? If it is wrong for children to use certain "dangerous" drugs, why isn't it also wrong for adults to use the same drugs? Should "immature" adults who abuse drugs and alcohol also be legally prohibited from using these substances? Support your answers.

3. Szasz rejects appeal to social tradition as a method of legitimizing public policy. Is he also committing the fallacy of appeal to tradition when he argues that we have a constitutional right to use drugs? Or can his argument for a "right of self-medication" stand without appeal to the Constitution? Support your answers.

4. Moonshining—the illegal production and sale of distilled spirits—is an underground art in some rural parts of the Atlantic provinces in Canada. Although moonshiners are not about to put the government liquor stores out of business, the Royal Canadian Mounted Police have been receiving a growing number of tips about the whereabouts of illegal stills, as well as complaints from public-spirited neighbors. Do laws that prohibit moonshining violate the right of citizens to exercise control over their own lives? Support your answer. Discuss how Szasz would respond to this question.

JAMES Q. WILSON

Against the Legalization of Drugs

James Q. Wilson is a professor of management and public policy at the University of California in Los Angeles and chairman of the National Advisory Council for Drug Abuse Prevention. He is also author of *The Moral Sense* and *Crime and Human Nature*. Wilson is particularly interested in the interplay of public policy and morality. In the following article, he rejects the libertarian view that citizens have the right to use drugs and to drink anything they want. Instead, Wilson argues that the harms of legalizing drugs outweigh the harms of prohibition.

Critical Reading Questions

1. What arguments does Wilson use to show that drug prohibition is morally justified?
2. According to Wilson, why are youth less likely to use heroin now than they were in 1972?
3. What is Wilson's view on the disease model of addiction? Has drug therapy been successful in reducing drug use?
4. What evidence does Wilson use to support his position that legalizing drugs would increase their use?
5. Which drugs does Wilson think should be prohibited and why? Is he opposed to the legalization of any drug or only of certain drugs?
6. What are some of the harmful effects of heroin and cocaine that, according to Wilson, justify their prohibition?
7. Why does Wilson reject the concept of drug abuse as a "victimless crime"?
8. Why is Wilson appalled by the argument that drug abusers should be allowed to kill themselves?
9. How does Wilson respond to the anti-prohibition argument that the illegality of drugs increases crime?
10. According to Wilson, what are some of the benefits of making drugs illegal?
11. According to Wilson, why would drug treatment be less successful if drugs were legal?
12. What is Wilson's view on the morality of tobacco use? What are the similarities and differences, according to Wilson, of tobacco use and cocaine use?
13. What is Wilson's view on the morality of alcohol use? What are some of its harms?
14. Why does Wilson dislike the "war on drugs" metaphor? What metaphor does he prefer?
15. According to Wilson, what is the role of science in helping us understand and cope with addiction?

"Against the Legalization of Drugs," *Commentary* 89, no. 2 (February 1990): 21–28.

In 1972, the President appointed me chairman of the National Advisory Council for Drug Abuse Prevention. Created by Congress, the Council was charged with providing guidance on how best to coordinate the national war on drugs. (Yes, we called it a war then, too.) In those days, the drug we were chiefly concerned with was heroin. When I took office, heroin use had been increasing dramatically. Everybody was worried that this increase would continue. Such phrases as "heroin epidemic" were commonplace.

That same year, the eminent economist Milton Friedman published an essay in *Newsweek* in which he called for legalizing heroin. His argument was on two grounds: as a matter of ethics, the government has no right to tell people not to use heroin (or to drink or to commit suicide); as a matter of economics, the prohibition of drug use imposes costs on society that far exceed the benefits. Others, such as the psychoanalyst Thomas Szasz, made the same argument. . . .

That was 1972. Today, we have the same number of heroin addicts that we had then—half a million, give or take a few thousand. Having that many heroin addicts is no trivial matter; these people deserve our attention. But not having had an increase in that number for over fifteen years is also something that deserves our attention. What happened to the "heroin epidemic" that many people once thought would overwhelm us?

The facts are clear: a more or less stable pool of heroin addicts has been getting older, with relatively few new recruits. In 1976 the average age of heroin users who appeared in hospital emergency rooms was about twenty-seven; ten years later it was thirty-two. More than two-thirds of all heroin users appearing in emergency rooms are now over the age of thirty. Back in the early 1970s, when heroin got onto the national political agenda, the typical heroin addict was much younger, often a teenager. . . .

Why did heroin lose its appeal for young people? When the young blacks in Harlem were asked why they stopped, more than half mentioned "trouble with the law" or "high cost" (and high cost is, of course, directly the result of law enforcement). Two-thirds said heroin hurt their health; nearly all said they had had a bad experience with it. We need not rely, however, simply on what they said. In New York City in 1973–75, the street price of heroin rose dramatically and its purity sharply declined, probably as a result of the heroin shortage caused by the success of the Turkish government in reducing the supply of opium base and of the French government in closing down heroin-processing laboratories located in and around Marseilles. These were short-lived gains for, just as Friedman predicted, alternative sources of supply—mostly in Mexico—quickly emerged. But the three-year heroin shortage interrupted the easy recruitment of new users. . . .

RELIVING THE PAST

Suppose we had taken Friedman's advice in 1972. What would have happened? We cannot be entirely certain, but at a minimum we would have placed the young heroin addicts (and, above all, the prospective addicts) in a very different position from the one in which they actually found themselves. Heroin would have been legal. Its price would have been reduced by 95 percent (minus whatever we chose to recover in taxes.) Now that it could be sold by the same people who make aspirin, its quality would have been assured—no poisons, no adulterants. Sterile hypodermic needles would have been readily available at the neighborhood drugstore, probably at the same counter where the heroin was sold. No need to travel to big cities or unfamiliar neighborhoods—heroin could have been purchased anywhere, perhaps by mail order.

There would no longer have been any financial or medical reason to avoid heroin use. Anybody could have afforded it. We might have tried to prevent children from buying it, but as we have learned from our efforts to prevent minors from buying alcohol and tobacco, young people have a way of penetrating markets theoretically reserved for adults. Returning Vietnam veterans would have discovered that Omaha and Raleigh had been converted into the pharmaceutical equivalent of Saigon.

Under these circumstances, can we doubt for a moment that heroin use would have grown exponentially? Or that a vastly larger supply of new users would have been recruited? . . .

But we need not rely on speculation, however plausible, that lowered prices and more abundant supplies would have increased heroin usage. Great Britain once followed such a policy and with almost exactly those results. Until the mid-1960s, British physicians were allowed to prescribe heroin to certain classes of addicts. (Possessing these drugs without a doctor's prescription remained a criminal offense.) For many years this policy worked well enough because the addict patients were typically middle-class people who had become dependent on opiate painkillers while undergoing hospital treatment. There was no drug culture. The British system worked for many years, not because it prevented drug abuse, but because there was no problem of drug abuse that would test the system.

All that changed in the 1960s. A few unscrupulous doctors began passing out heroin in wholesale amounts. One doctor prescribed almost 600,000 heroin tablets—that is, over thirteen pounds—in just one year. A youthful drug culture emerged with a demand for drugs far different from that of the older addicts. As a result, the British government required doctors to refer users to government-run clinics to receive their heroin.

But the shift to clinics did not curtail the growth in heroin use. Throughout the 1960s the number of addicts increased—the late John Kaplan of Stanford estimated by fivefold—in part as a result of the diversion of heroin from clinic patients to new users on the streets. An addict would bargain with the clinic doctor over how big a dose he would receive. The patient wanted as much as he could get, the doctor wanted to give as little as was needed. The patient had an advantage in this conflict because the doctor could not be certain how much was really needed. Many patients would use some of their "maintenance" dose and sell the remaining part to friends, thereby recruiting new addicts. As the clinics learned of this, they began to shift their treatment away from heroin and toward methadone, an addictive drug that, when taken orally, does not produce a "high" but will block the withdrawal pains associated with heroin abstinence.

Whether what happened in England in the 1960s was a mini-epidemic or an epidemic depends on whether one looks at numbers or at rates of change. Compared to the United States, the numbers were small. In 1960 there were 68 heroin addicts known to the British government; by 1968 there were 2,000 in treatment and many more who refused treatment. (They would refuse in part because they did not want to get methadone at a clinic if they could get heroin on the street.) Richard Hartnoll estimates that the actual number of addicts in England is five times the number officially registered. At a minimum, the number of British addicts increased by thirtyfold in ten years; the actual increase may have been much larger. . . .

The United States began the 1960s with a much larger number of heroin addicts and probably a bigger at-risk population than was the case in Great Britain. Even though it would be foolhardy to suppose that the British system, if installed here, would have worked the same way or with the same results, it would be equally foolhardy to suppose that a combination of heroin available from leaky clinics and from street dealers who faced only minimal law-enforcement risks would not have produced a much greater increase in heroin use than we actually experienced. My guess is that if we had allowed either doctors or clinics to prescribe heroin, we would have had far worse results than were produced in Britain, if for no other reason than the vastly larger number of addicts with which we began. We would have had to find some way to police thousands (not scores) of physicians and hundreds (not dozens) of clinics. If the British civil service found it difficult to keep heroin in the hands of addicts and out of the hands of recruits when it was dealing with a few hundred people, how well would the American civil service have accomplished the same tasks when dealing with tens of thousands of people?

BACK TO THE FUTURE

Now cocaine, especially in its potent form, crack, is the focus of attention. Now as in 1972 the government is trying to reduce its use. Now as then some people are advocating legalization. Is there any more reason to yield to those arguments today than there was almost two decades ago?*

I think not. If we had yielded in 1972 we almost certainly would have had today a permanent population of several million, not several hundred thousand, heroin addicts. If we yield now we will have a far more serious problem with cocaine.

Crack is worse than heroin by almost any measure. Heroin produces a pleasant drowsiness and, if hygienically administered, has only the physical side effects of constipation and sexual impotence. Regular heroin use incapacitates many users, especially poor ones, for any productive work or social responsibility. They will sit nodding on a street corner, helpless but at least harmless. By contrast, regular cocaine use leaves the user neither helpless nor harmless. When smoked (as with crack) or injected, cocaine produces instant, intense, and short-lived euphoria. The experience generates a powerful desire to repeat it. If the drug is readily available, repeat use will occur. Those people who progress to "bingeing" on cocaine become devoted to the drug and its effects to the exclusion of almost all other considerations—job, family, children, sleep, food, even sex. Dr. Frank Gawin at Yale and Dr. Everett Ellinwood at Duke report that a substantial percentage of all high-dose, binge users become uninhibited, impulsive, hypersexual, compulsive, irritable, and hyperactive. Their moods vacillate dramatically, leading at times to violence and homicide.

Women are much more likely to use crack than heroin, and if they are pregnant, the effects on their babies are tragic. . . . Cocaine harms the fetus and can lead to physical deformities or neurological damage. Some crack babies have for all practical purposes suffered a disabling stroke while still in the womb. The long-term consequences of this brain damage are lowered cognitive ability and the onset of mood disorders. Besharov estimates that about 30,000 to 50,000 such babies are born every year, about 7,000 in New York City alone. There

may be ways to treat such infants, but from everything we now know treatment will be long, difficult, and expensive. Worse, the mothers who are most likely to produce crack babies are precisely the ones who, because of poverty or temperament, are least able and willing to obtain such treatment. In fact, anecdotal evidence suggest that crack mothers are likely to abuse their infants.

The notion that abusing drugs such as cocaine is a "victimless crime" is not only absurd but dangerous. Even ignoring the fetal drug syndrome, crack-dependent people are, like heroin addicts, individuals who regularly victimize their children by neglect, their spouses by improvidence, their employers by lethargy, and their coworkers by carelessness. Society is not and could never be a collection of autonomous individuals. We all have a stake in ensuring that each of us displays a minimal level of dignity, responsibility, and empathy. We cannot, of course, coerce people into goodness, but we can and should insist that some standards must be met if society itself—on which the very existence of the human personality depends—is to persist. Drawing the line that defines those standards is difficult and contentious, but if crack and heroin use do not fall below it, what does? . . .

HAVE WE LOST?

Many people who agree that there are risks in legalizing cocaine or heroin still favor it because, they think, we have lost the war on drugs. "Nothing we have done has worked" and the current federal policy is just "more of the same." Whatever the costs of greater drug use, surely they would be less than the costs of our present, failed efforts.

That is exactly what I was told in 1972—and heroin is not quite as bad a drug as cocaine. We did not surrender and we did not lose. We did not win, either. What the nation accomplished then was what most efforts to save people from themselves accomplish: the problem was contained and the number of victims minimized, all at a considerable cost in law enforcement and increased crime. Was the cost worth it? I think so, but others may disagree. What are the lives of would-be addicts worth? I recall some people saying to me then, "Let them

---

* I do not take up the question of marijuana. For a variety of reasons—its widespread use and its lesser tendency to addict—it presents a different problem from cocaine or heroin.

kill themselves." I was appalled. Happily, such views did not prevail.

Have we lost today? Not at all. High-rate cocaine use is not commonplace. The National Institute of Drug Abuse (NIDA) reports that less than 5 percent of high-school seniors used cocaine within the last thirty days. . . . Medical examiners reported in 1987 that about 1,500 died from cocaine use; hospital emergency rooms reported about 30,000 admissions related to cocaine abuse. . . .

In some neighborhoods, of course, matters have reached crisis proportions. Gangs control the streets, shootings terrorize residents, and drug-dealing occurs in plain view. The police seem barely able to contain matters. But in these neighborhoods—unlike at Palo Alto cocktail parties—the people are not calling for legalization, they are calling for help. And often not much help has come. Many cities are willing to do almost anything about the drug problem except spend more money on it. The federal government cannot change that; only local voters and politicians can. It is not clear that they will.

It took about ten years to contain heroin. We have had experience with crack for only about three or four years. Each year we spend perhaps $11 billion on law enforcement (and some of that goes to deal with marijuana) and perhaps $2 billion on treatment. Large sums, but not sums that should lead anyone to say, "We just can't afford this any more."

The illegality of drugs increases crime, partly because some users turn to crime to pay for their habits, partly because some users are stimulated by certain drugs (such as crack or PCP) to act more violently or ruthlessly than they otherwise would, and partly because criminal organizations seeking to control drug supplies use force to manage their markets. These also are serious costs, but no one knows how much they would be reduced if drugs were legalized. Addicts would no longer steal to pay black-market prices for drugs, a real gain. But some, perhaps a great deal, of that gain would be offset by the great increase in the number of addicts. These people, nodding on heroin or living in the delusion-ridden high of cocaine, would hardly be ideal employees. Many would steal simply to support themselves, since snatch-and-grab, opportu-

nistic crime can be managed even by people unable to hold a regular job or plan an elaborate crime. Those British addicts who get their supplies from government clinics are not models of law-abiding decency. Most are in crime, and though their per-capita rate of criminality may be lower thanks to the cheapness of their drugs, the total volume of crime they produce may be quite large. Of course, society could decide to support all unemployable addicts on welfare, but that would mean that gains from lowered rates of crime would have to be offset by large increases in welfare budgets.

Proponents of legalization claim that the costs of having more addicts around would be largely if not entirely offset by having more money available with which to treat and care for them. The money would come from the taxes levied on the sale of heroin and cocaine.

To obtain this fiscal dividend, however, legalization's supporters must first solve an economic dilemma. If they want to raise a lot of money to pay for welfare and treatment, the tax rate on the drugs will have to be quite high. Even if they themselves do not want a high tax rate, the politicians' love of "sin taxes" would probably guarantee that it would be high anyway. But the higher the tax, the higher the price of the drug, and the higher the price the greater the likelihood that addicts will turn to crime to find the money for it and that criminal organizations will be formed to sell tax-free drugs at below-market rates. If we managed to keep taxes (and thus prices) low, we would get that much less money to pay for welfare and treatment and more people could afford to become addicts. There may be an optimal tax rate for drugs that maximizes revenue while minimizing crime, bootlegging, and the recruitment of new addicts, but our experience with alcohol does not suggest that we know how to find it.

THE BENEFITS OF ILLEGALITY

The advocates of legalization find nothing to be said in favor of the current system except, possibly, that it keeps the number of addicts smaller than it would otherwise be. In fact, the benefits are more substantial than that.

First, treatment. All the talk about providing "treatment on demand" implies that there is a demand for treatment. That is not quite right. There are some drug-dependent people who genuinely want treatment and will remain in it if offered; they should receive it. But there are far more who want only short-term help after a bad crash; once stabilized and bathed, they are back on the street again, hustling. And even many of the addicts who enroll in a program honestly wanting help drop out after a short while when they discover that help takes time and commitment. Drug-dependent people have very short time horizons and a weak capacity for commitment. These two groups—those looking for a quick fix and those unable to stick with a long-term fix—are not easily helped. Even if we increase the number of treatment slots—as we should—we would have to do something to make treatment more effective.

One thing that can often make it more effective is compulsion. Douglas Anglin of UCLA, in common with many other researchers, has found that the longer one stays in a treatment program, the better the chances of a reduction in drug dependency. But he, again like most other researchers, has found that drop-out rates are high. He has also found, however, that patients who enter treatment under legal compulsion stay in the program longer than those not subject to such pressure. . . . If for many addicts compulsion is a useful component of treatment, it is not clear how compulsion could be achieved in a society in which purchasing, possessing, and using the drug were legal. It could be managed, I suppose, but I would not want to have to answer the challenge from the American Civil Liberties Union that it is wrong to compel a person to undergo treatment for consuming a legal commodity.

Next, education. We are now investing substantially in drug-education programs in the schools. Though we do not yet know for certain what will work, there are some promising leads. But I wonder how credible such programs would be if they were aimed at dissuading children from doing something perfectly legal. We could, of course, treat drug education like smoking education: inhaling crack and inhaling tobacco are both legal, but you should not do it because it is bad for you. . . .

Again, it might be possible under a legalized regime to have effective drug-prevention programs, but their effectiveness would depend heavily, I think, on first having decided that cocaine use, like tobacco use, is purely a matter of practical consequences; no fundamental moral significance attaches to either. But if we believe—as I do—that dependency on certain mind-altering drugs *is* a moral issue and that their illegality rests in part on their immorality, then legalizing them undercuts, if it does not eliminate altogether, the moral message.

That message is at the root of the distinction we now make between nicotine and cocaine. Both are highly addictive; both have harmful physical effects. But we treat the two drugs differently, not simply because nicotine is so widely used as to be beyond the reach of effective prohibition, but because its use does not destroy the user's essential humanity. Tobacco shortens one's life, cocaine debases it. Nicotine alters one's habits, cocaine alters one's soul. The heavy use of crack, unlike the heavy use of tobacco, corrodes those natural sentiments of sympathy and duty that constitute our human nature and make possible our social life. To say, as does Nadelmann, that distinguishing morally between tobacco and cocaine is "little more than a transient prejudice" is close to saying that morality itself is but a prejudice.

THE ALCOHOL PROBLEM

. . . Alcohol, like heroin, cocaine, PCP, and marijuana, is a drug—that is, a mood-altering substance—and consumed to excess it certainly has harmful consequences: auto accidents, barroom fights, bedroom shootings. It is also, for some people, addictive. We cannot confidently compare the addictive powers of these drugs, but the best evidence suggests that crack and heroin are much more addictive than alcohol.

Many people, Nadelmann included, argue that since the health and financial costs of alcohol abuse are so much higher than those of cocaine or heroin abuse, it is hypocritical folly to devote our efforts to preventing cocaine or drug use. But as Mark Kleiman of Harvard has pointed out, this comparison is quite misleading. What Nadelmann is doing is showing that a *legalized* drug (alcohol) produces greater social harm than *illegal* ones (cocaine and heroin). But of course. Suppose that in the 1920s we had made heroin and cocaine legal and alcohol illegal. Can anyone doubt that Nadelmann would now be writing that it is folly to continue our ban on alcohol because cocaine and heroin are so much more harmful?

And let there be no doubt about it—widespread heroin and cocaine use are associated with all manner of ills. Thomas Bewley found that the mortality rate of British heroin addicts in 1968 was 28 times as high as the death rate of the same age group of non-addicts, even though in England at the time an addict could obtain free or low-cost heroin and clean needles from British clinics. Perform the following mental experiment: suppose we legalize heroin and cocaine in this country. In what proportion of auto fatalities would the state police report that the driver was nodding off on heroin or recklessly driving on a coke high? In what proportion of spouse-assault and child-abuse cases would the local police report that crack was involved? In what proportion of industrial accidents would safety investigators report that the forklift or drill-press operator was in a drug-induced stupor or frenzy? We do not know exactly what the proportion would be, but anyone who asserts that it would not be much higher than it is now would have to believe that these drugs have little appeal except when they are illegal. And that is nonsense.

An advocate of legalization might concede that social harm—perhaps harm equivalent to that already produced by alcohol—would follow from making cocaine and heroin generally available. But at least, he might add, we would have the problem "out in the open" where it could be treated as a matter of "public health." That is well and good, *if* we knew how to treat—that is, cure—heroin and cocaine abuse. But we do not know how to do it for all the people who would need such help. We are having only limited success in coping with chronic alcoholics. Addictive behavior is immensely difficult to change, and the best methods for changing it—living in drug-free therapeutic communities, becoming faithful members of Alcoholics Anonymous or Narcotics Anonymous—require great personal commitment, a quality that is, alas, in short supply among the very persons—young people, disadvantaged people—who are often most at risk for addiction.

Suppose that today we had, not 15 million alcohol abusers, but half a million. Suppose that we already knew what we have learned from our long experience with the widespread use of alcohol. Would we make whiskey legal? I do not know, but I suspect there would be a lively debate. The Surgeon General would remind us of the risks alcohol poses to pregnant women. The National Highway Traffic Safety Administration would point to the likelihood of more highway fatalities caused by drunk drivers. The Food and Drug Administration might find that there is a nontrivial increase in cancer associated with alcohol consumption. At the same time the police would report great difficulty in keeping illegal whiskey out of our cities, officers being corrupted by bootleggers, and alcohol addicts often resorting to crime to feed their habit. Libertarians, for their part, would argue that every citizen has a right to drink anything he wishes and that drinking is, in any event, a "victimless crime."

However the debate might turn out, the central fact would be that the problem was still, at that point, a small one. The government cannot legislate away the addictive tendencies in all of us, nor can it remove completely even the most dangerous addictive substances. But it can cope with harms when the harms are still manageable.

SCIENCE AND ADDICTION

One advantage of containing a problem while it is still containable is that it buys time for science to learn more about it and perhaps to discover a cure. Almost unnoticed in the current debate over legalizing drugs is that basic science has made rapid strides in identifying the underlying neurological processes involved in some forms of addiction. Stimulants such as cocaine and amphetamines alter the way certain brain cells communicate with one another. . . .

When dopamine crosses the synapse between two cells, it is in effect carrying a message from the first cell to activate the second one. In certain parts of the brain that message is experienced as pleasure. After the message is delivered, the dopamine returns to the first cell. Cocaine apparently blocks this return, or "reuptake," so that the excited cell and others nearby continue to send pleasure messages. When the exaggerated high produced by cocaine-influenced dopamine finally ends, the brain cells may (in ways that are still a matter of dispute) suffer from an extreme lack of dopamine, thereby making the individual unable to experience any pleasure at all. This would explain why cocaine users often feel so depressed after enjoying the drug. Stimulants may also affect the way in which other neurotransmitters, such as serotonin and noradrenaline, operate. . . .

Tragically, we spend very little on such research, and the agencies funding it have not in the past occupied very influential or visible posts in the federal bureaucracy. If there is one aspect of the "war on drugs" metaphor that I dislike, it is its tendency to focus attention almost exclusively on the troops in the trenches, whether engaged in enforcement or treatment, and away from the research-and-development efforts back on the home front where the war may ultimately be decided.

I believe that the prospects of scientists in controlling addiction will be strongly influenced by the size and character of the problem they face. If the problem is a few hundred thousand chronic, high-dose users of an illegal product, the chances of making a difference at a reasonable cost will be much greater than if the problem is a few million chronic users of legal substances. Once a drug is legal, not only will its use increase but many of those who then use it will prefer the drug to the treatment: they will want the pleasure, whatever the cost to themselves or their families, and they will resist—probably successfully—any efforts to wean them away from experiencing the high that comes from inhaling a legal substance.

Discussion Questions

1. Which model of addiction—the disease model or the moral-failing model—does Wilson adopt? Support your answer.

2. Wilson claims that both tobacco and cocaine corrode our natural sentiments of sympathy and duty. Do you agree? Should tobacco be made illegal across the board for people of all ages? Or is there a relevant moral distinction between cocaine and tobacco? Support your answers.

3. Compare and contrast Wilson's position on the legalization of drugs, for minors and for adults, with that of Thomas Szasz.

4. Preemployment drug screening and employee drug testing have become commonplace since the 1980s. The majority of Fortune 500 companies, for example, now have drug-testing programs.[54] Some colleges are also considering mandatory drug-screening programs for undergraduates. Would Wilson approve of mandatory drug testing in the workplace and on college campuses? How would Szasz respond to mandatory drug-testing programs? Support your answers.

5. Weigh the advantages and disadvantages of a drug/alcohol-testing program on your campus. Are there any circumstances in which mandatory drug and alcohol testing is morally justified?

6. Studies show that people under twenty-five are far more likely to binge on drugs and alcohol than people over twenty-five. Are people who engage in excessive drug and alcohol use simply morally immature? Support your answer in light of Lawrence Kohlberg's and Carol Gilligan's stages of moral development. If moral immaturity is a factor in drug and alcohol abuse, how might this knowledge be incorporated into a public or campus policy regarding drug use and drug education? Support your answers.

DOUGLAS N. HUSAK

A Moral Right to Use Drugs

Douglas Husak is a professor of philosophy at Rutgers University. In this article Husak critically analyzes the various arguments against drug use, including those based on harm and the virtue-based argument of James Q. Wilson. After dismissing these arguments, Husak concludes that there is nothing inherently immoral about drug use, apart from any harm it may cause. Therefore, adults have a moral right to use drugs recreationally. Husak concludes by suggesting that, instead of outlawing drugs, drug education programs should be used to combat harmful use.

Critical Reading Questions

1. According to Husak, what is the current status of the "war on drugs"?
2. How does Husak answer the question, Why do so many Americans use recreational drugs?
3. According to Husak, why has a war been declared on illegal drugs?
4. What does Husak mean when he says that "illegal drugs provide the perfect scapegoat"?
5. What is a "drug" and why is this term, as it is commonly used, confusing?
6. What is a "recreational drug"? How does it differ from a "nonrecreational drug"? What are some examples of nonrecreational uses of drugs?
7. What have been some of the consequences of the "get-tough" policy on drugs?
8. What are some of the arguments for the criminalization of drugs? How is paternalism used to support laws against drugs (LAD)? How is legal moralism used to support LAD?
9. On what grounds does Husak reject these arguments?
10. Why does Husak reject Wilson's virtue-based argument against the legalization of drugs?
11. What is the difference between maintaining that adults have a right to use drugs and advocating drug use?
12. Why does Husak reject the argument that legalizing drugs will send the wrong message to children?
13. What are the similarities, according to Husak, between his position on drugs and the pro-choice position on abortion?
14. What policy does Husak suggest regarding drug abuse?

"A Moral Right to Use Drugs" in *Drugs and Rights* (New York: Cambridge University Press, 1992), 10–22; 44–45; 56–68; 252–256. Some notes have been omitted.

Accurate or not, the perception that drug use is out of control has triggered an enormous state response. Illegal drugs have become the single most important concern of our criminal justice system. Although estimates are imprecise, tens of billions of dollars are probably spent to enforce LAD [laws against drugs] every year, and the less direct costs of the war on drugs are several times greater. Ronald Hamowy describes this war as "the most expensive intrusion into the private lives of Americans ever undertaken in the nation's history."

About 750,000 of the 28 million illegal drug users are arrested every year. Between one-quarter and one-third of all felony charges involve drug offenses. . . . As a result, courts have become clogged, and prison overcrowding is legendary. The U.S. Sentencing Commission has estimated that within fifteen years the Anti-Drug Abuse Act passed by Congress in 1986 will cause the proportion of inmates incarcerated for drug violations to rise from one-third to one-half of all defendants sentenced to federal prison. The costs of punishment threaten to drain the treasury, as each prisoner requires expenditures of between $10,000 and $40,000 per year. Since the average punishment for a drug conviction has risen to seventy-seven months in prison, each new inmate will cost taxpayers approximately $109,000 for the duration of the sentence.

Law enforcement officials continue to exercise broad discretion in arresting and prosecuting drug offenders. More than three-quarters of those arrested are eventually charged with possession, typically of marijuana. Many crimes of possession involve amounts that include a presumption of intent to distribute. Sometimes the quantity of drugs that creates this presumption is small. Moreover, the means used to measure the quantity of given drugs can be peculiar. Since statutes typically refer to a "mixture or substance containing a detectable amount" of a drug, the weight of the entire mixture or substance is included when calculating the quantity of a drug. If a tiny dose of LSD has been placed on a tab of paper or a cube of sugar, the weight of the tab or cube is included in the determination of the amount of the drug. The Supreme Court has recently held this practice to be constitutional.

The true extent of the war on drugs cannot be measured in quantities of dollars spent or numbers of defendants punished. The enforcement of drug laws has diminished precious civil liberties, eroding gains for which Americans have made major sacrifices for over two centuries. Increasingly common are evictions, raids, random searches, confiscations of driver's licenses, withdrawals of federal benefits such as education subsidies, and summary forfeitures of property. . . . Governor Douglas Wilder of Virginia proposes mandatory testing of college students for drug use. . . .

First, why do so many Americans use recreational drugs? Or, more specifically, why do so many Americans use the kinds of recreational drugs of which the majority disapproves? The power of drugs per se can only be part of the explanation. Illegal drug use is less prevalent in many countries where drugs are plentiful, inexpensive, and higher in quality than those available in America. A more viable strategy to combat drugs might attempt to identify and change the conditions peculiar to America that have led to widespread use. For present purposes, I am less concerned to attempt to identify these conditions than to ask why this issue has received so little attention from drug prohibitionists. It is hard to see how a long-term solution to the drug problem can be found without knowing why so many Americans are motivated to break the law in the first place. . . .

A second issue is typically neglected in understanding and evaluating the war on drugs: Why has war been declared on illegal drugs? The simplistic answer is that drugs pose a threat to American society comparable to that of an invading enemy. Self-protection requires the mobilization of resources equivalent to those employed in time of war. For reasons that will become clear, I do not believe that this answer can begin to explain the extraordinary efforts of the state in combating drugs. Few wars—and certainly not the war on drugs—can be understood as a purely rational response to a grave social crisis. . . .

The public fears that America is a nation in decline. Crime, poverty, poor education, corporate mismanagement, and an unproductive and unmotivated work force are cited as evidence of this deterioration. Who, or what, should be blamed? The political climate limits the range of acceptable answers. Conservatives will not allow liberals to blame institutional structures for our problems. The difficulty cannot be that government has failed to create the right social programs to help people. Nor will liberals allow conservatives to blame individuals for our problems. The difficulty cannot be that people are lazy, stupid, or egocentric. What alternative explanations remain?

Illegal drugs provide the ideal scapegoat. Drugs are alleged to be so powerful that persons cannot be blamed very much for succumbing to them, as they could be blamed for not studying or working. And drugs are so plentiful and easy to conceal that government cannot be blamed very much for failing to eliminate them. Even better, most drugs are smuggled from abroad, so Americans can attribute our decline to the influence of foreigners. In blaming drugs, politicians need not fear that they will antagonize a powerful lobby that will challenge their allegations and mobilize voters against them. Almost no organized bodies defend the interests of drug users. Illegal drugs represent a "no-lose" issue, the safest of all political crusades.

A scapegoat would be imperfect unless there were at least some plausibility in the accusations of drug prohibitionists. Perhaps illegal drug use *has* increased crime, contributed to poverty, exacerbated the decline of education, and decreased the productivity of workers. Sometimes it may have done so in dramatic ways. The stories of the most decrepit victims of drug abuse lend themselves to biographies and television docudramas that make a deep and lasting impression on viewers. Everyone has seen vivid images of persons who were driven by drugs to commit brutal crimes, abandon their children, steal from their friends, drop out of school, stop going to work, and perhaps even die. In light of these consequences, who can condone illegal drug use? . . .

A third and final issue about the war on drugs raises a matter that I will explore in greater depth: If there is to be a war on drugs, against which drugs should it be waged? . . .

How is "drug" defined by those who make the effort to define it at all? The answer depends on the discipline where an answer is sought. Perhaps the most frequently cited medical definition is "any substance other than food which by its chemical nature affects the structure or function of the living organism." Undoubtedly this definition is too broad. Nonetheless, I tentatively propose to adopt it until a better alternative becomes available.

Notice that this definition refers only to the pharmacological effect of a substance and not to its legal status. For two reasons, "drugs" must not be defined as synonymous with "illegal drugs." First, it would be absurd to suppose that a non-drug could become a drug, or that a drug could become a non-drug, simply by a stroke of the pen. A legislature can change the legal classification of a substance, but not the nature of that substance; it has no more power to decide that a substance is a drug than to decide that a substance is a food. Second, a philosophical study designed to evaluate the moral rights of drug users can hardly afford to rely uncritically on the existing legal status of substances, since the legitimacy of these determinations is part of what is under investigation. To suppose that "drugs" means "illegal drugs" begs important questions and concedes much of what I will challenge. In what follows, I will use the word "drug" to refer to both legal and illegal substances that satisfy the medical definition I cited.

No doubt this usage will create confusion. Despite the desirability of distinguishing "drugs" from "illegal drugs," there is ample evidence that the public tends to equate them. Surveys indicate, for example, that whereas 95 percent of adults recognize heroin as a drug, only 39 percent categorize alcohol as a drug, and a mere 27 percent identify tobacco as a drug. This tendency is pernicious. The widespread premise that only illegal substances are drugs lulls persons into accepting unsound arguments such as the following: Drugs are illegal; whatever is illegal is bad; we drink alcohol; what we do isn't bad; therefore, alcohol is not a drug. Clear thinking about this issue is impossible unless one realizes that whether a substance is a drug is a different question from whether that substance is or should be illegal. . . .

RECREATIONAL DRUG USE

As the examination of the Controlled Substances Act demonstrates, war has not really been declared on *drugs*. War has been declared on persons who make a certain *use* of drugs. I will describe this use as *recreational.*

By "recreational use," I mean consumption that is intended to promote the pleasure, happiness, or euphoria of the user. The more specific purposes that are encompassed under this broad umbrella include sociability, relaxation, alleviation of boredom, conviviality, feelings of harmony, enhancement of sexuality, and the like. Although borderline cases are numerous, paradigm examples of recreational drug use are plentiful. Interviews with users indicate that they are most likely to consume drugs on two general occasions. First, they use drugs to attempt to improve what they anticipate will be a good time. Hence drug use is frequent during parties, concerts, and sex. Second, they use drugs to attempt to make mindless and routine chores less boring. Hence drug use is frequent during house cleaning and cooking. I regard these as paradigm examples of recreational use.

The distinction between recreational and nonrecreational drug use does *not* purport to sort drugs into categories based on their pharmacological properties. Instead, this distinction sorts drug *use* into categories. The claim that a given drug is "recreational" can only mean that it is typically used for a recreational purpose. . . .

The concept of recreational use can be clarified by contrasting it with other purposes for using drugs. The most familiar nonrecreational reason to use drugs is medical. Although most drug use is either recreational or medical, these categories do not begin to exhaust the purposes for which drugs are consumed. Some persons take drugs for the explicit purpose of committing suicide. Others take drugs ceremonially, in the course of religious rituals. Still others take drugs in order to enhance their performance in competitive sports. Undoubtedly this list could be expanded, but I will make no attempt to provide a comprehensive account of the many reasons for using drugs. . . .

Undoubtedly my focus on recreational drug use will give rise to the criticism that my approach is academic, middle-class, and unresponsive to the realities of drug use in impoverished neighborhoods. Drug use in ghettos, it will be said, is not recreational. The less fortunate members of our society do not use drugs to facilitate their enjoyment at concerts but to escape from the harsh realities of their daily lives. Here, at least, gloom and despair play a central role in explaining the high incidence of drug use. . . .

The empirical facts are ambiguous in proving that illegal drug use is a special problem for the black community. Only 20 percent of all illegal drug users are black. Whites are more likely than blacks to have tried illegal drugs, and cocaine in particular, at some time in their lives. The more drug prohibitionists succeed in portraying drug use as a ghetto phenomenon, born of frustration and despair, the easier it is to lose sight of the repudiation of liberal values that LAD entails. As I will emphasize time and time again, too much of our policy about illegal drug use is based on generalizations from worst-case scenarios that do not conform to the reality of typical drug use. I hope to undermine the inaccurate stereotypes of drug use and drug users reinforced by this objection. LAD prohibits drug use by members of all races and classes; a legal policy applicable to all should not be based on the perceived problems of a few.

THE DECRIMINALIZATION MOVEMENT

. . . Courts and jails have become clogged as a result of "get-tough" policies toward drug offenders. The impact of drug offenses has led a number of commentators to speak of a collapse of the criminal justice system. Federal courts have become "drug courts," where narcotics prosecutions now account for 44 percent of all criminal trials, up 229 percent in the past decade. In many jurisdictions, delays in criminal cases not involving drugs or in the adjudication of civil disputes have become intolerable. The number of Americans behind bars has recently exceeded the one million mark and sets new records every day. Prisons cannot be built fast enough to accommodate drug offenders. . . . As a result of overcrowding by nonviolent drug offenders, violent criminals are less likely to serve long prison terms. . . .

Among the more serious effects of prohibition is discrimination against the poor, who increasingly consume a higher and higher percentage of illegal drugs. Although two-thirds of weekly drug users in New York State in 1987 were white, 91 percent of the persons convicted and sentenced to state prison for drug-related offenses were either black or Hispanic. Therapeutic treatment is frequently provided for middle- and upper-class users; prison is the preferred mode of "treatment" for the underprivileged. . . .

The enforcement of LAD has diminished precious civil liberties. Defense lawyers openly acknowledge the "drug exception" to the Bill of Rights. David Evans complains that "martial law has been declared in our inner cities."

Finally and most significantly, the war on drugs is counterproductive in making criminals of tens of millions of Americans whose behavior is otherwise lawful. Most drug users are lucky to escape detection. Others are less fortunate. Countless numbers of offenders have been forced to suffer long terms of imprisonment for violating laws that may not be morally justified. Even those who are eventually acquitted spend tremendous sums of time and money defending themselves in court. . . .

ARGUMENTS FOR CRIMINALIZATION

Defenses of and attacks against arguments for decriminalization have become so familiar that it is easy to forget that the burden of proof should be placed on those who favor the use of criminal penalties. When arguing about criminalization, most philosophers begin with a "presumption of freedom," or liberty, which places the onus of justification on those who would interfere with what a person wants to do. . . .

A second and equally familiar presumption cuts in the opposite direction. A "presumption in favor of the status quo" allocates the burden of proof on those who oppose any change in current laws against the use of recreational drugs. No one has any clear idea about what weight to assign to these "clashing presumptions." For this reason, it is probably unproductive to worry too much about who should bear the burden of proof on this issue. . . .

I assume without much argument that a respectable defense of criminal legislation must demonstrate that it is needed to prevent *harm*. Everyone agrees that persons lack a moral right to cause harm, so criminal laws that prohibit harmful conduct do not violate the basic principles I have described. Punishment of a person who causes harm can be justified by reference to the offender's desert. But in the absence of harm, criminal sanctions are undeserved and unjustified.

The least controversial rationale in favor of criminalization is that the conduct to be prohibited is harmful *to others*. Many legal philosophers, following the lead of [John Stuart] Mill, believe that harm to others is a necessary condition that any criminal law must satisfy in order to be justified. . . . A more controversial rationale in favor of criminalization is that drug use should be prohibited because it is harmful *to users* themselves. Although a number of philosophers are unsympathetic to this rationale, paternalistic arguments in favor of LAD are frequently defended. . . .

One common complaint about my strategy is misguided. Many philosophers are quick to point out that "no man is an island" and that whatever harms oneself also harms others or at least is capable of doing so. Perhaps there are no examples of "pure" or "unmixed" paternalism, that is, of an interference with liberty that is justifiable solely on the ground that the conduct to be prohibited harms the doer. I do not maintain otherwise. I do not suppose that a given activity can harm the doer but not others. The distinction between harm to oneself and harm to others is *not* a distinction between kinds of laws, but rather it is a distinction between *rationales* for laws. Any law might be defended by more than one rationale. I do not treat people as islands in using the distinction between harm to oneself and harm to others as an analytical device to help identify the best reasons for

LAD. The paternalistic rationale for LAD may be stronger than the nonpaternalistic rationale, or it may be weaker. In either event, the distinction between harm to oneself and harm to others must be drawn in order to evaluate each of the arguments in support of LAD. . . .

My premise that the use of the criminal sanction should require harm can be questioned. Perhaps arguments can be marshaled in support of LAD that do not depend on harm, either to oneself or to others. According to *legal moralism,* the wrongfulness of conduct per se, apart from its harmful effects, is a sufficient reason to impose criminal punishment.

Many drug prohibitionists resort to legal moralism in support of LAD. Bennett replies to the cost-benefit analyses of decriminalization theorists as follows: "I find no merit in the legalizers' case. The simple fact is that drug use is wrong. And the moral argument, in the end, is the most compelling argument." There can be no doubt that popular objections to illegal recreational drug use are often couched in the strongest possible moral terms. Drug use is frequently portrayed as sinful and wicked. . . .

For two reasons, however, I will have little to say about legal moralism here. First, this principle is extremely problematic. No one has presented a compelling case in favor of legal moralism; responses from philosophers have been almost entirely negative. One recurrent theme of their attack is that legal moralism might be used to enforce community prejudice. The requirement that criminal liability presupposes a *victim* who has been *harmed* helps to assure that persons will not be punished simply for doing what those with political power do not want them to do.

Second, the application of legal moralism to LAD is utterly baffling. Why would anyone believe the drug use per se is immoral, apart from any harm it might cause? . . . As long as moral reservations about drug use are presented as unsupported conclusions—or as feelings—they will prove resistant to criticism. Arguments, not conclusions, are the objects of philosophical evaluation.

What, exactly, do drug prohibitionists believe to be immoral about recreational drug use? Two alter-

natives are possible. Does the alleged wrong consist in the act of drug use per se, or in the alteration of consciousness that drug use produces? The former alternative seems unlikely. Suppose that the physiology of persons were altered so that a given drug no longer produced any psychological effect. Could anyone continue to believe that the use of that drug would still be immoral? In any event, contemporary Americans widely reject the view that the act of drug use is inherently wrong. Few condemn the moderate use of alcohol. The subdued moral opposition to alcohol heard today is light years away from the level of outrage expressed by zealots during the temperance movement.

The latter alternative seems no more attractive. Why should the alteration of consciousness produced by drug use be immoral, apart from any harm that might result? Some theorists have proposed that practices such as long-distance running and meditation can trigger natural neurological reactions that alter consciousness in respects that are phenomenologically indistinguishable from the effects of drug use. No one has suggested that such practices are immoral, and for good reason. There is ample reason to doubt that harmless experiences are among the kinds of things that *can* be immoral.

Perhaps many Americans share a vague conviction that some but not all ways of altering consciousness, by the use of some but not all drugs, is immoral. If this conviction could be defended, the particular experience of alcohol intoxication might be upheld as morally permissible, whereas the experiences of intoxication produced by various illegal drugs could be condemned. As it stands, however, this conviction is a conclusion in search of an argument. Typically, persons appeal to harm, either to oneself or to others, in attempts to differentiate between intoxication from alcohol and intoxication from illegal drugs. In this guise, the argument should be taken seriously. What is less clear is how to understand a version of this argument that does *not* appeal to harm. . . .

Moral objections to drug use might also be derived from an ideal of human excellence. Drug use might not be conducive to the attainment of a particular conception of virtue. These arguments are frequently endorsed by drug prohibitionists. According to Bennett, "Drug use degrades human character, and a purposeful, self governing society ignores its people's character at great peril." James Q. Wilson confines his virtue-based arguments to illegal drugs: "Tobacco shortens one's life, cocaine debases it. Nicotine alters one's habits, cocaine alters one's soul." What conception of virtue is employed here? . . . According to this tradition, drug use, like any other recreational activity, is suspect. Recreational activities are nonaltruistic and self-indulgent. . . .

The answer is that virtue-based arguments fail to support criminal punishment for recreational drug use. Bennett is correct that a society should not "ignore its people's character." But it does not follow that the protection of character is an appropriate objective of the criminal law. The prohibitions of the criminal law describe the minimum of acceptable behavior beneath which persons are not permitted to sink. Virtue-based considerations cannot be used to show that moderate self-indulgence, as well as any temporary impairment of rationality and autonomy brought about by most incidents of drug use, fall below this permissible level. The criminal law should not enforce a particular conception of human excellence, however attractive it may be. A theory of virtue might be applied to subject drug use to moral criticism. Opponents of LAD need not believe that drug use is beyond moral reproach. But no one should think that persons deserve to be punished as criminals because their behavior falls short of an ideal. . . .

MISINTERPRETATIONS

I have concluded that the arguments in favor of believing that adults have a moral right to use drugs recreationally are more persuasive than the arguments on the other side. This conclusion is easily misinterpreted. . . . The root of each misinterpretation is the supposition that rights exhaust the universe of moral discourse.

First, the conclusion that adults have a moral right to use drugs recreationally does not amount to advocating drug use. . . . This basic distinction is widely appreciated in most other contexts. Adults

have the moral right to preach communism or to practice Buddhism. Yet no one who defends this right would be misunderstood to recommend a conversion to communism or Buddhism.

Nonetheless, one of the most widely voiced objections to the proposal to repeal LAD is that it would express the wrong symbolism about drug use, especially among adolescents. John Lawn maintains: "Legalization of drugs would send the wrong message to our nation's youth. At a time when we have urged our young people to 'just say no' to drugs, legalization would suggest that they need only say no until they reach an appropriate age."[1] . . .

In order to dispel the impression that support for a right to use drugs is tantamount to encouraging drug use, those who reject LAD should be described as endorsing a *pro-choice* position on recreational drug use. This label has been carefully crafted by persons who uphold the right of women to terminate their pregnancies. These persons are not "pro-death," or "anti-life," as their critics would like the public to believe. Perhaps many of them would not elect abortion as their own solution to an unwanted pregnancy. Still, they believe that women have the right to make this choice for themselves. Misunderstanding would be avoided if the debate about the decriminalization of recreational drug use borrowed this terminology. The conclusion that adults have a moral right to use drugs recreationally should be described as the pro-choice position on recreational drug use. . . .

Should the rights of adults be infringed in order to ensure that the wrong message is not received by the public (to whom this argument extends very little credit)? The main problem is that this rationale for LAD would not allow the decriminalization of *any* activity that is less than exemplary. At bottom, this argument is simply another utilitarian defense of the status quo. The rights of some adults should not be sacrificed so that others do not misinterpret a message. This injustice is multiplied when the rights of millions of Americans are at stake. . . .

A second related but distinct misunderstanding of my position is as follows. The conclusion that adult use of recreational drugs is protected by a moral right does not entail that drug use is beyond moral reproach. The exercise of a moral right may be subject to criticism. Perhaps all recreational drug use, legal and illegal, is morally tainted. . . . In any event, some instances of recreational drug use are morally objectionable, beyond those in the special circumstances in which users create an impermissible risk of harm to others. These objectionable instances might be described by the pejorative term *drug abuse*. . . .

If the moral right to use drugs recreationally is to be respected, the need to minimize disutility leaves society with little choice but to discourage drug abuse. The process by which this goal is reached might loosely be described as "drug education." But this process differs from drug education as it is usually conceived. Most educational programs are prevention programs. As so designed, education has generally been deemed a failure, largely because it has not been shown to achieve its objective of decreasing drug use. Yet there may be more reason for optimism if the goal of education is to decrease drug abuse.

As so construed, drug education may never have been tried. No existing educational program has attempted either to separate use from abuse or to indicate how abuse might be avoided by means other than abstinence. The introduction of scientifically respectable materials in drug education programs has been politically unacceptable. As Chester Mitchell notes: "Because some parents insist that their children learn the official lies about the drug menace, well-informed teachers are caught in another superstition–science conflict except that the drug conflict has far greater legal repercussions for all involved than the evolution–creation debate."[2] Bruce Alexander adds: "The outrageously exaggerated scare stories about drugs that fill the electronic media are often called 'education' or 'prevention.'

These measures are part of the War on Drugs, not alternatives to it."[3] He proposes "domestication: learning to treat drugs with the same pragmatism that society applies to other familiar and sometimes dangerous household articles." . . .[4]

Since I make no attempt to solve America's drug problem as a matter of social policy, I will hazard only one final observation about the prospects for success that drug education as so conceived will minimize drug abuse. To demand that recreational drug users show restraint over the time, place, and quantity of their consumption is not to require the impossible. In fact, virtually every drug user exhibits some degree of control over her consumption. The means by which users manage to avoid abuse deserves careful study and extensive publicity. Perhaps a successful educational program should seek out responsible drug users. . . . To respect the moral right of adults to use recreational drugs may be painful, at least in the short run. But the protection of moral rights has a value to Americans that is not easily expressed in the utilitarian calculus of costs and benefits in which the decriminalization debate is usually cast.

NOTES

1. John Lawn, "The Issue of Legalizing Illicit Drugs," *Hofstra Law Review* 18 (1990): 703, 710.
2. Chester N. Mitchell, *The Drug Solution* (Ottawa: Carlton University Press, 1990), p. 307.
3. Bruce Alexander, *Peaceful Measures: Canada's Way out of the "War on Drugs"* (Toronto: University of Toronto Press, 1990), p. xi.
4. Ibid.

Discussion Questions

1. Virginia's Governor L. Douglas Wilder has proposed mandatory drug testing of all college students. Discuss some of the moral arguments for and against Wilder's proposal. Develop a policy on drug testing for your campus. What might some of the objections be? Discuss how you would defend your policy against objectors.
2. Does Husak present a convincing rebuttal of James Q. Wilson's argument against the legalization of drugs? Support your answer. Discuss how Wilson might respond to Husak's criticism.

3. Do you accept Husak's comparison of the right to use drugs and the pro-choice position in the abortion debate? Support your answer.
4. Do you agree with Husak that drug education, rather than LAD, is the best policy for dealing with drug abuse? Support your answer. Discuss what sort of drug education program would be most effective on your campus.
5. Florida State University in Tallahassee is one of many colleges working with local police and businesses to reduce alcohol abuse by its students. Recently, a bar near the university put on a "Valentine's Day 'No date, get drunk! Free beer all night'." The event was advertised at the college. How should universities, such as Florida State, respond to this type of aggressive advertising aimed at college students? What stance would Wilson and Husak each most likely take? Support your answers.

 THOMAS H. MURRAY

Drugs, Sports, and Ethics

Thomas H. Murray is a professor and the director of the Center of Biomedical Ethics at Case Western Reserve University in Cleveland, Ohio. In this paper, Murray argues against the use of performance-enhancing drugs, such as steroids, in sports. He begins by examining studies on the use of these drugs in professional and Olympic sports. After rejecting the standard arguments against the use of drugs in sports, Murray concludes that drug use in sports is still immoral because it restricts the free choice of competing athletes.

Critical Reading Questions

1. What is the difference between pleasure-enhancing and performance-enhancing drugs? What are some examples of the latter?
2. What are some examples of performance-enhancing drug use in sports?
3. What are anabolic and androgenic steroids? What are some of the desired effects of these drugs?
4. What are some of the other performance-enhancing drugs used in sports? What are some of the advantages and drawbacks of using high doses of these drugs?
5. Why do athletes take anabolic steroids? What are some of the risks of taking these drugs? Why are some athletes willing to take these risks?
6. According to Murray, what is the "inherent coerciveness" involved in the use of drugs in competitive sports?
7. According to Murray, why are the current policies prohibiting drugs in sports problematic and insufficient?

"Drugs, Sports, and Ethics" in *Feeling Good and Doing Better: Ethics and Nontherapeutic Drug Use,* ed. by Thomas H. Murray, Willard Gaylin and Ruth Macklin (Clifton, N.J.: Humana Press, 1984), 107–126. Some notes have been omitted.

8. What are the three reasons cited by ethicists that justify restriction of liberties?
9. According to Murray, under what circumstances can restrictions on certain liberties actually work to preserve liberty? Do these circumstances apply to the restriction of performance-enhancing drugs?
10. Why can't restrictions on performance-enhancing drugs be justified on the basis of harm to oneself? What is the relevance of Aristotle's concept of *eudaimonia,* or the good life, to the self-harm argument?
11. What does Murray mean by "free choice under pressure"? How does the use of performance-enhancing drugs violate this free choice?
12. According to Murray, who bears the primary responsibility for drug use among athletes?

Our images of the nonmedical drug user normally include the heroin addict nodding in the doorway, the spaced-out marijuana smoker, and maybe, if we know that alcohol is a drug, the wino sprawled on the curb. We probably do not think of the Olympic gold medalist, the professional baseball player who is a shoo-in for the Hall of Fame, or the National Football League lineman. Yet these athletes and hundreds, perhaps thousands, of others regularly use drugs in the course of their training, performance, or both. I am talking not about recreational drug use—athletes who use drugs for pleasure or relaxation probably no more or less than their contemporaries with comparable incomes—but about a much less discussed type of drug use: taking drugs to enhance performance.

It is a strange idea. . . . Performance-enhancing drug use is so common and so tolerated in some forms that we often fail to think of it as "drug" use. The clearest example is the (caffeinated) coffee pot, which is as much a part of the American workplace as typewriters and timeclocks. We drink coffee (and tea or Coke) for the "lift" it gives us. The source of "that Pepsi feeling" and the "life" added by Coke is no mystery—it is caffeine or some of its close chemical relatives, potent stimulants to the human central nervous system. Anyone who has drunk too much coffee and felt caffeine "jitters," or drunk it too late at night and been unable to sleep can testify to its pharmacological potency. Caffeine and its family, the xanthines, can stave off mental fatigue and help maintain alertness, very important properties when we are working around potentially dan-

gerous machines, fighting through a boring report, or driving a long stretch. In other words, caffeine can enhance our ability to perform tasks that would otherwise be so fatiguing that we might do them badly, or even harm ourselves or others in trying.

But is caffeine a drug? The fact that it is not under the control of doctors is irrelevant. . . .

About the only definition of "drugs" that would exclude things like caffeine and alcohol would be one that arbitrarily excludes them because of their wide availability and long and extensive history of use. Any reasonable definition of "drug" based on its effects on the human organism would have to include these two as well as nicotine and a number of other common substances.

Caffeine, then, is a performance-enhancing drug. . . . What the drug is used for and the intention behind the use—not the substance itself—determines whether we describe it as medical or nonmedical; as pleasure- or performance-, or health-enhancing.

DRUGS ON THE PLAYING FIELD

The area of human endeavor that has seen the most explosive growth in performance-enhancing drug use is almost certainly sport. At the highest levels of competitive sports, where athletes strain to improve performances already at the limits of human ability, the temptation to use a drug that might provide an edge can be powerful. Is this kind of drug use unethical? Should we think of it as an expression of liberty? Or do the special circumstances of sport affect our moral analysis? In particular, should liberty give way when other important values are threatened, and when no one's good is advanced? These questions frame the discussion that follows. . . .

Drugs did not enter sport in a major way until the 1960s. The 1964 Olympics were probably the first in which steroids were used. A group of steroids related to the masculinizing hormone testosterone was synthesized. These steroids are valued for two principal effects, which they have in varying proportions: androgenic, or masculinizing, and anabolic, or tissue-building. . . .

Those who lift or throw weights appear to have been the first to use steroids, and even today use them most. An informal, confidential survey of weight lifters revealed that between 90 and 100 percent used steroids. A recent study of power-lifters and body builders outside the Olympics, where athletes are a bit less reluctant to talk about their use of performance-enhancing drugs, found almost universal use of steroids as part of training. . . .

At about the same time that steroids were introduced into amateur sports, amphetamines and related stimulants were finding their way into professional sports. We know the most about professional baseball and football. But ignorance about other sports is just that—ignorance—and should not be taken to mean that performance-enhancing drugs are not used in those sports. . . .

WHY ATHLETES TAKE ANABOLIC STEROIDS

Many athletes persist in using performance-enhancing drugs despite official disapproval, possible disqualification, and even risk to their own health. They do so in the face of expert opinion that casts doubt on the effectiveness of the drugs they take. What leads them to jeopardize their futures as athletes, and possibly their very health, for what some medical people claim is an illusory advantage? The best case to illuminate these questions is steroid use among Olympic athletes. Nowhere else are the penalties greater, the efficacy more contended, or the possible health effects more serious. . . .

A recent report in *The Lancet* acknowledged, "Unquestionably, anabolics improve live weight gain, carcass weight, feed efficiency, and percentage meat in some species."[1] Although the report was referring to the practice of mixing steroids with livestock feed, it might have referred equally to humans. Aside from the genitals, the major active site for anabolic–androgenic steroids is skeletal muscles. The action of steroids on muscle tissue is probably related to their effect on nitrogen metabolism—dietary nitrogen is utilized more efficiently in androgenized tissue. There is even suggestive evidence that androgens may act directly on heart tissue; androgen receptors are found in atrial and ventrical myocardial cells.

Athletes also believe that anabolic–androgenic steroids make them more aggressive, and thus enable them to train harder. The case for this, as with most behavioral rather than physiological effects, is more elusive. . . .

AN UNSIGHTLY ARRAY OF RISKS

Along with the effects athletes desire to obtain from steroids come others not so welcome. Again, the lack of careful scientific information on chronic, high-dose usage forces us to rely on anecdotal reports and reasonable inferences. The anecdotes can be frightening. It is important to bear in mind that, despite being billed as "anabolic" steroids, all these drugs are related to testosterone and have a mix of anabolic and androgenic effects. . . . Therefore, any potent anabolic is also going to have a mix of androgenic effects. In male athletes this leads to a well-known decrease in fertility, since the synthetic androgen interferes with the normal feedback loop linking endogenous testosterone with sperm production. Other effects include acne (a real giveaway for steroid use, according to one athlete), and less visibly, cholesterol buildup and altered liver function. Athletes today are likely to have located a doctor who is willing to help them monitor some of the more subtle effects.

The impact on female athletes, like the East German swimmers, is more visible, and potentially catastrophic. Patricia Connelly, former Olympian and now coach, has lamented the use of steroids by women saying it robs them of their womanliness. The obvious changes—lowered voice, increased body hair, masculinized build—are probably reversible. Other changes are less well understood and potentially more dangerous. I have heard reports of two women, world champions in the 1970s, who appeared to age with stunning rapidity. One—in her early thirties—began to grow bald, developed age spots and wrinkles on her skin. . . .

Facing such an unpleasant, poorly understood, and unsightly array of risks, why do athletes persist in using steroids? The answer lies in the nature of international, or for that matter professional, athletic competition. In his Senate testimony, Harold Connelly said ". . . the overwhelming majority of the international track and field athletes I have known would take anything and do anything short of killing themselves to improve their athletic performance." The pressures are almost as intense in professional football. As one former player describes it: "It's hard to get violent every Sunday at 1 PM." Amphetamines permitted athletes to play with the necessary aggressive intensity. . . . The intense competition at the highest levels of sport calls for every effort the athletes can make, and pushes them to seek every possible advantage over their competitors. . . .

In a competitive endeavor, participants will be pressed to use any means available to achieve a competitive advantage. The higher the stakes, the more intense the competition, the more total the commitment, the more likely people are to use exceptional means. For the international amateur or professional athlete this has often come to include drugs. The pressure to use exists when people *believe* that something confers a competitive advantage, whether or not this is objectively true. There is, then, an *inherent coerciveness* present in these situations: when some choose to do what gives them a competitive edge, others will be pressed to do likewise, or resign themselves to either accepting a competitive disadvantage, or leaving the endeavor entirely. . . .

AN ETHICAL ACCOUNT

Now we can confront the fundamental ethical question: May athletes use drugs to enhance their athletic performance? The International Olympic Committee has given an answer of sorts by flatly prohibiting "doping" of any kind. This stance creates at least as many problems as it solves. It requires an expensive and cumbersome detection and enforcement apparatus, turning athletes and officials into mutually suspicious adversaries. It leads Olympic sports medicine authorities to proclaim that drugs like steroids are ineffective, a charge widely discounted by athletes, and thereby decreases the credibility of Olympic officials. Drug use is driven underground, making it difficult to obtain sound medical data on drug side-effects. . . .

Any argument for prohibiting or restricting drug use by Olympic athletes must contend with a very powerful defense of such use based on our concept of individual liberty. We have a strong legal and moral tradition of individual liberty that proclaims the right to pursue our life plans in our own way, to take risks if we so desire and, within very broad limits, to do with our own bodies what we wish. This right in law has been extended unambiguously to competent persons who wish to refuse even lifesaving medical care. More recently, it has been extended to marginally competent persons who refuse psychiatric treatment. Surely, competent and well-informed athletes have a right to use whatever means they desire to enhance their performance.

Those who see performance-enhancing drug use as the exercise of individual liberty are unmoved by the prospect of some harm. They believe it should be up to the individual, who is assumed to be a rational, autonomous, and uncoerced agent, to weigh probable harms against benefits, and choose accordingly to his or her own value preferences. It would be a much greater wrong, they would say, to deny people the right to make their own choices. Why should we worry so much about some probabilistic future harm for athletes when many other endeavors pose even greater dangers? High-steel construction work and coal-mining, mountain-climbing, hang-gliding, and auto-racing are almost certainly more dangerous than using steroids or other common performance-enhancing drugs.

Reasons commonly given to limit liberty fall into three classes: those that claim that the practice interferes with capacities for rational choice; those that emphasize harms to self; and those that emphasize harms to others. The case of performance-enhancing drugs and sport illustrates a fourth reason that may justify some interference with liberty, that given the social nature of the enterprise, performance-enhancing drug use in sport is inherently coercive. But first the other three reasons.

There is something paradoxical about our autonomy: we might freely choose to do something that would compromise our future capacity to choose freely. Selling yourself to slavery would be one way to limit liberty, making one's body the property of another person. If surrendering autonomous control over one's body is an evil and something we must refuse to permit, how much worse is it to destroy one's capacity to *think* clearly and independently? Yet that is one thing that might happen to people who abuse certain drugs. We may interfere with someone's desire to do a particular autonomous act if that act is likely to cause a general loss of the capacity to act autonomously. In this sense, forbidding selling yourself into slavery and forbidding the abuse of drugs likely to damage your ability to reason are similar *restrictions* on liberty designed to *preserve* liberty.

This argument applies only to things that do in fact damage our capacity to reason and make autonomous decisions. Although some of the more powerful pleasure-enhancing drugs might qualify, no one claims that performance-enhancing drugs like the steroids have any deleterious impact on reason. This argument, then, is irrelevant to the case of performance-enhancing drugs.

Destroying one's reasoning ability is a special kind of harm to oneself, but there are many other kinds of harm, and they constitute a potential argument in favor of curtailing liberty. Aristotle, in the Nichomachean Ethics, described a conception of *eudaimonia,* or the good life, in which the perfection of natural excellences was a central component. Our physical abilities, character traits, and above all our intellect were all to be perfected. We can infer from this that persons have a duty to do whatever is in their power to perfect their talents, and forsake whatever would interfere with that development. Aristotle might have no hesitation in condemning most or all pleasure-enhancing drug use, but his principle, which paraphrased is "People should develop their natural excellences," stumbles over the case of athletes and performance-enhancing drugs. Athletes use the drugs precisely to perfect their natural excellences. Our objection would have to be that drug use is an improper means to that end, since the end itself is especially commendable in the Aristotelian worldview. We could argue that drug use is wrong because, on balance, it hurts the pursuit of excellence more than it helps it. But then we are reduced to arguing about the facts—improved performances versus side effects. And if it turns out that the drugs work with minimal, reversible side effects, we would say that they are morally justified under the perfection-of-excellence principle.

Another way to put the Aristotelian objection is that we should not use unnatural means—drugs—to perfect natural excellences—athletic abilities. It is difficult to make this stick as a *moral,* and not merely an esthetic, objection. Although we recognize that certain means of perfecting our natural excellences are generally regarded as illegitimate and may be dismissed as "unnatural," the judgments are always with respect to specific ends. A prosthetic hand might be "unnatural" and unfair for the purpose of pitching baseball, but not objectionable if it allowed an injured novelist to operate a typewriter. Even in so narrow a case as drugs in sport, all depends on context. If we would not object to a diabetic athlete using insulin, could we object to a depressed one using an antidepressant, to an exhausted one using a stimulant? We can draw lines, but based on complex practical understandings, rather than solid, simple principles delineating the "natural" from the "unnatural." . . .

A second class of reasons to limit liberty says that we may interfere with some actions when they result in wrong to others. The wrong done may be direct. Lying, cheating, or other forms of deception are unavoidable when steroid use is banned, yet one persists in the practice. Of course, we could lift the ban, and then the steroid use need no longer be deceptive; it could be completely open to the same extent as other training aids. . . .

The wrong we do to others may be indirect. We could make ourselves incapable of fulfilling some duty we have to another person. For example, a male athlete who marries and promises his wife that they will have children makes himself sterile with synthetic anabolic steroids (a probable side effect). He has violated his moral duty to keep a promise. This objection could work, but only where the duty is clearly identifiable and not overly general, and the harm is reasonably foreseeable. . . . Except for cases like the sterile athlete reneging on his promise, instances where athletes make themselves incapable of fulfilling some specific duty to others would probably be rare. In any case, we cannot get a general moral prohibition on drug use in sports from this principle, only judgments in particular cases.

We may also do a moral wrong to others by taking unnecessary risks and becoming a great burden to family, society, or both. The helmetless motorcyclist who suffers severe brain damage in an accident is a prototypical case. Increasingly, people are describing professional boxing in very similar terms. Although this might be a good reason to require motorcyclists to wear helmets or to prohibit professional boxing matches, it is not a sound reason to prohibit steroid use. No one claims that the athletes using steroids are going to harm themselves so grievously that they will end up seriously brain-damaged or otherwise unable to care for themselves. Though the harms they do to themselves may be substantial, they are not disabling.

"FREE CHOICE UNDER PRESSURE"

So far we have not found any wrong done to others that is serious and likely to occur when athletes, at the top of the competitive ladder, commonly use performance-enhancing drugs. Let us look at the problem more closely. Olympic and professional sport, as a social institution, is an intensely competitive endeavor, and there is tremendous pressure to seek a competitive advantage. If some athletes are believed to have found something that gives them an edge, other athletes will feel pressed to do the same, or leave the competition. Unquestionably, coerciveness operates in the case of performance-enhancing drugs and sport. Where improved performance can be measured in fractions of inches, pounds, or seconds, and that fraction is the difference between winning and losing, it is very difficult for athletes to forego using something that they

believe improves their competitor's performance. Many athletes do refuse; but many others succumb; and still others undoubtedly leave rather than take drugs or accept a competitive handicap.

Under pressure, decisions to take performance-enhancing drugs are anything but purely "individual" choices. My alleged liberty to take performance-enhancing drugs, which is very hard to oppose from an individualistic conception of morality, is counterbalanced by the pressure I place on my fellow competitors. My "free" choice contains an element of coercion. If enough people like me choose to use performance-enhancing drugs, then the freedom of others not to use them is greatly diminished.

But can we say that "freedom" has actually been diminished because others are using performance-enhancing drugs? I still have a choice whether to participate in the sport at all. In what sense is my freedom impaired by what the other athletes may be doing? If we take freedom or liberty in the very narrow sense of noninterference with my actions, then my freedom has not been violated, because no one is prohibiting me from doing what I want, whether that be throwing the discus, taking steroids, or selling real estate. But if we take freedom to be one of a number of values, whose purpose is to support the efforts of persons to pursue reasonable life plans without being forced into unconscionable choices by the actions of others, then the coerciveness inherent when many athletes use performance-enhancing drugs and compel others to use the same drugs, accept a competitive handicap or leave the competition can be seen as a genuine threat to one's life plan. When a young person has devoted years to reach the highest levels in an event, only to find that to compete successfully he or she must take potentially grave risks to health, we have, I think, as serious a threat to human flourishing as many restrictions on liberty. . . .

My conclusions are complex. First, the athletes who are taking performance-enhancing drugs that have significant health risks are engaging in a morally questionable practice. They have turned a sport into a sophisticated game of "chicken." Most likely, each athlete feels pressed by others to take drugs, and does not feel he or she is making a free choice. The "drug race" is analogous to the arms race.

Second, since the problem is systemic, the solution must be too. The IOC has concentrated on individual athletes, and even then it has been inconsistent. This is the wrong place to look. Athletes do not use drugs because they like them, but because they feel compelled to. Rather than merely punishing those caught in the social trap, why not focus on the system? A good enforcement mechanism should be both ethical and efficient. To be ethical, punishment should come in proportion to culpability and should fall on *all* the guilty parties— not merely the athletes. Coaches, national federations, and political bodies that encourage, or fail to strenuously discourage, drug use, are all guilty. Current policy punishes only the athlete.

To be efficient, sanctions should be applied against those parties who can most effectively control drug use. Ultimately, it is the athlete who takes the pill or injection, so he or she ought to be one target of sanctions. But coaches are in an extraordinary influential position to persuade athletes to take or not to take drugs. Sanctions on coaches whose athletes are caught using drugs could be very effective. Coaches, not wanting to be eliminated from future competitions, might refuse to take on athletes who use performance-enhancing drugs.

Finally, although I am not in a position to elaborate a detailed plan to curtail performance-enhancing drug use in sports, I have tried to establish several points. Despite the claims of individual autonomy, the use of performance-enhancing drugs is ethically undesirable because it is coercive, has significant potential for harm, and advances no social value. Furthermore, any plan for eliminating its use should be just and efficient, in contrast to current policies.

Can we apply this analysis of drug use in sports to other areas of life? One key variable seems to be the social value that the drug use promotes, weighed against the risks it imposes. If we had a drug that steadied a surgeon's hand and improved his or her concentration so that surgical errors were reduced at little or no personal risk, I would not fault its use. If, on the other hand, the drug merely allowed the surgeon to operate more quickly and spend more time on the golf course with no change in surgical risk, its use would be at best a matter of moral indifference. Health, in the first case, is an important social value, one worth spending money and effort to obtain. A marginal addition to leisure time does not carry anywhere near the same moral value.

A careful, case-by-case, practice-by-practice weighing of social value gained against immediate and long-term risks appears to be the ethically responsible way to proceed in deciding the merits of performance-enhancing drugs.

NOTES

1. Editorial: "Anabolics in Meat Production," *Lancet,* March 27, 1982, pp. 721–722.

Discussion Questions

1. Compare and contrast Murray's position on drugs with that of a libertarian such as Thomas Szasz. Does the use of performance-enhancing drugs fall under Szasz's "right of self-medication"? Support your answer.
2. If we reject Aristotle's distinction between natural and unnatural means to perfection, could his virtue ethics and concept of *eudaimonia* be used to support the use of performance-enhancing drugs? If so, under what circumstances? For example, is it morally acceptable to use performance-enhancing drugs—such as caffeine, amphetamines, or other stimulants—before taking an exam, performing on stage, going to a job interview, or driving long distances at night? Support your answers.
3. What type of policy might Murray suggest regarding the use of performance-enhancing drugs in sports? How would it differ from current policies? Who would be penalized most severely by this policy? Who would benefit the most? Explain.

CASE STUDIES

1. FRATERNITIES AND ALCOHOL: THE DEATH OF BENJAMIN WYNNE[55]

Much of the criticism of binge drinking on college campuses is focused on the Greek system. A Harvard study found that 86 percent of fraternity-house residents are binge drinkers. Binge drinking can be deadly.

In August 1997 twenty-year-old Benjamin Wynne of Louisiana State University found out that he had been accepted as a pledge with the Sigma Alpha Epsilon fraternity. To celebrate the happy occasion, Wynne and the other pledges got rip-roaring drunk. The festivities started with an off-campus keg party in which beer was funneled through a rubber hose into the drinker's mouth. Following this, the Sigma Alpha Epsilon brothers headed down to Murphy's Bar, which was only a few hundred yards from the campus, and drank "Three Wise Men," a 151-proof drink made from rum, whiskey, and a liqueur. The festivities ended with the brothers wheeling the pledges back to campus in shopping carts because they were too drunk to walk.

Police were called to the fraternity house several hours later. They found almost two dozen men passed out on the living-room floor. By early morning Wynne was dead of alcohol poisoning, and three other brothers were hospitalized. The autopsy showed that Wynne had consumed the equivalent of twenty-four drinks the night before. When rescue workers arrived, he was already comatose. A few days later, his distraught parents had him removed from life support. This was not an isolated event. Fraternity pledge Scott Krueger died of alcohol poisoning the same semester after a Greek Week celebration at MIT; the previous May five students died in a North Carolina fraternity-house fire because they were too drunk to escape.

Discussion Questions

1. Who bears responsibility for the death of Benjamin Wynne? Did the brothers have a moral responsibility to intervene in order to keep the pledges from drinking in excess? Does the bartender who served Wynne bear part of the responsibility for his death? Would it make a difference if Wynne had used a fake ID to obtain alcohol? What would you have done had you been at Murphy's Bar that evening? Support your answers.

2. Is it morally acceptable for college students to use fake IDs to obtain alcohol? Support your answer.

3. Studies show that a permissive attitude on campus toward alcohol encourages students to drink more heavily than they otherwise would.[56] In response, several colleges and universities in the United States and Canada have limited or banned alcohol. Bishop's University in Quebec, once famous for its raucous partying, has outlawed all drinking games.

   On the other hand, outright prohibition isn't necessarily the answer. Louisiana State University had a no-alcohol policy in effect the day Wynne died. Create a policy for your campus regarding alcohol use. What moral concerns are most important in the creation of your policy? Given the fact that alcohol abuse is associated primarily with the Greek system, should fraternities and sororities be banned? Support your answers.

4. Some bars rely on college students for most of their business. These bars sometimes distribute handbills to students walking across campus and put fliers under doors in freshman dormitories. Should bars and alcohol companies be prohibited from advertising on college campuses?

5. Rutgers University has a dormitory especially for students who are recovering alcoholics and drug addicts and who wish to stay away from the drug-charged atmosphere of regular dorms. The cost of maintaining the dorm, which includes four people to run a substance-abuse program, is about $300,000 a year. Does the university have a duty to provide rehabilitative services to students who are alcoholics and drug abusers? If so, should these programs be voluntary or mandatory? Support your answers.

6. The primary justification of mandatory drug testing is the utilitarian argument that drug and alcohol use have a negative effect on productivity. Does this justify mandatory drug testing of college students? Support your answer. Discuss how Wilson and Husak might answer this question.

7. In response to the alarming increase in alcohol and drug abuse on college campuses, some police departments use undercover officers on campus. These officers live in dorms and attend classes like regular students in an attempt to gain information about illicit drug and alcohol use on campus and to bring offenders to justice. This approach has been very effective on some campuses in curtailing illicit drug dealing and underage drinking. Is this approach to the drug and alcohol problem morally justified? What would you do if you learned that your roommate or best friend was an undercover police officer? If you knew that another friend was selling drugs in your dorm, and the officer/roommate asked you if this person was selling drugs, what would you say? Support your answers.

   Discuss how both a Kantian and a utilitarian might respond to the morality of this approach.

---

2. BASEBALL STAR MICKEY MANTLE: SHOULD ALCOHOLICS RECEIVE LIVER TRANSPLANTS?

In 1995 sixty-three-year-old Yankee baseball star and Hall-of-Famer Mickey Mantle lay critically ill in a Dallas Hospital, his liver destroyed by forty years of alcohol abuse.

   Alcoholism is associated with a liver disease known as alcohol-related end-stage liver disease (ARESLD). In the United States, more than half of all deaths from liver disease are related to chronic alcoholism.[57] Mantle was given two to five weeks to live. The only hope for people with end-stage liver disease is a liver transplant. Livers are very scarce, however, and the waiting list is long. Only a fraction of those who need liver transplants ever get one.

   The night after Mantle was hospitalized, a suitable donor was found. Mantle was moved to the top of the recipient list and soon received a new liver. Mantle died shortly after of a failed liver transplant.

Discussion Questions

1. How should scarce resources, such as organs, be allocated? Should it be first come, first served? Is it fair to move to the top of an organ transplant list people who are

famous, or who still might make great contributions to society? Should the fact that a person's disease is related to lifestyle be taken into consideration in allocating scarce resources? Given the fact that there are not nearly enough livers even for people who do not have alcohol-related diseases, should alcoholics such as Mickey Mantle even be considered for liver transplants? Support your answer. Discuss how a supporter of the disease model of addiction and a supporter of the moral model of addiction might each answer these questions.

2. In 1991 the American Medical Association proposed as a general guideline that patients with alcohol-related liver disease should not compete equally with other people who need liver transplants.[58] Although they did not say that patients with ARESLD should *never* get liver transplants, they suggested that because livers are a scarce resource, patients with ARESLD be placed lower on the list than patients with nonalcohol-related liver disease. Is this fair? Support your answer. Should ex-alcoholics be treated differently than active alcoholics? Discuss your answer in light of the disease and moral models of addiction.

3. Who should be responsible for the medical costs incurred in Mickey Mantle's liver transplant? Studies show that the medical costs of alcohol and tobacco users are much higher than those of nonusers. Should private and public medical insurance plans cover these costs? Should alcohol and tobacco users have to cover the medical costs that are related to their use of these substances? Should tobacco companies have to foot the bill for diseases caused by tobacco use? Support your answers.

4. Some people argue that insurance companies should not cover the costs of substance-related care, because smokers and alcoholics have much higher medical costs. Others argue that this is unfair: Because smokers and alcoholics die much younger than nonusers, the cost of their health care over a lifetime is not much different than that of nonusers. Discuss how both Aristotle and a utilitarian might respond to these arguments.

5. Libertarian John Taylor argues that people such as Mickey Mantle and rock star Jerry Garcia, who died of a heart attack at age fifty-three, after decades of drug abuse and related health problems, have a right to choose their own ideal of the good life.[59] Abstaining from drugs and alcohol for the sake of longevity, he argues, may be overrated. Taylor writes that both Mantle and Garcia "choose lives that valued recklessness, intensity, sensation, and, in a word, fun over mere longevity. As a result they died at the onset of old age rather than at its outer limits." Do you agree with Taylor? Support your answer. Discuss how both a supporter and an opponent of the disease model of addiction might respond to Taylor's position.

6. Should the fact that Mantle chose the life he lived mean that he also forfeited his right to a liver transplant? Support your answer.

---

3. WINNING AT ALL COSTS: DRUGS IN SPORTS

You are the captain and star player on your college basketball team, which has made the finals. A wealthy entrepreneur, who is an avid basketball fan and alumnus of your college, has promised to make a $60 million donation to your school *if* your team wins the finals. Your college desperately needs the money. It is currently in serious financial trouble and has been forced to lay off faculty and cut back on academic programs.

A few weeks before the game, the wealthy entrepreneur offers you a banned performance-enhancing substance. He assures you that you will not get caught, because the substance has been slightly altered so that it cannot be detected. He also tells you that he will make a $60 million donation even if your team loses, but only on the condition that you take the drug for the next two weeks. The team you are playing in the finals is better than yours and has won the finals the past two years in a row. According to a noted sports analyst, the odds against your winning are eight to one.[60]

Discussion Questions

1. What should you do? Support your answer.
2. Would your answer be any different if the wealthy entrepreneur had also offered to give *you* $1 million if you agreed to use the drug? Would your answer be any different if you found out that the opposing team was going to be using performance-enhancing drugs? Explain your answers.
3. In a 1995 poll, 198 athletes, most U.S. Olympians or aspiring Olympians, were asked if they would take a banned performance-enhancing drug if the following two guarantees were made: (1) You would not be caught and (2) you will win. One hundred ninety-five of the athletes said yes; three said no. They were then asked if they would take the same drug with these two guarantees: (1) You will not be caught and (2) you will win every competition you enter for the next five years, then you will die from a side-effect of the drug. More than half replied that they would use the drug under these conditions. Does the fact that almost 99 percent of the athletes polled were willing to use drugs under certain circumstances undermine the argument that performance-enhancing drugs should be banned because they violate free choice? Does the prohibition of performance-enhancing drugs interfere more with athletes' free choice? Support your answers.
4. The cozy connection between sports and drugs goes beyond performance-enhancing drug use by athletes. Both the alcohol and the tobacco industries use professional sports to advertise their products. For every hour of professional sports programming, there are 2.4 alcohol commercials, many of which are very appealing to children and young adults.[61] Tobacco companies, such as Virginia Slims, also sponsor women's sporting events, thus encouraging girls to think that there is a connection between smoking and being slim, athletic, and liberated. The large number of teenage girls who have taken up smoking following its ad campaigns is a testimony to the success of Virginia Slims ads. Should alcohol and tobacco advertisements be more strictly regulated? Should alcohol and tobacco companies be forbidden to advertise? Should the sale of tobacco and alcohol be banned altogether? Support your answers.

---

4. PROZAC: ENHANCING MORALITY THROUGH DRUGS[62]

Although the role of drugs in lowering inhibitions against immoral behavior is widely acknowledged,[63] there is considerable resistance to the similar idea that certain drugs may actually enhance moral behavior. People who suffer from depression can become self-preoccupied to the point of seeming almost sociopathic in their indifference to the consequences of their actions for others. According to Peter Kramer, author of *Listening to*

Prozac, treatment with a drug such as Prozac can in some cases "turn a morally unattractive person into an admirable one."[64] Prozac can also numb feelings, however.

Kramer cites the case of Phillip, an undergraduate who was undergoing psychotherapy because of humiliation he had received from his parents. Initially, Phillip resisted the use of medication. As his depression became more severe, however, Phillip agreed to try Prozac. Although he felt better on the Prozac, he also hated it. He felt phony. Why? Because he had been robbed of his disdain, resentment, and rage without having to first work through it.[65]

Prozac is used not only by people who feel depressed or overwhelmed by the challenges of life; many use it as a means of self-transformation. According to Kramer, using Prozac can increase autonomy and life choices by "lend[ing] people courage and allow[ing] them to choose life's ordinary risky undertakings."[66]

Discussion Questions

1. Wilson argues that morality arises out of our natural sociability. In cases in which our natural sociability is deficient or suppressed by neurosis, would it be morally acceptable, or perhaps even morally obligatory, to use drugs to enhance it?

2. Is it morally admirable to use drugs in our quest to become better people? If we can find a shortcut to self-realization and moral maturity, shouldn't we take it? Support your answers. Discuss how both Aristotle and a Buddhist might respond to this question.

3. The use of mood-altering drugs such as Prozac has been criticized for masking our true personalities or essences, as well as for freeing us from having to "struggle with reality." Do you agree? What is meant by "essence" and "reality"?

4. Prozac use is more prevalent among women than among men. Unlike Valium, however, which made women more compliant, Prozac is described as the "feminist drug" because it seems to transform some people into assertive, self-confident high achievers who are socially adept. Given this, would it be morally desirable for women who put others' needs before their own to take Prozac? Is the assertiveness and self-confidence of women on Prozac morally equivalent to that of women who are at the postconventional stage of moral reasoning? Support your answers. Discuss how Carol Gilligan and care ethicist Nel Noddings might answer this question.

5. Is unhappiness or depression necessarily an indication of a moral failing? Discuss your answer in light of Phillip's experience.

6. Discuss the following statement by Peter Kramer, author of *Listening to Prozac:*

    > Working with Prozac has heightened my awareness of the extent to which compulsion is a basis for moral actions. Is it a sound basis? Surely one could make the case that what is compelled is inherently amoral; what characterizes moral action is choice. Still, in addressing this effect of Prozac [tempering compulsive behavior], we face the least irrational, most cogent aspect of pharmacological Calvinism: perhaps diminishing pain can dull the soul.[67]

    How might Szasz respond to Kramer's statement?

7. Apply the doctrine of the mean to the use of Prozac. Discuss when and under what conditions using a mood-altering drug such as Prozac may be a vice and when it may be a virtue.

5. THE ALCOHOLICS ANONYMOUS CONFESSION OF A DOUBLE MURDERER[68]

On New Year's Eve 1989, Donald Cox broke into a couples' bedroom and slashed their throats. The murder remained unsolved until Cox confessed his brutal crime at an AA meeting. Following the confession, one of the AA members called the police. Should this confession be admitted as evidence in a court of law?

According to Cox and his lawyers, the rules of AA obligate members to confess their transgressions. Because confession is part of the recovery process in AA, it should remain confidential, like confessions made to a priest or a psychiatrist. "It doesn't seem right," his lawyer Adele Walker argued, "It's like he's being punished for recovering." Furthermore, if confessions made during AA meetings did not remain confidential, AA would not be nearly as effective in helping alcoholics.

On the other hand, it is also an AA principle that alcoholics must accept responsibility for actions performed, even when they are drunk. Although Cox claimed that he was drunk at the time of the murders and tried the "drunken stupor–temporary insanity" defense at his trial, he had no trouble recalling what had happened on that tragic New Year's Eve.

Discussion Questions

1. Should the fact that Cox made his confession as part of his recovery absolve him of responsibility for his actions? Was he "sick," and hence not in control of his actions, when he committed the murders? Support your answers. Discuss how supporters of the disease model of addiction and the moral model of addiction might each respond to these questions.
2. Discuss what moral principles are in conflict when confidential confessions of murder or other horrific crimes—or plans to commit crimes—are made at AA meetings or to priests or psychiatrists. Which principles and moral concerns are most compelling?
3. Discuss what you would have done had you been at the AA meeting the night Cox confessed. Support your position.
4. Both Confucius and Aristotle maintain that a good government helps people to be good. Is the government partly responsible for the deaths of Cox's victims because it permits the sale and consumption of alcohol? Support your answer.
5. Should people who commit crimes under the influence of drugs or alcohol be given stiffer penalties, as in drunk-driving violations? Or should they be treated with greater leniency? Support your answers. Discuss how both a utilitarian as well as supporters of the disease model and the moral model might respond to these questions.

C H A P T E R   8

Homosexuality and Same-Sex Marriage

Comedian Ellen DeGeneres set the nation reeling when she "came out of the closet"[1] in a 1997 episode of her ABC sitcom *Ellen*. Ellen's coming out, after almost twenty years of being in the closet, was applauded by the gay and lesbian community. It also prompted other celebrities to follow suit, including her partner, actress Anne Heche. Others, however, were deeply offended by her frank disclosure. The gospel singers Angie and Debbie Winans, who strongly believe that homosexuality is against God's will, expressed their disapproval by writing the song "Not Natural." The Reverend Jerry Falwell denounced her as Ellen "DeGenerate."

Why did she choose to come out? "I never wanted to be the spokesperson for the gay community," DeGeneres replied. "I did it for my own truth."

BACKGROUND AND KEY TERMS

Ellen DeGeneres is one of approximately 2 to 10 percent (estimates vary) of people who identify themselves as homosexual.[2] Coming up with an accurate figure is complicated by two factors: (1) the lack of a sharp distinction between being exclusively homosexual or exclusively heterosexual, with many people falling somewhere between these two extremes, and (2) given the negative attitudes toward homosexuality in our culture, many homosexuals deny their orientation and may even adopt a heterosexual lifestyle. Indeed, a 1970s California survey revealed that one-fifth of gay men and more than a third of lesbians have been married.[3]

For the purposes of this chapter, we use the term *homosexual* for people whose sexual attraction is exclusively, or *almost* exclusively, to the opposite gender. Although the term *gender* is sometimes used to refer to socialized masculinity and feminity, in this chapter it denotes biological male and female.

RELIGIOUS AND CULTURAL ATTITUDES TOWARD HOMOSEXUALITY

Homosexuality is regarded as a violation of religious and cultural norms in much of the world. Homosexuality is forbidden in the Old Testament (Leviticus 18:22–23) as well as in the epistles of St. Paul (Romans 1:26–27). The three religions that accept the Old

KEY TERMS

heterosexual: a person whose sexual attraction is exclusively, or almost exclusively, toward members of the opposite gender.

homoeroticism: sexual attraction to members of one's own gender.

homosexual: a person whose sexual attraction is exclusively, or almost exclusively, toward members of his or her own gender.

bisexual: a person who is sexually attracted to both men and women.

gay: a male homosexual.

lesbian: a female homosexual.

same-sex marriage: marriage between two people of the same gender.

domestic partners: adult couples who live together, have a stable, intimate relationship, and are financially interdependent.

heterosexism: the belief that heterosexuals are morally superior to homosexuals.

homophobia: fear or hostility toward homosexuals, expressed or unexpressed.

outing: publicizing someone's homosexual orientation without their consent.

coming out: publicly and voluntarily embracing one's lesbian, bisexual, or gay identity.

passing: pretending that one's sexual orientation is different than it really is.

sodomy: sexual acts in which the genital organs of one partner come into contact with the mouth or anus of the other.

living in the closet: a metaphor describing the lives of homosexuals who choose to hide their sexual orientation.

Testament as part of their holy scripture—Judaism, Islam, and Christianity—condemn homosexuality. Saint Augustine called homosexuality a sin that should "in all times and places be detested and punished."[4] Ruse explores biblical teachings on homosexuality in great depth in his article. The prohibition against homosexuality was incorporated into the legal systems of most of the Western world. In seventeenth-century England, for example, male homosexuality was a capital crime.

Contemporary Judeo-Christian natural law ethicists condemn homosexuality as a violation of natural law. God created male and female as complementary natures, which, when united in marriage, constitute a unit that is more balanced and greater than the sum of its parts. Husbands and wives are called to "reflect the inner unity of the Creator."[5]

The role of the Christian Church as defenders of minorities has led to serious conflicts between the gay community and the Church's long-standing prohibition of homosexuality. Some of the more liberal Protestant churches now reject the traditional condemnation of homosexuality. Recently, conservative Protestant churches have begun toning down their antigay rhetoric. Rather than condemn homosexuals, they are ministering to them and offering programs to "redeem" them by helping them convert to heterosexuality.[6]

The Islam religion is clear in its condemnation of homosexuality, which is a capital offense in some Muslim countries. In Iran a fourth arrest for homosexuality brings the death penalty.[7] The international human rights organization Amnesty International estimates that more than three hundred people have been executed in Iran since 1990 for violation of laws prohibiting homosexuality.[8] In 1979, at the prompting of the Danish delegation, Amnesty International officially recognized people imprisoned because of their sexual orientation as "prisoners of conscience."

Most Asian countries have a more tolerant attitude toward homosexuality than Muslim and Judeo-Christian countries do. This is especially true in those cultures that subscribe to Confucian or Buddhist worldviews. Confucian philosophers, with their emphasis on family and filial piety, see homosexuality more as a threat to family continuity than as inherently immoral. In many Asian countries, men who are homosexual marry out of duty but have same-sex affairs on the side. This option, however, is not generally open to lesbians. Traditional Hindu countries such as India, Pakistan, and Bangladesh, in contrast, are more disapproving of homosexuality. In India homosexuality is condemned as a "deviant act, a sin, and a destructive life style."[9]

Homosexuality has been decriminalized in many of the non-Catholic European countries. Homosexual relations between consenting adults was decriminalized in England in 1967. Gay and lesbian couples in Denmark, Sweden, and Norway can now register as domestic partners, which confers the benefits of civic marriage.

Attitudes toward homosexuality tend to be more severe on this side of the Atlantic. In many Latin American countries, homosexuality is punishable by imprisonment. Some states in the United States have sodomy laws that punish homosexuality by up to twenty-five years in prison. The U.S. military goes beyond state sodomy laws, prohibiting even hand-holding and kissing between people with a "homosexual or bisexual orientation."

These laws reflect public disapproval of homosexuality. Americans are somewhat more tolerant of homosexuality than they were in 1982 when only 34 percent of Americans agreed to a Gallup Poll statement that "homosexuality should be considered an acceptable alternative lifestyle," compared to 45 percent who agreed with the same statement in 1999.[10] The increase in tolerance, however, is mainly due to an increased number of people in the 1999 poll having an opinion about homosexuality. About half of all Americans still believe, as they did in 1982, that homosexuality is not an acceptable lifestyle. Although Americans are slightly less opposed to homosexuality than they were almost twenty years ago, about half of Americans still believe that homosexuality is immoral. The shift in attitudes toward greater tolerance has occurred primarily in women, who are much more likely than men to view homosexuality as morally acceptable.

Despite the widespread "out of sight, out of mind" attitude, the message that homosexuality is immoral is pervasive in American society. Studies show that children are bombarded with antihomosexual messages from a young age; 97 percent of public school students report hearing antihomosexual remarks from their peers and 53 percent from their teachers. One study found that "the typical high school student hears anti-gay slurs as often as twenty-five times a day." In addition, 19 percent of gay and lesbian high school students are physically assaulted because of their sexual orientation. Teachers intervene in only 3 percent of the attacks.[11]

Attitudes on American college campuses reflect those of society. Despite the fact that several colleges now offer courses in gay and lesbian studies, homophobia is more widely accepted than sexism or racism. The annual Freshman Survey, run by the American Council on Education and the University of California at Los Angeles, found that 36.2 percent of freshmen in 1993 agreed with the statement "It is important to have laws prohibiting homosexual relationships."[12] This figure has remained relatively stable for several years with 33.3 percent of freshmen agreeing with the statement in the 1999 survey.[13]

HOMOSEXUALITY, THE LAW, AND SAME-SEX MARRIAGE

Holly Puterbaugh, fifty-four, and Lois Farnham, fifty-five, had been living together quietly for almost twenty-eight years when they decided to be joined in a ceremony of civil union before the minister of their church in a ceremony. However, after their request for a marriage license was denied, the two women, along with two other same-sex couples, brought suit against the state of Vermont.

Laws, especially civil rights laws, are important because they make a public statement about inclusion. In the past sodomy laws have been one of the primary vehicles for society to affirm its disapproval of homosexuality. In *Griswold v. Connecticut* (1965), the U.S. Supreme Court established that sexual relations between a husband and wife are protected by a right to privacy. The right of privacy was later extended to single heterosexuals in *Eisenstadt v. Baird* (1972). The same right, however, was later denied to homosexuals in *Bowers v. Hardwick* (1988) in which the Supreme Court upheld the constitutionality of a Georgia sodomy law.

Some gay and lesbian couples have tried to get around the sodomy laws by going through a marriage ceremony. Many homosexual couples also feel they should be eligible for the same benefits afforded to spouses, such as health-care benefits and Social Security. In the United States, the approach to legitimizing same-sex marriage has been mostly through piecemeal state legislation and litigation. The main obstacle has been public opposition (62 percent) to same-sex marriage.

In 1991 two lesbian couples and a gay couple filed a suit against Hawaii, stating that Hawaii's refusal to grant them marriage licenses was gender discrimination and, hence, violated the state constitution's Equal Rights Amendment. The court ruled against them. In 1993 the Hawaiian Supreme Court overturned the earlier ruling, arguing that the state had to show compelling reasons why three homosexual couples should be denied marriage licenses. The case subsequently became tied up in the courts. In 1998 Hawaiian voters voted overwhelmingly to amend the state constitution to prevent same-sex marriage, and in December 1999 the Hawaiian Supreme Court ruled that homosexual marriages do not get legal recognition.

Fearful that the initial ruling legalizing same-sex marriages would spark an influx of homosexual couples to Hawaii to exchange wedding vows, several states in the early and mid-1990s introduced bills to deny recognition of homosexual marriages. In the U.S. Congress, a Defense of Marriage Act was introduced as a preventive measure against the possibility that the Hawaiian court ruling would stand. The U.S. Senate approved the Defense of Marriage Act by an overwhelming majority. The bill was signed into law by President Clinton in September 1996. Under the new law, states are not obligated to

THE DEFENSE OF MARRIAGE ACT

United States Congress

September 21, 1996

No State, territory, or possession of the United States, or Indian tribe, shall be required to give effect to any public act, record, or judicial proceeding of any other State, territory, possession, or tribe respecting a relationship between persons of the same sex that is treated as a marriage under the laws of such other State, territory, possession, or tribe, a right or claim arising from such a relationship.

In determining the meaning of any Act of Congress, or of any ruling, regulation, or interpretation of the various administrative bureaus and agencies of the United States, the word "marriage" means only a legal union between one man and one woman as husband and wife, and the word "spouse" refers only to a person of the opposite sex who is a husband or wife.

recognize same-sex marriages performed in other states. Homosexual couples also remain ineligible for federal spousal benefits such as Social Security and Medicare. As of October 2000, thirty-three states and the federal government have adopted "defense of marriage" laws or constitutional amendments that restrict marriage to one man and one woman. Even California, by a resounding vote of 61 percent to 39 percent, approved a constitutional amendment in March 2000 banning same-sex marriages. Vermont is only one of three states whose Supreme Courts have struck down state marriage laws on the grounds that the laws discriminate against same-sex couples.

In the spring of 2000 Vermont passed a civil union law, the first of its kind in the nation. The law gives homosexual couples the right to enter into civil union, a legal status similar to marriage. The passing of this bill has touched off a heated debate about the morality of same-sex marriages.

The opposition to same-sex marriage has not been as strong in most other Western nations. In Canada the Ontario Human Rights Commission is urging the province to redefine marital status to include same-sex partners.[14]

Homosexuals in the United States also face discrimination in housing, employment, and the military. The Colorado Amendment 2, which was supported by the majority of voters, nullified antidiscrimination laws against homosexuals and prevented the passage of new ones. The amendment was appealed to the U.S. Supreme Court. John M. Finnis, whose article is included in the readings in this chapter, was one of the people who spoke in favor of retaining Colorado Amendment 2. In May 1996, however, the U.S. Supreme Court struck down Amendment 2, ruling that "A state cannot so deem a class of persons a stranger to its laws." Opponents of the Supreme Court ruling decried it as a blow against democracy and the wishes of the majority.

Marriage is not the only social institution in which homosexuals face legal discrimination. Since 1980 several thousand people have been discharged from the U.S. military

BOY SCOUTS OF AMERICA V. DALE (2000):
EXCERPTS FROM THE MAJORITY OPINION

Chief Justice Rehnquist delivering the opinion of the court:

The forced inclusion of an unwanted person in a group infringes the group's freedom of expressive association if the presence of that person affects in a significant way the group's ability to advocate public or private viewpoints. But freedom of expressive association, like many freedoms, is not absolute. . . .

To determine whether a group is protected by the First Amendment's expressive associational right we must determine whether the group engages "expressive Association." . . .

The general mission of the Boy Scouts is clear: "[T]o instill values in young people." The Boy Scouts seeks to instill these values by having its adult leaders spend time with the youth members, instructing and engaging them in activities like camping, archery, and fishing. During the time spent with the youth members, the scoutmasters and assistant scoutmasters inculcate them with the Boy Scouts' values—both expressly and by example. It seems indisputable that an association that seeks to transmit such a system of values engages in expressive activity. . . .

The values the Boy Scouts seeks to instill are "based on" those listed in the Scout Oath and Law. The Boy Scouts explains that the Scout Oath and Law provide "a positive moral code for living; . . . The Boy Scouts asserts that homosexual conduct is inconsistent with the values embodied in the Scout Oath and Law, particularly with the values represented by the terms "morally straight" and clean." . . .

The Boy Scouts asserts that it "teach[es] that homosexual conduct is not morally straight," and that it does "not want to promote homosexual conduct as a legitimate form of behavior." We accept the Boy Scouts assertion. . . .

As we give deference to an association's assertions regarding the nature of its expression, we must also give deference to an association's view of what would impair its expression. That is not to say that an expressive association can erect a shield against antidiscrimination laws simply by asserting that mere acceptance of a member from a particular group would impair its message. But here Dale, by his own admission, is one of a group of gay Scouts who have "become leaders in their community and are open and honest about their sexual orientation." Dale was the copresident of a gay and lesbian organization at college and remains a gay rights activist. Dale's presence in the Boy Scouts would, at the very least, force the organization to send a message, both to the youth members and the world, that the Boy Scouts accepts homosexual conduct as a legitimate form of behavior . . .

on the grounds that homosexuality was "incompatible with military service." In February 1994 the military formalized its ban on homosexuality in its controversial "Don't ask, don't tell" rule. The military discharged about five hundred people in the first year under the policy. Between 1994 and 1997 the number of military personnel discharged for homosexuality increased by 67 percent.[15] The "Don't ask, don't tell" rule has since been challenged as a violation of free speech and equal-protection rights.[16]

The gay rights movement suffered a setback in June 2000 when the U.S. Supreme Court ruled in a 5 to 4 vote that the Boy Scouts of America could legally expel a gay troop leader, because homosexuality was against the Scouts' "expressive message."[17]

THE DISEASE MODEL OF HOMOSEXUALITY

Homosexuality is a distinctly modern term, coined in 1869 by Hungarian Dr. Benkert as a category of scientific investigation.[18] Early researchers reported finding significant differences between heterosexual and homosexual people in their body type, lisping, angles at which they carried their arms, susceptibility to paranoia, and a variety of other physical and psychological traits.[19] These stereotypes, since disproved, remain today.

The belief that homosexuality is a deviation from the norm was reinforced by Freudian theory. In his *Three Essays on Sexuality* (1905), Sigmund Freud (1856–1939), put forth his theory that humans are basically bisexual. During their first four to six years of life children go through stages of sexual development. First their libidos are directed toward their mothers' breasts (the oral stage), then, narcissistically, toward their own bodies (the anal stage and the phallic stage). Following this, they go through a latency period until puberty. During puberty a boy gradually relinquishes his attraction to his mother, thus resolving his Oedipal complex. Freud was less clear on how this process worked in girls. One of the important developmental tasks of puberty, according to Freud, is to notice members of the opposite sex. Rather than violate the incest taboo, a boy gives up his sexual desire for his mother and redirects his libido toward females his own age.

Deviations from this natural developmental process, according to Freud, result in perversions in which the libido is misdirected, or neuroses when the libido is repressed. In male homosexuality the child fails to successfully resolve the Oedipal conflict and his early narcissism, thus misdirecting his libido toward members of the same gender. By loving males, the boy does not violate the incest taboo against his unresolved sexual desire for his mother.

For many decades the mental health community unquestioningly adopted Freud's assessment of homosexuality as a perversion and a mental disorder. Some state laws allowed homosexuals to be detained indefinitely for treatment as "sexual psychopaths." As with drug and alcohol addiction, homosexuality was caught in the net of the therapeutic revolution that swept the country in the mid-twentieth century. It wasn't until 1974 that the American Psychiatric Association removed homosexuality from its list of mental disorders.

The American Medical Association (AMA) was slower to relinquish the disease model of homosexuality. In 1981 the AMA adopted a policy paper aimed at changing the sexual orientation of homosexuals. This policy was revoked in 1994. The new policy called instead for a "nonjudgmental recognition of sexual orientation by physicians."[20] It also recognized that homosexuals may have "some unique mental health concerns" due to negative social attitudes regarding homosexuality. Despite the recent change in policy, the disease model is still pervasive. As of 1994 the World Health Organization (WHO) still classified homosexuality under mental disorders.

The new AMA policy has been challenged by a group called Exodus International, a nationwide coalition of ministers who believe that homosexuality is a symptom of deeper emotional and spiritual conflicts. Exodus claims to be very effective at helping people give up their homosexual identity. Bob Davies, a homosexual who underwent their program of therapy and prayer and has since been happily married for ten years, claims that although attraction to the same sex does not disappear, the program helps him manage his feelings and behavior. Others argue that conversion therapy is immoral and rarely successful in changing the behavior of homosexuals.[21] The American Psychological Association also opposes the use of reparative therapy, arguing that homosexuality is not a mental disorder and that there are possible harmful effects of the therapy on homosexuals.[22]

The high prevalence of AIDS (acquired immune deficiency syndrome), first diagnosed in 1977, in gay men has also fueled the belief that homosexuality is inherently unhealthy. Richard Mohr points out that gay self-hatred has been exacerbated by the AIDS crisis and the identification of AIDS as a "gay disease."[23] Despite the fact that AIDS is primarily a heterosexual disease in other countries, including many parts of Africa, AIDS became associated with the gay lifestyle in the United States. Former U.S. Secretary of Education William Bennett likened homosexuality to a fatal disease, pointing out that homosexual males are 430 times more likely than heterosexual males to be HIV positive.[24] In support of his argument that homosexuality is unhealthy, Bennett cited a study by Cameron that found the average life expectancy of a male homosexual to be only forty-three years compared with sixty-six years for a smoker and seventy-three years for the average American male. Cameron's study, however, has been challenged as being biased because it was based on the obituaries of gay men who died from AIDS, rather than a representative sample of gay men.[25]

The shift in new diagnoses of AIDS from primarily homosexual to primarily heterosexual populations has been accompanied by a shift away from the disease model of homosexuality. Although three-quarters of reported cases of AIDS in 1987 were in gay and bisexual men, in 1997 gay and bisexual men accounted for slightly less than half the new cases, with the largest increases appearing in men and women who acquired it through heterosexual contact.[26]

The recent announcement of the discovery of a "gay gene" as well as differences in the brains of gay and heterosexual men has reopened the debate about the medical status of homosexuality. Preliminary research suggests that there may be a "gay gene" on the q28 region of the X chromosome.[27] While some scientists maintain that evidence for a "gay gene" is flimsy, a University of California study published in 2000 strengthened the claim that homosexuality is at least partially genetic. Their research found that both gay men and lesbian women tend to have shorter index fingers, relative to their ring fingers, than do heterosexual men and women.[28] Despite some doubts from the scientific community about the existence of a gay gene, more and more Americans (34 percent in 1999 in contrast to 13 percent in 1997) believe that "homosexuality is something a person is born with" rather than due to upbringing or environment.[29]

Some people welcome the findings, which can help dispel Freudian-based myths about why some people have homoerotic tendencies. Other gay-rights activists, however, are suspicious about the ulterior motives in this research, fearing that it may be used to bolster the disease model by labeling homosexuality a genetic disorder.

The research also opens the possibility of using prenatal diagnosis to weed out fetuses who may have homoerotic tendencies. In a homophobic society, it is likely that a prenatal test for homosexuality will be favorably received. The military as well as employers could also demand genetic testing as a means of identifying people with homoerotic tendencies. In addition, these findings have not mitigated the moral disapproval of homosexuality. Even if homosexuality is genetic, giving in to one's homosexual urges could still be a moral failing.

HATE CRIMES

Unlike most other human-rights movements, the beneficiaries of the gay-rights movement are mostly invisible. Many gay and lesbian people prefer to pass as heterosexuals rather than face discrimination and hatred. The first gay-rights group in the United States was not organized until 1950, in Los Angeles. The first lesbian-rights group was established in San Francisco in 1955.[30]

Matthew Shepard, a student at the University of Wyoming, was beaten and left to die outside of town by two men who had targeted Matthew because he was gay. The two men are currently serving life sentences for their crime. Hate crimes are not new on campuses. Because colleges are not required under a federal law to report crimes unless they involve a major crime such as murder, aggravated assault, or a forcible sexual offense, most hate crime goes unreported. However, attacks on gay and lesbian students, threatening notes, and antihomosexual epithets scrawled across car windows or dormitory walls are not uncommon and are even on the rise on some campuses.[31]

Not surprisingly, many young people experience negative reactions to their coming out. One study of gay adolescent males found that 43 percent had strong negative reactions from their parents, and 41 percent from their friends. The majority of parents reported feelings of sadness, regret, depression, and/or concern for their child's well-being, as well as considerable family disruption as a result.[32]

Coming out also increases the risk of assault, especially for gay men. Almost half of all known gay teenagers report being physically assaulted in school and/or by family members. The U.S. Department of Justice has long included sexual-orientation assault as a category of hate crime; 13 percent of the hate crimes reported to the FBI in 1995 were based on sexual orientation. The perpetrators are generally young white males who, to use the words of one researcher, "conform to or are models of middle-class respectability." Hate crimes based on sexual orientation also tend to be more vicious than other hate crimes. Most gay beatings are "recreational"—that is, groups of adolescents or young men, bored and intoxicated, seek out a gay victim from a sense of adventure and because they believe that society has agreed to dislike homosexuals.[33] Hate crimes against homosexuals tend to be underreported because of concerns about being found out as well as fear of homophobic reactions from the police. In a Canadian study, in over half the cases in which gays sought police protection, the behavior of the responding officers was reported to have been "markedly unsatisfactory."[34]

Figures are somewhat lower on college campuses: 22 percent of gay and lesbian college students report that they have been physically assaulted as a result of their sexual orientation. This is four times as high as normal assault rates on campus.[35] On the other hand, the effects of remaining closeted can be also be devastating. Gay youths are two to three times more likely to commit suicide than their heterosexual peers.

Most gay activists believe that if more public figures would come out, it would help to dispel negative stereotypes regarding homosexuals. One of the solutions proposed by some radical gay groups for increasing the visibility of the gay and lesbian community is "outing." The term *outing* was coined by *Time* magazine following the publication of Michelangelo Signorile's article "The Secret Gay Life of Malcolm Forbes," which appeared a month after the millionaire's death in 1990.[36] Outing involves targeting prominent closeted homosexuals and publicly revealing, without their consent, their sexual orientation. Signorile and his supporters continue his crusade, outing other closeted public figures in New York, Hollywood, and Washington, D.C. The practice of outing has declined because of criticism from the gay community, but it is still a hotly debated issue with those who defend it; they argue that there simply is no other way to solve the country's gay problem. Supporters of outing maintain that closeted public figures who are desperate to pass as "one of the guys" are more likely to be vociferously homophobic than their straight counterparts. J. Edgar Hoover, for example, hunted down and expelled homosexuals from their government jobs before going home each night to his male lover.[37]

THE PHILOSOPHERS ON HOMOSEXUALITY

In *The Symposium,* a dialogue on love, Plato praises the ideals of masculine love. Like most ancient Greeks, however, including Socrates and Aristotle, he did not approve of the physical consummation of homosexual love: Homosexual feelings themselves are not wrong, but homosexual acts are wrong because they undermine the common good, an argument echoed in Finnis's article.

Like his philosophical predecessors Saint Augustine and Aristotle, natural law ethicist Thomas Aquinas also condemned homosexuality as immoral. According to natural law ethicists, legalizing homosexual relations is a denial of the true end of marriage, which is procreation, and an endorsement of the illusion that a same-sex relationship is no different than a relationship between a man and a woman. Although it is true that some husbands and wives, because of infertility, cannot have children, it is not inconsistent with the Church's claim that the primary purpose of marriage is procreation. Unlike heterosexual sex, even that which cannot result in procreation, homosexual acts are "radically and peculiarly non-marital" in that they can never form a "biological unit."[38] The natural end of the sexual act is the procreation of children. Because homosexual encounters cannot produce children, they are by definition a violation of natural law. Finnis adopts a natural law perspective on homosexuality in his article on the morality of homosexual relationships.

According to Immanuel Kant, homosexuality violates the categorical imperative because it involves using the body as a means only, rather than with the end of procreation of the species. Homosexual acts are hence an abuse of our sexuality and our very humanity.

John Stuart Mill came to the opposite conclusion regarding the morality of homosexuality. According to Mill, people have a liberty right to express their sexual preference so long as they are not harming others. Also, because pleasure is the greatest good, the pleasure gained through consensual homosexual acts is, prima facie, morally good. In the first two readings in this chapter, Michael Ruse and John M. Finnis go into greater detail on different philosophical views of homosexuality.

MORAL ISSUES

Personal Identity and Human Dignity

Personal identity or a sense of self emerges from the interaction between the individual and society. Because there is a presumption of heterosexuality in our society, remaining in the closet forces gay people to compromise their personal integrity and live a lie. Denying people the right to be open about their identity is an affront to their dignity as well as destructive to their self-image.

Michael Nava and Robert Dawidoff argue that marriage is important to a person's self-identity because it is a public declaration of commitment. In supporting Norway's 1993 Registered Partnerships for Homosexual Couples Act, the Ministry of Children and Family Affairs stated: "It can be detrimental for a person to have to suppress fundamental feelings concerning attachment and love for another person. Distancing oneself from these feelings or attempts to suppress them may destroy one's self-respect." Chesire Calhoun, in contrast, maintains that traditional heterosexual marriage, rather than affirming the dignity of women, is oppressive and should be resisted by lesbians.

Offensiveness

Many people believe that it is homosexuality itself, rather than lack of public affirmation of the right to be openly homosexual, that is an affront to dignity. Homosexuality is immoral because it is offensive and disgusting to those who are forced to witness public displays of homosexual affection. The public, and particularly children, have a right to be spared such scenes in places such as public lavatories, parks, and theaters. But as Finnis points out, the feeling of offense or moral indignation is not on its own sufficient grounds for declaring certain behaviors to be wrong.

Homosexuality Is Unnatural

One of the most common arguments against homosexuality is based on natural law ethics. Finnis, for example, argues that homosexuality is immoral because it is unnatural. The assumption underlying this argument is that the purpose of sex and marriage is the procreation of the species. Homosexuals have low self-respect and are unable to form stable relationships not because society is unaccepting of homosexuality, but because homosexual relationships are contrary to human nature and inherently immoral.

One weakness of this argument is the ambiguity of the term *unnatural*. Does "unnatural" mean contrary to the "laws of human nature"? Ruse points out that homosexual behavior is found throughout human societies as well as in other species of animals. Or does "unnatural" mean "uncommon"? This definition is also problematic: There are many types of uncommon behavior, such as great genius, beauty, or moral fortitude and compassion, that we regard as highly desirable, and "unnatural" in that sense does not mean immoral or bad.

Natural can also be defined in functional terms. The functional definition is based on the assumption that certain parts of our body were designed for specific functions. But why do we have to restrict ourselves to using something only for the function for which it was supposedly designed? Isn't part of human creativity the ability to see new possibilities in things? In addition, an appeal to design requires stating who designed the body, which in turn collapses into a religious argument against homosexuality and other sorts of sexual activity not aimed at procreation.

The modern counterpart of the natural law argument is that homosexuality is a sickness or, with the recent discovery of a "gay gene," a genetic disorder. If sickness is defined as a pathological condition that interferes with our everyday functioning, it appears on the surface that homosexuality may be a sickness. Most homosexuals have been "disabled" because of their sexual orientation. Advocates of gay and lesbian rights argue that it is not their sexual orientation per se that is disabling, but society's response to their sexual orientation. In this sense, homosexuality is no more a sickness than is having dark skin or being female, two other "conditions" that can interfere with everyday functioning.

Privacy

The right to privacy includes the right of adults to have consensual sex. This right comes into conflict with sodomy laws forbidding homosexuality. Those who support sodomy laws maintain that the common good is a more compelling moral concern in this case than are the privacy rights of active homosexuals.

The issue of privacy also arises in the controversy over outing. Does freedom of speech take precedence over the desire for privacy of closeted homosexuals? Claudia Card maintains that outing can be a profound violation of the most personal aspects of one's life.[39] Others, such as Richard Mohr, argue that the right to privacy does not protect or even address the freedom of closeted homosexuals because freedom is incompatible with suppressing a fundamental part of our identity.[40] Hence privacy rights conflict with the value of human dignity. Improving conditions for and advancing the rights of homosexuals as a group takes precedence over a personal right to privacy.

Consequentialist Considerations and Harm

Many of the arguments against homosexuality are based on beliefs regarding its harmful consequences. For example, it is argued that homosexuals tend to be child molesters and may seduce unsuspecting youngsters into adopting a homosexual lifestyle. Homosexuals are also a job risk because they are more likely to compromise their integrity in exchange for sexual favors or be blackmailed into divulging important corporate and military secrets. In addition, homosexuality has been condemned as promoting promiscuity which, in turn, increases the spread of sexually transmitted diseases (STDs), leads to loneliness and unhappiness, and precludes the possibility of a genuinely caring and personal relationship. Finally, homosexuality is seen as a threat to the very survival of the human race; if we all became homosexuals, there would be no future generations.

Most consequentialist arguments against homosexuality have proven to be groundless. Homosexuals are no more likely to be child molesters or pedophiles than are heterosexuals. Nor is there any evidence that a child's sexual orientation is influenced by contact with homosexuals, or that homosexuality will lead to an increase in the percentage of people who are homosexuals or the demise of the human race.[41]

Opponents of homosexuality also argue that the promiscuity associated with the gay lifestyle is harmful to social cohesiveness as well as a factor in the spread of AIDS. There is evidence that male homosexuals tend to be promiscuous. However, despite the stereotype of the gay bathhouse, there are no reliable studies that show that gay men are more promiscuous than heterosexual men.[42] Studies also show that gay men have trouble establishing stable relationships.[43] Although lesbians have more stable relationships than gay men, even their relationships generally break up within three years.[44] Even if homosexuals were more promiscuous, however, promiscuity itself is not inherently objectionable unless it harms others. In cases of harmful promiscuity, as in that which contributes to the spread of STDs, the sexual orientation of the promiscuous person is not morally relevant. A promiscuous heterosexual who knowingly puts his or her partner at risk for STDs is as morally culpable as a homosexual who does the same. Furthermore, supporters of homosexuality as a legitimate lifestyle counter that this is the effect of society's condemnation of homosexuality rather than inherent in homosexuality itself; it is difficult to establish open and stable caring relationships when doing so may cost people their jobs, alienate their families, and be met with disgust or even violence.

There is the further harm of hate crimes against homosexuals. In a homophobic society, being openly gay or lesbian can be dangerous. Few philosophers, if any, support the use of violence against homosexuals. Disapproval of violence or even most forms of discrimination against homosexuals, however, does not logically entail moral approval of homosexuality. But can the two be separated in actual practice? Is homophobia a normal consequence of public policies that discriminate against homosexuals? Some gay- and lesbian-rights activists maintain that the root of the problem is legislation that permits the violation of the rights of homosexuals. Opponents of homosexuality, such as Finnis, respond that, while it is regrettable that there is so much hostility, decriminalizing it is not the solution.

Justice and Discrimination

There is no doubt that homosexuals face discrimination. They have been denied housing, medical benefits, tax incentives, the opportunity to serve in the military or become members of the clergy, and the right to marry—all social privileges enjoyed by the heterosexual community. Discrimination is not inherently wrong; however, it must be based on morally relevant differences between two groups. For example, children are not allowed to drive automobiles. Discrimination against child drivers is based on the child's lack of maturity. Are there similar rational grounds for discriminating against people who are gay and lesbian?

The Common Good

Finnis claims that discrimination is justified because homosexual relations threaten the stability of the family and of society in general. Laws that prohibit same-sex marriage are justified on the grounds that they preserve the social fabric of the family. Because the primary purpose of marriage is to have children, homosexuals are not significantly harmed by not being able to marry. Nava and Dawidoff disagree, arguing that marriage, with its public acknowledgment of commitment, is integral to the goals of many homosexual couples. Marriage is important because of both the social benefits tied to the marital status, and the practical benefits such as retirement, Social Security, and medical coverage—benefits that are denied to homosexual couples. Calhoun responds that if the harms to women are taken into consideration, traditional heterosexual marriage is not in the common good. She suggests that the solution is not for homosexuals to buy into the institution of marriage, but to make the benefits, such as retirement and medical benefits, independent of it.

Do the purported social benefits of laws that discriminate against homosexuals offset the burdens imposed on them by these laws? Whether decriminalizing homosexuality and recognizing same-sex partnership will be destructive to social stability remains to be seen in countries, such as in Scandinavia, that now recognize homosexuality as legitimate.

CONCLUSION

The majority of Americans believe that homosexuality is immoral. The "tyranny of the majority" is problematic in a democracy when creating public policy regarding moral issues such as homosexuality, euthanasia, and abortion. Should the will of the people be reflected in the law? Or should democracy be superceded when it seems to run counter to what professional ethicists believe is the moral high ground? How should conflicts between rights claims on the part of disenfranchised groups be weighed against the will of the majority?

Being moral people entails more than simply giving lip service to the "politically correct" ideology while our actions continue to be informed by prejudice and ignorance. Virtue ethics and the duty of self-improvement direct us to examine our own views for doublethink. Those views that we cannot support on rational grounds should be discarded, both in our ideology and as a grounding for our everyday moral choices.

MICHAEL RUSE

Is Homosexuality Bad Sexuality?

Michael Ruse is a philosophy professor at the University of Guelph in Ontario. Ruse examines the argument that homosexuality is "bad sexuality" because it is unnatural and abnormal. After analyzing the philosophical views on homosexuality in ancient Greece and in the Judeo-Christian tradition, as well as other philosophical views on homosexuality, Ruse concludes that, although some people may see homosexuality as a perversion, it is not immoral. Furthermore, he suggests that if we cannot back up our negative feelings about homosexuality with rational arguments, we have a moral obligation to work on changing those feelings.

Critical Reading Questions

1. What were the conventions regarding homosexuality in ancient Greece?
2. What was Plato's view of homosexuality?
3. Why, according to Ruse, were both Socrates and Plato opposed to the physical consummation of homosexual relationships?
4. What does the Bible say regarding the morality of homosexuality?
5. Why, according to Thomas Aquinas, is homosexuality a violation of natural law?
6. What are the kinds of *crimina carnis*? How does Kant use the concept of *crimina carnis* in his analysis of the morality of homosexuality?
7. What was Jeremy Bentham's position on the morality of homosexuality? On what grounds does Bentham oppose outlawing it?
8. How does Bentham respond to the criticism that homosexuality "runs one down physically"? How does Bentham respond to the criticism that homosexuality among men "deprives women of sex and marriage"?
9. What is the source, according to Ruse, of the argument in Western philosophy that homosexuality is unnatural? How does Ruse respond to this argument?
10. According to Ruse, why do so many people regard homosexuality as a perversion? What does Ruse mean when he says that this kind of thinking involves a paradox?
11. On what grounds does Sara Ruddick argue that homosexuality is a perversion? How does Ruse respond to her argument?
12. How does Ruse define "naturalness" for humans? What is the relationship among naturalness, perversion, and morality?
13. Why do people find perversion so disgusting? What type of rules or values does perversion break?

"Is Homosexuality Bad Sexuality?" In *Homosexuality: A Philosophical Inquiry* (Oxford, England: Basil Blackwell, 1988), 179–192. Some notes have been omitted.

14. What does Ruse mean when he says that the question of the perversity of homosexuality is more of an empirical than a prescriptive matter?
15. What does Ruse mean when he says that perversion, when applied to homosexuality, is a relative concept?
16. What is the difference between moral indignation and disgust?

Is homosexuality, inclination and behavior, an acceptable way for a human being to feel and act, or is it pernicious? Undoubtedly, although there will be less unanimity on this matter today than there would have been (say) a hundred years ago, for a good many people the answer will seem obvious— that homosexuality is aesthetically revolting and morally gross; that in all its aspects it is wrong, and that this is a conclusion not merely confirmed by modern thought but underlined by the whole western religious/philosophical tradition. . . .

The Greeks, so the story would go, accepted and even promoted homosexual relations. Furthermore, this attitude is to be found in the greatest of their philosophers, most especially Plato. The Jews, however, both those of the Old and New Testaments, uniformly and unambiguously condemned all forms of homosexuality. It merited the punishment of man and of God. And it is this latter position which has prevailed ever since, thanks to the rise of Christianity, a religion which has such deep roots in Judaism.

But is this story true? Let us turn to the sources, beginning first with the Greeks. As is so often the case, popular opinion has a very inadequate grasp of the whole. It is indeed true that by the time of "classical Greece" . . . —a time which firmly includes the life span of the philosopher Plato (428–347 BC)—overt homosexuality was a well-established tradition and acceptable part of the Greek life style. But the sexuality of classical Greece was apparently not simply an unrestrained free-for-all, with any two or more people doing whatsoever they liked, to whomsoever they liked. Specifically, the homosexuality one hears about was very much an upper-class phenomenon, strongly associated with the enforced segregation of the sexes, and highly stylized, with emotions rather than actions playing a major role. The central focus was a bond which would be formed between a somewhat older and a somewhat younger man (ideally, a 25-year-old paired with a 15-year-old). It seems to have been rare indeed (and certainly not proper) for two men of exactly the same age to have fallen in love and to have had any kind of physical relationship. Moreover, after marriage the need for (and acceptability of) homosexual relations fell away rapidly. (It is assumed that an analogous story can be told about women, although we know far less about lesbianism. It seems, for some unknown reason, to have been a taboo subject for the male writers.)

The constraint about ages was accompanied also by a constraint about emotions. The older man (the *erastes* or lover) was expected to feel strong sexual emotion for the younger man or boy (the *eromenos* or loved one), admiring his beauty, wanting to get physically close to him, and being prepared to court him with gifts and favors. The boy, however, was not expected to feel the same kind of sexual attraction in response, but rather to admire his older lover, looking upon him as an ideal or model, and wanting to make him happy. This convention about love and ages helped dictate the nature of the physical sexual relations. Officially at least, sodomy was definitely taboo, not to mention things like fellatio. Being sodomized was considered far too degrading . . . Hence, the usual method of intercourse between upper-class lovers was somewhat limited, in a stylized manner. The erastes, the older, would push his penis between the thighs of the eromenos, the younger, and bring himself to ejaculation this way, "intercrurally." The boy was not supposed to ejaculate in return—indeed, he was supposed to find the whole business rather asexual, and to remain unaroused throughout. No doubt there was frequently a gap between the ideal and the actual.

Against this background we can understand Plato's position on homosexuality. . . . Plato, tradition has it, was unmarried and fairly exclusively homosexual in orientation. Be this as it may, [his teacher] Socrates and his (exclusively male) companions lived, thought, and behaved very much in the homosexual milieu described above as being the norm for upper-class Athenians. In Plato's early writings (which report, fairly authentically, on actual Socratic discussions or dialogues), we get repeated, unselfconscious references to the sexual pangs that an older man would feel for a boy or younger man, and the liaisons that would spring up between them. . . .

Although there is much talk of sexual desire, which seems even to be cherished, both Socrates and Plato unambiguously reject and condemn all taking of homosexual attraction to the point of intercourse and orgasm. . . .

Why were Socrates and Plato so strongly against physical homosexual relations? There is an obvious reason, which had nothing to do with homosexuality per se. Both Socrates and Plato were reflecting an important attitude of their society and class, namely a great respect for self-constraint and control. Emotions were seen as things which took control of one, and the man who could withstand them gained stature in his and his colleagues' eyes. . . .

For the mature Plato, therefore, control is essential. To read Plato's early and middle writings as providing a license for homosexual inclination and behavior is not to read them properly. Homosexual attraction is accepted and even venerated, but consummation is condemned. The man who lets his passions thus govern his reason is an object of pity. This, however, is not quite all that there is to Plato's treatment of homosexuality. Towards the end of his life he developed his ideas yet further, and indeed he arrived at a position by a line of argument that was profoundly to influence subsequent thinking on the matter of homosexuality. Simply and categorically Plato condemned homosexual behavior because it is "unnatural." It is not done by the animals. No more should it be done by us.

> Anyone who, in conformity with nature, proposes to re-establish the law as it was before Laios, declaring that it was right not to join with men and boys in sexual intercourse as with females, adducing as evidence the nature of animals and pointing out that [among them] male does not touch male for sexual purposes, since that is not natural, he could, I think, make a very strong case. (Plato, *Laws,* 836c–e, trans. Dover 1978: 166)

The opposition to homosexual acts becomes absolute. . . .

THE JUDAEO/CHRISTIAN TRADITION

Let us turn now to Judaism and its breakaway offspring, Christianity. Here, on the surface at least, popular opinion does seem closer to the truth. The primary source of information about the positions of the Jews and the early Christians is obviously the Bible, Old and New Testaments. In the Old Testament, there are two main sources of information about the position taken by God and his chosen people on the subject of homosexuality: the story of Sodom and Gomorrah, and various scattered dictates about homosexual practices. Both sources apparently tell the same tale: homosexual behavior is abhorrent in the eyes of the Lord and therefore morally barred to humankind. As it happens, the Sodom and Gomorrah story about the citizens of Sodom, who wanted to have homosexual intercourse with two of God's angels, has been the subject of much Biblical reinterpretation. Most pertinently, it has been argued that the homosexual theme of the Sodom and Gomorrah story is a later interpolation. But the "holiness Code" of Leviticus is unambiguous.

> Thou shalt not lie with mankind, as with womankind: it is abomination. (Leviticus xviii.22)

> If a man also lie with mankind, as he lieth with a woman, both of them have committed an abomination: they shall surely be put to death; their blood shall be upon them. (Leviticus xx.13)

In the New Testament, one likewise finds passages which categorically prohibit homosexual behavior. As is usual on matters of sex, it was not the founder himself who pronounced on these matters, but his chief proselytizer, Paul.

> the men, leaving the natural use of the woman, burned in their lust one toward another, men with men working unseemliness, and receiving in themselves that recompense of their error which was due. (Romans i.27)

> Be not deceived: neither fornicators, nor idolators, nor adulterers, nor effeminate, nor abusers of themselves with men, nor thieves, nor covetous, nor drunkards, nor revilers, nor extortioners, shall inherit the kingdom of God. (I Corinthians vi.9–10)

> law is not made for a righteous man, but for the lawless and unruly . . . for abusers of themselves with men . . . (I Timothy i.9–10)

Nor is lesbian behavior neglected.

> God gave them up unto vile passions: for their women changed the natural use into that which is against nature . . . (Romans i.26)

. . . The most detailed philosophical discussion of homosexuality by a Christian thinker is to be found in the writings of the thirteenth-century theologian St. Thomas Aquinas. Aquinas's treatment of homosexuality, as of most moral issues, depends crucially on the notion of "natural law." . . . Coming to sexuality, Aquinas (who was much influenced by Aristotle) did not ask the straightforward causal question, "How do things work?," but rather the teleological question, "What are things for? What end do they serve?" And the answer he gave is that sex exists for the procreation and raising of children. This is why God made us sexual beings, and this therefore is the end towards which we must strive if we are not to violate natural law, that area of the eternal law where we ourselves must make a contribution.

The consequence of Aquinas's position, as he thought, is that all sex outside marriage is wrong because it is a violation of natural law. Thus, quite apart from homosexuality's prohibition on Biblical grounds, for Aquinas it is necessarily barred as being against natural law: as being in conflict with "right reason." Homosexual encounters do not lead to children, therefore they must be wrong. But there

is rather more than this. All lust is immoral, but some acts are doubly to be condemned, because "they are in conflict with the natural pattern of sexuality for the benefit of the species." These are termed 'unnatural vices' ("*vitiae contra naturum*"). . . .

MODERN ETHICAL PHILOSOPHIES

Let us turn now to the modern era, the time after the scientific revolution. There are two major, secular moral philosophies, those of the German thinker, Immanuel Kant, and of the (primarily) British utilitarians. Both groups thought their views threw light on the status of homosexual behavior (again, feelings get short shrift). Let us take them in turn.

Kant thought humans are subject to an overriding and necessary moral law, a supreme directive, the "categorical imperative." It is this law which tells us what we ought to do; wherein lies our duty. . . .

As Kant himself recognized, at a quite general level sex and the categorical imperative have a rather uneasy relationship. The starting point to sex is the sheer desire of a person for the body of another. . . . This gets dangerously close to treating the other as a means to the fulfillment of one's own sexual desire—as an object, rather than as an end. And this, according to the categorical imperative, is immoral. To escape from this dilemma, and one surely must if the end of the human race is not to be advocated on moral grounds, one must go on to treat the object of one's sexual advances as an end. One does this by broadening one's feelings, so that the personhood of the object of one's desire is brought within one's attraction, and by giving oneself reciprocally—by yielding oneself, body and soul, one shows respect for the other as an end, and not just as a means.

But what about a sincere commitment between two people of the same sex, the sort of homosexual equivalent of heterosexual marriage? At this point Kant invokes the notion of a *crimina carnis,* an abuse of one's sexuality. There are two kinds. First, there are acts which are contrary to sound reason, *crimina carnis secundum naturam.* These are immoral acts which go against the moral code imposed upon us as humans, and include such things as adultery. Second, there are acts contrary to our animal nature, *crimina carnis contra naturam.* These include masturbation, sex with animals, and homosexuality. They are the lowest and most disgusting sort of vice, worse in a sense even than suicide, and they are practices that we hesitate to mention. . . .

> A second *crimen carnis contra naturam* is intercourse between *sexus homogenii,* in which the object of sexual impulse is a human being but there is homogeneity instead of heterogeneity of sex, as when a woman satisfies her desire on a woman, or a man on a man. This practice too is contrary to the ends of humanity; for the end of humanity in respect of sexuality is to preserve the species without debasing the person; but in this instance the species is not being preserved (as it can be by a *crimen carnis secundum naturam*), but the person is set aside, the self is degraded below the level of the animals, and humanity is dishonoured.[1]

Contrasting with Kantian ethics is that of the utilitarians, the most prominent of whom were Jeremy Bentham and the two Mills, James (father) and John Stuart (son). For them, the key to ethical theory is happiness: "The creed which accepts as the foundation of morals utility or the greatest happiness principle holds that actions are right in proportion as they tend to promote happiness; wrong as they tend to produce the reverse of happiness.". . .

Bentham thinks homosexual interactions as acceptable morally as Kant finds them pernicious. Such interactions give pleasure to the people engaged in them, and so by the greatest happiness principle they ought to be valued. "As to any primary mischief, it is evident that [a homosexual interaction] produces no pain in anyone. On the contrary it produces pleasure . . .". Bentham is not advocating homosexual behavior for everyone, only for those who want to so indulge. Then, there will be no harm. Nor is there any real problem stemming from the possibility that homosexual practices might incline or influence others into similar behavior. People who indulge homosexual appetites

seem to enjoy themselves; so at most one is inclining others to enjoyable practices.

What of the claim that homosexual behavior runs one down physically, thus as it were reducing one's long-term pleasure in life? Bentham's conclusion is that there is no evidence to this effect. In any case, being in line with medical opinion of the time, and accepting that masturbation is physically debilitating, Bentham pointed out the injustice of trying to eliminate homosexuality through the law, when one did (and obviously could) do nothing about self-abuse. What of the claim that homosexuality is a threat to the keeping of population numbers up to an acceptable level? (Bentham had no doubts that a sizeable population is a good thing.) Again Bentham saw no danger on this score. Men's sexual appetites and capabilities far exceed those of females, particularly in the sense that a man can fertilize many more times than a fertilized female can give birth. . . .

IS HOMOSEXUAL BEHAVIOR BIOLOGICALLY UNNATURAL?

. . . Plato, who introduced the argument, has had the greatest influence on western thought about the worth of homosexuality. Plato stated categorically that homosexuality (the behavior at least) is wrong because it is unnatural—it is not something done by the animals. . . .

It is biology which is the strongest plank in the barrier against the permissibility of same-gender sex. But should *we* condemn homosexual behavior as immoral because it is unnatural, in the sense of being against biology? Should we say that animals do not behave homosexually; therefore humans should not behave homosexually? Is it true that genitals were "designed" for heterosexual ends and that all other uses are a wicked corruption? We must try to answer these questions for ourselves, and to this end a number of points must be raised.

First, it is simply not true, if by "unnatural" one means "not performed by animals" or even "not commonly performed by animals," that homosexuality is unnatural. We know that in species after species, right through the animal kingdom, students of animal behavior report unambiguous evidence of homosexual attachments and behavior—in insects, fish, birds, and lower and higher mammals. . . . Whatever the moral implications of homosexuality and naturalness may be, it is false that homosexuality is immoral because it does not exist amongst animals. . . .

Even if it turns out that some kinds of sexual behavior have nothing to do with straight biology, even if it turns out that the homosexual is doing him/herself a biological disservice and perhaps even his/her race or species a similar disservice, this does not as such imply that anything sexual, including homosexual, is immoral. What moral obligation has the individual got to reproduce? What moral obligation has the individual got to help his/her species reproduce? It might be argued that any behavior which is so disruptive of society that society itself fails to reproduce is immoral; . . .

But, in reply, first of all it is obvious that homosexual activity today is not so disruptive of society as to prevent overall reproduction. Second, the moral importance of society's reproduction is not that obvious. We may have an obligation to future generations not so to pollute our planet that life for them becomes depressingly difficult, but do we have an obligation to produce future generations? . . .

My conclusions, therefore, are that once you strike out fallacious arguments about biological naturalness, and bring forward modern realizations of the possibilities for homosexuals of meaningful relationships, the Kantian and utilitarian positions come very much closer together. Certainly, at a minimum, there is moral worth in the close-coupled relationships of the Second Kinsey study, and probably more. . . .

SEXUAL PERVERSION

In theory, this should conclude our discussion at this point. Once you have strained out religious elements, once you have dropped outmoded scientific claims, once you have sorted through the proper relationship between "is" and "ought," once you

have discovered a little bit about what homosexuals are really like rather than what you think they might be like, moral conclusions start to fall fairly readily into place. Yet there is something about homosexual activity—and, indeed, the whole overt homosexual life style—that other people find disturbing and threatening; something which drives people to conclude that, for all of the fancy arguments of the philosophers, homosexual activity is a wrong: a moral evil. (The feeling is particularly strong for males, by males—an asymmetry to which I shall return.)

What is it about homosexuality—what is it about male homosexuality in particular—that brings forth such negative judgements? One thing, above all else, comes across. Listen to the eminent theologian Karl Barth (1980)[2]: "[Homosexuality] is the physical, psychological and social sickness, the phenomenon of perversion, decadence and decay, which can emerge when man refuses to admit the validity of the divine command in the sense in which we are now considering it" (p. 49). Forget about the sickness part of the complaint. God does not condemn the diabetic. What troubles Barth and his God—what troubles virtually all of those who hate homosexuality—is that they see it as a *perversion*. It is the epitome of wrongdoing, and therefore must be censored in the strongest possible way.

Obviously, from our perspective, we have seen a paradox. Homosexual behavior seems not very morally pernicious; yet, through the notion of perversion, this is precisely how it appears to many people—in our society, at least. How can we resolve it? Fortunately, some help is at hand, for the notion of perversion has been much discussed by analytic philosophers in recent years. Typical in many respects, certainly in that which ties in best with our previous discussion, is an analysis by Sara Ruddick. Trying to capture the concept, she turns to traditional arguments, claiming that what people have been arguing about down through the ages is less a moral question and more one of perversity. She suggests that the natural end of sex is reproduction: that all and only acts which tend to lead to reproduction are natural, and that all unnatural acts are perverted.

The ground for classifying sexual acts as either natural or unnatural is that the former type serve or could serve the evolutionary and biological function of sexuality—namely, reproduction. "Natural" sexual desire has as its "object" living persons of the opposite sex, and in particular their postpubertal genitals. The "aim" of natural sexual desire—that is, the act that "naturally" completes it—is genital intercourse. Perverse sex acts are deviations . . . (p. 91) [3]

. . . Naturalness keeps coming up. Perhaps the time has come to make it work for us, rather than against us. And indeed, this is a reasonable move, for people like Ruddick are surely right in thinking naturalness important. . . . Yet a biological definition will not do. Perhaps the time has come to make a break. We are human beings: that means we live in a cultural realm, unlike animals who are fundamentally trapped down at the level of pure biology. What I argue, therefore, is that naturalness ought to be defined in terms of culture and not simple biology. What is unnatural, and what is consequently in some important sense perverse, is what goes against or breaks with our culture. It is what violates the ends or aims that human beings think are important or worth striving for. This may include reproduction, but extends to all the things we hold dear, the things that make us happy and make life worth living generally. And this is why perversity is indeed a value laden term, because a perversion puts itself against human norms and values. . . .

This is the key to perversions: what I like to call the "Ugh! factor." A perversion involves a breaking not of a moral rule, but more of an aesthetic rule. We find perversions disgusting, revolting. But why is this? I would suggest the following reason. A perversion involves going against one of culture's values or ends or things considered desirable, and other members of society cannot understand why one would want to go against the value. . . .

We have come back to the original Platonic position—but with crucial shifts. Unnaturalness is connected to culture, not biology. (As a Darwinian, though, I would never deny that the former

comes from and is moulded by the latter. That is why many perversions do involve biologically unsavory acts—like eating feces.) And the values involved are not so much moral as aesthetic. So what about homosexuality? Are homosexual acts perverse acts, and is the inclination to such acts a perverse inclination? Acknowledging that I am trying to offer a descriptive rather than prescriptive analysis, I do not think there is any straightforward answer to these questions. But I look upon this as a strength of my analysis, not a weakness! I think the question of the perversity of homosexuality is to a great extent an empirical matter. How do people feel about homosexual behavior? Can they in some sense relate to it, whether or not they want to do it themselves and whether or not they have homosexual inclinations? . . . I suggest that for some people in our society homosexuality is not a perversion and for some it is. Some other societies have seen homosexuality totally as a perversion. Some other societies have not seen it as a perversion at all.

What I am arguing, therefore, is that, faced with divided opinion in our society about the perverted nature of homosexuality (inclination and behavior), neither side is absolutely right and neither side is absolutely wrong. There is a crucial element of subjectivity at work here, as with liking or disliking spinach. Perversion, especially as it applies to homosexuality, is a relative concept. . . . If one agrees that homosexuality is not immoral, then surely one ought to persuade people not to regard homosexuals and their habits with loathing. Certainly, one ought to persuade people not to confuse their disgust at a perversion with moral indignation. . . .

NOTES

1. Immanuel Kant, *Lectures on Ethics,* trans. L. Infield (New York: Harper & Row, 1963), p. 170.
2. Karl Barth, "Church Dogmatics." In E. Batchelor (ed.), *Homosexuality and Ethics* (New York: Pilgrim, 1980), pp. 48–51.
3. Sara Ruddick, "Better Sex." In R. Baker and F. Elliston (eds.), *Philosophy and Sex* (Buffalo: Prometheus, 1975), pp. 83–104.

Discussion Questions

1. Is it morally relevant that homosexuality has been and continues to be regarded as unnatural and morally deviant in many societies? Support your answer.
2. Does Ruse adequately respond to the argument that homosexuality is a disease? Does his concept of perversion allow for "healthy" perversions? Support your answers.
3. What stereotypes come to mind when you hear the terms *gay man, lesbian,* and *bisexual*? (These stereotypes do not have to be ones that you accept; this is just a brainstorming exercise.) Are these stereotypes based on fact? Discuss how these stereotypes affect your perception of gay, lesbian, and bisexual people, and how these stereotypes affect how people who are gay, lesbian, or bisexual feel about themselves. Discuss how these stereotypes limit the opportunities of people who are gay, lesbian, or bisexual. Are these limitations morally justified? Support your answers.
4. Do you agree with Ruse that if we cannot back up our negative feelings about homosexuality with rational arguments, we have a moral obligation to work on changing those feelings? Do we have a moral obligation to try to overcome doublethink? Relate your answer to the study mentioned in Chapter 1, which found that while slightly more than half of college students interviewed evaluated homosexuality in a positive light, stating that it was a personal preference, 92 percent of those same students also stated that it would not be morally acceptable or desirable if their own child was homosexual.[45]

JOHN M. FINNIS

Law, Morality, and "Sexual Orientation"

John Finnis is a professor of law and legal philosophy at Oxford University in England. A defender of Colorado Amendment 2 and the Defense of Marriage Act, Finnis argues that homosexuality is intrinsically immoral, not just because it is unnatural but because it is destructive to the common good. Because a stable family life is of fundamental importance to the community, the state has a compelling interest in denying that homosexual conduct is a valid and humane lifestyle. The high importance of the common good is expressed in sodomy laws that prohibit homosexual activity as well as laws that prohibit same-sex marriage and the adoption of children by homosexual couples.

"Law, Morality, and 'Sexual Orientation,'" *Notre Dame Law Review* 69 (1994): 1049–1057, 1063–1076. Some notes have been omitted.

Critical Reading Questions

1. What are the two components of the standard modern European position on the legal regulation of sexual conduct?
2. Why does the standard modern position reject outlawing discrimination based on sexual orientation?
3. What are the two things implied by the phrase *sexual orientation*? Which of these, according to Finnis, warrants discrimination and which does not?
4. On what grounds does Finnis oppose the adoption of laws that prohibit discrimination based on sexual orientation as a remedy for unjust discrimination against homosexuals?
5. Why did Plato, Aristotle, and Plutarch (c. A.D. 46–120) maintain that homosexual conduct is immoral?
6. What type of good, according to Saint Augustine, is the "good of marital communion"? Why does this good allow marriage of infertile heterosexual couples?
7. What is the position on the morality of extramarital sex in the Catholic encyclical *Veritatis Splendor*? How is this similar to the position of the ancient Greek philosophers?
8. According to Finnis, what are the two aspects of the "real common good" of marriage? Why can't these goods be realized in homosexual relations or in masturbation?
9. On what grounds does Finnis argue that he is not committing the naturalistic fallacy?
10. What is the difference between behavior that is merely offensive and behavior that is immoral? According to Finnis, what is it about homosexual conduct that makes it immoral rather than merely offensive?
11. How, according to Finnis, does the "gay ideology" treat human sexual capacities in a way that is an active threat to the stability of marriage?
12. What does it mean to say that a community has a common good? What are the three types of common goods in an open-ended community?
13. What does Aristotle mean when he speaks of the political community "making" people good? How, according to Finnis, should this be expressed in laws regulating sexual conduct?
14. According to Finnis, why would it be damaging to the common good to decriminalize homosexuality?

I.

During the past thirty years there has emerged in Europe a standard form of legal regulation of sexual conduct. . . . The standard modern European position has two limbs. On the one hand, the state is not authorized to, and does not, make it a punishable offense for adult consenting persons to engage, in private, in immoral sexual acts (for example, homosexual acts). On the other hand, states do have the authority to discourage, say, homosexual conduct and "orientation" (i.e. overtly manifested active willingness to engage in homosexual conduct). And typically, though not universally, they do so. That is to say, they maintain various criminal and administrative laws and policies which have as part of their purpose the discouraging of such conduct. Many of these laws, regulations, and policies discriminate (i.e. distinguish) between heterosexual and homosexual conduct adversely to the latter. . . .

III.

The standard modern position is part of a politico-legal order which systematically outlaws many forms of discrimination. Thus the European Convention on Human Rights (model for several dozen constitutions enacted over the past thirty-five years by the British authorities, for nations gaining independence) provides that the protection of the rights it sets out is to be enjoyed without discrimination on any ground such as "sex, race, colour, language, religion, political or other opinion, national or social origin, association with a national minority, property, birth or other status."

But the standard modern position deliberately rejects proposals to include in such lists the item "sexual orientation." The explanation commonly given (correctly, in my opinion) is this. The phrase "sexual orientation" is radically equivocal. Particularly as used by promoters of "gay rights," the phrase ambiguously assimilates two things which the standard modern position carefully distinguishes: (I) a psychological or psychosomatic disposition inwardly orienting one *towards* homosexual activity; (II) the deliberate decision so to orient one's public *behavior* as to express or *manifest* one's active interest in and endorsement of homosexual *conduct* and/or forms of life which presumptively involve such conduct. . . .

It is in fact accepted by almost everyone, on both sides of the political debate, that the adoption of a law framed to prohibit "discrimination on grounds of sexual orientation" would require the prompt abandonment of all attempts by the political community to discourage homosexual conduct by means of educational policies, restrictions on prostitution, non-recognition of homosexual "marriages" and adoptions, and so forth. . . .

IV.

The standard modern position involves a number of explicit or implicit judgments about the proper role of law and the compelling interests of political communities, and about the evil of homosexual conduct. Can these be defended by reflective, critical, publicly intelligible and rational arguments? I believe they can. Since even the advocates of "gay rights" do not seriously assert that the state can never have any compelling interests in public mo-

rality or the moral formation of its young people or the moral environment in which parents, other educators, and young people themselves must undertake this formation, I shall in this lecture focus rather on the underlying issue which receives far too little public discussion: What is wrong with homosexual conduct? . . .

Let me begin by noticing a too little noticed fact. All three of the greatest Greek philosophers, Socrates, Plato and Aristotle, regarded homosexual *conduct* as intrinsically shameful, immoral, and indeed depraved or depraving. That is to say, all three rejected the linchpin of modern "gay" ideology and lifestyle. . . .

The same Plato who in his *Symposium* wrote a famous celebration of *romantic* and *spiritual* man-boy erotic relationships, made very clear that all forms of sexual *conduct* outside heterosexual marriage are shameful, wrongful and harmful. This is particularly evident from his treatment of the matter in his last work, the *Laws,* but is also sufficiently clear in the *Republic* and the *Phaedrus,* and even in the *Symposium* itself. . . .

The core of this argument can be clarified by comparing it with Saint Augustine's treatment of marriage in his *De Bono Coniugali.* The good of marital communion is here an instrumental good, in the service of the procreation and education of children so that the intrinsic, non-instrumental good of friendship will be promoted and realized by the propagation of the human race, and the intrinsic good of inner integration be promoted and realized by the "remedying" of the disordered desires of concupiscence.[1] Now, when considering sterile marriages, Augustine had identified a further good of marriage, the natural *societas* (companionship) of the two sexes. Had he truly integrated this into his synthesis, he would have recognized that in sterile and fertile marriages alike, the communion, companionship, *societas* and *amicitia* of the spouses—their being married—*is* the very good of marriage, and is an intrinsic, basic human good, not merely instrumental to any other good. And this communion of married life, this integral amalgamation of the lives of the two persons, has as its intrinsic elements, as essential *parts* of one and the same good, the goods and ends to which the theological tradition, following Augustine, for a long time subordinated that communion. It took a long and gradual process of development of doctrine, . . . to bring the tradition to the position that procreation and children are neither the *end* (whether primary or secondary) to which marriage is instrumental (as Augustine taught), nor instrumental to the good of the spouses (as much secular and "liberal Christian" thought supposes), but rather: Parenthood and children and family are the intrinsic fulfillment of a communion which, because it is not merely instrumental, can exist and fulfill the spouses even if procreation happens to be impossible for them.

Now if, as the recent encyclical on the foundations of morality, *Veritatis Splendor,* teaches, "the communion of persons in marriage" which is violated by every act of adultery is itself a "fundamental human good,"[2] . . . Why cannot non-marital friendship be promoted and expressed by sexual acts? Why is the attempt to express affection by orgasmic non-marital sex the pursuit of an illusion? Why did Plato and Socrates, Xenophon, Aristotle, Musonius Rufus, and Plutarch, right at the heart of their reflections on the homoerotic culture around them, make the very deliberate and careful judgment that homosexual *conduct* (and indeed all extramarital sexual gratification) is radically incapable of participating in, actualizing, the common good of friendship?

Implicit in the philosophical and common-sense rejection of extra-martial sex is the answer: The union of the reproductive organs of husband and wife really unites them biologically (and their biological reality is part of, not merely an instrument of, their *personal* reality); reproduction is one function and so, in respect of that function, the spouses are indeed one reality, and their sexual union therefore can *actualize* and allow them to *experience* their *real common good—their marriage* with the two goods, parenthood and friendship, which (leaving aside the order of grace) are the parts of its wholeness as an intelligible common good even if, independently of what the spouses will, their capacity for biological parenthood will not be fulfilled by that act of genital union. But the common good

of friends who are not and cannot be married (for example, man and man, man and boy, woman and woman) has nothing to do with their having children by each other, and their reproductive organs cannot make them a biological (and therefore personal) unit. So their sexual acts together cannot do what they may hope and imagine. Because their activation of one or even each of their reproductive organs cannot be an actualizing and experiencing of the *marital* good—as marital intercourse (intercourse between spouses in a marital way) can, even between spouses who *happen* to be sterile—it can do no more than provide each partner with an individual gratification. For want of a *common good* that could be actualized and experienced *by and in this bodily union,* that conduct involves the partners in treating their bodies as instruments to be used in the service of their consciously experiencing selves; their choice to engage in such conduct thus dis-integrates each of them precisely as acting persons. . . .

In short, sexual acts are not unitive in their significance unless they are marital (actualizing the all-level unity of marriage) and (since the common good of marriage has two aspects) they are not marital unless they have not only the generosity of acts of friendship but also the procreative significance, not necessarily of being intended to generate or capable in the circumstances of generating but at least of being, as human conduct, acts of the reproductive kind— . . .

Does this account seek to "make moral judgments based on natural facts"? Yes and no. No, in the sense that it does not seek to infer normative conclusions or theses from non-normative (natural-fact) premises. Nor does it appeal to any norm of the form "Respect natural facts or natural functions." But yes, it does apply the relevant practical reasons (especially that marriage and inner integrity are basic human goods) and moral principles (especially that one may never *intend* to destroy, damage, impede, or violate any basic human good, or prefer an illusory instantiation of a basic human good to a real instantiation of that or some other human good) to facts about the human personal organism.

VI.

. . . Now, as I have said before, "homosexual orientation," in one of the two main senses of that highly equivocal term, is precisely the deliberate willingness to promote and engage in homosexual acts—the state of mind, will, and character whose self-interpretation came to be expressed in the deplorable but helpfully revealing name "gay." So this willingness, and the whole "gay" ideology, treats human sexual capacities in a way which is deeply hostile to the self-understanding of those members of the community who are willing to commit themselves to real marriage.

Homosexual orientation in this sense is, in fact, a standing denial of the intrinsic aptness of sexual intercourse to actualize and in that sense give expression to the exclusiveness and open-ended commitment of marriage as something good in itself. All who accept that homosexual acts can be a humanly appropriate use of sexual capacities must, if consistent, regard sexual capacities, organs and acts as instruments for gratifying the individual "selves" who have them. Such an acceptance is commonly (and in my opinion rightly) judged to be an active threat to the stability of existing and future marriages; it makes nonsense, for example, of the view that adultery is per se (and not merely because it may involve deception), and in an important way, inconsistent with conjugal love. A political community which judges that the stability and protective and educative generosity of family life is of fundamental importance to that community's present and future can rightly judge that it has a compelling interest in denying that homosexual conduct—a "gay lifestyle"—is a valid, humanly acceptable choice and form of life, and in doing whatever it *properly* can, as a community with uniquely wide but still subsidiary functions, to discourage such conduct.

VII.

. . . Every community is constituted by the communication and cooperation between its members. To say that a community has a common good is simply to say that communication and cooperation have a point which the members more or less concur in understanding, valuing and pursuing. There are three types of common good which each provide the constitutive point of a distinctive type of open-ended community and directly instantiate a basic human good: (1) the affectionate mutual help and shared enjoyment of the friendship and *communio* of "real friends"; (2) the sharing of husband and wife in married life, united as complementary, bodily persons whose activities make them apt for parenthood—the *communio* of spouses and, if their marriage is fruitful, their children; (3) the *communio* of religious believers cooperating in the devotion and service called for by what they believe to be the accessible truths about the ultimate source of meaning, value and other realities, and about the ways in which human beings can be in harmony with that ultimate source. . . .

The political community—properly understood as one of the forms of collaboration needed for the sake of the basic goods identified in the first principles of natural law—is a community cooperating in the service of a common good which is instrumental, not itself basic. . . . Its proper range includes the regulation of friendships, marriage, families, and religious associations, as well as of all the many organizations and associations which are dedicated to specific goals or which, like the state itself, have only an instrumental (e.g. an economic) common good. . . . [I]ts purpose must be to carry out the *subsidiary* (i.e. helping, from the Latin *subsidium*, help) function of assisting individuals and groups to coordinate their activities for the objectives and commitments they have chosen, and to do so in ways consistent with the other aspects of the common good of this community, uniquely complex, far-reaching and demanding in its rationale, its requirements of cooperation, and its monopolization of force: the political community. . . .

When Aristotle speaks of "making" people good, he constantly uses the word *poiesis* which he has so often contrasted with *praxis* and reserved for techniques ("arts") of manipulating matter.[3] But helping citizens to choose and act in line with integral human fulfillment must involve something which goes beyond any art or technique. For only individual acting persons can by their own choices make themselves good or evil. Not that their life should or can be individualistic; their deliberating and choosing will be shaped, and helped or hindered, by the language of their culture, by their family, their friends, their associates and enemies, the customs of their communities, the laws of their polity, and by the impress of human influences of many kinds from beyond their homeland. . . . And as members of all these communities they have some responsibility to encourage their fellow-members in morally good and discourage them from morally bad conduct.

To be sure, the political community is a cooperation which undertakes the unique tasks of giving coercive protection to all individuals and lawful associations within its domain, and of securing an economic and cultural environment in which all these persons and groups can pursue their own proper good. To be sure, this common good of the political community makes it far more than a mere arrangement for "preventing mutual injury and exchanging goods." But it is one thing to maintain, as reason requires, that the political community's rationale requires that its public managing structure, the state, should deliberately and publicly identify, encourage, facilitate and support the truly worthwhile (including moral virtue), should deliberately and publicly identify, discourage and hinder the harmful and evil, and should, by its criminal prohibitions and sanctions (as well as its other laws and policies), assist people with parental responsibilities to educate children and young people in virtue

and to discourage their vices. It is another thing to maintain that that rationale requires or authorizes the state to direct people to virtue and deter them from vice by making even secret and truly consensual adult acts of vice a punishable offence against the state's laws.

So there was a sound and important distinction of principle which the Supreme Court of the United States overlooked in moving from *Griswold v. Connecticut* (private use of contraceptives by *spouses*) to *Eisenstadt v. Baird* (*public distribution* of contraceptives to *unmarried* people). The truth and relevance of that distinction, and its high importance for the common good, would be overlooked again if laws criminalizing private acts of sodomy between adults were to be struck down by the Court on any ground which would also constitutionally require the law to tolerate the advertising or marketing of homosexual services, the maintenance of places of resort for homosexual activity, or the promotion of homosexualist "lifestyles" via education and public media of communication, or to recognize homosexual "marriages" or permit the adoption of children by homosexually active people, and so forth.

NOTES

1. St. Augustine, *De Bono Coniugali,* 9.9.
2. John Paul II, *Veritatis Splendor* ¶¶ 13, 48 (1984); *see also id.* at ¶¶, 50, 67, 78, 79.
3. *E.g.* Aristotle, *Nicomachean Ethics,* VI, 5: 1140a2; Aristotle, *Politics,* 1, 2. 1254a5.

Discussion Questions

1. Do you agree with Finnis that the common good and the promotion of virtue in the citizenry require outlawing homosexual activity? Would decriminalizing homosexuality be tantamount to the government promoting a homosexual lifestyle, as Finnis claims? Would decriminalizing homosexuality, in fact, lead to the deterioration of marriage and society, as Finnis claims? How might Aristotle and Confucius respond to these questions? How might Ruse respond to Finnis's concerns? Support your answers.
2. Does Finnis consider homosexuality a disease? Support your answer. What would Finnis's position most likely be on the use of conversion therapy to change sexual orientation?

3. In 1958, shortly after Mildred "Stringbean" Jetter and Richard Loving returned home to Virginia after their Washington, D.C., wedding, they were awakened by a sheriff flashing a light in their eyes. By living together as husband and wife, they violated the state's segregation laws. The subsequent prosecution of the interracial couple ended in 1967 when the U.S. Supreme Court ruled in *Loving v. Virginia* that Virginia's segregation law violated the equal protection clause of the Constitution. "There can be no doubt that restricting the freedom to marry solely because of racial classifications violates the central meaning of the equal protection clause . . . marriage is one of the 'basic civil rights of man,' fundamental to our very existence and survival." Is this case parallel to the current same-sex marriage? Are people like Finnis, who cite the common good and social stability in their opposition to same-sex marriage, simply betraying a cultural prejudice? Support your answers. Discuss how Finnis would respond to these questions.

4. The formula "Love the sinner, hate the sin" is often promoted by churches regarding homosexuality. Parents, clergy, and others should love the homosexual person while discouraging homosexual acts. Is this approach consistent with Finnis's position on homosexuality? Discuss the morality of this approach. Can we separate the person from the behavior? Is this approach demeaning to homosexuals or an assault on their integrity? Support your answers.

5. Forty percent of Americans believe that homosexuals should not be hired as clergy or as elementary school teachers.[46] Discuss whether Finnis's arguments support a public policy prohibiting homosexuals from entering these professions. Would it make a difference to Finnis if they were not "active" homosexuals? Support your answer. Discuss how Ruse might respond to this prohibition. Which person do you think presents the strongest argument? Support your answer.

6. Would Finnis approve of the current U.S. military policy on homosexuals? Support your answer.

7. In 1994 Finnis was invited to speak at Harvard; not everyone was glad to see him, however. His speech was interrupted by a group of gay-rights advocates who lowered a movie screen behind the podium. Across the screen in large letters was the word *HOMOPHOBE*. Scott Wiener, the student who led the protest, explained that Finnis was a "hate monger" because of his antihomosexual position. Inviting Finnis to campus, he maintained, was similar to inviting a Nazi or Grand Wizard of the Ku Klux Klan. If homophobia is to be stamped out and gay liberation is to become a reality, people such as Finnis must be silenced.[47] Do you agree with Wiener? How would you have responded had you been at the Finnis talk? Support your answers.

MICHAEL NAVA AND ROBERT DAWIDOFF

The Case for Gay Marriage

Michael Nava is a San Francisco lawyer and well-known novelist. Robert Dawidoff is a professor of history at the Claremont Graduate University in Claremont, California. Nava and Dawidoff argue that gay and lesbian couples should have the right to marry. Marriage as a legal and social institution is important to the goals of homosexual couples as well as heterosexual couples. Furthermore, prohibiting same-sex marriage harms not only gay and lesbian couples who wish to marry, but also impedes progress toward sexual equality.

Critical Reading Questions

1. What is the traditional American understanding of marriage? Why is marriage so important in our society?
2. What are some of the government-sponsored incentives that make marriage desirable?
3. Why do gays and lesbians want the right to marry? What are some of the consequences of denying them that right?
4. How do Nava and Dawidoff respond to the objection regarding gays' and lesbians' "inability" to form permanent attachments?
5. What is the significance, for arguments regarding gay and lesbian marriage, of studies showing that extended cohabitation before marriage increases the likelihood of divorce?
6. What evidence do Nava and Dawidoff use to support their argument that same-sex relationships play an important role in promoting "more equal relations between the sexes"?
7. What is the legal argument against gay and lesbian marriage? On what grounds do Nava and Dawidoff reject this argument?
8. How do Nava and Dawidoff respond to the argument that the chief purpose of marriage is procreation? What evidence do they offer for their argument that gays and lesbians make good parents? According to them, why would allowing same-sex marriage be an advantage to the children of these parents?
9. How do Nava and Dawidoff respond to the argument that allowing gays and lesbians to marry would encourage homosexuality and illegal sexual activity?
10. What is the purpose, according to Nava and Dawidoff, of outlawing homosexual activities?
11. According to Nava and Dawidoff, what are the ultimate goals of gays and lesbians? Why is marriage integral to these goals?
12. According to Nava and Dawidoff, who besides homosexuals is harmed by current laws outlawing same-sex marriage?

"The Case for Gay Marriage" in *Created Equal: Why Gay Rights Matter to America* (New York: St. Martin's Press, 1994), 144–157. Some notes have been omitted.

. . . Marriage is how society recognizes the intimate and lasting bond between two people and, in turn, it has become the cornerstone of the American family. Curiously, the American family as we know it is not "traditional" but innovative. Instead of inherited property or bloodlines or unquestioned patriarchal authority, the American family early on developed the view of marriage as a partnership between two consenting adults, not an agreement on their account by their parents or families. The churches that bless the marriage sacrament took their cue from secular, individualist America and, in general, endorse marriage as something entered into by the participants, if they are of age to contract, because they choose to make that commitment.

In the United States marriage is understood to be the decision of two people to live together and be a partnership, a unit, a family. Neither family nor church participates in the legal ceremony, and the religious wedding acquires legal force by the power vested in the officiant by the civil society; the religious ceremony confirms the civil arrangement. Marriage is not conditioned on the intention or the capacity to have children. Nothing in marriage, except custom, mandates partners of different genders. For example, John Boswell notes that in ancient Rome "marriages between males and between females were legal and familiar among the upper classes."[1] The institution of marriage in our society appears to be one that encourages monogamy as the basis for stable personal lives and as one aspect of the family. If we think about what marriage is for, it becomes clear that it is for people to find ways to live ordered, shared lives; it is intended to be the stablest possible unit of family life and a stable structure of intimacy.

Marriage is part of the formal and informal network of extended family, kinship, and friendship, and it is acknowledged in law as society's preferred way for consenting adults to connect their lives. Society recognizes that people have the right and the desire to have those connections solemnized according to their own beliefs; thus, religious ceremonies of all sorts, established or homemade, are encouraged as adjuncts to the civil bond. But it is the civil bond that the law acknowledges and that society encourages in all sorts of ways. No wonder many gay and lesbian Americans see marriage as their equal right. Marriage is society's way of making things easier and better for people who want to form permanent relationships, share their lives and property, and form families.

Marriage is not mere form. Society recognizes its importance not only rhetorically but with such benefits as preferential tax treatment, spousal Social Security and veteran's benefits, favorable immigration laws, property and support rights upon divorce, and intestate succession. In addition, according to Alissa Friedman, "both state and federal governments allocate a great many rights on the basis of marital status and have created powerful incentives for an individual to marry. Furthermore, private entities like insurance companies often provide special benefits and lower rates for married couples and legally recognized couples. Restrictions on the right to marry, therefore, affect both associational rights and a variety of societal entitlements."[2] . . .

Gays and lesbians want the right to marry for the same reasons other Americans do: to gain the moral, legal, social, and spiritual benefits conferred on the marrying couple and especially on their family unit. The material benefits of marriage are considerable, but it is the moral benefit that is especially attractive to many couples, including gay and lesbian ones. Marriage is, or can be, a moral commitment that two people make to one another. The marriage vow enshrines love, honor, respect, and mutual support and gives people access to resources and community acknowledgment that serve to strengthen their bond. Brought up and socialized as most Americans are, gays and lesbians also regard the prospect of marriage as reverently and respectfully as heterosexuals do. To mock and deny them is ultimately to mock and deny the institution of marriage. The impulse to marry, among gays, is essentially the same as it is among heterosexuals, and the capacity to do it well is probably the same. The only real difference is in the identity of the people who want to get married.

What is drastically different, of course, is that gay and lesbian unions get none of the support, encouragement, and benefits society regularly gives to heterosexual unions, however ill-advised. Instead, gays and lesbians are reviled for their "inability" to form permanent attachments. Of course, relationships between people that have to remain clandestine or have no foundation in law or social convention are just that much harder to maintain. Gay relationships can succeed, but always against heavy odds, odds not of the participants' making; heterosexual marriages fail all too often in spite of every conceivable social, familial, legal, and moral support.

The journal *Demography* recently published the results of a twenty-three-year study of the relationship of cohabitation to marriage; they suggest "the possibility that cohabitation weakens commitment to marriage as an institution." The authors of the study concluded that living together before marriage may not strengthen marriage; on the contrary, living together before marriage commonly produces "attitudes and values which increase the probability of divorce."[3] . . . If, as the *Demography* study indicates, marriage is a key ingredient in the longevity and solidity of intimate relationships, then denial of that most important advantage to one class of citizens on account of sexual orientation is cruelly unfair.

One of the ironies of our situation is that the American marriage that is so celebrated actually borrows from the historical character of gay relationships to describe itself. Far from being unnatural, gay and lesbian ways of living have played important roles in every human society. One almost universal function of those relationships has been to pioneer the more equal relations between the sexes. Long-standing relationships between men and between women are well known to history. Antiquity celebrated the bonds of friendship and loyalty between men, bonds that scholars tell us commonly included the sexual. The relationships among Greek soldiers and philosophers, which have played so critical a role in the traditional Western understanding of noble human relations (including the cohesion of the military unit), were modeled on love between men that regularly included sex.

The lifelong partnerships between middle-class or upper-class women in American history—the famous "Boston marriages"—also influenced decisively the understanding of marriage that American women derived from their colleges and their genteel upbringings. Female friendships played a critical role in the creation of the American institution of marriage as a partnership within which the woman was not owned but respected, not a human beast of burden and procreation but an equal source of authority and values for the family that marriage creates. . . .

The distinctive quality of modern American marriage and family is the equal and respectful relations between husband and wife as partners, friends, and co-parents, in the place of the economic, procreative, and kinship unit of traditional societies. Men and women are learning to treat one another as they more habitually treat favored members of their own gender—with confidence, trust, equality, respect, and sensitivity. Gays and lesbians are as capable of forming such relationships and making them work as heterosexual men and women are. . . .

Two main obstacles appear to gay marriage: legal definitions of marriage and the claim that marriage is chiefly for procreation or child-rearing. The legal argument boils down to the following: Marriage is a union of man and woman because it's always been that way. The civil law that governs marriage has its roots in ecclesiastical law, which reflects the biblical proscription of homosexuality. The statutes say that marriage is the union of man and woman, so that is what marriage must be. . . .

Even if we accept parenting as one important reason for the institution of marriage, shifting the model of marriage to include common if untraditional parenting units makes sense. Whatever was the case in the past, it is now common for gays and lesbians to be parents, not just to have fathered or borne children in heterosexual unions, but to be raising children as open gays and lesbians. In a survey of gay couples, Mary Mendola looked at gays and lesbians involved in a "gay marriage relationship," as she put it. She found that a quarter of the women and 17 percent of the men reported that they or their partners had children. Nearly 60 percent of the women reported that their children lived with them and their partners most of the time, while 39 percent reported that their children regularly visited. While only 3 percent of the men reported that their children lived with them and their partners, 53 percent reported that their children regularly visited them.[4] Mendola's report is a dozen years old; if anything the numbers have probably increased as more gays and lesbians are producing children by using artificial insemination (the so-called gayby boom) or adopting them or winning custody of them. If society is serious in its claim that marriage produces the best environment for raising children, then marriage must be extended to gays and lesbians who, in increasing numbers, are becoming parents.

Moreover, the studies available on gay parenting demonstrate that gays and lesbians make good parents; the children of gay families appear to do as well as the children of heterosexual ones. If, as it is sometimes argued, these children face difficulties among their peers because of negative attitudes toward homosexuality, the clear solution is to change those attitudes through education. Allowing same-sex marriage would be an important part of that change and would also promote family stability. If, in fact, that kind of stability is one of the reasons that marriage exists, it makes no sense to promote it in some families but not others by restricting marriage to heterosexuals.

Opponents of gay marriage finally arrive at the bedrock of their argument when they assert that allowing gays and lesbians to marry would encourage illegal sexual activity in the face of sodomy laws. . . . [This] implies a moral judgment against that activity (even in places where there are no sodomy laws), then allowing gays and lesbians to marry is contrary to acceptable morality. Of course, the whole point of gay and lesbian activism is to expose the underlying premise of immorality for the bigotry it is. Making an act illegal doesn't mean the act is inherently criminal. . . .

The quarter century of gay and lesbian political activism and openness has not resulted in a dramatic increase in the homosexual population (although it has dramatically increased the awareness of homosexuality and has also increased the numbers of lesbians and gays living openly). This points to the conclusion that this population is relatively stable and will always be a minority. Thus, punitive laws accomplish nothing but to intimidate a class of American citizens and deny them their constitutional rights. Denying gay and lesbian marriage will not eliminate gay and lesbian relationships; it will just make those relationships harder to sustain. If creating unnecessary suffering in the cause of popular prejudice is a permissible goal of legislation, then not only gay Americans are in for a bad time of it. . . .

Far from harming heterosexuals, gay marriage would give family-inclined gay men and lesbians the chance to fulfill this aspiration in conformity with their own natures. The legitimacy of gay marriage would save lives by creating the kind of respect for gays and lesbians that will work as a counterweight to bigotry and bashing. . . .

WHAT WE WANT

What do gays and lesbians want? What does any person want? Enough to live; basic protections; love, family, freedom. Beyond the basics, in the case of gays and lesbians, would be equal protection of the law, representation along with taxation. And what lies beyond that, it is the individual's place to say. We do not think there is a shared agenda among gays and lesbians that goes much beyond equality and freedom. But there are some other things that we imagine as human counterparts to legal protections.

It would be wonderful if families could see in their children the full range of the affectional possibilities that life in fact holds out. If girlish boys and boyish girls, who do not constitute the full range of homosexuality but who are often the ones targeted, could receive encouragement and praise and the love they deserve instead of derision, intimidation, and disappointment, their lives would be much improved. And it would improve the quality of the culture if these children could grow into adults who, because they were loved and valued, made rich contributions to the culture instead of expending that energy on overcoming the wounds that were inflicted on them.

It would also be wonderful if friends and colleagues of gay people would be as interested in their lives as they are in their company and counsel, if the walls came down and revealed each other's essential humanity. And it would be wonderful to see gay and lesbian judges, mayors, kindergarten teachers, construction workers, actors, fathers, brothers, mothers, sisters, musicians and clerics, all of them acknowledged and honored. In this utopia, little would appear changed, but there would be an addition rather than a diminution of freedom and well-being. . . .

NOTES

1. John Boswell, *Christianity, Social Tolerance and Homosexuality* (Chicago: University of Chicago Press, 1980), p. 82.

2. Alissa Friedman, "The Necessity for State Recognition of Same-Sex Marriage: Constitutional Requirements and Evolving Notions of Family," 3 *Berkeley Women's Law Journal* (1988), pp. 134–70.

3. William G. Axinn and Arland Thorton, "The Relationship Between Cohabitation and Divorce: Selectivity or Casual Influence?" *Demography* 29 (August 1992) 3:357, 361.

4. Mary Mendola, *The Mendola Report: A New Look at Gay Couples* (1980), p. 254.

Discussion Questions

1. Discuss how Finnis would most likely respond to Nava and Dawidoff's arguments for same-sex marriage.

2. Discuss whether natural rights ethicist John Locke would be more likely to agree with Finnis or with Nava and Dawidoff regarding the right of homosexuals to marry.

3. Former U.S. Secretary of Education William Bennett opposes same-sex marriage on the grounds that "broadening the definition of marriage to include same-sex unions would stretch it almost beyond recognition—and new attempts to expand the definition still further would surely follow."[48] Would legalizing same-sex marriage put us on the slippery slope to condoning incestuous marriages between a parent and child or between siblings, as Bennett claims? Can we, or ought we, draw a moral distinction between excluding people with a same-sex orientation from marriage and excluding people with a "same-family" orientation? Should consenting adults be able to marry whomever they want? Support your answers. Discuss how Nava and Dawidoff might respond to Bennett's argument.

4. Representative Bob Barr, the chief sponsor of the Defense of Marriage Act, stated that "America is not ready to change its definition of marriage."[49] Senator Phil Gramm of Texas agrees; he asks, "Are we so wise today that we are ready to reject five thousand years of recorded history? I don't think so."[50] Are these good reasons for supporting the bill, or are they based on fallacious reasoning? How should legislation on moral issues be decided if not by majority rule? Discuss your answers in light of John Stuart Mill's claim that one of the dangers of democracy is "tyranny of the majority."

5. William Bennett argues that marriage is not a blanket right. We do not, for example, allow polygamous, incestuous, or group marriage in the United States. Furthermore, heterosexual marriage is a right because it is the condition of the continuation of society. Discuss how Nava and Dawidoff would respond to Bennett's concerns. Who makes the best argument—Bennett, or Nava and Dawidoff? Support your answers.

MARGARET O'BRIEN STEINFELS

Marriage's True Ends

Margaret O'Brien Steinfels is editor of *Commonweal.* In her editorial, Steinfels addresses some of the moral and social issues raised by legalizing same-sex marriages. She concludes that legalizing same-sex marriage would erode the true ends of marriage primarily because it would weaken the traditional linkage in marriage between sexual love and procreation.

Critical Reading Questions

1. According to Steinfels, what are the two fundamental moral concerns at stake in deciding whether same-sex marriages should be legal?
2. Which of these two concerns is emphasized in contemporary society and what effect has this emphasis had on the traditional linkage between marriage and human procreation?
3. What are two of the arguments used to support same-sex marriages?
4. On what grounds does Steinfels reject the analogy between laws prohibiting same-sex marriages and miscegenation statutes?
5. Why does Steinfels think an analogy between same-sex marriage and polygamy is more fitting?
6. How does society define marriage?
7. What, according to the editorial, is marriage's true end? Why is it important to protect this ideal of marriage?
8. According to Steinfels, how would legalizing same-sex marriages contribute to the instability and trivialization of heterosexual marriage?
9. How does Steinfels respond to the argument that if we disapprove of same-sex marriages because they are nonprocreative then the state should also deny sterile and older heterosexual couples the right to marry?

There is every likelihood that Hawaii's Supreme Court will soon overturn that state's prohibition on same-sex marriage. The court's reasoning will be simple enough: Hawaii's constitution forbids discrimination on the basis of sex, and for the state to deny the benefits of marriage to same-sex couples without demonstrating a "compelling state interest" does precisely that. Should Hawaii license same-sex marriage, other states may be bound to recognize those marriages under the Full Faith and Credit clause of the Constitution. The U.S. Supreme Court, it seems certain, will eventually be asked to rule on the constitutionality of the heterosexual exclusivity of marriage.

For the state to license same-sex unions will entail a fundamental reappraisal of the nature of marriage and the balance struck between rights of individual self-determination and the integrity of basic social institutions such as the family. American society has much to gain from a fair-minded debate

Margaret O'Brien Steinfels, "Marriage's True Ends," editorial in *Commonweal,* May 17, 1996.

about such questions, and much to lose if we retreat further from reasoning together about the nature and aims of our common life.

Whether there are compelling enough reasons to preserve the heterosexual exclusivity of marriage is a question that arises in the wake of profound changes in how we think about sexual morality, procreation, and marriage. Historically, marriage forged a powerful connection between sexual love, procreation, and the care of children. However, contemporary understandings of marriage increasingly stress the primacy of individual self-fulfillment, not intergenerational attachments. Moreover, contraception and abortion have essentially severed any unwilled connection between sex and procreation. That connection has been further attenuated by technological advances allowing us to separate biological, gestational, and relational parenting at will. In this context, marriage's meaning seems anything but secure.

But is a further erosion of marriage's traditional linkage between sexual love and human procreation desirable? Advocates of same-sex marriage advance two arguments. First, denying same-sex couples the marriage rights enjoyed by heterosexual persons is discriminatory, an imposition of unjustified inequality. Second, same-sex marriage is presented as an embrace of, not an assault on, what is acknowledged to be a uniquely valuable social institution. If society wishes to promote the human goods of marriage—emotional fulfillment, lifelong commitment, the creation of families, and the care of children—marginalizing homosexuals by denying civil standing to their publicly committed relationships makes little sense, advocates argue.

In modern democratic societies wide latitude is given to individuals and groups pursuing often conflicting and incompatible conceptions of the good. Still, a broad tolerance and a high regard for individual autonomy cannot result in the equal embrace of every private interest or social arrangement. Economic freedom, for example, must be balanced against environmental concerns. Parents' rights to instill their own values in their children must accommodate the state's mandate to set educational standards for all children. The exclusive legal status of monogamous marriage, it is useful to

remember, was once challenged by Mormon polygamy. But polygamy was judged inimical to the value of individual dignity and social comity that marriage uniquely promotes.

Now we must weigh the implicit individual and social benefits of heterosexual marriage against those of same-sex unions. In this light, advocates of same-sex marriage often argue that laws prohibiting it are analogous to miscegenation statutes. But the miscegenation analogy fails. Miscegenation laws were about racial separation, not about the nature of marriage. Legalizing same-sex unions will not remedy a self-evident injustice by broadening access to the traditional goods of marriage. Rather, same-sex marriage, like polygamy, would change the very nature and social architecture of marriage in ways that may empty it of any distinctive meaning.

Recent social history can guide us here. Proponents of no-fault divorce argued that the higher meaning of marriage, and even the health of children, would be better served in making marriage easier to dissolve. Yet the plight of today's divorced women and their children refutes such claims. In fact, the loosening of marital bonds and expectations has contributed to the devaluation and even the abandonment of the marriage ideal by many, while encouraging unrealistic expectations of marriage for many more (*see* Barbara Dafoe Whitehead, p. 18).[1] How society defines marriage has a profound effect on how individuals think and act. And how individuals fashion their most intimate relationships has an enormous impact on the quality of our common life. The dynamic involved is subtle, but real.

Should marriage be essentially a contractual arrangement between two individuals to be defined as they see fit? Or does marriage recognize and embody larger shared meanings that cannot be lightly divorced from history, society, and nature—shared meanings and social forms that create the conditions in which individuals can achieve their own fulfillment? Popular acceptance of premarital sex and cohabitation gives us some sense of the moral and social trajectory involved. Both developments were welcomed as expressions of greater honesty and even better preparations for marriage. Yet considerable evidence now suggests that these newfound "freedoms" have contributed to the instability and trivialization of marriage itself, and have not borne the promises once made for them of happier lives. Similarly, elevating same-sex unions to the same moral and legal status as marriage will further throw into doubt marriage's fundamental purposes and put at risk a social practice and moral ideal vital to all.

The heterosexual exclusivity of marriage can be defended in the same way social policy rightly shows a preference for the formation of intact two-parent families. In both cases, a normative definition of family life is indispensable to any coherent and effective public action. Certainly, mutual love and care are to be encouraged wherever possible. But the justification and rationale for marriage as a social institution cannot rest on the goods of companionship alone. Resisting such a reductionist understanding is not merely in the interests of heterosexuals. There are profound social goods at stake in holding together the biological, relational, and procreative dimensions of human love.

"There are countless ways to 'have' a child," writes theologian Gilbert Meilaender of the social consequences and human meaning of procreation (*Body, Soul, & Bioethics,* University of Notre Dame Press, 1996). "Not all of them amount to doing the same thing. Not all of them will teach us to discern the equal humanity of the child as one who is not our product but, rather, the natural development of shared love, like to us in dignity. . . . To conceive, bear, give birth to, and rear a child ought to be an affirmation and a recognition: affirmation of the good of life that we ourselves were given; recognition that this life bears its own creative power to which we should be faithful."

Is there really any doubt that in tying sexual attraction to love and love to children and the creation of families, marriage fundamentally shapes our ideas of human dignity and the nature of society? Same-sex marriage, whatever its virtues, would narrow that frame and foreshorten our perspective. Marriage, at its best, tutors us as no other experience can in the given nature of human life and the acceptance of responsibilities we have not willed or chosen. Indeed, it should tutor us in respect for the given nature of homosexuality and the dignity of homosexual persons. With this respect comes a recognition of difference—a difference with real consequences.

Still, it is frequently objected that if the state does not deny sterile or older heterosexual couples the right to marry, how can it deny that right to homosexual couples, many of whom are already rearing children?

Exceptions do not invalidate a norm or the necessity of norms. How some individuals make use of marriage, either volitionally or as the result of some incapacity, does not determine the purpose of that institution. In that context, heterosexual sterility does not contradict the meaning of marriage in the way same-sex unions would. If marriage as a social form is first a procreative bond in the sense that Meilaender outlines, then marriage necessarily presupposes sexual differentiation, for human procreation itself presupposes sexual differentiation. We are all the offspring of a man and a woman, and marriage is the necessary moral and social response to that natural human condition. Consequently, sexual differentiation, even in the absence of the capacity to procreate, conforms to marriage's larger design in a way same-sex unions cannot. For this reason sexual differentiation is marriage's defining boundary, for it is the precondition of marriage's true ends.

NOTES

1. Whitehead, Barbara Dafoe, "The Abolition of Marriage: How We Lost the Right to a Lasting Love," *Commonweal* (May 17, 1996), vol. 123, no. 10, p. 18.

Discussion Questions

1. Discuss how Nava and Dawidoff would most likely respond to Steinfels's editorial. Which argument, in your view, is the strongest and why?

2. Which moral theories is Steinfels using to support her position? Discuss whether or not she does an adequate job in taking into account the different moral principles and concerns relating to the question of same-sex marriages.

3. A few states, such as Vermont, while prohibiting same-sex marriages, allow homosexual couples to enter into a civil union. Discuss what Steinfels would most likely think about the morality of granting homosexual couples the legal right to enter into a civil union. Does it overcome her objections to allowing homosexual couples to marry? Support your answer.

 CHESHIRE CALHOUN

Family's Outlaws: Rethinking the Connections Between Feminism, Lesbianism, and the Family

Cheshire Calhoun is an associate professor of philosophy and the director of women's studies at Colby College in Maine. Whereas many gay and lesbian activists, including Michael Nava and Robert Dawidoff, enthusiastically support same-sex marriage, others such as Calhoun have reservations about marriage itself and buying into "heterosexual norms."[51] Calhoun questions the assumption that marriage is a desirable social institution that should be extended to gay and lesbian couples. She points out that feminists have often raised concerns over the oppressive nature of heterosexual marriage. Instead, lesbians need to be aware of the problems with marriage before attempting to re-create traditional marriage and parenting practices among same-sex partners.

Critical Reading Questions

1. What arguments do feminists, offer for the claim that marriage is "a primary site of women's subordination to and dependence on men"?

2. According to Calhoun, why are lesbians uniquely positioned to avoid the problems of the traditional heterosexual family?

3. Why does Calhoun reject liberal efforts to redefine gay and lesbian families as functionally equivalent to heterosexual families?

4. How does lesbian motherhood differ from conventional heterosexual motherhood?

5. On what grounds does Calhoun argue that same-sex marriage does not necessarily revolutionize the traditional oppressive gender structure of marriage?

6. How does Calhoun respond to the argument that gay and lesbian couples lack access to benefits, such as medical insurance, enjoyed by married heterosexual couples?

"Family's Outlaws: Rethinking the Connections Between Feminism, Lesbianism, and the Family" in *Feminism and Families,* ed. by Hilde Lindemann Nelson (New York: Routledge, 1997), 131–150. Some notes have been omitted.

7. According to Calhoun, what are some of the differences between lesbian and hetero-sexual relationships, and how would extending marriage to same-sex couples, tend to diminish these differences?
8. Why, according to Calhoun, should lesbians resist buying into the traditional model of marriage?
9. How should lesbians and gays respond to laws that deny them the same privileges as heterosexuals?
10. What does Calhoun mean when she refers to lesbians and gays as "familial outlaws"?
11. What does the term *queer family* mean? Why does Calhoun claim that this term is op-pressive to gays and lesbians? What does she mean when she says that gay and les-bian families are "real families"?

How should we understand lesbians' relation to the family, marriage, and mothering? Part of what makes this a difficult question to answer from a feminist standpoint is that feminism has under-theorized lesbian and gay oppression as an axis of oppression distinct from gender oppression. As a re-sult, lesbians' *difference* from heterosexual women is often not visible—even oddly enough, within ex-plicitly lesbian-feminist thought. . . .

My aim is to suggest that lesbians' distinctive relation to the family, marriage, and mothering is better captured by attending to the social construc-tion of lesbians as familial outlaws than by attending exclusively to the gender structure of family, mar-riage, and mothering.

FEMINISM AND THE FAMILY

Feminist depictions and analyses of the family, marriage, and mothering have been driven by a deep awareness that the family centered around marriage, procreation, and child-rearing has his-torically been and continues to be a primary site of women's subordination to and dependence on men, and by an awareness that the gender ideology that rationalizes women's subordinate status is heav-ily shaped by assumptions about women's natural place within the family as domestic caretakers, as reproductive beings, and as naturally fit for moth-ering. It has been the task and success of feminism to document the dangers posed to women by fam-ily, marriage, and mothering in both their lived and ideological forms.

The ideology of the loving family often masks gender injustice within the family, including battery, rape, and child abuse. Women continue to shoul-der primary responsibility for both child-rearing and domestic labor; and they continue to choose occupations compatible with child care, occupa-tions which are often less well paid, more replace-able, and less likely to offer benefits and career-track mobility. The expectation that women within families are first and foremost wives and mothers continues to offer employers a rationale for pay-ing women less. Women's lower wages in the public workforce in turn make it appear economically rational within marriages for women to invest in developing their husband's career assets. . . . Wom-en's custody of children after divorce, their lower earning potential, the unavailability of low-cost child care, the absence of adequate social support for single mothers, and, often, fathers' failure to pay full child support combine to reduce divorced women's economic position even further, resulting in the feminization of poverty. The ideology of the normal family as the self-sufficient, two-earner, nu-clear family is then mobilized to blame single moth-ers for their poverty, to justify supervisory and psy-chological intervention into those families, and to rationalize reducing social support for them.

This picture, although generally taken as a pic-ture of women's relation to the family, marriage, and mothering, is not, in fact, a picture of *women's* relation to the family, but is more narrowly a picture of *heterosexual* women's relation to the family, marriage, and mothering. . . . Thus it fails to grasp lesbians' relation to the family.

LESBIAN FEMINISM, THE FAMILY, MOTHERING, AND MARRIAGE

In understanding what lesbians' relation to the family, motherhood, and marriage is and ought to be, lesbian feminists took as their point of departure feminist critiques of heterosexual women's experience of family, motherhood, and marriage. Lesbian feminists were particularly alive to the fact that lesbians are uniquely positioned to evade the ills of the heterosexual, male-dominated family. In particular, they are uniquely positioned to violate the conventional gender expectation that they, as women, would be dependent on men in their personal relations, would fulfill the maternal imperative, would service a husband and children, and would accept confinement to the private sphere of domesticity. Because of their unique position, lesbians could hope to be in the vanguard of the feminist rebellion against the patriarchal family, marriage, and institution of motherhood.

Family. . . . Lesbian-feminist interpretation of lesbians' relation to the family as nonparticipation in *heterosexual,* male-dominated, private families is then translated into nonparticipation in *any* form of family, including lesbian families. In a 1994 essay, for instance, Ruthann Robson argues against recent liberal legal efforts to redefine the family to include lesbian and gay families that are functionally equivalent to heterosexual ones. She argues that, in advocating legal recognition of lesbian families, "we have forgotten the lesbian generated critiques of family as oppressive and often deadly."[1] In particular we have forgotten critiques of the family as an institution of the patriarchal state, of marriage as slavery, and of wives as property within marriage. In her view, the category "family" should be abolished.

Motherhood. Feminist critiques of heterosexual women's experience also supplied the point of departure for lesbian-feminist critiques of lesbian motherhood. Lesbian motherhood, on this view, represents a concession to a key element of women's subordination—compulsory motherhood. By refusing to have children, or by giving up custody of their children at divorce, lesbians can refuse to participate in compulsory motherhood. They can thus refuse to accept the myth "that only family and children provide [women] with a purpose and place, bestow upon us honor, respect, love, and comfort."[2] Purpose and place is better found in political activities in a more public community of women. Lesbian feminists thus challenge lesbians contemplating motherhood to reflect more critically on their reasons for doing so and on the political consequences of participating in the present lesbian baby boom. . . .

Marriage. Like lesbian motherhood, lesbian (and gay) marriage seems antithetical to the lesbian-feminist goal of radically challenging conventional gender, sexual, and familial arrangements. Historically, the institution of marriage has been oppressively gender-structured. The historical and cross-cultural record of same-sex marriages does not support the claim that same-sex marriages will revolutionize the gender structure of marriage. On the contrary, same-sex marriages that have been legitimized in other cultures—for instance, African woman-marriage, Native American marriages between a berdache and a same-sex partner, and nineteenth-century Chinese marriages between women—have all been highly gender-structured. Thus there is no reason to believe that "'gender dissent' is inherent in marriage between two men or two women."[3]

Moreover, the attempt to secure legal recognition for lesbian and gay marriages is highly likely to work against efforts to critique the institution of marriage. In particular, by attempting to have specifically *marital* relationships recognized, advocates of marriage rights help to reinforce the assumption that long-term, monogamous relationships are more valuable than any other kind of relationship. As a result, the marriage rights campaign, if successful, will end up privileging those lesbian and gay relationships that most closely approximate the heterosexual norm over more deviant relationships that require a radical rethinking of the nature of families.

Finally, arguments for lesbian and gay marriage rights on the grounds that lesbians and gays lack privileges that heterosexual couples enjoy—such as access to a spouse's health insurance benefits—are insufficiently radical. Distributing basic benefits like health insurance through the middle-class family neglects the interests of poor and some working-class families as well as single individuals in having access to basic social benefits. If access to such benefits is the issue, then universal health insurance, not marriage, is what we should be advocating.

LESBIAN DISAPPEARANCE

The difficulty with the lesbian-feminist viewpoint is that it is one from which lesbian difference from heterosexual women persistently disappears from view.

First, the value of the family and marriage for *lesbians* is judged largely by evaluating the *heterosexual* nuclear family's effects on *heterosexual* women. Lesbians are to resist family and marriage because the family centered around the heterosexual married couple has been gender structured in a way that made marriage a form of slavery where heterosexual women could be treated as property and their labor appropriated by men. But to make this a principal reason for lesbians' not forming families and marriages of their own is to lose sight of the difference between lesbians and heterosexual women. Lesbian families and marriages are not reasonably construed as sites where women can be treated as property and where their productive and reproductive labor can be appropriated by men. It thus does not follow from the fact that heterosexual marriage and family has been oppressive for heterosexual women and a primary structure of patriarchy that *any* form of marriage or family, including lesbian ones, is oppressive for women and a primary structure of patriarchy. . . .

Both lesbians and heterosexual women have reason to resist the construction of mothering as an unpaid, socially unsupported task. Both have reason to reject women's confinement to the domestic sphere and reason to value participation in politically oriented communities of women. Both have

reason to resist their gender socialization into the myth of feminine fulfillment through mothering and to assert their deviance from the category of "woman." Both can have justice interests in objecting to a social and legal system that privileges long-term, monogamous relationships over all other forms of relationship and that does not provide universal access to basic benefits like health insurance. All of these are broadly feminist concerns. As a result, the lesbian-feminist perspective does not articulate any distinctively *lesbian* political tasks in relation to the family, marriage, and mothering. Instead, lesbians are submerged in the larger category "feminist."

Finally, the political relation between heterosexuals and nonheterosexuals and the ideologies of sexuality that support the oppression of lesbians and gays simply do not inform the lesbian-feminist analysis of lesbians' relation to the family, marriage, or mothering. What governs the lesbian-feminist perspective is above all the political relations between men and women, and to a lesser extent class relations and the political relations between those in normative long-term, monogamous relations (whether heterosexual or nonheterosexual) and all other human relations. As a result, the radicalness of lesbian and gay family, marriage, and parenting is measured on a scale that looks only at their power (or impotence) to transform gender relations, the privileging of long-term, monogamous relations, and class privilege. Not surprisingly, lesbian and gay families, marriages, and parenting fail to measure up. But this ignores the historical construction of lesbians and gays as outlaws to the natural family, as constitutionally incapable of more than merely sexual relationships, and as dangerous to children.

Within gender ideology, for instance, lesbians have not been and are not constructed as beings whose natural place is within the family as domestic caretakers, as reproductive beings, and as naturally fit mothers. On the contrary, the gender ideology that rationalizes the oppression of both lesbians and gays consists in part precisely in the assumption that both are aliens to the natural family, nonprocreative, incapable of enduring intimate ties, dangerous to children, and ruled by sexual instincts to the exclusion of parenting ones. . . .

Lesbians and gays are, for instance, denied the legal privileges and protections that heterosexuals enjoy with respect to their natural and familial relations. Among the array of rights related to marriage that heterosexuals enjoy but gays and lesbians do not are the rights to legal marriage, to live with one's spouse in neighborhoods zoned "single-family only," and to secure U.S. residency through marriage to a U.S. citizen; the rights to Social Security survivor's benefits, to inherit a spouse's estate in the absence of a will, and to file a wrongful death suit; the rights to give proxy consent, to refuse to testify against one's spouse, and to file joint income taxes.

Lesbians and gays similarly lack access to the privileges and protections that heterosexuals enjoy with respect to biological, adoptive, and foster children. Sexual orientation continues to be an over-riding reason for denying custody to lesbian and gay parents who exit a heterosexual marriage. Gays and lesbians fare equally poorly with respect to adoption and foster parenting. . . .

What comes into view in this picture of the legal inequities that lesbians and gays confront is the fact that the family, marriage, and parenting are a primary site of heterosexual privilege. The family centered around marriage, procreation, and child-rearing has historically been and continues to be constructed and institutionalized as the natural domain of heterosexuals only, and thus as a domain from which lesbians and gays are outlawed. . . .

FAMILIAL OUTLAWS

A constitutive feature of lesbian and gay oppression since at least the late nineteenth century has been the reservation of the private sphere for heterosexuals only. Because lesbians and gays are ideologically constructed as beings incapable of genuine romance, marriage, or families of their own, and because those assumptions are institutionalized in the law and social practice, lesbians and gays are displaced from this private sphere.

In what follows, I want to suggest that the historical construction of gays and lesbians as familial

outlaws is integrally connected to the history of social anxiety about the failure and potential collapse of the heterosexual nuclear family. In particular, I want to suggest that in periods where there was heightened anxiety about the stability of the heterosexual nuclear family because of changes in gender, sexual, and family composition norms within the family, this anxiety was resolved by targeting a group of persons who could be ideologically constructed as outsiders to the family, identifying the behaviors that most deeply threatened the family with those outsiders, and stigmatizing that group. . . . The construction of gays and lesbians as highly stigmatized outsiders to the family and as displaying the most virulent forms of family-disrupting behavior allayed anxieties about the potential failure of the heterosexual nuclear family in three ways. First, it externalized the threat to the family. As a result, anxiety about the possibility that the family was disintegrating from *within* could be displaced onto the spectre of the hostile outsider to the family. Second, stigma threatening comparisons between misbehaving members of the heterosexual family and the dangerous behavior of gays and lesbians could be used to compel heterosexual family members' compliance with gender, sexual, and family composition norms. Thirdly, by locating the genuinely deviant, abnormal, perverse behavior outside the family, members of heterosexual families were enabled to adjust to new, liberalized norms for acceptable gender roles and sexual behavior within families as well as new, liberalized norms for acceptable family composition. They could, in essence, reassure themselves with the thought: "At least we aren't like them!" . . .

NOT FOR HETEROSEXUALS ONLY

I have argued for the existence of a historical pattern in which anxiety about the stability of the family goes hand in hand with the ideological depiction of gays and lesbians as unfit for marriage, parenting, and family. The construction of lesbians and gays as natural outlaws to the family and the masking of heterosexuals' own family-disrupting behavior results in the reservation of the private sphere for heterosexuals only.

It is because being an outlaw to the family has been so central to the social construction of lesbianism that I think lesbians' relation to the family is better captured by attention to their outlaw status than to the gender structure of marriage and motherhood (as is characteristic of lesbian feminism). Indeed, on the historical backdrop of the various images of family outlaws—the mannish lesbian, the homosexual child molester, and their pretended family relationships—lesbian-feminist resistance to lesbian and gay marriages, lesbian motherhood, and the formation of lesbian and gay families looks suspiciously like a concession to the view of lesbians and gays as family outlaws. Because being denied access to a legitimate and protected private sphere has been and continues to be central to lesbian and gay oppression, the most important scale on which to measure lesbian and gay political strategies is one that assesses their power (or impotence) to resist conceding the private sphere to heterosexuals only. On such a scale, the push for marriage rights, parental rights, and recognition as legitimate families measures up.

For similar reasons, it seems to me a mistake to make advocacy of "queer families" *the* political goal for lesbians and gays. By "queer families" I mean ones not centered around marriage or children, but composed instead of chosen, adult, supportive relationships (which would include lesbian-feminist political communities of women).

Equating gay families with queer, nonmarital, and nonparenting families concedes too much to the ideology of gays and lesbians as family outlaws, unfit for genuine marriage and dangerous to children. In addition, describing families that depart substantially from traditional family forms as distinctively gay conceals the queerness of many heterosexual families. . . . Thus claiming that gay and lesbian families are (or should be) distinctively queer and distinctively deviant helps conceal the deviancy in heterosexual families, and thereby helps to sustain the illusion that heterosexuals are specially entitled to access to a protected private sphere because they, unlike their gay and lesbian counterparts, are supporters of the family.

All this is not to say that there is no merit in lesbian feminists' concern that normalizing lesbian motherhood will reinforce the equation of "woman" with "mother." Overcoming the idea that lesbian motherhood is a contradiction in terms may very well result in lesbians' being expected to fulfill the maternal imperative just as heterosexual women are. But this is just to say that the oppression of lesbians and gays is structurally different from gender oppression. Thus, strategies designed to resist *lesbian* oppression (such as pushing for the legal right to coadopt) are not guaranteed to counter *gender* oppression (which might better be achieved by resisting motherhood altogether). In gaining access to a legitimate and protected private sphere of mothering, marriage, and family, lesbians will need to take care that it does not prove to be as constraining as the private sphere has been for heterosexual women.

Nor have I meant to claim that there is no merit in both lesbian feminists' and queer theorists' concern that normalizing lesbian and gay marriage will reinforce the distinction between good, assimilationist gays and bad gay and heterosexual others whose relationships violate familial norms (the permanently single, the polygamous, the sexually nonmonogamous, the member of a commune, and so on). Overcoming the idea that lesbian and gay marriages are merely pretended family relationships may very well result in married lesbians and gays being looked upon more favorably than those who remain outside accepted familial forms. But this is just to say that countering lesbians' and gays' family outlaw status is not the same thing as struggling to have a broad array of social relationships recognized as (equally) valuable ones. . . . [L]esbians and gays who resist their construction as family outlaws are not bidding for access to one, highly conventional family form (such as the nuclear, two-parent, self-sufficient, procreative family). They are instead bidding for access to the same privilege that heterosexuals now enjoy, namely the privilege of claiming that *in spite of their multiple deviations* from norms governing the family, their families are nevertheless *real* ones and they are themselves naturally suited for marriage, family, parenting *however* these may be defined and redefined.

NOTES

1. Ruthann Robson, "Resisting the Family: Repositioning Lesbians in Legal Theory," *Signs* 19 (1994), pp. 975–996.

2. Irena Klepfisz, "Women Without Children/ Women Without Families/Women Alone," in *Politics of the Heart: A Lesbian Parenting Anthology,* ed. Sandra Pollack and Jeanne Vaughn (New York: Firebrand Books, 1987), p. 57.

3. Nancy D. Polikoff, "We Will Get What We Ask For: Why Legalizing Gay and Lesbian Marriage Will Not 'Dismantle the Legal Structure of Gender in Every Marriage'," *Virginia Law Review* 79 (1993), 1535–1550, p. 1538.

Discussion Questions

1. Do you agree with Calhoun that lesbians should not buy into traditional models of marriage and family? Support your answer.

2. Is Calhoun's argument compatible with Nava and Dawidoff's argument for the legalization of same-sex marriage? Does her argument imply that gay and lesbian couples who want to marry should not be allow to? Support your answers. Discuss how Calhoun and Nava and Dawidoff might respond to each other's arguments.

3. Do you agree with Calhoun that families with same-sex parents are "real families"? Should gay and lesbian couples have the same opportunities as heterosexual couples to adopt children or take in foster children? Support your answers. Discuss how Finnis might respond to Calhoun's argument.

4. Discuss how Calhoun would respond to Finnis's and Steinfels' argument that homosexuality is destructive to family stability and the common good.

5. Would Calhoun most likely support or oppose the granting of civil union domestic partnership status, as opposed to actual legal marital status, to homosexual couples? Discuss how Calhoun would most likely respond to the arguments against same-sex marriage put forth in the *Commonweal* editorial. Given Calhoun's qualms about the oppressiveness of traditional marriage, discuss whether or not Calhoun should support the legalization of same-sex marriage, on utilitarian grounds, if it could be shown that this would contribute to the instability and breakdown of traditional heterosexual marriage.

6. Is marriage inherently oppressive to women? Should the social institution of marriage be dismantled? If so, what should replace marriage as the family unit and the best means for raising children? Support your answers. Discuss how Calhoun and Nava and Dawidoff might answer these questions.

CASE STUDIES

1. THE "GAY GENE"

The Human Genome Project has opened the hunting grounds for geneticists trying to flush out genes associated with different human traits. Microbiologist Dean Hamer, referred to as a "big-gene hunter" by one journalist, is especially interested in learning more about the genetic basis of personality traits such as happiness, impulsiveness, depression—and sexual preference.

Hamer's preliminary studies had revealed that half the twins of homosexual men were themselves homosexual. This suggested that male homosexuality was partly genetic. Hamer also noted that homosexuality runs through the mother's line. Therefore he concentrated his search for the "gay gene" on the X chromosome, which is inherited from the mother. In 1993 Hamer announced that he had discovered a "gay gene" in the region of the X chromosome called q28. In a similar study of lesbian twins, however, he did not find a genetic basis for female homosexuality. Hamer concluded that female homosexuality might be more social and less genetically programmed than male homosexuality. An earlier study that looked at the prevalence of homosexuality in families and twins found that more than half of the identical twins of homosexual men are homosexual, compared with 22 percent of fraternal twins.

These studies have met with mixed reactions. Some scientists reject Hamer's claim that he has identified a "gay gene," while others are pondering the possible evolutionary value of a "gay gene, since nonreproductive same-sex sexual relationships are found among other animals as well."[52] Hamer's announcement was met with opposition from gay-rights activists as well as those who were opposed to homosexual rights.

Discussion Questions

1. Traditionally, scientific research has been regarded as morally neutral, but this view is being called into question. For example, Hamer's announcement was met with disapproval by those who were opposed to homosexual rights, because they fear that society might be more accepting of homosexuality if it could be shown to have a genetic basis. On the other hand, gay-rights activists fear that genetic research may be used to advance a heterosexist agenda. Rather than the contention that it is natural for some people, homosexuality can now be labeled a genetic disorder. Discuss the merits of the different views regarding the ethics of genetic research on the "gay gene."
2. What impact does the discovery of a "gay gene" have on the argument that homosexuality is immoral because it is unnatural? How might both natural law ethicist Thomas Aquinas and natural rights ethicist John Locke respond to this question? Because female homosexuality seems to have less of a genetic component, does this mean that the debate over male and female homosexuality should be treated differently?
3. If genetic engineers are able to identify a "gay gene" should parents have the right to use genetic engineering to replace this gene with a "heterosexual gene"? Discuss your answer in light of the different models of homosexuality.

2. DOMESTIC PARTNERSHIP: AN ALTERNATIVE TO MARRIAGE?

Domestic partnership was unheard of fifteen years ago. The number of Americans living together outside of marriage has increased dramatically since the 1970s. At the same time, the number of traditional two-parent families has been declining steadily.

In 1988 in the first federal lawsuit of its type, Sandra Rovira, the surviving lesbian partner of a deceased AT&T employee, sued AT&T for refusing to pay her the same benefits it would have paid to a husband. The couple had formalized their relationship in a ceremony in 1977, bought a house, and raised Rovira's two sons together. AT&T pointed out that its benefits are for legal spouses only. In addition, AT&T argued that because the law does not recognize same-sex marriages, neither should it.

Unlike AT&T, some companies, such as the ice cream company Ben & Jerry's, offer unmarried domestic partners the same benefits that married couples receive. Several local governments, including Seattle, Washington; Berkeley, California; and Tacoma Park, Maryland, have also set up domestic partner plans. Although domestic partnership is often seen as a gay issue, in fact, the majority of couples who take advantage of the domestic partnership plans are heterosexual. This may be in part because some homosexuals do not register for benefits because they don't want their sexual orientation made public.

Discussion Questions

1. Should the definition of family and marriage be expanded to include same-sex partners? Should homosexual couples be given domestic partner status by the government? Should domestic partners, even though they are not married, be eligible for the benefits given to legal spouses? Support your answers.
2. Would domestic partner status overcome the objections of those who are opposed to same-sex marriage? Support your answer. Discuss how Finnis, Calhoun, and Steinfels might each respond to this question.
3. Do benefits plans for unmarried domestic partners hurt the family? Support your answer.
4. Does the practice in the United States of tying benefits to marital status and unemployment strengthen the family? Or does this practice perpetuate discrimination against homosexuals and women? If the latter, what alternatives would you suggest for allocation of benefits? Support your answers.

3. THE LESBIAN MOTHER

It began as a routine child-custody battle between Suzanne Borden and her ex-husband, James Borden, over their two daughters. The battle turned nasty, however, when Suzanne Borden admitted to having a lesbian affair during her marriage. Judge Roy Moore gave temporary custody of the children to Mr. Borden, arguing that "The court strongly feels that the minor children will be detrimentally affected by the present lifestyle of [Mrs. Borden], who has engaged in a homosexual relationship during her marriage forbidden both by the state of Alabama and the laws of nature."[53] Moore insists that because God prohibits homosexual relations, so will he. He maintained that her lesbian affair was harmful to the children and to God's plan for the family.

After unsuccessfully trying to get Judge Moore to dismiss himself from the case, Suzanne Border turned to an American Civil Liberties Union lawyer, Janice Hart, who appealed the case to the Alabama Court of Civil Appeals. The court agreed that Moore should be dismissed from the case. Moore appealed the decision to the Alabama Supreme Court on the grounds that he was being discriminated against for his religious beliefs. Furthermore, Moore's lawyer pointed out, he did not need to appeal to his religious beliefs to support his ruling because lesbian relations are against Alabama's sodomy laws. The fact that his religious belief concurs with the law was not a reason to dismiss him from the case.

This is not the first time a court has ruled that homosexuals could not keep their children. In a 1993 ruling in Virginia, Judge Buford Parsons revoked custody of Sharon Bottoms's two-year-old son. Bottoms was living with her female lover. Parsons ruled that Bottoms's sexual orientation made her an unfit parent. The ruling was subsequently overturned by the Virginia Court of Appeals.

Discussion Questions

1. Should Suzanne Borden get custody, or at least joint custody, of her daughters? Support your answer.
2. Does the fact that Suzanne Borden violated the law make her an unfit mother? Does it make a difference what type of law she broke? What if she was a heroin dealer or a shoplifter, for example? Support your answers.
3. Most states do not allow openly homosexual couples to adopt children or take in foster children. Should such couples be allowed to adopt children or take in foster children? Would it make a difference if the couple were openly gay or lesbian? Support your answers. Discuss how Finnis, Steinfels, and Nava and Dawidoff might respond to these questions.
4. Studies show that children raised by homosexual couples actually have fewer psychological problems than those raised by a single heterosexual mother.[54] Is this finding morally relevant? Support your answer. Discuss how Finnis might respond to this finding.

---

4. AIDS TESTING

By 1995 AIDS had surpassed injuries and accidents as the leading killer of Americans from ages 25 to 44[55] and was the sixth-leading cause of death among fifteen to twenty-four year olds.[56] The Vancouver Project, initiated in 1995 and funded by Health Canada, is a three-year study of one-thousand gay and bisexual men with the purpose of learning more about HIV-infected men. During the first year of the study, 3 percent of the men who had tested HIV-negative at the beginning contracted the virus. According to Dr. Steffanie Strathdee, despite educational programs promoting "safe sex," there had actually been an increase in the first few years of the study in participants who practice unsafe anal sex. Strathdee surmises that, like most young people, young gay males see themselves as invincible. Deaths from AIDS began to decline in 1996, primarily because of the beneficial impact of new antiretroviral therapies.[57] The highly publicized "cocktails" for prolonging the lives of those who have AIDS have convinced some gay men that AIDS is a manageable disease, much like diabetes.

Discussion Questions

1. Why hasn't the Vancouver Project been more successful in curbing the spread of AIDS? What changes in the program might a utilitarian make for achieving this goal?

Does the end—lowering the incidence of AIDS—justify the means? Support your answers.

2. A 1995 study in California found that 33 percent of gay and bisexual men engaged in unprotected anal sex and 70 percent of HIV-positive gay and bisexual men were unaware of their HIV status.[58] Several groups, including prisoners, military personal, and immigrants applying for permanent U.S. residency, are already subject to mandatory AIDS testing. Should mandatory testing be extended to all men who are gay or bisexual? Is mandatory AIDS testing of gay men justified under utilitarian analysis?

3. The Centers for Disease Control estimates that 20 percent of new AIDS infections could be averted through confidential testing and counseling linked to partner notification.[59] Do people who engage in high-risk behavior have a social responsibility to get tested and to provide the names of previous contacts should the test results be positive? If so, should they be punished if they knowingly infect another person?[60] Or do we have a right not to know our HIV status or, if we do know, not to divulge it? Support your answers.

4. Some people, such as Dr. Bernard Ravinowitz, disagree that AIDS testing should be voluntary. Ravinowitz argues that the overriding moral obligation during an epidemic is protection of the uninfected. This has not been the case with the AIDS epidemic where, Ravinowitz writes, "we had endorsed the first legally protected epidemic in medical history . . . With AIDS the right to secrecy of a tiny minority were deemed ethically more important than the right of the huge uninfected majority."[61] Do you agree with Ravinowitz? Do the "right to secrecy" and the possibility of negative social consequences, especially for men who are gay, override the "right" of the government to institute mandatory testing for AIDS? Discuss your answer in light of the Vancouver Project.

5. Federal and state governments are now paying about 40 percent of AIDS-related medical expenses, amounting to several billion dollars a year. Discuss whether financial cost provides a justification for coercing people, or at least people at high risk for AIDS, into getting tested or notifying partners.

6. The Center for Disease Control estimates that in 1990 there were 10,000 to 35,000 college students in the United States who were HIV-positive,[62] meaning they were infected with the AIDS virus. Most students who are HIV-positive are not aware of their status until the first symptoms of AIDS are diagnosed. Should HIV testing be mandatory on college campuses for all students? Should it be mandatory only for "high risk" groups, such as gay and bisexual men and intravenous drug users? Support your answers.

---

5. GAYS IN THE MILITARY: "DON'T ASK, DON'T TELL"

The U.S. policy on homosexuals in the military is captured in the 1993 statement "Don't ask, don't tell."[63] Under this policy applicants will not be asked about their sexual orientation; they can, however, be discharged for homosexual conduct.[64]

As a protest against this policy, several colleges—including Massachusetts Institute of Technology and Yale University—have demanded that the Reserve Officer Training Corps (ROTC) be banned from their campuses until the military changes its policy. It is discriminatory, they argue, to have different standards for homosexuals and for heterosexuals. In response, in February 1996, Congress passed the ROTC Campus Access Act which cut off all Department of Defense funding to campuses that banned ROTC.[65]

The Young Americans Foundation, who actively worked to get the act passed by Congress applauds this move. They claim that banning ROTC on campuses unfairly discriminates against ROTC cadets and denies students the right to participate in ROTC programs on their campuses.[66] The ban also discriminates against poorer students, because ROTC has historically assisted economically disadvantaged students in attending college.

Discussion Questions

1. Discuss the arguments for and against banning ROTC. What (and whose) rights are at stake? How might this conflict of rights be resolved? Was the ban the best way to oppose the "Don't ask, don't tell" policy? Discuss what you would have done if you were the president of MIT or Yale.

2. Is the freedom to be open about our sexual orientation essential for ensuring self-respect and a sense of dignity? Discuss how Ruse and Finnis might each respond to this question in the context of the military.

3. In *Meinhold v. U.S. Department of Defense* (1994) the Court upheld the U.S. Navy's action in discharging Keith Meinhold after he said on television, "Yes, I am gay." The court ruled that openly declaring one's homosexual orientation demonstrates "a concrete, fixed, or expressed desire to commit homosexual acts despite their being prohibited."[67] Opponents of the decision argued that it is irrational to assume that because people are open about their homosexuality they will engage in homosexual activities while in the military.[68] Do you agree? Why is it important in a moral debate that arguments be based on rational premises? Use the arguments in the *Meinhold* case to illustrate your answer.

4. Some people argue that allowing gays in the military infringes on the privacy rights of heterosexuals, especially when it comes to housing. Women are housed in separate quarters because they have a right not to have their bodies looked at in a sexual manner by men. Do heterosexual men and women, likewise, have a right not to be looked at in a sexual manner by homosexuals? Does a right to privacy necessarily preclude allowing gay people in the military?

5. Discrimination is morally justified if it is based on rational criteria. Is this the case with the ban on homosexuality in the military? Support your answer. Discuss how both Ruse and Finnis might respond to this question.

6. A 1998 article reports that male students at the U.S. Naval Academy have a strong prejudice against gays as well as women in the military.[69] They justify their exclusionary attitudes on the grounds that group loyalty is paramount in the military and that the presence of gays threatens this cohesion. Does this argument, based on social concerns, justify discrimination against gays in the military? Support your answer. Discussion how Finnis might respond to this question.

6. JAMES DALE VERSUS THE BOY SCOUTS OF AMERICA

When the Boy Scouts of America (BSA) learned from a 1990 newspaper article that assistant scoutmaster James Dale was gay, they promptly expelled him from the organization. Dale, who had been a scout since childhood and had earned the rank of Eagle Scout, the highest honor given to a scout, decided to fight back. Dale claimed that his expulsion violated a New Jersey law barring sexual orientation-based discrimination in public places. The New Jersey high court agreed, ruling that the BSA was a "public accommodation" and therefore was bound by the antidiscrimination law.

The BSA appealed the decision. Banning gays, they argued, was necessary to maintaining the scout's express message of encouraging youths to lead a "morally straight" and "clean" life. The expression of this message, they further argued, was protected under their First Amendment governing free association and freedom of speech. The United States Supreme Court, in a June 28, 2000 ruling, agreed with the Boy Scouts, ruling that banning homosexuals was consistent with the BSA's right of free expression.

Discussion Questions

1. Discuss the morality of the Supreme Court ruling. Write two paragraphs stating what your ruling would have been if you had been a) a Supreme Court justice and b) a member of a specially appointed advisory ethics committee regarding the morality of expelling homosexuals in the Boy Scouts. Compare and contrast your rulings in the two cases. If your rulings differed, what course of action would a cultural relativist and a deontologist each advise you to take?
2. Many people prefer that gays and lesbians keep their identities secret. Do you believe that people who are homosexual, such as James Dale, should keep it to themselves? What about situations in which coming out would be detrimental to a career or would harm a person in other ways as happened in Dale's case. Support your answers. Discuss the question from the perspective of a virtue ethicist.
3. Imagine a scenario in which you learn from your college newspaper that your roommate's sexual orientation is different than you have previously been led to believe. What is your reaction? Discuss the effects of your discovery on concerns such as trust.
4. Imagine that you are Dale's friend and know that he is gay. However, Dale insists on passing as straight because he doesn't want to jeopardize his position in the Scouts. You encouraged Dale to come out because he is living a lie and also because you believe it is contributing to his depression. Also, you feel he would be a positive role model to other young gay men. Does Dale have a moral duty to come out? Discuss the moral issues involved in making a decision as to whether or not to out Dale.
5. Which is most morally compelling in this case: the duty of justice or the liberty right of freedom of speech? What other duties and rights are at stake in this case? Using both prima facie deontology and rights ethics, construct an argument analyzing the case.

C H A P T E R   9

Freedom of Speech

When Seth Greenberg, coach of the California State University at Long Beach basketball team, walked into the visitors' locker room in the Pan American Center at New Mexico State University, he was confronted by the greaseboard message, "SETH, GET READY FOR AN ASS-KICKING, YOU JEW BASTARD." The outpouring of hate continued during the game, with some of the fans yelling obscenities and racial epithets such as "Take one of the niggers out." After the game, the visibly upset coach Greenberg told television interviewers that the slurs were "a sad commentary on life and . . . a sad commentary on this university." A few days later, New Mexico State University Executive Vice President Michael Conroy sent a letter to the president of Long Beach State, demanding an apology from Greenberg and castigating him for impugning the reputation of the university and the entire state of New Mexico.

Who was in the wrong? Should Greenberg have been more tolerant of the racial slurs? Should college campuses have speech codes that restrict hate speech, or should hate speech be protected under freedom of speech? The primary focus of this chapter is not whether we ought to engage in hate speech, but whether we are morally justified in restricting the hate speech of others.

WHAT IS "FREEDOM OF SPEECH"?

Freedom of speech is a type of liberty right. We have a right to express our opinions without interference from the government or other people. The primary value of freedom of speech, according to most libertarians, is the promotion of truth.

Not all forms of verbal expression, however, are considered speech. Words can also be used as weapons. Yelling "Fire!" in a crowded theater; "fighting words" intended to inflame someone into committing violent actions; and slanderous, false rumors intended to ruin the reputation and livelihood of someone are not generally protected under freedom of speech.

Freedom of speech is generally distinguished from discriminatory conduct. Libertarians argue that, although discrimination is wrong, hate speech should be protected because we have a right to express our ideas. Others, such as Charles R. Lawrence III, reject this distinction, arguing that racist speech and discriminatory conduct are part of a totality that is incompatible with equality.

There are many gray areas in the freedom-of-speech debate. Doom cults, for example, are proliferating with the dawning of a new millennium. Should cults—such as

Heaven's Gate in California and David Koresh's cult in Waco, Texas—be allowed to freely disseminate their ideas? Should they be allowed to proselytize on college campuses? The community is even more deeply divided over the moral permissibility of hate speech. *Hate speech* is defined as "epithets conventionally understood to be insulting references to characteristics such as race, gender, nationality, ethnicity, religion, and sexual preference."[1] Should hate speech, which involves treating another person as a moral inferior, be censured?

LIMITATIONS ON FREEDOM OF SPEECH

Like most liberty rights, freedom of speech is not an absolute right but is limited by the rights of others to pursue their equal and similar interests. Freedom of speech does not mean that speech is immune from any sort of regulation, but that "no expression of opinion ought to be suppressed because the opinion itself is considered to be false, heretical, harmful, or subversive."[2]

Every society places limits on speech in order to prevent violence and civil disorder as well as to protect its citizens against fraud, threats, and harassment. Without some rules of order, discussions would degrade into chaos and frustration on the part of those who cannot get a word in edgewise. The question of how far these restrictions should extend is widely debated among ethicists and policy makers.

Liberals such as Jonathan Rauch argue that the government does not have a right to protect citizens from offensive speech; freedom of speech is meaningless if it does not include the right to offend. On the other hand, censorship can occur without legal sanctions. As both Alan M. Dershowitz and John Taylor point out in their articles on political correctness, the censorship of colleagues and political opinion can be just as oppressive.

Censorship has traditionally rested on the assumption that people in authority possess the truth and are able to make final judgments about what is right and good. Democracy, with its presumption that the truth is determined by the majority, is not immune from this type of censorship. During other periods in history, censorship was based on the assumption that certain positions were self-evidently true. People who expressed doubts about these truths were labeled heretics, foolish, dangerous, or insane. The oppression of great thinkers like Galileo illustrates how censorship can hold back progress.

Censorship is a normal practice in some parts of the world, such as China, a country that emphasizes social order over individual freedom. In 1978 Wei Jingsheng, an electrician at the Beijing zoo, posted a tract on Beijing's Democracy Wall advocating democracy in China. Despite the fact that the wall was supposedly a place where Chinese citizens could express their grievances, Wei was arrested, charged with high treason, and sentenced to fifteen years in prison. After his release in 1993, he resumed his advocation of democracy and was promptly arrested again. In 1997, Wei was forced into exile where he continues to criticize the Chinese government and advocate for human rights.

The United Nations has sought to combat what it regards as human-rights violations in the international community. The Universal Declaration of Human Rights was adopted by the United Nations in 1948 following World War II as a "common standard of achievement for all peoples and all nations." Article 19 of the declaration states that "Everyone has the right to freedom of opinion and expression; this right in-cludes freedom to hold opinions without interference and to seek, receive and impart information and ideas through any media and regardless of frontiers."

THE FIRST AMENDMENT TO THE U.S. CONSTITUTION

In the United States, freedom of speech is one of the most highly valued rights.[3] The contemporary belief that the First Amendment has been the backbone of American lib-erty, however, is a recent invention. It was not until 1931 that the U.S. Supreme Court first recognized freedom of expression as a constitutional right.

Before 1789 the only right of free speech was the right to speak in the legislature. The patriots in the Amercian Revolution were no more willing to recognize freedom of speech than the British were and had no qualms about repressing speech that was not favorable to their cause. Indeed, during the American Revolution many loyalists, Quakers, and other political dissenters fled to Canada in fear of their lives.

Nor is there any indication that the Bill of Rights was intended to prevent censor-ship and regulation of speech. The original purpose of the First Amendment was to dele-gate the power to restrict freedom of speech to the states; although the federal govern-ment could not restrict speech, the state and municipal governments could.

Freedom of speech, in other words, was not regarded as an end in itself, but rather as a means of informing the citizenry and promoting democracy. The most valued type of speech was political speech. "A popular government, without popular infor-mation, or the means of acquiring it," wrote James Madison, "is but a Prologue to a Farce or a Tragedy; or perhaps both. Knowledge will forever govern Ignorance: And a people who mean to be their own governors, must arm themselves with the power which knowledge gives." Alexander Hamilton, one of the great defenders of free expression, likewise wrote, "The liberty of the press consists in the right to publish, with impunity, truth, with good motives, and for justifiable ends, whether it respects government, mag-istracy, or individuals." Utterances that abused this liberty (that is, were not made with concern for the truth, or with good motives, or with justifiable ends) could be censored.

Following the Civil War, the power of the states, including their power to regulate speech, was increasingly restricted. World War I gave rise to new concerns about speech that endangered national security. Supreme Court Justices Oliver Wendell Holmes and Louis D. Brandeis were two of the great champions of freedom of speech in the early twentieth century; they believed that freedom of speech was not an absolute value, how-ever. In 1917 Holmes wrote the unanimous opinion of the Court on the constitutional-ity of the Congressional Espionage Act. It stated that speech is not protected by the First Amendment if it is "of such a nature as to create a clear and present danger" or if it "will bring about the substantive evils that Congress has a right to protect." Fear of harm, how-ever, is not sufficient to justify restrictions on freedom of speech. In his dissent in *Abrams v. the United States* (1919) Holmes defended freedom of speech on the grounds that so-ciety's ultimate good "is better reached by free trade of ideas—that the best test of truth is the power of the thought to get itself accepted in the competition of the marketplace." Holmes's concept of the free marketplace of ideas has had a major impact on the Su-preme Court's thinking about the role of freedom of speech in a democratic society.

THE FIRST AMENDMENT TO THE UNITED STATES CONSTITUTION

Congress shall make no law respecting an establishment of religion, or prohibiting the free exercise thereof; or abridging the freedom of speech, or of the press; or the right of the people to peaceably assemble, and to petition the Government for a redress of grievances.

Supreme Court Justice Brandeis wrote in the 1927 *Whitney v. California* decision: "Fear of serious injury cannot alone justify suppression of free speech and assembly. Men feared witches and burned women. It is the function of speech to free men from the bondage of irrational fears."

In the early 1950s Senator Joseph McCarthy of Wisconsin reported on his investigation of Communist subversion in the United States. His sensationalist report was followed by a series of public hearings in which the careers of many prominent Americans were ruined on the most flimsy, hearsay evidence. Defenders of McCarthyism argued that Communist ideas should be repressed to "protect freedom" and democratic values. According to editor and journalist William F. Buckley Jr., for a free market of ideas to thrive, people out to defraud the public with a defective product (Communism) must be exposed and sanctioned.[4]

In 1954 McCarthy was formally censured by the Senate. The demise of McCarthyism was followed by a rapid expansion of the First Amendment. Speech other than political speech—such as sexual speech and pornography, entertainment, commercial speech, nonverbal expressions such as nude dancing and flag burning, and emotional utterances—came to be included under freedom of speech.

More recently, the limits of freedom of speech have been tested in attempts to restrict protesters outside abortion clinics. In the 1997 *Schenck v. Pro-Choice Network* decision, the Supreme Court ruled that abortion protesters may be kept outside a fifteen-foot "bubble zone" protecting those entering and leaving the clinics, but may approach clients and workers on public property outside the clinics. In 2000 the United States Supreme Court in *Dale v. Boy Scouts of America* (BSA) ruled that the BSA's policy banning homosexuals from the Boy Scouts was protected under the First Amendment free association and freedom of speech (see page 369 for excerpts from this case).

FREEDOM OF SPEECH IN CYBERSPACE

Questions regarding freedom of speech have also arisen in the context of media violence. Who is responsible when viewers or readers commit horrendous acts based on crimes depicted in the media? Should the media be prohibited from portraying graphic violence because some suggestible people might copy what they see or read?

The Telecommunications Act of 1996 amended the Communication Act of 1934. One of the purposes of the large-scale revisions of the 1934 Act was to explicate and strengthen the marketplace of ideas and freedom of speech that have long been, and continue to be, debated in the communications industry.

Violence and hate speech have also found their way onto the Internet. In its first ruling on freedom of speech in cyberspace, the United States Supreme Court in 1997 ruled against President Clinton's Communications Decency Act, which required that online communication be reduced to a "safe for kids" level. The Court stated, "The interest in encouraging freedom of expression in a democratic society outweighs any theoretical but unproved benefit of censorship." Some educators protest that this ruling will limit students' educational opportunities, since schools will restrict student access to the Internet as a means of protecting students from inappropriate material.

By the year 2000 more than 200 million people were Internet users, a tenfold increase since 1996.[5] The rapid development of the Internet over the past decade has raised the question of whether the rules surrounding freedom of speech that apply to traditional forms of broadcast technology should apply to Internet speech. Internet technology is distinguished from traditional broadcast technology in that it is more democratic; anyone who has access to a computer can "broadcast" information to people around the world. Because the Internet is so accessible, it has been hailed as "the great equalizer," "the most participatory form of mass speech yet developed," and "the best advancement in democracy since universal suffrage."[6] In China, for example, the Internet gives people complete freedom to talk to people all over the world, a freedom previously denied by the Chinese government. On the other hand, as Chinese film director Zhang Xu points out, there is also a downside to the Internet. Web broadcast TV and radio may homogenize the thinking, interests, and tastes of people around the world. "There is a real possibility," she says, "that, in the future, the world will have only one culture."[7]

The ease of access to the Internet also means that children can gain access to the Internet through home computers. And unlike radio and television, where the hours of broadcast can be regulated, the material on the Internet is available twenty-four hours a day. On the other hand, offensive material on the Internet, unlike that on radio and television, is usually preceded by a title and description of the contents so it is easier for people to avoid being caught by surprise by offensive material.

Reno v. American Civil Liberties Union (1997) was the first United States Supreme Court decision according First Amendment protection to the Internet. The decision also rejected the government's argument that the Internet should be treated like the broadcast industry. The court struck down the Communications Decency Act (CDA) restrictions as they applied to the Internet stating that in the absence of any effective method for preventing minors from accessing offensive information on the Internet, the restriction of speech on the Internet would apply an undue restriction on adults' access to information.

In June 2000 a U.S. appellate court supported an injunction by a lower court against the 1998 Child Online Protection Act, which had been passed by Congress following the *Reno v. American Civil Liberties Union* decision. The Appellate court stated that the Act fell short of meeting First Amendment standards of freedom of speech.

The growing number of child pornography sites on the Internet has led to a corresponding proliferation of cyperspace sleuths—adults posing as children in an attempt to expose cyberpedophiles who prey on children. Critics of these self-appointed citizen sleuths point out that their techniques, because they involve deception, border on entrapment. Others who embrace a more utilitarian the-ends-justify-the-means approach applaud the success of these citizen sleuths in catching sex offenders and closing down child pornography sites.

In his article at the end of this chapter on "The First Amendment in Cyberspace" Cass Sunstein addresses some of the moral issues involved in regulating freedom of speech on the Internet.

HATE SPEECH AS PROTECTED SPEECH

As an Orthodox Jew, radio and television commentator Dr. Laura Schlessinger believes that homosexuals violate scriptural teachings and that homosexual sex is deviant behavior. And she's not afraid to make her views known to her audiences. Her views have incensed many homosexuals who have dubbed Dr. Schlessinger "the Queen of Hate Radio." Rather than an adversary whose ideas are to be debated in the free marketplace of ideas, she is viewed as a hateful person, a homophobic and defamer, who should be censored and silenced. The San Francisco Board of Supervisors has officially warned Schlessinger about "making inaccurate statements about gays and lesbians that incite violence and hate."[8] One supervisor compared her speech to yelling fire in a crowded building. However, do her antihomosexual views amount to dangerous hate speech that should be suppressed? Where do we draw the line between hate speech and speech, though offensive and perhaps even inaccurate, that should be tolerated in the name of freedom of speech?

In the United States, there is currently a trend away from laws and codes that ban hate speech. In the 1978 Skokie trial the American Civil Liberties Union (ACLU) defended the right of neo-Nazis to march in Skokie, Illlinois, a predominantly Jewish neighborhood in Chicago where a number of Holocaust survivors resided. The ACLU argued that the principle of justice required impartiality or neutrality in deciding whether a particular type of expression should be restricted or protected under freedom of speech. A particular type of expression should not be outlawed simply because some people find the content offensive.

In 1990 Robert A. Viktora and several other white teenagers fashioned a cross out of broken chair legs. They then held a Klan-type cross burning on the lawn of a black family who had just moved into a mostly white neighborhood in St. Paul, Minnesota. Viktora was convicted under the city's hate speech ordinance, which prohibited speech or expressions that were likely to provoke "anger, alarm or resentment in others on the basis of race, color, creed, religion or gender." The prohibition was meant to apply to "fighting words," which the Court had previously ruled in the 1942 *Chaplinsky v. New Hampshire* ruling were not protected speech. The doctrine of fighting words was defined to include only those words that are "inherently likely to provoke a violent reaction." Viktora challenged the verdict, arguing that it infringed on his right to free speech.

In the 1992 *R.A.V. v. St. Paul* ruling, the first U.S. Supreme Court ruling on hate speech, the Court agreed with Viktora that the St. Paul law violated his freedom of speech. Whereas laws restricting fighting words were constitutional, hate speech laws were not, because they exercised "content-based discrimination"; that is, they were aimed at preventing specific types of hate crimes such as racism. This narrow definition of fighting words has recently been questioned in the context of hate speech. Why should we protect speech that is so intimidating that the victim is unwilling or unable to fight back?

At the time of the *R.A.V. v. St. Paul* ruling, there were laws against hate speech in forty-six states. The Court declared most of these laws unconstitutional on the grounds that the First Amendment prohibits "laws silencing speech on the basis of its content." In a related

THE VILLAGE OF SKOKIE V. NATIONAL SOCIALIST PARTY OF AMERICA (1978):
EXCERPTS FROM THE MAJORITY OPINION

Honorable Joseph M. Wosik, Judge, Supreme Court of Illinois, delivering the opinion of the court:

Plaintiff, the village of Skokie, filed a complaint in the circuit court of Cook County seeking to enjoin defendants, the National Socialist Party of America (the American Nazi Party) and 10 individuals as "officers and members" of the party, from engaging in certain activities while conducting a demonstration within the village. . . .

It is alleged in plaintiff's complaint that the "uniform of the National Socialist Party of America consists of the storm trooper uniform of the German Nazi Party embellished with the Nazi swastika"; that the plaintiff village has a population of about 70,000 persons of which approximately 40,500 persons are of "Jewish religion or Jewish ancestry" and of this latter number 5,000 to 7,000 are survivors of German concentration camps; that the defendant organization is "dedicated to the incitation of racial and religious hatred directed principally against individuals of Jewish faith or ancestry and non-Caucasians"; and that its members "have patterned their conduct, their uniform, their slogan and their tactics along the pattern of the German Nazi Party." . . .

In defining the constitutional rights of the parties who come before this court, we are, of course, bound by the pronouncements of the United States Supreme Court in its interpretation of the United States Constitution. . . .

"It is firmly settled that under our Constitution the public expression of ideas may not be prohibited merely because the ideas are themselves offensive to some of their hearers" (*Bachellar v. Maryland* (1970) . . . and it is entirely clear that the wearing of distinctive clothing can be symbolic expression of a thought or philosophy. The symbolic expression of thought falls within the free speech clause of the first amendment (*Tinker v. Des Moines Independent Community School District* (1969) . . . and the plaintiff village has the heavy burden of justifying the imposition of a prior restraint upon defendants' right to freedom of speech (*Carroll v. President of Princess Anne County* (1968) . . .

The village of Skokie seeks to meet this burden by application of the "fighting words" doctrine first enunciated in *Chaplinsky v. New Hampshire* (1942). . . . That doctrine was designed to permit punishment of extremely hostile personal communication likely to cause immediate physical response, "no words being 'forbidden except such as have a direct tendency to cause acts of violence by the persons to whom, individually, the remark is addressed.'" . . .

In *Cohen* the Supreme Court restated the description of fighting words as "those personally abusive epithets which, when addressed to the ordinary citizen, are, as a matter of common knowledge, inherently likely to provoke violent reaction." . . . Plaintiff urges, and the appellate court has held, that the exhibition of the Nazi symbol, the swastika, addresses to ordinary citizens a message which is tantamount to fighting words. Plaintiff further asks this court to extend *Chaplinsky*, which upheld a statute punishing the use of such words, and hold that the fighting-words doctrine permits a prior restraint on defendants' symbolic speech. In our judgment we are precluded from doing so.

In *Cohen,* defendant's conviction stemmed from wearing a jacket bearing the words "Fuck the Draft" in a Los Angeles County courthouse corridor. The Supreme Court for reasons we believe applicable here refused to find that the jacket inscription constituted fighting words. That court stated:

> The constitutional right of free expression is powerful medicine in a society as diverse and populous as ours. It is designed and intended to remove governmental restraints from the arena of public discussion, putting the decision as to what views shall be voiced largely into the hands of each of us, in the hope that use of such freedom will ultimately produce a more capable citizenry and more perfect polity and in the belief that no other approach would comport with the premise of individual dignity and choice upon which our political system rests. . . .
>
> To many, the immediate consequence of this freedom may often appear to be only verbal tumult, discord, and even offensive utterance. These are, however, within established limits, in truth necessary side effects of the broader enduring values which the process of open debate permits us to achieve. That the air may at times seem filled with verbal cacophony is, in this sense not a sign of weakness but of strength. We cannot lose sight of the fact that, in what otherwise might seem a trifling and annoying instance of individual distasteful abuse of a privilege, these fundamental societal values are truly implicated "so long as the means are peaceful, the communication need not meet standards of acceptability," *Organization for a Better Austin v. Keefe,* (1971) . . .

The display of the swastika, as offensive to the principles of a free nation as the memories it recalls may be, is symbolic political speech intended to convey to the public the beliefs of those who display it. It does not, in our opinion, fall

ruling, the Wisconsin Supreme Court struck down the state's hate crime law on the grounds that a government "cannot criminalize bigoted thought with which it disagrees."[9]

The neutrality concept is challenged by Charles Lawrence, whose article is included in this chapter. He argues that the social context in which hate speech takes place is morally relevant to whether it should be tolerated. Rather than defending abstract principles such as impartiality, we should be more concerned with defending the real victims.

Canada and Britain also reject the neutrality argument and have laws restricting specific types of hate speech. Section 319(2) of the Canadian Criminal Code makes the willful promotion of hatred against an identifiable group a crime. Recently, the European Union, worried that racists and hate mongers might slip across borders, proposed a rule that would punish the dissemination of racist speech and the public incitement to discrimination or racial hatred.[10]

SPEECH CODES ON COLLEGE CAMPUSES

If colleges have a duty to promote moral development in students, should it include the enforcement of speech codes? In 1992, when the Supreme Court ruling overturned within the definition of "fighting words," and that doctrine cannot be used here to overcome the heavy presumption against the constitutional validity of a prior restraint.

Nor can we find that the swastika, while not representing fighting words, is nevertheless so offensive and peace threatening to the public that its display can be enjoined. We do not doubt that the sight of this symbol is abhorrent to the Jewish citizens of Skokie, and that the survivors of the Nazi persecutions, tormented by their recollections, may have strong feelings regarding its display. Yet it is entirely clear that this factor does not justify enjoining defendants' speech.

In summary, as we read the controlling Supreme Court opinions, use of the swastika is a symbolic form of free speech entitled to first amendment protections. Its display on uniforms or banners by those engaged in peaceful demonstrations cannot be totally precluded solely because that display may provoke a violent reaction by those who view it. Particularly is this true where, as here, there has been advance notice by the demonstrators of their plans so that they have become, as the complaint alleges, "common knowledge" and those to whom sight of the swastika banner or uniforms would be offensive are forewarned and need not view them. A speaker who gives prior notice of his message has not compelled a confrontation with those who voluntarily listen. . . .

Thus by placing the burden upon the viewer to avoid further bombardment, the Supreme Court has permitted speakers to justify the initial intrusion into the citizen's sensibilities.

We accordingly, albeit reluctantly, conclude that the display of the swastika cannot be enjoined under the fighting-words exception to free speech, nor can anticipation of a hostile audience justify the prior restraint. Furthermore, *Cohen* and *Erznoznik* direct the citizens of Skokie that it is their burden to avoid the offensive symbol if they can do so without unreasonable inconvenience. . . .

the St. Paul hate speech ordinance, more than a hundred colleges and universities in the United States had speech codes that placed restrictions on some forms of speech, such as hate speech, fighting words, or speech that violates civility codes.[11]

Campus speech codes evolved primarily out of the campus civil rights movement of the 1960s and 1970s and in response to the escalation of racist incidents on campuses in the 1980s. Sometimes dubbed the "politically correct" movement, these speech codes were intended to restrict offensive and bigoted forms of expression and encourage tolerance of diversity. The University of Wisconsin's speech code, for example, prohibited speech intended to "create a hostile learning environment" by demeaning another person's gender, race, sexual orientation, disability, creed, or ethnic background.

The politically correct movement was the most successful effort in American history to restrict hate speech. It was also one of the first times in history that students asked professors and administrators to place restrictions on offensive speech and conduct. Lawrence was a leader in the movement to curb hate speech on college campuses. His view was shaped by a 1981 boycott of a Harvard Law School course on "Race, Racism and American Law." A group of students demanded that the course be taught by a person of color. When the administration failed to accede to their demands, the students organized their own course. Lawrence was one of the guest lecturers. His ethical and legal expertise provided, in part, the sophisticated arguments needed to convince members of the college community, and in particular other professors, to support speech codes.

However, have campus speech codes gone too far? For example, one college has banned thirty offensive words and phrases including "lady," "history," and "slaving over a hot stove."[12] The words "lady" and "gentleman," so the rationale goes, have "class implications," while the word "history" has sexist implications. "Slaving over a hot stove" is considered racist.

Supporters of campus hate speech codes point out that colleges are residential. Because people should be able to feel secure in their own homes, there should be greater protection against hate speech harassment on campuses than might be necessary in a public setting. A college community is also a voluntary association. Agreeing to attend a particular college entails agreeing to abide by a certain set of rules, such as nondrinking rules, restrictions on visiting hours, smoking in dormitories, and restraints on certain forms of offensive speech. Taylor and Dershowitz disagree that campus speech codes are morally justified. They argue that the politically correct movement, which spawned these speech codes, has done more harm than good.

THE PHILOSOPHERS ON FREEDOM OF SPEECH

Although Aristotle did not believe that democracy was the best form of government for ancient Greece, he recognized the importance of liberty and freedom of speech in a democracy. He also believed that expression of violent and hateful thoughts might be cathartic and purge violent urges. Plato disagreed with his esteemed teacher. In his *Republic,* Plato argues that literature, art, verse, and even music that is "impious" and "self-contradictory" should be censored if the republic is to be well ordered. According to Plato, though some of this might appear innocuous in small doses, "lawlessness easily creeps in unobserved . . . in the guise of a pastime, which seems so harmless." A lawless spirit will eventually gain a foothold until it affects all of our dealings, ending by "overthrowing the whole structure of public and private life." The current debate over the morality of pornography and violence in the media depends to a large extent on whether one accepts Aristotle's or Plato's position on the benefits of free expression.

Libertarians maintain that freedom of speech is a necessary condition for other freedoms and, therefore, is a special right. John Locke, whose philosophy had a major influence on the writers of the U. S. Constitution, valued freedom of speech primarily as a political value. He writes, "He who takes away the Freedom [of debate in the legislature], . . . in effect takes away freedom of debate in the legislature, and puts an end to the Government."[13]

Like Locke, Ayn Rand argues that the right of free speech is a fundamental right. A person, she writes, "has the right to express his ideas without danger of suppression, interference or punitive action by the government."[14] John Rawls also regards freedom of speech as one of the basic liberties of citizens.[15]

John Stuart Mill is probably the most widely quoted—and misquoted—philosopher in the freedom of speech controversy. In his renowned essay "On Liberty," Mill argues that the state does not have the right to interfere with citizens' freedoms except where restriction is necessary to protect the person and property of others. According to him, the harm caused by censorship far outweighs any harm that might result from spreading vicious or false opinions. Truth, he notes, is often found not in the opinion of the status quo nor in the opinion of a dissenter, but in a combination of viewpoints. Therefore, freedom of speech and listening to opposing opinions, no matter how offensive they may be to some people, can allow a fuller truth to emerge.

According to the "marketplace of ideas" metaphor, ideas are like a product on the market. Just as the free market tends to deliver the best consumer goods, if everyone comes to the marketplace of ideas to express her or his opinions, the best opinions will eventually win out. Mill was not suggesting, however, that truth is like a product whose "goodness" is determined by how well it satisfies customer demand. When it comes to expression of ideas, Mill was well aware of the dangers of the tyranny of the majority over the minority. In a democracy, protection against the tyranny of government is not enough; "there needs protection also against the tyranny of the prevailing opinion and feeling, against the tendency of society to impose, by other means than civil penalties, its own ideas and practices as rules of conduct on those who dissent from them. . . ."[16] Although freedom of expression is a necessary condition for human progress, it is not a sufficient condition. We cannot assume that true opinions will triumph in a free marketplace of ideas. According to Mill, we must actively encourage the expression of minority viewpoints because of the tendency for the majority to coerce the minority into conforming. "It is the [opinion] which happens at the particular time and place to be in a minority . . . which, for the time being, represents the neglected interests, the side of human well-being which is in danger of obtaining less than its share."[17] Thus, rather than advocating passive tolerance of all forms of speech, Mill placed the highest value on the speech of those who have the least power in society.[18]

The concept of abstract rights that exist independently of a particular context is mostly a Western innovation. Buddhist virtue ethics, in contrast, is concerned with the development of a virtuous disposition, rather than abstract rights or legal prohibitions. Speech is one of the modes in which an evil disposition can be expressed. We have a moral obligation to avoid harsh, slanderous, and divisive speech and to cultivate speech that is truthful and trustworthy and that strengthens the bonds of friendship. Confucianism also emphasizes the virtue of sincerity in our speech and actions.

MORAL ISSUES

Social Order

One reason given for restrictions on the freedom of speech is to preserve public order. Members of a society must share certain core values if the society is to survive. For democracy to thrive, ideas that are subversive to democracy and freedom must be discouraged. Education, by its very nature, reinforces certain ideas over others. In the United States, for example, our schools routinely indoctrinate students in the virtues of democracy.

Campus speech codes maintain social order by keeping college campuses from turning into a pandemonium where the advantage goes to those who can shout the loudest and intimidate the most through their persistent expressions of hatred. On the other hand, speech codes can also intimidate and stifle anyone who has an idea that might be offensive to others. Restrictions on speech in the name of national social order can become overly restrictive. McCarthyism, for example, was carried out in the name of protecting freedom and democratic values against the "clear and present" danger of Communism.

Liberty Rights, Freedom of Speech, and Autonomy

Libertarians, such as Jonathan Rauch, argue that we cannot get rid of racist speech without destroying genuine freedom of speech. We do not have a right to be protected from offensive information. Therefore, we have to learn to live with prejudice. Hate speech is just another idea in the free marketplace of ideas. Some libertarians also believe that allowing hate speech to be freely expressed will contribute to the search for truth. Even racial slurs and hate speech are a type of information because they provide the target with information about the views, including the political views, of the person making the slur. It is better to let false or harmful ideas compete in the marketplace, where they are likely to fade when exposed to the light of truth, than to let the government or others in authority determine what is true and false and what is beneficial and harmful. Restriction of speech, even hate speech, stifles the free exchange of ideas by putting people on guard against making any jokes or statements that might be offensive to others. For example, Alan Dershowitz tapes his lectures on rape statutes, because he fears that someone in the class might interpret what he said as a form of sexual harassment.[19]

Lawrence counters that censoring hate speech is not an infringement on our right to free speech. Hate speech, he maintains, is not really speech because it is not an expression of an idea but an attack, designed to end discussion. Rather than being an example of free speech, hate speech is at odds with freedom of speech. Shouting racial slurs is like a slap in the face. Most hate speech is not an invitation to engage in dialogue but an attempt to silence dialogue through intimidation.

Proponents of restrictions on hate speech also point out that liberty rights exist to protect the autonomy of persons. One of the conditions of autonomy is rationality. For speech to be a moral right, the speaker must be coming from a position of reason and openness to judgment and rational dialogue. The purpose of speech, in the words of Supreme Court Justice Brandeis, is "to free men from the bondage of irrational fears." A speaker who attempts to monopolize the forum and prevent or intimidate others from speaking is not coming from a position of rationality. Therefore, hate speech is not morally protected because it oppresses autonomy rather than encouraging it.

Civility and Respect for Human Dignity

According to deontologists, rights stem from duties. A moral right, therefore, must be consistent with a commitment to treating others with dignity and respect and with the creation of conditions under which people can speak openly to each other without feeling threatened. Civility involves recognizing and respecting the dignity of other persons. Disrespect, in contrast, creates an atmosphere of distrust.

Hate speech creates a hostile environment and a message of exclusion. Rather than subjecting themselves to disrespect and assaults on their dignity, members of groups targeted by hate speech are likely to avoid these environments. For example, the rash of racist incidents on campuses in the 1980s was accompanied by a decrease in the college enrollment of black men. Thus hate speech thwarts the aims of education and diversity.

Rather than contributing to an open discussion of ideas, hate speech compromises the ability of those targeted by it to respond and to be equal participants in the debate.

Respect for human dignity requires that we as individuals refrain from using hate speech. On the other hand, it is not clear that this justifies legislating civility or placing restrictions on people's speech. There are many ways of treating people as moral inferiors—through ignoring or snubbing them, by interrupting them, or by avoiding them—all acts that few think should be legally banned. Furthermore, people cannot be forced into a subordinate position through hate speech in the way they can through segregation laws or discrimination in hiring. Although hate speech puts down its target as a moral inferior, it does not effect an actual change in the target's moral and legal status. Instead, hate speech essentially leaves the target's status unchanged.

Harm—Nonmaleficence

The primary justification usually given for restrictions on free speech is harm to others. Most ethicists agree that speech that directly results in physical harm should be prohibited. For example, it is illegal for a prankster to cry "Fire" in a crowded theater. Fraudulent and libelous speech is also restricted because of the harm it causes.

Does the principle of nonmaleficence also justify restrictions on hate speech? Although Mill uses the harm principle as a limit on freedom of speech, he is not clear on what constitutes harm to others. Is psychological distress sufficiently harmful to override freedom of speech? Lawrence claims that society has a moral duty to protect people from harm. Hate speech harms people by creating unequal opportunity in educational and workplace environments, thus depriving its targets of their freedom of speech by intimidating them into silence.

We may agree that hate speech is wrong because of the harm it imposes on its victims yet also believe that legal restrictions are not the best way to control it. Indeed, laws prohibiting hateful and abusive speech may harm the very groups they are meant to protect. One of the first people convicted under the 1976 British Race Relations Act was a black leader, who was sentenced to twelve months' imprisonment for verbally abusing the white community.[20]

The Slippery Slope

Some ethicists worry that restrictions on hate speech may become the sled that starts us down the proverbial slippery slope toward more and more restrictions on our freedom of speech. Because it is so difficult to decide what is and what isn't acceptable speech, laws and speech codes prohibiting hate speech might be expanded to embrace speech that is offensive to the powers that be, as happened during the McCarthy period.

Pluralism and Tolerance

Pluralism and multiculturalism require tolerance of individual and group differences. Lawrence maintains that tolerance of hate speech can conflict with pluralism and the elimination of racism. As a moral ideal, pluralism ensures that the most vulnerable groups of people have a place in society. Much of the motivation behind the politically correct movement and campus speech codes is to ensure that people who are not from the mainstream culture will be able to express their views without fear of intimidation.

On the other hand, restricting the freedom of speech of groups whose ideas are at odds with our own is to lay a trap for ourselves as well. Rauch argues that intellectual pluralism requires free exchange of ideas, even those that may be offensive or erroneous.

Impartiality, Equal Justice, and Discrimination

According to Lawrence, tolerance of hate speech conflicts with the elimination of discrimination and racism. He argues that the 1954 United States Supreme Court *Brown v. Board of Education* decision, which outlawed school segregation, was really about freedom of speech. Segregated schools are wrong because they communicate a message of unworthiness to black children. Similarly, prohibiting hate speech is necessary in order to ensure equal protection. Laws against racist speech would reaffirm the conviction that all people are equal. Some feminists also make the same argument: Permitting sexist speech is at odds with the more important goal of egalitarianism.

Those who feel that restrictions on freedom of speech should be content neutral base their argument on the principle of impartiality. Whereas the principle of impartiality in justice may be appropriate in an egalitarian society, in a society where racism and sexism are embedded in the very structure, it only serves to perpetuate inequalities.

Some Marxists argue that freedom of speech in a nonegalitarian society such as the United States can actually perpetuate injustice by empowering the status quo while repressing dissenters.[21] This is happening to some extent in the politically correct movement which, while extolling freedom of speech, oppresses, either through campus codes or through social disapproval, those who do not support the correct ideology.

CONCLUSION

One of the key issues is whether we should restrict hate speech, as the Canadians do, or continue to have no legal restrictions on it. Should freedom of speech outweigh the welfare rights of others, or does society have a moral obligation to protect people from assaults on their dignity? Regardless of whether we accept the libertarian position that hate speech should not be legally restricted, a libertarian public policy does not entail the claim that hate speech is morally acceptable or that we have a right to harm others. Hate speech is clearly inconsistent with respect for persons. We ought not to engage in it. As moral agents we also have a moral obligation to respond to hate speech. Alexander Hamilton once said that the greatest danger to freedom was not in restrictions on freedom of expression but an apathetic citizenry. Freedom of speech is not merely a negative concept of freedom from constraints on speech. Part of freedom of speech is a duty to speak out against hatred and bigotry.

CHARLES R. LAWRENCE III

If He Hollers Let Him Go: Regulating Racist Speech on Campus

Charles Lawrence III is a professor at the Georgetown University School of Law. In the following article, Lawrence examines the morality of regulating racist hate speech on college campuses. He concludes that the protection of racist speech is incompatible with the elimination of racism. Lawrence charges civil libertarians who invoke the First Amendment in defense of hate speech with fanning the flames of racism by protecting racist speech. Rather than encouraging the free exchange of ideas, the tolerance of hate speech silences and disvalues the ideas of minorities.

Critical Reading Questions

1. What does Lawrence mean by the "double consciousness" shared by minorities?
2. According to Lawrence, who is harmed more by oppressive speech: minorities who are targets of the speech, or those using hate speech?
3. On what grounds does Lawrence claim that many civil libertarians are actually fanning the flames of racism?
4. According to Lawrence, what is the relevance of the United States Supreme Court *Brown v. Board of Education* ruling to the regulation of racist speech?
5. Why does Lawrence insist that we view individual racist remarks as part of a totality rather than as discrete events?
6. According to Lawrence, why should the *Brown v. Board of Education* decision overrule the First Amendment when it comes to racist speech?
7. Why does Lawrence reject the distinction drawn by many libertarians between conduct and speech?
8. On what grounds does Lawrence claim that racist speech is the functional equivalent of fighting words?
9. What three types of injury does Lawrence argue are caused by racist speech?
10. Why don't blacks have as much faith in free speech as do whites?
11. According to Lawrence, what are some of the effects of racist speech on the marketplace of ideas?
12. On what grounds does Lawrence attack traditional civil libertarians?

"If He Hollers Let Him Go: Regulating Racist Speech on Campus," *Duke Law Journal* 431 (1990): 431–480. Notes have been omitted.

NEWSREEL*

Racist incidents at the University of Michigan, University of Massachusetts-Amherst, University of Wisconsin, University of New Mexico, Columbia University, Wellesley College, Duke University, and University of California-Los Angeles.

The campus ought to be the last place to legislate tampering with the edges of First Amendment protections.

University of Michigan:
"Greek Rites of Exclusion": Racist leaflets in dorms, white students paint themselves black and place rings in their noses at "jungle parties."

Silencing a few creeps is no victory if the price is an abrogation of free speech. Remember censorship is an ugly word too.

Northwest Missouri State University:
White Supremacists distribute flyers stating, "The Knights of the Ku Klux Klan are Watching You."

Temple University:
White Student Union formed.

Memphis State University:
Bomb Threats at Jewish Student Union.

The harm that censors allege will result unless speech is forbidden rarely occurs.

Dartmouth College:
Black professor called "a cross between a welfare queen and a bathroom attendant" and the Dartmouth Review purported to quote a black student, "Dese boys be sayin' that we be comin' here to Dartmut an' not takin' the classics. . . ."

Yes, speech is sometimes painful. Sometimes it is abusive. That is one of the prices of a free society.

Purdue University:
Counselor finds "Death Nigger" scratched on her door.

More speech, not less, is the proper cure for offensive speech.

Smith College:
African student finds message slipped under her door that reads, "African Nigger do you want some bananas? Go back to the Jungle."

Speech cannot be banned simply because it is offensive.

University of Michigan:
Campus radio station broadcasts a call from a student who "joked": "Who are the most famous black women in history? Aunt Jemima and Mother Fucker."

Those who don't like what they are hearing or seeing should try to change the atmosphere through education. That is what they will have to do in the real world after they graduate.

University of Michigan:
A student walks into class and sees this written on the blackboard: "A mind is a terrible thing to waste—especially on a nigger." . . .

INTRODUCTION

In recent years, American campuses have seen a resurgence of racial violence and a corresponding rise in the incidence of verbal and symbolic assault and harassment to which blacks and other traditionally subjugated groups are subjected. There is a heated debate in the civil liberties community concerning the proper response to incidents of racist speech on campus. Strong disagreements have

---

* The events that appear in this newsreel are gathered from newspaper and magazine reports of racist incidents on campuses. Each of them is followed by a statement, appearing in italics, criticizing proposals to regulate racism on campus. The latter have been garnered from conversations, debates, and panel discussions at which I have been present. Some I managed to record verbatim and are exact quotes; others paraphrase the sentiment expressed. I have heard some version of each of these arguments many times over.

arisen between those individuals who believe that racist speech, such as that contained in the Newsreel that opens this Article, should be regulated by the university or some public body and those individuals who believe that racist expression should be protected from all public regulation. At the center of the controversy is a tension between the constitutional values of free speech and equality. . . .

The "double consciousness" of groups outside the ethnic mainstream is particularly apparent in the context of this controversy. Blacks know and value the protection the First Amendment affords those of us who must rely on our voices to petition both government and our neighbors for redress of grievances. Our political tradition has looked to "the word," to the moral power of ideas, to change a system when neither the power of the vote nor that of the gun are available. This part of us has known the experience of belonging and recognizes our common and inseparable interest in preserving the right of free speech for all. But we also know the experience of the outsider. The Framers excluded us from the protection of the First Amendment. The same Constitution that established rights for others endorsed a story that proclaimed our inferiority. It is a story that remains deeply ingrained in the American psyche.

We see a different world than that which is seen by Americans who do not share this historical experience. We often hear racist speech when our white neighbors are not aware of its presence.

It is not my purpose to belittle or trivialize the importance of defending unpopular speech against the tyranny of the majority. There are very strong reasons for protecting even racist speech. Perhaps the most important reasons are that it reinforces our society's commitment to the value of tolerance, and that, by shielding racist speech from government regulation, we will be forced to combat it as a community. These reasons for protecting racist speech should not be set aside hastily, and I will not argue that we should be less vigilant in protecting the speech and associational rights of speakers with whom most of us would disagree.

But I am deeply concerned about the role that many civil libertarians have played, or the roles we have failed to play, in the continuing, real-life struggle through which we define the community in which we live. I fear that by framing the debate as we have—as one in which the liberty of free speech is in conflict with the elimination of racism—we have advanced the cause of racial oppression and have placed the bigot on the moral high ground, fanning the rising flames of racism. Above all, I am troubled that we have not listened to the real victims, that we have shown so little empathy or understanding for their injury, and that we have abandoned those individuals whose race, gender, or sexual orientation provokes others to regard them as second class citizens. These individuals' civil liberties are most directly at stake in the debate. . . .

BROWN V. BOARD OF EDUCATION: A CASE ABOUT REGULATING RACIST SPEECH

The landmark case of *Brown v. Board of Education* is not a case we normally think of as a case about speech. As read most narrowly, the case is about the rights of black children to equal educational opportunity. But *Brown* can also be read more broadly to articulate a principle central to any substantive understanding of the equal protection clause, the foundation on which all anti-discrimination law rests. This is the principle of equal citizenship. . . .

The key to this understanding of *Brown* is that the practice of segregation, the practice the Court held inherently unconstitutional, was *speech*. *Brown* held that segregation is unconstitutional not simply because the physical separation of black and white children is bad or because resources were distributed unequally among black and white schools. *Brown* held that segregated schools were unconstitutional primarily because of the *message* segregation conveys—the message that black children are an untouchable caste, unfit to be educated with white children. Segregation serves its purpose by conveying an idea. It stamps a badge of inferiority upon blacks, and this badge communicates a message to others in the community, as well as to blacks wearing the badge, that is injurious to blacks. Therefore, *Brown* may be read as regulating the content of racist speech. As a regulation of racist speech, the decision is an exception to the usual rule that regulation of speech content is presumed unconstitutional.

The Conduct/Speech Distinction

Some civil libertarians argue that my analysis of *Brown* conflates speech and conduct. They maintain that the segregation outlawed in *Brown* was discriminatory conduct, not speech, and the defamatory message conveyed by segregation simply was an incidental by-product of that conduct. . . . This objection to my reading of *Brown* misperceives the central point of the argument. . . .

Racism is both 100% speech and 100% conduct. Discriminatory conduct is not racist unless it also conveys the message of white supremacy—unless it is interpreted within the culture to advance the structure and ideology of white supremacy. Likewise, all racist speech constructs the social reality that constrains the liberty of non-whites because of their race. By limiting the life opportunities of others, this act of constructing meaning also makes racist speech conduct. . . .

RACIST SPEECH AS THE FUNCTIONAL EQUIVALENT OF FIGHTING WORDS

Much recent debate of the efficacy of regulating racist speech has focused on the efforts by colleges and universities to respond to the burgeoning incidents of racial harassment on their campuses. At Stanford, where I teach, there has been considerable controversy over the questions of whether racist and other discriminatory verbal harassment should be regulated and what form that regulation should take. Proponents of regulation have been sensitive to the danger of inhibiting expression, and the current regulation . . . manifests that sensitivity. It is drafted somewhat more narrowly than I would have preferred, leaving unregulated hate speech that occurs in settings where there is a captive audience, speech that I would regulate. But I largely agree with this regulation's substance and approach. I include it here as one example of a regulation of racist speech that I would argue violates neither First Amendment precedent nor principle. The regulation reads as follows:

Fundamental Standard Interpretation: Free Expression and Discriminatory Harassment

1. Stanford is committed to the principles of free inquiry and free expression. Students have the right to hold and vigorously defend and promote their opinions, thus entering them into the life of the University, there to flourish or wither according to their merits. Respect for this right requires that students tolerate even expression of opinions which they find abhorrent. Intimidation of students by other students in their exercise of this right, by violence or threat of violence, is therefore considered to be a violation of the Fundamental Standard.

2. Stanford is also committed to principles of equal opportunity and non-discrimination. Each student has the right to equal access to a Stanford education, without discrimination on the basis of sex, race, color, handicap, religion, sexual orientation, or national and ethnic origin. Harassment of students on the basis of any of these characteristics contributes to a hostile environment that makes access to education for those subjected to it less than equal. Such discriminatory harassment is therefore considered to be a violation of the Fundamental Standard.

3. This interpretation of the Fundamental Standard is intended to clarify the point at which protected free expression ends and prohibited discriminatory harassment begins. Prohibited harassment includes discriminatory intimidation by threats of violence, and also includes personal vilification of students on the basis of their sex, race, color, handicap, religion, sexual orientation, or national and ethnic origin.

4. Speech or other expression constitutes harassment by personal vilification if it:

a) is intended to insult or stigmatize an individual or a small number of individuals on the basis of their sex, race, color, handicap, religion, sexual orientation, or national and ethnic origin; and

b) is addressed directly to the individual or individuals whom it insults or stigmatizes; and

c) makes use of insulting or "fighting" words or non-verbal symbols.

In the context of discriminatory harassment by personal vilification, insulting or "fighting" words or non-verbal symbols are those "which by their very utterance inflict injury or tend to incite to an immediate breach of the peace," and which are commonly understood to convey direct and visceral hatred or contempt for human beings on the basis of their sex, race, color, handicap, religion, sexual orientation, or national and ethnic origin.

This regulation and others like it have been characterized in the press as the work of "thought police," but it does nothing more than prohibit intentional face-to-face insults, a form of speech that is unprotected by the First Amendment. When racist speech takes the form of face-to-face insults, catcalls, or other assaultive speech aimed at an individual or small group of persons, then it falls within the "fighting words" exception to First Amendment protection. The Supreme Court has held that words that "by their very utterance inflict injury or tend to incite to an immediate breach of the peace" are not constitutionally protected.

Face-to-face racial insults, like fighting words, are undeserving of First Amendment protection for two reasons. The first reason is the immediacy of the injurious impact of racial insults. The experience of being called "nigger," "spic," "Jap," or "kike" is like receiving a slap in the face. The injury is instantaneous. There is neither an opportunity for intermediary reflection on the idea conveyed nor an opportunity for responsive speech. The harm to be avoided is both clear and present. The second reason that racial insults should not fall under protected speech relates to the purpose underlying the First Amendment. If the purpose of the First Amendment is to foster the greatest amount of speech, then racial insults disserve that purpose. Assaultive racist speech functions as a preemptive strike. The racial invective is experienced as a blow, not a proffered idea, and once the blow is struck, it is unlikely that dialogue will follow. Racial insults

are undeserving of First Amendment protection because the perpetrator's intention is not to discover truth or initiate dialogue but to injure the victim.

The fighting words doctrine anticipates that the verbal "slap in the face" of insulting words will provoke a violent response with a resulting breach of the peace. When racial insults are hurled at minorities, the response may be silence or flight rather than fight, but the preemptive effect on further speech is just as complete as with fighting words. Women and minorities often report that they find themselves speechless in the face of discriminatory verbal attacks. This inability to respond is not the result of oversensitivity among these groups, as some individuals who oppose protective regulation have argued. Rather, it is the product of several factors, all of which reveal the non-speech character of the initial preemptive verbal assault. The first factor is that the visceral emotional response to personal attack precludes speech. Attack produces an instinctive, defensive psychological reaction. Fear, rage, shock, and flight all interfere with any reasoned response. Words like "nigger," "kike," and "faggot" produce physical symptoms that temporarily disable the victim, and the perpetrators often use these words with the intention of producing this effect. Many victims do not find words of response until well after the assault when the cowardly assaulter has departed.

A second factor that distinguishes racial insults from protected speech is the preemptive nature of such insults—the words by which to respond to such verbal attacks may never be forthcoming because speech is usually an inadequate response. . . .

The subordinated victim of fighting words also is silenced by her relatively powerless position in society. Because of the significance of power and position, the categorization of racial epithets as "fighting words" provides an inadequate paradigm; instead one must speak of their "functional equivalent." The fighting words doctrine presupposes an encounter between two persons of relatively equal power who have been acculturated to respond to face-to-face insults with violence. The fighting words doctrine is a paradigm based on a white male point of view. In most situations, minorities correctly perceive that a violent response to fighting words will result in a risk to their own life and limb. Since minorities are likely to lose the fight, they are forced to remain silent and submissive. This response is most obvious when women submit to sexually assaultive speech or when the racist name-caller is in a more powerful position—the boss on the job or the mob. . . .

The proposed Stanford regulation, and indeed regulations with considerably broader reach, can be justified as necessary to protect a captive audience from offensive or injurious speech. Courts have held that offensive speech may not be regulated in public forums such as streets and parks where a listener may avoid the speech by moving on or averting his eyes, but the regulation of otherwise protected speech has been permitted when the speech invades the privacy of the unwilling listener's home or when the unwilling listener cannot avoid the speech. Racist posters, flyers, and graffiti in dorms, classrooms, bathrooms, and other common living spaces would fall within the reasoning of these cases. Minority students should not be required to remain in their rooms to avoid racial assault. Minimally, they should find a safe haven in their dorms and other common rooms that are a part of their daily routine. I would argue that the university's responsibility for ensuring these students received an equal educational opportunity provides a compelling justification for regulations that ensure them safe passage in all common areas. . . .

Understanding the Injury Inflicted by Racist Speech

There can be no meaningful discussion about how to reconcile our commitment to equality and our commitment to free speech until we acknowledge that racist speech inflicts real harm and that this harm is far from trivial. I should state that more strongly: To engage in a debate about the First Amendment and racist speech without a full understanding of the nature and extent of the harm of racist speech risks making the First Amendment an instrument of domination rather than a vehicle of liberation. Not everyone has known the experience of being victimized by racist, misogynist, and homophobic speech, and we do not share equally the

burden of the societal harm it inflicts. Often we are too quick to say we have heard the victims' cries when we have not; we are too eager to assure ourselves we have experienced the same injury, and therefore we can make the constitutional balance without danger of mismeasurement. For many of us who have fought for the rights of oppressed minorities, it is difficult to accept that—by underestimating the injury from racist speech—we too might be implicated in the vicious words we would never utter. Until we have eradicated racism and sexism and no longer share in the fruits of those forms of domination, we cannot justly strike the balance over the protest of those who are dominated. My plea is simply that we listen to the victims. . . .

Again, *Brown v. Board of Education* is a useful case for our analysis. *Brown* is helpful because it articulates the nature of the injury inflicted by the racist message of segregation. When one considers the injuries identified in the *Brown* decision, it is clear that racist speech causes tangible injury, and it is the kind of injury for which the law commonly provides, and even requires, redress.

Psychic injury is no less an injury than being struck in the face, and is often far more severe. *Brown* speaks directly to the psychic injury inflicted by racist speech in noting that the symbolic message of segregation affected "the hearts and minds" of Negro children "in a way unlikely ever to be undone." Racial epithets and harassment often cause deep emotional scarring, and feelings of anxiety and fear that pervade every aspect of a victim's life. Many victims of hate propaganda have experienced physiological and emotional symptoms ranging from rapid pulse rate and difficulty in breathing, to nightmares, post-traumatic stress disorder, psychosis and suicide.

A second injury identified in *Brown* . . . is reputational injury. "[L]ibelous speech was long regarded as a form of personal assault . . . that government could vindicate . . . without running afoul of the Constitution." . . .

Brown is a case about group defamation. The message of segregation was stigmatizing to black children. To be labeled unfit to attend school with white children injured the reputation of black children, thereby foreclosing employment opportunities and the right to be regarded as respected members of the body politic. . . . *Brown* reflects that racism is a form of subordination that achieves its purpose through group defamation.

The third injury identified in *Brown* is the denial of equal educational opportunity. *Brown* recognized that black children did not have an equal opportunity to learn and participate in the school community if they bore the additional burden of being subjected to the humiliation and psychic assault that accompanies the message of segregation. University students bear an analogous burden when they are forced to live and work in an environment where, at any moment, they may be subjected to denigrating verbal harassment and assault. . . .

All three of these very tangible, continuing, and often irreparable forms of injury—psychic, reputational, and the denial of equal educational opportunity—must be recognized, accounted for, and balanced against the claim that a regulation aimed at the prevention of these injuries may lead to restrictions on important First Amendment liberties.

The Other Side of the Balance: Does the Suppression of Racial Epithets Weigh for or Against Speech?

In striking a balance, we also must think about what we are weighing on the side of speech. Most blacks—unlike many white civil libertarians—do not have faith in free speech as the most important vehicle for liberation. The First Amendment coexisted with slavery, and we still are not sure it will protect us to the same extent that it protects whites. It often is argued that minorities have benefited greatly from First Amendment protection and therefore should guard it jealously. We are aware that the struggle for racial equality has relied heavily on the persuasion of peaceful protest protected by the First Amendment, but experience also teaches us that our petitions often go unanswered until they disrupt business as usual and require the self-interested attention of those persons in power. . . .

Blacks and other people of color are equally skeptical about the absolutist argument that even the most injurious speech must remain unregulated because in an unregulated marketplace of ideas the best ideas will rise to the top and gain acceptance. Our experience tells us the opposite. We have seen too many demagogues elected by appealing to America's racism. We have seen too many good, liberal politicians shy away from the issues that might brand them as too closely allied with us. The American marketplace of ideas was founded with the idea of the racial inferiority of non-whites as one of its chief commodities, and ever since the market opened, racism has remained its most active item in trade.

But it is not just the prevalence and strength of the idea of racism that makes the unregulated marketplace of ideas an untenable paradigm for those individuals who seek full and equal personhood for all. The real problem is that the idea of the racial inferiority of non-whites infects, skews, and disables the operation of the market (like a computer virus, sick cattle, or diseased wheat). Racism is irrational and often unconscious. Our belief in the inferiority of non-whites trumps good ideas that contend with it in the market, often without our even knowing it. In addition, racism makes the words and ideas of blacks and other despised minorities less saleable, regardless of their intrinsic value, in the marketplace of ideas. It also decreases the total amount of speech that enters the market by coercively silencing members of those groups who are its targets.

Racism is an epidemic infecting the marketplace of ideas and rendering it dysfunctional. Racism is ubiquitous. We are all racists. Racism is also irrational. Individuals do not embrace or reject racist beliefs as the result of reasoned deliberation. For the most part, we do not recognize the myriad ways in which the racism pervading our history and culture influences our beliefs. In other words, most of our racism is unconscious. . . .

[John Stuart] Mill's vision of truth emerging through competition in the marketplace of ideas relies on the ability of members of the body politic to recognize "truth" as serving their interest and to act on that recognition. . . .

Prejudice that is unconscious or unacknowledged causes even more distortions in the market. When racism operates at a conscious level, opposing ideas may prevail in open competition for the rational or moral sensibilities of the market participant. But when an individual is unaware of his prejudice, neither reason nor moral persuasion will likely succeed.

Racist speech also distorts the marketplace of ideas by muting or devaluing the speech of blacks and other non-whites. An idea that would be embraced by large numbers of individuals if it were offered by a white individual will be rejected or given less credence because its author belongs to a group demeaned and stigmatized by racist beliefs. . . .

Finally, racist speech decreases the total amount of speech that reaches the market. I noted earlier in this Article the ways in which racist speech is inextricably linked with racist conduct. The primary purpose and effect of the speech/conduct that constitutes white supremacy is the exclusion of non-whites from full participation in the body politic. Sometimes the speech/conduct of racism is direct and obvious. When the Klan burns a cross on the lawn of a black person who joined the NAACP or exercised his right to move to a formerly all-white neighborhood, the effect of this speech does not result from the persuasive power of an idea operating freely in the market. It is a threat, a threat made in the context of a history of lynchings, beatings, and economic reprisals that made good on earlier threats, a threat that silences a potential speaker. The black student who is subjected to racial epithets is likewise threatened and silenced. Certainly she, like the victim of a cross-burning, may be uncommonly brave or foolhardy and ignore the system of violence in which this abusive speech is only a bit player. But it is more likely that we, as a community, will be denied the benefit of many of her thoughts and ideas. . . .

"WHICH SIDE ARE (WE) ON?"

. . . There is much about the way many civil libertarians have participated in the debate over the regulation of racist speech that causes the victims of that speech to wonder which side they are on. Those who raise their voices in protest against public sanctions of racist speech have not organized private protests against the voices of racism. It has been people of color, women, and gays who have held vigils at offending fraternity houses, staged candlelight marches, counter-demonstrations and distributed flyers calling upon their classmates and colleagues to express their outrage at pervasive racism, sexism, and homophobia in their midst and show their solidarity with its victims.

Traditional civil libertarians have been conspicuous largely in their absence from these group expressions of condemnation. Their failure to participate in this marketplace response to speech with more speech is often justified, paradoxically, as concern for the principle of free speech. When racial minorities or other victims of hate speech hold counter-demonstrations or engage in picketing, leafleting, heckling, or booing of racist speakers, civil libertarians often accuse them of private censorship, of seeking to silence opposing points of view. When both public and private responses to racist speech are rejected by First Amendment absolutists as contrary to the principle of free speech, it is no wonder that the victims of racism do not consider them allies. . . .

There is also a propensity among some civil libertarians to minimize the injury to the victims of racist speech and distance themselves from it by characterizing individual acts of racial harassment as aberrations, as isolated incidents in a community that is otherwise free of racism. When those persons who argue against the regulation of racist speech speak of "silencing a few creeps" or argue that "the harm that censors allege will result unless speech is forbidden rarely occurs," they demonstrate an unwillingness even to acknowledge the injury. Moreover, they disclaim any responsibility for its occurrence.

The recent outbreak of racism on our campuses in its most obvious manifestations provides an opportunity to examine the presence of less overt forms of racism within our educational institutions. But the debate that has followed these incidents has focused on the First Amendment freedoms of the perpetrator rather than the university community's responsibility for creating an environment where such acts occur. The resurgence of flagrant racist acts has not occurred in a vacuum. It is evidence of more widespread resistance to change by those holding positions of dominance and privilege in institutions, which until recently were exclusively white. Those who continue to be marginalized in these institutions—by their token inclusion on faculties and administrations, by the exclusion of their cultures from core curricula, and by commitment to diversity and multi-culturalism that seems to require assimilation more than any real change in the university—cannot help but see their colleagues' attention to free speech as an avoidance of these larger issues of equality.

When the ACLU enters the debate by challenging the University of Michigan's efforts to provide a safe harbor for its black, Hispanic, and Asian students (a climate that a colleague of mine compared unfavorably with Mississippi in the 1960s), we should not be surprised that non-white students feel abandoned. When we respond to Stanford students' pleas for protection by accusing them of seeking to silence all who disagree with them, we paint the harassing bigot as a martyred defender of democracy. When we valorize bigotry we must assume some responsibility for the fact that bigots are encouraged by their newfound status as "defenders of the faith." We must find ways to engage actively in speech and action that resists and counters the racist ideas the First Amendment protects. If we fail in this duty, the victims of hate speech rightly assume we are aligned with their oppressors.

Discussion Questions

1. What welfare rights, according to Lawrence, are violated by hate speech? Are you satisfied with Lawrence's suggestions for resolving the moral dilemma between welfare rights and liberty rights? Support your answers. Create a policy for your campus for resolving this conflict.

2. Lawrence argues that John Stuart Mill's marketplace of ideas does not include hate speech. Instead, Lawrence maintains that racist speech needs to be regulated because it has a "disruptive and disabling effect on the market of an idea [racism] that is ubiquitous and irrational." Do you agree with Lawrence? Given that one of the goals of colleges is to be a marketplace of ideas, discuss which would contribute more toward this goal—the tolerance of hate speech on your campus, or the regulation of hate speech.

   Discuss how Mill might respond to Lawrence's position on the regulation of racist speech.

3. Lawrence argues that the 1954 United States Supreme Court *Brown v. Board of Education* decision, which outlawed school segregation, was really about freedom of speech. Segregated schools are wrong because they communicate a message of unworthiness to black children. Similarly, prohibiting hate speech is necessary to ensure equal protection. Do you agree with Lawrence that the moral duty to promote equal justice outweighs the right to engage in hate speech? Support your answer.

4. Lawrence claims that "in most situations members of minority groups realize that they are likely to lose if they fight back, and are forced to remain silent and submissive." Do you agree with Lawrence that this justifies restrictions on hate speech? Or do members of minority groups, as well as others who hear hate speech being used, have a moral duty to stand up to it? Support your answers. Discuss how virtue ethicists, such as Aristotle and the Buddha, would answer these questions.

5. Do you agree with Lawrence that placing a higher value on freedom of speech than on the elimination of racism puts the bigot on the moral high ground? Support your answer.

J O N A T H A N   R A U C H

In Defense of Prejudice: Why Incendiary Speech Must Be Protected

Jonathan Rauch is author of *Kindly Inquisitors: The New Attacks of Free Thought* (1993). Rauch disagrees with the equation Lawrence draws between hate speech and physical violence and his call to censor hate speech. Instead, Rauch argues that we cannot get rid of racist speech without destroying genuine freedom of speech. We cannot protect some minorities by suppressing the opinions of other minorities. Instead we have to learn how to live with prejudice and hate speech. The way to cope with prejudice and hate speech is not to suppress it, but to openly correct and criticize it.

Critical Reading Questions

1. According to Rauch, why will there always be bigoted speech where there is freedom of speech?
2. What does Rauch think we should do about bigoted speech?
3. What does Rauch mean when he says that bigoted speech is integral to intellectual pluralism?
4. What is "purism"?
5. Why, according to Rauch, is the purist aim to eliminate prejudicial words and phrases futile?
6. What contribution does Rauch claim that modern feminism has made to the purist position?
7. What arguments does Rauch use to support his claim that purism poses a threat to education?
8. According to Rauch, why does purism pose a threat to minorities?
9. Why does Rauch reject the argument that oppressive speech is a form of violence?
10. What suggestions does Rauch make for dealing with violence that do not involve outlawing oppressive speech?

The war on prejudice is now, in all likelihood, the most uncontroversial social movement in America. Opposition to "hate speech," formerly identified with the liberal left, has become a bipartisan piety. In the past year, groups and factions that agree on nothing else have agreed that the public expression of any and all prejudices must be forbidden. On the left, protesters and editorialists have insisted that Francis L. Lawrence resign as president of Rutgers University for describing blacks as "a disadvantaged population that doesn't have that genetic, hereditary background to have a higher average." On the other side of the ideological divide, Ralph Reed, the executive director of the Christian Coalition,

"In Defense of Prejudice: Why Incendiary Speech Must Be Protected," *Harper's Magazine,* May 1995, pp. 37–46.

responded to criticism of the religious right by calling a press conference to denounce a supposed outbreak of "name-calling, scapegoating, and religious bigotry." Craig Rogers, an evangelical Christian student at California State University, recently filed a $2.5 million sexual-harassment suit against a lesbian professor of psychology, claiming that anti-male bias in one of her lectures violated campus rules and left him feeling "raped and trapped."

In universities and on Capitol Hill, in workplaces and newsrooms, authorities are declaring that there is no place for racism, sexism, homophobia, Christian-bashing, and other forms of prejudice in public debate or even in private thought. "Only when racism and other forms of prejudice are expunged," say the crusaders for sweetness and light, "can minorities be safe and society be fair." So sweet, this dream of a world without prejudice. But the very last thing society should do is seek to utterly eradicate racism and other forms of prejudice.

I suppose I should say, in the customary I-hope-I-don't-sound-too-defensive tone, that I am not a racist and that this is not an article favoring racism or any other particular prejudice. It is an article favoring intellectual pluralism, which permits the expression of various forms of bigotry and always will. Although we like to hope that a time will come when no one will believe that people come in types and that each type belongs with its own kind, I doubt such a day will ever arrive. By all indications, *Homo sapiens* is a tribal species for whom "us versus them" comes naturally and must be continually pushed back. When there is genuine freedom of expression, there will be racist expression. There will also be people who believe that homosexuals are sick or threaten children or—especially among teenagers—are rightful targets of manly savagery. Homosexuality will always be incomprehensible to most people, and what is incomprehensible is feared. As for anti-Semitism, it appears to be a hardier virus than influenza. If you want pluralism, then you get racism and sexism and homophobia, and communism and fascism and xenophobia and tribalism, and that is just for a start. If you want to believe in intellectual freedom and the progress of knowledge and the advancement of science and all those other good things, then you must swallow

hard and accept this: for as thickheaded and wayward an animal as us, the realistic question is how to make the best of prejudice, not how to eradicate it.

Indeed, "eradicating prejudice" is so vague a proposition as to be meaningless. Distinguishing prejudice reliably and nonpolitically from nonprejudice, or even defining it crisply, is quite hopeless. We all feel we know prejudice when we see it. But do we? At the University of Michigan, a student said in a classroom discussion that he considered homosexuality a disease treatable with therapy. He was summoned to a formal disciplinary hearing for violating the school's policy against speech that "victimizes" people based on "sexual orientation." Now, the evidence is abundant that this particular hypothesis is wrong, and any American homosexual can attest to the harm that the student's hypothesis has inflicted on many real people. But was it a statement of prejudice or of misguided belief? Hate speech or hypothesis? Many Americans who do not regard themselves as bigots or haters believe that homosexuality is a treatable disease. They may be wrong, but are they all bigots? I am unwilling to say so, and if you are willing, beware. The line between prejudiced belief and a merely controversial one is elusive, and the harder you look the more elusive it becomes. . . .

An enlightened and efficient intellectual regime lets a million prejudices bloom, including many that you or I may regard as hateful or grotesque. It avoids any attempt to stamp out prejudice, because stamping out prejudice really means forcing everyone to share the same prejudice, namely that of whoever is in authority. The great American philosopher Charles Sanders Peirce wrote in 1877: "When complete agreement could not be otherwise be reached, a general massacre of all who have not thought in a certain way has proved a very effective means of settling opinion in a country." . . . "Let all men who reject the established belief be terrified into silence," wrote Peirce, describing this system. "This method has, from the earliest times, been one of the chief means of upholding correct theological and political doctrines."

Intellectual pluralism substitutes a radically different doctrine: we kill our mistakes rather than each other. Here I draw on another great philosopher, the late Karl Popper, who pointed out that the critical method of science "consists in letting our hypotheses die in our stead." Those who are in error are not (or are not supposed to be) banished or excommunicated or forced to sign a renunciation or required to submit to "rehabilitation" or sent for psychological counseling. It is the error we punish, not the errant. By letting people make errors—even mischievous, spiteful errors (as, for instance, Galileo's insistence on Copernicanism was taken to be in 1633)—pluralism creates room to challenge orthodoxy, think imaginatively, experiment boldly. Brilliance and bigotry are empowered in the same stroke.

Pluralism is the principle that protects and makes a place in human company for that loneliest and most vulnerable of all minorities, the minority who is hounded and despised among blacks and whites, gays and straights, who is suspect or criminal among every tribe and in every nation in the world, and yet on whom progress depends: the dissident. I am not saying that dissent is always or even usually enlightened. Most of the time it is foolish and self-serving. No dissident has the right to be taken seriously, and the fact that Aryan Nation racists or Nation of Islam anti-Semites are unorthodox does not entitle them to respect. But what goes around comes around. As a supporter of gay marriage, for example, I reject the majority's view of family, and as a Jew I reject its view of God. I try to be civil, but the fact is that most Americans regard my views on marriage as a reckless assault on the most fundamental of all institutions, and many people are more than a little discomfited by the statement "Jesus Christ was no more divine than anybody else" (which is why so few people ever say it). Trap the racists and anti-Semites, and you lay a trap for me too. Hunt for them with eradication in your mind, and you have brought dissent itself within your sights.

The new crusade against prejudice waves aside such warnings. Like earlier crusades against anti-social ideas, the mission is fueled by good (if cocksure) intentions and a genuine sense of urgency. Some kinds of error are held to be intolerable, like pollutants that even in small traces poison the water

for a whole town. Some errors are so pernicious as to damage real people's lives, so wrongheaded that no person of right mind or goodwill could support them. Like their forebears of other stripe—the Church in its campaigns against heretics, the McCarthyites in their campaigns against Communists—the modern anti-racist and anti-sexist and anti-homophobic campaigners are totalists, demanding not that misguided ideas and ugly expressions be corrected or criticized but that they be eradicated. They make war not on errors but on error, and like other totalists they act in the name of public safety—the safety, especially, of minorities.

The sweeping implications of this challenge to pluralism are not, I think, well enough understood by the public at large. Indeed, the new brand of totalism has yet even to be properly named. "Multiculturalism," for instance, is much too broad. "Political correctness" comes closer but is too trendy and snide. For lack of anything else, I will call the new anti-pluralism "purism," since its major tenet is that society cannot be just until the last traces of invidious prejudice have been scrubbed away. Whatever you call it, the purists' way of seeing things has spread through American intellectual life with remarkable speed, so much so that many people will blink at you uncomprehendingly or even call you a racist (or sexist or homophobe, etc.) if you suggest that expressions of racism should be tolerated or that prejudice has its part to play.

The new purism sets out, to begin with, on a campaign against words, for words are the currency of prejudice, and if prejudice is hurtful then so must be prejudiced words. "We are not safe when these violent words are among us," wrote Mari Matsuda, then a UCLA law professor. Here one imagines gangs of racist words swinging chains and smashing heads in back alleys. To suppress bigoted language seems, at first blush, reasonable, but it quickly leads to a curious result. A peculiar kind of verbal shamanism takes root, as though certain expressions, like curses or magical incantations, carry in themselves the power to hurt or heal—as though words were bigoted rather than people. . . .

Faced with escalating demands of verbal absolutism, newspapers issue lists of forbidden words.

The expressions "gyp" (derived from "Gypsy") and "Dutch treat" were among the dozens of terms stricken as "offensive" in a much-ridiculed (and later withdrawn) *Los Angeles Times* speech code. The University of Missouri journalism school issued a *Dictionary of Cautionary Words and Phrases,* which included "*Buxom:* Offensive reference to a woman's chest. Do not use. See 'Woman.' *Codger:* Offensive reference to a senior citizen."

As was bound to happen, purists soon discovered that chasing around after words like "gyp" and "buxom" hardly goes to the roots of the problem. As long as they remain bigoted, bigots will simply find other words. If they can't call you a kike then they will say Jewboy, Judas, or Hebe, and when all those are banned they will press words like "oven" and "lampshade" into their service. The vocabulary of hate is potentially as rich as your dictionary, and all you do by banning language used by cretins is to let them decide what the rest of us may say. The problem, some purists have concluded, must therefore go much deeper than laws: it must go to the deeper level of ideas. Racism, sexism, homophobia, and the rest must be built into the very structure of American society and American patterns of thought, so pervasive yet so insidious that, like water to a fish, they are both omnipresent and unseen. The mere existence of prejudice constructs a society whose very nature is prejudiced.

This line of thinking was pioneered by feminists, who argued that pornography, more than just being expressive, is an act by which men construct an oppressive society. Racial activists quickly picked up the argument. Racist expressions are themselves acts of oppression, they said. "All racist speech constructs the social reality that constrains the liberty of nonwhites because of their race," wrote Charles R. Lawrence III, then a law professor at Stanford. From the purist point of view, a society with even one racist is a racist society, because the idea itself threatens and demeans its targets. They cannot feel wholly safe or wholly welcome as long as racism is present. Pluralism says: There will always be some racists. Marginalize them, ignore them, exploit them, ridicule them, take pains to make their policies illegal, but otherwise leave them alone.

Purists say: That's not enough. Society cannot be just until these pervasive and oppressive ideas are searched out and eradicated.

And so what is now under way is a growing drive to eliminate prejudice from every corner of society. I doubt that many people have noticed how far-reaching this anti-pluralist movement is becoming.

In universities: Dozens of universities have adopted codes proscribing speech or other expression that (this is from Stanford's policy, which is more or less representative) "is intended to insult or stigmatize an individual or small number of individuals on the basis of their sex, race, color, handicap, religion, sexual orientation or national and ethnic origin." Some codes punish only persistent harassment of a targeted individual, but many, following the purist doctrine that even one racist is too many, go much further. At Penn, an administrator declared: "We at the University of Pennsylvania have guaranteed students and the community that they can live in a community free of sexism, racism, and homophobia." Here is the purism that gives "political correctness" its distinctive combination of puffy high-mindedness and authoritarian zeal.

In school curricula: "More fundamental than eliminating racial segregation has to be the removal of racist thinking, assumptions, symbols, and materials from the curriculum," writes theorist Molefi Kete Asante. In practice, the effort to "remove racist thinking" goes well beyond striking egregious references from textbooks. In many cases it becomes a kind of mental engineering in which students are encouraged to see prejudice everywhere; it includes teaching identity politics as an antidote to internalized racism; it rejects mainstream science as "white male" thinking; and it tampers with history, installing such dubious notions as that the ancient Greeks stole their culture from Africa or that an ancient carving of a bird is an example of "African experimental aeronautics." . . .

Ah, but the task of scouring minds clean is Augean. "Nobody escapes," said a Rutgers University report on campus prejudice. Bias and prejudice, it found, cross every conceivable line, from sex to race to politics: "No matter who you are, no matter what the color of your skin, no matter what your gender or sexual orientation, no matter what you believe, no matter how you behave, there is somebody out there who doesn't like people of your kind." Charles Lawrence writes: "Racism is ubiquitous. We are all racists." If he means that most of us think racist thoughts of some sort at one time or another, he is right. If we are going to "eliminate prejudices and biases from our society," then the work of the prejudice police is unending. They are doomed to hunt and hunt and hunt, scour and scour and scour.

What is especially dismaying is that the purists pursue prejudice in the name of protecting minorities. In order to protect people like me (homosexual), they must pursue people like me (dissident). In order to bolster minority self-esteem, they suppress minority opinion. There are, of course, all kinds of practical and legal problems with the purists' campaign: the incursions against the First Amendment; the inevitable abuses by prosecutors and activists who define as "hateful" or "violent" whatever speech they dislike or can score points off of: the lack of any evidence that repressing prejudice eliminates rather than inflames it. But minorities, of all people, ought to remember that by definition we cannot prevail by numbers, and we generally cannot prevail by force. Against the power of ignorant mass opinion and group prejudice and superstition, we have only our voices. If you doubt that minorities' voices are powerful weapons, think of the lengths to which Southern officials went to silence the Reverend Martin Luther King Jr. (recall that the city commissioner of Montgomery, Alabama, won a $500,000 libel suit, later overturned in *New York Times v. Sullivan* [1964], regarding an advertisement in the *Times* placed by civil-rights leaders who denounced the Montgomery police). Think of how much gay people have improved their lot over twenty-five years simply by refusing to remain silent. Recall the Michigan student who was prosecuted for saying that homosexuality is a treatable disease, and notice that he was black. Under that Michigan speech code, more than twenty blacks were charged with racist speech, while no instance of racist speech by whites was punished. In Florida, the hate-speech law was invoked against a black man who called a policeman a "white cracker"; not

so surprisingly, in the first hate-crimes case to reach the Supreme Court, the victim was white and the defendant black. . . .

Here is the ultimate irony of the new purism: words, which pluralists hope can be substituted for violence, are redefined by purists *as* violence. "The experience of being called 'nigger,' 'spic,' 'Jap,' or 'kike' is like receiving a slap in the face," Charles Lawrence wrote in 1990. "Psychic injury is no less an injury than being struck in the face, and is often far more severe." This kind of talk is commonplace today. Epithets, insults, often even polite expressions of what's taken to be prejudice are called by purists "assaultive speech," "words that wound," "verbal violence." "To me, racial epithets are not speech," one University of Michigan law professor said. "They are bullets." In her speech accepting the 1993 Nobel Prize for Literature in Stockholm, Sweden, the author Toni Morrison said this: "Oppressive language does more than represent violence; it is violence."

It is not violence. I am thinking back to the moment on the subway in Washington, a little thing. I was riding home late one night and a squad of noisy kids, maybe seventeen or eighteen years old, noisily piled into the car. They yelled across the car and a girl said, "Where do we get off?"

A boy said, "Farragut North."
The girl: "*Faggot* North!"
The boy: "Yeah! Faggot North!"
General hilarity.

First, before the intellect resumes control, there is a moment of fear, an animal moment. Who are they? How many of them? How dangerous? Where is the way out? All of these things are noted preverbally and assessed by the gut. Then the brain begins an assessment: they are sober, this is probably too public a place for them to do it, there are more girls than boys, they were just talking, it is probably nothing.

They didn't notice me and there was no incident. The teenage babble flowed on, leaving me to think. I became interested in my own reaction: the jump of fear out of nowhere like an alert animal, the sense for a brief time that one is naked and alone and should hide or run away. For a time, one ceases to be a human being and becomes instead a faggot.

The fear engendered by these words is real. The remedy is as clear and as imperfect as ever: protect citizens against violence. This, I grant, is something that American society has never done very well and now does quite poorly. It is no solution to define words as violence or prejudice as oppression, and then by cracking down on words or thoughts pretend that we are doing something about violence and oppression. No doubt it is easier to pass a speech code or hate-crimes law and proclaim the streets safer than actually to make the streets safer, but the one must never be confused with the other. Every cop or prosecutor chasing words is one fewer chasing criminals. In a world rife with real violence and oppression, full of Rwandas and Bosnias and eleven-year-olds spraying bullets at children in Chicago and in turn being executed by gang lords, it is odious of Toni Morrison to say that words are violence.

Indeed, equating "verbal violence" with physical violence is a treacherous, mischievous business.

Not long ago a writer was charged with viciously and gratuitously wounding the feelings and dignity of millions of people. He was charged, in effect, with exhibiting flagrant prejudice against Muslims and outrageously slandering their beliefs. "What is freedom of expression?" mused Salman Rushdie a year after the ayatollahs sentenced him to death and put a price on his head. "Without the freedom to offend, it ceases to exist." I can think of nothing sadder than that minority activists, in their haste to make the world better, should be the ones to forget the lesson of Rushdie's plight: for minorities, pluralism, not purism, is the answer. The campaigns to eradicate prejudice—all of them, the speech codes and workplace restrictions and mandatory therapy for accused bigots and all the rest—should stop, now. The whole objective of eradicating prejudice, as opposed to correcting and criticizing it, should be repudiated as a fool's errand. Salman Rushdie is right, Toni Morrison wrong, and minorities belong at his side, not hers.

Discussion Questions

1. Discuss how Lawrence would most likely respond to Rauch's argument that we should tolerate rather than censor hate speech. Which person presents the more morally compelling argument? Support your answer.
2. According to Rauch, if all forms of hate speech were eliminated, freedom of expression in general would be severely limited. Describe what your campus would be like if hate speech were successfully eliminated by campus speech codes. Would it be a place of peace and harmony? Would it be a place of greater diversity and tolerance? Or would it be a place of tyranny and oppression? Support your answers.
3. Rauch claims that our goal should be to make the best of prejudice "rather than eradicate it." What does he mean by this? How can we make anything good out of prejudice? In terms of public policy, how could you implement Rauch's goal?
4. Unlike in the United States, Canadian criminal code makes the willful promotion of hatred against an identifiable group a crime. Has the outlawing of hate speech in Canada created a society, as Rauch envisions, where freedom of speech is severely limited? Or is the freedom of speech of minority groups more limited in the United States, as Lawrence claims? Canadians have traditionally placed less emphasis than Americans on liberty rights and more on welfare rights. Is this relevant to the type of public policy that might work best, from a moral point of view, in each country? Support your answers using specific examples.
5. Do you agree with Rauch that "the line between a prejudiced belief and a merely controversial one is elusive"? Even if the line between the two is elusive, does this

necessarily mean that there are not cases of clearly prejudiced hate speech? If so, would censorship be permissible for these extreme cases? Support your answers.

6. Discuss Rauch's claim that "brilliance and bigotry are empowered in the same stroke." Do you agree with Rauch? Use specific examples to illustrate your answer.

   J O H N   T A Y L O R

Are You Politically Correct?

Journalist John Taylor disagrees with people who argue that diversity is enhanced by restricting racist and other undesirable speech. He maintains that the politically correct movement on college campuses is reminiscent of the McCarthy era of the 1950s. Rather than encouraging diversity and free exchange of ideas, it is eroding our education system. The ultimate irony, he notes, is that the people who advocated free speech during the civil rights era are the very same people who are now trying to restrict speech on campus.

Critical Reading Questions

1. Why were Professors Thernstrom and Bailyn accused of being racists? How did students respond to what they regarded as racist speech on the part of these professors? Were the accusations justified, according to Taylor?
2. Who are the "new fundamentalists" on college campuses? Why does Taylor call them fundamentalists? What are some of the methods they use to restrict freedom of speech?
3. Why do the "new fundamentalists" believe that the doctrine of individual liberties is inherently oppressive? Does Taylor agree with them?
4. What does it mean to be "politically correct"? What is "false consciousness"? How do those who are politically correct invoke the concept of false consciousness to support censorship?
5. How does Taylor support his argument that the climate on today's college campus is similar to McCarthyism in the 1950s?
6. What does Taylor mean by "thought reform"? What are some of the examples of thought reform used by Taylor?
7. According to Taylor, why are the humanities a hotbed for political correctness and controversy?
8. What groups are assigned ethnic status by the "new fundamentalists"? What groups are assigned oppressed status? On what grounds does Taylor argue that these assignments are arbitrary?
9. What is the New Age caste system? Who is oppressed under this system?
10. Why does Paglia call gender feminism a "form of psychosis"?
11. How do gender feminists use the concept of false consciousness to attack heterosexuality?

"Are You Politically Correct?" *New York Magazine*, January 21, 1991, pp. 32–40.

12. On what grounds does Taylor reject the goals and ideologies of gender feminists?
13. Why is Taylor suspicious of reports on the prevalence of rape?
14. What group on campus is most involved in trying to restrict freedom of speech? Why do they want such restrictions?
15. In Taylor's view, how is political correctness eroding rationalism and education?

"Racist."

"Racist!"

"The man is a racist!"

"A *racist!*"

Such denunciations, hissed in tones of self-righteousness and contempt, vicious and vengeful, furious, smoking with hatred—such denunciations haunted Stephan Thernstrom for weeks. Whenever he walked through the campus that spring, down Harvard's brick paths, under the arched gates, past the fluttering elms, he found it hard not to imagine the pointing fingers, the whispers. Racist. There goes *the racist.* It was hellish, this persecution. Thernstrom couldn't sleep. His nerves were frayed, his temper raw. He was making his family miserable. And the worst thing was that he didn't know who was calling him a racist, or why.

Thernstrom, 56, a professor at Harvard University for 25 years, is considered one of the preeminent scholars of the history of race relations in America. He has tenure. He has won prizes and published numerous articles and four books and edited the *Harvard Encyclopedia of American Ethnic Groups.* For several years, Thernstrom and another professor, Bernard Bailyn, taught an undergraduate lecture course on the history of race relations in the United States called "Peopling of America." Bailyn covered the Colonial era. Thernstrom took the class up to the present.

Both professors are regarded as very much in the academic mainstream, their views grounded in extensive research on their subject, and both have solid liberal democratic credentials. But all of a sudden, in the fall of 1987, articles began to appear in the *Harvard Crimson* accusing Thernstrom and Bailyn of "racial insensitivity" in "Peopling of America." The sources for the articles were anonymous, the charges vague, but they continued to be repeated, these ringing indictments.

Finally, through the intervention of another professor, two students from the lecture course came forward and identified themselves as the sources for the articles. When asked to explain their grievances, they presented the professors with a six-page letter. Bailyn's crime had been to read from the diary of a southern planter without giving equal time to the recollections of a slave. This, to the students, amounted to a covert defense of slavery. Bailyn, who has won two Pulitzer Prizes, had pointed out during the lecture that no journals, diaries, or letters written by slaves had ever been found. He had explained to the class that all they could do was read the planter's diary and use it to speculate about the experience of slaves. But that failed to satisfy the complaining students. Since it was impossible to give equal representation to the slaves, Bailyn ought to have dispensed with the planter's diary altogether.

Thernstrom's failures, according to the students, were almost systematic. He had, to begin with, used the word *Indians* instead of *Native Americans.* Thernstrom tried to point out that he had said very clearly in class that *Indian* was the word most Indians themselves use, but that was irrelevant to the students. They considered the word racist. . . .

Even worse, they continued, Thernstrom had assigned a book to the class that mentioned that some people regarded affirmative action as preferential treatment. That was a racist opinion. But most egregiously, Thernstrom had endorsed, in class, Patrick Moynihan's emphasis on the breakup of the black family as a cause of persistent black poverty. That was a racist idea.

All of these words and opinions and ideas and historical approaches were racist. *Racist!* They would not be tolerated.

The semester was pretty much over by then. But during the spring, when Thernstrom sat down to plan the course for the following year, he had to think about how he would combat charges of racism should they crop up again. And they assuredly would. . . . And a charge of racism, however unsubstantiated, leaves a lasting impression. "It's like being called a Commie in the fifties," Thernstrom says. "Whatever explanation you offer, once accused, you're always suspect."

He decided that to protect himself in case he was misquoted or had comments taken out of context, he would need to tape all his lectures. Then he decided he would have to tape his talks with students in his office. He would, in fact, have to tape everything he said on the subject of race. It would require a tape-recording system worthy of the Nixon White House. Microphones everywhere, the reels turning constantly. That was plainly ridiculous. Thernstrom instead decided it would be easier just to drop the course altogether. "Peopling of America" is no longer offered at Harvard.

THE NEW FUNDAMENTALISM

When the Christian-Fundamentalist uprising began in the late seventies, Americans on the left sneered at the Bible thumpers who tried to ban the teaching of evolution in public schools, at the troglodytes who wanted to remove *The Catcher in the Rye* from public libraries. They heaped scorn on the evangelists who railed against secular humanism and the pious hypocrites who tried to legislate patriotism and Christianity through school prayer and the Pledge of Allegiance. This last effort was considered particularly heinous. Those right-wing demagogues were interfering with individual liberties! They were trying to indoctrinate the children! It was scandalous and outrageous, and unconstitutional too.

But curiously enough, in the past few years, a new sort of fundamentalism has arisen precisely among those people who were the most appalled by Christian fundamentalism. And it is just as demagogic and fanatical. The new fundamentalists are an eclectic group; they include multiculturalists, feminists, radical homosexuals, Marxists, New Historicists. What unites them—as firmly as the Christian fundamentalists are united in the belief that the Bible is the revealed word of God—is their conviction that Western culture and American society are thoroughly and hopelessly racist, sexist, oppressive. . . .

One of the marvels of the new fundamentalism is the rationale it has concocted for dismissing all dissent. Just as Christian fundamentalists attack nonbelievers as agents of Satan, so the politically correct dismiss their critics as victims of, to use the famous Marxist phrase, "false consciousness." Anyone who disagrees is simply too soaked in the oppressors' propaganda to see the truth. . . . "we are all the progeny of a racist and sexist society."

This circular reasoning enables the new fundamentalists to attack not just the opinions of their critics but the right of their critics to disagree. Alternate viewpoints are simply not allowed. Though there was little visible protest when Louis Farrakhan was invited to speak at the University of Wisconsin, students at the University of Northern Colorado practically rioted when Linda Chavez, a Hispanic member of the Reagan administration who opposes affirmative action and believes immigrants should be encouraged to learn English, was asked to talk. The invitation was withdrawn. Last February, Patrick Moynihan declared during a lecture at Vassar that America was "a model of a reasonably successful multiethnic society." Afterward, he got into an argument with a black woman who disagreed with him, and when she claimed the senator had insulted her, militant students occupied a school building until Moynihan returned his lecture fee. "The disturbing factor in the success of totalitarianism is . . . the true selflessness of its adherents," Hannah Arendt wrote in *The Origins of Totalitarianism*. "The fanaticized members can be reached by neither experience nor argument."

It is this sort of demand for intellectual conformity, enforced with harassment and intimidation, that has led some people to compare the atmosphere in universities today to that of Germany in the thirties. "It's fascism of the left," says Camille Paglia, a professor at the University of the Arts in Philadelphia and the author of *Sexual Personae*. "These people behave like the Hitler Youth."

It reminds others of America in the fifties. "This sort of atmosphere, where a few highly mobilized radical students can intimidate everyone else, is quite new," Thernstrom says. "This is a new Mc-

Carthyism. It's more frightening than the old Mc-Carthyism, which had no support in the academy. Now the enemy is within. There are students and faculty who have no belief in freedom of speech." . . .

Many schools—including Stanford, Pennsylvania, and the University of Wisconsin—have adopted codes of conduct that require students who deviate from politically correct thinking to undergo thought reform. When a student at the University of Michigan read a limerick that speculated jokingly about the homosexuality of a famous athlete, he was required to attend gay-sensitivity sessions and publish a piece of self-criticism in the student newspaper called "Learned My Lesson."

But is any of this so awful? In the minds of its advocates, thought reform is merely a well-intentioned effort to help stop the spread of the racial tensions that have proliferated in universities in recent years. "I don't know of any institution that is saying you have to adore everyone else," says Catharine Stimpson, dean of the graduate school at Rutgers. "They are saying you have to learn to live with everyone. They are taking insulting language seriously. That's a good thing. They're not laughing off anti-Semitic and homophobic graffiti."

After all, it is said, political indoctrination of one sort or another has always taken place at universities. Now that process is simply being overt. . . .

EVERYTHING IS POLITICAL

If the debate over what students should be taught has become an openly political power struggle, that is only because, to the politically correct, *everything* is political. And nothing is more political, in their view, than the humanities, where much of the recent controversy has been centered.

For most of the twentieth century, professors in the humanities modeled themselves on their counterparts in the natural sciences. They thought of themselves as specialists in the disinterested pursuit of the truth. . . .

That common sense of purpose began to fracture in the sixties. The generation of professors now acquiring prominence and power at universities . . . came of age during that period. They

witnessed its upheavals and absorbed its political commitments. . . .

In the view of such activists, the universities were hardly the havens of academic independence they pretended to be. They had hopelessly compromised their integrity by accepting contracts from the Pentagon, but those alliances with the reviled "military-industrial Establishment" were seen as merely one symptom of a larger conspiracy by white males. Less obviously, but more insidiously, they had appointed themselves guardians of the culture and compiled the list of so-called Great Books as a propaganda exercise to reinforce the notion of white-male superiority. "The canon of great literature was created by high-Anglican ass——s to underwrite their social class," Stanley Hauerwas, a professor at Duke's Divinity School, put it recently. . . .

That being the case, any attempt to assign meaning to art, literature, or thought, to interpret it and evaluate it, was nothing more than an exercise in political power by the individual with the authority to impose his or her view. It then followed that the only reason to require students to read certain books is not to "correct taste" or because the books were "the best that has been thought or written" but because they promoted politically correct viewpoints. That ideological emphasis also applied to scholarship generally. . . .

ETHNIC AND IDEOLOGICAL PURITY

The multicultural and ethnic-studies programs now in place at most universities tend to divide humanity into five groups—whites, blacks, Native Americans, Hispanics, and Asians. (Homosexuals and feminists are usually included on the grounds that, though they are not a distinct ethnic group, they, too, have been oppressed by the "white-male" . . . and prevented from expressing their "otherness.") These are somewhat arbitrary categories, and, in fact, the new fundamentalists have two contradictory views about just what constitutes an ethnic group and who can belong. . . .

This obsessive tendency to see oppression everywhere is creating a sort of New Age caste system. The Smith handout listed various categories of oppression that ranged from "classism" and "ageism" to "ableism" (identified as "oppression of the differently abled by the temporarily able") and "lookism," which was revealed to be "the construction of a standard for beauty/attractiveness; and oppression through stereotypes and generalizations of both those who do not fit that standard and those who do." Heightism may be next. In a joke now making the rounds, short people are demanding to be known as "the vertically challenged."

But joking isn't allowed! Even the most harmless, lighthearted remarks can lead to virulent denunciations. In October, Roderick Nash, a professor at the University of California at Santa Barbara, pointed out during a lecture on environmental ethics that there is a movement to start referring to pets as animal companions. (Apparently, domesticated animals are offended by the word *pet*.) Nash then made some sort of off-the-cuff observation about how women who pose for *Penthouse* are still called Pets (and not *Penthouse* Animal Companions). Inevitably, several female students filed a formal sexual-harassment complaint against him. Susan Rode, one of the signers, said, "Maybe this will make more people aware in other classes and make other faculty watch what they say."

Indeed, making people *watch what they say* is the central preoccupation of politically correct students. Stephan Thernstrom is not the only professor who has been forced to give up a course on race relations. . . .

THE GENDER FEMINISTS AND DATE RAPE

"Misogynist!"
   "Patriarchal!"
   "Gynophobic!"
   "Phallocentric!"

Last fall, Camille Paglia attended a lecture by a "feminist theorist" from a large Ivy League university who had set out to "decode" the subliminal sexual oppressiveness in fashion photography. The feminist theorist stood at the front of the room showing slides of fashion photography and cosmetics ads and exposing, in the style of Lacanian psychoanalysis, their violent sexism. She had selected a Revlon ad of a woman with a heavily made-up face who was standing up to her chin in a pool of water. When it came up on the screen, she exclaimed, "Decapitation!"

She showed a picture of a black woman who was wearing aviator goggles and had the collar of her turtleneck sweater pulled up. "Strangulation!" she shouted. "Bondage!"

It went on like this for the entire lecture. When it was over, Paglia, who considers herself a feminist, stood up and made an impassioned speech. She declared that the fashion photography of the past 40 years is great art, that instead of decapitation she saw the birth of Venus, instead of strangulation she saw references to King Tut. But political correctness has achieved a kind of exquisitely perfect rigidity among the group known as the gender feminists, and she was greeted, she says, "with gasps of horror and angry murmuring. It's a form of psychosis, this slogan-filled machinery. The radical feminists have contempt for values other than their own, and they're inspiring in students a resentful attitude toward the world."

Indeed, the central tenet of gender feminism is that Western society is organized around a "sex/gender system." What defines the system, according to Sandra Harding, a professor of philosophy at the University of Delaware and one of its exponents, is "male dominance made possible by men's control of women's productive and reproductive labor."

The primary arena for this dominance is, of course, the family, which Alison Jaggar, a professor at the University of Cincinnati and the head of the American Philosophical Association's Committee on the Status of Women in Philosophy, sees as "a cornerstone of women's oppression." The family, in Jaggar's view, "enforces heterosexuality" and "imposes the prevailing masculine and feminine character structures on the next generation." . . .

Women who have decided to get married and raise families, women who want to become mothers, are, naturally, victims of false consciousness. The radical feminists are fond of quoting Simone de Beauvoir, who said, "No woman should be authorized to stay at home and raise children . . . precisely because if there is such a choice, too many women will make that one." . . .

Unlike the pre-Copernican view that the Earth was at the center of the universe, androcentricity is not, in the view of the gender feminists, merely a flawed theory. It is a moral evil, dedicated to the enslavement of women. And since most of Western culture, according to this view, has been a testament to "male power and transcendence," it is similarly evil and must be discarded. This includes not only patriarchal books like the Bible and sexist subjects like traditional history, with its emphasis on great men and great deeds, but also the natural sciences and even the very process of analytical thinking itself. . . .

But is not just the coldly analytical and dualistic structures of male thinking that the gender feminists find so contemptible. It is males themselves, or at least heterosexual males. After all, heterosexuality is responsible for the subjugation of women, and so, in the oppressive culture of the West, any woman who goes on a date with a man is a prostitute. "Both man and woman might be outraged at the description of their candlelight dinner as prostitution," Jaggar has written. "But the radical feminist argues this outrage is simply due to the participants' failure or refusal to perceive the social context in which the dinner occurs." In other words, they are victims of—what else?—false consciousness.

This eagerness to see all women as victims, to describe all male behavior with images of rape and violation, may shed some light on the phenomenon of date rape, a legitimate issue that has been exaggerated and distorted by a small group with a specific political agenda. . . .

Much of this discussion starts off with the claim that one in four female students is raped by a date. The figure seems staggeringly high, and debate tends to focus on whether actual rape or merely the reporting of rape is on the rise. But the journalist Stephanie Gutmann has pointed out in *Reason* magazine the gross statistical flaws in the survey of date rape that produced this figure. According to Gutmann, "the real story about campus date rape is not that there's been any significant increase of rape on college campuses, at least of the acquaintance type, but that the word *rape* is being stretched to encompass any type of sexual interaction."

In fact, rape under the new definition does not have to involve physical assault at all. . . .

It is no surprise then that Catherine Nye, a University of Chicago psychologist interviewed by Gut-

mann, found that 43 percent of the women in a widely cited rape study "had not realized they had been raped." In other words, they were victims of, yes, false consciousness. But by the definition of the radical feminists, all sexual encounters that involve any confusion or ambivalence constitute rape. "Ordinary bungled sex—the kind you regret in the morning or even during—is being classified as rape," Gutmann says. "Bad or confused feelings after sex becomes someone else's fault." Which is fine with the feminists. "In terms of making men nervous or worried about overstepping their bounds, I don't think that's a bad thing," [Andrea] Parrot said. Indeed, since it encourages a general suspicion of all men, it's a good thing. As Parrot has put it, "Since you can't tell who has the potential for rape simply by looking, be on your guard with every man." . . .

MOONIES IN THE CLASSROOM

The supreme irony of the new fundamentalism is that the generation that produced the free-speech movement in Berkeley and rebelled against the idea of *in loco parentis*—that university administrators should act as surrogate parents—is now trying to restrict speech and control the behavior of a new generation of students. The enterprise is undertaken to combat racism, of course, and it is an article of faith among the politically correct that the current climate of racial hostility can be traced to the Reagan and Bush presidencies, to conservative-Republican efforts to gut civil-rights legislation and affirmative-action programs. However true that may be, scholars like Shelby Steele, a black essayist and English professor, have also argued that the separatist movements at universities—black dorms, Native American student centers, gay-studies programs, the relentless harping on "otherness"—have heightened tensions and contributed to the culture of victimization. "If you sensitize people from day one to look at everything in terms of race and sex, eventually they will see racism and sexism at the root of everything," says Alan Kors. "But not all the problems and frustrations in life are due to race and gender."

Furthermore, they say, instead of increasing self-esteem, schools that offer an Afrocentric education will only turn out students who are more resentful, and incompetent, than ever. Indeed, while the more rabid Afrocentrics have claimed that crack and AIDS are conspiracies by whites to eliminate blacks, it could just as easily be argued that white indulgence of Afrocentric education represents a conspiracy to provide blacks with a useless education that will keep them out of the job market.

Of course, to make such a statement is invariably to provoke a charge of racism. But part of the problem with this reaction is that it trivializes the debate. In fact, it makes debate impossible. But that is just as well, according to the new fundamentalists. Debate, and the analytic thinking it requires, is oppressive. It's logocentric. It favors the articulate at the expense of the inarticulate. It forces people to make distinctions, and since racism is the result of distinctions, they should be discouraged. "I have students tell me they don't need to study philosophy because it's patriarchal and logocentric," says Christina Sommers. "They're unteachable and scary. It's like having a Moonie in the classroom."

Resistance to this sort of robotic sloganeering is beginning. "Today, routinized righteous indigna-tion has been substituted for rigorous criticism,"[22] Henry Louis Gates, a black English professor at Duke, recently declared. . . .

A few emboldened administrators are actually suggesting that it is not unreasonable for Western culture to enjoy a certain prominence at American colleges. In an address to incoming Yale students in September, Donald Kagan, dean of the college, encouraged them to center their undergraduate studies around Western culture. He argued that the West "has asserted the claims of the individual against those of the state, limiting its power and creating a realm of privacy into which it cannot penetrate." The West's tradition of civil liberties has produced a "tolerance and respect for diversity unknown in most cultures."

But many of the Yale freshmen—or "freshpeople," as the *Yale Daily News* puts it—considered the dean's statements "quite disturbing." And the dean was denounced with the obligatory mind-numbing litany.

"Paternalistic!"

"Racist!"

"Fascist!"

Discussion Questions

1. Were the "racially insensitive" comments made by Professors Thernstrom and Bailyn examples of hate speech? Should people who use politically incorrect terms such as *Indian* instead of *Native American* be censured or reprimanded? If so, how should this be carried out; for example, should it be through exposés in student newspapers, as happened in this case, through speech codes, through laws, or through boycotts of classes? Support your answers.

2. What are some examples of "red flag" phrases and hate speech on your college campus? On what grounds do you consider them to be so? Discuss whether professors should censure students who use "red flag" phrases in their papers or who engage in hate speech in class.

3. Discuss Taylor's claim that the politically correct climate on today's campus is reminiscent of the McCarthyism of the 1950s. Would Lawrence agree with Taylor? Explain.

4. Do you find that you have to be careful of what you say on campus? Is it necessarily an undesirable thing that we should stop and think of the effects of our words before speaking? Support your answers.

5. Are multiculturalism and gender feminism divisive, as Taylor claims? Support your answer using examples from your own experience.

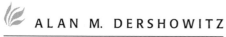

A L A N   M .   D E R S H O W I T Z

Political Correctness, Speech Codes, and Diversity

Alan Dershowitz is a law professor at Harvard University as well as one of the foremost defense lawyers and civil libertarians in the United States. His books include *Taking Liberties: A Decade of Hard Cases, Bad Laws, and Bum Raps,* and *The Abuse Excuse* (1994). In this article, Dershowitz examines the motives behind the political correctness movement. Like Taylor, he concludes that the speech codes promoted by the political correctness movement, while claiming to promote greater diversity, in fact limit diversity of expression.

Critical Reading Questions

1. According to Dershowitz, what are two of the basic tenets of the political correctness movement?
2. What is the primary purpose of campus speech codes? Is this purpose, according to Dershowitz, compatible with diversity of expression?
3. Why does Dershowitz question the real motives of the political correctness movement?
4. According to Dershowitz, what is the real motive behind the demand for more diversity on college campuses?
5. What group of people is pushing hardest for political correctness and speech codes?
6. What is the effect of speech codes on political speech?
7. How does Dershowitz respond to students who defend speech codes on the grounds that certain types of speech contribute to "bigotry, harassment and intolerance, and that it makes it difficult for them to learn"?
8. What has been the right-wing reaction to speech codes?
9. According to Dershowitz, what has been the effect of political correctness and speech codes on discussions and learning in the classroom?

There is now a debate among the pundits over whether the "political correctness" [P.C.] movement on college and university campuses constitutes a real threat to intellectual freedom or merely provides conservatives with a highly publicized opportunity to bash the left for the kind of intolerance of which the right has often been accused.

My own sense, as a civil libertarian whose views lean to the left, is that the "P.C." movement is dangerous and that it is also being exploited by hypocritical right wingers.

In addition to being intellectually stifling, the P.C. movement is often internally inconsistent. Among its most basic tenets are (1) the demand for "greater diversity" among students and faculty members; and (2) the need for "speech codes," so that racist, sexist and homophobic ideas, attitudes and language do not "offend" sensitive students.

"Political Correctness, Speech Codes, and Diversity," *Harvard Law Record,* September 20, 1991.

Is it really possible that the bright and well-intentioned students (and faculty) who are pressing the "politically correct" agenda do not realize how inherently self-contradictory these two basic tenets really are? Can they be blind to the obvious reality that true diversity of viewpoints is incompatible with speech codes that limit certain diverse expressions and attitudes?

I wonder if most of those who are pressing for diversity really want it. What many on the extreme left seem to want is simply more of their own: more students and faculty who think like they do, vote like they do and speak like they do. The last thing they want is a truly diverse campus community with views that are broadly reflective of the multiplicity of attitudes in the big, bad world outside of the ivory towers.

How many politically correct students are demanding—in the name of diversity—an increase in the number of Evangelical Christians, National Rifle Association members, and Right to Life advocates? Where is the call for more anti-communist refugees from the Soviet Union, Afro-Americans who oppose race-specific quotas, and women who are antifeminist?

Let's be honest: the demand for diversity is at least in part a cover for a political power grab by the left. Most of those who are recruited to provide politically correct diversity—Afro-Americans, women, gays—are thought to be supporters of the left. And historically, the left—like the right—has not been a bastion of diversity.

Now the left—certainly the extreme left that has been pushing hardest for political correctness—is behind the demands for speech codes. And if they were to get their way, these codes would not be limited to racist, sexist, or homophobic *epithets*. They would apply as well to politically incorrect *ideas* that are deemed offensive by those who would enforce the codes. Such ideas would include criticism of affirmative action programs, opposition to rape-shield laws, advocacy of the criminalization of homosexuality and defense of pornography.

I have heard students argue that the expression of such ideas—both in and out of class, both by students and professors—contributes to an atmosphere of bigotry, harassment and intolerance, and that it makes it difficult for them to learn.

The same students who insist that they be treated as adults when it comes to their sexuality, drinking and school work, beg to be treated like children when it comes to politics, speech and controversy. They whine to Big Father and Mother—the president or provost of the University—to "protect" them from offensive speech, instead of themselves trying to combat it in the marketplace of ideas.

Does this movement for political correctness—this intolerance of verbal and intellectual diversity—really affect college and university students today? Or is it, as some argue, merely a passing fad, exaggerated by the political right and the media?

It has certainly given the political right—not known for its great tolerance of different ideas—a hey day. Many hypocrites of the right, who would gladly impose their own speech codes if *they* had the power to enforce *their* way, are selectively wrapping themselves in the same First Amendment they willingly trash when it serves their political interest to do so.

But hypocrisy aside—since there is more than enough on both sides—the media is not exaggerating the problem of political correctness. It is a serious issue on college and university campuses. As a teacher, I can feel a palpable reluctance on the part of many students—particularly those with views in neither extreme and those who are anxious for peer acceptance—to experiment with unorthodox ideas, to make playful comments on serious subjects, to challenge politically correct views and to disagree with minority, feminist or gay perspectives.

I feel this problem quite personally, since I happen to agree—as a matter of substance—with most "politically correct" positions. But I am appalled at the intolerance of many who share my substantive views. And I worry about the impact of politically correct intolerance on the generation of leaders we are currently educating.

Discussion Questions

1. List some examples of politically correct ideology. Discuss the criteria you used for deciding whether a particular ideology was politically correct or politically incorrect. Are these criteria based on rational moral principles? Support your answer.
2. Some students confound morality with subscribing to the politically correct ideology. What is the difference between being a moral person and being politically correct? Does the politically correct movement encourage substituting ideology for true moral development? Support your answers.
3. What does diversity mean to you? Discuss whether diversity and freedom of speech are most likely to flourish on a college campus with, or without, speech codes. Use specific examples to illustrate your answer.
4. Ernst Zundel was brought before the Canadian Human Rights Tribunal in October 1997 on charges that he was printing lies about the Holocaust on his Web site.[23] He was accused of propagating hate by denying that the Nazis killed millions of Jews. Should Zundel be prohibited from printing lies about the Holocaust? Support your answer. How would Mill and Dershowitz each most likely respond to this question?
5. Discuss how Lawrence might respond to Dershowitz's objection to campus speech codes. Who makes the strongest argument—Dershowitz or Lawrence? Support your answer.

 CASS R. SUNSTEIN

The First Amendment in Cyberspace

Cass Sunstein is a professor of jurisprudence in the law school and the department of political science at the University of Chicago. In the following selection from his book *Free Markets and Social Justice,* Professor Cass explores the impact of the different interpretations of First Amendment freedom of speech on the regulation of cyberspace speech. He concludes that constitutionally based regulations on cyberspace speech should aim to foster democratic ends, including public debate, political equality, and even virtue.

Critical Reading Questions

1. What are the two models of the First Amendment free speech tradition?
2. What are the implications of these two models for the government regulation of speech?
3. Why does Sunstein prefer the Madisonian model over the marketplace model?
4. What are some of the new possibilities opened up by the new communication technology?

Cass R. Sunstein, "The First Amendment in Cyberspace," from *Free Markets and Social Justice* (New York: Oxford University Press, 1997), pp. 168–169, 172, 183, 187–191, 196–198, 200.

5. What are some of the dangers associated with the new communication technology?
6. According to Sunstein, why is universal access to the information superhighway important in a democracy?
7. According to Sunstein, what criteria should be used in deciding whether it is permissible for government to regulate cyberspace speech?
8. What is Sunstein's view on the regulation of obscene, indecent, and sexually explicit material on the Internet? How have the courts handled this in the past?
9. What analogy does Sunstein use in holding electronic mail servers liable for the distribution of unprotected speech?
10. According to Sunstein, what end(s) justify regulating speech in cyberspace?

. . . The existence of technological change promises to test the system of free expression in dramatic ways. What should be expected with respect to the First Amendment?

MARKETS AND MADISON

There have been in the United States two models of the First Amendment, corresponding to two free speech traditions.[1] The first emphasizes well-functioning speech markets. It can be traced to Justice Holmes's great *Abrams* dissent,[2] where the notion of a "market in ideas" received its preeminent exposition. . . .

The second tradition, and the second model, focuses on public deliberation. The second model can be traced from its origins in the work of James Madison, with his attack on the idea of seditious libel, to Justice Louis Brandeis, with his suggestion that "the greatest menace to freedom is an inert people,"[3] . . .

Under the marketplace metaphor, the First Amendment requires—at least as a presumption—a system of unrestricted economic markets in speech. Government must respect the forces of supply and demand. At the very least, it may not regulate the content of speech so as to push the speech market in its preferred directions. Certainly it must be neutral with respect to viewpoint. A key point for marketplace advocates is that great distrust of government is especially appropriate when speech is at issue. . . .

Those who endorse the marketplace model do not claim that government may not do anything at all. Of course, government may set up the basic rules of property and contract; it is these rules that make markets feasible. . . .

The law of free speech will ultimately have to make some hard choices about the marketplace and democratic models. It is also safe to say that the changing nature of the information market will test the two models in new ways. . . .

SPEECH, EMERGING MEDIA, AND CYBERSPACE

New Possibilities and New Problems: Referenda in Cyberspace and Related Issues

It should be unnecessary to emphasize that the explosion of new technologies opens up extraordinary new possibilities. As the Department of Commerce's predictions suggest, ordinary people are starting to be able to participate in a communications network in which hundreds of millions of people, or more, can communicate with each other and indeed with all sorts of service providers—libraries, doctors, accountants, lawyers, legislators, shopkeepers, pharmacies, grocery stores, museums, Internal Revenue Service employees, restaurants, and more. If you need an answer to a medical question, you may be able to push a few buttons and receive a reliable answer. If you want to order food for delivery, you may be able to do so in a matter of seconds. If you have a question about sports, music, or clothing, or about the eighteenth century, you can get an instant answer. People can now purchase many goods on their credit cards without leaving home. It may now be possible to receive a college education without leaving home. . . .

SOME POLICY DILEMMAS

A large question for both constitutional law and public policy has yet to receive a full democratic or judicial answer: To what extent, if any, do Madisonian ideals have a place in the world of new technologies or in cyberspace? Some people think that the absence of scarcity eliminates the argument for governmental regulation, at least if it is designed to promote attention to public issues, to increase diversity, or to raise the quality of public debate. If outlets are unlimited, why is regulation of any value? In the future, people will be able to listen to whatever they want, perhaps to speak to whomever they choose. Ought this not to be a constitutional ideal?

The question is meant to answer itself, but perhaps enough has been said to show that it hardly does that. Recall first that structural regulation, assigning property rights and making agreements possible, is a precondition for well-functioning markets. Laissez-faire is a hopeless misdescription of free markets. A large government role, with coercive features, is required to maintain markets. Part of the role also requires steps to prevent monopoly and monopolistic practices.

Moreover, Madisonian goals need not be thought anachronistic in a period of infinite outlets. In a system of infinite outlets, the goal of consumer sovereignty may well be adequately promoted. That goal has a distinguished place in both law and public policy, but it should not be identified with the Constitution's free speech guarantee. The Constitution does not require consumer sovereignty; for the most part, the decision whether to qualify or replace that goal with Madisonian aspirations should be made democratically rather than judicially. A democratic citizenry armed with a constitutional guarantee of free speech need not see consumer sovereignty as its fundamental aspiration. Certainly it may choose consumer sovereignty if it likes. But instead it may seek to ensure high-quality fare for children, even if this approach departs from consumer satis-

faction. It may seek more generally to promote educational and public-affairs programming. . . .

Analogies

An important issue for the future involves the use of old analogies in novel settings. The new technologies will greatly increase the opportunities for intrusive, fraudulent, harassing, threatening, libelous, or obscene speech. With a few brief touches of a finger, a speaker is now able to communicate to thousands or even millions of people—or to pinpoint a message, perhaps a commercial, harassing, threatening, invasive message, to a particular person. A libelous message, or grotesque invasions of privacy, can be sent almost costlessly. Perhaps reputations and lives will be easily ruined or at least damaged. There are difficult questions about the extent to which an owner of a computer service might be held liable for what appears on that service.

At this stage, it remains unclear whether the conventional legal standards should be altered to meet such problems. For the most part, those standards seem an adequate start and must simply be adapted to new settings. For purposes of assessing cyberspace, there are often apt analogies on which to draw. In fact, the legal culture has no way to think about the new problems except via analogies. The analogies are built into our very langauge: e-mail, electronic bulletin boards, cyberspace, cyberspaces, and much more. . . .

Access

The government has said that "universal access" is one of its goals for the information superhighway. The question of access has several dimensions. To some extent, it is designed to ensure access to broadcasting options for viewers and listeners. Here a particular concern is that poor people should not be deprived of access to a valuable good. Currently, the expense of Internet connections is prohibitively high for many families. This may entail a form of disenfranchisement. There is an additional problem of ensuring access for certain speakers who want to reach part of the viewing or listening public. In cyberspace, of course, people are both listeners and speakers.

Perhaps the goal of universal viewer or listener access should be viewed with skepticism. The government does not guarantee universal access to cars, housing, food, or even health care. It may seem puzzling to suggest that universal access to information technologies is an important social goal. But the suggestion is less puzzling than it appears. Suppose, for example, that a certain technology becomes a principal means by which people communicate with their elected representatives; suppose that such communications become a principle part of public deliberation and in that way ancillary to the right to vote. . . . Universal access could be seen to be part of the goal of political equality. More generally, universal access might be necessary if the network is to serve its intended function of promoting broad discussion between citizens and representatives. . . .

Protecting Against Obscene, Libelous, Violent, Commercial, or Harassing Broadcasting or Messages

New technologies have greatly expanded the opportunity to communicate obscene, libelous, violent, or harassing messages—perhaps to general groups via stations on (for example) cable television, perhaps to particular people via electronic mail. Invasions of privacy are far more likely. The Internet poses special problems on these counts. As a general rule, any restrictions should be treated like those governing ordinary speech, with ordinary mail providing the best analogy. If restrictions are narrowly tailored and supported by a sufficiently strong record, they should be upheld.

Consider in this regard a highly publicized case involving "cyberporn" at the University of Michigan. A student is alleged to have distributed a fictional story involving a fellow student, explicitly named, who was, in the story, raped, tortured, and finally killed. The first question raised here is whether state or federal law provides a cause of action for conduct of this sort. Perhaps the story amounts to a threat, or a form of libel, or perhaps the most plausible state law claim would be based on intentional infliction of emotional distress. The next question is whether, if a state law claim is available, the award

of damages would violate the First Amendment. At first glance, it seems that the question should be resolved in the same way as any case in which a writer uses a real person's name in fiction of this sort. . . .

What of a regulatory regime designed to prevent invasion of privacy, libel, unwanted commercial messages, obscenity, harassment, or infliction of emotional distress? Some such regulatory regime will ultimately make a great deal of sense. The principal obstacles are that the regulations should be both clear and narrow. It is easy to imagine a broad or vague regulation, one that would seize on the sexually explicit or violent nature of communication to justify regulation that is far broader than necessary. Moreover, it is possible to imagine a situation in which liability was extended to any owner or operator who could have no knowledge of the particular materials being sent. The underlying question, having to do with efficient risk allocation, involves the extent to which a carrier might be expected to find and to stop unlawful messages; that question depends on the relevant technology.

Consider, more particularly, possible efforts to control the distribution of sexually explicit materials on the Internet. Insofar as the government seeks to ban materials that are technically obscene and imposes civil or criminal liability on someone with specific intent to distribute such materials, there should be no constitutional problem. . . . On the other hand, many actual and imaginable bills would extend beyond the technically obscene, to include (for example) materials that are "indecent," "lewd," or "filthy." Terms of this sort create a serious risk of unconstitutional vagueness or overbreadth. At least at first glance, they appear unconstitutional for that reason.

The best justification for expansive terms of this kind would be to protect children from harmful materials. It is true that the Internet contains pornography accessible to children, some of it coming from adults explicitly seeking sexual relations with children. There is in fact material on the Internet containing requests to children for their home addresses. Solicitations to engage in unlawful activity are unprotected by the First Amendment, whether they occur on the Internet or anywhere else. . . .

But when government goes beyond solicitation and bans "indecent" or "filthy" material in general, the question is quite different. Here a central issue is whether the government has chosen the least restrictive means of preventing the relevant harms to children. In a case involving "dial-a-porn," for example, the Court struck down a ban on "indecent" materials on the ground that children could be protected in other ways.[4] . . . Under existing law, it seems clear that in order to support an extension beyond obscenity, Congress would have to show that less restrictive alternatives would be ineffectual. The question then becomes a factual one: What sorts of technological options exist by which parents or others can provide the relevant protection? To answer this question, it would be necessary to explore the possibility of creating "locks" within the Internet, for use by parents, or perhaps for use by those who write certain sorts of materials.

Different questions would be raised by the imposition of civil or criminal liability, not on the distributors having specific intent to distribute, but on carriers who have no knowledge of the specific materials at issue and could not obtain such knowledge without considerable difficulty and expense. It might be thought that the carrier should be treated like a publisher, and a publisher can of course be held liable for obscene or libelous materials, even if the publisher has no specific knowledge of the offending material. But in light of the relatively low costs of search in the world of magazine and book publishing, it is reasonable to think that a publisher should be charged with having control over the content of its publications. Perhaps the same cannot be said for the owner of an electronic mail service. Here the proper analogy might instead be the carriage of mail, in which owners of services are not held criminally or civilly liable for obscene or libelous materials. The underlying theory is that it would be unreasonable to expect such owners to inspect all the materials they transport, and the imposition of criminal liability, at least, would have an unacceptably harmful effect on a desirable service involving the distribution of a great deal of protected speech. If carriers were held liable for distributing unprotected speech, there would inevitably be an adverse effect on the dissemination of protected speech too. In other words, the problem with carrier liability in this context is that it would interfere with protected as well as unprotected speech. . . .

MADISON IN CYBERSPACE?

Do Madisonian ideals have an enduring role in American thought about freedom of speech? The Supreme Court has not said for certain; its signals are quite mixed; and the existence of new technologies makes the question different and far more complex than it once was. It is conceivable that in a world of newly emerging and countless options, the market will prove literally unstoppable, as novel possibilities outstrip even well-motivated government controls.

If so, this result should not be entirely lamented. A world in which consumers can select from limitless choices has many advantages. . . . If choices are limitless, people interested in politics can see and listen to politics; perhaps they can even participate in politics and in ways that were impossible just a decade ago. But that world would be far from perfect. It may increase social balkanization. It may not promote deliberation, but foster instead a series of referenda in cyberspace that betray constitutional goals.

My central point here has been that the system of free expression is not an aimless abstraction. . . . Rooted in a remarkable conception of political sovereignty, the goals of the First Amendment are closely connected with the founding commitment to a particular kind of polity: a deliberative democracy among informed citizens who are political equals. It follows that instead of allowing new technologies to use democratic processes for their own purposes, constitutional law should be concerned with harnessing those technologies for democratic ends—including the founding aspirations to public deliberation, citizenship, political equality, and even a certain kind of virtue. If the new technologies offer risks on these scores, they hold out enormous promise as well. . . .

Discussion Questions

1. Which of the two models of the First Amendment free speech tradition do you prefer and why? Discuss the moral principles and concerns, as well as other assumptions or premises, underlying the models. Discuss which model a rights ethicist, a utilitarian, and a Confucian philosopher would most likely support.

2. Discuss the moral issues raised by the University of Michigan "cyberporn" case. Imagine that you are the president of the University of Michigan. What action, if any, would you have taken if the case was brought to you by the fellow student who was the target of the offending message. Discuss how Charles Lawrence and Jonathan Rauch would most likely have responded had they been the president of the University of Michigan.

3. Analyze Sunstein's argument that electronic mail carriers should not be held liable for the distribution of libelous and obscene unprotected speech. Should this same protection apply to Internet service providers? Support your answer.

4. Do you agree with Sunstein that it may be permissible to regulate speech for democratic ends? Support your answer. Discuss how Ayn Rand and John Locke might respond to this question.

CASE STUDIES

1. *DOE VS. UNIVERSITY OF MICHIGAN*

The University of Michigan had one of the most restrictive campus speech codes. Its policy forbade all conduct that "stigmatizes or victimizes" students on the basis of "race, ethnicity, religion, sex and sexual orientation."[24] The University of Michigan code was created to cut down on the increasing frequency of racist, sexist, and other forms of hate speech.

Fearful that he would be charged as being sexist under the new speech code, a psychology teaching assistant who wanted to discuss mental differences between men and women and how these differences might influence career choices brought suit against the university. Known only as John Doe, he argued that the speech code violated his First Amendment right to freedom of speech. History Professor C. Vann Woodward supported Doe. Woodward noted:

> It simply seems unnatural to make a fuss about the rights of a speaker who offends the moral or political convictions passionately held by a majority. The far more natural impulse is to stop the nonsense, shut it up, punish it—anything but defend it. But to give rein to that inclination would be to make the majority the arbiters of truth for all. Furthermore, it would put the universities into the business of censorship.[25]

John Doe won his suit against the University of Michigan. The federal district court concluded that while it was "sympathetic to the University's obligation to ensure equal educational opportunities for all of its students, such efforts must not be at the expense of free speech."

Discussion Questions

1. Freedom of speech is highly valued in our society. Are there any moral limits to it? Discuss the nature of these limits.
2. Do we have a right not to be offended? How might Lawrence and Rauch each respond to this question?
3. How should "offensive" be defined? If there is a right not to be offended, how do we know when we have trampled on this right? Is there an objective criterion, or should we rely on people's subjective feelings? Are people's statements that they feel offended by, say, the use of *he* rather than *he or she* in a textbook sufficient to create a duty for a professor not to use that text? Support your answers.
4. Discuss how you could redraft the University of Michigan's speech code so that it did not infringe on freedom of speech.
5. Scholar Stanley Fish writes that "nowadays the First Amendment is the First Refuge of Scoundrels."[26] Do you agree with him? Discuss your answers using the different incidents cited in this case study.

---

2. THE *DARTMOUTH REVIEW*[27]

Dartmouth College in Hanover, New Hampshire, is a member of the Ivy League and one of America's most prestigious colleges. In 1972 this traditionally white, male, liberal arts college decided to admit women and encourage more diversity in the student population. The curriculum was also changed to reflect the new mission. Not everyone was pleased. The conservative independent school paper, the *Dartmouth Review,* vociferously opposed the affirmative action program and criticized the new nontraditional departments as "political indoctrination centers" making personal attacks on certain members of the college community. The *Dartmouth Review,* in turn, has been criticized for intimidating members of the community who disagreed with its views to the point where it oppressed freedom of speech and the open exchange of ideas.

For example, in 1983 the *Dartmouth Review* published an article in which it attacked Professor William Cole's music class, calling it the most "outrageous gut" course on campus. They also made personal attacks on Cole. Cole, one of the few black professors on campus, viewed the attacks as racist and demanded an apology. When this was not forthcoming, he filed a libel suit in U.S. district court. Cole charged that the *Dartmouth Review* was trying to interfere with his right to teach in whatever manner he chose. The *Dartmouth Review,* in turn, accused the college of being hostile to its ideas and of trying to restrict its freedom of speech; it had a right to publish whatever it wanted to publish. The case was eventually settled out of court.

The feud wasn't over, however. In 1988 the *Dartmouth Review* published a picture of Cole and another professor with the headline "Dartmouth's Dynamic Duo of Mediocrity." The accompanying article spoke of Cole's academic deficiencies and also contained a printed transcript of a telephone conversation between Cole and a member of the *Dartmouth Review* staff in which Cole allegedly called the staff members "racist dogs" and "scum of the earth." The story was published after four *Review* staffers attended one of Cole's classes in order to collect material for a follow-up story. Cole asked them to leave the class; they refused. There was a physical confrontation in which Cole shouted at them for invading his space and broke the flash off a camera when he grabbed it to prevent a staffer from taking pictures of the class. When confronted later about the incident, Cole claimed that the *Dartmouth Review* staff had harassed him into reacting.

Discussion Questions

1. Did the staff members of the *Dartmouth Review* do anything morally wrong? Support your answer.
2. Supporters of campus speech codes argue that hate speech interferes with the learning environment. Critics of speech codes, on the other hand, argue that such codes stifle professors and students who have ideas they fear may be offensive to others on campus. Discuss these two opposing views in light of the foregoing case study. If you were president of Dartmouth College, how would you resolve this case? Should restrictions be place on what school newspapers can print? Support your answers.
3. Should classrooms be open forums for the discussion of ideas? Do professors have a right to teach however they see fit? What happens if this right conflicts with students' freedom of speech? Was this the case in this case study? Support your answers.
4. Discuss what sort of policy Lawrence, Rauch, and Taylor might each suggest for dealing with the *Dartmouth Review*. Which policy do you think is best from a moral perspective? Support your answer.
5. What is the ideal classroom atmosphere? Is it a class where students can express any sort of opinions? Or is it one where only "rational" discussion of ideas occurs? Support your answers using specific examples.

---

3. THE SMOKING GUN: FREEDOM OF SPEECH AND CIGARETTE ADVERTISING

Commercial speech is protected because of its value in imparting accurate information to consumers about products. Marketing professor Jerry Kirkpatrick argues that advertising is one of the most effective means of combating ignorance and error. According to him, advertising provides us with important knowledge and guides us toward continuous economic progress. "Nothing, as far as I am concerned," Kirkpatrick writes, "could be more benevolent than advertising, beacon of free society."[28]

Not all advertising has such a benevolent goal, however. Some advertising, such as for cigarettes, does not convey information, but uses logical fallacies to make children and other potential consumers associate smoking with things they already desire, such as attractiveness, independence, economic success, and popularity.

In 1995 President Clinton initiated a campaign to prevent children from taking up smoking by severely restricting cigarette advertising on billboards, at sporting events, in magazines, and on promotional items. Clinton's proposal also sought to ban tobacco advertising within 1,000 feet of schools and to require tobacco companies pay for a $150 million advertising campaign aimed at convincing children and young people to stop smoking. Other countries, such as Brazil, have enacted similar laws against tobacco advertising. In the Czech Republic all cigarette advertising will be banned by April 2001, with Poland following suit in 2002. The European Union has also issued a directive phasing out tobacco ads beginning in July 2001.

The tobacco companies, including such giants as Philip Morris and R. J. Reynolds, have protested the U.S. government's restrictions on tobacco advertising as McCarthyism and an assault on their freedom of speech. Furthermore, they claim that the proposed restrictions would interfere with advertising for adults.

Discussion Questions

1. Does commercial speech deserve the same protection as political speech? Support your answer.
2. Natural rights ethicist and laissez-faire capitalist Ayn Rand opposes restrictions on the freedom of speech in the name of welfare rights. What policy, if any, would Rand most likely suggest regarding the regulation of tobacco advertising? Support your answer.
3. Do you agree with Kirkpatrick? Does cigarette advertising aimed at children combat ignorance and error? Should restrictions be placed on advertisements that are based on logical fallacies or that mislead customers? Or should the "buyer beware"? Support your answers.
4. Does paternalism and the protection of children (as well as adults) from potential harm justify restrictions on cigarette advertising, or is freedom of speech a more compelling moral concern in this case? Support your answer.

---

4. THE "MEAN WORLD SYNDROME" AND VIOLENCE IN THE MEDIA

Oscar Wilde once said that life imitates art. Perhaps he was right. Epidemiologist Brandon Centerwall of the University of Washington suggests that violence in the media has made us mean people—a situation he labels the "Mean World Syndrome."

In 1995 fourteen-year-old Sandy Charles of La Ronge, Saskatchewan, watched the movie *Warlock* at least ten times in the days leading up to the kidnapping and murder of seven-year-old Jonathan Thimpsen. The 1991 film depicted a satanic murder in which the victim's skull was crushed with a rock and then strips of flesh were peeled off the victim and boiled in liquid fat—the same method used in the murder of Thimpsen. In 1995, three days after the opening of the movie *Money Train,* in which a New York subway token clerk was doused with a flammable liquid and set on fire, two men who had seen the movie carried out a copycat crime, leaving token booth clerk Harry Kaufman in critical condition with burns over 75 percent of his body. In the next few days, two more token booth clerks were attacked or threatened in a similar manner. Copycat crimes have also been carried out based on Oliver Stone's blood-and-guts movie *Natural Born Killers.* A suit against his movie was recently dismissed by the courts.

This is not the first time lawyers tried to blame the media for murder. In 1977 fifteen-year-old Ronny Zamora shot and killed his eighty-two-year-old neighbor. Zamora's lawyers entered a "not guilty" plea, arguing that Zamora could no longer tell right from wrong. "If you judge Ronny Zamora guilty," his lawyer stated, "television would be an accessory."[29]

Murders have also been inspired by printed matter. In 1993 James Perry murdered Mildred Horn, her eight-year-old son, and the son's nurse. When they went through Perry's belongings police found two copies of books from Paladin Press, a Colorado publishing company specializing in the macabre. One of these books was entitled *Hitman:*

How to Make a Disposable Silencer, which contained in-depth information on the techniques of professional murder. There were twenty-two instances in which the book's "recommendations" matched actual details in the Perry murders.

The families of the murder victims brought a wrongful-death suit against the publisher, Paul Lind, who responded that the information they publish is protected under freedom of speech and that they are not responsible for how people use that information.[30]

Discussion Questions

1. Media violence disproportionately portrays minorities as victims, and young, lower-class Latino or foreign males as perpetrators. To what extent do you think these negative images are fueling hate speech? If there is a connection, would this justify the regulation of media on your campus as a step toward cutting down on hate speech and hate crime? Support your answers. Discuss how Lawrence and Rauch might each respond to these questions.

2. Should the media be held responsible if some people become violent after watching or reading violence? Or should the people who commit the crimes be held solely responsible? What if the killer is a child? How should the pain and death of the victims of copycat murders be weighed against freedom of speech?

3. There was a dramatic increase in violent crime in the United States not long after the introduction of television. A 1992 study in the *Journal of the American Medical Association* found that the average child in the United States will have watched 10,000 murders and 200,000 acts of violence by the age of eighteen. Epidemiologist Brandon Centerwall of the University of Washington hypothesizes that the sharp increase in murder rates in the United States beginning in 1955 is the result of viewing television. Reed Hundt, chairman of the Federal Communications Commission, estimated that without television there would be 10,000 fewer murders, 70,000 fewer rapes, and 700,000 fewer assaults in the United States every year.[31] Similar findings have been found in studies in Canada and Poland. Studies have also found that children and teenagers behave more aggressively after watching videos depicting aggression.[32] Many scholars believe that there is a causal connection between viewing violence and acting out hatred and aggression. Are these findings relevant to a decision about whether violence in the media, including the Internet, should be regulated? Support your answer.

4. Does the correlation between media and real-life violence justify limiting the freedom of speech of those who produce these shows? If the programming is harmful to children, would this justify regulating such programming for adults as well? Support your answers.

---

5. JOHN ROCKER: PITCHING HATE SPEECH

When Atlanta Braves pitcher John Rocker stated on a June 2000 television show that taking a train to Shea Stadium in New York was like "[riding through] Beirut next to some kid with purple hair next to some queer with AIDS right next to some dude who just got out of jail for the fourth time right next to some 20-year-old mom with four kids"[33] New Yorkers were outraged. Rocker later apologized saying, "I will put this situation behind me." He asked for others to do the same. However, the people of New York felt the appology was insincere and were not appeased.

When Rocker went in as a relief pitcher in the eighth inning, the crowd of 47,000 responded with deafening booing. Despite the presence of 600 riot police in the stands at least two projectile objects were hurled at the pitcher. The crowd did not calm down until Rocker left the field.

Discussion Questions

1. Was John Rocker exercising his freedom of speech in making the comments he did on the television show? Discuss your answer in light of the concept of liberty rights and legitimate interests.
2. Discuss how you would have responded to Rocker's statements. Examine the moral appropriateness of your response in light of the various moral theories, including virtue ethics, deontology, and utilitarian theory. Using role-playing, with students in the roles of Rocker, the manager of the Braves, and the spectators at the baseball game, come up with a response that is most consistent with moral principles and concerns. Discuss why this response was most morally appropriate.
3. Was the fact that Rocker did not intend to offend others by his comments on the television show morally relevant? Does he owe New Yorkers a duty of reparation? If so, how should he carry out this duty? Do those who booed him in the stadium owe him an apology? Is the fact that the baseball fans may have acted badly relevant to your decision about what Rocker ought to do? Support your answer.
4. Moral opposition to hate speech does not necessarily translate into support for laws banning hate speech. In keeping with the belief that a free marketplace of ideas is the best way to expose hatred for what it is, some maintain that public reaction is a sufficient deterrent. Discuss this statement, in light of the above case, as well as how Lawrence and Rauch would most likely respond to the case.

6. HATE AND SEXUAL PREDATION ON THE INTERNET

Hate groups are proliferating on the Internet. Racist groups have discovered that the Internet is an inexpensive way to get their message out to a large audience and to recruit new members.

Alt.support.loneliness was a popular twenty-four-hour Usenet newsgroup for people who were lonely or depressed; that is, until the South Carolina racist group Carolinian Lords of the Caucasus (CLOC) discovered the site. CLOC regularly surfs the Internet searching for new members. It also prides itself in driving people off the Internet with its race-baiting. After using the site to recruit new members, the CLOC postings on *alt. support.loneliness* turned nasty and threatening. Jay Dyson, who used to post messages on *alt.support.loneliness,* is concerned that such groups can invade a site so easily. "It's frightening because these [lonely] people are at their lowest point in their life," he points out, "and a drowning man will grasp at anything to keep from going under." A CLOC member with the screen name "racial theorist," says that his organization means no harm.

"What this thing is about is having fun. And shock value." Besides, they have just as much a right to air their views on the Internet as anyone else, he says.

Child pornography sites are also proliferating on the Internet. Cyberspace sleuth Nancy Casey, mother of two teenage daughters, spends up to eighteen hours a day at home on the Internet posing as young girls in an attempt to attract pedophiles cruising for teenagers and young girls on online-game rooms and chat rooms. Her undercover work has led to the conviction of seven male offenders.[34] While many people applaud her efforts and those of other citizen sleuths like her, others feel it is wrong for people to take the law into their own hands.

Discussion Questions

1. Defenders of the CLOC argue that the point of the Internet is that, unlike traditional media, a wide spectrum of viewpoints, even those that most people find offensive, is tolerated and even encouraged. Do you agree? How might Sunstein respond to defenders of CLOC? Support your answers.

2. Discuss the morality of the tactics used by cyberspace sleuths in tracking down online pedophiles.[35] In particular, discuss what Kant and Mill would most likely think of their tactics, particularly the use of deception in posing as children.

   Some of the pedophiles who are arrested by the police as a result of a sleuth's efforts argue in court that they have not committed a crime since they were merely engaging in fantasy, not an actual sex act. Furthermore, since the sleuths that nabbed them were adults, there was no child involved and hence no victim of the crime. Do you agree? Support your answer.

3. People who want the Internet regulated argue that freedom of speech is not an absolute value and it may well destroy the very environment that promotes it. People will stop using the Internet because of badgering by hate groups and sexual predators; also, many schools do not allow students direct access to the Internet because so much of the material there is deemed unsuitable for them. Should there be a code of ethics that prohibits Web sites promoting hatred and sexual predation?

4. In October 1997 Boston University sued eight companies that sell term papers on the Internet,[36] claiming that the companies encourage student plagiarism. In response the companies argued that the suit, which would close down their businesses, violated their First Amendment right to freedom of speech. They claimed that these papers are research material and, as such, are protected as academic expression. They have a right to print what they want.

   Do these companies have a moral right to publish term papers on the Internet even though they know how students will most likely use them? Or do the students bear moral responsibility for how they use the information from these companies? Do the colleges and the professors have a moral responsibility for making sure that students are not plagiarizing? Support your answers.

7. PUBLIC PRAYER

University of Colorado men's basketball coach, Richardo Patton, had been saying team prayers at the end of practice and after games for years. In February 2000 the American

Civil Liberties Union filed a complaint against the coach, stating that saying the prayers at a public university violated the constitutional separation of church and state.

Coach Patton countered that prohibiting his team from saying prayers violated their First Amendment Freedom of Speech. He pointed out that participation in the prayer is voluntary. To prevent the teams from praying is a direct violation of their First Amendment Freedom of Speech. Patton's critics responded that there is an implied coercion when a coach prays with his players. However, when the players were interviewed all of them supported the prayer ritual, supporting Patton's claim that the prayers were voluntary.[37]

In June 2000 the United States Supreme Court, in the case of *Santa Fe (Texas) Independent school districts vs. Jane Doe,* sided with those who want prayer out of public schools. The Supreme Court ruled that student prayers over loudspeakers before public school home football games violated the separation of church and state.

Most Americans disagree with the Supreme Court's decision. In a 1999 Gallup poll 83 percent of Americans agreed that students should be allowed to say prayers as part of graduation ceremonies. Not surprisingly, despite the Supreme Court ruling banning prayer, very few college administrators have plans to police their students and coaches or reprimand them for saying prayers at athletic events.

Discussion Questions

1. Is the fact that the majority of Americans oppose the Supreme Court ruling on prayer morally relevant? Support your answer. Discuss how a cultural relativist and a utilitarian would most likely answer this question.
2. Discuss how a court justice who was a natural law ethicist would most likely have ruled on the issue of prayer in public schools.
3. Patton maintains that "It's not just a coach's job to help these men run better and block better. It's our job to help them grow socially and spiritually." Discuss whether coaches and other educators have a moral right, or even obligation to help their students "grow socially and spiritually." Discuss the implications of your answer on the freedom of speech debate.
4. Identify and analyze the relevant moral principles and concerns in the above case study. Come to a conclusion on the morality of Coach Patton's actions.

C H A P T E R   1 0

Sexism, Pornography, and Violence Against Women

At dawn on January 24, 1989, Ted Bundy was put to death in the electric chair at a Florida state prison. Hundreds of spectators gathered outside the prison to cheer his execution. The handsome former law student had been sentenced to death for the sadistic murders of several women, including a twelve-year-old girl and two women in the Chi Omega sorority house at Florida State University, Tallahassee. According to some estimates, Bundy may have killed as many as one hundred women over the six-year period prior to his arrest.

Why did he murder these women? According to Bundy, hard-core pornography had fueled his impulse to brutalize women and inspired him to act out his fantasies through murder. He told a psychiatrist, "I know that if the police had . . . let me get drunk . . . and showed me some really hard-core pornography, I could have talked to them in that voice [the voice of a serial killer–torturer preparing to and committing his crimes]." Bundy also expressed surprise that "the vast majority of people can view the kind of so-called pornography I've been talking about and not be moved this way."[1]

SEXISM AND GENDER INEQUALITIES

In 1993 eight students from Lakewood High School in California were taken into custody for raping and molesting girls as young as ten years old. The boys, it turned out, belonged to a gang in which they won points through sexual conquest. Their activities were well known around the school and were even accepted as normal by some school authorities and members of the community: "Boys will be boys." When the boys were interviewed on a talk show and asked if they had any misgivings about what they did, they responded in the negative. What was more surprising was that they actually took pride in their conquests. "I'm definitely comfortable with myself and my self-esteem," one of the boys stated on *Dateline*. When asked if he liked himself, another boy answered, "Yeah, why wouldn't I? I mean, what's not to like about me?"[2]

Where do these boys get the idea that it is okay and even masculine to degrade females? Although most North Americans say that men and women should be equal, gender remains a significant determinant of a person's life opportunities. Women are more likely to earn lower wages, to have dull and dead-end jobs, to be raped or assaulted by their domestic partner, and to live in poverty. Only one out of every ten members of Congress in the United States is a woman. Although women now outnumber men as college students, once out in the job market women earn only about 75 percent of what men earn.[3] Throughout the world parents have a preference for sons, and the use of selective abortion and infanticide to weed out unwanted girls has led to a disproportionate number of boys in some areas of Asia. Thus it is not surprising that in most societies gender-related crimes, such as pornography, rape, sexual harassment, and domestic violence, are not taken seriously.

THE PHILOSOPHERS ON SEXISM AND WOMEN

Philosophers bear part of the responsibility for perpetuating sexism. Plato taught that man is the true humanity and that woman is a deviation. Woman exists as the result of evil and failure to control one's passions. Men's destinies are to use their rational human faculties. If a man fails to control his emotions, he lives unrighteously and will be reincarnated as a woman.

Aristotle continued the philosophical tradition of misogyny. According to him, heat is the fundamental principle of perfection in animals. Women are colder than men and, therefore, less perfect than men. Because nature always aims toward perfection, a female must be a deviation from nature. Aristotle concluded that a female embryo results when there is a deficiency in generative heat. A female, in other words, is a misbegotten male, a "monstrosity," a "mutilated male." Like Aristotle, Steven Goldberg in his article at the end of this chapter maintains that patriarchy has a basis in biology. Although not arguing that women are inferior, Goldberg does maintain that patriarchy is inevitable. Women are not biologically equipped to achieve equality with men in positions of power, authority, and status.

Despite their consensus on the inferiority of women, Plato and Aristotle had very different views on censorship. Plato would have supported censorship of pornography, not because pornography degrades women, but because he thought that art and literature were disruptive and irrational. Aristotle, on the other hand, believed that art forms that arouse strong negative emotions serve a socially useful cathartic effect by ridding potential rapists, harassers, and batterers of their violent sexual feelings.

The early Christian philosophers embraced the Platonic doctrine that women are inherently inferior to men. According to Augustine (354–430 A.D.), God created woman to be "in sex subjected to the masculine sex." The second creation story in Genesis, in which Eve was created from the rib of Adam, is used to reinforce the subservient role of women. In her article Judith Boss points out that domestic violence is more prevalent among people who subscribe to traditional religious views of the roles of men and women.

The philosophical view that privileges reason and equates male thinking with rationality continues to dominate much of Western philosophy. According to the Enlightenment philosophers, it is through reason that humanity progresses, socially and morally. Like his contemporary, French philosopher Jean-Jacques Rousseau, Immanuel Kant believed that women are deficient in reason. Consequently, women are deficient in the moral realm, because they are unable to comprehend moral imperatives. The "good" woman is modest and submits willingly to her husband's authority. A woman, because of her dangerous seductive and irrational nature, should remain confined within the domestic boundaries of home and family. Rousseau writes:

> Woman was made especially to please man. . . . This is the law of nature. If woman is formed to please and to live in subjection, she must render herself agreeable to man instead of provoking his wrath; her strength lies in her charms.

The belief that women's unbridled sexual passions and irrationality are a danger to men and society, and that women, therefore, are responsible for "provoking" men's wrath against them is still prevalent to this day. Because a woman is irrational, physical violence is justified to keep an unruly woman under control.

British philosopher Mary Wollstonecraft (1759–1797), wrote *A Vindication of the Rights of Woman* primarily as a response to Rousseau. Wollstonecraft argued that woman's nature is essentially the same as man's. Moral truths, such as equality, are universal and the same for both men and women.

John Stuart Mill also denounced patriarchal power, arguing that women need to be freed from subjection to men. The injustices perpetuated on women by an "almost despotic power of husbands over wives" need to be corrected by giving women the same rights and the same protection under the law as men.[4] Although Mill did not specifically address the issue of pornography, while he vigorously defended freedom of speech he also argued that speech could be restricted if it caused demonstrable harms to others and if it could be shown that these harms outweighed the harms of censorship.

In the end it was Sigmund Freud's theory of sexuality that won the day. Freud's claim that the moral development of men and women are significantly different reinforced the prevailing theories of female inferiority. According to Freud, woman's moral inferiority was the result of not so much a deficiency in intellectual development as in psychological development. Because of this, women are less capable of acting on the basis of justice. Despite his preoccupation with male sexuality and the all-important penis, Freud had little to say about rape and the use of the penis as a weapon.

Modern feminists reject theories claiming that women are morally inferior to men. In *The Second Sex*, French philosopher Simone de Beauvoir (1908–1986) accused the philosophical tradition of propagating the view of women as the "other," as deviant human beings. She argued that gender inequalities are primarily the result of upbringing.

Care ethicists, such as Nel Noddings and Carol Gilligan, agree with Beauvoir that gender inequalities are not natural, though rather than reject the belief that men and women are different, they accept it; they also argue, however, that both the feminine care approach and the male justice approach to morality are equally legitimate.

PORNOGRAPHY[5]

The debate over pornography in the past thirty years has moved from arguments over the morality of nonprocreative sex to arguments based on freedom of speech and concerns that pornography may contribute to gender discrimination, rape, and sexual harassment. This shift is due in part to the proliferation of pornography on the market since the late 1970s. More recently, the use of the Internet to distribute pornography has allowed those inclined to view sexual violence to do so without having to leave the comfort of their homes.

The 1971 film *Deep Throat* raked in millions of dollars, making it perhaps the most famous hard-core pornography film in history. In the late 1970s the U.S. Department of Justice prosecuted and convicted the three men who produced and distributed the X-rated film. During the 1970s and 1980s feminists began to document the systematic nature of violence against women, violence that they attributed in part to the rise of pornography.

Despite attempts to define pornography, reaching general agreement or establishing precise criteria has been difficult. Appeals to "offensiveness" run the risk of using subjective feelings or majority rule rather than rational criteria. Clearly, not everything that is offensive or repulsive—such as swear words, vomit, or dirty diapers—is harmful or should be legally restricted. Pornography is more about violence than offensiveness or even sexual pleasure. Indeed, the word *pornography* comes from the Greek term *porno* meaning "prostitution" or "female captives." Erotica, in contrast, involves a mutually pleasurable sexual expression; there is no clear conqueror or victim.[6] In 1986 the U.S. Attorney General's Commission on Pornography defined pornography as "the category of material featuring actual or unmistakably immolated or unmistakably threatened violence presented in sexually explicit fashion with a predominant focus on the sexually explicit violence." This definition of pornography is used in this chapter.

Canadians have been relatively consistent in their opposition to pornography. In 1978 the Canadian Standing Committee on Justice and Legal Affairs stated that "the clear and unquestionable danger of this type of material is that it reinforces some unhealthy tendencies in Canadian society [and] male-female stereotypes to the detriment of both sexes."[7] The Canadian Supreme Court reaffirmed this position in 1992, ruling that:

> the proliferation of materials which seriously offend the values fundamental to our society is a substantial concern which justifies restricting the otherwise full exercise of the freedom of expression. . . . [In addition,] if true equality between male and female persons is to be achieved, we cannot ignore the threat to equality resulting from exposure to audiences of certain types of violent and degrading material.[8]

In the United States, there have been mixed reactions to legal restrictions on pornography. In *Roth v. United States* (1957) the United States Supreme Court ruled that "obscene" material was not constitutionally protected speech. In 1970, however, the Commission on Obscenity and Pornography concluded that pornography was not harmful and recommended that all legal prohibitions against the sale of pornography between consenting adults be removed. In 1986 Attorney General Edwin Meese's Commission on Pornography recommended that pornography be censored, arguing that it contributes to sexual violence and antisocial attitudes.

One of the arguments used by Meese's opponents is the Aristotelian view that pornography acts as a catharsis or release for harmful, pent-up sexual urges.[9] There is no scientific evidence, however, that pornography has a cathartic effect. If anything, studies suggest that pornography provokes greater feelings of sexual aggression.

Although the evidence is inconclusive, some studies have found viewing violent pornography to be positively correlated to acts of violence against women.[10] Pornography may contribute to racist as well as sexist stereotypes. In a 1999 study of 209 vignettes in X- to XXX-rated videos, it was found that black women experienced more violence from both black men and white men than did white women.[11] In a study involving interviews with 114 convicted rapists, it was reported that "the scenes depicted in violent porn are repeated in rapists' accounts of their crimes."[12] Another study found that 51 percent of men, after watching violent pornography, stated that there was some possibility that they would commit rape if they could be assured they wouldn't be caught.[13] Pornography has also been identified by some researchers as one of the factors contributing to gang rape in fraternities, along with the view that coercion against women is normative and a sign of masculinity.[14] Other researchers, however, have failed to find a connection between pornography and rape.[15]

Catharine MacKinnon argues that pornography is immoral because it poses a substantial threat to women's equality and, therefore, directly harms women. The moral issues surrounding censorship of pornography came into the limelight in 1983, when MacKinnon and Andrea Dworkin drafted an antipornography ordinance for the city of Minneapolis, the first of its kind in the United States. Feminists from around the country traveled to Minneapolis to testify in support of the legislation. Among its supporters was Linda Marchiano, also known as Linda Lovelace, star of *Deep Throat*. Although the ordinance was approved by the city council, it was vetoed by Mayor Donald Fraser.

"PORNOGRAPHY IS THE THEORY, AND RAPE IS THE PRACTICE"

Like pornography, rape humiliates and degrades women. Former *Ms.* magazine editor Robin Morgan summarized her view of the relationship between pornography and rape in the slogan *Pornography is the theory, and rape is the practice*.[16] Rape seems to be a uniquely human phenomenon. Nonhuman animals, including other primates, living in their natural habitats have not been known to rape. Ethnologist Leonard Williams writes: "In monkey society there is no such thing as rape, prostitution, or even passive consent."[17]

Despite the prevalence of rape and violence against women, it wasn't until the past thirty years that rape became a topic of public discussion. In 1975 Susan Brownmiller, in her book *Against Our Will: Men, Women and Rape*, brought the issue into the open. She argued that rape is a crime of violence—a conscious process of intimidation by men to keep women in a state of fear—rather than an act of sexual passion.

A 1996 study of college men using the "Rape Myth Acceptance Scale" found that 34 percent of the men were inclined to rape as evidenced by their acceptance of rape myths, low empathy for victims of rape, gender stereotypes about women, and belief that interpersonal violence against women is acceptable.[18]

Rape is viewed more ambiguously than most crimes. Women who say they have been raped are often met with suspicion and insinuations that they must have somehow provoked it. Because of this, many women are reluctant to report rapes. Unlike most criminal acts, with rape cases courts generally require proof of resistance on the part of the victim. The woman's past sexual history, knowing the offender prior to the rape, her behavior prior to the rape such as drinking or how she dressed—all were seen as evidence of her complicity. "Rape shield laws," which have been passed in some states, shield alleged rape victims from being cross-examined about their sexual pasts.

In the 1960s the FBI reported that 20 percent of all rapes reported to the police "were determined by investigation to be unfounded." By the mid-1970s, the number of "false accusations" had dropped to 15 percent. When the City of New York put policewomen, instead of men, in charge of interviewing alleged victims of rape, the number of "false charges" dropped to 2 percent. Women, in other words, tend to believe other women whereas men do not.[19]

Rape has also been used as a weapon of war and oppression. Brownmiller documents her theory with examples of rape during the Second World War, the war in Vietnam, and the rape of Native American women and African slave women by white masters. In almost every war, soldiers have engaged in indiscriminate rape as a means of asserting their power and demoralizing the "enemy."

Most rapists, however, are known by their victims. This has prompted growing concern about both date rape and rape within marriage. A 1985 *Ms.* magazine article titled "A New Recognition of the Realities of 'Date Rape'" ignited a heated controversy over the problem of date rape on college campuses. Fraternities in particular have been called "rape-prone contexts." According to trial attorney Fray Tash, fraternity men are involved in more than 90 percent of all gang rapes on campuses.[20]

A survey in the *Ms.* article reported that one-fourth of all college women are victims of rape or attempted rape. Of the women defined as "rape victims," however, 75 percent did not define their experience as rape. In other words, they were victims according to someone else's criterion. In her article on date rape, Lois Pineau suggests that this simply shows that women have been socialized to see their oppression and violation as normal. Katie Roiphe disagrees, arguing that the problem lies in the definition of date rape used by the "rape crisis" feminists such as Pineau and MacKinnon. According to Roiphe, rather than helping women overcome oppression, the "rape crisis" approach buys into the archaic myth that women are naive, passive, innocent, and helpless and that women's virtue depends on their remaining sexually chaste.[21] These are the very stereotypes that modern women are trying to overcome.

Pineau rejects definitions of rape that require evidence of physical resistance. Instead, she defines date rape as nonconsensual sex that does not involve physical injury or the threat of physical injury. MacKinnon's definition of rape is even broader. "Politically," MacKinnon writes, "I call it rape whenever a woman has sex and feels violated."[22] In the mid-1990s the student government at Antioch College in Ohio instituted one of the strictest policies on date rape, based on "rape crisis" feminist definitions of date rape. The policy requires students to obtain explicit consent for every step of sexual intimacy.

SEXUAL HARASSMENT

The pornography industry normalizes and eroticizes sexual harassment as well as rape. The allegations of Anita Hill against Supreme Court Justice Clarence Thomas in 1991 and the Tailhook scandal in the military brought the problem of sexual harassment into the headlines. During the investigation into Hill's charges, several of Thomas's former colleagues and friends, as well as a Washington, D.C., video-rental store owner, stated that Thomas was interested in pornography and frequently rented X-rated videos.[23]

According to the National Organization for Women (NOW), 50 to 75 percent of employed women experience sexual harassment on the job,[24] in the great majority of cases by a man in a more powerful position.[25] The law has been slow to recognize sexual harassment as a form of discrimination against women. Although an amendment was added in 1972 to the Civil Rights Act specifically prohibiting sexual harassment, women are still reluctant to complain or sue because the costs of doing so are high, and in many cases courts have ruled against them.

The Protection from Harassment Act of 1997 gives employees legal power to claim damages and to obtain an injunction against further sexual harassment outside the workplace. In 1999, the United States Supreme Court, in *Davis v. Monroe County Board of Education,* further recognized the potential economic impact of sexual harassment as well as the responsibility of employers, in this case school authorities, to take steps to stop harassment by ruling that public schools can be required to pay damages for failing to stop student-on-student sexual harassment.

Many people believe that charges of sexual harassment are simply instances of miscommunication between men and women, or cultural differences, rather than a misuse of power.[26] They also believe that sexual harassment is a "woman's problem," or that women use charges to get back at men, or that it is an attempt to desexualize the workplace, or that women are just being too sexually repressed.

While not denying that sexual harassment can be a means of oppressing women, Roiphe questions the current definitions of sexual harassment. She argues that these definitions, like the "rape crisis" definitions of date rape, are so broad that they create distrust and suspicion among men and women by implying that men are sexual predators and that women are their helpless victims. While some types of sexual harassment should be curtailed, Roiphe argues that in many cases women just have to stand up to their harassers instead of playing the role of victim.

DOMESTIC VIOLENCE

In 95 percent of domestic assaults, men are the perpetrators and women are the victims. Every fifteen seconds a woman is physically assaulted in the United States, and 12 percent of all high school dating couples experience violence in their relationships.[27]

Domestic violence is the leading cause of injury to women in the United States.[28] Every day, four women are beaten to death. Of women visiting hospital emergency rooms, 40 percent are victims of domestic violence.[29] The incidence of injuries and deaths from domestic violence may be even higher. Because of the stigma attached to domestic violence, most victims attribute their injuries to accidents or delay seeking medical assistance. According to the American Medical Association (AMA), domestic violence is also a major cause of homelessness, homicide, child abuse, and suicide. Women who leave abusive partners run a greater risk of injury and death at the hands of the men they leave than those who stay in the abusive relationship.[30] Domestic violence also spills over into the workplace. The U.S. Bureau of National Affairs estimated that in 1997 domestic violence cost employers up to $5 billion a year in lost productivity.[31] This includes costs related to absenteeism and medical expenses.

In October 2000 Congress passed the Violence Against Women Act that allocated more than $3 billion over five years to programs to prevent domestic violence and to assist women victimized by domestic violence.[32] Of this money $140 million is earmarked for programs to stop violence against women on college campuses.

One of the gender myths underlying domestic violence is that men use physical violence to control "bad" women—those who are too assertive or "don't know their place." This myth has been perpetuated by philosophical views of women as less rational than and morally inferior to men. In her article on domestic violence, Boss points out that it is not assertive women who are most likely to be beaten up, but those who accept traditional definitions of womanliness. Furthermore, Boss notes, women who blame themselves for the violence or forgive unrepentant abusers place themselves at greater risk of further violence than do women who express moral indignation and resentment at their mistreatment.

MORAL ISSUES

Autonomy and Human Dignity

Sexism violates Kant's categorical imperative, because it defines women in relation to men, thus treating women as a means only. Pornography, rape, and other forms of violence against women dehumanize them. Rather than being portrayed as autonomous moral beings, women are viewed as instruments of men.

Pineau maintains that autonomy is essential in "good sex." Without consent, she argues, a woman's autonomy and dignity are compromised. Genuine sexual pleasure requires communication, which in turn entails communicating one's consent or lack thereof. Does autonomy, however, always require consent? Is it ever reasonable to assume that some women may agree to be coerced or pressured into sex, thus making it difficult, in her words, to distinguish at times between "assault and seduction, submission and enjoyment, or so we imagine"? Furthermore, is unsought sexual attention always bad? Do spontaneity and flirting necessarily constitute sexual harassment?

Freedom of Speech and Liberty Rights

Rape and other forms of direct violence against women are clearly not liberty rights, because they violate the dignity and legitimate interests of their victims. It is not clear, however, that the same is true of pornography or even some instances of sexual harassment. How should the dignity and autonomy of women be weighed against the freedom of pornographers to market their materials, or against the "right" of people to leer? Canadians place the dignity of women above freedom of speech in prohibiting pornography; Americans place a higher value on freedom of speech.

Libertarians focus primarily on abstract liberty rights, whereas radical feminists focus on women's dignity and autonomy. Radical feminists, such as MacKinnon, accuse libertarians of placing freedom of speech above women's well-being. They also argue that pornography restricts women's freedom of speech and, hence, cannot be defended on the grounds of freedom of speech. Furthermore, pornography has no value in the marketplace of ideas because it presents a distorted view of women and, hence, is based on a lie about women's sexuality. Other feminists, such as Katie Roiphe, disagree. They fear that repression of pornography may impede women's liberation by emphasizing women as victims.

Sexual harassment may also violate women's liberty rights by forcing them to leave their jobs or drop out of classes at college. The line between sexual harassment and harmless but obnoxious and boorish behavior, however, is fuzzy. Does sexual harassment have to involve pressure for sexual favors, or do other, less direct sexist actions also violate women's liberty rights by creating a hostile working or educational environment? Does freedom of speech give people the right to use sexist terms or to leer at another person? Are liberty rights violated only if the perpetrator of the harassment is in a position of greater power, or can a male student violate the liberty rights of a female professor?

Justice, Discrimination, and Gender Equality

MacKinnon argues that film and photographic pornography is a form of sex discrimination because it requires the abuse and coercion of women for its manufacture. Pornography is not like hate speech, which does not involve the compliance of its victims for its expression. Pornography does not just convey the idea that women are subordinate; it actually subordinates and silences them by putting them in a position of inferiority. Therefore, according to MacKinnon, legal restrictions on pornography are essential if women are to achieve full equality.

The expectation that women should have to take precautions against being assaulted—by being careful about what they wear, how much they drink, or walking alone at night—unfairly burdens women by denying them the same freedoms enjoyed by men. Laws pertaining to violence against women that place the burden of proof on women to prove they were raped, beaten, or harassed are also unjust, because laws against non-gender crimes do not place a similar burden on victims. Boss argues that the expectation that victims of domestic violence, rather than the perpetrators, should have to leave their homes and seek shelter discriminates against women as well.

Utilitarian Considerations: Harms and Benefits

Rape and domestic violence are clearly immoral because they seriously harm women. Domestic violence, though it may temporarily boost the self-esteem of the abuser, causes long-term harms to its victims, both women and children, and incurs millions of dollars in medical and social costs.

It is not as clear, however, how pornography can directly harm women. Furthermore, even though it may be a "lower" pleasure, pornography *is* pleasurable to those who use it. Unlike rape and domestic violence, where the direct and long-term harms to the victims clearly outweigh the pleasure of the perpetrators, the harms of pornography are not as clear. According John Stuart Mill, in order to justify censorship it must first be shown that the benefits of outlawing pornography would outweigh the harms of suppressing freedom of speech. Sexism in general harms men as well as women by creating an atmosphere of fear and distrust between the genders.

Feminists such as MacKinnon reject a purely abstract rights approach, arguing that it ignores the context of pornography and the realities of women's lives. Pornography, they argue, directly harms women by constructing a social environment that is harmful to women and that interferes with women's ability to participate fully and equally in social and political life. Some people, on the other hand, argue that pornography is actually beneficial because it is cathartic and provides pleasure for millions of consumers. As noted earlier, however, there is no evidence for this position.

The Slippery Slope

Some people agree that some pornography is harmful, but they still oppose censorship of it. To ban some types may lead to the slippery slope in which more and more material is included under the rubric of pornography, as happened with the censorship of novels like James Joyce's *Ulysses* and Valdimir Nabokov's *Lolita.* This in turn could lead to a serious erosion of freedom of speech. Roiphe argues that this has already happened with sexual harassment. The definition is now so broad that it includes relatively innocuous behavior such as leering or "reckless eyeballing." On the other hand, this erosion of freedom of speech does not seem to have occurred in Canada, where pornography is banned and sexual harassment is punishable by law.

Social Good

The Canadian argument for the legal regulation of pornography is based in part on the argument that the community has the right, as well as the duty, to enforce standards of public good. Pornography contributes to unhealthy attitudes and stereotypes and poses a treat to society because it weakens the principle of equality upon which society is founded.

On the other hand, this criterion also risks the danger of the "tyranny of the majority"; here the majority in the community impose their values on the minority. Hence, most ethicists in the United States believe that social good, on its own, is not a sufficient justification for outlawing certain types of behavior.

Human Nature

Ethical theories are grounded in certain philosophical assumptions about human nature. Assumptions about human nature, including the nature of men and women in particular, have a profound influence on what people regard as appropriate behavior and relationships. Although most people reject in theory the philosophical assumption that women are, by nature, inferior and subservient, these views are still embedded in gender stereotypes that degrade women. On the other hand, some people think that feminists have gone too far to the opposite extreme by promoting a false view of men as, by nature, oppressors of women. "The very term *women's liberation,*" one critic points out, is based on a denial of the "necessary relational bases of human nature."[33] Roiphe maintains that feminism also has a devalued view of women's nature. Where women were once defined as sex objects, feminists deny female sexuality. Goldberg also disagrees with feminist definitions of male and female nature. He maintains that patriarchy is natural and that society should be structured to reflect this reality. Feminist demands for equality are not only unreasonable but harmful to women. While not denying that men may be innately more aggressive, some feminists argue that this does not translate into an urge to rape or violently dominate women. Instead male violence against women is primarily the result of socialization.[34]

CONCLUSION

Sexism and violence against women permeate our society. Pornography, for example, is just one symptom of the disease of sexism. Because sexism is so pervasive, it is difficult to sort out the specific causes of violence against women and to come up with policies that counteract sexism without destroying other important liberties. How are we to deal with the root causes, rather than just the symptoms? Like many issues in social ethics, pornography brings up two distinct issues: First, what are the moral objections to pornography? Second, do these objections justify placing legal restrictions on pornography? It is not enough to show that pornography causes some harm, as there are many activities that harm people, such as smoking, eating a high-fat diet, driving on highways, binge drinking, and bungee jumping, that are legal. According to libertarians it must be shown that the harms are directly caused by pornography and that the harms are substantial. This has not yet been shown. What, then, is the government's obligation? Should public policy and laws, as in Canada, take a stand against misogyny? Or are people's attitudes outside the realm of law? Even if we accept a libertarian hands-off approach, virtue ethics requires that we respond personally to the problem of sexism and violence against women.

CATHARINE A. MACKINNON

Pornography, Civil Rights, and Speech

Catharine MacKinnon is a professor of law at the University of Michigan. MacKinnon argues that some pornography should be legally restricted. According to her, the harm of pornography outweighs the benefit of freedom of speech. The primary harm of pornography is not that it is offensive, but that it is a type of sexual discrimination. Pornography subordinates women. Rather than being harmless fantasy, pornography is a political practice that institutionalizes the sexuality of male supremacy. The end served by pornography is not pleasure but power. Pornography also contributes indirectly to violence against women and to their social and economic inequality.

Critical Reading Questions

1. What is the feminist "discovery" regarding the basic assumption of equality in our society?
2. What does the world look like from the feminist point of view?
3. According to MacKinnon, why don't very many people, including women, believe the feminist view of the world?
4. What is pornography? What view of women does pornography construct?
5. What does MacKinnon mean when she says, "What pornography *does* goes beyond its content"?
6. How does pornography harm women, according to MacKinnon?
7. What does MacKinnon mean when she calls sexuality and gender a "social construct"?
8. According to MacKinnon, why can't we consistently defend both pornography and the equality of the sexes?
9. How does pornography differ from obscenity?
10. What does MacKinnon mean when she says that pornography is a political practice?
11. What definition of pornography did MacKinnon and Dworkin use in drafting an antipornography ordinance for the city of Minneapolis?
12. On what grounds does MacKinnon argue that pornography is a type of sex discrimination that violates the guarantee of equal rights?
13. How does pornography harm women? According to MacKinnon, what is the connection between pornography, rape, and sexual harassment? What evidence does MacKinnon cite to support her claim?
14. What was the primary reason some people opposed MacKinnon and Dworkin's antipornography ordinance? How does MacKinnon respond to their concerns?
15. On what grounds does MacKinnon argue that antipornography laws do not violate, but rather promote, freedom of speech?

"Pornography, Civil Rights, and Speech," *Feminism Unmodified: Discourse on Life and Law* (Cambridge, Mass.: Harvard University Press, 1987), pp. 168–179, 193–195. Some notes have been omitted.

There is a belief that this is a society in which women and men are basically equals. Room for marginal corrections is conceded, flaws are known to exist, attempts are made to correct what are conceived as occasional lapses from the basic condition of sex equality. Sex discrimination law has concentrated most of its focus on these occasional lapses. It is difficult to overestimate the extent to which this belief in equality is an article of faith for most people, including most women, who wish to live in self-respect in an internal universe, even (perhaps especially) if not in the world. It is also partly an expression of natural law thinking: if we are inalienably equal, we can't "really" be degraded.

This is a world in which it is worth trying. In this world of presumptive equality, people make money based on their training or abilities or diligence or qualifications. They are employed and advanced on the basis of merit. In this world of just deserts, if someone is abused, it is thought to violate the basic rules of the community. If it doesn't, victims are seen to have done something they could have chosen to do differently, by exercise of will or better judgment. Maybe such people have placed themselves in a situation of vulnerability to physical abuse. Maybe they have done something provocative. Or maybe they were just unusually unlucky. In such a world, if such a person has an experience, there are words for it. When they speak and say it, they are listened to. If they write about it, they will be published. If certain experiences are never spoken about, if certain people or issues are seldom heard from, it is supposed that silence has been chosen. The law, including much of the law of sex discrimination and the First Amendment, operates largely within the realm of these beliefs.

Feminism is the discovery that women do not live in this world, that the person occupying this realm is a man, so much more a man if he is white and wealthy. This world of potential credibility, authority, security, and just rewards, recognition of one's identity and capacity, is a world that some people do inhabit as a condition of birth, with variations among them. It is not a basic condition accorded humanity in this society, but a prerogative of status, a privilege, among other things, of gender.

I call this a discovery because it has not been an assumption. Feminism is the first theory, the first practice, the first movement, to take seriously the situation of all women from the point of view of all women, both on our situation and on social life as a whole. The discovery has therefore been made that the implicit social content of humanism, as well as the standpoint from which legal method has been designed and injuries have been defined, has not been women's standpoint. Defining feminism in a way that connects epistemology with power as the politics of women's point of view, this discovery can be summed up by saying that women live in another world: specifically, a world of *not* equality, a world of inequality.

Looking at the world from this point of view, a whole shadow world of previously invisible silent abuse has been discerned. Rape, battery, sexual harassment, forced prostitution, and the sexual abuse of children emerge as common and systematic. We find that rape happens to women in all contexts, from the family, including rape of girls and babies, to students and women in the workplace, on the streets, at home, in their own bedrooms by men they do not know and by men they do know, by men they are married to, men they have had a social conversation with, and, least often, men they have never seen before. Overwhelmingly, rape is something that men do or attempt to do to women (44 percent of American women according to a recent study) at some point in our lives. Sexual harassment of women by men is common in workplaces and educational institutions. Based on reports in one study of the federal workforce, up to 85 percent of women will experience it, many in physical forms. Between a quarter and a third of women are battered in their homes by men. Thirty-eight percent of little girls are sexually molested inside or outside the family. Until women listened to women, this world of sexual abuse was *not spoken* of. It was the unspeakable. What I am saying is, if you *are* the tree falling in the epistemological forest, your demise doesn't make a sound if no one is listening. Women did not "report" these events, and overwhelmingly do not today, because no one is listening, because no one believes us. This silence does not mean nothing happened, and it does not mean consent. It is the silence of women of which Adrienne Rich has written, "Do not confuse it with any kind of absence."[1]

Believing women who say we are sexually violated has been a radical departure, both methodologically and legally. The extent and nature of rape, marital rape, and sexual harassment itself, were discovered in this way. Domestic battery as a syndrome, almost a habit, was discovered through refusing to believe that when a woman is assaulted by a man to whom she is connected, that it is not an assault. The sexual abuse of children was uncovered, Freud notwithstanding, by believing that children were not making up all this sexual abuse. Now what is striking is that when each discovery is made, and somehow made real in the world, the response has been: it happens to men too. If women are hurt, men are hurt. If women are raped, men are raped. If women are sexually harassed, men are sexually harassed. If women are battered, men are battered. Symmetry must be reasserted. Neutrality must be reclaimed. Equality must be reestablished.

The only areas where the available evidence supports this, where anything like what happens to women also happens to men, involve children—little boys are sexually abused—and prison. The liberty of prisoners is restricted, their freedom restrained, their humanity systematically diminished, their bodies and emotions confined, defined, and regulated. If paid at all, they are paid starvation wages. They can be tortured at will, and it is passed off as discipline or as means to a just end. They become compliant. They can be raped at will, at any moment, and nothing will be done about it. When they scream, nobody hears. To be a prisoner means to be defined as a member of a group for whom the rules of what can be done to you, of what is seen as abuse of you, are reduced as part of the definition of your status. To be a woman is that kind of definition and has that kind of meaning. . . .

What women do is seen as not worth much, or what is not worth much is seen as something for women to do. *Women* are seen as not worth much, is the thing. Now why are these basic realities of the subordination of women to men, for example,

that only 7.8 percent of women have never been sexually assaulted, not effectively believed, not perceived as real in the face of all this evidence? Why don't *women* believe our own experiences? In the face of all this evidence, especially of systematic sexual abuse—subjection to violence with impunity is one extreme expression, although not the only expression, of a degraded status—the view that basically the sexes are equal in this society remains unchallenged and unchanged. The day I got this was the day I understood its real message, its real coherence: *This is equality for us.*

I could describe this, but I couldn't explain it until I started studying a lot of pornography. In pornography, there it is, in one place, all of the abuses that women had to struggle so long even to begin to articulate, all the *unspeakable* abuse: the rape, the battery, the sexual harassment, the prostitution, and the sexual abuse of children. Only in the pornography it is called something else: sex, sex, sex, sex, and sex, respectively. Pornography sexualizes rape, battery, sexual harassment, prostitution, and child sexual abuse; it thereby celebrates, promotes, authorizes, and legitimizes them. More generally, it eroticizes the dominance and submission that is the dynamic common to them all. It makes hierarchy sexy and calls that "the truth about sex" or just a mirror of reality. Through this process pornography constructs what a woman is as what men want from sex. This is what the pornography means.

Pornography constructs what a woman is in terms of its view of what men want sexually, such that acts of rape, battery, sexual harassment, prostitution, and sexual abuse of children become acts of sexual equality. Pornography's world of equality is a harmonious and balanced place. Men and women are perfectly complementary and perfectly bipolar. Women's desire to be fucked by men is equal to men's desire to fuck women. All the ways men love to take and violate women, women love to be taken and violated. The women who most love this are most men's equals, the most liberated; the most participatory child is the most grown-up, the most equal to an adult. Their consent merely expresses or ratifies these preexisting facts.

The content of pornography is one thing. There, women substantively desire dispossession and cruelty. We desperately want to be bound, battered, tortured, humiliated, and killed. Or, to be fair to the soft core, merely taken and used. This is erotic to the male point of view. Subjection itself, with self-determination ecstatically relinquished, is the content of women's sexual desire and desirability. Women are there to be violated and possessed, men to violate and possess us, either on screen or by camera or pen on behalf of the consumer. On a simple descriptive level, the inequality of hierarchy, of which gender is the primary one, seems necessary for sexual arousal to work. Other added inequalities identify various pornographic genres or subthemes, although they are always added through gender: age, disability, homosexuality, animals, objects, race (including anti-Semitism), and so on. Gender is never irrelevant.

What pornography *does* goes beyond its content: it eroticizes hierarchy, it sexualizes inequality. It makes dominance and submission into sex. Inequality is its central dynamic; the illusion of freedom coming together with the reality of force is central to its working. Perhaps because this is a bourgeois culture, the victim must look free, appear to be freely acting. Choice is how she got there. Willing is what she is when she is being equal. It seems equally important that then and there she actually be forced and that forcing be communicated on some level, even if only through still photos of her in postures of receptivity and access, available for penetration. Pornography in this view is a form of forced sex, a practice of sexual politics, an institution of gender inequality.

From this perspective, pornography is neither harmless fantasy nor a corrupt and confused misrepresentation of an otherwise natural and healthy sexual situation. It institutionalizes the sexuality of male supremacy, fusing the erotization of dominance and submission with the social construction of male and female. To the extent that gender is sexual, pornography is part of constituting the meaning of that sexuality. Men treat women as who they see women as being. Pornography constructs who that is. Men's power over women means that the way men see women defines who women can

be. Pornography is that way. Pornography is not imagery in some relation to a reality elsewhere constructed. It is not a distortion, reflection, projection, expression, fantasy, representation, or symbol either. It is a sexual reality.

In Andrea Dworkin's definitive work, *Pornography: Men Possessing Women,* sexuality itself is a social construct gendered to the ground. Male dominance here is not an artificial overlay upon an underlying inalterable substratum of uncorrupted essential sexual being. Dworkin presents a sexual theory of gender inequality of which pornography is a constitutive practice. The way pornography produces its meaning constructs and defines men and women as such. Gender has no basis in anything other than the social reality its hegemony constructs. Gender is what gender means. The process that gives sexuality its male supremacist meaning is the same process through which gender inequality becomes socially real.

In this approach, the experience of the (overwhelmingly) male audiences who consume pornography is therefore not fantasy or simulation or catharsis but sexual reality, the level of reality on which sex itself largely operates. Understanding this dimension of the problem does not require noticing that pornography models are real women to whom, in most cases, something real is being done; nor does it even require inquiring into the systematic infliction of pornography and its sexuality upon women, although it helps. What matters is the way in which the pornography itself provides what those who consume it want. Pornography *participates* in its audience's eroticism through creating an accessible sexual object, the possession and consumption of which *is* male sexuality, as socially constructed; to be consumed and possessed as which, *is* female sexuality, as socially constructed; pornography is a process that constructs it that way.

The object world is constructed according to how it looks with respect to its possible uses. Pornography defines women by how we look according to how we can be sexually used. Pornography codes how to look at women, so you know what you can do with one when you see one. Gender is an assignment made visually, both originally and in everyday life. A sex object is defined on the basis of its looks, in terms of its usability for sexual pleasure, such that both the looking—the quality of the gaze, including its point of view—and the definition according to use become eroticized as part of the sex itself. This is what the feminist concept "sex object" means. In this sense, sex in life is no less mediated than it is in art. Men have sex with their image of a woman. It is not that life and art imitate each other; in this sexuality, they *are* each other. . . .

To defend pornography as consistent with the equality of the sexes is to defend the subordination of women to men as sexual equality. What in the pornographic view is love and romance looks a great deal like hatred and torture to the feminist. Pleasure and eroticism become violation. Desire appears as lust for dominance and submission. The vulnerability of women's projected sexual availability, that acting we are allowed (that is, asking to be acted upon), is victimization. Play conforms to scripted roles. Fantasy expresses ideology, is not exempt from it. Admiration of natural physical beauty becomes objectification. Harmlessness becomes harm. Pornography is a harm of male supremacy made difficult to see because of its pervasiveness, potency, and, principally, because of its success in making the world a pornographic place. Specifically, its harm cannot be discerned, and will not be addressed, if viewed and approached neutrally, because it *is* so much of "what is." In other words, to the extent pornography succeeds in constructing social reality, it becomes invisible as harm. If we live in a world that pornography creates through the power of men in a male-dominated situation, the issue is not what the harm of pornography is, but how that harm is to become visible.

Obscenity law provides a very different analysis and conception of the problem of pornography. In l973 the legal definition of obscenity became that which the average person, applying contemporary community standards, would find that, taken as a whole, appeals to the prurient interest; that which depicts or describes in a patently offensive way—you feel like you're a cop reading someone's *Miranda* rights—sexual conduct specifically defined by the applicable state law; and that which, taken as a whole, lacks serious literary, artistic, political or scientific value. Feminism doubts whether the average person gender-neutral exists; has more questions about the content and process of defining what community standards are than it does about deviations from them; wonders why prurience counts but powerlessness does not and why sensibilities are better protected from offense than women are from exploitation; defines sexuality, and thus its violation and expropriation, more broadly than does state law; and questions why a body of law that has not in practice been able to tell rape from intercourse should, without further guidance, be entrusted with telling pornography from anything less. Taking the work "as a whole" ignores that which the victims of pornography have long known: legitimate settings diminish the perception of injury done to those whose trivialization and objectification they contextualize. Besides, and this is a heavy one, if a woman is subjected, why should it matter that the work has other value? Maybe what redeems the work's value is what enhances its injury to women, not to mention that existing standards of literature, art, science, and politics, examined in a feminist light, are remarkably consonant with pornography's mode, meaning, and message. And finally—first and foremost, actually—although the subject of these materials is overwhelmingly women, their contents almost entirely made up of women's bodies, our invisibility has been such, our equation as a sex *with* sex has been such, that the law of obscenity has never even considered pornography a women's issue.

Obscenity, in this light, is a moral idea, an idea about judgments of good and bad. Pornography, by contrast, is a political practice, a practice of power and powerlessness. Obscenity is ideational and abstract; pornography is concrete and substantive. The two concepts represent two entirely different things. Nudity, excess of candor, arousal or excitement, prurient appeal, illegality of the acts depicted, unnaturalness or perversion are all qualities that bother obscenity law when sex is depicted or portrayed. Sex forced on real women so that it can be sold at a profit and forced on other real women; women's bodies trussed and maimed and raped and made into things to be hurt and obtained and accessed, and this presented as the nature of women in a way that is acted on and acted out, over and over; the coercion that is visible and the coercion that has become invisible—this and more bothers feminists about pornography. Obscenity as such probably does little harm. Pornography is integral to attitudes and behaviors of violence and discrimination that define the treatment and status of half the population.

At the request of the city of Minneapolis, Andrea Dworkin and I conceived and designed a local human rights ordinance in accordance with our approach to the pornography issue. We define pornography as a practice of sex discrimination, a violation of women's civil rights, the opposite of sexual equality. Its point is to hold those who profit from and benefit from that injury accountable to those who are injured. It means that women's injury—our damage, our pain, our enforced inferiority—should outweigh their pleasure and their profits, or sex equality is meaningless.

We define pornography as the graphic sexually explicit subordination of women through pictures or words that also includes women dehumanized as sexual objects, things, or commodities; enjoying pain or humiliation or rape; being tied up, cut up, mutilated, bruised, or physically hurt; in postures of sexual submission or servility or display; reduced to body parts, penetrated by objects or animals, or presented in scenarios of degradation, injury, torture; shown as filthy or inferior; bleeding, bruised, or hurt in a context that makes these conditions sexual. Erotica, defined by distinction as not this, might be sexually explicit materials premised on equality. . . .

To define pornography as a practice of sex discrimination combines a mode of portrayal that has a legal history—the sexually explicit—with an active term that is central to the inequality of the sexes—subordination. Among other things, subordination means to be in a position of inferiority or loss of power, or to be demeaned or denigrated. To be someone's subordinate is the opposite of being their equal. The definition does not include all sexually explicit depictions *of* the subordination of women. That is not what it says. It says, this which *does* that: the sexually explicit that subordinates women. To these active terms to capture what the pornography *does,* the definition adds a list of what

it must also contain. This list, from our analysis, is an exhaustive description of what must be in the pornography for it to do what it does behaviorally. Each item in the definition is supported by experimental, testimonial, social, and clinical evidence. We made a legislative choice to be exhaustive and specific and concrete rather than conceptual and general, to minimize problems of chilling effect, making it hard to guess wrong, thus making self-censorship less likely, but encouraging (to use a phrase from discrimination law) voluntary compliance, knowing that if something turns up that is not on the list, the law will not be expansively interpreted.

The list in the definition, by itself, would be a content regulation. But together with the first part, the definition is not simply a content regulation. It is a medium-message combination that resembles many other such exceptions to First Amendment guarantees. . . .

This law aspires to guarantee women's rights consistent with the First Amendment by making visible a conflict of rights between the equality guaranteed to all women and what, in some legal sense, is now the freedom of the pornographers to make and sell, and their consumers to have access to, the materials this ordinance defines. Judicial resolution of this conflict, if the judges do for women what they have done for others, is likely to entail a balancing of the rights of women arguing that our lives and opportunities, including our freedom of speech and action, are constrained by—and in many cases flatly precluded by, in, and through—pornography, against those who argue that the pornography is harmless, or harmful only in part but not in the whole of the definition; or that it is more important to preserve the pornography than it is to prevent or remedy of whatever harm it does. . . .

The harm of pornography, broadly speaking, is the harm of the civil inequality of the sexes made invisible as harm because it has become accepted as the sex difference. Consider this analogy with race: if you see Black people as different, there is no harm to segregation; it is merely a recognition of that difference. To neutral principles, separate but equal was equal. The injury of racial separation to

Blacks arises "solely because [they] choose to put that construction upon it." Epistemologically translated: how you see it is not the way it is. Similarly, if you see women as just different, even or especially if you don't know that you do, subordination will not look like subordination at all, much less like harm. It will merely look like an appropriate recognition of the sex difference.

Pornography does treat the sexes differently, so the case for sex differentiation can be made here. But men as a group do not tend to be (although some individuals may be) treated the way women are treated in pornography. As a social group, men are not hurt by pornography the way women as a social group are. Their social status is not defined as *less* by it. So the major argument does not turn on mistaken differentiation, particularly since the treatment of women according to pornography's dictates makes it all too often accurate. The salient quality of a distinction between the top and the bottom in a hierarchy is not difference, although top is certainly different. . . .

Free speech which only enhances the power of the pornographers while doing nothing substantively to guarantee the free speech of women, for which we need civil equality. The situation in which women presently find ourselves with respect to the pornography is one in which more *pornography* is inconsistent with rectifying or even counterbalancing its damage through speech, because so long as the pornography exists in the way it does there *will not be more speech by women.* Pornography strips and devastates women of credibility, from our accounts of sexual assault to our everyday reality of sexual subordination. We are stripped of authority and reduced and devalidated and silenced. Silenced here means that the purposes of the First Amendment, premised upon conditions presumed and promoted by protecting free speech, do not pertain to women because they are not our conditions. Consider them: individual self-fulfillment—how does pornography promote our individual self-fulfillment? How does sexual inequality even permit it? Even if she can form words, who listens to a woman with a penis in her mouth? Facilitating consensus—to the extent pornography does so, it does so one-sidedly by silencing protest over the injustice of sexual subordination. Participation in civic life—central to Professor Meiklejohn's theory—how does pornography enhance women's participation in civic life? Anyone who cannot walk down the street or even lie down in her own bed without keeping her eyes cast down and her body clenched against assault is unlikely to have much to say about the issues of the day, still less will she become Tolstoy. Facilitating change—*this law* facilitates the change that existing First Amendment theory had been used to throttle. Any system of freedom of expression that does not address a problem where the free speech of men silences the free speech of women, a real conflict between speech interests as well as between people, is not serious about securing freedom of expression in this country.

For those of you who still think pornography is only an idea, consider the possibility that obscenity law got one thing right. Pornography is more act-like than thoughtlike. The fact that pornography, in a feminist view, furthers the idea of the sexual inferiority of women, which is a political idea, doesn't make the pornography itself into a political idea. One can express the idea a practice embodies. That does not make that practice into an idea. Segregation expresses the idea of the inferiority of one group to another on the basis of race. That does not make segregation an idea. A sign that says "Whites Only" is only words. Is it therefore protected by the First Amendment? Is it not an act, a practice, of segregation because what it means is inseparable from what it does? *Law* is only words.

The issue here is whether the fact that words and pictures are the central link in the cycle of abuse will immunize that entire cycle, about which we cannot do anything without doing something about the pornography. As Justice Stewart said in *Ginsburg,* "When expression occurs in a setting where the capacity to make a choice is absent, government regulation of that expression may coexist with and *even implement* First Amendment guarantees."[2] I would even go so far as to say that the pattern of evidence we have closely approaches Justice Douglas' requirement that "freedom of expression can be suppressed if, and to the extent that, it is so closely brigaded with illegal action as to be an inseparable part of it."[3] Those of you who have been trying to separate the acts from the speech—that's an act, that's an act, there's a law against that act, regulate that act, don't touch the speech—notice here that the illegality of the acts involved doesn't mean that the speech that is "brigaded with" it *cannot* be regulated. This is when it *can* be.

I take one of two penultimate points from Andrea Dworkin, who has often said that pornography is not speech for women, it is the silence of women. Remember the mouth taped, the woman gagged, "Smile, I can get a lot of money for that." The smile is not her expression, it is her silence. . . .

Classically, opposition to censorship has involved keeping government off the backs of people. Our law is about getting some people off the backs of other people. The risks that it will be misused have to be measured against the risks of the status quo. Women will never have that dignity, security, compensation that is the promise of equality so long as the pornography exists as it does now. The situation of women suggests that the urgent issue of our freedom of speech is not primarily the avoidance of state intervention as such, but getting affirmative access to speech for those to whom it has been denied.

NOTES

1. Adrienne Rich, "Cartographies of Silence," in *The Dream of a Common Language* 16, 17 (1978).
2. Ginsburg v. New York, 390 U.S. 629, 649 (1968) (Stewart, J., concurring in result) (emphasis added).
3. Roth v. United States, 354 U.S. 476, 514 (Douglas, J., dissenting) (citing Giboney v. Empire Storage & Ice Co., 336 U.S. 490, 498 [1949]); Labor Board v. Virginia Power Co., 314 U.S. 469, 477–78 (1941).

Discussion Questions

1. Discuss MacKinnon's argument that censorship of pornography does not violate our freedom of speech. Has she successfully demonstrated that pornography violates Mill's harm principle? Discuss how a libertarian and feminist such as Mill might respond to MacKinnon's argument.
2. Discuss MacKinnon's claim that pornography is a type of sex discrimination that directly harms women. Discuss how MacKinnon might respond to the lack of evidence of a causal link between pornography and violence against women. Can her argument stand without it?
3. Does MacKinnon give an accurate description of male and female sexuality? Or does she buy into traditional stereotypes that emphasize chastity and female weakness? Support your answer.
4. Political analysts George F. Will and Ellen Willis warn that "if feminists define pornography per se as the enemy, the result will be to make a lot of women ashamed of their sexual feelings and afraid to be honest about them."[35] Do you agree? Support your answer. Discuss how MacKinnon might respond to this concern.
5. In 1960 Stanley Milgram ran an experiment to see how far people would go in obeying someone in authority. Much to his astonishment, he found that two-thirds of the subjects would administer what they thought was a potentially deadly electric shock to another person simply because someone in a position of authority urged them to do so. (See pages 1–2.) What are the implications of this study for the debate over whether to restrict access to pornography? Is pornography a type of "authority" on how to treat women? Support your answers.
6. Sexist attitudes also flourish in many religious groups, in advertisements, and in television shows. Indeed, this type of sexist message may be more pervasive and harmful

than that of pornography. If so, would sexist religious doctrines, ads, and televisions shows that demean women also be censored? Does the MacKinnon argument risk sending us down the slippery slope of all-out censorship? Support your answer. Discuss how MacKinnon might respond to this concern.

7. In 1990 Fort Lauderdale record-store owner Charles Freeman was arrested for selling to an undercover policeman a copy of 2 Live Crew's *As Nasty as They Wanna Be,* an album that had been deemed obscene by a federal court. After listening to it, the all-white jury decided that it was indeed obscene and convicted Freeman. Freeman was outraged. "They don't know nothing about the goddam ghetto, . . ." he fumed as he left the court. "The verdict does not reflect my community standards as a black man in Broward County."[36] Do you agree with Freeman? Does MacKinnon's proposed anti-pornography law demonstrate a white, upper-middle-class cultural bias? Or is pornography wrong no matter what the cultural context?

 LOIS PINEAU

Date Rape: A Feminist Analysis

Lois Pineau is a professor of philosophy at Kansas State University. Pineau defines date rape as nonconsensual sex that does not involve physical injury. The requirement by courts of evidence of physical injury, she argues, stems from myths that women are sexually provocative and asking for it, and that men's sexual desires are uncontrollable. Pineau rejects these myths as well as the contractual model of sex, arguing instead for a communicative model. According to Pineau, good sex requires communication. When sexuality is not communicative, the man cannot assume consent. To engage in sex without consent is rape.

Critical Reading Questions

1. How does Pineau define date rape?
2. Why is physical injury generally required to show that a sexual encounter was rape?
3. Why do courts, according to Pineau, usually shift the burden of proof onto the woman in cases of alleged rape?
4. What is the difference between *actus reas* and *mens reas*? What constitutes *mens reas* in order for a man to be guilty of rape? Why does Pineau find this account of rape unsatisfactory?
5. What are some of the myths underlying the criterion that an alleged rape victim must prove that she vigorously rejected the man's advances?
6. How does Pineau describe a possible date-rape scenario? Why, according to Pineau, do so many women experience paradoxical feelings in cases like these?
7. What are some of the myths about rape and sex in our culture?

"Date Rape: A Feminist Analysis," *Law and Philosophy* 8 (1989): 217–243. Some notes have been omitted.

8. What assumptions about male and female sexuality enforce the myth that women want to be raped? According to Pineau, why is this a myth?
9. According to Pineau, why is the contract, which supposedly exists when a woman acts provocatively, not binding?
10. Why doesn't a woman's consent given at the beginning of a sexual encounter necessarily establish the legitimacy of the whole encounter?
11. According to Pineau, what is the only way to establish the legitimacy of a sexual encounter?
12. What does Pineau mean by "communicative sexuality"? How does this model differ from the "contract" model? What is the role of consent in both of these models? Why does Pineau reject the contractual model in favor of the communicative model?
13. How would the communicative model change the way the judicial system currently approaches sexuality and the question of date rape?

The feminist recognition that dominant ideologies reinforce conceptual frameworks that serve patriarchal interests lies behind what must now be seen as a revolution in political analysis, one which for the first time approaches the problems that women face from a woman's point of view. One of those problems is the ongoing difficulty of dealing with a society that practices and condones violence against women. This is particularly the case with date rape.

Date rape is nonaggravated sexual assault, nonconsensual sex that does not involve physical injury, or the explicit threat of physical injury. But because it does not involve physical injury, and because physical injury is often the only criterion that is accepted as evidence that the *actus reas* is nonconsensual, what is really sexual assault is often mistaken for seduction. The replacement of the old rape laws with the new laws on sexual assault have done nothing to resolve this problem. . . .

THE PROBLEM OF THE CRITERION

The reasoning that underlies the present criterion of consent is entangled in a number of mutually supportive mythologies which see sexual assault as masterful seduction, and silent submission as sexual enjoyment. Because the prevailing ideology has so much informed our conceptualization of sexual interaction, it is extraordinarily difficult for us to distinguish between assault and seduction, submission and enjoyment, or so we imagine. . . . I therefore want to begin my argument by providing an example which shows both why it is so difficult to make this distinction, and that it exists. Later, I will identify and attempt to unravel the lines of reasoning that reinforce this difficulty.

The woman I have in mind agrees to see someone because she feels an initial attraction to him and believes that he feels that same way about her. She goes out with him in the hope that there will be mutual enjoyment and in the course of the day or evening an increase of mutual interest. Unfortunately, these hopes of *mutual* and *reciprocal* interest are not realized. We do not know how much interest she has in him by the end of their time together, but whatever her feelings she comes under pressure to have sex with him, and she does not want to have the kind of sex he wants. She may desire to hold hands and kiss, to engage in more intense caresses or in some form of foreplay, or she may not want to be touched. She may have reasons unrelated to desire for not wanting to engage in the kind of sex he is demanding. She may have religious reservations, concerns about pregnancy or disease, a disinclination to be just another conquest. She may be engaged in a seduction program of her own which sees abstaining from sexual activity as a means of building an important emotional bond. She feels she is desirable to him, and she knows, and he knows that he will have sex with her if he can. And while she feels she doesn't owe him anything, and that it is her prerogative to refuse him, this feeling is partly a defensive reaction against a deeply held belief that if he is in need, she should provide. If she buys into the myth of insistent male sexuality she may feel he is suffering from sexual frustration and that she is largely to blame.

We do not know how much he desires her, but we do know that his desire for erotic satisfaction can hardly be separated from his desire for conquest. He feels no dating obligation, but has a strong commitment to scoring. He uses the myth of "so hard to control" male desire as a rhetorical tactic, telling her how frustrated she will leave him. He becomes overbearing. She resists, voicing her disinclination. He alternates between telling her how desirable she is and taking a hostile stance, charging her with misleading him, accusing her of wanting him, and being coy, in short of being deceitful, all the time engaging in rather aggressive body contact. It is late at night, she is tired and a bit queasy from too many drinks, and he is reaffirming her suspicion that perhaps she has misled him. She is having trouble disengaging his body from hers, and wishes he would just go away. She does not adopt a strident angry stance, partly because she thinks he is acting normally and does not deserve it, partly because she feels she is partly to blame, and partly because there is always the danger that her anger will make him angry, possibly violent. It seems that the only thing to do, given his aggression, and her queasy fatigue, is to go along with him and get it over with, but this decision is so entangled with the events in process it is hard to know if it is not simply a recognition of what is actually happening. She finds the whole encounter a thoroughly disagreeable experience, but he does not take any notice, and wouldn't have changed course if he had. He congratulates himself on his sexual prowess and is confirmed in his opinion that aggressive tactics pay off. Later she feels that she has been raped, but paradoxically tells herself that she let herself be raped.

The paradoxical feelings of the woman in our example indicate her awareness that what she feels about the incident stands in contradiction to the prevailing cultural assessment of it. She knows that she did not want to have sex with her date. She is not so sure, however, about how much her own desires count, and she is uncertain that she has made her desires clear. Her uncertainty is reinforced by the cultural reading of this incident as an ordinary seduction.

As for us, we assume that the woman did not want to have sex, but just like her, we are unsure whether her mere reluctance, in the presence of high-pressure tactics, constitutes nonconsent. We suspect that submission to an overbearing and insensitive lout is no way to go about attaining sexual enjoyment, and we further suspect that he felt no compunction about providing it, so that on the face of it, from the outside looking in, it looks like a pretty unreasonable proposition for her.

Let us look at this reasoning more closely. Assume that she was not attracted to the kind of sex offered by the sort of person offering it. Then it would be *prima facie* unreasonable for her to agree to have sex, unreasonable, that is, unless she were offered some pay-off for her stoic endurance, money perhaps, or tickets to the opera. The reason is that in sexual matters, agreement is closely connected to attraction. Thus, where the presumption is that she was not attracted, we should at the same time presume that she did not consent. Hence, the burden of proof should be on her alleged assailant to show that she had good reasons for consenting to an unattractive proposition.

This is not, however, the way such situations are interpreted. In the unlikely event that the example I have described should come before the courts, there is little doubt that the law would interpret the woman's eventual acquiescence or "going along with" the sexual encounter as consent. But along with this interpretation would go the implicit understanding that she had consented because when all was said and done, when the "token" resistances to the "masterful advances" had been made she had wanted to after all. Once the courts have constructed this interpretation, they are then forced to conjure up some horror story of feminine revenge in order to explain why she should bring charges against her "seducer."

In the even more unlikely event that the courts agreed that the woman had not consented to the above encounter, there is little chance that her assailant would be convicted of sexual assault. The belief that the man's aggressive tactics are a normal part of seduction means that *mens rea* cannot be established. Her eventual "going along" with his advances constitutes reasonable grounds for his believing in her consent. These "reasonable" grounds attest to the sincerity of his belief in her consent. This reasonableness means that *mens rea* would be defeated even in jurisdictions which make *mens rea* a function of objective standards of reasonableness. Moreover, the sympathy of the court is more likely to lie with the rapist than with his victim, since, if the court is typical, it will be strongly inclined to believe that the victim had in some way "asked for it."

The position of the courts is supported by the widespread belief that male aggression and female reluctance are normal parts of seduction. Given their acceptance of this model, the logic of their response must be respected. . . .

RAPE MYTHS

The belief that the natural aggression of men and the natural reluctance of women somehow makes date rape understandable underlies a number of prevalent myths about rape and human sexuality. . . .

The claim that the victim provoked a sexual incident, that "she asked for it," is by far the most common defense given by men who are accused of sexual assault. Feminists, rightly incensed by this response, often treat it as beneath contempt, singling out the defense as an argument against it. . . .

The least sophisticated of the "she asked for it" rationales, and in a sense, the easiest to deal with, appeals to an injunction against sexually provocative behavior on the part of women. If women should not be sexually provocative, then, from this standpoint, a woman who is sexually provocative deserves to suffer the consequences. Now it will not do to respond that women get raped even when they are not sexually provocative, or that it is men who get to interpret (unfairly) what counts as sexually provocative. The question should be: Why shouldn't a woman be sexually provocative? Why should this behavior warrant any kind of aggressive response whatsoever?

Attempts to explain that women have a right to behave in sexually provocative ways without suffering dire consequences still meet with surprisingly tough resistance. Even people who find nothing wrong or sinful with sex itself, in any of its forms, tend to suppose that women must not behave sexually unless they are prepared to carry through on some fuller course of sexual interaction. The logic of this response seems to be that at some point a woman's behavior commits her to following through on the full course of a sexual encounter as it is defined by her assailant. At some point she has made an agreement, or formed a contract, and once that is done, her contractor is entitled to demand that she satisfy the terms of that contract. . . .

The rationale, I believe, comes in the form of a belief in the especially insistent nature of male sexuality, an insistence which lies at the root of natural male aggression, and which is extremely difficult, perhaps impossible to contain. At a certain point in the arousal process, it is thought, a man's rational will gives away to the prerogatives of nature. His sexual need can and does reach a point where it is uncontrollable, and his natural masculine aggression kicks in to assure that this need is met. Women, however, are naturally more contained, and so it is their responsibility not to provoke the irrational in the male. If they do go so far as that, they have both failed in their responsibilities, and subjected themselves to the inevitable. One does not go into the lion's cage and expect not to be eaten. Natural feminine reluctance, it is thought, is no protection against a sexually aroused male.

This belief about the normal aggressiveness of male sexuality is complemented by common knowledge about female gender development. Once, women were taught to deny their sexuality and to aspire to ideals of chastity. Things have not changed so much. . . . The assumption that women both want to indulge sexually, and are inclined to sacrifice this desire for higher ends, gives rise to the myth that they want to be raped. After all, doesn't rape give them the sexual enjoyment that they *really* want, at the same time that it relieves them of the responsibility for admitting to and acting upon what they want? And how then can we blame men, who have been socialized to be aggressively seductive precisely for the purpose of overriding female reserve? If we find fault at all, we are inclined to cast our suspicions on the motives of the woman. . . .

But if women really want sexual pleasure, what inclines us to think that they will get it through rape? This conclusion logically requires a theory about the dynamics of sexual pleasure that sees that pleasure as an emergent property of overwhelming male insistence. For the assumption that a raped female experiences sexual pleasure implies that the person who rapes her knows how to cause that pleasure independently of any information she might convey on that point. Since her ongoing protest is inconsistent with requests to be touched in particular ways in particular places, to have more of this and less of that, then we must believe that the person who touches her knows these particular ways and places instinctively, without any directives from her.

Thus we find, underlying and reinforcing this belief in incommunicative male prowess, a conception of sexual pleasure that springs from wordless interchanges, and of sexual success that occurs in a place of meaningful silence. The language of seduction is accepted as a tacit language: eye contact, smiles, blushes, and faintly discernible gestures. It is, accordingly, imprecise and ambiguous. It would be easy for a man to make mistakes about the message conveyed, understandable that he should mistakenly think that a sexual invitation has been made, and a bargain struck. But honest mistakes, we think, must be excused.

In sum, the belief that women should not be sexually provocative is logically linked to several other beliefs, some normative, some empirical. The normative beliefs are that (1) people should keep the agreements they make, (2) that sexually provocative behavior, taken beyond a certain point, gen-

erates agreements (3), that the peculiar nature of male and female sexuality places such agreements in a special category, one in which the possibility of retracting an agreement is ruled out, or at least made highly unlikely, [and] (4) that women are not to be trusted, in sexual matters at least. The empirical belief, which turns out to be false, is that male sexuality is not subject to rational and moral control.

DISPELLING THE MYTHS

The "she asked for it" justification of sexual assault incorporates a conception of a contract that would be difficult to defend in any other context, and the presumptions about human sexuality which function to reinforce sympathies rooted in the contractual notion of just deserts are not supported by empirical research.

The belief that a woman generates some sort of contractual obligation whenever her behavior is interpreted as seductive is the most indefensible part of the mythology of rape. In law, contracts are not legitimate just because a promise has been made. In particular, the use of pressure tactics to extract agreement is frowned upon. Normally, an agreement is upheld only if the contractors were clear on what they were getting into, and had sufficient time to reflect on the wisdom of their doing so. . . . But whatever the terms of a contract, there is no private right to enforce it. So that if I make a contract with you on which I renege, the only permissible recourse for you is through due legal process. . . .

Thus, even if we assume that a woman has initially agreed to an encounter, her agreement does not automatically make all subsequent sexual activity to which she submits legitimate. If during coitus a woman should experience pain, be suddenly overcome with guilt or fear of pregnancy, or simply lose her initial desire, those are good reasons for her to change her mind. Having changed her mind, neither her partner nor the state has any right to force her to continue. . . .

If the "she asked for it" contractual view of sexual interchange has any validity, it is because there is a point at which there is no stopping a sexual encounter, a point at which that encounter becomes the inexorable outcome of the unfolding of natural events. If a sexual encounter is like a slide on which I cannot stop halfway down, it will be relevant whether I enter the slide of my own free will, or am pushed.

But there is no evidence that the entire sexual act is like a slide. . . . Indeed, the available evidence shows that most of the activity involved in sex has to do with building the requisite level of desire, a task that involves the proper use of foreplay, the possibility of which implies control over the form that foreplay will take. Modern sexual therapy assumes that such control is universally accessible, and so far there has been no reason to question that assumption. Sexologists are unanimous, moreover, in holding that mutual sexual enjoyment requires an atmosphere of comfort and communication, a minimum of pressure, and an ongoing check-up on one's partner's state. . . .

Where the kind of sex involved is not the sort of sex we would expect a woman to like, the burden of proof should not be on the woman to show that she did not consent, but on the defendant to show that contrary to every reasonable expectation she did consent. The defendant should be required to convince the court that the plaintiff persuaded him to have sex with her even though there are no visible reasons why she should.

In conclusion, there are no grounds for the "she asked for it" defense. Sexually provocative behavior does not generate sexual contracts. . . . Secondly, all the evidence suggests that neither women nor men find sexual enjoyment in rape or in any form of non-communicative sexuality. Thirdly, male sexual desire is containable, and can be subjected to moral and rational control. Fourthly, since there is no reason why women should not be sexually provocative, they do not "deserve" any sex they do not want. . . .

COMMUNICATIVE SEXUALITY: REINTERPRETING THE KANTIAN IMPERATIVE . . .

In thinking about sex we must keep in mind its sensual ends, and the facts show that aggressive high-pressure sex contradicts those ends. Consensual sex in dating situations is presumed to aim at mutual enjoyment. It may not always do this, and when it does, it might not always succeed. There is no logical incompatibility between wanting to continue a sexual encounter, and failing to derive sexual pleasure from it.

But it seems to me that there is a presumption in favor of the connection between sex and sexual enjoyment, and that if a man wants to be sure that he is not forcing himself on a woman, he has an obligation either to ensure that the encounter really is mutually enjoyable, or to know the reasons why she would want to continue the encounter in spite of her lack of enjoyment. A closer investigation of the nature of this obligation will enable us to construct a more rational and a more plausible norm of sexual conduct.

Onara O'Neill has argued that in intimate situations we have an obligation to take the ends of others as our own, and to promote those ends in a non-manipulative and non-paternalistic manner.[1] Now it seems that in honest sexual encounters just this is required. . . .

But the obligation to promote the sexual ends of one's partner implies the obligation to know what those ends are, and also the obligation to know how those ends are attained. Thus, the problem comes down to a problem of epistemic responsibility, the responsibility to know. The solution, in my view, lies in the practice of a communicative sexuality, one which combines the appropriate knowledge of the other with respect for the dialectics of desire.

So let us, for a moment, conceive of sexual interaction on a communicative rather than a contractual model. . . .

The communicative interaction involved in conversation is concerned with a good deal more than didactic content and argument. Good conversationalists are intuitive, sympathetic, and charitable. Intuition and charity aid the conversationalist in her effort to interpret the words of the other correctly and sympathy enables her to enter into the other's point of view. Her sensitivity alerts her to the tone of the exchange. Has her point been taken good-humoredly or resentfully? Aggressively delivered responses are taken as a sign that *ad hominems* are at work, and that the respondent's self-worth has been called into question. Good conversationalists will know how to suspend further discussion until this sense of self-worth has been reestablished. . . .

Just as communicative conversationalists are concerned with more than didactic content, persons engaged in communicative sexuality will be concerned with more than achieving coitus. They will be sensitive to the responses of their partners. They will, like good conversationalists, be intuitive, sympathetic, and charitable. . . . Communicative sexual partners will not overwhelm each other with the barrage of their own desires. They will treat negative, bored, or angry responses, as a sign that the erotic ground needs to be either cleared or abandoned. Their concern with fostering the desire of the other must involve an ongoing state of alertness in interpreting her responses.

Just as a conversationalist's prime concern is for the mutuality of the discussion, a person engaged in communicative sexuality will be most concerned with the mutuality of desire. As such, both will put into practice a regard for their respondent that is guaranteed no place in the contractual language of rights, duties, and consent. . . .

CULTURAL PRESUMPTIONS

Now it may well be that we have no obligation to care for strangers, and I do not wish to claim that we do. Nonetheless, it seems that O'Neill's point about the special moral duties we have in certain intimate situations is supported by a conceptual relation between certain kinds of personal relationships and the expectation that it should be a communicative relation. Friendship is a case in point. It is a relation that is greatly underdetermined by what we usually include in our sets of rights and obligations. For the most part, rights and obligations disappear as terms by which friendship is guided. They are still there, to be called upon, in case the relationship breaks down, but insofar as the friendship is a friendship, it is concerned with fostering the quality of the interaction and not with standing on rights. . . .

But is there a similar conceptual relation between the kind of activity that a date is, and the sort

of moral practice that it requires? My claim is that there is, and that this connection is easily established once we recognize the cultural presumption that dating is a gesture of friendship and regard. Traditionally, the decision to date indicates that two people have an initial attraction to each other, that they are disposed to like each other, and look forward to enjoying each other's company. Dating derives its implicit meaning from this tradition. . . .

Explicit protest to the contrary aside, the conventions of dating confer on it its social meaning, and this social meaning implies a relationship which is more like friendship than the cutthroat competition of opposing teams. As such, it requires that we do more than stand on our rights with regard to each other. As long as we are operating under the auspices of a dating relationship, it requires that we behave in the mode of friendship and trust. But if a date is more like a friendship than a business contract, then clearly respect for the dialectics of desire is incompatible with the sort of sexual pressure that is inclined to end in date rape. And clearly, also, a conquest mentality which exploits a situation of trust and respect for purely selfish ends is morally pernicious. . . . The proper end of friendship relations is mutual satisfaction. But the requirement of mutuality means that we must take a communicative approach to discovering the ends of the other, and this entails that we respect the dialectics of desire.

But now that we know what communicative sexuality is, and that it is morally required, and that it is the only feasible means to mutual sexual enjoyment, why not take this model as the norm of what is reasonable in sexual interaction. The evidence of sexologists strongly indicates that women whose partners are aggressively uncommunicative have little chance of experiencing sexual pleasure. . . .

Thus, where communicative sexuality does not occur, we lack the main ground for believing that the sex involved was consensual. . . . All that is needed then, in order to provide women with legal protection from "date rape" is to make both reckless indifference and willful ignorance a sufficient condition of *mens rea* and to make communicative sexuality the accepted norm of sex to which a reasonable woman would agree. Thus, the appeal to communicative sexuality as a norm for sexual encounters accomplishes two things. It brings the aggressive sex involved in "date rape" well within the realm of sexual assault, and it locates the guilt of date rapists in the failure to approach sexual relations on a communicative basis. . . .

CONCLUSION

In sum, using communicative sexuality as a model of normal sex has several advantages over the "aggressive-acquiescence" model of seduction. The new model ties the presumption that consensual sex takes place in the expectation of mutual desire much more closely to the facts about how that desire actually functions. Where communicative sex does not occur, this establishes a presumption that there was no consent. The importance of this presumption is that we are able, in criminal proceedings, to shift the burden of proof from the plaintiff, who on the contractual model must show that she resisted or was threatened, to the defendant who must then give some reason why she should consent after all. The communicative model of sexuality also enables us to give a different conceptual content to the concept of consent. It sees consent as something more like an ongoing cooperation than the one-shot agreement which we are inclined to see it as on the contractual model. Moreover, it does not matter, on the communicative model, whether a woman was sexually provocative, what her reputation is, what went on before the sex began. All that matters is the quality of communication with regard to the sex itself.

But most importantly, the communicative model of normal sexuality gives us a handle on a solution to the problem of date rape. If noncommunicative sexuality establishes a presumption of nonconsent, then where there are no overriding reasons for thinking that consent occurred, we have a criterion for a category of sexual assault that does not require evidence of physical violence or threat. If we are serious about date rape, then the next step is to take this criterion as objective grounds for establishing that a date rape has occurred. The proper legislation is the shortest route to establishing this criterion.

There remains, of course, the problem of education. If we are going to change the rules about what is socially acceptable in sexual relations, then it is only fair to let the public know. In a mass media society, this is not hard to do. A public information campaign will spread the news in no time at all. The real problem is the reluctance of the mass media to deal with questions of sexual relations and sexual intimacy. Its politicians are still curiously reluctant to stand up to an increasingly small sector of society that is unwilling to admit, despite all the evidence to the contrary, that anyone but well-meaning husbands and wives ever have sex. I would not be surprised if this sort of puritanical holdout were the very source of the problem of rape. Certainly, sexual ignorance must contribute significantly to the kind of social environment conducive to rape.

NOTES

1. O'Neill, "Between Consenting Adults," *Philosophy and Public Affairs* **14**, 252–277.

Discussion Questions

1. Is Pineau's communicative model of sexuality the only desirable one? Are there times when it is reasonable for a man to believe that a woman has given her consent to sex even though she has not verbally communicated it? Support your answers using examples.
2. Are there times when women might really want to be sexually dominated by men? What about women who prefer not to discuss sex, or who prefer the man to take the initiative—much like patients who prefer to let their doctors make the decisions about their health care? Are these examples of "false consciousness" based on nega-

tive stereotypes about women? Or can there be "good sex" without communicative consensus? Support your answers. Discuss how Pineau might respond to these questions.

3. Catharine MacKinnon maintains that in a society where women are oppressed, communication alone is not sufficient to establish consent to sex. Do you agree? Are there times when a woman might consent out of a feeling of powerlessness, rather than a genuine desire for sexual intimacy? Support your answer using examples. Discuss how Pineau might respond to MacKinnon.

4. Discuss the implications of Pineau's definition of date rape on how such cases should be handled by the courts. Should policies such as that of Antioch College be instituted on all campuses? Support your answer.

5. In her book *The Morning After: Sex, Fear, and Feminism on Campus* (1993), Katie Roiphe critiques Pineau's approach. Roiphe argues that the fuss over date rape, rather than empowering and liberating women, perpetuates the stereotype of them as vulnerable, naive, and in need of protection. The emphasis on communicative consensus, rather than sexually liberating women, has thrown a damper on relationships and created an atmosphere of suspicion between men and women. Has the current focus on date rape empowered women, or made them more fearful? How has it affected the men on your campus and the heterosexual dating scene? Use examples to illustrate your answer.

6. A woman at a fraternity party gets very drunk. She is dressed in a low-cut blouse and short skirt. A man who is an acquaintance comes over and has a few drinks with her. He then leads her to his room. After making out for a while, he feels she is responding to him and, although no words are actually exchanged, they have intercourse. He then leaves her in the room, asleep or passed out. Is this an example of rape? Did she "ask for it"? Should women who get drunk and/or dress provocatively be expected to accept the consequences of their choices? Is sexual intercourse one of these consequences? Does drinking excuse what happened? If the woman was not responsible for her actions, is it fair that the man be held responsible for his when he had also been drinking? Support your answers. Discuss how Pineau might respond to this scenario.

7. Discuss how care ethicist Nel Noddings might respond to Pineau's communicative model of sex.

KATIE ROIPHE

Reckless Eyeballing: Sexual Harassment on Campus

Katie Roiphe is an author and a journalist. She argues that the current fear of rape and sexual harassment has been fueled by exaggerations of their actual incidence on campuses as well as by the rhetoric of "rape crisis feminists" such as MacKinnon and Pineau. The current broad definitions of sexual harassment and date rape used on college campuses, rather than empowering women, perpetuate stereotypes of women as both sexless and as powerless victims of male oppression.

Critical Reading Questions

1. What is the standard definition of sexual harassment? Why does Roiphe have concerns about this definition?
2. What is MacKinnon's view on sexual harassment, and what are its political implications?
3. Why does Roiphe maintain that the idea that a male student can sexually harass a female professor is insulting to women?
4. What view of men and women, according to Roiphe, is implied by the current rhetoric against sexual harassment?
5. According to Roiphe, why does such rhetoric create an atmosphere of suspicion and mistrust and reduce the number of meaningful contacts between students and faculty?
6. What does Roiphe mean by the "zookeeper school of feminism"?
7. How, according to Roiphe, do people from other countries view the concern with sexual harassment in the United States?
8. How does Roiphe explain the high incidence of sexual harassment in the United States?
9. What does Roiphe suggest women do instead of focusing so much on the dangers of sexual harassment?
10. On what grounds does Roiphe argue that "people have a right to leer" or, as she puts it, "engage in reckless eyeballing"? What, according to Roiphe, are appropriate moral responses to being leered at?
11. Where does Roiphe draw the line between harmless "harassment" and harassment that is a genuine abuse of power?
12. According to Roiphe, why might telling a woman who did not feel victimized that in fact she *has* been a victim of date rape or sexual harassment actually harm rather than empower her?

"Reckless Eyeballing: Sexual Harassment on Campus," in *The Morning After: Sex, Fear, and Feminism on Campus* (Boston: Little, Brown and Co., 1993), 85–112. Some notes have been omitted.

For generations, women have talked and written and theorized about their problems with men. But theories about patriarchy tumble from abstraction when you wake up next to it in the morning. Denouncing male oppression clashes with wanting him anyhow. From playgrounds to consciousness-raising groups, from suffragette marches to pro-choice marches, women have been talking their way through this contradiction for a long time.

Sometimes my younger sister and I go out for coffee and talk about our relationships. We analyze everything: why he acts that way, how unfair this is, how we shouldn't be waiting for his call, and how we have better things to do with our time anyway. How men are always like that, and we are always like this, and our conversation goes on, endless, pleasurable, interesting, over many refills, until we go home and wait for their calls.

Heterosexual desire inevitably raises conflicts for the passionate feminist, and it's not an issue easily evaded. Sooner or later feminism has to address "the man question." But this is more than just a practical question of procreation, more than the well-worn translation of personal into political. It's also a question for the abstract, the ideological, the furthest reaches of the feminist imagination.

Charlotte Perkins Gilman, a prominent feminist writing at the turn of the century, found a fictional solution to the conflict between sex and feminism in her utopian novel, *Herland.* Her solution is simple: there is no sexual desire. . . .

Many of today's feminists, in their focus on sexual harassment, share Gilman's sexual politics. In their videos, literature, and workshops, these feminists are creating their own utopian visions of human sexuality. They imagine a world where all expressions of sexual appreciation are appreciated. They imagine a totally symmetrical universe, where people aren't silly, rude, awkward, excessive, or confused. And if they are, they are violating the rules and are subject to disciplinary proceedings.

A Princeton pamphlet declares that "sexual harassment is unwanted sexual attention that makes a person feel uncomfortable or causes problems in school or at work, or in social settings."[1] The word "uncomfortable" echoes through all the literature on sexual harassment. The feminists concerned with this issue, then, propose the right to be comfortable as a feminist principle.

The difficulty with these rules is that, although it may infringe on the right to comfort, unwanted sexual attention is part of nature. To find wanted sexual attention, you have to give and receive a certain amount of unwanted sexual attention. Clearly, the truth is that if no one was ever allowed to risk offering unsolicited sexual attention, we would all be solitary creatures.

The category of sexual harassment, according to current campus definitions, is not confined to relationships involving power inequity. Echoing many other common definitions of sexual harassment, Princeton's pamphlet warns that "sexual harassment can occur between two people regardless of whether or not one has power over the other."[2] The weight of this definition of sexual harassment, then, falls on gender instead of status.

In current definitions of sexual harassment, there is an implication that gender is so important that it eclipses all other forms of power. The driving idea behind these rules is that gender itself is a sufficient source of power to constitute sexual harassment. Catharine MacKinnon, an early theorist of sexual harassment, writes that "situations of co-equal power—among co-workers or students or teachers—are difficult to see as examples of sexual harassment unless you have a notion of male power. I think we lie to women when we call it not power when a woman is come on to by a man who is not her employer, not her teacher."[3] With this description, MacKinnon extends the province of male power beyond that of tangible social power. She proposes using the words "sexual harassment" as a way to name what she sees as a fundamental social and political inequity between men and women. Following in this line of thought, Elizabeth Grauerholz, a sociology professor, conducted a study about instances of male students harassing their female professors, a phenomenon she calls "contra-power harassment."[4]

Recently, at the University of Michigan, a female teaching assistant almost brought a male student up on charges of sexual harassment. She was offended by an example he used in a paper about polls—a few sentences about "Dave Stud" entertaining ladies in his apartment when he receives a call from a pollster—and she showed the paper to the professor of the class. He apparently encouraged her to see the offending example as an instance of sexual harassment. She decided not to press charges, although she warned the student that the next time anything else like this happened, in writing or in person, she would not hesitate. The student wisely dropped the course. To understand how this student's paragraph about Dave Stud might sexually harass his teacher, when he has much more to lose than she does, one must recognize the deeply sexist assumptions about male-female relations behind the teaching assistant's charge.

The idea that a male student can sexually harass a female professor, overturning social and institutional hierarchy, solely on the basis of some primal or socially conditioned male power over women is insulting. The mere fact of being a man doesn't give the male student so much power that he can plow through social hierarchies, grabbing what he wants, intimidating all the cowering female faculty in his path. The assumption that female students or faculty must be protected from the sexual harassment of male peers or inferiors promotes the regrettable idea that men are natively more powerful than women.

Even if you argue, as many do, that *in this society* men are simply much more powerful than women, this is still a dangerous train of thought. It carries us someplace we don't want to be. Rules and laws based on the premise that all women need protection from all men, because they are so much weaker, serve only to reinforce the image of women as powerless.

Our female professors and high-ranking executives, our congresswomen and editors, are every bit as strong as their male counterparts. They have earned their position of authority. To declare that their authority is vulnerable to a dirty joke from someone of inferior status just because that person happens to be a man is to undermine their position. Female authority is not (and should not be seen as) so fragile that it shatters at the first sign of male sexuality. Any rules saying otherwise strip women, in the public eye, of their hard-earned authority.

Since common definitions of sexual harassment include harassment between peers, the emphasis is not on external power structures, but on inner landscapes. The boundaries are subjective, the maps subject to mood. According to the Equal Employment Opportunity Commission's definition, any conduct may be deemed sexual harassment if it "has the purpose or effect of unreasonably interfering with an individual's work or academic performance or creating an intimidating, hostile or offensive working or academic environment." The hostility or offensiveness of a working environment is naturally hard to measure by objective standards. Such vague categorization opens the issue up to the individual psyche.

The clarity of the definition of sexual harassment as a "hostile work environment" depends on a universal code of conduct, a shared idea of acceptable behavior that we just don't have. Something that makes one person feel uncomfortable may make another person feel great. At Princeton, counselors reportedly tell students, If you feel sexually harassed then chances are you were. At the university's Terrace Club, the refuge of fashionable, left-leaning, black-clad undergraduates, there is a sign supporting this view. It is downstairs, on a post next to the counter where the beer is served, often partially obscured by students talking, cigarettes in hand: "What constitutes sexual harassment or intimidating, hostile or offensive environment is to be defined by the person harassed and his/her own feelings of being threatened or compromised." This relatively common definition of sexual harassment crosses the line between being supportive and obliterating the idea of external reality.

The categories become especially complicated and slippery when sexual harassment enters the realm of the subconscious. The Princeton guide explains that "sexual harassment may result from a conscious or unconscious action, and can be subtle or blatant." Once we move into the area of the subtle and unconscious, we are no longer talking about a professor systematically exploiting power for sex. We are no longer talking about Hey, baby, sleep with me or I'll fail you. To hold people responsible for their subtle, unconscious actions is to legislate thought, an ominous, not to mention difficult, prospect.

The idea of sexual harassment—and clearly when you are talking about the subtle and unconscious, you are talking about an idea—provides a blank canvas on which students can express all of the insecurities, fears, and confusions about the relative sexual freedom of the college experience. Sexual harassment is everywhere: it crops up in dinner conversations and advertisements on television, all over women's magazines and editorial pages. No one can claim that Anita Hill is an unsung heroine. It makes sense that teenagers get caught up in the Anita Hill fury; they are particularly susceptible to feeling uncomfortable about sexuality, and sexual harassment offers an ideology that explains "uncomfortable" in political terms. The idea of sexual harassment displaces adolescent uneasiness onto the environment, onto professors, onto older men.

The heightened awareness of the potential for sexual encroachment creates an atmosphere of suspicion and distrust between faculty and students. Many professors follow an unwritten rule: never close the door to your office when you and a female student are inside. One professor told a male teaching assistant I know that closing the door to his office with a student inside is an invitation to charges of sexual harassment. . . .

The inflamed rhetoric against harassment implies that all women are potential victims and all men are potential harassers. "Men in the Academy," an essay in the book *Ivory Power*, vilifies the male academic so effectively that the author is forced to acknowledge that "nonetheless, not all male professors harass female students."[5] That this need even be said is evidence that this perspective is spiraling out of control.

The irony is that these open doors, and all that they symbolize, threaten to create barriers between faculty and students. In the present hypersensitive environment, caution and better judgment can lead professors to keep female students at a distance. It may be easier not to pursue friendships with female students than to risk charges of sexual harassment and misunderstood intentions. The rhetoric surrounding sexual harassment encourages a return to formal relations between faculty and students.

The university, with its emphasis on intellectual exchange, on the passionate pursuit of knowledge, with its strange hours and unworldly citizens, is theoretically an ideal space for close friendships. The flexible hours combined with the intensity of the academic world would appear to be fertile ground for connections, arguments over coffee. Recently, reading a biography of the poet John Berryman, who was also a professor at Princeton in the forties, I was struck by stories about his students crowding into his house late into the night to talk about poetry. These days, an informal invitation to a professor's house till all hours would be a breach of propriety. . . .

Feminists concerned with sexual harassment must fight for an immutable hierarchy, for interactions so cleansed of personal interest there can be no possibility of borders crossed. Although this approach to education may reduce the number of harmful connections between teachers and students, it may also reduce the number of meaningful connections. The problem with the chasm solution to faculty-student relations is that for graduate students, and even for undergraduates, connections with professors are intellectually as well as professionally important.

In an early survey of sexual harassment, a law student at Berkeley wrote that in response to fears of sexual harassment charges, "the male law school teachers ignore female students . . . this means that we are afforded [fewer] academic opportunities than male students."[6] Many male professors have confirmed that they feel more uncomfortable with female students than with male students, because of all the attention given to sexual harassment. They may not "ignore" their female students, but they keep them at arm's length. They feel freer to forge friendships with male students.

The overstringent attention given to sexual harassment on campuses breeds suspicion; it creates an environment where imaginations run wild, charges can seem to materialize out of thin air, and both faculty and students worry about a friendly lunch. The repercussions for the academic community, let alone the confused freshman, can be many and serious.

In an excessive effort to purge the university of sexual corruption, many institutions have violated the rights of the professors involved by neglecting to follow standard procedures. Since sexual harassment is a relatively recent priority, "standard procedures" are themselves new, shrouded, and shaky. Charges of sexual harassment are uncharted territory, and fairness is not necessarily the compass. . . .

The university has become so saturated with the idea of sexual harassment that it has begun to affect minute levels of communication. Like "date rape," the phrase "sexual harassment" is frequently used, and it does not apply only to extremes of human behavior. Suddenly everyday experience is filtered through the strict lens of a new sexual politics. Under fierce political scrutiny, behavior that once seemed neutral or natural enough now takes on ominous meanings. You may not even realize that you are a survivor of sexual harassment.

A student tells me that she first experienced sexual harassment when she came to college. She was at a crowded party, leaning against a wall, and a big jock came up to her, placed his hands at either side of her head, and pretended to lean against her, saying, So, baby, when are we going out? All right, he didn't touch me, she says, but he invaded my space. He had no right to do that.

She has carried this first instance of sexual harassment around in her head for six years. It is the beginning of a long list. A serious feminist now, an inhabitant of the official feminist house on campus, she recognizes this experience for what it was. She knows there is no way to punish the anonymous offender or everyone would be behind bars, but she thinks the solution is education. Like many feminists, she argues that discipline is clumsy, bureaucracy lumbering, and there is no hope for perfect justice in the university. She is more concerned with getting the message across, delineating acceptable behaviors to faculty and students alike, than in beheading professors. She subscribes to a sort of zookeeper school of feminism—training the beasts to behave within "acceptable" parameters.

Many foreigners think that concern with sexual harassment is as American as baseball, New England Puritans, and apple pie. Many feminists in other countries look on our preoccupation with sexual harassment as another sign of the self-indulgence and repression in American society.

Veronique Neiertz, France's secretary of state for women's rights, has said that in the United States "the slightest wink can be misinterpreted." Her ministry's commonsense advice to women who feel harassed by coworkers is to respond with "a good slap in the face."[7]

Once sexual harassment includes someone glancing down your shirt, the meaning of the phrase has been stretched beyond recognition. The rules about unwanted sexual attention begin to seem more like etiquette than rules. Of course it would be nicer if people didn't brush against other people in a way that makes them uncomfortable. It would also be nicer if bankers didn't bang their briefcases into people on the subway at rush hour. But not nice is a different thing than against the rules, or the law. It is a different thing than oppressing women. Etiquette and politics aren't synonyms.

Susan Teres of SHARE said, at the 1992 Take Back the Night march, that 88 percent of Princeton's female students had experienced some form of sexual harassment on campus. Catharine MacKinnon writes that "only 7.8% of women in the United States are not sexually assaulted or harassed in their lifetimes."[8] No wonder. Once you cast the net so wide as to include everyone's everyday experience, identifying sexual harassment becomes a way of interpreting the sexual texture of daily life, instead of isolating individual events. Sensitivity to sexual harassment becomes a way of seeing the world, rather than a way of targeting specific contemptible behaviors. In an essay attempting to profile the quintessential sexual harasser, two feminists warn in conclusion (and in all seriousness) that "the harasser is similar, perhaps disturbingly so, to the 'average man.'"[9]

As one peruses guidelines on sexual harassment, it's clear where the average man comes in. Like most common definitions, Princeton's definition of sexual harassment includes "leering and ogling, whistling, sexual innuendo, and other suggestive or offensive or derogatory comments, humor and jokes about sex."[10] MacKinnon's statistic includes obscene phone calls. These definitions of sexual harassment sterilize the environment. They propose classrooms that are cleaner than Sesame

Street and Mr. Rogers's neighborhood. Like the rhetoric about date rape, this extreme inclusiveness forces women into old roles. What message are we sending if we say We can't work if you tell dirty jokes, it upsets us, it offends us? With this severe a conception of sexual harassment, sex itself gets pushed into a dark, seamy, male domain. If we can't look at his dirty pictures because his dirty pictures upset us, it doesn't mean they vanish. It means he looks at them with a new sense of their power, their underground, forbidden, male-only value.

Instead of learning that men have no right to do these terrible things to us, we should be learning to deal with individuals with strength and confidence. If someone bothers us, we should be able to put him in his place without crying into our pillow or screaming for help or counseling. If someone stares at us, or talks dirty, or charges neutral conversation with sexual innuendo, we should not be pushed to the verge of a nervous breakdown. . . .

I would even go so far as to say that people have the right to leer at whomever they want to leer at. By offering protection to the woman against the leer, the movement against sexual harassment is curtailing her personal power. This protection implies the need to be protected. It paints her as defenseless against even the most trivial of male attentions. This protection assumes that she never ogles, leers, or makes sexual innuendos herself.

Interpreting leers and leer-type behavior as a violation is a choice. My mother tells me about the time she was walking down the street in the sixties, when skirts were short, with my older sister, who was then three. A construction worker made a comment to my mother, and my three-year-old sister leaned out of her carriage and said, "Hey, mister, leave my mother alone." My mother, never the conventional sort of feminist, told my sister that the construction worker wasn't hurting her, he was giving her a compliment.

Although my mother's reaction may not be everyone's, this is a parable about individual responses. There is spectrum of reactions to something like a leer. Some may be flattered, others distressed; some won't notice, and still others, according to some feminist literature, will be enraged and incapacitated. In its propaganda the movement against sex-

ual harassment places absolute value on the leer. According to its rules, whatever that construction worker said to my mother was violating, harmful, and demeaning. According to its rules, my three-year-old sister was right. By rallying institutional authority behind its point of view, by distributing these pamphlets that say leering always makes women feel violated, this movement propels women backward to a time when sexual attention was universally thought to offend. They are saying, as Catharine MacKinnon neatly summarizes it, that "all women live in sexual objectification the way fish live in water."[11] But I think it depends on where you learned to swim.

History offers an example of another time when looks could be crimes, but today feminists don't talk much about what happened to black men accused of "reckless eyeballing," that is, directing sexual glances at white women. Black men were lynched for a previous incarnation of "sexual harassment." As late as 1955, a black man was lynched for whistling at a white woman. Beneath the Jim Crow law about reckless eyeballing was the assumption that white women were the property of white men, and a look too hard or too long in their direction was a flouting of white power. Reckless eyeballing was a symbolic violation of white women's virtue. That virtue, that division between white women and black men, was important to the southern hierarchy. While of course lynchings and Jim Crow are not the current danger, it's important to remember that protecting women against the stray male gaze has not always served a social good. We should learn the lessons: looks can't kill, and we are nobody's property.

All of this is not to suggest that abuses of power are not wrong. They are. Any professor who trades grades for sex and uses this power as a forceful tool of seduction deserves to face charges. The same would be true if he traded grades for a thousand dollars. I'm not opposed to stamping out corruption; I only think it's important to look before you stamp. Rules about harassment should be less vague, and inclusive. They should sharply target serious offenses and abuses of power rather than environments that are "uncomfortable," rather than a stray professor looking down a shirt. The university's rules should not be based on the idea of female students who are pure and naïve, who don't harbor sexualities of their own, who don't seduce, or who can't defend themselves against the nonconditional sexual interests of male faculty and students. . . .

As feminists interested in the issue themselves argue, "Many have difficulty recognizing their experience as victimization. It is helpful to use the words that fit the experience, validating the depths of the survivor's feelings and allowing her to feel her experience was serious." [12] In other words, these feminists recognize that if you don't tell the victim that she's a victim, she may sail through the experience without fully grasping the gravity of her humiliation. She may get through without all that trauma and counseling. Buried within this description of helping students overcome the problem of "recognizing their experience as victimization" is the nagging concern that the problem may pass unnoticed, may dissolve without political scrutiny. To create awareness is sometimes to create a problem.

Education about sexual harassment is not confined to the space of freshman week. As sexual harassment is absorbed into public discussion, it enters grade schools as easily as colleges. An article in *New York* magazine documents the trickle-down effect: "After her first week at a reputable private school in Manhattan, 8-year-old Alexandra didn't want to go back. A 9-year-old boy had been harassing her: 'He said he wanted to hump me.' She wasn't sure what 'hump' meant." [13]

The article describes what happened when Alexandra discovered the name for her traumatic experience. She was listening to Anita Hill's testimony on the radio when she suddenly exclaimed: "'That's what happened to me! He didn't touch me, but his words upset me!'" The article concludes that "Alexandra's first lesson in sexual harassment may not be her last, but thanks to her parents, who listened to her, believed her and supported her, she'll at least be better prepared to deal with sexual abuse than the women and men of Anita Hill's generation." [14] As Alexandra grows up, will she be better able to deal with sexual abuse, or will she just see it everywhere she looks? Will she blur the line between childish teasing and sexual abuse for the rest of her life? The prospect of a maturing generation of Alexandras, sensitized from childhood to the issue of sexual harassment, is not necessarily desirable from the feminist point of view. As Joan Didion wrote in the sixties, certain segments of the women's movement can breed "women too sensitive for the difficulties of adult life, women unequipped for reality, and grasping at the movement as a rationale for denying that reality." [15]

Responding to sexual harassment in its most expansive definition purges the environment of the difficult, the uncomfortable, and the even mildly distasteful. Feminists concerned with sexual harassment reproduce their own version of Charlotte Perkins Gilman's *Herland*, based on the absence of messy sexual desire. Although it takes some imaginative leaps to get there, their version of Herland is a land without dirty jokes, leers, and other instances of "unwanted sexual attention." Whether or not visions of a universe free from "sexual harassment" are practical, the question becomes whether they're even desirable.

Mary Koss, author of the *Ms.* magazine survey of rape, writes that "experiencing sexual harassment transforms women into victims and changes their lives." [16] Koss sees this transformation into victimhood as something caused by sexual harassment, an external event. In Koss's paradigm, after the student has been harassed, her confidence is perilously shaken, her ability to function and trust men disrupted forever. She sees the "lecherous professor" as the agent of transformation. She does not see that it is her entire conceptual framework—her kind of rhetoric, her kind of interpretation—that transforms perfectly stable women into hysterical, sobbing victims. If there is any transforming to be done, it is to transform everyday experience back into everyday experience.

NOTES

1. "What You Should Know About Sexual Harassment." Princeton, N.J.: SHARE.

2. Ibid.

3. Catharine MacKinnon, *Feminism Unmodified* (Cambridge: Harvard University Press, 1987), 89.

4. *Chronicle of Higher Education,* 24 April 1991.

5. Sue Rosenberg Zalk, "Men in the Academy." In M. Paludi (ed.), *Ivory Power: Sexual Harassment on Campus* (Albany, NY: State University of New York, 1990), pp. 142–175.

6. "Sexual Harassment: A Hidden Issue." Washington, D.C.: Project on the Status and Education of Women, 1978.

7. *New York Times,* 3 May 1992.

8. MacKinnon, *Toward a Feminist Theory of the State* (Cambridge: Harvard University Press, 1989), 127.

9. Louise Fitzgerald and Lauren Weitzman, "Men Who Harass: Speculation and Data," in Paludi, 139.

10. Princeton, N.J.: SHARE.

11. MacKinnon, *Toward a Feminist Theory of the State,* 149.

12. Kathryn Quina, "The Victimization of Women," in Paludi, ed., 99.

13. *New York,* 16 November 1992.

14. Ibid.

15. Joan Didion, *The White Album* (New York: Farrar, Straus and Giroux, 1979), 116.

16. Mary Koss, "Changed Lives: The Psychological Impact of Sexual Harassment," in Paludi, ed., 73.

Discussion Questions

1. Discuss whether Roiphe believes that the current rhetoric on sexual harassment does more harm than good. Support your answer.

2. What does Roiphe mean when she says that broad definitions of sexual harassment "sterilize the environment"? Do you agree? Support your answers using examples from your campus.

3. Do you agree with the definition of sexual harassment now in common use? If so, explain why. If not, come up with a definition of sexual harassment that overcomes some of the problems in the current definition cited by Roiphe.

4. Do you agree with Roiphe that people have a right to leer? What are some of the pros and cons of including leering under the definition of sexual harassment? Support your answers. Discuss how a rights ethicist such as Ayn Rand might respond. Discuss how MacKinnon and Pineau might respond to these questions.

5. Discuss Roiphe's claim that feminists such as Pineau who tell victims of date rape that they have been "traumatized" are actually perpetuating the old ethos of female victimhood and contributing to the institutionalization of female weakness.

6. Discuss whether Roiphe adequately addresses the problem of sexual harassment as sexual discrimination and a violation of the right to equal opportunity. Does sexual harassment, even though it may not directly harm a particular woman, create a hostile working or academic environment which, in turn, limits women's opportunities and freedom? Support your answer.

7. Does sexual harassment violate Kant's categorical imperative? Support your answer. If so, discuss what policy should be adopted on your campus for dealing with it.

JUDITH A. BOSS

Throwing Pearls to the Swine: Women, Forgiveness, and the Unrepentant Abuser

Judith Boss is a philosopher, writer, and assistant director of Curriculum Affairs at Brown University Medical School. Boss argues that unconditional forgiveness in the context of domestic violence is incompatible with the principle of respect for persons. The proper moral response in the context of ongoing domestic violence is resentment rather than forgiveness. Until an abuser repents and changes his ways, it is not only imprudent but morally wrong for the woman to forgive. For a woman to fail to show resentment in the face of ongoing domestic violence is to show a lack of self-respect as well as a lack of proper respect for the basic human rights of all women.

Critical Reading Questions

1. Why does Boss reject the concept of forgiveness as a substantive virtue?
2. Why are women more likely than men to be the victims of domestic violence?
3. What is patriarchy? Why, according to Boss, does patriarchy encourage domestic violence?
4. What type of women are most likely to be abused by their partners?
5. What is the definition of forgiveness? What is the definition of resentment?
6. According to John Rawls, what is the purpose of resentment?
7. What, according to Kant, is our most fundamental moral duty? What is the relationship between self-respect, moral indignation, and resentment?
8. What is "repentance" in the context of domestic violence? What is remorse? How does repentance differ from remorse?
9. According to Boss, why can only the victim forgive the abuser?
10. What is Boss's view of the advice to victims of domestic violence "forgive and forget"?
11. What is Aristotle's view of people who fail to feel resentment?
12. What is the relationship between resentment and justice?
13. In what ways do well-meaning people, as well as self-help books, legitimate messages that degrade women who are victims of domestic violence? How do these messages contribute to self-blame and low self-esteem on the part of the victims?
14. What is Boss's view of the advice to victims of domestic violence that they must learn to forgive themselves?
15. According to Boss, why is it wrong for a woman to forgive an unrepentant abuser?
16. Why does Boss reject the advice to use forgiveness as a means of keeping the family intact? How does this advice contribute to child abuse?

"Throwing Pearls to the Swine: Women, Forgiveness, and the Unrepentant Abuser," in eds. Laurence Bove and Laura D. Kaplan, *Perspectives on Power and Dominance* (Netherlands: Rodolpi Press, 1997), 235–247. Some notes have been omitted.

17. According to Boss, why don't victims of domestic violence have a duty to forgive a repentant abuser?

To err is human; to forgive divine.
—Alexander Pope

Unconditional forgiveness, including forgiveness of an unrepentant wrongdoer, is often regarded as one of the highest virtues and as indicative of an exemplary moral character regardless of any actions that may follow as a consequence. . . . Victims of domestic violence who are unwilling to forgive are often viewed as bitter and vindictive and held to blame for their own emotional distress as well as for the breakdown of the family. . . .

The common concept of forgiveness as a substantive virtue—an act that is virtuous independently of its context—runs contrary to concerns for justice and respect for equal human dignity. Advocating forgiveness in the context of ongoing domestic violence is, instead, a means of maintaining and legitimating the current patriarchal power structure that elevates men to a position of power and superiority over women. Discussions of forgiveness in our culture, therefore, cannot be separated from gender politics.

Because of the inequality of power characteristic of the family and other institutions in our society, women find themselves the victims of oppression and violence far more often than men. Female battering in the "privacy" of the home is epidemic, not just in the United States, but in all patriarchal societies. Domestic violence, according to former Surgeon General C. Everett Koop, is the leading cause of injury to women in this country. More than 80 percent of the victims of family sexual abuse, spousal abuse, and elder abuse are women.[1] An estimated one in every three to four wives is beaten,[2] . . .

Domestic violence is not an isolated phenomenon, but exists within the context of a patriarchal superstructure. In a patriarchal society men's sense of self is grounded in feelings of entitlement, while women, who occupy a submissive status, often have a sense of self only in relationship to the men in their lives. Domestic violence, by its very nature, places women in a position of inferiority and subservience in relation to the abuser whose intention it is to diminish his victim's sense of worth.

Patriarchy as a norm is reinforced by religious and social institutions as well as by conventional moral wisdom that regards the virtuous woman as one who always puts others' needs before her own. Battered women are often advised, especially by pastoral counselors, to try to be more agreeable and submissive. Ironically, it is these very women who hold highly traditional views of the roles of men and women, and who try hardest to please their husbands, who are the most likely to be abused by their husbands and partners.[3]

DEFINING THE KEY TERMS: "FORGIVENESS," "RESENTMENT," AND "REPENTANCE"

Forgiveness, by definition, involves overcoming or being willing to overcome feelings of resentment toward someone who intentionally causes an injury. Resentment, in turn, is "the anger that one might properly feel at having been personally injured."[4] Resentment is not the same as vindictiveness or a desire to "get even" or to retaliate, as many people assume. Victims of domestic violence, according to counselor Maria Fortune, "rarely feel vengeful; they simply want the abuse to stop."[5]

Social philosopher John Rawls describes resentment as "a moral feeling (that) invokes the concept of right."[6] It is a "form of personal protest which expresses our respect for self, for others, and for morality."[7] By sending a message to the abuser that the victim will not tolerate such treatment, resentment serves to affirm the victim's own moral worth as well as to protect her from future abuse.

The cherished ideal that all humans have equal moral worth is central to Western morality. As beings with moral worth, all persons deserve to be treated by others with respect and dignity. The domination of one person by another runs contrary to the principle of respect. A dominant-submissive relationship also erodes self-respect which, as philosopher Immanuel Kant argues, is our most fundamental moral duty and the basis of respect for others.

Because respect for persons, including respect for oneself, is fundamental to morality, forgiveness can only be a virtue when it is compatible with self-respect. Just as moral indignation is the morally appropriate response in the face of the abuse and oppression of others—as occurred during the Nazi Holocaust and American slavery—so, too, resentment is appropriate in the face of one's own abuse and oppression. Both moral sentiments help to foster community by encouraging the victims and others to work toward moral reform rather than settling for the status quo. To put aside resentment or moral indignation and to forgive in the face of ongoing oppression absolves the oppressor of any need to change his or her behavior.

Forgiveness, in order to be consistent with self-respect and moral equality, is appropriate only when the offender ceases to hold a degraded view of his victim and repents of his wrongful actions. Repentance requires that the wrongdoer recognize and accept responsibility for his abusive actions. Sometimes an abuser will express remorse and seek to make up with his victim following a violent episode. Remorse is an emotional reaction of anguish in the face of guilt, in which the abuser seeks forgiveness "as an immediate way to be relieved of guilt for the wrongful actions."[8] Rather than stop the cycle of abuse, "acceptance of gifts or pleas for forgiveness [in response to the abuser's remorse] may simply perpetuate the man's abusive behavior."[9]

Repentance, in contrast to remorse, demands an actual change in a wrongdoer's attitudes and lifestyle. In repenting, the abuser sets himself apart from and condemns the harm he did. This is seldom possible "without some form of rehabilitative intervention and clear monitoring of change."[10] Genuine repentance offers assurance that the abusive behavior will not be repeated. Because the reason for resentment is negated by repentance, the abused can now forgive and at the same time maintain her self-respect.

As a moral virtue, then, forgiveness is bilateral and aimed at reestablishing moral equality between the two parties. Because forgiveness involves the overcoming of resentment toward the abuser, only the victim is in a position to forgive, just as only the wrongdoer is in a position to repent. . . .

Forgiving also differs from forgetting. The adage "forgive and forget" is rather odd, since one does not will to forget in the way one wills to forgive. Forgetting is something that happens to a person, whereas forgiving is an intentional act on the part of the victim. . . .

To tell the victim of a gross injustice and injury to "forgive and forget" is advocating something that is often not only impossible but also ignores their pain and who they are. Indeed, some writers urge people who have been oppressed in the past never to forgive or forget the horrors of events such as the Nazi Holocaust and American slavery. Resentment serves to protect the victims from future violence. To forget the past is to open the door for these horrors to be repeated in the future.

FORGIVENESS AND SELF-BLAME

The capacity to feel resentment is intimately linked with self-respect. Aristotle, in his *Nicomachean Ethics,* wrote regarding people who fail to feel resentment or justified anger:

> . . . people who are not angered by the right things, or in the right way, or at the right times, or towards the right people, all seem to be foolish. . . . Since he is not angered, he does not seem to be the sort to defend himself; and such willingness to accept insults to oneself or to overlook insults to one's family and friends is slavish.[11]

Rage and resentment against past wrongs motivates us to correct injustices and restore self-respect, even though our anger may make others uncomfortable. In many cases of domestic violence, however, it is not the intensity of the abused woman's anger or resentment that is morally problematic; it is the direction. Too often her anger is misdirected toward herself or sometimes even toward her children, rather than toward the wrongdoer.

Domestic violence can have a devastating effect on a woman's self-respect and self-esteem. This is precisely the "goal" of the abuser, who uses violence to bring the victim lower than himself by doing whatever he can to destroy her self-respect.[12] An abused woman's self-esteem may come to feel so low that she actually begins to believe that she deserved the abuse because she is so unworthy. "An abused woman," writes Ginny NiCarthy, co-director of a woman's counseling group in Seattle, Washington, "may have absorbed her former partner's stated view of her and developed a habit of verbal self-abuse."[13] If she were just more nurturing and caring, a "good enough" woman, she "could have loved him out of his violent ways." . . .

A woman who misdirects her anger and resentment inward toward herself does not resent her abuser. She is able to forgive him repeatedly because she does not hold him responsible for the abuse. Complying with one's degradation by excusing one's abuser boosts his self-esteem and invites further abuse when a man wants to feel better about himself. This leads to a cycle of violence where unconditional forgiveness reinforces the abusive behavior and makes it more likely to occur in the future.

Friends and families of abused women, and even some therapists, sometimes legitimate negative messages that degrade women and hold them responsible for their own distress. Often this takes the form of "helping" women who are victims of domestic violence to change their behavior in order to stop the abuse. This advice generally includes putting aside any negative feelings and taking that "final step of forgiveness"—letting bygones be bygones—so the family can get back to "normal."

By labeling resentment a "negative" feeling, blame is placed on the victim for her feelings as well as for the actions of the abuser. She is thus twice victimized while the true offender, the abuser, is transformed into the apparent victim of the woman's resentment. In urging a battered woman to "forgive" under these circumstances, or to praise her for her servility, one maintains the patriarchal *status quo* by denying that the resentment against the abuser was justified. It is a denial that the abuse was a violation of her human dignity. . . .

VICTIM-BLAMING AND "SELF-FORGIVENESS"

The advice that women who have been abused must learn to forgive themselves—that is, when the term "forgive" is not being used to mean "excuse"—suggests that women are somehow to blame for their own victimization. Talk of the "healing power of forgiveness" occurs in the context of counseling women who are victims of domestic violence and carries with it the implication that these women are sick or defective and in need of healing. Victims of other traumatic experiences such as the Holocaust or violent crimes outside the home are rarely seen as being in need of the "healing power of forgiveness." Instead, they are regarded as being in need of emotional support, comfort, and sympathy. . . .

A proliferation of "self-help" books aimed at a guilt-ridden female market capitalized on women's insecurity and low self-esteem. Women's feelings of anger and resentment, these authors alleged, were the result of women's own inadequacies, including their lack of forgiveness, rather than any "wrongdoing" on the part of another person. Promoting forgiveness as a substantive virtue and cure-all, advice to forgive was doled out without regard for the context. For example, Gerald Jampolsky, author of *Love Is Letting Go of Fear,* wrote:

> Forgiveness means correcting our misperception that the other person harms us. The unforgiving mind, contrasted with the forgiving mind, is confused, afraid and full of fear. It is certain of the interpretation it places on its perception of others. . . . It does not want the future to be different from the past. It thrives on conflict and on being right and it sees inner peace as its enemy.[14]

In this environment of victim-blaming, domestic violence came to be regarded by family therapists not as a crime *per se,* but as part of a "complementary pattern in the couple's relationship."[15] While the man was responsible for the violence, the woman was held responsible for protecting herself, to the extent that she could. Little recognition was given to the greatly increased risk of being killed that a woman puts herself and her children at when she attempts to leave a violent domestic situation or to the economic depravation that they often face without the husband's income. The belief that the woman should leave her home, rather than the abusive partner, also played into the cultural belief that the home is the "man's castle." In no other crime but domestic violence is the victim expected to leave the scene of the crime and go into hiding rather than the perpetrator.

Women who remained in violent situations and attempted to cope as best they could were regarded as co-conspirators, albeit unwitting ones, in their partners' violent behavior. Because women shared in the guilt of their own abuse, they too were in need of repentance and forgiveness—and therapy. To resent the abuser was regarded as a sign of arrogance and a denial of their own guilt. Rather than treating domestic violence as a crime against women, couples' therapy was recommended so partners could work out their unhealthy codependency, and learn to identify and avoid the "triggers" that provoked violence.

Family therapist, Claudia Bepko, on the other hand, maintains that the dependency on men that characterizes so many women who seem unable to break out of an abusive situation "reflects a disordered power arrangement embedded in gender." What is needed, according to Bepko, is a new feminist approach to the issue of female battering. This approach needs to acknowledge the causes of inequality by recognizing and validating women's realities and, at the same time, come up with a strategy for change.

The victim-blaming approach of the 1980s, fortunately, has been replaced in the past few years with laws in many states that require mandatory arrest for perpetrators of domestic violence. . . .

FORGIVENESS AS A MEANS OF KEEPING THE FAMILY INTACT

Women are sometimes urged to forgive their abusive partners "for the sake of the children." One of the myths that keeps women in abusive domestic situations is that a dysfunctional family is preferable to a "broken" family, that "children need two parents in order to develop to their fullest potential."[16] . . .

Because women are socialized to believe that to succeed as women they must do everything in their power to keep the family together, if the family breaks down, the woman is held to blame. Thus, any threat to the family integrity becomes a threat to the woman's own identity and self-esteem.

A woman may also be encouraged to forgive an abuser as a means of reforming him, thereby making him a better husband and father, thus keeping the family intact. By setting an example of what it means to be an exemplary moral person, she will shame him into a change of behavior. However, forgiving an unrepentant abuser with the intention of reforming him is more often than not perceived by the abuser as arrogance rather than "saintliness." This could lead to even more violence because the abuser now feels degraded and angered by his victim's apparent arrogance.

Domestic violence not only harms women, but also children and future generations. Over half of all men who abuse their wives also physically or sexually abuse their children.[17] Children who witness abuse or are victims of abuse are more likely to abuse their own spouse and children. Women in abusive situations are more likely than other mothers to abuse their children.[18] When a mother abuses her children, it is usually a direct response to her own abuse, feelings of powerlessness, and repressed resentment. Of course, this in no way excuses the child abuse. In the great majority of cases, however, the woman stops abusing her children when her abuser is no longer present.

Thus forgiving an abuser merely for the sake of keeping the family intact cannot be justified on the grounds of benefiting the children. Instead, advising forgiveness in this context constitutes a harm to the children as well as to the woman. When a victim of domestic violence responds with resentment and protests her mistreatment, she is no longer sending a mixed and confused message. Instead, she is letting the abuser know that what he has done is not morally acceptable and will not be tolerated in the home. In realizing that his behavior will no longer be tolerated, the abuser may be more likely to re-examine his behavior and come to regret what he has done.

IS THERE A DUTY TO FORGIVE A REPENTANT "ABUSER"?

If the abuser does come to regret what he has done and, in repenting, takes steps to change his behavior, does his former victim now have a moral obligation to forgive him? . . .

Clearly, the abuser has a duty to repent. He owes this to the woman since he took something away from her—her self-dignity. Even though a man may feel superior by abusing a woman, because he has disregarded the moral principle of equal respect for all persons, he has actually debased himself morally and put himself in his victim's debt. Until he repents, he remains indebted to her.

However, the concept of a victim being indebted to her former abuser, even though he may have repented, is somewhat odd. To suggest that victims of domestic violence have a duty to forgive their abusers implies that victims owe abusers something. To claim that a duty or debt to someone can stem from our own prior degradation or deprivation is like saying we are indebted to someone who robbed us and then, feeling remorse, decides to return the stolen goods. The purpose of repentance is not to put the reformed abuser in a higher position by having his former victim become morally indebted to him. Rather the primary purpose of repentance is to affirm their moral equality. As the person to whom the debt is owed, the woman should have the choice whether or not to accept the abuser's repentance and forgive him. Indeed, in cases of gross wrongdoing considerable effort may be required to even begin to overcome her resentment. She may just choose to put the whole matter behind her rather than have to deal again with the person who harmed her.

Thus, forgiveness of a repentant abuser, while it may be morally praiseworthy, cannot be regarded as a duty. Instead, forgiveness under these circumstances is a supererogatory action—that is, it is beyond the call of everyday morality. We do not ex-pect someone to forgive a gross wrongdoing, even when the wrongdoer has repented. To expect this would place a further burden on someone who has already been wronged. However, we admire them if they do forgive.

CONCLUSION

The concept of unconditional forgiveness as a virtue is incompatible with the most basic moral principle of equal respect for persons. Domestic violence, by its very nature, degrades the victim. A woman who forgives from this degraded position is tacitly condoning the violence and accepting her degraded status. . . .

Without repentance on the part of the abuser, encouraging forgiveness as a positive goal or as a therapeutic means for women to get over their feelings of resentment and anger merely compounds women's feelings of powerlessness, self-blame, and lack of self-respect. Under such circumstances, forgiveness is not morally commendable. For a woman to fail to feel resentment in the face of domestic violence is to show a lack of respect for herself and for the basic human rights of all women. If a woman respects herself as a person, then she *ought* to resent her own abuse and degradation, just as a person *ought* to feel indignation at any other degradation. In the absence of genuine repentance, forgiveness, that is, the putting aside of resentment, is a vice because it entails accepting the wrongdoer's degraded view of the victim.

Resentment, in the context of ongoing abuse, serves to protect the victim and her family as well as to call attention to the need for moral reform. Until an abuser repents of his wrongdoing, it is not only imprudent, but morally wrong for a woman to forgive him. Forgiveness, as a moral virtue, entails putting aside one's feelings of resentment only when they are no longer appropriate. The act of repentance "allows forgiveness and restoring of relationships because the insulting message is no longer present—no longer endorsed by the wrongdoer."[19]

In the absence of repentance, one might more appropriately counsel victims of domestic violence: To resent is divine, to forgive supine.

NOTES

1. Diane P. Holder and Carol M. Anderson, "Women and Serious Mental Disorders," in *Women and Families,* ed. Monica McGoldrick, Carol Anderson, and Froma Walsh (New York: Norton, 1989), p. 385.

2. Midred D. Pagelow and Pamela Johnson, "Abuse in the American Family: The Role of Religion," in *Abuse and Religion,* ed. Anne L. Horton and Judith A. Williamson (Lexington, Mass.: D.C. Heath, 1988), p. 2.

3. Claudio Bepko, "Disorders of Power: Women and Addiction in the Family," *Women and Families,* p. 412.

4. G. Haber, *Forgiveness* (Savage, Md.: Rowman and Littlefield, 1991). This definition is also used by McGary in "Forgiveness," pp. 343–351, and Jeffrie G. Murphy and Jean Hampton in *Forgiveness and Mercy* (New York: Cambridge University Press, 1988), p. 35.

5. Marie M. Fortune, "Justice-Making in the Aftermath of Woman-Battering," in *Domestic Violence on Trial,* p. 242.

6. John Rawls, *A Theory of Justice* (Cambridge, Mass.: Harvard University Press, 1971), p. 333.

7. Jeffrie Murphy, "Forgiveness and Resentment," in *Minnesota Studies in Philosophy: Social and Political Philosophy,* ed. Peter A. French, Theodore E. Uehling, Jr., and Howard K. Wettstein (Minneapolis: University of Minnesota Press, 1982), p. 507.

8. Lenore E. Walker, "Spouse Abuse: A Basic Profile," in *Abuse and Religion,* p. 19.

9. Lenore E. Walker, *The Battered Woman Syndrome* (New York: Springer, 1984).

10. Fortune, "Justice-Making in the Aftermath of Woman-Battering," p. 242.

11. Aristotle, *Nicomachean Ethics,* trans. Terence Irwin (Indianapolis: Hackett, 1985), v. 1126a, 44.

12. Walker, *The Battered Woman Syndrome.* See also R. Emerson Dobash and Russell P. Dobash, *Violence Against Wives* (New York: Free Press, 1979).

13. Ginny NiCarthy, "Building Self-Esteem: Overcoming Barriers to Recovery," in *Abuse and Religion,* p. 117.

14. Gerald Jampolsky, *Love Is Letting Go of Fear* (New York: Ballantine, 1988), p. 7.

15. Virginia Goldner, Peggy Penn, Marcia Sheinberg, and Gillian Walker, "Love and Violence: Gender Paradoxes in Volatile Attachments," *Family Process,* 29:4 (1990), p. 345.

16. Lewis Okun, *Woman Abuse* (Albany, N.Y.: State University of New York Press, 1986), p. 94.

17. Lenore Walker and Glenace E. Edwall, "Domestic Violence and Determination of Visitation and Custody in Divorce," in *Domestic Violence on Trial,* p. 135.

18. Daniel J. Sonkin, "The Assessment of Court-Mandated Male Batterers," in *Domestic Violence on Trial,* pp. 180–181.

19. J. M. Alsdurf and P. Alsdurf, "A Pastoral Response," in *Abuse and Religion: When Praying Isn't Enough,* ed. A. L. Horton and J. A. Williamson (Lexington, MA: Lexington, 1988), pp. 165–171.

Discussion Questions

1. Polaroid Corporation has a domestic violence assistance program that offers flexible work hours, short-term paid leave, and long-term unpaid leave, for employees in domestic violence situations. Discuss whether, and if so how, this program addresses the root causes of domestic violence. Discuss what type of program you would institute if you were in charge of coming up with a domestic violence assistance program for Polaroid or your university. Discuss what type of program for addressing domestic violence Boss might suggest for employers.

2. The gender-neutral term domestic violence was introduced to include violence against men as well. Discuss the moral implications of using a gender-neutral term

rather than one that focuses on violence against women. Discuss what Boss and Mac-Kinnon might each think of the use of these terms.

3. American bishops were silent about domestic violence until October 1992, when they produced their first official statement on the issue. The bishops expressed concern that Bible passages had been used to justify wife-beating and to coerce women into being subservient to abusive husbands. According to the statement, the Bible does not require women to submit to abusive husbands or to stay in abusive relationships. The statement also recommends that parishes educate their members about domestic violence, provide refuge to its victims, and offer help to the abusers. Critically analyze this approach. Discuss what Boss would most likely think of its recommendations.

4. Despite programs such as women's centers, counseling, and emergency shelters that help victims of domestic violence, its incidence does not seem to have diminished. Why do you think this is? Do these programs deal with the root cause of domestic violence, or do they perpetuate gender myths? Support your answers. Discuss how Boss might answer these questions. Formulate a policy for dealing with domestic violence in your community.

5. Many cities and states have adopted laws requiring mandatory arrests for spousal abuse. Under these laws, if a woman won't press charges against an abusive spouse, the state will press charges. Is this an adequate legal response to domestic violence? Or do mandatory-arrest laws violate the rights of battered women? Are restraining orders sufficient? Support your answers. Discuss how Boss might respond to these questions.

 STEVEN GOLDBERG

Male Aggression and the Attainment of Power, Authority, and Status

Steven Goldberg is chairman of the department of sociology of City College at the City University of New York (CUNY). Goldberg rejects the feminist argument that male dominance oppresses women. Male dominance and female submissiveness, Goldberg argues, are not simply the product of socialization and discrimination, but are rooted in inherent biological differences. Women are doomed by their biology to fail in their attempt to attain equality with men in achieving positions of power, authority, and status.

Critical Reading Questions

1. According to Goldberg, what are some of the inherent differences between men and women? What is the significance of these differences for society?
2. What is the primary difference between men and women, according to Goldberg?

"Male Aggression and the Attainment of Power, Authority, and Status," in *The Inevitability of Patriarchy* (New York: William Morrow & Co., 1973), 103–114. Notes have been omitted.

3. What explanation does Goldberg give for patriarchy and higher-status roles for men?
4. According to Goldberg, in what sort of society are the biological differences between men and women most likely to be given free play? How does Goldberg support his argument?
5. How does Goldberg respond to the feminist argument that men's greater power and status is a product of socialization rather than biological differences?
6. How does Goldberg support his argument that society should socialize women for maternal and nurturing roles and away from the roles that men attain through aggression? Why would socializing both girls and boys to compete in the job market or for positions of authority disadvantage women?
7. Would it be desirable, in Goldberg's view, if men and women achieved equality in positions of high authority?
8. How does Goldberg explain the discrepancy between women holding 51 percent of the vote and men holding almost all the positions of high authority in government? How does his explanation differ from that of feminists?
9. How does Goldberg explain what feminists view as the oppression of women?
10. According to Goldberg, why are men more successful than women in attaining desirable positions and roles in society? Why is it difficult for even aggressive women to achieve the same goals as men?
11. Why, according to Goldberg, is patriarchy inevitable?

IF MALE AGGRESSION WERE THE ONLY DIFFERENCE . . .

Having discussed the universality of patriarchy, male dominance, and male attainment of high-status roles and the biological factors that are relevant to these universals, we are now prepared to examine the mechanisms that *require* these biological factors to be manifested in these social institutions. In discussing these mechanisms we shall proceed as if the only inherent difference between men and women were their different hormonal systems, which leads to an inherent aggression advantage for the male. This does not imply that I doubt that there are positive female biological forces underlying the woman's extraordinary sensitivity and emotional powers or the mother's attentiveness to her infant and her protective reaction to her infant's vulnerability. . . . Such biological imperatives would have enormous significance in the development of male and female roles. Every society must care for its young and, if the need to care for and protect the young is greater in the female than the male, this would be reflected in thc social expectations of

men and women. If one accepts this female biological factor, he could utilize it to explain the universal sex-role differences I explain by differences in aggression and could use the same lines of reasoning I do without mentioning aggression. Likewise it is not unlikely that the neural factors underlying the male's sexual dominance come into play in social contacts between men and women; there may even be a female desire for men to dominate ("take the lead") that is a secondary manifestation of the neural factors directly relevant to female sexuality. Biological evidence indicates that there is a strong possibility that such dominance and submission factors exist in male and female physiologies, but, since such factors need not exist for the theory presented here to be correct, we will assume that they do not exist. If they do exist, of course, the theory presented here can be only strengthened.

Quite possibly all of these factors lead to the universal institutions we have discussed. *Aggression, however, is the only sexual difference that we can explain with direct (as opposed to convincing, but hypothetical) biological evidence.* Nothing is lost because the inevitable social manifestations of sexual differences in aggression are sufficient to explain the inevitability of patriarchy, male dominance, and male attainment of high-status roles. If the other biological directives do exist we have an example of a situation in which a factor (hormonal aggression) is *sufficient* to describe a reality (institutionalized sex differences), but not *necessary*. Maternal attentiveness, a male need to dominate, or a female desire for male political dominance would be sufficient even if there were no hormonal aggression differences, but none of these need exist for the theory proposed here to be correct.

Therefore, *we are assuming throughout this chapter that there are no differences between men and women except in the hormonal system that renders the man more aggressive.* This alone would explain patriarchy, male dominance, and male attainment of high-status roles; for the male hormonal system gives men an insuperable "head start" toward attaining those roles which any society associates with leadership or high status as long as the roles are not ones that males are biologically incapable of filling.

AGGRESSION AND ATTAINMENT . . .

As we shall see, this aggression "advantage" can be most manifested and can most enable men to reap status rewards *not* in those relatively homogeneous, collectivist primitive societies in which both male and female must play similar economic roles if the society is to survive or in the monarchy (which guarantees an occasional female leader); this biological factor will be given freest play in the complex, relatively individualistic, bureaucratic, democratic society which, of necessity, must emphasize organizational authority and in which social mobility is relatively free of traditional barriers to advancement. There were more female heads of state in the first two-thirds of the sixteenth century than in the first two-thirds of the twentieth.

The mechanisms involved here are easily seen if we examine any roles that males have attained by channeling their aggression toward such attainment. We will assume for now that equivalent women could *perform* the tasks of roles as well as men if they could attain the roles. Here we can speak of the corporation president, the union leader, the governor, the chairman of an association, or any other role or position for which aggression is a precondition for attainment. Now the environmentalist and the feminist will say that the fact that all such roles are nearly always filled by men is attributable not to male aggression but to the fact that women have not been allowed to enter the competitive race to attain these positions, that they have been told that these positions are in male areas, and that girls are socialized away from competing with boys in general. Women *are* socialized in this way, but again we must ask why. If innate male aggression has nothing to do with male attainment of positions of authority and status in the political, academic, scientific, or financial spheres, if aggression has nothing to do with the reasons why *every* society socializes girls away from those areas which are given high status and away from competition in general, then why is it never the *girls* in any society who are socialized toward these areas, why is it never the nonbiological roles played by women that have high status, why is it always boys who are told to compete, and why do women never "force" men into the low-status, nonmaternal roles that women play in every society?

These questions pose no problem if we acknowledge a male aggression that enables men to attain any nonbiological role given high status by any society. . . . Now I have no doubt that there is a biological factor that gives women the desire to emphasize maternal and nurturance roles, but the point here is that we can accept the feminist assumption that there is no female propensity of this sort and still see that a society must socialize women away from roles that men will attain through their aggression. For if women did not develop an alternative set of criteria for success their sense of their own competence would suffer intolerably. It is undeniable that the resulting different values and expectations that are attached to men and women will tend to work against the aggressive woman while they work for the man who is no more aggressive. But this is the unavoidable result of the fact that most men are more aggressive than most women so that this woman, who is as aggressive as the average man, but more aggressive than most women, is an exception. Furthermore, even if the sense of competence of each sex did not necessitate society's attaching to each sex values and expectations based on those qualities possessed by each sex, observation of the majority of each sex by the population would "automatically" lead to these values and expectations being attached to men and women.

SOCIALIZATION'S CONFORMATION TO BIOLOGICAL REALITY

Socialization is the process by which society prepares children for adulthood. The way in which its goals conform to the reality of biology is seen quite clearly when we consider the method in which testosterone generates male aggression (testosterone's serially developing nature). . . . The fetal alteration of the boy's brain by the testosterone that was generated by his testes has probably left him far more sensitive to the aggression-related properties of the testosterone that is present during boyhood than the girl, who did not receive such alteration. But let us for the moment assume that this is not the case. This does not at all reduce the importance of the hormonal factor. For even if the boy is more aggressive than the girl only because the society allows him to be, the boy's socialization still flows from society's acknowledging biological reality. Let us consider what would happen if girls have the same innate aggression as boys and if a society did not socialize girls away from aggressive competitions. Perhaps half of the third-grade baseball team would be female. As many girls as boys would frame their expectations in masculine values and girls would develop not their feminine abilities but their masculine ones. During adolescence, however, the same assertion of the male chromosomal program that causes the boys to grow beards raises their testosterone level, and their potential for aggression, to a level far above that of the adolescent woman. If society did not teach young girls that beating boys at competitions was unfeminine (behavior inappropriate for a woman), if it did not socialize them away from the political and economic areas in which aggression leads to attainment, these girls would

grow into adulthood with self-images based not on succeeding in areas for which biology has left them better prepared than men, but on competitions that most women could not win. If women did not develop feminine qualities as girls (assuming that such qualities do not spring automatically from female biology) then they would be forced to deal with the world in the aggressive terms of men. They would lose every source of power their feminine abilities now give them and they would gain nothing. . . .

DISCRIMINATION OF A SORT

If one is convinced that sexual biology gives the male an advantage in aggression, competitiveness, and dominance, but he does not believe that it engenders in men and women different propensities, cognitive aptitudes, and modes of perception, and if he considers it discrimination when male aggression leads to attainment of position even when aggression is not relevant to the task to be performed, then the unavoidable conclusion is that discrimination so defined is unavoidable. Even if one is convinced . . . that the differing biological substrates that underlie the mental apparatus of men and women *do* engender different propensities, cognitive aptitudes, and modes of perception, he will probably agree that the relevance of this to male attainment of male roles is small when compared to the importance of male biological aggression to attainment. Innate tendencies to specific aptitudes *would* indicate that at any given level of competence there will be more men than women or vice versa (depending on the qualities relevant to the task) and that the very best will, in all probability, come from the sex whose potentials are relevant to the task. Nonetheless, drastic sexual differences in occupational and authority roles reflect male aggression and society's acknowledgment of it far more than they do differences in aptitudes, yet they are still inevitable.

In addition, even if artificial means were used to place large numbers of women in authority positions, it is doubtful that stability could be maintained. Even in our present male bureaucracies problems arise whenever a subordinate is more aggressive than his superior and, if the more aggressive executive is not allowed to rise in the bureaucracy, delicate psychological adjustments must be made. Such adjustments are also necessary when a male bureaucrat has a female superior. When such situations are rare exceptions adjustments can be made without any great instability occurring, particularly if the woman in the superior position complements her aggression with sensitivity and femininity. It would seem likely, however, that if women shared equally in power at each level of the bureaucracy, chaos would result for two reasons. Even if we consider the bureaucracy as a closed system, the excess of male aggression would soon manifest itself either in men moving quickly up the hierarchy or in a male refusal to acknowledge female authority. But a bureaucracy is not a closed system, and the discrepancy between male dominance in private life and bureaucratic female dominance (from the point of view of the male whose superior is a woman) would soon engender chaos. Consider that even the present minute minority of women in high authority positions expend enormous amounts of energy trying *not* to project the commanding authority that is seen as the mark of a good male executive. It is true that the manner in which aggression is manifested will be affected by the values of the society in general and the nature of the field of competition in particular; aggression in an academic environment is camouflaged far more than in the executive arena. While a desire for control and power and a single-mindedness of purpose are no doubt relevant, here aggression is not easily defined. One might inject the theoretical argument that women could attain positions of authority and leadership by countering the male's advantage in aggression with feminine abilities. Perhaps, but the equivalents of the executive positions in every area of suprafamilial life in every society have been attained by men, and there seems no reason to believe that, suddenly, feminine means will be capable of neutralizing male aggression in these areas. And, in any case, an emphasis on feminine abilities is hardly what the feminists desire. All of this can be seen in a considerably more optimistic light, from the point of view of most women, if one considers that the biological abilities possessed only by women are complemented by biologically generated propensities directing women to roles that can be filled only by women. But it is still the same picture.

FIFTY-ONE PERCENT OF THE VOTE

Likewise, one who predicates political action on a belief that a society is oppressive until half of the positions of authority are filled by women faces the insuperable task of overcoming a male dominance that has forced every political and economic system to conform to it and that may be maintained as much by the refusal of women to elect widespread female leadership as by male aggression and ability. No doubt an exceptional configuration of factors will someday result in a woman's being elected president, but if one considers a society "sexist" until it no longer associates authority primarily with men and until a woman leader is no longer an exception, then he must resign himself to the certainty that all societies will be "sexist" forever. Feminists make much of the fact that women constitute a slight majority of voters but in doing so make the assumption that it is possible to convince the women who constitute this majority to elect equal female leadership. This is a dubious assumption since the members of a society will inevitably associate authority with males if patriarchy and male dominance are biologically inevitable. It would be even more dubious if there is an innate tendency for women to favor men who "take the lead." However, proceeding from this assumption and assuming that the feminists were successful, it is a sure bet that democracy—which obviously is not biologically inevitable (not patriarchy, which is)—would be eliminated as large numbers of males battled for the relatively small numbers of positions of power from which the rules that govern the battle are made. In any real society, of course, women can have the crucial effect of mobilizing political power to achieve particular goals and of electing those men who are motivated by relatively more life-sustaining values than other men just as mothers have the crucial effect of coloring and humanizing the values of future male leaders.

"OPPRESSION"

All of this indicates that the theoretical model that conceives of male success in attaining positions of status, authority, and leadership as *oppression* of the female is incorrect if only because it sees male aggressive energies as *directed toward* females and sees the institutional mechanisms that flow from the fact of male aggression as *directed toward* "oppressing" women. In reality these male energies are directed toward attainment of desired positions and toward succeeding in whatever areas a particular society considers important. The fact that women lose out in these competitions, so that the sex-role expectations of a society would have to become different for men and women even if they were not different for other reasons, is an inevitable byproduct of the reality of the male's aggression advantage and not the cause, purpose, or primary function of it. In other words, men who attain the more desired roles and positions do so because they channel their aggression advantage toward such attainment; whether the losers in such competitions are other men or women is important only in that—because so few women succeed in these competitions—the society will attach different expectations to men and women (making it more difficult for the exceptional, aggressive, woman to attain such positions even when her aggression is equal to that of the average man). Perhaps one could at least begin to de-

fend a model that stressed "oppression" if he dealt only with male dominance in dyadic relationships; here male energies are directed toward the female, but to call that which is inevitable "oppression" would seem to confuse more than clarify and, if one feels that male dominance is "oppressive," this model offers an illusory hope of change where there is no possibility of change. Male dominance is the emotional resolution (felt by both the man and the woman) of the difference between a man and a woman in the biological factors relevant to aggression; male authority in dyadic relationships, and the socialization of boys and girls toward this male authority, is societal conformation to this biological difference and a result of society's attempting to most smoothly and effectively utilize this difference. Note that all that I say in this paragraph—indeed, in this book—accepts the feminist assumption that women do not follow their own biologically generated imperatives, which are eternally different from those of men. I do this in an attempt to show the inadequacy of the feminist model and not because it is less than ludicrous to suppose that women do not hear their own drummer. This book does not pretend to explain female behavior, but merely to show that women would have to behave as they do if they were nothing more than less aggressive men. If one reversed the feminist model he could view the desire of the vast majority of women to have children as oppressing men by succeeding in an area in which men are doomed by their biology to fail. Such a theoretical model leaves much to be desired.

Discussion Questions

1. Do you agree with Goldberg that patriarchy is inevitable? Does civilization require patriarchy? Support your answers. Discuss how Brownmiller might respond to Goldberg's argument.
2. Goldberg assumes that civilization depends on aggressive competition for positions of status and power. Do you agree that civilization is incompatible with feminist goals? If so, is civilization, as we now know it, desirable? Can civilization be grounded in cooperation rather than competition? Support your answers.
3. Even if men are naturally aggressive and dominating, as Goldberg claims, does this justify patriarchy, or should this "instinct" be rechanneled toward "objects" other than

women or even repressed? Discuss whether pornography and/or prostitution are morally acceptable means for rechanneling it? Support your answers.

4. Discuss how Goldberg would explain the prevalence of date rape and sexual harassment on college campuses. What solution might he offer to these problems? Do you agree with this solution? Support your answers.

5. Discuss what Goldberg's position would most likely be on affirmative action for women as well as what sort of college curriculum and admissions program he might propose. Would he be in favor of coed colleges or would he recommend gender-segregated colleges? Should men and women be funneled into different majors?

6. Nicholas Davidson, author of *The Failure of Feminism,* maintains "Feminism is a failure as an explanation for male psychology and behavior . . . feminism makes all relations with men difficult, and good relations virtually impossible."[37] Do you agree? Would Goldberg? Support your answers. Discuss how Pineau, MacKinnon, and Roiphe might each respond to Davidson's criticism of modern feminism.

CASE STUDIES

1. *HUSTLER* PUBLISHER LARRY FLYNT: "FREE-SPEECH HERO"

The hard-core porn magazine *Hustler,* which has a monthy circulation of more than a million, is a popular source of sex education and socialization among teenage boys. In the world according to *Hustler,* rape is a normal part of male nature. One *Hustler* journalist instucts readers that men are "basically rapists, because we're created that way. We're irrational, sexually completely crazy. Our sexuality is more promiscuous, more immediate, and more fleeting, possibly less deep. We're like stud bulls that want to mount everything in sight."[38] *Hustler* also helps readers select vulnerable targets. For example, one issue had an article titled "Good Sex with Retarded Girls." *Hustler* also used to run a regular kiddie corner called "Chester the Molester."

In the 1996 film *The People vs. Larry Flynt,* producer Oliver Stone portrays *Hustler* magazine publisher Larry Flynt as a free-speech hero. *USA Today* called the movie "a civics lesson that will still be regaling film enthusiasts four decades hence."[39] The controversial film is about Flynt's legal battles against those who want to see pornography censored. Challenging the local obscenity law in Cincinnatti and rural Georgia, Flynt comes face-to-face in the Supreme Court with Jerry Falwell and the "religious right." The Supreme Court ruled that Flynt does indeed have a right to publish and sell pornography. Flynt has been declared by libertarians a free-speech hero and defender of civil liberties. Not everyone thinks so highly of the king of porn. Flynt's daughter, Tonya Flynt, whose father describes her as a "lying little wacko who I don't even know," claims that her father molested her as a child. This, however, was not addressed in the film.

Discussion Questions

1. Does freedom of speech apply to pornography? If so, does freedom of speech override the possible harms of pornography? Discuss the moral issues on both sides of the debate in light of this case study.

2. To what extent, if at all, do the "lessons" in pornography magazines such as *Hustler* harm and subordinate women? To what extent, if at all, do they harm men by socializing them to be sexually violent? Do these harms justify the legal regulation of pornography? Support your answers. Discuss how MacKinnon and Brownmiller might respond to these questions.

3. In response to the Supreme Court ruling, Jerry Falwell said, "Larry didn't save the First Amendment. The First Amendment saved him." What do you think Falwell meant by this? Do you agree with him? Support your answers. Discuss whether the First Amendment is consistent with "morality" in the Flynt ruling.

4. Does patriarchy and men's "natural aggression," as defined by Goldberg, imply that men are naturally prone to sexual violence? Are some men naturally rapists, or are they socialized to become rapists? Discuss your answer in light of the regulation-of-pornography debate. Discuss how Goldberg might respond to these questions.

2. GANG RAPE AND COLLEGE FRATERNITIES

Three UCLA undergraduates were arrested in June 1996 on charges for a rape that allegedly occurred during a Zeta Beta Tau fraternity retreat at a Palm Springs hotel.[40] The woman, a member of a UCLA sorority, claimed that she was gang-raped by the three men after she had gone to the hotel room late the previous night.

Although beer kegs at fraternity-sponsored events are a violation of the Interfraternity Council rules, there had been thirty to fifty kegs available that weekend. According to the alleged victim, she and the three men had been drinking alcohol and smoking marijuana in the room while playing a game called Master. During the game the three fraternity brothers began to undress her and then sexually assaulted her. She told them to stop but they ignored her protests. A fourth man watched while they raped her.

Following the rape, the distraught coed returned to her own room, where another student took her to a hospital emergency room. She filed charges with the police early the next morning. The police went to the hotel and arrested the three students. The students claimed in their defense that the sex was consensual. Their fraternity brothers stand by their story. The woman refused to speak to the press about the allegations, and her sorority requested that the media respect her desire for privacy.

Discussion Questions

1. Fraternity violence, including hazing, property destruction, and rape, has long been a problem. Some fraternities use women as bait to attract new members by having "Little Sisters," attractive undergraduates who attend and serve as hostesses at fraternity parties. Little Sisters are "sexual assets," and fraternities often promise prospective recruits sexual access to these women. The titles *Big Brothers* and *Little Sisters* reflect the subordinate status of women in fraternity life. The use of women as sexual objects and pawns in a game, some argue, encourage fraternities to see women as objects and rape as a sport.[41] Men are the predators, women their prey. Are fraternities breeding grounds for sexism and violence against women? Should the Little Sister programs be banned? Should fraternities themselves be banned? Support your answers. Discuss how MacKinnon and Pineau might answer these questions.

2. Brotherhood and loyalty are highly valued in fraternities as part of male bonding. In the great majority of rape cases, members of a fraternity will refuse to "rat on" or testify against their brothers. They may even make up stories to protect their brothers. Discuss the morality of this type of loyalty. Does the fourth man who watched the rape have a moral obligation to come forth and testify against his fraternity brothers? Is he morally culpable for not trying to stop the rape? Support your answers.

3. Fraternity gang rapes most often occur as part of a game or ritual. During these rituals brothers may "circle dance," during which other drunk and partially naked brothers entertain each other and guests by chanting, mimicking sexual acts, expressing verbal hostility toward women and gay men, and engaging in sexual banter with each other. The selected victim is sometimes referred to as a "nympho," suggesting that she "asked for it." Following fraternity gang rapes, the brothers generally celebrate their masculinity, heterosexual prowess, and group loyalty by drinking heavily together. Discuss how these gang rape rituals and games support gender myths that perpetuate sexism and violence against women. Discuss what policies Pineau and Roiphe might each suggest in response to these practices.

4. In fraternity gang rapes, men generally select women who are socially isolated, psychologically vulnerable, and either too intoxicated or too afraid to resist or complain to the authorities.[42] Discuss the extent, if any, to which our culture, including the college culture, socializes women to be victims of rape or to fear men. Do these norms also encourage or empower women who collaborate with men in the selection of victims? Discuss whether the refusal of the alleged victim and her sorority sisters to discuss the incident with the media perpetuates these norms, or empowers women. What suggestions might virtue ethicists such as Aristotle, Confucius, and Noddings offer for changing attitudes that contribute to rape on college campuses?

5. According to one survey, 26 percent of men who acknowledged committing sexual assault on a date say they were intoxicated at the time.[43] Women who are intoxicated are also less likely to successfully resist assault. According to policies like that at Antioch College, people who are intoxicated are unable to give consent to sex. Do you agree with this policy? Does this imply that men who rape while intoxicated are also not responsible for their actions? Discuss your answers in light of the UCLA case study.

---

3. PAULA JONES VERSUS THE PRESIDENT

In 1994 Paula Jones filed three civil charges against President Clinton alleging sexual harassment during a 1991 encounter at a hotel in Little Rock, Arkansas. At the time of the alleged incident, Clinton was governor of Arkansas and Jones a state employee. Although Jones claimed that the harassment affected her civil rights by affecting her job, her employment records show that she received the usual promotions and raises following the alleged incident. Jones also claimed that Clinton's behavior was so outrageous that it caused her serious emotional harm.

On April 1, 1998, U.S. District Judge Susan Wright Webber dismissed Jones's charges. Judge Webber based her decision on Jones's inability to prove that Clinton exposed himself and asked for oral sex. Judge Webber stated, "Although the governor's alleged conduct, if true, may certainly be characterized as boorish and offensive, even a most charitable reading of the record in the case fails to reveal a basis for a claim of sexual assault."[44]

The dismissal followed months of sensational charges of sexual misconduct by the president. Jones's lawyers appealed the decision. In December 1998, while the appeal was being heard, Clinton agreed to make a cash settlement to Jones, who then dropped the appeal.

Discussion Questions

1. Do you agree with Judge Webber's ruling? Support your answer. Discuss how MacKinnon and Roiphe might each respond to the ruling.
2. In the early 1990s a Massachusetts judge ruled that an election campaign collage, in which a male candidate distributed photocopies of the female opponent's face pasted on top of photographs of nude and seminude women in lewd positions, constitued sexual harassment and, therefore, could be legally prohibited. Do you agree with the judge's ruling that this a case of sexual harassment? Is the ruling a violation of freedom of speech? If not, should all attempts to degrade opponents in election campaigns be prohibited, or only those based on gender stereotypes? Support your answers. How might Roiphe and MacKinnon respond to these questions?
3. A group of women who worked at Stroh's Beer brought a lawsuit against the company, claiming sexual harassment on the basis of the sexist television ads used by Stroh's to sell its product. They argued that the sexist ads and the behavior of the male employees are connected, creating a hostile work environment for female employees. Do advertisements, calendars, and other graphic material that portray women as sex objects constitute sexual harassment? Support your answers. Discuss how Roiphe would respond to this question.
4. Is sexual harassment a problem on your campus? If so, why? How should women, such as Paula Jones, respond to sexual harassment in the workplace or on college campuses? Use specific examples to illustrate your answers. Discuss how Boss, MacKinnon, and Roiphe might each respond to the latter question.
5. Is sexual harassment inevitable if women insist on competing with men in schools and in the workplace? Discuss how Goldberg might respond to this question. What solution would he most likely propose to the problem of sexual harassment?

---

4. LORENA AND JOHN BOBBITT

The police had been called to the Virginia home of Lorena and John Wayne Bobbitt on several occasions because of domestic violence. On June 21, 1992, Lorena Bobbitt, a twenty-four-year-old native of Ecuador, requested a restraining order against her twenty-six-year-old husband. When she was told that she had to go to a judge to get one, she decided not to. Two days later Lorena took the law into her own hands. While her husband was asleep, she cut off his penis with a kitchen knife. She then fled the house with the severed penis, which she tossed out of her car window during her flight. The penis was found after an extensive search and reattached to John Bobbitt.

In defense of her actions, Lorena told the court that her husband had repeatedly raped her. She claims she acted out of rage and frustration. The attack was in retaliation for his sexual assault earlier that morning. "I was the victim of repeated emotional, physical, and sexual assaults. Everyone has a limit, and this was mine."

Lorena Bobbitt's defense lawyer pleaded temporary insanity. She acted on an "irresistible impulse" prompted by a temporary psychotic breakdown after her husband had raped her that morning. Although dozens of witnesses, including three court-appointed doctors, testified that her husband had been abusive, John Wayne Bobbitt testified that he had never abused his wife.

Judge Herman Whisenant Jr. acquitted Lorena Bobbitt by reason of temporary insanity and ordered her held for up to forty-five days of psychiatric evaluation at a mental-health facility.

Discussion Questions

1. Did Lorena Bobbitt act out of self-defense? Were the police or the justice system partly to blame for what happened in this case because they failed to protect her?
2. Do you agree with the verdict in the Bobbitt case? If not, what do you think the verdict should have been? Support your answers.
3. Several women's groups have hailed the verdict in the Bobbitt case as a victory for battered women, although they object to the fact that she was found temporarily insane. If the justice system does not treat women fairly, they may have to find justice in their own way. Some fear that Lorena Bobbitt's acquittal will encourage other women to engage in similar violence against men. Attorney Alan Dershowitz, for example, argues that what Lorena Bobbitt did was wrong and a part of the growing justification for vigilante justice on the part of those who do not receive justice from the legal system. Her actions will serve to encourage others to take the law into their own hands. Dissatisfaction with the legal system does not give us the right to exact revenge after the fact. Discuss the relative merits of the two positions.
4. Some philosophers and legal scholars want to do away with the insanity plea because, they claim, it is a denial of the autonomy and human dignity of the defendant. Do you agree? Was the verdict of temporary insanity an affront to Lorena Bobbitt's human dignity? What might Kant say about such a verdict? Do you think the fact that Lorena Bobbitt was both female and Hispanic contributed to the judge's verdict of temporary insanity? Support your answers.
5. Can rape occur within a marriage? Does the marriage contract imply consent to sexual intercourse at all times, or do a husband and wife (or domestic partners) have to consent anew each time they have sexual intercourse? Support your answers. Discuss how Pineau might answer these questions.

---

5. THE JEALOUS HUSBAND

On February 17, 1994, Kenneth Peacock, a thirty-six year-old long-distance truck driver, returned home unexpectedly because of a snow storm and found his wife in bed with another man. The enraged Peacock chased the other man out of the house at gunpoint. After several hours of drinking and arguing with his unfaithful wife, Peacock shot her with a hunting rifle.

As punishment for killing his wife in cold blood, Baltimore, Maryland, Judge Robert E. Cahill gave Peacock an eighteen-month jail sentence and ordered him to perform fifty hours of community service in a domestic-violence program. Judge Cahill expressed reluctance in having to sentence Peacock at all, stating that he gave him a prison sentence only "to make the system honest." "I seriously wonder," Cahill said at the sentencing, "how many married men—married five, four years—would have the strength to walk away without inflicting some corporal punishment."[45]

Discussion Questions

1. Who does Judge Cahill blame for Mrs. Peacock's murder? Does the sentence hold Mr. Peacock responsible for his actions, or does it imply that Mrs. Peacock is responsible for her own death? Was she "asking for it"? What sentence would you have given had you been the judge in this case? Explain why.
2. Historically, Western courts have been lenient toward men who committed so-called crimes of passion. Discuss, in the context of the Peacock case, the gender myths and philosophical views of men and women that support this practice.
3. Does Cahill's ruling reinforce the myth that women who are assaulted, raped, or murdered get what they deserve? Does Cahill's ruling discourage or encourage domestic violence against women? Support your answers. Discuss how Boss would most likely respond to these questions.
4. Compare and contrast the sentences received by Lorena Bobbitt and Kenneth Peacock. What sentence would Cahill most likely have given Lorena Bobbitt? Discuss ways in which the legal system might be made more gender equitable.

---

6. ANOREXIA NERVOSA AND BULIMIA: THE TYRANNY OF THINNESS

The myths that the female body and female sexuality are evil contributes to another type of violence against women's bodies: anorexia nervosa and bulimia. These two disorders, which were rare twenty-five years ago, have reached epidemic proportions today. According to the National Eating Disorders Screening Program, in 2001 more than five million Americans had eating disorders, including 15 percent of young women. About one hundred women die each year of anorexia nervosa.[46] In addition, an estimated 12 to 33 percent of college women are bulimic.[47]

Anorectics and bulimics strive to avoid all bodily contact. Both hunger and sexuality are disgusting and dirty. Anorectics and bulimics associate staying thin with being androgynous and, hence, not being a "temptation" to men. In fact, many victims of anorexia have been sexually abused as children.

In her book *Starving for Attention* (1982) Cherry Boone O'Neill describes her battle with bulimia. After her first romantic involvement, which never went beyond kissing, O'Neill wrote: "I feel secretive, deceptive, and . . . tainted by the ongoing relationship." Because sexuality and hunger are psychically connected, romantic encounters can bring on bingeing. O'Neill describes a late binge, eating scraps of leftovers from the dog's dish after spending the evening with her boyfriend:

I started slowly, relishing the flavor and texture of each marvelous bite. Soon I was ripping the meager remains from the bones, stuffing the meat into my mouth as fast as I could detach it.

[Her boyfriend surprises her, with a look of "total disgust" on his face.]

I had been caught red-handed . . . in an animalistic orgy on the floor, in the dark, alone. Here was the horrid truth for Dan to see. I felt so evil, so tainted, pagan. . . . In Dan's mind that day, I had been whoring after food.[48]

Whereas men are associated with the mind, women are associated with the body. In a society that degrades women, the body becomes alien—a cage or prison. The body is the enemy and an impediment to reason. Thinness is the triumph of mind over body. The ultimate goal of anorectics is to become completely free from their bodies by never having to eat again.

Discussion Questions

1. Discuss how myths about women, such as those described by Pineau, contribute to anorexia and bulimia. Are these myths generally accepted on your campus? If so, discuss what steps might be taken to counteract these myths.
2. Philosophical views, rather than being merely abstract ideas, have real-life consequences. Philosophers have traditionally associated women with the body and men with the mind. Discuss how this division, along with a degraded view of women, has contributed to women's negative views about their bodies.
3. In the scenario described by O'Neill, her boyfriend reacts with disgust to her gorging. She, in turn, perceives what she has done as "whoring after food." Discuss how these reactions reflect and reinforce negative societal views about women and their supposedly seductive and out-of-control sexuality.
4. The greatest fear of women today is not of a nuclear holocaust or environmental catastrophe, but of getting fat. In a recent survey, adults were asked what they feared most in the world; almost 40 percent replied, "Getting fat." Discuss how, if at all, pornography and sexism in the media contribute to this fear.
5. MacKinnon supports censorship of pornography on the grounds that it directly harms women. Has the increase in pornography in the past thirty years contributed to the rise of anorexia and bulimia in young women? Should advertisements and movies that set up impossible ideals of thinness for women be censored? How should freedom of speech be balanced against the harm principle in this case? Support your answers. Discuss how both MacKinnon and a libertarian such as John Stuart Mill might respond to these questions.
6. Do you have a moral obligation to try to help friends who are anorexic or bulimic? If so, what is the basis of this obligation? Imagine a situation in which a friend who is anorexic or bulimic comes to you for help. Discuss what you might say to her.

Racism and Affirmative Action

In October 1995 black celebrity O. J. Simpson was found not guilty of charges of murdering his white ex-wife Nicole Brown Simpson and her friend Ronald Goldman. Simpson's highly publicized trial focused public attention on the depth of the racial divide in the United States. Critics accused Simpson's defense team of playing the "race card" by capitalizing on the distrust many blacks feel toward the police. Indeed, polls consistently showed that the majority of blacks believed Simpson to be innocent, whereas the majority of whites thought he was guilty. Most people also thought that race influenced the decision of the jury and that the trial had harmed race relations in the United States. Almost half of those polled believed that Simpson would have been found guilty by the jury had he been white.[1] Following the verdict, *Newsweek* ran a story that asked if the United States was, in fact, one nation or two?[2] Is the United States more racially divided than it was twenty years ago?

DEFINING THE KEY TERMS

Race is a loose classification of groups of people based on physical characteristics. Race is more than just a set of physical characteristics, however; it is how people define themselves and others. As such, race is also a social construct. For example, although Jews were singled out as a distinct, inferior race in Nazi Germany, in the United States Jews are generally regarded as white. Hispanics, on the other hand, despite their physical and cultural diversity, are sometimes classified as a race in the United States.

Racism is an ideology or worldview that makes race one of the key defining characteristics of a person. Two fundamental premises of racism are (1) humans can be divided into distinct biological groups and (2) some of these groups are morally inferior to others. The Nazi worldview of Aryan superiority was based on an elaborate pseudo-scientific description of Jewish biological inferiority. Slavery was also bolstered by scientific theories of biological inferiority. Dr. W. H. Holcombe of Virginia wrote in 1861: "The Negro is not a white man with a black skin, but of a different species, . . . the hopeless physical and mental inferior [of the white, and] organically constituted to be an agricultural laborer in tropical climates—a strong animal machine."[3]

Because racial groups are seen as radically different, racism leads to an "us/other" mentality, thereby justifying granting privileges to certain groups while denigrating others. The "other" is also seen as contaminated and to be avoided. The "one drop" of blood criterion, which designates anyone as black who has even one black ancestor, and the scrutinizing of the pasts of Germans for Jewish ancestry illustrate this fear of racial contamination.

Racism implies prejudice. *Prejudice* is based on negative feelings and stereotypes rather than reason. *Racists* categorize people in such a way that they do not see the "other" as a person, but as an object of contempt. Racism is often supported and reinforced by other "isms" such as sexism and classism. Black women, for example, have been stereotyped since slavery as "mammies" or "breeders." This prejudice is perpetuated to this day in the stereotype of the black "welfare queen" who collects welfare checks and passes on her legacy of laziness and pathology to her many children. Another racist stereotype is that of the servile Asian woman who is satisfied being subservient to men. Stereotypes can also be used to justify war and police action, as in the stereotype of the "yellow peril" and the violent young black man.

Discrimination occurs when we treat people differently based on their group membership. Unjust discrimination occurs when we base our actions on prejudices rather than relevant differences. Racial discrimination can take many forms, from racially motivated hate speech to the use of Asian mail-order bride services by middle-aged American men who blame their problems with women on feminism.

Racism occurs on two levels—the personal and the institutional. *Multiculturalists* believe that racism is based primarily on individual ignorance and that education is the solution. *Antiracists,* on the other hand, define racism primarily in terms of power and institutions. Critical race theorists such as Mari Matsuda and Charles R. Lawrence III, for example, emphasize the political and social aspects of racism that privilege certain interpretations of history and everyday experience.[4] According to them, to dismantle racism we need to confront and oppose the dominant societal and institutional structures that maintain it. Economic systems, education, the family, religious organizations, and legal and political structures are all examples of social institutions.

Institutional racism, or *enforced discrimination,* occurs when the law or a social system is set up to provide advantages to one group of people at the expense of another. Institutional racism exists because of the actions of many individuals who either have the power to make and carry out discriminatory policies, or allow them to continue. Slavery and Jim Crow laws are two obvious examples of institutional racism. Schools also act as agents in perpetuating racism.[5] The myth that schools promote upward mobility among immigrant and minority groups is directly contradicted by the finding that the social mobility of second- and third-generation Hispanics is strictly downward.[6]

Institutional racism affects foreign as well as domestic policy. In South Korea and other Asian countries, for example, there are government-sanctioned "hospitality houses" or brothels for U.S. servicemen. The use of people in Third World nations for cheap labor sources as well as nonwhite immigrants for cheap labor in this country also reflects institutional racism. Indeed the very term *Third World* reflects the Western belief in the inferiority of non-Western countries.

Sometimes institutional racism is indirect. For example, the funding of schools with local, rather than state or federal, taxes means that children from poorer neighborhoods, which may be predominantly black, receive an inferior education. Patterns of environmental use, such as the destruction of American Indian lands by mining companies and the placement of toxic waste sites near minority communities, also reflect institutional racism.

Institutional racism is supported and perpetuated by the media as well as by legal and religious institutions. The 1915 film *The Birth of a Nation,* which is based on the best-selling book *The Clansman,* viciously degraded blacks and glorified the Ku Klux Klan. The movie was an instant hit, at least with some white people. When President Wilson saw the movie, he remarked, "It is like writing history with lightning and my only regret is that it is all so terribly true."

Like sexism, racism is embedded in our everyday language. The term *American* is assumed to mean white, usually white male. Other groups of Americans are distinguished from "real" Americans by the used of qualifying terms as in *African American, Asian American,* or *Native American.* In contrast, one rarely hears the term *European American.* Thus, language is used to perpetuate the colonial discourse, described by Uma Narayan in her article, that these "other" people are not true red-blooded Americans but rather exist as outsiders in American society.

THE PHILOSOPHERS ON RACISM

Although the ancient Greek philosophers did not directly address the issue, the elitist theories of Aristotle and Plato have been used—or, more correctly, misused—to justify racism. In his *Republic,* Plato argued that those with the greatest inherited capacity for moral and intellectual attainment should be educated to become the rulers. According to Aristotle's moral theory of perfection, certain humans are more highly developed or perfect in terms of virtue and reason. Those humans who are more perfected deserve more of what is good than those who are less perfected. Carrying this line of reasoning one step further, Aristotle concluded that those who are less perfected exist for the sake of and to serve those who are more perfected. Although Aristotle believed that some humans are "slaves by nature" and exist to serve the common good, he did not associate slavery with any particular race.

As with their complicity in endorsing sexism, philosophers are not immune to becoming servants of the status quo. During the seventeenth and eighteeth centuries, racism was incorporated into Western philosophy in part as a response to the need to morally justify European colonialism. John Locke's natural rights ethics, for example, while promoting a doctrine of equal human rights at the same time assumes the superiority of the white Europeans and the inferiority of the American Indians. Locke's version of natural rights theory became the basis of colonial rights discourse.

Swedish botanist Carolus Linnaeus (1707–1778), founder of taxonomy, was the first to scientifically classify plants and animals. In his *Systema Naturae* (1735), Linnaeus classified humans into varieties, or races, based on physical and psychological characteristics. According to his classification, Europeans are "light, active, ingenious"; Asians are "severe, haughty, miserly"; and Africans are "crafty, lazy, negligent . . . governed by whim." Most Western philosophers accepted Linnaeus's classifications without question. In his essay "National Character" (1748), David Hume alleged that all Negroes were of low intelligence.

In the early nineteenth century, the Lamarkian theory of the inheritance of acquired traits was used by scientists, theologians, and philosophers to explain the superiority of the white European race. It was generally agreed that the fair-skinned northern Europeans ("Aryans") were the superior race and that the dark-skinned Africans were the most inferior race. Indians and Asians were only slightly above Africans on the scale of moral value. Jean-Jacques Rousseau speculated that the great apes were really humans whose evolution toward civilization had been stunted by adverse environmental conditions. The people of Africa, because they shared a similar environment, were only slightly ahead of the great apes in their evolution. "Primitive" people, such as the African Bushmen and the Australian Aborigines, were studied by anthropologists in order to gain insight into the thinking and culture of prehistoric white men.

The Lamarkian theory was used to support the notion of the perfectibility of humans, which, in turn, justified both colonialization and slavery as a means of assisting "primitive" people in their evolution toward perfection and civilization. This racist worldview was incorporated into the ideals of colonial America. Like Hume and Locke, Thomas Jefferson (1743–1826) accepted the inequality of hereditary endowment in the different human races.

The institutionalization of racism was also justified on religious grounds. Most Europeans believed that they had a divine duty and right to "Christianize" savages. Indeed, many of the slave ships bore Christian names such as *Jesus* and *John the Baptist*.

The moral principle of equal respect for all persons was thus drowned out by the racist norms of cultural relativism. It was on the basis of these assumptions that the Europeans continued to exercise their "divine and natural right" to conquer, divide up, and exploit the rest of the world for the next two hundred years.

Modern Marxists link racism to capitalism and class exploitation. Ayn Rand disagrees with the Marxist analysis, arguing that racism is a product of collectivist thinking rather than capitalism.[7] Unlike capitalism, which judges people according to their individual merits, racism ascribes merit based on membership in a particular group or collective. The only antidote to racism, Rand argues, is laissez-faire capitalism and individualism, wherein each person is regarded as an independent, autonomous being.

The Marxist analysis of racism is problematic in that racism is also found in non-Western, noncapitalist economies. Racism is found in the Hindu caste system as well as in the nationalist Shinto religion of Japan. On the other hand, racism is inconsistent with Buddhism, which stresses the moral equality of all humans and the cultivation of the virtue of compassion or "true friendliness."

Perhaps one of the most insidious moral theories is cultural relativism, with its identification of morality with cultural norms. The incompatibility of cultural relativism with the moral condemnation of racism led to the rejection of cultural relativism by all but a few moral philosophers. The majority of Americans, however, still base their moral decisions on cultural relativism. In addition, the current popularity of ethical subjectivism, especially among college students, justifies racism and hatred as a personal choice.

THE ROOTS OF AMERICAN RACISM

Jesse Jackson once said, "America has never come to grips with slavery. It is a hole in the American soul." Although racism is found in many, if not most, cultures, this chapter focuses primarily on racism in the United States.

Racism in the United States is rooted in colonialism, slavery, and the systematic attempted extermination of the Americans Indians. In her article, Narayan explores the roots of racism in colonialism. The first record of African slaves arriving in the American colonies was in Jamestown, Virginia, in 1619. Although the slave trade was outlawed in 1808, the law was widely ignored. About 13 million slaves were brought from Africa to the Americas. Many who landed in the West Indies, Cuba, and Haiti were sold to slave-holders in the United States. The slave trade was both lucrative and brutal. About 10 to 15 percent of the 13 million slaves sent from Africa died en route to the New World.[8]

The American colonies eagerly took part in the slave trade. Although the framers of the Declaration of Independence and the U.S. Constitution briefly considered outlaw-ing the African slave trade (although not slavery itself), the idea was soon dropped be-cause several of them were slaveholders, including Thomas Jefferson, who owned hun-dreds of slaves.

During the early 1800s, more than a hundred thousand slaves escaped to northern states or found refuge among the Indians. Frustrated at the Native Americans' refusal to comply with orders to return the runaway slaves, southerners sought help from the fed-eral government to pass laws that would make it easier for them to retrieve slaves who had fled to free states. One of these laws, the Fugitive Slave Law of 1850, allowed any black person, even people who had been freed, to be returned to slavery. There was lit-tle protest in the North over the law, as even freed blacks were not particularly welcomed and were regarded by the whites as "a dangerous and useless element."

The number of white abolitionists in the United States was never very large. Most people either supported slavery or were indifferent to it. Many of those who were op-posed to slavery in principle hated and feared blacks. Frustrated and angry, the north-ern blacks, with the help of abolitionist groups such as the Quakers, set up the Under-ground Railroad that smuggled slaves from the United States over the border to Canada.

In 1857 Dred Scott, a slave who had moved with his master in the 1830s to a free ter-ritory, sued for his freedom. The Supreme Court ruled against Scott, arguing that blacks were strictly property and had no rights. The Court also ruled that the Missouri Com-promise, which made the territory free, was unconstitutional because it deprived white people of their right to enjoy their property.

When the Civil War broke out in 1861, the conflict was primarily over economic is-sues rather than slavery. In his 1861 inaugural address, Abraham Lincoln reassured the southern voters: "I have no purpose, directly or indirectly, to interfere with the institu-tion of slavery in the States where it exists. I believe I have no lawful right to do so, and I have no inclination to do so." The 1863 Emancipation Proclamation that freed the slaves, rather than being based on moral repugnance toward slavery, was more of a po-litical move calculated to weaken the Confederate forces and bring an end to the war. Two years later the Thirteenth Amendment to the Constitution guaranteed that "neither slavery nor involuntary servitude . . . shall exist."

Institutional racism did not end with the Thirteenth Amendment, however. The Ku Klux Klan (KKK) was formed in 1866 by a group of Tennessee Confederate veterans. They were soon joined by some of the South's leading businessmen and professionals. During the thirty years following the Civil War, the southern states passed "Jim Crow laws" reminiscent of the old "slave codes." These laws prevented blacks from owning property in certain areas, allowed employers to hunt down and whip troublesome black workers, and enforced segregation in restaurants, theaters, schools, public transporta-tion, hospitals, and even graveyards.

In 1896 the U.S. Supreme Court ruled in *Plessy v. Ferguson* that "separate but equal" segregation was constitutional. According to the Court, the Fourteenth Amendment,

EXCERPTS FROM U.S. SUPREME COURT *DRED SCOTT V. SANFORD* (1857)

In the opinion of the court, the legislation and histories of the times, and the language used in the Declaration of Independence, show, that neither the class of person that have been imported as slaves, nor their descendants, whether they had become free or not, were then acknowledged as part of the people, nor intended to be included in the general words used in the memorable instrument. . . .

They had for more than a century before been regarded as beings of an inferior order; and altogether unfit to associate with the white race, either in social or political relations; and so far inferior that they had no rights which the white man was bound to respect; and that the negro might be lawfully reduced to slavery for his own benefit. . . .

This opinion was at that time fixed and universal in the civilized portion of the white race. It was regarded as an axiom in morals as well as in politics which no one thought of disputing, or supposed to be open to dispute. . . . The state of public opinion has undergone no change [from] when the Constitution was adopted. . . .

Now the right of property in a slave is distinctly and expressly affirmed in the Constitution. . . . He is himself property in the strictest sense of the term. And the Government in express terms is pledged to protect it in all future time, if the slave escapes from his owner.

while guaranteeing political equality, does not guarantee social equality. The *Plessy v. Ferguson* ruling provided the legal justification for institutional racism for the next sixty years, until 1954, when the Supreme Court overturned the "separate but equal" ruling in *Brown v. Board of Education.*

During the late-nineteenth and early-twentieth centuries, thousands of blacks were raped, beaten, and brutally murdered. By 1880 alone, an estimated 130,000 people had been killed in the South either because they were black or because they sympathized with blacks. Unofficial "lynch laws" in the South allowed white mobs to torture and lynch blacks who couldn't be humbled and controlled by the other laws. The lynchings were advertised in the newspapers and became festive family outings for many white southerners. Even as late as the 1950s, black men could be beaten, jailed, or even lynched for the "reckless eyeballing" of white women.

Race riots followed the migration of southern blacks to the northern cities during the early twentieth century. Up to two hundred blacks were killed and six thousand driven from their homes in a 1917 race riot in East St. Louis, Illinois. With the increase in blacks living in the North, KKK activities spread northward as well. By 1924 the KKK had 4 million members.

Racial segregation continued to be the norm in the United States. There were separate professional leagues for black and white athletes. In Hollywood black actors performed in all-black shows. Although segregated neighborhoods had been ruled unconstitutional by the Supreme Court in 1917, "gentlemen's agreements" among realtors

BROWN V. BOARD OF EDUCATION OF TOPEKA

V.
SUPREME COURT OF THE UNITED STATES
1952

OPINION: MR. CHIEF JUSTICE WARREN delivered the opinion of the Court.

. . . Minors of the Negro race, through their legal representatives, seek the aid of the courts in obtaining admission to the public schools of their community on a nonsegregated basis. In each instance, they had been denied admission to schools attended by white children under laws requiring or permitting segregation according to race. This segregation was alleged to deprive the plaintiffs of the equal protection of the laws under the Fourteenth Amendment. In each of the cases . . . [the] court[s] denied relief to the plaintiffs on the so-called "separate but equal" doctrine announced by this Court in *Plessy v. Ferguson,* 163 U.S. 537. Under that doctrine, equality of treatment is accorded when the races are provided substantially equal facilities, even though these facilities be separate. . . .

The plaintiffs contend that segregated public schools are not "equal" and cannot be made "equal," and that hence they are deprived of the equal protection of the laws. . . .

In approaching this problem, we cannot turn the clock back to 1868 when the Amendment was adopted, or even to 1896 when *Plessy v. Ferguson* was written. We must consider public education in the light of its full development and its present place in American life throughout the Nation. Only in this way can it be determined if segregation in public schools deprives these plaintiffs of the equal protection of the laws.

Today, education is perhaps the most important function of state and local governments. Compulsory school attendance laws and the great expenditures for education both demonstrate our recognition of the importance of education to our democratic society. It is required in the performance of our most basic public responsibilities, even service in the armed forces. It is the very foundation of good citizenship. Today it is a principal instrument in awakening the child to cultural values, in preparing him for later professional training, and in helping him to adjust normally to his environment. . . . these days, it is doubtful that any child

and landlords ensured that neighborhoods—and schools—remained segregated. Few whites questioned the morality of segregation.

During the 1920s the growing "nativist" sentiment made it almost impossible for anyone but people from northern Europe to immigrate to the United States. Racial hatred and Klan activities expanded their targets to include Jews, Puerto Ricans, southern Europeans, Asians, Mexicans, and Native Americans. Following the Japanese attack on Pearl Harbor during World War II, thousands of Japanese Americans were removed from their homes and placed in federal internment camps, even though not a single case of sabotage involving Japanese Americans was ever discovered.

may reasonably be expected to succeed in life if he is denied the opportunity of an education. Such an opportunity, where the state has undertaken to provide it, is a right which must be made available to all on equal terms.

We come then to the question presented: Does segregation of children in public schools solely on the basis of race, even though the physical facilities and other "tangible" factors may be equal, deprive the children of the minority group of equal educational opportunities? We believe that it does.

In *Sweatt v. Painter, supra,* in finding that a segregated law school for Negroes could not provide them equal educational opportunities, this Court relied in large part on "those qualities which are incapable of objective measurement but which make for greatness in a law school." In *McLaurin v. Oklahoma State Regents, supra,* the Court, in requiring that a Negro admitted to a white graduate school be treated like all other students, again resorted to intangible considerations: ". . . his ability to study, to engage in discussions and exchange views with other students, and, in general, to learn his profession." Such considerations apply with added force to children in grade and high schools. To separate them from others of similar age and qualifications solely because of their race generates a feeling of inferiority as to their status in the community that may affect their hearts and minds in a way unlikely ever to be undone. The effect of this separation on their educational opportunities was well stated by a finding in the Kansas case by a court which nevertheless felt compelled to rule against the Negro plaintiffs:

> Segregation of white and colored children in public schools has a
> detrimental effect upon the colored children. The impact is greater
> when it has the sanction of the law; for the policy of separating the races
> is usually interpreted as denoting the inferiority of the negro group. A sense
> of inferiority affects the motivation of a child to learn. Segregation with the
> sanction of law, therefore, has a tendency to [retard] the educational and
> mental development of negro children and to deprive them of some of the
> benefits they would receive in a racial[ly] integrated school system.

. . . We conclude that in the field of public education the doctrine of "separate but equal" has no place. Separate educational facilities are inherently unequal. Therefore, we hold that the plaintiffs and others similarly situated for whom the actions have been brought are, by reason of the segregation complained of, deprived of the equal protection of the laws guaranteed by the Fourteenth Amendment. . . .

The 1950s ushered in what is called the Second Reconstruction. In 1954 the U.S. Supreme Court, in *Brown v. Board of Education of Topeka, Kansas,* ruled that school segregation was unconstitutional. The following year Rosa Parks of Montgomery, Alabama, refused to give up her seat on a bus to a white man as required by law. She was promptly arrested. Her act of nonviolent civil disobedience sparked a citywide bus boycott and the civil rights movement. In 1957 Congress created a Civil Rights Commission, which was followed by the passage of civil rights laws.

Martin Luther King Jr. (1929–1968) and Malcolm X (1925–1965) emerged as leaders of the movement. Both were assassinated because of their views. In 1963 Martin

Luther King Jr. led the March on Washington. In his famous "I Have a Dream" speech, King emphasized community between blacks and whites. The destiny of whites and blacks in the United States, he told the crowds, could not be separated.

The "Indian problem" was resolved primarily through genocide. By 1675, only fifty-five years after the Pilgrims landed at Plymouth, the Native Americans of New England, who once numbered in the thousands, were almost exterminated. During the early and mid-1800s, the U.S. government undertook the systematic removal of the Indians from their lands. The Bureau of Indian Affairs was created by Congress in 1824. Instead of being advocates for the Indians, however, the bureau was used to legitimate the takeover of their lands. The Cherokee, Choctaw, Chickasaw, Creek, and Seminole tribes in the South owned large tracts of fertile land. In addition to making the land available to the wealthy slaveowners in the South, the removal of the Indians would make it harder for slaves to escape, since the Indians regularly provided refuge for runaway slaves.

In 1830 Congress passed the Indian Removal Act. Although the law required the tribes' consent in order to be relocated, many were forced to move without consent. One-fourth of the Cherokee and half of the Creek died of starvation, exposure, and disease during the forced removal from their homes in the South to reservations in the West.

The near extermination of Native American populations by European settlers was justified as the fulfillment of Manifest Destiny—a divine plan for the expansion of the United States from coast to coast. The massacre of more than two hundred Sioux at Wounded Knee, South Dakota, in 1890 marked the final step in the conquest of Indians' homelands and their removal to reservations administered by the Bureau of Indian Affairs. The ultimate goal of the bureau was assimilation, and schools were set up on reservations so that Native American children could learn English and get a proper "white man's" education.

The American Indians were not the only group in the West to suffer from the slings and arrows of racism. During the mid-1800s thousands of Chinese came to the United States to work on the transcontinental railroad. Once the railroad was completed, they were no longer welcome by the whites. In 1882 Congress passed the Chinese Exclusion Act as a solution to the "Chinese problem" by stopping Chinese immigration and preventing resident Chinese from becoming U.S. citizens. Some of the Chinese, however, returned to China; others sought protection from anti-Chinese violence in segregated areas known as Chinatowns. The Chinese Exclusion Act remained in effect until 1943, when it was repealed by Congress as a gesture of friendship to China during World War II.

Although Mexicans are an ethnic rather than a racial group, the treatment of Mexicans and other Hispanics in the United States has followed a similar course of discrimination.

Federal initiatives to combat social problems are relatively recent. Under the banner of the Great Society, the Johnson administration in the mid-1960s declared war on poverty. Congress allocated $950 billion for the expansion of existing social services and the establishment of new programs such as Medicare, subsidized housing, and job training to help people break the cycle of poverty.

Following his election in 1980, President Ronald Reagan dismantled much of the Great Society legislation. Instead of viewing poverty as a result of institutional racism, the Reagan administration blamed the behavior and values of the poor. With the dismantling of legislation aimed at overcoming the social problems associated with institutional racism, the social conditions of blacks and other people of color also began to decline. By the late 1980s, black males were worse off than they were in the late 1960s on almost every socioeconomic measure, including employment rate and life expectancy.[9]

RACISM TODAY

Since the late 1980s, many of the positive gains of the civil rights era have been reversed. Blacks and whites continue to segregate themselves by race in their everyday decisions about housing, church attendance, vacations, and on college campuses. In 1992 housing was more segregated than in the mid-1960s.[10]

The gap between academic skills of black and white children has been widening since 1988.[11] Most of the schools in the United States are more segregated and unequal today than they were in 1954 at the time of the *Brown v. Board of Education* ruling.[12] Although segregation is now illegal, tracking, in which students are grouped according to performance on standardized tests, has had the effect of re-creating segregation within schools and holding black children to a lower educational level. There is currently a trend away from increasing efforts to integrating schools and toward increasing minority school funding instead.[13]

The percentage of blacks attending college began falling in 1980.[14] Indeed, young black men are now more likely to go to prison than to college. In 1990, 25 percent of all young black men ended up in the criminal justice system, compared with 10 percent of Hispanic men and 6 percent of white men.[15]

Hate Crimes

There has been a rise in racially motivated hate crimes since the mid-1980s. Between 1987 and 1989, hate crimes increased 41 percent in Los Angeles, 33 percent in Boston, and more than 100 percent in New York City. The majority of hate crimes are racially motivated, with antiblack crimes being by far the most common type.[16] In a February 2000 Gallup poll, 28 percent of non-white respondents said that they worried about becoming a victim of hate crime. The number of hate groups in the United States increased by 25 percent between 1996 and 2000.[17] Fewer than one-third of these groups are Klan affiliated, and most are not based in the South. In 1995 and 1996, there was a rash of fires at black churches—seventy-five in eighteen months, more than double the number in the previous five years.[18]

The number of racial incidents on college campuses has also been increasing since the mid-1980s.

At the turn of the millennium a rash of hate mail was sent to more than a dozen historically black colleges. The letters warned black students of their impending destruction stating that in 2000 there would be all out war against blacks.[19] As of June 2000, forty-one states have passed laws against hate crimes.

Racial Profiling

During the late 1990s another type of insidious racism known as racial profiling made the headlines. *Racial profiling* is the routine, and often unconscious, practice by police of targeting suspects on the basis of their race.[20] In a 1999 Gallup poll, 42 percent of blacks answered "yes" to the question: "Have you ever felt that you were stopped by the police just because of your race or ethnic background?" Only 6 percent of whites polled answered "yes" to the same question.[21]

Studies indicate that racial profiling is a common practice. A study by the New York Attorney General's office found that 50 percent of all police stops were of black New Yorkers, even though blacks make up only 25 percent of New York's population.

Law enforcement agencies claim that since blacks commit crimes at higher rates than whites, racial profiling is justified. However, whether blacks actually commit more crimes or are just more likely to be arrested and sentenced to jail for their alleged crimes remains under debate.[22] An April 2000 study on juvenile justice found that minorities were twice as likely as whites to be sentenced to prison, even when the youths had similar criminal histories.[23] Another study of U.S. Customs services practices found that black women were nine times more likely than white women to be x-rayed after a frisk or pat down, even though they "were less than half as likely to be found carrying contraband as white women."[24]

Asian Americans have also been the victims of racial profiling. For example, a U.S. Energy Department's inquiry has been accused of singling out Chinese Americans for investigation of security breaches. Both Edward T. Fei, one of the department's top experts on nuclear proliferation, and Wen Ho Lee, a Los Alamos scientist, have been aggressively investigated for security breaches despite lack of solid evidence to support the charges.[25]

Michael Levin in his article at the end of this chapter argues that practices such as racial profiling of African Americans are morally justified because of biological differences between the races. Bernard Boxill, in contrast, argues that color-conscious policies like this violate the principle of distributive justice. Color-conscious policies are justified only when they work toward creating more egalitarian public policy. Opponents of racial profiling also point out that it hurts not only its direct targets but leads to an erosion of trust in the government, especially in the justice system and the police, the very branches of government that are entrusted to protect citizens from injustice.

Affirmative Action

The first affirmative action legislation was passed in 1959. Affirmative action legislation was expanded in the 1960s during the civil rights era.

There are several ways to carry out affirmative action. A company or college may simply cast its net farther by advertising in minority newspapers to increase the pool of minority applicants. Another form of affirmative action involves giving preference to a minority person or a woman if that individual is equally qualified with a white male. A more controversial type involves giving preference to minorities and women who are less qualified than white male applicants. It is this type of strong affirmative action to which many affirmative action opponents object.

Some affirmative action programs set goals in terms of percentage of minority and female employees. These goals are usually ideals rather than requirements. Quotas, on the other hand, are fixed percentages or numbers set by a company or college for the hiring or admission of minorities and women. For example, a college might set aside a certain number of slots for blacks.

A basic assumption of affirmative action is that positive steps need to be taken to correct certain injustices against groups such as minorities and women. Because racism is institutional, it will not suffice to simply stop discriminating. Affirmative action benefits minorities by breaking the cycle of discrimination and racism. In addition, affirmative action programs bring together people from diverse racial backgrounds, thus creating a more tolerant and multicultural society.

While Gallup polls show that slightly more than half of blacks support it, affirmative action has never enjoyed popular support among whites in the United States.[26] Opponents of affirmative action point out that the most disadvantaged are not in a position to benefit from it. Affirmative action also creates resentment, especially among white males who are harmed by reverse discrimination.

In 1978 Allan Bakke, a white man, sued the University of California at Davis Medical School because his application was rejected while minorities with lower test scores were admitted. The Supreme Court agreed with Bakke, ruling that reverse discrimination was unconstitutional.

In November 1996, with the passage of Proposition 209, California became the first state to ban affirmative action in the public sector. Washington and Texas have also passed referendums banning affirmative action in college admissions.

The end of affirmative action at the University of California was accompanied by a dramatic drop in the number of minority students accepted in 1998. Despite initial concerns that minorities needed affirmative action programs to make up for past injustices, the enrollment of minorities at the University of California rebounded significantly in 2000.[27] However, the increase has been primarily at the satellite campuses. Minority enrollment at the elite flagship campuses at Berkeley, San Diego, and Santa Barbara are continuing to decline. This trend raises concerns that some state university campuses will become segregated institutions of higher learning.

MORAL ISSUES

Human Dignity and Individual Moral Worth

Racism, by definition, denies the moral worth of certain people based simply on their race. Jorge Garcia defines racism in terms of ill will and a disregard for the dignity and welfare of certain people based on their assigned race. He also argues that individual racism precedes and reinforces institutional racism. One of the problems in overcoming institutional racism is how to restore the dignity of groups that have suffered discrimination without violating the equal moral worth of members of groups who have historically benefited from that discrimination.

Justice and Equality

According to the principle of equality, "it is unjust to treat people differently in ways that deny them some significant social benefits unless we can show that there is a difference between them that is relevant to the differential treatment."[28] The principle of equality requires that differential treatment be based only on real and relevant differences.

Michael Levin argues that discrimination against blacks is justified based on, what he claims, are real differences between whites and blacks in terms of intelligence and aggressiveness. Ayn Rand, on the other hand, argues that even if it can be shown that members of one race are, on the average, more intelligent or more aggressive than members of another, this tells us nothing about a particular individual. The principle of equality requires that people be judged on their individual merits, not on their membership in a particular group.[29] Bernard R. Boxill questions whether color-conscious programs, such as affirmative action, are necessarily unjust. He maintains that there are times when race, like talent, is relevant in creating public policy.

Utilitarian Considerations

Racism hurts. In the 1954 *Brown v. Board of Education* ruling, the U.S. Supreme Court spoke of the irrevocable damage to the "hearts and minds" of black children who were compelled to attend segregated schools.

Affirmative action programs are both defended and opposed on utilitarian grounds. Some people argue that preferential treatment of minorities has actually worked against their best interests by fostering social tension and resentment against minorities. It also creates the impression that minorities can't make it on their own merits. Shelby Steele points out that in their enthusiasm to diversify, many universities have admitted minority students who are poorly qualified academically, thus setting them up for failure. Furthermore, it is argued, strong affirmative action programs waste the talents of those who are most qualified. Defenders of preferential hiring, in response, maintain that it helps minorities who are less qualified because of racism to develop their talents, thus creating a greater pool of qualified workers.

One of the problems of relying on a utilitarian calculus is the uncertainty of cause-and-effect relationships as well as the differing values people place on different outcomes. Utilitarian solutions can also run counter to considerations of human dignity and justice. Utilitarian cost/benefit analysis, for example, was used to justify slavery. Indeed, with the demise of slavery the economy of the South collapsed, leaving it the most economically backward region in the United States until after World War II.

Care Ethics

The analytical utilitarian approach is often contrasted with care ethics with its emphasis on sentiment and human relationships. Racism prevents the development of caring relationships between people of different races. Although caring is important, one of the weaknesses of care ethics is that it does not provide a strategy for overcoming racism in a segregated society. When a commitment to caring is absent, it is our commitment to an ideal or principle that must motivate us to do what is right. Care ethics, as Narayan points out, can also be used to justify paternalistic caring and colonialism.

Reparation

Reparations are payments made to a group of people for past harms. Affirmative action has been justified as one way of making reparations for such harms. Blacks, Native Americans, and Japanese Americans have all sought direct reparation from the U.S. government. In 1988 Congress passed the Civil Liberties Act authorizing the government to pay $20,000 to every living Japanese American who was interned in federal camps during World War II. No official apology, however, has been offered to blacks or American Indians.

What do we owe to blacks and Native Americans, if anything, for a legacy of slavery, genocide, and degradation? Is an apology enough? Should descendants of slaves be compensated monetarily, as were the Japanese Americans for their loss of freedom during World War II? Or do we owe only an indirect debt to contemporary blacks, since it was their ancestors, not them, who were brought to this country against their will? Should the U.S. government return Indian lands or monetarily compensate Indians for the loss of their lands? Or is it now time to make peace with the past and just put it behind us?

CONCLUSION

Because racism is woven into the very fabric of society and reinforced by personal prejudices, it is difficult to eliminate. We need to look past cultural interpretations and carefully analyze ways in which society today normalizes racism. The racism of the Jim Crow era seemed normal and rational to the great majority of white Americans, just as slavery was once regarded as part of the natural order, at least by those who benefited from it.

Some people argue that those affected by racist policies should take responsibility for changing the system. The problem of racism, however, is not a "black problem," or whatever group is seen as problematic; the problem is white racism. The people who created and maintain racism bear the main responsibility for eradicating it. Those who have the most power to change institutional racism are the very people who have the power to perpetuate it. In addition, all of us, whatever our race, need to resist the temptation to play the role of the innocent victim or to become racists ourselves by scapegoating members of other racial groups.

Racism needs to be addressed at all levels. Being "tolerant" or "color-blind" is not enough. The majority of whites state that they strongly believe in the ideal of racial equality; but, even though we may not personally feel racial hatred, our actions can be infected by the hatred of others. It is not enough to simply change our own personal attitudes. We cannot substitute a politically correct ideology for action. Action or behavior provides the link between personal attitudes and institutional racism. Unless we actively work toward eliminating racism, we are still part of the problem. Martin Luther King Jr. once said that "the choice is ours, and though we might prefer it otherwise, we *must* choose."

SHELBY STEELE

I'm Black, You're White, Who's Innocent?

Shelby Steele is a writer and professor of English at San Jose State University in California. Steele examines the origins of racism and conflict in race relations today. According to Steele, both black and white Americans have become trapped in placing color above character. Both have a deep sense of "racial vulnerability." Whites are charged with being racist, blacks with being inferior. Both have found a means of escape by retreating into "innocence" rather than adopting a true moral consciousness. Because of this, many contemporary social policies that were intended to decrease racism have only aggravated it.

Critical Reading Questions

1. According to Steele, why do blacks badger or provoke whites about race? Why did Steele have a hard time overcoming the impulse to do this to white liberals and even his own students?
2. What does Steele mean when he says that "black anger always, in a way, flatters white power"?
3. According to Steele, why is racism a power issue? How is innocence related to power and the feeling of entitlement?
4. On what grounds does Steele claim that both blacks and whites have a "hidden investment in racism"?
5. How do blacks lay claim to their racial "innocence"? What is problematic about claiming innocence through victim status? Why, according to Steele, is this form of power inconsistent with individual responsibility?
6. What explanation does Steele give for the deterioration in the conditions of blacks in America over the past twenty years?
7. What does Steele mean when he says that victimization and poverty have been the source of black power? Why is this type of power useless for overcoming poverty?
8. According to Steele, how should people try to gain real power in America?
9. How does Steele account for the high dropout rate of black college students?
10. Why is "seeing for innocence" more costly for blacks than for whites?
11. What is the difference, morally, between genuine and presumed innocence? What is the basis of genuine innocence? Which type of innocence characterized the early civil rights years?
12. What is the difference, according to Steele, between the racial consciousness that began in the mid-1960s and the moral consciousness of the early civil rights movement?

"I'm Black, You're White, Who's Innocent?" in *The Content of Our Character: A New Vision of Race in America* (New York: HarperCollins, 1991), 1–6; 14–20.

It is a warm, windless California evening, and the dying light that covers the redbrick patio is tinted pale orange by the day's smog. Eight of us, not close friends, sit in lawn chairs sipping chardonnay. A black engineer and I (we had never met before) integrate the group. A psychologist is also among us, and her presence encourages a surprising openness. But not until well after the lovely twilight dinner has been served, when the sky has turned to deep black and the drinks have long since changed to scotch, does the subject of race spring awkwardly upon us. Out of nowhere the engineer announces, with a coloring of accusation in his voice, that it bothers him to send his daughter to a school where she is one of only three black children. "I didn't realize my ambition to get ahead would pull me into a world where my daughter would lose touch with her blackness," he says.

Over the course of the evening we have talked about money, past and present addictions, child abuse, even politics. Intimacies have been revealed, fears named. But this subject, race, sinks us into one of those shaming silences where eye contact terrorizes.... Finally, the psychologist seems to gather herself for a challenge, but it is too late. "Oh, I'm sure she'll be just fine," says our hostess, rising from her chair. When she excuses herself to get the coffee, the psychologist and two sky gazers offer to help.

With four of us now gone, I am surprised to see the engineer still silently holding his ground. There is a willfulness in his eyes, an inner pride. He knows he has said something awkward, but he is determined not to give a damn. His unwavering eyes intimidate even me. At last the host's head snaps erect. He has an idea. "The hell with coffee," he says. "How about some of the smoothest brandy you've ever tasted?" An idea made exciting by the escape it offers. Gratefully, we follow him back into the house, quickly drink his brandy, and say our good-byes.

An autopsy of this party might read: death induced by an abrupt and lethal injection of the American race issue. An accurate if superficial assessment. Since it has been my fate to live a rather integrated life, I have often witnessed sudden deaths like this. The threat of them, if not the real-

ity, is a part of the texture of integration. In the late 1960s, when I was just out of college, I took a delinquent's delight in playing the engineer's role, and actually developed a small reputation for playing it well. Those were the days of flagellatory white guilt; it was such great fun to pinion some professor or housewife or, best of all, a large group of remorseful whites, with the knowledge of both their racism and their denial of it. The adolescent impulse to sneer at convention, to startle the middle-aged with doubt, could be indulged under the guise of racial indignation. And how could I lose? . . .

About a year of this was enough: the guilt that follows most cheap thrills caught up to me, and I put myself in check. But the impulse to do it faded more slowly. It was one of those petty talents that is tied to vanity, and when there were ebbs in my self-esteem the impulse to use it would come alive again. . . .

In the literature classes I teach I often see how the presence of whites all but seduces some black students into provocation. When we come to a novel by a black writer, say Toni Morrison, the white students can easily discuss the human motivations of the black character. But, inevitably, a black student, as if by reflex, will begin to set in relief the various racial problems that are the background of these characters' lives. This student's tone will carry a reprimand: the class is afraid to confront the reality of racism. Classes cannot be allowed to die like dinner parties, however. My latest strategy is to thank that student for his or her moral vigilance and then appoint the young man or woman as the class's official racism monitor. But even if I get a laugh—I usually do, but sometimes the student is particularly indignant, and it gets uncomfortable—the strategy never quite works. Our racial division is suddenly drawn in neon. Overcaution spreads like spilled paint. And, in fact, the black student who started it all does become a kind of monitor. The very presence of this student imposes new accountability on the class.

I think those who provoke this sort of awkwardness are operating out of a black identity that obliges them to badger white people about race almost on principle. . . . Race indeed remains a source of white shame; the goal of these provocations is to put whites, no matter how indirectly, in touch with this collective guilt. In other words, these provocations I speak of are *power* moves, little shows of power that try to freeze the "enemy" in self-consciousness. They gratify and inflate the provocateur. They are the underdog's bite. And whites, far more secure in their power, respond with a self-contained and tolerant silence that is itself a show of power. What greater power than that of nonresponse, the power to let a small enemy sizzle in his own juices, to even feel a little sad at his frustration just as one is also complimented by it. Black anger always, in a way, flatters white power. In America, to know that one is not black is to feel an extra grace, a little boost of impunity.

I think the real trouble between the races in America is that the races are not just races but competing power groups—a fact that is easily minimized, perhaps because it is so obvious. What is not so obvious is that this is true quite apart from the issue of class. Even the well-situated middle-class (or wealthy) black is never completely immune to that peculiar contest of power that his skin color subjects him to. Race is a separate reality in American society, an entity that carries its own potential for power, a mark of fate that class can soften considerably but not eradicate. . . .

But the human animal almost never pursues power without first convincing himself that he is *entitled* to it. And this feeling of entitlement has its own precondition: to be entitled one must first believe in one's innocence, at least in the area where one wishes to be entitled. By innocence I mean a feeling of essential goodness in relation to others and, therefore, superiority to others. Our innocence always inflates us and deflates those we seek power over. Once inflated we are entitled; we are in fact licensed to go after the power our innocence tells us we deserve. In this sense, *innocence is power.* Of course, innocence need not be genuine or real in any objective sense, as the Nazis demonstrated not long ago. Its only test is whether or not we can convince ourselves of it.

I think the racial struggle in America has always been primarily a struggle for innocence. White racism from the beginning has been a claim of white

innocence and therefore of white entitlement to subjugate blacks. And in the sixties, as went innocence so went power. Blacks used the innocence that grew out of their long subjugation to seize more power, while whites lost some of their innocence and so lost a degree of power over blacks. Both races instinctively understand that to lose innocence is to lose power (in relation to each other). To be innocent someone else must be guilty, a natural law that leads the races to forge their innocence on each other's backs. The inferiority of the black always makes the white man superior; the evil might of whites makes blacks good. This pattern means that both races have a hidden investment in racism and racial disharmony despite their good intentions to the contrary. Power defines their relations, and power requires innocence, which, in turn, requires racism and racial division.

I believe it was his hidden investment that the engineer was protecting when he made his remark—the white "evil" he saw in a white school "depriving" his daughter of her black heritage confirmed his innocence. . . . What none of us saw was the underlying game of power and innocence we were trapped in, or how much we need a racial impasse to play the game. . . .

Now the other side of America's racial impasse: How do blacks lay claim to their racial innocence?

The most obvious and unarguable source of black innocence is the victimization that blacks endured for centuries at the hands of a race that insisted on black inferiority as a means to its own innocence and power. Like all victims, what blacks lost in power they gained in innocence—innocence that, in turn, entitled them to pursue power. This was the innocence that fueled the civil rights movement of the sixties and that gave blacks their first real power in American life—victimization metamorphosed into power via innocence. But this formula carries a drawback that I believe is virtually as devastating to blacks today as victimization once was. It is a formula that binds the victim to his victimization by linking his power to his status as a victim. And this, I'm convinced, is the tragedy of black power in America today. It is primarily a victim's power, grounded too deeply in the entitlement derived from past injustice and in the innocence that

Western/Christian tradition has always associated with poverty.

Whatever gains this power brings in the short run through political action, it undermines in the long run. Social victims may be collectively entitled, but they are all too often individually demoralized. Since the social victim has been oppressed by society, he comes to feel that his individual life will be improved more by changes in society than by his own initiative. Without realizing it, he makes society rather than himself the agent of change. The power he finds in his victimization may lead him to collective action against society, but it also encourages passivity within the sphere of his personal life.

Not long ago, I saw a television documentary that examined life in Detroit's inner city on the twentieth anniversary of the riots there in which forty-three people were killed. A comparison of the inner city then and now showed a decline in the quality of life. Residents feel less safe, drug trafficking is far worse, crimes by blacks against blacks are more frequent, housing remains substandard, and the teenage pregnancy rate has skyrocketed. Twenty years of decline and demoralization, even as opportunities for blacks to better themselves have increased. This paradox is not peculiar to Detroit. By many measures, the majority of blacks—those not yet in the middle class—are further behind whites today than before the victories of the civil rights movement. But there is a reluctance among blacks to examine this paradox, I think, because it suggests that racial victimization is not our real problem. If conditions have worsened for most of us as racism had receded, then much of the problem must be of our own making. To admit this fully would cause us to lose the innocence we derive from our victimization. And we would jeopardize the entitlement we've always had to challenge society. We are in the odd and self-defeating position in which taking responsibility for bettering ourselves feels like a surrender to white power.

So we have a hidden investment in victimization and poverty. These distressing conditions have been the source of our only real power, and there is an unconscious sort of gravitation toward them, a complaining celebration of them. One sees evidence of this in the near happiness with which certain black leaders recount the horror of Howard Beach, Bensonhurst, and other recent instances of racial tension. As one is saddened by these tragic events, one is also repelled at the way some of the black leaders—agitated to near hysteria by the scent of victim power inherent in them—leap forward to exploit them as evidence of black innocence and white guilt. . . .

Seeing for innocence pressures blacks to focus on racism and to neglect the individual initiative that would deliver them from poverty—the only thing that finally delivers *anyone* from poverty. With our eyes on innocence we see racism everywhere and miss opportunity even as we stumble over it. About 70 percent of black students at my university drop out before graduation—a flight from opportunity that racism cannot explain. It is an injustice that whites can see for innocence with more impunity than blacks can. The price whites pay is a certain blindness to themselves. Moreover, for whites seeing for innocence continues to engender the bad faith of a long-disgruntled minority. But the price blacks pay is an ever-escalating poverty that threatens to make the worst off a permanent underclass. Not fair, but real. . . .

"Innocence is ignorance," Kierkegaard says, and if this is so, the claim of innocence amounts to an insistence on ignorance, a refusal to know. In their assertions of innocence both races carve out very functional areas of ignorance for themselves—territories of blindness that license a misguided pursuit of power. Whites gain superiority by not knowing blacks; blacks gain entitlement by not seeing their own responsibility for bettering themselves. The power each race seeks in relation to the other is grounded in a double-edged ignorance of the self as well as of the other. . . .

I think the civil rights movement in its early and middle years offered the best way out of America's racial impasse: in this society, race must not be a source of advantage or disadvantage for anyone. This is fundamentally a *moral* position, one that seeks to breach the corrupt union of race and power with principles of fairness and human equality: if all men are created equal, then racial difference cannot sanction power. The civil rights movement was conceived for no other reason than to redress that corrupt union, and its guiding insight was that only a moral power based on enduring principles of justice, equality, and freedom could offset the lower impulse in man to exploit race as a means to power. Three hundred years of suffering had driven the point home, and in Montgomery, Little Rock, and Selma, racial power was the enemy and moral power the weapon.

An important difference between genuine and presumed innocence, I believe, is that the former must be earned through sacrifice while the latter is unearned and only veils the quest for privilege. And there was much sacrifice in the early civil rights movement. The Gandhian principle of nonviolent resistance that gave the movement a spiritual center as well as a method of protest demanded sacrifice, a passive offering of the self in the name of justice. A price was paid in terror and lost life, and from this sacrifice came a hard-earned innocence and a credible moral power.

Nonviolent passive resistance is a bargainer's strategy. It assumes the power that is the object of the protest has the genuine innocence to respond morally, and puts the protesters at the mercy of that innocence. I think this movement won so many concessions precisely because of its belief in the capacity of whites to be moral. It did not so much demand that whites change as offer them relentlessly the opportunity to live by their own morality—to attain a true innocence based on the sacrifice of their racial privilege, rather than a false innocence based on presumed racial superiority. Blacks always bargain with or challenge the larger society; but I believe that in the early civil rights years, these forms of negotiation achieved a degree of integrity and genuineness never seen before or since.

In the mid-sixties all this changed. Suddenly a sharp *racial* consciousness emerged to compete with the moral consciousness that had defined the movement up to that point. Whites were no longer welcome in the movement, and a vocal "black power" minority gained dramatic visibility. Now suddenly the movement itself was using race as a means to power and thereby affirming the very union of race and power it was born to redress. In the end,

black power can claim no higher moral standing than white power. . . .

You hear it asked, why are there no Martin Luther Kings around today? I think one reason is that there are no black leaders willing to resist the seductions of racial power, or to make the sacrifices moral power requires. King understood that racial power subverts moral power, and he pushed the principles of fairness and equality rather than black power because he believed those principles would bring blacks their most complete liberation. He sacrificed race for morality, and his innocence was made genuine by that sacrifice. What made King the most powerful and extraordinary black leader of this century was not his race but his morality.

Black power is a challenge. It grants whites no innocence; it denies their moral capacity and then demands that they be moral. No power can long insist on itself without evoking an opposing power. Doesn't an insistence on black power call up white power? (And could this have something to do with what many are now calling a resurgence of white racism?) I believe that what divided the races at the dinner party I attended, and what divides them in the nation, can only be bridged by an adherence to those moral principles that disallow race as a source of power, privilege, status, or entitlement of any kind. In our age, principles like fairness and equality are ill-defined and all but drowned in relativity. But this is the fault of people, not principles. . . .

What both black and white Americans fear are the sacrifices and risks that true racial harmony demands. This fear is the measure of our racial chasm. And though fear always seeks a thousand justifications, none is ever good enough, and the problems we run from only remain to haunt us. It would be right to suggest courage as an antidote to fear, but the glory of the word might only intimidate us into more fear. I prefer the word effort—relentless effort, moral effort. What I like most about this word are its connotations of everyday-ness, earnestness, and practical sacrifice. No matter how badly it might have gone for us that warm summer night, we should have talked. We should have made the effort.

Discussion Questions

1. Steele starts by describing an incident at a party in which race comes up in the conversation. Why did the topic of race make people uncomfortable? Think of a similar incident in your own life. How did people respond?
2. Discuss Søren Kierkegaard's statement "innocence is ignorance" in the context of race. Relate your answer to the concept of resistance in Chapter 2, "Moral Reasoning."
3. Discuss Steele's claim that innocence is being used as a tool of power by both whites and blacks. To what extent do you, or others you know, engage in this type of power play? Give specific examples. Discuss steps you might take to replace presumed innocence with genuine innocence.
4. Mohandas ("Mahatma") Gandhi was once asked what he thought about Western civilization. He replied that he thought that it would be a good idea. Discuss why Gandhi might have thought that Western society was not truly civilized. What does it mean to be a civilization? Can a racist society be civilized? Support your answers.
5. Thirteen days after the O.J. Simpson verdict, Louis Farrakhan, a Nation of Islam minister, led the Million Man March in Washington, D.C. Several days before the rally, Farrakhan denounced Jews as "bloodsuckers"; a believer in black superiority, he regularly demonizes "blue-eyed devils." Farrakhan also believes in separatism and economic individualism and encourages black men to take personal responsibility for their actions. Discuss how Steele might respond to Farrakhan's teachings. Relate your answer to Steele's contrast of racial consciousness and moral consciousness.
6. Discuss ways in which you use "innocence" to maintain a position of moral superiority and to deny your complicity in racism.

 JORGE GARCIA

The Heart of Racism

Jorge Garcia is a professor of philosophy at Rutgers University. Garcia argues that the heart of racism is ill will and disregard for members of certain groups. Racism is rooted in intention rather than in action or simple belief. Garcia argues that his virtue-based definition of racism is not only more consistent with common usage than other definitions, but is better at accounting for interracial hostility. It also accounts for both individual and institutional racism, as well as the connection between the two. Garcia uses several examples to illustrate his concept of racism.

Critical Reading Questions

1. How does Garcia define racism? What is the essence of racism?
2. How does Garcia respond to the claim that because there are no races, there cannot be racism?

"The Heart of Racism," *Journal of Social Philosophy* 27, no. 1 (1996):5–45. Some notes have been omitted.

3. Can someone disapprove of a culture without being racist?

4. What is "higher order discrimination"?

5. Why does Garcia believe that racism is rooted in the heart rather than in action?

6. According to Garcia, why is racism always immoral? What moral duties and virtues does racism violate?

7. What is the relationship between individual racism and institutional racism? Which type does Garcia claim is of greater moral importance and why?

8. What is the connection between good intentions and racism? What does Garcia mean when he says that individual racism fundamentally lies in volition rather than in action or belief?

9. According to Garcia, can a person be a racist without ever acting on racist attitudes in a way that harms members of another race?

10. Does preferential treatment necessarily imply racism?

11. Is racial discrimination always conscious? What are some examples of unconscious racism?

12. How does Garcia's concept of racism apply to hate speech? What is the difference between hate speech and "racially offensive speech"?

13. On what grounds does Garcia find the gentle but paternal aristocracy of the antebellum period racist?

14. What is the "Kiplingesque" view? Why is the notion of the "white man's burden" racist?

15. Does Garcia think it is wrong for a white woman to avoid black teenagers on the street? How does his answer differ from that of Judith Lichtenberg?

16. Why does Garcia find it necessary to restrict the definition of institutional racism? How do the analogies of the "old boy network" and the alien missile attack on Africa support Garcia's position?

17. What point is Garcia making in the Smythe-Brown analogy?

18. Under what circumstance does Garcia find preferential hiring based on race morally justified?

19. According to Garcia, in what ways do individual and institutional racism reinforce each other? What does Garcia mean when he claims that institutional racism can continue even after individual racism has died out?

A VOLITIONAL CONCEPTION OF RACISM

Kwame Anthony Appiah rightly complains that, although people frequently voice their abhorrence of racism, "rarely does anyone stop to say what it is, or what is wrong with it" (Appiah, 1990: 3). This way of stating the program of inquiry we need is promising, because, although racism is not essentially "a moral doctrine," *pace* Appiah, it is always a moral evil (Appiah, 1990: 13). No account of what racism is can be adequate unless it at the same time makes clear what is wrong with it. How should we conceive racism, then, if we follow Appiah's advice "to take our ordinary ways of thinking about race and racism and point up some of their presuppositions"? (Appiah, 1990: 4). My proposal is that we conceive of racism as fundamentally a vicious kind of racially based disregard for the welfare of certain people. In its central and most vicious form, it is a hatred, ill-will, directed against a person or persons on account of their assigned race. In a derivative form, one is a racist when one either does not care at all or does not care enough (i. e., as much as morality requires) or does not care in the right ways about people assigned to a certain racial group, where this disregard is based on racial classification. Racism, then, is something that essentially involves not our beliefs and their rationality or irrationality, but our wants, intentions, likes, and dislikes and their distance from the moral virtues. Such a view helps explain racism's conceptual ties to various forms of *hatred* and contempt. (Note that "contempt" derives from "to contemn"—not to care [about someone's needs and rights].)

It might be objected that there can be no such thing as racism because, as many now affirm, "there are no races." This objection fails. First, that "race" is partially a social construction does not entail that there are no races. One might even maintain, though I would not, that race-terms, like "person," "preference," "choice," "welfare," etc., and, more controversially, such terms as "reason for action," "immoral," "morally obligatory," etc. may be terms that, while neither included within nor translatable into, the language of physics, nevertheless arise in such a way and at such a fundamental level of social or anthropological discourse that they should be counted as real, at least, for purposes of political and ethical theory. Second, as many racial anti-realists concede, even if it were true that race is unreal, what we call racism could still be real (Appiah, 1992: p. 45). What my account of racism requires is not that there be races, but that people make distinctions in their hearts, whether consciously or not, on the basis of their (or others') racial classifications. That implies nothing about the truth of those classifications.

Lawrence Blum [1991] raises a puzzling question about this. We can properly classify person S as a racist even if *we* do not believe in races. But what if S herself does not believe in them? Suppose S is a White person who hates Black people, but picks them out by African origin, attachment to African cultures, residence or rearing in certain U.S. neighborhoods, and so on. Should we call S racist if she does not hate Black people *as* such (i. e., on the basis of her assigning them to a Black race), but hates all people she thinks have been corrupted by their internalizing [of] undesirable cultural elements from Harlem or Watts, or from Nairobi, or the Bunyoro? I think the case underdescribed. Surely, a person can disapprove of a culture or a family of cultures without being racist. However, cultural criticism can be a mask for a deeper (even unconscious) dislike that is defined by racial classifications. If the person transfers her disapproval of the group's culture to contempt or disregard for those designated as the group's members, then she is already doing something morally vicious. When she assigns all the groups disliked to the same racial classification, then we are entitled to suspect racism, because we have good grounds to suspect that her disavowals of underlying racial classifications are false. If S hates the cultures of various Black groups for having a certain feature, but does not extend that disapproval to other cultures with similar features, then that strongly indicates racism.

Even if she is more consistent, there may still be racism, but of a different sort. Adrian Piper [1990] suggests that, in the phenomenon she calls "higher order discrimination," a person may claim to dislike members of a group because she thinks they have a certain feature, but really disapprove of the feature because she associates it with the despised group. This "higher order discrimination" would, of course, still count as racist in my account because the subject's distaste for the cultural element derives from and is morally infected by race-based disregard.

We should also consider an additional possibility. A person may falsely attribute an undesirable feature to people she assigns to a racial group because of her disregard for those in the group. This will often take the forms of exaggeration, seeing another in the worst light, and withholding from someone the benefit of the doubt. So, an anti-Semite may interpret a Jew's reasonable frugality as greed; a White racist may see indolence in a Black person's legitimate resistance to unfair expectations of her, and so on.

Thinking of racism as thus rooted in the heart fits common sense and ordinary usage in a number of ways. It is instructive that contemptuous, White racists have sometimes called certain of their enemies "Nigger-lovers." When we seek to uncover the implied contrast-term for this epithet, it surely suggests that enemies of those who "love" Black people, as manifested in their efforts to combat segregation, and so forth, are those who hate Black people or who have little or no human feelings toward us at all. This is surely born out by the behavior and rhetoric of paradigmatic White racists.

This account makes racism similar to other familiar forms of intergroup animosity. Activists in favor of Israel and of what they perceive as Jewish interests sometimes call anti-Semites "Jew-haters." . . . What is important for us is to note that *hostility* toward Jews is the heart of anti-Semitism.

Racism is always immoral. As Stephen Nathanson says, "Racism, as we ordinarily speak of it, . . . implies . . . a special disregard for other groups. Hence, there is a sense in which racism is necessarily immoral" (Nathanson, 1992: p. 9). Its immorality stems from its being opposed to the virtues of benevolence and justice. Racism is a form of morally insufficient (i.e., vicious) concern or respect for some others. It infects actions in which one (a) tries to injure people assigned to a racial group because of their XXXXX, or (b) objectionably fails to take care *not* to injure them (where the agent accepts harm to R1s because she disregards the interests and needs of R1s because they are R1s). We can also allow that an action is racist in a derivative and weaker sense when it is less directly connected to racist disregard, for example, when someone (c) does something that (regardless of its intended, probable, or actual effects) stems in significant part from a belief or apprehension about other people, that one has (in significant part) because of one's disaffection toward them because of (what one thinks to be their) race. Racism, thus, will often offend against justice, not just against benevolence, because one sort of injury to another is withholding from her the respect she is owed and the deference and trust that properly express that respect. Certain forms of paternalism, while benevolent in some of their goals, may be vicious in the means employed. The paternalist may deliberately choose to deprive another of some goods, such as those of (licit) freedom and (limited) self-determination in order to obtain other goods for her. Here, as elsewhere, the good end need not justify the unjust means. Extreme paternalism constitutes an instrumentally malevolent benevolence: one harms A to help her. . . .

My account of racism suggests a new understanding of racist behavior and of its immorality. This view allows for the existence of both individual racism and institutional racism. Moreover, it makes clear the connection between the two, and enables us better to understand racism's nature and limits. . . .

Some say that institutional racism is what is of central importance; individual racism, then, matters only inasmuch as it perpetuates institutional racism. I think that claim reverses the order of moral importance, and I shall maintain that the individual level has more explanatory importance.

At the individual level, it is in desires, wishes, intentions, and the like that racism fundamentally lies, not in actions or beliefs. Actions and beliefs are racist by virtue of their *coming from* racism in the desires, wishes, and intentions of individuals, not by virtue of their *leading to* these or other undesirable effects. . . .

How is institutional racism connected to racism within the individual? Let us contrast two pictures. On the first, institutional racism is of prime moral and explanatory importance. Individual racism, then, matters (and, perhaps, occurs) only insofar as it contributes to the institutional racism which subjugates a racial group. On the second, opposed view, racism within individual persons is of prime moral and explanatory import, and institutional racism occurs and matters because racist attitudes (desires, aims, hopes, fears, plans) infect the reasoning, decision-making, and action of individuals not only in their private behavior, but also when they make and execute the policies of those institutions in which they operate. I take the second view. Institutional racism, in the central sense of the term, occurs when institutional behavior stems from (a) or (b) above or, in an extended sense, when it stems from (c). Obvious examples would be the infamous Jim Crow laws that originated in the former Confederacy after Reconstruction. Personal racism exists when and insofar as a person is racist in her desires, plans, aims, etc., most notably when this racism informs her conduct. In the same way, institutional racism exists when and insofar as an institution is racist in the aims, plans, etc., that people give it, especially when their racism informs its behavior. Institutional racism begins when racism extends from the hearts of individual people to become institutionalized. What matters is that racist attitudes contaminate the operation of the institution; it is irrelevant what its original point may have been, what its designers meant it to do. . . .

Not only is individual racism of greater explanatory import, I think it is also more important morally. Those of us who see morality primarily as a matter of suitability responding to other people and to the opportunities they present for us to pursue value will understand racism as an offense against the virtues of benevolence and justice in that it is an undue restriction on the respect and goodwill owed people. (Ourselves as well as others; racism, we must remember, can take the form of self-hate.) Indeed, as follows from what I have elsewhere argued, it is hard to render coherent the view that racist hate is bad mainly for its bad effects. The sense in which an action's effects are bad is that they are undesirable. But that it is to say that these effects are evil things to want and thus things the desire for which is evil, vicious. Thus, any claim that racial disadvantage is a bad thing presupposes a more basic claim that race-hatred is vicious. What is more basic morally is also morally more important in at least one sense of that term. Of course, we should bear in mind that morality is not the same as politics. What is morally most important may not be the problem whose rectification is of greatest political urgency.

IMPLICATIONS AND ADVANTAGES

There are some noteworthy implications and advantages of the proposed way of conceiving of racism.

First it suggests that prejudice, in its strict sense of "pre-judgment," is not essential to racism, and that some racial prejudice may not be racist, strictly speaking. . . .

A person may hold prejudices about people assigned to a race without herself being racist and without it being racist of her to hold those prejudices. The beliefs themselves can be called "racist"

in an extended sense because they are characteristically racist. However, just as one may make a wise move without acting wisely (as when one makes a sound investment for stupid reasons), so one may hold a racist belief without holding it for racist reasons. One holds such a belief for racist reasons when it is duly connected to racial disregard: when it is held in order to rationalize that disaffection or when contempt inclines one to attribute undesirable features to people assigned to a racial group. One whose racist beliefs have no such connection to any racial disregard in her heart does not hold them in a racist way and if she has no such disregard, she is not herself a racist, irrespective of her prejudices.

Second, when racism is so conceived, the person with racist feelings, desires, hopes, fears, and dispositions is racist even if she never acts on these attitudes in such a way as to harm people designated as members of the hated race. (This is not true when racism is conceived as consisting in a system of social oppression.) It is important to know that racism can exist in (and even pervade) societies in which there is no systematic oppression, if only because the attempts to oppress fail. Even those who think racism important primarily because of its effects should find this possibility of inactive racism worrisome for, so long as this latent racism persists, there is constant threat of oppressive behavior.

Third, on this view, race-based preference (favoritism) need not be racist. *Preferential* treatment in affirmative action, while race-based, is not normally based on any racial disregard. This is a crucial difference between James Meredith's complaint against the University of Mississippi and Allan Bakke's complaint against the University of California at Davis Medical School (see Appiah, 1990: p. 15). Appiah says that what he calls "Extrinsic racism has usually been the basis [1] for treating people worse than we otherwise might, [2] for giving them less than their humanity entitles them to" (Appiah, 1992: 18). What is important to note here is that (1) and (2) are not at all morally equivalent. Giving someone less than her humanity entitles her to is morally wrong. To give someone less than we could give her, and even to give her less than we would if she (or we, or things) were different is to treat her "worse [in the sense of 'less well'] than we otherwise might." However, the latter is not normally morally objectionable. Of course, we may not deny people even gratuitous favors out of hatred or contempt, whether or not race-based, but that does not entail that we may not licitly choose to bestow favors instead on those to whom we feel more warmly. That I feel closer to A than I do to B does not mean that I feel hatred or callousness toward B. I may give A more than A has a claim to get from me and more than I give B, while nevertheless giving B everything to which she is entitled (and even more). Thus, race-based favoritism does not have to involve (2) and need not violate morality. . . .

As racist discrimination need not always be conscious, so it need not always be intended to harm. Some of what is called "environmental racism," especially the location of waste dumps so as disproportionally to burden Black people, is normally not intended to harm anyone at all. Nevertheless, it is racist if, for example, the dumpers regard it as less important if it is "only," say, Black people who suffer. However, it will usually be the case that intentional discrimination based on racist attitudes will be more objectionable morally, and harder to justify, than is unintentional, unconscious racist discrimination. Rac*ial* discrimination is not always rac*ist* discrimination. The latter is always immoral, because racism is inherently vicious and it corrupts any differentiation that it infects. The former—racial discrimination—is not inherently immoral. Its moral status will depend on the usual factors—intent, knowledge, motive, and so on—to which we turn to determine what is vicious.

This understanding of racism also offers a new perspective on the controversy over efforts to restrict racist "hate speech." Unlike racially *offensive* speech, which is defined by its (actual or probable) effects, racist *hate* speech is defined by its origins, i.e., by whether it expresses (and is thus an act of) racially directed hate. So we cannot classify a remark as racist hate speech simply on the basis of *what* was said, we need to look to *why* the speaker said it. Speech laden with racial slurs and epithets is presumptively hateful, of course, but merely voicing an opinion that members of R1 are inferior (in

some germane way) will count as racist (in any of the term's chief senses, at least) only if, for example, it expresses an opinion held from the operation of some predisposition to believe bad things about R1s, which predisposition itself stems in part from racial disregard. This understanding of racist hate speech should allay the fears of those who think that racial oversensitivity and the fear of offending the oversensitive will stifle the discussion of delicate and important matters beneath a blanket of what is called "political correctness." Racist hate speech is defined by its motive forces and, given a fair presumption of innocence, it will be difficult to give convincing evidence of ugly motive behind controversial opinions whose statement is free of racial insults.

SOME DIFFICULTIES

It may seem that my view fails to meet the test of accommodating clear cases of racism from history. Consider some members of the southern White aristocracy in the antebellum or Jim Crow periods of American history—people who would never permit racial epithets to escape their lips, and who were solicitous and even protective of those they considered "their Negroes" (especially Black servants and their kin), but who not only acquiesced in, but actively and strongly supported the social system of racial separatism, hierarchy, and oppression. These people strongly opposed Black equality in the social, economic, and political realms, but they appear to have been free of any vehement racial hatred. It appears that we should call such people racist. The question is: Does the account offered here allow them to be so classified?

This presents a nice difficulty, I think, and one it will be illuminating to grapple with. There is, plainly, a kind of hatred that consists in opposition to a person's (or group's) welfare. Hatred is the opposite of love and, as to love someone is to wish her well (i.e., to want and will that she enjoy life and its benefits), so one kind of hatred for her is to wish her ill (i.e., to want and will that she not enjoy them). It is important to remember, however, that not all hatred is wishing another ill for its own sake.

When I take revenge, for example, I act from hate, but I also want to do my enemy ill for a purpose (to get even). So too when I act from envy. (I want to deprive the other of goods in order to keep her from being better off than I, or from being better off than I wish her to be.) I have sometimes talked here about racial "antipathy" ("animosity," "aversion," "hostility," etc.), but I do not mean that the attitude in question has to be especially negative or passionate. Nor need it be notably ill-mannered or crude in its expression. What is essential is that it consists in either opposition to the well-being of people classified as members of the targeted racial group or in a racially based callousness to the needs and interests of such people.

This, I think, gives us what we need in order to see part of what makes our patricians racists, for all their well-bred dispassion and good manners. They stand against the advancement of Black people (as a group, even if they make an exception for "their Negroes"). They are averse to it as such, not merely doing things that have the *side* effect of setting back the interests of Black people. Rather, they *mean* to retard those interests, to keep Black people "in their place" relative to White people. They may adopt this stance of active, conscious, and deliberate hostility to Black welfare either simply to benefit themselves at the expense of Black people or out of the contemptuous belief that, because they are Black, they merit no better. In any event, these aristocrats and their behavior can properly be classified as racist. . . .

It may not be clear how the understanding of racism offered here accommodates the common-sense view that the attitudes, rhetoric, behavior, and representatives of the mindset we might characterize as the "white man's burden" view count as racist. One who holds such a Kiplingesque view (let's call her K) thinks non-Whites ignorant, backward, undisciplined, and generally in need of a tough dose of European "civilizing" in important aspects of their lives. This training in civilization may sometimes be harsh, but it is supposed to be for the good of the "primitive" people. Moreover, it is important, for our purposes, to remember that K may think that, for all their ignorance, lack of discipline and other intellectual and moral failings, individu-

als within the purportedly primitive people may in certain respects, and even on the whole, be moral superiors to certain of their European "civilizers." Thus, Kipling's notorious coda to "Gunga Din."

The matter is a complex one, of course, but I think that, at least in extreme instances, such an approach can be seen to fit the model of racism whose adoption I have urged. What is needed is to attend to and apply our earlier remarks about breaches of respect and the vice of injustice. An important part of respect is recognizing the other as a human like oneself, including treating her like one. There can be extremes of condescension so inordinate they constitute degradation. In such cases, a subject goes beyond more familiar forms of paternalism to demean the other, treating her as utterly irresponsible. Plainly, those who take it upon themselves to conscript mature, responsible, healthy, socialized (and innocent) adults into a regimen of education designed to strip them of all authority over their own lives and make them into "civilized" folk condescend in just this way. This abusive paternalism borders on contempt and it can violate the rights of the subjugated people by denying them the respect and deference to which their status entitles them. By willfully depriving the oppressed people of the goods of freedom even as part of an ultimately well-meant project of "improving" them, the colonizers act with the kind of instrumentally malevolent benevolence we discussed above. The colonizers stunt and maim in order to help, and therein plainly will certain evils to the victims they think of as beneficiaries. Thus, their conduct counts as a kind of malevolence insofar as we take the term literally to mean willing evils.

Of course, the Kiplinesque agent will not think of herself as depriving responsible, socialized people of their rights over their lives; she does not see them that way and thinks them too immature to have such rights. However, we need to ask why she regards Third World peoples as she does. Here, I suspect, the answer is likely to be that her view of them is influenced, quite possibly without her being conscious of it, by her interest in maintaining the social and economic advantages of having her group wield control over its subjects. If so, her beliefs are relevantly motivated and affected by (instrumental) ill-will, her desire to gain by harming others. When this is so, then her beliefs are racist not just in the weak sense that their content is the sort that characteristically is tied to racial disaffection, but in the stronger and morally more important sense that her own acceptance of these beliefs is partially motivated by racial disaffection. She is *being* racist in thinking as she does. I conclude that the account of racism offered here can allow that, and help explain why, many people who hold the "white man's burden" mentality are racist, indeed, why they may be racist in several different (but connected) ways. . . .

SOME CASES . . .

What should we say of some different cases . . . in which a person who herself harbors no racial disregard or disrespect, nonetheless accedes to others' racism by refusing to hire, promote, or serve those assigned to a targeted racial group? Here the agent's action is infected, poisoned by racial hatred. It has such hate in its motivational structure, and that is the usual hallmark of racist behavior. I think what crucially distinguishes this agent's behavior is that it is not *the agent's own* hatred. I suggest that in addition to the two forms of racial disaffection we have already identified—the core concept of racial malevolence and the derivative concept of a race-based insufficiency of good-will—we can allow that an action may be called racist in an extended sense of the term when it is poisoned by racism, even where the racial disaffection that corrupts it does not lie in the agent's own heart but in those to whom the agent accedes. Thus, the agent in our example, while not herself a racist, performs an action that is in an important way infected by other people's racism. I doubt we should simply say without qualification that her own action is racist, but it is surely morally objectionable. . . . Consider a person who denies service, or promotion, or admission, or employment to people assigned to group G1 in order to appease people with a racial disaffection directed against them. Now suppose further that she herself cooperates in the latter's malevolence by *trying* to harm those classified as G1s in

order to placate their enemies. (This would be a form of what moral theologians have called "formal cooperation.") When the agent goes that far, she has internalized racist malice into her own intentions, and thus corrupted her actions in a more grievous way than has the person who merely goes along with neighboring racists in her external actions. This is so whether or not her *feelings* toward people assigned to G1 are hostile.

What should we say of a case Judith Lichtenberg raises, in which, acting from racial fear, a White person crosses the street to avoid Black pedestrians she perceives as possible dangers? Lichtenberg thinks it acceptable for the fearful (and prejudiced?) White person to cross the street in order to avoid proximity with the Black teenagers who approach her at night ([1992] p. 4). She sensibly suggests that this is not racist if the person would respond in the same way with White teenagers. "She might well do the same if the teenagers were white. In that case her behavior does not constitute racial discrimination." (Of course, her behavior now raises a question of age discrimination, but, like Lichtenberg, I will not pursue that topic.) Helpfully, Lichtenberg cites several factors she thinks relevant to deciding when it is unjust to take race into account. How much harm does the victim suffer? How much does the agent stand to suffer if she does not discriminate? Is the person who discriminates acting in a public or official capacity?

Lichtenberg maintains that the Black teenagers suffer "a minimal slight—if it's even noticed." She even suggests that the White person might spare their feelings "by a display of ulterior motivation, like [pretending to] inspect the rosebushes on the other side" of the street in order to make it look as if it were her admiration for the flowers, and not her fear of Black people, that motivated her to cross the street. The latter pretense is, in my judgment, insulting and unlikely to succeed. More important, this appears to be a guilty response, as if the person is trying to cover up something she knows is wrong. I think that fact should cause Lichtenberg and her imagined agent to reconsider the claim that the action is unobjectionable. It is also quite wrongheaded to think that the harm of insult is entirely a matter of whether a person has hurt feelings. Does it make a difference that the victims suffer little direct and tangible harm? Some, but not much. After all, by that criterion, egregiously racist behavior such as engaging in caricatures or telling jokes that mock Black people would be justified if done in an all-White setting.

According to Lichtenberg, it is acceptable for the White woman to try to avoid the Black teenager on the street, but much harder to justify her racially discriminating when he applies for a job. It will be difficult to maintain this position, however. How is this woman—so terrified of contact with young Black males that she will not walk on the same side of the street with them—simply to turn off this uneasiness when the time comes for her to decide whether to offer a job to the Black male? Suppose that the job is to help out in her family's grocery store, and that this is likely to mean that the woman and the teenager will be alone in the store some evenings? Lichtenberg's advice that the woman indulge her prejudice in her private life but rigorously exclude it from their official conduct, seems unstable. Indeed, Lichtenberg seems to assume that the woman can take refuge in bureaucracy, that she will be the personnel officer who does the hiring, while it is other people who will actually have to work in proximity with the new employee. It is the worst of liberal bad faith, however, for this woman to practice her tolerance in official decision-making, but only on the condition that it is other people who will have to bear the burden of adjusting to the pluralistic environment those decisions create and of making that environment work. (Compare the liberal politician who boldly integrates the public schools while taking care to "protect" her own kids in all-White private schools.)

Lichtenberg assumes that private discrimination is less serious morally, but this is doubtful. The heart is where racism, like all immorality, begins and dwells. Even if some moral *virtue*-traits were differentially distributed along racial lines (and even if that were for genetic rather than historical reasons), each individual would still retain the right to be given the benefit of the probability that she is *not* herself specially inclined toward vice. Of course, this sort of racial discrimination need not be racist, since it can be entirely unconnected to any racial

disaffection, just as it may not be irrational if it is a response to a genuine statistical disparity in risk. (Similarly, there need be nothing immoral in age-based discrimination should the woman seek to avoid being on dark streets alone with teenagers but not with the elderly.) Nevertheless, such conduct runs substantial risk of reinforcing some of the ugly racial stereotypes that are used to rationalize racial antipathy, and there is reason to avoid relying upon it.

Our view of institutional racism is both narrower and wider than some others that have been offered. To see how it is narrower, that is, less inclusive, let us consider the practice of "word-of-mouth" job-recruitment, in which people assigned to a privileged racial group, who tend to socialize only with one another, distribute special access to employment benefits to social acquaintances similarly assigned. Some deem this institutional racism, because of its adverse impact on those considered members of the disadvantaged group. . . .

Consider . . . the so-called "old boy network." Person F, upon hearing of an opening at his place of employment, tells the people he thinks of (who are all White males like himself) about the job and recommends one of them (Person G) to the boss, who hires him. Ignoring the exaggeration in calling anything so informal an "institution," let us explore whether this "institution" of the "old boy network" is racist. Is F (or F's behavior) racist? Is G (or G's behavior) racist? Some are ready to offer affirmative answers. What should we say? First, G cannot be racist just for receiving the job; that's not sufficiently active. What about G's act of *accepting* the job? That can be racist. I think, however, that it is racist only in the exceptional circumstance where the institutions are so corrupt that G should have nothing to do with them. Second, F may be racist insofar as his mental process skips over some possible candidates simply because the stereotypes he uses (perhaps to mask his racial disaffection from himself and others) keep him from thinking of them as possible job candidates. Third, one needs some further reason not yet given to label racist the practice of the "old boy network." It may work "systematically" to the detriment of Black people. That, however, merely shows that, in our society, with our history of racism, Black people can be disadvantaged by many things other than race-based factors. . . . What is important to note is that it is misleading to call all these things racist, because that terminology fails to differentiate the very different ways in which and reasons for which they disadvantage people. This classification and broad use of the term, then, fails adequately to inform us and, of more practical importance, it fails to direct our attention (and efforts) to the source of the difficulty. It doesn't identify for us *how* things are going wrong and thus *what* needs to be changed.

Some accounts of institutional racism threaten to be excessively broad in other ways. Some implicitly restrict institutional racism to operations *within* a society—they see it as one group maintaining its social control over the other. This is too narrow, since it would exclude, for example, what seem to be some clear cases of institutional racism, such as discrimination in immigration and in foreign assistance policies. However, if this restriction to intragroup behavior is simply removed from these accounts, then they will have to count as instances of institutional racism some actions which do not properly fall within the class. Suppose, for example, the government of a hostile planet, free of any bigotry toward any Earthling racial group, but unenamored of all Earthlings, launches a missile to destroy the Earth. Suppose it lands in Africa. This institutional (governmental) action has a disproportionally adverse impact on Black people, but it is silly to describe it as racist. (It remains silly even if the aliens decide to target *all* their attacks on the same continent—say, because of size or subterranean mineral deposits make it easier for their tracking systems to locate—and the effect thus becomes "systematic.") Talk of racism here is inane because the action, its motivation, and its agents are entirely untainted by any racial disaffection or prejudice. By the same token, however, although the agents of many earthly institutions *are* tainted by racism (e.g., in the U.S. government), that fact cannot suffice, even in combination with adverse impacts, to make its actions institutionally racist. The racism has first to *get into* the institutional conduct somehow by informing the conduct of individual agents. In contrast, proponents of expansive accounts of insti-

tutional racism, by focusing on the action's effects, end up in the untenable position of claiming that racism somehow *comes out of* institutional behavior, while simultaneously denying that it must ever even get into the action at the action's source in the aims, beliefs, desires, hopes, fears, and so on of the agents who execute institutional policy.

We can also profitably turn our account to an interesting case Skillen offers. He writes:

> Suppose Dr. Smythe-Browne's surgery has been ticking over happily for years until it is realized that few of the many local Asians visit him. It turns out that they travel some distance to Dr. Patel's surgery. Dr. Smythe-Browne and his staff are upset. Then they realize that, stupidly, he has never taken the trouble to make himself understood by or to understand the Asians in his area. His surgery practices have had the effect of excluding or at least discouraging Asians. Newly aware, he sets out to fix the situation.
>
> By the same token as his practices have been "consequentially," not "constitutively" discriminatory, they have been "blind," lacking in awareness.
>
> The example shows the possibility of a certain sort of "racism" that, if we must attribute blame, is a function of a lack of thought (energy, resources, etc.). If that lack of thought is itself to be described as "discriminatory" it would need to be shown Dr. Smythe-Browne showed no such lack of attention when one of the local streets became gentrified. . . . In such cases, it is not racial sets as such that are the focus of attention, but race as culturally 'inscribed'. In other words, one is concerned with people in respect of how they identify themselves and are identified by others (for example, intimidating institutions or outright racists). (Skillen [1993], p. 81)

Despite what Skillen implies, that an institution intimidates some racial groups ("sets") does not make it racist. Flew is right about the insufficiency (even the irrelevance) of mere effects to establish racism, as he is right about the sufficiency of racism to establish immorality. Otherwise, the interplanetary attacks in our earlier example would count as instances of institutional racism. Moreover, that Smythe-Browne was thoughtless about what might be needed to attract Asians in no way shows his conduct was racist, not even if he was more sensitive and interested in how to attract "yuppies" brought close by local gentrification. Insensitivity to certain race-related differences is not racist, even if one is sensitive to class-related differences or to differences associated with other racial differences. Smythe-Browne does not so much "discourage" Asians as fail to encourage them. Psychologically and ontologically, that is a very different matter, and those differences are likely to correlate with moral differences as well. (Failure to encourage is likely merely to be at worst an offense of *non*benevolence rather of *male*volence.) *Perhaps* the Asians were "invisible" to Smythe-Browne in a way that he is culpable for. To show this, however, more would need to be said about why he did not notice them, their absence, and their special interests. Is it that he cares so little about Asians and their well-being? If there is nothing like this involved, then there is no racism in Smythe-Browne's professional behavior, I say. And if there is something like this involved, then Smythe-Browne's conduct is not purely "'consequentially' . . . discriminatory." It is corrupted by its motivation in racial disaffection. . . .

Skillen . . . adds further detail to his case, asking us to suppose that Dr. Smythe-Browne "decides that the only way to cope with the situation is to get an Asian doctor, preferably female, onto the staff. He advertises the job and, finding a good person of the sort he needs, she joins the practice, whereas a number of, in other respects at least, equally good applicants (white, male for the most part) do not. Is this 'racism'?" Skillen thinks not, and I think he argues his point well. . . . "Dr. Smythe-Browne's criteria remain medical. His selection is legitimate insofar as we accept that medicine is a human and communicative 'art' in respect of which socially significant variables are relevant. In that sense it is simply not the case that bypassed candidates with better degree results were necessarily 'better candidates'" (Skillen [1993], p. 82).

With this understanding and assessment, I agree wholeheartedly. Dr. Smythe-Browne's hiring prefer-

ence here seems to me to exemplify the sort of race-based distinction that is in its nature and its morality quite different from racist discrimination. . . .

Skillen is correct to observe that oftentimes institutions shape individual intentions and actions. Institutional racism will often exist in reciprocal relation to individual racism. The racism of some individual (or individuals) first infects the institution, and the institution's resultant racism then reinforces racism in that individual or breeds it in others. Once individual racism exists, institutional racism can be a powerful instrument of its perpetuation. This reciprocity of casual influence, however, should not blind us to the question of origins. Individual racism can come into the world without depending on some prior institutionalization. (It could come to be, say, as a result of some twist in one person's temperament.) The converse is not true. Institutional racism can reinforce and perpetuate individual racism. Unless an institution is corrupted (in its ends, means, priorities, or assumptions) by a prior and independent racism in some individual's heart, however, institutional racism can never come to exist.

Nevertheless, we should take care not to overstate the dependence of institutional racism upon individuals. Institutional racism appears to be capable of continuing after individual racism has largely died out. Think of a case where, for example, officials continue, uncomprehendingly, to implement policies originally designed, and still functioning, to disadvantage those assigned to a certain racial group. Indeed, I strongly doubt that the qualifier "and still functioning" is necessary. Institutional racism can exist without actually functioning to harm anyone. Suppose, a few generations back, some R1s designed a certain institutional procedure P specifically to harm R2s, an oppressed racial group, though the designers were never explicit about this aim. Later, anti-R2 feeling among R1s faded away, and in time real social equality was achieved. The R1s, however, are a traditionalist lot, and they continue faithfully to execute P out of deference to custom and their ancestors. P no longer specially harms R2s. (Perhaps it excludes from various privileges those who come from some specific, traditionally poor R2 neighborhoods, and

R2s are no longer disproportionally represented in those neighborhoods, which, perhaps, are also no longer disproportionally poor.)

In that case, it appears that the racism of the earlier generation persists in the institutional procedure P, even though P no longer specially harms R2s. This indicates that institutional racism, no less than individual racism, can be either effective or ineffective, either harmful or innocuous. Institutional racism, then, is a bad thing; but it is a bad thing not because of its actual effects, but sometimes merely because of its aims. The study of people's aims directs the social theorist's attention to their hearts, to what they care about, to what they have set themselves on having, or being, or making, or doing. Such is the stuff of the moral virtues, of course. Neither the social theorist nor the moral theorist can continue to neglect them if she wishes to understand the world. Or to change it.

CONCLUSION

These reflections suggest that an improved understanding of racism and its immorality calls for a comprehensive rethinking of racial discrimination, of the preferential treatment programs sometimes disparaged as "reverse discrimination," and of institutional conduct as well. They also indicate the direction such a rethinking should take, and its dependence on the virtues and other concepts from moral psychology. That may require a significant change in the way social philosophers have recently treated these and related topics.

REFERENCES

Appiah, Anthony. "Racisms." In *Anatomy of Racism*, pp. 3–17. Ed. D. T. Goldberg. Minneapolis: University of Minnesota Press, 1990.

——. *In My Father's House: Africa in the Philosophy of Culture.* Oxford: Oxford University Press, 1992.

Blum, Lawrence. "Antiracism, Multiculturalism, and Interracial Community: Three Educational Values for a Multicultural Society." Office of Graduate Studies and Research, University of Massachusetts at Boston, 1991.

Lichtenberg, Judith. "Racism in the Head, Racism in the World." *Philosophy and Public Policy* (Newsletter of the Institute for Philosophy and Public Policy, University of Maryland), Vol. 12 (1992).

Nathanson, Stephen. "Is Patriotism Like Racism?" *APA Newsletter on Philosophy and the Black Experience* 91 (1992): 9–11.

Piper, Adrian M. "Higher Order Discrimination." In *Identity, Character, & Morality,* pp. 285–309. Ed. Owen Flanagan and Amelie Rorty. Cambridge: MIT Press, 1990.

Skillen, Anthony. "Racism: Flew's Three Concepts of Racism." *Journal of Applied Philosophy.* vol. 10 (1993): 73–89.

Discussion Questions

1. Do you agree with Garcia's definition of a racist? According to Garcia's definition, does being a nonracist necessarily entail white people lowering the standards for their children's educations so that nonwhite children can get a better education? Are white people who take advantage of better schools in affluent white neighborhoods racist by definition? Are people who oppose state or federal (instead of local) funding for schools racists? Support your answers.

2. According to Garcia, people who act in ways that retard the interests of blacks, even though they claim to feel no ill will toward them, are racist. Do you agree? Illustrate your answer using affirmative action as an example.

3. Discuss ways in which your actions may be infected by racism even though you yourself may bear no ill will or racial hatred. Use specific examples to illustrate your answer.

4. Do you agree with Lichtenberg that private discrimination is less serious than public discrimination? Compare and contrast Lichtenberg's and Garcia's analyses of the

white woman crossing the street to avoid the black teenager. Which person do you think provides the best analysis? Support your answers.

5. Discuss ways in which the "old boy network" advantages whites and disadvantages blacks and other minorities on your campus. Use specific examples to illustrate your answer.

6. In the Smythe-Browne case study, Garcia argues that the fact that some racial groups are intimidated by an institution does not necessarily make it a racist institution. Do you agree? Discuss you answer in light of Steele's description of minority experience and in light of certain college institutions such as the Greek system.

7. Discuss the implications of Garcia's analysis of racism for affirmative action. What type of affirmative action, if any, might Garcia support? Discuss, in particular, how Garcia might respond to affirmative action in college admissions.

8. Garcia claims that his definition of racism is better than others at explaining interracial antagonism. In the United States, there is often antagonism among minority groups. Following the 1992 Rodney King verdict, riots broke out in Los Angeles among blacks, Hispanics, and Koreans. More than twelve thousand arrests were made in one week. Property damage was estimated at $400 million. Koreans suffered the most damage at the hands of rioters, with more than a thousand Korean-owned businesses burned or looted. Discuss whether Garcia's definition of racism accounts for this type of violence among minorities.

 BERNARD R. BOXILL

The Color-Blind Principle

Bernard Boxill is a philosophy professor at the University of North Carolina in Chapel Hill. Boxill rejects the assumption that law and morality should always be color-blind. Whereas some color-conscious policies, such as Jim Crow laws, are clearly unjust, there are other times, he argues, when it is morally justified to base public policy on color-conscious principles. Discrimination is not necessarily unjust. As with differences in talent, differences in color can sometimes justly be considered in circumstances such as hiring.

Critical Reading Questions

1. Who was Homer Plessy and why was he arrested in 1892? On what grounds did Plessy defend his actions? What was the U.S. Supreme Court ruling on the Plessy case?

2. What did Justice John Marshall Harlan mean when he said, "Our Constitution is color-blind"?

3. Why do some liberals maintain that the "I didn't notice" kind of color-blindness is a worthy ideal?

"The Color-Blind Principle," in *Blacks and Social Justice* (Totowa, N.J.: Rowman & Allanheld, 1984), 9–18. Some notes have been omitted.

4. What is the essence of a color-conscious policy and what are some examples of such policies?
5. What are the main arguments used by advocates of the color-blind principle?
6. What is the difference between the racist's and the black nationalist's view on the importance of color? Why, as Boxill notes, do some people say that the slogan *Black is beautiful* rings hollow?
7. What is the "responsibility criterion" and how is it used to support legal color-blind policies? Why does Boxill claim that this can be a false and confusing criterion for creating egalitarian public policies?
8. According to Boxill, why does the fact that race is arbitrary and not freely chosen make color-blind policies unjust?
9. Why does racial discrimination subordinate the best interests of minority communities?
10. According to Boxill, why are color-conscious principles no less discriminatory than the principles of meritocracy?
11. On what grounds does Boxill argue that "adopting a color-blind principle entails adopting a talent-blind principle"? How does Boxill use this argument to support his conclusion that color-conscious policies can be just?
12. How does Boxill respond to the objection that affirmative action leads to reverse discrimination against whites?

PLESSY

In 1892, Homer Plessy, an octoroon, was arrested in Louisiana for taking a seat in a train car reserved for whites. He was testing a state law which required the "white and colored races" to ride in "equal but separate" accommodations, and his case eventually reached the Supreme Court.

Part of Plessy's defense, though it must be considered mainly a snare for the opposition, was that he was "seven-eighths Caucasian and one-eighth African blood," and that the "mixture of colored blood was not discernible in him." The bulwark of his argument was, however, that he was "entitled to every right, privilege and immunity secured to citizens of the white race," and that the law violated the Fourteenth Amendment's prohibition against unequal protection of the laws. Cannily, the court refused the snare. Perhaps it feared—and with reason—that the ancestry of too many white Louisianans held dark secrets. But it attacked boldly enough Plessy's main argument that the Louisiana law was unconstitutional. That argument, Justice Henry Billings Brown wrote for the majority, was

unsound. "Its underlying fallacy," he averred, was its "assumption that the enforced separation of the two races stamps the colored race with a badge of inferiority." "If this be so," Brown concluded, "it is not by reason of anything found in the act, but solely because the colored race chooses to put that construction upon it."

Only one judge dissented from the court majority—Justice John Marshall Harlan. It was the occasion on which he pronounced his famous maxim: "Our Constitution is color-blind." In opposition to Justice Brown, Justice Harlan found that the "separation of citizens on the basis of race [was a] badge of servitude . . . wholly inconsistent [with] equality before the law."

Plessy's is the kind of case which makes the color-blind principle seem indubitably right as a basis for action and policy, and its contemporary opponents appear unprincipled, motivated by expediency, and opportunistic. This impression is only strengthened by a reading of Justice Brown's tortuously preposterous defense of the "equal but separate" doctrine. It should make every advocate of color-conscious policy wary of the power of arguments of expediency to beguile moral sense and subvert logic. Yet I argue that color-conscious policy can still be justified. The belief that it cannot is the result of a mistaken generalization from *Plessy*. There is no warrant for the idea that the color-blind principle should hold in some general and absolute way.

"I DIDN'T NOTICE" LIBERALS

In his book *Second Wind*, Bill Russell recalls how amazed he used to be by the behavior of what he called "I didn't notice" liberals. These were individuals who claimed not to notice people's color. If they mentioned someone Russell could not place, and Russell asked whether she was black or white, they would answer, "I didn't notice." "Sweet and innocent," Russell recalls, "sometimes a little proud." Now, the kind of color-blindness the "I didn't notice" liberals claim to have may be a worthy ideal—Richard Wasserstrom, for example, argues that society should aim toward it—but it is absolutely different from the color-blind principle which functions as a basis for policy. Thus, while Wasserstrom supports color-conscious policies to secure the ideal of people not noticing each others' color, the principle of color-blindness in the law opposes color-conscious policies and does not necessarily involve any hope that people will not notice each others' color. Its thesis is simple: that no *law* or *public policy* be designed to treat people differently because they are of a different color.

COLOR-BLIND AND COLOR-CONSCIOUS POLICIES

The essential thing about a color-conscious policy is that it is designed to treat people differently because of their race. But there are many different kinds of color-conscious policies. Some, for example the Jim Crow policies now in the main abolished, aim to subordinate blacks, while others, such as busing and preferential treatment, aim at elevating blacks.

Some color-conscious policies explicitly state that persons should be treated differently because of their race, for example the segregation laws at issue in *Plessy;* others make no mention of race, but are still designed so that blacks and whites are treated differently, for example, the "grandfather clauses" in voting laws that many states adopted at the turn of the century. . . .

Advocates of the belief that the law should be color-blind often argue that this would the best means to an ideal state in which people are color-blind. They appeal to the notion that, only if people notice each other's color can they discriminate on the basis of color and, with considerable plausibility, they argue that color-conscious laws and policies can only heighten people's awareness of each other's color, and exacerbate racial conflict. They maintain that only if the law, with all its weight and influence, sets the example of color-blindness, can there be a realistic hope that people will see through the superficial distinctions of color and become themselves color-blind.

But this argument is not the main thesis of the advocates of legal color-blindness. Generally, they eschew it because of its dependency on the empirical. Their favorite argument, one that is more direct and intuitively appealing, is simply that it is wicked, unfair, and unreasonable to penalize a person for what he cannot help being. Not only does this seem undeniably true, but it can be immediately applied to the issue of race. No one can help being white or being black, and so it seems to follow that it is wicked, unfair, and unreasonable to disqualify a person from any consideration just because he is white or black. This, the advocates of color-blindness declare, is what made Jim Crow law heinous, and it is what makes affirmative action just as heinous.

The force of this consideration is enhanced because it seems to account for one peculiar harmfulness of racial discrimination—its effect on self-respect and self-esteem. For racial discrimination makes some black people hate their color, and succeeds in doing so because color cannot be changed. Furthermore, a racially conscious society has made color seem an important part of the individual's very essence, and since color is immutable it is easily susceptible to this approach. As a result, the black individual may come, in the end, to hate even himself. . . . The black nationalist agrees with the racists' view that his color is an important and integral part of his self, but affirms, in opposition to the racists, that it has value. This strategy, which is exemplified by the slogans "black is beautiful" and "black and proud," has the obvious advantage of stimulating pride and self-confidence. Nevertheless, it is no panacea. For one thing, it has to contend with the powerful propaganda stating that black is *not* beautiful. And there is a more subtle problem. Since the black cannot choose *not* to be black, he cannot be altogether confident that he would choose to *be* black, nor, consequently, does he really place a special value in being black. Thus, some people, black and white, have expressed the suspicion that the slogan "black is beautiful" rings hollow, like the words of the man who protests too loudly that he loves the chains he cannot escape. In this respect the black who can pass as white has an advantage over the black who cannot. For, though he cannot choose not to be black, he can choose not to be *known* to be black.

THE RESPONSIBILITY CRITERION

A final argument in favor of legal color-blindness is related to, and further develops, the point that people do not choose to be, and cannot avoid being, black or white. This links the question of color-blindness to the protean idea of individual responsibility. Thus, William Frankena writes, that to use color as a fundamental basis for distributing "opportunities, offices, etc." to persons is "unjust in itself," because it is to distribute goods on the basis of a feature "which the individual has not done, and can do nothing about; we are treating people differently in ways that profoundly affect their lives because of differences for which they have no responsibility."[1] Since this argument requires that people be treated differently in ways which profoundly affect their lives only on the basis of features for which they are responsible, I call it the responsibility criterion.

The responsibility criterion also seems to make the principle of color-blindness follow from principles of equal opportunity. Joel Feinberg takes it to be equivalent to the claim that "properties can be the grounds of just discrimination between persons only if those persons had a fair opportunity to acquire or avoid them."[2] This implies that to discriminate between persons on the basis of a feature for which they can have no responsibility is to violate the principle of fair opportunity. But color (or sex) is a feature of persons for which they can have no responsibility.

The responsibility criterion may seem innocuous because, though, strictly interpreted it supports the case for color-blindness, loosely interpreted it leaves open the possibility that color-conscious policies are justifiable. Thus, Frankena himself allows that color could be an important basis of distribution of goods and offices if it served "as [a] reliable sign[s] of some Q, like ability or merit, which is more justly employed as a touchstone for the treatment of individuals."[3] This sounds like a reasonable compromise and is enough to support some arguments for color-conscious policies. For example, it could support the argument that black and white children should go to the same schools because being white is a reliable sign of being middle-class, and black children, who are often lower-class, learn better when their peers are middle-class. Similarly, it might support the argument that preferential hiring is compensation for the harm of being discriminated against on the basis of color, and that being black is a reliable sign of having been harmed by that discrimination.

But however loosely it is interpreted, the responsibility criterion cannot be adduced in support of all reasons behind color-conscious policies. It cannot, for example, sustain the following argument, sketched by Ronald Dworkin, for preferential admission of blacks to medical school. "If quick hands count as 'merit' in the case of a prospective surgeon this is because quick hands will enable him to serve the public better and for no other reason. If a black skin will, as a matter of regrettable fact, enable another doctor to do a different medical job better, then that black skin is by the same token 'merit' as well."[4] What is proposed here is not that a black skin is a justifiable basis of discrimination because it is a reliable sign of merit or some other factor Q. A closely related argument does make such a proposal, viz., that blacks should be preferentially admitted to medical school because being black is a reliable sign of a desire to serve the black community. But this is not the argument that Dworkin poses. In the example quoted above what he suggests is that being black is in *itself* merit, or, at least, something very like merit.

According to the responsibility criterion, we ought not to give A a job in surgery rather than B, if A is a better surgeon than B only because he was born with quicker hands. For if we do, we treat A and B "differently in ways that profoundly affect their lives because of differences for which they have no responsibility." This is the kind of result which puts egalitarianism in disrepute. It entails the idea that we might be required to let fumblers do surgery and in general give jobs and offices to incompetents, and this is surely intolerable. But, as I plan to show, true egalitarianism has no such consequences. They are the result of applying the responsibility criterion, not egalitarian principles. Indeed, egalitarianism must scout the responsibility criterion as false and confused.

Egalitarians should notice first that, while it invalidates the merit-based theories of distribution that they oppose, it also invalidates the need-based theories of distribution they favor. For, if people are born with special talents for which they are not responsible, they are also born with special needs for which they are not responsible. Consequently, if the responsibility criterion forbids choosing A over B to do surgery because A is a better surgeon because he was born with quicker hands, it also forbids choosing C rather than D for remedial education because C needs it more than D only because he was born with a learning disability and D was not.

At this point there may be objections. First, that the responsibility criterion was intended to govern only the distribution of income, not jobs and offices—in Feinberg's discussion, for example, this is made explicit. Second, that it does not mean that people should not be treated differently because of differences, good or bad, which they cannot help, but rather that people should not get less just because they are born without the qualities their society prizes or finds useful. This seems to be implied in Frankena's claim that justice should make the "same proportionate contribution to the best life for everyone" and that this may require spending more on those who are "harder to help"—probably the untalented—than on others. Qualified in these ways, the responsibility criterion becomes more plausible. It no longer implies, for example, that fumblers should be allowed to practice surgery, or that the blind be treated just like the sighted. But with these qualifications it also becomes almost irrelevant to the color-blind issue. For that issue is not only about how income should be distributed. It is also about how jobs and offices should be distributed.

Most jobs and offices are distributed to people in order to produce goods and services to a larger public. To that end, the responsibility criterion is irrelevant. For example, the purpose of admitting people to medical schools and law schools is to provide the community with good medical and legal service. It does not matter whether those who provide them are responsible for having the skills by virtue of which they provide the goods, or whether the positions they occupy are "goods" to them. No just society makes a person a surgeon just because he is responsible for his skills or because making him a surgeon will be good for him. It makes him a surgeon because he will do good surgery.

Accordingly, it may be perfectly just to discriminate between persons on the basis of distinctions they are not responsible for having. It depends on whether or not the discrimination serves a worthy end. It may be permissible for the admissions policies of professional schools to give preference to those with higher scores, even if their scores are higher than others only because they have higher native ability (for which they cannot, of course, be considered responsible), if the object is to provide the community with good professional service. And, given the same object, if for some reason a black skin, whether or not it can be defined as merit, helps a black lawyer or doctor to provide good legal or medical service to black people who would otherwise not have access to it, or avail themselves of it, it is difficult to see how there can be a principled objection to admissions policies which prefer people with black skins—though, again, they are not responsible for the quality by virtue of which they are preferred.

JUSTICE AND THE RESPONSIBILITY CRITERION

A further point needs to be made in order to vindicate color-conscious policies. The principles of justice are distributive: Justice is concerned not only with increasing the total amount of a good a society enjoys, but also with how that good should be distributed among individuals. Generally, judicial principles dictate that people who are similar in ways deemed relevant to the issue of justice, such as in needs or rights, should get equal amounts of a good, and people who are dissimilar in these regards should get unequal amounts of the good. In terms of these principles certain laws and rules must be considered unjust which would not otherwise be thought unjust. Consider, for example, a policy for admitting persons to medical school which resulted in better and better medical service for white people, but worse and worse medical service for black people. This policy would be unjust, however great the medical expertise—certainly a good—it produced, unless color is relevant to the receiving of good medical attention.

In a case like this, where it is not, the theoretical circumstance outlined by Dworkin, in which black skin might be considered a "merit," becomes viable. It is true, of course, that color is not, precisely, merit. But to insist on strict definition in this context is to cavil. The point is that if black clients tend to trust and confide more in black lawyers and doctors, then color—functioning as merit—enables a good to be produced and distributed according to some principle of justice.

If these considerations are sound, then the responsibility criterion thoroughly misconstrues the reasons for which racial discrimination is unjust.

Racial discrimination against blacks is unjust because it does not enable goods to be produced and distributed according to principles of justice. It is not unjust because black people do not choose to be black, cannot *not* be black, or are not responsible for being black. This is completely irrelevant. For example, a policy denying university admission to people who parted their hair on the right side would be unjust because the way in which people part their hair is irrelevant to a just policy of school admission. It does not matter in the least, in relation to the nature and object of education, that they choose how they part their hair. Similarly, even if black people could choose to become white, or could all easily pass as white, a law school or medical school that excluded blacks because they were black would still act unjustly. Nothing would have changed.

The arguments in support of color-blindness tend to make the harmfulness of discrimination depend on the difficulty of avoiding it. This is misleading. It diverts attention from the potential harmfulness of discrimination that *can* be avoided and brings the specious responsibility criterion into play. Suppose again, for example, that a person is denied admission to law school because he parts his hair on the right side. Though he, far more easily than the black person, can avoid being unfairly discriminated *against,* he does not thereby more easily avoid being the object, indeed, in a deeper sense, the victim, of unfair discrimination. If he parts his hair on the left side he will presumably be admitted to law school. But then he will have knowingly complied with a foolish and unjust rule and this may well make him expedient and servile. Of course, he will not be harmed to the same extent and in the same way as the victim of racial discrimination. For example, he probably will not hate himself. Unlike color, the cause of his ill-treatment is too easily changed for him to conceive of it as essential to himself. Moreover, if he chooses to keep his hair parted on the right side and thus to forego law school, he *knows* that he is not going to law school because he freely chose to place a greater value on his integrity or on his taste in hairstyles than on a legal education. He knows this because he knows he could have chosen to change his hairstyle. As I noted earlier, this opportunity for self-assertion, and thus for self-knowledge and self-confidence, is denied the black who is discriminated against on the basis of his color.

Nevertheless, as I stated earlier, the considerations that stem from applying the responsibility criterion to a judgment of racial discrimination are secondary to understanding its peculiar harmfulness. Suppose, for example, that a person is not admitted to medical school to train to be a surgeon because he was born without fingers. If all the things he wants require that he have fingers, he may conceivably come to suffer the same self-hatred and self-doubt as the victim of racial discrimination. Yet his case is different, and if he attends to the difference, he will not suffer as the victim of racial discrimination suffers. The discrimination that excludes him from the practice of surgery is not denigrating his interests because they are his. It is a policy that takes into account a just object—the needs of others in the community for competent surgery. Allowing him to be a surgeon would rate other, equally important, interests below his. But racial discrimination excludes its victims from opportunities on the basis of a belief that their interests are ipso facto less important than the interests of whites. The man without fingers may regret not being born differently, but he cannot resent how he is treated. Though his ambitions may be thwarted, he himself is still treated as a moral equal. There is no attack on his self-respect. Racial discrimination, however, undermines its victims' self-respect through their awareness that they are considered morally inferior. The fact that racial discrimination, or any color-conscious policy, is difficult to avoid through personal choice merely adds to its basic harmfulness if it is in the first place unjust, but is not the *reason* for its being unjust.

It remains to consider Feinberg's claim that if people are discriminated for or against on the basis of factors for which they are not responsible the equal opportunity principle is contravened. This I concede. In particular, I concede that color-conscious policies giving preference to blacks place an insurmountable obstacle in the path of whites, and since such obstacles reduce opportunities, such policies may make opportunities unequal. But this gives no advantage to the advocates of color-blind policies. For giving preference to the competent has exactly the same implications as giving preference to blacks. It, too, places obstacles in the paths of some people, this time the untalented, and just as surely makes opportunities unequal. Consequently, an advocate of color-blindness cannot consistently oppose color-conscious policies on the grounds that they contravene equal opportunity and at the same time support talent-conscious policies. Nor, finally, does my concession raise any further difficulty with the issue of equal opportunity. As I argue later, equal opportunity is not a fundamental principle of justice, but is derived from its basic principles. Often these basic principles require that opportunities be made more equal. Invariably, however, these same principles require that the process of equalization stop before a condition of perfect equality of opportunity is reached.

To conclude, adopting a color-blind principle entails adopting a talent-blind principle, and since the latter is absurd, so also is the former. Or, in other words, differences in talent, and differences in color, are, from the point of view of justice, on a par. Either, with equal propriety, can be the basis of a just discrimination. Consequently, the color-blind principle is not as simple, straightforward, or self-evident as many of its advocates seem to feel it is. Color-conscious policies can conceivably be just, just as talent-conscious policies can conceivably be—and often are—just. It depends on the circumstances.

NOTES

1. William Frankena, "Some Beliefs About Justice," in *Justice,* ed. Joel Feinberg and Hyman Gross (Encino, Calif.: Dickenson, 1977), 49.

2. Joel Feinberg, *Social Philosophy* (Englewood Cliffs, N.J.: Prentice-Hall, 1973), 49.

3. Frankena, "Some Beliefs About Justice," 49.

4. Ronald Dworkin, "Why Bakke Has No Case," *New York Review of Books,* 10 Nov. 1977, 14.

Discussion Questions

1. Does Boxill's argument support affirmative action policies in college admissions? Support your answer.
2. Discuss what Boxill would most likely think of the current trend to create minority curriculums in colleges.
3. Alan Bloom in *The Closing of the American Mind* (1987) writes: "The black [college] student who wishes to be just a student and to avoid allegiance to the black group has to pay a terrific price, because he is judged negatively by his black peers and because his behavior is atypical in the eyes of whites."[30] Do you agree with Bloom? Support your answer using examples from your own college experience. Discuss whether color-conscious policies like those advocated by Boxill encourage stereotyping as well as the isolation of students who prefer a color-blind environment.
4. Several civil rights and Native American groups have protested the use of Indian mascots and symbols by professional sports teams such as the Washington Redskins and the Atlanta Braves. Is this practice morally justified under the color-blind principle? Support your answer. Discuss what Boxill would most likely think of this practice.
5. Discuss how Boxill might respond to Louis Farrakhan's color-conscious philosophy.
6. Koreans, like other Asian immigrants, are sometimes referred to as "model minorities"—a term they don't particularly like. Despite the fact that most Koreans living in the United States are relative newcomers, nearly 40 percent of them own businesses. During the 1992 Los Angeles riots, more than a thousand Korean stores were burned or ransacked; black resentment of Koreans was cited as the one of the reasons for that. Blacks say they have a harder time getting bank loans, a claim that appears to be true, and that the schools in black neighborhoods are worse. Why might this be the case? Discuss how Boxill might answer this question. What does it mean to be called a "model minority," and why do some Asians dislike this designation?

 MICHAEL LEVIN

Race, Biology, and Justice

Michael Levin was a professor of philosophy at City College of New York. Levin argues that the attainment gap between whites and blacks is due not to racism but to genetic differences between the races. Levin cites various studies to support his claim of racial differences in intelligence and temperament. He argues that affirmative action and other compensatory programs are wrong because, rather than advancing blacks, they annul the natural advantage whites have over blacks.

"Race, Biology, and Justice," *Public Affairs Quarterly* 8, no. 3 (1994): 267–282. Some notes have been omitted.

Critical Readings Questions

1. Why aren't possible biological differences between races openly discussed? Why do some people who say that there are differences between races deny that such differences would matter? Does Levin think genetic differences matter?
2. What are some documented differences between whites and blacks?
3. What does the Smith/Jones analogy illustrate? What is compensatory justice? In what ways is affirmative action compensatory?
4. What is the "bias-fighting rationale" behind affirmative action? What assumption is integral to this argument?
5. On what grounds does Levin reject Boxill's position on affirmative action?
6. How does Levin account for the attainment gap between blacks and whites?
7. What evidence does Levin use to argue that racism isn't a plausible explanation for the attainment?
8. What is the relationship between IQ and job attainment? According to Levin, how do differences in IQ between whites and blacks undermine the claim that racism is the cause of the attainment gap? How do racial IQ differences affect educational attainment?
9. According to Levin, what temperamental characteristics of blacks lead to a propensity toward poverty?
10. On what grounds does Levin discount the role that environment plays in IQ?
11. Why, according to Levin, must the burden of proof be shifted onto blacks who claim that racism has brought about their failure?
12. How does Levin answer the charge that distributive justice requires greater racial equality?
13. How does Levin respond to the argument that slavery and segregation have left blacks disadvantaged?
14. On what grounds does Levin reject Rawls's "natural lottery" as irrelevant to racial differences?
15. How does Levin use Rawls's difference principle, as well as utilitarian considerations, to support his position?

Genetic black/white differences have played almost no role in recent discussions of interracial justice. This paper explores the relevance of these differences to issues of compensation and distribution.

One reason for the neglect of group differences, of course, is the belief that any talk of them is "racist." Obviously, though, the wickedness of mentioning a phenomenon does not diminish its logical bearing on any issue that may present itself.

At the same time, many writers who do admit the possibility of genetic race differences deny that they would matter if found. One of two reasons is usually offered for this conclusion: 1) it might prove possible to suppress genetic differences by manipulating the environment, or 2) moral principles such as a right to equal treatment are independent of the empirical traits of individuals and groups. . . .

RACE DIFFERENCES

The most thoroughly documented race difference is that in intelligence. It is accepted by every competent student of the subject that blacks score about one standard deviation (SD) below whites on all tests of intelligence; under the conventional scaling of IQ, the mean IQ of whites is 100 and that of blacks a bit below 85.[1] A literature survey by the National Academy of Science concluded "The largest difference in group averages [exists] between blacks and whites on all given tests and at all grade levels." . . . The idea that IQ measures immersion in white culture is contradicted by the performance of Japanese and Chinese on IQ tests, which exceeds that of whites and blacks. Finally, IQ associates with numerous variables unrelated to socialization. . . .

It would be hasty to suppose that blacks and whites differ in intelligence only. Many writers[2] claim that blacks are on average less inclined to defer gratification, a conjecture consistent with psychometric data. Black self-esteem is higher than white,[3] a common assumption to the contrary notwithstanding, and black scores on the Minnesota Multiphasic Personality Inventory are elevated in the direction of greater impulsivity.[4] Because they are more conjectural, however, race differences in temperament play only a minor role in what follows.

COMPENSATORY JUSTICE

When Jones limps into court to demand compensation from Smith for his broken leg, there are a number of defenses Smith should avoid. Denial that anyone can put a price-tag on a sound leg is pettifogging; appeal to the statute of limitations—the claim that Jones was harmed too long ago to deserve anything now—is legalistic; complaints about the cost of compensation are beside the point, the point being Jones' entitlement. Concentrating too heavily on the immediate cause of injury may be misdirection; Smith is still guilty if Jones broke his leg slipping on ice after being stranded by Smith on a frozen lake. Finally, concern that a large settlement may blunt Jones' zeal for rehabilitation sounds disingenuous coming from Smith.

Smith's best defense is to challenge the factual claim that he directly or indirectly broke Jones' leg. If Jones' lameness is not his doing, Smith is off the hook, morally and legally. No one is liable for what he did not do. . . .

The parallel with race is patent. Blacks limp behind whites at virtually all prestigious and remunerative tasks. This deficit is blamed on whites; blacks are said to fail because discrimination and racism have stifled their competitive ability. Given the principle of compensation—a person damaged by a wrong deserves what he lost, and is owed it by the wrong-doer—whites owe blacks the positions blacks would have occupied but for discrimination. In practical terms, redress means preferring blacks over whites when they compete.

Many defenders of preference deny they are demanding compensation. They are often the first to agree that the whites being asked to step aside now never discriminated against anyone, and that blacks receiving preference now never experienced discrimination. Yet the arguments intended to fill the resulting void are often compensatory in character. For instance, many preference advocates insist that innocent contemporary whites still benefit from past wrongs, and that anyone better off because of a wrong must surrender his illicit advantage to those the wrong has left worse off. So this new rationale for preference, like the original one, represents preference as putting blacks and whites where they would have been but for the misdeeds of (other) whites. Whether this new argument is called "compensatory," it too assumes that the black attainment deficit is the fault of (some) whites.

Or consider the argument that affirmative action provides role models for young blacks. The obvious question is, what is wrong with the present number of role models? Why not let role models distribute themselves race neutrally? Because, role-model theorists usually reply, blacks have fewer role models and lower aspirations than they would have had but for oppression. Whites should step aside for blacks so that young blacks may have hopes they should have developed. So understood, the role-model argument is patently compensatory.

Affirmative action is sometimes deemed necessary to counteract present discrimination, as revealed by the continued statistical underrepresentation of blacks in desirable positions. . . . [T]he bias-fighting rationale, while not compensatory, also assumes black ability is roughly equal to that of whites.

Now, just as Smith should not defend himself against Jones with technicalities and subterfuges, critics of affirmative action should not dodge their issue either. . . .

Smith retains the moral high ground only by showing that he did not break Jones' leg. So too, critics of quotas can retain the high ground only by showing that "racism" did not cause the attainment gap. Enter the race difference in intelligence (and, perhaps, motivation), which explains black failure better than "racism."

RACE DIFFERENCES AND THE ATTAINMENT GAP

Quite apart from the plausibility of its rivals, "racism" as a catch-all hypothesis has been eroded by the sheer passage of time. Slavery ended 130 years ago, school segregation 40 years ago; blacks have enjoyed full civil rights protection since 1964 and the ever-expanding privileges of quotas since 1970. Yet blacks are not doing appreciably better now than in 1954, and by some measures, such as marital stability, far worse. To take one of many striking examples, the National Science Foundation has spent over $1.5 billion on programs reserved for blacks since 1972, yet "20 years later, matters have barely improved" with regard to blacks in science.[5]

It is difficult to argue that blacks were too heavily burdened for gains to appear in thirty or forty years. Equally burdened groups, notably Chinese in the US and Jews in many places, have made longer strides in less time. The Germans and Japanese, whose countries lay destroyed in 1945, were again world economic powers by 1970. To explain differential responses to adversity by attributing to some groups a "tradition of hard work" begs the question of black failure to develop that tradition. Post-war Europe did receive Marshal Plan aid, and it has become something of a cliché that American blacks need a domestic Marshal Plan, but in fact the net transfer of resources to blacks under Aid to Families with Dependent Children and other subsidies already amounts to a Marshal Plan every three years.

Given the weakness of "racism" as an explanation, one turns naturally to endogenous black traits, such as lower levels of intelligence and self-restraint, to account for the attainment gap. . . .

Compensation theorists might reply that talk of *the* cause of the attainment gap is an oversimplification. The proper question is *how much* of the gap is explained by race differences, for whatever portion of the gap is left unexplained by race differences might be due to compensable racism. . . .

The reader should think of IQ in the black and white populations as represented by overlapping bell curves, with the mean of the black curve lying one SD to the left of the white mean. . . . Thus, assuming the black SD equals the white SD, about 16% of all blacks have IQs of 100 or more, while about 50% of whites do, so there are about 1/3 as many blacks as whites whose IQs exceed 100. As the normal distribution is nonlinear, this ratio varies with IQ. There is 1 black for every 8 whites whose IQs exceed 115, and 1 black for every 18 whites whose IQs exceed 130. . . .

The recruitment gap is explained by the IQ difference alone, without reference to slavery or segregation. More generally, discrimination apparently explained a minute proportion at most of black vocational failure in 1970, and by 1980 has ceased to be a factor altogether. On the evidence, black representation caught up with ability some time after World War II and before affirmative action, by which point the effects of slavery and discrimination—whatever they may once have been—had been attenuated to non-existence. If so, the present competitive abilities of blacks are what they would have been had slavery and discrimination never happened, and no white enjoys any significant wrongful advantage over his black competitors because of them. Hence, no white is required by compensatory justice to forego any of his competitive advantage.

Black academic failure, usually blamed wholly on whites, is also explicable by the race difference in IQ. The correlation between IQ and academic performance exceeds .6 in the lower grades, where the population is most diverse and the race difference most pronounced.[6] The correlation, along with the variance, decreases as one ascends the academic hierarchy, but it still suffices to explain the absence of blacks from graduate education. In

1990, 838 blacks earned the Ph.D.[7] Jensen cites an IQ of 130 as predicting the ability to earn a Ph.D.,[8] and, if the mean IQ in a population is 100, 2.3% of its members have IQs $\geq$ 130. As there are about 420,000 blacks in any one-year cohort, proportionality requires that .023 $\times$ 420,000 = 9600 blacks earn the Ph.D. annually. In fact, however, only .13% of blacks have IQs $\geq$ 130, leading to a prediction of .013 $\times$ 420,000 = 575 blacks annually capable of earning a Ph.D., close to the actual figure. . . .

The high rejection rate for blacks in the NIH competition is actually one instance of a general tendency for whites to outperform blacks when credentials are held constant—whites outearn blacks when occupation and years of schooling are controlled for.[9] This discrepancy strongly suggests bias, but it too can be explained as a statistical artifact. . . . Since wages correlate with IQ within as well as between occupations, the average income of whites exceeds that of blacks in the same jobs and with the same schooling. Proportionately fewer black scientists are outstanding scientists, capable, for instance, of conceiving research projects which win grants in blind competition.

I know of no study like Gottesman's of the relation of black temperament to poverty, but many commentators—including some preference advocates—see a link.[10] Banfield (op. cit.) blames most of the problems of the slums on preference for immediate payoffs. Boxill, who supports quotas, acknowledges that black "chronic tardiness" and other "habits or cultural traits which are debilitating and unproductive" (op. cit.). Black sociologist William J. Wilson has consistently found that ghetto males look down on jobs which don't produce a lot of money for relatively little effort.[11] Richard J. Hernstein and James Q. Wilson report that a pervasive attitude in black slums is that "Straight jobs" are for "suckers." "Every boy interviewed [in a study cited] had been employed at one time, but the turnover was very high. When asked why they left a job, they typically answered that they found it monotonous or low paying. . . [B]eing able to 'make it' while avoiding the 'work game' is a strong, pervasive, and consistent goal."[12] Such attitudes obviously impede attainment.

AN OBJECTION

There is an objection so likely to be raised at this point that it seems less an objection than a decisive refutation of my entire argument. Virtually everyone with whom I have ever discussed race differences has raised it, and it has probably occurred to the reader. Perhaps the *immediate* cause of low black attainment is lower intelligence (and greater impulsiveness), but if this difference is itself a result of racism, whites are still responsible at one remove for black failure, and the competitive edge enjoyed by whites today remains illicit. (Smith was not exonerated because he merely left Jones on the slippery ice without actually tripping him.) While some writers do not take overt or "institutional" discrimination to be the immediate cause of black failure, more thoughtful compensation theorists recognize that blacks are now objectively less able than whites. In Lyndon Johnson's famous comparison of blacks to a once-shackled runner, no one is restraining the shackled runner. He is slower than his competitors. But he is slower *because* of what has been done to him, and so deserves a head start. Likewise, if blacks are less intelligent than whites because of past discrimination, or denial of proper nutrition, or because racism discourages blacks from stimulating their children, they would still deserve a head start of some sort. It may be superior mental ability that gives whites their advantage over blacks, but the advantage should be annulled if the cause of this advantaging factor was a wrong. . . .

The only environmental factor that does seem capable of explaining the systematic character of black failure are disadvantages imposed on blacks by the majority society. . . .

GENETIC DIFFERENTIATION

The evidence strongly suggests that the race difference in intelligence is due significantly, perhaps primarily, to genetic differences. To begin with, the interindividual heritability of intelligence is quite high, between .5 and .7.[13] Operationally, this means that if everyone were raised in the same environment, the average difference between the IQs of different individuals would be almost as large as it is at present. . . . The difference between Africa and Alaska, great as it may be, does not explain the difference in height between Masai and Eskimos; no one expects a Masai baby raised by Eskimos in Alaska to grow up short and stocky. Mathematically speaking, the higher the heritability of a phenotype, the greater the difference must be between the mean environments of two groups for environment to explain completely a fixed mean group phenotypic difference. . . . I know of no scalable environmental variable on which blacks and whites differ that widely, and the worlds of American blacks and whites—the language they speak, the movies and television shows they see, the school subjects they are exposed to, the technology available to them—appear quite similar. Black slums are admittedly less stimulating than white suburbs, but, as a neighborhood is the work of its inhabitants, the slum/suburb difference must count as an effect, not a cause, of race differences.

There are three sources of direct evidence of genetic influences on the race difference in intelligence. The first is the performance of African blacks on the most culture-free IQ tests, which averages about 70 to 75.[14] The second is transracial adoption. Were blacks genetically identical to whites with respect to intelligence, black adoptees raised from infancy in upper-middle class white families should develop the mean IQ of whites. The Minnesota Transracial Adoption Study[15] found the reverse in a sample of about 100 such adoptees. By late adolescence, their mean IQ was 89. By contrast the mean IQ of whites adopted by the same families was 105, and that of the natural children of these families was 109. In a reanalysis of this study, I estimate that genetic variation explains 60% to 70% of the between-race variance in intelligence.[16] . . .

BURDENS OF PROOF

It cannot be proven beyond a shadow of a doubt that intelligence is a valid construct, or that IQ measures it. A genetic explanation of race differ-

ences is inherently more conjectural still than the race differences themselves. . . . Yet these uncertainties weaken my argument less than might be supposed.

Claims of damage must be *sustained*. Jones cannot simply storm into court, accuse Smith of breaking his leg, and expect to collect. He must *show* that Smith broke his leg. As this is a civil action, the standard he must meet is the relatively undemanding one of the preponderance of the evidence; he need only show it is more likely than not that Smith broke his leg. But show it he must—which means that, to defend himself successfully, Smith need not *prove* that he did not break Jones' leg. Smith need only show it is more likely that he did not break Jones' leg than that he did. Just so, white failure to prove the accusations against them false does not by itself leave them liable to compensatory damages. Since those who demand compensation are obliged to show that their accusations are plausible, whites are vindicated by a showing that black failure is *less likely* to be due to racism than to phenotypic race differences due in turn to genetic factors. The hereditarian analysis need not be certain, just more probable than "racism"—as I believe any disinterested examination of the evidence will find it to be.

Lest it seem legalistic in its own right to force the accuser of whites to carry the burden of proof, the reader should reflect that over the last quarter-century a great many whites have watched jobs and resources go to less qualified blacks because of the "racism" theory. It is only fair to ask that this theory be shown to be more likely than its rivals before more sacrifices from whites are demanded in its name.

DISTRIBUTIVE JUSTICE

It might be argued that greater racial equality is a requirement, not of compensatory, but of distributive justice, understood as what is obligatory in the initial distribution of goods. Many contemporary social philosophers seem to treat equality as the inertial distributive state, deviation from which needs justifying. Black and white shares are plainly unequal, hence prima facie wrong.

. . . Rather than repeat that the effects of these [past] inequalities have lingered, it is more pertinent to distribution to remark that past inequalities almost certainly did not leave blacks with smaller shares than they would have had in Africa. Slavery was common in Africa—white slavers bought blacks from tribal chiefs who had captured them—and no indigenous black society developed democracy, which blacks at least witnessed in the antebellum South. It is unlikely that blacks left on their own would shape conditions more conducive to mental growth than the ones they have been exposed to, for no indigenous black society ever developed an educational system remotely comparable in quality to the segregated schools of the Jim Crow era or the de facto segregated public schools of today. . . .

It may be replied that the benchmark of equality is not what would have been available for blacks in Africa, but what is available where they are, the US. This might be true when "what is available" refers to natural resources, but schools, housing and wealth—the goods blacks are commonly said to have too little of—are produced by human effort. The work of human hands should presumably go to the hands that did the work. By that standard, black holdings in the US seem less like inequity than white generosity.

Rawls cites the arbitrariness of the "natural lottery" to divorce an individual's contribution to wealth from his distributive share in it. The exceptional individual is said to have no right to the fruits of his talents because those talents, having been caused by fortuitous circumstances, are undeserved. His talents belong to everyone,[17] and he should keep only as much of what he produces as is needed as an incentive to keep him active. Rawls' argument has not to my knowledge been applied explicitly to race, probably out of reluctance to admit race differences in talent, but the obviousness of the application may help explain the popularity of *A Theory of Justice*.

At one level Rawls' inference from determinism to socialism collapses without a shove from empirical data, for it patently confuses *entitlement* with *entitlement to entitlement*. I may not deserve to spot a gold nugget in a stream, but this hardly implies that

I do not deserve the nugget once I do spot it. Perhaps I deserve to be a finder of nuggets only by cultivating habits of alertness, but all I have to do to deserve the *nugget* is find it. I don't have to be entitled to find it.

At a deeper but still logical level, Rawls confuses the contradictory of "The natural lottery is required by justice" with one of its contraries. From the clear truth that "The natural distribution [of ability] is neither just nor unjust" (op. cit.) Rawls infers the wrongness of capitalizing on natural abilities. But the fact that a situation is "not just," in the sense of not *required* by justice, does not leave it *forbidden* by justice. Precisely as Rawls says, the natural lottery is neither just *nor unjust*. So, while whites may not *deserve* to have been made cleverer than blacks by the processes of evolution, it hardly follows that there is any *unfairness* in evolution having done this. If there is no positive reason to accept the consequences of evolution, there is also—unless equality is already assumed desirable—no positive reason to resist them. . . .

Second, Rawls' system is far from egalitarian: his difference principle, that the lot of the better off can be improved only when doing so helps the worst off, accords the worst off a veto power denied to other groups. Assuming blacks among the worst off in American society, the difference principle would seem to give priority to helping them. The ghetto has first claim on the next dollar spent on education. . . . Yet given the relevant facts, the difference principle may imply quite another conclusion. Technical innovations, which originate from the high tail of the bell curve, have historically benefited the worst off more than anyone else. The computer, the latest product of Caucasoid ingenuity, most dramatically boosts the productivity and with it the marketability of workers whose talents confine them to routine clerical tasks. Vacuum cleaners most benefited those women unable to afford domestic help.[18] If giving that next dollar to the—almost entirely white and Asian—gifted would benefit blacks more than giving it to blacks, the difference principle says give it to the gifted.

The findings of the best-known enrichment programs for black children[19] do not settle the issue. The Milwaukee Project produced short-term gains in the IQ of black children at a cost of $23,000 per point. The net benefit of the Perry Preschool Program, as measured by such factors as increased chances of employment, was $250 per IQ point in the first year (and negative thereafter). . . . Yet what the Rawlsian needs to know is whether these programs did more for blacks than would have been done for blacks by investing the same resources in the—mostly non-black—gifted. Utilitarians need similar data, since for them the disposition of that next dollar hinges on a straight bang-for-the-buck comparison of the educability of black and non-black children. The studies needed to apply maximin and utilitarian criteria have not been done, and it is far from clear what their outcome would be.

THE FINAL REMARK

Having returned to reasons for studying race differences, I would repeat the main one.

The right to cite truths in one's own defense is very nearly absolute. This right emphatically includes the marshaling of truths that embarrass one's accuser. A man asked to pay for a wrong he did not commit may repel the accusation even if to do so raises questions his accuser would rather not answer. Jones may wish to avoid thinking about his misshapen leg. He may be ashamed that this deformity runs in his family. He may not want anyone to call attention to it. *But if he accuses Smith of having broken it, Smith is entitled to talk about Jones' leg all day long.* If Jones isn't prepared to have his leg talked about, he shouldn't open the topic by hurling accusations. If racial egalitarians hurl immoderate charges at whites, they open the topic of race differences by forcing whites to defend themselves.

NOTES

1. See A. Shuey, *The Testing of Negro Intelligence* (New York: Social Science Press, 1966); J. S. Coleman, et al., *Equality of Educational Opportunity.* Washington, D.C.: U.S. Department of Health, Education, and Welfare, 1966. A. Jensen, and

R. Figueroa, "Forward and Backward Digit-Span Interaction with Race and IQ: Predictions from Jensen's Theory." *Journal of Educational Psychology*, vol. 67 (1975), pp. 882–93. Entry for "Negro Intelligence," in R. J. Sternberg, ed., *Encyclopedia of Intelligence* (New York: Macmillan, 1993).

2. E.g., E. Banfield, *The Unheavenly City Revisited* (Boston: Little Brown, 1974).

3. A. Tashakkori, "Race, Gender and pre-Adolescent Self-Structure: A Test of Construct-Specificity Hypothesis [sic]." *Personality and Individual Differences,* vol. 14 (1993).

4. W. Dahlstrom, et al., *MMPI Patterns of American Minorities* (Minneapolis: University of Minnesota Press, 1986).

5. E. Culotta, "What Went Wrong: Why Programs Failed," *Science,* vol. 258 (1992), pp. 1185–190.

6. A. Jensen, *Bias in Mental Testing* (New York: The Free Press, 1980), p. 343.

7. A. DePalma, "Drop in Black Ph.D.'s Brings Debate on Aid to Foreigners," *New York Times,* April 21, 1992, p. A18.

8. *Bias in Mental Testing,* p. 112.

9. See G. Jaynes, and R. Williams, eds., *A Common Destiny: Blacks in American Society* (Washington D.C.: National Academy Press, 1989), pp. 288, 301.

10. I. I. Gottesman, "Biogenetics of Race and Class," in M. Deutch, I. Katz, and A. R. Jensen (eds.), *Social Class, Race, and Psychological Development* (New York: Holt, Rinehart, and Winston, 1968).

11. William J. Wilson, *The Truly Disadvantaged: The Inner City, the Underclass and Public Policy* (Chicago: University of Chicago Press, 1987).

12. R. Hernstein, and J. Wilson, *Crime and Human Nature* (New York: Simon and Schuster, 1985), pp. 304, 335.

13. Plomin favors .5, see R. Plomin, *Nature and Nurture* (Belmont, CA: Wadsworth, 1990), and "The Role of Inheritance in Behavior," *Science,* vol. 248 (1990), pp. 183–88. T. J. Bouchard, Jr., et al., "Sources of Human Psychological Differences: The Minnesota Study of Twins Reared Apart," *Science,* vol. 250 (1990), favor .7. The

heritabilities of traits of temperament are generally .4–.6.

14. See e.g., K. Owen, "The Suitability of Raven's Standard Progressive Matrices for Various Groups in South Africa," *Personality and Individual Differences,* vol. 13 (1992), pp. 149–59.

15. R. Weinberg, S. Scarr, and I. Waldman, "The Minnesota Transracial Adoption Study: A Follow-up of IQ Test Performance at Adolescence," *Intelligence,* vol. 16 (1992).

16. M. Levin, "Comment on the Minnesota Transracial Adoption Study," *Intelligence,* vol. 19 (1994).

17. J. Rawls, *A Theory of Justice* (Cambridge, MA: Harvard University Press, 1971), pp. 101–102.

18. See J. Fulda, *Are There Too Many Lawyers?* (Irvington, NY: The Foundation for Economic Education, 1993), pp. 1–3.

19. See H. Spitz, *The Raising of Intelligence* (Hillsdale, NJ: Erlbaum, 1986).

Discussion Questions

1. Is Levin a racist? Support your answer. Discuss how Garcia might answer this question.

2. Has Levin adequately demonstrated that there is empirical support for differences between the races? If so, do these differences justify differential treatment? Does Levin support a color-blind or a color-conscious approach?

3. Discuss how Shelby Steele would most likely respond to Levin's claim that the attainment gap between whites and blacks is primarily due to genetic differences between the races. Which person presents the stronger argument? Support your answer.

4. Levin disagrees with Boxill's support of affirmative action. Discuss how Boxill might respond to Levin's criticism of his position.

5. In his article "Response to Race Differences in Crime,"[31] Levin argues that because there is a one-in-four chance that a young black male is a felon, a jogger who sees a black male on the path in front of him is justified in turning around and running away. He also believes that police are justified in racial profiling even on campuses. Do you agree with Levin that this differential treatment of black men is morally justified? Discuss how Garcia and Boxill would each answer this question.

6. The United States spends about ten times more money imprisoning black men than educating them. Is this justified on utilitarian grounds? Discuss how both Levin and Boxill might respond to this question.

7. When Levin tried to find a publisher for his controversial manuscript *Why Race Matters: Race Differences and Their Implications,* dozen of publishers rejected it, including several academic publishers. Other authors, who have attempted to publish "politically incorrect" views on race differences, such as Arthur Jensen, a preeminent psychometrician, have met similar obstacles in finding publishers.[32] Do publishers have a moral obligation to publish books that they find objectionable? Or does freedom of the press give publishers the right to choose not to publish certain material? Does publishing controversial ideas on alleged differences between the races work to diminish or increase racism? What is the relationship, if any, between freedom of the press, and the perpetuation of the status quo and institutional racism? Support your answers. Discuss how John Stuart Mill might answer these questions.

UMA NARAYAN

Colonialism and Its Others: Considerations on Rights and Care Discourses

Uma Narayan is a professor of philosophy at Vassar College. Narayan shows how colonial care discourse and rights discourse were used to enable colonizers to justify themselves in relationship to "inferior" colonized subjects. She concludes that improvements in both justice and care discourse are needed to make this a world more conducive to human flourishing.

Critical Reading Questions

1. What were the primary elements in the colonial rights discourse and care discourse?
2. How was paternalism and its rhetoric of responsibility and care used by colonists to justify their practices? How did colonists sustain the paternalistic moral vision of colonialism?
3. Why did colonists feel the need to justify colonialism?
4. According to Narayan, in what ways are colonial stereotypes similar to gender stereotypes? What purpose did these stereotypes serve?
5. According to Narayan, what does colonialism teach us about rights discourse? What does it teach us about care discourse?
6. What is the "the white man's burden"? How was this notion used to morally justify colonialism?
7. How did liberal political theory use rights discourse to support colonialism?
8. What views of moral agency are embedded in colonial discourse? How is the "colonialized Other" defined in terms of relationship to the colonizer? How has the "Other" challenged this definition and the colonists' worldview?
9. In what ways have some anticolonial movements reinforced other relationships of power?
10. What is the "doctrine of disqualification" and how is it used to maintain unequal social relationships?
11. Why is Joan Tronto concerned about the widespread adoption of a theory of care? How does Narayan respond to her concerns?
12. What does Narayan mean when she states that we need improvements along the dimensions of both justice and care in order to provide "enabling conditions" for the provision of care? In what ways, according to her, can greater attention to justice foster more-adequate forms of care?

"Colonialism and Its Others: Considerations on Rights and Care Discourses," *Hypatia* 10, no. 2 (1995), 138–140. Some notes have been omitted.

I wish to think about certain aspects of the roles played by rights and care discourses in colonial times. I shall start with the following question: How did the vast majority of people in the colonizing countries motivate themselves to participate in the large-scale phenomena of slavery and colonialism, not only embracing the idea that distant lands and peoples should be subjugated, but managing to conceive of imperialism as an *obligation,* an obligation taken so seriously that by 1914 Europe "held a grand total of roughly 85 percent of the earth as colonies, protectorates, dependencies, dominions, and commonwealths"? (Said 1993, 8).

The answer to this question forces us to attend to the self-serving collaboration between elements of colonial rights discourse and care discourse. Pervasive racist stereotypes about the negative and inferior status of enslaved or colonized Others were used both to justify denial of the rights enjoyed by the colonizers, and to construct the colonized as childish and inferior subjects, in need of the paternalistic guidance and rule of their superiors. In general terms, the colonizing project was seen as being *in the interests of, for the good of,* and as *promoting the welfare of* the colonized—notions that draw our attention to the existence of a *colonialist* care discourse whose terms have some resonance with those of some contemporary strands of the ethic of care. Particular colonial practices were seen as concrete attempts to achieve these paternalistic ends. Coercive religious conversion was seen as promoting the *spiritual* welfare of the "heathen." Inducting the colonized into the economic infrastructures of colonialism was seen as conferring the *material* benefits of western science, technology and economic progress, the *cultural* benefits of western education, and the *moral* benefits of the work ethic. There were often marked gender dimensions to these projects—colonial attempts to get "native women" to conform to Victorian/Christian norms of respectable dress, sexuality, and family life were regarded as in the moral interests of the women.

I am not denying there were powerful economic motivations underlying colonialism and slavery. However, justifications for colonialism and slavery in terms of crude self-interest alone seem to have been rare. These enterprises were made morally palatable by the rhetoric of responsibility and care for enslaved and colonized Others. Though such justifications have often been seen as attempts to convince the dominated of the appropriateness of their domination, I would argue that the central purpose of such arguments often is to make domination morally palatable to those engaged in the infliction of domination. While much of the contemporary discourse on an ethics of care focuses on the import of one's relationships to *particular others,* thinking about care-discourse in the colonial context highlights, in contrast, the roles it has historically played in justifying relationships of power and domination between *groups of people,* such as colonizers and colonized. The paternalistic moral vision of colonialism was sustained by the discourses of religion, philosophy, science, and art—cultural practices that collaborated to make a sense of western superiority part of the collective world view of people in the colonizing countries. (A large segment of western women's movements and working class movements of the time, such as those in England, were pro-empire.)

Colonial stereotypes about the hierarchy of races had similarities to existing theories of the hierarchy of gender—where attributes such as physical "weakness," smaller craniums, deficient rationality, and moral frailty were ascribed to western women, constructing them as the "weaker sex" in need of the care, support, and guidance of western men, not unlike the colonized. However, while western women's care-taking labor, namely domestic work and childcare responsibilities, were often rendered invisible qua work by being depicted as expressions of love and care for their families, the toil and labor of exploited slaves and colonized workers were often effaced instead by depicting their products as results of the efforts of colonial capitalists. John Stuart Mill provides a vivid example in *Principles of Political Economy:*

> These [outlying possessions of ours] are hardly to be looked upon as countries, but more properly as outlying agricultural or manufacturing estates. . . . Our West Indian colonies, for example, cannot be regarded as countries with a productive capital of their own,

. . . [but are rather] the place where England finds it convenient to carry on the production of sugar, coffee and a few other tropical commodities. All the capital employed is English capital. (Mill 1965, 693)

What does attending to the colonial context teach us about discourses of rights and care? Among the more obvious lessons is that rights discourse was only seemingly universal, not extending to the colonized, among others. Another lesson is that care discourse can sometimes function ideologically, to justify or conceal relationships of power and domination. While it has been pointed out that much of the responsibility for informal as well as institutionalized caring falls on subordinate and relatively powerless members of society—often working class and minority women—I want to add that "paternalistic caring" of the sort found in colonial discourse can also be wielded as a form of control and domination by the powerful and privileged. The colonial notion of "the white man's burden" included both a sense of obligation to confer the benefits of western civilization on the colonized, and a sense of being burdened with the responsibility for doing so—an obligation and responsibility rooted in a sense of being agents who had a world-historic mission to bring the light of civilization and progress to others inhabiting "areas of darkness"!

The seemingly universal, free, equal, independent, separate, and mutually disinterested individual of contract theory and of rights discourse has been criticized as being contrary to the experiences of most women. I wish to add that the contractual focus on relationships between equals, and on agents as independent, separate and mutually disinterested was only *part* of the liberal story. Another part of the story was that these same subjects had paternalistic obligations and responsibilities to "inferior Others," whether women in their own families or distant colonial peoples. Rights-discourse was constructed during the historical time when western countries were becoming increasingly interdependent with, unseparate from, and anything but disinterested in their unfree and unequal colonies, and most liberal political theorists had no difficulty endorsing colonialism. We would be

mistaken if we read liberal rights-theorists as concerned only with contractual relationships between equals, or if we focus only on notions of agency pertinent to that side of their thought, since we would be ignoring their support for colonialism, and the more "missionary" notions of agency embedded in that facet of their worldview. If we recognize that the agent of liberal rights theory was also the agent of the colonial project, its independence, separateness and disinterestedness appear to be more qualified properties than the picture of the same agent that emerge if we ignore the colonial dimensions of liberal theory.

In the colonial worldview, white women too had their own version of the "white man's burden," in which caretaking roles played a large part. Many white women went to the colonies as wives, whose presence was meant to shield their husbands from the lurking dangers of miscegenation and of "going native." White women had their own brand of paternalistic roles towards the colonized, and often shared in roles that constructed the "natives" as children.

Many aspects of the self-perceptions of the colonizers seem to have depended heavily on their relationship to the colonized. The world-view of colonialism, as well as the moral and socio-political world-views of many colonized cultures, subscribed to a picture where several large groups of people were normatively defined in terms of their relationships as inferiors and subordinates vis-a-vis members of dominant groups. To be a slave, a colonized Other, an untouchable, a woman, has often been meant as having one's entire existence defined in terms of one's "proper place" with respect to those with power, which entailed obligations to acquiesce to relationships of domination.

This suggests that strands in contemporary care discourse that stress that we are all essentially interdependent and in relationship, while important, do not go far enough if they fail to worry about the *accounts* that are given of these interdependencies and relationships. The colonizers and the colonized, for example, while both acutely conscious of their relationship to each other, had very different accounts of what the relationship and its interdependencies amounted to, and whether they were morally justified. Many social movements and struggles on the part of subordinate groups, though often couched in terms of individual rights, were also attempts to renegotiate and change the prevailing relationships between social groups.

While I do not endorse reducing the value of any moral theory to its ideological uses, I would argue that we must attend to the ideological functions served by various moral theories. Pervasive structural relationships of power and powerlessness between groups, such as those between colonizers and the colonized, tend to foster ideological justifications for the maintenance of such relationships. While aspects of care discourse have the potential virtue of calling attention to vulnerabilities that mark relationships between differently situated persons, care discourse also runs the risk of being used to ideological ends where these "differences" are defined in self-serving ways by the dominant and powerful. Notions of differences in vulnerabilities and capabilities should be recognized as *contested terrain,* requiring critical attention to who defines these differences as well as their practical implications.

Ideological pictures of the nature of Self and Others, and of one's relationship to Others are problematic pictures shared by large historically constituted groups of individuals. It is not clear to me that any moral theory is immune to such ideological deployment, nor am I convinced that there is any moral faculty or set of moral practices, neither Humean "reflection" nor Kantian "reason," whose careful and sustained cultivation *necessarily* liberates particular individuals from the historical effects of such ideologies. It seems to me that what such ideological pictures often yield to are not primarily theoretical moral self-corrections, based either on reason or on enlarged sympathies with Others, but to political contestations and moral challenges by groups who are victimized by the status quo. To challenge the paternalistic construction of femininity and of colonial subjectivity, western women and the colonized had to resort to insurgencies, rebellions, and protests, and had to *prove* themselves to be moral and political agents in order to make plausible their claims to such agency.

Two broad strategies were used both by western women and by the colonized in these contestations: (a) there were frequent assertions that western women or the colonized possessed the capacities and capabilities that entitled them to the same rights as white male colonizers, and (b) there were frequent redescriptions of the "paternalistic protective project" as one based instead on force and exploitation, inflicting misery on the powerless, and brutalizing those with power. The powerful role played by rights discourse in these emancipatory movements should not lead us to ignore their concurrent critique of the paternalistic colonial care-discourses that operated as justifications for their domination.

The alternative moral visions of the agency of women or of the colonized that developed in such political contestations, though they challenge the moral picture of the world held by the powerful, are not themselves immune to creating or reinforcing other relationships of power. A great deal has been written on how, for instance, the contemporary feminist movement has tended to be focused on the interests of middle-class white women, and about how drawing attention to the problems of women of color remains an ongoing problem. Anticolonial nationalist movements often displayed similar problems—in that nationalist discourses often constructed issues in a manner that marginalized colonized women. Several strands of Indian nationalism, for instance, associated Indian women with the preservation of Indian traditions, culture, and spirituality—a function that simultaneously gave them an *imagined function* in the nationalist agenda, but excluded them from *real participation* in many areas of work, politics, and public culture (Chatterjee 1990, 243). Thus, though I believe large-scale political movements have been historically crucial in bringing about certain forms of moral change and progress, these movements too generate problematic moral narratives. I would conclude that moral theories need to be evaluated not only in terms of their theoretical adequacy in accounting for the range of phenomena in our moral lives but also with regard to the instrumental political uses to which they lend themselves at concrete historical junctures.

I shall end with a few reflections on the relationship between rights and care discourses. The perspectives of colonialism, as well as those of many colonized cultures, and of many contemporary societies, provide several examples of what John Ladd refers to as the "Doctrine of Moral Disqualification," whereby groups with social power define members of other groups in ways that disqualify them for full membership in the moral community (Ladd 1991, 40). These definitions have been repeatedly used to justify the denial of rights to members of "disqualified" groups. These definitions have also been used to justify the failure to be genuinely attentive and responsive to the needs, interests, and welfare of the members of these groups. Dominant social definitions of what an untouchable or a slave was, did not encourage the powerful to care for the less powerful; and the same definitions were in fact inimical to the well-being of the less powerful, who were not, by these definitions, entitled to the means and opportunities for flourishing.

Justice concerns have been central to many social and political movements because asserting and gaining rights have been instrumental in transforming certain groups of people, however imperfectly, into fellow citizens whose concerns mattered, into people whose human worth mattered. However, as many slave-narratives well illustrate, much of the moral and political work that was necessary to change the "moral disqualification" inflicted on powerless groups consisted not only of claims to rights, but of attempts to call attention to the *suffering* inflicted on the powerless by the status quo. These political depictions of suffering can be seen as attempts to elicit the attentiveness and moral responsiveness of those with power, by redescribing the life situations of the powerless in ways that challenged the rationalizations of the powerful. The discourses of slave narratives, for example, make it difficult for members of dominant groups to continue to believe in the myth of happy slaves, content with their lot.

Joan Tronto may well be right in arguing that "one of the practical effects of the widespread adoption of a theory of care may be to make our concerns for justice less central" (Tronto 1995). I would like to add the converse claim, that a more serious commitment to and enforcement of the claims of justice might, at least in some cases, be a precondition for the possibility of adequately caring for and about some people. Tronto herself acknowledges that "*until* we care about something, the care process cannot begin" (Tronto 1995). Social relationships of domination often operate so as to make many who have power unable to *genuinely* care about the marginalized and powerless.

Although I am very sympathetic to the idea of a politics and of public policies that are more sensitive to *needs,* I am not sure we can arrive at what Tronto calls "a full account of human needs" without serious attention to considerations of justice that would enable the powerless to seriously participate in the social and political discourse where such needs are contested and defined. Once again, adequate attention to justice may, in some instances, be a precondition for adequately caring policies. . . .

Carol Gilligan's work suggests that rights and care perspectives provide alternative accounts of moral problems and decisions, and that shifting to a care perspective foregrounds moral issues of preserving and maintaining relationships that are often not well illuminated by a rights perspective. I understand . . . Tronto . . . as arguing that the care perspective is a wider or possibly more foundational framework, within which considerations of rights and justice constitute a subset—though admittedly an important one.

I would like to suggest yet another possibility. Improvements along dimensions of justice and rights might, in some cases such as the issue of fatal neglect of female children, provide what I shall call "enabling conditions" for the provision of adequate care. In other cases, improvements along care dimensions, such as attentiveness to and concern for human needs and human suffering, might provide the "enabling conditions" for more adequate forms of justice. For instance, attention to the needs, predicaments and suffering of the impoverished and destitute in affluent western societies might result in social policies that institutionalize welfare rights, rights to adequate medical care, and so forth.

I suggest that this is one possible dimension of the relationships between care and justice considerations, and not an over-arching account of their relationship. I am suggesting that, in particular contexts, struggles for greater justice may foster more adequate or richer forms of care and that in others, the cultivation of a care perspective might foster enhanced forms of justice. In some situations at least, justice and care perspectives might be seen less as contenders for theoretical primacy or moral and political adequacy and more as collaborators and allies in our practical and political efforts to make our world more conducive to human flourishing.

REFERENCES

Chatterjee, Partha. 1990. The nationalist resolution of the women's question. In *Recasting women: Es-says in Indian colonial history,* ed. Kumkum Sangari and Suresh Vaid. New Brunswick: Rutgers University Press.

Ladd, John. 1991. The idea of collective violence. In *Justice, law and violence,* ed. James A. Brady and Newton Garver. Philadelphia: Temple University Press.

Mill, John Stuart. 1965. *Principles of political economy,* Vol. 3. ed. J. M. Robson. Toronto: University of Toronto Press.

Said, Edward. 1993. *Culture and imperialism.* New York: Alfred A. Knopf.

Tronto, Joan. 1995. Care as a basis for radical political judgements. *Hypatia* 10(2): pp. 141–149.

Discussion Questions

1. Discuss ways in which colonial care discourse has contributed to contemporary institutional racism, citing examples from the previous readings.
2. What does Narayan mean when she argues that we need to attend to the ideological functions served by moral theories? Discuss how, if at all, currently popular moral theories, such as liberal rights ethics, can be used to serve the ideology of racism.
3. Narayan points out that both rights discourse and care discourse can be used to justify racism and conceal relationships of power and domination. Discuss examples of situations in which contemporary institutional racism is currently being justified on the grounds of "paternalistic caring."
4. The brutal government removal of Native Americans from their lands in the 1800s was justified as being in their best interest. Examine ways in which colonial care discourse and colonial rights discourse are still embedded in U.S. public policy regarding Native Americans.
5. Shelby Steele maintains that because many well-meaning whites are fearful of being labeled racists, they try to establish their innocence of this charge by becoming "angels of mercy" and embracing policies such as affirmative action that help blacks overcome their victimization. Discuss the extent, if any, to which this strategy recreates a colonial care discourse similar to the old concept of the "white man's burden."
6. Compare and contrast Narayan's concept of colonial care discourse with Garcia's analysis of paternalistic racism.
7. Princeton political scientist John DiIulio suggests that certain current social policies, promoted as solutions to racial problems by both conservatives and liberals, are in fact

manifestations of ongoing institutional racism. He questions whether the war on drugs and high rate of imprisonment of young black men is a rational response to urban crime and disorder. Antipoverty programs that treat the inner city as an island, he claims, also isolate inner-city blacks and downplay the strategic economic location of inner-city neighborhoods and their connection to the wider community. In addition, DiIulio questions whether making publicly funded abortions more widely available to poor black women is really "an act of enlightened social compassion" or "an unspeakably ugly act of kill-now-rather-than-help-later social control."[33] Do you agree or disagree with DiIulio? Does the fact that blacks believe that the criminal justice system unfairly discriminates against them, and the fact that whites are significantly more in favor of legalized abortion than blacks, add weight to DiIulio's argument? Are these "solutions" simply a manifestation of an ongoing colonial care discourse and rights discourse? How might Narayan respond to these questions? Support your answers.

CASE STUDIES

1. *CHERYL J. HOPWOOD V. THE STATE OF TEXAS*[34]

In 1992 Cheryl Hopwood's application to the University of Texas Law School was turned down despite the fact that she had better grades and LSAT scores than many of the minority students who were admitted. At the time, the University of Texas (UT) had a quota system that gave preferential treatment to both African American and Mexican American applicants. Hopwood sued the State of Texas on the grounds that the policy violated the equal protection clause of the Fourteenth Amendment, which "prevent[ed] the States from purposefully discriminating between individuals on the basis of race."[35]

In ruling in favor of Hopwood, the federal circuit court stated that UT's admissions policy was discriminatory in that it treated minorities as a group rather than as individuals. Hopwood's victory against the State of Texas brought an end to affirmative action at UT and changed college admissions policies across the country.

The State of Texas appealed the ruling. The United States Supreme Court, however, rejected the appeal, agreeing with the circuit courts' ruling that "the law school has presented no compelling justification under the Fourteenth Amendment or Supreme Court precedent that allows it to continue to elevate some races over others, even for the wholesome purposes of correcting perceived racial imbalance in the student body."[36]

Discussion Questions

1. In its ruling, the circuit court acknowledged that Texas had a "long history of racially discriminatory practices in its primary and secondary schools" and that "remedial action is necessary" to correct past injustices against minority groups in the state.[37] The court also agreed that "obtaining the educational benefits that flow from a racially and ethnically diverse student body" is a desirable goal. Referring to the readings, discuss ways in which this goal might be achieved.

2. Hopwood had been accepted at Princeton for undergraduate school but couldn't afford to attend. Instead she worked her way through school at a community college, graduating with a 3.8 grade-point average. Is it fair that minorities who come from

well-off families be given preferential treatment over white people, like Hopwood, who come from economically disadvantaged families? Support your answer. Discuss how Steele and Boxill might each respond to this question.

3. Studies indicate that minority enrollment in the top colleges would drop significantly without affirmative action.[38] Does the promotion of diversity justify reverse discrimination? Discuss in light of Ross's prima facie duties as well as Rawls's two principles of justice.

4. Compare and contrast the equal protection clause of the Fourteen Amendment with Kant's categorical imperative. Discuss whether the affirmative action policy of UT violated the categorical imperative.

5. Did Hopwood have a moral duty to protest her rejection by UT? If so, what is the source of this duty?

6. Former senator Bob Dole is opposed to affirmative action. "We ought to do away with preferences," he stated in a 1996 speech. "This is America. It ought to be based on merit." Discuss Dole's position. How might Garcia respond to Dole?

7. Many colleges already extend preferences to athletes. Compare and contrast this policy with the affirmative action policy at UT.

---

2. WEARING THE CONFEDERATE FLAG

The Confederate flag had been banned at the mostly white Robert E. Lee high school in Tyler, Texas, in 1971 following a race riot. Undeterred, a sophomore wore a T-shirt to school that featured a Confederate flag with the slogan *It's a white thing, you wouldn't understand.* Other students had been wearing T-shirts with the same slogan but without the flag. The T-shirts had been allowed because they were regarded as a takeoff on a T-shirt, which was popular among blacks as well as some whites, that showed two black youths dressed in fashionable baggy clothes with the slogan *It's a black thing, you wouldn't understand.*

When the rebellious sophomore was told by principal Eddie Milham to change his shirt, he refused, arguing that it was his right to self-expression. A television news crew that happened to be at the school was quick to jump on the story, which appeared on the evening news. Although classes were disrupted for the next few days, students were not sorry that this incident had occurred. They said there was already a lot of racial stuff under the surface and this just helped bring it to light.

Discussion Questions

1. Is wearing the Confederate flag a racist action? Discuss whether the wearing of racist symbols should be protected as freedom of speech or prohibited as promoting racism. Support your answer.

2. Many of the students claimed that they got their racist attitudes from their parents and other adults in their lives and that education has done little to resolve it. Indeed, the principal has a picture of Robert E. Lee in his office in full Confederate regalia. Is this inconsistent with the intent of the ban of the Confederate flag in the school? Should everyone in the school community, and perhaps even in the town, be held to the same standards as the students? Support your answers.

3. Should symbols and names associated with slavery be removed from public schools? Several schools in the South that are named after slaveholders, such as Thomas Jefferson and George Washington, are changing their names. Do you agree with this policy? Compare and contrast this policy to one forbidding swastikas and Nazi symbolism in schools.

4. At the University of Mississippi, several students and alumni insist on their right to wave the Confederate flag at the Ole Miss football games. College officials have asked them to stop. Do they have the right? Support your answer.

5. The flag of Mississippi, with its Confederate emblem, has recently come under fire from civil rights groups who want the state to remove the emblem which, the groups argue, symbolizes oppression of blacks. Defenders of the flag maintain that the Confederate symbol is part of the state's heritage and, as such, should remain on the flag. Discuss which moral principles and concerns are most relevant in deciding whether or not the state has a moral obligation to remove the Confederate emblem.

3. COLIN FERGUSON AND THE "BLACK RAGE" DEFENSE

Maryanne Philips was one of hundreds of commuters who took the Long Island Railroad to and from work in New York City. On December 7, 1993, she watched in horror as Colin Ferguson came down the aisle of her train car, pulled out a semiautomtic handgun, and shot twenty-five people, killing six. At the time of his arrest, Ferguson, a Jamaican immigrant, had notes in his pockets that expressed hatred of whites, Asians, and "Uncle Tom Negroes." Ferguson, who had a long history of angry encounters with whites, had earlier been involved in an incident in which he shouted at his perceived enemies: "Black rage will get you!"

Ferguson's lawyers decided to use black rage in their client's defense. The term *black rage* stems from a 1968 study by two psychiatrists who argued that racism has made blacks mistrustful and suspicious of outsiders. Rage is a response to racism. According to Ronald Kuby, one of Ferguson's lawyers, "Being exposed to racist treatment over a long period of time drove Ferguson to violence."[39] "If you treat people as second-class citizens, they're going to snap," added Kuby's law partner William Kunstler.[40] Ferguson is not responsible for his actions. Like the people he killed, Ferguson is also a victim—a victim of white racism.

A survey of eight hundred people before Ferguson's trial found that 68 percent of blacks and 45 percent of whites believed that a compelling defense could be made on rage stemming from long-term racism. The jury, however, didn't buy the black-rage defense. Ferguson received two hundred years in prison for the murders.

Discussion Questions

1. Should the black-rage defense be taken into consideration in sentencing Ferguson? If so, is long-term imprisonment the appropriate response, or should Ferguson have received counseling?

2. Is Ferguson a victim? Discuss how Shelby Steele might respond to Ferguson's black-rage defense. Relate your answer to Steele's notion of innocence.

3. Journalist Jonathan Alter once asked, "Where does acknowledgment of pain stop and excuse-making begin?" Discuss this question in light of the Ferguson case. Is the lack of rage a sign of servility? Compare and contrast the black-rage defense with the battered-woman defense.

4. Attorney Alan Dershowitz argues that the black-rage excuse is an "insult to millions of law-abiding black Americans." The vast majority of African Americans, he points out, do not use "the mistreatment they have suffered as an excuse to mistreat others."[41] Do you agree with Dershowitz? How should people respond to mistreatment?

5. Dershowitz also suggests that the argument that blacks as a group have more rage than other people, and hence are more prone to violence, instead of helping blacks overcome racism merely reaffirms racism and the fear of many white Americans that crime is a "black problem." Do you agree with Dershowitz? Discuss how Michael Levin and Bernard Boxill might each respond to Dershowitz's concerns.

6. Compare and contrast how libertarian Ayn Rand and a Marxist might each respond to Ferguson's case and his black-rage defense. Which analysis of the case—the libertarian or the Marxist—do you find more compelling from a moral point of view?

---

4. AMADOU DIALLO: A DEADLY CASE OF RACIAL PROFILING

Amadou Diallo, a twenty-two-year-old unarmed West African immigrant with no criminal record, was standing in the doorway of his Bronx apartment building when police approached him. What began as a routine patrol ended in tragedy when the police shot and killed Diallo, hitting him with nineteen of the forty-one shots they fired at him, after mistaking the wallet he pulled from his pocket for a gun. The police were members of an aggressive Street Crimes Unit that conducted stop-and-frisk searches of persons whom they suspected of carrying guns.

When the case went to trial the jury ruled that the police were guilty of making a tragic mistake, but not murder. The National Association for the Advancement of Colored People disagreed, calling the incident "excessive force at its worst."

Discussion Questions

1. Should the police in this case be held morally responsible for their actions and, if so, to what extent? Support your answer. Is the fact that the police were acting on the belief that Diallo was pulling a gun from his pocket morally relevant? Discuss how both Kant and Aristotle might respond to these questions.

2. Discuss what a utilitarian would most likely think of racial profiling.

3. A study in 2000 found that the Street Crimes Unit disproportionately targeted Blacks and Hispanics, even when the higher crime rates in minority neighborhoods were taken into account. Less than a third of their searches were conducted in response to victim identification. Discuss how Levin and Boxill might each respond to this practice of racial profiling.

4. Using Rawls's principles of justice, develop a policy for reducing crime in high-crime neighborhoods. What criteria should police in Street Crimes Units use in determin-

ing whether to stop-and-frisk a particular person? Or should they only respond to actual crimes in the act of commission? Support your answers.

---

5. KKK GRAND WIZARD DAVID DUKE: POLITICS AND RACISM

In a democratic society, where the majority rules, minorities have the deck stacked
against them. In 1984 and 1988, Jesse Jackson became the first black person to run for
president, although neither the Republican nor the Democratic Party supported his can-
didacy. Jackson lost the election by a huge margin. Racists, on the other hand, seem to
have better luck.

In 1988 David Duke was elected to the Louisiana House of Representatives. Unlike
Jackson, who calls for racial unity, Duke is openly racist. Duke, a former grand wizard of
the KKK, believes that blacks have "inherited tendencies . . . to act in anti-social ways." A
defender of Nazi ideology as well, Duke expressed great admiration for Nazi war criminals Rudolf Hess and Dr. Josef Mengele. After his election, Duke continued to maintain
ties with white supremacist organizations. In 1990 Duke ran for the U.S. Senate with a
campaign based on "affirmative action for whites" and "upholding Western European,
Christian values." Unlike Jackson, who lost by a huge margin, Duke lost by only a few percentage points. David Duke is now focusing his efforts on spreading his message over the
Internet. His name appears on hundreds of Web sites. He also has a radio program that
is broadcast around the world twenty-four hours a day.[42]

Duke is not the only racist with political power. During a trip to the Soviet Union in
1988, President Reagan was asked about the American Indians. He responded that the
United States may have "made a mistake" in allowing Indians to retain their own cultures.
"Maybe we should not have humored them in that, wanting to stay in that kind of primitive lifestyle," Reagan told a Soviet audience. "Maybe we should have said: 'No, come join
us. Be citizens with the rest of us.'" He also claimed that American Indians had become
rich because of oil on some of the reservations.

Discussion Questions

1. Does democracy reinforce racism and cultural relativism? How can the "tyranny of the
   majority" be counteracted in the United States? Would a meritocracy, as promoted by
   Aristotle and Plato, less likely be racist?
2. *Apartheid* is an Afrikaan word meaning "apartness." Does the United States have apartheid? Does democracy institutionalize apartheid? Is apartheid desirable? Support
   your answers. Discuss Levin's response to these questions.
3. Political analyst George Will writes that, as a true believer, Duke's "reputation is supposedly redeemed, at least a little bit, by 'sincerity,' considered inherently virtuous in
   an age so committed to subjectivism that it firmly believes only in believing."[43] Does
   the fact that Duke sincerely believed in racism morally justify his racist actions? If not,
   why not? Support your answers. Discuss how an ethical subjectivist would respond to
   these questions.

4. Were Reagan's remarks about American Indians racist? Is it morally acceptable, or even morally required, for a president to be racist if the majority of the electorate supports racism? Discuss how a cultural relativist and a deontologist would answer these questions.

5. During his trip to Africa in the spring of 1998, President Clinton made an unofficial apology for American slavery and for complicity in apartheid, as well as for U.S. inaction in the face of the genocide in Rwanda. Should President Clinton have apologized? Is an apology sufficient reparation? Support your answers.

6. Many people regard the United States as a "melting pot." Multiculturalists, on the other hand, think of the United States as a stew where different groups of people have their own customs, experiences, and even languages. What does *melting pot* imply? Is the concept racist? Is multiculturalism consistent with democratic ideals? Should minorities in the United States be encouraged to assimilate by adopting the values of the majority? Support your answers.

---

6. "NOT IN MY BACKYARD": FIGHTING A TOXIC-WASTE INCINERATOR[44]

The poor and minorities, like everyone else, don't want a toxic-waste dump in their back yards. So why does toxic waste more often than not end up in their neighborhoods? In 1991 Chemical Waste Management (Chem Waste), the country's largest hazardous-waste company, received approval to build California's first commercial toxic-waste incinerator at its Kettleman Hills dump site in the San Joaquin Valley.

Weeks after receiving approval, Chem Waste, the state, and the county were slapped with a lawsuit claiming discrimination and violation of the residents' civil rights. The suit, which was filed by People for Clean Air & Water, alleges that the decision to place the toxic-waste incinerator in the almost entirely Hispanic community was part of a national pattern of situating hazardous-waste facilities near minority areas. Chem Waste admitted that most of its toxic-waste sites were in largely minority areas but nevertheless claimed that it didn't engage in discriminatory siting, because the sites it uses already had incinerators or landfills when it acquired them.

Minority activists, in response, maintained that minorities bear the burden of the nation's toxic waste disposal because minorities lack the clout to keep it out of their neighborhoods and that they have studies to support their claims. Indeed, Chem Waste's other three incinerators are located in poor, black neighborhoods in Chicago; Suget, Illinois; and Port Arthur, Texas. In December 1991 the people of Kettleman City won their civil rights lawsuit against Chem Waste.

Discussion Questions

1. Discuss whether this case study is an illustration of institutional racism.

2. According to University of California professor Robert Bullard, minority and poor communities are the least likely to fight back against toxic-waste sites. Indeed, some poor communities welcome waste sites in their areas, because they create much needed jobs and tax revenue. Would the placement of toxic-waste sites in poor areas be justified under utilitarianism? Would it be justified under John Rawls's two principles of justice? Support your answers.

3. Discuss whether toxic-waste disposal should be regulated by government or left to private enterprise. Discuss how Ayn Rand might respond to this question. Develop a public policy for toxic-waste disposal.

4. Some philosophers suggest that racism, patriarchy, and the domination of nature are all interconnected. Furthermore, the judgment by those in power that certain racial groups are "socially polluted" is used to justify environmental pollution of minority communities. Discuss this explanation of environmental racism.

5. Using a utilitarian calculus, decide whose "backyards" companies should use as toxic-waste dumps. Should the people who contribute the most to society also recieve the most protection from toxic waste? Discuss how Levin would answer this question.

C H A P T E R   1 2

Nonhuman Animals and the Environment

In the fall of 1995, Lisa Simpson, one of television's most famous cartoon characters, became a vegetarian with a little help from her friends Linda and Paul McCartney. The episode, watched by 10 million Americans, opened with the Simpsons visiting a petting zoo. That evening the family had lamb chops for dinner, and Lisa faced a moral crisis as she made the connection between the lambs she had been petting at the zoo and the meat on her plate. Lisa decided to quit eating meat. She soon discovered, however, that being a vegetarian wasn't all that easy in a society of carnivores. Her brother, Bart, tormented her mercilessly. Lisa faced another crisis when her father, Homer, hosted a pig roast. When Lisa's offer of vegetarian gazpacho as an alternative was rejected, she destroyed the barbecue and fled in disgust at her family's indifference to animal suffering.

Lisa found solace and moral support from her friends the McCartneys, who were visiting Apu, a vegan from India. Lisa confided in Apu that she eats cheese. "You must think I'm a monster," Lisa said. "Indeed I do," Apu responded. "But I have learned long ago to tolerate others rather than forcing my beliefs on them." Lisa realized that one cannot convert others through force but only through reason and example.

THE LEGAL AND MORAL STATUS OF NONHUMAN ANIMALS

Do humans have obligations toward other animals? Do other animals have rights that we ought to respect? Most people, when asked, say that they like animals and disapprove of animal cruelty. They draw the line, however, when it comes to animals having rights. When there is a conflict between animal interests and human interests, no matter how trivial, human interests almost always win out. We eat meat, visit zoos, wear leather shoes, use cosmetics and drugs that have been tested on captive animals, and abandon our dogs and cats at animal shelters when they inconvenience us. Most of the debate on the moral and legal status of animals has centered around meat-eating and the use of nonhuman animals in experiments.

Suggestions that other animals have rights that we ought to respect are generally met with ridicule. When Mary Wollstonecraft first published *A Vindication of the Rights of Woman* in 1792, her ideas were also ridiculed. One critic wrote that if the idea of equality was applied to women, why shouldn't it also hold for "brutes"? Because the idea of granting rights to dogs and cats and other animals is absurd, therefore, the critic concluded, it is also absurd to grant rights to women. Women have since been granted rights under the law, although it took more than a century. "Brutes," however, still have a long way to go.

The animals-rights movement is relatively new. In the past twenty-five years, dozens of books and hundreds of articles have been written on animals rights. There are thousands of animal-rights and vegetarian groups that have also proliferated; most colleges have at least one animals-rights group on campus.

In many Asian countries, such as India, vegetarianism has long been the norm. According to Hindu and Buddhist ethics, meat-eating violates the principle of *ahiṃsā,* or nonviolence. Meat-eating also contributes to a mentality of violence and has negative karmic consequences. With the arrival of Christian and Islam colonists, the moral ideal of vegetarianism began to erode. Nevertheless, much of the inspiration for the current animals-rights movement in the West has come from Eastern philosophy. Gandhi's philosophy, in particular, has had an enormous influence on both the American civil rights movement and the animal-rights movement.

Unlike India, in most Western countries nonhuman animals have only instrumental value and are regarded primarily as commodities, as the property of people. One meat-company manager, for example, described a breeding sow as "a valuable piece of machinery whose function is to pump out baby pigs like a sausage machine."[1] For at least ten months out of the year, the pregnant and nursing breeding sow or "mother machine" is isolated in a narrow pen in which she is unable to turn around. She is impregnated forcefully either by being tethered to a "rape rack" for easy access or through "the surgical transplant of embryos from 'supersows' to ordinary sows."[2]

Although animal-rights groups in England have been somewhat effective in changing attitudes and legislation, this fourteen-year trend reversed in 1991 with the advent of biotechnology, which will likely revolutionize agriculture and medicine.[3] Through genetic engineering, scientists can create new forms of animals by introducing genes from one species to another. The ability of humans to create new forms of animal life will very likely lead to the further commidification of nonhuman (and possibly human) animals.

The Animal Welfare Act was enacted in the United States in 1970 and has since undergone many amendments. The act is not concerned, however, with protecting the welfare of rats, mice, birds, reptiles, frogs, or animals raised for food; nor does it include genetically altered animals. In addition, animal welfare laws are paternalistic at best and do not give animals rights. Under legal welfarism almost all animal interests can be sacrificed to even the most trivial human interest. Concern for animal suffering is based primarily on the concept of "necessary suffering." Suffering is wrong ("unnecessary") only when it does not advance human interests, or at least the interests of the status quo.

Not everyone accepts legal welfarism. Ethical positions regarding public policy can be divided into the abolitionist, reformist, and status quo positions. *Abolitionists* argue that we should stop using animals altogether as a source of food and as tools in scientific experiments. They oppose zoos, circuses, and keeping animals as house pets. Their position is supported by animal-rights activists such as Tom Regan. Although few Western philosophers accept this position, it is more generally accepted in Eastern philosophies such as Hinduism, Buddhism, and Jainism, which are based on respect for all living beings.

Reformists accept meat-eating and animal experimentation, but think that we need to improve these institutions. Unlike abolitionists, who sometimes work outside the law, reformist organizations such as humane societies work within the system, promoting reform and legislative initiatives on behalf of animals. Animal-welfare laws that require certain sized cages for animals in laboratories but do not oppose animal experimentation itself are based on the reformist position.

The *status quo* position maintains that no changes are necessary in the way humans treat other animals. The status quo position is supported by traditional Western philosophies, which regard nonhuman animals as lacking moral value. This philosophical tradition has been one of the most deeply rooted obstacles to any serious consideration of the moral rights of both nonhuman animals and the environment.

THE LEGAL AND MORAL STATUS OF THE ENVIRONMENT

The environmental ethics movement is a relative newcomer on the philosophical scene. Environmental ethics is concerned with the moral basis of environmental responsibility, including the moral value of nonhuman nature, pollution, population control, food production, and preservation of the wilderness and species diversity.

In 1967 history professor Lynn White published an article in *Science* in which he blamed Christian anthropocentric thinking for creating an ecological crisis. According to Judeo-Christian tradition, earth was created by God for the benefit of humans. "By destroying pagan animism," White wrote, "Christianity made it possible to exploit nature in a mood of indifference to the feelings of natural objects."[4] The article created an uproar, especially among religious thinkers.

Philosophers entered the fray in the early 1970s. Their attention was initially focused primarily on Aldo Leopold's essay on land ethics, excerpts of which are included at the end of this chapter. This essay was first published in his 1949 *A Sand County Almanac* but did not become widely available until 1970. In the essay Leopold attacks the anthropocentric relationship between humans and environment that is based on humans as the conquerors of the land. He calls on us to replace the old paradigm with a new ecocentric paradigm in which humans are viewed as members, rather than conquerors, of the greater biotic community.

The *deep ecology* movement began in the mid-1970s. Deep ecology is generally regarded as a *radical environmental ethic*. The central concern of deep ecologists, such as Arne Naess, George Sessions, and Bill Devall, is to cultivate a sense of identification with nature and an awareness of our interconnectedness. The goal of environmental consciousness is self-realization based on unity between self and the world.

Ecofeminism emerged as an important movement in the 1980s. Ecofeminists such as Karen Warren link environmental ethics to feminism and animal rights, arguing that oppression of women, oppression of nonhuman animals, and oppression of nature are all grounded in the same logic of dominance.

As in the animal rights debate, the *status quo* position, which is presented by Richard Watson in his article at the end of this chapter, is based on an anthropocentric worldview that regards nonhuman nature as a resource for human consumption. Most Americans accept an anthropocentric view of nature. The primary purpose for protecting nonhuman nature, according to this view, is to preserve it for ourselves and future generations. While support for environmental protection varies somewhat according to the strength of the economy, there is increasing public support for it. A 2000 Gallup Poll found that

70 percent of Americans felt that protection of the environment should be given priority over economic growth. This is up from 62 percent in 1995.[5]

THE PHILOSOPHERS ON THE MORAL VALUE OF NONHUMAN ANIMALS AND THE ENVIRONMENT

Ancient Greek philosophers were divided on the issue of the moral value of nonhuman nature. The Pythagoreans, who were vegetarians, taught that other animals should be treated with respect. Aristotle, on the other hand, thought that other animals had only instrumental moral value. Contemporary views on the moral value of nonhuman animals have been shaped primarily by Aristotle's anthropocentric philosophy.

The split between humans and nonhuman nature in Western thought began with the acceptance of the ancient Greek dualism, which split reality into nonthinking material substances (body) and nonmaterial thinking substances (mind or soul). Aristotle argued that reason is an activity of the soul. Humans have a soul; nonhuman animals don't. Because moral value depends on the ability to reason, only humans have intrinsic moral value. Other animals are inferior beings whom nature has made "for the sake of man." We can use other animals for food, clothing, labor, and entertainment.[6] Likewise, we can use inanimate nature to serve human purposes.

Aristotle's worldview was Christianized by Thomas Aquinas. "Humans," according to Aquinas, "are the highest in the order of material beings, yet the lowest in the order of spiritual beings . . . the progression from the non-living to humans is one of increasing perfection . . . schematically, humans are at the apex of material creation."[7]

Aquinas backs up his teaching with biblical scripture. According to Genesis 1:26, "God said, 'let us make man in our image, after our likeness; and let them have dominion over the fish of the sea, and over the birds of the air, and over the cattle . . . and over all the earth.'" The world was created by God for humans. Nature and other animals exist only to the extent that they benefit humans. According to this worldview, humans have a radically different nature that sets us apart from other animals. Humans, as beings created in the image of God, are rational and free and, therefore, have intrinsic moral worth. Nonhuman animals, on the other hand, are irrational, mechanistic, and lack moral worth.

The belief that other humans are separate from, and morally superior to, other animals was affirmed by René Descartes, the "father of modern philosophy." Carrying the hierarchical worldview of his predecessors even further, Descartes concluded that nonhuman animals are merely organic machines, much like clocks, without souls, free will, or consciousness. Because of this, it is not immoral to kill and eat them.

French philosopher Voltaire (1694–1778) disagreed. "What a pitiful, what a sorry thing," he wrote of Descartes's philosophy, "to have said that animals are machines bereft of understanding and feeling," arguing that animals have thought, feelings, and souls just like humans. Rousseau thought that our moral concerns should extend beyond animals to include care for plants and all living beings. In the end, however, Descartes's view prevailed.

John Locke based his natural rights theory on the belief that humans are a special and unique creation of God. To base rights on equal consideration for the interests of all living beings, rather than on the so-called special nature of humans, is to deny the "natural" order of creation. Locke's anthropocentric, theologically based worldview of humans not only disallows the possibility of nonhuman beings having rights but grants humans the inalienable right to exploit nonhuman nature with impunity.

Francis Bacon (1561–1626), one of the founders of the scientific method, unquestionably accepted the prevailing philosophical views on nonhuman animals. Bacon enthusiastically advocated vivisection—the dissection of live animals—for the pure joy of learning. Because of the tremendous success of science in generating results and new technologies, few people bothered to question the morality of sacrificing nonhuman animals to achieve some of these successes.

In his lectures on ethics, Immanuel Kant taught that we have no direct duties toward animals because they lack rationality and, hence, are nonpersons. We should, however, according to Kant, "practice kindness towards animals, for he who is cruel to animals becomes hard also in his dealings with men." Cruelty toward animals purely for sport cannot be morally justified because it hardens us. While Kant did not regard other animals or nonhuman nature as having intrinsic worth, he emphasized the importance of the aesthetic experience of nature to human well-being. Just as cruelty toward other animals is wrong because it damages our character, destroying a beautiful area of wilderness is wrong because it damages our human sensibilities. On the other hand, because "animals must be regarded as man's instruments," we can use them for scientific experiments and for food just as we can use plants and the natural environment for justifiable human purposes.

The impassioned battle for equal rights for all groups of humans during the various civil rights movements fueled a similar demand for respect for the rights of other animals as well. Mohandas Gandhi, Mary Wollstonecraft, Susan B. Anthony, Elizabeth Cady Stanton, and Horace Greeley, to name only a few human-rights advocates, also spoke out on behalf of other animals. The utilitarians were among the first advocates for the rights of nonhuman animals. According to Jeremy Bentham, it is not reason but the capacity to suffer that is morally relevant.[8] The utilitarian's concern for the happiness of all sentient beings—regardless of their race, gender, or species—reflects the moral ideal of equality that was so important during the late eighteenth century. This ideal gave rise to both the American and French Revolutions. The utilitarians hoped that this moral ideal would someday be extended to all sentient beings—both human and nonhuman. In the selection from his book *Animal Liberation,* utilitarian Peter Singer maintains that to not grant equal consideration to other animals of equal cognitive ability is to engage in speciesism.

Charles Darwin (1809–1882) also rejected anthropocentricism. Darwin attacked the assumption that only humans are capable of reason. Reason, by definition, involves the ability to form general rules from particular experiences. That other animals are clearly capable of reasoning seemed obvious to Darwin and to many of the other naturalists of his time. "Only a few persons now dispute that animals possess some power of reasoning, he wrote in *The Descent of Man* (1871). Animals may constantly be seen to pause, deliberate, and resolve. It is a significant fact, that the more the habits of any particular animals are studied by a naturalist, the more he attributes to reason and the less to unlearnt instincts."[9] But Darwin underestimated the power of tradition. Indeed, his theory of evolution was reinterpreted not only to justify the oppression of non-Western people, but to justify the exploitation of other animals and nature by placing humans at the apex of evolution, thus scientifically legitimating the religious view that humans are a special creation.

Feminist philosophers are divided on the issue of animal rights. Nel Noddings argues that we do not have moral obligations toward nonhuman animals because they are incapable of being in reciprocal caring relationships with humans. Other feminists, such as Karen Warren, argue that the domination of women and the domination of nonhuman animals are part of the same patriarchal paradigm. Women can achieve autonomy only by rejecting the dualistic ideology that allows humans to subordinate other animals.

Not all cultures, as we have already noted, share the Western view of nonhuman animals. Some Native American cultures, as well as the Australian Aborigines, regard the earth and all living beings on earth as a sacred whole. Other animals deserve to be treated with respect; accordingly, we should take no more from nature than we need for our survival. Buddhist philosophers also believe that all life is interconnected and that we have to extend moral respect to all living beings if we are ever to have a peaceful world.

ANIMAL FARMING, ENVIRONMENTAL DEGRADATION, AND VEGETARIANISM

Our eating habits are our most direct interaction with the Earth. Americans are steeped in the Jeffersonian tradition that regards farmers as "the chosen People of God" and as our "most valued citizens."[10] Farming, Jefferson claimed, ennobles humans by keeping them in touch with living nature. However, modern agriculture is not a natural process but a cultural institution shaped by cultural beliefs that prescribe our relationships to the environment. Critics of modern agricultural practices maintain that exploitation of the Earth and other animals through agriculture does not ennoble us, as Kant would hope, but instead disrupts our sense of connection and blunts our feelings, particularly of empathy.[11] That agriculture has become one of the major causes of environmental degradation is not surprising given our culture's degraded view of both the environment and other animal species.

Most people are unaware of the extent to which human practices affect other animals. Each year almost 7 billion animals are killed in the United States in laboratories, for their fur, by sports hunters, and in slaughterhouses. Of these animals, 95 percent are killed for food. The average per-capita consumption of meat in the United States, Canada, and Australia is two hundred pounds per year.[12] On an average day in the United States, 130,000 cattle, 7,000 calves, 360,000 pigs, and 24 million chickens are killed.[13]

The affluence boom that followed World War II was accompanied by an increase in meat-eating, which was regarded as a status symbol. By the early 1970s, rich nations were feeding more grain to their livestock than all the people of China and India (who make up more than two-thirds of the world's population) consumed directly.

Intensive farming of animals also began in the United States shortly after the war. Intensive farming involves raising animals indoors in large, automated "factories." Several thousand chickens or pigs may be housed in one building. Confining animals in buildings requires less land and less labor. Intensive farming also makes it easier to collect the animal products and to dispose of animal waste. The modern factory farm reflects the traditional Western view of nonhuman animals as machines.

The institution of animal agriculture is one of the greatest sources of suffering for nonhuman animals. Animals in the modern factory farm are raised in large buildings in crowded cages or stalls. Today almost all of egg production comes from caged birds in automated factory buildings.[14] Journalist Joy Williams writes:

> Factory farmers are all Cartesians. Animals are no more than machines—milk machines, piglet machines, egg machines—production units converting themselves into profits. . . . The factory farm today is a crowded, stinking bedlam, filled with suffering animals that are quite literally insane, sprayed with pesticides and fattened on a diet of growth stimulants, antibiotics, and drugs. Two hundred and fifty thousand laying hens are confined within a single building. (The high mortality rate caused by overcrowding is economically acceptable; nothing is more worthless than an individual chicken.)[15]

Eating affects all of us; we need to eat to stay alive. We do have a choice, however, in what to eat. Humans do not need meat in their diets. Indeed, heavy reliance on meat is one of the leading causes of disease and obesity in the United States, England, Australia, and Canada.[16]

More and more people in these countries are becoming vegetarians. A *vegetarian* is a person who refrains from eating the flesh of animals, although some vegetarians eat fish. *Vegans*, on the other hand, abstain from all animal products including eggs and milk. A 1977/78 survey by the U.S. Department of Agriculture found that 1.2 percent of Americans identified themselves as vegetarians. In a 1997 survey, 5 percent of Americans identified themselves as vegetarians. About one-third to one-half of these people are vegans.[17] While the number of vegetarians who abstain from red meat has remained about the same, the percent of vegans, as well as people who eat no poultry or fish, has more than doubled in the past three years.[18] Asian Americans are the most likely to be vegetarians and whites the least likely to be vegetarians. Women are twice as likely as men to be vegetarians.[19]

Ethical vegetarians maintain that nonhuman animals have moral value. Although meat-eating might be justified if we needed meat for survival, the human taste for animal flesh does not justify killing and eating animals. Ethical vegetarians also point to the tremendous animal suffering by modern farming methods. Those who believe that animals should be treated with moral respect require us to expand our moral community to include other animals as well as humans. This requires giving up certain practices, such as meat-eating and wearing leather or fur. Those who defend meat-eating, such as Jan Narveson, on the other hand, deny that animals have either moral status or rights that we have to respect.

Environmental ethicists do not have a unified position on agriculture. Aldo Leopold did not reject agriculture but instead judged it against a holistic model of its impact on the entire biotic community. While many environmental ethicists advocate for the more humane treatment of nonhuman animals, a few support a move toward intensive farming of "farm" animals, blaming grazing "livestock" for the destruction of wildlife habitat. This has led to criticism that environmentalists who identify nature with the pristine wilderness have created an artificial divide not only between humans and nonhuman nature but between "domestic" and "wild" animals. The increased use of genetic engineering in agriculture may further exacerbate this divide if genetically engineered plants and animals are viewed as legal property of their human creators.

Many people adopt a vegetarian lifestyle primarily out of concern for the environment. Green political parties in Europe and Great Britain advocate a vegetarian diet for environmental and political reasons. Animal farming is tremendously damaging to the environment. They point out that if we gave up animal farming, there would be enough food for everyone in the world. Many of the world's environmental problems would also be resolved by the elimination of animal agriculture. A meat-based diet uses three times as much fossil fuel as a vegetarian diet. Much of the water pollution, depletion of topsoil, and deforestation is the result of animal agriculture. In the United States, most of the agricultural land is dedicated to raising beef. One acre of land can produce 40,000 pounds of potatoes or 250 pounds of beef.[20]

POLLUTION AND GLOBAL WARMING

Issues of pollution, global warming, and hazardous waste disposal are of central importance to applied environmental ethics. Some of the substances that contribute to atmospheric pollution, such as gases from volcanic explosions, are not of human origin. However, most of the air pollution that is contributing to global warming and acid rain is of human origin.

Global warming is of particular concern to environmentalists. Based on a one thousand-year record, the 1990s was the warmest decade and the twentieth century the warmest century.[21] Of the one hundred fifty glaciers in Glacier National Park one hundred have melted in the past one hundred fifty years, with much of the glacial runoff eventually ending up in the already swollen Mississippi River. Areas as large as Connecticut have broken off of the Antarctic ice shelf in the last few years. The melting ice, in turn, contributes to rises in sea levels.

While some areas of the world will experience significant warming, global warming may also alter ocean currents which may, in turn, plunge temperatures in Northern Europe twenty degrees in the next ten years.[22] This, along with the clearing of rain forests for agriculture and timber, has already contributed to the extinction or threatened extinction of hundreds, perhaps even thousands, of species of plants and animals.

Solid waste disposal also contributes to environmental degradation and human disease. While population growth in the Third World has been blamed for many of the environmental problems we are currently facing, in fact, affluent Westerners are responsible for much of this pollution. The average American produces much more household waste and is responsible for more industrial and agricultural pollution than anyone else in the world. Hazardous waste disposal, including the disposal of nuclear waste, is particularly problematic. There are currently over twelve hundred hazardous waste sites in the United States, most of them located in poor, minority neighborhoods and on Native American homelands.

ANIMAL EXPERIMENTATION

An estimated 100 million nonhuman animals are killed every year in scientific experiments in the United States alone.[23] As with animal agriculture, the practice of animal experimentation is based on an anthropocentric paradigm.

The U.S. Food and Drug Administration (FDA) requires that all new chemical products be tested. Most of these tests are performed on nonhuman animals. One of the more common tests is the Draize eye irritancy test, which was developed by J. H. Draize, who worked for the FDA. The Draize test involves placing a rabbit's head in a restraining

---

EXPERIMENTS USING NONHUMAN ANIMALS[24]

- **Acute toxicity test.** This test involves force-feeding enormous quantities of a substance to a group of animals, either orally or through a tube. The purpose is to determine the lethal dose at which a given percentage of animals die within two weeks. The tests can cause convulsions, vomiting, diarrhea, paralysis, and rupture of internal organs.

- **Chronic toxicity test.** Animals are force-fed smaller quantities of a substance over time to determine if continuous exposure is lethal.

- **Skin and eye irritation tests.** Animals are immobilized in restraining devices and chemicals are applied to raw skin or sprayed in the eyes.

- **Acute inhalation toxicity test.** Animals are subjected to large amounts of spray from aerosol preparations. They are then killed and their tissues examined.

- **Psychology research.** Animals are used in experiments that include electric shock, "punishment," induced fighting and killing, brain damage, mutilation, drug addiction, maternal deprivation, and overcrowding.

- **Weapons tests.** Animals are used to study the effects of atomic blasts, radiation, chemical warfare, and laser weapons on the body.

- **Biotechnology.** Animals are genetically engineered for use in medical experiments, to produce drugs for human use, and for organ transplants.

---

device and then putting in one of their eyes a substance such as bleach, shampoo, nail polish, chemical cleaning substances, or weed killer. These experiments are extremely painful. Some rabbits snap their necks in their frantic attempts to escape.

The medical field, the defense industry, and universities also make extensive use nonhuman animals in their research. The different types of animal experiments are outlined above.

Probably the biggest increase in the use of animals in experiments has been in biotechnology and genetic engineering. Scientists are using genetic engineering to create "designer" animals for specific purposes. It may not be long before pigs, genetically altered to contain human genes, will be mass produced as drug factories and to provide organ transplants for humans. Those who defend the status quo, such as Carl Cohen, argue that animals have no rights that we are bound to respect. They also point out the benefits that animal experimentation has brought to humans.

On the other hand, the results of experiments on one species do not necessarily carry over to humans. Millions of dollars are wasted every year on pointless or repetitive experiments. Eliminating these types of experiments would rule out some animal experimentation, but it would not rule out all of it. Unlike reformists, abolitionists oppose all animal experimentation, even if it can be shown to greatly benefit humans. We cannot use other animals to advance human interests. In England scientific experimentation on dogs and puppies was outlawed as part of the government's preelection promise to implement a far-reaching ban on animal experimentation.

Both abolitionists and reformists encourage the use of alternatives to animal research. These alternatives include observation of patients, clinical tests, tissue and cell cultures, the use of cadavers, mechanical models, and computer-generated models. Some college students have also refused to participate in dissection and the use of animals in experiments in class.[25]

Although some scientists believe that the advent of biotechnology will increase the demand for animal experimentation, others argue that the completion of the Human Genome Project may render much of animal experimentation obsolete. The new field of pharmogenetics, for example, which studies the effects of genetics on an individual's reactions to drugs, will increase the likelihood that medications will be tailored for each individual based on their particular genome rather than on animal models.[26]

MORAL ISSUES

The Moral Standing of Nonhuman Animals and Nature

To attribute moral standing to a being is to claim that it is worthy of moral respect and protection. A common approach for determining moral standing is to ask if a being has cognitive qualities similar to those of a rational and autonomous human adult. The more the being is like a human adult in these respect, the higher its moral standing. Applying this line of reasoning, traditional philosophers and scientists maintain that other animals lack reason and the ability to be autonomous and, therefore, have little, if any, moral standing. Narveson and Cohen represent this view on the moral standing of nonhuman animals. Singer, on the other hand, argues that some adult mammals are sufficiently like humans in their cognitive abilities to warrant moral consideration.

One of the problems in this approach is in knowing the mental life and intentions, if any, of other animals. Furthermore, although lack of certain cognitive abilities may exclude a being from being a moral agent, it does not logically follow that it should be denied moral standing because of this. Regan, for example, argues that nonhuman animals may not be moral agents, but they can still be moral patients; that is, they have interests, and therefore rights, that we ought to respect. For example, a cat companion may not have any moral duties toward us, but we, as moral agents, have a duty to provide her with food and shelter. According to Regan, both moral agents and moral patients, as beings that are subjects of life, have inherent value.

Utilitarians, such as Singer, maintain that sentience, not reason, is the relevant criterion for assigning moral standing. It is wrong to cause suffering no matter what the cognitive level of the being. Singer also employs anthropocentric criteria, however, attributing higher moral standing to those animals, such as adult mammals, that are most like adult humans in their cognitive abilities. Hindu and Buddhist philosophers, on the other hand, cast the net wide enough to include all living beings in the moral community.

The primary divide in the environmental rights movement is between ecocentrism and anthropocentrism. Ecocentrists and biocentrists, such as Leopold, maintain that nature has moral standing and that we have a duty to preserve the integrity of the biotic community. Environmental ethicists such as Watson, on the other hand, maintain that the ecocentric arguments are misguided and possibly even misanthropic. While there are good reasons for preserving nonhuman nature, they argue, these reasons are based on human interests. We by necessity operate from a human-centered perspective. Human beings, by their very nature, cannot help but treat nature instrumentally in order to use resources from the natural world. Caring for nature is good, not because nature has intrinsic worth, but because identification with nature expands and humanizes us.

Social Contract Theory

According to social contract theorists, such as Narveson, morality is a type of voluntary contract among people. We have moral obligations only toward those who have entered into this agreement. Because nonhuman animals, plants, and inanimate objects such as mountains cannot enter into a social contract, we have no direct moral obligations toward them. Instead we have direct duties only toward other humans. For example, we ought not to kill or destroy someone else's pet, not because the pet has a right to life, but because we have a duty toward the human not to destroy her property. A pet owner, however, may decide to rid herself of her pet.

The Principle of Utility

What matters, according to utilitarians, is whether animals can feel pain, not whether they can reason. Singer and Regan graphically illustrate the pain and torment caused to nonhuman animals by human practices. The moral duty to minimize pain and maximize pleasure militates against most human use of animals. The pleasure humans may get from the taste of meat does not outweigh the suffering caused to animals by farming.

We also need to weigh the benefits to humans of animal experimentation against the animals' interests in living a pain-free life. On the other hand, if our concern is to benefit humans, it could be argued that it would be preferable to use brain-damaged humans rather than nonhuman animals, because the results would be more accurate. Indeed, the use of certain "nonproductive" groups of humans, such as elderly people and children who are mentally retarded, has been justified on utilitarian grounds by researchers in the past. Most people find this implication of utilitarian reasoning morally repugnant.

Another problem with relying on utilitarian criteria is the definition of "necessary" suffering." The concepts of necessary and unnecessary suffering, used by Cohen to justify the use of nonhuman animals in experiments, are notoriously vague as well as biased in favor of human interests. Suffering is generally regarded as unnecessary only when it does not facilitate human ends or well-being. People who torture their dogs are seen as despicable cowards; scientists who conduct painful experiments on dogs are seen as promoting human progress. Furthermore, the suffering caused to one hundred dogs by an experiment might be labeled "necessary," whereas the suffering from performing the same experiment on one severely retarded human would probably be deemed morally unacceptable. Thus, utilitarian talk of benefits and necessary suffering often serves to mask a view of other animals as property and lack of genuine concern for them. The tremendous disparity in power of scientists and agribusiness also ensures that the interests of humans will always be given greater weight than the interests of other animals. The principle of *ahiṃsā*, in contrast, states that the suffering of nonhuman animals cannot be justified by its benefits to humans.

Many environmental ethicists, including the deep ecologists and ecofeminists, reject both the utilitarian and the stewardship models. Because they focus on sentience as conferring moral worth, they believe that utilitarians define the "common good" too narrowly. While many environmental ethicists embrace a concept of the common good it includes all of nature, not just sentient beings. To use the words of Leopold, "a thing is right when it tends to preserve the stability, integrity, and beauty of the biotic community." In addition, the stewardship model, like Singer's utilitarian theory, is hierarchical, placing more value on beings who are the most sentient. Land and nonhuman nature have value beyond their usefulness to humans.

Rights

One of the weaknesses of utilitarianism is that it does not guarantee that animals—human or nonhuman—cannot be used as a means only. Animal-rights advocates argue that just as we ought to respect humans' intrinsic worth, regardless of their utility, we should also treat other animals as ends-in-themselves. Animals welfarists, while acknowledging that animals have welfare rights such as health care, proper nutrition, and a clean living space, do not generally recognize other animals' liberty rights or right to life. Animal-rights advocates, on the other hand, claim that nonhuman animals have both welfare and liberty rights.

Traditional Western philosophy supports a model of rights based on self-assertion. This position is defended by Cohen. According to the self-assertion model, a right is a claim or potential claim that one being may exercise against another. Rights arise only among beings that can make moral claims against one another. Because nonhuman animals presumably lack the capacity for moral choice, they lack moral rights.

In contrast, the model of rights adopted by animal-rights advocates, such as Regan, is based on interests. The existence of interests is based on the capacity for suffering and for enjoyment. All sentient animals, including humans, have an interest in doing that which brings pleasure, as well as an interest in avoiding harm and suffering. Under this model of rights, benefits to oneself and others are morally acceptable only if no one else's rights have been violated in achieving these benefits.

On the other hand, advocates of deep ecology have been accused of being eco-fascists. There is concern that ecocentrism may motivate the state to be overly coercive and restrictive of the activities of humans for the sake of the greater environmental good.

Justice, Speciesism, and the Principle of Equality

The principle of equality states that it is unjust to treat beings differently unless we can show that there is a difference between them that is relevant to the differential treatment. Singer claims that "speciesism," which he defines as "a prejudice or attitude of bias in favor of the interests of members of one's own species and against those of members of another species,"[27] violates the principle of equality. His rule of thumb for avoiding speciesism is that "we should give the same respect to the lives of animals as we give to the lives of those humans at a similar mental level." Both Singer and Warren relate discrimination against other animals to discrimination based on racism and sexism.

The moral equality of sentient beings does not entail that human and nonhuman animals have the same rights. Different species have different interests. There are distinctly human rights, such as the right to religious freedom and the right to a formal education, that other animals lack because they have no interest in either organized religion or formal schooling. All sentient animals, however—including humans, cats, mice, and frogs—have an interest in not being tortured, starved, or held captive, not because they are capable of rational thought, but because they have the ability to feel pain.

To most people, speciesism doesn't seem as bad as racism or sexism. In fact, many people find the comparison offensive. Whereas gender or skin color is arbitrary and of no moral importance, they argue, the difference in our treatment of humans and other species is based on morally relevant differences. Only humans, as rational autonomous beings, are able to participate in the moral community.

On the other hand, as Singer points out, there are humans who are neither rational nor autonomous. Including these people in the moral community while excluding other animals of equal or greater cognitive capacity seems to violate the principle of equality because it involves basing moral treatment on group membership rather than on individual differences. Also, the claim that no other animals are capable of reason seems empirically wrong. There would be no point in using nonhuman animals, such as monkeys and rats, in some learning experiments if they were incapable of reason. Indeed, as Singer points out, the reason why we use other animals in learning and medical experiments is precisely because they are so much like us.

The environmental justice movement emerged in the United States in the 1980s as an outgrowth of the movement for social justice for politically disenfranchised groups of people. Its focus has been on the urban environment rather than on the wilderness. As such this movement has radically redefined the meaning of environment to include the broader framework of economic, racial, and social justice. The movement's primary concerns have been on ending environmental racism and on promoting tighter government regulation of industrial pollution and waste disposal.

Natural Law

Defenders of meat-eating point out that other animals eat meat. The human practice of meat-eating is simply part of the natural order. This argument is also used in support of hunting. But because humans are omnivores, an argument based on nature can go either way and hence is not particularly useful in resolving the question regarding the moral acceptability of meat-eating. Opponents of meat-eating maintain that humans are not physiologically suited for a meat-based diet. Indeed many of our modern ailments are due to our meat-eating habits. This argument also commits the naturalist fallacy: Just because humans can and do eat meat does not mean that they ought to.

CONCLUSION

Gandhi once said that "the greatness of a nation can be judged by the way its animals are treated." Even if we don't accept the claim that other animals have inherent moral worth, we ought to stop and consider the ways in which our lifestyles cause suffering to other animals. The case for vegetarianism, especially when almost all the animals we use for food are now raised on factory farms, is strong whichever position we accept on the moral status of nonhuman animals. Morality requires that we be able to justify actions that affect others. Human beings have the power to exploit or to live in harmony with other species and the environment. It is up to each of us to decide how we want to use this power.

TOM REGAN

The Moral Basis of Vegetarianism

Tom Regan is an animal-rights activist and professor of philosophy and religion at North Carolina State University. In the following selection, Regan provides a rights-based argument for vegetarianism. He begins by responding to traditional philosophical arguments that deny moral value and rights to nonhuman animals. After analyzing and rejecting these arguments, Regan concludes that the current differential treatment of human and nonhuman animals cannot be morally justified. All animals that are experiencing subjects of their own lives have inherent value.

Critical Reading Questions

1. How did Gandhi's life and writings influence Regan's thinking on vegetarianism?
2. On what grounds does Regan reject Descartes's view of nonhuman animals?
3. Why does Regan reject the traditional view that language is necessary for experiencing pain?
4. According to Regan, why is the principle of nonmaleficence morally relevant to our treatment of nonhuman animals?
5. How does Regan respond to the argument that humans have certain natural rights that animals lack?
6. How does Regan respond to the argument that only humans have the ability to reason?
7. How does Regan respond to the argument that animals cannot have rights because they lack the ability to claim them? How does he respond to the argument that granting rights to animals is absurd as they are not capable of making moral decisions?
8. What is Regan's position on the use of "intensive rearing methods"? What is the purpose and result of these modern farming techniques? Who, according to Regan, is morally responsible for their continuation?
9. How does Regan respond to the argument that meat-eating may be justified if the meat is bought from farms where intensive rearing methods are not used?
10. How does Regan respond to the argument that meat-eating would no longer be morally objectionable if we could find ways to raise and kill animals painlessly?
11. On what grounds does Regan reject the natural rights argument that "all and only human beings have an equal right to life"?
12. Why does Regan claim that the burden of justification rests on the shoulders of meat-eaters rather than on vegetarians?
13. Does Regan oppose all taking of the lives of animals? Under what circumstances might it be morally justifiable to take the life of a nonhuman animal?
14. According to Regan, what would be necessary to justify the differential treatment of humans and nonhuman animals?

"The Moral Basis of Vegetarianism," in *All That Dwell Therein: Animal Rights and Environmental Ethics* (Berkeley: University of California Press, 1982), 1–36. Notes have been omitted.

My initial interest in vegetarianism grew out of my study of the life and writings of Mahatma Gandhi. Gandhi, as is well known, was an advocate of nonviolence (ahimsā), not only in political affairs but in the conduct of one's life generally. The extreme pacifistic position he advocated, from which he derived the obligatoriness of vegetarianism, struck me as inadequate, and I sought a less radical moral basis for vegetarianism, one that those of us in the Western world would find more hospitable. Since the leading theories were (and remain) one or another version of utilitarianism, on the one hand, and, on the other, theories that proclaim basic moral rights, it seemed to me that the moral basis of vegetarianism would have to be found somewhere among these options. That such a basis may be provided by a rights-based theory is what "The Moral Basis of Vegetarianism" attempts to show. Both the moral right not to be caused gratuitous suffering and the right to life, I argue, are possessed by the animals we eat if they are possessed by the humans we do not. To cause animals to suffer cannot be defended merely on the grounds that we like the taste of their flesh, and even if animals were raised so that they led generally pleasant lives and were "humanely" slaughtered, that would not insure that their rights, including their right to life, were not violated. Despite the Western custom of supposing that vegetarians must defend their "eccentric" way of life, the essay attempts to shift the burden of proof onto the shoulders of those who should bear it—the nonvegetarians.

Now, there can be no doubt that animals sometimes appear to be in pain. On this point, even Descartes would agree. In order for us to be rationally entitled to abandon the belief that they actually do experience pain, therefore, especially in view of the close physiological resemblances that often exist between them and us, we are in need of some rationally compelling argument that would demonstrate that this belief is erroneous. Descartes's principle argument in this regard fails to present a compelling case for his view. Essentially, it consists in the claim that, since animals cannot speak or use a language, they do not think, and since they do not think, they have no minds; lacking in these respects, therefore, they have no consciousness either. Thus, since a necessary condition of a creature's being able to experience pain is that it be a conscious being, it follows,

given Descartes's reasoning, that animals do not experience pain. . . .

Imagine a person whose vocal chords have been damaged to such an extent that he no longer has the ability to utter words or even make inarticulate sounds, and whose arms have been paralyzed so that he cannot write, but who, when his tooth abscesses, twists and turns on his bed, grimaces and sobs. We do not say, "Ah, if only he could still speak, we could give him something for his pain. As it is, since he cannot speak, there's nothing we need give him. For he feels no pain." We say he is in pain, despite his loss of the ability to say so.

Whether or not a person is experiencing pain, in short, does not depend on his being able to perform one or another linguistic feat. Why, then, should it be any different in the case of animals? It would seem to be the height of human arrogance, rather than of . . . "superstition," to erect a double standard here, requiring that animals meet a standard not set for humans. If humans can experience pain without being logically required to be able to say so, or in any other ways to use a language, then the same standard should apply to animals as well. . . .

Now, an essential part of any enlightened morality is the principle of noninjury. What this principle declares is that we are not to inflict pain on, or otherwise bring about or contribute to the pain in, any being capable of experiencing it. This principle, moreover, is derivable from the more general principle of nonmaleficence, which declares that we are not to do or cause evil, together with the value judgment that pain, considered in itself, is intrinsically evil. . . .

Given the intrinsic evil of pain, and assuming further that pleasure is intrinsically good, it is clear that cases can arise in which the evil (pain) caused to animals is not compensated for by the good (pleasure) caused humans. The classical utilitarians—Bentham, Mill, and Sidgwick—all were aware of this . . .

It has already been pointed out that the pain an animal feels is just as much pain, and just as much an intrinsic evil, as a comparable pain felt by a human being. So, if there is any rational basis for rendering conflicting judgments about the two practices, it must be looked for in some other direction.

The most likely and, on the face of it, the most plausible direction in which to look is in the direction of rights. "Humans," this line of reasoning goes, "have certain natural rights that animals lack, and that is what makes the two practices differ in a morally significant way. For in the case of the practice involving humans, their equal natural right to be spared undeserved pain is being violated, while in the case of the practice involving animals, since animals can have no rights, *their* rights are not being ignored. That is what makes the two cases differ. And that is what makes the practice involving humans an immoral one, while the practice involving animals is not."

Natural though this line of argument is, I do not think it justifies the differential treatment of the animals and humans in question. For on what grounds might it be claimed that the humans, but not the animals, have an equal natural right to be spared undeserved pain? Well, it cannot be, as it is sometimes alleged, that all and only human beings have this right because all and only humans reason, make free choices, or have a concept of their identity. These grounds will not justify the ascription of rights to all humans because some humans—infants and the severely mentally defective, for example—do not meet these conditions. Moreover, even if these conditions did form the grounds for the possession of rights; and even if it were true that all human beings met them; it still would not follow that *only* human beings have them. For on what grounds, precisely, might it be claimed that no animals can reason, make free choices, or form a concept of themselves? What one would want here are detailed analyses of these operative concepts together with rationally compelling empirical data and other arguments that support the view that all nonhuman animals are deficient in these respects. It would be the height of prejudice merely to assume that man is unique in being able to reason. To the extent that these beliefs are not examined in the light of what we know about animals and animal intelligence, the supposition that *only* human beings have these capacities is just that—a supposi-

tion, and one that could hardly bear the moral weight placed upon it by the differential treatment of animals and humans. . . .

Two objections should be addressed before proceeding. Both involve difficulties that are supposed to attend the attribution of rights to animals. The first declares that animals cannot have rights because they lack the capacity to *claim* them. Now, this objection seems to be a variant of the view that animals cannot have rights because they cannot speak, and, like this more general view, this one too will not withstand a moment's serious reflection. For there are many human beings who annot speak or claim their rights—tiny infants, for example—and yet who would not be denied the right in question, assuming, as we are, that it is supposed to be a right possessed by *all* human beings. Thus, if a human being can possess this (or any other right) without being able to demand it, it cannot be reasonable to require that animals be able to do so, if they are to possess this (or any other) right. The second objection is different. It declares that the attribution of rights to animals leads to absurdity. For if, say, a lamb has the natural right to be spared undeserved pain, then the wolf, who devours it unmercifully, without the benefit of anesthetic, should be said to violate the lamb's right. This, it is alleged, is absurd, and so, then, is the attribution of rights to animals. Well, absurd it may be to say that the wolf violates the lamb's right. But even supposing that it is, nothing said here implies that such deeds on the part of the wolf violate the lamb's rights. For the lamb can have rights only against those beings who are capable of taking the interests of the lamb into account and [are] trying to determine, on the basis of its interests, as well as other relevant considerations, what, morally speaking, ought to be done. In other words, the only kind of being against which another being can have rights is a being that can be held to be morally responsible for its actions. Thus, the lamb can have rights against, say, most adult human beings. But a wolf, I think it would be agreed, is not capable of making decisions from the moral point of view; nor is a wolf the kind of being that can be held morally responsible; neither, then, can it make sense to say that the lamb has any rights against the wolf. This situation has its counterpart in human affairs. The severely mentally feeble, for example, lack the requisite powers to act morally; thus, *they* cannot be expected to recognize our rights, nor can *they* be said to violate our rights, even if, for example, they should happen to cause us undeserved pain. For as they are not the kind of being that can be held responsible for what they do, neither can they be said to violate anyone's rights by what they do. . . .

Animals who are raised to be eaten by human beings very often are made to suffer. Nor is it simply that they suffer only when they are being shipped to the slaughterhouse or actually being slaughtered. For what is happening is this: The human appetite for meat has become so great that new methods of raising animals have come into being. Called intensive rearing methods, these methods seek to insure that the largest amount of meat can be produced in the shortest amount of time with the least possible expense. In ever increasing numbers, animals are being subjected to the rigors of these methods. Many are being forced to live in incredibly crowded conditions. Moreover, as a result of these methods, the natural desires of many animals often are being frustrated. In short, both in terms of the physical pain these animals must endure, and in terms of the psychological pain that attends the frustration of their natural inclinations, there can be no reasonable doubt that animals who are raised according to intensive rearing methods experience much nontrivial, undeserved pain. Add to this the gruesome realities of "humane" slaughter and we have, I think, an amount and intensity of suffering that can, with propriety, be called "great."

To the extent, therefore, that we eat the flesh of animals that have been raised under such circumstances, we help create the demand for meat that farmers who use intensive rearing methods endeavor to satisfy. Thus, to the extent that it is known that such methods will bring about much undeserved, nontrivial pain on the part of the animals raised according to these methods, anyone who purchases meat that is a product of these methods— and almost everyone who buys meat at a typical supermarket or restaurant does this—is *causally implicated* in a practice that causes pain that is both nontrivial and undeserved for the animals in question. On this point too, I think there can be no doubt. . . .

Now, there are, as I mentioned earlier, two further objections that might be raised, both of which, I think, uncover important limitations in the argument of this section. The first is that a meat eater might be able to escape the thrust of my argument by the simple expedient of buying meat from farms where the animals are not raised according to intensive rearing methods, a difficult but not impossible task at the present time. For despite the widespread use of these methods, it remains true that there are farms where animals are raised in clean, comfortable quarters, and where the pain they experience is the natural result of the exigencies of animal existence rather than, to use an expression of Hume's, of "human art and contrivance." . . .

The [second] objection that reads thus: "Granted, the amount of pain animals experience in intensive rearing units is deplorable and ought to be eliminated as far as is possible; still, it does not follow that we ought to give up meat altogether or to go to the trouble of hunting or buying it from other farmers. After all, all we need do is get rid of the pain and our moral worries will be over. So, what we should do is this; we should try to figure out how to *desensitize* animals so that they do not feel any pain, even in the most barbarous surroundings. Then, if this could be worked out, there would not be any grounds for worrying about the 'morality' of eating meat. Remove the animals' capacity for feeling pain and you thereby remove the possibility of their experiencing any pain that is gratuitous."

Now, I think it is obvious that nothing that I have said thus far can form a basis for responding to this objection, and though I think there are alternative ways in which one might try to respond to it, the case I try to make against it evolves out of my response to the first objection; I try to show, in other words, that an adequate response to this objection can be based upon the thesis that *it is the killing of animals, and not just their pain, that matters morally.*

. . .

Let us begin, then, with the idea that all humans possess an equal natural right to life. And let us notice, once again, that it is an *equal natural* right that we are speaking of, one that we cannot acquire or have granted to us, and one that we all are supposed to have just because we are human beings. On what basis, then, might it be alleged that all and only human beings possess this right to an equal extent? Well, several familiar possibilities come immediately to mind. It might be argued that all and only human beings have an equal right to life because either (*a*) all and only human beings have the capacity to reason, or (*b*) all and only human beings have the capacity to make free choices, or (*c*) all and only human beings have a concept of "self," or (*d*) all and only human beings have all or some combination of the previously mentioned capacities. And it is easy to imagine how someone might argue that, since animals do not have any of these capacities, *they* do not possess a right to life, least of all one that is equal to the one possessed by humans.

I have already touched upon some of the difficulties such views must inevitably encounter. Briefly, it is not clear, first, that no nonhuman animals satisfy any one (or all) of these conditions, and, second, it is reasonably clear that not all human beings satisfy them. The severely mentally feeble, for example, fail to satisfy them. Accordingly, *if* we want to insist that they have a right to life, then we cannot also maintain that they have it because they satisfy one or another of these conditions. Thus, *if* we want to insist that they have an equal right to life, despite their failure to satisfy these conditions, we cannot consistently maintain that animals, because they fail to satisfy these conditions, therefore lack this right.

Another possible ground is that of sentience, by which I understand the capacity to experience pleasure and pain. But this view, too, must encounter a familiar difficulty—namely, that it could not justify restricting the right *only* to human beings. . . .

The onus of justification lies not on the shoulders of those who are vegetarians but on the shoulders of those who are not. If the argument of the present section is sound, it is the nonvegetarian who must show us how he can be justified in eating meat, when he knows that, to do so, an animal has had to be killed. It is the nonvegetarian who must show us how his manner of life does not contribute

to practices that systematically ignore the right to life which animals possess, if humans are supposed to possess it on the basis of the most plausible argument considered here. And it is the nonvegetarian who must do all this while being fully cognizant that he cannot defend his way of life merely by summing up the intrinsic goods—the delicious taste of meat, for example—that come into being as a result of the slaughter of animals.

This is not to say that practices that involve taking the lives of animals cannot possibly be justified. . . . For example, perhaps they are satisfied in the case of the Eskimo's killing of animals and in the case of having a restricted hunting season for such animals as deer. But to say that this is (or may be) true of *some* cases is not to say that it is true of all, and it will remain the task of the nonvegetarian to show that what is true in these cases, assuming that it is true, is also true of any practice that involves killing animals which, by his actions, he supports. . . .

Even if it should turn out that there are no natural rights, that would not put an end to many of the problems discussed here. For even if we do not possess natural rights, we would still object to practices that caused nontrivial, undeserved pain for some human beings if their "justification" was that they brought about this or that amount of pleasure or other forms of intrinsic good for this or that number of people; . . . and we would still object to any practice that involved the killing of human beings, even if killed painlessly, if the practice was supposed to be justified in the same way. But this being so, what clearly would be needed, if we cease to invoke the idea of rights, is some explanation of why practices that are not right, when they involve the treatment of people, can be right (or at least permissible) when they involve the treatment of animals. What clearly would be needed, in short, is what we have found to be needed and wanting all along—namely, the specification of some morally relevant feature of being human which is possessed by *all* human beings and *only* by those beings who are human. Unless or until some such feature can be pointed out, I do not see how the differential treatment of humans and animals can be rationally defended, natural rights or no.

Discussion Questions

1. Do you have a moral obligation to be a vegetarian? Support your argument.
2. Some "vegetarians" eat free-range animals, including fish, especially on holidays such as Thanksgiving, Easter, and Passover. Does eating only free-range animals overcome Regan's objection to meat-eating? Support your answer.
3. Discuss how Regan would stand on the morality of keeping animals in zoos. Do their educational value and protection of endangered species justify the existence of zoos? Support your answer.
4. Regan is opposed to animal experimentation no matter how much it benefits humans. Do you agree with Regan's position? Discuss how Aquinas and Kant might respond to Regan's abolitionist position.
5. Would Regan approve or disapprove of the human practice of keeping pets and, if so, under what conditions? Support your answer. Discuss how Regan might stand on the euthanasia of sick and elderly animal companions.
6. In his 1982 essay, "The Nature and Possibility of an Environmental Ethics,"[28] Regan explores the possibility that there is an "inherent goodness" in natural objects that we should respect. This respect should lead us to adopt a "preservation principle" of "nondestruction and noninterference." Do you agree with Regan? Analyze Regan's premises and conclusion.

 JAN NARVESON

Animal Rights Revisited

Jan Narveson is a philosophy professor at the University of Waterloo. Narveson argues that it is not clear that utilitarianism requires us to adopt a vegetarian lifestyle. Furthermore, he argues, under social contract theory, animals, being nonrational and lacking language, are not capable of entering into a contractual agreement. Therefore under the social contract, they have no rights that we are morally bound to respect. Although it may be unfortunate for animals that we make meals out of them, we are morally justified in doing so.

Critical Thinking Questions

1. What are the three possible options listed by Narveson regarding our moral obligations to nonhuman animals?
2. What assumptions does Narveson make regarding the utility of nonhuman animals?
3. Why, according to Narveson, do nonhuman animals have less utility than humans?
4. On what grounds does Narveson argue that raising nonhuman animals for food might actually increase the total utility for that species?

"Animal Rights Revisited," in eds. Harlan B. Miller and William H. Williams, *Ethics and Animals* (Clifton, N.J.: Humana Press, 1993), 45–59.

5. According to Narveson's interpretation of contractarian theory, what characteristics must a being have to be included in a social contract?
6. Why, according to Narveson, can't nonhuman animals be included in a social contract?
7. What is the connection between being included in a social contract and having moral rights?
8. According to Narveson, what abilities are required to be eligible for moral consideration?
9. On what grounds does Narveson claim that our dealings with other animals need only be based on our own self-interest?
10. How does Narveson respond to the "marginal cases" objection?

What do we owe to the animals? What, that is to say, do we owe them *qua* animal, rather than in their various possible roles as pets, watchdogs, potential sources of protein, or potential sources of knowledge on various matters of medical interest? Our usual repertoire of moral ideas does not give us a very clear answer to this question, for those ideas have been framed for dealing with our fellow humans, by and large. When we address ourselves to this nonstandard case, then, we must scrutinize those ideas rather closely. . . .

It may be well to begin by trying to assemble the options, though even to do this is assuredly to begin to do moral theory. Here, then, are the main ones as I see it:

(1) The moral status of animals is simply that of things, potentially useful or dangerous in various ways; the proper way to deal with them is simply whatever way is dictated by our interests in such things.

(2) Animals are in the same moral boat as we are: to wit, they have the capacity to suffer or prosper, to be better or worse off, and we ought to attach the same weight to a given degree of well- or ill-being on their part as we do to our own, endeavoring to do the best we can for all concerned.

(3) Animals are in the same moral boat as we are, but it is a different boat: to wit, they have the right to lead their lives as they choose, without interference from us—but also, without *help* from us, if we do not wish to give it.

This list of options is not exhaustive of the logical possibilities, obviously. I have come to suspect, however, that it exhausts all the *interesting* possibilities. And curiously enough, those are the same possibilities that obtain with respect to our moral dealings with our fellow humans. . . .

What assumptions is it reasonable to make about the utility of animals? It seems very reasonable indeed to suppose that animals can feel pain and pleasure. It seems reasonable to attribute to them some degree of intelligence (but unclear just what we are attributing to them in doing so, nor whether it is a capacity of the same sort we attribute to humans). Does that matter? Mill thought it did. It is tempting to say that he thought that the utility of intelligent beings counts more than the utility of less intelligent ones, but that surely will not do. What we must say instead, and what Mill really does say (I think), is that intelligent beings have a greater capability of utility than less intelligent ones: the satisfaction of a satisfied Socrates (if that is possible) involves a great deal more utility than the satisfaction of a satisfied pig. For that matter, even the satisfactions of a dissatisfied Socrates outweigh those of the pig. One question to worry about is: Is Mill right, or even believable, about that? Another is: What follows if he is? . . .

We do, certainly, make judgments of the form "people would in general be happier if . . . " Although there is a good deal of disagreement about such judgments, it may also be admitted that we are not entirely out in left field in making them. The problem is to make judgments of the form, "people *and animals* would be happier if . . . ," and that is trickier. It is acutely trickier in just the cases we have to worry about in the present paper—all the cases wherein there is a genuine conflict between the interests of us and the animals: namely, if our main interest in animals is realized, then their interest in *whatever* they may be interested in is thwarted, because they end up on our dinner plates. And that is a loss of utility that, in the case of humans, would certainly not be thought to be outweighed by the gourmet's interest in them, however powerful that interest might be. So we would surely be headed for vegetarianism if there were no reason for downrating the animals' utility quite substantially.

Actually, there are two sorts of "downrating." One way is to claim that the utility of animals, although admittedly quite comparable to ours, simply does not count, or that it counts very little: as if, for instance, we were allowed to multiply the animal's utility score by 0.01. The other way is to claim that animals have very little utility, really, at least by comparison with our own. As we have noted, utilitarianism must surely take the latter tack. It is axiomatic, after all, that everyone counts for one and none for more (or less).

What might reasonably (as opposed to just self-interestedly) persuade us that animals *do* have a lesser capacity for utility than we? Many would point to their supposedly lesser intelligence as a justification for treating them as we do. But they may or may not have in mind intelligence as a factor influencing utility. They may instead be thinking of it as an intrinsic good. Can we find a reason for supposing that intellect affects capacity for utility, then?

One thing that has long intrigued me in this connection is the involvement of intelligent beings with their own, or indeed, any futures. We are acutely aware of the future stretching out before us, and of the past in the other direction. We are, indeed, often so involved with time that we might be accused of neglecting our present. And we can at least conjecture that with animals things are different. Perhaps it is still excessively anthropomorphic to think so, but we do seem to think that animal awareness of their own future, indeed of their own identity in general, is rather dim; this despite homing pigeons and whatnot, who certainly seem to

have a clear idea where to go next. But we do suppose that they are, as the saying goes, guided by instinct rather than reason. . . .

Still, *why* might this matter? I have suggested that animals might "experience only more or less isolated sensations and uninterpreted feelings. If such beings are killed, all that happens is that a certain series of such feelings which would otherwise have occurred, do not occur . . . When beings having a future are killed, they lose that future; when beings lacking it are killed, they do not. So no interest in continued life is lost in their case."[1] Well, setting aside the critical question of whether some such thing is true of animals, there remains the question just why it might make the kind of difference I supposed it did *on utilitarian grounds*. If two beings, one of whom has and one of whom lacks a future, each had a nonutilitarian-type right to its future, then we could agree that if we painlessly killed each of them, we would have violated one creature's rights, but not the other's. Unfortunately, utilitarians are not entitled to nonutilitarian rights. So if this difference is to make a difference, it must be because beings with futures experience more utility than beings without. . . .

What we need to think, therefore, if we are to remain utilitarians *and* we think that normal humans are much greater in their capacity for utility than animals, is that at each typical moment in the sentient life of a human, he or she is chalking up a much higher utility score than a beast at any typical moment for it. And what the basis of this judgment would be is, again, unclear. There is certainly the danger of anthropocentric bias here . . .

Perhaps this affords some hold on the matter in the following way. If utility is based on preference, then perhaps we could say that if being X is able to have in mind more possible states of affairs over which to exercise preference than Y then X has a greater capacity for utility. As stated, this raises some rather kinky problems about individuating states of affairs so that we can get a fair count; and there is a lingering suspicion that the whole idea is wrong anyway, and utility should not really be thought of as preference at all. But it might offer some explanation of how we manage to account for so great a proportion of the universe's known supply of utility, or at least why we think we do.

If that amount of elitism is accepted, what about vegetarianism? It is axiomatic that some beings may, in principle, be sacrificed for others, on the utilitarian view. But may animals be sacrificed merely in order to enable humans to have a wider variety of gustatory pleasures? In order for it to be so, the marginal increment of such pleasure for humans has to exceed the marginal cost to the animals. Consider, then, the case of Kentucky Fried Chicken. Suppose that one chicken feeds three people for one meal. We might suppose that the cost of this is all the utility that the chicken might have experienced had it been allowed to live to a ripe old age. But wrongly. For that is only the cost to *that* chicken. But it is also reasonable to believe that, under the carnivorous regime we are investigating, this chicken will be replaced by another one which would not have existed at all if its predecessor were not eaten. In fact, the plot is thicker than that, for . . . its predecessor would most likely not have existed either, were it not for the prospect of *its* being eaten. Given that we in fact raise animals to be eaten, it is not unreasonable to believe that the total utility of the animal population is enormously higher than it would be if we did not eat them, because so comparatively few would exist at all otherwise. And if we count that way, then the marginal cost to any given animal is the wrong thing to weigh against the marginal benefit to us of eating it. Viewed globally, those costs are very handily outweighed by the total utility increase in question.

That, of course, is to assume that we can apply "total" rather than average or some other sort of utilitarianism here. If we do not, and insist that it is the average utility of animals that should be our sole concern, the prospects for animal rights are much better, perhaps. Or are they? For now we also must reckon the cost of upkeep and care for the animals, which is born by people. Their cost would certainly not be born, in fact, if the animals were not beneficial to people in this way. Chickens would be raised only to lay eggs, cows for milk; but most would have little if any use. It might be argued that the loss in utility to people from having to care for

useless beasts would exceed the loss to the beasts if they were (painlessly) killed. So even on average principles, it is far from clear that maximization would preclude the eating of animals.

Of course, if we do use total utilitarianism, then we have another small matter to contend with. Animals are, in fact, quite an inefficient source of food. If humans ate only vegetarian diets, it would be possible for there to be a great many more of *them*. And if, as has been imagined above, each human is so much larger a source of utility than any animal, it might seem that the tables are turned again, since the large animal population is keeping the human population smaller, and yet the human population is so much more efficient a source of utility than the animal one. But that, in turn, is to assume that the marginal utility change associated with the addition of each further human is in fact positive, and it can be argued that *that* is not so. Perhaps a world with two billion humans would have more total utility than one with ten billions. If so, we would have a global justification of carnivorousness from the above arguments.

I am sure that no one will think me excessively conservative if I conclude with the observation that the situation regarding the ethics of our treatment of animals is not entirely clear if we opt for utilitarianism. This is not exactly a surprise, but it is of some importance that it should be so. The vegetarians do not have things all their way on that theory; and it is, I think, the theory that offers the best prospects for animal rights among those I am considering. . . .

On the contract view of morality, morality is a sort of agreement among rational, independent, self-interested persons, persons who have something to gain from entering into such an agreement. It is of the very essence, on such a theory, that the parties to the agreement know who they are and what they want—what they in particular want, and not just what a certain general class of beings of which they are members generally tend to want. Now, Rawls' theory has his parties constrained by agreements that they would have made if they *did not* know who they were. But if we can have that constraint, why should we not go just a little further and specify that one is not only not to know *which* person he or she is, but also whether he or she will be a person *at all:* reason on the assumption that you might turn out to be an owl, say, or a vermin, or a cow. We may imagine that *that* possibility would make quite a difference . . . (Some proponents of vegetarianism, I believe, are tempted by it, and do extend the veil of ignorance that far.)

The "agreement" of which morality consists is a voluntary undertaking to limit one's behavior in various respects. In a sense, it consists in a renunciation of action on unconstrained self-interest. It is, however, self-interested overall. The idea is to come out ahead in the long run, by refraining, contingently on others' likewise refraining, from certain actions, the general indulgence in which would be worse for all and therefore for oneself. There are well-known problems generated by this characterization, and I do not claim to have solutions for them. I only claim that this is an important and plausible conception of morality, worth investigating in the present context.

A major feature of this view of morality is that it explains why we have it and who is a party to it. We have it for reasons of long-run self-interest, and parties to it include all and only those who have *both* of the following characteristics: (1) they stand to gain by subscribing to it, at least in the long run, compared with not doing so, and (2) they are *capable* of entering into (and keeping) an agreement. Those not capable of it obviously cannot be parties to it, and among those capable of it, there is no reason for them to enter into it if there is nothing to gain for them from it, no matter how much the others might benefit.

Given these requirements, it will be clear why animals do not have rights. For there are evident shortcomings on both scores. On the one hand, humans have nothing generally to gain by voluntarily refraining from (for instance) killing animals or "treating them as mere means." And on the other, animals cannot generally make agreements with us anyway, even if we wanted to have them do so. Both points are worth expanding on briefly.

(1) In saying that humans have "nothing generally to gain" from adopting principled restraints against behavior harmful to animals, I am in one

respect certainly overstating the case, for it is possible that animal food, for instance, is bad for us, or that something else about animals, which requires such restraint from us, would be for our long-term benefit. Those are issues I mostly leave on one side here . . .

(2) What about the capability of entering into and keeping such agreements? . . .

There remains a genuine question about the eligibility of animals for morality on the score of their abilities. A very few individuals among some animal species have been enabled, after years of highly specialized work, to communicate in fairly simple ways with people. That does not augur well for animals' entering quite generally into something as apparently sophisticated as an agreement. But of course agreements can be tacit and unwritten, even unspoken. Should we postulate, at some such inexplicit level, an "agreement" among humans, it is largely tacit there. People do not enter into agreements to refrain from killing each other, except in fairly specialized cases; the rule against killing that we (virtually) all acknowledge is one we adopt out of common sense and antecedent inculcation by our mentors. Still, it is reasonable to say that when one person does kill another one, he or she is (among other things) taking *unfair advantage* of the restraint that one's fellows have exercised with regard toward one over many years. But can any such thing be reasonably said of animals? I would think not.

On the whole, therefore, it seems clear that contractarianism leaves animals out of it, so far as rights are concerned. They are, by and large, to be dealt with in terms of our self-interest, unconstrained by the terms of hypothetical agreements with them. Just exactly what our interest in them is may, of course, be matter for debate; but that those are the terms on which we may deal with them is, on this view of morality, overwhelmingly indicated.

There is an evident problem about the treatment of what I have called "marginal cases" on this view, of course: infants, the feeble-minded, and the incapacitated are in varying degrees in the position of the animals in relation to us, are they not? True: but the situation is very different in several ways. For one thing, we generally have very little to gain from treating such people badly, and we often have much to gain from treating them well. For another, marginal humans are invariably members of families, or members of other groupings, which makes them the object of love and interest on the part of other members of those groups. Even if there were an interest in treating a particular marginal person badly, there would be others who have an interest in their being treated well and who are themselves clearly members of the moral community on contractarian premises. Finally, it does have to be pointed out that there is genuine question about the morality of, for instance, euthanasia, and that infanticide has been approved of in various human communities at various times. On the whole, it seems to me not an insurmountable objection to the contractarian account that we grant marginal humans fairly strong rights.

It remains that we may think that suffering is a bad thing, no matter whose. But although we think so, we do not think it is so bad as to require us to become vegetarians. Here by 'we,' of course, I mean most of us. And what most of us think is that, although suffering is too bad and it is unfortunate for animals that they are turned into hamburgers at a tender age, we nevertheless are justified on the whole in eating them. If contractarianism is correct, then these attitudes are not inconsistent. And perhaps it is.

NOTES

1. Jan Narveson, "Animal Rights," *Canadian Journal of Philosophy,* vol. 7 (1977), 161–178.

Discussion Questions

1. Narveson argues that by breeding animals destined for our plates we are increasing their overall utility, as they would not have had any existence otherwise. How might Jeremy Bentham respond to this argument? Could this argument also be used to justify the breeding or cloning of humans for slavery or organ transplants?
2. Narveson admits that the criteria we use for eliminating nonhuman animals from moral consideration also eliminates some humans. How does he overcome this criticism? Are you satisfied with his response? Support your answers.
3. Narveson bases much of his argument against vegetarianism on John Rawls's social contract theory. Rawls said, however, that his was "not a complete contract theory . . . since it would seem to include only our relationship with other persons and to leave out of account how we are to conduct ourselves toward animals and the rest of nature." Because of this, "it does not follow [from social contract theory] that there are no requirements at all in regard to [animals], nor in our relations with the natural order."[29] Has Narveson engaged in fallacious logic in concluding that animals lack rights because they cannot be included in a social contract? Discuss how Rawls might respond to Narveson's argument.
4. Discuss how Regan and an ecocentric environmental ethicist would respond to Narveson's defense of meat-eating. Whose position do you find more convincing from a moral point of view?

PETER SINGER

Animal Liberation

Australian philosopher Peter Singer is director of the Centre for Human Bioethics at Monash University in Melbourne. He is also actively involved in the animal-liberation movement. Singer argues that utilitarian theory requires that the interests of all sentient beings be given equal weight. The pain humans feel and the pain other animals feel should be given equal moral consideration. To not take the pain and interests of other animals seriously is to engage in what Singer calls "speciesism." Singer compares speciesism to racism and sexism.

Critical Reading Questions

1. What is the principle of equality?
2. What is "speciesism"? Why is speciesism wrong, according to Singer?
3. What criteria does Singer suggest we use to avoid speciesism?
4. According to Singer, what kind of lives have greater moral value than others?
5. Why does Singer claim that most humans are speciesists? What does he mean when he says that speciesism is analogous to racism and sexism?
6. What is the moral significance of sentience, or the ability to feel pain? In what ways do humans inflict suffering on other animals?
7. According to Singer, what is the moral significance of a being's level of cognitive ability? Does his argument make it morally permissible to experiment on humans with low-level cognitive functioning?
8. What do we need to do, according to Singer, to avoid speciesism? Does a rejection of speciesism imply that all lives are of equal worth?
9. Why, according to Singer, has opposition to experimentation on animals made such little headway?
10. Why do psychological experiments that use animals pose a dilemma for researchers who claim that other animals are not like us cognitively?
11. In what ways does a pattern of animal experimentation become self-reinforcing?
12. According to Singer, when, if ever, is animal experimentation morally justified?
13. What question does Singer think experimenters must be able to answer in the affirmative to justify the use of animals?
14. Why does Singer claim that the controversy over the benefits derived from animal experimentation is essentially irrelevant?

Animal Liberation (New York: Random House, 1990), 5–94. Notes have been omitted.

Jeremy Bentham, the founder of the reforming util-itarian school of moral philosophy, incorporated the essential basis of moral equality into his system of ethics by means of the formula: "Each to count for one and none for more than one." In other words, the interests of every being affected by an action are to be taken into account and given the same weight as the like interests of any other being. . . .

It is an implication of this principle of equality that our concern for others and our readiness to consider their interests ought not to depend on what they are like or on what abilities they may possess. Precisely what our concern or considera-tion requires us to do may vary according to the characteristics of those affected by what we do: concern for the well-being of children growing up in America would require that we teach them to read; concern for the well-being of pigs may re-quire no more than that we leave them with other pigs in a place where there is adequate food and room to run freely. But the basic element—the tak-ing into account of the interests of the being, what-ever those interests may be—must, according to the principle of equality, be extended to all beings, black or white, masculine or feminine, human or nonhuman. . . .

It is on this basis that the case against racism and the case against sexism must both ultimately rest; and it is in accordance with this principle that the attitude that we may call "speciesism," by anal-ogy with racism, must also be condemned. Species-ism—the word is not an attractive one, but I can think of no better term—is a prejudice or attitude of bias in favor of the interests of members of one's own species and against those of members of other species. It should be obvious that the fundamental objections to racism and sexism made by Thomas Jefferson and Sojourner Truth apply equally to spe-ciesism. If possessing a higher degree of intelli-gence does not entitle one human to use another for his or her own ends, how can it entitle humans to exploit nonhumans for the same purpose?

Many philosophers and other writers have pro-posed the principle of equal consideration of inter-ests, in some form or other, as a basic moral prin-ciple; but not many of them have recognized that this principle applies to members of other species as well as to our own. Jeremy Bentham was one of the few who did realize this. In a forward-looking passage written at the time when black slaves had been freed by the French but in the British domin-ions were still being treated in the way we now treat animals, Bentham wrote:

> The day *may* come when the rest of the animal creation may acquire those rights which never could have been withholden from them but by the hand of tyranny. The French have already discovered that the blackness of the skin is no reason why a human being should be abandoned without redress to the caprice of a tormentor. It may one day come to be recognized that the number of the legs, the villosity of the skin, or the termination of the *os sacrum* are reasons equally insufficient for abandoning a sensitive being to the same fate. What else is it that should trace the insuperable line? Is it the faculty of reason, or perhaps the faculty of discourse? But a full-grown horse or dog is beyond comparison a more rational, as well as a more conversable animal, than an infant of a day or a week or even a month, old. But suppose they were otherwise, what would it avail? The question is not, Can they *reason*? nor Can they *talk*? but, Can they *suffer*?

In this passage Bentham points to the capacity for suffering as the vital characteristic that gives a being the right to equal consideration. The capacity for suffering—or more strictly, for suffering and/or enjoyment or happiness—is not just another char-acteristic like the capacity for language or higher mathematics. Bentham is not saying that those who try to mark "the insuperable line" that determines whether the interests of a being should be consid-ered happen to have chosen the wrong characteris-tic. By saying that we must consider the interests of all beings with the capacity for suffering or en-joyment Bentham does not arbitrarily exclude from consideration any interests at all—as those who draw the line with reference to the possession of reason or language do. The capacity for suffering and enjoyment is *a prerequisite for having interests at all*, a condition that must be satisfied before we can speak of interests in a meaningful way. It would be nonsense to say that it was not in the interests of a stone to be kicked along the road by a schoolboy. A stone does not have interests because it cannot suffer. Nothing that we can do to it could possibly make any difference to its welfare. The capacity for suffering and enjoyment is, however, not only necessary, but also sufficient for us to] say that a being has interests—at an absolute minimum, an interest in not suffering. A mouse, for example, does have an interest in not being kicked along the road, because it will suffer if it is. . . .

Racists violate the principle of equality by giving greater weight to the interests of members of their own race when there is a clash between their interests and the interests of those of another race. Sexists violate the principle of equality by favoring the interests of their own sex. Similarly, speciesists allow the interests of their own species to override the greater interests of members of other species. The pattern is identical in each case.

Most human beings are speciesists. . . . Ordinary human beings—not a few exceptionally cruel or heartless humans, but the overwhelming majority of humans—take an active part in, acquiesce in, and allow their taxes to pay for practices that require the sacrifice of the most important interests of members of other species in order to promote the most trivial interests of our own species. . . .

Do animals other than humans feel pain? How do we know? Well, how do we know if anyone, human or nonhuman, feels pain? We know that we ourselves can feel pain. We know this from the direct experience of pain that we have when, for instance, somebody presses a lighted cigarette against the back of our hand. But how do we know that anyone else feels pain? We cannot directly experience anyone else's pain, whether that "anyone" is our best friend or a stray dog. Pain is a state of consciousness, a "mental event," and as such it can never be observed. Behavior like writhing, screaming, or drawing one's hand away from the lighted cigarette is not pain itself; nor are the recordings a neurologist might make of activity within the brain observations of pain itself. Pain is something that

we feel, and we can only infer that others are feeling it from various external indications.

In theory, we *could* always be mistaken when we assume that other human beings feel pain. It is conceivable that one of our close friends is really a cleverly constructed robot, controlled by a brilliant scientist so as to give all the signs of feeling pain, but really no more sensitive than any other machine. We can never know, with absolute certainty, that this is not the case. But while this might present a puzzle for philosophers, none of us has the slightest real doubt that our close friends feel pain just as we do. This is an inference, but a perfectly reasonable one, based on observations of their behavior in situations in which we would feel pain, and on the fact that we have every reason to assume that our friends are beings like us, with nervous systems like ours that can be assumed to function as ours do and to produce similar feelings in similar circumstances.

If it is justifiable to assume that other human beings feel pain as we do, is there any reason why a similar inference should be unjustifiable in the case of other animals?

Nearly all the external signs that lead us to infer pain in other humans can be seen in other species, especially the species most closely related to us— the species of mammals and birds. The behavioral signs include writhing, facial contortions, moaning, yelping or other forms of calling, attempts to avoid the source of pain, appearance of fear at the prospect of its repetition, and so on. In addition, we know that these animals have nervous systems very like ours, which respond physiologically as ours do when the animal is in circumstances in which we would feel pain: an initial rise of blood pressure, dilated pupils, perspiration, an increased pulse rate, and, if the stimulus continues, a fall in blood pressure. Although human beings have a more developed cerebral cortex than other animals, this part of the brain is concerned with thinking functions rather than with basic impulses, emotions, and feelings. These impulses, emotions, and feelings are located in the diencephalon, which is well developed in many other species of animals, especially mammals and birds.

We also know that the nervous systems of other animals were not artificially constructed—as a robot might be artificially constructed—to mimic the pain behavior of humans. The nervous systems of animals evolved as our own did, and in fact the evolutionary history of human beings and other animals, especially mammals, did not diverge until the central features of our nervous systems were already in existence. A capacity to feel pain obviously enhances a species' prospects of survival, since it causes members of the species to avoid sources of injury. It is surely unreasonable to suppose that nervous systems that are virtually identical physiologically, have a common origin and a common evolutionary function, and result in similar forms of behavior in similar circumstances should actually operate in an entirely different manner on the level of subjective feelings. . . .

Other differences between humans and animals cause other complications. Normal adult human beings have mental capacities that will, in certain circumstances, lead them to suffer more than animals would in the same circumstances. If, for instance, we decided to perform extremely painful or lethal scientific experiments on normal adult humans, kidnapped at random from public parks for this purpose, adults who enjoy strolling in parks would become fearful that they would be kidnapped. The resultant terror would be a form of suffering additional to the pain of the experiment. The same experiments performed on nonhuman animals would cause less suffering since the animals would not have the anticipatory dread of being kidnapped and experimented upon. This does not mean, of course, that it would be *right* to perform the experiment on animals, but only that there is a reason, which is *not* speciesist, for preferring to use animals rather than normal adult human beings, if the experiment is to be done at all. It should be noted, however, that this same argument gives us a reason for preferring to use human infants—orphans perhaps—or severely retarded human beings for experiments, rather than adults, since infants and retarded humans would also have no idea of what was going to happen to them. So far as this argument is concerned nonhuman animals and infants and retarded humans are in the same category; and if we use this argument to justify experiments on nonhuman animals we have to ask ourselves whether we are also prepared to allow experiments on human infants and retarded adults; and if we make a distinction between animals and these humans, on what basis can we do it, other than a bare-faced—and morally indefensible—preference for members of our own species?

There are many matters in which the superior mental powers of normal adult humans make a difference: anticipation, more detailed memory, greater knowledge of what is happening, and so on. Yet these differences do not all point to greater suffering on the part of the normal human being. Sometimes animals may suffer more because of their more limited understanding. If, for instance, we are taking prisoners in wartime we can explain to them that although they must submit to capture, search, and confinement, they will not otherwise be harmed and will be set free at the conclusion of hostilities. If we capture wild animals, however, we cannot explain that we are not threatening their lives. A wild animal cannot distinguish an attempt to overpower and confine from an attempt to kill; the one causes as much terror as the other.

It may be objected that comparisons of the sufferings of different species are impossible to make and that for this reason when the interests of animals and humans clash the principle of equality gives no guidance. It is probably true that comparisons of suffering between members of different species cannot be made precisely, but precision is not essential. Even if we were to prevent the infliction of suffering on animals only when it is quite certain that the interests of humans will not be affected to anything like the extent that animals are affected, we would be forced to make radical changes in our treatment of animals that would involve our diet, the farming methods we use, experimental procedures in many fields of science, our approach to wildlife and to hunting, trapping and the wearing of furs, and areas of entertainment like circuses, rodeos, and zoos. As a result, a vast amount of suffering would be avoided. . . .

Just as most human beings are speciesists in their readiness to cause pain to animals when they would not cause a similar pain to humans for the same reason, so most human beings are speciesists in their readiness to kill other animals when they would not kill human beings. . . .

This does not mean that to avoid speciesism we must hold that it is as wrong to kill a dog as it is to kill a human being in full possession of his or her faculties. The only position that is irredeemably speciesist is the one that tries to make the boundary of the right to life run exactly parallel to the boundary of our own species. Those who hold the sanctity of life view do this, because while distinguishing sharply between human beings and other animals they allow no distinctions to be made within our own species, objecting to the killing of the severely retarded and the hopelessly senile as strongly as they object to the killing of normal adults.

To avoid speciesism we must allow that beings who are similar in all relevant respects have a similar right to life—and mere membership in our own biological species cannot be a morally relevant criterion for this right. Within these limits we could still hold, for instance, that it is worse to kill a normal adult human, with a capacity for self-awareness and the ability to plan for the future and have meaningful relations with others, than it is to kill a mouse, which presumably does not share all of these characteristics; or we might appeal to the close family and other personal ties that humans have but mice do not have to the same degree; or we might think that it is the consequences for other humans, who will be put in fear for their own lives, that makes the crucial difference; or we might think it is some combination of these factors, or other factors altogether.

Whatever criteria we choose, however, we will have to admit that they do not follow precisely the boundary of our own species. We may legitimately hold that there are some features of certain beings that make their lives more valuable than those of other beings; but there will surely be some nonhuman animals whose lives, by any standards, are more valuable than the lives of some humans. A chimpanzee, dog, or pig, for instance, will have a higher degree of self-awareness and a greater capacity for meaningful relations with others than a severely retarded infant or someone in a state of advanced senility. So if we base the right to life on these characteristics we must grant these animals a right to life as good as, or better than, such retarded or senile humans.

This argument cuts both ways. It could be taken as showing that chimpanzees, dogs, and pigs, along with some other species, have a right to life and we commit a grave moral offense whenever we kill them, even when they are old and suffering and our intention is to put them out of their misery. Alternatively one could take the argument as showing that the severely retarded and hopelessly senile have no right to life and may be killed for quite trivial reasons, as we now kill animals. . . .

What we need is some middle position that would avoid speciesim but would not make the lives of the retarded and senile as cheap as the lives of pigs and dogs now are, or make the lives of pigs and dogs so sacrosanct that we think it wrong to put them out of hopeless misery. What we must do is bring nonhuman animals within our sphere of moral concern and cease to treat their lives as expendable for whatever trivial purposes we may have. At the same time, once we realize that the fact that a being is a member of our own species is not in itself enough to make it always wrong to kill that being, we may come to reconsider our policy of preserving human lives at all costs, even when there is no prospect of a meaningful life or of existence without terrible pain.

I conclude, then, that rejection of speciesism does not imply that all lives are of equal worth. While self-awareness, the capacity to think ahead and have hopes and aspirations for the future, the capacity for meaningful relations with others and so on are not relevant to the question of inflicting pain—since pain is pain, whatever other capacities, beyond the capacity to feel pain, the being may have—these capacities are relevant to the question of taking life. It is not arbitrary to hold that the life of a self-aware being, capable of abstract thought, of planning for the future, of complex acts of communication, and so on, is more valuable than the life of a being without these capacities. . . .

The practice of experimenting on nonhuman animals as it exists today throughout the world reveals the consequences of speciesism. Many experiments inflict severe pain without the remotest prospect of significant benefits for human beings or any other animals. Such experiments are not isolated instances, but part of a major industry. In Britain, where experimenters are required to report the number of "scientific procedures" performed on animals, official government figures show that 3.5 million scientific procedures were performed on animals in 1988. In the United States there are no figures of comparable accuracy. . . .

Among the tens of millions of experiments performed, only a few can possibly be regarded as contributing to important medical research. Huge numbers of animals are used in university departments such as forestry and psychology; many more are used for commercial purposes, to test new cosmetics, shampoos, food coloring agents, and other inessential items. All this can happen only because of our prejudice against taking seriously the suffering of a being who is not a member of our own species. Typically, defenders of experiments on animals do not deny that animals suffer. They cannot deny the animals' suffering, because they need to stress the similarities between humans and other animals in order to claim that their experiments may have some relevance for human purposes. The experimenter who forces rats to choose between starvation and electric shock to see if they develop ulcers (which they do) does so because the rat has a nervous system very similar to a human being's, and presumably feels an electric shock in a similar way.

There has been opposition to experimenting on animals for a long time. This opposition has made little headway because experimenters, backed by commercial firms that profit by supplying laboratory animals and equipment, have been able to convince legislators and the public that opposition comes from uninformed fanatics who consider the interests of animals more important than the interests of human beings. But to be opposed to what is going on now it is not necessary to insist that all animal experiments stop immediately. All we need to say is that experiments serving no direct and urgent purpose should stop immediately, and in the remaining fields of research, we should, whenever possible, seek to replace experiments that involve animals with alternative methods that do not. . . .

This attitude is illustrated by the following autobiographical statement . . . [that] appeared in *New Scientist:*

> When fifteen years ago I applied to do a degree course in psychology, a steely-eyed interviewer, himself a psychologist, questioned me closely on my motives and asked me what I believed psychology to be and what was its principal subject matter? Poor naïve simpleton that I was, I replied that it was the study of the mind and that human beings were its raw material. With a glad cry at being able to deflate me so effectively, the interviewer declared that psychologists were not interested in the mind, that rats were the golden focus of study, not people, and then he advised me strongly to trot around to the philosophy department next door. . . .

Perhaps not many psychologists would now proudly state that their work has nothing to do with the human mind. Nevertheless many of the experiments that are performed on rats can only be explained by assuming that the experimenters really are interested in the behavior of the rat for its own sake, without any thought of learning anything about humans. In that case, though, what possible justification can there be for the infliction of so much suffering? It is certainly not for the benefit of the rat.

So the researcher's central dilemma exists in an especially acute form in psychology: either the animal is not like us, in which case there is no reason for performing the experiment; or else the animal is like us, in which case we ought not to perform on the animal an experiment that would be considered outrageous if performed on one of us. . . .

Once a pattern of animal experimentation becomes the accepted mode of research in a particular field, the process is self-reinforcing and difficult to break out of. Not only publications and promotions but also the awards and grants that finance research become geared to animal experiments. A proposal for a new experiment with animals is something that the administrators of research funds will be ready to support, if they have in the past supported other experiments on animals. New methods that do not make use of animals will seem less familiar and will be less likely to receive support.

All this helps to explain why it is not always easy for people outside the universities to understand the rationale for the research carried out under university auspices. Originally, perhaps, scholars and researchers just set out to solve the most important problems and did not allow themselves to be influenced by other considerations. No doubt some are still motivated by these concerns. Too often, though, academic research gets bogged down in petty and insignificant details because the big questions have been studied already and they have either been solved or proven too difficult. So the researchers turn away from the well-plowed fields in search of new territory where whatever they find will be new, although the connection with a major problem may be remote. It is not uncommon, as we have seen, for experimenters to admit that similar experiments have been done many times before, but without this or that minor variation; and the most common ending to a scientific publication is "further research is necessary." . . .

When are experiments on animals justifiable? Upon learning of the nature of many of the experiments carried out, some people react by saying that all experiments on animals should be prohibited immediately. But if we make our demands as absolute as this, the experimenters have a ready reply: Would we be prepared to let thousands of humans die if they could be saved by a single experiment on a single animal?

This question is, of course, purely hypothetical. There has never been and never could be a single experiment that saved thousands of lives. The way to reply to this hypothetical question is to pose another: Would the experimenters be prepared to carry out their experiment on a human orphan under six months old if that were the only way to save thousands of lives?

If the experimenters would not be prepared to use a human infant then their readiness to use nonhuman animals reveals an unjustifiable form of discrimination on the basis of species, since adult apes, monkeys, dogs, cats, rats, and other animals are more aware of what is happening to them, more self-directing, and, so far as we can tell, at least as sensitive to pain as a human infant. (I have specified that the human infant be an orphan, to avoid the complications of the feelings of parents. Specifying the case in this way is, if anything, overgenerous to those defending the use of nonhuman animals in experiments, since mammals intended for experimental use are usually separated from their mothers at an early age, when the separation causes distress for both mother and young.)

So far as we know, human infants possess no morally relevant characteristic to a higher degree than adult nonhuman animals, unless we are to count the infants' potential as a characteristic that makes it wrong to experiment on them. Whether this characteristic should count is controversial—if we count it, we shall have to condemn abortion along with experiments on infants, since the potential of the infant and the fetus is the same. To avoid the complexities of this issue, however, we can alter our original question a little and assume that the infant is one with irreversible brain damage so severe as to rule out any mental development beyond the level of a six-month-old infant. There are, unfortunately, many such human beings, locked away in special wards throughout the country, some of them long since abandoned by their parents and other relatives, and, sadly, sometimes unloved by anyone else. Despite their mental deficiencies, the anatomy and physiology of these infants are in nearly all respects identical with those of normal humans. If, therefore, we were to force-feed them with large quantities of floor polish or drip concentrated solutions of cosmetics into their eyes, we would have a much more reliable indication of the safety of these products for humans than we now get by attempting to extrapolate the results of tests on a variety of other species. The LD50 tests, the Draize eye tests, the radiation experiments, the heatstroke experiments, and many others could have told us more about human reactions to the experimental situation if they had been carried out on severely brain-damaged humans instead of dogs or rabbits.

So whenever experimenters claim that their experiments are important enough to justify the use of animals, we should ask them whether they would be prepared to use a brain-damaged human being at a similar mental level to the animals they are planning to use. I cannot imagine that anyone would seriously propose carrying out the experiments described in this chapter on brain-damaged human beings. Occasionally it has become known that medical experiments have been performed on human beings without their consent; one case did concern institutionalized intellectually disabled children, who were given hepatitis. When such harmful experiments on human beings become known, they usually lead to an outcry against the experimenters, and rightly so. They are, very often, a further example of the arrogance of the research worker who justifies everything on the grounds of increasing knowledge. But if the experimenter claims that the experiment is important enough to justify inflicting suffering on animals, why is it not important enough to justify inflicting suffering on humans at the same mental level? What difference is there between the two? Only that one is a member of our species and the other is not? But to appeal to that difference is to reveal a bias no more defensible than racism or any other form of arbitrary discrimination. . . .

No doubt there are some fields of scientific research that will be hampered by any genuine consideration of the interests of animals used in experimentation. No doubt there have been some advances in knowledge which would not have been attained as easily without using animals. Examples of important discoveries often mentioned by those defending animal experimentation go back as far as Harvey's work on the circulation of blood. They include Banting and Best's discovery of insulin and its role in diabetes; the recognition of poliomyelitis as a virus and the development of a vaccine for it; several discoveries that served to make open heart surgery and coronary artery bypass graft surgery possible; and the understanding of our immune system and ways to overcome rejection of transplanted organs. The claim that animal experimentation was essential in making these discoveries has been denied by some opponents of experimentation. I do not intend to go into the controversy here. We have just seen that any knowledge gained from animal experimentation has made at best a very small contribution to our increased lifespan; its

contribution to improving the quality of life is more difficult to estimate. In a more fundamental sense, the controversy over the benefits derived from animal experimentation is essentially unresolvable, because even if valuable discoveries were made using animals, we cannot say how successful medical research would have been if it had been compelled, from the outset, to develop alternative methods of investigation. Some discoveries would probably have been delayed, or perhaps not made at all; but many false leads would also not have been pursued, and it is possible that medicine would have developed in a very different and more efficacious direction, emphasizing healthy living rather than cure.

In any case, the ethical question of the justifiability of animal experimentation cannot be settled by pointing to its benefits for us, no matter how persuasive the evidence in favor of such benefits may be. The ethical principle of equal consideration of interests will rule out some means of obtaining knowledge. There is nothing sacred about the right to pursue knowledge. We already accept many restrictions on scientific enterprise. We do not believe that scientists have a general right to perform painful or lethal experiments on human beings without their consent, although there are many cases in which such experiments would advance knowledge far more rapidly than any other method. Now we need to broaden the scope of this existing restriction on scientific research.

Finally, it is important to realize that the major health problems of the world largely continue to exist, not because we do not know how to prevent disease and keep people healthy, but because no one is putting enough effort and money into doing what we already know how to do. The diseases that ravage Asia, Africa, Latin America, and the pockets of poverty in the industrialized West are diseases that, by and large, we know how to cure. They have been eliminated in communities that have adequate nutrition, sanitation, and health care. . . .

It does not seem likely that any major Western democracy is going to abolish all animal experimentation at a stroke. Governments just do not work like that. Animal experimentation will only be ended when a series of piecemeal reforms have reduced its importance, led to its replacement in many fields, and largely changed the public attitude to animals. The immediate task, then, is to work for these partial goals, which can be seen as milestones on the long march to the elimination of all exploitation of sentient animals. All concerned to end animal suffering can try to make known what is happening at universities and commercial laboratories in their own communities. Consumers can refuse to purchase products that have been tested on animals—especially in cosmetics, alternatives are now available. Students should decline to carry out experiments they consider unethical. Anyone can study the academic journals to find out where painful experiments are being carried out, and then find some way of making the public aware of what is happening. . . .

The exploitation of laboratory animals is part of the larger problem of speciesism and it is unlikely to be eliminated altogether until speciesism itself is eliminated. Surely one day, though, our children's children, reading about what was done in laboratories in the twentieth century, will feel the same sense of horror and incredulity at what otherwise civilized people could do that we now feel when we read about the atrocities of the Roman gladiatorial arenas or the eighteenth-century slave trade.

Discussion Questions

1. Do you agree with Singer that most humans are speciesists? If you are a speciesist, on what grounds do you morally justify it? In what ways does your lifestyle contribute to the suffering of the members of other species?

2. Do you agree with Singer that speciesism is similar to sexism and racism? Support your answer. Discuss how both Adams and Narveson might respond to Singer's claim.

3. Singer wants to seek a "middle position that would avoid speciesism but would not make the lives of the retarded and senile as cheap as the lives of pigs and dogs now are, or make the lives of pigs and dogs so sacrosanct that we think it wrong to put them out of hopeless misery." Can he morally justify drawing the line at this point? Or is this middle point arbitrary? Support your answers.

4. Like Singer, R. G. Frey opposes species membership as the criterion of moral standing. Instead Frey uses the quality of life as the criterion of moral worth. He maintains that the lives of certain cognitively impaired humans are such that they may have a lower moral value than that of many nonhuman animals.[30] Whereas Singer concludes that the principle of equality should preclude experimentation on nonhuman animals whose cognitive capacity is equivalent to that of human infants or cognitively impaired humans, Frey draws the opposite conclusion. Humans with an impoverished cognitive life can be used in experiments in the same way we use animals. Discuss Frey's argument as well as how Singer might respond to him.

5. Is Singer, as a utilitarian, being inconsistent when he argues that the benefits derived from animal experimentation are morally irrelevant? Support your answer. Discuss how Jeremy Bentham or John Stuart Mill might respond to this question.

6. Do the benefits of experimentation ever justify the use of nonconsenting humans or nonhuman animals in experiments? Support your answer.

CARL COHEN

Do Animals Have Rights?

Carl Cohen is a philosophy professor at the University of Michigan. Cohen defends the traditional Kantian view of moral agency and rights. According to Cohen, rights are based on self-assertion rather than on interests. Because only moral agents can assert moral claims, only moral agents have rights. Therefore, we do not violate the rights of nonhuman animals by doing research on them. Cohen also argues that we have a moral obligation to increase the use of nonhuman animals in research because doing so benefits humans.

Critical Reading Questions

1. Why is the question of whether animals have rights of great importance?
2. How does Cohen define the term *right*?
3. What are some of the ways in which experimentation using nonhuman animals has benefited humans?
4. Why does Cohen reject Regan's argument that animals have rights?
5. According to Cohen, what is the relationship between rights and obligations?
6. Why can't nonhuman animals be the bearers of rights? How does Cohen use the example of the baby zebra and the lioness to illustrate his position?
7. How does Cohen interpret Regan's concept of nonhuman animals as being moral patients?
8. According to Cohen, where do human rights come from?
9. How does Cohen respond to the objection that, under his definition, human infants and other cognitively impaired humans don't have rights? How does he support his position that all and only humans have rights?
10. Why does Cohen claim that only humans can commit crimes? How does Cohen use Kant's philosophy to support his position?
11. What fallacy does Cohen accuse Regan of committing in his use of the term *inherent value*? According to Cohen, how does this fallacy invalidate Regan's conclusion that animals have rights?
12. What is Cohen's conclusion regarding the use of nonhuman animals in medical experiments?

Whether animals have rights is a question of great importance because if they do, those rights must be respected, even at the cost of great burdens for human beings. A right (unlike an interest) is a valid claim, or potential claim, made by a moral agent, under principles that govern both the claimant and the target of the claim. Rights are precious; they are dispositive; they count.

You have a right to the return of money you lent me; we both understand that. It may be very convenient for me to keep the money, and you may have no need of it whatever; but my convenience

"Do Animals Have Rights?" *Ethics and Behavior* 7, no. 2 (1997): 103–111.

and your needs are not to the point. You have a *right* to it, and we have courts of law partly to ensure that such rights will be respected.

If you make me a promise, I have a moral right to its fulfillment—even though there may be no law to enforce my right. It may be very much in your interest to break that promise, but your great interests and the silence of the law cut no mustard when your solemn promise—which we both well understood—had been given. Likewise, those holding power may have a great and benevolent interest in denying my rights to travel or to speak freely—but their interests are overridden by my rights.

A great deal was learned about hypothermia by some Nazi doctors who advanced their learning by soaking Jews in cold water and putting them in refrigerators to learn how hypothermia proceeds. We have no difficulty in seeing that they may not advance medicine in that way; the subjects of those atrocious experiments had rights that demanded respect. For those who ignored their rights we have nothing but moral loathing.

Some persons believe that animals have rights as surely as those Jews had rights, and they therefore look on the uses of animals in medical investigations just as we look at the Nazi use of the Jews, with moral loathing. They are consistent in doing so. If animals have rights they certainly have the right not to be killed, even to advance our important interests.

Some may say, "Well, they have rights, but we have rights too, and our rights override theirs." That may be true in some cases, but it will not solve the problem because, although we may have a weighty *interest* in learning, say, how to vaccinate against polio or other diseases, we do not have a *right* to learn such things. Nor could we honestly claim that we kill research animals in self-defense; they did not attack us. If animals have rights, they certainly have the right not to be killed to advance the interests of others, whatever rights those others may have.

In 1952 there were about 58,000 cases of polio reported in the United States, and 3,000 polio deaths; my parents, parents everywhere, trembled in fear for their children at camp or away from home. Polio vaccination became routine in 1955,

and cases dropped to about a dozen a year; today polio has been eradicated completely from the Western Hemisphere. The vaccine that achieved this, partly developed and tested only blocks from where I live in Ann Arbor, could have been developed *only* with the substantial use of animals. Polio vaccines had been tried many times earlier, but from those earlier vaccines children had contracted the disease; investigators had become, understandably, exceedingly cautious.

The killer disease for which a vaccine now is needed most desperately is malaria, which kills about 2 million people each year, most of them children. Many vaccines have been tried—not on children, thank God—and have failed. But very recently, after decades of effort, we learned how to make a vaccine that does, with complete success, inoculate mice against malaria. A safe vaccine for humans we do not yet have—but soon we will have it, thanks to the use of those mice, many of whom will have died in the process. To test that vaccine first on children would be an outrage, as it would have been an outrage to do so with the Salk and Sabin polio vaccines years ago. We use mice or monkeys *because there is no other way*. And there never will be another way because untested vaccines are very dangerous; their first use on a living organism is inescapably experimental; there is and will be no way to determine the reliability and safety of new vaccines without repeated tests on live organisms. Therefore, because we certainly may not use human children to test them, we will use mice (or as we develop an AIDS vaccine, primates) *or we will never have such vaccines*.

But if those animals we use in such tests have rights as human children do, what we did and are doing to them is as profoundly wrong as what the Nazis did to those Jews not long ago. Defenders of animal rights need not hold that medical scientists are vicious; they simply believe that what medical investigators are doing with animals is morally wrong. Most biomedical investigations involving animal subjects use rodents: mice and rats. The rat is the animal appropriately considered (and used by the critic) as the exemplar whose moral stature is in dispute here. Tom Regan is a leading defender of the view that rats do have such rights, and may not be used in biomedical investigations. He is an honest man. He sees the consequences of his view and accepts them forthrightly. In *The Case for Animal Rights* (Regan, 1983) he wrote,

> The harms others might face as a result of the dissolution of [some] practice or institution is no defense of allowing it to continue. . . . No one has a right to be protected against being harmed if the protection in question involves violating the rights of others. . . . No one has a right to be protected by the continuation of an unjust practice, one that violates the rights of others. . . . Justice *must* be done, though the . . . heavens fall. (pp. 346–347)

That last line echoes Kant, who borrowed it from an older tradition. Believing that rats have rights as humans do, Regan (1983) was convinced that killing them in medical research was morally intolerable. He wrote,

> On the rights view, [he means, of course, the Regan rights view] we cannot justify harming a single rat *merely* by aggregating "the many human and humane benefits" that flow from doing it. . . . Not even a single rat is to be treated as if that animal's value were reducible to his *possible utility* relative to the interests of others. (p. 384)

If there are some things that we cannot learn because animals have rights, well, as Regan (1983) put it, so be it.

This is the conclusion to which one certainly is driven if one holds that animals have rights. If Regan is correct about the moral standing of rats, we humans can have no right, ever, to kill them—unless perchance a rat attacks a person or a human baby, as rats sometimes do; then our right of self-defense may enter, I suppose. But medical investigations cannot honestly be described as self-defense, and medical investigations commonly require that many mice and rats be killed. Therefore, all medical investigations relying on them, or any other animal subjects—which includes most studies and all the most important studies of certain kinds—will have to stop. Bear in mind that the

replacement of animal subjects by computer simulations, or tissue samples, and so on, is in most research a phantasm, a fantasy. Biomedical investigations using animal subjects (and of course all uses of animals as food) will have to stop.

This extraordinary consequence has no argumentative force for Regan and his followers; they are not consequentialists. For Regan the *interests* of humans, their desire to be freed of disease or relieved of pain, simply cannot outweigh the *rights* of a single rat. For him the issue is one of justice, and the use of animals in medical experiments (he believes) is simply not just. But the consequences of his view will give most of us, I submit, good reason to weigh very carefully the arguments he offers to support such far-reaching claims. Do you believe that the work of Drs. Salk and Sabin was morally right? Would you support it now, or support work just like it saving tens of thousands of human children from diphtheria, hepatitis, measles, rabies, rubella, and tetanus (all of which relied essentially on animal subjects)—as well as, now, AIDS, Lyme disease, and malaria? I surely do. If you would join me in this support we must conclude that the defense of animal rights is a gigantic mistake. I next aim to explain why animals *cannot* possess rights.

WHY ANIMALS DO NOT HAVE RIGHTS

Many obligations are owed by humans to animals; few will deny that. But it certainly does not follow from this that animals have rights because it is certainly not true that every obligation of ours arises from the rights of another. Not at all. We need to be clear and careful here. Rights entail obligations. If you have a right to the return of the money I borrowed, I have an obligation to repay it. No issue. If we have the right to speak freely on public policy matters, the community has the obligation to respect our right to do so. But the proposition *all rights entail obligations* does not convert simply, as the logicians say. From the true proposition that all trees are plants, it does not follow that all plants are trees. Similarly, not all obligations are entailed by rights. Some obligations, like mine to repay the money I borrowed from you, do arise out of rights.

But many obligations are owed to persons or other beings who have no rights whatever in the matter.

Obligations may arise from commitments freely made: As a college professor I accept the obligation to comment at length on the papers my students submit, and I do so; but they have not the right to *demand* that I do so. Civil servants and elected officials surely ought to be courteous to members of the public, but that obligation certainly is not grounded in citizens' rights.

Special relations often give rise to obligations: Hosts have the obligation to be cordial to their guests, but the guest has not the right to demand cordiality. Shepherds have obligations to their dogs, and cowboys to their horses, which do not flow from the rights of those dogs or horses. My son, now 5, may someday wish to study veterinary medicine as my father did; I will then have the obligation to help him as I can, and with pride I shall—but he has not the authority to demand such help as a matter of right. My dog has no right to daily exercise and veterinary care, but I do have the obligation to provide those things for her.

One may be obliged to another for a special act of kindness done; one may be obliged to put an animal out of its misery in view of its condition—but neither the beneficiary of that kindness nor that dying animal may have had a claim of right.

Beauchamp and Childress (1994) addressed what they called the "correlativity of rights and obligations" and wrote that they would defend an "untidy" (pp. 73–75) variety of that principle. It would be very untidy indeed. Some of our most important obligations—to members of our family, to the needy, to neighbors, and to sentient creatures of every sort—have no foundation in rights at all. Correlativity appears critical from the perspective of one who holds a right; your right correlates with my obligation to respect it. But the claim that rights and obligations are *reciprocals,* that *every* obligation flows from another's right, is false, plainly inconsistent with our general understanding of the differences between what we think we *ought* to do, and what others can justly *demand* that we do.

I emphasize this because, although animals have no rights, it surely does not follow from this that one is free to treat them with callous disregard.

Animals are not stones; they feel. A rat may suffer; surely we have the obligation not to torture it gratuitously, even though it be true that the concept of a right could not possibly apply to it. We humans are obliged to act humanely, that is, being aware of their sentience, to apply to animals the moral principles that govern us regarding the gratuitous imposition of pain and suffering; which is not, of course, to treat animals as the possessors of rights.

Animals cannot be the bearers of rights because the concept of rights is essentially *human;* it is rooted in, and has force within, a human moral world. Humans must deal with rats—all too frequently in some parts of the world—and must be moral in their dealing with them; but a rat can no more be said to have rights than a table can be said to have ambition. To say of a rat that it has rights is to confuse categories, to apply to its world a moral category that has content only in the human moral world.

Try this thought experiment. Imagine, on the Serengeti Plain in East Africa, a lioness hunting for her cubs. A baby zebra, momentarily left unattended by its mother, is the prey; the lioness snatches it, rips open its throat, tears out chunks of its flesh, and departs. The mother zebra is driven nearly out of her wits when she cannot locate her baby; finding its carcass she will not even leave the remains for days. The scene may be thought unpleasant, but it is entirely natural, of course, and extremely common. If the zebra has a right to live, if the prey is just but the predator unjust, we ought to intervene, if we can, on behalf of right. But we do not intervene, of course—as we surely would intervene if we saw the lioness about to attack an unprotected human baby or you. What accounts for the moral difference? We justify different responses to humans and to zebras on the ground (implicit or explicit) that their moral stature is very different. The human has a right not to be eaten alive; it is, after all, a human being. Do you believe the baby zebra has the *right* not to be slaughtered by that lioness? That the lioness has the *right* to kill that baby zebra for her cubs? If you are inclined to say, confronted by such natural rapacity—duplicated with untold variety millions of times each day on planet earth—that neither is right or wrong, that neither has a *right* against the other, I am on your side. Rights are of the highest moral consequence, yes; but zebras and lions and rats are totally amoral; there is no morality for them; they do no wrong, ever. In their world there are no rights.

A contemporary philosopher who has thought a good deal about animals, referring to them as "moral patients," put it this way:

> A moral patient lacks the ability to formulate, let alone bring to bear, moral principles in deliberating about which one among a number of possible acts it would be right or proper to perform. Moral patients, in a word, cannot do what is right, nor can they do what is wrong. . . . Even when a moral patient causes significant harm to another, the moral patient has not done what is wrong. Only moral agents can do what is wrong. (Regan, 1983, pp. 152–153)

Just so. The concepts of wrong and right are totally foreign to animals, not conceivably within their ken or applicable to them, as the author of that passage clearly understands.

When using animals in our research, therefore, we ought indeed be humane—but we can never violate the rights of those animals because, to be blunt, they have none. Rights do not *apply* to them.

But humans do have rights. Where do our rights come from? Why are we not crudely natural creatures like rats and zebras? This question philosophers have struggled to answer from earliest times. A definitive account of the human moral condition I cannot here present, of course. But reflect for a moment on the kinds of answers that have been widely given:

- Some think our moral understanding, with its attendant duties, to be a divine gift. So St. Thomas said: The moral law is binding, and humans have the power, given by God, to grasp its binding character, and must therefore respect the rights that other humans possess. God makes us (Saint Augustine said before him) in his own image, and therefore with a will that is free, and gives us the power to recognize that, and therefore, unlike other creatures, we must choose between good and evil, between right and wrong.

- Many philosophers, distrusting theological justifications of rights and duties, sought the ground of human morality in the membership, by all humans, in a moral community. The English idealist, Bradley, called it an organic moral community; the German idealist, Hegel, called it an objective ethical order. These and like accounts commonly center on human interrelations, on a moral *fabric* within which human agents always act, and within which animals never act and never can possibly act.

- The highly abstract reasoning from which such views emerge has dissatisfied many; you may find more nearly true the convictions of ethical intuitionists and realists who said, as H. A. Prichard, Sir David Ross, and my friend and teacher C. D. Broad, of happy memory, used to say, that there is a direct, underivative, intuitive cognition of rights as possessed by other humans, but not by animals.

- Or perhaps in the end we will return to Kant, and say with him that critical reason reveals at the core of human action a uniquely moral will, and the unique ability to grasp and to lay down moral laws for oneself and for others—an ability that is not conceivably within the capacity of any nonhuman animal whatever.

To be a moral agent (on this view) is to be able to grasp the generality of moral restrictions on our will. Humans understand that some things, which may be in our interest, *must not be willed;* we lay down moral laws for ourselves, and thus exhibit, as no other animal can exhibit, moral autonomy. My dog knows that there are certain things she must not do—but she knows this only as the outcome of her learning about her interests, the pains she may suffer if she does what had been taught forbidden. She does not know, cannot know (as Regan agrees) that any conduct is wrong. The proposition *It would be highly advantageous to act in such-and-such a way, but I may not because it would be wrong* is one that no dog or mouse or rabbit, however sweet and endearing, however loyal or attentive to its young, can ever entertain, or intend, or begin to grasp. Right is not in their world. But right and wrong are the very stuff of human moral life, the ever-present awareness of human beings who can do wrong, and who by seeking (often) to avoid wrong conduct prove themselves members of a moral community in which rights may be exercised and must be respected.

Some respond by saying, "This can't be correct, for human infants (and the comatose and senile, etc.) surely have rights, but they make no moral claims or judgments and can make none—and any view entailing that children can have no rights must be absurd." Objections of this kind miss the point badly. It is not individual persons who qualify (or are disqualified) for the possession of rights because of the presence or absence in them of some special capacity, thus resulting in the award of rights to some but not to others. Rights are universally human; they arise in a *human moral world,* in a moral *sphere.* In the human world moral judgments are pervasive; it is the fact that all humans including infants and the senile are members of that moral community—not the fact that as individuals they have or do not have certain special capacities, or merits—that makes humans bearers of rights. Therefore, it is beside the point to insist that animals have remarkable capacities, that they really have a consciousness of self, or of the future, or make plans, and so on. And the tired response that because infants plainly cannot make moral claims they must have no rights at all, or rats must have them too, we ought forever put aside. Responses like these arise out of a misconception of right itself. They mistakenly suppose that rights are tied to some identifiable individual abilities or sensibilities, and they fail to see that rights arise only in a community of moral beings, and that therefore there are spheres in which rights do apply and spheres in which they do not.

Rationality is not at issue; the capacity to communicate is not at issue. My dog can reason, if rather weakly, and she certainly can communicate. Cognitive criteria for the possession of rights, Beauchamp said, are morally perilous. Indeed they are. Nor is the capacity to suffer here at issue. And, if *autonomy* be understood only as the capacity to choose this course rather than that, autonomy is not to the point either. But *moral autonomy*—that is, *moral self-legislation*—is to the point, because moral autonomy is uniquely human and is for animals out of the question, as we have seen, and as Regan and I agree. In talking about autonomy, therefore, we must be careful and precise.

Because humans do have rights, and these rights can be violated by other humans, we say that some humans commit *crimes.* But whether a crime has been committed depends utterly on the moral state of mind of the actor. If I take your coat, or your book, honestly thinking it was mine, I do not steal it. The *actus reus* (the guilty deed) must be accompanied, in a genuine crime, by a guilty mind, a *mens rea.* That recognition, not just of possible punishment for an act, but of moral duties that govern us, no rat or cow ever can possess. In primitive times humans did sometimes bring cows and horses to the bar of human justice. We chuckle at that practice now, realizing that accusing cows of crimes marks the primitive moral view as inane. Animals never can be criminals because they have no moral state of mind.

Mistakes parallel to this in other spheres may be helpful to think about. In the Third Part of *The Critique of Pure Reason,* Immanuel Kant explained with care the metaphysical blunders into which we are led when we misapply concepts of great human import. In our human experience, for example, the concepts of time and space, the relations of cause and effect, of subject and attribute, and others, are essential, fundamental. But, forgetting that these are concepts arising only within the world of our human experience, we sometimes are misled into asking: Was the world caused, or is it uncaused? Did the world have a beginning in time, or did it not? Kant explained—in one of the most brilliant long passages in all philosophical literature—why *it makes no sense to ask such questions.* Cause applies to phenomena we humans encounter *in* the world, it is a category of our experience and cannot apply to the world as a whole. Time is the condition of our experience, not an absolute container in which the world could have begun. The antinomies of pure reason, and after those the paralogisms of pure reason, Kant patiently exhibited as confusions arising from the misapplication of the categories of experience. His lesson is powerful and deep. The misapplication of concepts leads to error and, sometimes, to nonsense. So it is with rights also. To say that rats have rights is to apply to the world of rats a concept that makes good sense when applied to humans, but which makes no sense at all when applied to rats.

WHY ANIMALS ARE MISTAKENLY BELIEVED TO HAVE RIGHTS

From the foregoing discussion it follows that, if some philosophers believe that they have proved that animals have rights, they must have erred in the alleged proof. Regan is a leader among those who claim to *argue* in defense of the rights of rats; he contends that the best arguments are on his side. I aim next to show how he and others with like views go astray. Bear in mind that Regan's book is long, its argument tortuous and at times convoluted. In what follows I must compress the report of his views, obviously; but I promise to be fair and to hold Regan responsible for nothing that he does not clearly say. We know—if we are agreed that rats are not the holders of rights—that Regan must have got off the track. Examining *The Case for Animal Rights,* let us see if we can find the faulty switch.

Much of Regan's (1983) book is devoted to a general treatment of the nature of ethical thinking and theory, to discussions of animal consciousness and animal awareness, and to detailed critiques of the views of others whom he thinks in error. Regan sought to show, patiently and laboriously, that the common belief that we do have obligations to animals, although they have no rights, has not been defended satisfactorily. That belief cannot be justified, he contended, by direct duty views of which he finds two categories: those depending on the obligation to be kind or not to be cruel, and those depending on any kind of utilitarian calculation.

None of this counterargument could possibly establish his conclusion that animals do have rights, unless Regan had proved that his listing of all alternative conflicting views was exhaustive, which it was not, and unless he had proved conclusively that every such candidate is untenable, which he did not do. . . .

The case is built entirely on the principle that allegedly *carries over* almost everything earlier claimed about human rights to rats and other animals. What principle is that? It is the principle, put in italics but given no name, that equates moral agents with moral patients:

> *The validity of the claim to respectful treatment, and thus the case for the recognition of the right to such treatment, cannot be any stronger or weaker in the case of moral patients than it is in the case of moral agents.* (Regan, p. 279)

But hold on. Why in the world should anyone think this principle to be true? Back where Regan first recounted his view of moral patients, he allowed that some of them are, although capable of experiencing pleasure and pain, lacking in other capacities. But he is interested, he told us there, in those moral patients—those animals—that are like humans in having *inherent value.* This is the key to the argument for animal rights, the possession of inherent value. How that concept functions in the argument becomes absolutely critical. I will say first briefly what will be shown more carefully later: *Inherent value* is an expression used by Regan (and many like him) with two very different senses—in one of which it is reasonable to conclude that those who have inherent value have rights, and in another sense in which that inference is wholly unwarranted. But the phrase *inherent value* has some plausibility in both contexts, and thus by sliding from one sense of inherent value to the other Regan appears to succeed . . . in making the case for animal rights.

The concept of inherent value first entered the discussion in the seventh chapter of Regan's (1983) book, at which point his principle object is to fault and defeat utilitarian arguments. It is not (he argued there) the pleasures or pains that go "into the cup" of humanity that give value, but the "cups" themselves; humans are equal in value because they are humans, having inherent value. So we are, all of us, equal—equal in being moral agents who have this inherent value. This approach to the moral stature of humans is likely to be found quite plausible. Regan called it the "postulate of inherent value"; all humans, "The lonely, forsaken, unwanted, and unloved are no more nor less inherently valuable than those who enjoy a more hospitable relationship with others" (p. 237). And Regan went on to argue for the proposition that all moral agents are "equal in inherent value." Holding some such views we are likely to say, with Kant, that all humans are beyond price. Their inherent value gives them moral dignity, a unique role in the moral world, as agents having the capacity to act morally and make moral judgments. This is inherent value in Sense 1.

The expression *inherent value* has another sense, however, also common and also plausible. My dog has inherent value, and so does every wild animal, every lion and zebra, which is why the senseless killing of animals is so repugnant. Each animal is unique, not replaceable in itself by another animal or by any rocks or clay. Animals, like humans, are not just things; they live, and as unique living creatures they have inherent value. This is an important point, and again likely to be thought plausible; but here, in Sense 2, the phrase *inherent value* means something quite distinct from what was meant in its earlier uses.

Inherent value in Sense 1, possessed by all humans but not by all animals, which warrants the claim of human rights, is very different from inherent value in Sense 2, which warrants no such claim. The uniqueness of animals, their intrinsic worthiness as individual living things, does not ground the possession of rights, has nothing to do with the moral condition in which rights arise. Regan's argument reached its critical objective with almost magical speed because, having argued that beings with inherent value (Sense 1) have rights that must be respected, he quickly asserted (putting it in italics lest the reader be inclined to express doubt) that rats and rabbits also have rights because they, too, have inherent value (Sense 2).

This is an egregious example of the fallacy of equivocation: the informal fallacy in which two or more meanings of the same word or phrase have been confused in the several premises of an argument (Cohen & Copi, 1994, pp. 143–144). Why is this slippage not seen at once? Partly because we know the phrase *inherent value* often is used loosely, so the reader is not prone to quibble about its introduction; partly because the two uses of the phrase relied on are both common, so neither signals danger; partly because inherent value in Sense 2 is in-

deed shared by those who have it in Sense 1; and partly because the phrase *inherent value* is woven into accounts of what Regan (1983) elsewhere called the *subject-of-a-life criterion,* a phrase of his own devising for which he can stipulate any meaning he pleases, of course, and which also slides back and forth between the sphere of genuine moral agency and the sphere of animal experience. But perhaps the chief reason the equivocation between these two uses of the phrase *inherent value* is obscured (from the author, I believe, as well as from the reader) is the fact that the assertion that animals have rights appears only indirectly, as the outcome of the application of the principle that moral patients are entitled to the same respect as moral agents—a principle introduced at a point in the book long after the important moral differences between moral patients and moral agents have been recognized, with a good deal of tangled philosophical argument having been injected in between.

I invite readers to trace out this equivocation in detail; my limited space here precludes more extended quotation. But this assurance I will give: there is no argument or set of arguments in *The Case for Animal Rights* that successfully makes the case for animal rights. Indeed, there *could* not be, any more than any book, however long and convoluted, could make the case for the emotions of oak trees, or the criminality of snakes.

Animals do not have rights. Right does not apply in their world. We do have many obligations to animals, of course, and I honor Regan's appreciation of their sensitivities. I also honor his seriousness of purpose, and his always civil and always rational spirit. But he is, I submit, profoundly mistaken. I conclude with the observation that, had his mistaken views about the rights of animals long been accepted, most successful medical therapies recently devised—antibiotics, vaccines, prosthetic devices, and other compounds and instruments on which we now rely for saving and improving human lives and for the protection of our children — could not have been developed; and were his views to become general now (an outcome that is unlikely but possible) the consequences for medical science and for human well-being in the years ahead would be nothing less than catastrophic.

Advances in medicine absolutely require experiments, many of which are dangerous. Dangerous experiments absolutely require living organisms as subjects. Those living organisms (we now agree) certainly may not be human beings. Therefore, most advances in medicine will continue to rely on the use of nonhuman animals, or they will stop. Regan is free to say in response, as he does, "so be it." The rest of us must ask if the argument he presents is so compelling as to force us to accept that dreadful result.

REFERENCES

Beauchamp, T. L., & Childress, J. F. (1994). *Principles of biomedical ethics* (4th ed.). New York: Oxford University Press.

Cohen, C., & Copi, I. M. (1994). *Introduction to logic* (9th ed.). New York: Macmillan.

Regan, T. (1983). *The case for animal rights.* Berkeley: University of California Press.

Discussion Questions

1. Most rights ethicists maintain that rights are correlatives of duties or obligations. Cohen acknowledges that inhumane treatment of nonhuman animals is wrong when we can achieve the same results using alternative methods. Is his claim that researchers have a moral obligation to treat nonhuman animals humanely inconsistent with his claim that animals have no rights? Can we have an obligation to animals if they have no rights? Support your answers.

2. Is Cohen a speciesist? Discuss how Singer might respond to Cohen's claim that all and only humans have rights, even those who lack reason and moral autonomy.

3. Cohen admits that nonhuman animals feel pain and that researchers should not subject them to unnecessary suffering. What does he mean by unnecessary suffering? To what extent does this criterion limit the type of research that is morally permissible? Does this criterion oblige Cohen to limit the type of research that he sanctions? Compare and contrast Cohen's and Singer's positions on the significance of suffering in the moral justification of experiments using nonhuman animals. Who presents the more compelling argument? Support your answers.

4. Does Cohen do an effective job of discrediting Regan's argument that nonhuman animals have rights? Support your answer. Discuss how Regan might respond to Cohen's criticism of his position.

5. Do you agree with Cohen's claim regarding the qualitative gap between humans and other animals? Discuss how Cohen might respond to Singer's argument that scientists who justify using nonhuman animals in psychology and learning experiments on the grounds that they are not like humans find themselves in a moral dilemma, because there would be no point in using them if they were not like us.

6. Discuss whether Cohen's argument supports factory farming and meat-eating.

ALDO LEOPOLD

The Land Ethic

Aldo Leopold (1887–1948) was a forester and wildlife manager with the U.S. Forest Service and a professor of wildlife management at the University of Wisconsin. In his highly influential essay "The Land Ethic," Leopold expresses concern about the detrimental impact of human activities on the environment. He argues that instead of seeing the environment primarily in terms of its value to humans (anthropocentrism), we should see ourselves as part of the natural world (ecocentrism).[31]

Critical Reading Questions

1. What does Leopold mean when he talks of the "extension of ethics"?
2. What is the premise of current ethics?
3. In what ways does a land ethics change the role of humans in the land community?
4. Why does Leopold reject an ethics based on a conservation system?
5. What is the land pyramid? Where are humans in Leopold's land pyramid?
6. What attitudes toward the land are required in order for humans to have an ethical relationship with the land?
7. According to Leopold, how does evolution of species take place?
8. What are some of the obstacles impeding the evolution of a land ethics?
9. What strategies does Leopold suggest for overcoming these obstacles?
10. According to Leopold, what are the fundamental criteria for determining if something is ethically right?

When god-like Odysseus returned from the wars in Troy, he hanged all on one rope a dozen slave-girls of his household whom he suspected of misbehavior during his absence.

This hanging involved no question of propriety. The girls were property. The disposal of property was then, as now, a matter of expediency, not of right and wrong.

Concepts of right and wrong were not lacking from Odysseus' Greece: . . . The ethical structure of that day covered wives, but had not yet been extended to human chattels. During the three thousand years which have since elapsed, ethical criteria have been extended to many fields of conduct, with corresponding shrinkages in those judged by expediency only.

THE ETHICAL SEQUENCE

This extension of ethics, so far studied only by philosophers, is actually a process in ecological evolution. Its sequences may be described in ecological as well as in philosophical terms. An ethic, ecologically, is a limitation on freedom of action in the struggle for existence. An ethic, philosophically, is a differentiation of social from anti-social conduct. These are two definitions of one thing. The thing

---

Aldo Leopold, "The Land Ethic," from *A Sand County Almanac: And Sketches Here and There* (New York: Oxford University Press, 1949 and 1977), pp. 201–226.

has its origin in the tendency of interdependent individuals or groups to evolve modes of co-operation. The ecologist calls these symbioses. . . .

The first ethics dealt with the relation between individuals; the Mosaic Decalogue is an example. Later accretions dealt with the relation between the individual and society. The Golden Rule tries to integrate the individual to society; democracy to integrate social organization to the individual.

There is as yet no ethic dealing with man's relation to land and to the animals and plants which grow upon it. Land, like Odysseus' slave-girls, is still property. The land-relation is still strictly economic, entailing privileges but not obligations.

The extension of ethics to this third element in human environment is, if I read the evidence correctly, an evolutionary possibility and an ecological necessity. . . .

THE COMMUNITY CONCEPT

All ethics so far evolved rest upon a single premise: that the individual is a member of a community of interdependent parts. His instincts prompt him to compete for his place in that community, but his ethics prompt him also to co-operate (perhaps in order that there may be a place to compete for).

The land ethic simply enlarges the boundaries of the community to include soils, waters, plants, and animals, or collectively: the land.

This sounds simple: do we not already sing our love for and obligation to the land of the free and the home of the brave? Yes, but just what and whom do we love? Certainly not the soil, which we are sending helter-skelter downriver. Certainly not the waters, which we assume have no function except to turn the turbines, float barges, and carry off sewage. Certainly not the plants, of which we exterminate whole communities without batting an eye. Certainly not the animals, of which we have already extirpated many of the largest and most beautiful species. A land ethic of course cannot prevent the alteration, management, and use of these "resources," but it does affirm their right to continued existence, and, at least in spots, their continued existence in a natural state.

In short, a land ethic changes the role of *Homo sapiens* from conqueror of the land-community to plain member and citizen of it. It implies respect for his fellow-members, and also respect for the community as such. . . .

SUBSTITUTES FOR A LAND ETHIC

When the logic of history hungers for bread and we hand out a stone, we are at pains to explain how much the stone resembles bread. I now describe some of the stones which serve in lieu of a land ethic.

One basic weakness in a conservation system based wholly on economic motives is that most members of the land community have no economic value. Wildflowers and songbirds are examples. . . .

Lack of economic value is sometimes a character not only of species or groups, but of entire biotic communities: marshes, bogs, dunes, and "deserts" are examples. Our formula in such cases is to relegate their conservation to government as refuges, monuments, or parks. . . .

Industrial landowners and users, esecially lumbermen and stockmen, are inclined to wail long and loudly about the extension of government ownership and regulation to land, but (with notable exceptions) they show little disposition to develop the only visible alternative: the voluntary practice of conservation on their own lands.

When the private landowner is asked to perform some unprofitable act for the good of the community, he today assents only with outstretched palm. If the act costs him cash this is fair and proper, but when it costs only forethought, open-mindedness, or time, the issue is at least debatable. The overwhelming growth of land-use subsidies in recent years must be ascribed, in large part, to the government's own agencies for conservation education: the land bureaus, the agricultural colleges, and the extension services. As far as I can detect, no ethical obligation toward land is taught in these institutions.

To sum up: a system of conservation based solely on economic self-interest is hopelessly lopsided. It tends to ignore, and thus eventually to eliminate, many elements in the land community that lack commercial value, but that are (as far as we know) essential to its healthy functioning. It assumes, falsely, I think, that the economic parts of the biotic clock will function without the uneconomic parts. It tends to relegate to government many functions eventually too large, too complex, or too widely dispersed to be performed by government.

An ethical obligation on the part of the private owner is the only visible remedy for these situations.

THE LAND PYRAMID

An ethic to supplement and guide the economic relation to land presupposes the existence of some mental image of land as a biotic mechanism. We can be ethical only in relation to something we can see, feel, understand, love, or otherwise have faith in.

The image commonly employed in conservation education is "the balance of nature." For reasons too lengthy to detail here, this figure of speech fails to describe accurately what little we know about the land mechanism. A much truer image is the one employed in ecology: the biotic pyramid. I shall first sketch the pyramid as a symbol of land, and later develop some of its implications in terms of land-use.

Plants absorb energy from the sun. This energy flows through a circuit called the biota, which may be represented by a pyramid consisting of layers. The bottom layer is the soil. A plant layer rests on the soil, an insect layer on the plants, a bird and rodent layer on the insects, and so on up through various animal groups to the apex layer, which consists of the larger carnivores.

The species of a layer are alike not in where they came from, or in what they look like, but rather in what they eat. Each successive layer depends on those below it for food and often for other services, and each in turn furnishes food and services to those above. Proceeding upward, each successive layer decreases in numerical abundance. Thus, for every carnivore there are hundreds of his prey, thousands of their prey, millions of insects, uncountable plants. The pyramidal form of the system reflects this numerical progression from apex to base. Man shares an intermediate layer with the bears, raccoons, and squirrels which eat both meat and vegetables. . . .

Land, then, is not merely soil; it is a fountain of energy flowing through a circuit of soils, plants, and animals. Food chains are the living channels which conduct energy upward; death and decay return it to the soil. The circuit is not closed; some energy is dissipated in decay, some is added by absorption from the air, some is stored in soils, peats, and long-lived forests; but it is a sustained circuit, like a slowly augmented revolving fund of life. . . .

This interdependence between the complex structure of the land and its smooth functioning as an energy unit is one of its basic attributes.

When a change occurs in one part of the circuit, many other parts must adjust themselves to it. Change does not necessarily obstruct or divert the flow of energy; evolution is a long series of self-induced changes, the net result of which has been to elaborate the flow mechanism and to lengthen the circuit. Evolutionary changes, however, are usually slow and local. Man's invention of tools has enabled him to make changes of unprecedented violence, rapidity, and scope. . . .

THE OUTLOOK

It is inconceivable to me that an ethical relation to land can exist without love, respect, and admiration for land, and a high regard for its value. By value, I of course mean something far broader than mere economic value; I mean value in the philosophical sense.

Perhaps the most serious obstacle impeding the evolution of a land ethic is the fact that our educational and economic system is headed away from, rather than toward, an intense consciousness of land. Your true modern is separated from the land by many middlemen, and by innumerable physical gadgets. He has no vital relation to it; to him it is the space between cities on which crops grow. Turn him loose for a day on the land, and if the spot does not happen to be a golf links or a "scenic" area, he is bored stiff. If crops could be raised by hydroponics instead of farming, it would suit him very well. Synthetic substitutes for wood, leather, wool, and other natural land products suit him better than the originals. In short, land is something he has "outgrown."

Almost equally serious as an obstacle to a land ethic is the attitude of the farmer for whom the land is still an adversary, or a taskmaster that keeps him in slavery. Theoretically, the mechanization of farming ought to cut the farmer's chains, but whether it really does is debatable. . . .

The case for a land ethic would appear hopeless but for the minority which is in obvious revolt against these "modern" trends.

The "key-log" which must be moved to release the evolutionary process for an ethic is simply this: quit thinking about decent land-use as solely an economic problem. Examine each question in terms of what is ethically and esthetically right, as well as what is economically expedient. A thing is right when it tends to preserve the integrity, stability, and beauty of the biotic community. It is wrong when it tends otherwise.

It of course goes without saying that economic feasibility limits the tether of what can or cannot be done for land. It always has and it always will. The fallacy the economic determinists have tied around our collective neck, and which we now need to cast off, is the belief that economics determines *all* land-use. This is simply not true. An innumerable host of actions and attitudes, comprising perhaps the bulk of all land relations, is determined by the land-users' tastes and predilections, rather than by his purse. The bulk of all land relations hinges on investments of time, forethought, skill, and faith rather than on investments of cash. As a land-user thinketh, so is he. . . .

The evolution of a land ethic is an intellectual as well as emotional process. Conservation is paved with good intentions which prove to be futile, or even dangerous, because they are devoid of critical understanding either of the land, or of economic land-use. I think it is a truism that as the ethical frontier advances from the individual to the community, its intellectual content increases.

The mechanism of operation is the same for any ethic: social approbation for right actions: social disapproval for wrong actions.

By and large, our present problem is one of attitudes and implements. We are remodeling the Alhambra with a steam-shovel, and we are proud of our yardage. We shall hardly relinquish the shovel, which after all has many good points, but we are in need of gentler and more objective criteria for its successful use.

Discussion Questions

1. Discuss Leopold's assumption about the evolution of ethics toward a land ethics. Is it indeed morally desirable, as Leopold claims, to expand our concept of moral community to include the environment? Support your answer.
2. Discuss whether or not Leopold's land ethics is compatible with the Judeo-Christian view of creation and our place as human beings in the universe.
3. What does Leopold mean when he says: "A thing is right when it tends to preserve the integrity, stability, and beauty of the biotic community. It is wrong when it tends otherwise"? Discuss the implications of this statement on your own lifestyle and on public policy regarding the environment.
4. In his essay, "Thinking Like a Mountain," Leopold describes watching the death of a wolf he just shot. "We reached the old wolf in time to watch a fierce green fire dying in her eyes. I realized then, and have known ever since, that there was something new to me in those eyes—something known only to her and to the mountain. I was young then, and full of trigger-itch; I thought that because fewer wolves meant more deer, that no wolves would mean a hunter's paradise. But after seeing the green fire die, I sensed that neither the wolf nor the mountain agreed with such a view."[30] Do you agree with Leopold? Support your answer. Discuss Leopold's experience in light of your own experience.

5. Discuss the implications of Leopold's land ethics for our eating habits and the use of nonhuman animals in medical experiments. How would Tom Regan, Peter Singer, Jan Narveson, and Carl Cohen each most likely respond to Leopold's land ethics?

 BILL DEVALL AND GEORGE SESSIONS

Deep Ecology

Bill Devall is a sociology professor at Humboldt State University in Arcata, California. George Sessions is a philosophy professor at Sierra College in Rocklin, California. Their book has been called a manifesto for the deep ecology movement. In this selection, the authors present the eight principles of deep ecology, as originally put forth by George Sessions and Norwegian philosopher Arne Naess. They also contrast deep ecology with the dominant worldview.

Critical Reading Questions

1. What is the essence of "deep ecology"?
2. Who is Arne Naess?
3. What is the difference between "deep" and "shallow" ecology?
4. What are the foundations of deep ecology?
5. How does the deep ecology worldview differ from the dominant worldview? What are the implications of both of these worldviews for what it means to be human and our place in nature?
6. What are the two ultimate norms of deep ecological consciousness?
7. What is the deep ecology sense of self, and how can society help nurture this self?
8. What is "biocentric equality" and how is it related to self-actualization?
9. What are the eight basic principles of deep ecology, and what is the meaning of each of these principles?
10. What is a biosphere?
11. According to Devall and Sessions, what are the implications of deep ecology for human population growth and our relationship to nature?

The term *deep ecology* was coined by Arne Naess in his 1973 article, "The Shallow and the Deep, Long-Range Ecology Movements." Naess was attempting to describe the deeper, more spiritual approach to Nature exemplified in the writings of Aldo Leopold and Rachel Carson. He thought that this deeper approach resulted from a more sensitive openness to ourselves and nonhuman life around us. The essence of deep ecology is to keep asking more searching questions about human life, society, and Nature as in the Western philosophical tradition of Socrates. As examples of this deep questioning, Naess

Bill Devall and George Sessions, "Deep Ecology," from *Deep Ecology: Living as if Nature Mattered* (Salt Lake City: Peregrine Smith Books, 1985), pp. 65–73. Notes have been omitted.

points out "that we ask why and how, where others do not. For instance, ecology as a science does not ask what kind of a society would be the best for maintaining a particular ecosystem—that is considered a question for value theory, for politics, for ethics." Thus deep ecology goes beyond the so-called factual scientific level to the level of self and Earth wisdom.

Deep ecology goes beyond a limited piece-meal shallow approach to environmental problems and attempts to articulate a comprehensive religious and philosophical worldview. The foundations of deep ecology are the basic intuitions and experiencing of ourselves and Nature which comprise ecological consciousness. Certain outlooks on politics and public policy flow naturally from this consciousness. . . .

Many of these questions are perennial philosophical and religious questions faced by humans in all cultures over the ages. What does it mean to be a unique human individual? How can the individual self maintain and increase its uniqueness while also being an inseparable aspect of the whole system wherein there are no sharp breaks between self and the *other*? An ecological perspective, in this deeper sense, results in what Theodore Roszak calls "an awakening of wholes greater than the sum of their parts. In spirit, the discipline is contemplative and therapeutic."

Ecological consciousness and deep ecology are in sharp contrast with the dominant worldview of technocratic-industrial societies which regards humans as isolated and fundamentally separate from the rest of Nature, as superior to, and in charge of, the rest of creation. But the view of humans as separate and superior to the rest of Nature is only part of larger cultural patterns. For thousands of years, Western culture has become increasingly obsessed with the idea of *dominance:* with dominance of humans over nonhuman Nature, masculine over the feminine, wealthy and powerful over the poor, with the dominance of the West over non-Western cultures. Deep ecological consciousness allows us to see through these erroneous and dangerous illusions.

For deep ecology, the study of our place in the Earth household includes the study of ourselves as part of the organic whole. Going beyond a narrowly

materialist scientific understanding of reality, the spiritual and the material aspects of reality fuse together. While the leading intellectuals of the dominant worldview have tended to view religion as "just superstition," and have looked upon ancient spiritual practice and enlightenment, such as found in Zen Buddhism, as essentially subjective, the search for deep ecological consciousness is the search for a more objective consciousness and state of being through an active deep questioning and meditative process and way of life.

Many people have asked these deeper questions and cultivated ecological consciousness within the context of different spiritual traditions—Christianity, Taoism, Buddhism, and Native American rituals, for example. While differing greatly in other regards, many in these traditions agree with the basic principles of deep ecology. . . .

From this most basic insight or characteristic of deep ecological consciousness, Arne Naess has developed two *ultimate norms* or intuitions which are themselves not derivable from other principles or intuitions. They are arrived at by the deep questioning process and reveal the importance of moving to the philosophical and religious level of wisdom. They cannot be validated, of course, by the methodology of modern science based on its usual mechanistic assumptions and its very narrow definition of data. These ultimate norms are *self-realization* and *biocentric equality*.

I. SELF-REALIZATION

In keeping with the spiritual traditions of many of the world's religions, the deep ecology norm of self-realization goes beyond the modern Western *self* which is defined as an isolated ego striving primarily for hedonistic gratification or for a narrow sense of individual salvation in this life or the next. This socially programmed sense of the narrow self or social self dislocates us, and leaves us prey to whatever fad or fashion is prevalent in our society or social reference group. We are thus robbed of beginning the search for our unique spiritual/biological personhood. Spiritual growth, or unfolding, begins when we cease to understand or see ourselves as isolated and narrow competing egos and begin to identify with other humans from our family and friends to, eventually, our species. But the deep ecology sense of self requires a further maturity and growth, an identification which goes beyond humanity to include the nonhuman world. We must see beyond our narrow contemporary cultural assumptions and values, and the conventional wisdom of our time and place, and this is best achieved by the meditative deep questioning process. Only in this way can we hope to attain full mature personhood and uniqueness.

A nurturing nondominating society can help in the "real work" of becoming a whole person. The "real work" can be summarized symbolically as the realization of "self-in-Self" where "Self" stands for organic wholeness. This process of the full unfolding of the self can also be summarized by the phrase, "No one is saved until we are all saved," where the phrase "one" includes not only me, an individual human, but all humans, whales, grizzly bears, whole rain forest ecosystems, mountains and rivers, the tiniest microbes in the soil, and so on.

II. BIOCENTRIC EQUALITY

The intuition of biocentric equality is that all things in the biosphere have an equal right to live and blossom and to reach their own individual forms of unfolding and self-realization within the larger Self-realization. This basic intuition is that all organisms and entities in the ecosphere, as parts of the interrelated whole, are equal in intrinsic worth. Naess suggests that biocentric equality as an intuition is true in principle, although in the process of living, all species use each other as food, shelter, etc. Mutual predation is a biological fact of life, and many of the world's religions have struggled with the spiritual implications of this. Some animal liberationists who attempt to side-step this problem by advocating vegetarianism are forced to say that the entire plant kingdom including rain forests have no right to their own existence. This evasion flies in the face of the basic intuition of equality. Aldo Leopold expressed this intuition when he said humans are "plain citizens" of the biotic community, not lord and master over all other species.

Biocentric equality is intimately related to the all-inclusive Self-realization in the sense that if we harm the rest of Nature then we are harming ourselves. There are no boundaries and everything is interrelated. But insofar as we perceive things as individual organisms or entities, the insight draws us to respect all human and nonhuman individuals in their own right as parts of the whole without feeling the need to set up hierarchies of species with humans at the top.

The practical implications of this intuition or norm suggest that we should live with minimum rather than maximum impact on other species and on the Earth in general. Thus we see another aspect of our guiding principle: "simple in means, rich in ends." . . .

A fuller discussion of the biocentric norm as it unfolds itself in practice begins with the realization that we, as individual humans, and as communities of humans, have vital needs which go beyond such basics as food, water, and shelter to include love, play, creative expression, intimate relationships with a particular landscape (or Nature taken in its entirety) as well as intimate relationships with other humans, and the vital need for spiritual growth, for becoming a mature human being.

Our vital material needs are probably more simple than many realize. In technocratic-industrial societies there is overwhelming propaganda and advertising which encourages false needs and destructive desires designed to foster increased production and consumption of goods. Most of this actually diverts us from facing reality in an objective way and from beginning the "real work" of spiritual growth and maturity.

Many people who do not see themselves as supporters of deep ecology nevertheless recognize an overriding vital human need for a healthy and high-quality natural environment for humans, if not for all life, with minimum intrusion of toxic waste, nuclear radiation from human enterprises, minimum acid rain and smog, and enough free flowing wilderness so humans can get in touch with their sources, the natural rhythms and the flow of time and place.

Drawing from the minority tradition and from the wisdom of many who have offered the insight of interconnectedness, we recognize that deep ecologists can offer suggestions for gaining maturity and encouraging the processes of harmony with Nature, but that there is no grand solution which is guaranteed to save us from ourselves.

The ultimate norms of deep ecology suggest a view of the nature of reality and our place as an individual (many in the one) in the larger scheme of things. They cannot be fully grasped intellectually but are ultimately experiential. . . .

As a brief summary of our position thus far, figure 5-1 summarizes the contrast between the dominant worldview and deep ecology.

Figure 5-1

Dominant Worldview	*Deep Ecology*
Dominance over Nature	Harmony with Nature
Natural environment as resource for humans	All nature has intrinsic worth/biospecies equality
Material/economic growth for growing human population	Elegantly simple material needs (material goals serving the larger goal of self-realization)
Belief in ample resource reserves	Earth "supplies" limited
High technological progress and solutions	Appropriate technology; nondominating science
Consumerism	Doing with enough/recycling
National/centralized community	Minority tradition/bioregion

III. BASIC PRINCIPLES OF DEEP ECOLOGY

In April 1984, during the advent of spring and John Muir's birthday, George Sessions and Arne Naess summarized fifteen years of thinking on the principles of deep ecology while camping in Death Valley, California. In this great and special place, they articulated these principles in a literal, somewhat neutral way, hoping that they would be understood and accepted by persons coming from different philosophical and religious positions.

Readers are encouraged to elaborate their own versions of deep ecology, clarify key concepts and think through the consequences of acting from these principles.

Basic Principles

1. The well-being and flourishing of human and nonhuman Life on Earth have value in themselves (synonyms: intrinsic value, inherent value). These values are independent of the usefulness of the nonhuman world for human purposes.

2. Richness and diversity of life forms contribute to the realization of these values and are also values in themselves.

3. Humans have no right to reduce this richness and diversity except to satisfy *vital* needs.

4. The flourishing of human life and cultures is compatible with a substantial decrease of the human population. The flourishing of nonhuman life requires such a decrease.

5. Present human interference with the nonhuman world is excessive, and the situation is rapidly worsening.

6. Policies must therefore be changed. These policies affect basic economic, technological, and ideological structures. The resulting state of affairs will be deeply different from the present.

7. The ideological change is mainly that of appreciating *life quality* (dwelling in situations of inherent value) rather than adhering to an increasingly higher standard of living. There will be a profound awareness of the difference between big and great.

8. Those who subscribe to the foregoing points have an obligation directly or indirectly to try to implement the necessary changes.

Naess and Sessions Provide Comments on the Basic Principles:

RE (1). This formulation refers to the biosphere, or more accurately, to the ecosphere as a whole. This includes individuals, species, populations, habitat, as well as human and nonhuman cultures. From our current knowledge of all-pervasive intimate relationships, this implies a fundamental deep concern and respect. . . .

The term "life" is used here in a more comprehensive nontechnical way to refer also to what biologists classify as "nonliving"; rivers (watersheds), landscapes, ecosystems. For supporters of deep ecology, slogans such as "Let the river live" illustrate this broader usage so common in most cultures.

Inherent value as used in (1) is common in deep ecology literature ("The presence of inherent value in a natural object is independent of any awareness, interest, or appreciation of it by a conscious being.")

RE (2). More technically, this is a formulation concerning diversity and complexity. From an ecological standpoint, complexity and symbiosis are conditions for maximizing diversity. So-called simple, lower, or primitive species of plants and animals contribute essentially to the richness and diversity of life. They have value in themselves and are not merely steps toward the so-called higher or rational life forms. The second principle presupposes that life itself, as a process over evolutionary time, implies an increase of diversity and richness. . . .

Complexity, as referred to here, is different from complication. Urban life may be more complicated than life in a natural setting without being more complex in the sense of multifaceted quality.

RE (3). The term "vital need" is left deliberately vague to allow for considerable latitude in judgment. Differences in climate and related factors, together with differences in the structures of societies as they now exist, need to be considered (for some Eskimos, snowmobiles are necessary today to satisfy vital needs).

People in the materially richest countries cannot be expected to reduce their excessive interference with the nonhuman world to a moderate level overnight. . . . But the longer we wait the more drastic will be the measures needed. Until deep changes are made, substantial decreases in richness and diversity are liable to occur: the rate of extinction of species will be ten to one hundred times greater than any other period of earth history.

RE (4). The United Nations Fund for Population Activities in their State of World Population Report (1984) said that high human population growth rates (over 2.0 percent annum) in many developing countries "were diminishing the quality of life for many millions of people." . . .

Most of the nations in the developing world (including India and China) have as their official government policy the goal of reducing the rate of human population increase, but there are debates over the types of measures to take (contraception, abortion, etc.) consistent with human rights and feasibility.

The report concludes that if all governments set specific population targets as public policy to help alleviate poverty and advance the quality of life, the current situation could be improved.

As many ecologists have pointed out, it is also absolutely crucial to curb population growth in the so-called developed (i.e., overdeveloped) industrial societies. Given the tremendous rate of consumption and waste production of individuals in these societies, they represent a much greater threat and impact on the biosphere per capita than individuals in Second and Third World countries.

RE (5). . . . The slogan of "noninterference" does not imply that humans should not modify some ecosystems as do other species. Humans have modified the earth and will probably continue to do so. At issue is the nature and extent of such interference.

The fight to preserve and extend areas of wilderness or near-wilderness should continue and should focus on the general ecological functions of these areas (one such function: large wilderness areas are required in the biosphere to allow for continued evolutionary speciation of animals and plants). Most present designated wilderness areas and game preserves are not large enough to allow for such speciation.

RE (6). Economic growth as conceived and implemented today by the industrial states is incompatible with (1)-(5). There is only a faint resemblance between ideal sustainable forms of economic growth and present policies of the industrial societies. And "sustainable" still means "sustainable in relation to humans."

Present ideology tends to value things because they are scarce and because they have a commodity value. There is prestige in vast consumption and waste (to mention only several relevant factors).

Whereas "self-determination," "local community," and "think globally, act locally," will remain key terms in the ecology of human societies, nevertheless the implementation of deep changes requires increasingly global action—action across borders. . . .

RE (7). Some economists criticize the term "quality of life" because it is supposed to be vague.

But on closer inspection, what they consider to be vague is actually the nonquantitative nature of the term. One cannot quantify adequately what is important for the quality of life as discussed here, and there is no need to do so.

RE (8). There is ample room for different opinions about priorities: what should be done first, what next? What is most urgent? What is clearly necessary as opposed to what is highly desirable but not absolutely pressing?

Discussion Questions

1. Discuss Devall and Sessions's claim that biocentric equality is intuitively true. How would Cohen most likely respond to this claim?
2. What does self-realization mean to you? Discuss Devall and Sessions's position that self-realization and spiritual growth are enhanced by going beyond the traditional view of humans to the view espoused by deep ecology. What view of human nature are deep ecologists presupposing in making this claim? Discuss how Kant and Buddha would each most likely respond to the deep ecologist view of human nature and self-realization.
3. Discuss the implications of each of the eight basic principles, both for your lifestyle and for public policy.
4. In his book, *Earth in the Balance,* former vice-president Al Gore argues that modern civilization is dysfunctional because it assumes a radical separation between humans and nature. This dysfunction is manifested in spiritual malaise as well as in our addiction to consuming ever larger quantities of oil, trees, top soil, and other "substances we rip from the crust of the earth."[32] However, Gore rejects deep ecology claiming that it incorrectly portrays humans in the "role of pathogens, a kind of virus giving the earth a rash and a fever, threatening the planet's vital life functions."[33] Gore argues instead that we need to seek a balance between our needs and preservation of the global environment. Our proper role is as God's stewards of the earth. Analyze these two approaches to environmental ethics. Discuss how might Devall and Sessions might respond to Gore.

RICHARD WATSON

A Critique of Anti-Anthropocentric Ethics

Richard Watson is professor of philosophy at Washington University in St. Louis. Watson maintains that biocentric ethics, as put forth by people such as Aldo Leopold, George Sessions, and Arne Naess is neither egalitarian nor fully biocentric. He concludes that human interest in survival is the best foundation for achieving ecological balance that is good for both humans and the whole biological community.

Critical Reading Questions

1. What is "anthropocentrism"? How does it differ from "biocentrism"?
2. What is Tom Regan's "preservation principle"?
3. What is meant by "hands-off-nature"? Who, according to Watson, supports this view?
4. What is "ecosophy"? Why does Watson reject it?
5. What are the five principles of anti-anthropomorphic biocentrism as delineated by Watson?
6. According to Watson, what are some of the internal contradictions in biocentrism?
7. On what grounds does Watson accuse biocentrists of anthropocentric thinking?
8. According to Watson, what are some of the logical conclusions regarding human activities if we accept biocentrism?
9. On what grounds does Watson reject the biocentrists' claim that humans are too destructive of the environment and that these "destructive" human activities should be limited or curtailed?
10. What does Watson mean when he says that "there are anthropocentric foundations in most environmental and ecosophical literature"?
11. What approach does Watson consider best for preserving a rich and balanced ecology?

I

Anthropocentric is defined specifically as the position "that considers man as the central fact, or final aim, of the universe" and generally "conceiv[es] of everything in the universe in terms of human values."[1] In the literature of environmental ethics, anti-anthropocentric biocentrism is the position that human needs, goals, and desires should not be taken as privileged or overriding in considering the needs, desires, interests, and goals of all members of all biological species taken together, and in general that the Earth as a whole should not be interpreted or managed from a human standpoint. According to this position, birds, trees, and the land itself considered as the biosphere have a right to be and to live out their individual and species' potentials, and that members of the human species have no right to disturb, perturb, or destroy the ecological balance of the planet.

Richard Watson, "A Critique of Anti-Anthropocentric Ethics," *Environmental Ethics,* Vol. 5, no. 3, Fall 1983, pp. 245–256. Some notes have been omitted.

An often quoted statement of this right of natural objects to continue to be as they are found to be occurs in John Rodman's "The Liberation of Nature?":

> To affirm that "natural objects" have "rights" is symbolically to affirm that ALL NATURAL ENTITIES (INCLUDING HUMANS) HAVE INTRINSIC WORTH SIMPLY BY VIRTUE OF BEING AND BEING WHAT THEY ARE.[2]

In "On the Nature and Possibility of an Environmental Ethic," Tom Regan follows an implication of this view by presenting a "preservation principle":

> By the "preservation principle" I mean a principle of nondestruction, noninterference, and, generally, nonmeddling. By characterizing this in terms of a principle, moreover, I am emphasizing that preservation (letting-be) be regarded as a moral imperative.[3]

Support for this hands-off-nature approach is provided by George Sessions in his "Spinoza, Perennial Philosophy, and Deep Ecology," where, among other things, he describes how Aldo Leopold moved from a position considering humans as stewards or managers of nature to one considering humans as "plain members" of the total biotic community.[4] As Leopold himself puts it:

> A thing is right when it tends to preserve the integrity, stability, and beauty of the biotic community. It is wrong when it tends otherwise.[5]

According to Sessions, Leopold reached this position in part as a result of his dawning realization that ecological communities are internally integrated and highly complex. He saw how human activities have disrupted many ecological communities and was himself involved in some unsuccessful attempts to manage communities of animals in the wild. These failures led Leopold to conclude that "the biotic mechanism is so complex that its workings may never be fully understood."[6]

Like many other environmentalists, Sessions associates Leopold's position with Barry Commoner's first law of ecology: "Everything is connected to everything else,"[7] according to which "any major man-made change in a natural system is likely to be *detrimental* to that system."[8] . . .

Sessions, at least, is not naive about some of the problems that arise from these pronouncements. He says that if an environmental ethic is to be derived from ecological principles and concepts, this raises

> the old problem of attempting to derive moral principles and imperatives from supposedly empirical fact (the "is-ought problem"). The attempt to justify ecosystem ethics on conventional utilitarian or "rights and obligations" grounds presents formidable obstacles. And, so far, little headway has been made in finding other acceptable grounds for an ecosystem ethics other than a growing intuitive ecological awareness that *it is right.*[9]

Sessions by no means advocates or thinks possible a simple return to pre-Socratic religion or pantheism. But what, on the basis of ecological principles and concepts, is the underlying motif or guiding ideal today for "a correct understanding of God/Nature"?[10] According to [Arne] Naess, the proper position is an *ecosophy* defined as "a philosophy of ecological harmony or equilibrium."[11] Thus, while deploring the Greek contribution to the present desacralization of nature, these ecosophers do acknowledge the Stoic and Epicurean contributions to the philosophy of balance, harmony, and equilibrium. They present a holistic vision of the Earth circling in dynamic ecological equilibrium as the preferred and proper contemplative object of right-thinking environmental man.

In pursuing a statement of anti-anthropomorphic biocentrism, then, I have exposed five principles of the movement:

(1) The needs, desires, interests, and goals of humans are not privileged.

(2) The human species should not change the ecology of the planet.

(3) The world ecological system is too complex for human beings ever to understand.

(4) The ultimate goal, good, and joy of humankind is contemplative understanding of Nature.

(5) Nature is a holistic system of parts (of which man is merely one among many equals) all of which are internally interrelated in dynamic, harmonious, ecological equilibrium.

The moral imperative derived from this "ecosophy" is that human beings do not have the right to, and should not, alter the equilibrium.

II

I do not intend to challenge the controversial naturalistic assumption that some such environmental ethic can be derived from ecological principles and concepts. Whatever the logical problems of deriving value from fact, it is not (and probably never has been) a practical problem for large numbers of people who base their moral convictions on factual premises.

Nevertheless, it must be obvious to most careful readers that the general position characterized in section 1 suffers from serious internal contradictions. I think they are so serious that the position must be abandoned. In what follows I detail the problems that arise in the system, and then offer an alternative to the call for developing a new ecosophic ethic.

To go immediately to the heart of the matter, I take anti-anthropocentrism more seriously than do any of the ecosophers I have quoted or read. If man is a part of nature, if he is a "plain citizen," if he is just one nonprivileged member of a "biospherical egalitarianism," then the human species should be treated in no way different from any other species. However, the entire tone of the position outlined in section 1 is to set man apart from nature and above all other living species. Naess says that nonhuman animals should be "cared for in part for their own good."[12] Sessions says that humans should curb their technological enthusiasms to preserve ecological equilibrium.[13] Rodman says flatly that man should let nature be.[14]

Now, the posing of man against nature in any way is anthropocentric. Man is a part of nature.[15] Human ways—human culture—and human actions are as natural as are the ways in which any other species of animals behaves. But if we view the state of nature or Nature as being natural, undisturbed, and unperturbed only when human beings are *not* present, or only when human beings are curbing their natural behavior, then we are assuming that human beings are apart from, separate from, different from, removed from, or above nature. It is obvious that the ecosophy described above is based on this position of setting man apart from or above nature. (Do I mean even "sordid" and "perverted" human behavior? Yes, that is natural, too.)

To avoid this separation of man from nature, this special treatment of human beings as other than nature, we must stress that man's works (yes, including H-bombs and gas chanbers) are as natural as those of bower birds and beavers.

But civilized man wreaks such havoc on the environment. We disrupt the ecology of the planet, cause the extinction of myriad other species of living things, and even alter the climate of the Earth. Should we not attempt to curb our behavior to avoid these results? Indeed we should as a matter of prudence if we want to preserve our habitat and guarantee the survival of our species. But this is anthropocentric thinking.

Only if we are thinking anthropocentrically will we set the human species apart as *the* species that is to be thwarted in its natural behavior. Anti-anthropocentric biocentrists suggest that other species are to be allowed to manifest themselves naturally. They are to be allowed to live out their evolutionary potential in interaction with one another. But man is different. Man is *too* powerful, *too* destructive of the environment and other species, *too* successful in reproducing, and so on. What a phenomenon is man! Man is so wonderfully bad that he is not to be allowed to live out his evolutionary potential in egalitarian interaction with all other species.

Why not? The only reason is anthropocentric. We are not treating man as a plain member of the biotic community. We are not treating the human species as an equal among other species. We think of man as being better than other animals, or worse, as the case may be, because man is so powerful.

One reason we think this is that we think in terms of an anthropocentric moral community. All other species are viewed as morally neutral; their behavior is neither good nor bad. But we evaluate human behavior morally. And this sets man apart. If we are to treat man as a part of nature on egalitarian terms with other species, then man's behavior must be treated as morally neutral, too. It is absurd, of course, to suggest the opposite alternative, that we evaluate the behavior of nonhuman animals morally.

Bluntly, if we think there is nothing morally wrong with one species taking over the habitat of another and eventually causing the extinction of the dispossessed species—as has happened millions of times in the history of the Earth—then we should not think that there is anything morally or ecosophically wrong with the human species dispossessing and causing the extinction of other species.

Man's nature, his role, his forte, his glory and ambition has been to propagate and thrive at the expense of many other species and to the disruption—or, neutrally, to the change—of the planet's ecology. I do not want to engage in speculation about the religion of preliterate peoples, or in debates about the interpretation of documented non-Judeo-Christian-Platonic-Aristotelian religions. I am skeptical, however, of the panegyrics about pantheism and harmonious integration with sacred Nature. But these speculations do not matter. The fact is that for about 50,000 years human beings (*Homo sapiens*) have been advancing like wildfire (to use an inflammatory metaphor) to occupy more and more of the planet. A peak of low-energy technology was reached about 35,000 years ago at which time man wiped out many species of large animals. About 10,000 years ago man domesticated plants and animals and started changing the face of the Earth with grazing, farming, deforestation, and desertification. About 200 years ago man started burning fossil fuels with results that will probably change the climate of the planet (at least temporarily) and that have already resulted in the extinction of many species of living things that perhaps might otherwise have survived. In 1945 man entered an atomic age and we now have the ability to desertify large portions of the Earth and perhaps to cause the extinction of most of the higher forms of life.[16]

Human beings do alter things. They cause the extinction of many species, and they change the Earth's ecology. This is what humans do. This is their destiny. If they destroy many other species and themselves in the process, they do no more than has been done by many another species. The human species should be allowed—if any species can be said to have a right—to live out its evolutionary potential, to its own destruction if that is the end result. It is nature's way.

This is not a popular view. But most alternative anti-anthropocentric biocentric arguments for preserving nature are self-contradictory. Man is a part of nature. The only way man will survive is if he uses his brains to save himself. One reason why we should curb human behavior that is destructive of other species and the environment is because in the end it is destructive of the human species as well.[17]

I hope it is human nature to survive because we are smart. But those who appeal for a new ethic or religion or ecosophy based on an intuitive belief that they know what is right not only for other people, but also for the planet as a whole, exhibit the hubris that they themselves say got us in such a mess in the first place.[18] If the ecosphere is so complicated that we may never understand its workings, how is it that so many ecosophers are so sure that they know what is right for us to do now? Beyond the issue of man's right to do whatever he can according to the power-makes-right ecosophic ethic outlined by Naess, we may simply be wrong about what is "good" for the planet. Large numbers of species have been wiped out before, e.g., at the time the dinosaurs became extinct. Perhaps wiping out and renewal is just the way things go. Of course, a lot of genetic material is lost, but presumably all the species that ever existed came out of the same primordial soup, and could again. In situations where genetic material was limited, as in the Galapagos Islands or Australia, evolutionary radiation filled the niches. Even on the basis of our present knowledge about evolution and ecology, we have little ground to worry about the proliferation of life on Earth even if man manages to wipe out most of the species now living. Such a clearing out might be just the thing to allow for variety and diversity. And why is it that we harp about genetic banks today anyway?

For one thing, we are worried that disease might wipe out our domesticated grain crops. Then where would *man* be?

Another obvious anthropocentric element in ecosophic thinking is the predilection for ecological communities of great internal variety and complexity. But the barren limestone plateaus that surround the Mediterranean now are just as much in ecological balance as were the forests that grew there before man cut them down. And "dead" Lake Erie is just as much in ecological balance with the life on the land that surrounds it as it was in pre-Columbian times. The notion of a climax situation in ecology is a human invention, based on anthropocentric ideas of variety, completion, wholeness, and balance. A preference for equilibrium rather than change, for forests over deserts, for complexity and variety over simplicity and monoculture, all of these are matters of human economics and aesthetics. What *would* it be, after all, to think like a mountain as Aldo Leopold is said to have recommended?[19] It would be anthropocentric because mountains do not think, but also because mountains are imagined to be thinking about which human interests in their preservation or development they prefer.[20] The anthropocentrism of ecosophers is most obvious in their pronouncements about what is normal and natural. Perhaps it is not natural to remain in equilibrium, to be in ecological balance.

As far as that goes, most of the universe is apparently dead—or at least inanimate—anyway. And as far as we know, the movement of things is toward entropy. By simplifying things, man is on the side of the universe.

And as for making a mess of things, destroying things, disrupting and breaking down things, the best information we have about the origin of the universe is that it is the result of an explosion. If we are going to derive an ethic from our knowledge of nature, is it wrong to suggest that high-technology man might be doing the right thing? . . .

III

[U]nlike many ecosophers, I do not believe that we can return to religion, or that given what we know about the world today we can believe in pantheism or panpsychism, I think it is a mistake to strive for a new environmental ethic based on religious or mystical grounds. And I trust that I have demonstrated both how difficult it is to be fully biocentric, and also how the results of anti-anthropocentric biocentrism go far beyond the limits that ecosophers have drawn. Ecosophers obviously want to avoid the direct implications of treating the human species in the egalitarian and hands-off way they say other species should be treated. It is nice that human survival is compatible with the preservation of a rich planetary ecology, but I think it is a mistake to try to cover up the fact that human survival and the good life for man *is* some part of what we are interested in. There is very good reason for thinking ecologically, and for encouraging human beings to act in such a way as to preserve a rich and balanced planetary ecology: human survival depends on it.[21]

NOTES

1. *Webster's New World Dictionary,* 2nd ed. (Cleveland: William Collins and World Publishing Co., 1976), p. 59.

2. John Rodman, "The Liberation of Nature?" *Inquiry* 20 (1977): 108 (quoted with emphasis in capitals by George Sessions in *Ecophilosophy III,* p. 5a).

3. Tom Regan, "The Nature and Possibility of an Environmental Ethic," *Environmental Ethics* 3 (1981): 31–32.

4. George Sessions, "Spinoza, Perennial Philosophy, and Deep Ecology," unpublished, p. 15.

5. Aldo Leopold, *A Sand County Almanac* (Oxford: Oxford University Press, 1966), p. 240 (quoted by George Sessions in "Spinoza, Perennial Philosophy, and Deep Ecology," unpublished, p. 15).

6. Ibid.

7. Barry Commoner, *The Closing Circle: Nature, Man, and Technology* (New York: Alfred A. Knopf, 1971), p. 33 (quoted by George Sessions in "Panpsychism versus Modern Materialism: Some Implications for an Ecological Ethics," unpublished, p. 35).

8. Ibid., p. 41.

9. George Sessions, "Shallow and Deep Ecology: A Review of the Philosophical Literature," unpublished, p. 16.

10. See note 14.

11. Arne Naess, "The Shallow and the Deep, Long-Range Ecology Movement. A Summary," *Inquiry* 16 (1973): 99.

12. Arne Naess, "Environmental Ethics and Spinoza's Ethics. Comments on Genevieve Lloyd's Article," *Inquiry* 23 (1980): 319.

13. George Sessions, "Spinoza and Jeffers on Man and Nature," *Inquiry* 20 (1977): 482.

14. See note 2.

15. Richard A. Watson and Patty Jo Watson, *Man and Nature: An Anthropological Essay in Human Ecology* (New York: Harcourt Brace and World, 1969).

16. Ibid.

17. Biocentrism does not imply radical anti-anthropocentrism, for what is best for man may also be best for the whole biological community. See, e.g., J. Baird Callicott, "Elements of an Environmental Ethic: Moral Considerability and the Biotic Community," *Environmental Ethics* 1 (1979): 71–81. See also R. and V. Routley, "Against the Inevitability of Human Chauvinism," in K. E. Goodpaster and K. M. Sayre, eds. *Ethics and Problems of the 21st Century* (Notre Dame: University of Notre Dame Press, 1979). Sophisticated arguments in diverse fields support the view that cooperation leading to ecological balance is best for the whole biologic community, see, e.g., Robert Axelrod and William D. Hamilton, "The Evolution of Cooperation," *Science* 211 (1981): 1390–96.

18. See note 9.

19. Susan Flader, *Thinking Like a Mountain: Aldo Leopold and the Evolution of an Ecological Attitude toward Deer, Wolves, and Forests* (Columbia: University of Missouri Press, 1974).

20. Christopher D. Stone, *Should Trees Have Standing? Toward Legal Rights for Natural Objects* (Los Altos, Calif.: William Kaufmann, 1974).

21. See note 17.

Discussion Questions

1. Discuss whether Watson's summary of the five principles of "anti-anthropomorphic biocentrism" are consistent with the eight principles of deep ecology put forth by Naess and Sessions.

2. Discuss how Devall and Sessions would most likely respond to Watson's claim that biocentrism (deep ecology) contains serious internal contradictions.

3. In his article "A Defence of the Deep Ecology Movement,"[34] Arne Naess takes exception to Watson's claim that biocentrists set humans apart from nature by viewing humans as destructive to nature. Naess points out that every species, including humans, alters ecosystems. However, humans have a special responsibility because of our capacity to pose the problem of long-term consequences. Thus, it is an expression of our human nature to act responsibly in our relationships with the environment. Is this an adequate rebuttal of Watson's argument that biocentrism is anthropocentric? Discuss how Watson might reply to Naess.

4. What would Watson most likely think about the morality of the practice of cutting down rain forests to create grazing land for cattle? Role-play a discussion between Watson, Regan, and Sessions on this issue. Which person presents the best argument? Support your answer.

KAREN J. WARREN

The Power and the Promise of Ecological Feminism

Karen Warren is a philosophy professor at Macalester College in St. Paul, Minnesota. Warren argues that the domination of women and the domination of nature are both grounded in the same logic of domination and value-hierarchy thinking. Therefore, feminism and environmental ethics are conceptually inseparable.

Critical Reading Questions

1. What is "ecological feminism"?
2. What types of issues are "feminist issues"? Which of these issues are conceptual ones?
3. What is a "conceptual framework"?
4. What is an "oppressive conceptual framework"? What are the three significant features of oppressive conceptual frameworks?
5. What is a "logic of domination"? What are the assumptions supporting it?
6. How is a logic of domination used to justify both oppression of women and oppression of nature?
7. What is "naturism"?
8. According to Warren, why is the first-person narrative an effective means of raising important issues in environmental ethics?
9. What is the difference between the "loving eye" and the "arrogant eye"? Which type of perception is compatible with ecofeminism?
10. Why is ecofeminism anti-naturalist?
11. What does Warren mean when she says that ecofeminism is a contextualist ethic?
12. What does Warren mean when she says that ecofeminism is pluralistic and inclusivistic?
13. What is the ecofeminist view of what it means to be human and to behave ethically?

Ecological feminism (ecofeminism) has begun to receive a fair amount of attention lately as an alternative feminism and environmental ethic. As I use the term in this paper, ecological feminism is the position that there are important connections—historical, experiential, symbolic, theoretical—between the domination of women and the domination of nature, an understanding of which is crucial to both feminism and environmental ethics. I argue

that the promise and power of ecological feminism is that *it provides a distinctive framework both for reconceiving feminism and for developing an environmental ethic which takes seriously connections between the domination of women and the domination of nature.* I do so by discussing the nature of a feminist ethic and the ways in which ecofeminism provides a feminist and environmental ethic. I conclude that any feminist theory *and* any environmental ethic which fails to

Karen J. Warren, "The Power and the Promise of Ecological Feminism," *Environmental Ethics,* Vol. 12, No. 2, Summer 1990, pp. 123–146. Some notes have been omitted.

take seriously the twin and interconnected dominations of women and nature is at best incomplete and at worst simply inadequate.

FEMINISM, ECOLOGICAL FEMINISM, AND CONCEPTUAL FRAMEWORKS

Whatever else it is, feminism is at least the movement to end sexist oppression. It involves the elimination of any and all factors that contribute to the continued and systematic domination or subordination of women. While feminists disagree about the nature of and solutions to the subordination of women, all feminists agree that sexist oppression exists, is wrong, and must be abolished.

A "feminist issue" is any issue that contributes in some way to understanding the oppression of women. Equal rights, comparable pay for comparable work, and food production are feminist issues wherever and whenever an understanding of them contributes to an understanding of the continued exploitation or subjugation of women. . . .

Feminist philosophers claim that some of the most important feminist issues are *conceptual* ones: these issues concern how one conceptualizes such mainstay philosophical notions as reason and rationality, ethics, and what it is to be human. Ecofeminists extend this feminist philosophical concern to nature. They argue that, ultimately, some of the most important connections between the domination of women and the domination of nature are conceptual. To see this, consider the nature of conceptual frameworks.

A *conceptual framework* is a set of *basic* beliefs, values, attitudes, and assumptions which shape and reflect how one views oneself and one's world. It is a socially constructed lens through which we perceive ourselves and others. It is affected by such factors as gender, race, class, age, affectional orientation, nationality, and religious background.

Some conceptual frameworks are oppressive. An *oppressive conceptual framework* is one that explains, justifies, and maintains relationships of domination and subordination. When an oppressive conceptual framework is *patriarchal,* it explains, justifies, and maintains the subordination of women by men.

I have argued elsewhere that there are three significant features of oppressive conceptual frameworks: (1) value-hierarchical thinking, i.e., "up-down" thinking which places higher value, status, or prestige on what is "up" rather than on what is "down"; (2) value dualisms, i.e., disjunctive pairs in which the disjuncts are seen as oppositional (rather than as complementary) and exclusive (rather than as inclusive), and which place higher value (status, prestige) on one disjunct rather than the other (e.g., dualisms which give higher value or status to that which has historically been identified as "mind," "reason," and "male" than to that which has been historically identified as "body," "emotion," and "female"); and (3) logic of domination, i.e., a structure of argumentation which leads to a justification of subordination.

The third feature of oppressive conceptual frameworks is the most significant. A logic of domination is not *just* a logical structure. It also involves a substantive value system, since an ethical premise is needed to permit or sanction the "just" subordination of that which is subordinate. This justification typically is given on grounds of some alleged characteristic (e.g., rationality) which the dominant (e.g., men) have and the subordinate (e.g., women) lack. . . .

For ecofeminism, that a logic of domination is explanatorily basic is important for at least three reasons. First, without a logic of domination, a description of similarities and differences would be just that—a description of similarities and differences. Consider the claim, "Humans are different from plants and rocks in that humans can (and plants and rocks cannot) consciously and radically reshape the communities in which they live; humans are similar to plants and rocks in that they are both members of an ecological community." Even if humans are "better" than plants and rocks with respect to the conscious ability of humans to radically transform communities, one does not *thereby* get any *morally* relevant distinction between humans and nonhumans, or an argument for the domination of plants and rocks by humans. To get *those* conclusions one needs to add at least two powerful assumptions, viz., (A2) and (A4) in argument A below:

(A1) Humans do, and plants and rocks do not, have the capacity to consciously and radically change the community in which they live.

(A2) Whatever has the capacity to consciously and radically change the community in which it lives is morally superior to whatever lacks this capacity.

(A3) Thus, humans are morally superior to plants and rocks.

(A4) For any X and Y, if X is morally superior to Y, then X is morally justified in subordinating Y.

(A5) Thus, humans are morally justified in subordinating plants and rocks.

Without the two assumptions that *humans are morally superior* to (at least some) nonhumans, (A2), and that *superiority justifies subordination,* (A4), all one has is some difference between humans and some nonhumans. This is true *even if* that difference is given in terms of superiority. Thus, it is the logic of domination, (A4), which is the bottom line in ecofeminist discussions of oppression.

Second, ecofeminists argue that, at least in Western societies, the oppressive conceptual framework which sanctions the twin dominations of women and nature is a patriarchal one characterized by all three features of an oppressive conceptual framework. Many ecofeminists claim that, historically, within at least the dominant Western culture, a patriarchal conceptual framework has sanctioned the following argument B:

(B1) Women are identified with nature and the realm of the physical; men are identified with the "human" and the realm of the mental.

(B2) Whatever is identified with nature and the realm of the physical is inferior to ("below") whatever is identified with the "human" and the realm of the mental; or, conversely, the latter is superior to ("above") the former.

(B3) Thus, women are inferior to ("below") men; or, conversely, men are superior to ("above") women.

(B4) For any X and Y, if X is superior to Y, then X is justified in subordinating Y.

(B5) Thus, men are justified in subordinating women.

If sound, argument B establishes *patriarchy,* i.e., the conclusion given at (B5) that the systematic domination of women by men is justified. But according to ecofeminists, (B5) is justified by just those three features of an oppressive conceptual framework identified earlier: value-hierarchical thinking, the assumption at (B2); value dualisms, the assumed dualism of the mental and the physical at (B1) and the assumed inferiority of the physical vis-à-vis the mental at (B2); and a logic of domination, the assumption at (B4), the same as the previous premise (A4). . . .

Ecofeminists insist that the sort of logic of domination used to justify the domination of humans by gender, racial or ethnic, or class status is also used to justify the domination of nature. Because eliminating a logic of domination is part of a feminist critique—whether a critique of patriarchy, white supremacist culture, or imperialism—ecofeminists insist that *naturism* is properly viewed as an integral part of any feminist solidarity movement to end sexist oppression and the logic of domination which conceptually grounds it.

CLIMBING FROM ECOFEMINISM TO ENVIRONMENTAL ETHICS

Many feminists and some environmental ethicists have begun to explore the use of first-person narrative as a way of raising philosophically germane issues in ethics often lost or underplayed in mainstream philosophical ethics. Why is this so? What is it about narrative which makes it a significant resource for theory and practice in feminism and environmental ethics? . . .

Consider the following first-person narrative about rock climbing:

For my very first rock climbing experience, I chose a somewhat private spot, away from other climbers and on-lookers. After studying "the chimney," I focused all my energy on making it to the top. I climbed with intense determination, using whatever strength and skills I had to accomplish this challenging feat. By midway I was exhausted and anxious. . . . I was determined to make it to the top. With renewed confidence and concentration, I finished the climb to the top.

On my second day of climbing, I rappelled down about 200 feet from the top of the Palisades at Lake Superior to just a few feet above the water level. I could see no one—not my belayer, not the other climbers, no one. I unhooked slowly from the rappel rope and took a deep cleansing breath. I looked all around me—really looked—and listened. I heard a cacophony of voices—birds, trickles of water on the rock before me, waves lapping against the rocks below. I closed my eyes and began to feel the rock with my hands—the cracks and crannies, the raised lichen and mosses, the almost imperceptible nubs that might provide a resting place for my fingers and toes when I began to climb. At that moment I was bathed in serenity. I began to talk to the rock in an almost inaudible, child-like way, as if the rock were my friend. I felt an overwhelming sense of gratitude for what it offered me—a chance to know myself and the rock differently, to appreciate unforeseen miracles like the tiny flowers growing in the even tinier cracks in the rock's surface, and to come to know a sense of *being in relationship* with the natural environment. It felt as if the rock and I were silent conversational partners in a longstanding friendship. I realized then that I had come to care about this cliff which was so different from me, so unmovable and invincible, independent and seemingly indifferent to my presence. I wanted to be with the rock as I climbed. Gone was the determination to conquer the rock, to forcefully impose my will on it; I wanted simply to work respectfully with the rock as I climbed. And as I climbed, that is what I felt. I felt myself *caring* for this rock and feeling thankful that climbing provided the opportunity for me to know it and myself in this new way.

There are at least four reasons why use of such a first-person narrative is important to feminism and environmental ethics. First, such a narrative gives voice to a felt sensitivity often lacking in traditional analytical ethical discourse, viz., a sensitivity to conceiving of oneself as fundamentally "in relationship with" others, including the nonhuman environment. It is a modality which *takes relationships themselves seriously.* It thereby stands in contrast to a strictly reductionist modality that takes relationships seriously only or primarily because of the nature of the *relators* or parties to those relationships (e.g., relators conceived as moral agents, right holders, interest carriers, or sentient beings). . . .

Second, such a first-person narrative gives expression to a variety of ethical attitudes and behaviors often overlooked or underplayed in mainstream Western ethics, e.g., the difference in attitudes and behaviors toward a rock when one is "making it to the top" and when one thinks of oneself as "friends with" or "caring about" the rock one climbs. These different attitudes and behaviors suggest an ethically germane contrast between two different types of relationship humans or climbers may have toward a rock: an imposed conqueror-type relationship, and an emergent caring-type relationship. This contrast grows out of, and is faithful to, felt, lived experience.

The difference between conquering and caring attitudes and behavior in relation to the natural environment provides a third reason why the use of first-person narrative is important to feminism and environmental ethics: it provides a way of conceiving of ethics and ethical meaning as *emerging out of* particular situations moral agents find themselves in, rather than as being *imposed on* those situations (e.g., as a derivation or instantiation of some predetermined abstract principle or rule). . . . As a reflection of and on felt, lived experiences, the use of narrative in ethics provides a stance from which ethical discourse can be held accountable to the historical, material, and social realities in which moral subjects find themselves.

Lastly, and for our purposes perhaps most importantly, the use of narrative has argumentative significance. . . . Narrative has argumentative force by suggesting *what counts* as an appropriate conclusion to an ethical situation. One ethical conclusion suggested by the climbing narrative is that what counts as a proper ethical attitude toward mountains and rocks is an attitude of respect and care (whatever that turns out to be or involve), not one of domination and conquest.

In an essay entitled "In and Out of Harm's Way: Arrogance and Love," feminist philosopher Marilyn Frye distinguishes between "arrogant" and "loving" perception as one way of getting at this difference in the ethical attitudes of care and conquest.[1] Frye writes:

> The loving eye is a contrary of the arrogant eye.
>
> The loving eye knows the independence of the other. It is the eye of a seer who knows that nature is indifferent. It is the eye of one who knows that to know the seen, one must consult something other than one's own will and interests and fears and imagination. One must look at the thing. One must look and listen and check and question.
>
> . . . The loving eye does not make the object of perception into something edible, does not try to assimilate it, does not reduce it to the size of the seer's desire, fear and imagination, and hence does not have to simplify. It knows the complexity of the other as something which will forever present new things to be known. The science of the loving eye presuppose[s] The Endless Interestingness of the Universe.[2]

. . . An ecofeminist perspective about both women and nature involves this shift in attitude from "arrogant perception" to "loving perception" of the nonhuman world. Arrogant perception of nonhumans by humans presupposes and maintains *sameness* in such a way that it expands the moral community to those beings who are thought to resemble (be like, similar to, or the same as) humans in some morally significant way. Any environmental movement or ethic based on arrogant perception builds a moral hierarchy of beings and assumes some common denominator of moral considerability in virtue of which like beings deserve similar treatment or moral consideration and unlike beings do not. Such environmental ethics are or generate a "unity

in sameness." In contrast, "loving perception" presupposes and maintains *difference*—a distinction between the self and other, between human and at least some nonhumans—in such a way that perception of the other as other *is* an expression of love for one who/which is recognized at the outset as independent, dissimilar, different. . . .

"Loving perception" of the nonhuman natural world is an attempt to understand what it means *for humans* to care about the nonhuman world, a world *acknowledged* as being independent, different, perhaps even indifferent to humans. Humans *are* different from rocks in important ways, even if they are also both members of some ecological community. A moral community based on loving perception of oneself *in relationship with* a rock, or with the natural environment as a whole, is one which acknowledges and respects difference, whatever "sameness" also exists. . . .

ECOFEMINISM AS A FEMINIST AND ENVIRONMENTAL ETHIC

A feminist ethic involves a twofold commitment to critique male bias in ethics wherever it occurs, and to develop ethics which are not male-biased. Sometimes this involves articulation of values (e.g., values of care, appropriate trust, kinship, friendship) often lost or underplayed in mainstream ethics. Sometimes it involves engaging in theory building by pioneering in new directions or by revamping old theories in gender sensitive ways. What makes the critique of old theories or conceptualizations of new ones "feminist" is that they emerge out of sex-gender analyses and reflect whatever those analyses reveal about gendered experience and gendered social reality.

. . . It is a feminism that critiques male bias wherever it occurs in ethics (including environmental ethics) and aims at providing an ethic (including an environmental ethic) which is not male biased—and it does so in a way that satisfies the preliminary boundary conditions of a feminist ethic.

First, ecofeminism is quintessentially anti-naturist. Its anti-naturism consists in the rejection of any way of thinking about or acting toward nonhuman nature that reflects a logic, values, or attitude of domination. Its anti-naturist, anti-sexist, anti-racist, anti-classist (and so forth, for all other "isms" of social domination) stance forms the outer boundary of the quilt: nothing gets on the quilt which is naturist, sexist, racist, classist, and so forth.

Second, ecofeminism is a contextualist ethic. It involves a shift *from* a conception of ethics as primarily a matter of rights, rules, or principles predetermined and applied in specific cases to entities viewed as competitors in the contest of moral standing, *to* a conception of ethics as growing out of . . . relationships conceived in some sense as defining who one is. . . .

For an ecofeminist, *how* a moral agent is in relationship to another becomes of central significance, not simply *that* a moral agent is a moral agent or is bound by rights, duties, virtue, or utility to act in a certain way.

Third, ecofeminism is structurally pluralistic in that it presupposes and maintains difference—difference among humans as well as between humans and at least some elements of nonhuman nature. Thus, while ecofeminism denies the "nature/culture" split, it affirms that humans are both members of an ecological community (in some respects) and different from it (in other respects). Ecofeminism's attention to relationships and community is not, therefore, an erasure of difference but a respectful acknowledgment of it.

Fourth, ecofeminism reconceives theory as theory in process. It focuses on patterns of meaning which emerge, for instance, from the storytelling and first-person narratives of women (and others) who deplore the twin dominations of women and nature. The use of narrative is one way to ensure that the content of the ethic—the pattern of the quilt—may/will change over time, as the historical and material realities of women's lives change and as more is learned about women-nature connections and the destruction of the nonhuman world.

Fifth, ecofeminism is inclusivist. It emerges from the voices of women who experience the harmful domination of nature and the way that domination is tied to their domination as women. It emerges from listening to the voices of indigenous peoples such as Native Americans who have been dislocated from their land and have witnessed the attendant undermining of such values as appropriate reciprocity, sharing, and kinship that characterize traditional Indian culture. It emerges from listening to voices of those who, like Nathan Hare, critique traditional approaches to environmental ethics as white and bourgeois, and as failing to address issues of "black ecology" and the "ecology" of the inner city and urban spaces.[3] . . .

Sixth, as a feminism, ecofeminism makes no attempt to provide an "objective" point of view. It is a social ecology. It recognizes the twin dominations of women and nature as social problems rooted both in very concrete, historical, socioeconomic circumstances and in oppressive patriarchal conceptual frameworks which maintain and sanction these circumstances.

Seventh, ecofeminism makes a central place for values of care, love, friendship, trust, and appropriate reciprocity—values that presuppose that our relationships to others are central to our understanding of who we are. . . .

Lastly, an ecofeminist ethic involves a reconception of what it means to be human, and in what human ethical behavior consists. Ecofeminism denies abstract individualism. Humans are who we are in large part by virtue of the historical and social contexts and the relationships we are in, including our relationships with nonhuman nature. . . .

By making visible the interconnections among the dominations of women and nature, ecofeminism shows that both are feminist issues and that explicit acknowledgement of both is vital to any responsible environmental ethic. Feminism *must* embrace ecological feminism if it is to end the domination of women because the domination of women is tied conceptually and historically to the domination of nature.

NOTES

1. Marilyn Frye, "In and Out of Harm's Way: Arrogance and Love," *The Politics of Reality* (Trumansburg, New York: The Crossing Press, 1983), pp. 66–72.

2. Ibid., pp. 75–76.

3. Nathan Hare, "Black Ecology," in *Environmental*

Ethics, ed. K. S. Shrader-Frechette (Pacific Grove, Calif.: Boxwood Press, 1981), pp. 229–36.

Discussion Questions

1. Analyze Warren's argument that a logic of domination justifies the oppression of both women and nature. For example, are her premises acceptable? Has she left out any important premises? Does her conclusion logically follow from her premises?

2. Discuss Warren's claim that being a feminist entails being an ecofeminist. How might Leopold and Cohen each respond to this claim?

3. Care ethicist Nel Noddings, in her article at the end of Chapter 1, maintains that we cannot have meaningful caring relationships with nonhuman animals or the environment. How might Warren respond to Noddings? Discuss which person presents the more compelling argument and why.

4. Using the first-person narrative, describe a recent experience you had in the "outdoors." Does the use of the narrative make you aware, or more aware, of your relationship with the environment? Discuss some of the philosophical and ethical issues raised by your narrative.

5. Compare and contrast Warren's concept of naturism with Singer's concept of speciesism. Is naturism a logical extension of speciesism? Discuss how both Warren and Singer might respond to this question.

6. Some ecofeminists criticize deep ecology as being patriarchal or embodying masculine egoism.[35] Do you agree? Support your answer.

CASE STUDIES

1. ANIMAL LIBERATION IN THE SCIENCE LAB

Founded in England in the mid-1970s, the Animal Liberation Front (ALF) is a loose organization of radical animal-rights activists who target science laboratories, slaughterhouses, and the fur industry. On May 24, 1984, five members of the ALF broke into the Experimental Head Injury Lab at the University of Pennsylvania and stole files and videotapes of experiments done in the lab. The videotapes showed gruesome scenes of terrified baboons in vises with their heads being smashed by pistons while the researchers joked around. Operations were shown being performed on primates without regard for their pain or for standard research procedures. After taking the videotapes, the ALF ransacked the lab.

In the controversy that followed the release of the tapes to the public, Dr. Thomas Gennarelli, the director of the lab, defended the research, claiming that the animals had been properly treated. He also accused the ALF of setting back medical research. Both the university and the National Institutes of Health (NIH), which gave the lab a new grant to repair the damage, supported Dr. Gennarelli.

The ALF responded to the accusation by comparing the lab experiments to those conducted by Nazi Dr. Joseph Mengele on Jews in concentration camps. Protesters supported the ALF by staging demonstrations on campuses and at the offices of the NIH. In 1985 the secretary of Health and Human Services stopped federal funding for the head injury program. The university also agreed to pay a fine for violating the Animal Welfare Act and promised to pay more attention to the welfare of the animals used in experiments. The members of the ALF were not prosecuted for their actions.

Discussion Questions

1. Were stealing the tapes and ransacking the lab morally justified? Should the ALF have been punished for its actions? Support your answers. Discuss how a utilitarian, such as Peter Singer, might respond to these questions.
2. Morally speaking, does it make a difference, because of their similarity to humans, that primates were used in the experiments? Support your answer. Discuss how both Singer and Cohen would respond to this question.
3. Discuss how an abolitionist, a reformist, and a status quo person would respond to this case. What solutions would each of them most likely propose?
4. Would the experiments have been morally justified if Dr. Gennarelli had not violated that Animal Welfare Act and if it could be shown that thousands of human lives have been saved as a result of these experiments? Support your answer.
5. Discuss the analogy made by the ALF between Dr. Gennarelli and Dr. Mengele.
6. During the 1993 Christmas season, the ALF protested the selling of furs by planting battery-and-paper-bag incendiary devices in three large Chicago department stores. Although no one was hurt, the FBI reported that it was considering classifying the ALF along with dozens of other animals-rights groups as terrorist organizations. Is the ALF a terrorist organization? Do you agree with the ALF that the selling and wearing of fur and leather clothing is immoral? If so, do clerks employed in stores that sell fur and leather have a moral obligation to protest this practice? Support your answers.
7. The Animal Rights Direct Action Coalition has targeted MacDonald's restaurants. They drive up to a MacDonald's in a pickup truck with a dead cow in the back and a sign reading "Here's your lunch." Discuss the moral implications of these tactics.

---

2. USING ANIMALS FOR XENOTRANSPLANTS

There are about 44,000 people in the United States waiting for organ transplants, according to the United Network for Organ Sharing, which oversees organ donations. Most of these people will die before a suitable donor is found. More than 28,000 people, for example, die each year from liver failure.[36] Xenotransplants, the transplanting of organs from one species of animal into another, may offer a solution to this shortage.

The first animal-to-human transplant occurred in 1906, when French physician Mathieu Jaboulay transplanted a kidney from a pig into a woman. Neither the woman nor the pig survived the procedure. Since then several people have received organs from pigs and baboons. Although baboons are genetically closer to humans, many researchers prefer pigs for xenotransplants because pigs are anatomically very similar to humans. They are also healthier, less likely to carry viruses, and easier to breed. At Duke University scientists are genetically engineering pigs with human genes so that their livers will be more compatible with humans.

In 1995 researchers at the University of California at San Francisco injected an AIDS patient with baboon bone marrow. Because baboons are resistant to HIV, it was hoped that the bone marrow would provide a replacement for the patient's damaged immune system. Earlier that year, doctors at Lahey Hitchcock Medical Center in Massachusetts injected cells from fetal pig brains into patients with Parkinson's disease.

Discussion Questions

1. Although many people have ethical qualms about using baboons for xenotransplants, because of their similarity to humans, they have fewer objections to using pigs because pigs are already slaughtered for food. Is the fact that pigs are slaughtered for food morally relevant? Is the fact that pigs are not primates morally relevant, or are we being speciesists in making such a distinction? Support your answers.
2. At what point do animals genetically engineered to have human genes become human, and, as such, deserving of the moral respect we normally give other humans? Support your answer. Discuss how Cohen might respond to this question.
3. Xenotransplants raise the possibility of outbreaks of new infectious diseases. Retroviruses that may be harmless in other species can be potentially deadly in humans. For example, many researchers believe that AIDS was transmitted to humans from monkeys. If xenotransplants might endanger healthy human populations, should they be banned or more closely regulated? Does the possibility of contracting a disease from another species weaken the anthropocentric argument that humans are a special creation? Support your answers.
4. Weigh the rights, if any, of nonhuman animals such as pigs and baboons against those of humans who need organ transplants. Is it morally acceptable to sacrifice the lives of other animals for humans whose organs have been damaged by their destructive lifestyles, such as heavy drinking or smoking? Support your answer. Discuss how Cohen and Singer might respond to this question.

---

3. BRITAIN SAYS "TALLY-NO" TO FOX HUNTING

One of the most colorful images of rural England is the hunters in scarlet-and-black jackets riding through the green patchwork countryside, accompanied by their packs of hounds in pursuit of the elusive fox. All this may soon come to an end. In November 1997 the British Parliament voted overwhelmingly to ban fox and deer hunting with dogs. Under the bill, hunters and people who allow hunting with dogs on their land would be liable to maximum sentences of six months and fines of up to $8,400. The bill is currently being challenged by hunting organizations and legislators.[37]

Labour Party lawmaker Mike Foster, who sponsored the bill, said that the intention of the bill is "to protect wild mammals from cruelty and from the unnecessary pain and suffering inflicted in the name of a so-called sport." Although Foster acknowledges that foxes can be a nuisance, he says that hunting them down in this manner is not the answer.

Those who protest the ban argue that it will bring about the end of twenty-seven thousand rural jobs, such as for gamekeepers and saddle makers, as well as destruction of the twenty thousand hounds that are used for hunting. They also point out that much of England's unique patchwork countryside, with its hedges and woodlands, is maintained specifically for field sports.

Discussion Questions

1. Fox hunting has long had its critics in England. In the 1890s playwright Oscar Wilde called it "the unspeakable in full pursuit of the uneatable." Are fox hunting and other types of hunting justified if it is done for food?

2. Sir Brian Mawhinner, a conservative lawmaker who opposes the ban, argues that "the freedom of the individual to hunt with hounds is no different in principle from the freedom of each individual to or not to: fish, shoot, eat meat, use tobacco, drink, gamble or worship, as he or she chooses." Analyze Mawhinner's argument.

3. Supporters of fox and deer hunting argue that bans are an unjustified restriction on their freedom, because foxes and deer are not part of the social contract. People have the right to pursue their lifestyle activities without hindrance from the government so long as those activities do not restrict the personal freedom of or cause harm to another member of society. Opponents of hunting must show that hunting is contrary to the public interest or that it interferes with the freedom of other members of society. Anti-hunting legislation does not meet these requirements and, hence, is a violation of human rights. Do you agree with this argument? Support your answer. Discuss how both Narveson and Regan might respond to the social contract argument for hunting.

4. Tory lawmaker John Gummer argues that the ban on hunting violates that "predatory chain" of nature. "The fox has its own animals which it is a predator of, but we are the predator upon the fox, and we need, therefore, within that predatory chain, to carry out our role."[38] Discuss the merits of Gummer's argument.

5. Fox hunting with hounds is also practiced in Australia, New Zealand, Italy, Portugal, and the United States. In the United States and Australia, hunters pursue foxes but usually do not kill them. Is fox hunting morally justified so long as the fox isn't killed? Discuss how a utilitarian might respond to this question.

6. Oregon recently outlawed for being inhumane using dogs to track and tree cougars which are then shot at close range. With more cougar habitat being lost to development and agriculture every year, this has resulted in increased conflicts with humans as more cougars are roaming into residential areas. Do you agree with Oregon voters that sport-hunting tactics that put the animal at such an unfair disadvantage are inhumane? Is it morally justifiable to shoot cougars for killing livestock? For "trespassing" into residential areas? Support your answers.

---

4. THE ABANDONED CAT[39]

David had always wanted a cat but couldn't have one because his father was allergic to them. Although pets were forbidden in his dormitory, shortly after he moved to college David went to the local animal shelter and adopted a young cat which he kept confined in his room. At the end of the year, David moved back home and left the cat to fend for herself.

After several weeks of wandering around campus, the cat was taken in by one of the department secretaries, who took pity on it. By this time the cat was near starvation; she also had a rash that had caused her to lose much of her fur. The secretary knew that one of the professors in the department, Professor Carey, was thinking of getting a cat. Professor Carey agreed to take the cat home.

After the cat's rash did not clear up, Professor Carey took her to the veterinarian. The vet told the professor that the cat had multiple allergies and would have to receive cortisone shots as well as eat a special diet. In addition, the cat had an overactive thyroid that would require an expensive operation or else medication for the rest of her life. The medication would cost approximately $30 a month and would have to be given to the cat three times a day at six-hour intervals. After thinking about it, Professor Carey decided that the expense and inconvenience was not worth it. She asked the veterinarian to euthanize the cat.

Discussion Questions

1. What are the professor's moral obligations, if any, toward the cat? Support your answer.
2. Is it morally acceptable to euthanize the cat? Or does the cat's interest in staying alive outweigh the professor's inconvenience? Are there any conditions under which it is morally acceptable to have an animal companion euthanized? Support your answers. Discuss how both Narveson, Cohen, and Singer might respond to this question.
3. About seventy thousand kittens and puppies are born each day in the United States. More than 70 percent of people who adopt them end up giving them away, abandoning them, or giving them to shelters. More than half of these animals—about 17 million annually—are destroyed.[40] Do dogs and cats have a right to have kittens and puppies? Or, given these statistics, is it morally irresponsible for humans to allow cats and dogs in their care to breed? Support your answers.
4. Was it morally acceptable for David to adopt a cat from the animal shelter, knowing that it was against the rules to keep a cat in the dormitory and knowing that he could not take her home with him once the school year ended? Did he have a moral obligation to find another home for the cat when he moved out of the dormitory? Support your answers.
5. Some animal-rights activists, such as Regan, argue that owning house pets (animals that are kept inside or allowed outside only on a leash or in an enclosure) is a type of slavery. Do you agree? Can having a pet or animal companion be compatible with respect? Support your answers.
6. A lot of animal shelters do not allow college students to adopt cats and dogs. Is this policy a violation of the autonomy of college students? Support your answer.

---

5. ZOOS: PRISONS OR HAVENS?

Zoos are a relatively new phenomenon. The first modern zoos were established in Europe in the nineteenth century. Britain's famous London Zoo was opened in the nineteenth century to house the collection of animals brought back from the British colonies around the world.

In the early 1990s, the London Zoo became mired in a financial crisis because of the mismanagement of funds and a steady drop in attendance. Like other zoos around the world, it had also been under attack by animal-rights activists. One of these groups, Zoo Check, wanted to see zoos closed and the money used for conservation instead.

In 1993 it was announced that the London Zoo would have to close down. A high-profile "Save Our Zoo" campaign, however, raised enough money to keep the zoo going. Supporters of the zoo argued that zoos are often the first contact young people have with "wild animals." They also pointed out the important role that the London Zoo plays in educating people about conservation and in saving endangered species.

Opponents responded by pointing out that watching captive and anguished animals is hardly a good introduction. The use of documentaries of animals in their natural habitat is a more realistic way to educate young people about other animals. They also argued that conservation, including the preservation of endangered species, should take place within the animals' natural habitats. According to Wills Travers of Zoo Check, as many black rhinos in zoo-based captive breeding programs die as are bred.

Discussion Questions

1. Are zoos ever morally justified? If so, under what conditions? What about safari parks, such as Six Flags or Disney's Animal Kingdom, where animals roam free, within limits, and the people remain in their cars? Support your answers.
2. While it may be possible to protect some of these species, such as the black rhino, within their natural habitats, in other cases the habitats have been destroyed by human encroachment. The destruction of the rain forests in Central and South America for agricultural land has already resulted in the extinction of hundreds of species of animals. Does the preservation of endangered species, in these cases, morally justify the continuation of zoos as a means of preserving endangered species? Support your answer. Discuss how Leopold, Devall, and Sessions might each respond to this question.
3. Discuss the institution of zoos in light of Warren's ecofeminist analysis. What would Warren's position on zoos most likely be? In what ways, if any, do zoos, and the continued justification of zoos, illustrate a dualistic, patriarchal ideology? Compare and contrast the institution of zoos to other patriarchal institutions such as colonialism, slavery, sexism, and meat-eating.

---

6. THE "BAMBI BOOM"

The Teneja family were on the way to the College of William and Mary where 19-year-old Baninder Teneja was starting a summer research project. As they exited Interstate 95 on a side trip to nearby Lake Anna, a panicked deer struck and careened off a van ahead of them and came crashing through their front window. Baninder, who was riding in the back seat, was fatally injured when she was struck by the decapitated head of the deer before it smashed through their back window.

This was just one of over four thousand vehicle/deer collisions that occurred in Virginia in 1999, up from six hundred in 1997. In Michigan the state police alone logged in 67,669 deer/vehicle collisions in 1999. According to the National Highway Traffic Safety Administration, there were 182 human fatalities from vehicle/deer collisions in 1998, up from 139 in 1996.[41]

The increase in vehicle/deer accidents is causing concern especially since the deer population in the United States is growing at an unprecedented rate. In many parts of the United States the deer population is two to four times what it was in pre-European times. This population explosion is due to a number of factors, including the milder winters we've had in the last decade and a decline in the number of natural predators such as the wolf.

Humans aren't the only ones being negatively impacted by the "Bambi boom." Some scientists predict that the deer population, if left unchecked, could lead to the catastrophic disintegration of certain biotic communities. Overbrowsing by deer not only damages their own habitat but reduces vegetation that butterflies and songbirds use. Their eating habits are also threatening plant species such as orchids and lilies and eastern hemlock and white cedar trees.

The use of an organic deer contraceptive has had only limited success. Fencing has also been unsuccessful. Many people feel that the only way to control the deer herds is through culling—hunting deer with the goal of thinning out the herds.

Discussion Questions

1. Many animal-rights activists oppose the use of hunting to control deer populations, arguing that hunting is inconsistent with the belief that other animals have inherent worth. Do you agree? Discuss solutions that Singer and Regan might suggest to the Bambi boom.
2. Discuss how a utilitarian might approach the problem of the growing deer population. Are you satisfied with this solution? Support your answer.
3. Aldo Leopold supported the "harvesting" of deer herds to control their population. If what is right is defined in terms of preserving the "integrity, stability and beauty of the biotic community," would the land ethic also justify the culling of human populations where overpopulation is threatening the integrity of the biotic environment? Support your answer. Discuss how both Leopold and Watson might respond to this question.
4. Discuss how an ecofeminist, such as Karen Warren, might respond to the use of hunting to control the deer population.
5. Working in small groups, develop an ethical public policy for dealing with the Bambi boom.

7. BIOTECHNOLOGY AND AGRICULTURE

Biotechnology offers farmers increased food production and reduced unit costs. In particular, it may offer substantial benefits to developing countries in terms of reducing malnutrition, starvation, and poverty.

On the other hand, there are concerns about the safety of genetically modified (GM) food both for humans and the environment. There is the possibility of gene transfer to other closely related natural species through cross-pollination as well as through the buildup of resistance in insects and viruses to the insect-resistant and virus-resistant strains of GM crops. This could prove disastrous to naturally occurring plants. The pollen of genetically engineered plants might also be harmful to species such as the Monarch butterfly.

So far the United States, with 72 percent of the world's GM plantings, is the primary user of GM crops. There is strong opposition to GM food in the European Union, which has placed severe restrictions on the use of GM crops and imports from the United States containing GM food products. In Asia, only China has significant areas planted with GM crops. India has not approved the use of any GM crops. In Thailand research programs are looking at conventional breeding, rather than using GM seeds, as a way to develop desirable new crop varieties from their own biodiversity.[42]

Discussion Questions

1. Biotechnology has been offered as a solution to increasing food needs in areas where population growth and urbanization have outstripped food production. Is this solution environmentally and morally sound? Discuss how an ecocentric environmental ethicist might respond to this proposed solution.
2. There is concern that biotechnology advances in food production may create a sort of "scientific apartheid" in which the rich countries have access to technological advances that are not available in poorer countries. Discuss this concern from a justice perspective.
3. Genetic engineering is already used in animal agribusiness. In the United States, pigs are bred with an extra human growth hormone. Broiler chickens now grow so fast that their legs can't support their own body weight. Cows are being bred to produce more milk as well as milk that contains therapeutic drugs for human use. These biological alterations place great stress on the animal's bodies. Is it morally acceptable to genetically alter other animals to increase their utility for human consumption? Support your answer. Discuss how both Narveson and Warren might respond to this question.
4. Are genetically modified foods "unnatural"? What criteria should we use to draw the line between what is "natural" and what is "unnatural"? If humans are technologists by nature, should the products of our technology be considered part of the natural world, just as modifications to the environment by animals such as beaver, oak trees, or volcanoes are considered natural? Support your answers. Discuss how Watson and Devall and Sessions might answer these questions.

---

8. ANTARCTICA: PRESERVING PRISTINE NATURE

Antarctica has been called "the world's most pristine environment."[43] And it's no wonder it has remained untouched by human activities for so long. With temperatures as low as 100 degrees below zero, the climate here is so hostile that life—tiny microbes/organisms—take refuge inside the pores of the ancient rock merely inches below the surface where they are safe.

In 1959 twelve nations signed a treaty agreeing to reserve the area south of latitude 60°S just above the Antarctic Circle for peaceful scientific purposes. By 1984 there were thirty-three full-time bases with a population of five thousand in summer and seven hundred who wintered over. In 1985 thirty-two nations agreed to limit access of humans to Antarctic to specific research sites.

Despite the bleak climate and restrictions on their travel, Antarctica is fast becoming a fashionable tourist destination, at least for those who can afford to pay the up to $25,000 for a tour. In 1999–2000 13,370 tourists visited the continent; 3,500 people visit America's McMurdo Station each year.

Environmentalists are concerned about the effect of humans on Antarctica's unique ecology. Adélie penguins, who are not used to looking upwards, fall over backwards when airplanes fly overhead. The delicate Antarctic lichens, which are only a few millimeters thick, can be destroyed by one carelessly placed boot. While some want to limit tourism, others propose more radical solutions. Scott Base staffer Lana Hastie says that no humans should be allowed in Antarctica; instead, it should be left the way it is.

Discussion Questions

1. The high cost of a tour to Antarctica makes it prohibitive for all but the rich. Given deep ecology's directive that we ought to cultivate a sense of identification and interconnectedness with nature, is it fair that only the rich can visit the most pristine area of nature in the world? Isn't this limiting the nonaffluent's chance for self-realization? On the other hand, if we make Antarctica and other pristine wilderness areas more accessible to everyone, will we destroy the very reason for visiting them in the first place? Support your answers. Discuss how deep ecologists Devall and Sessions would respond to these questions.

2. Discuss Hastie's proposal that all human visitation, including scientific expeditions and tourism, be stopped. Is the fact that humans are not, as far as we know, native to Antarctica morally relevant? Should migration of other species to new areas be halted as well? Is Hastie's argument consistent with evolutionary theory, or is Hastie adopting an anthropocentric view that places humans outside of nature? Support your answers. Discuss how Watson might answer these questions.

3. Humans do not have to visit the Antarctic to alter its ecology. The ozone hole over the Antarctic is getting bigger each year. Do we have a moral obligation to preserve faraway environments? If so, is this obligation direct or indirect—that is, does our obligation stem from respect for the inherent value of the Antarctic biosphere or because of the indirect effects of global warming on humans? Support your answers.

4. The Antarctica is a massive storehouse of fresh water—containing over 70 percent of the earth's fresh water. Do icebergs have inherent moral worth or only instrumental worth? Discuss the moral implications of harvesting the icebergs for fresh water for human agriculture and drinking water.

9. EARTH'S DWINDLING FORESTS

People, like other animals, need to use nature in order to survive. We use trees for lumber to build our homes, the soil for growing crops, the earth as a source of minerals and energy. However, are there limits to how much we ought to use and, if so, what is the justification for these limits?

Most of the world's forests have been cleared by humans. Tropical rain forests have been bulldozed to create land for cattle grazing, mining operations, hydroelectric dams, and for growing export plants such as coffee. Destruction of the rain forest throughout the world has been implicated in the extinction, or threatened extinction, of thousands of species of animals and plants. In addition to destruction of wildlife habitat, the lifestyles as well as the lives of indigenous people living in the Amazon rain forests have been threatened by the clearing operations and by epidemics such as measles.

The rain forests are not the only forests that are being destroyed at an alarming rate. In the United States, the U.S. Forest Service has long regarded assisting the logging industry as one of its primary roles. There is little wilderness left in our national forests that is not crisscrossed with logging roads. With the exception of 34 million acres designated as wilderness, most accessible tracts of public forests have already been logged. In some cases the logging has threatened bird species with extinction and destroyed recreational areas, creating animosity between environmentalists, and businesses and workers whose livelihood depends on harvesting natural resources.

Discussion Questions

1. Discuss the prevailing attitude and practices regarding using natural resources in light of the ecofeminists concept of the logic of dominance. What policy might Warren suggest for the human use of rain forests and our national forests?

2. Americans drink one-third of the world's coffee.[44] Much of this coffee is grown on land that used to be rain forests. This is because coffee plants grown on bare land are much more productive than coffee plants that are shade-grown. However, some environmentalists are encouraging coffee drinkers to buy only shade-grown coffee, which does not require the destruction of surrounding trees, even though it is more expensive and harder to find at the stores. Discuss whether or not we have a moral obligation either to give up coffee drinking or to drink only shade-grown coffee.

3. Role-play a discussion between Warren and Watson on our current policy of allowing logging in national forests. Which person presents the strongest argument? Support your answer.

4. One of the primary reasons for clearing rain forests is to raise beef for the U.S. market. Discuss your moral obligation, if any, to modify your lifestyle in order to use fewer natural resources. If you do have such an obligation, what is the source of this moral obligation? Discuss how Regan, Narveson, Leopold, and Watson might each answer this question.

A P P E N D I X I

Writing a Paper in Moral Philosophy

Most of you will be asked to write at least one paper as part of your course requirement. Expressing your ideas in a paper allows you to develop, more fully and systematically, your understanding of a particular moral issue. Writing a paper also gives you an opportunity to demonstrate your ability to analyze concepts in moral philosophy. Because many of you may never have written a paper in philosophy, this appendix is designed to help you through the process.

GETTING STARTED

1. *Define your goals.* First determine what you want to accomplish by writing this paper. Your goals should be simple and achievable and should include the following:

- Complete the paper on time.
- Fulfill the requirements of the assignment.
- Get a good grade on the paper.

You may want to post your goals above your desk or write them on your assignment sheet. Clearly defining your goals will help you focus on the task at hand instead of going off on tangents that can be costly in time and energy. Keep in mind that the purpose of writing an undergraduate paper in moral philosophy is not to become an expert on the topic or to win a Pulitzer Prize for writing.

2. *Have a clear idea of your assignment.* If you are given written directions for the assignment, read them carefully. If the directions were given orally, make sure you have an accurate version of them. Some professors are notoriously vague in giving directions ("Whatever length you need to say it" or "Any issue in moral philosophy"). If you are not sure what the professor wants, ask him or her to be more specific.

Your professor may ask you to write one of several types of papers. Most papers in moral philosophy are *thesis papers* where you are expected to defend a particular position or thesis, such as support for capital punishment. If you are writing a thesis paper, stay focused on the actual argument and premises that support your conclusion. Don't get sidetracked into a sociological survey of how people feel about the issue, a history of the issue, or a discussion of the legal issues.

Instead of a thesis paper, your professor may ask you to *compare and contrast* two views, such as the pro and con capital punishment arguments. In this type of paper you present summaries of the arguments for the opposing sides of the issue, a discussion of the weakness and strengths of the arguments and, finally, a concluding paragraph about which position is the strongest and why.

The *survey* paper is less frequently assigned in a moral issues course. This assignment may include, in addition to a survey of the different philosophical views and arguments on an issue, a history of the legal status of the issue.

If you are not clear about what is expected, put together an outline or a half-page summary of your proposed paper and show it to the professor before starting.

3. *Know your audience.* Effective writers keep their audience or prospective readers in mind when writing. Unlike most "real-world" writing, in writing a college paper in moral philosophy you are writing for an expert audience of one—your professor. Ask yourself "What are my professor's expectations?" Your primary purpose is not generally to try to persuade your professor of a particular position. Instead the professor, in most cases, wants to know that you understand moral theory and concepts and can apply them to a particular moral issue.

4. *Identify and develop your own writing style.* The mandate "Know thyself" forms the cornerstone of philosophy. Often we flounder in college life because we have not taken the time to first learn about ourselves, our thinking, and our writing styles. Indeed, nationwide about 40 percent of people who start college drop out. Knowing your personality type allows you to compensate for your weaknesses and capitalize on your strengths.

The conventional way of writing a paper is to start with an outline; however, recent research indicates that not all people write best this way. Different personality types learn best and are most productive under different conditions. What might be stressful and counterproductive to one personality type when it comes to writing a paper may be enjoyable and productive for another type. Some people do well by outlining first, but for others an outline impedes the creative flow.

In the 1950s Katheryn Briggs and Isabel Myers, a mother-daughter team, developed a personality-type test based on psychologist Carl Jung's work. They came up with four pairs of personality types or preferences. Each member of the pair is represented by a single letter. The pairs of preferences represent dichotomies, and all of us fall somewhere on the line between the two ends of each of the four dichotomies. For example, someone who is more extroverted (E) than introverted, more of an intuitive (N) person than one who relies on sense experience, more of feeler (F) than a thinker when making decisions, and more organized (J) than spontaneous is known as an ENFJ.

You can use the box "Personality Types and Learning Styles" to identify your personality type. More complete tests are available in books such as David Keirsey and Marilyn Bates, *Please Understand Me: Character & Temperament Types.*[1] Also check with your student services office on campus; they often keep copies of the Myers-Briggs test on file.

Each of the eight preference types has their own learning and writing style. **Extroverts (E),** for example, write best when they have an opportunity to bounce their ideas off others. They are most productive if they first discuss the issue with several other people in class. E's tend to neglect introverted tasks like reading and writing, and they may be inefficient at completing papers because they jump into tasks without planning.

PERSONALITY TYPES AND LEARNING STYLES[2]

The Four Pairs of Preferences

Introvert (I)
Works best alone; reflective; thinks before speaking.

Extrovert (E)
Works best in groups; outgoing activity-oriented; speaks before thinking.

Sensing (S)
Focuses on concrete here-and-now; fact and detail oriented; practical and realistic.

Intuitive (N)
Focuses on abstract ideas; speculative; imaginative; prefers theory to facts; dislikes routine and details.

Thinking (T)
Logical; systematic; thing-oriented; does best when others acknowledge their competence.

Feeling (F)
Caring; people-oriented; tends to write from the heart; does best with personal encouragement.

Judgment (J)
Disciplined; good at setting goals and meeting deadlines; dislikes change and ambiguity.

Perceptive (P)
Spontaneous; flexible; dislikes structure; open-ended; tends to be unorganized.

E's write best if they do a quick first draft before doing an outline; however, because they tend to write by trial and error, their first drafts may be confusing. Because E's tend to write before thinking out their ideas, it is important that they periodically seek feedback from others. Because they are easily distracted by social activities, they also need to plan ahead to get the most out of their study time. They are most productive when they schedule a lot of breaks, especially breaks that involve social activities with other people.

For **introverts (I)** reflection is more important than activity. They prefer to sit back and assimilate the material quietly rather than discussing their moral issue with others. I's need time alone to reflect before beginning a paper and tend to plan extensively, anticipate problems, and even rehearse what they are going to say before writing down an idea on paper. I's may spend too much time contemplating a writing assignment and too little time doing it. When they write, they stop often to think about where their ideas are leading them, so they usually spend more time between drafts than extroverts. Unlike extroverts, I's do well with long stretches of solitary study rather than a lot of breaks. They also prefer to work without interruption in their own space, rather than in a public area like a library. Although I's can read for long periods of time, they have to be careful not to let the reading propel them into a daydream. Stretch breaks or solitary walks tend to refresh introverts, so they can get back to their writing.

Sensing (S) types are great at collecting the facts needed for writing a paper. They also pay close attention to the mechanics of writing, such as spelling and grammar; however, they tend to avoid theory and instead focus too much on details. Because they tend to ignore theory, they often fail to consider how the facts fit in with a particular theory or the larger picture. This can be a real handicap in writing papers in moral philosophy. In fact, S's tend to do well in high school, but they are more likely to drop out of college than are N's.

Intuitives (N) have a much easier time writing a philosophy paper. They write quickly and write their best when they let one idea trigger another. N's are great at understanding and writing about abstract concepts and theories, but they are poor at backing up their positions with facts. N's also tend to go with their first impression rather than thoroughly researching a particular issue. For example, they may base their entire argument in favor of capital punishment on the belief that capital punishment is an effective deterrent without ever bothering to check out the relevant studies. As a result, N's may have to redo an assignment because they neglected important details. S's and N's can benefit greatly from going over their drafts with each other. N's can help free up the thinking of S's ("What if . . . ," "How does that relate to . . . ?"), while S's can help anchor the N's writing ("Be realistic . . ." "The fact is . . .")

Thinking (T) types like to have a clear set of expectations before they begin writing a paper, and they write best when they make and follow an outline. Unlike F's, T's prefer writing assignments where they can keep an emotional distance. They feel uncomfortable when writing in the first person. T's are especially good at analytical thinking and drawing conclusions from a list of premises. On the other hand, they tend to assume that other people are as good at logic as they are and, hence, may fail to adequately explain in writing how they arrived at their conclusions. They tend to forget that they are writing for an audience, and instead write for themselves. If you are a T, make an effort to put yourself in your audience's shoes—in this case your professor's.

Feeling (F) types write best when they are asked to write about their personal values. They want to know how the assignment can be used in helping others or in their own personal development. Because they are people-oriented, F's are good at writing with their audience in mind. On the other hand, they are easily bored with dry, uninteresting readings and tend to neglect assignments that do not personally engage them. They tend to be weak in objective, analytical skills, instead relying on their personal viewpoints and feelings in backing up a particular position. Like S's and N's, T's and F's would do well to seek out each other for going over early drafts of their papers.

Judgment (J) types are well organized and highly motivated. They write well with outlines and meet their deadlines by systematically completing one task at a time. They also tend to be highly structured and inflexible, and they may get in a rut that ultimately impedes their productivity. For example, because they are so goal oriented, J's may complete their research too quickly and hence get confused in later readings. They need to schedule in some flexibility and also allow more time for preliminary research.

Perceptive (P) people feel stifled by outlines and schedules. They tend to procrastinate about the actual writing of the paper and, hence, miss deadlines. On the other hand, they are better at doing a thorough job at researching a topic. They tend to select very broad topics when doing a paper and dive right into the research before narrowing down the topic. P's need to pay more attention to narrowing their topics and setting a deadline for no more research. Their papers tend to be rambling, weak in spelling and grammar, and include too much. P's are the most likely of all the types to drop or flunk out of college. If you are a P you may want to attend some of the study skill sessions that are offered by most colleges or seek feedback from your professor before turning in the final copy.

Knowing your personality type can also help you in setting goals for yourself. Some people can identify with a particular type simply by reading the descriptions in the above diagrams.

5. *Make a schedule.* Time management means different things to the different personality types. However you choose to proceed, your schedule should include time for:

- selecting the topic
- researching
- writing the first draft or outline
- revising
- writing the final draft
- proofreading
- printing out the final draft

In making your schedule, start with the due date and work backwards. Allow time for unforeseen emergencies or activities. How much time you should allot to each of the above tasks will depend on your writing style and the time you have available to complete your paper. If you are a P, plan to finish your paper well before the due date and set a strict limit on the time you are going to spend researching the paper. J's, on the other hand, should allow more time for research and not be so concerned with finishing the paper early. N's may need to allow time to go back and check the facts. S's need to allow more time for reading theoretical pieces but, unlike P's, need minimal time to proofread for grammar and spelling. E's, T's, and F's should all try to schedule time for others to proofread their papers.

Even if the paper is not due for a few months, begin working on it right away—start the first draft, brainstorm with others, allow time for reflecting on the topic, research, or to make up an outline. Doing something the day the paper is assigned, even if it is only talking to friends about the assignment, is a good way to get your ideas flowing.

RESEARCHING

1. *Choosing your topic.* In some ethics classes the research topic is assigned by the professor. Even so, you may have to *narrow down the topic.* Make sure your topic is manageable within the time frame allowed for completing the paper. Students often waste a lot of time writing on a topic that is too broad or inappropriate. It is tempting to keep the topic broad (for example, freedom of speech, homosexuality, euthanasia), thinking that it will be easier to find material on the topic. This approach, however, can be costly in terms of time and effort. It is often more work to write on a broad topic, such as euthanasia, than it is to take the time at the beginning to focus in on a particular aspect of the topic, such as assisted suicide, or involuntary euthanasia, or same-sex marriage.

Choose a topic that involves a moral controversy. There is no point in defending a position that is self-evident, such as the immorality of rape or domestic violence. Issues such as outing in the gay community, hate speech on college campuses, assisted suicide, mandatory AIDS testing of college students, and human cloning, on the other hand, are rife with moral conflicts.

Choose a topic appropriate for a paper in moral philosophy. Because most college students are cultural relativists, they tend to confuse moral issues with legal issues or with public consensus. If you are writing on a topic that is also a legal controversy, such as capital

---

 QUICK REFERENCE BOX

Research

Do

- Choose a topic that is appropriate for a moral issues course.
- Make sure your topic is neither too broad nor too narrow.
- Check out the available resources for researching your paper.
- Read up on the topic before you begin writing the paper.
- Use only reputable resources.
- Keep track of your sources as you're doing your research.
- Stick to your schedule for completing your research.

Do Not

- Try adapting a paper from another class.
- Choose a topic that you find uninteresting or too complex.

---

punishment or abortion, make sure you stay focused on the moral arguments, unless your topic is specifically to analyze the moral arguments in the laws and court rulings.

You should also avoid topics that deal primarily with related psychological or sociological issues. Because the sensing (S) personality types prefer descriptive facts to abstract theory, they are the most likely to make this error. A paper on the incidence and causes of rape or domestic violence would make an interesting psychology or sociology paper. However, while there are moral implications involved in these topics, the morality of these two types of violence is hardly a controversial issue. Writing a paper inappropriate for a moral issues course can happen when a student tries to adapt a paper written for another course. This tactic rarely works because moral philosophy demands a type of analytical thinking that is generally not required in more descriptive subjects, such as political science, sociology, or psychology.

Choose a topic that holds your interest. Choose a topic that interests you and that you can defend in good conscience. If you are a feeling (F) personality type, pick a topic, such as date rape, vegetarianism, or racism on campus, that engages you on a personal level. Otherwise, you are likely to get bored and put off completing the paper. Thinking (T) types, on the other hand, do better with more abstract topics such as genetic engineering or capital punishment.

Have a basic understanding of the topic. It's helpful if you have the background for understanding the facts underlying the issue. For example, if you have no background in biology, you should probably avoid doing a paper on cloning and organ transplants.

Check out available resources on your proposed topic. Set aside time to go to the library and check out what is written on the topic. Half a day may be plenty if you are an organized (J) personality type. Intuitive (N) personality types, on the other hand, have a tendency to jump the gun and go with their first idea rather than checking out the topic first. If you are an N, you should probably allow a few days for this task. Because perceptive (P) personality types enjoy leisurely browsing through the stacks, they might, if time permits, even allow themselves the luxury of two or three days for this part of the assignment.

Your topic should be neither too narrow nor too broad. If you find yourself overwhelmed by the sheer volume of resources and books on the topic, your subject is probably too broad. On the other hand, your topic might be too narrow. For example, your proposed topic may be the cloning of humans for medical research. However, an initial survey of your library resources may reveal that very little has been published on the moral aspect of this issue. If this is the case, try making your topic a bit broader.

2. *Background Research.* Once you have chosen your topic, you are ready to do the actual research on the paper. Set aside a block of time for researching your paper. Remember that personality style plays an important role in how a person researches a paper. Researching your paper can be one of the most enjoyable parts of preparing a paper if you approach it in a systematic and organized manner.

Read up on your topic. Good writers spend a lot of time reading on their topic. Read some of the current articles and browse through books on your chosen topic. Take notes or make photocopies of particularly relevant articles and book excerpts.

Use reputable sources. Choose your sources carefully. Who are the most respected authorities in this field? Also check the copyright dates. This is especially important if you are writing about a timely issue, such as assisted suicide or cloning. If you are going to make empirical claims in your argument, you will, in most cases, need to back them up with reliable sources. For example, if you are going to use the utilitarian argument that capital punishment is a deterrent or that affirmative action has been successful in helping women and minorities, you will need reputable statistics to back up your claim.

Keep track of your sources. Selections from another author, even if it is only a sentence, should always be put in quotes and cited in a footnote or endnote. Do not assume that you will remember where you found a particular quote or statistic. Keep track of your sources as you are doing your research. You can do this on index cards; or you can set up a bibliography page on your computer.

Available Resources. Modern technology has made research much easier. The following are some of the many resources that can help you in your research.

a. *Library catalogs.* Library catalogs can be invaluable in locating a particular book. Most library catalogs now are electronic and online. However, do not depend solely on the catalogs for a list of books. Take time to browse in the stacks. Ethics is found under BJ in the Library of Congress classification and in the 170 category in the Dewey decimal classification. If your library does not have a particular book or journal that you want, you can usually get it through interlibrary loan. However, allow enough time—usually one to two weeks—for books to be sent to your library. Journal articles can be faxed, in most cases, within a week.

b. *The Philosopher's Index.* There are several research resources that are geared specifically toward philosophy. The most useful of these is the *Philosopher's Index,* a quarterly subject-author index of philosophical books and articles from almost 600 philosophical journals. Abstracts are available for the majority of references. The years covered are 1940 to present for journals, and 1980 to present for books. Because the index is updated only quarterly, you may still want to look through the new journals in the periodical room of the library.

This *Philosopher's Index* is an excellent place to start your research. Copies of the *Philosopher's Index* are usually available in the reference section of the library or on CD-ROM. If possible use the electronic (CD-ROM), rather than the hard copy, version of *Philosopher's Index.* This index can be invaluable in helping you focus on a particular topic because the computerized version allows you to do a more comprehensive subject search using a keyword that may appear in the title or in the description of the entry. The CD-ROM also makes it easier for you to narrow your search by using a combination of keywords.

   c. *Philosophical Journals.* If your library does not have *Philosopher's Index,* you can go straight to the journals themselves. Of course this will take more time and should be a second option. Many of the philosophical journals contain articles in ethics. Some of the journals to start with are *Ethics, Journal of Value Inquiry, Philosophy and Public Affairs, Public Affairs Quarterly, Hypatia, Environmental Ethics, Criminal Justice Ethics, Hastings Center Report, Kennedy Institution of Ethics Journal, Journal of Medicine and Philosophy, Free Inquiry,* and *Journal of Medical Ethics.* The current issues of these journals are generally kept in the periodicals room of your library. Use the lists of references at the end of the more current articles to find other articles and books on the topic.

   d. *Encyclopedias.* Both the *Encyclopedia of Philosophy* and the *Encyclopedia of Bioethics* can be useful in researching your paper. In addition, a new ten-volume encyclopedia, the *Routledge Encyclopedia of Philosophy,* is available in both print and electronic formats.

   The *Encyclopedia of Philosophy* is an eight volume encyclopedia that covers general topics such as "ethics, problems of." The encyclopedia itself is over twenty-five years old and is geared primarily toward traditional Western philosophy. Despite these drawbacks, the *Encyclopedia of Philosophy* can be very helpful to students, especially in clarifying some of the more theoretical aspects of ethics.

   The *Encyclopedia of Applied Ethics* is a great place to start your research on a moral issue. The four-volume encyclopedia includes 630 ethics titles, including readings in media and biomedical ethics, and in law and politics. Each article includes definitions of key terms, glossaries, and bibliographies.

   The *Encyclopedia of Bioethics* is also a great place to start your research if you are considering writing about an issue that is even remotely related to bioethics. Unlike the *Encyclopedia of Philosophy,* which is concerned primarily with theoretical philosophy, the *Encyclopedia of Bioethics* covers both moral theory and applied ethics. The 1995 revised edition of the *Encyclopedia of Bioethics* contains excellent articles on topics, such as abortion, vegetarianism, capital punishment, assisted suicide, and environmental racism, as well as articles covering moral issues from the perspectives of non-Western philosophies such as Buddhism and Confucianism. Following each article is an extensive bibliography.

   e. *General Academic Indexes.* If your library does not have *The Philosopher's Index,* the major philosophical journals are also covered in several other academic indexes. The following are only a few of the more than 600 periodical indexes that are now available in hard copy and/or online.

   Humanities Index (HumanitiesIn) indexes more than 300 publications in the humanities, including publications in philosophy, from 1994 to the present. In addition to feature articles, this index includes book reviews, interviews, original works of fiction, bibliographies, and reviews of movies, plays, and television performances. *Humanities Index* is available in both hard copy and online.

   Expanded Academic Index is an online interdisciplinary database that mostly covers the humanities, including philosophy, current events, and the social sciences. This massive database covers over 1,500 general interest and academic periodicals, including many of the major philosophical journals, from 1980 to the present. The *Expanded Academic Index* is a gold mine of information. Unlike the *Philosopher's Index,* the *Expanded Academic Index* frequently includes the whole article rather than just an abstract. And, unlike the *Philosopher's Index,* it is also available at most college libraries.

Academic Search FULLTEXT ELITE is another full-text database that indexes more than 3,000 scholarly journals. The full text is available for articles in more than 1,000 of these journals. *Academic Search* is updated on a daily basis. Its major drawback is that it is a relatively new database and only covers journals from 1996 to the present.

f. *MedLine* is an author-subject index of about 3,700 international biomedical journals from 1966 to present. About 75 percent of the citations include abstracts. In addition to including citations from the philosophy journals in medical ethics, MedLine includes excellent articles in medical ethics from prominent medical journals, such as the *Journal of the American Medical Society* (JAMA) and the *New England Journal of Medicine,* that are not indexed in the *Philosopher's Index.* This index, which is updated monthly, is invaluable if you are doing a paper on a timely issue in medical ethics, such as cloning, genetic engineering, or assisted suicide. *MedLine* is available on CD-ROM in many college libraries, and it is also available free of charge on the Web through PubMed (http://www.ncbi.nih.gov/PubMed).

g. The *Internet* offers a rich, although somewhat unpredictable, source of information. For a comprehensive list of the different sites in moral philosophy start by typing in the term "philosophy WWW internet."

One of the best Internet sites for scholarly research in philosophy is the WWW Virtual Library: Philosophy (http://www.bris.ac.uk/Depts/Philosophy/VL/). This site offers links to thousands of high-quality Internet resources that have been selected and described by academic librarians and subject specialists. The American Philosophical Association Web site (http://www.apa.udel.edu/apa/resources/) also provides links to web resources such as journals, philosopher sites, bibliographies, and electronic texts.

For a summary of a particular topic in ethics, the *Internet Encyclopedia of Philosophy* (http://www.utm.edu/research/iep/) has a well-organized key word index that will bring up the encyclopedia article on the topic entered. You can also type in a search term, such as "environmental ethics" or "freedom of speech" to find out what other articles in the encyclopedia address the topic.

In addition to its *Encyclopedia of Philosophy,* Routledge has an online Philosophy Resource Center (http://www.routledge.com/philosophy/rprcmain.html). The center offers an easy-to-use source of information on all of their philosophy publications. Their Web resource center can also link you to other philosophy-related sites, including ethics Web sites.

Also check out the Web pages at philosophy departments at different colleges and universities. The Philosophy Department at Earlham College, for example, has a "Guide to Philosophy on the Internet" (http://www.earlham.edu/~peters/philinks.htm) that includes links to journals, newsgroups, topics, quotations, and bibliographies.

The Database *NetFirst* is also helpful in philosophy research. NetFirst is an authoritative database of Internet-accessible resources on all subjects. It includes WWW pages, Internet groups, FTP and Gopher sites, electronic journals, and newsletters. *NetFirst* is updated weekly with about 2,000 records being added each week. *NetFirst* provides up-to-date information on the latest scientific and legislative developments in particular, as well as an overview of the moral issues involved in these developments.

For a more comprehensive listing of resources in philosophy, see *Philosophy: A Guide to the Reference Literature* by Hans Bynagle (1997). This user-friendly guide is written for both students and professional philosophers and contains short descriptions of 572 available references, including bibliographies, research guides, general and specialized dictionaries, encyclopedias and handbooks, general indexes and abstracts, and professional organizations.

WRITING THE PAPER

For earlier drafts use the writing instrument that you are most comfortable using—pencil, tape recorder, or word processor. Some people work best with index cards; others prefer the cut and paste method; others prefer to work on a word processor right from the first moment an idea pops into their head.

Word processors make rewrites easier. If you do not own one, most colleges and universities have computers available in the library's computer centers or in the dormitories. Most colleges also offer mini-courses in word processing. If you are using a word processor, remember to save your work frequently on a diskette or floppy disk. Also make a backup file either on the hard drive or another diskette. Make a printout of each draft.

Most papers in moral philosophy are thesis papers. The purpose of a thesis paper is to analyze and present a well thought out argument for a particular position. Philosophical analysis of a moral issue is *not* the same as stating your sincerely held opinions, no matter how eloquently and sincerely you may do so. Some students think that ethics is simply a matter of voicing their opinion; they become upset when they get poor grades on their papers. If you have a weak background in logic, review Chapter 2, "Moral Reasoning," before writing your paper.

A thesis paper in moral philosophy has at least five parts: (1) the introduction, (2) the presentation of the arguments, (3) the presentation of objections or counterarguments, (4) a response to these objections, and (5) the conclusion. Some professors require a bibliography as well. For papers longer than four or five pages, consider using subtitles. Subtitles make a paper more readable. For example, the subtitle for the second part of your paper might read "Arguments in Support of Same-Sex Marriages."

Sometimes it is easiest to start in the middle of the paper. If you are having trouble with your introduction, try starting by writing out your arguments first. Don't worry about your grammar or spelling in your first draft. What is important is that you get your ideas down on paper. You can clean up the paper later.

1. *Introduction.* The opening paragraph serves as the introduction to your paper. It should contain a thesis statement and an explanation of your thesis.

Statement of your thesis. The thesis statement tells the reader what position or conclusion you are going to defend in your paper. Do not draft your thesis statement until *after* you have done your research. As the conclusion of your argument, the thesis statement should evolve as a result of your research of the various arguments on the issue. If

---

QUICK REFERENCE BOX

Writing the Paper

Do

- Keep a backup of your work on a diskette.
- Clearly state your thesis.
- Clearly define all your key terms.
- Include only material that is relevant to your argument.
- Use subtitles if the paper is more than 5 pages long.
- Choose the strongest 3 or 4 arguments and counterarguments.
- Use only the strongest premises in your arguments and counterarguments.
- Present each argument and counterargument in a separate paragraph.
- Respond to the counterarguments in order.
- Check your paper for logical fallacies.
- Try out your arguments on other people.

Do Not

- Write an opinion paper.
- Avoid taking a stand.
- Use inflammatory or sexist language.
- Repeat arguments.

---

you begin your research with the purpose of defending a particular position, you are likely to get caught up in rhetoric, reading only those arguments that support your initial opinion rather than approaching the issue with an open mind.

The thesis should be stated clearly as a *normative* or *value statement*. For example:

"Abortion on demand is morally wrong."

"Affirmative action in college admissions is morally justifiable."

"It is wrong to use animals in experiments."

Thesis statements should *not* be in the form of empirical claims, as in the following statements: "Abortion is a constitutional right," or "Affirmative action discriminates against white males," or "Cosmetic experiments cause pain to animals." These statements may be used later in your paper in support of your thesis, but they are not conclusions about the morality of particular practices. In fact, many people who believe that abortion is morally acceptable acknowledge that it causes pain to the fetus; and most people who support affirmative action agree that it involves discriminating against white males.

Keep in mind that philosophy papers are not forums for airing your personal opinions. *Avoid* thesis statements such as "In my opinion abortion is morally wrong" or "I feel that animal experimentation is morally justifiable."

Your thesis statement should *clearly state the position you intend to support.* Some people who haven't thought through an issue or who fear confrontation and criticism may try to avoid taking a stand by fence-straddling, as in the following statement: "As far as the

THE FIVE PARTS OF A PAPER IN MORAL PHILOSPHY

1. Introduction
   a. statement of thesis
   b. explanation of thesis
2. Presentation of arguments that support the thesis
3. Presentation of objections to the thesis
4. Response to objections to the thesis
5. Conclusion
   a. restatement of the thesis
   b. a summary of the argument
6. Bibliography

morality of abortion is concerned, I can see both sides of the issue." This sort of non-committal position may be acceptable as a starting point prior to doing your research, but it is not a thesis statement. Also avoid fatalistic statements such as "Abortion is a controversial issue that will probably never be resolved." This is lazy thinking and simply a way of dismissing an issue. Take the issue seriously. Remember, for centuries people talked this way about slavery! As long as most people think this way about an issue, it is unlikely to be resolved. Your goal in a thesis paper is not to remain on the sidelines but to critically analyze all sides of the issue and then to decide which position is the best.

Even though you have done your research, *your initial thesis statement may still change as you get more into your paper.* This is fine—you can always go back and fine tune the thesis statement later. For example:

"Abortion for sex selection is morally wrong."

"Affirmative action in college admissions is morally justifiable only in cases where the applicants are also economically and socially disadvantaged."

"It is wrong to use sentient nonhuman animals, such as rabbits, in cosmetic experiments."

Explanation of the thesis statement and definition of key terms. Before you defend your thesis statement, first explain what it means. Include a brief summary and explanation of your argument as in the following example:

In stating that abortion on demand is morally unacceptable, I mean that it is prima facie wrong to kill the fetus because, as I shall argue, the fetus is a person. Killing a person, except in cases of self-defense, violates the categorical imperative as well as the fundamental moral principle of non-maleficence. Abortion, therefore, when practiced, has to be morally justified.

If you qualify your thesis statement, as in "Abortion-on-demand may or may not be morally wrong depending on the circumstances," explain exactly what these circumstances are. Don't make the reader second guess you.

For more complex issues, you may have to inform the reader about the nature of the issue you intend to defend. Most people, for example, are not clear about what cloning entails or how it is currently being used. Many people are also not aware of the purpose and types of tests cosmetic companies perform on nonhuman animals. Make your explanation as concise as possible, presenting only the information that is necessary in order for the reader to follow your argument.

Define the key terms in your thesis statement. While most people agree on the definitions of abortion and capital punishment, terms and phrases such as *abortion-on-demand, selective abortion, pornography, rape, outing, euthanasia, hate speech, environment, person,* and even *right* and *immoral,* have several shades of meaning. *Abortion-on-demand* for some people means that abortion is morally permissible for any reason at any time of the pregnancy; others who claim to support abortion-on-demand draw the line at sex selection or abortion for convenience during the last trimester. Similarly, for some people *pornography* includes any sort of nudity, while others define pornography more narrowly as involving violence or coercion against women and/or children. Explain to the reader exactly how you will be using these terms in your paper.

The definitions should be clear, concise, and acceptable to most people. Clearly defining the key terms at the beginning of your paper will keep you from getting bogged down in verbal disputes. The definition "sentience is the capacity to experience pain and pleasure," for example, is clear, concise, and the one used by most people, including philosophers. Defining "hate speech" as "saying hurtful things," on the other hand, is much too vague as well as too broad to be useful in a philosophical analysis of the issue. Find a definition that most people who write on the issue would find acceptable. In her article "Pornography, Civil Rights, and Speech," for example, Catharine MacKinnon uses a modified version of the definition of pornography from the Minneapolis Code of Ordinances Relating to Civil Rights (Dec. 30, 1983). If you are using someone else's definition, make sure you cite the source. Whatever definitions you use for your key terms, make sure you use them in a consistent manner throughout the paper.

2. *Presenting arguments to support the thesis.* The arguments supporting your thesis make up the greater part of your paper. In presenting your arguments, use only premises that are logically compelling. Remember, the purpose of your paper is to convince the reader, in this case your professor, to accept your thesis.

Make a list of possible arguments. This list will be expanded into paragraphs in later revisions. Don't worry about the exact wording right now; just get your ideas down. Do not limit your arguments to one philosophical tradition. One of the purposes of a paper in moral philosophy is to demonstrate that you have a understanding of how the different moral theories apply to moral issues. Jot down notes regarding both empirical and theoretical support for these arguments. This will help you in choosing the best arguments.

Using the thesis statement "It is wrong to use sentient nonhuman animals, such as rabbits, in cosmetic experiments," the following arguments, among others, might appear on your initial list:

1. It is wrong to cause unnecessary pain to sentient beings (Utilitarianism; principle of non-maleficence; Buddhist principle of *ahiṃsā*).

2. Animal experimentation infringes on the liberty rights of the subjects (Rights ethics; animals' freedom to pursue their legitimate interests, Tom Regan).

3. Polls show that most Americans oppose using of rabbits in cosmetic experiments (Gallup Polls).

4. People should be happy the way they are rather than use cosmetics in order to feel good about themselves (my opinion).

5. Animal experimentation, in this case, violates the principle of equality (Peter Singer and Jeremy Bentham).

6. The use of other animals as things reinforces a hierarchy that also degrades certain groups of humans (Ecofeminism).

7. The pain caused animals by cosmetic experiments is not outweighed by the benefit to humans (the principle of utility).

Choose the strongest three or four arguments that support your position. Numbers three and four in the preceding list can be eliminated. Number 3 is based on the fallacy of popular appeal, and number 4 is irrelevant to your argument; however, numbers 1, 2, 5, 6, and 7 look promising.

Do not repeat arguments. Each argument should be different, not a rehash of an earlier argument. Do not reword earlier arguments and present them as new arguments in order to make the paper longer. Such tactics are guaranteed to irritate your professor who has to waste valuable time reading the same argument twice. Examine each argument in your list. In the preceding list, for example, numbers 1 and 7 are basically the same argument and should be combined.

Do not get sidetracked by irrelevant material. Do not go off on tangents about the legal status of pornography or sociological studies on the prevalence of pornography in this country no matter how interesting these tangents may be; remember, this is a paper in moral philosophy, not in law, psychology, sociology, or politics.

Clearly state the premises in each argument. The premises of each of your arguments will consist of both moral principles and empirical statements. In presenting premises based on moral theory, state which principles, duties, and/or rights are involved. Sensing (S) personality types tend to neglect theory. Do not limit yourself to one philosophical tradition; draw from as many of the universal moral theories as possible, such as deontology, utilitarianism, rights ethics, or care ethics. Avoid cultural relativism and ethical subjectivism, however; they are both very weak moral theories that are rejected by the great majority of moral philosophers.

Do not make claims you cannot support. This is most likely to happen with Intuitive (N) personality types who tend to assume that their claims are intuitively true. If you use empirical facts to support your claim make sure you can back them up with reputable sources. For example, if you claim that capital punishment is morally acceptable because capital punishment acts as a deterrent, you should have facts that show that capital punishment does have a deterrent effect. If you are arguing for selective abortion, do not simply assume that people with disabilities or children of the "wrong" gender would rather not have been born.

Do not put more than one argument in a paragraph. If each argument is more than one paragraph long you may want to *number the arguments.* The opening sentence or two of each paragraph should contain a summary of the argument and definitions of ambiguous key terms that have not already been defined in the introduction to the paper.

Begin by making a list of your premises for each argument. Put any thoughts you may have about each premise in parentheses after the premise. Do not worry about the exact wording right now. It is more important for you to get your ideas down first. For example, in the first argument "It is wrong to cause unnecessary pain to sentient beings," a rough outline might go as follows:

Premises: 1. Rabbits, because they are sentient beings, can feel pain. (define "sentient")

2. Some cosmetic experiments, such as the Draize test, are so painful that some rabbits will break their backs trying to escape. (cite source; explain Draize test)

3. The pain is unnecessary, *because* (3a) many of these tests can be done by computer simulations and *because* (3b) cosmetics are not necessary for human well being or pleasure. (cite source)

4. According to the principle of utility, we should try to maximize pleasure and minimize pain. (utilitarian theory)

5. The principle of non-maleficence requires us to avoid harm. (deontological theory)

6. The principle of *ahiṃsā* requires us to avoid harming any living beings. (Buddhist and Taoist ethics)

Conclusion: It is wrong to cause unnecessary pain to sentient beings.

The first three premises are empirical statements; the last three premises are moral principles. The conclusion of each argument will become a sub-conclusion or one of the premises for your final conclusion or thesis statement, "It is wrong to use sentient nonhuman animals, such as rabbits, in cosmetic experiments."

Avoid the use of inflammatory language. How we say something is as important as what we say. In presenting your arguments, use neutral language as much as possible. Referring to capital punishment as "state sanctioned murder" or homosexuality as a "sexual perversion" does not promote rational discussion of opposing positions. Similarly, calling people who experiment on nonhuman animals "sadists" or people who are opposed to gay marriage "homophobic" does little to create an atmosphere in which these issues can be openly discussed. Also avoid sexist language. Do not use the term "him" or "men" for the generic human; instead use "he/she" or another gender neutral term.

Check your arguments for logical fallacies. After you have completed a draft of your paper, go back and check your arguments for fallacies. If you are unsure of what the fallacies are, review the section on logical fallacies in Chapter 2 on "Moral Reasoning." If you find that your arguments contain fallacies, get rid of them, no matter how convincing they may sound to you. They are only going to weaken your overall argument.

Ask yourself if your premises really do support your conclusion. For example, the premise "human life is sacred or has intrinsic moral worth" may mean two different things in the context of euthanasia. To one person it implies that humans should be kept alive as long as possible; to another person it implies that humans should have the right to choose when to terminate their lives. In this case you may want to add additional premises regarding the meaning of intrinsic moral worth. Thinking (T) personality types are good at logical analysis, but they have a tendency to leave out premises, assuming that they are self-evident. Feeling (F) types, on the other hand, tend to substitute personal experience for analysis. In checking over your arguments, be aware of the weaknesses associated with your personality type.

Apply the reasonable person criteria. This criteria is also known as the "test of publicity." In applying this criteria, ask yourself if a well-informed, reasonable person would be convinced by your arguments. If you are unsure of the answer, try out your arguments on someone. Then go back and polish your arguments.

Polish your arguments. In your final draft, your premises and arguments should not be in list form. Eliminate any fallacies, inflammatory language, or weak arguments before you begin the final draft of your paper. Make each argument as concise as possible. Eliminate any redundant or superfluous words and phrases. If the argument you are presenting overlaps with another argument, simply mention that you will be elaborating on the other argument later in the paper. Start out with your strongest, and longest, supporting argument. In presenting the first argument begin with a summary of your thesis statement as well as the conclusion of your first argument. Then give a summary of the premises for the argument as in the following draft:

> **Argument 1.** *Cosmetic experiments on sentient animals are wrong because they cause unnecessary pain.* The moral imperative to avoid harm or pain is fundamental to systems of moral philosophy throughout the world. According to utilitarians, pain is the greatest evil and pleasure the greatest good. The principle of utility states that we should minimize pain and maximize pleasure for the greatest number. In both Buddhism and Taoist philosophy, the duty of *ahiṃsā* requires us to avoid harming any living beings. The duty of non-maleficence in deontological theories also states that we should avoid harm. Although most deontologists, such as Immanuel Kant, do not extend this consideration to nonhuman animals, I will argue in this paper that this duty should be extended to certain nonhuman animals, such as rabbits.
>
> As sentient beings, rabbits are capable of feeling pain. Many of the cosmetic tests are extremely painful. For example, the commonly used Draize test involves putting potentially toxic substances in a rabbit's eyes. The Draize test is so painful that rabbits will sometimes break their backs attempting to escape the excruciating pain.[3]
>
> According to utilitarians, causing pain may be morally justified *if* it is the only means to bring about a greater good. However, the pain caused to rabbits and other sentient beings by cosmetic experiments is unnecessary for two reasons. First, these tests can now be carried out by using computer simulation programs.[4] Secondly, cosmetics are not necessary for human well-being. The pain caused to the rabbits in these experiments, in contrast, is intense and life threatening. Therefore, the pain caused to animals in cosmetic experiments cannot be morally justified.

3. *Presentating objections to the thesis.* It is generally best to do this part of the paper after you have completed at least a rough draft of your supporting arguments. Most of the advice for presenting your supporting arguments applies to this part of the paper.

Step into your opponent's shoes for a while and ask yourself what are some of the arguments against your thesis statement. Go back and review your research materials by philosophers or others who disagree with your thesis statement. Make a list of the objections or counterarguments. Select the three or four strongest objections or counterarguments. If you numbered your arguments you should also number the counter arguments; for example, **Objection 1.**

Resist the temptation to use only the weaker counterarguments in an attempt to make your own position look more compelling. Remember that your audience, your professor, is most likely familiar with the arguments on both sides of the issue; he or she is interested in how you respond to the stronger counterarguments, not with how deftly you avoid them.

The counterarguments should address, as much as possible, the issues brought up in the arguments presented in the previous section. For example, some philosophers argue that rationality, rather than sentience, is the necessary criteria for personhood. Many rights ethicists, especially natural rights ethicists, argue that only humans have rights. Both of these counterarguments need to be addressed if you are doing a paper on the morality of using nonhuman animals in cosmetic experiments. Present the counterarguments in the most convincing form possible. Save your objections to the counterarguments for the next part of the paper.

4. *Responding to objections to the thesis.* Respond to objections one at a time. If you numbered your counterarguments, refer to each one by its number, for example, **Response to Objection 1.** Avoid the temptation to dismiss the objections or counterarguments by using fallacies. If you cannot come up with a reasonable response, consider going back and modifying your own position during the next rewrite of your paper. If the objection is a good one but you do not change your thesis, you should explain why the moral concerns that support your thesis statement are *morally* more compelling.

5. *Conclusion.* The conclusion sums up your paper. It should include the following:

a restatement of the thesis

a brief summary of argument

The following is an example of a conclusion:

> In conclusion, the use of sentient nonhuman animals, such as rabbits, in cosmetic experiments cannot be morally justified. The pain caused to these animals clearly outweighs the benefits to humans. Even if it is conceded that humans have a right to use other animals for our benefit, cosmetic experiments are not necessary to the well-being of humans. Futhermore, I have argued that rights should be based on interests rather than self-assertion. Sentient animals have an interest in freedom of movement and the avoidance of pain, interests that are thwarted by using them in cosmetic experiments. Furthermore, animal experimentation violates the principle of equality because it is considered morally repugnant to use humans of the same mental capacity as rabbits for cosmetic experiments. Albert Schweitzer once said that we are not truly civilized if we concern ourselves only with the relation of humans to other humans. What is important is the relation of humans to all life.[5] Ending animal testing in cosmetic experiments is one step on the road to becoming truly civilized.

6. *Bibliography and footnotes.* Any references or works used from other sources should be cited either in footnotes at the bottom of each page, or in endnotes. In citing books and articles, include the author's name, the title of the work, and information about the publication such as edition, volume number, page number, publisher, and date of publication. The professor may also require a bibliography of sources used in writing the paper. The bibliography should include, at a minimum, all the references mentioned in the footnotes.

There are different forms for citing works. Some professors have a clear preference for one particular style; others ask only that you be consistent in your form. There are several books available on writing papers. One of the most popular for undergraduates is Kate Turabian's *A Manual for Writers of Term Papers, Theses, and Dissertations* (University of Chicago Press).

PREPARING THE FINAL DRAFT

1. *Reread and edit.* Once you have completed a satisfactory draft of your paper, put it aside for a few days. Then, go back and reread what you have. Ask yourself "What am I trying to say?" Once you are clear on what you want to say, reread the paragraph and answer the question "Have I said it? If so, have I said it clearly and as concisely as possible?" Who is your audience? Imagine your professor reading your paper. Put yourself in his or her shoes. Make notes in the margin of your draft. After reflection, some of your arguments may appear weak or redundant. You may also have come up with some new stronger arguments for your position or have found new information on your topic.

Some people have an easier time writing than speaking about ideas. Other people, especially extroverts (E), speak well but may have difficulty putting their ideas down on paper. If you are one of these people, read your paper out loud to yourself—or even better, find a willing listener (I read all my manuscripts to my cat!). Reading aloud will bring out the weaknesses. In fact, you may even find yourself paraphrasing a particular sentence to make it clearer.

Cut out all superfluous words and sentences. "Clutter," writes editor and author William Zinsser, "is the disease of American writing. We are a society strangling in unnecessary words, circular constructions, pompous frills, and meaningless jargon."[6] College students are no exception. Clutter is the result of unclear thinking, as the writer meanders back and forth rather than moving clearly toward the goal. Most people's first drafts, including those by professional writers, can be cut by 50 percent. Perceptive (P) personality types are especially prone to turning out long, rambling papers. Philosophy papers are not the place for embellishment. Be as succinct as possible. Go back through your first draft and cross out all redundant and superfluous words, especially extra adverbs and adjectives.

2. *The final touches.* Writing is more than just putting ideas down on paper. *Your paper should meet the style guidelines set by the professor.* If you are using footnotes or have a bibliography, make sure they are in the correct style. If the professor did not state a preference for a particular style, make sure you use the same style throughout.

Check your paper for grammar and spelling. Before typing out your final copy, check your paper for grammar and spelling. Most computers have spell checks, and some programs also check for grammar; however, these programs are not flawless and you should recheck the paper yourself as well.

3. *Printing the final draft.* Allow at least a few days for getting the final draft printed out. Printers can malfunction, and you may have to find another printer at the last minute. If you are not going to type your own final draft, allow plenty of time for someone else to type it for you. Be prepared for possible contingencies. Remember Murphy's Law of writing: the machinery is not going to work when you need it! Professors are not impressed by students who complain that their paper is not ready because the printer broke down or their word processor crashed. Such excuses only show lack of organization and foresight on your part rather than genuine hardship.

QUICK REFERENCE BOX

Preparing the Final Draft

Do

- Cut out all superfluous words and sentences.
- Check your paper for spelling and grammar.
- Follow the style guidelines.
- Type your paper double-space on 8½-by-11 inch, 20 pound white paper.
- Leave 1-inch margins at the bottom and sides, and 1½-inch margins at the top of each page.
- Make sure your name is on the first page of the paper.
- Use legible size 12-point font.
- Number your pages.
- Attach your pages.
- Make a backup copy of your paper.

Do Not

- Make changes in pencil or pen on the final copy.
- Wait until the last day to print out your final copy.
- Use small or fancy fonts.

Final drafts should be typed. Your paper should be double-spaced on 8½-by-11 inch, 20 pound white paper. Leave 1-inch margins on the sides and bottom, and 1½-inch at the top of each page. Each page should be numbered. Use a letter quality printer with a font that is easy on the eye, such as Times Roman 12-point font. Avoid fancy or smaller fonts because they are hard to read. Always make a backup of your final draft in case the professor's copy gets misplaced or lost.

Once your paper is printed, check to make sure that all the pages are there and in the right order. If your paper is longer than five pages, you may want to include a title page. For shorter papers, unless the professor states a preference, it is usually best to staple the pages rather than use a paper clip because paper clips tend to come off or get caught on other people's papers. Longer papers can be put in a binder, but make sure the binder holds the pages securely.

Writing a paper in moral philosophy can be a wonderful learning experience as well as an opportunity to hone your analytical and writing skills. Many of the skills used in writing a paper in moral philosophy can be transferred to other types of writing.

Debating Moral Issues

A philosopher who is not taking part in discussion is like a boxer who never goes into the ring.

—Ludwig Wittgenstein, *Conversation* (1930)

One who refuses to participate in a debate almost automatically lowers his personal standing and the credibility level of his position unless the reasons for the refusal are exceptionally good.

—Ray Nadeau, *A Basic Rhetoric of Speech Communication* (1969)

In a democracy the citizens hold the power and authority to make decisions that affect the public welfare. This places upon us the responsibility not only to think and write critically but to be able to debate topics of moral importance. In writing we have an opportunity to clarify our ideas on a topic. However, there is seldom any direct confrontation. In debates on moral issues our justifications may be called into question in ways which we did not expect. Thus, debates demand a level of preparedness and skill in analysis that papers or reading philosophical arguments do not.

In the final analysis, however, it is majority rule that decides the course of our nation. Therefore, in a democracy it is not enough that we are able to critically analyze moral issues and support a position that we believe to be moral; we must be able to convince others and be willing to engage in debate on important issues that affect our welfare and change our minds, if necessary.

U.S. historian and educator Henry Steele Commager once wrote: "When a nation silences criticism and dissent, it deprives itself of the power to correct its errors." Trying out our ideas in a classroom debate hones our skills to participate effectively in a democracy through the sharing of ideas. By learning how to present and critically analyze ideas we can improve our own moral reasoning as well as discover and remedy the errors in our thinking.

Many students balk at classroom debates, saying they are too shy or that morality is a private matter. However, in a democracy where the people decide important issues such as who shall be free and who shall be slaves, do we merely have a right to express our views or do we also have a duty to debate our views and subject them to critical analysis? Philosopher Edmund Burke warned us that "The only thing necessary for evil to triumph is for good people to do nothing." Refusing to openly express our views or listen to the views of others is, in effect, to do nothing.

There are several misconceptions about debates. First of all, a debate is not simply a sharing of opinions. In a debate we are expected to support our position as well as to modify it in light of constructive criticism. Nor is a debate a contest in the sense that there is a winner and a loser. Of course, debates may point out that someone is wrong about their facts and that their conclusion does not logically follow from their premises. While this may be a somewhat humbling experience at the time, on a more positive note, learning this about our position is an excellent opportunity to revise our position or even change it if we can no longer support it. Indeed position papers written after the topic has been debated in class tend to be much stronger than the pre-debate versions. Remember, the purpose of a debate in moral philosophy is not to rigidly stick to your position and refuse to change your view on an issue. Debating instead is a dynamic process that allows both parties to be better prepared to deal effectively with a particular issue and to develop a position that is the most morally acceptable, given the options.

One of the biggest temptations in debates is to engage in rhetoric. While the term *rhetoric* is sometimes used to refer to any type of persuasive argumentative strategy, rhetoric is being used here in the narrower sense to mean a strategy whose primary or only goal is to persuade rather than to find truth. This type of rhetoric involves beginning with a "conclusion" and then presenting only those arguments that support that conclusion while ignoring the rest. Philosophical debate, in contrast, is based on moral reasoning. While one may be assigned a particular position, this position is not written in stone. Unlike rhetoric, where a person's sole mission is to persuade the audience of his or her position, in debate the initial position is merely a stepping off point on the journey to discovering truth. Thus, debate encourages convergence and finding common ground on an issue, rather than maintaining a rigid division between pro and con.

Philosophical debates are also different from casual uncritical discussions of moral issues, where people often end up frustrated or dismiss differences with clichés about respecting differences of opinions. Philosophical debates on moral issues require that the participants carefully and rationally present and defend their positions. The good debater is able to take this into account and modify, or even reverse, his or her initial position if it is found to be faulty or if an opponent has a stronger argument.

Most of the guidelines for writing papers also apply to preparing for a debate. Your key terms should be clearly defined and your argument should follow from your premises. Debates, however, are structured differently than papers. Classroom debates are generally done with two or three people taking each side of a position and include a moderator. The moderator's primary task is to keep order. The moderator makes sure that everyone stays within his or her time limits and does not speak out of turn but waits to be called on. The moderator may also request clarification on a point or make notes on the board regarding points made by the two sides. However, he or she does not take a position or actively debate the issue with the other participants.

The debate itself usually has four parts. Debates generally begin with an initial timed presentation by each of the participants. The presentations are followed by an opportunity for each presenter to respond to the other presenters. After the presenters respond to each other, the debate is generally thrown open for questions and answers. Finally, each side pulls together a summary statement in which they may decide to maintain, modify, or even reject their position based on the debate.

Unlike ordinary discussions of moral issues, which often consist of an uncritical airing of opinion, formal debates on moral issues require that the participants carefully and rationally present and defend their positions. This involves preliminary preparation of a well-thought out argument that can stand up to challenges. If it turns out that your argument is weak, you should be willing to revise it by incorporating the strengths of your opponent's argument. Unlike papers, debates involve everyone in the class, including an audience (the class) that critically analyzes the two positions.

In preparing for a debate make a list of the primary moral principles and concerns. Which ones are relevant to the issue you are discussing? Avoid inconsistency when debating particular moral issues. People may use one moral principle, "it is wrong to kill innocent humans," when arguing about abortion but completely ignore this principle when arguing about the ethics of war. A man may be an advocate of equal human rights when at work, but at home expect his wife to put his needs before her own. This is called doublethink.

The following are some additional guidelines to help you be a more effective debater:

1. *Coordinate group presentations.* If you are doing a debate with more than one person defending each position, work together as a group. Divide up the arguments among each participant. Each person in the group should have a chance to read or listen to presentations of the others in their group before doing the presentation in front of the class. Make sure that all the main arguments are covered; at the same time be careful to avoid redundancy.

2. *Do a practice run.* Try out your presentation before giving it in class. If you feel uncomfortable giving it in front of other people, try it out in front of a mirror, or let your cat or dog be your trial audience. In most debates the different presenters are limited to a specific time—usually 2 to 10 minutes. Make sure your presentation falls within the time allotted. This way you won't be cut short and forced to leave out key arguments during the actual debate.

3. *Make your presentation interesting.* Stand when you are presenting. Look at your audience. Speak clearly so the people in the back of the room can hear you. Be enthusiastic. Avoid sarcasm or demeaning comments about your opponents' position.

4. *Know your topic.* Do not simply prattle off a list of premises or, even worse, read someone else's argument from a book or journal. It is fine to use notes, as well as short quotes and statistics. However, you should know your position well enough so you can use your notes for guidance rather than reading them verbatim.

5. *Try to predict, beforehand, the arguments that will be used by your opponents.* This will give you an opportunity to prepare counterarguments or, if the opposing arguments are valid, to modify your own position to take them into account.

6. *Question the facts.* If your opponents have not done so, ask them for the sources of any factual statements. For example, if they say that capital punishment has been proven to be an effective deterrent, ask them to support this statement. Make sure that their sources are reputable and not just based on someone's opinion or personal anecdotes. If you disagree with your opponents' facts, be prepared with counter facts.

7. *Stay focused on the topic.* Do not let the debate wander into related topics. When a person is uncertain of their position they may try to subtly change the topic in order to avoid defending their position. Although the moderator should nip this in the bud,

debaters sometimes find themselves inadvertently debating a different subject. For example, a debate on abortion may meander over into a debate on child neglect and the strain of motherhood. However, people who are opposed to abortion are not saying that the woman must also raise the child. In cases such as these, a good debater is skilled at drawing the opponent back to the topic under debate.

8. *Avoid the use of fallacies.* While it may be tempting to use fallacies in order to persuade the other side or the class of your opinion, the victory is generally short lived. Also, be alert to the use of fallacies by your opponents. A list of fallacies is included in Chapter 2, "Moral Reasoning."

9. *Avoid rhetoric.* In our competitive society, it is tempting to slip into rhetoric during open discussion, thus turning a debate into a competition rather than a cooperative search for truth. Don't be afraid to moderate your position or to admit that the opponent has made a good point. Think of ways that your best arguments and their best arguments can be melded to form an even stronger position, even though this may involve modifications to both positions. For example, in a debate over freedom of speech is there a way that the libertarians' concern for liberty rights can still be honored while protecting people from hate speech?

10. *Be open to the other side's arguments.* Debating is not a contest where there is a winner and a loser. Hopefully both sides will come out winners. Be willing to accept the opponent's argument or those aspects of their argument that are stronger than yours. Stubbornness or close-mindedness is not a virtue! A good philosopher is always open-minded and willing to revise his or her position if there is good reason for doing so. You only hurt your own credibility by continuing to defend a position that is weak. Being open-minded can turn an otherwise stressful win-lose situation into a positive learning experience where all sides win.

Endnotes

CHAPTER 1

1. *Obedience* is available on both film and video.

2. Stanley Milgram, *Obedience to Authority* (New York: Harper & Row, 1969), 6.

3. Elliot Turiel, Carolyn Hildebrandt, and Cecilia Wainryb, "Judging Social Issues: Difficulties, Inconsistencies, and Consistencies," *Monographs of the Society for Research in Child Development* vol. 56, no. 2, 1991.

4. Lawrence Kohlberg, *The Philosophy of Moral Development* (New York: Harper & Row, 1981).

5. This is not to say that religious people are necessarily cultural relativists; many people who are religious believe that morality exists independently of religion; religious teachings confirm, rather than create, morality.

6. Stephen A. Satris, "Student Relativism," *Teaching Philosophy* 9, no. 3 (1986): 193–200.

7. Gontran de Poncins, *Kabloona* (New York: Reynal & Hitchcock, 1941).

8. Nancy L. Jacobs, Alison Landes, and Mark A. Siegd (eds.), *Capital Punishment — Cruel and Unusual* (Wylie, Tex.: Information Plus, 1996), 85.

9. Elliot Turiel et al., "Judging Social Issues."

10. Satris, "Student Relativism," 193–200.

11. Carol Gillian, *In a Different Voice* (Cambridge, Mass.: Harvard University Press, 1982).

12. Adapted from Lawrence Kohlberg, *The Philosophy of Moral Development* (San Francisco: Harper & Row, 1984), 510–511.

13. From Norma Haan, *On Moral Grounds: The Search for Practical Morality* (New York: New York University Press, 1985).

14. Paul M. Valliant, "Personality, Peer Influence, and Use of Alcohol and Drugs by First-Year University Students," *Psychological Reports* 77, no. 2 (1995): 401–402.

15. For more on moral development in college students see Alexander Astin and Gregory Blimling, "Developing Character in College Students," *NASPA Journal* 27, no. 4 (1990): 268; and Dwight Boyd, "The Condition of Sophomoritis and Its Educational Cure," *Journal of Moral Education* 1 (1980): 24–39.

16. Eva Skoe and Rhett Diessner, "Ethic of Care, Justice, Identity, and Gender: An Extension and Replication," *Merrill-Palmer Quarterly* 40, no. 2 (1994): 272–289.

17. Carol Gilligan and Jane Attanucci, "Two Moral Orientations: Gender Differences and Similarities," *Merrill-Palmer Quarterly* 34, no. 3 (1988): 223–227; R. Blotner and D. J. Bearison, "Developmental Consistencies in Socio-Moral Knowledge: Justice Reasoning and Altruistic Behavior," *Merrill-Palmer Quarterly* 30, no. 4, (1984): 349–357; Nancy Stiller and Linda Forrest, "An Extension of Gilligan and Lyon's Investigation of Morality: Gender Differences in College Students," *Journal of College Student Development* 31, no. 1 (1990): 54–63.

18. Children by the age of four, regardless of their culture, recognize the duty of justice, even though they mostly apply it egocentrically, protesting only when they are unjustly treated. William Damon, *The Moral Child* (New York: Free Press, 1993), 36.

19. The film *Obedience* on the Milgram study is an excellent example of this occurring.

20. James Rest, "Research on Moral Development: Implications for Training the Counseling Psychologist," *The Counseling Psychologist* 12, no. 2 (1984): 26.

21. Study by William Damon of Stanford University.

22. Although Confucianism and Buddhism are sometimes included under the rubric of religion, they are philosophies.

23. An excellent debate on this question is found in Plato's *Euthyphro*.

24. An exception here is fundamentalist religion, such as fundamentalist Christianity or Islam, in which the

Bible and the Koran are interpreted literally and are regarded as the final word on certain moral issues such as drinking and homosexuality.

25. See Kwame Gyekye, *An Essay on African Philosophical Thought: The Akan Conceptual Scheme* (New York: Cambridge University Press, 1964), 184–185.

26. John Stuart Mill, "Utilitarianism," in *Utilitarianism*, ed. by Mary Warnock (New York: Meridian, 1962), 257.

27. John Rawls, *A Theory of Justice* (Cambridge, Mass.: Belknap Press, 1971), 30.

28. Chang Wing-tsit, *A Source Book in Chinese Philosophy* (Princeton, New Jersey: Princeton University Press, 1963), bk. 3:1.

29. Elliot Turiel et al., "Judging Social Issues."

30. Immanuel Kant, "Duties to Oneself," in *Lectures on Ethics* (Indianapolis: Hackett, 1775–1780/1963), 123.

31. Jeane Kirkpatrick, "Establishing a Viable Human Rights Policy," *World Affairs* (winter 1980/81): 323–34.

32. Confucius, *The Analects*, bk. 2:1.

33. Adapted from Aristotle's *Nicomachean Ethics*, bk. 2.

34. Virginia Held, "The Meshing of Care and Justice," *Hypatia* 10, no. 2 (1995): 128–132.

CHAPTER 2

1. Judy Monroe, "Binge Drinking," *Current Health* 2, 22, no. 9 (1996): 26.

2. Based on the findings of the United Nations International Panel on Climate Change (1997).

3. Richard G. Majors and Jacob U. Gordon, eds., *The American Black Male: His Present Status and His Future* (Chicago: Nelson-Hall, 1994), 156.

4. Allan Bloom, *The Closing of the American Mind* (New York: Simon & Schuster, 1987), 25.

5. Daniel Hart and Susan Chmiel, "Influence of Defense Mechanisms on Moral Judgment Development: A Longitudinal Study," *Developmental Psychology* 28, no. 4 (1992): 722–729.

6. The term *rhetoric* is being used in the more narrow sense of Sophist-type rhetoric, rather than in the broad sense of *any* type of persuasive argument.

7. Stanley Milgram, *Obedience to Authority* (New York: Harper & Row, 1974).

8. Arthur Jensen, "How Much Can We Boost IQ and Scholastic Achievement?" *Harvard Educational Review* 39 (winter 1969): 1–23.

CHAPTER 3

1. ABC Nightly News, 16 January 1998.

2. "U.S. Abortion Rate is Lowest Since '75," *New York Times*, 7 January 2000, p. 16.

3. Marji Gold, Denis Luks, and Matthew R. Anderson, "Medical Options for Early Pregnancy Termination," *American Family Physician* 56, no. 2 (1997): 533.

4. Gold, et al., "Medical Options," 533.

5. "Abortion Surveillance: Preliminary Data—United States, 1993 (From the Centers for Disease Control and Prevention)," *JAMA, The Journal of the American Medical Association*, 275, no. 14 (1996): 1073; and Vrazo Fawn, "Abortions Drop Significantly, Study Reports," *Knight-Ridder/Tribune News Service*, 19 June 1994; "Experts Try to Explain Declining Abortion Rate," *CQ Researcher* 44, no. 44 (1997): 1038.

6. Julia Duin, "'Millennials' Are Coming (Survey about College Freshman)," *Insight on the News* 15, no. 9, p. 40.

7. Brief of 281 American Historians as *Amici Curiae* Supporting the Appellees in *Webster v. Reproductive Services*, 1988.

8. James C. Mohr, *Doctors and the Law: Medical Jurisprudence in Nineteenth-Century America* (New York: Oxford University Press, 1993): 42–43.

9. Reva Siefel, "Reasoning from the Body: A Historical Perspective on Abortion Regulation and Questions of Sexual Protection," *Stanford Law Review* 44 (1992): 286.

10. Elizabeth Cady Stanton, "Child Murder," *The Revolution* 1, no. 10 (1868): 146–147.

11. Susan B. Anthony, "Marriage and Maternity," *The Revolution* 1, no. 1 (1869): 4.

12. Elizabeth Cady Stanton, "Infanticide," *The Revolution* 1, no. 4 (1868): 57–58.

13. Judith Blake, "Abortion and Public Opinion: The 1960–1970 Decade," *Science* 171 (1971): 540–48.

14. The Gallup Organization (http://www.gallup.com/poll/indicators/indabortion.asp), July 2000.

15. George Gallup Jr., *The Gallup Poll 1996:* 112–113.

16. *ABC Nightly News*, 16 January 1997.

17. "Fewer Doctors Performing Abortions," *Facts on File World News Digest*, 12 October 1995, p. 766-B2.

18. For more on the Islamic Perspective, see "Abortion: Religious Traditions," Warren T. Reich, *Encyclopedia of Bioethics*, vol. I (New York: Simon & Schuster; New York: Macmillan, 1995), 38–42.

19. Gold, et al., "Medical Options," 533–539.

20. "Advocate Lied on Late-Term Method," *Facts on File World News Digest*, 20 March 1997, p. 195-F3.

21. Robert J. White, "Partial-Birth Abortion: A Neurosurgeon Speaks," Testimony by U.S. House Committee on the Judiciary, 19 June 1996.

22. For a defense of this definition of personhood, see Baruch Brody, "The Morality of Abortion," in *Abortion and the Sanctity of Human Life: A Philosophical View* (Cambridge, Mass.: MIT Press, 1975).

23. Clifford Grobstein, *Science and the Unborn* (New York: Basic Books, 1988), 109.

24. Bernard Dickens, "Prenatal Diagnosis and Female Abortion: A Case Study in Medical Law and Ethics," *Journal of Medical Ethics* 12 (1986): 144.

25. "Ultrasound Effects," *The Economist* 336, no. 7926, (1996): 34(1).

26. "Ultrasound Effects," 34(1).

27. Dorothy Wertz and John Fletcher, "Ethics and Medical Genetics in the United States," *American Journal of Medical Genetics* 29 (April 1988): 815–827.

28. See Chapter 8, "Homosexuality," for more on genetic research on a "gay gene."

29. See Chapter 4 for a summary of the cloning process.

30. "The Right Ear," *Human Events* 53, no. 45 (1997): 24.

31. Deroy Murdock, "United Nations' Social Welfare Produces Scant Results," *Headway* 9, no. 10 (1997): 20.

32. Diane M. Gianelli, "AMA Report: Third trimester Abortions 'Rarely Necessary,'" *American Medical News* 40, no. 20 (1997): 1–4.

33. "Ultrasound Effects," 34(1).

34. Paul A. Logli, "Drugs in the Womb: The Newest Battlefield in the War on Drugs," *Criminal Justice Ethics* (winter/spring 1990): 25.

35. Paul A. Logli, "Drugs in the Womb," 23–24.

36. "Supreme Court: Debates Pregnancy Drug Testing Policy," *American Health Line,* 29 February 2000.

37. Katherine Beckett, "Fetal Rights and 'Crack Moms': Pregnant Women in the War on Drugs," *Contemporary Drug Problems* 22, no. 4 (1995): 587–612.

38. J. M. Lawrence, "Police Say Arsonist Set N.H. Abortion Clinic Fire," *Boston Herald,* 30 May 2000, p. 2.

39. "Blasts Probed at Atlanta Family Clinics," *US News & World Report,* 16 January 1997.

40. "Abortion-Related Crime Increased in 1997," *Providence Journal,* 18 January 1998, p. F5.

CHAPTER 4

1. Plato, *Republic,* bk. III: 410; bk. IV: 456–461.

2. In actual fact, as of 2000, about 1% of the human genome remains uncertain; but, for all practical purposes, the genome is "ready for use." See Nicholas Wade, "Researchers Unlock Genetic Code Secrets," *Providence Journal,* 27 June 2000, p. A6.

3. Sheryl Bay Stolberg, "A Small Leap to Designer Babies," *New York Times,* 1 January 2000, p. E7.

4. *Ibid.*

5. Nicholas Wade, "Researchers Unlock Genetic Code Secrets," *The Providence Journal,* 27 June 2000, p. A1.

6. "Cloning Success Spurs Debate; Other Developments," *Facts on File World News Digest,* 3 April 1997, p. 235-E2.

7. Mitochondria are slender microscopic filaments that provide energy to the cell.

8. James Webb, "Cloning Plans Breed Skepticism, Outrage," *Providence Journal Bulletin,* 8 January 1998, pp. A1, A11.

9. Sharon Kirkey, "Making Babies," *The Ottawa Citizen,* 15 October 1999, p. A1.

10. *The Opinion of the Advisers to the President of the European Commission on the Ethical Implications of Biotechnology,* 28 May 1997.

11. "Vatican Condemns Birth Technologies," *Facts on File World News Digest,* 13 March 1987, p. 158-F1.

12. Richard A. McCormick, "Blastomere Separation: Some Concerns," *Hastings Center Report* 24, no. 2 (1994): 14–16.

13. Allen Bushanan, Dan W. Brock, Norman Daniels, Daniel Wikler, *From Chance to Choice: Genetics and Justice* (Cambridge, UK: Cambridge University Press, 2000), pp. 160–161.

14. Quoted in Bob Harris, "Second Thoughts about Cloning Humans," *The Humanist* (May/June 1997): 43.

15. Aisling Irwin, "Cloning Can Save Giant Panda, Claim Chinese," *The Daily Telegraph* (London), 7 October 1999, p. 10.

16. Quoted in Charles Marwick, "Put Human Cloning on Hold, Say Bioethicists," *The Journal of the American Medical Association* 278, no. 1 (1997): 14.

17. Terence Chea, "Going Whole Hog for Cloning: Biotech Firm Plans Its Use in Breeding Farm Animals," *The Washington Post,* 5 August 2000, p. E1.

18. "Many U.S. Animals Pregnant with Clones," *Providence Journal,* 28 June 1997, p. A4.

19. John Travis, "Cloning Extends Life of Cells—and Cows?" *Science News,* 29 April 2000, 157, no. 18, p. 279.

20. Judith B. Hall, "Mendel Might Get Dizzy," *Canadian Medical Association Journal* 157, no. 12 (1997): 1669–1670.

21. Frederick Hutt, *Animal Genetics* (New York: John Wiley & Sons, 1982), 108.

22. Clive Cookson and David Firn, "Dolly's Creators to End Pig Cloning Project," *Financial Times* (London), 15 August 2000, p. 2.

23. Stephen S. Hall, "The Recycled Generation," *New York Times Magazine,* 30 January 2000. Section 6: p. 30.

24. Roger Dobson, "Cloning of Pigs Bring Xenotransplants Closer," *British Medical Journal,* Volume 320, March 2000, p. 826.

25. Mark Johnson, "From Hubris and Hysteria, A Global Furor Over Cloning," *New York Times,* 24 January 1998, p. A1.

26. "The Bad Seed," editorial, *New York Times,* 9 January 1998.

27. Mark Johnson, "Hubris," p. A1.

28. Wendy Cole, "Seed of Controversy: Will This Unemployed Physicist be First to Clone Humans?" *Time,* 11 January 1999, v. 153, p. 77.

29. "Company Gets Funds to Clone Baby," *Science,* 29 September 2000.

30. Mark Johnson, "Hubris," p. A1.

31. *Ibid.,* p. A5.

32. "The Moo Two: Any Way You Splice It," *Newsweek,* 2 February 1998, 65.

33. Roger Dobson, "Cloning of Pigs Bring Xenotransplants Closer," *British Medical Journal,* 320, March 2000, p. 826.

34. This is a fictional case study set in the future.

35. Glenn Zorpette, "Off With Its Head!" *Scientific American,* January 1998, 41.

36. Anthony Ramirez, "A Case of Letting the Gene Out of the Bottle," *New York Times,* 14 May 2000, Section 4: p. 5.

37. Gloria Goodale, "Mammoth Mystery," *The Christian Science Monitor,* 10 March 2000, p. 17.

38. This is based on correspondence to British geneticist and author Dr. Patrick Dixon, November 1997.

CHAPTER 5

1. Quoted in Sogyal Rinpoche, *The Tibetan Book of Living and Dying* (San Francisco: HarperCollins, 1992), 375.

2. One exception was David Hume who, in his 1783 essay "On Suicide," argued that suicide may sometimes be part of our duty to society.

3. Robert Jay Lifton, *The Nazi Doctors: Medical Killing and the Psychology of Genocide* (New York: Basic Books, 1986), 63.

4. George Gallup Jr., *The Gallup Poll: Public Opinion 1996* (Wilmington, Del.: Scholarly Resources Inc., 1997), 197.

5. Faye Girsh, "Death with Dignity: Choices and Challenges," *USA Today Magazine,* March 2000, 1228, no. 2658, p. 62.

6. Gallup Poll Releases, March 24, 1999; A. Albanese, "A Question of Human Rights," *The Sydney Morning Herald,* 27 September 1996, p. 11.

7. Carol Daniel, "Killing with Kindness," *New Statesman,* 15 August 1997, 16.

8. M. Cuttini et al., "End of Life Decisions in Neonatal Intensive Care: Physician's Self-Reported Practices in Seven European Countries," *The Lancet* 355, no. 9221, p. 2112.

9. Katherine K. Young, "Death: Eastern Thought," *Encyclopedia of Bioethics,* vol. 1, p. 497.

10. Studies cited in Barbara Dority, "The Ultimate Liberty," *The Humanist* 57, no. 4 (1997): 16–20.

11. Sharon Fraser and James Walters, "Death—Whose Decision?" *Journal of Medical Ethics,* April 2000, 26, no. 2, p. 121.

12. Wim Weber, "Dutch Proposal for Children's Right to Euthanasia Withdrawn," *The Lancet* 356, no. 9226, 22 July 2000, p. 322.

13. *Ibid.*

14. Layne Cameron, "Death Becomes Him," *The American Legion Magazine,* October 1997, 64.

15. Cameron, "Death Becomes Him," 33, 64.

16. Martha L. Twaddle, "Hospice Care," in *Dignity and Dying,* ed. by John F. Kilner, Arlene F. Miller, and Edmund D. Pellegrino (Grand Rapids, Mich.: William B. Eerdmans, 1996), 183.

17. Cicely Saunders, "A Commitment to Care," *Raft, The Journal of Buddhist Hospice Trust* 2 (winter 1989/90): 10.

18. Donna White, "Death on Trial," *US News & World Report,* 25 April 1994, 31–41.

19. Stuart N. Davidson, "Pain and Opiophobia," *Healthcare Forum Journal* (May/June 1997): 64–67.

20. Sarah Ramsay, "Debate Continues on End-of-Life Issues," *The Lancet* 355, no. 9206, 4 March 2000, p. 811.

21. *Ibid.*

22. *Ibid.*

23. Raymond S. Duff, and A. G. M. Campbell, "Moral and Ethical Dilemmas in the Special-Care Nursery," *New England Journal of Medicine* 289 (1973): 890–894.

24. "Dutch, U.S. Doctors' Views on Assisted Suicide Vary," *Star Tribune* (Minneapolis, MN), 23 January 2000, p. 5E.

25. White, "Death on Trial," 34.

26. Timothy Quill, "Death and Dignity: A Case of Individualized Decision Making," *New England Journal of Medicine* (March 7, 1991).

27. Harry A. Cole and Martha M. Jablow, *One in a Million* (Boston: Little, Brown, 1993).

28. Quoted in Steve Hallock, "Physician-Assisted Suicide: 'Slippery Slope' or Civil Right?" *The Humanist* 56, no. 4 (1996): 7–14.

29. Tom Koch, "Living Versus Dying 'With Dignity': A New Perspective on the Euthanasia Debate," *Cambridge Quarterly Healthcare Ethics* 5, no. 1 (1996): 50–61.

30. Richard Selzer, "A Question of Mercy," *The New York Times Magazine,* 22 September 1991, 32–38.

31. Jack Kevorkian, *Prescription: Medicide* (Buffalo, N.Y.: Prometheus, 1991).

32. Case study adapted from Judith A. Boss, *Perspectives on Ethics* (Mountain View, Calif.: Mayfield Publishing Co., 1997), 312.

33. "Kevorkian Charged in Assisting 3 Suicides," *Patriot Ledger* (Quincy, Mass.), 1 November 1996, p. 11.

34. Doreen Iudica Vigue, "The Top 10 Local News Stories of 1996," *Boston Globe*, 1 January 1997, p. B1.

35. Derek Humphry, "Prisoner of Conscience," Dr. Jack Kevorkian, Prisoner #284797," http://www.finalexit.org/drkframe.html, 29 January 2000.

36. John Stuart Mill, "Utilitarianism," in *Utilitarianism*, ed. by Mary Warnock (New York: Meridian Books, 1962), 308.

37. Kim Murphy, "Graphic How-to Program on Suicide to Air on TV in Oregon, Sparking Debate," *Los Angeles Times*, 1 February 2000, p. A-13.

38. *Ibid.*

39. Sharon Doyle Driedger, "Should Latimer Go Free?" *Maclean's*, 17 November 1997.

CHAPTER 6

1. InterPress/globalinfro.org—4/18/00.

2. Robert F. Drinan, "Catholics and the Death Penalty," *America* 170 (June 1994): 13–15.

3. Bureau of Justice Statistics, "Capital Punishment," December 1999, NCJ-179012.

4. George Pettinico, "Crime and Punishment: America Changes its Mind," *Public Perspective* (Sept./Oct. 1994): 29–32.

5. Bureau of Justice Statistics, "Capital Punishment," December 1999, NCJ-179012.

6. U.S. Department of Justice, "Bureau of Justice Statistics: Capital Punishment Statistics," www.ojp.usdoj.gov/bjs/, 23 June 2000.

7. Kathleen Maguire, Ann L. Pastore, and Timothy J. Flanagen (eds.), *Sourcebook of Criminal Justice Statistics 1992*, U.S. Department of Justice, Bureau of Justice Statistics (Washington, D.C.: USGPO, 1993), 357.

8. George Pettinico, "Crime and Punishment," 29–32.

9. Bureau of Justice Statistics, "Corrections Compendium" and "The Sentencing Project," 2000.

10. Gallup Poll, (http://www.gallup.com/poll/indicators/inddeath_pen.asp), July 2000.

11. Ernest van den Haag, "The Ultimate Punishment: A Defense," *Harvard Law Review* 99 (1986): 1662–1669.

12. Helen Prejean, *Dead Man Walking* (New York: Random House, 1993), 47.

13. *The Gallup Poll*, 1991 (Wilmington, DE: 1992), pp. 130–131.

14. Tom Morganthau, "The Lull Before the Storm," *Newsweek*, 4 December 1995, 40.

15. Office of Juvenile Justice and Delinquency Prevention, "Juvenile Offenders and Victims: 1999 National Report," 1999.

16. Leoro Broydo, "Crackdown on Kids," *Utne Reader*, September/October 1998, no. 89, p. 16.

17. *The World Almanac and Book of Facts 1996* (Mahwah, N.J.: Funk & Wagnalls, 1995), 960.

18. Leah Brumer, "Lethal Objection," *New Physician* (Jan./Feb. 1997): 52.

19. *Ibid.*

20. *Ibid.*

21. *Ibid.*

22. John Locke, *The Second Treatise of Government* (Indianapolis: Bobbs-Merrill, 1952), ch. 2.

23. Jeremy Bentham, *An Introduction to the Principles of Morals and Legislation*, in Mary Warnock (ed.), *Utilitarianism* (Cleveland: Meridian, 1962).

24. John Stuart Mill, "Parliamentary Debate on Capital Punishment Within Prisons Bill," in *Hansard's Parliamentary Debates*, 3d ser. (London: Hansard, 1868).

25. Immanuel Kant, *The Philosophy of Law*, pt. II, trans. by W. Hastie (Edinburgh: T. T. Clark, 1887), 194–198.

26. Prejean, *Dead Man Walking*, 110.

27. *The Death Penalty* (London: Amnesty International Publications, 1987), 18.

28. Ted Gest, "A House Without a Blueprint," *US News & World Report*, 8 July 1996, 41–42.

29. Stanley Rothman and Stephen Powers, "Execution by Quota," *The Public Interest* 116 (summer 1994): 3–17.

30. Eric M. Freedman, "The Case Against the Death Penalty," *USA Today* (magazine), March 1997, 48–50.

31. Albert Camus, "Reflexions sur la Guillotin," in *Reflexions sur la Peine Capital* (Paris: Calmann-Levy, 1957).

32. Freedman, "Death Penalty," 48–50.

33. "Study Reveals Flaws in U.S. Death Sentences," *Facts On File* 60, no. 3106, 15 June 2000, p. 404.

34. Lawrence Kohlberg, P. Scharf, and J. Hickey, "The Justice Structure of the Prison: A Theory and Intervention," *Prison Journal* 51 (1972): 3–14.

35. Clarence Darrow, *Crime and Criminals* (Charles H. Kerr & Co., 1902).

36. Prejean, *Dead Man Walking*, 122.

37. Dan Malone, "Views from Death Row," *Providence Sunday Journal*, 25 May 1997, p. D1.

38. Case study and questions adapted from Judith A. Boss, *Perspectives on Ethics* (Mountain View, Calif.: Mayfield Publishing Co., 1998), 362.

39. Albert Camus, *Reflections sur la Pein Capital* (Paris: Calmann-Levy, 1957), 199.

40. "Study Reveals Flaws in U.S. Death Sentences," *Facts On File* 60, no. 3106, 15 June 2000, p. 404.

41. Jill Smolowe, "Not in My Backyard!" *Time,* 5 September 1994, 59.

42. John Larrabee, "At 21, RI Serial Killer Soon Will Go Free," *USA Today,* 6 June 1994, p. A8.

43. Normal males have one X and one Y chromosome (XY). About one in every one thousand males, however, is born with an extra Y chromosome (XYY).

44. Juan Williams, "Violence, Genes, and Prejudice," *Discover Magazine* (November 1994): 92–101.

45. Patricia B. Sutker, C. E. Moran, and Albert N. Allain, "Assessment of Cognitive Control in Psychopathics and Normal Prisoners," *Journal of Behavioral Assessment* 5 (1983): 275–287.

46. Malone, "Views from Death Row," p. D5.

CHAPTER 7

1. *Global Health Research, Drugs and Beyond* (Alberta, Canada: Global Health, 1995), 7.

2. Jerome Jaffe's definition, quoted in Francis F. Seeburger, *Addiction and Responsibility* (New York: Crossroad, 1996), 48.

3. Listed are the effects of small or moderate amounts of these drugs. Excessive amounts may be accompanied by other, sometimes harmful, effects.

4. Jean Kinney and Gwen Leaton, *Understanding Alcohol* (St. Louis: Mosby Year Book, 1992), 17.

5. George B. Wood, *A Treatise on Therapeutics, and Pharmacology, or Materia Medica,* 3d ed., vol. 1 (Philadelphia: J. B. Lippincott, 1868), 712.

6. For an excellent history of drug and alcohol use in the United States, see David R. Musto, *The American Disease* (New Haven: Yale University Press, 1973) and his article "Legal Control of Harmful Substances," in the *Encyclopedia of Bioethics,* vol. 5 (New York: Simon & Schuster, 1995), 2439–2443.

7. "It's Time to Open the Doors of Our Prisons, *Newsweek* 133, no. 16, 19 April 1999, p. 10.

8. Chris Wood, "'This Was Global,' The RCMP Shuts Down a Major Illicit Drug Lab," *Maclean's,* October 1996, 58.

9. Barry Stimmel, *Drug Abuse and Social Policy in America* (New York: Haworth, 1996), 3.

10. Stimmel, *Drug Abuse,* 6.

11. "Picture of Drug Use by Young is Mixed," *The San Diego Union-Tribune,* 1 September 2000, Page A-6.

12. Gallup Poll, September 23–26, 1999, http://gallup.com/poll/indicators/indtobacco.asp.

13. "Tobacco Pervades Teen World, CDC Finds," *The Atlanta Journal and Constitution,* 13 October 2000, p. 1G.

14. R. Gary Edwards and Jon Hughes, "Twenty-nine percent of Canadians Smoke, 75% Consume Alcohol," *Gallup Poll,* 4 June 1997, p. 1.

15. J. B. Treaster, "Drugs Not Just an Urban Problem, Study Finds," *New York Times,* 1 October 1991, p. B1.

16. Stimmel, *Drug Abuse,* 9.

17. Adam Cohen, "Battle of the Binge," *Time,* 8 September 1997, 55.

18. Cohen, "Binge," 55.

19. "Clean up Campuses," *Maclean's,* September 1996, 14.

20. Henry Wechsler et al., "Health and Behavioral Consequences of Binge Drinking in College. A National Survey of Students at 140 Campuses," *The Journal of the American Medical Association* 272 (1994): 1672–1677.

21. Wechsler et al., "Health and Behavioral Consequences," 1672–1677.

22. Mary E. Larimer, Daniel L. Irvine, Jason R. Kilmer, and G. Alan Mariatt, "College Drinking and the Greek System: Examining the Role of Perceived Norms for High-Risk Behavior," *Journal of College Student Development* 38, no. 6 (1997): 587–598.

23. Claudia Kalb, "Drinking and Dying: A Death at MIT Puts Campuses on Edge," *Newsweek,* 13 October 1997, 69.

24. Nweze Nnakwe, "Anabolic Steroids and Cardiovascular Risk in Athletes," *Nutrition Today* 31, no. 5 (1996): 206–208.

25. Lucy Ward, "Pushers Target Campuses," *Times Educational Supplement,* 19 April 1996, p. A27.

26. Henry Wechsler et al., *Secondary Effects of Binge Drinking on College Campuses* (Newton, Mass.: Higher Education Center for Alcohol and Other Drug Prevention, 1996).

27. Antonia Abbey et al., "Alcohol and Dating Risk Factors for Sexual Assault Among College Women," *Journal of Women Quarterly* 20, no. 1 (1996): 147–169.

28. Study supporting the United States Crime Awareness and Campus Security Act, 1990.

29. Kalb, "Drinking and Dying," 69.

30. Keith F. Durkin et al., "College Students' Use of Fraudulent Identification to Obtain Alcohol," *Journal of Alcohol and Drug Education* 41, no. 2 (1996): 92–104.

31. "Picture of Drug Use by Young Is Mixed," *The San Diego Union-Tribune,* 1 September 2000, Page A-6.

32. Julia Duin, "'Millennials' Are Coming (Survey about College Freshman)," *Insight on the News* 15, no. 9, 8 March 1999, p. 40.

33. "Steroid Cloud Mars Baseball," *Milwaukee Journal Sentinel,* 15 October 2000, p. 1C.

34. See E. M. Jellinek, *The Disease Concept of Alcoholism* (Highland Park, N.J.: 1960).

35. Alison M. Goate, "Molecular Biology," *Alcohol Health and Research World* 19, no. 3 (1995): 217–220.

36. Mark Edward Lender and James Kirby Martin, *Drinking in America* (New York: Free Press, 1987), 200–201.

37. Lender and Martin, *Drinking*, 96.

38. Aristotle, *Nicomachean Ethics,* bk. 3, ch. 5.

39. *Encyclopedia of Religion,* vol. 12, ed. Mircea Eliade (New York: Macmillan, 1987), 129.

40. John Stuart Mill, *On Liberty* (Indianapolis: Hackett, 1859/1978), 9.

41. H. Thomas Milhorn, *Drug and Alcohol Abuse* (New York: Plenum, 1994), 3.

42. E. Webb, C. H. Ashton, P. Kelly, and F. Kamali, "Alcohol and Drug Use in UK University Students," *The Lancet* 348, no. 9032 (1996): 922–925.

43. Jean Kinney and Gwen Leaton, *Understanding Alcohol* (St. Louis: Mosby Year Book, 1992), 20.

44. Cohen, "Binge," 54–56.

45. G. Alan Marlatt, "Harm Reduction: Come as You Are," *Addictive Behaviors* 21, no. 6 (1996): 779–788.

46. "Alcohol Illness Cited as Big Cost," *New York Times,* 12 September 1993, A22.

47. Mark S. Gold, "Addiction and Dependence," ed. Warren T. Reich, in *Encyclopedia of Bioethics,* vol. 5 (New York: Simon & Schuster, 1995), 2145.

48. Stimmel, *Drug Abuse,* 14.

49. William W. Latimer, Ken C. Winters, and Randy D. Stinchfield, "Screening for Drug Abuse Among Adolescents in Clinical and Correctional Settings Using the Problem-Oriented Screening Instrumentation for Teenagers," *American Journal of Drug and Alcohol Abuse* 23, no. 1 (1977): 79–98.

50. Kevin Marron, "High Times Doing Hard Time," *Maclean's,* March 1996, 50.

51. S. C. Gfroerer and M. C. Brodsky, "Frequent Cocaine Users and Their Use of Treatment," *American Journal of Public Health* 83 (1993): 1149–1154.

52. Lonn Lanza-Kaduce, Donna M. Bishop, and Lawrence Winner, "Risk/Benefit Calculations, Moral Evaluations, and Alcohol Use: Exploring the Alcohol-Crime Connection," *Crime and Delinquency* 43, no. 2 (1997): 222.

53. Stimmel, *Drug Abuse,* 17.

54. Gold, "Addiction and Dependence," 2416.

55. Cohen, "Binge," 54–56.

56. H. Wesley Perkins and Henry Wechsler, "Variation in Perceived College Drinking Norms and Its Impact on Alcohol Abuse: A Nationwide Study," *Journal of Drug Issues* 26, no. 4 (1996): 961–974.

57. Clayton L. Thomas, ed., *Taber's Cyclopedic Medical Dictionary,* 16th ed. (Philadelphia: F. A. Davis, 1989), 1045.

58. Alvin H. Moss and Mark Siegler, "Should Alcoholics Compete Equally for Liver Transplants?" *Journal of the American Medical Association* 265, no. 10 (1991): 1295–1297.

59. John Taylor, "Live and Let Die: In Praise of Mickey, Jerry, and the Reckless Life," *Esquire,* December 1995, 120.

60. This case study is based on questions used in a 1995 poll of U.S. Olympians or aspiring Olympians as reported in Michael Bamberger and Don Yaeger, "Over the Edge," *Sports Illustrated,* April 1997, 60–67.

61. Stimmel, *Drug Abuse,* 41.

62. Case study adapted from Judith A. Boss, *Perspectives on Ethics* (Mountain View, Calif.: Mayfield Publishing Co., 1998), 222–223.

63. Drugs and crime are closely connected. The majority of prison inmates are serving time for drug-related crimes. See Ted Gup, "Drugs and Crime," *Cosmopolitan,* July 1996, 180.

64. Peter D. Kramer, *Listening to Prozac* (New York: Viking, 1993), 294.

65. Kramer, *Prozac,* 291.

66. Kramer, *Prozac,* 258.

67. Kramer, *Prozac.*

68. This case study is adapted from "AA Made Me Confess," in Alan Dershowitz, *The Abuse Excuse* (Boston: Little, Brown & Co., 1994), 69–71.

CHAPTER 8

1. For definitions of *coming out* and *living in the closet,* see the "Key Terms" box on page 365.

2. Different studies have arrived at different figures. See Robert P. Cabaj and Terry S. Stein (eds.), *Textbook of Homosexuality and Mental Health* (Washington, D.C.: American Psychiatric Press, 1996), 57, and Michael Ruse, *Homosexuality: A Philosophical Inquiry* (Oxford: Basil Blackwell, 1988).

3. Richard A. Posner, *Sex and Reason* (Cambridge: Harvard University Press, 1992), 417.

4. Augustine, *Confessions,* VIII:1–15.

5. The Vatican, "Declaration on Sexual Ethics," 19 December 1975.

6. Chris Bull, "From Damnation to Salvation," *The Advocate,* 20 January 1998, 72–75.

7. Elizabeth Llorente, "Homosexuals Seek U.S. Political Asylum," *The Report,* 11 August 1996, p. A1.

8. Gary Pool, "Human Rights Watch," *The Humanist,* November/December 1997, 38–40.

9. K. C. Abraham and Ajit K. Abraham, "Homosexuality: Some Reflections from India," *The Ecumenical Review,* January 1998, 22–29.

10. "Gallup Poll Topics: Homosexual Relations," The Gallup Organization, http://www.gallup.com/poll/indicators/indhomosexual.asp.

11. "Grading Schools on the Treatment of Gays," *USA Today Magazine,* December 1997, 11.

12. Gary D. Malaney, Elizabeth A. Williams, and William W. Geller, "Assessing Campus Climate for Gays, Lesbians, and Bisexuals at Two Institutions," *Journal of College Student Development,* July/August 1997, 367.

13. Julia Duin, "'Millennials'" Are Coming (Survey about College Freshman)," *Insight on the News* 15, no. 9, 8 March 1999, p. 40.

14. "Gay and Lesbian Rights," *Maclean's,* July 1997, 35.

15. Gregory L. Vistica and Evan Thomas, "Backlash in the Ranks," *Newsweek* 131, no. 16, 20 April 1998, page 27.

16. "Military Homosexual Policy Overturned; Other Developments," *Facts on File World News Digest,* 6 April 1995, p. 251-D1.

17. U.S. Supreme Court, *Boy Scouts of America v. Dale,* 28 June 2000.

18. Ken Plummer, "Homosexualities," in Adam Kuper and Jessica Kuper (eds.), *The Social Science Encyclopedia,* 2d ed. (London: Routledge, 1996), 373.

19. See Timothy F. Murphy, *Gay Science: The Ethics of Sexual Orientation Research* (New York: Columbia University Press, 1997).

20. American Medical Association policy paper, "Health Care Needs of Gay Men and Lesbians in the U.S.," 6 December 1994.

21. "AMA Reverses Policy on Gays and Lesbians," *San Francisco Examiner,* 22 December 1994, p. A1.

22. APA, "Homosexuality Doesn't Need Treatment," *Mental Health Weekly* 7, no. 33 (1997): 8.

23. Richard Mohr, "Mandatory AIDS Testing," in *Gays/Justice: A Study of Ethics, Society, and Law* (New York: Columbia University Press, 1988).

24. *Good Morning America,* 9 November 1997.

25. Andrew Sullivan, "False Bennett: Gay Bashing by the Numbers," *The New Republic,* Jan. 1998, 15–16.

26. U.S. Centers for Disease Control and Prevention, "Update: Trends in AIDS Incidence," *The Journal of the American Medical Association,* 278, no. 18 (1997): 1485–1486.

27. Dean Hammer, et al., "A Linkage Between DNA Markers on the X Chromosome and Male Sexual Orientation," *Science* 261 (1993): 321–327.

28. Bill Ghent, "The Nation," *Advocate,* 9 May 2000, p. 14.

29. "Gallup Poll Topics: Homosexual Relations," The Gallup Organization, http://www.gallup.com/poll/indicators/indhomosexual.asp.

30. John D'Emilio, *Making Trouble: Essays on Gay History, Politics, and the University* (New York: Routledge, 1992), 129.

31. Patrick Healy, "A Rally Against Hate Crimes," *The Boston Globe,* 1 October 2000, p. C20.

32. Robert P. Cabaj and Terry S. Stein, *Textbook of Homosexuality and Mental Health* (Washington, DC: American Psychiatric Press, 1996), 274–275.

33. G. D. Comstock, *Violence Against Lesbians and Gay Men* (New York: Columbia University Press, 1991), 171–172.

34. Comstock, *Violence,* 151–162.

35. Comstock, *Violence,* 31–55.

36. The article appeared in the March 1990 issue of *Outweek.*

37. Daniel Cohen, "A Defense of 'Outing,'" *College Hill Independent,* 3 January 1998.

38. See Richard F. Duncan, "Homosexual Marriage and the Myth of Tolerance: Is Cardinal O'Connor a 'Homophobe'?" *Notre Dame Journal of Law, Ethics, and Public Policy* 10 (1996), 587–607.

39. Claudia Card, "Other People's Secrets: The Ethics of Outing," in *Lesbian Choices* (New York: Columbia University Press, 1995), 194–217.

40. Richard Mohr, "The Outing Controversy: Privacy and Dignity in Gay Ethics," in *Gay Ideas: Outing and Other Controversies* (Boston: Beacon Press, 1992), 11–48.

41. For a more in-depth discussion of the arguments against homosexuality, see Burton Leiser, *Liberty, Justice, and Morals: Contemporary Value Conflicts* (New York: Macmillan, 1979), ch. 2.

42. Martha Nussbaum, "Lesbian and Gay Rights: Pro," in eds. Michael Leahy and Dan Cohn-Sherbok, *The Liberation Debate* (London: Routledge, 1996), 104.

43. Martin Hoffman, *The Gay World* (New York: Harper & Row, 1965), 166.

44. Marcel T. Saghir and Eli Robins, *Male and Female Homosexuality: A Comprehensive Investigation* (Baltimore: Williams & Wilkins, 1973), 64.

45. Elliot Turiel, Carolyn Hildebrandt, and Cecilia Wainryb, "Judging Social Issues: Difficulties, Inconsistencies, and Consistencies," *Monographs of the Society for Research in Child Development* 56, no. 2, 1991.

46. George Gallup Jr., *The Gallup Poll: Public Opinion* 1996 (Wilmington, Del.: Scholarly Resources Inc., 1997), 48–49.

47. See Scott Wiener, "Homophobia Cannot Be Tolerated," *Harvard Law Record* (29 April 1994), 11.

48. William Bennett, "Leave Marriage Alone," *Newsweek,* 3 June 1996, 27.

49. "House Passes Gay Marriage Recognition Ban," *Facts on File World News Digest,* 18 July 1996, p. 499-D3.

50. *CNN U.S. News,* 10 September 1996.

51. Gabriel Rotello, "To Have and to Hold: The Case for Gay Marriage," *Nation,* June 1996, 11.

52. Roger Highfield, "Strange But True," *Sunday Telegraph* (London), 31 October 1999, p. 19.

53. Laurie A. Lattimore, "Bias on the Bench," *Liberty,* May/June 1997, 6–9.

54. Posner, *Sex and Reason,* 418.

55. "AIDS is Leading Killer of Americans from Age 25 to 44," *Jet,* 20 February 1995, 22.

56. "The Growing Specter of AIDS in the Young," *Medical Update,* 17, no. 9 (1994): 3.

57. "Update: Trends in AIDS Incidence," *The Journal of the American Medical Association* 278, no. 18 (1997): 1485–1486.

58. John K. Watters, "HIV Testing: Moral and Ethical Aspects," *The Lancet* 346, no. 8971 (1995): 326–327.

59. D. R. Hotgrave et al., "Human Immunodeficiency Virus Counselling, Testing, Referral, and Partner Notification Services: A Cost/Benefit Analysis," *Archives of International Medicine* 153 (1993): 1225–1230.

60. In a 1988 study, almost 25 percent of sexually active people said that if they tested positive for the AIDS virus they would not inform casual sexual partners of their status. Study cited in Ronald Munson, *Intervention and Reflections: Basic Issues in Medical Ethics,* 4th ed. (Belmont, Calif.: Wadsworth, 1992), 220.

61. Bernard Rabinowitz, "The Great Hijack," *British Medical Journal* 313, no. 7060 (1996): 826.

62. "College HIV Rate Holds Steady, but Risk of Exposure Remains High," *AIDS Alert* 9, no. 11 (1994): 153–156.

63. 10 USCA s. 654(b).

64. See "Don't Ask, Don't Tell: Homosexuals and the Military," *Congressional Digest* 75, no. 11 (1996): 262.

65. "MIT Tries a New Approach in the Battle over ROTC," *Chronicle of Higher Education,* 31 May 1996, p. A23 (1).

66. "Foundation, ROTC Students Defeat Campus Leftists," *Liberatus,* March/April 1996.

67. *Meinhold v U.S. Department of Defense,* 34 F 3d 1469 at 1479 (9th Cir. 1994).

68. For more on legal cases involving sexual orientation and the military, see Robert Wintemute, *Sexual Orientation and Human Rights* (Oxford, England: Clarendon, 1995), 78–83.

69. Bruce Fleming, "Gay Poets, Women, and Other Threats to Group Loyalty at the Naval Academy," *Chronicle of Higher Education,* 30 January 1998, p. B45.

CHAPTER 9

1. Larry Alexander, "Banning Hate Speech and the Sticks and Stones Defense," *Constitutional Commentary* 13, no. 1 (1996): 71.

2. Burton Leiser, "Truth and Civil Rights," *Intellect,* February 1973, 311.

3. For a history of free speech and the First Amendment, see O. Lee Reed, "Is Commercial Speech Really Less Valuable than Political Speech?" *American Business Journal* 34, no. 1 (1996): 1–37.

4. William F. Buckley Jr., and L. Brent Bozell, *McCarthy and His Enemies* (Chicago: Henry Regnery, 1954).

5. Russell Weaver, "Free Speech, Crime, and the Challenge of Advancing Technology," *International Review of Law, Computers & Technology* 14, no. 1, March 2000, p. 25.

6. Reid Goldsborough, "Free Speech in Cyberspace—Both a Privilege and a Burden," *Community College Week* 12, no. 1, 23 August 1999, p. 27.

7. Kevin Platt, "With a Click, Chinese Vault Cultural Walls," *Christian Science Monitor* 92, no. 133, 1 June 2000, p. 1.

8. John Leo, "Watch What You Say," *U.S. News & World Report* 128, no. 11, 20 March 2000, p. 18.

9. "Supreme Court Overturns 'Hate-Speech' Law," *Facts on File World News Digest,* 25 June 1992, p. 464-D1.

10. "Free Speech and Europe," *The Economist,* 16 December 1995, 15.

11. Phil Cox, "The Disputation of Hate: Speech Codes, Pluralism, and Academic Freedoms," *Social Theory and Practice* 21, no. 1 (1995): 113.

12. Martin Bentham, "College Guide Bans 'Lady' and 'History' as Offensive Words," *Sunday Telegraph* (London), 11 June 2000, p. 3.

13. John Locke, *The Second Treatise of Government* (New York: Cambridge University Press, 1960), 457.

14. Ayn Rand, "Man's Rights," in *The Virtue of Selfishness* (New York: Penguin, 1964), 114.

15. John Rawls, *A Theory of Justice* (Cambridge, Mass.: Harvard University Press, 1971).

16. John Stuart Mill, "On Liberty," in *Collected Works of John Stuart Mill* (Toronto: University of Toronto Press, 1977), 220.

17. Mill, "On Liberty," 224.

18. For more on this interpretation of Mill's theory of free speech, see Jill Gordon, "John Stuart Mill and the 'Marketplace of Ideas,'" *Social Theory and Practice* 23, no. 2 (1997).

19. "Forbidden Thoughts: A Roundtable on Taboo Research," *The American Enterprise,* January/February 1995, 69.

20. D. F. B. Tucker, *Law, Liberalism and Free Speech* (Totowa, N.J.: Rowman & Allanheld, 1985), 141.

21. Herbert Marcuse, "Repressive Tolerance," in *A Critique of Pure Tolerance,* ed. by Robert Paul Wolff and Herbert Marcuse (Boston: The Beacon Press, 1969).

22. Henry Louis Gates Jr., "Let Them Talk: Why Civil Liberties Pose No Threat to Civil Rights," *The New Republic,* 20 September 1993, 37–49.

23. "Hate on the Web," *Maclean's,* October 1997, 25.

24. *Doe v University of Michigan,* 721 F. Supp. 852 (E.D.Mich. 1989).

25. *New York Times,* 15 October 1986, p. A27.

26. This is a paraphrase of Samuel Johnson's famous statement, "Patriotism is the first refuge of scoundrels."

27. For a more complete description of this case study, see Christopher McMahon, "Preserving the Bastion: The Case of the *Dartmouth Review,*" in eds. Milton Heumann and Thomas W. Church, *Hate Speech on Campus* (Boston: Northeastern University Press, 1997), 192–212.

28. Jerry Kirkpatrick, *In Defense of Advertising: Arguments from Reason, Ethical Egoism, and Laissez-Faire Capitalism* (Westport, Conn., Quorum, 1994), 154.

29. Scott Stossel, "The Man Who Counts the Killings," *The Atlantic Monthly,* May 1997, 86.

30. See Calvin Reid, "Appeals Court Reviewing 'Hitman' Ruling," *Publishers Weekly,* 19 May 1997, 14.

31. Brandon S. Centerwall, "Exposure to Television as a Cause of Violence," in ed. G. Comstock, *Public Communication and Behavior,* vol. 2 (Orlando: Academic, 1989), 1–58.

32. Richard B. Felson, "Mass Media Effects on Violent Behavior," *Annual Review of Sociology* 22 (1996): 103–128.

33. Kevin Grace, "Eclectia," *Report/Newsmagazine* (Alberta Edition), 27, no. 6, 24 July 2000, p. 33.

34. Joshua Quittner, "Home Pages for Hate: A Campaign to Limit the Voices of White Supremacists on the Internet Has Defenders of the First Amendment Worried," *Time,* 22 January 1996, 69.

35. Alissa Quart, "The Sex Avengers," *Time* 5, no. 5, September 2000.

36. See Sharon Machlis, "University Sues Over Internet Term-Paper Site," *Computerworld,* October 1997, 3; and Julianne Basinger and Kelly McCollum, "Boston U. Sues Companies for Selling Term Papers Over the Internet," *Chronicle of Higher Education,* 31 October 1997, pp. A34–35.

37. Dylan B. Tomlinson and Adam Thompson, "Freedom of Speech: Both Sides of the Prayer Debate in College Sports Point to the First Amendment for Justification," *The Denver Post,* 21 June 2000, Page D-1.

CHAPTER 10

1. Polly Nelson, *Defending the Devil: My Story as Ted Bundy's Last Lawyer* (New York: William Morrow and Co., 1994), pp. 17–18.

2. Joan Didion, "Trouble in Lakewood," *The New Yorker,* July 1993, 50.

3. "USA," *Christian Science Monitor* 91, no. 45, 1 February 1999, p. 20.

4. John Stuart Mill, *On Liberty* (Indianapolis: Hackett, 1978/1859), 104.

5. For an excellent coverage of this issue see Susan Dwyer, *The Problem of Pornography* (Belmont, Calif.: Wadsworth, 1995).

6. See Gloria Steinem, "Erotica and Pornography: A Clear and Present Difference," *Ms.* magazine, November 1978, for a more in-depth discussion of the difference between erotica and pornography.

7. House of Commons, Standing Committee on Justice and Legal Affairs, *Report on Pornography,* no. 18, 22 March 1978, p. 4.

8. "Canada: Pornography Limits Upheld," *Facts on File World News Digest,* 12 March 1992, p. 176-D3.

9. Ronald J. Berger, Patricia Searles, and Charles E. Cottle, *Feminism and Pornography* (New York: Praeger, 1991), 4.

10. Cynthia A. Stark, "The War Against Pornography," *Social Theory and Practice* 23, no. 2 (1997): 279.

11. Elizabeth Monk-Turner and Christine Purcell, "Sexual Violence in Pornography: How Prevalent is It?" *Gender Issues* 17, no. 2, Spring 1999, p. 58.

12. Study by Diana Scully, reported in *Newsweek,* 18 March 1985, p. 65.

13. See Sarah J. McCarthy, "Pornography, Rape, and the Cult of Macho," *The Humanist,* September/October 1980, 18.

14. Julie K. Ehrhart and Bernice R. Sandler, *Campus Gang Rape: Party Games?* (Washington, D.C.: Association of American Colleges, 1985).

15. See N. B. McCormick, *Sexual Salvation: Affirming Women's Sexual Rights and Pleasures* (Westport, Conn.: Praeger, 1994).

16. Robin Morgan, "Theory and Practice: Pornography and Rape," in L. Lederer, ed., *Take Back the Night* (New York: Morrow, 1980), 139.

17. Susan Brownmiller, *Against Our Will: Men, Women and Rape* (New York: Simon & Schuster, 1975), 13.

18. Julie Osland, Marguerite Fitch, and Edmond Willis, "Likelihood to Rape in College Males," *Sex Roles* 35, nos. 3 and 4 (1996): 171–175.

19. Brownmiller, *Against Our Will,* 378.

20. See Patricia Yancey Martin and Robert A. Hummer, "Fraternities and Rape on Campus," *Gender and Society* 3, no. 4, 1989.

21. See especially Katie Roiphe, *The Morning After: Sex, Fear, and Feminism on Campus* (Boston: Little, Brown and Co., 1993).

22. Catharine MacKinnon, *Feminism Unmodified* (Cambridge: Harvard University Press, 1987), 82.

23. "Book Revisits Thomas-Hill Affair," *Facts on File World News Digest,* 24 November 1994, p. 877-F1.

24. T. J. Wallis, "Sexual Harassment on the Job," *Career World* 28, no. 5, Feb/March 2000, p. 16.

25. Ronni Sandoff, "Sexual Harassment: The Inside Story," *Working Woman,* June 1992.

26. Vaughana Macy Feary, "Sexual Harassment: Why the Corporate World Still Doesn't 'Get It'," *Journal of Business Ethics* 13 (1994): 648–662.

27. Statistics from the Rhode Island Coalition Against Domestic Violence, 1997.

28. John Q. Kelley, "Emerging from the Shadows: Domestic Violence as a Medical Issue," *Vital Speeches* 6, no. 24 (1997): 748–752.

29. Rhode Island Coalition, 1997.

30. Kelley, "Emerging from the Shadows," 748–752.

31. Larry Reynolds, "Fighting Domestic Violence in the Workplace," Article no. 8738, *HRFocus,* November 1997.

32. "New Law Offers Stronger Weapons Against Domestic Violence," *The Providence Journal,* 29 October 2000, p. A4.

33. See Nicholas Davidson, *The Failure of Feminism* (Buffalo, N.Y.: Prometheus, 1988).

34. Sarah McCarthy, "Pornography, Rape, and the Cult of the Macho," *The Humanist,* September/October 1980, pp. 11–20.

35. Keith Burgess-Jackson, "Justice and the Distribution of Fear," *The Southern Journal of Philosophy* 32 (1994): 367–388.

36. "Mapplethorpe or 2 Live Crew: 'As Nasty as They Wanna Be'?" *Newsweek,* 15 October 1990, p. 74.

37. Davidson, *The Failure of Feminism,* 295–296.

38. Quoted by Sarah J. McCarthy, "Pornography, Rape, and the Cult of Macho," in *The Humanist,* September/October 1980, 15.

39. Oliver L. North, "Constitution Rights are Latest Wares Hustled by Hollywood," *Insight on the News,* 24 February 1997, p. 29.

40. Marie Blanchard, "Students Arrested in Alleged Rape Case," *Daily Bruin Online,* 6 June 1996.

41. Patricia Yancey Martin and Robert A. Hummer, "Fraternities and Rape on Campus," *Gender and Society* 3, no. 4, 1989.

42. Naomi B. McCormick, "Fraternity Gang Rape: Sex, Brotherhood, and Privilege on Campus," *Archives of Sexual Behavior* 24, no. 3 (1994): 355–358.

43. Jill Rhynard, Marlene Krebs, and Julie Glover, "Sexual Assault in Dating Relationships," *Journal of School Health* 67, no. 3 (1997): 89–93.

44. *Providence Journal,* 2 April 1998, pp. A1, A8.

45. "Sentence in Maryland Wife Murder Stirs Row," *Facts on File World News Digest,* 17 November 1994, p. 859-D3.

46. American Anorexia Bulemia Association, Inc., www.aabainc.org/general.

47. For more on this issue see Susan Bordo, "Anorexia Nervosa: Psychopathology as the Crystallization of Culture," in eds. Ann Garry and Marilyn Pearsall, *Women, Knowledge, and Reality: Explorations in Feminist Philosophy* (New York: Routledge, 1996), 388–418.

48. Cherry Boone O'Neill, *Starving for Attention* (New York: Dell, 1982), 131.

CHAPTER 11

1. George Gallup, Jr., *The Gallup Poll 1995* (Wilmington, DE: Scholarly Resources, Inc. 1996), 265.

2. Mark Whitaker, "White v. Blacks," *Newsweek,* 16 October 1995, p. 28; and "O.J. and Race: Will the Verdict Split America?, *Time,* 9 October 1995.

3. William H. Holcombe, "Characteristics and Capabilities of the Negro Race," *Southern Literary Messenger* vol. 33 (1986): 401–410.

4. See Chapter 9 on "Freedom of Speech."

5. See Jonathan Kozol, *Savage Inequalities: Chidren in America's Schools* (New York: Crown Publishers, Inc., 1991).

6. Barbara Kantrowitz and L. Rosado, "Falling Further Behind: A Generation of Hispanics Isn't Making the Grade," *Newsweek,* 19 August 1991, p. 60.

7. Ayn Rand, "Racism," in *The Virtue of Selfishness* (New York: Penguin Books, 1964), 147–161.

8. Jonathan Alter, "The Long Shadow of Slavery," *Newsweek,* 8 December 1997, p. 62.

9. Ronald L. Taylor, "Black Males and Social Policy: Breaking the Cycle of Disadvantage," in *The American Black Male: His Present Status and His Future,* eds. Richard G. Majors and Jacob U. Gordon (Chicago: Nelson-Hall Publishers, 1994), 148–166.

10. Linda Mizell, *Think About Racism* (New York: Walker & Co., 1992), 156.

11. Stephan Thernstrom and Abigail Thernstrom, *America in Black and White* (New York: Simon & Schuster, 1997), 357–359.

12. Kozol, *Savage Inequalities.*

13. Gallup Poll Topics: Race Relations, 24 September–16 November, 1999. http://www.gallup.com/poll/indicators/indrace.asp.

14. Carroll P. Horton and Jessie Carney, eds., *Statistics Record of Black America* (Detroit: Gale Research, 1990).

15. Mizell, *Think About Racism,* 160–161.

16. *Uniform Crime Reports: Hate Crime—1995,* U.S. Department of Justice, FBI, Criminal Justice Information Services Division.

17. "Hate Springs Eternal," *Harper's Magazine* 3000, no. 1978, March 2000, p. 96.

18. "Burned Churches, Fiery Politics," *Christian Century* (December 1996): 1243–1254.

19. "Time to Tell Hate, 'Not on Our Campus,'" *Black Issues in Higher Education* 16, no. 27, 2 March 2000, p. 48.

20. "Race, Crime and Justice," *Christian Century* 117, no. 11, 5 April 2000, p. 379.

21. Gallup Poll Topics: Race Relations, 24 September– 16 November, 1999. http://www.gallup.com/poll/ indicators/indrace.asp.

22. Jeffrey Prescott, "New Facts on Racial Profiling," *Christian Science Monitor* 92, no. 118, 10 May 2000, p. 8.

23. *Ibid.*

24. *Ibid.*

25. Michael Isikoff, "A Question of Profiling," *Newsweek* 136, no. 12, 18 September 2000, p. 68.

26. See the Gallup polls.

27. Herbert I. London, "Minority Enrollment Rebounds at California Schools," *Human Events* 56, no. 24, 30 June 2000, p. 24.

28. Barbara MacKinnon, *Ethics: Theory and Contemporary Issues* (Belmont, Calif.: Wadsworth, 1995), 238.

29. Ayn Rand, "Racism," in *The Virtue of Selfishness* (New York: Penguin, 1964), 147–161.

30. Alan Bloom, *The Closing of the American Mind* (New York: Simon & Schuster, 1987), 95.

31. Michael Levin, "Response to Race Differences in Crime," *Journal of Social Philosophy* 23, no. 1 (1992): 5–29.

32. Kevin Lamb, "IQ and PC," *National Review*, 27 January 1997, pp. 39–42.

33. John J. DiIulio, "State of Grace," *National Review*, 22 December 1997, p. 63.

34. *Cheryl J. Hopwood v. The State of Texas*, 78 F.3d 932 (5th Cir. 1996).

35. *Hopwood v. Texas*, p. 939.

36. *Hopwood v. Texas*, p. 934.

37. *Hopwood v. Texas*, p. 939.

38. Kim Strosnider, "Minority Law-School Enrollment Would Drop Without Affirmative Action, Study Finds," *Chronicle of Higher Education* 43, no. 21, 1997, p. A-28.

39. Quoted in Sophfronia Scott Gregory, "Black Rage: In Defense of a Mass Murderer," *Time*, 6 June 1994, p. 31.

40. Quoted in Alan Dershowitz, *The Abuse Excuse* (Boston: Little, Brown and Company, 1994).

41. Dershowitz, *The Abuse Excuse.*

42. Ward Harkavy, "Left Behind," *Village Voice* 45, no. 19, 16 May 2000, pp. 41–43.

43. George Will, "The Bad Seed of Our Politics," *Newsweek*, 8 October 1990, p. 80.

44. "Environmental Racism: Hispanics Fight a Toxic Waste Incinerator," *Business Week*, 20 May 1991.

CHAPTER 12

1. David Coats, *Old MacDonald's Factory Farm* (New York: Continuum, 1989), 32.

2. Coats, *Factory Farm*, p. 34.

3. The Vegetarian Society, "Gene Genius?" *The Vegetarian,* spring 1993.

4. Lynn White, "The Historical Roots of Our Ecological Crisis, *Science* 155, 10 March 1967, p. 1205.

5. http://www.gallup.com/poll/indicators/inenviron ment.asp.

6. Aristotle, "Politics," I, ch. 8. *The Oxford Translation of Aristotle,* trans. by Benjamin Jowett (Oxford: Oxford University Press).

7. Thomas Aquinas, *Summa Contra Gentiles,* bk. III, pt II, ch. CXII, trans. by the English Dominican Father (Chicago: Benziger Brothers, 1928).

8. Jeremy Bentham, *Principles of Morals and Legislation* (London: Clarendon Press, 1907), 1.

9. Charles Darwin, *The Descent of Man,* excerpt from Tom Regan and Peter Singer, eds., *Animal Rights and Human Obligations* (Englewood Cliffs, N.J.: Prentice-Hall, 1989), 30.

10. Thomas Jefferson, *Writings* (New York: Literary Classics of the United States, 1984), pp. 290 and 818.

11. See Judith Boss, "Treading on Harrowed Ground: The Violence of Agriculture," in *Institutional Violence,* eds. Deane Curtin and Robert Litke (Amsterdam: Rodopi, 1999), pp. 263–277.

12. *Discussing Vegetarianism with a Meat-Eater: A Hindu View* (Kapaa, Hawaii: Himalayan Academy Publications).

13. Joy Williams, "The Inhumanity of the Animal People," *Harper's*, August 1997, p. 65.

14. Jim Mason and Peter Singer, *Animal Factories* (New York: Crown, 1990), 3.

15. Williams, "Inhumanity," p. 61.

16. See John Robbins, *Diet for a New America* (Walpole, N.H.: Stillpoint, 1987).

17. "How Many Vegetarians Are There?" *Vegetarian Journal* 16, no. 5, Sept./Oct. 1997.

18. John Fetto, "It Ain't Easy Eating Greens," *American Demographics* 22, no. 5, May 2000, p. 13.

19. *Ibid.,* p. 13.

20. *Discussing Vegetarianiasm* (Kapaa).

21. Andrew Weaver, "Earth, Not Debate, Heating Up," *The Gazette* (Montreal), 8 December 2000, p. B3.

22. Sharon Begley, "The Mercury's Rising," *Newsweek,* 4 December 2000, p. 52.

23. Peter Singer, *Animal Liberation* (New York: Random House, 1990), 37.

24. Adapted from *PETA Factsheet on Animal Experiments,* no. 1.

25. See Rutgers Animals Rights Law Center, *1996 Supplement to Vivisection and Dissection in the Classroom.*

26. "The President of Europeans for Medical Advancement Responds to the Prediction that the Mapping of the Human Genome Will Increase Animal Experimentation," *The Independent* (London), 28 June 2000, p. 2.

27. Singer, *Animal Liberation,* p. 6.

28. Tom Regan, "The Nature and Possibility of an Environmental Ethics," in *All That Dwell Therein: Animals Rights and Environmental Ethics* (Berkeley: University of California Press, 1982).

29. John Rawls, *A Theory of Justice* (Cambridge, Mass.: Harvard University Press, 1971), 17, 512.

30. R. G. Frey, "Moral Community and Animal Research in Medicine," *Ethics and Behavior* 7, no. 2 (1997): 123–136.

31. Aldo Leopold, *A Sand County Almanac* (New York: Ballantine Books, 1982), pp. 138–39.

32. Al Gore, *Earth in the Balance: Ecology and the Human Spirit* (Boston: Houghton Mifflin Co., 1992), p. 221.

33. Al Gore, *Earth in the Balance: Ecology and the Human Spirit,* p. 216.

34. Arne Naess, "A Defence of the Deep Ecology Movement," *Environmental Ethics* 6, no. 3, Fall 1984, pp. 265–270.

35. See Val Plumwood, *Feminism and the Mastery of Nature* (New York: Routledge, 1993).

36. Rebecca D. Williams, "Organ Transplants from Animals: Examining the Possibilities," *FDA Consumer,* June 1996.

37. Sir David Goodall, "An Opportunity to Rethink Hunt Bill," *New York Times,* February 26, 2001.

38. Quotes from Robert Barr, "Tally-No! House of Commons Votes to Ban Fox Hunting," *Athens Daily News,* 29 November 1997.

39. This is based on a true story. However, the professor in question—the author—did not have the cat euthanized.

40. "Companion Animals, Pets or Prisoners?" *PETA Factsheet,* no. 19.

41. Sean Paige, "Hunting a Solution to the Bambi Boom," *Insight on News,* 3 July 2000, http://www.findarticles.com.

42. Per Pinstrup Andersen, "Biotechnology: A Matter of Life or Starvation," *Bangkok Post,* 26 November 2000.

43. NAAP Bernie, "Rules for Our Slice of the Ice," *The Evening Post* (Wellington, NZ), 5 December 2000, p. 7.

44. Steve La Rue, "More Retailers Warming to Rainforest-Friendly Coffee," *The San Diego Union-Tribune,* 5 November 2000, p. B-1.

APPENDIX I

1. Keirsey, David, and Bates, Marilyn. *Please Understand Me* (Del Mar, Calif.: Prometheus Nemesis Books, 1978).

2. For more information on these personality types and learning styles see: Provost, Judith A. and Anchors, Scott. *Applications of the Myers-Briggs Type Indicator in Higher Education* (Consulting Psychologists Press, Inc., 1987).

3. Peter Singer, *Animal Liberation* (New York: Random House, 1990), 55.

4. Andrew N. Rowan, "The Alternatives Concept," *Animal Welfare Information Newsletter* 2 (1991).

5. Albert Schweitzer, *The Philosophy of Civilization* (New York: Macmillan, 1949).

6. Zinsser, William, *On Writing Well* (New York: Harper & Row Publishers, 1985), p. 7.

Credits

Index